PEACE · THROUGH · UNDERSTANDING ·

AMERICAN
PRESIDENTIAL
FAMILIES

AMERICAN PRESIDENTIAL FAMILIES

WITH
POLITICAL ESSAYS BY HUGH BROGAN
AND FAMILY ESSAYS BY CHARLES MOSLEY

BIOGRAPHICAL DETAILS AND DESCENDANTS TABLES
COMPILED BY CHARLES MOSLEY

MACMILLAN PUBLISHING COMPANY, NEW YORK
MAXWELL MACMILLAN CANADA, TORONTO
1993

American Presidential Families editorial address:
Ballaghmore Castle, Borris-in-Ossory, Co. Laois, Ireland

Published by Macmillan Publishing Company, 866 Third Avenue, New York, NY 10022 and
Maxwell Macmillan Canada, 1200 Eglinton Avenue East, Suite 200, Don Mills, Ontario M3C 3N1

Library of Congress Cataloguing-in-Publication Data

American presidential families / with political essays by Hugh Brogan
and family essays by Charles Mosley : biographical details and
descendants tables compiled by Charles Mosley.
    p.   cm.
   ISBN 0-02-897305-4 : $95.00
    1. Presidents--United States--Biography.   I. Brogan. Hugh.
II. Mosley, Charles.
E176. 1. A6555 1993
973' .099--dc20
  [B]   93-32206
                                             CIP

PUBLISHER'S NOTE

ISBN 0-02-897305-4

Typeset in Perpetua by Bookcraft, Stroud, Gloucestershire, England
Designed by Alan Sutton Publishing, Far Thrupp, Stroud, Gloucestershire, England
Printed by Tien Wah Press, Singapore

CONTENTS

ACKNOWLEDGEMENTS

Thanks are due to the following: Marie Altzinger, who, having completed a joint American Studies Project at University College Dublin and the National Library of Ireland, was of the greatest help in undertaking research; Donal Begley, Chief Herald of Ireland, who provided a copy of President John F. Kennedy's coat of arms and an explanation of why its constituent parts were chosen; John Button, whose skill in typesetting and information retrieval allowed us to mail out to so many presidential descendants with the greatest efficiency and ease; Liam Cody, printer; Jeff Danziger, cartoonist of the *Christian Science Monitor*, who supplied valuable information when we were monitoring presidential candidates; John Funchion, whose design of the forms for mailing to presidential descendants so enhanced that process; Liz FitzPatrick, formerly of the Carroll Institute, London, whose experience in researching the ancestry of Charles Carroll of Carrollton (1737-1832), the celebrated Signer of the Declaration of Independence, made her invaluable as an editorial assistant; Fergus Gillespie, Pursuivant at the Chief Herald of Ireland's Office; Olivia Hamilton (great-great-granddaughter of Admiral Pascual Cervera, who commanded the fleet that fought so gallantly, yet in vain, against Commodore Winfield S. Schley — whose uncle married a Washington — at the Battle of Santiago Bay in the Spanish-American War of 1898) for her tireless labours as archivist and assembler of much of the material into essays on Presidents Grant, Benjamin Harrison, McKinley and Wilson; Archbishop Bruno Heim, for help in ascertaining whether Countess Rose Kennedy was granted armorial bearings; R. Hoffman, of the Carter Center, Ga.; Malcolm Innes of Edingight, CVO, WS, Lord Lyon King of Arms (whose grandfather's third cousin married President Monroe's niece and whose father's fourth cousin married President Theodore Roosevelt's sister) for help in ascertaining whether Presidents Monroe and Buchanan were armigerous.

Desmond Leslie, whose mother's friendship with Alice Roosevelt Longworth made him a valuable source of information on the Oyster Bay branch of the Roosevelts; Father Martin McCarthy, of the Apostolic Nunciature in London, for help with details of Countess Rose Kennedy's ennoblement; Brian MacDermot; Gerald Morgan, Jr, Secretary of The Monticello Association (descendants of President Jefferson) and its members generally; Bawn O'Beirne-Ranelagh, without whose hospitality in London, expertise in information technology and intimate knowledge of the American psyche gained from both part-American ancestry and education at Vassar this book would have been especially deficient; Roisin O'Doherty, librarian at the US Embassy, Dublin; Professor Gary Owens; Monsignor Rino Passigato, of the Apostolic Nunciature in Washington, DC, for help with details of Countess Rose Kennedy's ennoblement; Henry Paston-Bedingfeld, Rouge Croix Pursuivant of Arms, for help in ascertaining whether President Jefferson applied for a grant of arms; Ronald D. Patkus, Archivist of the Archdiocese of Boston, for help with details of Countess Rose Kennedy's ennoblement; Hugh Peskett, doyen of European genealogists expert in presidential families; R. Andrew Pierce, volunteer at the New England Historic Genealogical Society, for help with the Kennedy ancestry; Homan Potterton, formerly Director of the National Gallery of Ireland; John Ranelagh, whose magisterial book on the CIA and personal friendship with members of President Taft's family were so useful; Gary Boyd Roberts, of the New England Historic Genealogical Society, whose life's work has been the unravelling of presidential ancestries and who has been unstinting with information and help; the Countess of Rosse (whose 17th-century kinsmen include Nathaniel Fiennes, defender of Bristol in the English Civil War internally against Robert Yeamans, a royalist conspirator from whom Charles Mosley, co-author of this book, descends, and externally against Henry Washington, President Washington's first cousin several generations back), who drew the cartouche which adorned our writing paper and forms for this project and which managed charmingly to combine a castellated Hibernian atmosphere with that of an antebellum plantation mansion; Professor Robert Schuettinger; Rex W. Scouten, Curator of the White House; and Alfred Shaughnessy, a relative of President Polk who provided much interesting material on the Polks.

We would like to acknowledge the kind permission of Duane L. C. M. Galles, author, and J. P. Brook-Little, CVO, Norroy and Ulster King of Arms, editor of the Heraldry Society magazine *The Coat of Arms*, to reproduce the article from No. 161, 'American Orders of Chivalry'.

The illustrations appear by permission of:

Associated Press (plate 105)

Bettmann (plate 124)

Hulton Deutsch Collection Limited (plates 3, 4, 34, 45, 48, 52, 54, 55, 56, 57, 58, 59, 64, 75, 78, 82, 86, 87, 89, 90, 91, 94, 95, 96, 98, 99, 100, 101, 106, 107, 108, 109, 110, 111, 117, 118, 119, 121, 123, 125, 126, 130, 132, 133)

Library of Congress (plates 8, 9, 10, 11, 12, 13, 14, 15, 16, 17, 18, 19, 21, 22, 23, 24, 25, 26, 27, 28, 29, 30, 31, 32, 33, 35, 36, 37, 38, 39, 40, 41, 42, 43, 44, 46, 49, 50, 51, 53, 60, 61, 62, 65, 66, 67, 68, 69, 71, 72, 73, 74, 76, 79, 80, 83, 84, 85, 88, 104, 116, 120, 124, 128, 129)

National Museum of American Art, Smithsonian Institution (plate 1)

Peter Newark's Western Americana, Bath, UK (plates 2, 5, 6, 7, 20, 47, 63, 70, 77, 81, 92, 93, 97, 103, 112, 113, 114, 115, 122)

Popperfoto (plate 102)

Ronald Reagan Library (plate 127)

The White House (plate 131)

ABBREVIATIONS

*	living descendant of a President or current spouse of living descendant of a President	BBC	British Broadcasting Corporation
		BC	British Columbia
		BCh	Bachelor of Surgery
a	*ante* (*i.e.*, before)	BCL	Bachelor of Civil Law
AB	Bachelor of Arts	BD	Bachelor of Divinity
ABA	American Bar Association	Bd	Board
ac	acre(s)	Bde	Brigade
Acad	Academy	BE	Bachelor of Engineering
actg	acting	BFA	Bachelor of Fine Arts
ADC	Aide-de-Camp	BL	Bachelor of Law
addl	additional	bldg	building
Adj	Adjutant	Bn	Battalion
Admin	Administration	Bp	Bishop
Adml	Admiral	Brig	Brigadier
Advsr	Advisor	Brig-Gen	Brigadier-General
advsy	advisory	bro	brother
AEF	American Expeditionary Force	BS	Bachelor of Science or Surgery
Affrs	Affairs	BSc	Bachelor of Science
Ag	Agriculture/agricultural	BSEE	Bachelor of Science in Electrical Engineering
Agy	Agency		
AICE	American Institute of Consulting Engineers	BSEng	Bachelor of Science in Engineering
		BSM	Battery Sergeant-Major
a.k.a.	also known as	*bur*	buried
AM	Master of Arts	*c*	circa (around, used of a date)
Amb	Ambassador	Capt	Captain
Am Bd Educ	American Board of Education	CB	Companion of the Order of the Bath
apptd	appointed		
Apt	Apartment	CBE	Commander of the Order of the British Empire
AQMG	Assistant Quarter-Master General		
Arty	Artillery	Cdr	Commander
Assist	Assistant	Cdre	Commodore
Assoc	Associate/Association	CE	Civil Engineer
Atty	Attorney	centl	central
b	born	Cert Ed	Certificate of Education
BA	Bachelor of Arts	Ch	Chief
bapt	baptized	Ch Ch	Christ Church
Bart	Baronet	Ch-Engr	Chief-Engineer
BBA	Bachelor of Business Administration	Chllr	Chancellor

Chm	Chairman
CIA	Central Intelligence Agency
CIE	Companion of the Order of the Indian Empire
C-in-C	Commander-in-Chief
CMG	Companion of the Order of St Michael and St George
cmmdg	commanding
Cmmn	Commission
Cmmr	Commissioner
Cncl	Council
Co	County or Company
Col	Colonel
Coll	College
Conf	Conference
Confed	Confederation
Conventn	Convention
Corp	Corporation
CPA	Certified Public Accountant
Cpl	Corporal
cr	created
Ctee	Committee
CVO	Commander of the Royal Victorian Order
D	Democrat
d	died
DA	District Attorney
DAR	Daughters of the American Revolution
dau	daughter
DBA	Doctor of Business Administration
DCh	Doctor of Surgery
DCL	Doctor of Civil Law
DD	Doctor of Divinity
DDS	Doctor of Dental Surgery
DE	Doctor of Engineering
Del	Delegate
Delegn	Delegation
Dept	Department
Depy	Deputy
Devpt	Development
DHL	Doctor of Humane Letters
Dir	Director
Dist	District
Div	Division
DL	Deputy Lieutenant
DLit	Doctor of Letters
DM	Doctor of Medicine
DMus	Doctor of Music
Dr	Doctor
DSC	Distinguished Service Cross
DSc	Doctor of Science
DSM	Distinguished Service Medal
DSO	Distinguished Service Order
DVM	Doctor of Veterinary Medicine
econ	economic
ed	editor
educ	educated
educn	education
Engr	Engineer
engrg	engineering
er	elder
est	eldest
Exec	Executive
Expedy	Expeditionary
FA	Field Artillery
FAAAS	Fellow American Association for the Advancement of Science
FBA	Fellow of the British Academy
FBI	Federal Bureau of Investigation
FCPath	Fellow of the College of Pathologists
Fedl	Federal
Fedlst	Federalist
Fell	Fellow
FInstBiol	Fellow of the Institute of Biology
fl	flourished
Fl-Lt	Flight-Lieutenant
Fndn	Foundation
Fndr	Founder
For	Foreign
FRCP	Fellow of the Royal College of Physicians
FRCS	Fellow of the Royal College of Surgeons
FRGS	Fellow of the Royal Geographical Society
FRS	Fellow of the Royal Society
FSA	Fellow of the Society of Antiquaries
GBE	Knight or Dame Grand Cross of the Order of the British Empire
GCB	Knight or Dame Grand Cross of the Order of the Bath

GCVO	Knight or Dame Grand Cross of the Royal Victorian Order	KCVO	Knight Commander of the Royal Victorian Order
Gd	Guard	KG	Knight of the Order of the Garter
gdau	granddaughter	Kt	Knight
gdn	garden	ldr	leader
Gen	General	Lectr	Lecturer
ggdau	great-granddaughter	LHD	Doctor of Letters; Doctor of Humanities
gggdau	great-great-granddaughter	LittD	Doctor of Letters
ggggdau	great-great-great-granddaughter	LLB	Bachelor of Laws
ggggs	great-great-great-grandson	LLD	Doctor of Laws
gggs	great-great-grandson	LLM	Master of Laws
ggs	great-grandson	LSE	London School of Economics
gn	great-nephew/great-niece	Lt	Lieutenant
Gnds	Grounds	Lt-Col	Lieutenant-Colonel
Govr	Governor	Lt-Gen	Lieutenant-General
govt	government	*m*	married
govtal	governmental	MA	Master of Arts
gp	group	*ma*	missing in action
Gren	Grenadier	Maj	Major
gs	grandson	Maj-Gen	Major-General
HEW	Dept of Health, Education and Welfare	MArch	Master of Architecture
HH	His/Her Highness	MB	Bachelor of Medicine
HIH	His/Her Imperial Highness	MBA	Master of Business Administration
HM	His/Her Majesty('s)	MBE	Member of the Order of the British Empire
Hon	(The) Honourable/Honorable	MBSc	Master of Business Science
hosp	hospital	MC	Military Cross
House of Reps	House of Representatives	MD	Doctor of Medicine
HRH	His/Her Royal Highness	ME	Master of Engineering
HSH	His/Her Serene Highness	MEd	Master of Education
husb	husband	med	medical
Inc	Incorporated	MEE	Master of Electrical Engineering
info	information	memb	member
Infy	Infantry	meml	memorial
Insp	Inspector	MFA	Master of Fine Arts
Inst	Institute	mfr	manufacturer
Insur	Insurance	Mgr	Monsignor
JD	Doctor of Jurisprudence	mi	mile(s)
JP	Justice of the Peace	Mily	Military
Jr	Junior	Min	Minister
Jt	Joint	Miny	Ministry
JUD	Doctor of Both Laws (Canon & Civil)	MIT	Massachusetts Institute of Technology
k	killed	Mlle	Mademoiselle
ka	killed in action	MP	Member of Parliament
KC	King's Counsel	MPH	Master of Public Health
KCB	Knight Commander of the Order of the Bath		

MRCP	Member Royal College of Physicians	Rep	Representative
MS	Master of Surgery; Master of Science	ret	retired
		Revd	Reverend
MSc	Master of Science	Revy	Revolutionary
MSciMed	Master of Scientific Medicine	RFD	Rural Free Delivery
MSW	Master of Social Work	rlwy	railway
MVO	Member of the Royal Victorian Order	RMC	Royal Military College
		RN	Royal Navy
NAACP	National Association for the Advancement of Colored People	ROTC	Reserve Officer Training Corps
		Rt	Right
Nat	National	s	son
NATO	North Atlantic Treaty Organization	SAS	Special Air Service
nr	near	SB	Bachelor of Science
OBE	Officer of the Order of the British Empire	ScD	Doctor of Science
		Sch	School
offr	officer	SEC	Security Exchange Commission
OM	Order of Merit	Sec	Secretary
ops	operations	Sen	Senator
OSS	Office of Strategic Studies	Serv	Service
p	*post* (i.e., after)	Sgt	Sergeant
Parly	Parliamentary	sis	sister
Paymr	Paymaster	SJ	Society of Jesus
Perm	Permanent	slr	solicitor
PhB	Bachelor of Philosophy	SMU	Southern Methodist U
PhD	Doctor of Philosophy	Soc	Society
Pncpl	Principal	Sqdn	Squadron
POW	Prisoner of War	Sr	Senior
Pres/pres	President	STD	Doctor of Sacred Theology
Presdtl	Presidential	stepf	stepfather
Prof	Professor	Supt	Superintendant
Pte	Private	Surg	Surgeon
ptnr	partner	TD	Territorial Decoration
QMG	Quarter-Master General	Tresr	Treasurer
qv	*quod vide* (i.e., which see)	Tst	Trust
R	Republican	Tstee	Trustee
RAF	Royal Air Force	U	University
RAMC	Royal Army Medical Corps	UCLA	U of California at Los Angeles
RCAF	Royal Canadian Air Force	unc	uncle
RCMP	Royal Canadian Mounted Police	UNESCO	United Nations Educational, Scientific and Cultural Organiation
REA	Rural Electrification Administration		
Regd	Registered	UNO	United Nations Organization
Regn	Region	USAAC	United States Army Air Corps
Regnl	Regional	USAAF	United States Army Air Force
Regt	Regiment	USAF	United States Air Force
Regtl	Regimental	USARC	United States Army Recruiting Command
rels	rels		

ABBREVIATIONS

USN	United States Navy	V-Pres/v-pres	Vice-President
USNR	United States Naval Reserve	w	wife
Utd	United	WCC	World Council of Churches
V-Adml	Vice-Admiral	yr	younger
VOA	Voice of America	yst	youngest
Vol(y)	Volunteer/voluntary		

STATE ABBREVIATIONS

The first column contains the standard abbreviations now preferred by the postal authorities. The second column contains the older and — to many people — more familiar abbreviations. Because these older, more familiar abbreviations make the location of a town or city immediately apparent they have usually been retained in all contexts other than postal addresses. Occasionally a still fuller version is used to help readers unfamiliar with American usage.

AK	Alaska	Alaska	MT	Mont.	Montana
AL	Ala.	Alabama	NC	N. Carolina	North Carolina
AR	Ark.	Arkansas	ND	N. Dak.	North Dakota
AZ	Ariz.	Arizona	NE	Nebr.	Nebraska
CA	Calif.	California	NH	New Hampshire	New Hampshire
CO	Colo.	Colorado	NJ	New Jersey	New Jersey
CT	Conn.	Connecticut	NM	N. Mex.	New Mexico
DC	DC	District of Columbia	NV	Nev.	Nevada
DE	Del.	Delaware	NY	New York	New York
FL	Fla.	Florida	OH	Ohio	Ohio
GA	Ga.	Georgia	OK	Okla.	Oklahoma
HI	Hawaii	Hawaii	OR	Oreg.	Oregon
IA	Iowa	Iowa	PA	Pa.	Pennsylvania
ID	Idaho	Idaho	RI	Rhode Island	Rhode Island
IL	Ill.	Illinois	SC	S. Carolina	South Carolina
IN	Ind.	Indiana	SD	S. Dak.	South Dakota
KS	Kans.	Kansas	TN	Tenn.	Tennessee
KY	Ky.	Kentucky	TX	Tex.	Texas
LA	La.	Louisiana	UT	Utah	Utah
MA	Mass.	Massachusetts	VA	Va.	Virginia
MD	Md.	Maryland	VT	Vt.	Vermont
ME	Maine	Maine	WA	Wash.	Washington
MI	Mich.	Michigan	WI	Wis.	Wisconsin
MN	Minn.	Minnesota	WV	W. Va.	West Virginia
MO	Mo.	Missouri	WY	Wyo.	Wyoming
MS	Miss.	Mississippi			

The following common abbreviations for English counties will be found

Beds	Bedfordshire	Middx	Middlesex (roughly what is now Greater London)
Glos	Gloucestershire		
Hants	Hampshire	Northants	Northamptonshire
Herts	Hertfordshire	Warwicks	Warwickshire
Lancs	Lancashire		

READER'S GUIDE

The material on each President constitutes a chapter. First comes one essay on the political career (except with Clinton, where it is too early to evaluate his presidency), then one on the family. Next follows a pattern similar to that for the families in BURKE'S PEERAGE & BARONETAGE: the principal person concerned (in BURKE'S the current peer, here the President) is described in a resumé of his birth date, education, career and details of his wife or wives. Next follows a table of his children, grandchildren and other descendants. Next comes an account of his family history, predominantly in the male line. Lastly (and here we depart from BURKE'S), there is a chart showing his entire ancestry both through the mother and father.

Each successive generation of a president's ancestors or descendants is usually indented a further space to the right. (The exception is where there is only one member of each generation.) Each multi-member generation has its own form of numbering (roman numerals, arabic ones, arabic ones in brackets and so on). The only occasion when members of the same generation in a single family are not listed in the order they were born is when we have no precise dates. Usually that means at least 100 years ago or more. If males are listed before females on such occasions it reflects the system that existed in those days, when male primogeniture was supreme. *It is not an expression of editorial policy toward women as such.*

An asterisk before a name means the person is, as far as we know, still living. Exceptions are divorced spouses of presidential descendants, and a living President or ex-President. Unless instructed otherwise by the individuals concerned we have described married women as having taken their husbands' names, *i.e.*, when Jane Smith marries John Brown she becomes Mrs John Brown. When a male marries, his wife's forenames only are given initially where we have information on her father's surname. Thus John Brown marries Jane, daughter of Peter Smith and his wife Mary. A deceased person is assumed to have died unmarried unless stated otherwise.

The word *sic* in square brackets means the form of wording just before it is the one intended. Human nature is such that different members of a single family may have different ways of spelling or hyphenating their surname.

Each President's political party is mentioned in his biographical resumé. It can be assumed that he held all his other positions — *e.g.*, Congressman, State Governor — as a representative of that party unless stated otherwise. Sobriquets, *e.g.*, Andrew ('Old Hickory') Jackson, are put in brackets in inverted commas. Mere abbreviations — Bill for William — are in brackets without inverted commas.

Various titles of honour crop up. For a full description of British ones see the introduction to the 1956 edition of BURKE'S PEERAGE & BARONETAGE, pp. cxx-cxxviii. Barons are in Britain the lowest rank of the peerage; next come Viscounts, next Earls, next Marquesses and at the top Dukes. Baronetcies are hereditary titles but do not strictly speaking confer nobility, nor a seat in the House of Lords. On the Continent of Europe the hierarchy is (in ascending order) Baron (German *Freiherr*), Viscount (French *Vicomte*), Count (German *Graf*, Italian *Conte*, French *Comte*), Marquis (Italian *Marchese*), Duke (French *Duc*). The title of Prince(ss) is more complicated, but is certainly considered superior to that of a Count. Sometimes the reader is referred to BURKE'S PEERAGE & BARONETAGE for the history of a family. Unless otherwise stated the 105th edition is the one referred to. The title of a family can be different from the family name and if so this title reference will be given, *e.g.*, Jenny Jerome marrying Lord Randolph Churchill (*see* BURKE'S PEERAGE & BARONETAGE, Marlborough), where the dukedom of Marlborough is held by the (Spencer-)Churchill family. If the title is not included in the reference it may be assumed to be the same as the family name, *e.g.*, Sophie May marrying Peter Gerard (*see* BURKE'S PEERAGE & BARONETAGE), for here the barony of Gerard is held by a family of the same name.

Well-known cities such as Chicago or San Francisco are given without the state they are located in; where several mentions of the same town occur, only the first mention appears together with the state. New York is assumed to be the city rather than state where a specific occurrence such as a birth is mentioned. But if a person is mentioned as buying a farm in New York then of course it is the state that is intended. In the genealogical charts a question mark before a date or person's name indicates possibility; one after indicates probability. An either/or date is given prior to 1752 for births and deaths because the change from the Julian to the Gregorian calendar did not take place in Britain or British North America until then. Before that, the new year commenced either in January according to the new Gregorian calendar or March according to the older Julian calendar.

Where family trees take up more than one page the generation furthest back from the President on the right-hand page is split in two, between the President's father's ancestors and his mother's ancestors, and repeated on the left-hand page. Thus the right-hand section of each of the two columns on a left-hand page is identical with either the top section or bottom section of the left-hand column of ancestors on the right-hand page.

We cordially invite all presidential descendants to notify us of any changes in their family circumstances, whether of birth, address, marriage, divorce or death. Write to American Presidential Families, Ballaghmore Castle, Borris-in-Ossory, Co. Laois, Ireland.

Plate 1   George Washington, sculpture by Horatio Greenough 1840

INTRODUCTION

BY CHARLES MOSLEY

This book examines the ancestors, descendants and immediate families of every US President. Because the presidency is a prize that theoretically goes to merit alone, not to people with good connections, it might seem a bizarre approach. Americans are citizens of a republic established in defiance of King George III specifically and royalty generally (though nowadays citizens of that republic adore British royalty). One would have expected Americans to be indifferent to anything concerning genealogy, hereditary distinctions and ceremonial in their own country. Many are of course. But one has only to look around a well-stocked genealogical library to observe how prominent are the various American societies devoted to ancestry. Also how many books there are — published privately or in limited editions — detailing a particular American family's descent from Charlemagne or some other, similarly remote European monarch. (No very exclusive ancestry, incidentally, since it has been calculated that about half of all Europeans are descended from Charlemagne.) In that library one will also observe how prominent in the United States are societies whose membership is or has nearly always been hereditary: the Society of the Cincinnati, the Sons of the American Revolution, the Daughters of the American Revolution, the Mayflower Society. Their prestige is out of all proportion to their generally rather small membership, though with the Sons numbering over 20,000 and the Daughters over 200,000 'small' is a relative term. Odder still than their existence at all in an egalitarian society is the way most were founded a century ago, just when the hereditary principle was being called in question back in Europe. Perhaps it was a response by the formerly dominant group of Protestants, descended from settlers of British Isles origins, to the waves of immigrants from very different cultures. Yet there must have been a consciousness of ancestry throughout the entire mass of the American people, for when the World's Columbian Exposition of 1893 was held at Chicago the senior living descendant of Christopher Columbus — Cristóbal, Duke of Veragua — was invited along. It was rather as if the entire USA had been founded in 1492, on the lines of an Oxford college in England, and founder's kin, as at Oxford, was to be honoured. The tendency continues today. The present Duke visited New York to attend the Columbus Day celebrations a few years ago.

The institution at the summit of American public life, the presidency, has been shaped by such influences. Indeed it has been shaped by many of the same traditions as monarchy in Europe, and monarchy there is above all a family institution. Virginia was a cradle of the Revolution in the late 18th century, but its revolution was conducted very largely by landowners who, if not quite 'gentry' in the English sense of the term (it was easier in Virginia to become a large landowner for one thing), had the confidence, the military experience and the leadership ability of a ruling class. Moreover this ruling class had a strong sense of family, one that survives in the southern states today. Families rallied round when it was a question of giving material help to less fortunate relations, or educating them or bringing up children when those children's parents had died young. (They did in all classes until recently. The difference is, the ruling class in Virginia could offer more substantial help than most.) An astonishing

19

number of people by today's standards chose marriage partners from among their relatives. Virginia was an odd place to be a cradle of Revolution. Only a few generations earlier its royalism had been so intense that when news of Charles I's execution in London reached America the Virginia Assembly promptly declared Charles II king. It took another 11 years before England got around to doing so. The former hotbed of royalism became a staunch upholder of the new republic, however. Virginia, in the late 18th century the richest and most populous state, furnished four of the first five Presidents, a group which became known as the 'Virginia Dynasty', as if they were related. As it happens, all of them — Washington, Jefferson, Madison, Monroe — were. True, the kinship was usually by marriage rather than blood. But in Europe also there have been dynasties with much the same loose connection between successive rulers — the Julio-Claudians who ruled the Roman Empire in the 1st century AD, or the Antonines a century later.

Compared with European influences on the presidency the native American institution of the tribe, with its chieftains, is of far less account. When the President enters a room and the Marines band plays 'Hail to the Chief', the title may conjure up in bystanders some cloudy vision of a Red Indian chief. During the 1920 election the federated Indian chief Red Fox Skiuhushu made Warren Gamaliel Harding a member of his tribe. Calvin Coolidge once donned Indian head dress — and was embarrassed by the episode ever afterward. That is all. Earlier Presidents — Andrew Jackson, William Henry Harrison or Zachary Taylor for instance — made a name for themselves by exterminating Indians, not by emulating them. Europe then, not America, is the fountainhead. Early kings back in Europe were chosen from among men whose principal qualification was prowess in warfare, just as Washington was when it came to selecting a President. In 19th-century America a successful military career was one of the surest ways to capture the presidency. Presidents Jackson, Taylor and Grant, as well as Washington, owed their elections to it. Even in the 20th century there has been the case of Eisenhower, and although talk of MacArthur as a presidential candidate came to nothing, while talk of Colin Powell or Norman Schwarzkopf as presidential candidates has — so far — proved equally hypothetical, it is safe to say that none of them would even have been mentioned if they had not been successful soldiers. Most of the post-Civil War Presidents found that distinguished military service was highly advantageous in pushing their claims to the job. Teddy Roosevelt won national fame principally by his exploits in the Spanish-American War. Even Lincoln, a pacific man personally and self-deprecatory about his meagre soldiering experience, actually led troops in combat on one occasion while President.

Nor were sovereign leaders back in Europe originally so very different from American Presidents in other ways. For instance, in the Celtic parts of Britain and Ireland — and nearly all the early American colonists came from one or the other island, sometimes both, lingering in Ireland on their way from Scotland to the New World for a few generations — chieftains were elected from among the most suitable of the senior clan members. The new chieftain was by no means always the eldest son of the last one, or even a son at all. And his position was no empty honour. He had to be a law-giver, administrator, commander-in-chief, settler of disputes — rather like a President. Even in England the crown remained to a certain degree elective, though from a restricted pool of members of the same family, until the early 13th century. It is because that crown had not yet started to descend according to strict male primogeniture that King John's assumption of the crown on the death of his elder brother Richard I in 1199 was not out-and-out usurpation, even though Arthur, the young son of an intermediate brother, Geoffrey, was living. (King John, incidentally, was the ancestor of Presidents Washington, Jefferson, Madison, John Quincy Adams, both Harrisons, Taylor, Cleveland, both Roosevelts, Coolidge, Hoover, Nixon, Ford and Bush.)

The American Revolution was a struggle against the British king but only accidentally against kingship as such. Lewis Nicola (1717-1807), a Pennsylvania man of Irish-Huguenot ancestry who was active in public affairs and a former commander of the Invalid Regiment during the Revolution, had done particularly useful work in compiling manuals for military training. In May 1782 he begged Washington to assume the crown of the United States as King George I, saying "the war must have shown to all, but to military men in particular, the weakness of republics." Washington spurned the suggestion. Another man might not have done, however. And Nicola claimed to be writing on behalf not just of himself but of a group of army officers.

Almost the moment the republic had been established there were doubts as to the wisdom of the breach with Britain and its monarchy. Political activity was now carried on chiefly by the Federalists and Republicans. The former, who favoured a strong central authority, were suspected of supporting a restoration. Certainly when the new French republic sent over as its minister Edmond Genet there were pro-monarchists who reacted to the extreme republican reception of him with a banquet where toasts to George III and his son the Prince of Wales were offered. In the 1790s the Society of the Cincinnati agitated in favour of hereditary distinctions. The Cincinnati was founded by the Continental Army's chief of artillery Henry Knox, later the first Federal US Secretary of War, and was open only to those officers who had served during the Revolution for at least three years or were serving officers at the end of the Revolution, together with their descendants. Eligibility for membership in the 20th century has continued to depend on one's being a male descendant of such an officer.

Washington, though opposed to the pretensions of the Cincinnati, was when President treated in some ways like a king. (Adams too, though to more ribaldry from his opponents.) Martha Washington on entering New York was accorded a salute of 13 guns. Her husband's official residence was likened to a palace and the etiquette there to that of Versailles: servants wore livery, guests full dress. Everybody stood in the presence of the head of state. At one ball Washington sat upon a sofa resembling a throne. With Jefferson one of American history's periodic reactions got under way. Jefferson criticised levees, birthday celebrations and processions among other examples of ceremonial in the new republic. In a letter of 11 October 1798 he had even claimed to fear the presidency was about to be made hereditary. At his own Inauguration on 4 March 1801 he is said to have ridden to the Capitol without any attendants, not even a servant, and to have hitched his mount to the palisade around the building before entering to deliver his Inaugural address. Another account has him walking to the Capitol, though accompanied by both soldiery and civilians. When in office he introduced hand-shaking at receptions in place of the stiff bows of Washington's and Adams's day. He also tried to restrain members of the diplomatic corps from going in too religiously for bows and curtseys, saying these were servile and trivial. The Danish minister once paid a formal call on him and was shocked to find the President in his slippers. The British Minister, Merry, was even more put out when Jefferson breached the rules of precedence by taking the wrong woman into dinner. For a while Merry even refused further invitations to the Presidential residence.

But subsequent Presidents have redressed the balance. It has not been easy. If a President has been too formal he has been accused of monarchical ambitions, if too folksy he has been sneered at as a hick. Recently the presidency has become more enshrouded with ceremony and protocol than at any time in the last half-century, although back in FDR's time Dean Acheson, later Harry Truman's Secretary of State, was already likening the President's levees to Louis XIV's. And Sir Denis Brogan, the celebrated historian of America and father of Professor Hugh Brogan, co-author of this book, used to advise anyone posted to Washington to read *The memoirs of the Duc de Saint-Simon* rather than De Tocqueville's *Democracy in America* because, he argued, they were going to attend at a court. As one might expect, Republican presidents have been more ritualistic, Democratic ones less so. There have been exceptions, however. Truman adored the ceremonial side of his job and for his 1949 Inauguration, as well as wearing the regulation top hat and striped pants (trousers in British usage), designed new versions of the presidential seal and flag, rather as George IV in England spent his declining years designing new uniforms for the Guards. It was Eisenhower, a Republican, who made the great break with tradition, much to Congress's chagrin, by adopting short jacket and homburg hat for his Inauguration rather than top hat and club coat (morning coat in British usage). He was presumably unworried by the thought of what too casual an approach to Inaugural dress had done to President William H. Harrison (for details of which *see* the essay on his political career). Ronald Reagan reintroduced the wearing of a club coat, striped pants and grey vest (waistcoat) at Inaugurations. He did not go to the extent of donning a top hat, however, and Kennedy remains, somewhat surprisingly, the last President to do so. Nixon wore morning dress at his Inauguration but Johnson did not at his (though when attending Nixon's he did so out of courtesy to Nixon). Nor did Jimmy Carter at his, both LBJ and Carter preferring ordinary suits. Reagan also reintroduced full dress diplomatic receptions, with envoys wearing white tie and tails and decorations.

The new American republic could not shake off European influence, then, even though it repudiated monarchy. Not surprisingly it looked to a European model of republic in the shape of ancient Rome. Ancient Rome was in fashion anyway. Washington's relatives the Lees chose names for their children such as Brutus and Cassius. It was with Ancient Rome in mind that the name 'Senate' was chosen for one of the legislative houses of the new United States, a choice which has sometimes led the Senate to regard itself as superior to the House of Representatives. The fashion for antiquity led to the laying out of a capital city on classical lines. Hence also a taste for portraits and sculptures showing contemporary heroes such as Washington dressed in a toga and posed in attitudes reminiscent of classical figures (*see* Plate 1). George M. Troup, US Congressman from Georgia (and later the state's governor), publicly declared Andrew Jackson's 1815 victory at New Orleans as worthy of Homer, and a speech of almost Gibbonian orotundity in the House of Representatives in 1817 by the future President William H. Harrison conveys the flavour even better. Harrison was proposing that a national militia be established: "The ancient Republics, from which we have drawn many of the choicest maxims upon which to found our civil institutions, will furnish also a most perfect model for our system of national defense. The whole secret of ancient military glory [here he threw in references to Sparta, Roman legions and Athens's resistance to Persian invasion] will be found in the military education of the youth. The victories of Marathon and Plataea, of Cynocephale and Pydna, were the practical results of the exercise of the Campus Martius and Gymnasia."

Such influences were not confined to America. They were sweeping Europe, notably France. But then France fell under Napoleon, who replaced the republic with a hereditary empire. The Roman republic had become a hereditary empire too, even though the title of king long remained anathema to Romans. America, some men thought, might go that way. Washington wanted to retire after a single term in 1792, fearing he might die in office, when Adams would automatically become President — a move smacking too much of monarchical succession. Yet Washington was the sort of man who might well have become a monarch a thousand years earlier — or right then if he had operated three-and-a-half thousand miles further east in Europe, where not only Napoleon himself but his family and some of his successful marshals were picking up crowns. The only new monarch among them to survive, Bernadotte, King of Sweden, was a man very like Washington, being chosen by the Swedes to found a dynasty because he had ability as a commander of troops in the field yet was moderate in governing. The Bonapartes themselves have shown less staying ability. Oddly enough, the only one to win any kind of political power this century has been a US Cabinet member, the Hon Charles J Bonaparte, who was made Attorney-General by Teddy Roosevelt. He seems to have shared his famous relative's fondness for spying on his countrymen (Napoleon is more truly the architect of the police state than Lenin, Stalin or Hitler): he founded the FBI.

In America the idea of a hereditary head of state died. Washington's childlessness, a quirk of fate that is nothing if not genealogical (it has also been suggested he was sterile), was one reason why. There was of course no reason why a country should not have a leader chosen according to some sort of hereditary principle even if it repudiated crowns and kingship. That is just as true today. Several

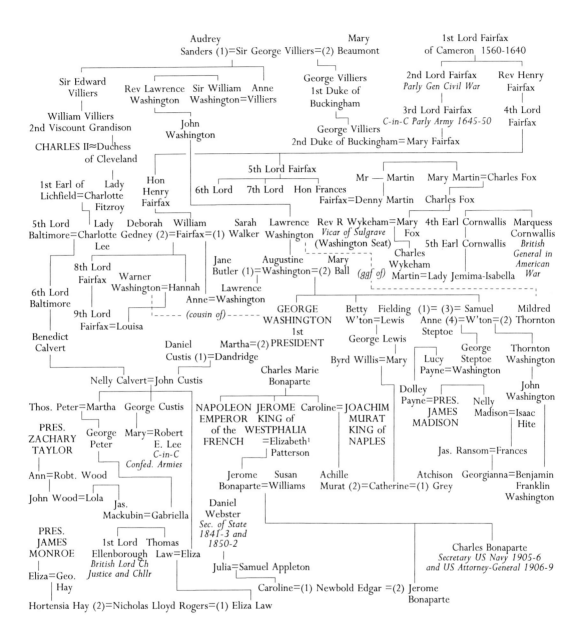

Fig. 1   Kinship chart showing how George Washington was connected to six of the most celebrated military commanders in history, three other Presidents, an emperor (who was of course also one of the military commanders), three kings and various statesmen both British and American. Names of heads of state are in capital letters; holders of clerical, military or government posts in italics. Glossary: = means married; ≈ means liaison.

[1] *Elizabeth Patterson's bro Robert m as her 1st husb Marianne Caton, gdau of Charles Carroll, a Signer of the Declaration of Independence. Marianne m 2nd Marquess Wellesley, whose bro the Duke of Wellington defeated Napoleon at Waterloo and who m Catherine Pakenham. Her bro Sir Edward Pakenham was the British commander defeated by Andrew Jackson at the Battle of New Orleans.*

20th-century republics have had a succession of leaders from the same family, and not always just because they were dictatorships such as North Korea. There is India, for example. Conversely, one could have a purely elective monarchy, as Poland did and as the Holy Roman Empire did throughout its existence, for though the imperial crown became settled in the Habsburg family it was not always so. Europe's only surviving absolute sovereign is elected — the Pope. And over the last 100 years or so the crowns of one or two Balkan or Central European countries have on several occasions been hawked round among various European notables — mostly British — as if they were sets of encyclopaedias. In America such expressions as 'Father of His Country', used of Washington, and 'Founding Fathers', used of the group of men who set up the republic, reflected a notion that the family was a natural unit of government. Inasmuch as a modern presidential candidate's private life comes under scrutiny the moment he announces his intention of running, it still is. And although in the 19th century many a President was suspected of kingly ambitions or manners and sharply attacked, many more Americans have never quite thrown off the feeling that politically active fellow citizens who have a past family connection with the presidency partake of a moral right, on occasion even a duty, to aspire.

The most famous instances are those where the close relative of a previous incumbent actually captured the presidency: John Quincy Adams, son of the 2nd President, John Adams, who lived to see that son succeed him; the 23rd President, Benjamin Harrison, whom popular memories of his grandfather 'Old Tippecanoe' William Henry Harrison, the 9th President, helped ease into the White House; and the 32nd, Franklin Roosevelt, whose very career was launched by his having the same surname as his cousin and uncle-by-marriage Theodore, the 26th President. But there are many other cases where a President's relative reached for, or was edged toward, the prize. He might fail. Sometimes he only just failed. But often the fact of his being presidential kin meant he was under active consideration. There were Charles Francis Adams, President John Quincy Adams's son; Robert Lincoln, Abraham Lincoln's son; James Rudolph Garfield, President James A. Garfield's son; Teddy Roosevelt's son Ted, Jr; John Roosevelt and James Roosevelt, FDR's sons (Franklin, Jr, just as ambitious politically as the other two, would presumably have been precluded from the presidency itself by having been born on Campobello Island, outside US territory); Robert Taft, William Howard Taft's son; Milton Eisenhower, Ike's brother; Bobby and Teddy Kennedy. Even Presidents' sons-in-law have found the connection a useful springboard, either to public service in the first place or to a more active public career than they would otherwise have enjoyed: Nicholas Longworth, who married Teddy Roosevelt's daughter 'Princess' Alice; Senator William McAdoo, who married Woodrow Wilson's daughter Eleanor; Charles Robb, who married LBJ's daughter Lynda Bird. Andrew Jackson's adopted son and nephew-by-marriage Andrew Jackson Donelson was the Know Nothing Vice-Presidential candidate in 1856. There have been American political dynasties at a lower level too: the Adlai Stevensons of Illinois; the Cabot Lodges of Boston; the Poindexters; the Dulleses.

So much for conspicuous family ties between Presidents. In addition, 26 out of 41 Presidents (63.4%) have been a cousin, around the sixth or seventh degree of kinship at the furthest, of at least one other President. Some were much closer: Madison and Zachary Taylor (second cousins), Van Buren and Theodore Roosevelt (third cousins), Van Buren and Franklin Roosevelt (third cousins). The interrelationships can be numerous as well as close. George Bush and Franklin Roosevelt have 15 other Presidents among their cousins (including each other); Gerald Ford and William Howard Taft have 14; Calvin Coolidge 13; Millard Fillmore 10; Richard Nixon and Herbert Hoover nine; Grover Cleveland and Benjamin Harrison eight; John Quincy Adams and Rutherford B. Hayes seven; Ulysses Grant six; Franklin Pierce and Warren Gamaliel Harding five; and so on. If one is prepared to go back to medieval English royalty to find a common ancestor between two Presidents, one can even include Jefferson, who otherwise has no near traceable direct kinship with the others. (But one should not get too excited over this last link; as with Charlemagne, millions of Britons and other Americans with British ancestry descend from medieval English royalty too.)

This web of interrelated presidents exists because in the early days of the republic most of the white male population which made up the electorate descended from a handful of well-documented 17th-century immigrants to New England or one of the other 13 colonies along the eastern seaboard. Indeed so small was the ruling class in the late 18th century that one can trace family links between George Washington and (1) Lord Cornwallis, his opponent at Yorktown, (2) both the men who came to dominate Europe militarily in the decade and a half after Washington's death — Napoleon and the Duke of Wellington, (3) Presidents Madison, Monroe, Van Buren and Taylor and beyond them Jefferson, Tyler, William H. and Benjamin Harrison, through the last two of whom one can reach Presidents Jackson and Polk. Moreover through Jefferson there is a family link with General John Burgoyne, the British commander who surrendered at Saratoga. In addition Washington has family links with General Robert E. Lee and Daniel Webster. The last of these might seem unremarkable enough — many leading American politicians have had family connections to a President — until one realises that one of the two connections is through Napoleon and his brother-in-law Murat (*see* Fig. 1). As well as ancestral links those between Presidents' descendants play a part. That sort of link is more readily traced than links between Presidents' ancestors because the population of the United States has continually grown and records of births, deaths and marriages have become more plentiful. Other factors come into play. The difficulty of travel in a huge country in the early days of the republic, together with the politician's habit of marrying into another politician's family, also accounts for the links between various descendants of early Presidents. But by the 20th century, after the massive late 19th-century immigration of such disparate groups as Germans, Irish, Italians, Jews and Scandinavians and the opening up of the American continent to easy and rapid travel, it is surprising to find that Calvin Coolidge, for instance, is as near kin as third cousin to John Adams; likewise that Herbert Hoover is fourth cousin to Franklin Pierce; that Carter and Nixon should be sixth cousins when they were both from provincial homes far apart and Carter's rural Georgia birthplace was a backwater explored by few outsiders; and that George Bush is as closely related to James Garfield as to be a fourth cousin.

If one looks closer other common patterns emerge besides descent from a small group of well-documented settlers. One feature is parental or grandparental involvement in politics. And Presidents can be grouped into social categories. Some have belonged to what one might reasonably call landed proprietor families: Washington, Jefferson, Madison, Monroe, William Henry Harrison, John Tyler, Zachary Taylor, Benjamin Harrison, even at a pinch, in our own time, Jimmy Carter. There are the men from patrician mercantile, legal or financial families: both Roosevelts, Bush. In addition Kennedy, whose membership of the category dates from one generation back, and Van Buren, who qualified in his own generation, can be included here. There are families where the practice of law is so entrenched as almost to constitute what in France was once called the *nobless de robe*: the Tafts. There are Presidents from an intellectual, clerical or academic elite: the Adamses, Woodrow Wilson. If one leaves out the military heroes already mentioned — and military heroes are a special case, as we have seen — Presidents of genuinely humble background are remarkably few: Nixon, Lyndon Johnson, Truman, Hoover, Harding, Andrew Johnson, Lincoln, Fillmore, Clinton — only just over a fifth of the total. Many even of these got to the White House after making socially advantageous (or what used to be called 'good') marriages.

It is worth stressing these points because the notion persists that the presidency is open to any American citizen with a little drive, whereas in class-conscious Britain — the society inevitably chosen as a foil because it shares the same language and numerous cultural traditions with the USA, besides being the source of most presidential ancestors — anybody wanting to be prime minister has until recently had to come from the 'right' background. Undoubtedly in Britain the ruling class (as opposed to the upper class, a slightly different thing) was until recently less easy to enter than that in America, but not excessively so. More to the point, it was seldom as narrow-minded. Britain has had a Jewish prime minister in Disraeli over a century ago, an illegitimately born one in Ramsay MacDonald over half a century ago and a divorced one in Anthony Eden 35 years ago. In the USA no one, with such a background, would in the equivalent period have stood a chance of becoming President in the USA. Even nowadays the dice would be loaded against them. (Ronald Reagan is the obvious exception here, but although he was divorced, he had acquired his second wife sufficiently long before winning the presidency for it not to be held against him, and in any case his relationship with Nancy has been so uxurious it has virtually excluded any other relationship, even with the rest of the family, if their daughter Patti is to be believed.) More generally British politicians, despite the titles conferred on them when they retire, have not necessarily come from 'grander' backgrounds than American ones. Lord Sidmouth, British prime minister in the early years of the 19th century, was the son of a country doctor, then a despised calling; Canning, appointed prime minister in 1827, was the son of an actress, a calling then regarded as little better than prostitute and one that was used against him politically. (Not that this stopped Canning being one of the chief mockers of Sidmouth as a parvenu.) Lord Melbourne, Queen Victoria's first prime minister, was the grandson of a country attorney, a calling little less despised than doctors. It is true that mid- and late 19th-century prime ministers tended to be of genuine magnate status — Derby, Palmerston, Rosebery, Salisbury. But then Britain reverted to men like Gladstone, scion of a mercantile slavetrading family (the equivalent socially of, say, Benjamin Harrison, though Harrison's lineage is traceable further back); Asquith, a self-made lawyer (marginally more parvenu than his exact contemporary Taft); Lloyd George, a lower middle class radical with Celtic Fringe associations (more akin socially — sexually too — to Harding, with whom he overlaps in time at the end of his premiership, than to the fastidious Woodrow Wilson, his opposite number during his heyday); and Bonar Law, a colonial compared with whom Calvin Coolidge was of good family. Indeed Coolidge was of good family compared with most people.

As the 20th century proceeds the pattern becomes more symmetrical: patricians-with-the-popular-touch in FDR and Churchill (the two men were even related, being seventh cousins), then businessmen's sons enjoying marriage connections to the great house of Cavendish, Dukes of Devonshire, in the case of Kennedy and Macmillan (one a Roman Catholic, the other a near convert to Roman Catholicism when young). Both Churchill and Macmillan, superficially the most British of men, had American mothers. It is true that good family connections have not been vital to the ambitious American politician. But they haven't been vital to the British one either. On the other hand, they have certainly done no harm; sometimes they have been very useful. It is a mistake to think, as most British people and many Americans probably do, that in a republic there is no such thing as a hereditary ruling class. The history of Ancient Rome, Venice and the Netherlands in the days of the Dutch Republic would disprove such a notion even if the USA had never existed. As it is, in both leaders and language the two great English-speaking western democracies are not so very dissimiliar.

Readers will have noticed Britain being called "the source of most presidential ancestors". How many? If one takes only the male lineage, then every President but Van Buren, the two Roosevelts, Hoover and Eisenhower, or 36 out of 41 (87.8%), descends from Americans who emigrated from either England, Ireland, Scotland or Wales, that is to say the British Isles (using the term 'British' in a purely geographical sense, not a political one). But of course concentrating on the male lineage is insufficient. When one speaks of a peerage family in Britain being old, meaning the male line goes back a long way even though the mother's family may be untraceable only a generation or two back, there is some justification, for in such a case inheritance is usually by male primogeniture. With American Presidents no such considerations operate. Besides, with many of them the mother's role in shaping the future statesman is actually more important than the father's. Reagan is a case in point. True, this book devotes more attention to a President's male lineage. That is because in society as it has actually been constituted for the last few centuries a person's surname derives from his or her male parent. But we have not neglected the family tree's other branches. After all, if a man with a Spanish father such as Eamon De Valera can embody Ireland's aspirations to self-determination and dominate the country's political life once it becomes independent, first as prime minister then as President, his father's lineage is hardly the principal point to dwell on. (Even De Valera's grasp of the Spanish language was weak.) Clearly one needs to look at every ancestral strand comprising a single US President before pronouncing on his ancestry. As a result the picture becomes more complex.

For a start, the best documented ancestors of US Presidents are those who settled first in New England or Virginia, with New England having a slight edge. And because ancestors with birth places in the British Isles are more easily traced in the case of New England settlers than Virginia ones, many presidential ancestors known to have specific origins in England are of dissenting stock (*i.e.*, non-Anglicans). That in turn is because the men and women of European origin who first settled New England tended to be Puritans and of the artisan class. In contrast, Virginia resembled traditional English society more, with a landed gentry class at the top, clergy of the Established Church a rung or two below them and so on. Because the early dissenter immigrants to New England from old England were predominantly from the counties of Essex and Suffolk, with the West Country and Yorkshire in third and fourth places, it would be tempting to claim that the primary origins of most Presidents with English ancestry are from those areas. That would be a mistake. For instance, we don't even know for sure the maiden name of George Washington's mother's mother, though she was probably an Englishwoman born in one of the southern counties of England. The same problem occurs with Monroe. With Andrew Jackson things are even worse: we know the full names of only one of his four grandparents. Until recently only one of Andrew Johnson's grandparents could be traced at all and the identity of a second still awaits full acceptance by America's leading genealogists.

Moreover, one needs to be cautious before assuming that a surname is any guide to the place of origin of ancestors. Changing one's surname did not start with Central European refugees from Hitlerian persecution arriving at Ellis Island and acquiring Anglo-Saxon plumage in order to make the country club set. Take the romantic-sounding Clarissa Montfort. Clarissa, who died in 1845 in Virginia a mere seven years after her marriage to the maternal grandfather of the wife of the Revd James Bush, George Bush's great-grandfather, sounds as if she might have belonged to an old Creole family, with Norman origins and related to Simon de Montfort, who had fled the French Revolution to settle in the Old South, perhaps after the period of a generation spent in somewhere like Martinique. She sounds, in fact, a bit too good to be true. That is precisely the case. Her father started life as the more prosaic Munford. Still, we shouldn't be too hard on Clarissa. At the same period people back in England were discreetly suborning genealogists into bringing out reference works which ascribed their origins to Norman barons who came over to Sussex with the Conqueror. It is in fact fairly unlikely that exotic strains crept into presidential ancestries, for most of the settlers on the Eastern seaboard up to the early 19th century were from Britain and Ireland, though even that statement needs qualification. After all, Britain itself has been a bit of a melting pot, with French Huguenots, Dutch, Germans, Italians and Sephardic Jews going to live there from the Continent of Europe in appreciable numbers from the 17th century on. Ireland, though with its own distinct identity, was not so very different, being settled by Huguenots too, and Northern Ireland was in many ways different from the South as early as the 17th century, when numerous Scots Presbyterians came over to Ulster. Something of all this was inevitably reflected in America when it still consisted of 13 British colonies: Charleston, South Carolina, for instance, was not just a town infused with Huguenots (one of whom, Louis Ogier, originally from Lower Poitou in France, was an ancestor of LBJ). It was also the site of one of the first Jewish settlements in North America.

As long as one bears the above in mind, it is still possible, though obviously with many qualifications, to state that nearly all the Presidents' ancestors are from Britain or Ireland. (1) Washington (mostly

England with a dash of Huguenot, plus remote Irish and Scottish ancestors, also possibly Norman and Scandinavian ones); (2) John Adams (around nine-tenths English with a possible Spanish ancestor in the late 16th century); (3) Jefferson (all known ancestors English except for a German infusion in the mid-16th century); (4) Madison (entirely English); (5) Monroe (his father's line only is Scottish; the names of the rest suggest England); (6) John Quincy Adams (same as John Adams except for a possible Norman-French ancestress in the early 17th century); (7) Andrew Jackson (all known ancestors Northern Irish); (8) Van Buren (wholly Dutch); (9) William Henry Harrison and Benjamin Harrison (the former entirely English, the latter almost entirely English with minute particles of Irish and Scots-Irish); (10) Tyler (mostly English but with a paternal grandmother of Huguenot stock and a half-Huguenot maternal grandmother); (11) Polk (Scots and Northern Irish); (12) Zachary Taylor (wholly English); (13) Fillmore and Pierce (both almost entirely English with just a smidgeon of Welsh); (14) Buchanan (Scots Northern Irish, Irish and Scottish); (15) Lincoln (English and northern Irish — that is, from Donegal, in the northernmost part of what is now the Republic of Ireland); (16) Andrew Johnson (Irish?); (17) Grant (Scots-Northern Irish, Irish?, Walloon, French, Welsh?, the rest English); (18) Hayes (wholly English); (19) Garfield (mostly English but with a Huguenot strain through his mother, whose maiden name was Ballou); (20) Arthur (English, Irish, Scottish and Welsh in more or less equal quantities); (21) Cleveland (mostly English but with Irish, German and Channel Island infusions); (22) McKinley (Irish or Northern Irish, also Scottish?); (23) Theodore Roosevelt (mostly Dutch of course, but very nearly as much Scottish; moreover a Yates ancestor was English but married into a Dutch family and the descendants for a generation or two are documented as having Dutch forenames although the surname remained Yates; Roosevelt was also a little bit French, Irish and Welsh); (24) Taft (English); (25) Woodrow Wilson (almost entirely Scottish, though with a Northern Irish-Scots infusion; yet his mother, though genetically Scottish, if one may employ such a relatively sweeping term, was brought up in England and was regarded as English); (26) Harding (on the face of it English, but the only ancestors traceable back to Europe were Dutch); (27) Coolidge (judging by the names of his ancestors almost entirely English, but none apart from the male line has been traced back to Europe); (28) Hoover (only the father's line German, his mother's being English until a thin German strain appears far back in one of her maternal ancestors); (29) FDR (the father's paternal line certainly Dutch but even here a preponderance of English surnames, also a Baltic and Scottish infusion; as for the mother, apart from the Delano line, which was ultimately Walloon, they were mostly English); (30) Truman (certainly Scottish plus possibly Welsh and English on his father's side; a surprisingly strong German showing on the mother's side); (31) Eisenhower (predominantly German, though with a link to the frontiersman Daniel Boone, whose ancestors were from Devon, also to the corporate raider T. Boone Pickens, through his Stover mother); (32) Kennedy (purely Irish as far as one can see, though even here the Fitzgerald strain might ultimately prove to be from the Cambro-Norman family of the same name, a member of which invaded Ireland in the 12th century along with Strongbow); (33) LBJ (a surprisingly strong German showing, plus Huguenot, Scottish, Swiss and Irish elements, also presumably English ones judging by surnames); (34) Nixon (strong Irish descent, plus a Welsh and English strain); (35) Ford (Scottish, French-Huguenot and presumably English and Dutch judging by surnames); (36) Carter (Irish strains on both sides of his family, plus mostly English, also a little Dutch); (37) Reagan (Irish on father's side, English and Scottish on mother's); (38) Bush (surprisingly exotic given his reputation as an archetypal WASP: possibly Dutch and French strains, a fair amount of Northern Irish and German, a touch of English); (39) and lastly, Clinton (initial research suggests a strong southern states of America English and Irish background, with a possible German infusion).

So far we have discussed the presidency in terms of the family stretched up and down many generations. But the immediate family of wife and children, plus occasionally in-laws and grandchildren, clusters round a President more closely. J. B. West, who was Chief Usher at the White House from

1941 to 1969, observed that the Presidents he had known tended when in office to draw closer to their families because they became so isolated from former friends and colleagues. In the 19th century the immediate family had in some ways a more explicitly political role: it was accepted practice to use one's close relatives as private secretaries. The President was given no public money beyond his salary, so had to pay his staff out of his own pocket. Appointing a son, son-in-law or nephew probably saved money. That was a negative advantage. A positive one was that it diminished jealousy and in-fighting between other close associates of the President. James Buchanan Henry, President Buchanan's nephew and private secretary, records the 15th President's dislike of nepotism, but such dislike was unusual. Buchanan expressed his distaste so forcibly that his relatives refrained from asking for positions. Yet, as James B. Henry put it, "Public policy clearly indicates the propriety and desirability of the President's private secretary being, if possible, a blood relation, upon the ground that the honor and interests of the President and his high office can be most safely entrusted to one having an interest in his good name and fame, and therefore more guarded against temptation of any kind. I therefore do not consider the selection of myself, or my cousin Mr James Buchanan, who followed me, as any exception to what I have stated."

Modern notions of what constitutes political suitability look to the candidate's wife just as much as to the candidate. Not only can a wife shield her husband from the stress of the job and the importunities of office-seekers and other nuisances, she helps set the social tone of the administration and smooth over relations with home-grown politicians and foreign dignitaries by her skills as a hostess. This concept of the political family is not confined to America. In Britain, for instance, where the prime minister is only a chief executive not head of state as well, and where in consequence the spouse does not shoulder such a burden of ceremonial and entertaining as the First Lady, prime ministerial spouses are nevertheless very much in the public eye. But there is more to it than utilitarian considerations. The man who would be President must have a wife who, like Caesar's, is above suspicion in that she must have no character flaws. Oddly enough that would have eliminated large numbers of Presidents in the past. And not just those, such as Lincoln, whose wives were unbalanced. Nowadays it is inconceivable that a bachelor could be elected President of the United States, as Buchanan was. Yet Buchanan was far from being the only President with, in effect, no wife to undertake full-fledged presidential entertaining. Whether because of a wife's dislike of the capital city, physical or nervous debility (can the notorious Washington climate have contributed?), or simply because she had died, an astonishingly large number of 19th-century Presidents had at one point or other either to operate socially at half-throttle or rope in a daughter, daughter-in-law, sister or niece to do the honours: Jefferson, Monroe, Van Buren, Tyler, Fillmore, Pierce, Buchanan, Lincoln, Andrew Johnson, Arthur, Cleveland, Benjamin Harrison, McKinley.

A minor but intriguing aspect of presidential families is the role of the dog. This is not facetiousness. Every Hollywood or Madison Avenue depiction of the all-American family features a dog and if Hollywood or Madison Avenue doesn't know what constitutes the all-American family, who does? In *Two Sisters*, by Gore Vidal (himself a First Lady's step-brother and a persistent and highly entertaining chronicler, albeit in fiction, of presidential families), a character called Hiram Backhouse puts forward a theory that dogs in George Eliot's novels play a crucial role in illuminating character. So too with the presidency. Nixon's Checkers was far from being the first of these, though he remains the most famous. Nixon reveals in his memoirs that it was a piece of whimsy by FDR that inspired him to drag in Checkers when trying to save his own bacon in 1952. On 23 Sept 1944 Roosevelt opened his campaign for a fourth term with a speech to a Teamsters' Union banquet. After laying in to the Republicans he said: "These Republican leaders have not been content to make personal attacks upon me — or my wife — or my sons. They now include my little dog, Fala [a Scottie given FDR by his cousin and confidante Daisy Suckley]. Unlike the members of my family, Fala resents this. When he learned that the Republican fiction writers had concocted a story that I had left him behind on an Aleutian island and had sent a destroyer back to find him — at a cost to the taxpayer of two or three or twenty million dollars — his Scotch soul was furious. He has not been the same dog since. I am accustomed to hearing malicious falsehoods about myself . . . But I think I have a right to object to libelous statements about my *dog*." Fala proved a howling success. For a while the cartoonist Alan Foster drew a series of cartoons in *Collier's* called 'Fala of the White House'. A few months later, when a dog called Blaze was flown over from England to Elliott Roosevelt's third wife, the actress Faye Emerson, the Republicans made a meal of it, drawing attention to the waste and favouritism involved. Harry Truman summed the position up more succinctly: "If you want a friend in Washington — get yourself a dog." As for Nixon eight years later, he had a temporary success, but as so often happened with him, was reviled throughout the rest of his life simply for copying what another President, here FDR, had got away with. Later, in 1972, he was more successful: the *Saturday Evening Post* ran a feature on him during the presidential election which included a picture of him playing with his Irish setter; even here a typically Nixonian element of subterfuge was involved — the dog's real name was 'King', but since this might smack too much of monarchism the caption pretended he was called 'Timahoe'.

Even Roosevelt had not been the first President to woo the public using a dog. Harding distributed publicity photographs of himself and his Airedale, Laddie Boy. Once a publicity-hungry owner of a performing dog, Tige, wrote to Laddie Boy inviting him to see his show. A presidential publicity agent returned thanks on Laddie Boy's behalf in a letter ending with a "cordial wag and friendly sniff". Laddie Boy marched at the head of a parade during Be Kind to Animals Week and was reported as sitting in on Cabinet Meetings. For Herbert Hoover the dog was a blacker beast. At the low point of his presidency his publicity agents advised him to be photographed feeding his pet dog. It would, they said, counteract the damaging public view of him as cerebral and morose, too little gifted with the human touch to do anything effective about the Depression. The ploy backfired. Hoover still came over as morose and the picture of him giving good food to a dog enraged thousands of Americans for whom a square meal was now a luxury.

Heidi, the Eisenhowers' Weimeraner, was relatively uncontroversial except when she made a mess on one of the carpets before an important reception, temporarily driving Mamie Eisenhower demented. Her (Mamie's that is) husband's famous short temper was held in check by David Eisenhower's terrier Skunky, which kept the President's favourite White House putting green clear of squirrels. The temporary rapprochement between Russia and America in Kennedy's time was symbolized by Pushinka, a gift to the Kennedy family from Nikita Khrushchev, and JFK's nephew William Kennedy Smith at the time of his 1992 rape trial succeeded in scrubbing his public image clean by being photographed with his labrador bitch Mitzie and a nine-week old puppy McShane to demonstrate that he was just folks. In the '60s LBJ publicly picked up one of the Johnsons' beagles (there were two, called Him and Her) by its ears. It would be an exaggeration to say he was electorally doomed from then on, but many dog-lovers who might have tolerated further carnage in Vietnam began to look on their President with disfavour. Lady Bird Johnson enlisted Lassie, the television and film star collie, to help publicize her Beautify America campaign and in May 1967 had herself photographed shaking hands/paws with the nation's top dog. A poster featuring Lassie urged the public to keep America free from litter. Given dogs' contribution to the general mess, it was an odd way of cleaning up the environment, but the 1960s was still in many ways, to borrow a phrase from Edith Wharton, the age of innocence.

The Fords were frequently photographed with their golden retriever, Liberty, which served to remind the public how wholesome they were. The retriever was the preferred traditional breed as far as the Fords were concerned — they had had two others already — and Liberty was bought by Ford's daughter Susan to distract him from the anguish caused by his wife's operation for breast cancer. In the early 1990s the Bush administration won friends in hitherto unexpected quarters after Mrs Bush published the memoirs of Millie, more pompously Mildred Kerr Bush, one of two springer spaniels belonging to the Bushes (the other was called Ranger). The Bushes' 1991 tax return showed *Millie's Story* had earned around $900,000. When George Bush was Vice-President, Barbara Bush published *C. Fred's Story*, the biography of another spaniel. It was during a tour by Mrs Bush of the USA to promote it that her husband was alleged to have had an affair with a secretary of his, a story bandied about during the 1992 re-election campaign by political opponents to show that the Republicans' support for family values was no greater than the Democrats'. (To which one might add that although there can have been no greater philanderer President than the Democrat John Kennedy, the only President actually to have been divorced — Reagan — has been a Republican, and the only President known with virtual certainty to have fathered an illegitimate child — Warren Harding — was a Republican too, for although the Democrat President Grover Cleveland gallantly accepted the paternity of his former mistress's child she was too friendly with too many other men for it to be certain the child was his.)

Even this doggy aspect of the presidency followed a precedent set by the British monarchy. In June 1910 Hodder & Stoughton published a book entitled *Where's Master?, by Caesar the King's Dog*, the king in question being Edward VII, who had recently died. It ran to at least nine editions in the next two months. Caesar, or at any rate his ghost, wrote "I've no history, I've no pedigree, I'm not highborn. But . . . he [the sovereign] didn't care how humble man or beast may be as long as they did their best and were faithful." As the present book shows, not all Presidents have been without pedigree by any means, even though, being politicians in a democracy, they have usually pretended otherwise. (If it comes to that Edward VII himself, like many American Presidents, was a curious mixture of breeding and vulgarity.) Perhaps not all Presidents have done their very best and kept the purest faith with their sovereign — the American people. Nevertheless, it is difficult to think of a President who has deliberately set out from the very start of his career to cheat the American people, though several have been less than straightforward once caught up in the pressure cooker of high politics. All in all, Caesar's words would make a good epigraph for the American presidency.

PREFACE

BY HUGH BROGAN

The presidency is so inextricably mixed up with American history, has both shaped and been shaped by it to such a degree, that no one can ever finish exploring all the ramifications. Nor is it easy to know where to start. Even the second article of the Constitution, which is the founding charter of the presidency, is too short and cryptic to be really helpful. It must be read by any student of the presidency; but it has to be read in conjunction with the rest of the Constitution, which raises a hundred more difficulties; and in itself is no more than a sketch which it has taken over 200 years to fill out.

The presidency is the child of the American Revolution, which began with the Stamp Act crisis in 1765 and ended in 1789 when General George Washington took the oath of office as first President. The Revolution was a complex movement; two aspects particularly concern us. The first is the overthrow of the authority of the British King and Parliament, the force which had previously served to provide some sort of common government for Americans; the second is the attempt to substitute for the British Empire an American Union of states. This Union was originally little more than an alliance of 13 rebel colonies, kept together chiefly by the need to fight Britain ("we must hang together or hang separately" said Benjamin Franklin), but it quickly became the settled view of almost all the revolutionaries that the gains of the Revolution — peace, freedom, republican government — would be jeopardized unless the Union was made permanent. There were plenty of issues for the newly independent states to quarrel about, even to the point of war; there must be some centralizing force to resolve them peaceably. Besides, there was already a feeling (arising largely out of the common sufferings and achievements of the Revolution) that state identities were now secondary, that a new American nation had come into being and needed expression in formal institutions. So the Union became a shibboleth; and a long search was begun for the appropriate instruments for perfecting it.

It is important to understand that there was no intention of abolishing the states. One or two voices suggested some such radical measure; but loyalty to the states was too strong for the majority to contemplate it for a moment. If the Union was one shibboleth, states' rights was another. The Constitution that eventually emerged was an attempt to combine the two principles. It succeeded remarkably well, until slavery brought on a collision. But even after the predominance of the Union had been established by Northern victory in the Civil War, the states continued, and continue, to exercise great powers, and to command powerful loyalty among their citizens.

The presidency, however, has from the beginning been the supreme embodiment of the Union. This was not altogether intended by the Founding Fathers, who drew up the Constitution in 1787 at Philadelphia. They laid it down that the President was to be chosen by an electoral college consisting of delegates chosen by each state in proportion to its representation in Congress (one elector for each Senator, one for each Congressman). Had the machinery worked as intended, the President would have been much more the creature of the states than of the nation. But from the first the electoral college has been little better than a fiction; its last moment of real importance was in 1888, when the popular vote went one way, the electoral vote the other. George Washington, every American's hero, was the first President (it is more than doubtful if the Fathers would have created such an office, a sort of modernized monarchy, if such an excellent candidate had not been there to fill it) and clearly owed nothing to the electoral college. The third presidential election, in 1796, was the first to be disputed. It might have been the moment for the electoral college to come into its own, but instead the electors were chosen by strict party competition, and were obliged to vote according to their party loyalties. Thus John Adams, the Federalist candidate, became the first partisan President. He was followed by three more, but by 1820 there were misleading signs that political parties were on the wane. In 1824 party lines were sufficiently confused to make a decision in the electoral college impossible, so the election was thrown into the House of Representatives, as laid down by the Constitution. It never happened again. The spread of universal white male suffrage meant that political party organizations were absolutely necessary if ambitious men were to be sure of getting the object of their desire (the presidency has always exerted a powerful pull on politicians' imaginations); successful party organizations were necessarily national. All presidential elections since 1828 have been partisan, and the victorious candidates have claimed a special authority because they express the will of the national majority.

But if they have had authority, they have not always exercised much power. The strength of the presidency has ebbed and flowed. It was strong between George Washington and Andrew Jackson, because each of the first seven Presidents (with the possible exception of Monroe) was a man of great personal prestige and ability. Even their failures did not diminish their office. A surprising amount of authority and power survived to cling to the weaker Presidents who followed Jackson, but they were hampered by the very instrument which elected them. The great political parties of those years, the Jacksonian Democrats and the Whigs, were enormous organisations, tightly disciplined for the battle for power. They contested not merely presidential, but congressional, state and local elections as well. To keep up the spirits of their members, and to pay for the vast expenses of electioneering, the public service was taken over. "To the victor the spoils!" proclaimed one of Jackson's followers, and thus gave the name to what was called the spoils system. By this, every election was followed, if the presidency changed hands, by a general expulsion of the losers from their official posts — in the Treasury, the State Department, the Post Office and so on — and their replacement by the winners, who enjoyed the official salaries until the next election. They had to pay over part of their wages to the party chest and work hard for the party candidates when required. It meant that elections were taken very seriously, but it also diminished the President's power in a vital respect. He was no longer able to choose his subordinates to please himself and his own ideas of what the public service required. Instead he had to consult the good of the party and in practice that meant consulting Congress.

It was no wonder then, that in the half century or so before the Civil War the powers of Congress tended to increase. It was above all in Congress that the great struggle over slavery was fought out before it transferred to the battlefield. Slavery was a relic of a past that most Americans wanted to put behind them, but to the Southern states it seemed indispensable both economically and as the only tolerable solution to the problem of race relations. Southern whites united increasingly in defence of the 'peculiar institution'. They imposed the Missouri Compromise of 1820, under which slavery, to be sure, would not be allowed to extend westward north of a line, but under which, also, every new free state admitted to the Union would have to be balanced by a slave state — Maine by Missouri, Michigan by Arkansas, and so on. In the 1830s Southerners were able to force a reduction in the national tariff by threatening either disobedience or rebellion otherwise; and in the last of the great compromises, that of 1850, they exacted a vigorous Fugitive Slave Law, which entitled them to go hunting slave runaways in the free states, in return for allowing California to enter the Union as a free state and some other points. These episodes were highly dramatic and increasingly fraught with the threat of disunion; it is noteworthy how marginal a part the Presidents played in each of them. Andrew Jackson, in 1832, issued a fierce proclamation and wanted to march an army into South Carolina to subdue that recalcitrant state, but the terms on which peace was made were actually hammered out in Congress. The parts played by other Presidents in other such crises were occasionally useful, seldom crucial.

When at last the slavery question got quite out of hand, when the question of whether the 'peculiar institution' would be allowed to spread onto what had always been 'free soil' generated, first, a small civil war in Kansas, and then an all-out war to preserve the sacred Union against Southern secessionists, then the presidency revived. This was the work partly of Abraham Lincoln but chiefly of circumstances. In time of war the President's power and authority always increase. Lincoln extended them both enormously. He was head of the government, head of the governing party, commander in chief, *de facto* (as well as by diplomatic courtesy) head of state. He embodied the American nation in its hour of greatest trial; its victory was his victory (and largely his work); his death was the nation's martyrdom; he gave the presidency an added aura which it has never quite lost. They say he haunts the White House; certainly his lying-in-state there made the presidential mansion, once and for all, the true shrine of each patriot's devotion.

The end of the war, the furious quarrels of Andrew Johnson's presidency, the scandals of Grant's, soon undid the work of Lincoln. The spoils system, now more flagrantly corrupt than ever, was at its height; the presidency was, if not at its lowest, certainly at something like it. The impeachment of Andrew Johnson, had it succeeded, might have emasculated the office for good, so that it became something like the presidency of the third French Republic; however it did not succeed. Nevertheless it was a long, slow business before the presidency regained its old strength. The Presidents of the late 19th century were honest men, but not of outstanding ability. Theodore Roosevelt, at the beginning of the 20th century, was able and exciting enough, and started the work both of modernizing the office and ending congressional ascendancy; but it took another war, in the time of Woodrow Wilson, to restore national leadership to the presidency. Even then there was a setback: Wilson endured shattering political defeat over the Treaty of Versailles (1919-20), and during the 1920s matters seemed to revert to their old fashion, with the question of tariff policy taking up most of the time of Congress, and the presidency sinking into second place again. The coming of the Great Depression put a stop to this tendency. Herbert Hoover was an active if unsuccessful President, founding such important executive agencies as the Reconstruction Finance Corporation. Franklin Roosevelt finally assured the ascendancy of the executive branch both by the policies he carried out during the Depression and by his conduct of World War II. After his death came the Cold War, which continued the strengthening of the presidency, largely because of the enormous military expenditure and ceaseless diplomatic activity it entailed. Some commentators, especially after the unpopular war in Vietnam, spoke of the Imperial Presidency. But the defeat in Vietnam and, even more, the miserable Watergate affair, produced a corrective. After 1975, with the replacement of Richard Nixon by Gerald Ford, the presidency seemed a much more humdrum job than for decades. Congress, to be sure, did not show itself capable of taking on the national leadership, but it seemed likely that only another great crisis (which nobody wanted) could restore the full measure of presidential authority.

The crisis, however, occurred sooner rather than later, but in thoroughly paradoxical fashion; Jimmy Carter's presidency was wrecked by the so-called hostage crisis, a ramification of the Iranian Revolution, and Carter was replaced by an immensely popular Republican, Ronald Reagan. The presidency resumed its ascendancy with astonishing completeness and speed, and it was not seriously weakened either by the Iran-Contra affair or by Reagan's retirement in 1989.

It should be clear from the foregoing that presidential powers, functions and actions are largely determined by circumstances outside presidential control: the state of the American economy, for example, or America's international involvements, or the strength (nowadays more usually the decrepitude) of the political parties. There is nevertheless at all times a wide sphere of presidential liberty, and having surveyed the whole line I am more than ever impressed by the wisdom of Woodrow Wilson's remark that "the President is at liberty to be as big a man as he can". The test of a President is his ability to master events. It is true that Abraham Lincoln once remarked "I claim not to have controlled events, but confess plainly that events have controlled me." But no student of the Civil War is going to take that remark at its face value. Lincoln meant by it chiefly that he had never acted except when it was necessary or inevitable; his policies were not lightly or wilfully adopted. The truth is that the presidency is above all a test of character, which Lincoln passed successfully. He had the courage and goodwill to face appalling challenges, the humility and intelligence to see them for what they were and react accordingly. No training, and no mere intellectual brilliance, let alone the cheap skills of day-to-day politics, will serve a President so well as these gifts of wisdom.

Unhappily character is not enough. My closing reflection is melancholy. There have been several Presidents of outstanding gifts — above all Herbert Hoover — who have failed because their gifts were inappropriate to the actual needs of the moment. In other words, there have been some undeservedly unlucky Presidents, just as there have been some undeservedly lucky ones (Calvin Coolidge). Napoleon always wanted to know of a general if he was lucky. It is depressing to think that such a quality as luck, so entirely outside human control, should matter so much, but it clearly does. The comfort is that in the worst crises the luck of the nation has taken over (the United States is a favourite of chance) and a Lincoln or a Roosevelt has seized the helm. The discomfort is that the crises have often been caused, or at any rate intensified, by inept Presidents. Every election to the office is a gamble. Happily, the Americans are a betting nation. There is no sign that they want a safer institution. The presidency will be with us for a long time yet.

Plate 2   George Washington, portrait by Rembrandt Peale 1795

GEORGE WASHINGTON

1732-99
1ST PRESIDENT OF THE UNITED STATES OF AMERICA
1789-97

Father of his Country. The hallowed phrase expresses everything that was unique about President Washington. For all other Presidents — even Thomas Jefferson — the office was the climax of their lives, their greatest opportunity for fame. Washington alone was greater than his post. He had to make decisions for the first time, and thus lay down guidelines for the future. He set the precedents that others would have to follow. His greatest precedent was himself. Without him there might not have been a presidency at all. The Founding Fathers might have settled for some form of collective leadership or cabinet government. And then, although he had a characteristically modest idea of what the President should be and do, the fact that their great man had found the job worth undertaking enhanced its value in the eyes of all Americans. The fact that he did it so well reinforced the effect, by showing that there would always be some useful work for an honourably ambitious President. Washington, in short, created the presidency in his own image, and handed it on, a precious burden, to his successors, as perhaps his greatest memorial.

He was a remarkable man, but even he could not have done so much if the times had not favoured him. His countrymen desperately needed a hero. In the dark days of the Revolutionary War (and for most of the time they were very dark) only the inflexible figure of General Washington offered any hope. Benjamin Franklin might be having his diplomatic triumphs as the American representative in Paris, but Paris was a long way away. The General was near at hand, visibly struggling with his country's foes, not only the British; he also had to deal with traitors; with mutinous, ill-trained, ill-disciplined troops; with a dilatory Congress; corrupt suppliers; and, worst of all, with incredibly short-sighted, mean, incompetent state legislatures which were, nevertheless, his source of pay and supplies. Groaning inwardly, Washington stood firm, and in due course had his reward, when the British surrendered at Yorktown. That was the turning point, although the war dragged on for another two years. In 1783 Washington returned to New York in triumph, thus blotting out the memory of his rapid retreat from the city in 1776. Then he lost no time in resigning his commission and hurrying home to Virginia; but his glory followed him. He had given the Americans faith in themselves, and notably justified it. They could not forget him. He was inevitably recalled to be the first head of the new government.

His achievements as President did nothing to diminish his fame in the long run, although for a few years party warfare did not spare even his great name. His first cabinet was one of the strongest in American history, with John Adams as Vice-President, Alexander Hamilton as Secretary of the Treasury, and Thomas Jefferson as Secretary of State (dealing with foreign affairs). Over the full eight years of Washington's two terms in office Adams was perhaps the most useful to him of these men, sharing as he did Washington's straightforward patriotism and personal loyalty, as well as his strong common sense. But Hamilton and Jefferson left the greater mark, Hamilton especially, pushing through Congress a series of measures, such as a national tariff and a national bank, which tended to strengthen the financial credit, and therefore the political institutions of the United States. Unfortunately, Hamilton and Jefferson were devoted enemies, both personal and ideological, and it was more than Washington could do to prevent them from eventually running off to lead opposing political parties — the Federalists and the Republicans. The wonder is that he was able to put off the break for so long. Jefferson did not resign until 1793, Hamilton until 1795. Forced to choose, Washington backed Hamilton, as the more conservative of the two, and because he believed in Hamilton's vision of America as a great power, rich as well as republican (Jefferson called him senile for his pains). But he understood very well that the United States also needed Jefferson's vision of democracy. It is a pity that the two rivals lacked his breadth of view.

Then there was the great crisis of the French Revolutionary wars. From America these looked to be merely the latest in the long series of struggles between the national ally, France, and the national enemy, Britain. France had purged herself of the sin of monarchy, while Britain had not. So there was much enthusiasm for the French cause, not altogether dampened by news of the Jacobin Reign of Terror of 1793-94, and the so-called 'Citizen' Genet was sent to America as a French emissary to exploit it. The British had not helped themselves by refusing to carry out all the provisions of the 1783 peace treaty: in particular, they still occupied a string of forts (among them Detroit) in the American North-West, and their blockade of French ports seriously interfered with US commerce.

Nonetheless, it was clear to Washington, Jefferson and the cabinet that strict neutrality was the country's best course, and the President stuck to this view even when others began to drift away from it. Neutrality during a war on the Atlantic did not protect American shipping against British interference, but participation in the war would injure it far more. The country would not be united whichever side was chosen, and in many ways it had scarcely recovered from the Revolutionary War. Finally, what did it matter to America which side won? The ideological claims of both belligerents were bogus: they were quarrelling over power, not principle. Let America then stay at peace.

With this in mind, Washington opened negotiations with Great Britain for the settlement of outstanding differences; the result was Jay's Treaty (1794). Britain conceded as little as possible to the US; but it did agree to move its troops from American soil. After anguished hesitation, Washington sent the treaty to the Senate for ratification, and after a sharp struggle it was passed by a just-sufficient majority. It was perhaps the hardest battle of his career; Federalists and Republicans used the episode to further their own ambitions, which the President regarded with deep distaste. But today nobody seriously questions his action.

Knowledge of this might have comforted him; as it was, beneath a marble exterior he was a sensitive man and suffered deeply under the responsibilities, controversies and denunciations that went with his office. His inner life became one of dignified discontent. It is hard not to pity him. Undoubtedly as a young man he had been ambitious for wealth, fame and power. In this he was like the other two most successful soldiers of the age, Napoleon Bonaparte and Arthur Wellesley. But whereas the path before the future Duke of Wellington was clear, and suited his temperament exactly, and whereas Napoleon found in a revolutionary age the perfect opportunity for his stormy genius, Washington, their inferior as a general but their superior as a statesman, had to subdue himself ruthlessly to a not altogether congenial environment. He had to swallow the humiliation of rejection when, as a young officer of volunteers, he applied for a regular commission in the British army; he had to apply himself doggedly to farming in Virginia for 20 years, earnestly studying to avoid the bankruptcy with which exhausted soil and expensive tastes threatened all the great tobacco planters; as General, he had to control his hot temper for eight years when dealing with the difficulties, mostly human, already mentioned; and as President he had to do all he could to avoid the imputation that he was an autocrat with monarchical ambitions. If he had not been a good man as well as a great one, the strain would have been too much for him, and he would either have left his fellow citizens to look after themselves or indulged in ambitious plotting. As it was, he reminded himself of his duty, and soldiered on.

Plate 3   George Washington with family: l-r George Custis (step-grandson), the 1st President,
Nellie Custis (younger step-granddaughter), Martha Washington and an attendant William Lee;
a plan of the new capital city of Washington is on the table before them

But he really only enjoyed life at his beloved Mount Vernon, his beautiful plantation above the River Potomac. In Philadelphia, where the capital of the United States was established during most of his time, it was all labour and keeping up appearances. His idea of how the President of the United States should appear was austerely grand. He went everywhere in coach and horses; he wore rich black clothes; he held levees, like George III; and he gave formal dinner parties of stupefying boredom. Washington himself had no small talk, and his wife Martha, though a cheerful soul, was as dull as her husband seemed. Besides, the President was always in agony from his false teeth. His real ones had long since started to fall out and for years he had been struggling without much success to get satisfactory substitutes. He possessed two sets made partly of hippopotamus ivory, which he tried to preserve by soaking in port wine when not in use. It was in these circumstances that the most famous portraits of him were painted by Gilbert Stuart. One at least of them is a masterpiece, but it does not do justice either to Washington's character or to his appearance in his prime. Instead it shows brilliantly what he felt like during his presidency.

By 1796 he had had enough. Besides, if he agreed to serve for another term he might well die in office, and then there was a risk that the presidency would become an office always held for life, which was scarcely desirable. He would set his last precedent, and retire after two terms. He got into his coach and drove down to Congress with a personal message — his Farewell Address. This had been written up from his suggestions by Alexander Hamilton, but it was Washington's own long-pondered thought, and he had revised it carefully. Earnestly he adjured his countrymen to maintain the union of the states, to respect the Constitution, check party spirit and the encroachments of government on liberty, follow an honest and frugal policy of public expenditure and steer clear of the wiles of foreign

Plate 4   The Death of Washington,
painted by J. Mortimer Lichtenauer for the Bicentennial Washington Celebration 1932

powers. Then he said good-bye, anticipating, as he put it, a happy retirement while enjoying the benign influence of good laws under a free government. He waited impatiently for the day of his release, and when, in March 1797, his successor John Adams took the oath of office, he rode thankfully back to Mount Vernon, with an air, as Adams noted, of triumph, as if to say "Ay! I am fairly out and you fairly in! See which of us is the happiest!"

GEORGE WASHINGTON'S FAMILY

"Washington came of very good blood — aw, quite good — I b'lieve."
Attributed by his classmates to Amory Blaine in F. Scott Fitzgerald's *This Side of Paradise*

The Washingtons are of unusual antiquity in European terms, let alone American ones. A direct male ancestry has been traced back to William de Wessington or Wessyngton (*i.e.*, Washington, a town in Tyne and Wear, formerly County Durham, in northern England), who was living in the late 12th century. The remoter ancestry is not absolutely certain but a detailed argument has been put forward for William de Wessington's descent in the male line from Eochu Mugmedon, High King of Ireland in the mid-4th century, through his son Niall of the Nine Hostages. Niall reigned as King of Ireland at a time when the Romans had not yet gone home to Italy from across the water in Britain. Indeed he may have been the Irish king who waged war on Stilicho, father-in-law of the Emperor Honorius who was the last Roman ruler of Britain. From Eochu and Niall descend the O'Neills, the oldest family traceable in the male line in Europe. If the link between William de Wessington and Eochu is accepted, it makes

Washington the first of many American Presidents with direct male line Irish ancestry, though he must have been the only one not to boast about it to win votes.

In 1264 William de Wessington's grandson (or conceivably son) Sir Walter de Washington fought on King Henry III's side against Simon de Montfort at the battle of Lewes, where he was killed. So far George Washington's ancestors had been the senior male line, but after Sir Walter's son they descend through a junior branch. This branch seems to have maintained the family loyalty to the kings of England. Robert, Sir Walter's grandson, chose as his wife Joan de Stirkeland, a member of a north country family who have supplied several sheriffs of their county, a deputy lieutenant of their county, the bearer of the banner of St George at the Battle of Agincourt during the Hundred Years War against the French and a leader of a royalist infantry regiment at the Battle of Edgehill in the Civil War of the 17th century.

Despite their marrying several heiresses this junior branch of Washingtons could not arrest the decline over the next two centuries of their own younger sons — and George Washington's recent ancestors descended from a younger branch of a younger branch. By the mid-16th century this junior branch of Washingtons was settled at Sulgrave in the English Midland county of Northamptonshire. Even now they enjoyed the status of lesser gentry (Robert Washington in 1584 inherited 1,250 acres, a respectable property). George Washington, however, descends from a fifth son of Lawrence Washington, who predeceased his father, the Robert who had inherited 1,250 acres, after having sold the bulk of the estate at Sulgrave in 1605, perhaps under some financial pressure. This fifth son became a parson but was expelled from his parish as a royalist by the Parliamentarians during the Civil War. It was therefore understandable that the parson's son Colonel John Washington should emigrate to America. There he eventually acquired 6,000 acres (including 700 as his wife's dowry), which was more than respectable by English standards.

Colonel John's son Captain Lawrence Washington, as High Sheriff in Virginia in 1692, continued the long family tradition of supporting the Crown, albeit in an American context. He married Mildred Warner, granddaughter of a one-time acting governor of Virginia and a descendant of the medieval Lords Kyme, whose loyalty to their king was not always total. It would be downright fanciful to trace George Washington's disaffection toward the Hanoverian George III to a remote ancestor's quarrels with the Plantagenets. Yet the link between Washington and Plantagenet high politics was not as tenuous as might be supposed. Because of the vagaries of English peerage law Washington was a potential heir to the Kyme title, which had become abeyant (very roughly, fallen into disuse) in 1381. He was almost certainly not aware of this, although since he remained technically King George's subject till the Treaty of Paris in 1783 (and certainly till the end of 1775, when two thirds of his life was over) and titles of nobility were only dropped in the United States in 1795 after some discussion as to whether to introduce native American ones, the historical might-have-beens are intriguing to say the least.

Captain Lawrence Washington died when his son Augustine was only three, whereupon Augustine's mother, Mildred, remarried. Her new husband, George Gale, was from the northwestern English county of Cumberland and took the family back to England. When Mildred died in childbirth a year later Gale took over the care of her three children by Captain Lawrence Washington. Mildred had left Gale £1,000 but the Washingtons contested her will, claiming she had alienated Washington property. As a result the children were awarded to the care of a cousin on their father's side, John Washington, and returned to America.

Augustine died when his son George was only 11 and the boy spent the next six or so years, some of them at Mount Vernon, with relatives. The Mount Vernon estate at this time belonged to his elder half-brother Lawrence, whom George greatly admired, for Lawrence had been educated in England and had acquired what the 18th century called an easy address (i.e., geniality), together with graceful manners. Lawrence eventually willed the estate to George. (Augustine had left over 10,000 acres altogether.) In Virginia the English system of entail was widespread. Entail allowed estates to be kept whole by being passed to a single heir, usually the eldest male, at the expense of younger sons and females. It was only abolished after the Revolution (by Thomas Jefferson as it happened). Lawrence had married a cousin of the Lords Fairfax, who owned large estates in Virginia, and his father-in-law Colonel William Fairfax was a powerful influence on the young George Washington. Lawrence's half-sister-in-law married George Washington's cousin Warner Washington and Sally Cary, the great love of George's youth, married Mrs Lawrence Washington's eldest brother George William Fairfax. Strong links therefore developed between the Fairfaxes and Washingtons (which were confirmed a generation later when Warner's daughter Louisa married the 9th Lord Fairfax). It was through these links that George Washington in 1748 took part in a survey of the Fairfax lands in Virginia.

In an age when 'interest' (*i.e.*, personal influence) was virtually a necessity to get a young man a start in life, that of a nobleman like Lord Fairfax counted for much. It could have led to a naval career for Washington but his mother was highly possessive right up to her death in 1789 and her anguish at the prospect of his leaving her made it out of the question. He did take a brief voyage, however. When Lawrence went to Barbados for the sake of his health in 1751 George accompanied him. There he caught small-pox, but survived and was subsequently immune to the disease. This was a considerable blessing for the United States since small-pox was one of the chief scourges of the troops in the Revolutionary War.

When, a few years after the end of that war, the young republic's new, stronger form of government was set up, Washington could probably have assumed the Crown if he had wanted. Given his ancestry, character and military reputation, he would have been an ideal candidate. But the times were not auspicious for hereditary monarchy. Indeed the particular year in which the presidency was inaugurated — 1789 — saw the beginning of the French Revolution, after which kings could never feel wholly safe on their thrones again. America's transition from a number of colonies over which a king ruled, however distantly, to an independent republic involved one or two little awkwardnesses. For instance, although the US Constitution was remarkably well designed and Washington as near an ideal first President as one could hope for, protocol problems cropped up, such as how to address the new President. The Senate deliberated and suggested 'His Highness, the president of the United States of America, and Protector of their Liberties'. (Oliver Cromwell when Protector of England had also been addressed as 'His Highness'.) It never caught on, but that didn't prevent numerous citizens over the next century writing to the President as "His Majesty", "His Lordship" or "His Excellency", as President Benjamin Harrison testifies in his book on the presidency.

In a republic the President's name may live on after him but his family are more likely than royalty to sink into obscurity. The proof of this is that the most famous other Washington, Booker T., is no relation. But George Washington's nephew Bushrod Washington was an associate justice of the Supreme Court from 1798 to 1829 when that institution was at perhaps its greatest importance in shaping the young republic. He was considered to have a slow mind and he may also have had poor judgement in worldly matters (he was enthusiastic about the Society of the Cincinnati in correspondence with his famous uncle). But he made up for that with the clarity of his legal judgements. His uncle bequeathed Bushrod his library and personal papers. Eventually (after Martha's death) Bushrod inherited Mount Vernon itself. He oversaw preparation of John Marshall's five-volume work *The Life of Washington* (1804-7). Another nephew, George Augustine Washington, son of the 1st President's younger brother Charles by a cousin, Mildred Thornton, managed the Mount Vernon estate during his uncle's first term as President. He married Martha Washington's favourite niece, Fanny Bassett, but died in 1793, whereupon George Washington invited Fanny to stay on at Mount Vernon. He also offered to educate their eldest surviving son, George Fayette Washington. When the Whiskey Rebellion erupted in 1794 and Washington called out the militia to suppress it, five of his Washington nephews served in the Virginia contingent. Of these nephews Colonel William A. Washington, the older surviving son of

*Plate 5 George Washington's mother Mary Ball,
from the original painting by Captain Charles Middleton*

*Plate 6 George Washington's wife Martha
Dandridge, from an engraving in Jared Sparks's*
Life of Washington, *after a painting by John
Wollaston (d 1770)*

*Plate 7 Martha Dandridge Custis Washington
when older*

George's younger brother Austin, showed more than ordinary military talent. President Monroe in his autobiography mentions William Washington as having shown promise as early in the Revolutionary War as 1776, when he was chosen to lead the attack on Trenton. Monroe served as his lieutenant on that occasion and took over the command when William Washington was badly wounded. In December 1780 William Washington tricked a loyalist detachment in South Carolina into surrendering by the use of what was called a 'Quaker gun' — a log balanced on three of its branches to resemble artillery.

George Washington's marriage to Martha Dandridge Custis ultimately brought him outright possession of about $100,000, making him one of the richest men in the American colonies (he died owning over 33,000 acres and was worth about $500,000). At that time a married woman had no independent property rights, even though she might have been married before and have children by her first husband. It was a system that might have been designed to encourage avaricious stepfathers but Washington was no Mr Murdstone: he had considerable affection for his step-children, and the death aged 18 of the youngest, Patsy, particularly saddened him, even though her considerable property now passed to her mother and therefore to Washington himself. His stepson John Custis, Martha's spoiled favourite and an intractable puppy who shirked military service during the Revolutionary War as well as cheating his stepfather of various small sums, had a seventh and youngest child, George Washington Parke Custis, who was the author of a book, *Recollections and Private Memoirs of Washington* (1861). It is rich in traditional stories about Washington but not necessarily accurate. Other biographies of Washington include one by President Woodrow Wilson — stigmatized as silly by a recent scholarly study — and one by Henry Cabot Lodge, friend of President Theodore Roosevelt and a member of the famous Boston Brahmin family. George Custis's daughter Anna married the Confederate commander Robert E. Lee, whose father, General 'Light Horse Harry' Lee, composed the encomium on Washington "First in war, first in peace, first in the hearts of his countrymen".

BIOGRAPHICAL DETAILS

WASHINGTON, GEORGE, *b* Pope's Creek, Westmoreland Co, Va., 22 Feb 1732 (11 Feb 1731/2 Julian Calendar); *educ* as surveyor (surveyor's licence from William and Mary College 1749); Official Surveyor Culpeper Co, Va., 1749, military: Adj-Gen Virginia (with rank of Maj) 1752, Lt-Col Virginia Regt 1754 (resigned commission 5 Nov when offered captaincy on Virginia Regt's being split up into companies), ADC to Maj-Gen Edward Braddock (Cdr British Forces America) and Col Virginia Regt and C-in-C Virginia forces 1755 (resigned commission 1758), Commanding Gen Continental Army 1775-83 (Lt-Gen 1780), V-Adml of France 1780, Lt-Gen and C-in-C of All the Armies of the United States 1798, civil: Memb House of Burgesses, Virginia Assembly, for Fredericksburg Co 1759, JP Fairfax Co, Va., 1770, Delegate Williamsburg Convention 1773, Memb 1st Virginia Provincial Convention 1774, Virginia Delegate 1st Continental Congress 1774 (also attended 2nd Continental Congress 1775 as Virginia Delegate), Virginia Delegate to proposed convention of States 1787, Pres Federal Convention 1787, Congressional Medal (for capturing Boston) 1776, Hon Dr of Laws: Harvard 1776, Yale 1781, Pennsylvania U 1783, Washington Coll (Chesterton, Md.) 1789, Brown U 1790, Chllr William and Mary College (Williamsburg, Va.) 1788, 1st Pres-Gen Soc of Cincinnati 1783, Pres Potomac Company (Alexandria, Va.) 1785, 1st President of the USA 1789-97, author: *The Journal of Major John Washington* (1754); *m* New Kent Co, Va., 6 Jan 1759 Martha (*b* New Kent Co 21 June 1731; *d* Mount Vernon 22 May 1802, *bur* there), est dau of Col John Dandridge, of New Kent Co, and his *w* Frances (dau of Orlando Jones) and widow of Col Daniel Parke Custis (by whom she was mother, together with other issue, of John (Jack) Parke Custis (1754-81); *m* 1774 Nelly, dau of Benedict Calvert, himself illegitimate *s* of 6th Baron Baltimore (*see* BURKE'S PEERAGE & BARONETAGE, Eden, section entitled Eden, Bart, of Maryland) and was father of, with other issue, a dau Elizabeth, who *m* Thomas Law, bro of 1st Baron Ellenborough (*see* BURKE'S PEERAGE & BARONETAGE), and another dau, Nelly, for whom *see* the section Washington Male Line Ancestry and Collateral Descendants); President Washington *d* Mount Vernon 14 Dec 1799 of pneumonia (*bur* there 18 Dec), leaving no issue

MALE LINE ANCESTRY AND COLLATERAL DESCENDANTS

Note: Sources for George Washington's male line ancestry before 1600 are highly contradictory and confused and for the 17th and 18th centuries only somewhat less so. The following account represents a synthesis of the most authoritative and latest findings.

DUNCAN, Lay Abbot (*i.e.*, protector of the Abbey) of Dunkeld (to the north of Perth in what subsequently became the Scottish county of Perthshire); *k* at the battle of Duncrub, in which Duff, eldest son of MALCOLM I King of Scots, defeated Colin, representative of the rival royal line of Aodh, *c* 965. Duncan the Lay Abbot, who was an adherent of Colin's, is believed to descend from the Cenél Conaill (the collective name for the descendants of Niall of the Nine Hostages by Niall's fifth son Conall Gulban, King of Tír Conaill — otherwise the 'Land of Conall', subsequently Tyrconnell or roughly what is now called Donegal in northwest Ireland). Niall was King of Ireland and was living in the year 400. He was son of Eochu, High King of Ireland (living 360), and his wife Carina, an Ancient Briton princess (*see* BURKE'S PEERAGE & BARONETAGE, O'Neill). DUNCAN the Lay Abbot's est s:

DUNCAN, Lord and Mormaor (a Gaelic word meaning high steward) of Athole (modern Atholl, north-northwest of Dunkeld), was also Lay Abbot of Dunkeld; commanded the Scottish left wing at the battle of Luncarty (*c* 990), where the Danes were so crushingly defeated that their raids on that part of what subsequently became Perthshire, hitherto periodic and devastating, were terminated. He had three s:

I CRINAN, for whom *see below*

II Grim, Thane (hereditary tenant of the Crown) of Strathearn (west of Perth) and Baillie (a functionary with judicial powers) of Dule; *k* 1010 at the battle of Mortlach, where MALCOLM II King of Scots (reigned 1005-34) defeated the invading Norsemen

III Duncan, ancestor of the Irvings of Dumfries and Forbes Irvines of Drum

The est s,

CRINAN, Mormaor of Athole, Lay Abbot of Dunkeld and Steward of the Western Isles (what are now known as the Hebrides); *m c* 1000 Bethoc, er dau of King MALCOLM II (*see above*) and was *k* 1045 in battle against MACBETH (the historic figure who murdered Crinan's er s, King DUNCAN I, and subsequently is portrayed as having usurped the Scottish throne, most famously by Shakespeare), leaving issue:

I DUNCAN I The Gracious, King of Scots 1034-40, King of Strathclyde 1018-34

II MALDRED, Lord of Allerdale, Regent of the Kingdom of Strathclyde 1034-45, for whom *see below*

The er s,

DUNCAN I, *b c* 1001; *m c* 1030 Sibylla, dau of Bjorn Bearsson (probably also f or gf of Siward Earl of Northumbria, who eventually defeated MACBETH, paving the way for the restoration of the line of Duncan to the Scottish throne), succeeded to his gf's throne on the latter's death in 1034 and was murdered at Bothnagowan (modern Pitgaveny), nr Elgin, northeast Scotland, 14 Aug 1040 (*bur* isle of Iona, 30 miles west of Oban, western Scotland), leaving issue:

I MALCOLM III Canmore ('Great Chief'), King of Scots 1058-93, *b c* 1031; *m* 1st *c* 1059 Ingibrorg (*d* before 1070), widow of Thorfin (gs through his mother of MALCOLM II, King of Scots), Jarl (a noble Scandinavian rank, forerunner of the word Earl) of Orkney and Earl of Caithness; Ingibrorg was dau of Finn Arnason, Jarl of Halland, and his w Bergljot (herself dau of Halfdan Sigurdsson, half-bro of OLAV II 'The Fat', Saint and King of Norway); MALCOLM III and Ingibrorg had (with other issue):

  1 DUNCAN II, King of Scots May-Nov 1094, *b c* 1060; *m c* 1090 his 2nd cousin Æthelreda, dau of Gospatric (I) (*see below*), and was murdered 12 Nov 1094, leaving issue (*see below*)

I (cont.) MALCOLM III *m* 2nd Dunfermline 1070 Margaret (*b* probably in Hungary *c* 1045; *d* Edinburgh Castle 16 Nov 1093), Saint (canonized by INNOCENT IV 1250; feast day 10 June, changed to 8 July in 1584, then back to 10 June in 1693 by INNOCENT XII at request of the exiled JAMES II (and VII) to mark birthday of his s, the titular James III (and VIII), the Old Pretender) and dau of Edward Atheling (s of EDMUND II 'Ironside', King of England) and Edward's w Agatha, niece of the Holy Roman Emperor HENRY II. MALCOLM III was *k* on a raid into Northumberland at Alnwick 13 Nov 1093. By his 2nd w he left (with other issue):

  2 EDGAR, King of Scots 1097-1107   3 ALEXANDER I 'The Fierce', King of Scots 1107-24

  4 DAVID I, Saint and King of Scots 1124-53

  1 Edith, later known as Matilda, *b* Dunfermline 1079; *m* Westminster Abbey 11 Nov 1100, as his 1st w, HENRY I, King of England, and *d* 1 May 1118, having had issue:

    (1) William, Duke of Normandy; drowned young in the wreck of the White Ship 1120   (2) Richard; *d* with his er bro
    (1) MATILDA, Lady of the English, *b c* 1102; *m* 1st 1114 The Holy Roman Emperor HENRY IV (*d* 1125); *m* 2nd 1127 Geoffrey Plantagenet, Count of Anjou and Maine, through whom she was ancestress of the Plantagenet Dynasty together with their successors as rulers of England the Houses of Tudor, Stuart, Hanover, Saxe-Coburg and Gotha, and Windsor

II DONALD III Ban (perhaps Bán, meaning 'white', *i.e.*, that he lived to a hoary old age) or Bane ('murderer' — there is a suggestion that he killed his grandfather), King of Scots 1093-94 and 1094-97, succeeded his er bro MALCOLM III

DUNCAN I's yr bro,

MALDRED, Lord of Allerdale etc, *m* Ealdgyth or Aldgyth, dau of Ughtred or Uchtred Earl of Northumberland or Northumbria and Ughtred's 3rd w Elgiva or Ælfgifu, herself dau of ETHELRED II 'The Unready', King of England 979-1013 and 1014-16; Maldred and Ealdgyth had issue:

I GOSPATRIC (I), for whom *see below*
II Maldred, ancestor of the Nevills, Marquesses of Abergavenny (*see* BURKE'S PEERAGE & BARONETAGE)

The er s,

GOSPATRIC (I), *b* 1040-48; installed 1068/9 by WILLIAM I The CONQUEROR, King of England, as Earl (then still predominantly an administrative post) of Northumberland after his payment of a heavy fine or what would now be thought of as an entrance fee (though his hereditary claim through his maternal gf also played a part), later (Oct or Nov 1072) deprived of the earldom on a charge of having taken part in a massacre at Durham; fled to Scotland, where his cousin MALCOLM III granted him the Mormaorship of Dunbar; *m* ——, sister of one Edmund; *d* and *bur* Ubbanford (modern Norham, Northumberland, on the border with Scotland) *c* 1075, leaving (with several other daus):

I Dolfin (son)   II Waltheof, living *c* 1126; *m* Sigrid   III GOSPATRIC (II), for whom *see below*
I Æthelreda, *m c* 1090 DUNCAN II, King of Scots

The 3rd s,

GOSPATRIC (II), known to have been living *c* 1115, when he was a signatory to the Charter of Scone by which the Abbey of Scone was founded, generally accounted 1st Earl of Dunbar (as opposed to his f, also Gospatric (*see above*), who is thought to have lived at a time before the emergence of earldoms, although he is referred to in a monumental inscription as "Gospatric Comes" — *Comes* being the Latin for Count, the Continental European equivalent of Earl); *m* —— and was *k* fighting against the English at the battle of the Standard (nr Northallerton, N Yorks) 23 Aug 1138, having had 2 s:

I Alan; *d* after 16 Aug 1139 without surviving male issue
II GOSPATRIC (III); may have been illegitimate but was recognized as (2nd) Earl of Dunbar; *m* Derdere and *d* between 1156 and 1166, having had at least one s, Waltheof, who is said by some sources to have *d* without male issue before 1200, but by others to have exercised the functions of (3rd) Earl of Dunbar, married Aline (*d* 20 Aug 1179) and died 1182, leaving a s Patrick, (4th) Earl of Dunbar

The late George Sydney Horace Lee Washington, a cousin several times removed of the 1st President of the USA, has argued for a blood link between Gospatric (III) and one William de Hertburn, who Mr Washington has suggested was probably another son of Gospatric (III) and who *c* 1182 acquired the manor of Wessyngton, Wessington or Washington, Co Durham. William de Hertburn was undoubtedly an ancestor of the Washington family. To support his argument Mr G. S. H. L. Washington points out that William de Hertburn, who is also referred to as William de Wessington or Washington (he will henceforth be called William (I) de Washington), also owned the adjacent manor of Offerton, whose previous lord had been a Sir Patric. Mr Washington identifies Sir Patric with Patric of Dunbar, *i.e.*, Gospatric (III), 2nd Earl of Dunbar. Again, William de Washington's grandson Sir Walter de Washington bore as his coat of arms not the celebrated bars and molets which George Washington 1st President of the USA employed as a bookplate, but the Dunbar lion 'differenced' (*i.e.*, with a slight modification to signify such circumstances as its being used by a younger branch of the family, as may have been the case here).

William (I) de WASHINGTON, thought to be a s of Gospatric, 2nd Earl of Dunbar, *d* in or after 1220, having had issue:

I Walter, predeceased his father, leaving no issue, *c* 1210
II William (II) de WASHINGTON; inherited his father's manor of Washington; *m* 1211 Alice de Lexington and *d* in or after 1239, leaving issue:

1 Sir Walter (I) de WASHINGTON, for whom *see below*
2 Robert (I) de WASHINGTON (but possibly identical with Robert (II) de WASHINGTON, for whom *see below*), mentioned in Plea Rolls as holding Routhworth from the barony (at this time a feudal territorial entity, with no suggestion of any representation as a lord of Parliament) of Kendal 1278

William (II) de Washington's er(?) s,

Sir Walter (I) de WASHINGTON, *b c* 1212 (but according to Mr G. S. H. L. Washington the s of William (I) de Washington, not of William (II)); inherited manor of Washington; *m* Joan or Juliana (*d* in or after 1266), dau of Sir Robert de Whitchester and sister and heiress of Sir Roger de Whitchester, Keeper of the Rolls and Canon of St Paul's Cathedral in London, and in right of his wife came into possession of landed property in Northumberland; a seal of his shows the Dunbar arms of *Argent, a lion rampant Gules, over all a bend compony Argent and Azure*, which has been held to be yet another piece of evidence supporting the theory of a family link between the Earls of Dunbar and the Washingtons; Sir Walter (I) was *k* in battle 14 May 1264, leaving (with four other s and three daus):

Sir William (III) de WASHINGTON; inherited manor of Washington; *m* Margaret, sister and co-heiress of Sir Robert de Morville, of Helton Flecket, Westmorland, and *d* between 1288 and 1290, leaving (with other issue) a yr s:

Robert (II) de WASHINGTON (according to Mr G. S. H. L. Washington the s not of Sir William (III) de Washington but of William (II) de Washington and a third s rather than yr s); acquired as well as Routhworth (*see above*) a moiety of the manor of Carnforth, Lancashire; MP for Westmorland 1300; *m* 1st Amice, by whom he had no children and who *d* 12——; *m* 2nd 1292 Joan, dau of Sir William de Stirkeland or Strickland, of Sizergh Castle, Westmorland, and his *w* Elizabeth, dau and heiress of Ralph Deincourt, and *d* 1324, leaving issue:

Robert (III) de WASHINGTON (according to Mr G. S. H. L. Washington it was this Robert who was MP for Westmorland in 1320 and *m* Joan de Stirkeland); *m* Agnes, only dau and heiress of Ranulf le Gentyl, and *d* between 1346 and 1348, leaving issue:

I Robert (IV) de WASHINGTON; witness 1386 for Sir Robert Le Grosvenor in the quarrel between the latter and Lord Scrope of Bolton as to which of them was entitled to bear the coat of arms *Azure, a bend Or* (*see* BURKE'S PEERAGE & BARONETAGE, Westminster). It has been suggested that from Robert (IV) descended a line of Washingtons who in the person of one James Washington migrated about the end of the 17th century to the Continent of Europe:

1 One branch is said to have settled at Rotterdam in the Netherlands, becoming extinct in the male line with Captain Jacob Washington, of the Royal Dutch Navy, who *d* 1845 in the East Indies.

2 Another line, stemming also from James Washington, apparently settled in southern Germany and Austria. According to this claim, James Washington (*see* preceding para.) had as gs William or James Washington. Certainly a James Washington, of a family of English origin, was *b* 1778 and served Kings MAXIMILIAN and LUDWIG I of Bavaria as Hofmarschall (Marshal of the Court) and aide-de-camp and as Lt-Gen in the Bavarian Army. This James von Washington, as Bavarian envoy, brought to a conclusion the treaty between Britain and Bavaria which was signed 7 June 1815 at Brussels (the Duke of Wellington representing Britain). He was raised to the rank of *Freiherr* (Baron) 8 Dec 1830 by LUDWIG I, acquired the Lordship of Notzing, Upper Bavaria, and was decorated with the Order of the Bavarian Crown, the Greek Order of the Saviour and the French Legion of Honour. On 12 July 1843 a Lt-Gen William von Washington, in the service of the King of Bavaria, was created an honorary Knight Commander of the Order of the Bath by Queen VICTORIA. It is assumed that this William and James were one and the same. Baron von Washington *d* Munich 5 Aug 1848, leaving issue:

(1) Maximilian Emanuel, 2nd Baron von Washington, *b* Notzing 2 Aug 1829; *m* at Rastede 15 Aug 1855 Her Highness Duchess Friederike of Oldenburg (*b* Oldenburg 8 June 1820; *d* Pöls, nr Graz, Styria, Austria, 20 March 1891), yr dau of HRH AUGUST, Grand Duke of Oldenburg (reigned 1829-53), by his 1st *w* Adelheid, 2nd dau of VIKTOR II Prince of Anhalt-Bernburg-Schaumburg and his *w* Princess Amalie of Nassau-Weilburg; HH Duchess Friederike was a 1st cousin twice removed of Princess Mary of Teck, who *m* King GEORGE V of Great Britain and Ireland; Baron (Maximilian Emanuel) von Washington *d* Graz 3 July 1903, leaving issue:

1a George, 3rd Baron von Washington, *b* Schloss Pöls, Graz, 31 July 1856; Cavalry Capt (ret before 1914), Hon Kt Prussian Order of St John; *m* Pöls 27 March 1883 Countess Gisela (*d* Pöls 1 July 1913), dau of Count Vincenz Welser von Welserheimb, and *d* 1929 without issue

(2) Baron Karl von Washington, *b* Notzing 27 Oct 1833; Royal Bavarian Chamberlain and Lt-Col; *m* at Gries bei Bozen 18 April 1893 Countess Marie, dau of Theobald, Count (of the Holy Roman Empire, created 1681; of Bavaria 1812) Butler von Clonebough (of a cadet branch of the Anglo-Norman Butlers settled in Ireland from the 12th century, who at various times have been Earls, Marquesses and Dukes of Ormonde), and *d* before 1929 without issue

II A son

III John (I) de WASHINGTON, *m* 1st 1363 Eleanor or Alina (*d* 1370), *née* Garnet, widow of Sir William de Lancaster, of Howgill, Westmorland; *m* 2nd 1382 Joan, dau and heiress of John de Croft, of Tewitfield in Warton (north of Lancaster), Lancashire, and *d* 1407/8; by his 2nd *w* (who *m* 2nd her cousin Sir John de Croft) he had a *s*, John (II) de Washington

John (I) de Washington's *s*,

   John (II) de WASHINGTON, *b c* 1385; enjoyed possession of the manor of Tewitfield and other lands in his mother's lifetime, she having made them over to him 1408; *m* 13—— or 14—— and *d* 1423, leaving issue:

Robert (V) WASHINGTON, of Tewitfield; *m* Margaret, widow of John Lambertson, of Warton, and *d* 7 Dec 1483, leaving (with other issue) a 2nd *s*:

Robert (VI) WASHINGTON, of Warton, *b c* 1455; it is recorded in the great hall of Sulgrave Manor, which in the 16th century became the seat of the Washingtons, that Robert (VI) Washington bore as a coat of arms *Argent two bars and in chief three molets gules, in fesse point a crescent for difference gules; for crest, on a wreath argent and gules, a coronet or, and issuant therefrom a raven's head sable*; *m* 1st Elizabeth, dau of John Westfield, of Overton, Lancs, and had issue:

I John (III) WASHINGTON, for whom *see below*   II Thomas WASHINGTON   III Ellen Washington, *m* James MASON, of Warton, and had issue

Robert (VI) Washington *m* 2nd Jane, dau of Miles or Myles Whittington, of Borwick Hall, Lancs, and with her had issue:

IV Robert (VII) WASHINGTON, ancestor of a line of Washingtons who became settled at Compton, Surrey   V Miles WASHINGTON

Robert (VI) Washington *m* 3rd Agnes Bateman, of Heversham, Westmorland, and *d* in or after 1528 (will dated 6 Sept), having with her had issue:

VI Anthony Washington, *d* before 1529   VII Matthew Washington, *b* 1493; became a priest; *d* in or after 1532

Robert (VI) Washington's est s by his 1st w,

John (III) WASHINGTON, of Warton, *b c* 1478; is recorded in the great hall of Sulgrave Manor as having born arms (for him and his wife) *Argent two bars and in chief three molets gules, in fesse point a crescent for difference gules; impaling Sable, three lucies haurient argent, a chief or*; *m* Margaret, dau of Robert Kytson, also of Warton, and sister of Sir Thomas Kytson, whose dau Katherine *m* Sir John Spencer, of Wormleighton, Warwicks, and was thereby ancestress of both Sir Winston Churchill and the Princess of Wales; John (III) Washington *d* before 1528 (predeceasing his father), leaving issue (together with a dau, Jane, who *m* Humphrey Gardiner, of Cockerham, Lancs):

I Lawrence (I) WASHINGTON, for whom *see below*   II Nicholas WASHINGTON

III Leonard WASHINGTON; *m* Elizabeth Croft and had issue   IV Peter WASHINGTON

V Thomas WASHINGTON, *b c* 1520; apprenticed to his maternal uncle Sir Thomas Kytson (a Freeman of the Mercers' Company) 1541, member of the company of Merchant Adventurers in Antwerp 1550; *m* 15— ——— and *d* Colchester, Essex, 17 April 1583, leaving (with other issue):

1 Revd Lawrence (II) WASHINGTON, MA, DD; rector of Colmer, Hants, 1565-1609; *m* 1st ———; *m* 2nd Faith, sister of Thomas Bilson, Bp of Worcester 1596-97 and of Winchester 1597-1616, and dau of Herman Bilson, gs of Arnold Bilson by a woman who is said by the antiquary Anthony à Wood to have been a dau of the Duke of Bavaria; thus Mrs Lawrence Washington may have been a remote kinswoman of her distant cousin-by-marriage's royal patron two-and-a-half centuries later, *see above* under descendants of Robert (IV) Washington)

John (III) Washington's est s,

Lawrence (I) WASHINGTON, *b c* 1500; *educ* Gray's Inn; was by 1529 bailiff in Warton to William, Lord Parr of Horton (uncle of HENRY VIII's 6th and last Queen, Katharine Parr), the Parr family having acquired the castle and a part of the barony of Kendal (from which, it will be recalled, Robert (I?) de Washington was holding Routhworth over two centuries earlier) by marriage to a de Ros heiress in the reign of RICHARD II; Lawrence (I) Washington *m* 1st 1530 Elizabeth, widow of William Gough, a prosperous mercer of Northampton, with whom he had no children; soon afterward Lawrence Washington went to live in Northampton, where his w had property and business connections; was Mayor of Northampton 1532 and 1545; built Sulgrave Manor, Northants, having received as outright owner (he having previously been the tenant in right of his wife) the manor of Sulgrave, formerly the property of the Priory of St Andrew in Northampton, by grant from HENRY VIII 10 March 1539 at the time of the Dissolution of the Monasteries; is recorded in the great hall of Sulgrave Manor as having born arms (for him and his 2nd w) *Argent two bars and in chief three molets gules, in fesse point a crescent for difference gules; impaling Barry of four or and sable, three mascles counterchanged*; *m* 2nd Amy (*d* 6 Oct 1564), 3rd dau of Robert Pargiter, of Greatworth, nr Sulgrave, and his w Anne Knight, and *d* 19 Feb 1584 (*bur* Sulgrave), having acquired through marriage other properties, including the manor and rectory of Stuchbury, Northants; with his 2nd w he had issue:

I Robert (VIII) WASHINGTON, for whom *see below*

II Lawrence (III) WASHINGTON; *educ* Magdalen Coll, Oxford (BA 1567), Gray's Inn (barrister 1582, bencher 1599); Registrar High Court of Chancery, MP Maidstone 1604-11; *m* 1st 31 Jan 1578 Martha, dau of Clement Newce, of Great Hadham, Herts, and with her had issue:

1 Sir Lawrence (IV) WASHINGTON, of Garsdon, Wilts, *bapt* 5 April 1579; *educ* Balliol Coll, Oxford; knighted 24 July 1627; *m* 1609 his cousin Anne (*d* 18 June 1645), dau of William Lewyn, DCL, MP and Chancellor of the Diocese of Rochester, of Otterden, Kent, and sister of Sir Justinian Lewyn, and *d* Oxford 14 May 1643 during the Civil War in the service of King CHARLES I, leaving issue:

(1) Lawrence (V) WASHINGTON; *m* Eleanor, dau of William Guise, Sheriff of Glos 1647 and MP for Glos 1654-55, of Elmore, Glos, and his w Cecilia, herself dau of John Dennis, of Pucklechurch (northeast of Bristol), and had an only dau and heiress:

1a Elizabeth (I) Washington, *b* 1655/6; *m* 28 Dec 1671, as his 1st w, Sir Robert Shirley, 7th Bart, *cr* Earl Ferrers 1711 (*b* 20 Oct 1650; *d* 25 Dec 1717) and *d* 2 Oct 1693, having had 10 s and seven daus; from her descend subsequent Earls Ferrers (*see* BURKE'S PEERAGE & BARONETAGE), many of whom have Washington or Lawrence among their Christian names

(2) Elizabeth (II) Washington, dau of a Sir Lawrence Washington, of Garsdon, Wilts, presumably the Sir Lawrence (IV) above; *m* as his 1st w Christopher GUISE (later Sir Christopher Guise, *cr* a Bart 1661), est s of William Guise (*d* 26 Aug 1653), of Elmore, Glos, and er bro of Eleanor, w of Lawrence (V) Washington above, and *d* without issue before 1654

2 Martha Washington, *b c* 1580; *m* as his 2nd w Sir John TYRRELL, TIRRELL or TYRELL, 21st in the direct male line from Sir Walter Tirrell (whom some suppose to have been the assassin of WILLIAM II Rufus, King of England) and *d* 17 Dec 1670, aged 90, having had issue:

(1) Laurence TYRRELL; *d* without issue   (2) John TYRRELL, his father's heir; *cr* a Bart 22 Oct 1666
(3) Thomas TYRRELL; *d* without issue   (4) Charles TYRRELL; *d* without issue
(5) Martha Tyrrell; *m* Sir Benjamin AYLOFFE, 4th Bart, of Braxted, Essex (*d* 5 March 1722) and had a s (*d* without issue) and two daus

III Christopher WASHINGTON, alive 1587; left issue

IV George WASHINGTON, of Malmesbury, Wilts; *m* 20 July 1601 Dame Joan Hall and *d* 1625 (*bur* 2 May), having had a s, Lawrence (VI) WASHINGTON, who *d* without issue

I Amy Washington; *m* Edmund FORSTER, of Wolf's Place, Hanslope, Bucks, and had issue Sir Guy FORSTER
II Frances Washington; *m* John THOMPSON, of Sulgrave
III Elizabeth Washington; *m* Henry MARSHALL, of Evenley, Northants, and had issue:

1 Amy Marshall; *m* Simon HAYNES, of Turweston, Bucks
2 Frances Marshall; *m* George YORKE, of Brackley, Northants

IV Barbara Washington; *m* Simon BUTLER, of Appletree, Northants, ancestor of the Butlers of Appletree and Aston le Walls, among whom were the Revd Alban Butler, author of *The Lives of the Saints*
V Magdalen Washington; *m* 1st Nicholas CLARKE, of Culworth, Northants; *m* 2nd Anthony HUMFREY, of Sulgrave
VI Margaret Washington; *m* Gerard HAWTAYNE, of Easington, Oxon, 2nd s of Edward Hawtayne, of the Lea
VII Mary Washington; *m* Abel MAKEPEACE (*d* 1602), of Chipping Warden, Northants, and *d* 1622, having had issue:

1 Lawrence MAKEPEACE, *b* 1586; *educ* Brasenose Coll, Oxford (BA 1603); bought reversion to (*i.e.*, deferred ownership of) Sulgrave Manor 1 March 1610 from his cousin Lawrence (VII) Washington (*see below*); Registrar High Court of Chancery and barrister Inner Temple; *m* Elizabeth Croker, gdau of Sir Gerald Croker, of Hook Norton, Oxon, and *d* 24 Nov 1640, leaving issue:

(1) Abel MAKEPEACE; sold Sulgrave Manor 1659-60 to Revd Moses Hodges

Lawrence (I) Washington's est s,
    Robert (VIII) WASHINGTON, *b c* 1544; is recorded in the great hall of Sulgrave Manor as having born arms (for him and his wife) *Argent two bars and in chief three molets gules, in fesse point a crescent for difference gules; impaling Gules, a chevron between three swans their wings elevated argent; m* 1st *c* 1565 Elizabeth (*d c* 1599), dau of Walter Lyte or Light, of Radway Grange, Warwicks, and Brackley, Northants, and his w Ursula Woodford; by his marriage to Elizabeth Robert (VIII) acquired the manor of Radway and title to the manors of Horley and Hornton in Oxfordshire; he had issue:

I Lawrence (VII) WASHINGTON, for whom *see below*
II Robert (IX) WASHINGTON, *b* after 1569; leased house at Great Brington, Northants, from his cousin Sir John Spencer, of Althorp, just before 16 April 1599, also leased manor of Sandy, Beds; *m* 19 Feb 1596 Elizabeth (*d* 19 March 1623), dau of Giles Chishull, of Little Bardfield, Essex, and *d* 10 March 1623
III Walter WASHINGTON; *m* as her 1st husb Alice, dau of John Murden, of Morton Morell, Warwicks (she *m* 2nd John Woodward, of Stratford-on-Avon, and *d* there on or before 22 May 1647), and *d* on or before 23 April 1597, leaving issue:

1 John (IV) WASHINGTON, *b* 15—; inherited Radway Grange under testamentary bequest of his ggf Walter Lyte; suffered for his Royalism in and after Civil War and obliged to sell Radway 1654; *m* 1614 Anne, dau of George Danvers, of Upton, Warwicks (s and heir of John Danvers, of Colthorpe) and had five s and five daus
2 Katherine Washington; *m* 30 July 1616 Thomas STAUNTON, of Wolverton Hall, Warwicks

IV Christopher WASHINGTON, *b* 1573; *educ* Oriel Coll, Oxford; *m* Margaret Palmer, of Radway
V William WASHINGTON, *b* 1577; *educ* Oriel Coll, Oxford; *d* in or after 1620
VI Thomas WASHINGTON; *d* in or after 1620
I Amy Washington; *m* 1588 Alban WAKELYN (*d* 1603), of Nether Boddington, Northants (which manor he sold in 1600 to his f-in-law Robert (VIII) Washington), afterward of Henley-on-Thames, Oxon
II Ursula Washington; *m* Thomas ADCOCK, of Swinford, Leics
III Elizabeth Washington; *m* Lewis RICHARDSON, of Turvey, Beds

Robert (VIII) Washington *m* 2nd before 25 March 1599 Anne Fisher (*bur* East Haddon, Northants, 16 March 1652) and *d* probably at Nether Boddington 1620 (will dated 7 Feb 1620, proved 3 Jan 1621), having had issue by her also.

Robert (VIII) Washington's est s by his 1st w,
    Lawrence (VII) WASHINGTON, *b c* 1568; sold on 20 Aug 1605 the bulk of the Sulgrave estate of *c* 1,000 ac to Thomas Atkins, of Over Winchendon, Bucks, but kept the manor house and 7 acres of land until 1 March 1610, when (his f consenting) he sold the reversion to his cousin Lawrence Makepeace; *m* Aston-le-Walls, Northants, 3 Aug 1588 Margaret (*d* 1652), dau of William Butler, of Tyes Hall, Cuckfield, Sussex, and his w Margaret Greeke, of Palsters, Lancs, and London; Lawrence (VII) *d* Brington, Northants, 13 Dec 1616, predeceasing his father, having had issue:

I Robert (X) WASHINGTON, *b* 15—; *d* before 1610
II Sir John (V) WASHINGTON, of Thrapston Manor, Northants, and Stanbridge Earls, Hants, *b c* 1592; knighted 21 Feb 1622/3 at Newmarket, was his gf's heir, Gentleman of the Privy Chamber to CHARLES II; *m* 1st 14 June 1621 Mary Curtis (*d* 1 Jan 1625), thought to have been sister of Philip Curtis, of Islip, Northants (Sir John (V)'s sis Amy's husband), and had issue:

1 Mordaunt WASHINGTON, *b* 1621 or 1622; *educ* Pembroke Coll, Oxford; fought as a Royalist in Civil War, when *k*
2 John (VI) WASHINGTON, *b* 1623; *d* in or after 1673

II (cont.) Sir John (V) *m* 2nd 1629 Dorothy (*d* 1678), widow of Gerard Kirkby, of Stanbridge Earls, Hants (which property passed to Sir John by his marriage with Dorothy), and est dau of William Pargiter, of Greatworth, Northants (descended from Robert Pargiter, f-in-law of Lawrence (I) Washington, for whom *see above*), and *d* without surviving issue on or before 18 May 1668
III Sir William WASHINGTON, of Leckhampstead, Bucks, and subsequently of Wicke Hall, Isleworth, Middx, knighted at Theobalds, Herts, 17 Jan 1622; *m* 1614 Anne (*d* 1643), 2nd dau of Sir George Villiers and his 1st w Audrey and half-sister

to George Villiers, Duke of Buckingham, the celebrated favourite of JAMES I, and *d* 1643 (*bur* St Martin's-in-the-Fields, London, 22 June), having with her had issue:

1 Henry WASHINGTON, *b c* 1615 (baptized 21 March); served under Prince Rupert at the successful Royalist siege of Bristol 1643 in the English Civil War, personally effecting a breach in the defences with a handful of infantry; Actg Govr during the siege of Worcester 1646 by the Parliamentarians until ordered to surrender by his sovereign; *m* Elizabeth (who *m* 2nd Col Samuel Sandys, of Ombersley, Worcs, and *d* 1699), only dau of Sir John Pakington, 1st Bart (*see* BURKE'S PEERAGE & BARONETAGE, Hampton), of Aylesbury, Bucks, and his *w* Frances, dau of Sir John Ferrers, of Tamworth, Staffs, and *d* 1664, leaving four daus

2 Susanna Washington, *b* in or before 1618; *m* Reginald GRAHAM, *s* of Fergus Graham and his *w* Sibill and brother of Sir Richard Graham, 1st Bart (*see* BURKE'S PEERAGE & BARONETAGE, Graham of Esk), and *d* without issue 26 Feb 1699

3 Elizabeth Washington, *b* 1619; *m* 2 March 1642 Col William LEGGE (*d* 1672), Keeper of the King's Wardrobe and Groom of the Bedchamber to King CHARLES I, and *d* in or after 1647, having had issue:

(1) George LEGGE, *b* 1647; *cr* 2 Dec 1682 Baron Dartmouth (*see* BURKE'S PEERAGE & BARONETAGE)

4 George WASHINGTON, *b* in or before 1620; *d* in or after 1643

IV Richard WASHINGTON, *b* 1600; *d* in or after 1610
V Revd Lawrence (VIII) WASHINGTON, for whom *see below*
VI Thomas WASHINGTON, *b* 1605; page to Prince of Wales (afterward CHARLES I) during his visit to Spain with the Duke of Buckingham seeking a Spanish princess as bride; *d* Madrid before 15 Aug 1623
VII George WASHINGTON, *b* in or before 1608; *d* on or before 4 Dec 1626
I Elizabeth Washington; *m* St Mary Le Strand, London, 26 May 1615 Francis MEWCE (*d* 1654), of Holdenby, Northants, and *d* between 11 Aug and 12 Dec 1676
II Joan Washington; *m* Francis PILL, of Maidford, Northants, and subsequently of Wicken Manor, Northants, tutor in the household of his wife's distant kinsman 1st Lord Spencer (of the 1603 creation) to his lordship's sons William (later 2nd Lord Spencer) and John Spencer
III Margaret Washington; *m* 1st 1621 Sir Robert SANDYS, of Stretham, Cambs, one of the seven sons of Sir Myles Sandys, 1st Bart, of Wilburton, Cambs, and his *w* Elizabeth, dau of Edward Cook; *m* 2nd 8 Oct 1640 Samuel THORNTON, of Soham, Cambs, and *d* on or before 15 Oct 1678
IV Alice Washington; *m* 17 May 1628 Revd Robert SANDYS, MA, Rector of Boddington, Northants, and nephew of Sir Myles Sandys, 1st Bart, for whom *see above*
V Frances Washington; *m* Robert GARGRAVE, of London
VI Amy Washington; *m* 8 Aug 1620 Philip CURTIS, of Islip, Northants (*see* entry for Sir John (V) Washington, above)
VII Jane Washington; *m* Richard SEYMOUR, of Savoy, London (*d* on or after 13 April 1641)

Lawrence (V) Washington's fifth *s*,

Revd Lawrence (VIII) WASHINGTON, *b* Sulgrave Manor *c* 1602; *educ* Brasenose Coll Oxford (BA 1623, Fellow 1624, MA 1626, Proctor and Lector (in philosophy) 1631, Bachelor of Divinity 1634); Rector of Purleigh, Essex (said to have been a particularly well-endowed living) 1632/3 to 1643, when ejected from his living for Royalism, subsequently Rector of Little Braxted, Essex; *m* probably at Purleigh between March and Dec 1633 Amphyllis (*bapt* Spratton, Northants, 2 Feb 1601/2; *bur* Tring, Herts, 19 Jan 1655), dau and co-heiress of John Twigden, of Little Creaton, Northants, and his *w* Anne (who subsequently *m* Andrew Knowling, of Tring), dau of William Dickens, of Great Creaton, Northants, and his *w* Anne, sister of Thomas Thornton, of Brockhall, Northants, and *d* on or before 21 Jan 1653 (*bur* that day at Maldon, Essex), having had issue:

I John (VII) WASHINGTON, for whom *see below*
II Lawrence (IX) WASHINGTON, *bapt* Tring 18 June 1635; emigrated to America and settled in Virginia by 27 Sept 1667; *m* 1st in England 26 June 1660 Mary (*d c* 1666), dau of Edmund Jones, of Luton, Beds, and had issue:

1 Mary Washington, *bapt* Luton 22 Dec 1663; inherited land from her *f* at Tring and Luton; *m* Revd Edward GIBSON, MA (*d* 1732), Vicar of Hawnes, Beds, and *d* on or before 23 Oct 1721, leaving issue
2 Charles WASHINGTON, *b* Luton on or before 22 Nov 1665 (when baptized); *d* 16— or 17—

II (cont.) Lawrence (IX) WASHINGTON *m* 2nd, as her 2nd husb, *c* 1668 Joyce (*d* 1685, having *m* as her 3rd husb James Yeats), widow of Capt Alexander Fleming, JP, of Westphalia, Essex Co, Va., and *d* before 6 June 1677, having had further issue:

3 John (VIII) WASHINGTON, *b* 2 April 1671; Under-Sheriff, Westmoreland Co, Va., 1692, JP and High Sheriff Stafford Co, Va., 1717; *m* 15 March 1692 Mary (*d* 1 April 1728), dau and coheiress of Needham Langhorne, of Newton Bromswold, Northants, and had (with other issue, who did not survive):

(1) Lawrence (X) WASHINGTON; High Sheriff Stafford Co; *m* Sarah, dau and coheiress of Thomas Lund, and *d* before 1727
(2) Capt John (IX) WASHINGTON; JP Stafford Co; *m* Mary (*d* on or before 11 May 1746), dau of Capt Dade Massey, High Sheriff Stafford Co, and *d* on or before 27 Feb 1743, leaving issue

(3) Robert WASHINGTON, of Westmoreland Co, *b* 16 Sept 1700; *m c* 1744 Sarah, gdau of Col Richard Fossaker, JP and Burgess of Stafford Co, and *d* 1756, leaving issue:

1a John (X) WASHINGTON; *d* 1787, leaving issue

2a Susanna Washington, *m* 1st 1 March 1763 her cousin Lawrence (XII) WASHINGTON (*b* on or before 10 Feb 1744; *d* 1774), of Mattox Hall, Westmoreland Co, Va., only s of Henry Washington and his w Elizabeth Storke, and had issue (with two daus):

1b Henry WASHINGTON, *b* 1765; sold Mattox Hall to his cousin William Augustine Washington 1797, Ensign Revolutionary War; *m* Sarah (*d* 22 Jan 1831), dau of John Ashton, of Mount Lebanon, King George Co, Va., and his w Hannah West, and *d* 20 May 1812, leaving (with other issue):

1c Lawrence (XI) WASHINGTON, *b* Westmoreland Co 26 Feb 1791; *m* 26 Oct 1819 Haywood, Va., his 5th cousin Sarah Tayloe Washington (*b* Haywood 14 April 1800; *d* 20 Dec 1886), 7th child of William Augustine Washington, 3rd s of President WASHINGTON's half-bro Austin Washington, and *d* 15 March 1875, having had eight s and three daus

2c Henry WASHINGTON, *b* 27 Nov 1792; helped draw up Kentucky's first constitution; *m* 15 May 1817 Catherine Robinson Bate (*d* 30 Nov 1875), ggdau of John Robinson, Treasurer and Speaker Virginia House of Burgesses, whose 1st cousin Peter's gs John Robinson was *cr* a Baronet 21 Sept 1854 (*see* BURKE'S PEERAGE & BARONETAGE, Robinson of Toronto)

3c Mary West Washington, *b* 1 June 1802; *m* 14 Oct 1828 William JAMES

4c Richard Conway WASHINGTON, of Alexandria, Va., and later of Washington, DC, *b* 22 March 1804; *m* 1st 13 Oct 1825 Mary Smith (*d* 10 Dec 1827); *m* 2nd 8 Jan 1829 Sophia May (*d* 3 Feb 1892), dau of Hon John Roberts, twice Mayor of Alexandria, and *d* 24 May 1867, leaving issue:

1d Llewellyn WASHINGTON, *b* 11 May 1830; *d* 26 July 1902

2d Florence Washington, *b* 31 Aug 1834; *m* 3 Feb 1859 Frederick SCHLEY (*d* 1875), of Frederick, Md. (uncle of Adml Winfield Scott Schley (1839-1909), commander of the US squadron against Adml Cervera (*see* Acknowledgements) at the Battle of Santiago in the Spanish-American War of 1898), and *d* 1928

3d Richard WASHINGTON, *b* 12 April 1837; Pay Dir and Inspector-Gen US Navy; *m* 1st Katherine (*b* 17 April 1842; *d* 4 Aug 1865), dau of Col Robert Meldrum Lee, of Philadelphia, and had issue:

1e Horace Lee WASHINGTON, *b* 4 June 1864; US Consul-Gen London 1924-28, FRGS; *m* 22 Sept 1897 Helen Stewart, dau of George Sydney Williams, of Chicago and York Harbor, Maine, and his w Hannah McKibben, dau of Gen Hart L. Stewart, of Chicago, and *d* 27 Aug 1938, having had issue:

1f George Sydney Horace Lee WASHINGTON, *b* England 6 April 1910; *educ* Harrow and Trinity Coll, Cambridge (BA 1934, MA 1938); family historian and genealogist, Fellow Society of Antiquaries; *d* before 1989

2f Helen Lawrence Lee Washington, *b* 21 Feb 1912; *m* 1940 Arthur Norris KENNARD, only s of Sir Howard Kennard, GCMG, CVO, British Ambassador to Poland 1934-41, and 3rd cousin of Sir Coleridge Kennard, 1st Bart (*see* BURKE'S PEERAGE & BARONETAGE)

3d (cont.) Richard Washington *m* 2nd 1867 Thomasine (*d* 1921), dau of Capt Abraham Barker, of New Bedford, Mass., and *d* 1895

4d Sophia Washington, *b* 20 May 1839; *m* 8 Aug 1861 Samuel Eliot MIDDLETON, of Woodley, Washington, DC, and *d* 11 Aug 1872, leaving issue:

1e Richard Washington MIDDLETON, *b* 2 Sept 1862

5d Rose Maria Washington, *b* 9 June 1844; *m* Lt Albert ASTON, USN, and *d* 15 June 1921

2a (cont.) Susanna Washington *m* 2nd Col Thomas JETT; *m* 3rd Col John SKINKER and *d* 1822

(4) Townshend WASHINGTON, *b* 16 Sept 1705; *m* 22 Dec 1726 Elizabeth (*d* 1778), dau of Thomas Lund, of Green Hill, Stafford Co, and *d* on or before 31 Dec 1743, having had issue

III William WASHINGTON, *bapt* Tring 14 Oct 1641; apprenticed to a London weaver 1653

I Elizabeth Washington, *bapt* 17 Aug 1636; *m* William RUMBALL, of London

II Margaret Washington; *m* 27 Feb 1663 George TALBOT, of London, and *d* 1710

III Martha Washington, emigrated to Virginia 1678; *m* there Samuel HAYWARD, JP, Burgess and Clerk of Stafford Co, s of Nicholas Hayward, a merchant, of London, and *d* between 6 May and 8 Dec 1697

The Revd Lawrence (VIII) Washington's est s,

Colonel John (VII) WASHINGTON, *b* probably at Purleigh, Essex, *c* 1634; settled in what became Washington Parish, Westmoreland Co, Virginia, 1656-57; Col commanding Virginian Forces in alliance with Maryland Forces against Seneca tribe in Indian War 1675, Memb Virginia House of Burgesses for Westmoreland County; *m* 1st Westmoreland Co, 1 Dec 1658, Anne (*d* Westmoreland Co *c* 1668), dau of Lt-Col Nathaniel Pope, JP (*b c* 1610; emigrated to Maryland from Bristol *c* 1637, resettled in Virginia *c* 1650; *d* between 16 May 1659 and 26 April 1660), of The Cliffs, Westmoreland Co, and his w Lucy (*d* after 1660), and had issue:

I Lawrence (XII) WASHINGTON, for whom *see below*

II John (XI) WASHINGTON, *b c* 1661; of Mattox Hall, Westmoreland Co, and Hylton, Stafford Co; *m*, as her 1st husb, Anne (she *m* 2nd 1700 Col Charles Ashton and *d* England 1704), sister of Henry Wycliffe, and *d* Feb 1698, leaving issue:

1 Lawrence (XIII) WASHINGTON, *d* before 31 March 1708

2 Nathaniel WASHINGTON, *m* Mary Dade, gdau of Maj John Dade, Speaker Virginia House of Burgesses, and had issue

3 John (XII) WASHINGTON

4 Capt Henry WASHINGTON; JP, of Mattox Hall and Hylton, High Sheriff Stafford Co; *m* Mary, gdau of Basil Bailey and his w Anne, sister of Maj Caleb Butler, and *d* on or before 22 Oct 1748, leaving (with other issue):

(1) Henry WASHINGTON, of Mattox Hall; *m* 18 May 1743, as her 1st husb, Elizabeth (she *m* 2nd 1749 Col Robert Vaux, of Vaux Hall, and 3rd 1757 Col Thomas Jett, of Walnut Hill), dau of William Storke, and *d* 1745, leaving issue Lawrence (XIV) WASHINGTON, for whom *see above* under Susanna Washington

(2) Bailey WASHINGTON, of Stafford Co; JP; *m* Catherine, dau of William Storke, and had issue:

1a Henry Augustine WASHINGTON, *b* 1749; *d* 1825; ancestor of Walter Owen Washington, sometime resident of Brownsville, Tex.

2a Gen William WASHINGTON, *b* 1752; cavalry officer in Revolutionary War; *m* —— and *d* 1819 leaving issue:

1b William WASHINGTON, *b* 1785; barrister Inner Temple, London, UK, 1804; *m* Martha, dau of Gen Blake and had issue

3a Col Bailey WASHINGTON, *b* 1754; *m*, as her 1st husb, Euphan Dandridge Wallace (she *m* 2nd Daniel Carroll Brent) and *d* 17— or 18—, having had issue:

1b Bailey WASHINGTON; Sr Surg USN; *m* Jane Matilda Lee (*d* 1880), cousin of Gen Robert E. Lee, and *d* 1854

2b John Macrae WASHINGTON, AQM to Gen Winfield Scott Florida War 1838-39, served with artillery Mexican War 1846-48, Govr Territory of New Mexico 1848-49; *d* 1853

III Ann Washington, *b c* 1662; *m c* 1680 Maj Francis WRIGHT, of Kingcopsico, Westmoreland Co, and *d* 1698, leaving issue

Col John (VII) Washington *m* 2nd Frances (who herself *m* 2nd Capt William Hardidge) and *d* probably in Washington Parish (named after him in honour of his public services), Va., 1677

His er s,

Capt Lawrence (XII) WASHINGTON, *b* Washington Parish, Westmoreland Co, Sept 1659; Memb Virginia House of Burgesses 1685, High Sheriff 1692; *m* probably at Warner Hall, Gloucester Co, Va., *c* 1689 Mildred (*b* probably Warner Hall *c* 1671; *m* 2nd 16 May 1700 George Gale, of Whitehaven, Cumberland, England; *d* and was *bur* there 26 March 1701), dau of Col Augustine Warner, Jr (*b* 3 June 1642; *d* 19 June 1681), of Warner Hall, Speaker Virginia House of Burgesses and Memb Govr's Cncl, and his w Mildred (*d c* 1694), dau of George Reade (*b* Linkenholt, Hants, England, 25 Oct 1608; *d* before 21 Nov 1674), sometime Actg Govr Virginia; Capt Lawrence (XII) Washington *d* Westmoreland Co Feb 1697/8, having had issue:

I Maj John (XIII) WASHINGTON, of High Gate, Gloucester Co, Va., *b* 12 Nov 1692; *m* 9 July 1716 Catherine (*d* 7 Feb 1743), dau of Hon Henry Whiting, Memb Govr's Cncl and Treasurer of Virginia, and *d* 1 Sept 1746, leaving issue:

1 Col Warner WASHINGTON, of High Gate and subsequently of Fairfield, Clarke Co, *b* 22 Sept 1722; *m* 1st 1 Dec 1747 Elizabeth, dau of Col William Macon, and had issue:

(1) Warner WASHINGTON, of Fairfield, *b* 15 April 1751, ancestor of Bowden Washington, sometime resident of Philadelphia

1 (cont.) Col Warner Washington *m* 2nd 10 May 1764 Hannah, yst dau of Hon William Fairfax and sister of 8th Lord Fairfax of Cameron (*see* BURKE'S PEERAGE & BARONETAGE) and had issue:

(2) Fairfax WASHINGTON, *b* 1767; *m* 1804 Sarah, dau of Col William Armistead, and had issue

(3) Mildred Washington, *m* 22 Feb 1799, as his 1st w, Mordecai THROCKMORTON (*see* BURKE'S PEERAGE & BARONETAGE), of Meadow Farm, Loudoun Co, Va. (*b* 10 March 1777; *d* 7 April 1838), 3rd s of Hon Thomas Throckmorton, of Frederick Co, Va., and his 2nd w Mary Anne Hooe, and had issue:

1a Mathew Reade THROCKMORTON, *b* 1 Aug 1802; *m* Frances Everhart

(4) Louisa Washington, *m* Feb 1798, as his 2nd w, her cousin 9th Lord FAIRFAX of CAMERON, of Vaucluse, Fairfax Co, Va. (*b* 1762; *d* 21 April 1846), and *d* 28 April 1798

2 Catherine Washington, *b* 11 Feb 1724; *m* as his 1st w Col Fielding LEWIS, of Kenmore

3 Henry WASHINGTON, of Hampstead, Middlesex Co, Va., *b* 13 Sept 1728; *m* 1st 9 Jan 1749 Anne, dau of Col Edwin Thacker, and with her had surviving issue:

(1) Thacker WASHINGTON, of Spy Hill, King George Co, Va., *m* 12 Oct 1776, as her 1st husb, Harriet (she *m* 2nd Col Francis Whiting), dau of 'Sir John Peyton, Bart' [there is some doubt as to whether this gentleman's assumption of the baronetcy was valid], of Isleham, Gloucester Co, Va., and had issue:

1a Henry Thacker WASHINGTON, of Spy Hill; *m* 4 April 1802 Mary, dau of Col Robert Stith, and had (with other issue):

1b Henry Thacker WASHINGTON, of Windsor, King George Co, Va.; *m* 31 March 1829 Virginia (*d* 1871), dau of Gen William Fitzhugh Grymes, and had issue a son, who *m* and had issue William Henry WASHINGTON, sometime resident of Windsor, Va.

(2) Anne Washington; *m* Thomas or John PEYTON, only surviving (and probably illegitimate) s of 'Sir John Peyton, Bart' (for whom *see above*) and *d* 10 Jan 1777

3 (cont.) Henry Washington *m* 2nd 3 March 1760, as her 2nd husb, Charlotte (she *m* 3rd 6 Oct 1769 Col Charles Nelson), widow of John Montague

II Capt Augustine WASHINGTON, for whom *see below*

III Mildred Washington, *b* 1696; made over to her brother Augustine 26 May 1726 the Epsewasson estate (later known as Mount Vernon); *m* 1st 1705 Roger GREGORY (*d* 1730) with whom she had at least one child:

1 Frances Gregory, *b* 17—; *m* 17— Francis THORNTON and had issue at least one child:

(1) John THORNTON, *b* Spotsylvania Co, Va., *c* 1747; Col; *m* Milbank, King George Co, Va., 1784 his second cousin Jane (*b* Wakefield April 1756; *d* Thornton Hill, Rappahannock Co, Va., Oct 1833), 3rd dau of President WASHINGTON's half-bro Augustine Washington and his w Anne Aylett, and had two s and three daus

III (cont.) Mildred Washington Gregory *m* 2nd 23 Jan 1733 Col Henry WILLIS

Capt Lawrence (XII) Washington's yr s,

Capt Augustine WASHINGTON, *b* Westmoreland Co, Va., *c* 1694; *educ* Appleby Sch, Westmorland, England; JP and High Sheriff in Virginia 1727, plantation manager and owner and director of iron mine (at Fredericksburg, Va.); *m* 1st 20 April 1715 Jane (*b* Westmoreland Co 24 Dec 1699; *d* probably Pope's Creek, Westmoreland Co, 24 Nov 1729), dau and heiress of Major Caleb Butler, JP, of Westmoreland Co, and had issue:

President Washington's half-brothers
I Butler WASHINGTON, *b* Bridge's Creek, Va., 1716; *d* before 1729
II Lawrence (XV) WASHINGTON, *b* Bridge's Creek 1718; *educ* in England; Adj-Gen of Virginia, Burgess for Fairfax County, Pres of Ohio Company, served in West Indies 1740-42 under Adml Vernon (commemorated in the name Mount Vernon when the Epsewasson estate which Lawrence's aunt Mildred had made over to his father Augustine was rechristened); *m* 19 July 1743, as her 1st husb, Anne (*b* 1728; *m* 2nd 16 Dec 1752 Col George Lee, of Mount Pleasant, nephew of Hon Thomas Lee, Actg Govr Virginia, and *d* 14 March 1761), est dau of Hon William Fairfax, of Belvoir, Pres of Govr's Cncl in Virginia, and his 1st w Sarah Walker, and half-sis of 8th Lord Fairfax of Cameron (*see* BURKE'S PEERAGE & BARONETAGE), and *d* Mount Vernon 22 July 1752 probably of consumption, having had issue:

Half-brother's children
1 Jane WASHINGTON, *b* Mount Vernon 27 Sept 1744; *d* there Jan 1745/6
2 Fairfax WASHINGTON, *b* Mount Vernon 22 Aug; *d* there Oct 1747
3 Mildred WASHINGTON, *b* Mount Vernon 28 Sept 1748; *d* there 1749
4 Sarah WASHINGTON, *b* Mount Vernon 7 Nov 1750; *d* there late 1752

President Washington's half-brother
III Augustine (Austin) WASHINGTON, *b* Bridge's Creek 1720; *educ* in England; Col Virginia Militia, Memb Virginia Assembly; *m* 1743 Anne (*b* 1726; *d* Wakefield, Va., Dec 1773), dau and co-heiress of Col William Aylett, Burgess for King William Co, and his 1st w Anne, herself dau of Col Henry Ashton and his 1st w Elizabeth, who in her turn was dau and heiress of Capt William Hardidge by his w Frances, widow of Col John (VII) Washington (with his bro the first Washington to settle in America (*see above*)); Col Augustine Washington *d* 1762, having had issue:

Half-brother's children
1 Lawrence (XVI) WASHINGTON, *b c* 1745; *d* in infancy   2 Augustine WASHINGTON, *b c* 1747; *d* in infancy
3 Elizabeth Washington, *b* Wakefield 15 Nov 1749; *m* 15 Feb 1769 Brig-Gen Alexander SPOTSWOOD, Virginia Militia, of Nottingham, Spotsylvania Co (so named in honour of the Spotswood family), Va. (*b* New Post, Va., 16 Oct 1746; *d* Nottingham 20 Dec 1818), s of John Spotswood and his w Mary Dandridge and gs of Gen Alexander Spottiswood (*see* Appendix, II), apptd Govr of Virginia 1710 (and himself ggs of John Spottiswood, Archbishop of St Andrews in Scotland 1615-61 and the prelate who crowned King CHARLES I at Holyrood in 1633); Elizabeth Washington Spotswood *d* 20 Oct 1814, having had issue (with six s and six other daus) a 6th dau:

Half-brother's grandchildren
(6) Henrietta Brayne Spotswood, *b* Spotsylvania Co 29 Aug 1786; *m* 14 Aug 1806 her 1st cousin Bushrod WASHINGTON (*see below*, *b* Haywood, Westmoreland Co, Va., 4 April 1785; *educ* Harvard; *d* Mount Eagle, Fairfax Co, Va., 16 April 1831), 2nd s of Col William Augustine Washington (3rd s of Austin Washington) and *d* Baltimore 10 Aug 1869, having had issue:

Half-brother's great-grandchildren
1a Ann Eliza Washington, *b* Mount Zephyr, Fairfax Co, 17 Sept 1807; *m* Washington, DC, 15 March 1831 Revd William Philander Chase JOHNSON (*b* Bucks Co, Pa., 5 Nov 1806; *d* Clinton, La., Nov 1852), s of James Johnson, and *d* Jackson, Miss., 18 April 1851, having had eight s and two daus
2a Jane Mildred WASHINGTON, *b* Mount Zephyr 25 Nov 1809; *d* Fairfax Co 19 Sept 1839 (*bur* Mount Vernon)
3a Spotswood Augustine WASHINGTON, of Watseka, Iroquois Co, Ill., *b* Mount Zephyr 17 July 1811; *m* Kalamazoo,

Mich., 9 April 1837 Evaline Fletcher (*b* Romney, W. Va., 6 Dec 1815; *d* Watseka 28 Dec 1877) and *d* Watseka 25 Aug 1865, leaving issue (with two other children, who *d* in infancy):

Half-brother's great-great-grandchildren
1b Bushrod DeLaneau WASHINGTON, *b* Kalamazoo 20 Sept 1841; *m* Chicago 12 Aug 1866 Martha Jane (*b* Macon, Ga., 31 May 1842; *d* Chicago Oct 1912), dau of Daniel McRae and his w Anne Adams, and *d* Chicago 21 Dec 1918, leaving issue:

Half-brother's great-great-grandchildren's children
1c Estella Evaline Washington, *b* Chicago 28 Aug 1867; *m* 1st *c* 1896 Lewis NIEMAN (*d* Pittsburgh, Pa., 1913) and had one dau (*d* young); *m* 2nd 22 Feb 1916 John Rudisill WITHERS (*b* Chicago; *d* there 25 April 1927) and *d* Chicago *c* 1931

Half-brother's great-great-grandchildren
2b James Fletcher WASHINGTON, *b* Kankakee, Ill., 4 July 1846; *m* 1st Carthage, Jasper Co, Ill., 25 Nov 1871 Caroline (*b* Newton Co, Mo.; *d* Chicago *c* 1890), dau of Daniel McRae and his w Anne Adams and sister of Mrs Bushrod DeLaneau Washington (*see above*), and had issue:

Half-brother's great-great-grandchildren's children
1c Martha Ella Washington, *b* Watseka 17 March 1873; *m* Chicago Aug 1896 Charles Halden BARNARD (*b* Lafayette, Ind., 12 Oct 1866; *d* Chicago 10 Oct 1926) and *d* Pittsburgh 12 Jan 1951, having had three s and two daus
2c Orra May WASHINGTON, *b* Chicago 18 Feb 1881; *d* Watseka 15 July 1883

Half-brother's great-great-grandchildren
2b (cont.) James F. Washington *m* 2nd 29 Dec 1896 Mary R. Bryant (*b* Canada 1859; *d* Chicago 31 July 1926), widow of —— Horne, and *d* Chicago 15 Jan 1924, having with her had issue:

Half-brother's great-great-grandchildren's children
3c Lee Richardson WASHINGTON, *b* Chicago 29 July 1897; *m* 1st 1 May 1919 (divorce 1950) Lucienne Audette (*b* Ontario, Canada, 21 April 1897; *d* 1963) and had issue:

Half-brother's great-great-grandchildren's grandchildren
1d *Odelle Lee Washington [Mrs Ernest C Hanson, 111 145th Avenue, Madeira Beach, St Petersburg, FL 33708, USA; 415 Lakeview Street, Orlando, FL 32804, USA], *b* 20 April 1921; *m* 1st 28 Nov 1940 (divorce 1947) Charles KETCHEL; *m* 2nd 28 April 1948 *Ernest Chrest HANSON (*b* 8 Dec 1917) and has issue:

Half-brother's great-great-grandchildren's great-grandchildren
1e *Brynda Leigh Hanson, *b* 3 Dec 1948; *m* 23 Dec 1972 *Michael KELLY
2e *Victoria Louise HANSON, *b* 28 March 1954

Half-brother's great-great-grandchildren's children
3c (cont.) Lee R. Washington *m* 2nd *c* 1957 Mary Kelly, widow of —— English, and *d* Olma, Fla., *c* 1970

Half-brother's great-great-grandchildren
3b William Augustine WASHINGTON, *b* Watseka July 1849; atty; *m* Watseka 3 July 1872 Louise Jane (*b* Fountain Co, Ind., 14 March 1852; *d* Kankakee 30 Aug 1927), dau of Ebenezer Hooker and his w Marie Hastings, and *d* Kankakee 24 March 1913, having had issue (with two other children, who *d* in infancy):

Half-brother's great-great-grandchildren's children
1c Inez Louisa Washington, *b* Watseka 18 March 1873; *m* 1st Kankakee 1894 (divorce) Dr James GUTHRIE; *m* 2nd Kankakee 28 June 1905 Thomas Akers BEEBE (*b* 12 Oct 1862; *d* Aug 1920) and *d* Kankakee 9 Aug 1955
2c Evaline Edna WASHINGTON, *b* Danville, Ill., 17 Aug 1874; *d* 14 March 1875
3c Spotswood Corbin WASHINGTON, *b* Danville 1 Feb 1876; carpenter and decorator; *m* 12 April 1905 Bertha Wilhelmina (*b* Bonfield, Ill., 7 April 1878; *d* Quincy, Ill., 16 June 1974), dau of Ludwig Nowack and his w Johannah Haase, and *d* Kankakee 13 May 1948, leaving issue:

Half-brother's great-great-grandchildren's grandchildren
1d *William Augustine WASHINGTON [2 Andrews Court, Bradley, IL 60915, USA], *b* Kankakee 28 Jan 1906; tool and die and modelmaker; *m* Kankakee 11 Nov 1927 *Hazel Marie (*b* Fairmount, Ill., 13 June 1910), dau of Albert A. Craver and his w Mary Zettie Myers, and has issue:

Half-brother's great-great-grandchildren's great-grandchildren
1e *Joyce Eileen Washington [Mrs John De Valk, 2061 Surrey Lane, Tucson, AZ 85704, USA], *b* Kankakee 26 Oct 1928; *m* there 25 June 1950 *John C. De VALK (*b* Chicago 26 Dec 1926), s of Corneil De Valk and his w Florence Brewer, and has issue:

Half-brother's great-great-grandchildren's great-great-grandchildren
1f *John C. De VALK, Jr, *b* 4 Oct 1953
2f *Dan(iel) Wayne De VALK [177 South Fulton Avenue, Bradley, IL, USA; 1791 N Riverside Drive, Momence, IL, USA], *b* 19 May 1955
3f *Lana Joyce De VALK, *b* 6 July 1966

Half-brother's great-great-grandchildren's great-grandchildren

2e *Inez Gay Washington [Mrs Ewald Kunde Jr, RR 2, Box 228X, Tower Drive, Kankakee, IL 60915, USA; 1850 West Tower Rd, Kankakee, IL, USA], *b* Kankakee 21 Feb 1934; *m* 27 Sept 1953 *Ewald KUNDE, Jr (*b* Kankakee 30 Aug 1930), s of Ewald E. Kunde and his w Elsie Pearl Yancey, and has two adopted children:

   a *Julie Ann KUNDE, *b* 27 July 1963
   b *Steven Lee KUNDE [245 S Fraser Ave, Kankakee, IL, USA], *b* 15 April 1967; *m* 19— *Mary ——

Half-brother's great-great-grandchildren's grandchildren

2d *Florence Evaline Washington, *b* Kankakee 14 Aug 1909; *m* Peotone, Ill., 21 Aug 1930 *Frederick Henry NEMITZ (*b* Kankakee 14 Dec 1905), s of Frank Nemitz and his w Bertha Doberstein, and has issue:

   Half-brother's great-great-grandchildren's great-grandchildren
   1e *Gerald Frederick NEMITZ, *b* Kankakee 26 Dec 1931; certified public accountant; *m* 19— *Janet Hicks
   2e *Beverly Ann Nemitz [Mrs Dale Irps, 7784 S 8500 E Rd, St Anne, IL 60964, USA], *b* Kankakee 10 April 1933; *m* 1st ——; *m* 2nd 19— *Dale R. IRPS
   3e *William Corbin NEMITZ, *b* Kankakee 15 Nov 1935; *m* 19— *Phyllis Lehnus

Half-brother's great-great-grandchildren's children

4c Fannie Evaline Washington, *b* Danville 22 June 1878; *m* 12 Feb 1904 Robert Gregory MORRIS (*b* 1874; *d* St Louis, Mo., 31 Dec 1936) and *d* St Louis 26 April 1931
5c A child, *b* 19 April, *d* 15 Sept 1880
6c Julia Henrietta WASHINGTON, *b* 17 March, *d* 27 Sept 1884

Half-brother's great-great-grandchildren

4b Estella Henrietta Washington, *b* Watseka 27 Sept 1852; *m* there 12 Sept 1871 Delbert Brooks KICE (*b* Illinois 24 March 1851; *d* Chicago 13 Feb 1892) and *d* Chicago 18 Feb 1892, having had four s and three daus

Half-brother's great-grandchildren

4a Bushrod Corbin WASHINGTON, *b* Mount Zephyr 14 Dec 1813; *d* before 1826
5a George William WASHINGTON, *b* Mount Zephyr 4 Sept 1816; *educ* West Point; *m* 18— and *d* between 1850 and 1869
6a John WASHINGTON, *b* Mount Zephyr 15 Jan 1818; *d* between 1839 and 1850
7a Mary Randolph WASHINGTON, *b* Mount Zephyr Jan 1819; *d* before 1824
8a Martha D. WASHINGTON, *b* Mount Zephyr 1821; *d* before 1831 (*bur* Mount Vernon)
9a Mary Henrietta WASHINGTON, *b* 10 May 1824; *d* Watseka 30 March 1863
10a Corbin WASHINGTON, *b* 20 April 1826; *d* Georgetown, DC, 27 Nov 1871
11a Frances Louisa Augusta Washington, *b* 17 Feb 1828; *m* 1st 8 Oct 1856, as his 2nd w, Revd Daniel MOTZER (*b* Pennsylvania *c* 1818; *d* 1 Nov 1864); *m* 2nd 24 April 1872 Myron L. FINCH, of Brooklyn, New York (*d c* 1880), and *d* Georgetown, DC, 15 March 1900
12a Hannah Bushrod WASHINGTON, *b* 6 June 1830; *d* in infancy (*bur* Mount Vernon)

Half-brother's children

4 Anne Washington, *b* Wakefield 2 April 1752; *m* 19 Dec 1768, as his 1st w, Col Burdett ASHTON, of Chestnut Hill, Westmoreland Co, Va. (*b* 21 Nov 1747; Memb Virginia Convention 1788 and Virginia Assembly; *d* King George Co, Va., 8 March 1814), s of Charles Ashton and his w Sarah Butler, and *d* 3 June 1777, having had two s and two daus
5 Jane Washington, *b* 1756; *m* 1784 her 2nd cousin Col John THORNTON (*see above*)
6 William Augustine WASHINGTON, *b* Wakefield 25 Nov 1757; Lt-Col 3rd Continental Dragoons, Brig-Gen US Army; *m* 1st 25 Sept 1777 his half-1st cousin Jane (*b* Bushfield, Westmoreland Co, 20 June 1759; *d* Sweet Springs, Va., 16 Aug 1791), est dau of John Augustine Washington (*see below*), 7th child and 6th s of Capt Augustine Washington, and had issue:

Half-brother's grandchildren

(1) Hannah Bushrod WASHINGTON, *b* 7 Aug 1778; *d* May 1797
(2) Augustine WASHINGTON, *b* 15 June 1780; *d* 9 Feb 1798
(3) Ann Aylett Washington, *b* Haywood, Westmoreland Co, 11 Feb 1783; *m* Westmoreland County 8 Oct 1800, as his 1st w, her 5th cousin William ROBINSON, of Bunker Hill, Westmoreland Co (*b* 1 June 1782; *d* 17 Aug 1857), s of William Robinson and his w Margaret, dau of Dr Walter Williamson and his w Mildred Washington (widow of Langhorne Dade), and *d* Alexandria, Va., 12 Sept 1804, having had three children (all of whom *d* in infancy)
(4) Bushrod WASHINGTON, of Mount Zephyr, *m* 14 Aug 1806 his 1st cousin Henrietta Brayne (*see above*)
(5) Corbin Aylett WASHINGTON, *b* Haywood 11 May 1787; *d* Nov 1788
(6) George Corbin WASHINGTON, of Dumbarton House, Georgetown, DC, *b* Haywood 20 Aug 1789; *educ* Harvard; Memb Maryland Legislature and House of Reps, Pres Chesapeake and Ohio Canal Co; *m* 1st Dumbarton 1 Sept 1807 Elizabeth Ridgely (*b* 22 Nov 1786; *d* Georgetown 1 July 1820), dau and co-heiress of Col Thomas Beall, of Rock of Dumbarton, and his w Anne Orme, and had issue:

Half-brother's great-grandchildren

1a Thomas Beall Augustine WASHINGTON, *b* 7 June 1808; *d* 2 Feb 1809
2a George Thomas Beall WASHINGTON, *b* 26 Feb 1810; *d* young
3a Augustine Bushrod WASHINGTON, *b* 10 June 1811; *d* 12 Feb 1812

4a Lewis William WASHINGTON, of Beall Air, Jefferson Co, Va., *b* Georgetown, DC, 30 Nov 1812; Col US Army, captured by John Brown during his notorious raid on Harper's Ferry; *m* 1st Baltimore 17 May 1836 Mary Ann (*b* 19 Oct 1817; *d* Beall Air 16 Nov 1844), dau of James Barroll, of Baltimore, and his *w* Mary Ann Crockett, and had issue:

Half-brother's great-great-grandchildren
1b George Corbin WASHINGTON, *b* Baltimore 20 March 1837; *d* there 20 Sept 1843
2b James Barroll WASHINGTON, *b* Baltimore 26 Aug 1839; Maj Confederate States Army; *m* Montgomery, Ala., 23 Feb 1864 Jane Bretney (*b* 15 Feb 1842; *d* Atlantic City, New Jersey, 1 June 1901), widow of Dr Powhatan Bolling Cabell and dau of Major William Lewis Lanier and his *w* Lucy Elizabeth Virginia Armistead, and *d* Pittsburgh 6 March 1900, having had issue:

Half-brother's great-great-grandchildren's children
1c William Lanier WASHINGTON, *b* Montgomery, Ala., 30 March 1865; Pres and Gen Manager Pittsburgh Sheet Steel Mfrg Co; *m* 1st New York 6 June 1906 (divorce 19——) May Bruce (*b* Louisville, Ky., 28 June 1873), formerly *w* of Lewis Jane Shallcross and dau of Thomas Brennan, of Louisville, and his *w* Anna Virginia Bruce; *m* 2nd 7 July 1919 (divorce 19——) Ida Alice Holland, and with her had issue:

Half-brother's great-great-grandchildren's grandchildren
1d Winston Lanier WASHINGTON, *b* 6 May 1920; *d* 17 Sept 1921

Half-brother's great-great-grandchildren's children
1c (cont.) William L. Washington *m* 3rd St Louis, Mo., 3 July 1923 Augusta Adeline (*b* 18 April 1895), dau of William Koblank and his *w* Elizabeth von Heiser, and *d* 11 Sept 1933
2c Benjamin Cabell WASHINGTON, *b* Baltimore 16 Nov 1866; *d* Allegheny, Pa., 23 Sept 1881
3c Lewis William WASHINGTON, *b* Baltimore 20 Nov 1869; *m* London, UK, 12 Nov 1904 Anne Raymond Cox and *d* Nice, France, 15 May 1906
4c Mary WASHINGTON, *b* Baltimore 4 Oct 1871; *d* there 25 Aug 1872

Half-brother's great-great-grandchildren
3b Mary Ann Washington, *b* Baltimore 1 June 1841; *m* there 17 Nov 1864 Henry Irvine KEYSER, of Baltimore (*b* 17 Dec 1837; *d* 7 May 1916), s of Samuel S. Keyser and his *w* Elizabeth Wyman, and *d* 8 Dec 1931, having had five s and one dau
4b Elizabeth Ridgeley Beall Washington, *b* Beall Air 16 Nov 1844; *m* Baltimore 25 April 1865 Elias Glenn PERINE (*b* 14 June 1829; *d* 15 June 1922), s of David Maulden Perine and his *w* Mary, and *d* 28 Jan 1919, having had six s and seven daus

Half-brother's great-grandchildren
4a (cont.) Col Lewis W. Washington *m* 2nd at Clover Lea, Hanover Co, Va., 6 Nov 1860 Ella More (*b* Eltham, New Kent Co, Va., 7 Sept 1834; *d* New York 17 Jan 1908), 5th dau of George Washington Bassett and his *w* Betty Burnett, 4th dau of Robert Lewis, himself 8th s of Col Fielding Lewis and his *w* Betty Washington (*see below*), and *d* Jefferson Co, Va., 1 Oct 1871, having with her had issue:

Half-brother's great-grandchildren
5b Betty Lewis WASHINGTON, *b* Clover Lea 26 Aug 1861; *d* there 25 July 1862
6b William de Hertburn WASHINGTON, *b* Clover Lea 29 June 1863; *d* New York 30 Aug 1914

Half-brother's great-grandchildren
5a Bushrod WASHINGTON, *b* Dec 1814; *d* Aug 1815
6a Harriet Ann Bushrod WASHINGTON, *b* 16 March 1816; *d* 4 Dec 1817
7a Cornelia Adelaide WASHINGTON, *b* between March 1817 and March 1821; *d* young

Half-brother's grandchildren
(6) (cont.) George C. Washington *m* 2nd 25 Oct 1821 Ann Thomas Beall (*b* Georgetown, DC, 1 May 1800; *d* there 3 Feb 1861), dau of Col John Peter and his *w* Eleanor Orme, and *d* Georgetown 17 July 1854, having with her had issue:

Half-brother's great-grandchildren
8a Eleanor Ann WASHINGTON, *b* Georgetown 30 Oct 1822; *d* there 13 April 1849

Half-brother's children
6 (cont.) William A. Washington *m* 2nd Westmoreland Co 10 July 1792 his half-1st cousin Mary (*b* 28 July 1764; *d* 2 Nov 1795), est dau of Richard Henry Lee and his 1st *w* Anne Aylett; *m* 3rd 11 May 1799 Sarah (*b* 5 March 1765; *d* Princeton, New Jersey, 3 Sept 1834), dau of Col John Tayloe, of Mount Airy, Va., and his *w* Rebecca Plater, and *d* Georgetown, DC, 2 Oct 1810, having with her had issue:

Half-brother's grandchildren
(7) Sarah Tayloe Washington, *b* Haywood 14 April 1800; *m* there 26 Oct 1819 her 4th cousin Lawrence (XI) WASHINGTON (*see above*)
(8) A son, *b* and *d* 12 April 1803
(9) William Augustine WASHINGTON, *b* Haywood 30 Aug 1804; *m* 7 Oct 1823 Juliet Elizabeth (*b* 4 March 1806; *d* 16 Dec 1865), dau of Samuel J. Bayard, of Princeton, New Jersey, and *d* Haywood 26 June 1830, having had issue:

Half-brother's great-grandchildren
1a A child, *b* Washington, DC, 28 July, *d* there 30 July 1824
2a Martha WASHINGTON, *b* 2 Jan 1826; *d* 21 Feb 1828
3a William Augustine WASHINGTON, *b* 15 April 1828; *d* 21 Feb 1833
4a Julia Augusta Washington, *b* Princeton, New Jersey, 1 Sept 1830; *m* 19 Nov 1855 Dabney Carr WIRT (*b* Richmond Co, Va., 2 March 1817; *d* Westmoreland Co 27 March 1893), s of William Wirt, and *d* 24 April 1888

Half-brother's children
7 George WASHINGTON, *b* Wakefield *c* 1760; *d* March 1781

President Washington's half-sister
IV Jane WASHINGTON, *b* Bridge's Creek 1722; *d* 17 Jan 1734/5

Capt Augustine WASHINGTON *m* 2nd 6 March 1731 Mary (*b* Lancaster County, Va., *c* 1708/9; *d* Fredericksburg 25 Aug 1789 of breast cancer), only dau of Col Joseph Ball (*b* England 24 May 1649; *d* Epping Forest, Lancaster Co, between 25 June and 11 July 1711) and his 2nd w Mary (*d* 1721), widow of William Johnson, of Norwich, Middlesex Co, Va. (she *m* 3rd Richard Hewes); Capt Augustine Washington *d* Ferry Farm, King George Co, Va., 12 April 1743, having with his 2nd w had issue:

V GEORGE WASHINGTON, 1st PRESIDENT of the UNITED STATES of AMERICA
VI Betty Washington, *b* Wakefield, Westmoreland Co, 20 June 1733; *m* 7 May 1750, as his 2nd w, Col Fielding LEWIS, of Kenmore, Fredericksburg, Va. (*b* Warner Hall, Gloucester Co, Va., 7 July 1725; *d* Fredericksburg Dec 1781; s of John Lewis and his w Frances Fielding, and *d* Western View, Culpeper Co, 31 March 1797, having had nine s and two daus; the fourth s:

President Washington's nephew
4 George LEWIS, of Marmion, King George Co, *b* 1757; Maj; *m* Catherine Daingerfield and *d* 1821, having had (with other issue):

Great-niece
(1) Mary Willis Lewis, *b* 1781; *m* Col Byrd Charles WILLIS (*b* 1781; *d* 1846) and *d* 1834, having had (with other issue) an eldest dau:

Great-niece's children
1a Catherine Daingerfield Willis, *b* Jefferson Co, Fla., 1803; *m* 1st Atchison GRAY (*d* in or before 1826); *m* 2nd Tallahassee, Fla., 12 July 1826 Achille Charles Louis Napoléon (alias Napoléon Achille) MURAT, 2nd Prince MURAT (*b* Paris, France, 21 Jan 1801; Duke of Clèves 15 March 1806-1 Aug 1808, Crown Prince of Naples 1 Aug 1808-19 May 1815; *d* Jefferson Co, Fla., 15 April 1847), er s of Joachim Murat (*b* La Bastide-Fortunière (since renamed La Bastide-Murat), Guyenne, France, 25 March 1767, 11th child of an innkeeper; one of Napoleon's cavalry commanders, a Marshal of the (Napoleonic or First) Empire, a Grand Admiral of the Empire, King of Naples as GIOACCHINO NAPOLEONE 1808-15; tried by court martial and shot Castello di Pizzo, Calabria, Italy, 13 Oct 1815) and his w CAROLINE (*b* Ajaccio, Corsica, 25 March 1782; assumed title Countess Lipona after losing her throne in 1815; *d* Florence, Italy, 18 May 1839), sixth and yst dau of Charles Marie Bonaparte and his w Marie Laetitia Ramolino (from 1804 Her Imperial Highness Madame Mère de l'Empereur) and sister of the Emperor NAPOLEON BONAPARTE; Princess (Catherine Daingerfield Willis) Murat *d* without issue Aug 1867

President Washington's nephew
7 (Betty Washington Lewis's seventh s) Lawrence LEWIS, *b* 4 April 1767; *m* 1st 17— ——; *m* 2nd Mount Vernon 22 Feb 1799 Eleanor (Nelly) Parke Custis (*b* Abingdon, Va., 31 March 1779; *d* Audley, Clarke Co, Va., 15 July 1852), fourth dau of John (Jack) Parke Custis (*see* Washington Biographical Details), and *d* Arlington 20 Nov 1839, having with his 2nd w had issue:

Great-niece
(1) Frances Parke Lewis, *b* Mount Vernon 27 Nov 1799; *m* Woodlawn, Fairfax Co, Va., 4 April 1826 Col Edward George Washington BUTLER, 3rd Dragoons US Army (*b* Tellico Plains, Tenn., 22 Feb 1800; *d* St Louis, Mo., 5 Sept 1888), s of Capt Edward Butler and his w Isabella Fowler, and *d* Pass Christian, Miss., 20 June 1875, having had issue:

Great-niece's children
1a Edward George Washington BUTLER, *b* 4 Dec 1826; *d* 23 Sept 1827
2a and 3a Twin daus, *b* and *d* 29 Feb 1828
4a Edward George Washington BUTLER, *b* Woodlawn 4 June 1829; *educ* U of Virginia and Harvard; Sec US Legation Berlin, Maj Confederate States Army; *ka* Belmont, Mo., 7 Nov 1861
5a Eleanor Angela Isabella Butler, *b* Louisiana 7 Feb 1832; *m* 9 or 12 May 1854, as his 1st w, Col George McWillie WILLIAMSON, of Shreveport, La. (*b* S Carolina 22 Sept 1829; US Min Central America; *d* 29 Jan 1882), s of Thomas Taylor Williamson and his w Tirzah Ann McWillie, and *d* 9 Jan 1867, leaving issue:

Great-niece's grandchildren
1b Isabel Butler Williamson, *b* 4 Nov 1855; *m* 1881 Arthur HODGE and *d* 1909, having had issue:

Great-niece's great-grandchildren
1c Evelyn Angela Isabel HODGE, *b* 24 July 1884; drowned in Twelve-Mile Bayou, nr Shreveport, 3 May 1903

Great-niece's grandchildren
2b George McWillie WILLIAMSON, Jr, of DeSoto Parish, La., *b* La. 1857; *m* 1882 Adine Eatman (*b* 1859; *d* 1912) and had issue:

Great-niece's great-grandchildren
1c George McWillie WILLIAMSON III, *b* 14 April 1884
2c Isabel Butler Williamson, *b* DeSoto Parish 21 March 1888; *m* 19— James CUMMINGS or CUMMING and *d* 19—
3c Sarah Leigh Williamson, *b* 19 Sept 1892; *m* 19— Joseph A. BECKER, of Brookhaven, Miss., and *d* 19—, having had issue:

Great-niece's great-great-grandchildren
1d *Mary Adine Becker, *b* 19—; *m* 19— *Chester W. HILL and has issue:

Great-niece's great-great-grandchildren's children
1e *Mary Lee HILL, *b c* 1947
2e *Jackson Becker HILL, *b c* 1950

Great-niece's great-grandchildren
4c *Mary Alice WILLIAMSON, *b* 10 Jan 1898
5c *Caro Butler WILLIAMSON, *b* 3 July 1900

Great-niece's grandchildren
3b Evelyn Angela WILLIAMSON, *b* La. 22 Feb 1859?; teacher as Sister Marie Angela at Port of Spain, Trinidad, 1905; *d* 19—
4b William McWillie WILLIAMSON, *b* La. 17 March 1861; *m* Nannie Lemon and *d* Central America May 1894, having had issue:

Great-niece's great-grandchildren
1c Matelle WILLIAMSON; *d* in infancy

Great-niece's grandchildren
5b Anne McWillie Williamson, *b* La. *c* 1863; *m* 1900 George Herbert FREEMAN and *d* 19—
6b Caroline Butler Williamson, *b* Shreveport 11 June 1865; *m* 1887 Philip Bernard FRIERSON, of Frierson, La., (*b* 1859; *d* 1903), s of Gen George Philip Frierson, of S Carolina, and *d* before 1909, leaving issue:

Great-niece's great-grandchildren
1c Anne Leigh Frierson, *b* 12 June 1891; *m* 1st 19— Thomas B. WILSON; *m* 2nd 19— John A. SEWALL, Jr
2c *George Philip FRIERSON, *b* 16 Nov 1893
3c *Dorothy Witten FRIERSON, *b* 3 Feb 1896
4c *Edward Butler FRIERSON, *b* 3 Dec 1898
5c *Mary Eleanor FRIERSON, *b* 9 March 1900

Great-niece's children
6a Caroline Swanwick Butler, *b* 21 Aug 1834; *m* 9 May 1853 William Barrow TURNBULL, sugar cane planter, of Turnbull Island, nr Simmesport, La. (*b* 8 Aug 1829; drowned 11 Nov 1856), and *d* 1876 (*bur* Pass Christian, Miss.), leaving issue:

Great-niece's grandchildren
1b William Butler TURNBULL, of Boston, *b* 8 April 1854; *m* 1st after 1889 (divorce 18— or 19—) Sarah, formerly w of —— Barrow and dau of Col Robert H. Barrow; *m* 2nd Sarah (?) Hill, of New York, and *d* after 1935, leaving issue by her:

Great-niece's great-grandchildren
1c *Caro Turnbull; *m* 19— and has issue
2c *Thelma TURNBULL

Great-niece's grandchildren
2b Daniel Parke TURNBULL, of Mandan, N. Dak., *b* 25 May 1856; *educ* Washington and Lee U; attorney; *m* after 1889 ——, a widow, and had issue:

Great-niece's great-grandchildren
1c Daniel Park TURNBULL, Jr, *b* 1898; *d* 5 Feb 1920

Great-niece's children
7a Lawrence Lewis BUTLER, *b* Denbayne Plantation, La., 10 March 1837; *educ* U of Virginia; Maj Confederate States Army; *m* 1st 11 March 1869 Mary Susan (*b* Plaquemine, La., 1847; *d* St Louis, Mo., 26 March 1882), dau of Edward James Gay, of Plaquemine, and his w Lavinia Hynes, and had issue:

Great-niece's grandchildren
1b Frances Park Butler, *b* St Louis 27 Dec 1869; *m* 28 Aug 1895 Maj John EWENS, of Vicksburg, Miss., and *d* St Louis 21 April 1929, leaving issue:

Great-niece's great-grandchildren
1c *Frances Parke Butler Ewens, b St Louis 19 Dec 1898; m 1922 *Col Edward Francis TWISS and has issue:

Great-niece's great-great-grandchildren
1d Nan Betty TWISS, b London, UK, 4 May 1923; d 31 Dec 1987
2d *Col Edward Francis TWISS [Goatley Farmhouse, Church Hanborough, Oxon OX8 8AB, UK], b Sheringham, Norfolk, 7 Oct 1925; educ Shrewsbury; regular army offr (ret); m 1st 21 April 1951 Veronica Aletheia Knott and has issue:

Great-niece's great-great-grandchildren's children
1e *Candida Twiss, b Hong Kong 3 Dec 1954; m 13 Feb 1988 *Colin HOLMES and has issue:

Great-niece's great-great-grandchildren's grandchildren
1f *Adam Twiss HOLMES, b 10 Aug 1989

Great-niece's great-great-grandchildren's children
2e *Edward Jeremy TWISS, b Hong Kong 3 Jan 1956; m July 1982 *Ruth Margaret Broadhead

Great-niece's great-great-grandchildren
2d (cont.) Col Twiss m 2nd 22 Oct 1989 *Frances Mary Brigstocke Burke, née Hitchings

Great-niece's grandchildren
2b Edward Gay BUTLER, of Boyce, Va., b St Louis 18 June, 1872; m 7 June 1898 Emily Mansfield (b 18 Jan 1874; d 26 Aug 1952) and d 8 Feb 1953
3b Lavinia Hynes Butler, b St Louis 30 May 1875; m 28 Oct 1896 Wyatt SHALLCROSS, of Kirkwood, St Louis (b Louisville, Ky., 5 March 1865; d 18— or 19—), and had issue:

Great-niece's great-grandchildren
1c *Eleanor Custis SHALLCROSS, b 7 Dec 1898
2c *Nan Butler Shallcross [Mrs Cyril Clemens, 841 N Kirkwood Road, MT, USA], b 5 April 1901; m 18 Oct 1933 *Cyril C. CLEMENS, s of Dr James R. Clemens, of St Louis, and his w Katherine Boland
3c *Lawrence Butler SHALLCROSS, b St Louis 10 Nov 1907
4c *Wyatt SHALLCROSS, Jr, b St Louis May 1910
5c *(Mary) Sue SHALLCROSS, b St Louis 20 April 1919

Great-niece's grandchildren
4b Anna Gay Butler, b St Louis 1 Aug 1877; m 30 Nov 1904 Richard Cheatham PLATER, of New York (b Nashville, Tenn., 4 Feb 1872; d Louisiana 30 Jan or 6 Feb 1955), s of Thomas Plater and his w Mary Louise Bugg, and d Nashville 3 July 1961, leaving issue:

Great-niece's great-grandchildren
1c *Richard Cheatham PLATER, Jr [Acadia Plantation PO Box 110, Thibodeaux, LA 70302, USA], b Nashville 20 May 1908; educ The Taft Sch and Williams Coll; banker, life insurance executive, psychotherapist, National Labor Relations Board investigator and sugarcane planter; m 1st 4 June 1932 Eleanore (d North Adams, Mass., 7 Aug 1937), dau of Dr Henry Sabin Leake, of New York, and his w Gertrude Munde, and has issue:

Great-niece's great-great-grandchildren
1d *(Richard) Ormonde PLATER [1453 Arabella, New Orleans, LA 70115, USA], b New York 6 Sept 1933; educ Vanderbilt and Tulane Us; newspaper reporter 1955-59, college teacher 1966-71, Episcopal Deacon 1971-; m Albany, New York, 19 July 1957 *(Elizabeth) Kathleen, dau of Ralph A Treadway and his w Elizabeth C. Bakeman, and has issue:

Great-niece's great-great-grandchildren's children
1e *Nancy Eleanore PLATER [720 Betz Ave, Jefferson, LA 70121, USA], b Albany, New York, 2 March 1958
2e *Elizabeth Treadway Plater [Mrs Charles C Cropp, 604 Nashville Ave, New Orleans, LA 70115, USA], b New Orleans 15 June 1959; m 8 April 1988 *Charles C. CROPP and has issue:

Great-niece's great-great-grandchildren's grandchildren
1f *Isabelle Mathilde CROPP, b New Orleans 19 Jan 1993

Great-niece's great-great-grandchildren's children
3e *George Ormonde PLATER [974 Eolus Ave, Encinitas, CA 92024, USA], b 16 Aug 1960; m 1st 8 Sept 1983 (divorce 1987) Dawn Benner; m 2nd 20 June 1987 (divorce 1993) Giovanna Valverde

Great-niece's great-great-grandchildren
2d *(David) Dunboyne PLATER [425 Easy St, Thibodeaux, LA 70301, USA], b Nashville, Tenn., 3 May 1936; m 26 March 1962 *Sheela Burke and has issue:

Great-niece's great-great-grandchildren's children
1e *Bryan Butler PLATER, b 4 Nov 1964; m 1988 *Elizabeth Harn
2e *Christopher T. S. PLATER, b 28 March 1966
3e *Juliana Hite Plater, b 10 Sept 1967; m 1990 *Robert WOHLSEN

Great-niece's great-grandchildren

1c (cont.) Richard Cheatham Plater, Jr, *m* 2nd 6 Sept 1941 *Pamela Quarles, dau of R. G. Robinson

2c Louise Plater, *b* Nashville 31 Jan 1910; *m* 29 Sept 1934 R(obert) Walter HALE, Jr (*b* 9 April 1906; *d* 21 Aug 1987), s of Robert Walter Hale and his w Allie Crook, and *d* 16 May 1982, leaving issue:

Great-niece's great-great-grandchildren

1d *Nancy Plater Hale [Mrs William V Hoyt, Mountain Lake PO Box 832, Lake Wales, FL 33859-0832, USA; 79 Harbor Dve #315, Stamford, CT 06902-7448, USA], *b* Nashville, Tenn., 16 Feb 1941; *educ* Wellesley; *m* Nashville, Tenn., 17 Aug 1963 *William Vernor HOYT (*b* Norwalk, Conn., 17 Feb 1937; *educ* Cornell, Newark Coll of Engrg and Harvard Business Sch), s of Fred Fisher Hoyt and his w Lois Grace MacNeill, and has issue:

Great-niece's great-great-grandchildren's children

1e *William Hale HOYT [101 Eaton Court, Stafford, VA 22554, USA], *b* New York 17 July 1966; *m* Michigan 15 Feb 1992 *Moira Jean (*b* 30 Aug 1961), dau of John McKinnie and his w Moira

2e *Edward Plater HOYT, *b* Naples, Italy, 28 Feb 1968; *educ* West Point and Oxford, UK (Marshall Scholar); US Army; *m* Va. 4 Feb 1992 *Carolyn Ann (*b* England 22 Feb 1967; *educ* West Point and Oxford, UK (Rhodes Scholar)), dau of Richard Ford and his w Jeanette Burger

3e *Walter MacNeill HOYT, *b* Norwalk, Conn., 8 May 1969; *educ* Colgate U

Great-niece's great-great-grandchildren

2d *Robert Walter Hale III [426 Ellendale, Nashville, TN 37205, USA], *b* Nashville, 2 Dec 1943; *educ* Princeton and U of Pennsylvania Wharton Sch of Business; *m* San Antonio, Tex., 21 June 1969 *Janin L. Sinclair and has issue:

Great-niece's great-great-grandchildren's children

1e *Virginia Phillips HALE, *b* 12 April 1970

2e *Patrick Sinclair HALE, *b* 18 April 1974

Great-niece's great-great-grandchildren

3d *Vianda Plater Hale [Mrs Nicholas Hill, 203 Lynwood Blvd, Nashville, TN 37205, USA], *b* Nashville 18 Feb 1948; *educ* Vanderbilt U; *m* Nashville 11 Sept 1971 *Nicholas Lorraine Edmund HILL, s of Michael Lorraine Alan Hill (*b* England) and his w Christiane Goemans (*b* Belgium), and has issue:

Great-niece's great-great-grandchildren's children

1e *Nicki HILL, *b* 9 Feb 1977

2e *Christiane Louise HILL, *b* 9 Aug 1982

Great-niece's grandchildren

5b Mary Suzanne Butler, *b* St Louis 19 Oct 1880; *m* there 12 Feb 1901 George Armistead WHITING, of Roland Park, Baltimore (*b* there 3 Nov 1879; *d* there 7 Sept 1947), s of Clarence Carlyle Whiting and his w Marian Gordon Armistead, and had issue:

Great-niece's great-grandchildren

1c Eleanor Custis Whiting, *b* Baltimore 3 Jan 1902; *m* 1st 1923 (divorce 19—) William Francis FitzGERALD, Jr, s of William Francis FitzGerald and his w Mary E. O'Leary, and had issue:

Great-niece's great-great-grandchildren

1d *Mary Carlyle FitzGERALD, *b* 4 Oct 1925

Great-niece's great-grandchildren

1c (cont.) Mrs Eleanor FitzGerald *m* 2nd Jackson, Wyo., 8 Aug 1949 *Baron Leopold Ludwig James Wulff Mogens von PLESSEN (*b* Darmstadt, Germany, 13 June 1894), 3rd s of Ludwig Mogens Gabriel, 1st Count von Plessen-Cronstern (creation of the Prussian crown 1898), and his w Countess Leopoldine Hoyos, and *d* San Francisco 1 Sept 1949

2c Lawrence Lewis Butler WHITING, *b* Catonsville, Md., 9 April 1906; *educ* Johns Hopkins (MD); orthopaedic surg; *m* 26 Oct 1931 Katherine Ahern (*b* Chestertown, Md., 7 March 1912; *d* Baltimore 5 Sept 1948), dau of David Ford and his w Anna Ahern, and *d* Pensacola, Fla., 26 Jan 1950, having had issue:

Great-niece's great-great-grandchildren

1d George Armistead WHITING, *b* 23 Jan 1935; *d* 5 Sept 1948

2d *Suzanne Lewis WHITING, *b* 13 June 1936

3d *Lewis Butler WHITING, *b* 3 Aug 1940

4d David Ford WHITING, *b* 8 June, *d* 13 June 1941

Great-niece's great-grandchildren

3c *Betty Washington WHITING [4221 Greenway, Baltimore, MD, USA], *b* Elkridge, Md., 4 Oct 1912

Great-niece's children

7a (cont.) Maj Lawrence Lewis Butler *m* 2nd 1886 Sue Martin, of Huntsville, Ala. (*d* St Louis, Mo., 1893), and *d* St Louis 3 June 1898

Great-niece and -nephews
(2) Martha Betty LEWIS, *b* Mount Vernon 19 Aug 1801; *d* there 17 June 1802
(3) Lawrence Fielding LEWIS, *b* and *d* Western View, Culpeper Co, Va., 5 Aug 1802
(4) Lorenzo LEWIS, *b* Woodlawn 13 Nov 1803; *m* 6 June 1827 Esther Maria (*b* 1804; *d* Audley, Clarke Co, Va., 23 June 1885), dau of Dr John Redman Coxe, of Philadelphia, and *d* Audley 27 Aug 1847, leaving issue:

Great-nephew's children
1a George Washington LEWIS, *b* Philadelphia 12 Feb 1829; *educ* Virginia Mily Inst; Commissary Officer Confederate States Army; *m* Baltimore 25 March 1852 Emily Contee (*b* 31 July 1832; *d* 8 April 1909), dau of Reverdy Johnson, of Baltimore (*b* 21 May 1796; *educ* St John's Coll, Md.; lawyer, Maryland State Senator 1821-25, US Senator (Whig) 1845-49 and 1863-68, US Atty-Gen 1849-50 and US Min to UK 1868-69; *d* 10 Feb 1876), and his w Mary Mackall Bowie, and *d* Monterey, Clarke Co, Va., 5 Feb 1885, having had issue:

Great-nephew's grandchildren
1b Lorenzo LEWIS, *b* Baltimore 11 March 1853; *m* 28 Feb 1885 Rose Ellzey (*b* 21 July 1855; *d* 21 Feb 1948), dau of Col Francis McCormick, of Berryville, Va., and his w Rosanna Mortimer Ellzey, and *d* Frankford, Va., 27 Feb 1887, leaving issue:

Great-nephew's great-grandchildren
1c George Washington LEWIS, *b* Clarke Co, Va., 22 July 1886; lawyer; *m* 12 Dec 1916, as her 1st husb, Sylvia Ishbel De Beck, of New York (she *m* 2nd —— Israel), and *d* Braddock, Va., 2 Oct 1918, leaving issue:

Great-nephew's great-great-grandchildren
1d *Lorenzo Custis LEWIS, *b* Braddock, 18 Nov 1917

Great-nephew's grandchildren
2b Reverdy Johnson LEWIS, *b* Audley 25 April, *d* there 1 May 1854
3b Mary Bowie LEWIS, *b* Monterey, Va., 17 July 1855; *d* Hoboken, New Jersey, 25 April 1886
4b Esther Maria Lewis, *b* Monterey 6 Aug 1856; *m* Berryville 7 Dec 1882 Samuel McCORMICK, of Berryville (*b* Frankford 5 July 1849; lawyer, Clerk Clarke Co Court 1904-12; *d* 17 Feb 1937), s of Col and Mrs Francis McCormick and bro of Mrs Lorenzo Lewis (*see above*), and *d* Four Winds, Berryville, 28 July 1931, having had issue:

Great-nephew's great-grandchildren
1c Emily Contee McCORMICK, *b* Monterey 15 Sept 1885; librarian; *d* 19—
2c Mary Lewis McCORMICK, *b* Norwood, Va., 11 Oct 1887; *d* there 17 July 1888
3c Edward Lewis McCORMICK, *b* Berryville 22 May 1895; *educ* Virginia Mily Inst; *d* 19—

Great-nephew's grandchildren
5b Emily Contee Lewis, *b* Monterey 29 Dec 1857; *m* Berryville 28 Oct 1879 Col Edwin Augustus STEVENS, Jr, of Castle Point, Hoboken, New Jersey (*b* Philadelphia 14 March 1858; *d* Washington, DC, 8 March 1918), s of Edwin Augustus Stevens and his 2nd w Martha Bayard Dod, and *d* Bedminster, New Jersey, 25 Oct 1931, having had issue:

Great-nephew's great-grandchildren
1c John STEVENS VI, *b* 28 Jan 1881; *d* 27 Aug 1932
2c Edwin Augustus STEVENS III, *b* Hoboken 15 Aug 1882; *educ* Stevens Inst; marine engr in New York, with US Shipping Bd World War I; *d* Hoboken 1 Dec 1954
3c Washington Lewis STEVENS, *b* 26 Sept 1883; *educ* Princeton (AB 1905); *m* 28 Oct 1905 (divorce 1916) Nannie Nye Jackson and *d* 5 March 1946
4c Bayard STEVENS, *b* 20 July 1885; *m* Berryville 11 Oct 1910 Mary Green (*b* Anchorage, Ky., 9 March 1887; *d* Berryville Jan 1966), dau of William Naylor McDonald, of Berryville, and his w Catherine S. Gray, and *d* Short Hills, New Jersey, 15 Nov 1927, leaving issue:

Great-nephew's great-great-grandchildren
1d John STEVENS VII, *b* Hoboken 8 Jan 1912; *educ* Princeton and Columbia U; writer; *d* New York 16 April 1941
2d *Bayard McDonald STEVENS [73 Goetze Street, Bay Head, NJ 08742, USA], *b* Hoboken 9 March 1916; *educ* Princeton (AB 1939) and New York U (AM); *m* Morristown, New Jersey, 24 May 1940 *Mary Louise Whitney (*b* 30 Sept 1918) and has issue:

Great-nephew's great-great-grandchildren's children
1e *Elizabeth Alexander Stevens, *b* New York 10 April 1942; *m* 20 May 1972 *Benjamin BERGSTEIN
2e *Bayard McDonald STEVENS, Jr [206 East 34th Street, New York, NY 10016, USA], *b* New York 27 June 1945

Great-nephew's great-great-grandchildren
3d *Nancy Gray Stevens, *b* Short Hills, New Jersey, 29 May 1925; *m* Berryville 25 Aug 1945 *Douglas Brooke ALLEN (*b* 1 Oct 1923) and has issue:

Great-nephew's great-great-grandchildren's children
1e *Catherine MacDonald ALLEN, *b* 19—
2e *Nancy Bayard ALLEN, *b* 1 Dec 1951

Great-nephew's great-grandchildren
5c Martha Bayard STEVENS, *b* Castle Point, Hoboken, 30 Dec 1886; *d* there 3 April 1888
6c Basil Martiau STEVENS, *b* Castle Point 28 Dec 1888; US Commissioner Dist of New Jersey 1932-36, Special Master in Chancery New Jersey 1933-47, Commissioner Supreme Court New Jersey 1933-47, Lt-Col Nat Gd New Jersey; *m* Newcastle, Pa., 28 Oct 1913 Helen Clendenin (*b* Newcastle 5 March 1891; *d* 2 Dec 1943), dau of Edward Hatnett Ward and his w Mary Clendenin, and *d* 7 Nov 1957, leaving issue:

> Great-nephew's great-great-grandchildren
> 1d Emily Custis Lewis Stevens, *b* Hoboken 22 May 1915; *m* 3 July 1948 *James Vincent de Paul TULLY [16 Prospect Avenue, Montclair, NJ 07042, USA] (*b* James Britt at Bayonne, New Jersey, 21 Sept 1910), s of John Britt and his w Emma Hall, and *d* Montclair 9 Feb 1980
> 2d Edwin Augustus STEVENS IV, *b* Bernardsville, New Jersey, 8 March 1917; *educ* Colorado U (AB, BEd 1941) and U of S California (MS, PhD); *m* Beverly Hills 14 Aug 1954 *Mary Susanne Leake (*b* 9 July 1928) and *d* Whittier, Calif., 26 Sept 1959, leaving issue:

>> Great-nephew's great-great-grandchildren's children
>> 1e *Edwin Augustus STEVENS V [316 19th Street, Santa Monica, CA 90402, USA], *b* 17 July 1955
>> 2e *Mary Stuyvesant STEVENS, *b* 9 Feb 1957
>> 3e *William Leake STEVENS, *b* 5 July 1959

Great-nephew's great-grandchildren
7c Lawrence Lewis STEVENS, *b* Castle Point, Hoboken, 29 Nov 1889; *m* Philadelphia 2 April 1913 Anne D. Malpass (*b* Philadelphia 22 Aug 1890; *d* May 1974) and *d* 1957, leaving issue:

> Great-nephew's great-great-grandchildren
> 1d *Lawrence Lewis STEVENS, Jr [462 Montgomery Avenue, Haverford, PA 19041, USA], *b* Philadelphia 29 July 1915; *educ* Pennsylvania U: *m* 19— *Dorothy A. Poole and has issue:

>> Great-nephew's great-great-grandchildren's children
>> 1e *Edward M. STEVENS [370 East 76th Street, New York, NY 10021, USA]
>> 2e *Mark L. STEVENS, *b* 19—; *educ* Susquehanna

Great-nephew's great-grandchildren
8c Emily Custis Lewis STEVENS, *b* Bernardsville 27 June 1896; *d* 8 May 1963

Great-nephew's grandchildren
6b Reverdy Johnson LEWIS, *b* Monterey, Va., 3 June 1859; *m* Alice Powers (*b* 23 Feb 1854; *d* 12 Oct 1934) and *d* Berryville 14 Dec 1928
7b Louise Travers LEWIS, *b* Monterey 3 March 1861; *d* 17 Aug 1863
8b Charles Conrad LEWIS, *b* Monterey 14 June 1862; *m* 1st 14 Feb 1895 Alice Maud Hough (*b* 1 Oct 1865; *d* 4 April 1902); *m* 2nd Cranford, New Jersey, 4 Sept 1912 Mabel Eleanor (*b* Philadelphia 30 July 1876), dau of William Henry Boyer and his w Sally Coxe, and *d* Fielding, Va., 7 March 1930, having with her had issue:

> Great-nephew's great-grandchildren
> 1c *Charles Conrad LEWIS, Jr [421 East Pall Mall, Winchester, VA 22601, USA], *b* Fielding 9 Feb 1918

Great-nephew's grandchildren
9b Louise Travers LEWIS, *b* Monterey 10 Oct 1863; *d* Rome, Italy, 20 Jan 1912
10b William Travers LEWIS, *b* Monterey 14 March 1865; lawyer, Commonwealth Atty Clarke Co; *m* Dec 1902 Maria Garnett McGuire (*b* 11 March 1867; *d* 19—) and *d* 17 May 1929, having had issue:

> Great-nephew's great-grandchildren
> 1c William Travers LEWIS, Jr, *b* 17 July, *d* 31 July 1904

Great-nephew's grandchildren
11b Ella Johnson Lewis, *b* Monterey 16 May 1868; *m* 1 June 1898 James McKenney WHITE (*b* 4 Dec 1873; *d* 19—) and *d* 18 May 1941
12b Robert Edward Lee LEWIS, of New York, *b* Monterey 17 Sept 1869; *educ* Sewanee Coll and Columbia Law Sch; lawyer; *m* 24 Nov 1896 Johanna Elizabeth Mathilde Gossler (*b* 24 May 1870; *d* 1952) and *d* Avon, New Jersey, 19 Oct 1946, leaving issue:

> Great-nephew's great-grandchildren
> 1c *Edwin Stevens LEWIS [Skyhill, Delaplane, VA 22025, USA], *b* 1898
> 2c *Robert Edward Lee LEWIS, Jr [Twyford, Old Tavern Road, Farmingdale, NJ 07727, USA; 913 Riverview Drive, Brielle, NJ 08730, USA], *b* 10 May 1903; *m* 4 June 1928 *Alice McKim Voss (*b* 28 April 1903) and has issue:

>> Great-nephew's great-great-grandchildren
>> 1d *Eleanor Custis LEWIS, *b* 19—
>> 2d *Sandra V. LEWIS, *b* 1933

Great-nephew's grandchildren

13b Maude Lewis, *b* Monterey 4 March 1871; *m* 31 Aug 1891 Fenton Peterkin WHITING, of Berryville, Va. (*b* 19 Dec 1853; *d* 6 June 1921), s of Francis Henry Whiting, and *d* 18 April 1925

14b Eleanor Parke Custis LEWIS, *b* Monterey 25 May, *d* there 23 Aug 1872

Great-nephew's children

2a John Redman Coxe LEWIS, *b* Audley, Va., 18 April 1834; accompanied Cdre Perry's expedition to Japan 1853, Offr US Revenue Cutter Service, Col Confederate States Army; *m* Richmond, Va., 12 Dec 1863, Maria Bradfute (*b* Lynchburg, Va., 24 May 1838; *d* 1920), dau of John Freeland, of Richmond, and his w Rose Bradfute and sister of Mrs Henry Lewellyn Daingerfield Lewis (*see below*), and *d* 1898, leaving issue:

Great-nephew's grandchildren

1b Lawrence Fielding LEWIS, *b* Richmond 7 Oct 1864; *m* 9 June 1891 Jane Hollins Nicholas and *d* 18— or 19—, leaving issue:

Great-nephew's great-grandchildren

1c *Janet Hollins Lewis, *b* Baltimore 27 April 1895; *m* 19— *Harry MANVELL, of Washington, DC, and has issue:

Great-nephew's great-great-grandchildren

1d *Harry MANVELL, Jr, *b* 19—

2d *Jean MANVELL, *b* 19—

Great-nephew's grandchildren

2b John Redman Coxe LEWIS, Jr, *b* Richmond 13 June 1870; *d* Virginia U 26 Feb 1905

3b Marie Stuart Lewis, *b* Richmond 25 Jan 1875; *m* Lexington, Va., 24 Nov 1908 St Julien Ravenel MARSHALL, of New York (*b* Portsmouth, Va., 23 Nov 1881), s of Col Richard Coke Marshall and his w Mary Catherine Wilson, and *d* 19—, having had issue:

Great-nephew's great-grandchildren

1c *St Julien Ravenel MARSHALL, Jr [521 East 14th Street, New York, NY 10003, USA], *b* Ruxton, Md., 24 July 1910; *educ* Columbia; *m* 23 June 1936 *Rebecca Stone, dau of Col Harold C. Fiske, and has issue:

Great-nephew's great-great-grandchildren

1d *Louise Ravenel Marshall [Mrs Carleton Rosenburgh, Scarsdale, NY 10583, USA], *b* 19—; *m* 1962 *Carleton Francis ROSENBURGH, Jr, s of Carleton Francis Rosenburgh

2d *Virginia Fiske MARSHALL, *b* 19—

Great-nephew's great-grandchildren

2c John Lewis MARSHALL, *b* Washington, DC, 23 June 1912; *d* New York 25 May 1927

Great-nephew's grandchildren

4b Duncan Freeland LEWIS, *b* Richmond 18 Feb 1876; *d* Washington, DC, 12 Feb 1914

Great-nephew's children

3a Lawrence Fielding LEWIS, *b* Audley, Va., 18 April 1834 (twin with John Redman Coxe Lewis); *d* 25 Jan 1857

4a Edward Parke Custis LEWIS, *b* Audley 7 Feb 1837; Col Confederate States Army, US Min Portugal; *m* 1st 23 March 1858 Lucy Belmain (*b* 1839; *d* Audley 28 Aug 1866), dau of Josiah William Ware, of Berryville, and his w Frances Toy Glassell, and had issue:

Great-nephew's grandchildren

1b Eleanor Angela LEWIS, *b* 25 July 1859; *d* 18 Feb 1860

2b Lawrence Fielding LEWIS, *b* 1861; *d* in infancy

3b John Glassell LEWIS, *b* 1862; *d* in infancy

4b Edward Parke Custis LEWIS, *b* Aug 1864; *d* 22 March 1866

5b Lucy Ware Lewis, *b* Audley 26 Aug 1866; *m* 31 Dec 1893 Charles Treadwell Ayres McCORMICK, of Berryville (*b* 11 March 1861; *d* 16 March 1932), and *d* 8 Nov 1944, having had issue:

Great-nephew's great-grandchildren

1c Charles Treadwell Ayres McCORMICK, Jr; served World War I with US Marine Corps; *ka* Soissons, France, 1918

2c Mary Elizabeth McCORMICK, *b* 6 Aug 1899; *d* 16 Aug 1908

Great-nephew's children

4a (cont.) Edward P. Lewis *m* 2nd Baltimore 1 June 1869 Mary Picton (*b* Philadelphia 19 May 1840; *d* Bernardsville, New Jersey, 21 Sept 1903), widow of Gen Muscoe Russell Hunter Garnett and dau of Edwin Augustus Stevens and his 1st w Mary B. Picton (also half-sister of Col Edwin Augustus Stevens, Jr, for whom *see above*), and *d* Hoboken 3 Sept 1892, having with his 2nd w had issue:

Great-nephew's grandchildren

6b Edwin Augustus Stevens LEWIS, *b* Pau, France, 15 March 1870; lawyer; *m* 7 Jan 1899 Alice Stuart (*b* New York

24 Nov 1877; *d* Baltimore 22 Nov 1973), dau of Gen Henry Harrison Walker, Confederate States Army, and his w Mary Stuart Mercer, and *d* 5 Sept 1906, leaving issue:

Great-nephew's great-grandchildren
1c Edward Parke Custis LEWIS; *b* Hoboken 13 Feb 1900; *d* Baltimore 21 July 1973
2c *Henry Harrison Walker LEWIS [103 St John's Road, Baltimore, MD 21210, USA], *b* Hoboken 10 Feb 1904; lawyer; *m* 7 Oct 1938 *Eleanor Randall (*b* Pottsville, Pa., 3 Oct 1914), dau of John Marbury Nelson, Jr, and his w Ellen Cheston McIlvaine, and has issue:

Great-nephew's great-great-grandchildren
1d *Edwin Augustus Stevens LEWIS, *b* Baltimore 4 March 1940; *m* 27 Jan 1968 *Mary Ann (*b* 15 July 1938), dau of Donald Glasgo, and has issue:

Great-nephew's great-great-grandchildren's children
1e *Catherine Bell LEWIS, *b* Hartford, Conn., 7 Feb 1970
2e *Walker LEWIS, *b* Schenectady, New York, 23 Nov 1972

Great-nephew's great-great-grandchildren
2d *John Nelson LEWIS, *b* Baltimore 16 March 1942; *m* 11 Aug 1973 *Jo Deweese (*b* 21 Dec 1945)
3d *Fielding LEWIS, *b* Pasadena, Calif., 11 March 1945; *m* 12 June 1976 *Elizabeth Ann (*b* 10 Aug 1948), dau of Leland H. Pence
4d *Henry McIlvaine LEWIS, *b* Baltimore 10 March 1947; *m* 22 Nov 1969 *Deborah Ann (*b* 13 June 1949), dau of Charles B. Sanders, and has issue:

Great-nephew's great-great-grandchildren's children
1e *Kelly Lynn LEWIS, *b* Princeton, New Jersey, 21 Nov 1971
2e *Erin Evenson LEWIS, *b* Worcester, Mass., 22 Sept 1974
3e *Megan McIlvaine LEWIS, *b* Medfield, Mass., 19 March 1978

Great-nephew's grandchildren
7b Esther Maria Lewis, *b* Geneva, Switzerland, 17 June 1871; *m* 19 May 1894 Charles Merrill CHAPIN, of Cleveland, Ohio, and New York City (*b* 19 April 1871; *d* 1932), and *d* Bernardsville, New Jersey, 21 June 1959, leaving issue:

Great-nephew's great-grandchildren
1c Mary Stevens Chapin, *b* 10 Nov 1895; *m* 1 July 1916 Dr Shepard KRECH, of New York (*b* St Paul, Minn., 22 Feb 1891; *d* East Hampton, Long Island, 15 Dec 1968), s of Alvin William Krech and his w Caroline Shepard, and *d* East Hampton 23 Sept 1967, leaving issue:

Great-nephew's great-great-grandchildren
1d *Dr Shepard KRECH, Jr [PO Box 779, Easton, MD 21601, USA], *b* New York 24 April 1918; *educ* Groton, Yale and Columbia; physician 1944-75, environmentalist 1975-; *m* 14 Aug 1940 *Nora, dau of Clarkson Potter and his w Amy Holland, and has issue:

Great-nephew's great-great-grandchildren's children
1e *Amy Krech [Mrs Thomas B Knowles Jr, PO Box 13, Islamorada, FL 33036, USA], *b* New York 1 Oct 1941; *m* Easton, Md., 21 Dec 1963 *Thomas Barnes KNOWLES, Jr, and has issue:

Great-nephew's great-great-grandchildren's grandchildren
1f *Barnes KNOWLES, *b* 19—
2f *Carter Shepard KNOWLES, *b* 19—

Great-nephew's great-great-grandchildren's children
2e *Professor Shepard KRECH III [84 Keene St, Providence, RI 02906, USA], *b* New York 22 Feb 1944; *educ* Groton, Yale (BA), Oxford, UK (BLitt), and Harvard (PhD); Prof Anthropology Brown U; *m* 1st 1970 (divorce 1982) Minette Dill, dau of Gordon Grand, and has issue:

Great-nephew's great-great-grandchildren's grandchildren
1f *Kerry Dill KRECH, *b* Cambridge, Mass., 19 Jan 1970
2f *Teal Chapin KRECH, *b* Cambridge 14 March 1973

Great-nephew's great-great-grandchildren's children
2e (cont.) Prof Shepard Krech III *m* 2nd 23 Sept 1983 *Sheila, dau of Peter ffolliott and his w Gertrude

Great-nephew's great-great-grandchildren
2d *(Merrill) Chapin KRECH [1537 Saragossa Avenue, Coral Gables, FL 33134, USA], *b* New York 18 Sept 1919; *educ* Yale; *m* East Hampton 27 July 1946 *Cynthia Smathers Haynes
3d *Mary Esther Krech [Mrs Lyttleton Gould Jr, Brush Hill Rd, Hadlyme, CT 06439, USA], *b* Boston 12 Dec 1921; *m* 1st 26 July 1941 William Brinckelhoff JACKSON and has issue:

Great-nephew's great-great-grandchildren's children
1e *Mary Stevens JACKSON, *b* 19—
2e *Barbara JACKSON, *b* 19—

Great-nephew's great-great-grandchildren

3d (cont.) Mary Krech Jackson *m* 2nd 21 June 1947 *Lyttleton Bowen Purnell GOULD, Jr, s of Lyttleton Bowen Purnell Gould, and has further issue:

Great-nephew's great-great-grandchildren's children

3e *Lyttleton Bowen Purnell GOULD III [1330 Massachusetts Avenue, Washington, DC, USA], *b* 6 March 1948

4e *Isabel Cynthia GOULD, *b* 28 Oct 1950

Great-nephew's great-great-grandchildren

4d *Alvin William KRECH [PO Box 330, Big Pine Key, FL 33043, USA], *b* New York 10 Jan 1925; *educ* Goddard Coll; *m* Thomasville, Ga., 16 June 1948 *Virginia Groover, dau of William Thomas Mardre, of Boston, Ga.

Great-nephew's great-grandchildren

2c *Charles Merrill CHAPIN, Jr, *b* 27 May 1898; *m* 1st 7 July 1925 Cynthia Meldrum Robinson (*d* 1934); *m* 2nd 19— *Katherine, formerly w of Charles Huntington Erhart and dau of George Edward Kent, of Jericho, New York, and has two children

Great-nephew's grandchildren

8b Julia Stevens Lewis, *b* Hoboken 4 March 1874; *m* 4 June 1898 James Millar CUMMING, of Newark, New Jersey (*b* Kilmarnock, Scotland, 28 March 1876), s of Robert Cumming, of Ayrshire, Scotland, and his w Elizabeth Aitken Millar, and had issue:

Great-nephew's great-grandchildren

1c *Dr Robert A. CUMMING, *b* Bernardsville 5 July 1900; *educ* Edinburgh U; *m* Feb 1929 *Elizabeth Jean (*b* 17 April 1901), dau of William Knox, of Edinburgh, and has issue:

Great-nephew's great-great-grandchildren

1d *Grace Kirk CUMMING, *b* 11 April 1931

2d *Julia Stevens Lewis CUMMING, *b* 19—

3d *Robert CUMMING, *b* 19—

Great-nephew's great-grandchildren

2c *Edward Parke Custis Lewis CUMMING [Rock Hill, Oyster Bay, Long Island, NY 11771, USA], *b* Newark, New Jersey, 25 June 1905; *educ* Emmanuel Coll, Cambridge, UK; *m* 4 June 1927 (divorce 19—) Lucy Barney, dau of Walter Gurnee, of Oyster Bay, Long Island, and has issue:

Great-nephew's great-great-grandchildren

1d *Edward Parke Custis Lewis CUMMING, Jr, *b* 19—; *m* 16 April 1955 *Kerrin Bartlett Gjellerup

Great-nephew's grandchildren

9b Elinor Parke Custis Lewis, *b* 28 March 1876; *m* 1st 14 Jan 1905 (divorce 19—) Thomas Bloodgood PECK, Jr, of New York (*b* 22 Feb 1875; *d* after 1912), s of Thomas Bloodgood Peck; *m* 2nd 19— Dr Baron Zdenko von DWORZAK, of Florence, Italy (*b* 1875; *d* 19—), and *d* 19—

Great-nephew's children

5a Charles Conrad LEWIS, *b* Audley 28 Oct 1839; *d* U of Virginia 7 March 1859

6a Henry Llewellyn Daingerfield LEWIS, *b* Audley 25 April 1843; *educ* Virginia Mily Inst; memb staff of Govr Fitzhugh Lee of Virginia; *m* 26 April 1871 Carter Penn (*b* Richmond, Va., 11 March 1853; *d* Charlotte, N Carolina, 3 Dec 1915), dau of John Freeland, of Richmond, and his w Rosalie Warwick Bradfute (also sister of Mrs John Redman Coxe Lewis, for whom *see* above), and *d* Audley 17 Dec 1893, having had issue:

Great-nephew's grandchildren

1b Rosalie Warwick Lewis, *b* Berryville 21 July 1872; *m* there 21 June 1893, as his 1st w, Frank Vincit TILFORD, of Washington, DC (*b* New York 30 Nov 1871; *d* 1932), s of John Boyle Tilford and his w Florinda Jones Hammond, and *d* Berryville 28 Sept 1895

2b Lorenzo Conrad LEWIS, *b* 18 July 1874; *d* 20 Nov 1879

3b James Freeland LEWIS, of St Petersburg, Fla., *b* Berryville 31 Oct 1875; *m* 1907 Page Ellyson, of Newport News, Va. (*b* 31 Aug 1886; *d* 19—), and *d* St Petersburg 8 Aug 1952, leaving issue:

Great-nephew's great-grandchildren

1c *James Freeland LEWIS, Jr [2214 River Road, Maumee, OH 43537, USA], *b* 19—; *m* and has issue:

Great-nephew's great-great-grandchildren

1d *Moaste Fielding LEWIS, *b* 19—

Great-nephew's great-grandchildren

2c *Page Ellyson LEWIS, *b* 19—

Great-nephew's grandchildren

4b Henry Llewellyn Daingerfield LEWIS, Jr, of Hewlett, Long Island, *b* Richmond 17 June 1877; *educ* Virginia Mily Inst; *m* 1st 1916 (divorce 1924) Lucy Reis; *m* 2nd 2 May 1925 Jessie Somerville Knox Voss and *d* Hewlett, Long Island, 9 Jan 1938

5b Edward Parke Custis LEWIS, b 2 May 1879; d Lexington, Va., 10 March 1896

6b Esther Maria Lewis, b Audley, Va., 26 March 1881; m Winchester, Va., 3 Oct 1906 Dr (Alexander) Wylie MOORE, of Charlotte, N Carolina (b Chester, S Carolina, 23 Feb 1878; d c 1950), s of Eli Peyton Moore and his w Annie Wylie, and d c 1944

7b Mary Picton LEWIS, b 27 May 1883; d 17 Jan 1905

8b Carter Penn Lewis, b Audley 2 July 1885; m 19— William Henry WILEY, of Hackensack, New Jersey, and d Wilmington, Del., 4 July 1963, leaving issue:

Great-nephew's great-grandchildren

1c *Carter Penn Wiley, b 19—; m 19— *—— DESBERNINE

2c *Mary Patricia Wiley [Mrs Harold Brown, Chadd's Ford, PA 19317, USA], b 19—; m 19— *Harold G. BROWN

Great-nephew's grandchildren

9b John Freeland LEWIS, b 18 March 1887; d 15 June 1894

10b Margaret Byrd Lewis, b 1889; m 27 Oct 1917, as his 1st w, Thomas Bolling BYRD, of Winchester, Va. (b 4 Sept 1889), s of Richard Evelyn Byrd and his w Elinor Bolling Flood, and d Charlotte, N Carolina, 13 April 1920, leaving issue:

Great-nephew's great-grandchildren

1c *Margaret Lewis Byrd, b Charlotte, N Carolina, 13 April 1920; m 19— *Harry F. STIMPSON, Jr, s of Harry F. Stimpson

Great-nephew's grandchildren

11b Fielding LEWIS, of Charlotte, N Carolina, and Tampa, Fla., b Audley 28 Oct 1890; d before 1952

12b William McGuire LEWIS, b 14 March 1892; d 14 April 1893

Great-nieces and -nephews

(5) Eleanor Agnes Freire LEWIS, b Woodlawn 8 Aug 1805; d Philadelphia 28 Aug 1820

(6) Fielding Augustine LEWIS, b Woodlawn 12 July 1807; d 27 March 1809

(7) George Washington Custis LEWIS, b Woodlawn 14 Feb 1810; d 16 Dec 1811

(8) Mary/Martha Eliza/Eleanor Angela Lewis, b Woodlawn 1 April 1813; m there 30 July 1835 Charles Magill CONRAD (b Winchester, Va., 24 Dec 1804; US Senator 1842-43, Congressman 1849-50, Sec of War 1850-53, Memb Confederate Congress 1862-64, Brig-Gen Confederate States Army; paralysed by a stroke while testifying in court and d New Orleans 11 Feb 1878), s of Federick Conrad and his w Frances Thruston, and d Pass Christian, Miss., 21 Sept 1839, having had issue:

Great-niece's children

1a Angela Lewis CONRAD, b New Orleans 17 March 1836; d 25 March 1837

2a Charles Angelo Lewis CONRAD, b Bay St Louis 14 Aug 1837; m 1867 Norma (d 28 Sept 1915), dau of Alfred Penn, of Lynchburg, Va., and his w Evelyn Bradfute, and d New Orleans 23 Sept 1892

3a Lawrence Lewis CONRAD, b Pass Christian 3 July 1839; m 18— Sallie Howard Worthington, of Baltimore (b 26 April 1842; d 2 June 1917), and d 7 Aug 1883, leaving issue:

Great-niece's grandchildren

1b Charles Angelo Lewis CONRAD, b 8 Jan 1873; d 1 March 1911

2b Marie W. Conrad, b 4 April 1884; m, as his 1st w, Dr Louis C. LEHR, of Baltimore (b 19 Feb 1876; d 20 Feb 1930), and d 6 June 1921

President Washington's nephew

8 (Betty Washington Lewis's 8th s) Robert LEWIS, b 1769; m 17— or 18— and d 1829, having had at least four daus; the fourth:

Great-niece

(4) Betty Burnett, b 17— or 18—; m 18— George Washington BASSETT and d 18— having had at least five children, all daus; the fifth:

Great-niece's children

5a Ella More Bassett, b Eltham, New Kent Co, Va., 7 Sept 1834; m Clover Lea, as his 2nd w, Col Lewis William WASHINGTON (b 1812; d 1871), 4th s of George Corbin Washington (see above under issue of Capt Augustine Washington's first marriage, i.e., President WASHINGTON's half-brothers and sisters)

VII Samuel WASHINGTON, of Harewood, Jefferson Co, Va., b Wakefield, Westmoreland Co, Va., 16 Nov 1734; Col Virginia Militia, JP and High Sheriff in pre-Revolutionary Virginia; m 1st c 1754 Jane (d c 1755), dau of Col John Champe, of Lamb's Creek, King George Co; m 2nd c 1756 his 1st cousin once-removed Mildred (b c 1741; d c 1762), dau of Col John Thornton, of Caroline County, Va., and his w Mildred, dau and co-heiress of Roger Gregory by his w Mildred Washington, President WASHINGTON's aunt, and with her had issue:

President Washington's nephew

1 Thornton WASHINGTON, b Stafford County, Va., c 1758; m 1st Charles Co, Md., 26 Dec 1779 his 4th cousin Mildred (b c 1760; d c 1785), dau of Thomas Berry and his w Elizabeth Washington, and had issue:

Great-nephews

(1) Thomas Berry WASHINGTON, *b c* 1780; *d* 1794

(2) John Thornton Augustine WASHINGTON, of Cedar Lawn, Jefferson Co, Va., *b* Berkeley Co 20 May 1783; *m* Shepherdstown 24 Sept 1810 Elizabeth Conrad (*b* Shepherdstown 27 Sept 1793; *d* Cedar Lawn 21 Oct 1837), dau of Maj Daniel Bedinger and his w Sarah Rutherford and sister of Hon Henry Bedinger, US Min to Denmark, and *d* Cedar Lawn 9 Oct 1841, having had issue:

Great-nephew's children

1a Lawrence Berry WASHINGTON, *b* Cedar Lawn 26 Nov 1811; lawyer and writer, Lt Virginia Militia Mexican War; *d* Missouri 21 Sept 1856

2a Daniel Bedinger WASHINGTON, *b* Cedar Lawn 8 Feb 1814; Col Confederate States Army; *m* Harper's Ferry, Va., 24 Oct 1843, his half-1st cousin Lucy Anne (*b* 9 Dec 1811; *d* 22 Aug 1885), widow of Dr John James Wharton and dau of Samuel Washington (*see below*), and *d* 28 Dec 1887, having had issue:

Great-nephew's grandchildren

1b Samuel Thornton WASHINGTON, *b* Cedar Lawn 23 Dec 1844; *d* Buffalo, Putnam Co, W. Va., 15 Nov 1850

2b Catharine Townsend WASHINGTON, *b* Cedar Lawn 11 Sept 1846; *d* Garden City, Cass Co, Mo., 27 Oct 1919

3b Elizabeth Bedinger Washington, *b* Red House, Putnam Co, 3 Sept 1848; *m* Index, Cass Co, Mo., 26 May 1881 Clark CRAIG (*b* Buffalo, W. Va., 20 Oct 1837; *d* there 15 May 1904) and *d* Poca, Putnam Co, 28 Oct 1931, leaving one s and two daus

4b Thornton Augustine WASHINGTON, *b* Buffalo, W. Va., 23 April 1854; *d* Garden City 10 Aug 1935

5b Marian Wallace WASHINGTON, *b* Otterville, Johnson Co, Mo., 17 June 1856; *d* Cass Co 18 July 1948

Great-nephew's children

3a Virginia Thornton WASHINGTON, *b* Cedar Lawn 22 May 1816; *d* Jefferson Co, Va., 13 Nov 1838

4a Sarah Eleanor WASHINGTON, *b* Cedar Lawn 7 April 1818; *d* Cass Co 21 Jan 1858

5a Benjamin Franklin WASHINGTON, *b* Cedar Lawn 17 April 1820; author, Collector of the Port of San Francisco; *m* Charles Town, Va., 22 Oct 1845 Georgianna Hite (*b* Jefferson Co *c* 1822; *d* San Francisco 3 Dec 1860), dau of James Lackland Ransom and his w Frances Madison Hite, niece of President MADISON, and *d* San Francisco 22 Jan 1872, having had issue:

Great-nephew's grandchildren

1b John Thornton WASHINGTON, *b* Charles Town 26 July 1846; *d* San Francisco 22 Feb 1929

2b Franklin Bedinger WASHINGTON, *b* Charles Town 13 June 1848; *m* Mill Valley, Calif., 14 June 1898 Alice Maria Bacon (*b* San Francisco 30 Oct 1858; *d* Palo Alto, Calif., 25 April 1939) and *d* Oakland, Calif., 12 May 1915, leaving issue:

Great-nephew's great-grandchildren

1c *Lawrence WASHINGTON [868 Northampton Drive, Palo Alto, CA 94303, USA], *b* San Francisco 30 May 1899; *m* Berkeley, Calif., 24 Jan 1942 *Eileen Louise McCall (*b* Portland, Oreg., 6 Sept 1907) and has issue:

Great-nephew's great-great-grandchildren

1d *Margot Elise Washington, *b* Berkeley 9 Nov 1942; *m* 22 Nov 1962 *David Clarence HALL (*b* 18 May 1939) and has issue:

Great-nephew's great-great-grandchildren's children

1e *Daniel Lawrence Washington HALL, *b* 14 June 1963

2e *Wendy Lynn HALL, *b* 24 Feb 1965

3e *Timothy David HALL, *b* 29 March 1966

Great-nephew's grandchildren

3b Fanny Madison Washington, *b* San Francisco 13 Aug 1853; *m* there 8 April 1876 Capt Daniel DELEHANTY, USN (*b* 12 Dec 1845; *d* 2 Feb 1918), and *d* 4 June 1930, having had three s and four daus

4b Lillian WASHINGTON, *b* San Francisco 12 July 1856; *d* Charles Town 26 March 1857

5b Bertha James Washington, *b* San Francisco 2 March 1858; *m* 1st 8 Sept 1880 Sherwood CALLAGHAN (*d* London, UK, *c* 1890) and had four daus; *m* 2nd London *c* 1891 William Robert SULLIVAN (*b* 14 Dec 1860; *d* Los Angeles Feb 1916) and *d* 29 June 1935

Great-nephew's children

6a Georgeanna Augusta Washington, *b* Cedar Lawn 3 March 1822; *m* there 20 Nov 1851 Col John Wheeler SMITH, US Army (*b* 14 May 1825; *d* 23 Dec 1892), s of Samuel Mansfield Smith and his w Eliza, and *d* Little Rock, Ark., 26 Oct 1895, leaving two s and three daus

7a Mary Elizabeth Washington, *b* Cedar Lawn 11 March 1824; *m* Johnson County, Mo., 17 Aug 1858 Squire ASBURY (*b* 16 March 1821; *d* 10 March 1896) and *d* Pleasant Grove, Ark., 3 March 1898, having had one s and two daus

8a Thornton Augustine WASHINGTON, *b* Cedar Lawn 22 Jan 1826; Maj and Assist Adj-Gen Confederate States Army; *m* San Antonio, Tex., 8 March 1860 Olive Ann (*b* Detroit 8 Sept 1839; *d* Washington, DC, 1 April 1922), dau of Enoch Jones and his w Olive Ann, and *d* Washington, DC, 10 July 1894, leaving issue:

Great-nephew's grandchildren

1b Flora May WASHINGTON, *b* Indianola, Tex., 1 May 1861; *d* Washington, DC, 17 June 1927

2b George Thornton WASHINGTON, *b* San Antonio 13 April 1863; *m* 13 Dec 1889 Catherine La Vallee (*b* New Orleans 24 Feb 1865; *d* there Nov 1953) and *d* New Orleans 11 Oct 1938

3b Lee Howard WASHINGTON (dau), *b* San Antonio 17 April 1865; *d* Washington, DC, 3 Oct 1930

4b Sarah WASHINGTON, *b* San Antonio 12 April 1867; *d* 27 Dec 1909

5b Lawrence Berry WASHINGTON, *b* San Antonio 23 July 1869; *m* 8 Oct 1908 Ruth Bird and *d* Tulsa, Okla., 16 Aug 1919

6b Olive Ann Washington, *b* Galveston, Tex., 12 Sept 1875; *m* Washington, DC, 5 Sept 1905 Frank COBURN (*b* 21 May 1862; *d c* 1946) and *d* June 1954, having had one s and one dau

7b Elizabeth Washington, *b* 17 March 1877; *m* Washington, DC, 8 Oct 1902 Vernon Goldsborough OWEN (*b* Gaithersburg, Md., 1 May 1879; *d* Washington, DC, 20 Feb 1944) and *d* Washington, DC, 8 May 1963, having had one s and one dau

Great-nephew's children

9a Mildred Berry WASHINGTON, *b* Cedar Lawn 3 Sept, *d* there 12 Sept 1827

10a Mildred Berry Washington, *b* Cedar Lawn 28 March 1829; *m* there 8 Feb 1854 Solomon Singleton BEDINGER (*d* 8 Feb 1873), s of Henry Clay Bedinger and his 2nd w Judith Singleton, and *d* Lewisburg, Conway Co, Ark., 8 Nov 1871, having had three s and two daus

11a George WASHINGTON, *b* Cedar Lawn 9 Dec 1830; Judge Johnson Co, Mo.; *m* Otterville, Johnson Co, 11 April 1871 Mary Virginia (*b* Cooper Co, Md., 23 May 1844; *d* 1931), dau of William Rowland Dempsey and his w Mahala, and *d* 20 Nov 1890, having had issue:

Great-nephew's grandchildren

1b Robert WASHINGTON, *b* Centerview, Johnson Co, 17 March 1872; *d* in infancy

2b Mary Virginia WASHINGTON, *b* Centerview 14 July 1873; *d* there 24 April 1882

3b Vernon de Hertburn WASHINGTON, *b* Centerview 27 July 1876; *d* Eldorado Springs, Mo., 23 Aug 1941

Great-nephew's children

12a Susan Ellsworth Washington, *b* Cedar Lawn 1 April 1833; *m* 22 May 1857 Henry Clay BEDINGER, of Lewis Co, Ky. (*b* 5 Sept 1832; *d* 27 July 1908), s of Henry Clay Bedinger and his 2nd w Judith Singleton and bro of Solomon Singleton Bedinger (*see above*), and *d* 28 July 1893, having had three s and five daus

13a Henrietta Gray WASHINGTON, *b* Cedar Lawn 10 Sept 1835; *d* 18 Dec 1838

President Washington's nephew

1 (cont.) Thornton Washington *m* 2nd, King George Co, 2 April 1786, as her 1st husb, Frances Townshend (*b* 18 April 1767; *m* 2nd King George Co 14 June 1788 Col Griffin Stith; *d* before 1808), dau of Lawrence Washington and his w Elizabeth Dade, and *d* Berkeley Co 1787, having with her had issue:

Great-nephew

(3) Samuel WASHINGTON, of Delraine, Culpeper Co, Va., and Newport, Ky., *b* Berkeley Co 14 Feb 1787; *m* 18— his 2nd cousin Catherine Townshend (*b* 25 Aug 1790; *d* Delhi, Hamilton Co, Ohio 4 Sept 1869), dau of John Washington and his w Martha Massey, and *d* Delhi 18 March 1867, leaving issue (with three other children, all of whom *d* young):

Great-nephew's children

1a Lucy Anna Washington, *b* Culpeper Co 9 Dec 1811; *m* 1st there 2 April 1834 Dr John James WHARTON, of Greenville, Culpeper Co (*b* London, UK, 1807; *d* St Louis, Mo., *c* 1839), s of Dr John Wharton and his w Ann (widow of —— Abbott), and had one son and one dau; *m* 2nd 24 Oct 1843 her half-first cousin Daniel Bedinger WASHINGTON (*see above*) and *d* Index, Mo., 22 Aug 1885, having had further issue

2a John Thornton Augustine WASHINGTON, *b* Virginia 1812; commission merchant Memphis, Tenn., and Newport, Ky.; *m* Lexington, Ky., 20 Jan 1839 Adelaide Josephine (*b c* 1822; *d* Newport 13 April 1893), dau of Thomas Tibbatts, of Lexington, and *d* Newport 8 May 1888, having had issue:

Great-nephew's grandchildren

1b Mary Elizabeth WASHINGTON, *b* 23 Nov 1839; *d* after 1866

2b Elizabeth Washington, *b* Newport, Ky., 15 March 1842; *m* Campbell Co, Ky., 18 June 1962 Col John Barry TAYLOR (*b c* 1837; *d* Newport 22 Dec 1914) and *d* Newport 22 May 1917

3b Francis Townsend WASHINGTON, *b* 14 Oct 1844?; *m* 18— or 19— Josephine Russell (*d* Englewood, New Jersey, 7 July 1930) and *d* 6 Nov 1917

4b John Thornton WASHINGTON, of St Louis, Mo., *b* 14 Oct 1852; *m* 1886 Agatha (*b* Baltimore *c* 1863; *d* Cincinnati, Ohio, 17 Dec 1941), dau of Jerome Bonaparte Timmonds and his w Kathryn Ayers, and *d* London Bridge, Princess Anne Co, Va., 30 Jan 1910, having had issue:

Great-nephew's great-grandchildren

1c Betty Washington, *b* St Louis, Mo., 23 May 1892; *m* Newport, Ky., her 2nd cousin Dr Herbert Hoffman TRUESDELL (*b* Campbell Co, Ky., 8 Feb 1873; *d* Newport 9 June 1963), s of George Fletcher Truesdell and his w Lucy Ella, herself dau of George Washington Carmack and his w Martha Dandridge Washington (*see below*), and had issue:

Great-nephew's great-great-grandchildren
1d *Patricia Truesdell, b 20 Feb 1922; m *Kenneth DAVIS and has one dau

Great-nephew's great-grandchildren
2c John Taylor WASHINGTON, b 18— or 19—; d aged 18
3c Adelaide Estelle WASHINGTON, b St Louis, Mo., 16 Oct 1906; d 14 March 1942

Great-nephew's grandchildren
5b Florence May WASHINGTON, b Newport, Ky., 8 May 1856; d 15 July 1926

Great-nephew's children
3a Frances T. WASHINGTON, b c 1813; d Delraine, Culpeper Co, Va., June 1830
4a George WASHINGTON, of Newport, Ky., b Culpeper, Va., 2 Jan 1815?; steamboat captain; m 1st 28 Sept 1837 Mary Elizabeth (b 4 March 1814; d Covington, Ky., 12 Jan 1839), dau of Benjamin Wharton and his w Elizabeth Finney Gray, and had issue:

Great-nephew's grandchildren
1b Thomas Wharton WASHINGTON, b 1 Jan, d 20 Aug 1839

Great-nephew's children
4a (cont.) Capt George Washington m 2nd Campbell Co, Ky., 10 May 1842 Martha Ann (b Ohio c 1823; d 1876), dau of John Doxon and his w Elizabeth Nolan, and d Newport, Ky., 1857, having with her had issue:

Great-nephew's grandchildren
2b George WASHINGTON, of Knoxville, Tenn., and Newport, Ky., b Newport 25 Dec 1843; lawyer, Chm Kentucky Constitutional Convention 1890; m Memphis, Tenn., 1867 Jane Todd (b Tenn. 6 Oct 1847; d Tex. 29 Oct 1924), dau of Dr Francis Alexander Ramsey and his w Anne Maria Breck, and d Newport 23 Aug 1905, having had issue:

Great-nephew's great-grandchildren
1c Ramsey WASHINGTON, b Memphis, Tenn., 4 Feb 1869; County Atty Campbell Co, Ky.; m 1st 27 Dec 1897 Eunice E. Barbee, of Ohio; m 2nd Ida M. Hughes and d 19 Sept 1923
2c Bushrod WASHINGTON, b May? 1870; d before 1877
3c Anne Lee Washington, b Knoxville, Tenn., 6 Oct 1872; m 14 Sept 1904 Ezekiel Field CLAY, Jr, of Lexington, Ky. (b 16 June 1871; d 1915), s of Col Ezekiel Field Clay and his w Mary Letitia Woodford and gggs of Gen William Woodford and his w Mary Thornton, dau of John Thornton and Mildred Gregory, 1st cousin of President WASHINGTON), and d 1922, leaving one s
4c Alfred Rogers WASHINGTON, b Knoxville, Tenn., 24 Feb 1876; m 17 March 1904 Katherine Montgomery Lucas, of Paris, Ky., and d San Francisco 1925
5c Revd William Morrow WASHINGTON, b Knoxville 7 June 1877; Rector of St Thomas's Episcopal Church, Detroit; m Tex. 25 June 1902 Janet Margaret Thomas (b Newport, Ky., 25 June 1877; d Washington, DC, 21 April 1954) and d 6 Feb 1942, having had issue:

Great-nephew's great-great-grandchildren
1d Janet WASHINGTON, b 1907; d 1907 or 1908
2d George Thomas WASHINGTON, b Ohio 24 June 1908; educ Yale and Oxford, UK (Rhodes Scholar); Prof Law Cornell, Assist US Slr-Gen, Judge US Circuit Court of Appeals for DC; m 18 July 1953 *Helen Goodner (b 17 June 1909) and d Santa Barbara, Calif., 21 Aug 1971
3d *Katherine Elizabeth Washington [Mrs Donald Scheurer, 204 Garden Court, Falls Church, VA, USA], b Ohio 10 Oct 1909; m 19— *Cdr Donald Bertram SCHEURER, USN, and has issue:

Great-nephew's great-great-grandchildren's children
1e *Janet Washington SCHEURER, b 12 Feb 1942
2e *Andrea M. SCHEURER, b 16 July 1947

Great-nephew's great-grandchildren
6c Elizabeth Taylor WASHINGTON, b Knoxville, Tenn., 17 Sept 1878; d 4 May 1895
7c John WASHINGTON; d in infancy

Great-nephew's grandchildren
3b Alice Washington, b 17 July 1846; m Gettys SCOTT, Pncpl Sch for Deaf Mutes, Austin, Tex., and d 1901, leaving six children
4b Ernest WASHINGTON, b 14 May 1849; d 23 June 1852

Great-nephew's children
5a Martha Dandridge Washington, b Va. Aug 1817; m 1st Culpeper Co, Va., 1832 Allen Thomas JOHNSON and had one s; m 2nd Campbell Co, Ky., 14 May 1838 George Washington CARMACK (b nr Knoxville, Tenn., June 1812; d Alexandria, Campbell Co, Ky., April 1895) and d 18 May 1881, having had a further five s and two daus
6a Marion W. Washington, b Culpeper Co, Va., 19 March 1819; m Hamilton Co, Ohio, 11 May 1854 Dr John M. MACKENZIE (b Columbiana Co, Ohio, 14 March 1816; d Delhi, Ohio, 20 April 1891), s of James Mackenzie and his w Ellen Burrowes, and d Delhi 15 Jan 1889
7a Maria Washington, b 1823; m Campbell Co 17 March 1847 James E. PERRY, of Newport, Ky., and d Newport

1901, having had two s and five daus

8a John Francis WASHINGTON, of Memphis, Tenn., *b* Va. *c* 1826; *m* Hamilton Co, Ohio, 28 June 1854 Eleanor *b* Mackenzie (*b* Ohio *c* 1837; *d* Memphis 5 Oct 1878) and *d* Memphis 23 Sept 1897, having had issue:

Great-nephew's grandchildren

1b Mary Washington, *b* Alexandria, Campbell Co, 7 April 1855; *m* William M. CARR (*b c* 1849; *d* 16 March 1900) and *d* 31 Oct 1937, having had two daus

2b George WASHINGTON, *b* Ky. *c* 1857; *d* 3 Nov 1888

3b Vernon Delraine WASHINGTON; *d* in infancy

Great-nephew's children

9a Catherine Townshend Washington, *b* Culpeper Co, Va., 20 April 1834; *m* Newport, Ky., 23 April 1855 James Bausman DUKE (*b c* 1827; *d c* 1866), s of Dr Alexander Duke and his w Mary Mackall Broome, and *d* St Louis, Mo., 30 Nov 1916, leaving one s and two daus

10a Ella WASHINGTON; *d* young

President Washington's nephew

2 Tristram WASHINGTON, *b c* 1760; *d* before 1768

VII (cont.) Col Samuel Washington *m* 3rd *c* 1762 Louisa (*b* 29 June 1743; *d c* 1763), dau of Nathaniel Chapman, of Fairfax Co, Va., and his w Constantia Pearson; *m* 4th 24 March 1764 Anne (*b* 10 Oct 1737; *d* Harewood 14 March 1777), widow of Willoughby Allerton, of the Narrows, and dau of Col James Steptoe, of Homing Hall, and his 1st w, and with her had issue:

President Washington's nephews and niece

3 Ferdinand WASHINGTON, *b* Stafford Co, Va., 15 July 1767; *m* —— and *d* Lancaster Co, Va., Feb 1788

4 Frederick Augustus WASHINGTON, *b* Stafford Co, Va., 4 June 1768; *d* there 23 April 1769

5 Lucinda WASHINGTON, *b* Stafford Co, Va., 29 Nov 1769; *d* Harewood 3 Nov 1770

6 George Steptoe WASHINGTON, *b* Harewood 17 Aug 1771; *m* Philadelphia 20 May 1793 Lucy (*b* Hanover Co, Va., *c* 1772; *m* 2nd the White House, Washington, DC, 29 March 1812 Hon Thomas Todd, Assoc Justice US Supreme Court; *d* Megwillie, Jefferson Co, 29 Jan 1846), dau of John Payne, of Philadelphia, and his first w Mary Coles and sister-in-law of President MADISON, and *d* Augusta, Ga., 10 Jan 1809, having had issue:

Great-nephews

(1) George WASHINGTON, *b* Harewood *c* 1795; *d* in infancy

(2) Dr Samuel Walter WASHINGTON, *b* Harewood 20 March 1797; *m* Philadelphia 3 Aug 1820 Louisa (*b* 4 Sept 1805; *d* 14 Feb 1882), dau of Thomas Green Clemson, of Philadelphia, and his w Elizabeth Baker, and *d* Harewood 12 Oct 1831, having had issue:

Great-nephew's children

1a A son, *b* and *d* 23 Jan 1822

2a Lucy Elizabeth Washington, *b* Harewood 2 July 1823; *m* Baltimore 3 March 1840 John William Bainbridge PACKETT (*b* 18 Feb 1817; *d* Locust Hill, Jefferson Co, W. Va., 18 Nov 1872), s of John Packett and his w Fanny Hammond, and *d* 14 April 1881, having had three s and five daus

3a George Lafayette WASHINGTON, of Harewood and Claymont, Del., *b* Harewood 12 Jan 1825; *m* Claymont, Del., 29 April 1859, as her 1st husb, Anna Bull (*b* 18 June 1833; *m* 2nd Samuel Roberts; *d* 28 June 1914), dau of Revd John Baker Clemson and his 1st w Margaretta Jacobs Bull, and *d* Siegfried's Bridge, Pa., 7 Feb 1872, having had issue:

Great-nephew's grandchildren

1b Margaretta WASHINGTON, *b* 11 June 1860; medical textbook illustrator; *d* 11 Jan 1917

2b Louisa Clemson WASHINGTON, *b* 29 April 1862; *d* June 1864

3b John Clemson WASHINGTON, *b* 5 Jan 1865; *d* 1 Oct 1881

4b Martha WASHINGTON, of Philadephia, *b* 29 Aug 1867; Herald Plantagenet Soc; *d* 13 Aug 1956

5b Anne Harewood Washington, *b* 26 Nov 1869; *m* 6 June 1906, as his 2nd w, Edwin Fairfax NAULTY (*b* 16 March 1869; *d* 19—) and *d* 31 Jan 1951, leaving one dau

6b Elizabeth Fisher WASHINGTON, *b* 20 Dec 1871; miniature- and landscape-painter, Regent-Gen Nat Soc Magna Carta Dames; *d* 30 Aug 1953

Great-nephew's children

4a Christian Maria Washington, *b* Harewood 16 Dec 1826; *m* Philadelphia 20 Nov 1844 her 3rd cousin Richard Scott Blackburn WASHINGTON (*b* Blakeley, Jefferson Co, W. Va.,, 2 Nov 1822; *d* Charles Town 15 Oct 1910), yst s of John Augustine Washington, of Mount Vernon (gn of President WASHINGTON), and his w Jane Charlotte Blackburn, and *d* 10 June 1895, having had issue:

Great-nephew's grandchildren

1b Elizabeth Clemson Washington, *b* Blakeley 21 Aug 1845; *m* Jefferson Co, W. Va., 23 Jan 1868, as his 2nd w, George Hite FLAGG (*b* Jefferson Co 9 April 1832; *d* Charles Town 25 March 1900), s of John R. Flagg and his w Susan Rutherford Hite, and *d* Charles Town 3 Oct 1911

2b John Augustine WASHINGTON, *b* Blakeley 27 May 1847; *m* Jefferson Co, W. Va., 26 Nov 1890 Jane Keyes (*b* there 8 Feb 1862; *d* there 4 July 1891), est dau of Revd Charles Edward Ambler and his 2nd w Susan West Keyes, and *d* Charles Town 14 Aug 1923

3b Anna Maria Thomasina Blackburn WASHINGTON, *b* Blakeley 1 Nov 1849; *d* 22 Sept 1852

4b Louisa Clemson WASHINGTON, *b* Blakeley 17 Nov 1851; *d* 22 Sept 1852

5b Samuel Walter WASHINGTON, *b* Blakeley 1 Nov 1853; *m* Rock Hall, Jefferson Co, W. Va., 11 Oct 1900 Elizabeth Ryland (*b* there 24 Jan 1870; *d* Washington, DC, 6 Feb 1960), est dau of Nathaniel Hite Willis and his w Jane Charlotte Washington (for whom *see below*), and *d* Charles Town 16 July 1923, leaving issue:

Great-nephew's great-grandchildren

1c Samuel Walter WASHINGTON, *b* Charles Town 30 Sept 1901; *educ* Virginia Mily Inst, Lexington, and Hertford Coll, Oxford, UK (Rhodes Scholar); with State Dept 1926-53, Prof Us of Virginia and Puerto Rico 1954-69; *m* 1st Tokyo, Japan, 29 Sept 1933 (divorce 1956) Simone Cécile (*b* Paris, France, 1 Sept 1905; *d* Washington, DC, 18 Dec 1973), widow of —— Stecker and dau of Benjamin Wilfred Fleisher and his w Blanche Blum, and had issue:

Great-nephew's great-great-grandchildren

1d *Dr John Augustine WASHINGTON II [3304 Mayowood Hills Drive SW, Rochester, MN 55901, USA], *b* Istanbul, Turkey, 29 May 1936; *educ* U of Virginia and Johns Hopkins (MD); Head Clinical Microbiology Section Mayo Clinic and Prof Microbiology and Laboratory Medicine Mayo Medical Sch; *m* Princeton, New Jersey, 11 July 1959 *Maaja (*b* Tallin, Estonia, 21 Jan 1938), dau of Eugen Härms and his w Gerda Elisabeth Pauming, and has issue:

Great-nephew's great-great-grandchildren's children

1e *Stephen Lawrence WASHINGTON, *b* Bethesda, Md., 28 March 1964

2e *Richard Ryland WASHINGTON, *b* Washington, DC, 12 Feb 1967

3e *Mikaela Ann WASHINGTON, *b* Rochester, Minn., 25 Sept 1970

Great-nephew's great-grandchildren

1c (cont.) Samuel W. Washington *m* 2nd New York 6 June 1958 *Dr Adriana Cornelia (*b* Amsterdam, The Netherlands, 27 Sept 1919), widow of —— and dau of Pieter Fenenga and his w Josephine Bource, and *d* 3 April 1978

2c *John Augustine WASHINGTON [Harewood, Charles Town, WV 25414, USA], *b* Charles Town 12 Oct 1903; *educ* Virginia Mily Inst and Johns Hopkins (MD); paediatrician; *m* Georgetown, DC, 24 Sept 1942 *Margaret Hayes (*b* Germantown, Pa., 10 May 1908), er dau of Henry Justice Kenderdine and his w Margaret McKinney, and has issue:

Great-nephew's great-great-grandchildren

1d *Samuel Walter WASHINGTON, *b* Washington, DC, 1 April 1948; *educ* Carlton Coll, Northfield, Minn., and American U, Washington, DC

Great-nephew's grandchildren

6b Richard Scott Blackburn WASHINGTON, *b* Blakeley 21 March 1856; *m* Louisville, Ky., 19 Nov 1884 Nannie (*b* there 14 June 1859; *d* Brant Beach, New Jersey, 25 April 1947), only surviving dau of Edward Tyler Sturgeon and his w Margaret Dye Fielder, and *d* Woodbury, New Jersey, 13 Oct 1922, having had issue:

Great-nephew's great-grandchildren

1c Margaret Sturgeon Washington, *b* Georgetown, N. Mex., 7 Sept 1885; *m* Woodbury, New Jersey, 2 March 1905 George Pepper ROBINS (*b* Philadelphia 3 March 1882), s of William Bowdoin Robins and his w Ann Bronson Reed, and *d* Wilmington, Del., 27 Dec 1970, having had three daus

2c Richard Scott Blackburn WASHINGTON, *b* Georgetown, N. Mex., 16 Sept 1887; *m* Richmond, Va., 9 May 1918 Eliza Mayo Atkinson (*b* Charles Town, W. Va., 27 July 1897; *d* Binghamton, New York, 24 March 1965), only dau of Dr Van Lear Perry and his w Elizabeth Travers Green, and *d* Binghamton 29 Sept 1964, leaving issue:

Great-nephew's great-great-grandchildren

1d *Bessie Van Lear Washington [Mrs Harry Goodwin, 1113 Colonial Avenue, Andalusia, Cornwells Heights, PA 19020, USA], *b* Germantown, Pa., 10 Feb 1919; *m* there 5 July 1941 Harry Berger GOODWIN (*b* Philadelphia 14 March 1916; *d* 29 Aug 1989), s of Ralph Althouse Goodwin and his w Ida Berger, and has issue:

Great-nephew's great-great-grandchildren's children

1e *Barbara Jean Goodwin [Mrs Barbara Goodwin Ceballos, 17 Oakbridge Dve, Binghamton, NY 19020, USA], *b* Chestnut Hill, Pa., 2 Jan 1943; *m* Philadelphia 30 June 1962 (divorce 1985) Dr Mario CEBALLOS-MEJIA (*b* Antioquia, Colombia, 13 Feb 1934), s of Dr Julio Ceballos and his w Matilde Mejia, and has issue:

Great-nephew's great-great-grandchildren's grandchildren

1f *Daniel Harry CEBALLOS [216 Benson, Santa Clara, CA 95053, USA], *b* Bogotá, Colombia, 23 April 1963; assist dir residential life Santa Clara U

2f *John Miguel CEBALLOS [48 Crescent Ave, Malden, MA 02148, USA], *b* Binghamton 16 July 1966

3f *David Scott CEBALLOS, *b* Binghamton 22 Dec 1971

4f *Cristina Marie CEBALLOS, *b* Binghamton 6 Sept 1974

Great-nephew's great-great-grandchildren's children
2e *Harry Washington GOODWIN [11711 Lanett Road, Philadelphia, PA 19154, USA], b Chestnut Hill, Pa., 21 Nov 1945; m Philadelphia 27 Sept 1969 *Constance Anne (b there 15 Dec 1948), dau of Robert Patrick Meehan and his w Anne Livingston, and has issue:

Great-nephew's great-great-grandchildren's grandchildren
1f *Jennifer Anne GOODWIN, b Philadelphia 25 Sept 1970
2f *James Andrew GOODWIN, b Philadelphia 10 Nov 1971

Great-nephew's great-great-grandchildren
2d *Nannie Sturgeon Washington [Mrs William Dall, 417 South Carlisle Street, Philadelphia, PA 19146, USA], b Germantown 19 Feb 1920; artist; m Philadelphia 17 April 1943 Prof William DALL (formerly Dall Connor), management consultant and labour arbitrator (b Brookline, Mass., 5 May 1913; d Philadelphia 6 May 1964), s of Charles Connor and his w Marian Dall
3d *Richard Scott WASHINGTON [11222 South Shore Drive, Reston, VA 22070, USA], b Germantown 26 May 1923; m Philadelphia 27 April 1946 *Lola Louise (b Wilmington, Del., 15 June 1917), widow of Maxwell Case, Jr, and dau of William Osborne Barnhill and his w Grace Elizabeth Pleasanton, and has issue:

Great-nephew's great-great-grandchildren's children
1e *Lawrence Scott WASHINGTON [Woodcrest Park Apartments B-12, RD1, Tilton Road, Pleasantville, NJ 08232, USA; 1307 Rosebay Pl, Mays Landing, NJ, USA], b Philadelphia 22 Sept 1948; m 19— *——— and has a s and dau
2e *Elizabeth Washington [Mrs John Keane Jr, 1854 Patten Terrace, McLean, VA 22101, USA; 7839 Altboro Drive, Springfield, VA, USA], b Philadelphia 28 Feb 1951; m Reston, Va., 18 Sept 1971 *John Joseph KEANE, Jr (b Washington, DC, 11 June 1934), s of John Joseph Keane and his w Irene Antoinette Buscher, and has issue:

Great-nephew's great-great-grandchildren's grandchildren
1f *Katherine Irene KEANE, b Arlington, Va., 2 March 1973
2f *Erin Kelly KEANE, b Oct 1976

Great-nephew's great-great-grandchildren's children
3e *Lola Louise Washington [Mrs Mark Monroe, 2702 Paoli Pike Apt 52, New Albany, IN 47150, USA], b Philadelphia 30 Dec 1952; m Reston, Va., 23 June 1973 *Mark Patrick MONROE (b Ridgecrest, Calif., Jan 1949), s of Henry Lawrence Monroe and his w Cecilia Mary Lynch, and has two daus

Great-nephew's great-grandchildren
3c John Augustine WASHINGTON, b Albuquerque, N. Mex., 19 March 1891; m Clarksburg 13 Nov 1917 *Elise Sill (b Columbus, Mont., 3 Oct 1896; m 2nd Baltimore 21 Sept 1933 Chesney Michael Carney, of Clarksburg; d Clarksburg 9 June 1955), 2nd dau of Francis Sprigg Gibson and his 1st w Sevilla Shaffner Friend, and d LeRoy, New York, 5 Oct 1928, leaving issue:

Great-nephew's great-grandchildren
1d *John Augustine WASHINGTON, Jr [4208 Rosemary Street, Chevy Chase, MD 20015, USA], b Clarksburg 4 May 1920; educ Hotchkiss Sch and Harvard; manager Washington, DC, office Alex Brown & Sons, investment bankers; m Washington, DC, 3 Sept 1960 *Alice Claire (b San Diego, Calif., 3 Oct 1925), er dau of Capt Henry Richard Lacey, USN, and his w Edith Helen Johnson, and has issue:

Great-nephew's great-great-grandchildren's children
1e *Edith Lacey WASHINGTON [1512 Spruce St, Philadelphia, PA 19102, USA], b Washington, DC, 11 Dec 1961
2e *John Augustine WASHINGTON [708 South Barrington Ave, Los Angeles, CA 90049, USA], b Washington 15 July 1963

Great-nephew's twin great-grandchildren
4c Christian Maria WASHINGTON, b and d Harewood 20 June 1893
5c George Lafayette WASHINGTON, of Overbrook, Montgomery Co, Pa., b Harewood 20 June 1893; m Winchester, Va., 17 July 1913 Katherine Parke (b Boston 26 Feb 1891; d 1978), dau of Joseph Blanchard Ames and his w Helen B., and d Bryn Mawr 10 Feb 1968, leaving issue:

Great-nephew's great-great-grandchildren
1d Helen Ames Washington, b Woodbury, New Jersey, 22 Sept 1914; m 1st Upper Darby, Pa., 16 May 1935 (divorce 1946), as his 1st w, Berthold John HELLER, Jr, s of Berthold John Heller, and had issue:

Great-nephew's great-great-grandchildren's children
1e *Eugene Washington HELLER [2424 South First Ave, Sioux Falls, SD 57105, USA], b Bryn Mawr, Pa., 9 Dec 1935; m Philadelphia 10 July 1965 (divorce 28 July 1986) Vivian (b Fall River, Mass., 10 Aug 1938), dau of Wilfred Joseph Vaudreuil and his w Aurore Levasseur, and has issue:

Great-nephew's great-great-grandchildren's grandchildren
1f *Laura Eugenie Heller, *b* Philadelphia 27 July 1966; *m* Sioux Falls, S. Dak., 12 May 1990 *Terry LARSON (*b* there 13 Feb 1968), s of Robert Larson and his w Shirley, and has issue:

Great-nephew's great-great-grandchildren's great-grandchildren
1g *Kathryn Lynda LARSON, *b* Sioux Falls 4 July 1991

Great-nephew's great-great-grandchildren's grandchildren
2f *Eugenie Vivian HELLER, *b* Philadelphia 24 Nov 1967

Great-nephew's great-great-grandchildren
1d (cont.) Mrs Helen Heller *m* 2nd Philadelphia 9 Jan 1971 Carlton Converse DAY (*b* Picture Rocks, Pa., 3 Jan 1912; *d* between 1975 and 1984), s of Howard Edgar Day and his w Anna May Converse, and *d* Dec 1984
2d Marie Blackburn Washington, *b* Boston 23 Feb 1917; *m* Philadelphia 25 Nov 1939 (divorce 1958), as his 1st w, John Yocum Randolph CRAWFORD (*b* 4 Aug 1915; *d* 14 Feb 1976) and *d* Philadelphia 17 July 1973, leaving three daus

Great-nephew's grandchildren
7b Christine Maria WASHINGTON, *b* Blakeley 13 June 1858; *d* Charles Town 15 May 1937
8b George Steptoe WASHINGTON, *b* Blakeley 7 June 1860; *m* Philadelphia 28 Oct 1886 May Tome (*b* Lancaster, Pa., 21 Aug 1865; *d* Riverton 29 March 1959), dau of James King Alexander and his w Elizabeth Old Hopkins, and *d* Riverton 17 June 1943, having had issue:

Great-nephew's great-grandchildren
1c Richard Blackburn WASHINGTON, *b* Philadelphia 29 Aug 1887; *d* Riverton 15 April 1898
2c Elizabeth Alexander Washington, *b* Philadelphia 31 Aug 1888; *m* Riverton 10 Jan 1912 Revd William Hudson CUMPSTON (*b* Leeds, UK, 16 April 1878; *d* Riverton 5 May 1960), s of Thomas Bowser Cumpston and his w Annie Martha Carter, and *d* Mount Holly, New Jersey, 6 May 1980, leaving issue:

Great-nephew's great-great-grandchildren
1d *May Alexander Cumpston [Mrs Howland Dudley Jr, 125 Providence Ave, Doylestown, PA 18901, USA], *b* Riverton 23 July 1913; *educ* St Mary's Hall, Burlington, and Moore Inst, Sch of Design, Philadelphia; Jr Lt USNR World War II; *m* Riverton 20 Sept 1947 *Howland DUDLEY, Jr (*b* Belmont, Mass., 6 Feb 1910), s of Howland Dudley and his w Helen Fuller, and has issue:

Great-nephew's great-great-grandchildren's children
1e *Anne Carter Dudley [Mrs Philip Charles, 20 Davenant Rd, Oxford, OX2 8BX, UK], *b* Glen Ridge, New Jersey, 29 Dec 1948; *educ* U of Arizona; computer programmer: U of California 1977-79, Oxford U (UK) 1981-87, Royal Greenwich Observatory, UK, 1988-92, Rutherford Appleton Laboratory, Oxford, UK, 1993-; *m* Bedminster, Pa., 20 Sept 1975 *Philip Allan CHARLES (*b* Fareham, Hants, UK, 24 Nov 1950), s of A(llan) Robert J(oseph) Charles and his w Maisie Eileen Wise, and has issue:

Great-nephew's great-great-grandchildren's grandchildren
1f *William Wise CHARLES, *b* Oxford 18 Feb 1984
2f *Thomas Cumpston CHARLES, *b* Oxford 18 Feb 1984

Great-nephew's great-great-grandchildren's children
2e *Sarah Fuller Dudley [Mrs Sarah Staub, 69 Meadowbrook Rd, North Wales, PA 19454, USA], *b* Glen Ridge 23 March 1951; *m* Hilltown 14 Sept 1974 (divorce 19—) Michael Joseph STAUB (*b* Philadelphia 4 July 1952), s of Michael Joseph Staub and his w Elsie Lagler, and has issue:

Great-nephew's great-great-grandchildren's grandchildren
1f *Michael Jeremiah STAUB, *b* Doylestown, Pa., 9 April 1977

Great-nephew's great-great-grandchildren's children
3e *Elizabeth Washington Dudley [Mrs Edward Bibic, 209 Morwood Rd, Telford, PA 18969, USA], *b* Glen Ridge, New Jersey, 16 Oct 1953; *m* Hilltown, Pa., 4 March 1978 *Edward BIBIC, Jr (*b* Sellersville, Pa., 4 Sept 1953), s of Edward Bibic and his w Dorothy Fosbennner, and has issue:

Great-nephew's great-great-grandchildren's grandchildren
1f *Katherine Elizabeth BIBIC, *b* Doylestown, Pa., 7 Sept 1982
2f *Jonathan Edward BIBIC, *b* Doylestown 2 March 1985

Great-nephew's great-great-grandchildren's children
4e *Laura Howland Dudley [Mrs Gerald Ricci, 54 Whitney Dve, Woodstock, NY 12498, USA], *b* Glen Ridge, New Jersey, 30 Dec 1955; *m* 1st Bedminster, Pa., 18 June 1977 (divorce 1979) John DUNCAN (*b* Boston 26 Sept 1955), s of Walter Duncan and his w Jean Dinsmore; *m* 2nd Kingston, New York, 8 Feb 1992 *Gerald RICCI (*b* 3 Oct 1946), s of Victor Ricci and his w Ella Martin

Great-nephew's great-great-grandchildren
2d *George Steptoe Washington CUMPSTON [PO Box 981, Swansboro, NC 28584-0981, USA], *b* Riverton 25

July 1918; *educ* St Andrew's Sch, Middletown, Del.; manufacturer's rep 1946-73; *m* Riverton 7 June 1952 *Eileen Marie (*b* 4 Feb 1920), dau of Harry William Bagnall and his w Mary Teresa, and has issue:

Great-nephew's great-great-grandchildren's children
1e *William Hudson CUMPSTON [3402 Huggins, Flint, MI 48566, USA], *b* Lima, Peru, 26 March 1957

Great-nephew's great-grandchildren
3c Christine Maria Washington, *b* Riverton 31 July 1891; *m* there 7 Feb 1912 George Lincoln RIDLEY (*b* Hyde Park, Mass., 23 Nov 1888; *d* Washington, DC, 23 Nov 1963), s of George Lewis Ridley and his w Elizabeth Horton Sears, and *d* Riverton 15 May 1961, leaving three daus
4c Howard Alexander WASHINGTON, *b* Riverton 17 July 1893; *m* 1st Augusta, Ga., 11 April 1923 Lily Kate (*b* there 3 Feb 1896; *d* Avalon, New Jersey, 3 Oct 1946), dau of Henry Balk and his w Florence McCarrell; *m* 2nd Winter Haven, Fla., 5 April 1948 Jane (*b* Boston, Ga., 5 July 1905; *d* 19——), formerly w of —— Bradshaw and dau of John Hawkins McIntosh and his w Lawson Turner, and *d* Riverton 17 Feb 1981, having adopted his stepson:

   a *William BRADSHAW

Great-nephew's great-grandchildren
5c George Steptoe WASHINGTON, *b* Riverton 3 Nov 1900; *d* Charles Town 15 Sept 1901
6c William de Hertburn WASHINGTON, *b* Riverton 21 Sept 1902; *educ* Shenandoah Valley Acad and Lehigh U; Capt US Army; *d* Richboro, Pa., 4 June 1992

Great-nephew's grandchildren
9b William de Hertburn WASHINGTON, *b* Jefferson Co, W. Va., 14 Feb 1864; *m* Pearce, Ariz., 1 Feb 1901 Alice Lee (*b* Kimble Co, Tex., 5 March 1880; *d* Douglas, Ariz., 24 Dec 1960), dau of Paschal C. Lemons and his w Luella J. Tulk, and *d* Douglas 12 Feb 1937, leaving issue:

Great-nephew's great-grandchildren
1c Richard Scott Blackburn WASHINGTON, *b* Pearce 25 Oct 1901; *m* Douglas 28 May 1929 *Mabel Anne [Mrs Richard Washington, 3621 Woodcrest Road, Sacramento, CA 95821, USA; 809 WEI Camino Avenue, Sacramento, CA, USA] (*b* Coeur d'Alene, Idaho, 20 July 1903), dau of Jacob Hansen Wiks and his w Marie Louise Larsen, and *d* Douglas 23 July 1966, leaving issue:

Great-nephew's great-great-grandchildren
1d *Richard Scott WASHINGTON [3405 Klamath Woods Place, Concord, CA 94518, USA], *b* Douglas 13 Oct 1930; *m* there 8 Nov 1953 *Patricia Anne (*b* there 27 July 1930), dau of Frank William Sharpe, Jr, and his w Edith Jones, and has issue:

Great-nephew's great-great-grandchildren's children
1e *Kathleen Lee Washington [Mrs Mark Costa, 11959 Montana Avenue #5, Los Angeles, CA 90049, USA], *b* Douglas 17 Jan 1956; *m* 16 Dec 1978 *Mark COSTA
2e *Richard Scott WASHINGTON, *b* Douglas 27 Dec 1956
3e *Suzanne WASHINGTON, *b* Douglas 23 July 1958
4e *Mark Sharpe WASHINGTON [1510 Hill Road #20, Novato, CA 94947, USA], *b* Douglas 22 Jan 1960; *m* Concord, Calif., 6 Oct 1979 *Teresa (*b* Walnut Creek, Calif., 17 Feb 1960), dau of Hugh Lyle
5e *Timothy Edward WASHINGTON, *b* Alamogordo, N. Mex., 14 Sept 1961
6e *Steven Patrick WASHINGTON, *b* Mountain View, Calif., 28 May 1965

Great-nephew's children
5a Annie Steptoe Clemson Washington, *b* Harewood 8 Sept 1831; *m* Philadelphia 17 Oct 1854 Thomas Augustus BROWN (*b* Charleston, W. Va., 20 Dec 1822; *d* 23 May 1909), s of William Brown and his w Elizabeth Forrest, and *d* 19 July 1911, having had one s and five daus

Great-nephew
(3) William Temple WASHINGTON, of Megwillie, Jefferson Co, and Inglewood, Stafford Co, *b* Harewood 16 July 1800; *m* Lexington, Ky., 3 Aug 1821 Margaret Calhoun (*b* there 1805; *d* Falmouth, Va., 9 Jan 1865), dau of Gen Thomas Fletcher (s of Charles François-Joseph, Count de Fléchir) and his w Margaret Calhoun, and *d* Stafford Co 20 April 1877, having had issue:

Great-nephew's children
1a Lucy WASHINGTON, *b* Lexington, Ky., 8 Oct 1822; *d* 17 Oct 1825
2a Millissent Fowler Washington, *b* Bath Co, Ky., 4 Aug 1824; *m* Megwillie, Jefferson Co, 10 Dec 1840 Robert Grier McPHERSON (*b* Md. 26 March 1819; *d* 13 Nov 1899) s of Robert Grier McPherson and his w Maria, and *d* 17 Nov 1893, having had four s and four daus
3a William Temple WASHINGTON, *b* Lexington, Ky., 7 Jan 1827; *m* 1846 Lucy Herndon (*b* c 1829; *d* Indiana 1850) and *d* 18—— or 19——
4a Thomas West WASHINGTON, *b* Megwillie 17 March 1829; *d* Missouri 12 April 1849
5a Jean Charlotte Washington, *b* Megwillie 29 June 1834; *m* Falmouth, Va., 12 April 1868 Thomas Gascoigne MONCURE (*b* 24 Feb 1837; *d* 5 July 1906), s of Richard Cassius Lee Moncure and his w Mary Butler Washington Conway, and *d* 2 Aug 1916, having had three s and one dau

6a Eugenia Scholay WASHINGTON, *b* Megwillie 24 June 1838; First Memb and Registrar-Gen DAR; *d* Washington, DC, 30 Nov 1900

7a Ferdinand Steptoe WASHINGTON, *b* Megwillie 22 Jan 1843; *d* Arkansas 22 Aug 1912

Great-nephew
(4) George Steptoe WASHINGTON, *b* Harewood 15 Oct 1806; *m* Frankfort, Ky., 2 May 1827 Gabriella Augusta (*b* Bourbon Co, Ky., 25 Jan 1810; *m* 2nd Col Leo Tarleton; *d* after 1898), dau of Thomas Wyatt Hawkins and his *w* Ann Eleanor Gerrard, and *d* Belvidere, Va., 13 Oct 1831

President Washington's nephew
7 Lawrence Augustine WASHINGTON, *b* Harewood 11 April 1774; *m* Winchester 6 Nov 1797 Mary Dorcas (*b* 6 Nov 1781; *d* Ohio Co, W. Va., 9 Nov 1835), dau of Robert Wood and his *w* Comfort Welch, and *d* Ohio Co 15 Feb 1824, leaving issue:

Great-nephews and -niece
(1) Robert Wood WASHINGTON, *b* Winchester, Va., 1808; *d* Ohio Co 1843
(2) Emma Tell WASHINGTON, *b* Red House Shoals, Mason Co, Va., 22 Sept 1812; *d* 1838
(3) Dr Lawrence Augustine WASHINGTON, *b* Red House Shoals 3 Dec 1814; *m* Charleston, W. Va., 21 Nov 1839 Martha Dickinson Shrewsbury (*b* there 16 March 1820; *d* Denison, Tex., 29 July 1891) and *d* Denison 11 Aug 1882, having had issue:

Great-nephew's children
1a Lawrence Augustine WASHINGTON, *b* Kanawha Co 21 March 1841; *d* Denison 20 Aug 1852
2a Walter Good WASHINGTON, *b* Mason Co, W. Va., 21 Feb 1843; *m* Silver Cliff, Colo., 4 March 1885 Olive Eleanor Lawrence (*b* Rock Island, Ill., 10 July 1857; *d* Pueblo, Colo., 14 Sept 1894) and *d* Guerida, Colo., 2 April 1904, having had issue (with a son and dau, both of whom *d* in infancy):

Great-nephew's grandchildren
1b Winifred Lee Washington, *b* Silver Cliff, Colo., 6 Aug 1889; *m* 1st 10 Jan 1906 (divorce 1915) William Charles FALKENBERG (*b* 25 July 1870) and had issue:

Great-nephew's great-grandchildren
1c Walter Washington FALKENBERG, *b* 8 Oct 1907; *d* 25 Dec 1929

Great-nephew's grandchildren
1b (cont.) Mrs Winifred Falkenberg *m* 2nd 24 Feb 1931 Robert Scott WHEATLEY (*b* 21 April 1889)
2b Anna Louise Washington, *b* 27 April 1891; *m* 1st 1915 James Henry FITZPATRICK (*b* 1880; *d* 11 Nov 1928); *m* 2nd 15 June 1941 Albert Henry LYBARGER (*b* 12 Nov 1887; *d* 31 Jan 1947)

Great-nephew's children
3a John Shrewsbury WASHINGTON, *b* Mason Co, W. Va., 27 April 1845; *d* Denison, Tex., 1 Aug 1898
4a James Turner WASHINGTON, *b* Mason Co, W. Va., 3 March 1847; *m* Brownwood, Tex., 29 Nov 1874 Josephine Clara (*b* Indiana 4 Feb 1857; *d* Proctor 1 Nov 1943), dau of —— Burroughs and his *w* Mary Jane Hines, and *d* Proctor 1 May 1926, having had issue:

Great-nephew's grandchildren
1b Martha Washington, *b* Comanche Co, Tex., 6 Nov 1875; *m* 1st 22 July 1896 William Edgar McCAMPBELL (*b* 12 Aug 1865; *d* 28 Feb 1904) and had issue:

Great-nephew's great-grandchildren
1c Ruth Washington McCampbell, *b* 11 Nov 1900; *m* 19— (divorce 19—) Robert Chauncey OVERTON (*d* 10 May 1971) and *d* 7 July 1973, leaving issue:

Great-nephew's great-great-grandchildren
1d *Elizabeth Overton; *b* before 23 March 1934; *m* 19— (divorce 19—) Jim STAPLETON and has had issue:

Great-nephew's great-great-grandchildren's children
1e Ed Stapleton, *b* 19—; *m* 19— (divorce 19—) Alger WAITES and *d* 1979, leaving issue:

Great-nephew's great-great-grandchildren's grandchildren
1f *Sue WAITES, *b* 19—

Great-nephew's great-great-grandchildren
2d *Sarah Hayes Overton, *b* 23 March 1934; *m* 1st 19— (divorce 19—) Jerry LAKE and has issue:

Great-nephew's great-great-grandchildren's children
1e *Kirk Allen LAKE, *b* 27 Feb 1955

Great-nephew's great-great-grandchildren
2d (cont.) Mrs Sarah Lake *m* 2nd 19— *Kenneth ARNOLD (*b* 29 Oct 1929) and has further issue:

Great-nephew's great-great-grandchildren's children
2e *Holly Ann ARNOLD, *b* 3 Feb 1961

Great-nephew's great-grandchildren
2c William Washington McCAMPBELL, *b* 1 May 1904; *d* 5 Jan 1972

Great-nephew's grandchildren
1b (cont.) Mrs Martha McCampbell *m* 2nd 12 June 1917 Richard Francis MOORE (*b* 1 March 1861; *d* 6 May 1921) and *d* Dallas 1961
2b A son, *b* and *d* 19 May 1878
3b Mary Estelle Washington, *b* Denison, Tex., 21 July 1879; *m* 1st 23 March 1902 Dr John Wilson ROARK (*b* Tennessee 29 May 1872; *d* 17 Dec 1938) and had one child who *d* in infancy; *m* 2nd 22 Oct 1947 James S. HAIR (*b* Bartlett, Tex., 15 June 1878; *d* April 1954) and *d* 17 Jan 1976
4b Wood Elliot Washington, *b* Proctor, Tex., 23 Feb 1882; *m* 1st 2 July 1904 (divorce *c* 1917) Amos Hardin PLUMMER (*b* 14 March 1873; *d* 19—) and had one s and one dau; *m* 2nd 15 May 1944 Charles KINCAID (*b* Wallace, W. Va., 8 Feb 1875; *d* Feb 1951) and *d* Abilene, Tex., 1955
5b Frances Marion WASHINGTON, *b* Proctor 23 March, *d* there 12 Nov 1885
6b James Turner WASHINGTON, *b* Proctor 20 May 1887; *d* there 7 Feb 1950
7b George Patrick WASHINGTON, *b* Proctor 7 Oct 1890; *m* Dallas 6 June 1920 *Arlee Myrtle [Mrs George Washington, 2704 Parkview Apt 2103, Bedford, TX 76022, USA] (*b* Lewisville, Tex., 14 June 1897), dau of Isaac Emery and his w Annette Ratliff, and *d* Hurst 19 Dec 1965, leaving issue:

Great-nephew's great-grandchildren
1c *Shirley Annette Washington [Ms Shirley Scott, 12 Lone Star, Wimberley, TX 78676, USA], *b* Roanoke, Tex., 3 Aug 1921; *m* 14 Feb 1941 (divorce 1969) Jack SCOTT (*b* 1 March 1921) and has issue:

Great-nephew's great-great-grandchildren
1d *Suzanne Scott [Mrs Suzanne Goodwin, 6736 Mesa Dve, Fort Worth, TX 76180, USA], *b* 29 June 1944; *educ* N Texas State U; registrar Tarrant Co Jr Coll; *m* 1971 (divorce 1974) Larry GOODWIN and has issue:

Great-nephew's great-great-grandchildren's children
1e *Carrie Lisa GOODWIN, *b* 2 Aug 1972

Great-nephew's great-great-grandchildren
2d *John Mark SCOTT [8603 Midway Rd, Dallas, TX 75209, USA], *b* Corpus Christi, Tex., 4 June 1948; *educ* North Texas State U (BS 1972); art dir

Great-nephew's great-grandchildren
2c *Mary George Washington [Mrs William Southwell, 308 Highland Lake Drive, Lewisville, TX 75087, USA], *b* Denton, Tex., 7 April 1923; *educ* Handley High Sch, U of Texas at Arlington, Baylor U Sch of Nursing; *m* 4 Dec 1944 *William Alexander SOUTHWELL (*b* 13 Feb 1920), s of Carrol Edward Southwell and his w Catherine Taylor, and has issue:

Great-nephew's great-great-grandchildren
1d *William Alexander SOUTHWELL II [9100 FM 2181 #14J, Denton, TX 76205, USA], *b* Fort Worth., Tex., 12 Dec 1945; *m* Irvington, Tex., 19— (divorce 19—) Vicki Lynne Gipson (*b* 12 Dec 1952) and has issue:

Great-nephew's great-great-grandchildren's children
1e *Brandi Lynne SOUTHWELL, *b* 6 Feb 1979
2e *William Alexander SOUTHWELL III, *b* 17 Aug 1981
3e *Kristine Diane SOUTHWELL, *b* 26 Aug 1983

Great-nephew's great-great-grandchildren
2d *Steven Carrol SOUTHWELL [5180 Hildring Dve E #155, Fort Worth, TX 76132, USA], *b* Dallas 23 May 1952

Great-nephew's great-grandchildren
3c *Paul Emery WASHINGTON [22727 Cielo Vista, San Antonio, TX 78255, USA], *b* Santa Maria, Tex., 2 Aug 1926; *educ* Baylor U (BS 1951); *m* Denton, Tex., 22 Aug 1948 *Jo Delle (*b* Groesbeck, Tex., 27 Aug 1927), dau of Ernest Robertson Trotter and his w Esther Lurline Webb, and has issue:

Great-nephew's great-grandchildren
1d *Julianne Washington, *b* Waco, Tex., 6 July 1949; *m* 1st San Antonio, Tex., 5 Nov 1967 (divorce 1973) Gary Robert SPENCER (*b* Indianapolis, Ind., 3 Nov 1933), s of Sylvester Spencer and his w Viola McNay, and has issue:

Great-nephew's great-great-grandchildren's children
1e *Shelley SPENCER, *b* San Antonio, Tex., 6 Feb 1970

Great-nephew's great-great-grandchildren
1d (cont.) Mrs Julianne Spencer *m* 2nd 23 Dec 1979 (divorce 1980) Kelly E. AXTELL; *m* 3rd Texas 6 April 1985 *Robert L. COONS and has further issue:

Great-nephew's great-great-grandchildren's children
2e *Robert L. COONS III, *b* 3 April 1987

Great-nephew's great-great-grandchildren
2d *Richard Trotter WASHINGTON, *b* Waco, Tex., 16 April 1952; *m* Texas 5 June 1976 *Michaele Shelnutt and has issue:

Great-nephew's great-great-grandchildren's children
1e *Conner Paul WASHINGTON, *b* 14 Dec 1991

Great-nephew's great-great-grandchildren
3d *Bill Emery WASHINGTON, *b* Corpus Christi, Tex., 29 Dec 1953; *educ* N Texas U
4d *Jack Webb WASHINGTON, *b* Corpus Christi 1 Aug 1956; *m* 1st San Antonio 22 Nov 1972 (divorce 1973) Winona Carol (*b* Wiesbaden, Germany, 11 April 1956), dau of William Charles Herm and his w Marilyn Joan Bruce, and has issue:

Great-nephew's great-great-grandchildren's children
1e *David Michael WASHINGTON, *b* Corpus Christi, Tex., 14 April 1973

Great-nephew's great-great-grandchildren
4d (cont.) Jack W. Washington *m* 2nd 23 Oct 1987 *Brenda Ann Hardesty and has further issue:

Great-nephew's great-great-grandchildren's children
2e *Taylor Ann WASHINGTON, *b* 6 Sept 1990

Great-nephew's great-grandchildren
4c Carolyn Sue Washington, *b* Handley, Tex., 5 Oct 1931; *m* 19— (divorce 19—) William YEATTS and *d* 18 Nov 1983, leaving issue:

Great-nephew's great-great-grandchildren
1d *Mark Emery YEATTS, *b* 8 Sept 1962

Great-nephew's grandchildren
8b *Elizabeth Bryan Washington, *b* Proctor, Tex., 3 July 1893; *m* 16 June 1918 Edward Campbell KEAN (*b* Abilene, Tex., 24 May 1888; *d* March 1964) and has issue:

Great-nephew's great-grandchildren
1c *Dr James Edward KEAN, *b* Dallas 5 June 1922; *m* 1st 6 Sept 1947 (divorce 19—) Mary Ella Denning (*b* Bryson, Tex., 7 Aug 1925) and has issue:

Great-nephew's great-great-grandchildren
1d *Mary Elizabeth KEAN, *b* Austin, Tex., 16 Dec 1948

Great-nephew's great-grandchildren
1c (cont.) Dr James E. Kean *m* 2nd *Maxine Wolf and with her has issue:

Great-nephew's great-great-grandchildren
2d *Michelle KEAN, *b* 28 Aug 1954
3d *James KEAN, *b* 7 July 1956

Great-nephew's grandchildren
9b Paul Gray WASHINGTON, *b* Proctor, Tex., 6 March 1898; served 9th FA US Infy World War I; *d* 1 Oct 1923

Great-nephew's children
5a Emma Tell Washington, *b* Mason Co, W. Va., 27 Sept 1848; *m* Eagle Lake, Tex., 16 Sept 1865 George Lewis PATRICK (*b* Springville, Ala.; *d* 1914), s of George Washington Patrick and his w Margaret, and *d* 18 Dec 1907, having had three s and six daus
6a Julia Wood Washington, *b* Columbus, Tex., 29 May 1850; *m* there 19 June 1873 Sydney Thruston FONTAINE (*b* Houston 28 Nov 1838; *d* Galveston, Tex., 5 Sept 1912), s of Judge Henry Whiting Fontaine and his w Susan Elizabeth Bryan, and *d* New York 1 Oct 1936, having had four s and two daus
7a Mary Wood Washington (adopted name Cecil Wood WASHINGTON), *b* Colorado Co, Tex., 1 Jan 1858; *m* 1st 1877 Capt Richard Saunders (*d* Denison, Tex., July? 1878) and had one s; *m* 2nd Sherman, Tex., 29 Sept 1885 (divorce 18—) Joshua E. Howard, of Denison; *m* 3rd Sherman 7 March 1897, as his 1st w, George McLagan, of Pueblo, Colo., and Los Angeles (*b* 9 Oct 1859; *d* Hollywood 26 June 1945), and *d* San Diego, Calif., 16 Dec 1916, leaving a further dau

Great-niece
(4) Mary Dorcas WASHINGTON, *b* Mason Co, W. Va., 10 April 1817; *d* Colorado Co, Tex., 15 Nov 1861

President Washington's niece
8 Harriott Washington, *b* Harewood 2 Aug 1776; *m* Richmond, Va., 15 July 1796 Col Andrew PARKS, of Baltimore and Fredericksburg, later of Kanawha Salines, Va. (now Malden, W. Va.), (*b* 10 Aug 1773; *d* Kanawha Co 1836), s of John Parks and his w Margaret Gibson, and *d* Kanawha Co 3 Jan 1822, having had five s and three daus

VII (cont.) Col Samuel Washington *m* 5th *c* 1778 Susannah (*b* 27 June 1753; *d* Harewood 5 March 1783), widow of George Holden and dau of John Ferrin, of Gloucester Co, Va., and *d* Harewood 26 Sept 1781, having with her had issue:

President Washington's nephew

9 John Perrin WASHINGTON, *b* Harewood *c* 1779; *d* there 1783

VIII John Augustine WASHINGTON, of Bushfield, Westmoreland Co, Va., *b* Stafford Co, Va., 13 Jan 1735/6; Col Virginia Militia, Memb Virginia Conventions 1775-76; *m* Westmoreland Co 14? April 1756 Hannah (*b* Bushfield *c* 1738; *d* there 1801), er dau and co-heiress of Col John Bushrod, of Bushfield, JP and Burgess, and only dau by his 1st w Jane, dau of Hon Gawin Corbin, Pres Govr's Cncl, and *d* Bushfield 8? Jan 1787, having had issue:

President Washington's nieces and nephews

1 Mary WASHINGTON, *b* probably Mount Vernon *c* 1757; *d* probably Bushfield *c* 1762

2 Jane Washington, *b* Bushfield 20 June 1759,; *m* 25 Sept 1777, as his 1st w, her half-1st cousin Col William Augustine WASHINGTON, of Wakefield (*b* 25 Nov 1757; *d* 2 Oct 1810), 3rd s of Augustine Washington, himself 3rd est half-bro of President WASHINGTON, and *d* Sweet Springs, Va., 16 Aug 1791, leaving issue (*see above*)

3 Bushrod WASHINGTON, of Mount Vernon, *b* Bushfield 5 June 1762; *educ* William and Mary Coll; Memb Virginia House of Delegates 1787 and Virginia State Convention 1788, Assoc Justice US Supreme Court 1798-1829, 1st Pres (elected 1816) American Colonization Soc which founded Liberia, LLD; *m* Rippon Lodge, Prince William Co, Va., Oct 1785 Julia Ann (*b* there *c* 1768; *d* Derby, Pa., 28 Nov 1829 while travelling from Philadelphia to Mount Vernon to attend her husb's funeral), 2nd dau of Col Thomas Blackburn, of Rippon Lodge, ADC to Gen Washington in Revolutionary War, and his w Christian Scott, and *d* Philadelphia (*bur* Mount Vernon) 26 Nov 1829

4 Corbin WASHINGTON, of Walnut Farm, Westmoreland Co, and later of Selby, Fairfax Co, Virginia, *b* Bushfield 1764; *m* Chantilly, Westmoreland Co, 10 May 1787 Hannah (*b* there 1765; *d* Alexandria, Va., 23 Nov 1801), 2nd dau of Richard Henry Lee and his 1st w Anne Aylett and sister of the 2nd Mrs William Augustine Washington (*see above*), and *d* Bushfield 10 Dec 1799, leaving issue:

Great-nephews

(1) Richard Henry Lee WASHINGTON, of Prospect Hill, Jefferson Co, W. Va., *b* Walnut Farm 1788; *d* Mount Vernon 17 Sept 1817

(2) John Augustine WASHINGTON, of Blakeley, Jefferson Co (which he built), later also of Mount Vernon, *b* Walnut Farm 6 Aug 1789; *m* Rippon Lodge 14 Nov 1811 Jane Charlotte (*b* Rippon Lodge 23 Aug 1786; *d* Blakeley 6 Sept 1855), est dau and co-heiress of Maj Richard Scott Blackburn, of Rippon Lodge (himself bro of Mrs Bushrod Washington, for whom *see above*), and his 1st w Judith Ball, and *d* Mount Vernon 13 June 1832, having had issue:

Great-nephew's children

1a Anne Maria Thomasina Blackburn Washington, *b* Blakeley 4 Nov 1816; *m* Mount Vernon 15 May 1834, as his 1st w, Dr William Fontaine ALEXANDER (*b* Mount Ida, nr Alexandria, Va., 31 Oct 1811; *d* Walnut Farm 7 Jan 1862), 2nd s of Charles Alexander, of Mount Ida, and his w Mary Bowles Armistead, and *d* Blakeley 29 March 1850, having had three s and four daus

2a George WASHINGTON, *b* Blakeley 7 March 1818; *d c* 1827

3a Christian Scott WASHINGTON, *b* Blakeley 5 Jan, *d* 18 May 1820

4a John Augustine WASHINGTON, of Mount Vernon (sold by him 1858 to the Mount Vernon Ladies Association of the Union, who have maintained it ever since), and later of Waveland, Fauquier Co, Va., *b* Blakeley 3 May 1821; Lt-Col Confederate States Army and ADC to Gen Robert E. Lee; *m* Exeter, Loudoun Co, Va., 16 Feb 1843 Eleanor Love (*b* probably there 12 April 1824; *d* Waveland 9 Oct 1860), only dau and heiress of Col Wilson Cary Selden, of Exeter, and his w Louisa Elizabeth Fontaine Alexander (sister of Dr William Fontaine Alexander, for whom *see above*), and was *k* in a skirmish during the Civil War at Cheat Mountain, Randolph Co, W. Va., 13 Sept 1861, leaving issue:

Great-nephew's grandchildren

1b Louisa Fontaine Washington, *b* Mount Vernon 19 Feb 1844; *m* Blakeley 15 Aug 1871 Col Roger Preston CHEW, Confederate States Army, of Charles Town, Jefferson Co, W. Va. (*b* Loudoun Co, Va., 9 April 1843; *d* Charles Town 16 March 1921), s of Roger Chew and his w Sarah West Aldridge, and *d* Charles Town 1 July 1927, having had three s and three daus (all of whom *d* without issue)

2b Jane Charlotte Washington, *b* Mount Vernon 26 May 1846; *m* Blakeley 13 Jan 1869 Nathaniel Hite WILLIS, of Rock Hall, Jefferson Co, W. Va. (*b* there 25 March 1842; *d* Charles Town 26 Oct 1914), only surviving s of Thomas Hite Willis and his w Elizabeth Ferguson Ryland, and *d* Charles Town 7 Aug 1924, having had three s and five daus

3b Eliza Selden Washington, *b* Blakeley 17 July 1848; *m* 6 Oct 1895, as his 3rd w, Maj Robert Waterman HUNTER, Confederate States Army, of Winchester and Alexandria, Va. (*b* 12 July 1837; *d* 2 April 1916), and *d* Charles Town 28 Aug 1909

4b Anna Maria Washington, *b* Mount Vernon 17 Nov 1851; *m* Charles Town 22 July 1873 Beverley Dandridge TUCKER, DD, Bishop of Southern Virginia (*b* Richmond, Va., 9 Nov 1846; *d* Norfolk, Va., 17 Jan 1930), s of Nathaniel Beverley Tucker and his w Jane Shelton Ellis, and *d* Norfolk, Va., 7 Jan 1927, leaving nine s and four daus

5b Lawrence WASHINGTON, of Waveland, Fauquier Co, Va., and later of Washington, DC, *b* Mount Vernon 14 Jan 1854; *m* Charles Town 14 June 1876 Fannie (*b* Riverside, Jefferson Co, W. Va., 17 May 1855; *d* Washington, DC, 26 March 1953), dau of Thomas Griggs Lackland, of Charles Town, and his w Martha Ellen Willis (sister of Nathaniel Hite Willis, for whom *see above*), and *d* Washington, DC, 28 Jan 1920, leaving issue:

Great-nephew's great-grandchildren

1c John Augustine WASHINGTON, of Logan, Logan Co, W. Va., *b* Waveland 20 Jan 1878; *m* 1st Lawson Hall,

Cabell Co, W. Va., 8 Nov 1905 Eleanor Guye (*b* 20 Oct 1873; *d* Logan 16 May 1949), dau of Simon Slade Altizer and his w Roxye Lawson, and had issue:

Great-nephew's great-great-grandchildren

1d *Eleanor Altizer Washington [Mrs Douglas Lilly, 715 Southwest 27th Way, Boynton Beach, FL 33435, USA], *b* Logan 20 Sept 1906; *m* there 8 Jan 1931 Clifford Douglas LILLY (*b* Logan 3 March 1904), s of William Riley Lilly and his w Martha Ellen McGinnis, and has two adopted children:

 a *John Douglas LILLY, *b* 12 June 1944

 b *Linda Washington Lilly [Mrs Donald Kelly, 37 Kings Highway, Huntington, WV 25705, USA], *b* 31 Dec 1947; *m* Boynton Beach, Fla., 4 Nov 1972 Donald Wendell KELLY (*b* Cincinnati 27 May 1931), s of Donald Bartley Kelly and his w Elsie Yorke

Great-nephew's great-great-grandchildren

2d *John Augustine WASHINGTON [Holley Hotel, 1008 Quarrier Street, Charleston, WV 25330, USA], *b* Logan 15 March 1913; *m* there 7 Sept 1950 (divorce 19—) Virginia Dare (*b* Beckley, Raleigh Co, W. Va., 20 May 1923), dau of —— Knighton and formerly w of Max Welton Stell, and has issue:

Great-nephew's great-great-grandchildren's children

1e *John Augustine WASHINGTON [4341 Southwest 129th Place, Miami, FL 33165, USA], *b* Miami 27 Dec 1952

Great-nephew's great-grandchildren

1c (cont.) John A. Washington *m* 2nd Jesup, Wayne Co, Ga., 30 May 1952 *Sybil Mildred [Mrs John Washington, Barnabus, Logan Co, WV 25609, USA] (*b* Logan 21 April 1919), dau of George Cleveland Steele and his w Ora Gustava Curry and formerly w of Robson Roake Sage II, and *d* Logan 5 Nov 1962

2c Lawrence WASHINGTON, *b* Waveland 9 Aug 1879; *m* Northfork, McDowell Co, W. Va., 4 Feb 1913 Nell McKay (*b* Falls Mills, Va., 13 May 1890; *d* Bluefield, W. Va., 1 July 1931), dau of William Edward Dudley and his w Margaret Gillespie, and *d* Northfork 20 Nov 1953, leaving issue:

Great-nephew's great-great-grandchildren

1d *Frances Lackland WASHINGTON [1120 Virginia Avenue, Bluefield, VA 24605, USA], *b* Northfork 4 July 1916

Great-nephew's great-grandchildren

3c Patty Willis WASHINGTON, *b* Waveland 1 Oct 1880; *d* Alexandria, Va., 22 Feb 1971

4c Anne Madison WASHINGTON, *b* Waveland 27 May 1882; *d* Arlington, Va., 17 Oct 1966

5c Louisa Fontaine Washington, *b* Waveland 14 Nov 1883; *m* Washington, DC, 14 June 1921 Philip DAWSON (*b* Cameron, Fairfax Co, Va., 30 July 1880; *d* Alexandria, Va., 20 June 1963), s of Nicholas Dawson and his w Virginia Mason Cooper, and *d* 24 Feb 1976, leaving issue:

Great-nephew's great-great-grandchildren

1d *Virginia Cooper Dawson [Mrs John Beebe, PO Box 287, White Stone, VA 22578, USA], *b* Lynchburg, Va., 2 April 1922; *m* Alexandria, Va., 4 Sept 1948 *John BEEBE (*b* Washington, DC, 10 Sept 1920), s of Lawrence Laverne Beebe and his w Alma Pearl Lattin, and has issue:

Great-nephew's great-great-grandchildren's children

1e *(Eliza)Beth Lattin Beebe [Mrs Gregory Schlickenmaier, 10233 Dunfries Rd, Vienna, VA 22181, USA], *b* Washington, DC, 13 Dec 1952; *m* 1980 *Greg(ory) SCHLICKENMAIER and has issue:

Great-nephew's great-great-grandchildren's grandchildren

1f *Matthew Lee SCHLICKENMAIER, *b* 1983

2f *Sarah Elixabeth SCHLICKENMAIER, *b* 1986

Great-nephew's great-great-grandchildren's children

2e *Louisa Fontaine Beebe [Mrs Kenneth Quesenberry, 8725 Arley Dve, Springfield, VA 22153, USA], *b* Washington, DC, 21 Nov 1953; *educ* Mary Washington Coll (BA 1975); elementary sch teacher 1975-79, computer programmer 1980-83, pre-sch teacher 1983-; *m* 21 April 1979 *Kenneth Lee QUESENBERRY, s of Roscoe Quesenberry and his w Thelma Maxine Noble, and has issue:

Great-nephew's great-great-grandchildren's grandchildren

1f *Andrew Noble QUESENBERRY, *b* Alexandria, Va., 31 Dec 1982

2f *Katherine Beebe QUESENBERRY, *b* Fairfax, Va., 22 April 1987

Great-nephew's great-great-grandchildren's children

3e *Virginia Cooper Beebe [Mrs Veillette, Box 57, Studley, VA 23162, USA], *b* Washington 30 June 1956; *educ* Virginia Polytechnic U (BS 1978); *m* 10 June 1979 *Thomas Joseph VEILLETTE, s of Leo Joseph Veillette and his w Margaret Ann Pera, and has issue:

Great-nephew's great-great-grandchildren's grandchildren

1f *Ross Thomas VEILLETTE, *b* N Carolina 27 Nov 1986

2f *Anne Rebecca VEILLETTE, *b* N Carolina 2 Jan 1988
3f *Marie Virginia VEILLETTE, *b* N Carolina 14 Sept 1989

Great-nephew's great-great-grandchildren's children
4e *John Washington BEEBE [1919 Fruitdale Ave, Apt I 304, San Jose, CA 95128, USA], *b* Alexandria, Va., 8 June 1963

Great-nephew's great-great-grandchildren
2d *Louisa Fontaine Washington Dawson [Mrs John Smucker III, 108 North Quaker Lane, Alexandria, VA 22304, USA], *b* Lynchburg, Va., 9 March 1925; *educ* Randolph Macon Women's Coll; *m* Alexandria, Va., 28 June 1958 *Revd John Reed SMUCKER III (*b* Kansas City, Mo., 20 April 1928), s of John Reed Smucker, Jr, and his w Dorothy Gorton, and has issue:

Great-nephew's great-great-grandchildren's children
1e *Anne Mason SMUCKER [505 Park Plaza, Charlottesville, VA 22902, USA], *b* Detroit 19 July 1959; *educ* Swarthmore; financial offr Innisfree Inc
2e *Philip Gorton SMUCKER, *b* Grosse Pointe, Mich., 31 Aug 1961; journalist

Great-nephew's great-grandchildren
6c Richard Blackburn WASHINGTON, *b* Waveland 3 March 1885; *m* 1st Alexandria, Va., 27 March 1912 Agnes Harwood (*b* Markham, Fauquier Co, Va., 1 Aug 1884; *d* Arlington, Va., 18 April 1947), dau of Dr Jaquelin Ambler Marshall (gs of Ch Justice John Marshall of the US Supreme Court) and his w and cousin Mary Douthat (ggdau through her mother of Ch Justice John Marshall), and had issue:

Great-nephew's great-great-grandchildren
1d Lawrence WASHINGTON, *b* Alexandria 29 Jan 1913; librarian Library of Congress; *m* 1st Alexandria 28 Feb 1934 Mary Katherine (*b* Stafford Co, Va., 16 May 1915; *d* Alexandria 29 Nov 1971), dau of Dwight Lee Armstrong and his w Lilla Payne, and had issue:

Great-nephew's great-great-grandchildren's children
1e *Mary Katherine Washington [Mrs Edward Shaffner Jr, 1602 Revere Drive, Alexandria, VA 22308, USA], *b* Alexandria 19 July 1936; *m* there 16 June 1954 *Edward Ervin SHAFFNER, Jr (*b* Washington, DC, 7 Oct 1932), s of Edwin Ervin Shaffner and his w Frances Lincoln Stevens, and has issue:

Great-nephew's great-great-grandchildren's grandchildren
1f *Pamela Kay Shaffner [Mrs Thomas R Dent, 14200 Fall Brook Lane, Woodbridge, VA 22193, USA], *b* St Petersburg, Fla., 17 March 1955; *m* Mt Vernon, Va., 8 May 1982 *Thomas Richard DENT and has issue:

Great-nephew's great-great-grandchildren's great-grandchildren
1g *Richard Edward DENT, *b* 9 Oct 1985
2g *Lawrence Marshall DENT, *b* 4 March 1988

Great-nephew's great-great-grandchildren's grandchildren
2f *Patricia Kay Shaffner [Mrs Shannon M Mann, 214 3rd St, Shenandoah, VA 22849, USA], *b* St Petersburg 17 March 1955; *m* Va. 11 Nov 1983 *Shannon Mervin MANN and has issue:

Great-nephew's great-great-grandchildren's great-grandchildren
1g *Katherine Elizabeth MANN, *b* 18 May 1984
2g *David Christopher MANN, *b* 23 June 1986

Great-nephew's great-great-grandchildren's grandchildren
3f *(Eliza)Beth Darleen Shaffner, *b* Washington, DC, 16 Jan 1958; *m* Alexandria, Va., 19 Feb 1977 *Bryce Alan HANSON (*b* Columbus, Ohio, 18 Sept 1954), s of Kenneth Parker Hanson and his w Rexa Golden, and has issue:

Great-nephew's great-great-grandchildren's great-grandchildren
1g *Ryan Alan HANSON, *b* Alexandria 14 May 1978
2g *Courtenay Rebecca HANSON, 9 Feb 1981

Great-nephew's great-great-grandchildren's grandchildren
4f *Lawrence (Larry) Washington SHAFFNER [1602 Revere Dve, Alexandria, VA 22308, USA], *b* Washington, DC, 22 Aug 1960; *m* Feb 1983 *Cynthia Ellen Stanley and has issue:

Great-nephew's great-great-grandchildren's great-grandchildren
1g *Amber Rene SHAFFNER, *b* 17 Sept 1983
2g *Ashlee Nicole SHAFFNER, *b* 22 Aug 1987

Great-nephew's great-great-grandchildren
1d (cont.) Lawrence Washington *m* 2nd Alexandria 21 April 1973 *Muriel Florence ('Woody') [Mrs Lawrence Washington, 127 Longview Dve, Alexandria, VA 22314, USA] (*b* Cambridge, Mass., 23 Dec 1923), dau of Herbert Bradford Woodruff and his w Georgia Frances Wade and formerly w of Howard Acton, Jr, and *d* Alexandria 9 Oct 1979
2d *Revd Jaquelin Marshall WASHINGTON [5232 15 Street, Lubbock, TX 79416, USA], *b* Alexandria 19 Dec

1914; *educ* Duke U and Virginia Episcopal Theological Seminary; Rector St Paul's Church-on-the-Plains, Lubbock, 1956-84; *m* 1st Fairfax, Fairfax Co, Va., 17 Jan 1942 Frances Blanche (*b* Manassas, Va., 15 Oct 1915; *d* Lubbock 29 Nov 1962), dau of Francis Norvell Larkin and his w Marie Herrell; *m* 2nd Lubbock 14 July 1974 (divorce 7 July 1978) Louise (*b* Greeneville, Tex., 15 Sept 1915), dau of Cary Alvin Fagg and widow of Charles Maedgen

3d *Richard Blackburn WASHINGTON, Jr [3350 South Elm Street, Denver, CO 80222-7313, USA], *b* Alexandria 16 Jan 1917; *educ* Episcopal High Sch; formerly with United Airlines; *m* 1st Alexandria 14 Jan 1941 (divorce Jan 1944) Dorothy Jean Catrow; *m* 2nd Key West, Fla., 7 Jan 1944 (divorce Jan 1972) Mildred Frances (*b* Wellington, Ala., 12 Feb 1920), dau of Joseph Homer Smith and his w Huldah Frances Prickett, and with her has issue:

> Great-nephew's great-great-grandchildren's children
> 1e *Richard Blackburn WASHINGTON III [PO Box 253, Fork Union, VA 23055, USA], *b* Fort Pierce, St Lucie Co, Fla., 2 Nov 1944; instructor Fork Union Mily Acad, Va.; *m* 1st Eads, Colo., 27 Dec 1979 (divorce Aug 1981) Arita Arlene Blooding; *m* 2nd Fork Union 1 Oct 1981 *Joanne Headen
> 2e *Rilla Washington [Ms Rilla Prickett Marshall, 8692 Briarwood Blvd, Englewood, CO 80112, USA], *b* Berlin, New Hampshire, 23 April 1946; *educ* Radford Coll; software engr 1980- ; *m* 18 Jan 1975 (divorce Nov 1982) Bohuslav Oliver PANSKY (*b* Prague, Czechoslovakia, 2 Nov 1948), s of Bohuslav Pansky and his w Eva, and with him has issue:

>> Great-nephew's great-great-grandchildren's grandchildren
>> 1f *Cedric Oliver PANSKY, *b* Denver, Colo., 23 Jan 1980

Great-nephew's great-great-grandchildren
3d Richard B. Washington Jr *m* 3rd Burlington, Kans., 14 June 1975 *Louise Marie Sanders (*b* there 9 April 1912; retired grade sch teacher)

4d *Agnes Harwood Washington [Mrs Walter Hougas, Rte3 Box 90, N 2947 Hiawatha Rd, Monroe, WI 53566, USA], *b* Alexandria, Va., 15 Dec 1919; *educ* Sch of Nursing U of Virginia; registered nurse; *m* Arlington 3 Oct 1948 *Walter Dean HOUGAS (*b* Pembina, N. Dak., 21 Oct 1924), s of Harley Jay Hougas and his w Maud Alberta Richardson, and has issue:

> Great-nephew's great-great-grandchildren's children
> 1e *Anne Harwood Hougas [Mrs Richard Watman, 21945 Mayrose Blvd, Brookfield, WI 53045, USA], *b* Madison, Wis., 8 Aug 1952; *m* 1st 19— ——; *m* 2nd 19— ——; *m* 3rd Wisconsin 3 April 1987 *Richard WATMAN
> 2e *Walter Dean HOUGAS [2465 Hillpoint Rd, McFarland, WI 53558, USA], *b* Madison 26 June 1955; *m* Wisconsin 19 Oct 1985 *Angeline (Angie) Lamb and has issue:

>> Great-nephew's great-great-grandchildren's grandchildren
>> 1f *Max(well) John HOUGAS, *b* 14 Dec 1988

> Great-nephew's great-great-grandchildren's children
> 3e *Robert Hayer HOUGAS [2516 N 67th St, Wauwatosa, WI 53213, USA], *b* Elgin, Ill., 25 Sept 1960; *m* 29 Sept 1984 *Sherry Liebnow and has issue:

>> Great-nephew's great-great-grandchildren's grandchildren
>> 1f *Nicholas HOUGAS, *b* 29 March 1989

Great-nephew's great-great-grandchildren
5d *John Augustine WASHINGTON [19117 Bloomfield Road, Olney, MD 20832, USA], *b* Alexandria, Va., 9 Dec 1921; purchasing agent Atomic Energy Commission (ret); *m* Lynchburg, Va., 24 Dec 1952 *Geraldine Farrar (*b* Brookneal, Va., 15 Nov 1932), dau of Robert Lawrence Peake and his w Bernice Smith Puckett, and has issue:

> Great-nephew's great-great-grandchildren's children
> 1e *(John Au)Gus(tine) WASHINGTON, Jr [566 Prospect St, Maplewood, NJ 07040, USA], *b* Alexandria 8 Jan 1959; *educ* Georgetown Law Sch; atty with Mudge, Rose, Alexander, Guthrie & Ferdan; *m* 19— *Cheryl —— and has issue:

>> Great-nephew's great-great-grandchildren's grandchildren
>> 1f *Jack WASHINGTON, *b* 1992

Great-nephew's great-great-grandchildren
6d *Lt-Col Fielding Lewis WASHINGTON, USAF (ret) [1506 Oxford Court, Denton, TX 76201, USA], *b* Alexandria, Va., 23 Jan 1924; *educ* George Washington U (JD 1949); USAF Judge Advocate Dept 1950-71, atty Seguin, Tex., 1979-90; *m* Lubbock, Tex., 23 May 1945 *Jacqueline (*b* Texico, N. Mex., 26 Oct 1923), dau of Clarence Vernon Young and his w Ola Mae Jackson, and has issue:

> Great-nephew's great-great-grandchildren's children
> 1e *Jacqueline Marshall Washington [Mrs Stanley M Bode, 2207 Longmeadow St, Denton, TX 76201, USA], *b* Lubbock 10 Sept 1951; *educ* San Antonio Coll of Medical Assistants; medical assist 1972-76, medical insur specialist 1978-89, legal sec 1990- ; *m* Seguin 23 June 1973 *Stanley Martin BODE (*b* there Nov 1953), s of Henry Robert Bode and his w Hulda Ann Barth, and has issue:

Great-nephew's great-great-grandchildren's grandchildren
1f *Sarah Michelle BODE, *b* N Richland Hills, Tex., 26 Aug 1984

Great-nephew's great-great-grandchildren
7d *Thomas Lackland WASHINGTON [1026 Revere Drive, Oconomowoc, WI 53066, USA], *b* Alexandria, Va.,
8 Oct 1926; *educ* Purdue U (BSATE 1950); salesman Bingham Co 1958-89 (ret 1989); *m* Alexandria 15 June 1948
*Reva Fay (*b* Langhorne, Pa., 30 Dec 1927; *educ* Purdue U (BSHE)), adopted dau of Dr Charles Everand Reeves
and his *w* Frances Fugate, and has issue:

Great-nephew's great-great-grandchildren's children
1e *Thomas Ryland WASHINGTON [3912 Bach Blvd, Carrollton, TX 75007, USA], *b* Richmond, Va., 4 June
1956; *educ* U of Wisconsin (BBA); staff auditor Arthur Andersen & Co Milwaukee 1979-82, corporate auditor
American Airlines Inc Fort Worth, Tex., 1982-84, controller Great Southwest Cos Dallas 1984-86, V-Pres
Finance and Ch Financial Offr Combined American Properties Dallas 1986, self-employed CPA 1987-89, sr
consultant Coopers & Lybrand Dallas 1989-, Treasurer Denton Co Mental Health and Mental Retardation Bd
of Tstees 1987-90; *m* Fontana, Wis., 6 March 1982 *Vivian Marie (*b* Preston, Minn., 20 Oct 1957; *educ* U of
Wisconsin (BS 1979)), dau of Fritz Rudolph Behm and his *w* Herta Hedwig Hoedl (dau of Paul Georg Hoedl,
sometime Austrian Ambassador to UK), of Williams Bay, Wis., and has issue:

Great-nephew's great-great-grandchildren's grandchildren
1f *Andrew Thomas WASHINGTON, *b* Dallas 5 Dec 1985
2f *Alexandra Marie WASHINGTON, *b* Carrollton, Tex., 10 July 1991

Great-nephew's great-great-grandchildren's children
2e *Elaine Frances Washington [Mrs Edward Kilpatrick, 716 Mansfield Ct, Hartland, WI 53029, USA], *b*
Richmond 23 Jan 1958; *m* Anniston, Ala., 25 June 1977 *Edward Nicholas KILPATRICK (*b* 18 April 1950), *s*
of Edward Nicholas Kilpatrick and his *w* Marie Fiore, and has issue:

Great-nephew's great-great-grandchildren's grandchildren
1f *Kathleen Marie KILPATRICK, *b* Fort McClellan, Ala., 16 March 1978

Great-nephew's great-great-grandchildren's children
3e *Patricia Anne WASHINGTON [7193 Dover Lane Rt2 Box 359, Mazomanie, WI 53560, USA], *b* Baltimore
26 March 1966; *educ* MATC, Madison; certified surgical technologist, Richland Hosp, Richland Center, Wis.

Great-nephew's great-grandchildren
6c (cont.) Richard B. Washington *m* 2nd Hagerstown, Md., 18 Sept 1948 Lillian Margaret (*b* Needville, Tex., 9
Dec 1905; *d c* 1972 ?Pittsburgh, Pa., in a car accident), dau of William Franklin Banker and his *w* Louise Cramer
and formerly *w* of —— Alexander, and *d* Dunn Loring, Va., 8 Dec 1961
7c Willis Lackland WASHINGTON, *b* Waveland 17 Jan 1887; *m* 13 March 1958 *Mrs Mabel Miller [Mrs Willis
Washington, Route 1, Box 146A, Foristell, MO 63348, USA] (*b* 6 June 1895), dau of William Briggs Rogers, and
d Front Royal, Va., 21 June 1972
8c Frances Jaquelin Washington, *b* Waveland 14 June 1888; *m* Washington, DC, 25 April 1917 Owen Batchelder
LEWIS (*b* Richmond, Va., 22 Jan 1889; *d* Germantown, Pa., 17 April 1954), *s* of Louis Lewis and his *w* Jane
Elizabeth Owen, and *d* Charles Town, W. Va., July 1967, having had one *s* (*d* in infancy) and adopted a girl:

a *Betty Lewis [Mrs John Leser, 318 Manheim St, Philadelphia, PA, USA], *b* 19—; *m* 19— *Revd John LESER

Great-nephew's great-grandchildren
9c Wilson Selden WASHINGTON, *b* Waveland 13 Sept 1889; Memb Virginia House of Delegates; *m* Washington,
DC, 14 April 1920 *Irene Watkins [Mrs Wilson Washington, Goodwin House, 4800 Fillmore Avenue, Alexandria,
VA 22311, USA] (*b* East Radford, Montgomery Co, Va., 18 March 1896), dau of James Whitefield Tinsley and his
w Nancy James, and *d* Alexandria 21 July 1953, leaving issue:

Great-nephew's great-great-grandchildren
1d *Nancy James Washington [Mrs Kingston McCoy, 3000 Tanglewood Court, Williamsburg, VA 23185, USA],
b Alexandria 16 June 1922; *m* there 21 July 1956 *Kingston Chandler Ware McCOY (*b* Marietta, Ohio, 19 Aug
1906), *s* of Asa Davis McCoy and his *w* Mary Rebecca Hancock, and has issue:

Great-nephew's great-great-grandchildren's children
1e *John Washington McCOY, *b* Washington, DC, 29 June 1958
2e *Chandler Ware McCOY, *b* Washington 25 Dec 1959

Great-nephew's great-great-grandchildren
2d Wilson Selden WASHINGTON, *b* Alexandria 11 June 1925; *educ* American U, Washington, DC, and Princeton;
Assist Dir Honolulu Acad of Arts from 1969; *m* Washington 8 Sept 1956 *Barbara, dau of Charles Silas Baker
and his *w* Elizabeth Lambert, and *d* 19—

Great-nephew's great-grandchildren
10c Preston Chew WASHINGTON, *b* The Plains, Fauquier Co, Va., 30 Aug 1892; *m* Huntington, W. Va., 24
April 1917 *Lucille Hite [Mrs Preston Washington, 505 Eleventh Avenue, Huntington, WV 25701, USA] (*b*

Chapmanville, Logan Co, W. Va., 21 Nov 1897), dau of George Brammer and his w Roxie Anne Butcher, and *d* Huntington 24 July 1968

11c Julian Howard WASHINGTON, *b* Alexandria 8 March 1894; *m* Richmond, Va., 23 Oct 1933 Mary Edna Eleanor (*b* Washington, DC, 31 Oct 1907; *d* Baltimore 1963), dau of John Warwick Daniel, Jr, and his w Edna Bishop, and *d* Benedict, Md., 12 Nov 1956

12c Francis Ryland WASHINGTON, *b* Alexandria 18 Aug 1897; *m* Annapolis, Md., 30 Aug 1930 Rebecca Holmes (*b* 29 July 1903; *d* 19—), dau of Revd Charles Noyes Tyndell and his w Rebecca Holmes Lewis, and *d* 19—, having had one child (*d* in infancy)

Great-nephew's grandchildren

6b Eleanor Love Selden Washington, *b* Mount Vernon 14 March 1856; *m* Warsaw, Va., 5 May 1880 Julian Smith HOWARD, of Richmond, Va. (*b* 10 July 1853; *d* Warsaw 17 May 1884), s of Charles Howard and his w Sarah Anne Smith, and *d* Alexandria 7 Nov 1937, leaving one dau

7b George WASHINGTON, *b* Mount Vernon 26 July 1858; *m* Charles Town, W. Va., 16 Feb 1886 Emily Serena (*b* Jefferson Co, W. Va., 3 May 1863; *d* Charles Town 10 Nov 1944), dau of Col George Alexander Porterfield and his w Emily Terrill, and *d* Charles Town 31 Dec 1905, having had issue:

Great-nephew's great-grandchildren

1c Revd Richard Blackburn WASHINGTON, SJ, *b* Charles Town 5 Feb 1887; Pastor of the Shrine of the Sacred Heart, Hot Springs, Va.; *d* Philadelphia 14 March 1962

2c Louisa Fontaine WASHINGTON, *b* Charles Town 15 Jan 1889; *d* there 8 Sept 1898

Great-nephew's children

5a Richard Scott Blackburn WASHINGTON; *m* 20 Nov 1844 Christian Maria, 2nd dau of Dr Samuel Walter Washington, and had issue (for whom *see above*)

Great-nephew

(3) Bushrod Corbin WASHINGTON, of Claymont (which he built), Jefferson Co, W. Va., *b* Walnut Farm 25 Dec 1790; Memb Virginia House of Delegates; *m* 1st Rippon Lodge 1810 Anna Maria Thomasina (*b* there 30 Oct 1790; *d* Washington, DC, 24 Sept 1833), 2nd dau and co-heiress of Richard Scott Blackburn, of Rippon Lodge, and his 1st w Judith Ball (also sister of Mrs John Augustine Washington, for whom *see above*), and had issue:

Great-nephew's children

1a Hannah Lee Washington, *b* Rippon Lodge 19 May 1811; *m* June 1835 (divorce 1854), as his 2nd w, William Pearson ALEXANDER (*b* King George Co, Va., *c* 1803; *d* Alexandria, Va., *c* 1862), s of Thomas Pearson Alexander and his w Sarah Mustin (and 1st cousin once removed of Dr William Fontaine Alexander, for whom *see above*), and *d* Charles Town 12 Jan 1881, having had five s and three daus

2a Thomas Blackburn WASHINGTON, of Claymont, *b* Rippon Lodge 19 Aug 1812; *m* 28 Feb 1837 Rebecca Janet (*b* Richlands, Frederick Co, Md., 13 Nov 1820; *m* 2nd Revd Edward William Syle and *d* London, UK, 23 Sept 1890), dau of James Cunningham and his w Catherine Campbell, and *d* Alexandria 3 Aug 1854, leaving issue:

Great-nephew's grandchildren

1b Bushrod Corbin WASHINGTON, *b* Claymont 14 May 1839; *m* 1st Weehaw, Clarke Co, Va., 21 July 1864 his 2nd cousin once-removed Catherine Thomas (*b* Weehaw 25 Nov 1840; *d* Braddock 15 Sept 1876), dau of Dr Richard Scott Blackburn and his w Sarah Ann Eleanor Thomas, and had issue:

Great-nephew's great-grandchildren

1c Bushrod Corbin WASHINGTON, *b* Claymont 28 Dec 1865; *m* 1st 12 Oct 1887 Emma (*b* Balclutha, Clarke Co, Va., 17 June 1864; *d* Branford, Conn., 27 Aug 1934), dau of William Temple Allen and his w Mary Elizabeth Bayly, and had issue:

Great-nephew's great-great-grandchildren

1d *Katharine Cunningham Washington, *b* Balclutha 13 Aug 1888; *m* 13 Dec 1912 (divorce 19—) Matthew Smith HOPKINS (*b* White Hall, Howard Co, Md.), s of Samuel Hopkins and his w Martha Tyson Smith, and has had issue:

Great-nephew's great-great-grandchildren's children

1e Matthew Smith HOPKINS, *b* Washington, DC, 31 Jan 1914; lost at sea when SS *Jacksonville* sunk off Irish coast 30 Aug 1944

2e *Bushrod Washington HOPKINS [6761 Haviland Mill Road, Clarksville, MD 21029, USA], *b* Reading, Pa., 31 July 1915; *m* Washington, DC, 26 Dec 1953 *Mary Jozie (*b* Burkburnett, Tex., 7 July 1921), dau of Henry George Spence and his w Lola May Sides, and has two adopted children:

a *Bushrod Washington HOPKINS, *b* 12 April 1955; *m* Ellicott City, Md., 17 Aug 1974 *Donna Carol (*b* 1956), dau of Calvin Stanley Bassler and his w Diane

b *Glenn Spence HOPKINS, *b* 1 Oct 1957

Great-nephew's great-great-grandchildren's children

3e *Samuel Ellicott HOPKINS [Route 3 Box 77, Centreville, MD 21617, USA], *b* Reading, Pa., 7 May 1917;

m Centreville 30 Aug 1951 *Susan Green (*b* Queenstown, Md., 20 July 1915), dau of R. Carter Bryan and his w Mary Green, and has two adopted children:

    a *George Ellicott Tyson HOPKINS, *b* 14 Feb 1952
    b *Betty Jean HOPKINS, *b* 12 Aug 1953

Great-nephew's great-great-grandchildren's children

4e Katharine Blackburn Hopkins, *b* Reading, Pa., 4 April 1919; *m* 1st (divorce 19——) Gilbert Ward LEWIS, s of Charles Venable Lewis and his w —— Motley, and had one dau; *m* 2nd 12 Oct 1942, as his 2nd w, James Knox Polk MILLS (*b* Princeton, Mercer Co, W. Va., 1915; *d* July 1944), s of B. T. Mills, and had a further dau; *m* 3rd Santa Barbara, Calif., 16 Sept 1945 (divorce 1958), as his 3rd w, Andrew Jackson LINEBARGER (*b* Santa Paula, Calif., 23 Jan 1903), s of John George Linebarger, and had a further three s and one dau; *m* 4th Merced, Calif., *Pedro MARTINEZ and *d* there Oct 1963

5e *Eleanor Blackburn Hopkins [Mrs Leon Sisson, 5925 Damascus Road, Gaithersburg, MD 20720, USA], *b* Reading, Pa., 26 Jan 1921; *m* Silver Spring, Md., 18 Oct 1949 *Leon Wesley Arnold Gray SISSON (*b* Lynchburg, Va., 18 July 1907), s of William Sisson and his w Roberta Odessa Gray, and has issue:

    Great-nephew's great-great-grandchildren's grandchildren
    1f *Leon Gray SISSON, *b* Queenstown, Md., 5 Feb 1951
    2f *Odessa Gray SISSON, *b* Sandy Spring, Md., 25 Feb 1953
    3f *Sharon Gray SISSON, *b* Sandy Spring 6 Sept 1954
    4f *Byron Gray SISSON, *b* Bethesda, Md., 22 July 1956
    5f *Glenda Joy SISSON, *b* Frederick, Md., 17 Feb 1958

Great-nephew's great-great-grandchildren's children

6e *John Marsh Smith HOPKINS [421 India Creek Drive, Cocoa Beach, FL 32931, USA], *b* Washington, DC, 17 May 1929; *m* 1st Biloxi, Miss., 17 June 1952 (divorce 19——) Helen Krzwic-Ostoai; *m* 2nd Cocoa Beach 17 July 1966 *Jean Ada (*b* Orlando, Fla., 18 March 1931), dau of Arthur Ira Gould and his w Florence Ward and formerly w of —— Risher, and with her has issue:

    Great-nephew's great-great-grandchildren's grandchildren
    1f *Martha Ann HOPKINS, *b* Cocoa Beach 6 Nov 1968

Great-nephew's great-great-grandchildren

2d Emma Allen Washington, *b* Balclutha 22 April 1890; *m* Washington, DC, 26 Sept 1917 Chester Carmen BAXTER (*b* Allen Co, Ohio, 1 June 1886; *d* Winter Haven 2 Oct 1967), s of James Baxter and his w Clara MacBride, and *d* 1 June 1983, having had issue:

G-nephew's great-great-grandchildren's children

1e Jane Blackburn BAXTER, *b* Washington, DC, 29 Jan 1919; *d* Merchantville, New Jersey, 20 Aug 1929

2e *James BAXTER [Rt 3 Box 193, Kinderhook Rd, Columbia, PA 17512, USA], *b* Philadelphia 20 April 1920; *educ* Lafayette Coll; metallurgical engr; *m* Columbia 23 April 1950 *Beth Lane (*b* Oak Hill, Fayette Co, W. Va., 2 Feb 1928), dau of Kent Bailey Williams and his w Margaret Lucile Johnson, and has issue:

    Great-nephew's great-great-grandchildren's grandchildren
    1f *James (Jim) Chester BAXTER [242 Plainsfield Pl, Jackson, TN 38305, USA], *b* São Paulo, Brazil, 4 Aug 1951; *educ* U of Tennessee; material handling equipment distributor; *m* Lexington, Tenn., 2 July 1977, as her 2nd husb, *Deborah Ann, da of Harold Anderson and his w Eddy Sue, and has issue:

        Great-nephew's great-great-grandchildren's great-grandchildren
        1g *Megan Elizabeth BAXTER, *b* Jackson, Tenn., 29 Jan 1979
        2g *Adam Carmen BAXTER, *b* Jackson 23 March 1982

    Great-nephew's great-great-grandchildren's grandchildren
    2f *Christopher Hale BAXTER [Rt1 361-T, Carthage, TN 37030, USA], *b* New Haven, Conn., 31 July 1955; *educ* U of Tennessee; *m* Fairfield, Iowa, 26 Aug 1978 *Connie Fry

    3f *Stephen (Steve) Allen BAXTER [104 Friar Tuck Drive, Dickson, TN 37055, USA], *b* New Haven 1 Jan 1959; *m* 19 Dec 1983 *Carol, dau of Homer W. Cresong and his w June Collin, and has issue:

        Great-nephew's great-great-grandchildren's great-grandchildren
        1g *Amy Michelle BAXTER, *b* Tennessee 4 Aug 1983

Great-nephew's great-great-grandchildren's children

3e *William Temple Allen BAXTER [2105 Parkside Place, Indian Harbor Beach, FL 32937, USA], *b* Philadelphia 19 Sept 1921; *educ* Lafayette Coll; personnel manager RCA 1940-70, with US Civil Service Commission 1974-84; *m* Wilmington, N Carolina, 6 Oct 1943 *Irene Blanche (*b* Martins Creek, Pa., 13 June 1924), dau of William Jennings Karabinus and his w Blanche Sinaly, and has issue:

    Great-nephew's great-great-grandchildren's grandchildren
    1f *Jane Blackburn Baxter, *b* Camden, New Jersey, 17 Dec 1946; *m* Gainesville, Fla., 17 March 1973 *Paul Stephen HUGHES (*b* Oneonta, New York, 28 April 1949), s of Raymond Archie Hughes and his w Audrey

Louise Donovan
2f *William ('Bucky') Temple Allen BAXTER, Jr [3891 Knight Dve, White's Creek, TN 37189, USA], *b* Melbourne, Fla., 8 March 1955; musician; *m* 1st Vienna, Va., 10 July 1981 (divorce 19—) Claudia Kritini and has issue:

   Great-nephew's great-great-grandchildren's great-grandchildren
   1g *Brooke Claire BAXTER
   2g *Rayland Allen BAXTER

Great-nephew's great-great-grandchildren's grandchildren
   2f (cont.) William T. Baxter *m* 2nd 19— (divorce 19—) ——

Great-nephew's great-great-grandchildren
3d Bushrod Corbin WASHINGTON, *b* Balclutha 25 Nov 1892; *m* Washington, DC, 5 April 1920 Edith (*b* Washington, DC, 1 Jan 1895), dau of Jesse E. Eastlack and his w Martha Featherer, and *d* 29 Sept 1974, leaving issue:

   Great-nephew's great-great-grandchildren's children
   1e *Bushrod Corbin WASHINGTON [2509 Popkins Lane, Alexandria, VA 22506, USA], *b* Washington, DC, 1 Oct 1920; *m* there 15 June 1946 *Lydia Elizabeth (*b* Fayetteville, N Carolina, 20 Aug 1925), dau of Lonnie Thomas Brown and his w Lena Burke, and has issue:

      Great-nephew's great-great-grandchildren's grandchildren
      1f *Lydia Dianne WASHINGTON, *b* Washington, DC, 21 Jan 1951
      2f *Sharon Rose WASHINGTON, *b* Washington 27 July 1953
      3f *Bushrod Corbin WASHINGTON [2622 New Banner Lane, Herndon, VA 22071, USA], *b* Alexandria, Va., 22 April 1956

   Great-nephew's great-great-grandchildren's children
   2e *Mary Martha Washington [Mrs Bruce Sparling, 3106 Pulaski Pike NW, Huntsville, AL 35810, USA], *b* Norristown, Pa., 8 Dec 1927; *m* Arcadia, Calif., 2 Aug 1950 *Bruce Enoch SPARLING (*b* Muscatine, Iowa, 9 July 1927), s of Enoch Albert Sparling and his w Lulu Mae, and has issue:

      Great-nephew's great-great-grandchildren's grandchildren
      1f *Edith Mae Sparling, *b* Washington, DC, 17 Jan 1952; *m* Huntsville, Ala., 27 Sept 1974 *Howard Ray ATCHLEY (*b* Atlanta, Ga., 12 Oct 1950), s of James Howard Atchley and his w Betty Wells
      2f *Bruce Edward SPARLING, *b* Washington, DC, 4 Oct 1956

Great-nephew's great-great-grandchildren
4d Eleanor Blackburn Washington, *b* Balclutha 15 Dec 1896; *m* Alexandria, Va., 25 April 1919, as his 1st w, Stuart Kaen JOICE, s of John K. Joice, and *d* Washington, DC, 13 Aug 1920, having had a s (*d* in infancy)
5d *Elizabeth Temple Washington [Mrs Charles Phillips, Apartado 1694, Ensenada, Baja California, Mexico], *b* Washington, DC, 8 Nov 1902; *m* 1st 9 Nov 1920 (divorce 19—), as his 1st w, Samuel Oliver BALDWIN (*b* 22 Sept 1900); *m* 2nd Washington, DC, 6 Nov 1926 *Charles William PHILLIPS (*b* Reading, Pa., 20 Oct 1903), s of Nathan Phillips and his w Emma Pauline Hettinger, and has issue:

   Great-nephew's great-great-grandchildren's children
   1e *Charles Washington PHILLIPS [165 Delta Lane, Arcadia, CA 91006, USA], *b* Birmingham, Ala., 26 Oct 1927; *m* 1st San Francisco 6 Oct 1950 Patricia June (*b* Baltimore 18 June 1932; *d* 15 Feb 1956), dau of Irving Douglas Ross and his w Lillian Mae Fowler, and has issue:

      Great-nephew's great-great-grandchildren's grandchildren
      1f *Charles Washington PHILLIPS, *b* Fort Lewis, Wash., 8 July 1951; *m* Charleston, S Carolina, 20 May 1973 *Susan Louise Buckley (*b* Santa Monica, Calif., 31 Oct 1951), dau of Charles Burres Buckley and his w Mary Nind Lacy, and has issue:

         Great-nephew's great-great-grandchildren's great-grandchildren
         1g *Kimberley Shannon PHILLIPS, *b* Lexington Park, Md., 26 July 1974

      Great-nephew's great-great-grandchildren's grandchildren
      2f *Robert Ross PHILLIPS, *b* 24 Oct 1953

   Great-nephew's great-great-grandchildren's children
   1e (cont.) Charles W PHILLIPS *m* 2nd Arcadia, Calif., 7 Aug 1968 *Sharon Margaret (*b* Glendale, Calif., 14 May 1939), formerly w of —— Blecha and dau of Russell W. Harris and his w Ruth Audrey O'Dell, and has an adopted dau:

      a *Marla Dell PHILLIPS, *b* 17 June 1963

Great-nephew's great-grandchildren
1c (cont.) Bushrod C. WASHINGTON *m* 2nd 20 Oct 1934 Ruby (*b* White Post, Clarke Co, Va., 1 Jan 1884; *d* Hendersonville, N Carolina, 31 Dec 1945), dau of —— McDonald and widow of Taylor Stringer, and *d* Oteen, N Carolina, 15 June 1954

2c Eleanor Blackburn Washington, *b* Claymont 15 Aug 1867; *m* 26 Aug 1889, as his 1st w, John Saunders CASTLEMAN (*b* Clarke Co, Va., 12 Feb 1851; *d* Leesburg, Va., 27 March 1923), s of William Saunders Castleman and his w Mary Emily Sinclair, and *d* Charles Town 25 Oct 1894, leaving issue (with an er s):

Great-nephew's great-great-grandchildren
1d Corbin Washington CASTLEMAN, *b* Charles Town, W. Va., 24 Oct 1893; insurance agent; *m* 1st 19— Vergie Ellen Scott (*d* Woodburn, Oreg., 24 Dec 1926) and had issue:

Great-nephew's great-great-grandchildren's children
1e 2e *Ellen E. Castleman [Mrs James Looker, 6915 Willow Ave, Lincoln, NE 68507, USA], *b* 26 July 1919; Memb DAR; *m* San Francisco 25 May 1946 *Dr James Howard LOOKER, s of —— Looker and his w Lalah Martha, and has issue:

Great-nephew's great-great-grandchildren's grandchildren
1f *Dan(iel) James LOOKER [3301 Twana Dve, Des Moines, IA 50310, USA], *b* Columbus, Ohio, 10 Aug 1947; *m* Lincoln, Nebr., 28 Nov 1968 *Joan McCullough and has issue:

Great-nephew's great-great-grandchildren's great-grandchildren
1g *Marie LOOKER, *b* 18 Jan 1973
2g *Maureen Carol LOOKER, *b* 22 Aug 1977
3g *Nathaniel Thomas LOOKER, *b* 2 Aug 1989

Great-nephew's great-great-grandchildren's grandchildren
2f *Revd Ronni Sue Looker [Revd Ronni S Verboom, 25653 Willow Springs Rd, Mondelein, IL 60060, USA], *b* Lincoln 13 Nov 19—; *m* Nebraska 14 June 1970 *Gilles VERBOOM and has issue:

Great-nephew's great-great-grandchildren's great-grandchildren
1g *Natalie Ellen VERBOOM, *b* 2 Sept 1971
2g *Andrea Missette VERBOOM, *b* 8 Nov 1974
3g *Julien VERBOOM, *b* 22 Oct 1977

Great-nephew's great-great-grandchildren's children
2e *Emma Lou(ise) Castleman [Mrs Everett Shelby, 16720 6th Ave W #J201, Lynnwood, WA 98037-8168, USA], *b* Lambert, Mont., 24 July 1921; *educ* Washington State U, Ewa U and U of Washington; teacher 1941-74, supervisor insurance co 1975-83, nanny 1984-; *m* 7 Aug 1941 *Everett SHELBY and has issue:

Great-nephew's great-great-grandchildren's grandchildren
1f *Jeffrey Alan SHELBY [4812-196 SE, Bothell, WA 98012, USA], *b* Nebraska 30 Dec 1960; *m* Seattle 16 July 1983 *Heather Philips

Great-nephew's great-great-grandchildren's children
3e *Alice CASTLEMAN, *b* 22 Aug 1922
4e *Frances CASTLEMAN, *b* 26 Jan 1926

Great-nephew's great-great-grandchildren
1d (cont.) Corbin W. Castleman *m* 2nd 19— (divorce 19—), as her 2nd husb, his half-uncle Nathaniel Willis Washington's widow Gladys (*b* Port Orchard, Wash., 29 Aug 1890; *d* Spokane, Wash., 13 June 1969), dau of Francis Duane Fuller and his w Nancy Jane Tate; *m* 3rd 19— *Hildra Hughes and *d* Seattle, Wash., 22 May 1989

Great-nephew's great-grandchildren
3c Janet Fairleigh WASHINGTON, *b* Claymont 28 Dec 1868; *d* Ephrata, Wash., 4 Aug 1911
4c Catherine Blackburn Washington, *b* Claymont 5 Sept 1870; *m* 30 Oct 1902 Charles Henry WARD, Jr (*b* Colorado 14 July 1873; *d* Colorado Springs, Colo., 13 Dec 1927), s of Charles Henry Ward and his w Hannah Ogden, and *d* Spokane, Wash., 2 July 1940, having had issue (with two daus):

Great-nephew's great-great-grandchildren
1d *Gerald WARD [PO Box 689, Edmonds, WA 98020, USA], *b* 19—

Great-nephew's great-grandchildren
5c Hannah Lee WASHINGTON, *b* Braddock, W. Va., 30 Dec 1871; *d* Spokane 16 Jan 1917
6c Richard Scott Blackburn WASHINGTON, *b* Braddock 4 Sept 1873; *m* Durango, Mexico, 7 July 1915 Guadalupe (*b* Durango 17 Feb 1891; *d* there 21 May 1916), dau of Juan I. Reyes and his w Jovita Natera, and *d* there 1 June 1938, leaving issue:

Great-nephew's great-great-grandchildren
1d *Guadalupe Washington [Señora Guadalupe Arzac, Florida 1215, PTE, Durango, Durango, Mexico), *b* Durango 4 May 1916; *m* 8 Sept 1941 Ulpiano ARZAC (*b* Mazatlán, Sinaloa, Mexico, 7 Nov 1916; *d* Durango 6 March 1969), s of Ulpiano Arzac and his w Adriana Rodreguez, and has issue:

Great-nephew's great-great-grandchildren's children
1e *Ulpiano ARZAC [Florida 1213 Pte, Durango, Dgo 34000, Mexico], *b* Mazatlán 4 Nov 1942; *educ* Catholic U of Chile; businessman; *m* May 1984 *Guillermina, dau of Guillermo Castillo and his w Margarita Fernandez de Castro, and has issue:

Great-nephew's great-great-grandchildren's grandchildren
1f *Andrea ARZAC CASTILLO, *b* Durango 28 Oct 1985

Great-nephew's great-great-grandchildren's children
2e *Ricardo ARZAC WASHINGTON [Florida 1213, Durango, Durango 34000, Mexico], *b* Mexico Federal District, Mexico, 20 March 1944; *m* 8 July 1967 (divorce 19——) Elena Maria (*b* Torreón, Coahuila, Mexico, 3 Nov 1947), dau of Jesus Max Romo and his w Refugio Zozaya, and has issue:

Great-nephew's great-great-grandchildren's grandchildren
1f *Ricardo ARZAC ROMO, *b* Torreón 2 Nov 1969
2f *Inigo ARZAC ROMO, *b* Torreón 2 June 1976

Great-nephew's great-great-grandchildren's children
2e (cont.) Ricardo Arzac Washington *m* 2nd 19— *Martha Reyes and with her has issue:

Great-nephew's great-great-grandchildren's grandchildren
3f *Rodrigo Ulpiano ARZAC REYES, *b* 25 April 1988
4f *Alonso ARZAC REYES, *b* 22 April 1990

Great-nephew's great-great-grandchildren's children
3e *Ernesto ARZAC [Francisco de Ibarra 1125, Durango, Durango, Mexico], *b* Mexico Federal District, Mexico, 1 April 1945; *m* 19 April 1973 *Virginia (*b* Chihuahua 1 Aug 1954), dau of Raul Lozoya and Mercedes Uribe, and has issue:

Great-nephew's great-great-grandchildren's grandchildren
1f *Ernesto ARZAC, *b* 19 Sept 1974

Great-nephew's great-great-grandchildren's children
4e *Maria de Lourdes ARZAC [Señora Maria Garza, Florida 1215b, PTE, Durango, Durango, Mexico], *b* Mexico Federal District, Mexico, 31 March 1948; *m* 13 Sept 1969 Rodolfo GARZA (*b* San Pedro, Coahuila, Mexico, 12 Sept 1935), s of Rodolfo Garza Martinez and his w Josefina Sada, and has issue:

Great-nephew's great-great-grandchildren's grandchildren
1f *Rodolfo GARZA ARZAC, *b* 15 July 1970
2f *Alfredo GARZA ARZAC, *b* 1 Jan 1973

Great-nephew's great-great-grandchildren's children
5e *Sergio ARZAC, *b* Moclova, Coahuila, Mexico, 19 Oct 1955; *educ* Instituto Tecnologico de Monterrey, Monterrey, Mexico

Great-nephew's great-grandchildren
7c Thomas Campbell WASHINGTON, *b* Braddock, W. Va., 9 Feb 1875; *m* Mattapoisett, Mass., 7 Sept 1910 Elizabeth Harlow (*b* there 28 May 1885; *d* Annandale, Va., 13 April 1967), dau of Judge Lemuel LeBaron Holmes and his w Elizabeth Warren Harlow, and *d* Washington, DC, 3 Aug 1946, leaving issue:

Great-nephew's great-great-grandchildren
1d *Thomas Campbell WASHINGTON [300 West Columbia Street, Falls Church, VA 22046, USA], *b* Washington, DC, 24 Sept 1911; architect; *m* Washington 27 April 1942 *Marguerite (*b* Oak Crest, Md., 1 June 1913), dau of Eugene Lewis Culver and his w Florence Owna Bridges
2d *Lt-Col Richard Blackburn WASHINGTON (ret) [181 Via Chiquita, Los Cruces, NM 88005, USA], *b* Washington, DC, 14 Dec 1915; *educ* George Washington U and Benjamin Franklin U; US Army offr to 1960, supervisory contracting offr USN to 1980; *m* Washington, DC, 5 June 1943 *Joan Barbara (*b* New York 13 July 1925), yr dau of Robert Lister Macneil, The Macneil of Barra, 45th Chief of Clan Niall and 25th of Barra, and his 1st w Kathleen Gertrude Metcalf; The Macneil of Barra was 45th in descent, as the Macneils claim, from Niall of the Nine Hostages (*see* the beginning of the section Washington Male Line Ancestry); Col and Mrs Richard B. Washington have issue:

Great-nephew's great-great-grandchildren's children
1e *Lyn Metcalf Washington [Mrs Lyn Washington, 1727 Foxglove Dve, St Charles, MO 63303, USA], *b* Washington, DC, 27 Dec 1946; *educ* Boston and St Louis Us (BLA 1984); financial analyst and accountant 1985-92, independent consultant with Mary Kay Cosmetics 1993-; *m* Marbledale, Conn., 4 Oct 1969 (divorce 1985) Francis Joseph KEANE (*b* Cambridge, Mass., 15 Sept 1945), s of Francis Thomas Keane and his w Honora Kennelly, and has issue:

Great-nephew's great-great-grandchildren's grandchildren
1f *Carlyn Corbin KEANE, *b* Nuremberg, Germany, 9 Sept 1973; *educ* Boston Coll, Mass.
2f *Courtney Washington KEANE, *b* Cleveland, Ohio, 15 Oct 1977

Great-nephew's great-great-grandchildren's children
2e *Jan Blackburn Washington [Mrs Jan Stodte, 1732 Monument St, Concord, MA 01742, USA], *b* Frankfurt, Germany, 18 July 1948; *educ* U of Massachusetts; registered nurse 1989, certified yoga instructor; *m* Darmstadt,

Germany, 17 March 1970 *Karsten Günther STODTE, architect (b Cologne, Germany, 8 June 1937), s of Dr Gunther O. Stodte and his w Gertrud Richardson, and has issue:

Great-nephew's great-great-grandchildren's grandchildren
1f *Maya (b Maja) STODTE, b Darmstadt 14 Jan 1973; educ Reed Coll, Portland, Oreg.

Great-nephew's great-great-grandchildren's children
3e *Richard Corbin WASHINGTON [18071 Heritage Trail, Strongsville, OH 44136, USA], b Heidelberg, Germany, 11 Aug 1949; educ Brown and Case Western Reserve Us; lawyer and banker; m Alliance, Ohio, 6 July 1974 *Georgeta (b Faragas, Romania, 20 Jan 1953), dau of George Blebea and his w Helen Livia Leancu, and has issue:

Great-nephew's great-great-grandchildren's grandchildren
1f *Tiffany Elena WASHINGTON, b Cleveland, Ohio, 4 Feb 1978
2f *John Blackburn WASHINGTON, b Cleveland 20 Sept 1981

Great-nephew's great-great-grandchildren
3d *LeBaron Holmes WASHINGTON [7044 Cindy Lane, Annandale, VA 22003, USA], b Washington, DC, 9 April 1921; educ Cornell and U of Iowa; instrumentation engineer; m 26 Dec 1942 *Dorothy Helen (b Hickory Point, Tenn., 20 Dec 1924), dau of William Reid Tucker and his w Ruby R. Blackwell, and has issue:

Great-nephew's great-great-grandchildren's children
1e *Carol Reid Washington [Mrs Robert Mongelli, 5-J Eastway, Greenbelt, MD 20770, USA], b Arlington, Va., 3 Jan 1946; m Hyattsville, Md., 14 Jan 1967 *Robert Charles MONGELLI (b Washington, DC, 12 July 1940), s of Charles Mongelli and his w Mary Ondus, and has issue:

Great-nephew's great-great-grandchildren's grandchildren
1f *Brian Joseph MONGELLI, b Silver Spring, Md., 23 Dec 1968
2f *Eric LeBaron MONGELLI, b Washington, DC, 26 Sept 1970

Great-nephew's great-great-grandchildren's children
2e *Faye Holmes Washington [Mrs Robert Weyant Jr, 7802 Windy Point Court, Springfield, VA 22153, USA], b Alexandria, Va., 19 Aug 1953; m Annandale, Va., 1 June 1974 *Robert Nelson WEYANT, Jr (b Windber, Pa., 8 Sept 1947), s of Robert Nelson Weyant and his w Victoria Madeline Kieta, and has issue:

Great-nephew's great-great-grandchildren's grandchildren
1f *Patrick Randall WEYANT, b Woodbridge, Va., 9 March 1981

Great-nephew's great-great-grandchildren's children
3e *Bradley Tucker WASHINGTON [2311 Pimmit Dve #1408-E, Falls Church, VA 22043, USA], b Alexandria, Va., 19 Nov 1955; m Arlington, Va., 26 Oct 1985 *Monique Carlson (b Hamburg, Germany, 6 April 1948), dau of Theodor Pflumm and his w Rose Konstanzer

Great-nephew's great-great-grandchildren
8c Anne Washington, b Braddock, W. Va., 1 Sept 1876; m St Louis, Mo., 2 April 1901 John Taylor HOPKINS, Jr (b Hopkinsville, Christian Co, Ky., 23 Oct 1878; d Madison, Fla., 17 Jan 1947), s of John Taylor Hopkins and his w Elizabeth Edwards Hickman, and d Washington, DC, 4 March 1971, having had issue (with another dau, deceased, and a s):

Great-nephew's great-great-grandchildren
1d *Elizabeth HOPKINS [212 Cromwell Ave, Tarboro, NC 27886, USA], b 19—

Great-nephew's grandchildren
1b (cont.) Bushrod C. Washington m 2nd Charles Town 14 Nov 1878 Emma Edwards (b Rock Hall, Jefferson Co, W. Va., 12 Nov 1843; d Ephrata, Wash., 16 Oct 1930), 7th dau of Thomas Hite Willis and his 1st w Elizabeth Ferguson Ryland (also sister of Nathaniel Hite Willis, for whom see above), and d Almira, Wash., 24 Feb 1919, having with her had issue:

Great-nephew's great-grandchildren
9c Nathaniel Willis WASHINGTON, b Charles Town 6 April 1881; m Bremerton, Wash., 13 Aug 1913 Gladys (see above against Corbin Washington Castleman) and d Douglas Co, Wash., 10 July 1926, having had issue:

Great-nephew's great-great-grandchildren
1d *Nathaniel Willis WASHINGTON [42 C Street NW, Ephrata, WA 98823, USA], b Coulee City, Wash., 2 May 1914; educ U of Washington; atty and Memb Washington State Senate 1951-79; m Tucson, Ariz., 24 April 1945 *Wanda Florence Wells (née Sokolska, from which she changed it by legal instrument) (b Brooklyn, New York, 3 Jan 1918), dau of Andrew Sokolski and his w Mary Magdalene Kotik, and has issue:

Great-nephew's great-great-grandchildren's children
1e *Nathaniel Willis WASHINGTON [9925 NE 1st St, Bellevue, WA 98004, USA], b Spokane 3 May 1946; m Seattle, Wash., 11 Aug 1973 *Lisa Gale (b 8 Aug 1952), dau of Harold Chadwick and his w Geneva, and has issue:

Great-nephew's great-great-grandchildren's grandchildren
1f *Sarah Elizabeth WASHINGTON, *b* Portland, Oregon 2 July 1972
2f *Rebekah Ann WASHINGTON, *b* Seattle 15 May 1976
3f *Johanna Lynn WASHINGTON, *b* Seattle 15 May 1976

Great-nephew's great-great-grandchildren's children
2e *Thomas Fuller WASHINGTON [11918 NE 143 Pl, Kirkland, WA 98034, USA], *b* Spokane 8 March 1949; *m* Seattle, Wash., 11 Aug 1973 *Lois (*b* 27 April 1951), dau of Louie Mueller and his w Wilma

Great-nephew's great-great-grandchildren
2d Francis Duane WASHINGTON, *b* Coulee City 25 Feb, *d* there 28 Feb 1916
3d *Roberta Ryland Washington [Mrs James Williams, Riddle, OR 97469, USA], *b* Ephrata 21 Oct 1917; *m* Spokane 21 Sept 1936 *James Barclay WILLIAMS (*b* there 20 Jan 1912), s of Jay Carl Williams and his w Rose Butler, and has issue:

Great-nephew's great-great-grandchildren's children
1e *James Donald WILLIAMS [50 Reliance Rd, Rock Springs, WY 82901, USA], *b* Spokane 26 May 1937; *m* Greenacres, Wash., 31 July 1954 *Sharon Naomi (*b* Tacoma, Wash., 9 April 1937), dau of Roderick Peter Forrest, Jr, and his w Minnie Grenville, and has issue:

Great-nephew's great-great-grandchildren's grandchildren
1f *Rannah Louise Williams [Mrs Stanley Hall, 2740 University Street, Eugene, OR 97403, USA; 678 W 5th Ave, Eugene, OR 97402, USA], *b* Spokane 17 March 1955; *m* 3 April 1976 *Stanley Wayne HALL (*b* Roseburg, Oreg., 8 March 1954), s of Leland Verne Hall and his w Morene Marjorie Moore, and has issue:

Great-nephew's great-great-grandchildren's great-grandchildren
1g *Jessica Chani HALL, *b* Eugene 7 Nov 1977

Great-nephew's great-great-grandchildren's grandchildren
2f *David Allen WILLIAMS, *b* Spokane 18 Nov 1957
3f *Eugene Scott WILLIAMS, *b* Oxnard, Calif., 14 June 1960
4f *Frederick Russell WILLIAMS, *b* Grants Pass, Oreg., 19 July 1963

Great-nephew's great-great-grandchildren's children
2e *Glenora Susanne Williams [Mrs Duane Flick, Box 593, Cashmere, WA 98115, USA], *b* Spokane 29 Joly 1938; *m* Greenacres 16 Nov 1956 *Duane Donald FLICK (*b* Leavenworth, Wash., 16 Oct 1934), s of Ezra Earl Flick and his w Jennie Dolores Latimer, and has issue:

Great-nephew's great-great-grandchildren's grandchildren
1f *Robert Alan FLICK, *b* Spokane 26 Sept 1957; *m* 19— and has one dau
2f *Dale Duane FLICK, *b* Spokane 4 Nov 1958

Great-nephew's great-great-grandchildren's children
3e *Nathaniel Robert WILLIAMS [Apt 201 6810 Walker Mill Road, District Heights, MD 20027, USA], *b* Spokane 3 April 1943; *m* 1st Houston, Tex., 19 Sept 1965 (divorce 19—) Vermeda Louise Birmingham (*b* Arkansas 1945); *m* 2nd Weslaco, Tex., 29 April 1967 *Judith Ann (*b* there 5 Feb 1947), dau of Glen Ernest Adams and his w Mary Jane Wilson, and with her has issue:

Great-nephew's great-great-grandchildren's grandchildren
1f *Jacque Leanne WILLIAMS, *b* Corpus Christi, Tex., 18 Aug 1968
Mr and Mrs Nathaniel R. Williams also have an adopted s:
a *Jeffery Brian WILLIAMS, *b* Panama City, Fla., 12 May 1971

Great-nephew's great-great-grandchildren's children
4e *Carl Willis WILLIAMS [1038 West Providence Avenue, Spokane, WA 99205, USA], *b* Spokane 18 March 1944; *m* there 9 Feb 1968 *Rita Lou (*b* there 10 April 1944), dau of John Andrew Hull and his w Margaret Alda McMillan and formerly w of Joseph Occhipinti, and has issue:

Great-nephew's great-great-grandchildren's grandchildren
1f *Joy Tracy WILLIAMS, *b* Spokane 27 Aug 1969

Great-nephew's great-great-grandchildren's children
5e *Roberta Ann Williams, *b* Spokane 10 Dec 1945; *m* Opportunity, Wash., 27 Aug 1966 *John Martin BLOOM (*b* Sedro Woolley, Wash., 22 Sept 1946), s of John Frederick Bloom and his w Susie Marie Vander Laan
6e *Patrick Orville WILLIAMS [Apt 1 715 Cherry Street, Suisun City, CA 94585, USA], *b* Spokane 6 Sept 1950; *m* Berkeley, Calif., 14 Feb 1971 *Bonnie Janine Billecci (*b* 22 April 1953 but later took stepf's name), dau of —— Alben and his w —— Willenberg, and step-dau of Andrew Billecci, and has issue:

Great-nephew's great-great-grandchildren's grandchildren
1f *Paris Beckett WILLIAMS, *b* Moscow, Idaho, 12 July 1972

Great-nephew's great-great-grandchildren's children
7e *Hugh Jay WILLIAMS [1819 Salisbury Dve, Fairfield, CA 94533, USA], b Spokane 4 Feb 1954; m 11 Jan 1980 *Palesteen ——

Great-nephew's great-great-grandchildren
4d *Glenora Gertrude Washington [Mrs Deming Brown, 602 Oswego Street, Ann Arbor, MI 48014, USA], b Ephrata 21 Oct 1917; m there 18 June 1941 *Deming Bronson BROWN (b Seattle, Wash., 26 Jan 1919; Prof Slavic Languages and Literature U of Michigan 1959- and memb faculty 1957-), s of Kirk Charles Brown and his w Lois Bronson, and has issue:

Great-nephew's great-great-grandchildren's children
1e *Kate Deming BROWN, b New York 9 May 1947
2e *Sarah Fuller BROWN, b Evanston, Ill., 30 Sept 1951

Great-nephew's great-grandchildren
10c James Cunningham WASHINGTON, b Charles Town 9 March 1883; d Douglas Co, Wash., 10 July 1926
11c Peachey Ryland WASHINGTON, b Charles Town 3 July 1884; d Douglas Co 10 July 1926

Great-nephew's grandchildren
2b George WASHINGTON, b Claymont 22 Feb 1842; ka during Civil War nr Brownsburg, Va., 30 June 1863
3b Catherine Campbell WASHINGTON, b Claymont 28 Sept 1845; d there 20 Aug 1847
4b James Cunningham WASHINGTON, b Claymont 14 Sept 1847; d military prison Washington, DC, during Civil War 28 Feb 1865
5b Thomas Blackburn WASHINGTON, b Claymont 11 Jan 1851; m 5 Nov 1874 his 2nd cousin once-removed Eleanor Thomas (b Clarke Co, Va., 22 Oct 1844; d Washington, DC, 1 Sept 1921), dau of Dr Richard Scott Blackburn and his w Sarah Ann Eleanor Thomas, and d 9 Aug 1923, having had issue:

Great-nephew's great-grandchildren
1c Rebecca Janet WASHINGTON, b Knoxville, Md., 3 Dec 1875; d Washington, DC, 8 March 1939
2c Eleanor Thomas Washington, b Braddock, W. Va., 30 April 1878; m 5 Jan 1904 Harris Lightfoot FORBES (b Annapolis, Md., 5 Feb 1877; d after 1953), s of Joseph Harris Forbes and his w Fanny Lightfoot, and d Montrose, Calif., 28 Oct 1953, leaving one s
3c John Sinclair WASHINGTON, b Charles Town 12 Jan, d there 13 Jan 1880
4c Sarah Watts Washington, b Charles Town 3 Aug 1883; m Washington, DC, 3 Aug 1905 Walter Howell LEE (b there 3 Jan 1880; d there 8 July 1928), s of Mandeville Girard Lee and his w Frances Knapp, and d Westmoreland Hills, Montgomery Co, Md., 11 Jan 1939, leaving two s and two daus

Great-nephew's grandchildren
6b Anne Maria Thomasina Blackburn Washington, b Claymont 22 Oct 1854; m Tokyo, Japan, 14 May 1879, as his 1st w, Prof James Alfred EWING, CB, FRS (Edin) (later Sir Alfred Ewing, KCB, JP, DL, FRS, MInstCE) (b Dundee, Scotland, UK, 27 March 1855; Prof Mechanical Engineering and Physics Imperial U of Tokyo 1878-83, Prof Engineering U of Dundee 1883-90, Prof Mechanism and Applied Mechanics Cambridge (UK) 1890-1903, Dir Naval Educn Admiralty 1903-16, supervised deciphering of German signals during World War I in 'Room 40' of the Admiralty 1914-17, Principal and V-Chllr Edinburgh U 1916-29; d Cambridge, UK, 7 Jan 1935), 3rd and yst s of Revd James Ewing, of Dundee, and his w Marjory Ferguson, and d Crockham Hill, nr Edenbridge, Kent, UK, 10 April 1909, leaving one s and one dau

Great-nephews and -nieces
(3) (cont.) Bushrod C. Washington m 2nd Leesburg, Va., 29 Jan 1835 Maria Powell (b 27 July 1791; d 4 Nov 1847), dau of Matthew Harrison, and d Albany, New York, 27 July 1851
(4) Jane Mildred WASHINGTON, b Walnut Farm c 1793; d Mount Vernon Sept or Oct 1807
(5) Mary Lee Washington, b Walnut Farm c 1796; m Mount Vernon Nov 1813 Noblet HERBERT (b c 1784; d Mount Vernon 15 Aug 1825), s of Thomas Herbert and his w Sarah, and d Blakeley 16 Oct 1827, having had four s and one dau (all d in infancy or unmarried)
(6) Corbin Thomas WASHINGTON, b Selby, Fairfax Co, Va., c 1798; d c 1802

President Washington's nephew and niece
5 William Augustine WASHINGTON, b Bushfield c 1767; d c Feb 1784
6 Mildred C. Washington, b Bushfield c 1769; m Westmoreland Co, Va., 15 Oct 1788, as his 2nd w, Thomas LEE, of Parke Gate, Prince William Co, Va. (b Chantilly, Westmoreland Co, 20 Oct 1758; d Belmont, Loudoun Co, Va., 7 Sept 1805), est s of Richard Henry Lee and his w Anne Aylett (also bro of Mrs Corbin Washington and the 2nd Mrs William Augustine Washington), and d Va. 1797

IX Charles WASHINGTON, of Happy Retreat, Jefferson Co, W. Va., b Stafford Co, Va., 2 May 1738; founded Charles Town, Col Virginia Militia; m probably Spotsylvania Co, Va., 1757 his 1st cousin once-removed Mildred (b Spotsylvania Co c 1739; d Happy Retreat 1804), dau of Col Francis Thornton, of Fall Hill, Spotsylvania Co, and his w Frances, dau and co-heiress of Roger Gregory and his w Mildred Washington, and d Happy Retreat c 16 Sept 1799, having had issue:

President Washington's nephew

1 George Augustine WASHINGTON, *b c* 1759; Maj US Army; *m* Mount Vernon 15 Oct 1785 Frances (*b* probably Eltham, New Kent Co, Va., 19 Dec 1767; *m* 2nd, as 2nd of his three ws, Tobias Lear, sec to President WASHINGTON; *d* Mount Vernon *c* 24 March 1796), niece of Martha Dandridge Washington and dau of Col Burwell Bassett and his w Anna Maria Dandridge; George Augustine Washington *d* Mount Vernon 5 Feb 1793, having had issue:

Great-nephews and -niece

(1) George Fayette WASHINGTON, *b* Mount Vernon 10 April, *d* there 25 April 1787

(2) Anna Maria Washington, *b* Mount Vernon 3 April 1788; *m* Culpeper Co, Va., 20 Sept 1810 her 1st cousin once-removed Capt Reuben THORNTON (*b* Spotsylvania Co 21 Oct 1780; *d* Woodville, Wilkinson Co, Miss., 23 April 1815), s of Maj George Thornton and his w Mary Alexander, and gs of Col Francis Thornton and his w Frances Gregory, and *d* Woodville 23 Jan 1816, leaving two s

(3) George Fayette WASHINGTON, *b* Mount Vernon 17 Jan 1790; *m* Charles Town, W. Va., 18 Nov 1813 Maria (*b* there Oct 1793; *d* Waverly, Va., Feb 1860), dau of Matthew Frame, of Charles Town, and his w Massey Gibbs, and *d* Waverly in or after 1829, having had issue:

Great-nephew's children

1a Charles Augustine WASHINGTON, of Wellington, Fairfax Co, Va., *b* Charles Town 9 Aug 1814; *d* Georgetown, DC, Feb 1861

2a Francis Massey WASHINGTON, *b* Charles Town 21 Jan 1816; *d* before 1846

3a A child, *b* Charles Town *c* 1819; *d* in infancy

4a George Fayette WASHINGTON, *b* Charles Town 21 Feb 1823; *d* Waverly 6 Nov 1853

5a Matthew Burwell Bassett WASHINGTON, of Waverly, *b* Charles Town 15 Aug 1830; *m* Albemarle Co, Va., 20 March 1862 Anna Bird Dandridge (*b* Md. 18 Aug 1833; *d* Washington, DC, 27 April 1920), dau of Thomas Ely Buchanan and his w Ann Spotswood Dandridge, and *d* Waverly 1 Aug 1868, leaving issue:

Great-nephew's grandchildren

1b Nannie Bird WASHINGTON, *b* Winchester, Frederick Co, Va., 17 March 1864; *d* Waverly 31 Dec 1919

Great-nephew

(4) Charles Augustine WASHINGTON, *b* Mount Vernon 3 Nov 1791; *d* Cadiz, Spain, 5 July 1811

President Washington's niece and nephew

2 Frances Washington, *b* 4 June 1763; *m* 1st 7 April 1781, as his 2nd w, Col Burgess BALL (*b* Lancaster Co, Va., 28 July 1749; *d* Springwood, Loudoun Co, Va., 7 March 1800), widower of Mary Chichester and s of Jeduthan Ball and his w Elizabeth Burgess, and had four s and four daus; *m* 2nd 7 April 1802 Dr Francis H. PEYTON (*d* Leesburg, Loudoun Co, Va., 5 Dec 1808), s of Col Francis Peyton and his w Frances Dade, and *d* Middleburg, Va., Feb 1815, having had another dau (*d* young)

3 Samuel WASHINGTON, of Fredericksburg, Va., later of Kanawha Co, W. Va., *b* probably Fredericksburg *c* 1770; Capt US Army; *m* probably Fall Hill, Spotsylvania Co, *c* 1795 his 1st cousin Dorothea (*b* probably Fall Hill 6 May 1778; *d* Fredericksburg 27 Dec 1813), dau of Francis Thornton, of Fall Hill, and his w Ann Thompson, and gdau of Francis Thornton and his w Frances Gregory, and *d* Kanawha Co, W. Va., 10 Aug 1831, having had issue:

Great-niece and -nephew

(1) Mildred Ann WASHINGTON, *b* 17 Aug 1797; *d* Fredericksburg 15 Nov 1799

(2) Samuel Thompson WASHINGTON, *b* Culpeper Co, Va., 18 Feb 1806; *m* Kanawha Co, W. Va., 18 Feb 1829 Wilhelmina Judith (*b* Rose Hill, Kanawha Co, 7 July 1811; *d* West Columbia, Mason Co, W. Va., 27 July 1855), dau of Jesse Hudson and his w Martha, and *d* Mountain City, Hays Co, Tex., 1869, having had issue:

Great-nephew's children

1a William Meade WASHINGTON, *b* Coals Mouth (now St Albans), Kanawha Co, 19 Jan 1831; *m* Mason Co, W. Va., 11 September 1856 Martha Ann (*b* there 20 Jan 1837; *d* there 11 Nov 1880), dau of Calvin Somerville and his w Margaret Matilda Hogg, and *d* West Columbia, Mason Co, 3 Jan 1884, having had issue:

Great-nephew's grandchildren

1b Wilhelmina Matilda Washington, *b* Mason Co 27 June 1857; *m* 20 Oct 1880 John JOHNSON (*b* 1849; *d* Huntington, W. Va., 12 April 1907), s of Eli Johnson and his w Catherine Yeager, and *d* Huntington 4 Oct 1907, leaving one s

2b Mary Louise Washington, *b* Mason Co 9 April 1859; *m* 10 June 1888 George Newton YEAGER (*b* Mason Co 6 Nov 1854; *d* there 17 March 1945), s of Joseph Yeager and his w Barbara Eckard, and *d* Mason Co 19 Sept 1934

3b Alice Jane WASHINGTON, *b* Mason Co 24 Dec 1860; *d* Huntington, W. Va., 12 March 1943

4b Robert Custis WASHINGTON, *b* Mason Co 20 Jan 1863; *m* 4 Sept 1890 Mary Ellen (*b* Mason Co 7 Aug 1866; *d* Middleport, Ohio, 26 Sept 1962), dau of John Zerckel and his w Edith, and *d* Middleport 13 Jan 1948, leaving issue:

Great-nephew's great-grandchildren

1c Claude Custis WASHINGTON, *b* West Columbia, Mason Co, 8 Nov 1891; *m* 26 Nov 1919 Esther Viola (*b* Middleport, Ohio, 15 May 1896; *d* Virginia Beach, Va., 5 Feb 1952), only child of Paul Clifford Jones and his w Laura Alderman Dumble, and *d* Gallipolis, Ohio, Feb 1973

2c Edith Lorena Washington, *b* West Columbia 26 Dec 1895; *m* 4 Sept 1923 Floyd Everett DAVIS (*b* Pomeroy,

Ohio, 20 May 1895; *d* 19—) and *d* 19—

3c *Nannie Louise Washington, *b* West Columbia 31 Oct 1900; *m* 13 June 1923 Harold Matthew MOORE (*b* Bellaire, Ohio, 21 Oct 1899; *d* Dallas 8 Nov 1925) and has issue:

Great-nephew's great-great-grandchildren
1d *Marguerite Elizabeth Moore, *b* Summerfield, Ohio, 5 Feb 1925; *m* 19—, as his 2nd w, —— *HAWLEY

Great-nephew's great-grandchildren
4c *Elizabeth Virginia Washington [Mrs James Mourning, 266 South Fountain Street, Springfield, OH, USA], *b* West Columbia 31 Oct 1900; *m* 28 Dec 1920 *James Herman MOURNING (*b* Point Pleasant, W. Va., 27 May 1898), s of Robert Mourning

Great-nephew's grandchildren
5b Margaret Elizabeth Washington, *b* Mason Co 8 Jan 1865; *m* 10 Sept 1924, as his 2nd w, her 2nd cousin Lewis Jamison BUMGARNER (*b* 11 April 1866; *d* New Haven, Mason Co, 3 July 1952), s of John Wesley Bumgarner and his w Catherine Barbara Somerville, and *d* Cheshire, Ohio, 14 Jan 1956
6b Judith Frances Washington, *b* Mason Co 1 Jan 1867; *m* 17 Sept 1890 George F. BUMGARNER (*b* 17 March 1862), s of Seth Bumgarner and his w Mary A. Capehart, and *d* 1 April 1891
7b Virginia Susan Washington, *b* Mason Co 5 Jan 1870; *m* 23 Nov 1892 William Richard POWELL (*b* Clifton, Mason Co, 18 Dec 1869; *d* Huntington, W. Va., 1917), s of Samuel Powell and his w Ann Miller, and *d* Charleston, W. Va., 29 May 1956, having had three s and one dau
8b Samuel Thomas WASHINGTON, *b* Mason Co 15 July 1872; *m* 23 Aug 1899 Martha L. (*b* Mason Co 15 July 1871; *d* 12 April 1937), dau of Eugene Chamberlain, and *d* Mason Co 23 Feb 1942, having had issue:

Great-nephew's great-grandchildren
1c *Geneva Marie Washington [Mrs Dewey Swisher, Cheshire, OH, USA], *b* Mason Co 21 May 1900; *m* 29 May 1942 *Dewey Elmo SWISHER (*b* 25 March 1898)
2c Paul Thomas WASHINGTON, *b* Mason Co 1 Feb 1904; *m* 24 Dec 1933 *Maxine Charlotte Heaton [Mrs Paul Washington, Letart, WV 25260, USA] (*b* Letart 30 April 1914) and *d* Letart 21 May 1974, leaving issue:

Great-nephew's great-great-grandchildren
1d *Paul Thomas WASHINGTON, *b* Mason Co 23 Sept 1935
2d *Patricia Louise Washington, *b* Mason Co 27 April 1940; *m* 8 Sept 1962 *Robert Ray HARRIS, USN, s of Frank Harris and his w Elizabeth

Great-nephew's great-grandchildren
3c Helen Louise WASHINGTON, *b* 11 Nov 1906; *d* 8 May 1927

Great-nephew's grandchildren
9b William Calvin WASHINGTON, of Lavallette, W. Va., *b* Mason Co 5 July 1874; *m* Scarbro, W. Va., 1 March 1912 Dulcie (*b* Clifftop, W. Va., 14 April 1891; *d* 13 March 1983), dau of John Bragg and his w Flora Huddleston, and *d* Huntington, W. Va., 8 Nov 1947, having had issue:

Great-nephew's great-grandchildren
1c *Mary Louise Washington, *b* Scarbro 4 Feb 1913; MD; *m* 26 Aug 1960 *Dr Kenneth CLARKE
2c *William Calvin WASHINGTON, Jr [6181 Rosalind Road, Huntington, WV 25705, USA], *b* Scarbro 12 Aug 1914; *educ* Oakhill High; store clerk 1936, truck-driver 1936-40, USN World War II (gunner at Pearl Harbor, saw action in the Philippines, awarded Congressional Medal, discharged 1946); *m* Greenup, Ky., 15 Jan 1955, as her 2nd husb, *Dorothy Marie Brown, dau of Milford and Maggie Davis, and has issue:

Great-nephew's great-great-grandchildren
1d *Martha Anne Washington, *b* 3 Nov 1958; *m* 14 May 1980 *Larry HECK and has issue:

Great-nephew's great-great-grandchildren's children
1e *Chastity Dawn HECK, *b* 31 Aug 1980

Great-nephew's great-great-grandchildren
2d *Thomas William WASHINGTON, *b* 12 Oct 1960

Great-nephew's great-grandchildren
3c Robert Edward WASHINGTON, *b* Scarbro 4 June 1916; *m* Huntington 8 Jan 1944 *Mary Olive Wolfe (*b* 4 July 1915) and *d* 19—
4c *Howard Raymond WASHINGTON, *b* Oak Hill, W. Va., 27 Jan 1918; *m* 29 Sept 1946 *Mary Louise Weir (*b* 19 Feb 1926) and has issue:

Great-nephew's great-great-grandchildren
1d *Susan Dianne WASHINGTON, *b* 23 Dec 1949
2d *Carolyn Louise WASHINGTON, *b* 8 Nov 1951
3d *William Robert WASHINGTON, *b* 30 Dec 1952
4d *Joanne Gale WASHINGTON, *b* 14 April 1959

Great-nephew's great-grandchildren
5c Martha Ann WASHINGTON, *b* Oak Hill 14 Oct 1919; *d* 14 Oct 1920

Great-nephew's grandchildren
10b Arvilla Lorena WASHINGTON, *b* Mason Co 1 Feb 1877; *d* 1 Aug 1963
11b A child, *b* and *d* Mason Co 11 Nov 1880

Great-nephew's children
2a Jesse David WASHINGTON, of Caldwell Co, Mo., later of West Plains, Howell Co, Mo., *b* Kanawha Co, W. Va., 26 March 1833; *m* 25 Dec 1857 Sarah Maria (*b* Kanawha Co 16 Aug 1835; *d* West Plains 23 April 1926), dau of Daniel Dusenberry Bateman and his w Sarah Baker, and *d* West Plains 28 Jan 1899, having had issue:

Great-nephew's grandchildren
1b Custis WASHINGTON, *b* 26 Dec 1857; *d* 29 March 1912
2b Eulala Washington, *b* 14 Aug 1861; *m* 1 Jan 1891, as his 1st w of four, John Harrison WILLIAMS (*b c* 1865) and *d* Phoenix, Ariz., 31 Dec 1911, leaving four s and one dau
3b Zelle Dixie WASHINGTON, *b* 28 Aug 1862; *d* West Plains, Mo., 7 Feb 1946
4b Robert Hudson WASHINGTON, *b* 5 June 1863; *d* 11 Nov 1865
5b George Dusenberry WASHINGTON, of Cull, West Plains, Mo., *b* Chillicothe, Mo., 3 June 1866; *m* Springfield, Mo., 21 April 1892 Kate Catherine (*b* Rolla, Mo., 5 May 1868; *d* West Plains *c* 1962), dau of Patrick Mullin and his w Catherine Davis, and *d* 18 Oct 1933, leaving issue:

Great-nephew's great-grandchildren
1c *Sarah Dixie Washington, *b* 27 Oct 1895; *m* 1 April 1918 Perry Everrett ROUINTREE (*b* 16 Nov 1891; *d* 19—) and has two daus
2c *Chorea Rosalind Washington, *b* 21 Sept 1897; *m* 1 Aug 1946 William Lee SELBY (*b* Linn Creek, Camden Co, Mo., 7 Nov 1878; *d* 19—)
3c *Lee Patrick WASHINGTON, *b* 1 July 1899; *m* 1st 26 Aug 1930 Elsie Elizabeth Bridges (*b* 17 Dec 1905; *d* 17 Jan 1934) and has issue:

Great-nephew's great-great-grandchildren
1d *Lee Patrick WASHINGTON, *b* 28 Aug 1931

Great-nephew's great-grandchildren
3c (cont.) Lee P. Washington *m* 2nd *Maxine Lorene Barrett (*b* 27 Aug 1911), widow of —— Chesnut, and with her has issue:

Great-nephew's great-great-grandchildren
2d *Janet Louise WASHINGTON, *b* 7 Oct 1940

Great-nephew's great-grandchildren
4c Edward Hudson WASHINGTON, *b* 26 March 1901; *m* 18 April 1925 Ellen Jane Barr (*d* 19—) and *d* 19—, having had issue:

Great-nephew's great-great-grandchildren
1d *Glenn Edward WASHINGTON, *b* 29 March 1926; *m* 12 July 1952 *Marcella Ann Heimos (*b* Lemay, St Louis Co, Mo., 29 Sept 1934)
2d *Eugene Hudson WASHINGTON, *b* 24 Dec 1931
3d *Bobby Dean WASHINGTON, *b* 13 Jan 1935

Great-nephew's great-grandchildren
5c *Kate Catherine Washington, *b* 19 Sept 1902; *m* Cloverdale, Calif., 14 Jan 1929 (divorce 19—) Richard Moor ROBERTSON (*b* 16 Feb 1897)
6c Robert Dusenberry WASHINGTON, *b* 8 March 1904; *m* 15 Aug 1939 *Laura Maye Garrett (*b* 16 Oct 1911) and *d* 5 May 1965, leaving issue:

Great-nephew's great-great-grandchildren
1d *Connie Sue Washington, *b* Aug 1941; *m* 19— *Dennis WELLESLEY and has issue:

Great-nephew's great-great-grandchildren's children
1e *Stephanie WELLESLEY, *b* 26 May 1963
2e *Scott WELLESLEY, *b* 8 May 1965
3e *Whitney WELLESLEY, *b* 24 May 1968

Great-nephew's great-great-grandchildren
2d *Paul Robert WASHINGTON, *b* 15 Oct 1945

Great-nephew's great-grandchildren
7c *Georgia Marie Washington, *b* 16 Dec 1906; *m* 1st 8 July 1939 Harry Earl STRONG (*b* 6 Jan 1890; *d* 7 March 1943); *m* 2nd 11 Dec 1947 *William Francis GREENE (*b* Boston 16 July 1906)
8c Wayne Kenneth WASHINGTON, *b* 16 Oct 1909; *m* 4 July 1936 *Mary Guagliardo and *d* 4 March 1948, leaving issue:

Great-nephew's great-great-grandchildren
1d *Kenneth WASHINGTON, *b* 18 July 1938
2d *Marilyn Diane WASHINGTON, *b* 1 May 1940
3d *Arlene Josephine WASHINGTON, *b* 18 July 1943
4d *Darlene Catherine WASHINGTON, *b* 18 July 1943
5d *Georgia Ann WASHINGTON, *b* 2 Dec 1944

Great-nephew's great-grandchildren
9c *Russell Lowell WASHINGTON, *b* 10 April 1912; *m* 18 April 1936 *Nancy Catherine Garrett (*b* 29 May 1918) and has issue:

Great-nephew's great-great-grandchildren
1d *Russell Neale WASHINGTON, *b* 12 Aug 1941
2d *Norman Garrett WASHINGTON, *b* 20 June 1947

Great-nephew's great-grandchildren
10c *Dorothea Louise Washington, *b* 11 Dec 1915; *m* 14 Oct 1938 *Garnett Gilbert SELLS (*b* 28 Oct 1915) and has one s

Great-nephew's grandchildren
6b Daniel Samuel WASHINGTON, *b* Caldwell Co, Mo., 13 June 1869; *m* West Plains, Mo., 26 Oct 1890 Charlotte Matilda Hooper (*b* 26 Oct 1871; *d* West Plains 20 June 1947) and *d* West Plains 22 May 1936, leaving issue:

Great-nephew's great-grandchildren
1c Jesse David WASHINGTON, *b* West Plains 12 Aug 1891; *m* there 19 July 1913 Mary Arissa Buford (*b* 4 Jan 1890) and *d* 12 Feb 1960, leaving issue:

Great-nephew's great-great-grandchildren
1d *Jesse Buford WASHINGTON, *b* 28 June 1914; *m* 12 June 1937 *Amy Leona Dix (*b* 5 Aug 1915) and has issue:

Great-nephew's great-great-grandchildren's children
1e *Jesse Claude WASHINGTON, *b* 25 Oct 1938

Great-nephew's great-great-grandchildren
2d Margaret Maxine Washington, *b* West Plains 30 Oct 1916; *m* 1st 25 March 1935 (divorce 1938) Barney Leon LITTLE (*b* 11 Sept 1912) and had issue:

Great-nephew's great-great-grandchildren's children
1e *Rose Mary Little, *b* 6 March 1936; took stepf's surname of STEWART

Great-nephew's great-great-grandchildren
2d (cont.) Mrs Margaret Little *m* 2nd 14 Jan 1946 *William Everett STEWART [4551 Reed Avenue S, Springfield, MO 65804, USA] (*b* 6 Dec 1914)
3d *Mary Sue Washington, *b* 8 July 1919; *m* 13 Sept 1937 *Raymond Edward CRABTREE (*b* 12 April 1919) and has three daus
4d *Dorothy Irene WASHINGTON, *b* 21 Dec 1921

Great-nephew's great-grandchildren
2c William Daniel WASHINGTON, *b* West Plains 9 April 1894; *m* April 1927 Bertha Ann Bolch (*b* 28 Nov 1888; *d c* 1972) and *d* 17 May 1943
3c *Charles Ramsay WASHINGTON, *b* West Plains 9 July 1896; *m* 29 Sept 1920 *Florence Yocky (*b* 22 Aug 1899)
4c George Samuel WASHINGTON, *b* West Plains 24 Jan 1899; *m* 5 Nov 1921 *Thelma Nancy Crandell (*b* Delta, Colo., 21 Oct 1904) and *d* leaving issue:

Great-nephew's great-grandchildren
1d *George Daniel WASHINGTON, *b* Fort Collins, Colo., 22 Aug 1922; *m* 16 Jan 1946 *Wilma Pauline Weeks (*b* Eldorado, Okla., 22 Sept 1927)
2d *Thelma Jean Washington, *b* West Plains, Mo., 25 May 1924; *m* 21 April 1943 *Royal Clyde HUFF (*b* Delta, Colo., 25 May 1924) and has one s and one dau
3d *William Walter WASHINGTON, *b* West Hollywood, Calif., 26 Nov 1928
4d *Donald Lee WASHINGTON, *b* West Hollywood 16 Dec 1930

Great-nephew's great-grandchildren
5c Dixy Hooper WASHINGTON, *b* West Plains 6 June 1901; *m* 30 Oct 1927 Billy Ruth Farrell (*b* 10 May 1905) and *d* 19—, having had issue:

Great-nephew's great-great-grandchildren
1d *Charles Judson WASHINGTON, *b* 4 Dec 1928
2d *Dixy Hooper WASHINGTON, *b* 7 Dec 1929

3d *Martha Pauline WASHINGTON, *b* 28 Feb 1935
4d *Virginia Ruth WASHINGTON, *b* 12 May 1939

Great-nephew's great-grandchildren

6c *Ova Matilda Washington, *b* West Plains 11 Oct 1903; *m* 4 Aug 1921 *John Wesley DIGGS (*b* Paris, Tenn., 25 April 1896) and has two s and one dau
7c *Martha Ola Washington, *b* West Plains 12 April 1907; *m* 4 May 1928 *Hollys Arlington FARRELL (*b* 5 July 1907), brother of Mrs Dixy Hooper Washington (*see above*), and has one dau

Great-nephew's children

3a Samuel Edward WASHINGTON, *b* Kanawha Co, W. Va., 20 March 1836; *d* White Co, Ark., 3 May 1852
4a Martha Mary Washington, *b* Cabell Co, W. Va., 24 July 1838; *m* Pomeroy, Ohio, 19 Aug 1858, as his 2nd w, Andrew Jackson SOMERVILLE (*b* Mason Co, W. Va., 10 April 1827; *d* there Jan 1907), s of Samuel Somerville, Jr, and his w Margaret Eckard and unc of Mrs William Meade Washington (for whom *see above*), and *d* Mason Co 6 Feb 1884, having had five s and four daus
5a Robert James WASHINGTON, *b* 16 Feb 1839-42; *d* of wounds after Gettysburg 1863
6a Judith Rebecca Washington, *b* W. Va. 30 Oct 1843; *m* Mason Co 5 April 1877 Samuel Paul SOMERVILLE (*b* Mason Co 10 Feb 1853; *d* Richmond, Ohio, 18 Sept 1936), s of Samuel Jamison Somerville and his w Mary Chamberlain, and nephew by marriage of his w's aunt, Mrs Andrew Jackson Somerville (for whom *see above*) as well as 1st cousin of Mrs William Meade Washington (for whom also *see above*), and *d* Ten-Mile Creek, Mason Co, 24 Oct 1901, leaving two s and three daus
7a Champlin WASHINGTON, *b* Mason Co, 31 May 1847; *m* West Columbia, Mason Co, *c* 1885 Martha Jane (*b* 19 Jan 1853; *d* Huntington, W. Va., 23 Feb 1937), dau of Eli Johnson and his w Catherine Yeager and sister of John Johnson, who *m* Wilhelmina Matilda Washington (for whom *see above*), and *d* Fraziers Bottom, W. Va., 12 Sept 1920, leaving issue:

Great-nephew's grandchildren

1b Katherine C. Washington, *b* Fraziers Bottom Nov 1887; *m c* 1921, as his 1st w, Handley PAUL, of Lincoln Co, W. Va., and *d* there *c* 1923
2b Bessie Blanche Washington, *b* Fraziers Bottom 25 Sept 1889; *m* 29 Dec 1907 Granville WILCOXEN (*b* 19 June 1882) and *d* there 19—, having had four s and three daus
3b Alta (Allie) Ethel Washington, *b* Fraziers Bottom Oct 1890; *m* 1st 19— (divorce 19—) Andrew PRICE; *m* 2nd 19— Noah STEWART and *d* 19—
4b Anna Mae Washington, *b* Fraziers Bottom July 1893; *m* 19—, as his 1st w, Clarence SCOTT, of Ashton, Mason Co, and *d c* 1937, leaving two s and three daus
5b Birta (Birdie) Gazelle WASHINGTON, *b* Fraziers Bottom March 1897; *d* there 6 March 1917

Great-niece and -nephew

(3) Augusta Clifford WASHINGTON, *b c* 1809; *d* 1823
(4) George Fayette WASHINGTON, *b* Jefferson Co, W. Va., *c* 1811; *m* 1st W. Va. 1842 Frances A. (*b c* 1823; *d c* 1855), dau of Zachariah Garten, and had issue:

Great-nephew's children

1a Zachariah WASHINGTON, *b c* 1846; served Union Army Civil War; *d* 18 Dec 1864

Great-nephew

(4) (cont.) George Fayette Washington *m* 2nd Putnam Co, W. Va., *c* 1858 Mary L. (*b* Putnam Co *c* 1825; *d* 3 Aug 1885), widow of —— Hayes, with whom she had had one s and three daus, and dau of Thomas McGraw, and *d* Putnam Co 1871, having with her had issue:

Great-nephew's children

2a Samuel T. WASHINGTON, *b* Putnam Co 1861; *m c* 1880 Catherine (who *m* 2nd —— Parsons and *d* Hansford, W. Va., *c* 1914), dau of Henry Hedrick, and *d* Putnam Co 1881, leaving issue:

Great-nephew's grandchildren

1b Albert Maywood WASHINGTON, *b* Putnam Co 16 June 1881; *m* 1st Kanawha Co 16 June 1906 Ernie Lewis (*b* Putnam Co *c* 1884; *d* Standard, W. Va., 29 June 1908) and had issue:

Great-nephew's great-grandchildren

1c *Mary Catherine Washington, *b* Standard 27 Aug 1907; *m* Kanawha Co 25 Dec 1925 *John CLARK (*b* 18 Nov 1908) and has one dau

Great-nephew's grandchildren

1b (cont.) Albert M. Washington *m* 2nd Mucklow, W. Va., 8 Oct 1914 Mary Frances Kincaid (*b* Kanawha Co 11 Oct 1895; *m* 2nd H. S. Libbee) and *d* Spencer, W. Va., 18 Aug 1925, having with her had issue:

Great-nephew's great-grandchildren

2c Clarence Russell WASHINGTON, *b* Montgomery, W. Va., 5 Oct; *m* Charleston, W. Va., *c* 1935 *Lola —— and *d* Cabin Creek, Kanawha Co, 22 Aug 1950, leaving issue:

Great-nephew's great-great-grandchildren
1d *Patty WASHINGTON, *b c* 1936
2d *William Ray WASHINGTON, *b* 1 Jan 1939
3d *Clarence Russell WASHINGTON, *b c* 1941

Great-nephew's great-grandchildren
3c Georgia Azeline WASHINGTON, *b* Page, W. Va., 22 July 1916; *d* Charleston, W. Va., 20 April 1932

Great-nephew's children
3a Robert Franklin WASHINGTON, *b* Putnam Co 19 April 1864; *m* there 24 Oct 1886 Cora Dell (*b* 8 July 1867; *d* Charleston, W. Va., 24 Nov 1951), dau of Edward Older and his w Catherine Aultz, and *d* Charleston 25 Dec 1932, having had issue:

Great-nephew's grandchildren
1b Lola Catherine Washington, *b* 4 Oct 1887; *m* Reuben J. HASKINS and *d* 1973, leaving three s
2b Callie Frances Washington, *b* 9 May 1889; *m* 1st 19— (divorce 19—) W. S. C. HOLT and had one s and one dau (both *d* in infancy); *m* 2nd 9 Jan 1917 Homer Vane SMITH (*b* 18 Jan 1893; *d* 19—) and had two more s and one more dau
3b George Franklin WASHINGTON, of Charleston, W. Va., *b* 7 Sept 1891; *m* 19— (divorce 19—) Ethel Ruth Kidey Sedessi and *d* 1957, leaving issue:

Great-nephew's great-grandchildren
1c Charles Robert WASHINGTON, of Charleston, *b* 19—; *m* 19— Margaret Rohrer and *d* 19—
2c Ruth Washington, *b* 19—; *m* 1st 19— ——— (*d* 19—); *m* 2nd ——— BEAGARIE and *d* 19—

Great-nephew's grandchildren
4b *Goldie Ethel Washington, *b* nr Charleston, W. Va., 25 Feb 1894; *m* there 1 April 1917 Samuel Stillman CUTLIP (*b* 27 April 1891; *d* 8 Sept 1956) and has two s
5b Robert Lawrence WASHINGTON, *b* 10 Feb 1896; *d* 19—
6b *Leslie Madison WASHINGTON, *b* 7 Jan 1898; *m* 23 Nov 1928 *Nina Dow Hudson (*b* 29 April 1908)
7b Harley Leonard WASHINGTON, *b* 18 Feb 1900; *m* Charleston, W. Va., 21 Jan 1923 *Ira Carmon McNealy (*b* 14 July 1902) and *d* 19—, having had issue:

Great-nephew's great-grandchildren
1c *Charles Bushrod WASHINGTON, *b* Charleston, W. Va., 5 Nov 1923; *m* Cheltenham, Gloucestershire, UK, 21 Sept 1945 *Ethel Mary James (*b* there 7 April 1927) and has issue (with three other children):

Great-nephew's great-great-grandchildren
1d *Gary James WASHINGTON, *b* Richmond, Ind., 29 Sept 1946

Great-nephew's great-grandchildren
2c *Harley Leonard WASHINGTON, *b* Charleston 24 Jan 1925; *m* 19— and has issue
3c *George Elwood WASHINGTON, *b* West Alexandria, Ohio, 24 Oct 1928; *m* 19— and has issue

Great-nephew's grandchildren
8b Wilbur Watson WASHINGTON, *b* 3 May 1902; *d* 7 July 1903
9b *Martha Custis Washington, *b* 16 April 1906; *m* 22 July 1928 *Alton Ree FORTNEY (*b* 16 Jan 1905) and has one s and two daus
10b *Dorothy Lenora Washington, *b* 30 June 1911; *m* 9 July 1933 *John Wesley JAMES, Jr (*b* 9 July 1914), and has one s

Great-nephew
(5) Francis Augustine WASHINGTON, *b c* 1811 (twin with George Fayette Washington); *m* Mason Co, W. Va., 20 Feb 1842 Melvina (*b c* 1826; *d* 15 April 1894), dau of Zachariah Garten and sister of Mrs George Fayette Washington (for whom *see above*), and *d* Midway, W. Va., 4 Aug 1872, having had issue:

Great-nephew's children
1a Francis Augustus WASHINGTON, of Putnam Co, *b* 25 Aug 1845; *m* 21 Oct 1868 Lucy Joanna Walters (*b* 2 April 1849; *d* 13 Nov 1884) and *d* 2 Nov 1913, having had issue:

Great-nephew's grandchildren
1b Ora Blanch Washington, *b* 10 Aug 1869; *m* 18— or 19— John Alexander GRANT, of Fraziers Bottom, W. Va. (*b* 22 April 1869; *d* 15 Dec 1908), and *d* 1947, leaving one s and one dau
2b Ladonia WASHINGTON (s), *b* 4 Sept 1870; *d* 28 Oct 1947
3b Oliver Franklin WASHINGTON, *b* and *d* Aug 1871
4b Edith Ona Washington, *b* 14 Sept 1872; *m* 18— or 19— Edgar Leander ERWIN (*b* 30 Jan 1879; *d* 15 Dec 1928) and had one s and two daus
5b Mae Forester Washington, *b* 2 Dec 1873; *m* 9 April 1905 Stephen HODGES (*b* 20 Nov 1884; *d* 19—) and *d* 2 Dec 1926, having had one s and three daus
6b Lillie Belle Washington, *b* 14 Oct 1875; *m* 5 June 1898 Ralph Ames GILLISPIE (*b* 11 May 1877; *d* 19—) and *d* 1 Oct 1954, having had three s and two daus

7b Ocie Gaynelle Washington, *b* 29 March 1877; *m* 4 June 1919 John Daniel BOWEN, of Dexter, Ohio (*b* Ohio 12 Dec 1866; *d* 20 April 1948) and *d* 1 Oct 1948

8b Otho Oscar WASHINGTON, *b* 15 Oct 1879; *m* 18— or 19— Iva Pierce and *d* 3 Oct 1945, having had issue:

Great-nephew's great-grandchildren
1c Mervin Francis WASHINGTON, *b* 18 Dec 1903; *m* 27 June 1922 Mary Strong (*b* 13 Sept 1901; *m* 2nd Elwood Nelson, of Dexter, Ohio; *d* 19—) and *d* 29 Sept 1928, having had issue:

Great-nephew's great-great-grandchildren
1d *Hester Marie Washington, *b* 4 Feb 1924; *m* 25 Nov 1950 *Woodrow Wilson ADAMS, of Ky. (*b* 23 Oct 1914), and has one s and one dau
2d Oscar Eugene WASHINGTON, *b* 3 Oct 1925; *d* 18 Jan 1927
3d *Pauline Fern Washington, *b* 15 Feb 1926; *m* 4 March 1950 *Ronald Edward DAVIS (*b* 19 May 1926)
4d Marvel Edith WASHINGTON, *b* 1 Feb 1929; *d* 1 Aug 1930

Great-nephew's great-grandchildren
2c *Melvin Augustus WASHINGTON, of Huntington, W. Va., *b* 19—; *m* 19— *Jewell Young and has issue:

Great-nephew's great-great-grandchildren
1d *Avalee WASHINGTON, *b* 19—
2d *Lloyd WASHINGTON, *b* 19—
3d *James WASHINGTON, *b* 19—

Great-nephew's great-grandchildren
3c *Villa Washington, *b* 19—; *m* 19— *Samuel RIDDLES, of St Albans, W. Va., and has two s and three daus
4c *Velva Jewell Washington, *b* 1 July 1910; *m* 19— *Clay GRANT (*b* 7 Feb 1906) and has four s and eight daus
5c *Violet Washington, *b* 19—; 19— *Arnold GRANT, of Hurricane, W. Va., bro of Clay Grant, and has 10 children
6c Millard Freeman WASHINGTON, *b* 19—; *d* 19— in infancy
7c *Vonda Washington, *b* 19—; *m* 19— *Mervin GRANT, bro of Clay and Arnold Grant, and has eight children
8c *Valeria Washington, *b* 19—; *m* 19— *James JOHNSON, of Huntington, W. Va., and has four children

Great-nephew's-grandchildren
9b Luther Thornton WASHINGTON, of Hurricane, W. Va., *b* 29 Dec 1880; *m* 13 Aug 1903 Mary Elizabeth Hodges (*b* 13 Aug 1886; *d* 19—), sister of Stephen Hodges (who *m* Mae Forester Washington, for whom *see above*), and *d* 19—, having had issue:

Great-nephew's great-grandchildren
1c Norma Ellen WASHINGTON, *b* and *d* 5 May 1904
2c *Orga Virginia Washington, *b* 23 May 1905; *m* 18 May 1927 *Ivan Edison DAVIS (*b* 22 June 1902) and has one s and one dau
3c Martha Onesida WASHINGTON, *b* 2 March 1918; *d* 26 May 1919
4c *Billy Lee WASHINGTON, of Lexington, Ky., *b* Hurricane 5 July 1926; *m* Huntington July 1947 *Lola McVey and has issue:

Great-nephew's great-great-grandchildren
1d *Mary Annette WASHINGTON, *b* 1949
2d *William Lee WASHINGTON, *b* 1952
3d *Kent Alan WASHINGTON, *b* 1955

Great-nephew's-grandchildren
10b Sallie Anne Washington, *b* 9 March 1883; *m* 16 June 1912 Daniel Webster GRANT (*b* 14 Sept 1881; *d* 19—), bro of John Grant (who *m* Ora Blanch Washington, for whom *see above*) and *d* 19—, having had two s

Great-nephew's children
2a Viola WASHINGTON, *b* 1847; *d* nr Little Rock, Ark., *c* 1853
3a Dorothy A. Washington, *b c* 1856; *m c* 1877 her 1st cousin James HUGHEY, of Rings Hollow, Hernshaw, nr Marmet, Kanawha Co, W. Va. (*d c* 1921), s of James Hughey and his w Judith Garten, and *d* 1903, having had six s and one dau

President Washington's niece
4 Mildred Gregory Washington, *b* probably Fredericksburg, Va., 2 Oct 1772; *m* probably at Happy Retreat, Berkeley Co (now Jefferson Co), Va. (now W. Va.), 20 April 1797, as his 2nd w of three, Col Thomas HAMMOND (*b* Ireland *c* 1770; *d* Charles Town, W. Va., 18 April 1820) and *d* Happy Retreat, having had three s (all *d* in infancy)

X Mildred WASHINGTON, *b* Wakefield, Westmoreland Co, Va., 21 June 1739; *d* there 23 Oct 1740

Robert Washington[1]
c 1544-1620/1

Elizabeth Light/Lyte
d c 1599

  Lawrence Washington
  c 1568-1616

William Butler
fl c 1588

Margaret Greeke

  Margaret Butler
  a 1568-*c* 1652

        ?Lawrence Ball

        — —

Thomas Twigden
d 1579/80

— Watts

  John Twigden
  d 1610/1

William Dickens
d 1583/4

Anne Thornton
d c 1614

  Anne Dickens
  d 1637

        ?Thomas Atherold

        — —

?Thomas Vesey

?Elizabeth Gardiner

?John Church

— —

        ?Thomas Vesey

        ?Elizabeth Church

William Warner?
1540-*c* 1610/1

Mary —?
d c 1616

  Thomas Warner?
  c 1580/1-16—

Augustine Sotherton?
d 1585

Ann Peck?
b c 1553

  Elizabeth Sotherton?
  c 1582/4-p 1629

Lawrence Towneley
d 1597/8

Margaret Hartley

  Lawrence Towneley
  d 1654/5

John Halstead
d 1601

Elizabeth —
d 1612

  Jennet Halstead
  d c 1623?

Andrew Reade
d 1623

Alice Cooke
d 1606

  Robert Reade
  c 1551/71-*c* 1627

Sir Thomas Windebank
d 1607

Frances Dymoke

  Mildred Windebank
  c 1584-*c* 1630

  Nicholas Martiau
  c 1591-*c* 1656/7

  ?Jane —
  d a 1646

[1] For lineage further back *see* Male Line Ancestry section

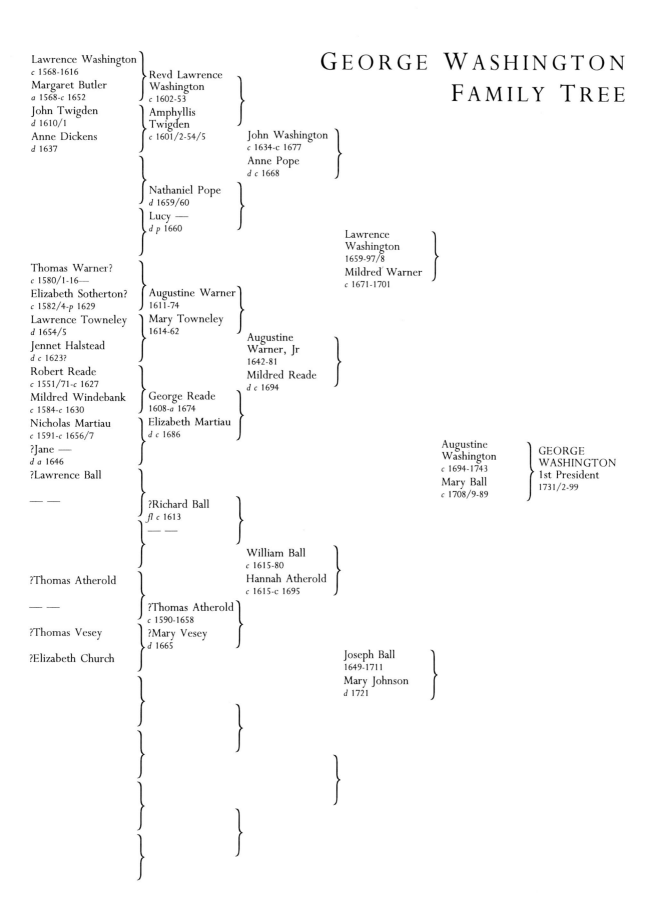

GEORGE WASHINGTON FAMILY TREE

Lawrence Washington
c 1568-1616

Margaret Butler
a 1568-*c* 1652

John Twigden
d 1610/1

Anne Dickens
d 1637

Revd Lawrence
Washington
c 1602-53

Amphyllis
Twigden
c 1601/2-54/5

John Washington
c 1634-*c* 1677

Anne Pope
d c 1668

Nathaniel Pope
d 1659/60

Lucy —
d p 1660

Lawrence
Washington
1659-97/8

Mildred Warner
c 1671-1701

Thomas Warner?
c 1580/1-16—

Elizabeth Sotherton?
c 1582/4-*p* 1629

Lawrence Towneley
d 1654/5

Jennet Halstead
d c 1623?

Augustine Warner
1611-74

Mary Towneley
1614-62

Augustine
Warner, Jr
1642-81

Mildred Reade
d c 1694

Robert Reade
c 1551/71-*c* 1627

Mildred Windebank
c 1584-*c* 1630

Nicholas Martiau
c 1591-*c* 1656/7

?Jane —
d a 1646

George Reade
1608-*a* 1674

Elizabeth Martiau
d c 1686

Augustine
Washington
c 1694-1743

Mary Ball
c 1708/9-89

GEORGE
WASHINGTON
1st President
1731/2-99

?Lawrence Ball

— —

?Richard Ball
fl c 1613

— —

William Ball
c 1615-80

Hannah Atherold
c 1615-*c* 1695

?Thomas Atherold

— —

?Thomas Vesey

?Thomas Atherold
c 1590-1658

?Mary Vesey
d 1665

?Elizabeth Church

Joseph Ball
1649-1711

Mary Johnson
d 1721

Plate 8   John Adams

JOHN ADAMS

1735-1826
2ND PRESIDENT OF THE UNITED STATES OF AMERICA
1797-1801

If Washington is marble, John Adams is New England granite. The metaphor tells us two important things about him; he had the same staunch character, the same broad patriotism as his illustrious predecessor, and he was thoroughly provincial, in the best meaning of that term. He judged the world as a Puritan should, and if the world frequently failed the trial, that does not prove 'Honest John Adams' wrong.

Of his devotion to the ideals laid down in Washington's Farewell Address there can be no doubt, nor of his wish to live up to Washington's example. Unfortunately this was in some respects difficult. Washington had been tall and magnificent; Adams was short and stout. (When he was Vice-President, and worried about how high American officials should be addressed, some unkind person suggested that he be known as 'His Rotundity'.) Adams was very nearly Washington's age, and was in fact senior to him as an American revolutionary; he had been deeply involved in the Stamp Act crisis of 1765, in which Washington had played little part. But his services to his country, though highly meritorious (he had been the one to propose that Washington be given command in 1775, and he had played a part second only to that of Benjamin Franklin in the diplomacy of the Revolution), had not been of the kind to give him the sort of aura which surrounded Washington. Nor was his skin any thicker than Washington's (though as a veteran politician he usually recovered quickly from the smartest wound) and he was far less able to disguise his mortification when under scurrilous attack. He was not so rich as Washington; he had to give up many of the more lavish trappings of the presidency. All in all, the superficial observer might be pardoned for thinking that the second President was a sad come-down. However, the superficial observer would have been wrong.

For Adams had qualities that fully equipped him for his post. Revolutionary Massachusetts and the revolutionary Congress had been an excellent school in the rough and tumble of politics. As minister to France, the Netherlands and Britain he had got to know the scene of international politics thoroughly, and as Vice-President for eight years he had been able to study the workings of the new Constitution from a point of vantage (although he bitterly complained that "My country has in its wisdom contrived for me the most insignificant office that ever the invention of man contrived or his imagination conceived"). Furthermore, he was a highly capable lawyer (he had successfully defended the British soldiers responsible for the Boston Massacre in 1770), and knowledge of the law has always been an advantage to a President. In his charming, intelligent, high-spirited wife Abigail he had a far greater asset than most other Presidents have enjoyed in their wives. Lastly, his character — brave, peppery, proud, stubborn, upright, shrewd and devoted — made him an excellent instrument to carry on Washington's policies. He could not be intimidated and he would not be fooled for very long.

Attempts were made at both. Adams was called a Federalist, but he had as low an opinion of party politics as Washington, and if he belonged to any faction it was really to the old patriotic Whig party of his youth in Boston. He would have been quite ready to patch things up with Jefferson, his competitor for the presidency and successor as Vice-President: the two men were old collaborators, and in fact served together on the committee which drafted the Declaration of Independence. But the intrigues of Hamilton now kept them apart. Hamilton did worse. He conspired to seize control of the government from the President, whom he wished to reduce to a mere figurehead. He was nearly able to succeed in this, thanks to his mastery of the Federalist party, a mastery which he maintained although he held no public office and was rapidly losing ground in his own state of New York to the Republicans led by Aaron Burr.

The Hamiltonian schemes threatened more than John Adams. Hamilton was so committed to the conservative and British side in the continuing war that he wanted the United States to join the alliance against France. This policy risked reducing the United States to a position of a mere satellite of Britain; war would be expensive and cruel in itself; and it would bitterly divide the country. It might even break up the Union and the new Constitution, both of them still fairly tender plants. Once Adams perceived what was involved, he fought steadily against the impending calamity. But he left it rather late, and the Hamiltonians were able to push through the Alien and Sedition Acts, which harassed immigrant groups and the free press, in the name of national security. These acts in turn provoked the Resolutions of the Kentucky and Virginia legislatures (secretly drafted by Jefferson and James Madison respectively) which hinted, none too delicately, that if matters went much further rebellion or disunion might have to come. Nor were matters helped by the French, who treated American emissaries with contempt, demanding handsome bribes before they would negotiate. To cap it all, Adams discovered that several members of the Cabinet (then quite a small body) were taking orders from Hamilton, not himself. Undeclared war with France was raging at sea; on land an army was to be formed. Washington was induced to emerge from his retirement to command it, and insisted on Hamilton for his second-in-command. It looked as if the President had lost control of events.

Grimly Adams fought back. Thanks to his persistence in offering negotiations, and to their own realization that war with America was unwise, the French agreed to settle their differences, and the threat of war, rebellion or coup d'etat receded. The Cabinet was purged. Peace approached in Europe. Calmer waters were ahead.

Unhappily for Adams he was not to remain at the helm. His break with Hamilton wrecked the Federalists; the Republicans were solidly united. In the election of 1800 Adams came third in the electoral vote. By a muddle, the Republican candidates, Jefferson and Burr, got exactly the same number of votes and since under the Constitution as it then stood no distinction was made between presidential and vice-presidential candidates, the election was thrown into the House of Representatives.

By now the Federal government had moved to the new city of Washington (Abigail hung up her laundry to dry in the East Room of the unfinished President's House, or Executive Mansion); the struggle for the presidency made a dramatic opening to the city's history, and Adams watched it, not without hope. But the election could not decently be denied to one of the Republican candidates, and Hamilton, with unusual good sense, made sure that the Federalist votes went to Jefferson, as the lesser of two evils.

Adams had long come to regard Jefferson as a danger, and he now saw a chance to limit the threat he posed. The Chief Justiceship of the United States was vacant. He hurried to confer it on his Secretary of State, John Marshall, which turned out to be as valuable an action as any of his presidency, for Marshall was the greatest of American judges. He also tried to fill some new judgeships with sound Federalists, but the incoming administration was able to circumvent him. However, by that time John Adams had left the scene of his defeat. He had no wish to see Jefferson sworn in. He retired to his home at Quincy, Massachusetts.

It is pleasant to record that he lived for another 25 years, very happily on the whole, even though his adored Abigail died in 1818. He had his vanity, and disliked being rated below George Washington, Thomas Jefferson and (especially) Benjamin Franklin, but essentially he was too warmhearted and sincere to sulk for very long. In old age his nature grew even sweeter, like an apple kept in store. He was reconciled to Jefferson by a common friend in 1811; lived to see his son John Quincy Adams elected to the presidency and died on the same day as Jefferson, which happened to be the Fourth of July, 1826.

JOHN ADAMS'S FAMILY

The Adamses are so far the only family where a father and son became President. Another Massachusetts family, the Kennedys, came near to providing a pair of brothers. Massachusetts is the heart of New England and arguably, if not the heart, at any rate a lifegiving artery of the United States inasmuch as the Pilgrim Fathers disembarked there. That is worth remembering given the currency of a phrase such as the 'Virginia Dynasty', used of Southerners who dominated the early presidency. In addition Adamses had been settled in America for longer — as far as we can tell — than the family of any other early President. And in Samuel Adams, a second cousin who was one of the first as well as most energetic opponents of British colonial rule, the Adamses could claim a purer republicanism than any other family in America.

Adams reckoned his parents' marriage had been unequal, with his mother socially a cut above his father and lifting the Adamses from provincial obscurity. Certainly she was more citified, being from Brookline, then still separate from Boston but an agreeable residential district in its own right. But financially, if only at a local level, Adams's father was predominant. His son wrote of him that by his death almost all Braintree's commerce was in his hands. The father was able to leave a couple of farms in his will. A third of his estate went to his widow, who then married again (her son implies she was rather flighty). The other two-thirds went to the three sons, John getting a smaller share than his brothers Peter and Elihu because he had had a good education. Adams was close to his brothers, working hard in the early 1760s to get Peter made Deputy Sheriff of Braintree, although privately he recorded his misgivings that the easy-going young man was not up to the job.

Yet for all the Adamses' republican credentials, whereas Washington was addressed by his compatriots with reverence, Adams was dubbed 'the Duke of Braintree' and accused, as Washington had never plausibly been, of wanting to restore hereditary monarchy and set up a native aristocracy. Adams did indeed put faith in what he called "the efficacy of pageantry" but he seems to have regarded it as a means to the end of good government: "If government cannot be had nor laws obeyed without some parade, as I fully believe we must have some parade or no laws." In the circumstances this did not go down well. And Abigail Adams, who maintained the starchy protocol started by Martha Washington, was called by one critic 'Her Majesty'. But then Abigail Adams had a longer penance to perform as wife of a leading public figure than Martha Washington, with whom she personally got on very well. And the Adamses as the Second Family were expected to entertain almost as much as the President, yet on less than half his salary.

Adams was unfortunate in other ways. Where Washington could get away with riding to his Inauguration in a gilded coach drawn by six cream horses (and according to Abigail Adams rode out always while President in a six-horse carriage with four servants and two gentlemen going before him), when Adams did so he was seen as aping George III. He could hardly complain. If one said, as he did, "A royal, or at least a princely title will be found indispensably necessary to maintain the reputation, authority and dignity of the President" and talked of styling the President "His Most Benign Highness"

Plate 9   Abigail Smith Adams

one was bound to attract a few brickbats. What Adams truly believed in, however, was less aristocracy (he disapproved of the Society of the Cincinnati and was perturbed when his only surviving daughter got engaged to a member of it) than meritocracy. The belief in merit has turned out reasonable enough in the circumstances — the family has supplied America with a multitude of scholars and public servants.

John and Abigail Adams, who were third cousins, were married by Abigail's father. This marriage too was thought a misalliance, at any rate by Adams's mother-in-law Elizabeth, *née* Quincy, who regarded the Smiths as grander than the Adamses. His marriage brought Adams into contact with the leading Massachusetts families early in life. He greatly admired his wife's grandfather, John Quincy, who dominated Braintree in Adams's youth as well as being a member of the Governor's Council, Colonel of Militia and Speaker of the Massachusetts Assembly (a position he held for 40 years, dying at the advanced age of nearly 78). Through Abigail subsequent Adamses enjoy a remote family connection with the Downing baronets in England who gave their name to both Downing Street in London, where the British prime minister resides, and Downing College at Cambridge. She possessed energy, wit and political influence with her husband. She also wrote superb letters, with she and Adams calling each other Lysander and Diana, and managed the family property while he was away in Europe. When Adams was President she acted in a capacity that one historian has termed near that of minister-without-portfolio, writing a series of semi-official letters emphasising some aspect or other of her husband's policy. Hers was the distinction of being the first First Lady to entertain in the White House (though the terms 'First Lady' and 'White House' were neither of them yet current) when she presided over a reception on New Year's Day 1801.

Of their five children, the eldest, Abigail (Nabby to her family), married a New York congressman, Col William Smith, the spoiled younger son of a large and supercilious New York family who patronized her. Unfortunately he lost much of his money in land speculation. Nabby's two eldest sons, William and John, acted as secretary to their uncle John Quincy Adams, Adams's eldest son and a future President, when he was on diplomatic missions. Adams's middle son Charles married William Smith's sister Sally, also speculated unsuccessfully and died at 30, weakened by drink. Sally and the children, who had on one occasion been temporarily abandoned by Charles, moved in with Nabby and later, after Charles died, with her parents-in-law John and Abigail. Adams's youngest son, Thomas, was a neurasthenic but somehow got himself made chief justice of the Massachusetts supreme court. Thomas and his family eventually came to live with Adams after the latter became a widower, as did Susanna, Charles's elder daughter, with her daughter Susanna Maria. This was despite the Adams family's disapproval of Susanna's husband Charles T. Clark. Susanna's daughter's great-granddaughter married a cousin of Thomas Jefferson's — a neat Montagu-Capulet touch given Adams's huffy attitude toward Jefferson when the latter succeeded as President.

BIOGRAPHICAL DETAILS AND DESCENDANTS

ADAMS, JOHN, *b* North Precinct of Braintree (from 1792 Quincy, named after his grandfather-in-law, John Quincy), Norfolk Co, Mass., 19/30 Oct 1735; *educ* Harvard (BA 1755); schoolmaster in Worcester, Mass., admitted Massachusetts Bar 1758, Surveyor of Highways Braintree (elective post) 1761, Memb Massachusetts Legislature 1768, Boston Rep Massachusetts General Court 1770, Memb Revolutionary Congress of Massachusetts 1774 and Massachusetts Delegate to 1st Continental Congress 1774-78 (Head Board of War and Ordnance 1776), Commissioner to France 1777, Braintree Rep Massachusetts Constitutional Convention 1779, Minister Plenipotentiary: for negotiating peace and treaty of commerce with Great Britain 1779, to the Netherlands 1780 (Minister to the Netherlands 1781), to the Court of St James's 1785, Massachusetts Delegate to Continental Congress 1788, 1st V-President USA 1789-97, 2nd President of the USA 1797-1801, Quincy Rep Massachusetts Constitutional Convention 1820; author: *A Dissertation on the Canon and Feudal Law* (1768), *Thoughts on Government* (1776), *A Defence of the Constitution of Government of the United States* (1787), *Discourses on Davila* (1805), *Correspondence of the Late President Adams* (1810), *Novanglus and Massachusettensis* (1819), *Correspondence Between the Hon John Adams and the Late William Cunningham, Esq* (1823); *m* Weymouth, Suffolk Co, Mass., 25 Oct 1764 Abigail (*b* Weymouth 11/22 Nov 1744; *d* Quincy 28 Oct 1818 of a stroke), 2nd dau of Revd William Smith, Jr (*b* Charlestown, Mass., 29 Jan 1706/7; *d* Weymouth 17 Sept 1783), and his *w* Elizabeth Quincy (*bapt* Braintree 17 Dec 1721; *d* Weymouth 1 Oct 1775) and *d* Quincy 4 July 1826 of a stroke, having had issue:

President Adams's daughter

I Abigail (Nabby) Adams, *b* Braintree 14 July 1765; *m* London, Great Britain, by the Bishop of St Asaph 12 June 1786 Col William Stephens SMITH (*b* Long Island, New York, 8 Nov 1755; Memb US House of Reps from New York 1813-15; *d* Lebanon, New York, 10 June 1816), s of John Smith and his *w* Margaret Stephens, and *d* Braintree 30 Aug 1813 of breast cancer, having had issue:

Grandchildren

1 William Steuben SMITH, *b* London 30 April 1787; *educ* Harvard and Columbia U; sec to his uncle John Quincy Adams when latter US Min to Russia; *m* 1813 Catherine Maria Frances (*d* 1869), 5th dau of Hon Joshua Johnson, of Baltimore, US Consul-Gen London 1785-99, and his *w* Catherine Nuth, and sister of Mrs John Quincy Adams, and *d* 12 May 1850, having had issue:

Great-grandchildren
(1) Caroline Amelia SMITH, *b* Russia 1814; *d* New York *c* 1 July 1815

Grandchildren

2 John Adams SMITH, *b* Long Island, New York, 10 Nov 1788; sec to his uncle John Quincy Adams when latter Envoy Extraordinary and Min Plenipotentiary to UK 1815-17, lawyer, postmaster Hamilton, New York; *d* 1854
3 Thomas Hollins SMITH, *b* Sept 1790; *d* 1791
4 Caroline Amelia Smith, *b* 27 Jan 1795; *m* 11 Sept 1814 John Peter De WINDT (*b* 19 Oct 1786; *d* 18 Nov 1870) and drowned in Hudson River 28 July 1852 as a result of a catastrophe involving a steamboat, having had issue:

Great-grandchildren
(1) Caroline Elizabeth de Windt, *b* 19 Oct 1815; *m* 1st 7 June 1838 Andrew Jackson DOWNING (*b* Newburgh, New York, 30 Oct 1815; drowned 28 July 1852 with his mother-in-law), s of Samuel Downing and his w Eunice Bridge; *m* 2nd 16 Feb 1860 Judge John James MONELL (*d* 22 April 1885) and *d* 1896?
(2) Julia de Windt, *b* 24 Sept 1817; *m* 27 Sept 1842 William Alexander VAN WAGENEN (*b* 1816; *d* 5 June 1871) and *d* 22 Oct 1889, having had issue:

Great-great-grandchildren
1a Samuel Whittemore VAN WAGENEN, *b* 25 May 1843; *d* 24 Oct 1856
2a Julia Carmer VAN WAGENEN, *b* 15 Nov 1844; *d* 19 Jan 1895
3a Caroline Adams VAN WAGENEN, *b* Beacon, New York, 1847; *d* Essex Falls, New Jersey, 7 March 1939
4a Charles VAN WAGENEN, *b* 18—; *m* Nettie Burke and had one dau (*d* young)
5a William Alexis VAN WAGENEN, *b* 18—; *m* Flora Whitbeck (*b* 1853; *d* 25 April 1881) and had issue:

Great-great-grandchildren's children
1b Percy VAN WAGENEN; *d* 26 Oct 1882 in infancy
2b Hazel Van Wagenen, *b* 18—; *m* Henry Cleveland WELLMAN (*b* Yonkers, New York, 18 June 1872; *d* Ossining, New York, 3 May 1951) and *d* 30 Dec 1920, leaving issue:

Great-great-grandchildren's grandchildren
1c *Henry Hamilton WELLMAN, *b* 7 Feb 1910; *m* 19— *Harriet Lambie and has issue:

Great-great-grandchildren's great-grandchildren
1d *William Hamilton WELLMAN, *b* 27 March 1941
2d *Barbara Lambie WELLMAN, *b* 3 Feb 1944

Great-great-grandchildren
6a Jessie Van Wagenen, *b* 20 July 1859; *m* June 1888 John Gorham LOW (*b* 2 April 1840; *d* 26 Nov 1907) and *d* 20 Dec 1951, having had issue:

Great-great-grandchildren's children
1b Julia de Windt LOW, *b* 22 April 1890; *d* 19—
2b Mary Langdon Low, *b* 10 Aug 1892; *m* 14 Sept 1928 William Prichard BROWNE and had issue:

Great-great-grandchildren's grandchildren
1c *William Prichard BROWNE, *b* 2 July 1930; *m* 27 Nov 1954 *Frances Ann Kiehn
2c *Mary Langdon BROWNE, *b* 26 March 1934

Great-great-grandchildren's children
3b John Gorham LOW, Jr, *b* 20 May 1894; *m* 19— *Frances Fiesenius and *d* June 1953, leaving issue:

Great-great-grandchildren's grandchildren
1c *John Gorham LOW III, *b* 19—; *m* Sept 1952 *Elizabeth ——
2c *David Nicholson LOW, *b* 19—; *m* 19 Feb 1955 *Betty Bright Page

Great-great-grandchildren's children
4b *Rebecca Cordis LOW, *b* 2 Jan 1896
5b *Caroline Van Wagenen Low, *b* 10 Sept 1898; *m* 1st 19— (divorce 19—) Lawrence MANLEY and has issue:

Great-great-grandchildren's grandchildren
1c *Mary Louise Manley, *b* 19—; *m* June 1951 *Coley RHODES and has issue:

Great-great-grandchildren's great-grandchildren
1d *Coley RHODES, Jr, *b* Feb 1954

Great-great-grandchildren's grandchildren
2c *Emma Hall Manley, *b* 19—; *m* March 1951 *Lee HANNER and has issue:

Great-great-grandchildren's great-grandchildren
1d *Dale Robert HANNER, *b* Oct 1953

Great-great-grandchildren's children
5b (cont.) Mrs Caroline Manley *m* 2nd 19— *John R. BURTON
6b Alexander Van Wagenen LOW, *b* 18—; *d* 1900

Great-grandchildren
(3) Elizabeth de Windt, *b* 23 Sept 1819; *m* 10 Oct 1843 her 2nd cousin once-removed Revd Christopher Pearse CRANCH (*b* Alexandria, Va., 8 March 1813; Unitarian Minister and painter practising mostly in Paris and Italy, Memb Nat Acad of Design; *d* Cambridge, Mass., 20 Jan 1892, s of William Cranch and his w Anna Greenleaf and gs of Judge Richard Cranch and his w Mary Smith (sister of Mrs John Adams), and had issue:

Great-great-grandchildren
1a George William CRANCH, *b* 11 March 1847; *d* 18 Sept 1867

2a Leonora Cranch, *b* 4 June 1848; *m* 20 June 1872 Col Henry Bruce SCOTT (*b* 15 March 1839; *d* 22 Feb 1921) and *d* 8 Dec 1933, having had issue

Great-great-grandchildren's children
1b George Cranch SCOTT, *b* 17 July 1873; *m* 1 June 1905 Mary Kennard (*b* 16 Feb 1877; *d* 18 April 1960) and *d* 28 April 1958, having had issue:

Great-great-grandchildren's grandchildren
1c Henry Bruce SCOTT, *b* 19—; *d* in infancy
2c *Mary Adams Scott, *b* 2 Sept 1908; *m* 26 June 1935 Emerson EVANS (*b* 1 Sept 1904; *d* 8 Jan 1969) and has issue:

Great-great-grandchildren's great-grandchildren
1d *Robert Scott EVANS, *b* 24 May 1939
2d *Martha Pickering Evans, *b* 17 Jan 1945; *m* 4 April 1964 *John KERNS (*b* 14 Feb 1943) and has issue:

Great-great-grandchildren's great-great-grandchildren
1e *John KERNS, Jr, *b* 26 Aug 1964
2e *Scott Emerson KERNS, *b* 26 Aug 1965
3e *Jennifer KERNS, *b* 7 March 1969

Great-great-grandchildren's grandchildren
2c *George Cranch SCOTT, Jr, *b* 25 Aug 1911; *m* 18 Sept 1943 *Emily Rice (*b* 29 Aug 1919) and has issue:

Great-great-grandchildren's great-grandchildren
1d *Emma Scott, *b* 19 Oct 1945; *m* 3 Aug 1974 *Douglas Evans HOLMES (*b* 1945)
2d *Henry Bruce SCOTT, *b* 23 Oct 1946; *m* 11 Dec 1971 *Margaret Louise Morley and has issue:

Great-great-grandchildren's great-great-grandchildren
1e *Gregory Kennard SCOTT, *b* Aug 1975

Great-great-grandchildren's great-grandchildren
3d *Mary Adams SCOTT, *b* 3 Sept 1948
4d *George Gordon SCOTT, *b* 27 Jan 1950

Great-great-grandchildren's grandchildren
3c *Dr Oliver Kennard SCOTT [Boston, MA, USA; 940 East 3rd Street, Casper, WY 82601, USA; 10750 Bessemer Bend Rd, Casper, WY, USA], *b* 3 Sept 1914; *m* 4 July 1942 *Deborah Ann Hubbard (*b* 13 March 1916) and has issue:

Great-great-grandchildren's great-grandchildren
1d *Charles Kennard SCOTT, *b* Aug 1945; *m* 20 Dec 1975 *Elaine Fenton
2d *Hustace Hubbard SCOTT, *b* Sept 1947
3d *George Cranch SCOTT III, *b* 20 Jan 1950; *m* 18 Nov 1972 *Millicent Louise Klein
4d *Clifford Belcher SCOTT, *b* 12 Jan 1951

Great-great-grandchildren's children
2b Henry Russell SCOTT, *b* 19 Nov 1874; *m* 23 May 1910 Mary Derby Peabody (*b* 28 Jan 1881; *d* 19—) and *d* 23 March 1952
3b Sarah Carlisle SCOTT, *b* 9 March 1877; *d* Oct 1954
4b Richard Gordon SCOTT, *b* 25 July 1880; *m* 1st 28 Feb 1908 (divorce 1933) his 2nd cousin Grace Cranch Eliot (*b* 13 Sept 1875; *d* 26 Oct 1973) and had issue:

Great-great-grandchildren's grandchildren
1c *Henry Eliot SCOTT [1 Lincoln Place, Weehawken, NJ 07087, USA], *b* 26 Feb 1909; *m* 25 Jan 1947 (divorce 1960) Florentia Elizabeth Metzger (*b* 9 Aug 1912) and has issue:

Great-great-grandchildren's great-grandchildren
1d *Florentia Louise Scott, *b* 3 April 1948; *m* 25 July 1970 *Jacques JANSON Count De TUMBA (*b* Bordeaux, France, 16 Feb 1944) and has issue:

Great-great-grandchildren's great-great-grandchildren
1e *Frederick Scott JANSON, Viscount de St-POL, *b* Montreal, Canada, 27 April 1972
2e *Jacques Jarvis JANSON, *b* Montreal 20 March 1974

Great-great-grandchildren's great-grandchildren
2d *Elizabeth Ann SCOTT, *b* 14 Oct 1952

Great-great-grandchildren's grandchildren
2c *Richard Cranch SCOTT, *b* 1 June 1910; *m* 1st 22 June 1935 (divorce 19—) Madeleine Leonie Erhard (*b* 7 June 1912) and has issue:

Great-great-grandchildren's great-grandchildren
1d *Richard Cranch SCOTT, Jr, *b* 6 Sept 1938; *m* 1st 10 Oct 1964 (divorce 1972) Barbara Foulkrod (*b* Nov 1942) and has issue:

Great-great-grandchildren's great-great-grandchildren
1e *Kristen Jean SCOTT, *b* 20 July 1966
2e *Erica Madeleine SCOTT, *b* 22 Nov 1968

Great-great-grandchildren's great-grandchildren
1d (cont.) Richard Cranch Scott, Jr, *m* 2nd 25 Aug 1973 *Mrs Sisa Axelrod, *née* Sternbach (*b* Ecuador 11 Oct 1939)

Great-great-grandchildren's grandchildren
2c (cont.) Richard C. Scott, Sr, *m* 2nd Tokyo, Japan, 4 Dec 1967 *Mrs Lucille Evans, *née* Claus (*b* 6 Feb 1909)
3c *Abigail Adams Scott, *b* 9 Feb 1912; *m* 28 July 1939 *J. Henry KORSON (*b* 9 Jan 1910) and has issue:

Great-great-grandchildren's great-grandchildren
1d *Thomas Eliot KORSON, *b* 4 Feb 1942; *m* 24 July 1971 *Mary Jane Mullarkey (*b* 28 Sept 1943)

Great-great-grandchildren's grandchildren
4c Peter Chardon SCOTT, *b* 9 Feb 1917; *d* 12 May 1934

Great-great-grandchildren's children
4b (cont.) Richard G. Scott *m* 2nd 1934 (divorce 1936) Effie Cuthbert; *m* 3rd Oct 1937 Mrs Daisy Jarvis Gossett (*b* 12 April 1893) and *d* 16 April 1966
5b Christopher Pearse SCOTT, *b* 19 Sept 1883; *m* 1st 25 June 1910 (divorce 19—) Julia Reichman (*b* 25 July 1886; *d* 19 Nov 1958) and had issue

Great-great-grandchildren's grandchildren
1c *Bruce Chardon SCOTT, *b* 7 March 1912
2c Jean Elizabeth Scott, *b* 23 Sept 1913; *m* 25 June 1936 *Francis COAN (*b* 22 Jan 1913) and *d* Dec 1939, having had issue:

Great-great-grandchildren's great-grandchildren
1d David Scott COAN, *b* 19—; *d* in infancy

Great-great-grandchildren's grandchildren
3c Josephine SCOTT, *b* 22 Nov 1914; *d* March 1925
4c *Margaret Scott, *b* 5 Jan 1919; *m* 26 Sept 1942 *Norman Charles JENSEN (*b* 17 Sept 1916) and has issue:

Great-great-grandchildren's great-grandchildren
1d *Norman Scott JENSEN, *b* 12 May 1946
2d *Barbara Ellen Jensen, *b* 15 April 1947; *m* 18 June 1968 *Philip PHILLIPS (*b* 14 Oct 1946) and has issue:

Great-great-grandchildren's great-great-grandchildren
1e *Ellen Margaret PHILLIPS, *b* 1 May 1973
2e *Eric PHILLIPS, *b* Aug 1975

Great-great-grandchildren's great-grandchildren
3d *Elizabeth Ann Jensen, *b* 5 Oct 1948; *m* 20 July 1970 *Darrell MEEKS (*b* 13 Oct 1947) and has issue:

Great-great-grandchildren's great-great-grandchildren
1e *Jane Emily MEEKS, *b* 22 Nov 1972
2e *Sarah Elizabeth MEEKS, *b* Nov 1975

Great-great-grandchildren's grandchildren
5c *Ruth Carlisle Scott, *b* 15 Dec 1920; *m* Nov 1943 George Edward GARVEY (*b* 31 July 1916; *d* 10 Dec 1970) and has issue:

Great-great-grandchildren's great-grandchildren
1d *Margaret Garvey, *b* 3 Feb 1946; *m* 28 April 1973 *Alan TOTH (*b* 1 Feb 1943)
2d *Deborah GARVEY, *b* 28 June 1947
3d *Susan Garvey, *b* 28 June 1947; *m* 4 Aug 1973 *Joseph BAILEY II (*b* 10 Nov 1946) and has issue:

Great-great-grandchildren's great-great-grandchildren
1e *Joseph BAILEY III, *b* Nov 1975

Great-great-grandchildren's great-grandchildren
4d *Richard Scott GARVEY, *b* 26 Nov 1951; *m* 1 Feb 1974 *Mary Jane Cajka (*b* 7 Feb 1951)

Great-great-grandchildren's children
5b (cont.) Christopher P. Scott *m* 2nd 1924 (divorce *c* 1940) Mrs Beulah Ivon Leach, *née* Young (*d* 25 July 1974); *m* 3rd Mrs Margaret —— (*d* after 1954) and *d* 4 July 1954
6b Elizabeth Rose Scott, *b* 5 Feb 1886; *m* 9 Oct 1920 (divorce 1936) Ernest GARFIELD (*b* 1 March 1884; *d* 1 July 1959) and *d* 13 Dec 1965, having had issue:

Great-great-grandchildren's grandchildren
1c Margaret Scott Garfield, *b* 8 Sept 1922; *m* 18 June 1949 *Robert Allen CUNNINGHAM and *d* 19—, having adopted a s

   a *Jonathan CUNNINGHAM, *b* 1960

Great-great-grandchildren's grandchildren
2c *William Ernest GARFIELD, *b* 13 July 1924
3c *Nancy Greenleaf Garfield, *b* 8 Aug 1926; *m* Sept 1951 (divorce 1965) Howard RISDON and has issue:

   Great-great-grandchildren's great-grandchildren
   1d *Linde RISDON, *b* 27 Feb 1955
   2d *Claudia RISDON, *b* 27 March 1957

Great-great-grandchildren's children
7b Margaret Scott, *b* 23 April 1889; *m* 11 Sept 1911 Edward Lewis LINCOLN (*b* 10 Oct 1886; *d* 29 May 1959) and *d* 4 Jan 1919, leaving issue:

Great-great-grandchildren's grandchildren
1c *Leonora Cranch Lincoln, *b* 16 Nov 1912; *m* 7 Sept 1935 Richard Fremont ESTES (*b* 1 Feb 1912; *d* 11 Feb 1965) and has issue:

   Great-great-grandchildren's great-grandchildren
   1d *Richard Fremont ESTES, Jr, *b* 29 June 1936; *m* July 1960 *Cynthia Helen Love (*b* 28 Jan 1937) and has issue:

      Great-great-grandchildren's great-great-grandchildren
      1e *Scott David ESTES, *b* 19 April 1964

   Great-great-grandchildren's great-grandchildren
   2d *Margaret Lincoln Estes, *b* 17 May 1938; *m* 19 April 1968 *Llewellyn James GRIFFITH and has issue:

      Great-great-grandchildren's great-great-grandchildren
      1e *Catherine GRIFFITH, *b* 11 Aug 1970
      2e *Peter GRIFFITH, *b* 26 Sept 1971
      3e *Daniel GRIFFITH, *b* 25 April 1973

   Great-great-grandchildren's great-grandchildren
   3d *Jere ESTES, *b* 19 Oct 1942; *m* July 1965 *Angela Grovino and has adopted two s:

      a *Eric Scott ESTES, *b* 1969
      b *Christopher Lee ESTES, *b* 1970

Great-great-grandchildren's grandchildren
2c Elizabeth Scott Lincoln, *b* 10 Feb 1914; *m* Nov 1936 *Byron FAIRCHILD (*b* 29 June 1912) and *d* 5 Jan 1962, leaving issue:

   Great-great-grandchildren's great-grandchildren
   1d *Martha Bond Fairchild, *b* 20 Oct 1938; *m* 26 June 1964 *Joseph Robert SHEPLER (*b* 29 July 1937) and has issue:

      Great-great-grandchildren's great-great-grandchildren
      1e *Robert Alexander SHEPLER, *b* 12 May 1968
      2e *William Byron SHEPLER, *b* 5 Feb 1970

   Great-great-grandchildren's great-grandchildren
   2d *Margaret Graham Fairchild, *b* 26 Nov 1942; *m* 1 July 1966 *Ronald LeGrand ARMS (*b* 3 Jan 1933) and has issue:

      Great-great-grandchildren's great-great-grandchildren
      1e *Joseph LeGrand ARMS, *b* 20 Nov 1967
      2e *Oliver Graham ARMS, *b* 26 Jan 1970
      3e *Sarah Lincoln ARMS, *b* 26 Aug 1975

   Great-great-grandchildren's great-grandchildren
   3d *Lincoln FAIRCHILD, *b* 12 Aug 1945; *m* 3 Sept 1967 *Margaret Anne Wachstein (*b* 22 Jan 1947) and has issue:

      Great-great-grandchildren's great-great-grandchildren
      1e *Elizabeth Alden FAIRCHILD, *b* 15 Oct 1969

Great-great-grandchildren
3a Caroline Amelia CRANCH, *b* 7 May 1853; painter; *d* 30 June 1931
4a Quincy Adams CRANCH, *b* Aug 1855; *d* 15 Nov 1875

Great-grandchildren
(4) Louisa W. de Windt, *b* 1 Sept 1821; *m* 1st Aug 1840 Samuel WHITTEMORE and had issue:

Great-great-grandchildren
1a John de Windt WHITTEMORE, *b* 15 Sept 1841; *m* 11 Oct 1869 Ella Carroll Hoyt (*d* 16 Oct 1890), sister of Mrs Frank Adams de Windt (for whom *see below*), and *d* 10 June 1899, having had issue:

Great-great-grandchildren's children
1b Louis Hoyt WHITTEMORE, *b* 13 Sept 1871; *m* 1st Sept 1903 Eliza Dietrich; *m* 2nd 9 Sept 1931 Ethel Gardner and *d* 19—
2b Grace Carroll Whittemore, *b* March 1873; *m* 10 June 1899 DeLancey Verplank NEWLIN and had issue:

Great-great-grandchildren's grandchildren
1c Grace DeLancey NEWLIN, *b* 1900; *d* 1930

Great-great-grandchildren's children
3b Samuel WHITTEMORE, Jr, *b* 24 Oct 1876; *d* 8 April 1893
4b Mabel Thurston Whittemore, *b* 9 Nov 1879; *m* Frederick ROTH and *d* 25 Aug 1929
5b Harold WHITTEMORE, *b* 25 June 1885; *d* 16 March 1903

Great-great-grandchildren
2a Caroline Louisa WHITTEMORE, *b c* 1834; *d c* 1859

Great-grandchildren
(4) (cont.) Louisa De Windt Whittemore *m* 2nd 26 Oct 1852 Clarence Chatham COOK (*b* 1828; *d* 1900) and had further issue:

Great-great-grandchildren
3a Clara COOK, *b* 4 Feb 1853; *d* 25 July 1854

Great-grandchildren
(5) Anna Maria DE WINDT, *b* 9 Dec 1823; *d* 15 June 1848
(6) John Adams DE WINDT, *b* 4 Aug 1825; *m* 3 June 1854 Mary Elizabeth Smith (*b* 1 May 1830; *d* 12 Nov 1912) and *d* 24 Sept 1874, leaving issue:

Great-great-grandchildren
1a John Peter Heyliger DE WINDT, *b* 12 Nov 1855; *m* 1st 18— (divorce 18— or 19—) Millie Etta (*b* 1 Nov 1859; *d* 8 March 1945), dau of Forrest Berry, and had issue:

Great-great-grandchildren's children
1b John Peter Heyliger DE WINDT, Jr, *b* Andover, Mass., 7 Aug 1883; *m* Randolph, Mass., 1902 Lucie (*b* Suffield, Conn., 21 Jan 1883; *d* Bayside, New York, 1 Oct 1970), dau of William H. Spencer and his *w* Mary L. Kellogg, and *d* Bayside 15 July 1948, having had issue:

Great-great-grandchildren's grandchildren
1c *Florence Spencer de Windt [Mrs Philip Dowdell, 519 North Overlook Drive, Alexandria, VA 22305, USA], *b* New York 29 Dec 1902; *m* Jamaica, New York, 12 March 1925 *Philip Higbee DOWDELL (*b* Watsontown, Pa., 15 Dec 1900), s of Thomas Dowdell and his *w* Della Higbee Fulmer, and has issue:

Great-great-grandchildren's great-grandchildren
1d *Florence Higbee Dowdell, *b* Danville, Pa., 20 Jan 1926; *m* Lewisburg, Pa., 12 April 1948 *Richard Warg LINS (*b* Milton, Pa., 15 Feb 1922), s of Charles R. Lins and his *w* Dorothy Warg, and has issue:

Great-great-grandchildren's great-great-grandchildren
1e *Christine Deming LINS, *b* Flushing, New York, 25 June 1950
2e *Douglas Warg LINS, DDS, *b* Butler, Pa., 24 March 1952; *m* 22 Nov 1978 *Amy Lou, dau of Paul Sampson and his *w* Betty
3e *Adele Bradford LINS, *b* Pittsburgh, Pa., 31 Oct 1953
4e *Katherine Ann LINS, *b* Gary, Ind., 4 Nov 1960
5e *Steven Gray LINS, *b* Gary 22 Oct 1962

Great-great-grandchildren's great-grandchildren
2d *Thomas de Windt DOWDELL, *b* Danville 22 July 1930; *m* Vineland, New Jersey, 16 June 1951 *Phyllis Ann (*b* there 1 April 1929), dau of Fred Davis Snyder and his *w* Alma, and has issue:

Great-great-grandchildren's great-great-grandchildren
1e *Linda Jane Dowdell, *b* Vineland, New Jersey, 14 Feb 1953; *m* Saranac Lake, New York, 14 July 1974 *Edward Livingston HOE (*b* Poughkeepsie, New York, 9 Aug 1952)
2e *Ann Phyllis DOWDELL, *b* Philadelphia 6 Dec 1955
3e *Thomas de Windt DOWDELL, Jr, *b* Chestnut Hill, Pa., 23 Oct 1959
4e *Andrew Reeves DOWDELL, *b* Chestnut Hill 26 June 1963

Great-great-grandchildren's grandchildren

2c John Peter Heyliger DE WINDT III, *b* Suffield, Conn., 3 July 1908; *m* 1st 19— (divorce 19—) Helene Poey; *m* 2nd 1939 Dorothy Kilbourn (*b* Aug 1912; *d* 15 or 16 Sept 1989) and *d* 30 Dec 1966, leaving further issue:

> Great-great-grandchildren's great-grandchildren
> 1d *John Peter Heyliger DeWINDT IV [1039 Prospect Blvd, Elgin, IL 60120, USA], *b* 15 July 1940
> 2d *Spencer Worth DeWINDT [1055 Debeck Dve, Rockville, MD 20851, USA], *b* 26 Jan 1947
> 3d *David Adams DeWINDT [Rt3 Box 915, Salisbury, MD 21801, USA], *b* Salisbury 7 Aug 1953; *educ* Bennett Sr High Sch; served US Army, now in trucking business; *m* 24 April 1976 *Elizabeth Cecelia, dau of Sabine Puopulo and Evelyn Crosher French, and has issue:
>
> > Great-great-grandchildren's great-great-grandchildren
> > 1e *Jennifer Adams DeWINDT, *b* Maryland 22 April 1978

Great-great-grandchildren's grandchildren

3c Adele Adams de Windt, *b* 14 May 1910; *m* 8 Jan 1935 *William Harold HAYWARD and *d* 30 July 1936
4c *Mary Louise de Windt [Mrs Harry Dunkerton, 249 Hillside Avenue, Kentfield, CA 94904, USA], *b* New Haven, Conn., 3 Jan 1913; secretary 1931-35; *m* Bayside, New York, 24 Aug 1934 *Harry Fitzmaurice DUNKERTON (*b* New York 18 Feb 1910), s of T. Henry Dunkerton and his w Elizabeth Bouse, and has issue:

> Great-great-grandchildren's great-grandchildren
> 1d *Gail Spencer Dunkerton, *b* Flushing, New York, 30 Oct 1936; *m* Frankfurt, West Germany, 1 Oct 1966 *Klaus ECKRICH (*b* Klein Auheim, Germany, 5 Sept 1943), s of Rudolph Eckrich, and has issue:
>
> > Great-great-grandchildren's great-great-grandchildren
> > 1e *Harry Rudolph ECKRICH, *b* Frankfurt 13 Aug 1967
> > 2e *Linda Gail ECKRICH, *b* Frankfurt 30 Jan 1969
>
> Great-great-grandchildren's great-grandchildren
> 2d *Virginia Anne Dunkerton [Mrs Clement Newbold Jr, Box 832, Lake Wales, FL 33859, USA], *b* Flushing 18 June 1939; *m* Short Hills, New Jersey, 25 May 1963 *Clement Buckley NEWBOLD, Jr (*b* Jenkintown, Pa., 26 July 1934), s of Clement Buckley Newbold and his w Marianne Meade Morris, and has issue:
>
> > Great-great-grandchildren's great-great-grandchildren
> > 1e *Pamela de Windt NEWBOLD, *b* Jenkintown 23 Oct 1964
> > 2e *Mariamne Meade NEWBOLD, *b* Jenkintown 30 Nov 1965
> > 3e *Clement Buckley NEWBOLD III, *b* Jenkintown 30 Nov 1969
>
> Great-great-grandchildren's great-grandchildren
> 3d *Linda de Windt Dunkerton [Mrs Jonathan H Gates, 249 Hillside Ave, Kentfield, CA 94904, USA], *b* Mineola, New York, 8 July 1944; *m* Ross, Calif., 23 July 1966 *Jonathan Hubert GATES (*b* Clinton, Mass., 26 June 1941), s of John Randall Gates and his w Ann Charlotte Lafayette, and has issue:
>
> > Great-great-grandchildren's great-great-grandchildren
> > 1e *Quintin Garner GATES, *b* Mountain View, Calif., 12 March 1967
> > 2e *Andrea Lins GATES, *b* Japan 14 Feb 1970
> > 3e *Althea Ora GATES [8639 Centerton Lane, Manassas, VA 22111, USA], *b* Japan 14 Feb 1970
>
> Great-great-grandchildren's great-grandchildren
> 4d *Kathy Elizabeth Dunkerton [Mrs Edwin Barry, 22 Endeavor Dve, Corte Madera, CA 94925, USA], *b* Summit, New Jersey, 6 March 1946; *m* 1st Jackson, Miss., 1 April 1972 (divorce 1984) Harry Remone CRIMM, s of Harry R. Crimm and his w Susan, and has issue:
>
> > Great-great-grandchildren's great-great-grandchildren
> > 1e *Abigail Amanda CRIMM, *b* Jackson 31 May 1973
> > 2e *Harry Nicholas CRIMM, *b* Alexandria, La., 14 Nov 1978
>
> Great-great-grandchildren's great-grandchildren
> 4d (cont.) Mrs Kathy Crimm *m* 2nd Ross, Calif., 28 Aug 1988 *Edwin BARRY (*b* 30 April 1945), s of Arthur John Barry and his w Marjorie Burdick Hand

Great-great-grandchildren's grandchildren

5c Garrett Girard DE WINDT, *b* Birmingham, Ala., 16 Aug 1915; *d* Jamaica, New York, 1918
6c *Arthur Kellogg DE WINDT [148 Laurel Hill Road, Mountain Lakes, NJ 07046, USA], *b* 22 April 1920; *m* 1st 19— (divorce 19—) Angela de Menceni; *m* 2nd 19— *Margaret Bonner (*b* 21 Feb 1922) and with her has issue:

> Great-great-grandchildren's great-grandchildren
> 1d *Keith Adams DE WINDT, *b* 17 May 1951
> 2d *Bonnie Day DE WINDT, *b* 29 Nov 1954

Great-great-grandchildren's grandchildren

7c *Forrest Berry DE WINDT [Jamaica, Long Island, NY 11431 or 11101, USA], *b* 19 Dec 1923

Great-great-grandchildren's children
2b Mary Elizabeth de Windt, *b* 1887; *m* 11 April 1911 John Odell HAUSER (*b* 18—; *d* Feb 1941) and had issue:

Great-great-grandchildren's grandchildren
1c *Revd John Henry HAUSER [626 Pomona Rd, Coronado, CA 91720, USA], *b* 2 May 1912; *m* 19— *Ruth Arbenz and has issue:

Great-great-grandchildren's great-grandchildren
1d *Virginia Arbenz HAUSER, *b* 19—
2d *John Odell HAUSER, *b* 19—
3d *Millie Keith HAUSER, *b* 19—

Great-great-grandchildren's grandchildren
2c Peter de Windt HAUSER, *b* 8 Oct 1914; *m* 19— *Lydia Smith [Mrs Peter Hauser, 1835 Edgehill Road, Abington, PA 19001, USA] and *d* 19—, having had issue:

Great-great-grandchildren's great-grandchildren
1d *Jana Smith HAUSER, *b* 19—
2d *Peter Keith HAUSER, *b* 19—

Great-great-grandchildren's grandchildren
3c *Doris Hauser, *b* 21 Dec 1918; *m* 19— *Webster Fairbanks WILLIAMS, Jr, s of Webster Fairbanks Williams and his w Rachel Nichols, and has issue:

Great-great-grandchildren's great-grandchildren
1d *Elizabeth de Windt WILLIAMS, *b* 19—
2d *Webster Fairbanks WILLIAMS III, *b* 19—

Great-great-grandchildren's children
3b Carolyn Girard Adams de Windt, *b* Hempstead, New York, 3 Feb 1893; *m* 19— Harlan B. HAYS and *d* 1919, leaving issue:

Great-great-grandchildren's grandchildren
1c *Elizabeth de Windt Hays, *b* 14 Nov 1914; *m* 19— *William A. FISHER (*b* 17 Dec 1905) and has issue:

Great-great-grandchildren's great-grandchildren
1d *Carolyn Hays FISHER, *b* 7 July 1940
2d *Robert Ward FISHER, *b* 22 Oct 1945

Great-great-grandchildren
1a (cont.) John P. de Windt *m* 2nd Susan J. Anderson and *d* 9 March 1936

Great-grandchildren
(7) William Stephens DE WINDT, *b* 30 Jan, *d* 23 Sept 1827
(8) Isabella Adams de Windt, *b* 23 Sept 1828; *m* 25 June 1848 Gabriel FURMAN and *d* 18— or 19—, having had issue:

Great-great-grandchildren
1a William Stephens FURMAN, *b* 18—; *m* 18— or 19— and *d* 3 Jan 1925
2a Susan Booth Furman, *b* 14 Aug 1850; *m* 26 Aug 1875, as his 2nd w, Charles Elliott LORD (*b* 8 Feb 1843; *d* 14 April 1883) and *d* 17 May 1916, having had issue:

Great-great-grandchildren's children
1b Susan Isabel Lord, *b* 16 July 1877; *m* 12 April 1898 Henry T. ALLEY (*b* 19 Sept 1866; *d* 18— or 19—) and *d* 15 Feb 1927, leaving issue:

Great-great-grandchildren's grandchildren
1c Isabel E. Alley, *b* 18 Aug 1899; *m* 16 Nov 1920 Thornton EMMONS and *d* 15 Feb 1935, leaving issue:

Great-great-grandchildren's great-grandchildren
1d *Virginia Emmons, *b* 23 Oct 1923; *m* 19— *William Harrison KALTHOOF, Jr, s of William Harrison Kalthoof, and has issue:

Great-great-grandchildren's great-great-grandchildren
1e *Craig Emmons KALTHOOF, *b* 27 Nov 1952

Great-great-grandchildren's great-grandchildren
2d George T. EMMONS, *b* 6 March 1928; *d* 27 Aug 1939

Great-great-grandchildren's children
2b Sarah Lord, *b* 9 March 1879; *m* 8 Feb 1911 Arthur MURPHY (*b* 19 Dec 1876; *d* 25 Nov 1911) and had issue:

Great-great-grandchildren's grandchildren
1c *Arthur Lord MURPHY, *b* 28 Dec 1911; *m* 24 Dec 1938 *Eleanor Harlee (*b* 22 Nov 1910) and has issue:

Great-great-grandchildren's great-grandchildren
1d *Arthur Lord MURPHY, Jr, *b* 1952
2d *Gloria MURPHY, *b* 1954

Great-great-grandchildren's children
3b Henry LORD, *b* 18 Nov 1880; *d* 12 Nov 1886

Great-great-grandchildren
3a Amelia Seaman FURMAN, *b* after 1850; *d* 18— or 19—

Great-grandchildren
(9) Emily Augusta de Windt, *b* 9 July 1830; *m* 30 May 1855 Frederick Clarke WITHERS (*b* 4 Feb 1828; *d* 7 Jan 1901) and *d* 1 July 1863, leaving issue:

Great-great-grandchildren
1a Frank WITHERS, *b* 18—; *d* 18— or 19—
2a Alice Withers, *b* 18—; *m* 18— or 19— J. Foster JENKINS and *d* 18— or 19—

Great-grandchildren
(10) Arthur DE WINDT, *b* 28 July 1832; *m* 8 May 1855 Georgiana T. Rich (*b* 1836; *d* 7 May 1900) and *d* 30 Sept 1907, leaving issue:

Great-great-grandchildren
1a Heyliger Adams DE WINDT, *b* Fishkill, New York, 17 Feb 1858; *m* 1st New Bedford, Mass., 10 Sept 1889 Bertha Williams (*b* New Bedford 8 Aug 1867; *d* Winnetka, Ill., 27 July 1907), dau of Thomas Mandell, and had issue:

Great-great-grandchildren's children
1b Heyliger DE WINDT, *b* Chicago 3 Aug 1890; *m* 10 Sept 1914 Clara Swigart (*b* 1892; *d* 19—) and *d* 19—
2b Delano DE WINDT, *b* Chicago 30 Oct 1892; *m* Great Barrington, Mass., 17 June 1916 Ruth (*d* 4 March 1982), dau of John H. C. Church and his w Mary Loop, and *d* Albany, New York, 10 Nov 1953, leaving issue:

Great-great-grandchildren's grandchildren
1c *Ruth de Windt [Mrs Archibald Hoxton Jr, Route 1 Box 52, Fruit Hill, Shepherdstown, WV 25443, USA], *b* New Bedford 24 April 1917; *educ* Barrington Sch, Garland, S Carolina; sometime clerical worker in New York; *m* Great Barrington 16 Aug 1941 *Archibald Robinson HOXTON, Jr (*b* Alexandria, Va., 20 April 1916), s of Archibald Robinson Hoxton and his w Sarah Purvis Taylor, and has issue:

Great-great-grandchildren's great-grandchildren
1d *Archibald Robinson HOXTON III [Box E Shepherdstown, WV 25443, USA], *b* Washington, DC, 21 Oct 1943; *m* N Carolina 25 July 1964 *Constance Congdon and has issue:

Great-great-grandchildren's great-great-grandchildren
1e *Archibald Robinson HOXTON IV, *b* Erwin, Tenn., 22 Feb 1965
2e *Frederick Clayborne HOXTON, *b* Erwin 31 Oct 1966

Great-great-grandchildren's great-grandchildren
2d *Ann Hoxton [Mrs Michael F Taylor, Route 1 Box 52, Shepherdstown, WV 25443, USA], *b* Washington, DC, 13 Sept 1946; *educ* Sweetbriar Coll and U of Colorado; Sec of Corp, Michael F. Taylor Inc; *m* Shepherdstown 29 Aug 1970 *Michael Frank TAYLOR, of Denver, Colo., s of Pete Taylor and his w Juanita J., and has issue:

Great-great-grandchildren's great-great-grandchildren
1e *Anna Sorrel TAYLOR, *b* Winchester, Va., 26 Dec 1977
2e *Leah Michael TAYLOR, *b* Winchester 19 March 1982

Great-great-grandchildren's grandchildren
2c *Mary de Windt [Mrs William Speers, 50 Willow Road, London NW3, UK], *b* New Bedford, Mass., 14 Aug 1918; *m* Great Barrington, Mass., 1947 *William Archer SPEERS (*b* New York 1918), s of William Speers and his w Olive Archer, and has issue:

Great-great-grandchildren's great-grandchildren
1d *Susan Archer Speers, *b* New York 1948; *m* Sept 1972 *R. Leith HERMANN, s of Robert Henry Hermann, and has issue:

Great-great-grandchildren's great-great-grandchildren
1e *William de Windt HERMANN, *b* Baltimore 25 July 1976
2e *Virginia Galleher HERMANN, *b* Baltimore 21 Nov 1978

Great-great-grandchildren's great-grandchildren
2d *Joan Adams Speers, *b* New York 1950; *m* London, UK, 4 Nov 1978 *Roger M. L. MEARS (*b* 16 Feb 1944)

Great-great-grandchildren's grandchildren
3c *Edward Mandell DE WINDT [25299 Cedar Road, Lyndhurst, OH 44124, USA], *b* Great Barrington, Mass., 31 March 1921; *m* Englewood, New Jersey, 21 June 1941 *Elizabeth (Betsy) (*b* Long Island, New York, 15 July 1921), dau of Harold Bope and his w Elizabeth Baird, and has issue:

Great-great-grandchildren's great-grandchildren
1d *Pamela de Windt, *b* Battle Creek, Mich., 15 Oct 1942; *m* 1st Cleveland, Ohio, 5 Sept 1964 Peter Charles STECK (*b* Cleveland 30 June 1942), s of William Steck and his w Elizabeth, and has issue:

> Great-great-grandchildren's great-great-grandchildren
> 1e *Heather Baird STECK, *b* Cleveland 30 April 1967
> 2e *Megan Lloyd STECK, *b* Cleveland 27 Aug 1969
> 3e *Elizabeth de Windt STECK, *b* Cleveland 29 Jan 1972

Great-great-grandchildren's great-grandchildren
1d (cont.) Mrs De Windt Steck *m* 2nd 19— *Daniel BURKE
2d *Delano DE WINDT II, *b* Battle Creek 21 Feb 1944; *m* 3 March 1973 *Adriane (*b* Bloomfield Hills, Mich., 19—), dau of Maynard Rudolph Andreae and his w Patricia, and has issue:

> Great-great-grandchildren's great-great-grandchildren
> 1e *Allison Andreae DE WINDT, *b* Detroit 18 Nov 1976
> 2e *Delano DE WINDT III, *b* Detroit 20 May 1979

Great-great-grandchildren's great-grandchildren
3d *Dana DE WINDT, *b* Cleveland, Ohio, 12 May 1948; *m* there 19 June 1971 *Kathy (*b* there 1949), dau of Victor Gelb and his w Joan Freeman, and has issue:

> Great-great-grandchildren's great-great-grandchildren
> 1e *Cullen Adams DE WINDT, *b* Stuart, Fla., 3 Oct 1975
> 2e *Gavin DE WINDT, *b* Stuart 10 Aug 1978

Great-great-grandchildren's great-grandchildren
4d *Elizabeth (Lisa) de Windt, *b* Cleveland 5 Oct 1953; *m* there 15 Dec 1979 *Martin Joseph KELLY (*b* Bridgeport, Conn., 28 Oct 1957), s of Neil Kelly and his w Mildred
5d *Edward Mandell DE WINDT, Jr, *b* Cleveland 8 Jan 1962

Great-great-grandchildren's grandchildren
4c *Ann de Windt [Mrs Frederick R Schroeder Jr, 1010 West Muirlands Dve, La Jolla, CA 92037, USA], *b* Great Barrington, Mass., 7 April 1924; secretary; *m* Great Barrington 5 Feb 1944 *Frederick R. (Ted) SCHROEDER, Jr (*b* Newark, New Jersey, 20 July 1921; *educ* Glendale High Sch, Calif., and Stanford U (BA Econ 1942); served USN World War II; US Junior Singles Tennis Champion 1939, US Singles Champion 1942, US Doubles Champion 1940, 1941 and 1947, Wimbledon Singles Champion 1949, V-Pres Kold Hold Pacific Sales Co 1949), s of Frederick Rudolph Schroeder and his w Helen Heath, and has issue:

> Great-great-grandchildren's great-grandchildren
> 1d *John Laurence SCHROEDER, *b* Great Barrington 12 Nov 1945; *m* Saginaw, Mich., 2 Aug 1969 *Kathleen (*b* Saginaw 5 May 1947), dau of Dr Donald Kelly and his w Elizabeth, and has issue:
>
> > Great-great-grandchildren's great-great-grandchildren
> > 1e *Patricia SCHROEDER, *b* San Diego, Calif., 18 Feb 1974
> > 2e *Molly SCHROEDER, *b* San Diego 17 April 1976
> > 3e *Jennifer Kelly SCHROEDER, *b* San Diego 13 Nov 1979
>
> Great-great-grandchildren's great-grandchildren
> 2d *Richard Frederick SCHROEDER, *b* Glendale, Calif., 30 June 1946; *m* Los Angeles 25 Nov 1978 (divorce) Debbie —— (*b* 7 June 1953) and has issue:
>
> > Great-great-grandchildren's great-great-grandchildren
> > 1e *Nicholas SCHROEDER, *b* San Diego, Calif., 26 Oct 1983
> > 2e *Emily SCHROEDER, *b* San Diego 28 Dec 1985
>
> Great-great-grandchildren's great-grandchildren
> 3d *Robert Edward SCHROEDER, *b* Glendale 19 Nov 1956; *m* 1st 8 June 1979 (divorce 19—) Kellie Tennison (*b* 27 Oct 1959); *m* 2nd Dale City, Va., 20 Oct 1990 *Mary Walbridge and has issue:
>
> > Great-great-grandchildren's great-great-grandchildren
> > 1e *Justin T. SCHROEDER, *b* Colorado Springs, Colo., 7 April 1992

Great-great-grandchildren's children
3b *Caroline de Windt, *b* 24 Aug 1900; *m* 10 June 1922 (divorce 19—) Albert Sellner GARDNER and has issue:

Great-great-grandchildren's grandchildren
1c *Carol Gardner, *b* 21 April 1923; *m* 1st 15 June 1946 (divorce 19—) James Edward THOMPSON and has issue:

> Great-great-grandchildren's great-grandchildren
> 1d *Carol Ann THOMPSON, *b* 19—

Great-great-grandchildren's grandchildren
1c (cont.) Mrs Carol Thompson *m* 2nd 16 July 1950 *Orville E. GOWER and has further issue:

Great-great-grandchildren's great-grandchildren
2d *April GOWER, *b* 19—
3d *Bretton Lee GOWER, *b* 19—
4d *Candice GOWER, *b* 19—

Great-great-grandchildren's grandchildren
2c *William Alfred GARDNER, *b* 10 June 1925; *m* 20 Jan 1950 *Joan Carolyn Arnold and has issue:

Great-great-grandchildren's great-grandchildren
1d *Deborah Ann GARDNER, *b* 19—
2d *William Alfred GARDNER, Jr, *b* 30 April 1955

Great-great-grandchildren's children
4b *Alice de Windt [Mrs Randolph Owsley, 16345 Redington Drive, Redington Beach, St Petersburg, FL 33708, USA], *b* 27 Sept 1902; *m* 4 Oct 1924 *Randolph Gibson OWSLEY (*b* Dallas 18 Sept 1900; banker, Lt-Cdr USNR), s of William Lucius Owsley and his w Virginia Marion (Maybird) Gibson, and a descendant of William Randolph of Turkey Island, Va., and has had issue:

Great-great-grandchildren's grandchildren
1c Alicia Owsley, *b* Lake Forest, Ill., 21 Jan 1928; *m* 194- *William CUNNINGHAM and *d* 1949
2c *Randolph Gibson OWSLEY, Jr, *b* Lake Forest 4 Sept 1929; *m* 22 Nov 1961 *Barbara Ann Jones (*b* Kansas City 15 Feb 1939) and has issue:

Great-great-grandchildren's great-grandchildren
1d *Laura Alice OWSLEY, *b* Chicago 6 July 1962
2d *Randolph Gibson OWSLEY III, *b* Evanston, Ill., 25 June 1963
3d *Barbara Adams OWSLEY, *b* Kansas City 11 Jan 1966

Great-great-grandchildren
1a (cont.) Heyliger A. de Windt *m* 2nd 16 March 1912 Alice Greene Arnold (*b* 20 June 1871; *d* 16 May 1944) and *d* 17 Nov 1941

Great-grandchildren
(11) Francis (Frank) Adams DE WINDT, *b* 9 June 1834; *m* 15 Jan 1857 Emily Adele Hoyt (*d* 16 Oct 1890), sister of Mrs John de Windt Whittemore (for whom *see above*), and *d* 8 Aug 1866, leaving issue:

Great-great-grandchildren
1a Francis Adams DE WINDT, Jr, *b* 18—; *m* 18— or 19— Eliza Counhoven (*b* 4 Jan 1849; *d* 8 May 1919) and *d* 1926, leaving issue:

Great-great-grandchildren's children
1b Katherine Belden de Windt, *b* 11 Oct 1882; *m* 18— or 19— William Brewster WERNER (*b* 11 Nov 1881; *d* 19—) and *d* 19—, leaving issue:

Great-great-grandchildren's grandchildren
1c *Edith Natalie Werner, *b* 5 June 1905; *m* 19— *William Louis ALEXANDER (*b* 13 July 1904) and has issue:

Great-great-grandchildren's great-grandchildren
1d *William de Windt ALEXANDER, *b* 5 April 1923; *m* 19— *Elva Virginia De Voe (*b* 19 April 1920) and has issue:

Great-great-grandchildren's great-great-grandchildren
1e *Nancy Virginia ALEXANDER, *b* 21 Sept 1944

Great-great-grandchildren's great-grandchildren
2d *Richard Bruenig ALEXANDER, *b* 20 Nov 1937

Great-great-grandchildren's children
2b Marjorie Counhoven DE WINDT, *b* 19 April 1884; *d* 18— or 19—

Great-great-grandchildren
2a Cornelia (Nina) DE WINDT, *b* 18—; *d* 18— or 19—
3a Elizabeth (Bessie) de Windt, *b* 18—; *m* 18— or 19— Forest GREENFIELD and *d* 18— or 19—
4a Adele de Windt, *b* 18—; *m* 18— or 19— Van VORHIS and *d* 18— or 19—
5a Garrett (Gary) Sprevit DE WINDT, *b* 25 Jan 1864; *m* 4 Feb 1931 Maude Hunter and *d* 21 June 1937

Great-grandchildren
(12) Mary Catherine de Windt, *b* 5 Dec 1838; *m* 5 June 1861 George Allen SEAMAN and *d* 26 March 1881, having had issue:

Great-great-grandchildren
1a Caroline Amelia SEAMAN, *b* 22 March 1862; *d* 2 Aug 1863

2a Emily de Windt SEAMAN, *b* 9 June 1865; *d* 21 July 1931

3a George Williams SEAMAN, *b* 11 Nov 1868; *m* 1st 18 Nov 1896 Caroline Ward Halgin (*b* 14 June 1873; *d* 14 May 1899); *m* 2nd 9 June 1903 Irmingarde Van Horne Freeman (*b* 2 April 1878; *d* 19—) and *d* Beacon, New York, 27 Feb 1942, having had issue:

Great-great-grandchildren's children

1b *Sarah Corvinus Seaman, *b* 9 May 1904; *m* 24 Dec 1940 *A. P. MULLAN (*b* 5 Sept 1892)

2b George Hurtin SEAMAN, *b* 5 Oct 1905; *d* 1 March 1907

3b Ogden Van Horne SEAMAN, *b* 28 May 1908; *d* 12 Feb 1923

4b *Margaret Osborne Seaman, *b* 20 July 1910; *m* 10 Nov 1939 *Artimus Whitaker JONES (*b* 12 Nov 1905)

5b *Elizabeth Hurtin Seaman, *b* 23 Nov 1911; *m* 13 May 1938 *Robert Campbell BARRY (*b* 28 Dec 1912) and has issue:

Great-great-grandchildren's grandchildren

1c *Michael Van Horne (Robert) BARRY, *b* 19 Oct 1940

2c *Gail Stuart BARRY, *b* 15 Dec 1942

3c *Christopher Quinn BARRY, *b* 15 March 1946

4c *Paul Corbett BARRY, *b* 15 March 1946

Great-great-grandchildren's children

6b *Anne Ogden SEAMAN, *b* 13 Feb 1914

7b *Emily de Windt Seaman, *b* 21 Oct 1917; *m* 11 June 1942 *Lawrence Henry HADLAND (*b* 16 Nov 1919) and has issue:

Great-great-grandchildren's grandchildren

1c *Janet Ruth HADLAND, *b* 4 May 1943

2c *Richard Manning HADLAND, *b* 14 Aug 1944

3c *Judy Anne HADLAND, *b* 13 July 1948

4c *Kenneth Lawrence HADLAND, *b* 17 July 1949

5c *Marie Patricia HADLAND, *b* 16 Sept 1951

6c *George Robert HADLAND, *b* 16 Sept 1951

Great-great-grandchildren's children

8b *Mary Patricia Seaman, *b* 20 Sept 1920; *m* 5 June 1948 James Robinson DANIELS (*b* Wilson, N Carolina, 13 March 1905; *d* Sylva, N Carolina, 18 June 1961)

Great-great-grandchildren

4a Charles Henry SEAMAN, *b* 15 March 1870; *m* 22 Oct 1901 Grace Beulah Aldridge (*b* 14 Nov 1880; *d* 14 Aug 1926) and *d* 11 Oct 1949, leaving issue:

Great-great-grandchildren's children

1b *Harriet Elizabeth Seaman, *b* 14 April 1903; *m* 1 April 1927 *Joseph James DOYLE and has issue:

Great-great-grandchildren's grandchildren

1c *Joseph James DOYLE, Jr, *b* 19 May 1928

2c *Thomas Henry DOYLE, *b* 21 Oct 1930

3c *Grace Pauline Doyle, *b* 7 Dec 1932; *m* 19— *Edward George GREGER (*b* 27 Oct 1929) and has issue:

Great-great-grandchildren's great-grandchildren

1d *Pauline Elizabeth GREGER, *b* 16 July 1953

2d *Katherine Johanna GREGER, *b* 17 Sept 1954

Great-great-grandchildren's grandchildren

4c *Harry DOYLE, *b* 1 July 1938

Great-great-grandchildren's children

2b *Mary Catherine Seaman, *b* 8 April 1904; *m* 17 July 1923 Dr Samuel Benajah LINK (*b* 7 July 1900; *d* Stamford, Conn., 31 March 1961) and has issue:

Great-great-grandchildren's grandchildren

1c *Patricia Ann Link, *b* 31 Oct 1925; *m* 1st 1 May 1944 Robert J. CAVANAUGH (*d* Dec 1944); *m* 2nd Nov 1947 *Thomas Christopher MURPHY and has issue:

Great-great-grandchildren's great-grandchildren

1d *Thomas Christopher MURPHY, Jr, *b* 26 Aug 1948

2d *Brian MURPHY, *b* 5 Jan 1950

3d *Sally Elizabeth MURPHY, *b* 31 Dec 1952

Great-great-grandchildren's grandchildren

2c *Sally Elizabeth Link, *b* 17 Jan 1927; *m* March 1947 *Robert BILDER and has issue:

Great-great-grandchildren's great-grandchildren

1d *Cynthia Curtis BILDER, *b* 9 Nov 1950

Great-great-grandchildren's grandchildren
3c *Samuel Adams LINK, *b* 29 June 1932
4c *Walker Gordon LINK, *b* 11 Aug 1934; *m* 19— *Joyce Elliott (*b* 17 June 1934) and has issue:

Great-great-grandchildren's great-grandchildren
1d *Michael Elliott LINK, *b* 7 Feb 1952
2d *Catherine Ann LINK, *b* 16 July 1954

Great-great-grandchildren's children
3b *Charles Henry SEAMAN, Jr, *b* 2 June 1916; *m* 19— *Barbara Tunison (*b* 11 Sept 1914) and has issue:

Great-great-grandchildren's grandchildren
1c *Gary Adams SEAMAN, *b* 25 Aug 1949

Great-great-grandchildren
5a Mary Groebe Seaman, *b* 1 July 1872; *m* 1 July 1903 George KETCHUM (*d* 1940) and *d* 7 Jan 1947, leaving issue:

Great-great-grandchildren's children
1b *Mary Catherine Wolfe Ketchum, *b* 29 Aug 1904; *m* 19— *Ernest Cluett WALKER (*b* 19 Feb 1905) and has had issue:

Great-great-grandchildren's grandchildren
1c Richard Seaman WALKER, *b* 17 March 1931; *d* April 1953

Great-great-grandchildren's children
2b *George Miller KETCHUM, *b* 4 Dec 1906; *m* 4 Dec 1929 *Grace Doughty (*b* 2 May 1908) and has issue:

Great-great-grandchildren's grandchildren
1c *Jacqueline Joan KETCHUM, *b* 30 May 1932

Great-great-grandchildren's children
3b *Morris KETCHUM, *b* 20 Nov 1909; *m* 1 Feb 1936 (divorce 19—) Jessie Nisbit (*b* 2 June 19—) and has issue:

Great-great-grandchildren's grandchildren
1c *Joy Anne KETCHUM, *b* 20 Nov 1936
2c *Morris George KETCHUM, *b* 24 May 1941

Great-great-grandchildren
6a Richard Heber SEAMAN, *b* 17 Jan, *d* 13 July 1881

President Adams's children
II JOHN QUINCY ADAMS, 6th PRESIDENT of the UNITED STATES of AMERICA
III Susanna ADAMS, *b* Boston 28 Dec 1768; *d* there 4 Feb 1770
IV Charles ADAMS, *b* Boston 29 May 1770; *educ* Harvard; *m* 29 Aug 1795 Sarah (Sally) (*b* 6 Nov 1769; *d* 8 Aug 1828), dau of John Smith and his w Margaret Stephens and sister of Charles's bro-in-law Col William Stephens Smith, and *d* New York 30 Nov 1800, leaving issue:

Grandchildren
1 Susanna Boylston Adams, *b* New York 8 Aug 1796; *m* 1st 3 Aug 1817 Lt Charles Thomas CLARK (*b* 1793; *d* 14 April 1819) and had issue:

Great-grandchildren
(1) Susanna Maria Clark, *b* Quincy, Mass., 2 March 1818; *m* 13 May 1839 Adoniram Judson CRANE, of Richmond, Va. (*b* 2 Nov 1817; *d* 3 Jan 1867), and *d* Philadelphia 27 Aug 1853, having had issue:

Great-great-grandchildren
1a Abigail Louisa CRANE, *b* 17 Feb 1840; *d* 8 Feb 1843
2a Charles Thomas CRANE, *b* 12 April 1842; *d* 1 Aug 1843
3a Charles Thomas Clark CRANE, *b* 9 Jan 1844; *m* 1st 18 Sept 1867 Annie Louise Levering (*b* 22 July 1845; *d* 12 July 1906) and *d* 18— or 19—, having had issue:

Great-great-grandchildren's children
1b Charles Levering CRANE, *b* 1868; *d* 1902
2b Clinton CRANE, *b* 1870; *d* 1871
3b Elizabeth CRANE, *b* 1871; *d* 1872
4b Louis Woods CRANE, *b* 1873; *d* 1879
5b Churchill CRANE, *b* 1875; *d* 1876
6b Robert Treat CRANE, *b* Baltimore 9 June 1880; *educ* Johns Hopkins; *m* 20 June 1908 Maria Louise (*b* St Louis, Mo., 6 Oct 1882), dau of George Washington Riggs and his w Kate Cheesman, and had issue:

Great-great-grandchildren's grandchildren
1c *Robert Treat CRANE, Jr [1341 Monk Rd, Gladwyne, PA 19035, USA], *b* Montreal, Canada, 25 Aug 1909; *m* 31 Dec 1934 *Virginia Mary Ladd and has had issue:

Great-great-grandchildren's great-grandchildren
1d Mary Truesdell CRANE, *b* 28 June 1938; *d* 9 June 1940
2d *Robert Treat CRANE III, *b* 27 Dec 1939
3d *Sanford Ladd CRANE, *b* 28 July 1943
4d *Maria Louisa CRANE, *b* 27 Dec 1945

Great-great-grandchildren's grandchildren
2c *George Levering CRANE, *b* Washington, DC, 6 Oct 1911; *m* 1st 19— (divorce 19—) Ruth Carrington and has issue:

Great-great-grandchildren's great-grandchildren
1d *Elizabeth Louise CRANE, *b* 30 Dec 1939
2d *Ruth Carrington CRANE, *b* 30 Dec 1941

Great-great-grandchildren's grandchildren
2c (cont.) George L. Crane *m* 2nd 2 Aug 1947 *Lyle· Long and has further issue:

Great-great-grandchildren's great-grandchildren
3d *Marion Long CRANE, *b* 8 Jan 1949
4d *George Levering CRANE, Jr, *b* 18 June 1950
5d *Susan Adams CRANE, *b* 21 Dec 1953
6d *Thomas Francis CRANE, *b* 21 Dec 1953

Great-great-grandchildren's grandchildren
3c *Charles Thomas CRANE [7 Temple Street, Stonington, CT 06378, USA], *b* Ann Arbor, Mich., 20 Dec 1913
4c Lawrason Riggs CRANE, *b* Ann Arbor 20 Dec 1913; *d* 18 Oct 1922
5c *Kate Cheesman CRANE [7 Temple Street, Stonington, CT 06378, USA], *b* Ann Arbor 26 Feb 1918
6c *Matlack Cheesman CRANE, *b* Ann Arbor 26 Feb 1918; *m* 19— *———

Great-great-grandchildren's children
7b John Alden CRANE, *b* St George Island, Md., 2 Dec 1885; *educ* Johns Hopkins; artillery offr US Army; *m* 21 Oct 1908 Mary Sterrett, dau of Sterrett McKim, of Baltimore, and *d* 19—, having had issue:

Great-great-grandchildren's grandchildren
1c *John Alden McKim CRANE, *b* Fort McKinley, the Philippines, 2 Aug 1909; *m* 28 July 1950 *Eva D. Rabbitt
2c *Mary McKim CRANE, *b* Baltimore 6 Oct 1917

Great-great-grandchildren
3a (cont.) Charles T. Crane *m* 2nd 26 Oct 1907 Gertrude Jackson and *d* 23 March 1920
4a Maria Louisa Crane, *b* 15 Sept 1846; *m* Daniel C. WOODS and *d* 18— or 19—

Grandchildren
1 (cont.) Susanna Adams Clark *m* 2nd 1833 William R. H. TREADWAY, of Richmond, Va. (*b* 1795; *d* 1836), and *d* 21 Jan 1846
2 Abigail Louisa Smith Adams, *b* 8 Sept 1798; *m* 14 Oct 1814 Alexander Bryan JOHNSON, of Utica, New York (*b* Gosport, Hants, Great Britain, 29 May 1786; *d* 9 Sept 1867), and *d* 4 July 1838, having had issue:

Great-grandchildren
(1) John Adams JOHNSON, *b* 3 Oct 1815; *d* 29 Oct 1820
(2) Alexander Smith JOHNSON, *b* Utica, New York, 30 July 1817; judge; *m* 8 Nov 1852 Catherine (*b* 19 April 1833; *d* 5 Feb 1898), dau of —— Crysler, of St Catherine, Ontario, Canada, and *d* Nassau, the Bahamas, 26 Jan 1878, leaving issue:

Great-great-grandchildren
1a Catherine Maria Crysler Johnson, *b* 1 Aug 1853; *m* 1st 2 June 1878 Harvey Doolittle TALCOTT (*b* 1844?; *d* 18—) and had issue:

Great-great-grandchildren's children
1b Margaret Talcott; *b* 18—; *m* —— CORBIN and *d* 18— or 19—, having had issue:

Great-great-grandchildren's grandchildren
1c *Margaret CORBIN, *b* 18— or 19—

Great-great-grandchildren
1a (cont.) Catherine Johnson Talcott *m* 2nd 14 June 1881 Judge George Edmund OTIS, of Redlands, Calif. (*b* 1846; *d* 1906), and had further issue:

Great-great-grandchildren's children
2b Elsie Gansevoort Otis, *b* San Francisco 13 July 1882; *m* 30 Aug 1913 her 1st cousin Horatio SEYMOUR, Jr (*b* Marquette, Mich., 14 July 1883; *educ* Yale; Capt US Army 1918-20; *d* 19—), only s of Horatio Seymour and his w Abigail Adams Johnson (*see below*), and *d* 19—, having had issue:

Great-great-grandchildren's grandchildren
1c *Horatio SEYMOUR III, *b* Bronxville, New York, 9 March 1915
2c *John Forman SEYMOUR, *b* Bronxville 13 June 1917

Great-great-grandchildren
2a Abigail Adams Johnson, *b* 23 Nov 1855; *m* 12 Oct 1880 her 1st cousin Horatio SEYMOUR (*b* 8 Jan 1844; *d* 21 Feb 1907), s of John Forman Seymour (whose bro Horatio was Democratic presidential candidate against Ulysses Grant 1868) and his w Frances Ancil Tappan, and *d* 6 Jan 1915, leaving issue:

Great-great-grandchildren's children
1b Mary Ledyard Seymour, *b* 30 Sept 1881; *m* 23 Oct 1901 Henry ST ARNAULD (*b* 26 Jan 1846; *d* 19—) and *d* 19—, having had issue:

Great-great-grandchildren's grandchildren
1c *Marie Alice Gansevoort St Arnauld [Mrs Lewis Fowler, 131 Higby Road, Utica, NY 13501, USA], *b* 23 Sept 1902; *m* 26 Feb 1922 *Lewis George FOWLER, atty, and has issue:

Great-great-grandchildren's great-grandchildren
1d *Jane Marie Fowler, *b* 16 Feb 1926; *m* 7 Sept 1946 *Russell F. HOFFMAN and has issue:

Great-great-grandchildren's great-great-grandchildren
1e *Stephen Lewis HOFFMAN, *b* 7 Aug 1947; *educ* Syracuse U; civil servant
2e *Valerie Jane HOFFMAN, *b* 27 Oct 1953; *educ* Union Coll and Boston Coll of Law; atty in Chicago

Great-great-grandchildren's great-grandchildren
2d George Ledyard FOWLER, *b* 16 Feb 1926; *m* 16 Oct 1948 *Helen Frankl and *d* 26 Nov 1976, leaving issue:

Great-great-grandchildren's great-great-grandchildren
1e *Gail Marie Fowler, *b* 9 Aug 1949; *m* 27 Aug 1972 *Gary BARTNICK and has issue:

Great-great-grandchildren's great-great-grandchildren's children
1f *Todd Michael BARTNICK, *b* 31 March 1975
2f *Jill Stacy BARTNICK, *b* 24 March 1978

Great-great-grandchildren's great-great-grandchildren
2e *George Ledyard FOWLER, Jr [27 Larchmont Dve, New Harford, NY 13413, USA], *b* 11 July 1950; *educ* Morrisville Sch; technician with Welton Motors 1971-82 and Clinton Auto Servs 1982-; *m* 12 June 1976 *Linda, dau of John Gelfuso and his w Maxine, and has issue:

Great-great-grandchildren's great-great-grandchildren's children
1f *Curt Ledyard FOWLER, *b* 5 March 1979
2f *Alan George FOWLER, *b* 11 March 1981

Great-great-grandchildren's children
2b *Horatio SEYMOUR, Jr, for whom *see above* against the preceding 2b

Great-great-grandchildren
3a A dau, *b* 23 Nov 1855; *d* in infancy
4a Alexander Bryan JOHNSON III, *b* 16 Sept 1860; *m* Louise Tilden White (*d* 1921) and *d* 1916, leaving issue:

Great-great-grandchildren's children
1b Louise Alexandra Adams Johnson, *b* Dec 1908; *m* 1931 *William Rankin DURYEE [3241 North Woodrow St, Arlington, VA 22207, USA], descended from Samuel Huntington (1731-96), Pres Continental Congress 1776, Signer of the Declaration of Independence and Govr Connecticut 1786, and *d* 30 Jan 1983, leaving issue:

Great-great-grandchildren's grandchildren
1c *Sanford Huntington DURYEE [Apt E248 1952 Ormond Blvd, Destrehan, LA 70047, USA], *b* Washington, DC, 10 Aug 1950; *educ* Prince George's Coll and U of Maryland; operator Goddard Space Flight Computer 1972-75, systems engr Singer-Link 1980-86, simulation engr MSI Industs; *m* Oxon Hill, Md., 15 April 1969 (divorce 22 Dec 1975) Janet Louise, dau of James Milton Brown and his w Margaret Chase, and has issue:

Great-great-grandchildren's great-grandchildren
1d *Margot Katharine Duryee, *b* Washington, DC, 2 Aug 1971; *m* New Hampshire 23 Jan 1993 *Scott Timothy SMITH, of Milford, New Hampshire

Great-great-grandchildren's children
2b Alexander Bryan JOHNSON V, *b* New York 15 July 1911; *educ* Deerfield Acad and Yale; investment advisor with Cyrus J. Lawrence in New York; *m* 25 May 1934 *Henriette Louise [Mrs Alexander B Johnson, Vicar's Landing Box H-306, Ponte Vedra Beach, FL 32082, USA], dau of H. Thurston Huntting and his w Florence Allen, and *d* 24 Aug 1991, having had issue:

Great-great-grandchildren's grandchildren
1c *Alexander Bryan JOHNSON VI [4830 NE 43rd St, Seattle, WA 98105, USA], *b* New York 29 May 1938; *m* Duncan, British Columbia, Canada, 28 Jan 1967 *Daphne Sheila Stewart Williams and has issue:

Great-great-grandchildren's great-grandchildren
1d *Victoria Anne Johnson [Mrs Jeffry Pereverzoff, 236 Ranchland Court, Kelowna, BC, Canada VIV 183], *b* Seattle, Wash., 28 June 1968; *m* there 1 Aug 1992 *Jeffry PEREVERZOFF
2d *Adrienne Diane JOHNSON, *b* 14 Nov 1969

Great-great-grandchildren's grandchildren
2c Thurston Huntting JOHNSON, *b* Jan, *d* May 1945
3c *John Adams JOHNSON [16 Mead St, New Canaan, CT 06840, USA], *b* New York 26 April 1947

Great-great-grandchildren
5a Alice Gansevoort JOHNSON, *b* 8 Jan 1867; *d* 1919

Great-grandchildren
(3) Bryan JOHNSON, *b* Utica, New York, 30 April 1819; *d* New York 28 Oct 1837
(4) John Adams JOHNSON, *b* Utica 28 Feb 1821; *d* there 12 Sept 1839
(5) William Clarkson JOHNSON, *b* Utica 16 Aug 1823; *m* 1st 1 Nov 1847 Henrietta Maria, dau of —— Douw, of Albany, New York, and had issue:

Great-great-grandchildren
1a Alexander Bryan JOHNSON, *b* 1848; *m* 18— Mary Knight Brown and *d* Windsor Hotel, New York, 1899 in a fire

Great-grandchildren
(5) (cont.) William C. Johnson *m* 2nd 30 June 1853 his 2nd cousin Mary Louisa (*b* 2 Dec 1828; *d* 16 July 1859), er dau of John Adams II and his w Mary Catherine Hellen (for whom *see* under President JOHN QUINCY ADAMS), and with her had issue:

Great-great-grandchildren
2a Mary Adams Johnson, *b* 1854; *m* 1875 Charles Andrew DOOLITTLE, of Utica, New York, and *d* 1920, having had issue:

Great-great-grandchildren's children
1b Julia Tyler Sherman Adams Doolittle, *b* Utica 22 Nov 1876; *m* Dr John Nelson TEETER and *d* 10 June 1903
2b William Clarkson Johnson DOOLITTLE, *b* Utica 16 April 1879; *m* there 1st 17 June 1902 Amelia Lowery (*b* Utica 4 Aug 1879; *d* there 16 Oct 1922) and had issue:

Great-great-grandchildren's grandchildren
1c *William Clarkson Johnson DOOLITTLE, Jr, *b* Utica 24 July 1903; *m* 1st 192- (divorce 1935) Gladys Louise Hamblin and has issue:

Great-great-grandchildren's great-grandchildren
1d *William Clarkson Johnson DOOLITTLE III, *b* Utica 22 Sept 1930; *m* 1st 15 May 1951 (divorce 195-) Frances Louise Council; *m* 2nd 1 June 1955 (divorce 1967) Elaine Nadine Moye, and with her has issue:

Great-great-grandchildren's great-great-grandchildren
1e *Gary Raymond DOOLITTLE, *b* Reno, Nev., 22 April 1956
2e *William Joseph DOOLITTLE, *b* 20 Feb 1958; *m* 4 Dec 1978 *Julia Woodfield
3e *Georgia Patricia Doolittle, *b* 6 Jan 1959; *m* 26 Nov 1977 *Mark JOHNSON and has issue:

Great-great-grandchildren's great-great-grandchildren's children
1f *Ryan Michael JOHNSON, *b* 13 May 1978

Great-great-grandchildren's great-great-grandchildren
4e *Julie Ann DOOLITTLE, *b* 31 Jan 1960
5e *Donald Patrick DOOLITTLE, *b* 20 Aug 1961
6e *Colleen Marie DOOLITTLE, *b* 6 Oct 1963

Great-great-grandchildren's great-grandchildren
1d (cont.) William C. Doolittle III *m* 3rd 10 April 1977 *Lena Fox
2d *Judith Adams Doolittle, *b* Los Angeles 23 Nov 1933; *m* 2 Feb 1954 *Jerry Albert PLANTE and has issue:

Great-great-grandchildren's great-great-grandchildren
1e *Michael Thomas PLANTE, *b* 11 Oct 1954; *m* 20 March 1972 *Barbara Louise Clancy and has issue:

Great-great-grandchildren's great-great-grandchildren's children
1f *Dustin Michael PLANTE, *b* 20 Aug 1972
2f *Michael Thomas PLANTE, *b* 29 Dec 1974
3f *William Edward Joseph PLANTE, *b* 2 July 1976

Great-great-grandchildren's great-great-grandchildren
2e *Laurence William PLANTE, *b* 30 Oct 1955
3e *Erik Charles PLANTE, *b* 13 Oct 1956; *m* 6 July 1978 *Toby Lynn Weinstein and has issue:

Great-great-grandchildren's great-great-grandchildren's children
1f *Harry Jason PLANTE, *b* 14 Nov 1979

Great-great-grandchildren's great-great-grandchildren
4e *Anthony PLANTE, *b* 21 Sept 1967

Great-great-grandchildren's grandchildren
1c (cont.) William C. Doolittle, Jr, *m* 2nd 9 April 1947 *Dorothea Justine Claessens
2c *Julia Tyler Sherman Doolittle, *b* Utica 25 Sept 1904; *m* 4 Oct 1924 Henry Bradley OGDEN (*b* New Hartford, New York, 15 Aug 1896; *d* Utica 15 May 1951) and has issue:

Great-great-grandchildren's great-grandchildren
1d *Amelia Lowery Ogden, *b* Utica 21 Aug 1925; *m* there 16 Aug 1947 *Stanley Mason BABSON (*b* Orange, New Jersey, 13 July 1925) and has issue:

Great-great-grandchildren's great-great-grandchildren
1e *Bradley Ogden BABSON, *b* Orange 15 Feb 1950; *m* Hingham, Mass., 4 Aug 1972 *Katharine Partridge Earle
2e *Mary Darby BABSON, *b* Orange 6 May 1951
3e *James Gorham BABSON, *b* Orange Jan 1957

Great-great-grandchildren's great-grandchildren
2d *Elizabeth Clark Ogden, *b* Utica 14 Nov 1927; *m* 25 Sept 1948 (divorce 1972) Richard Jarvis BROWN (*b* 25 May 1925) and has issue:

Great-great-grandchildren's great-great-grandchildren
1e *Elizabeth Gale BROWN, *b* Utica 9 March 1950
2e *Cynthia Allen Brown, *b* Utica 28 Nov 1951; *m* New Hartford, New York, 23 Sept 1972 *Donald MAJOR and has issue:

Great-great-grandchildren's great-great-grandchildren's children
1f *Tonia Kirstin MAJOR, *b* New Hartford 25 Dec 1972

Great-great-grandchildren's great-great-grandchildren
3e *Philip Henry BROWN, *b* Utica 30 March 1954
4e *Allison Ogden BROWN, *b* Utica 25 Feb 1958

Great-great-grandchildren's grandchildren
3c Marklove Lowery DOOLITTLE, *b* Utica 1 Sept, *d* there 6 Nov 1906
4c *Mary Adams Doolittle, *b* Utica 12 Nov 1909; *m* Valley Forge, Pa., 3 July 1933 *Aubrey Morgan EVANS (*b* Scranton, Pa., 13 May 1902) and with him has adopted two children:

a *Daniel Adams EVANS, *b* Boston 8 Oct 1935
b *Bradley Beattie EVANS, *b* Boston 18 Oct 1937; *m* Nutley, New Jersey, 3 Aug 1963 *Beatrice Conde Blackwell (*b* 6 Dec 1941) and has issue:

i *Kimberley Ann EVANS, *b* Nutley 26 March 1964
ii *John Blackwell EVANS, *b* Nutley 18 March 1966

Great-great-grandchildren's grandchildren
4c (cont.) Mr and Mrs Aubrey M Evans also have issue:

Great-great-grandchildren's great-grandchildren
1d *James Stewart EVANS, *b* St Louis, Mo., 14 Dec 1940
2d *Jenner Lowery EVANS, *b* Utica 30 Oct 1947

Great-great-grandchildren's grandchildren
5c *John Quincy Adams DOOLITTLE [Menands Road, Menands, Albany, NY 12204 or 12211, USA], *b* Utica 8 March 1911; *m* Albany, New York, 20 June 1936 *Mary-Arthur (*b* Albany 7 Feb 1916), dau of Hiland Garfield Batcheller and his w Jessie Jackson, great-niece of President ARTHUR, and has issue:

Great-great-grandchildren's great-grandchildren
1d *John Quincy Adams DOOLITTLE, Jr, *b* Albany 24 Jan 1938; *m* Montclair, New Jersey, 18 June 1966 *June Kathleen Dallery (*b* 6 Oct 1940) and has issue:

Great-great-grandchildren's great-great-grandchildren
1e *John Quincy Adams DOOLITTLE III, *b* Newport, Rhode Island, 29 Nov 1967
2e *Andrew Carleton DOOLITTLE, *b* Newport 26 Oct 1969
Mr and Mrs John Doolittle, Jr, also have an adopted dau:
a *Lauren Tamlen DOOLITTLE, *b* 8 June 1974

Great-great-grandchildren's great-grandchildren
2d *Mary-Arthur Doolittle, *b* Albany 13 May 1940; *m* there 15 June 1963 *John Wickersham BEEBE (*b* Albany 29 March 1937) and has issue:

Great-great-grandchildren's great-great-grandchildren
1e *Jean Louise BEEBE, b Albany 28 Feb 1966
2e *Mary-Arthur BEEBE, b Albany 7 April 1968

Great-great-grandchildren's great-grandchildren
3d *Hiland Garfield Batcheller DOOLITTLE [31 Upper Loudon Rd, Loudonville, NY, USA], b Albany 25 June 1945; m there 2 Aug 1969 *Judith Ruth Anderson (b Waterford, New York, 20 Feb 1946) and has issue:

Great-great-grandchildren's great-great-grandchildren
1e *Judith Ashley DOOLITTLE, b Albany 9 June 1974
2e *Hiland Garfield Batcheller DOOLITTLE, Jr, b Albany 13 Oct 1975
3e *Abigail Adams DOOLITTLE, b Albany 29 Aug 1979

Great-great-grandchildren's great-grandchildren
4d *Peter Lowery DOOLITTLE, b Albany 8 April 1949; m there 29 June 1974 *Susan Rose Kolodny (b Albany 27 Dec 1949) and has issue:

Great-great-grandchildren's great-great-grandchildren
1e *Jason Lowery DOOLITTLE, b Albany 12 Jan 1979

Great-great-grandchildren's children
2b (cont.) William C. Doolittle m 2nd New York 23 Oct 1923 Georgette (b Kansas City, Mo., 8 Dec 1904; m 2nd Asheville, N Carolina, Aug 1970 Edward K. Parmelee; d 6 July 1971), dau of George A. Leiter, and d Utica 26 Aug 1967, having with her had issue:

Great-great-grandchildren's grandchildren
6c *James Carrington Leiter DOOLITTLE [Route 28, Barneveld, NY 13304, USA], b Utica 13 Sept 1925; m 1st Menlo Park, Calif., 1948 (divorce 19—) Lois Hawley (who m 2nd James Wilson) and has issue:

Great-great-grandchildren's great-grandchildren
1d *Graham WILSON, b 194- or 195-; changed name from Doolittle when adopted by step-father James Wilson

Great-great-grandchildren's grandchildren
6c (cont.) James C. Doolittle m 2nd Barneveld, New York, 20 June 1953 *Susan Rockwell Bray (b Utica 14 Aug 1933) and with her has issue:

Great-great-grandchildren's great-grandchildren
2d *William Johnson Hitchcock DOOLITTLE [RD2, Barneveld, NY, USA], b Utica 17 Nov 1953
3d *Edward Kimball Cowles DOOLITTLE, b Utica 3 April 1955; m Carmel, New York, 5 Aug 1978 *Susan Louise Andres (b Mount Kisco, New York, 31 Aug 1955)
4d *Abigail Adams Doolittle, b Utica 8 March 1956; m Barneveld 29 March 1980 *Robert Grant RUHLMAN (b Euclid, Ohio, 19 April 1956)
5d *Katharine Leiter DOOLITTLE, b Utica 7 Sept 1960
6d *James Carrington Leiter DOOLITTLE, Jr, b New Hartford, New York, 6 Oct 1964

Great-great-grandchildren's grandchildren
7c *George Leiter DOOLITTLE [RD2 Box 257, Holland Patent, NY 13354, USA], b Utica 13 April 1934; educ U of Virginia (BA); V-Pres Marine Midland Bank 1977-; m 1st Charlottesville, Va., 4 Feb 1956 (divorce 1964) Susan Faulkner Johnson and has issue:

Great-great-grandchildren's great-grandchildren
1d *Thomas Cary Johnson DOOLITTLE [Rt1 Box 137, Mason, WI 54856, USA], b Augusta, Ga., 9 Nov 1958; m 19— —— (divorce 19—) and has issue:

Great-great-grandchildren's great-great-grandchildren
1e *Britton Sonia Leiter DOOLITTLE, b 1 March 1981
2e *Keenan Bayard DOOLITTLE, b 24 March 1985

Great-great-grandchildren's great-grandchildren
2d *Jane Leiter Doolitle [Mrs John Brouilette, PO Box 501, New Hartford, NY 13413, USA], b Utica 29 Nov 1962; m 6 July 1991 *John BROUILLETTE

Great-great-grandchildren's grandchildren
7c (cont.) George L. Doolittle m 2nd Clinton, New York, 5 March 1966 *Alaric Marshall Bray Burke (b Utica 29 June 1938), dau of Edward K. Parmelee and his w Bertha Hitchcock, and with her has issue:

Great-great-grandchildren's great-grandchildren
3d *George Andrew Leiter DOOLITTLE [Apt 401 1240 N Rolfe, Arlington, VA 22209, USA], b New Hartford, New York, 5 Nov 1967; educ George Washington U (MA)
Mr George Leiter Doolittle has also adopted his step-daus:
a *Heather Ann Burke [Mrs James P Hanna, 10373 Ridge Crest Rd, Utica, NY 13502, USA], b Evanston, Ill., 28 Dec 1961; m 10 Aug 1985 *James P. HANNA and has issue:

    i *Baily Ann HANNA, *b* 10 June 1991
    ii *Lydia Marie HANNA, *b* 28 Sept 1992

b *Elizabeth Hitchcock Burke [Mrs Ronald Davies, Rt 28 Barneveld, NY 13304, USA], *b* Asheville, N Carolina, 24 May 1963; *m* 20 Sept 1986 *Ronald DAVIES and has issue:

    i *Jason Christopher DAVIES, *b* 4 Oct 1987

Great-great-grandchildren's children
3b Charles Andrew DOOLITTLE, Jr, *b* Utica 31 Dec 1881; *m* Eleanor Shotter (*d* 29 June 1965) and *d* New York 19 Oct 1935, having had issue:

  Great-great-grandchildren's grandchildren
  1c Peter DOOLITTLE; *d* in infancy
  2c *Eleanor Doolittle; *m* Waldo Cory Melrose JOHNSTON and has issue

Great-great-grandchildren's children
4b John Quincy Adams DOOLITTLE, *b* Utica 7 Feb 1884; *k* on golf course there 28 June 1900 by lightning
5b Ebenezer Brown Sherman DOOLITTLE, *b* Utica 24 Sept 1889; *m* 19— Alice Watson Lowery (*b* Utica 20 July 1891; *d* Boston 11 Feb 1961) and *d* Washington, DC, 9 April 1944, leaving issue:

  Great-great-grandchildren's grandchildren
  1c *Alice Parkinson Doolittle, *b* 26 June 1925; *m* 19— *Henry BROOKS and has issue:

    Great-great-grandchildren's great-grandchildren
    1d *Alice Shearman BROOKS, *b* 19—
    2d *Woody BROOKS, *b* 19—

  Great-great-grandchildren's grandchildren
  2c *Lois Andrews Doolittle, *b* Boston 12 March 1928; *m* 19— *J. Carter INCHES and has issue:

    Great-great-grandchildren's great-grandchildren
    1d *David INCHES, *b* 27 Nov 1961.
    2d *Louisa Adams INCHES, *b* 7 Nov 1962

Great-great-grandchildren
3a Louisa Catherine Adams Johnson, *b* Washington, DC, 29 March 1856; *m* 18— Erskine CLEMENT, of Boston, and *d* 1948, having had issue:

  Great-great-grandchildren's children
  1b Mary Louisa Adams CLEMENT, *b* 18—; *d* 23 Sept 1950
  2b Clarence Erskine CLEMENT, *b* 1884; *m* 19— Bianca, formerly w of —— Harrington and dau of —— Cogswell, and *d* 1927, leaving issue:

    Great-great-grandchildren's grandchildren
    1c *Louisa Catherine Adams Clement [Mrs Harry Hull, Uplands, Highland Avenue, Manchester, MA 01944, USA], *b* 1922; *m* 19 Aug 1943 *Rear-Adml Harry HULL, Jr, USN (ret) (*b* Athens, Ga., 18 Jan 1912), s of Harry Hull and his w Ann Spann Burnett, and has issue:

      Great-great-grandchildren's great-grandchildren
      1d *Lt Harry HULL III, USN, *b* 4 March 1945; *m* 19—
      2d *Kimball Erskine Clement HULL, *b* 28 Nov 1947
      3d *Louisa Catherine Adams HULL, *b* 10 Nov 1952

Great-great-grandchildren
4a John Quincy Adams JOHNSON, *b* Washington, DC, 12 Feb 1859; *m* 1st 1884 Caroline (*b* 1862; *d* 1932), dau of —— Curtiss, of Yonkers, New York, and had issue:

  Great-great-grandchildren's children
  1b William Curtiss JOHNSON, *b* 1884; *m* 1920 Jessie, dau of —— Farrington, of Yonkers, and *d* Point Pleasant, New Jersey, 17 April 1940
  2b John Quincy Adams JOHNSON, Jr, *b* Yonkers 1887; *m* 1913 Marian, dau of —— Thomas, of Dayton, Ohio, and *d* Yonkers 8 Dec 1953, leaving issue:

    Great-great-grandchildren's grandchildren
    1c *Winters Adams JOHNSON, *b* 1914; *m* 1948 *Evelyn Walsh and has issue:

      Great-great-grandchildren's great-grandchildren
      1d *Eric Winters JOHNSON, *b* 1951

    Great-great-grandchildren's grandchildren
    2c *John Quincy Adams JOHNSON III, *b* 1917; *m* 1944 *Helen Brady and has issue:

      Great-great-grandchildren's great-grandchildren
      1d *Sherry Ann JOHNSON, *b* 1945

2d *John Quincy Adams JOHNSON IV, *b* 1949
3d *Allen Curtiss JOHNSON, *b* 1951

Great-great-grandchildren's grandchildren
3c *Marjorie Adams JOHNSON, *b* 1919

Great-great-grandchildren's children
3b Alexander Bryan JOHNSON IV, *b* 8 Aug 1890; *m* 1st 1915 (divorce 1934) Corinne, dau of ——— Carver, of Yonkers, and had issue:

Great-great-grandchildren's grandchildren
1c *Nancy Corinne Johnson, *b* 1916; *m* 1936 *Frank QUIRK and has issue:

Great-great-grandchildren's great-grandchildren
1d *Dana QUIRK, *b* 1938
2d *Kathleen QUIRK, *b* 1945

Great-great-grandchildren's grandchildren
2c *Alexander Bryan JOHNSON VI, *b* 1918; *m* 1st 1940 (divorce 1942) Flavia Ellen Bensing; *m* 2nd 1942 (divorce 1946) Eleanor Wagner and with her has issue:

Great-great-grandchildren's great-grandchildren
1d *Alexander Bryan JOHNSON VII, *b* 1944

Great-great-grandchildren's grandchildren
2c (cont.) Alexander B. Johnson VI *m* 3rd 1951 *Alese Psenicki and with her has issue:

Great-great-grandchildren's great-grandchildren
2d *Wendy Alese JOHNSON, *b* 1952

Great-great-grandchildren's grandchildren
3c *Audrey Curtiss Johnson, *b* 1922; *m* 1944 *Robert Stolte BAILEY and has issue:

Great-great-grandchildren's great-grandchildren
1d *David BAILEY, *b* 1945
2d *Barbara BAILEY, *b* 1949

Great-great-grandchildren's children
3b (cont.) Alexander B. Johnson IV *m* 2nd 1934 *Helen Moore Earle and *d* 19——, leaving further issue:

Great-great-grandchildren's grandchildren
4c *Alexandra Adams JOHNSON, *b* 1936

Great-great-grandchildren's children
4b Caroline Curtiss JOHNSON, *b* 1893; *d* 1920
5b *Charles Adams JOHNSON, Jr, *b* 1896; *m* 1926 *Katharyn, dau of ——— Starr, of Woodbury, New Jersey, and has had issue:

Great-great-grandchildren's grandchildren
1c *Charles Adams JOHNSON III, *b* 1927; *m* 1952 *Lida Forsythe Wilson and has issue:

Great-great-grandchildren's great-grandchildren
1d *Cynthia Starr JOHNSON, *b* 1953

Great-great-grandchildren's grandchildren
2c Lewis Starr JOHNSON, *b* 1929; *d* 1949

Great-great-grandchildren's children
6b *Abigail Adams Johnson, *b* 1902; *m* 1944 *Bradley KELLY
7b *Mary Louisa Adams Johnson, *b* 1903; *m* 1934, as his 2nd w, *Henry J. DIETRICH, former husband of her twin sister Martha
8b Martha Johnson, *b* 1903; *m* 1927, as his 1st w, *Henry J. DIETRICH and *d* 1933, leaving issue:

Great-great-grandchildren's grandchildren
1c *Henry Curtiss DIETRICH, *b* 1928; *m* 1950 *Betty Jane Anderson and has issue:

Great-great-grandchildren's great-grandchildren
1d *Arthur Curtiss DIETRICH, *b* 1950
2d *Jane Kirsten DIETRICH, *b* 1953

Great-great-grandchildren's grandchildren
2c *Robert Gregory DIETRICH, *b* 1930; *m* 1952 *Ann Rowling and has issue:

Great-great-grandchildren's great-grandchildren
1d *Martha Ann DIETRICH, *b* 1952
2d *Melinda Adams DIETRICH, *b* May 1954

Great-great-grandchildren

4a (cont.) John Q. Johnson *m* 2nd 1933 Caroline (*b* 1859; *d* 1950), dau of —— Sutherland, of Washington, DC, and *d* 9 April 1938

Great-grandchildren

(5) (cont.) William C. Johnson *m* 3rd 30 July 1860 Mary Cornelia Nicholson and *d* New York 28 Jan 1893, having with her had issue:

Great-great-grandchildren

5a Abigail Adams Johnson, *b* Newbury, Mass., 1861; *m* there 1889 Milton Strong THOMPSON (*b* 1855; *d* 1933) and *d* Newbury, Mass., Feb 1947, having had issue:

Great-great-grandchildren's children

1b Sarah Elizabeth THOMPSON, *b* Newbury, Mass., 1890; *d* Connecticut 1973
2b Gardiner THOMPSON, *b* Newbury 1892; served World War I and *ka* France 1918
3b Alexander Bryan THOMPSON, *b* Newbury 1896; *d* there 1900
4b *Milton Strong THOMPSON, Jr, *b* Newbury 1901; *m* 19— *Elizabeth, widow of —— May
5b Abigail Adams Thompson, *b* Newbury 1903; *m* there 1932 Joseph Whitmore KNAPP (*b* 1887; *d* 19—) and *d* 9 Nov 1951

Great-great-grandchildren

6a Elizabeth Lispenard Johnson, *b* Newbury 1865; *m* 1st 1887 Walter Bell PHISTER, of Maysville, Ky. (*b* 1858; *d* Newbury 1912), s of Charles Phister and his w Margaret, and had issue:

Great-great-grandchildren's children

1b Mary Cornelia Phister, *b* Newbury 1888; *m* 1916 Dr Dana Winslow Atchley (*b* 1892; *d* Englewood, New Jersey, 27 June 1982), s of William A. Atchley and his w Florence Ames, and *d* Englewood 4 May 1982, leaving issue:

Great-great-grandchildren's grandchildren

1c *Dana Winslow ATCHLEY, Jr [Granville Road, Lincoln, MA 01773, USA], *b* New York 27 Oct 1917; *m* 1st 26 Aug 1939 (divorce 1953) Barbara Welch and has issue:

Great-great-grandchildren's great-grandchildren

1d *Dana Winslow ATCHLEY III, *b* 1941
2d *Mary Babcock ATCHLEY, *b* 1942
3d *Elizabeth Ross ATCHLEY, *b* 1946
4d *Sarah Ross ATCHLEY, *b* 19—

Great-great-grandchildren's grandchildren

1c (cont.) Dana W. Atchley, Jr, *m* 2nd 1 May 1954 *Barbara Payne and by her has issue:

Great-great-grandchildren's great-grandchildren

5d *Marion Woodward ATCHLEY, *b* 4 May 1955
6d Abigail Adams ATCHLEY, *b* 19—; *d* 19—
7d *Cornelia Phister ATCHLEY, *b* 19—
8d *Katherine Saltonstall ATCHLEY, *b* 19—

Great-great-grandchildren's grandchildren

2c *Dr John Adams ATCHLEY [961 Main St, West Newbury, MA 01985, USA], *b* Baltimore 30 May 1920; *m* 27 Sept 1942 *Martha Welch and has issue:

Great-great-grandchildren's great-grandchildren

1d *Susan ATCHLEY, *b* 1944
2d *John Adams ATCHLEY, Jr, *b* 1947
3d *Peter Ross ATCHLEY, *b* 1949

Great-great-grandchildren's grandchildren

3c *Dr William Ames ATCHLEY [1721 Mar West, Tiburon, CA 94920, USA], *b* New York 1922; *m* 1st Cleveland, Ohio, 14 April 1945 (divorce 1955) Anstis Manton, dau of Russell Burwell, of Cleveland, and his w Aubrey, and has had issue:

Great-great-grandchildren's great-grandchildren

1d *Mark Ames ATCHLEY, *b* New York 14 Jan 1948
2d Anthony Burwell ATCHLEY, *b* and *d* 1950

Great-great-grandchildren's grandchildren

3c (cont.) Dr William A. Atchley *m* 2nd Carmel, Calif., 23 Oct 1955 (divorce 29 Nov 1973) Margaret Feiring, dau of Jesse Feiring Williams and his w Gertrude, and with her has issue:

Great-great-grandchildren's great-grandchildren

3d *William Ames ATCHLEY, Jr, *b* San Francisco 22 April 1958

Great-great-grandchildren's grandchildren

3c (cont.) Dr William A. Atchley *m* 3rd 1974 (divorce 1980), as her 3rd husb, Sandol Milliken, dau of Carlos Stoddard and his w Caroline, and previously w of —— Warburg and —— Dollard; *m* 4th Tiburon, Calif., 9 Aug 1981, as her 2nd husb, *Anna Elisabeth, dau of Karl Georg Vischer and his w Catherina Elizabeth Heringa and previously w of —— Pesl

Great-great-grandchildren's children

2b Lispenard Bache PHISTER, *b* Chicago 1896; *d* 24 Nov 1985

Great-great-grandchildren

6a (cont.) Elizabeth Johnson Phister *m* 2nd 1916 Spencer Gobel LANE, of Manila, the Philippines (*b* 1865; *d* 1922), and *d* San Francisco 23 Aug 1948

Great-grandchildren

(6) Charles Adams JOHNSON, *b* 1825

(7) Sarah Adams Johnson, *b* Utica, New York, 27 April 1827; *m* 28 April 1848 James Stoughton LYNCH (*b* 18—; *d* Utica 3 April 1889) and had issue:

Great-great-grandchildren

1a Abigail Louisa Johnson LYNCH, *b* 31 March 1850; *d* 1932

2a Johnson LYNCH, *b* 21 Nov 1852; *d* in infancy

3a Johnson Livingston LYNCH, *b* 1 April 1854; *d* 3 Oct 1883

4a Sarah Leah Lynch, *b* 7 June 1856; *m* 7 July 1878 Wilbur H. BOOTH and *d* 15 Feb 1882

5a Anne Margaret LYNCH, *b* 6 Feb 1858; *d* 1942

6a Catherine Gertrude LYNCH, *b* 27 Jan 1861; *d* 1942

7a Frances LYNCH *b* 8 Aug 1863; *d* in infancy

8a James DePeyster LYNCH, *b* 17 May 1868; *m* 20 June 1898 Julia Henrietta Wright and *d* April 1917, having had issue:

Great-great-grandchildren's children

1b James DePeyster LYNCH, Jr, *b* 17 June 1899; *d* in infancy

2b Andrew Green LYNCH, *b* Utica, New York, 3 Oct 1902; *educ* Harvard; US Ambassador to Somalia 1960-62; *m* *Jean Adele Bidwell and *d* Barneveld, New York, 25 Jan 1966

3b Leah LYNCH, *b* 4 March 1906; *d* 4 July 1924

4b *Bryan Johnson LYNCH [Reading, VT 05062, USA], *b* 24 Oct 1907; *m* 23 Feb 1935 *Alicia Maria Calvo and has issue:

Great-great-grandchildren's grandchildren

1c *James Stoughton LYNCH, *b* 4 June 1938

Great-grandchildren

(8) Arthur Breese JOHNSON, *b* Utica 3 Dec 1829; *m* 12 May 1859 Eliza Stringham, dau of Justice Ward Hunt, and *d* 3 Nov 1883, leaving issue:

Great-great-grandchildren

1a Ward Hunt JOHNSON, *b* Utica 9 May 1864; *d* 18— or 19—

2a Mary Savage JOHNSON, *b* Utica 28 June 1866; *d* New Haven, Conn., Aug 1952

3a Laura Savage Johnson, *b* Utica 24 April 1870; *m* there 10 Oct 1901 Walter Hedden MORTON (*b* Springfield, Mass., 12 June 1869; *d* Cambridge, Mass., 2 Feb 1945), s of James Hodges Morton and his w Elizabeth Hall Ashmun, and *d* 26 Jan 1933, leaving issue:

Great-great-grandchildren's children

1b *George Ashmun MORTON [1122 Skycrest Dve Apt 6, Walnut Creek, CA 94595, USA], *b* New Hartford, New York, 24 March 1903; *educ* MIT (BS 1926, MS 1928, PhD 1932); electronic research physicist with David Sarnoff Research Center Princeton (RCA) 1933-68; *m* Boston 15 Sept 1934 *Lucy Mitchell (*b* Massena, New York, 29 Nov 1909), dau of Benjamin F. Groat and his w (Harriet) Grace Mitchell, and has issue:

Great-great-grandchildren's grandchildren

1c *Walter Groat MORTON [Harbor View, San Pedro, CA, USA], *b* Camden, New Jersey, 21 June 1935

2c *George Ashmun MORTON, Jr [787 West 14th St, San Pedro, CA 90731, USA], *b* Camden 22 July 1937; *m* 1979 *Donna Lea, dau of Joseph Green and his w Clara June Funkhouser, and has issue:

Great-great-grandchildren's great-grandchildren

1d *Heather Grace MORTON, *b* San Pedro, Calif., 13 March 1974

Great-great-grandchildren's grandchildren

3c *Grace Mitchell Morton [Mrs Raymond Solomonoff, 26 JFK St, Cambridge, MA 02138, USA], *b* Camden 1 July 1938; *m* 19— *Raymond SOLOMONOFF

4c *Lewis Hunt MORTON [42 Walden Park Rd, Woking, Surrey, UK], *b* Princeton, New Jersey, 3 July 1944

Great-great-grandchildren's children

2b *Eliza Stringham Morton [Mrs James Borland, 135 Llewsac Lodge, 106 Billerica Rd, Bedford, MA 01730, USA], b New Hartford, New York, 15 March 1904; m Cambridge, Mass., 15 Oct 1932 James Post BORLAND (b Oakland, New Jersey, 22 Feb 1900; d 16 June 1979), s of Charles R. Borland and his w Elizabeth Post, and has issue:

Great-great-grandchildren's grandchildren

1c *Elizabeth Morton Borland [Mrs Andrew Roderick, 1578 Virginia Street East, Charleston, WV 25311, USA], b Cambridge, Mass., 5 Jan 1939; educ Radcliffe; proprietor Roderick's Painting and Papering Service and financial manager women's health centre 1978-; m 1st Cambridge 17 June 1960 (divorce 1977) Gardner Murray STULTZ (b Boston 11 Oct 1937), s of Irving W. Stultz and his w Marjorie MacEachern, and has issue:

Great-great-grandchildren's great-grandchildren

1d *Laura Katherine Stultz, b Hartford, Conn., 6 April 1964; m Charleston, W. Va., 4 Dec 1992 *Juan Pablo CLAUDE

2d *Karen Elizabeth STULTZ, b Hartford 29 Dec 1966

3d *Janet Lynn STULTZ, b Charleston, W. Va., 24 Jan 1972

Great-great-grandchildren's grandchildren

1c (cont.) Mrs Elizabeth Stultz m 2nd 2 May 1977 *Andrew Valarius RODERICK (b Frederick, Md., 19 March 1923)

2c *Charles Randolph BORLAND [15 Woodland Ave, Glen Ridge, NJ 07028, USA], b 1 Nov 1940; m Dec 1963 *Prudence Mahala Price and has issue:

Great-great-grandchildren's great-grandchildren

1d *Gillian Beecher BORLAND, b Oct 1966

2d *Isabel Breese BORLAND, b 28 March 1969

3d *Mahala Carlock BORLAND, b 5 Feb 1972

Great-great-grandchildren's children

3b *Montgomery Hunt MORTON [PO Box 433F, Marathon, FL 33050, USA], b New Hartford, New York, 10 Dec 1905

Great-great-grandchildren

4a Montgomery Hunt JOHNSON, b 12 April 1872; m 3 Oct 1906 Frances Lillian Munger (b 15 Nov 1878; d 19—) and d 7 Feb 1952, leaving issue:

Great-great-grandchildren's children

1b *Montgomery Hunt JOHNSON, Jr [19002 Dodge Avenue, Santa Ana, CA 92705, USA], b 21 Nov 1907; m 6 April 1946 *Gwyneth Mary Johnson (b 13 Jan 1915) and has issue:

Great-great-grandchildren's grandchildren

1c *Sarah Langhorne JOHNSON, b 1 Jan 1947

2c *Gwyneth Mary Johnson, b 15 April 1948; m 26 Dec 1967 (divorce 1971) Costas LYMBERIS

Great-great-grandchildren's children

2b *Francis Munger JOHNSON, b 28 Oct 1908; m 30 April 1931 *Dorothy Elizabeth Ely

3b *Greig Adams JOHNSON, b 31 March 1911; m 1st 19— (divorce 194-) Marilyn Twite and has issue:

Great-great-grandchildren's grandchildren

1c *Greig Adams JOHNSON, Jr, b 7 Sept 1941; m 1965 *Christine Gonsalves and has issue:

Great-great-grandchildren's great-grandchildren

1d *Greig Adams JOHNSON III, b 25 Jan 1966

2d *Julie JOHNSON, b 21 Feb 1967

3d *Amy JOHNSON, b 6 Oct 1970

Great-great-grandchildren's children

3b (cont.) Greig A. Johnson m 2nd 1 July 1950 *Ann (b 4 Jan 1921), dau of —— Whitcomb and formerly w of ——, and with her has issue:

Great-great-grandchildren's grandchildren

2c *Mary Frances JOHNSON, b 21 Nov 1951

Greig A. Johnson has also adopted his step-s:

a *William JOHNSON, b 19—

Great-great-grandchildren

5a Louise Eliza JOHNSON, b 11 Nov 1873; d 8 June 1875

6a Leon Arthur JOHNSON, b 11 Nov 1877; d 23 Aug 1909

Great-grandchildren

(9) Louisa Ann Smith Johnson, b Utica, New York, 24 Nov 1832; m 19 April 1852 George Bolton ALLEY (b 22 March 1831; d 1883), s of Saul Alley, and d 29 Nov 1929, leaving issue:

Great-great-grandchildren
1a Alexander Bryan ALLEY, *b* 1853; *m* Mary Gibb (*d* 1937) and *d* 8 Sept 1926, leaving issue:

Great-great-grandchildren's children
1b John Gibb ALLEY; *m* Dec 1928 Frances Ziegler and *d* 19—

Great-great-grandchildren
2a William Shaw ALLEY; *m* Josephine Demarest and *d* 1911, leaving issue:

Great-great-grandchildren's children
1b *George Bolton ALLEY II; *m* and has issue:

Great-great-grandchildren's grandchildren
1c *William Shaw ALLEY; *m* 1956 *Mary Argyle Kent

Great-great-grandchildren's children
2b *William Shaw ALLEY, Jr

Great-great-grandchildren
3a Harriet Douw Alley, *b* 9 Aug 1856; *m* 19 Dec 1877 Thomas Parmellee WICKES (*b* 17 April 1853) and *d* 27 May 1899, leaving issue:

Great-great-grandchildren's children
1b Henry Parmellee WICKES, *b* 7 Dec 1878; *m* 21 Nov 1896 Ethel Catlin Kinney and had issue:

Great-great-grandchildren's grandchildren
1c *Bradford WICKES, *b* 1 Sept 1897

Great-great-grandchildren's children
2b Marie Louise WICKES, *b* 18 Dec 1881; *d* 19—

Great-great-grandchildren
4a Mary Alley, *b* 18—; *m* William Robert NEAL and *d* 26 Nov 1942, having had issue:

Great-great-grandchildren's children
1b Dorothy NEAL
2b Herbert NEAL, *b* 1884; *m* 19— Ann Peebles and *d* 7 Oct 1951, leaving issue:

Great-great-grandchildren's grandchildren
1c *Mary Ann NEAL, *b* 29 Oct 1942

Great-great-grandchildren
5a Abigail Louise Alley, *b* 1860; *m* Edward Martin TALBOT (*b* 1854; *d* 1927) and *d* Aug 1940, leaving issue:

Great-great-grandchildren's children
1b Abigail Adams Talbot, *b* New York 1884; *educ* Barnard; *m* 20 Feb 1905 Reuben HALLETT (*b* 1883; *d* 1944) and *d* Mattapoisett, Mass., 12 May 1952, leaving issue:

Great-great-grandchildren's grandchildren
1c *Priscilla Alden Hallett, *b* 20 Oct 1906; *m* 1930 *Ira R. HILLER II (*b* 15 Nov 1905) and has issue:

Great-great-grandchildren's great-grandchildren
1d *Priscilla Alden HILLER, *b* 11 Feb 1933
2d *Charles Mathew HILLER, *b* 21 April 1937
3d *Ira R. HILLER III, *b* 23 Sept 1940

Great-great-grandchildren's grandchildren
2c *Marion Marcus Hallett, *b* 1909; *m* 1933 *Edwin LOVEJOY and has issue:

Great-great-grandchildren's great-grandchildren
1d *Edward Clinton LOVEJOY, *b* 12 Feb 1936
2d *Stephen Frederick LOVEJOY, *b* 23 April 1941

Great-great-grandchildren's grandchildren
3c Reuben HALLETT, Jr, *b* 1912; *m* 26 Nov 1936 *Berenice Regula and *d* before 1952, leaving issue:

Great-great-grandchildren's great-grandchildren
1d *Noel HALLETT, *b* 8 Sept 1940
2d *Neil HALLETT, *b* 7 Jan 1942
3d *Ann Amory Jill HALLETT, *b* 12 Sept 1946

Great-great-grandchildren's grandchildren
4c *Abigail Adams Hallett, *b* 1914; *m* 1934 *Harold WARNER and has issue:

Great-great-grandchildren's great-grandchildren
1d *Alden Talbot WARNER, *b* 15 Jan 1935

2d *George Harold WARNER, *b* 27 Oct 1937
3d *Janet WARNER, *b* 18 Oct 1939
4d *Robert WARNER, *b* 13 Sept 1944
5d *Abigail Adams WARNER, *b* 25 Nov 1948
6d *Marianne WARNER, *b 1950*

Great-great-grandchildren's children
2b Edwina Charlotte Talbot, b 1888; m 19— Reginald D. TAYLOR and d 19—, having had issue:

Great-great-grandchildren's grandchildren
1c *Edwina Charlotte TAYLOR, b 1912
2c *Katherine Taylor, b 1914; m 19— *J. Pearce MANNING, Jr, s of J. Pearce Manning
3c *Reginald D. TAYLOR, Jr, b 1915; m 19— *Marion Reynolds and has issue:

Great-great-grandchildren's great-grandchildren
1d *Marion TAYLOR, b 1938
2d *Sandra TAYLOR, b 1947

Great-great-grandchildren's grandchildren
4c *Dorothy Quincy Taylor, b 1918; m 1941 *James Kenny McMAHON and has issue:

Great-great-grandchildren's great-grandchildren
1d *Barbara Vernon McMAHON, b 1942
2d *Martin William McMAHON, b 1943
3d *James Kenny McMAHON, Jr, b 1944
4d *Charles Reginald McMAHON, b 1946

Great-great-grandchildren's children
3b John Alden TALBOT, b 12 Aug 1890; m June 1919 Priscilla Peabody (b 29 Feb 1896; d Aug 1938) and d Nassau, the Bahamas, 25 Dec 1962, leaving issue:

Great-great-grandchildren's grandchildren
1c *John Alden TALBOT, Jr, b 30 March 1920; m 22 Feb 1952 *Patricia, dau of ——— Potter and formerly w of ——— Jessup, and has issue:

Great-great-grandchildren's great-grandchildren
1d *John Alden TALBOT III, b 22 Jan 1953
2d *Henry Adams TALBOT, b 12 Jan 1954

Great-great-grandchildren's children
4b *Adrian Bancker TALBOT, b 25 Jan 1896; m 1st 19— Jeanette Butler Strong (b 1905; d 1938) and has issue:

Great-great-grandchildren's grandchildren
1c *Virginia Wayne Talbot, b 15 Dec 1930; m 15 Aug 1953 *William Henry HARBAUGH (b 1920)
2c *Gail Adams Talbot, b 16 Aug 1932; m 1956 *Middleton ROSE, Jr, s of Middleton Rose

Great-great-grandchildren's children
4b (cont.) Adrian B. Talbot m 2nd 1938 or 1939 *Constance Burr (b 1915) and with her has issue:

Great-great-grandchildren's grandchildren
3c *Barbara TALBOT, b 16 March 1940
4c *Edward Richmond TALBOT, b 16 July 1943
5c *Deborah TALBOT, b 13 May 1945

Great-great-grandchildren
6a Georgina Alley, b 27 Oct 1862; m Edwin Cameron FFOULKES and d 18 Jan 1954

Great-grandchildren
(10) Frances Elizabeth Johnson, b Utica, New York, 7 Nov 1835; m 10 Sept 1856 Charles Platt WILLIAMS, of Boonville, New York (b 27 Nov 1829; d 26 Dec 1901), and d 22 Nov 1902, leaving issue:

Great-great-grandchildren
1a Sarah Adams Williams, b Forestport, New York, 17 April 1859; m Rouen, France, 1 Aug 1885 James Edgar BULL (b New Jersey Aug 1857; d New York 2 Oct 1923), s of Richard Harrison Bull and his w Mary Ann Scouten, and d New York 5 July 1955, having had issue:

Great-great-grandchildren's children
1b Marion Frances Bull, b New York 3 March 1888; m there 16 Oct 1912 Butler WHITING (b Larchmont, New York, 6 Oct 1882; d Deep River, Conn., 7 Jan 1948), s of Eliot Butler Whiting and his w Florence Daisy Day, and d Middletown, Conn., 29 Jan 1962, having had issue:

Great-great-grandchildren's grandchildren
1c Florence Day Whiting, b New York 27 April 1914; m New Rochelle, New York, 29 Jan 1938 *Adml John

Joseph HYLAND, Jr, USN (ret) [4946 Kolohala St, Honolulu, Hawaii 96816, USA] (*b* Philadelphia 1 Sept 1912), s of Capt John Joseph Hyland, USN, and his w Josephine Walker, and *d* Honolulu, Hawaii, 16 Feb 1990, having had issue:

Great-great-grandchildren's great-grandchildren
1d *Capt John Joseph HYLAND III, USN (ret) [1105 Priscilla Lane, Alexandria, VA 22308, USA], *b* San Diego, Calif., 20 Aug 1939; *educ* Kent Sch, US Naval Acad and Inst of Political Studies, Paris, France; *m* Westover Air Force Base, Mass., 1 Feb 1964 *Sandra Ann (*b* Bisbee, Ariz., 29 Nov 1942), dau of Thomas Philip Coleman and his w Ann Marie Barnett, and has issue:

Great-great-grandchildren's great-great-grandchildren
1e *John Joseph HYLAND IV [2448 Hawkwood Drive, Chino Hills, CA 91709, USA], *b* New London, Conn., 3 Oct 1965; *m* Calif. Feb 1990 *Monica Menotti and has issue:

Great-great-grandchildren's great-great-grandchildren's children
1f *Hanna Marie HYLAND, *b* Chino Hills 4 March 1992

Great-great-grandchildren's great-great-grandchildren
2e *Thomas Philip HYLAND, *b* Kittery, Maine, 19 Oct 1966
3e *Anne-Marie HYLAND, *b* Honolulu, Hawaii, 22 Nov 1968
4e *Martine Nalani HYLAND, *b* Kailua, Hawaii, 29 Sept 1975

Great-great-grandchildren's great-grandchildren
2d *Nancy Hyland [Mrs Thomas Arnold Jr, Box 682, Waverly, VA 23890, USA], *b* Washington, DC, 19 Aug 1944; *m* Washington, DC, 1966 *Thomas St John ARNOLD, Jr, s of Thomas St John Arnold and his w Betty Waddill Christian, and has issue:

Great-great-grandchildren's great-great-grandchildren
1e *Robert Watson ARNOLD, *b* Richmond, Va., 26 Dec 1969

Great-great-grandchildren's great-grandchildren
3d *Pamela Hyland [Mrs James Trenholme, 27 Pinewood Dve, Spencerport, NY 14559, USA], *b* 14 Feb 1947; *m* 1971 James Harvey TRENHOLME
4d *Whiting Walker HYLAND [649 Ululani Street, Kailua, HI 96734, USA], *b* Honolulu 28 April 1955; *m* Alton, Ill., 9 Feb 1991 *Rachel, dau of Charles L. Morgan and his w Joann

Great-great-grandchildren's grandchildren
2c *Sarah Adams Whiting [Mrs Robert Baylis, Box 667, Madison, CT 06443, USA], *b* New York 15 Aug 1915; *educ* Sarah Lawrence; *m* Pelham Manor, New York, 10 June 1938 *(James) Robert BAYLIS (*b* 13 July 1910), s of Albert Wilbur Baylis and his w Ellen Grubb Cleland, and has issue:

Great-great-grandchildren's great-grandchildren
1d *Butler Whiting BAYLIS [21 Key Largo Course, Corte Madera, CA 94925, USA], *b* St Augustine, Fla., 27 Sept 1944; *m* Towson, Md., 7 Aug 1971 *Elizabeth Jenkins (*b* Baltimore 22 Nov 1946), dau of Joseph Jenkins Mack and his w Elaine Hartt, and has issue:

Great-great-grandchildren's great-great-grandchildren
1e *Sarah Adams BAYLIS, *b* San Francisco 1 July 1976
2e *Katherine Harwood Mack BAYLIS, *b* San Francisco 1 May 1979

Great-great-grandchildren's great-grandchildren
2d *James Edgar BAYLIS [7 Packet Landing, Orleans, MA 02653, USA], *b* New Rochelle, New York, 17 Nov 1947; *m* Towson, Md., 7 Aug 1971 *Penelope Wakefield (*b* New York 16 Oct 1946), dau of William Whitson Crabb and his w Elizabeth Brown, and has issue:

Great-great-grandchildren's great-great-grandchildren
1e *Kristen Wakefield BAYLIS, *b* New York 31 March 1974
2e *Whitson Whiting BAYLIS, *b* Mt Kisco, New York, 22 Feb 1978

Great-great-grandchildren's great-grandchildren
3d *Linda Baylis [Mrs Robert P Zanes III, RR2 Box 299, Gooseneck Hill Rd, Canterbury, CT 06331, USA], *b* New Rochelle, New York, 2 March 1952; *m* Madison, Conn., 18 Sept 1976 *Richard Parker ZANES III (*b* 30 Aug 1951), s of Dr Robert P. Zanes and his w Edwina Atteridge

Great-great-grandchildren's grandchildren
3c *Edgar Bull WHITING, *b* New York 17 July 1917; *m* 1st Scarsdale, New York, 22 Aug 1953 Gladys Dils deCoppet (*b* Toledo, Ohio, 7 July 1911; *d* Boca Raton, Fla., 27 March 1990), dau of David Henry Dils and his w Cora Imo Jagua; *m* 2nd Clearfield, Pa., 30 April 1992 *Mary M. Waterworth
4c Butler WHITING, Jr, *b* 3 Aug 1921; *d* 23 Dec 1943

Great-great-grandchildren's children
2b Richard Harrison BULL, *b c* 1891; *d* in infancy

3b Priscilla Mullins Bull, *b* New York 28 April 1894; *m* there 7 Nov 1914 Leonard Jarvis WYETH IV (*b* New York 4 Aug 1890; *d* there 17 March 1968), s of Leonard Jarvis Wyeth III and his *w* Louisa Alley Hopkins, and *d* Sharon, Conn., 18 July 1981, having had issue:

Great-great-grandchildren's grandchildren
1c *Priscilla Mullins Wyeth [Mrs Arthur Gray, 152 Fontaine Drive, Tavernier, FL 33070, USA; The Chateau 2726 Pleasant Hill Rd, Pleasant Hill, CA 94523, USA], *b* New York 1 Oct 1916; *m* there 6 Nov 1940 *Arthur Zabriskie GRAY (*b* New York 30 May 1915), s of Arthur Romeyn Gray and his *w* Laura Ferguson, and has issue:

Great-great-grandchildren's great-grandchildren
1d *Priscilla Adams Gray, *b* New York 30 April 1941; *m* Armonk, New York, 2 April 1966 *C. David BAXTER, s of C. David Baxter and his *w* Constance, and has issue:

Great-great-grandchildren's great-great-grandchildren
1e *David Edward BAXTER, *b* Portland, Oreg., 22 Feb 1967
2e *Alexandra Wyeth BAXTER, *b* Portland 24 March 1969

Great-great-grandchildren's great-grandchildren
2d *Alexandra Romeyn Gray [Mrs Donald P Hines, 4861 Montevista Rd, Sarasota, FL, USA], *b* New York 19 Dec 1946; *m* Armonk, New York, 11 Nov 1967 *Donald Price HINES (*b* Dobbs Ferry, New York, 20 Sept 1934), s of Joseph B. Hines and his *w* Mary Price, and has issue:

Great-great-grandchildren's great-great-grandchildren
1e *Dana Wyeth HINES, *b* Mount Kisco, New York, 12 March 1971
2e *Marni Alexandra HINES, *b* Mount Kisco 1973

Great-great-grandchildren's great-grandchildren
3d *Leonora Ferguson Gray [Mrs Michael Smith, Rt 2 Box 468, Hendersonville, NC 28792, USA], *b* White Plains, New York, 2 Aug 1952; *m* Homestead Air Force Base, Fla., 26 May 1973 *Michael SMITH, s of Guy Smith and his *w* Ann, and has issue:

Great-great-grandchildren's great-great-grandchildren
1e *Dustin SMITH
2e *Jennifer SMITH
3e *Daniel SMITH

Great-great-grandchildren's grandchildren
2c *Leonard Jarvis WYETH V [Gander Run, 417 Salmon Kill Rd, PO Box 393, Lakeville, CT 06039, USA], *b* New York 9 Jan 1918; *m* Buenos Aires 18 Oct 1941 *Pamela Isabel (*b* Buenos Aires 26 Sept 1921), yr dau of Tyrrell Langley Evans (gs of Revd Tyrrell Evans and his *w* Elizabeth, gdau of Sir William Godfrey, 1st Bart (*see* BURKE'S PEERAGE & BARONETAGE)) and his *w* Elsie Canning (widow of Leonard Sworn), and has issue:

Great-great-grandchildren's great-grandchildren
1d *Pamela Isabel Wyeth, *b* Buenos Aires 9 July 1942; *m* 1st Dayton, Ohio, 6 July 1963 (divorce 1967) Dr Charles Klaus BAYER (*b* 4 June 1927), s of Hans Bayer, of Göttingen, Germany, and his *w* Charlotte; *m* 2nd Boston 5 July 1969 (divorce 197-) Charles B. MARGOLIS (*b* Boston 18 March 1944), s of Samuel O. Margolis, of Chelsea, Mass., and his *w* Marion
2d *Christina Langley Wyeth, *b* Dayton 12 March 1950; *m* New York 28 Feb 1977 (divorce 19——) Alexis Coster MANICE
3d *Leonard Jarvis WYETH VI, *b* Dayton 24 March 1953; *educ* Brooks Sch, Syracuse U (BA) and U of Virginia (MA); architect; *m* Cornwall, Conn., 30 June 1990 *Susan Edler (*b* Brooklyn 2 Nov 1956) and has issue:

Great-great-grandchildren's great-great-grandchildren
1e *Leonard Jarvis WYETH VII, *b* New Haven, Conn., 5 April 1991

Great-great-grandchildren
2a Frances Elizabeth WILLIAMS, *b* Forestport, New York *c* 1862; *d* young
3a Harriet Eaton Williams, *b* Forestport 2 March 1864; *m* 1st Rouen, France, 15 Jan 1889 James Ronald WATSON (*b* Rouen 13 May 1866; *d* London, UK, 18 May 1899) and had issue:

Great-great-grandchildren's children
1b Maud Emma WATSON, *b* London 22 Oct 1889; *d* Brighton, Sussex, UK, 25 June 1962

Great-great-grandchildren
3a (cont.) Harriet Williams Watson *m* 2nd London 22 Dec 1902 Herbert Charles Walter JONES (*d* London 23 Jan 1909) and *d* Shoreham, UK, 4 March 1942

President Adams's son
V Thomas Boylston ADAMS, *b* Penns Hill Farm, Braintree, Mass., 15 Sept 1772; *educ* Harvard; Ch Justice Massachusetts Supreme Court; *m* 1805 Ann Harrod (*b* 1774; *d* 1846) and *d* 13 March 1832, having had issue:

Grandchildren
1 Abigail Smith Adams, *b* 1806; *m* 1831 John ANGIER and *d* 1845
2 Elizabeth Coombs ADAMS, *b* 1808; *d* 1903
3 Thomas Boylston ADAMS, Jr, *b* 1809; Lt 2nd US Artillery; *d* 1837
4 Frances Foster ADAMS, *b* 1811; *d* 1812
5 Isaac Hull ADAMS, *b* 1813; *d* 1900
6 John Quincy ADAMS, *b* 1815; lost at sea 1854 when on voyage aboard USS *Albany*
7 Joseph Harrod ADAMS, *b* 1817; *d* aboard USS *Powhattan* 1853 during expedition commanded by Commodore Perry

MALE LINE ANCESTRY AND COLLATERAL DESCENDANTS

John ADAMS, of Barton St David, Somerset, mentioned in a muster roll (list of men performing military service) of 1539 as being among the billmen (soldiers whose chief weapon was a concave axe on a long wooden handle) whose duty it was to furnish harness, had a brother, Robert, of Butleigh, Somerset, who was a working farmer and who died between 8 April and 2 Aug 1557. John Adams had issue:

Henry ADAMS, of Barton St David, *b c* 1531; farmer; *m* 15— Rose? —— (*bur* Barton St David 20 Sept 1598) and *d* shortly before 12 Aug 1596, leaving issue:

John ADAMS, of Barton St David, *b c* 1555; *m c* 1576 Agnes (*bur* Barton St David 15 Jan 1615/16), possibly dau of John Stone and his w Agnes, and *d* on or before 22 March 1603/4, leaving issue (with an er s and two daus):

Henry ADAMS, *b* Barton St David 21 Jan 1583; emigrated to America 1638, settling at Braintree, Massachusetts; *m* Charlton Mackrell, Somerset, England, 19 Oct 1609, as her 1st husb, Edith (baptized Charlton Mackrell 29 May 1587; *m* 2nd *c* 1651 John Fussell, of Weymouth and Medfield, Mass; *d* 21 Jan 1672/73), dau of Henry Squire, of Charlton Mackrell and Kingweston, Somerset, and sister of (1) Ann Squire, who *m* Aquila Purchase and with him was ancestor of President FILLMORE, and (2) of Margaret Squire, who *m* John Shepard and with him was ancestor of President TAFT; Henry Adams *d* Braintree on or before 6 Oct 1646, leaving issue (with seven other s and one dau) a 7th s:

Joseph ADAMS, Sr, of Braintree, *b* Kingweston, Somerset, England, 9 Feb 1626; farmer and maltster; *m* Braintree 2 Nov 1650 Abigail (*b* Roxbury, Mass., Sept 1634; *d* Braintree 27 Aug 1692), dau of Gregory Baxter and his w Margaret Paddy, and *d* Braintree 6 Dec 1694, having had issue (with three yr s and five daus):

  I Joseph ADAMS, Jr, for whom *see below*
  II John ADAMS, of Boston, *b* 1661; *m* 16— or 17— and *d* 1702, having had at least one s:

    1 Samuel ADAMS; as a rich and politically active Bostonian was a member of the Caucus or Caulker's Club (said to be the origin of the term caucus used in American politics); *m* 17— Mary Fifield and *d* 17—, having had issue:

      (1) Hon Samuel ADAMS, *b* 1722; *educ* Harvard (AM 1743); maltster, political journalist, tax-collector 1756-64, Boston Rep to Lower House of Massachusetts Gen Court 1765-74 (clerk there from 1766), Delegate to Continental Congress 1774-81, Memb Massachusetts Constitutional Convention 1779-80, Memb Massachusetts Convention to ratify US Constitution 1788, Lt-Govr Massachusetts 1789-94 and Govr Massachusetts 1794-97; *m* and *d* Boston 2 Oct 1803, having had issue, his ggs, W. V. Wells, being author of *Life and Public Services of Samuel Adams*, 3 vols (1865)

Joseph Adams Sr's est s,
  Joseph ADAMS, Jr, *b* Braintree 24 Dec 1654; *m* 1st 1682 Mary (*b* 27 Aug 1662; *d* 14 June 1687), dau of Josiah Chapin, and had 2 daus; *m* 2nd *c* 1688 Hannah (*b* Braintree 22 June 1667; *d* there 24 Oct 1705), dau of John Bass and his w Ruth (dau of John Alden, who with his first w Priscilla Mullins sailed to America on the *Mayflower* 1620), and with her had five s and three daus; *m* 3rd *c* 1708 Elizabeth (*d* 13 Feb 1739), dau of Caleb Hobart, and *d* 12 Feb 1737. His 2nd s by his 2nd w:

John ADAMS, *b* Braintree 28 Jan/8 Feb 1690/91; cordwainer and farmer, served as deacon at the Puritan meeting house in Braintree; *m* 23 Nov 1734, as her 1st husb, Susanna (*b* Brookline, Mass., 5 March 1708/9; *m* 2nd John Hall; *d* Quincy (as Braintree had now been renamed) 17 April 1797), dau of Peter Boylston and his w Ann, dau of Benjamin White, and *d* Braintree 25 May 1761 of influenza during an epidemic, leaving issue:

  I JOHN ADAMS, 2nd PRESIDENT of the UNITED STATES of AMERICA
  II Capt Peter Boylston ADAMS, *b* Braintree 16 Oct 1738; Deputy Sheriff Braintree *c* 1761; *m* 1768 Mary Crosby and *d* 1823, having had one s and three daus. He has no living descendants
  III Capt Elihu ADAMS, of Randolph, Mass., *b* Braintree 29 May 1741; *m* 1765 Thankful White (*b* 1747) and *d* Boston 18 March 1776, leaving issue (with two er s, both of whom *m* and had issue):

President Adams's niece
1 Susanna Adams, *b* 1766; *m* Aaron HOBART and *d* 1826, having had (with at least one other s):

Great-nephew
(1) Aaron HOBART, *b* 1787; Judge and Memb Congress; *d* 1858

Great-great-great-great grandparents on the father's side

Henry Adams
c 1531-96
?Rose —
d 1598

John Adams
c 1555-1603/4

?John Stone
d 1597
?Agnes —
d c 1597

Agnes ?Stone
d 1615/6

Revd William Squire?
-*c* 1567?
— —

Henry Squire
b c 1563
— —

William Savil
— —

William Mullins
d p Feb 1620/1
Alice —
d 1620/1

Great-great-great-great grandparents on the mother's side

Henry Boylson/Boylston
d 1592
— —
d c 1592

Edward Boylston
see (a) J Q Adams tree
d 1625

Thomas Bastian/Baston
d c 1597
Sara Wright
c 1559/60-1607

Anne Bastian
see (b) J. Q Adams tree
c 1595-1621

Thomas Gardner
d 1638
— —
d 1658

Edward Cogswell
d c 1615/6
Alice —
d 1615/6

John Cogswell
c 1592-1669

Revd William Thompson
d 1623
Phyllis —
d 1608

Elizabeth Thompson
d 1676

John Hawke
— —

Adam Hawkes
c 1605-71/2

?Edward Brown
fl 1590/1-1612/3
?Jane Lide

Mrs Ann ?Brown/Hutchinson
1595-1669

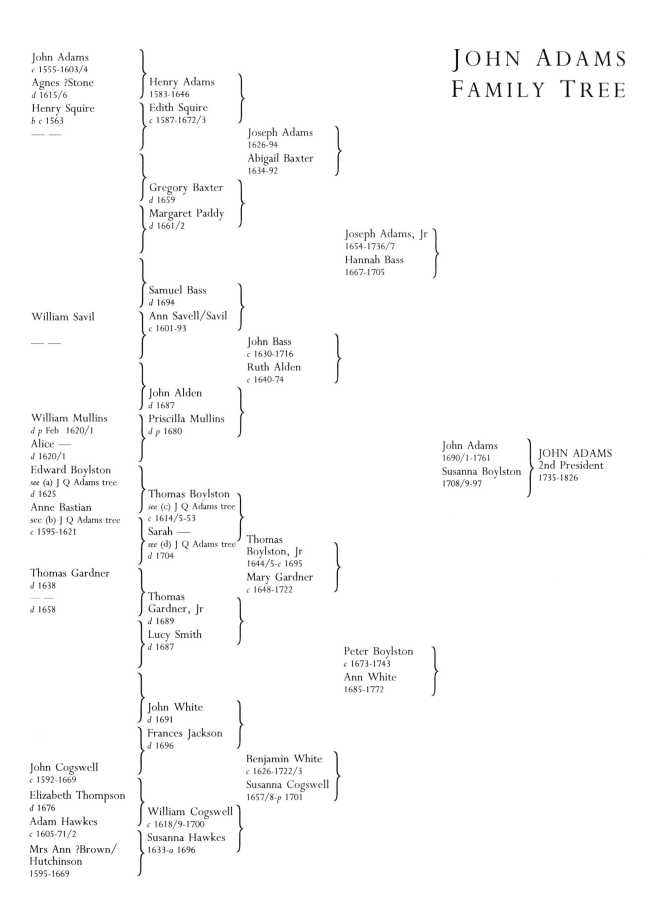

JOHN ADAMS
FAMILY TREE

John Adams
c 1555-1603/4
Agnes ?Stone
d 1615/6
Henry Squire
b c 1563
— —

Henry Adams
1583-1646
Edith Squire
c 1587-1672/3

Joseph Adams
1626-94
Abigail Baxter
1634-92

Gregory Baxter
d 1659
Margaret Paddy
d 1661/2

Joseph Adams, Jr
1654-1736/7
Hannah Bass
1667-1705

William Savil
— —

Samuel Bass
d 1694
Ann Savell/Savil
c 1601-93

John Bass
c 1630-1716
Ruth Alden
c 1640-74

John Alden
d 1687
Priscilla Mullins
d p 1680

William Mullins
d p Feb 1620/1
Alice —
d 1620/1
Edward Boylston
see (a) J Q Adams tree
d 1625
Anne Bastian
see (b) J Q Adams tree
c 1595-1621

Thomas Boylston
see (c) J Q Adams tree
c 1614/5-53
Sarah —
see (d) J Q Adams tree
d 1704

Thomas
Boylston, Jr
1644/5-*c* 1695
Mary Gardner
c 1648-1722

John Adams
1690/1-1761
Susanna Boylston
1708/9-97

JOHN ADAMS
2nd President
1735-1826

Thomas Gardner
d 1638
— —
d 1658

Thomas
Gardner, Jr
d 1689
Lucy Smith
d 1687

Peter Boylston
c 1673-1743
Ann White
1685-1772

John White
d 1691
Frances Jackson
d 1696

Benjamin White
c 1626-1722/3
Susanna Cogswell
1657/8-*p* 1701

John Cogswell
c 1592-1669
Elizabeth Thompson
d 1676
Adam Hawkes
c 1605-71/2
Mrs Ann ?Brown/
Hutchinson
1595-1669

William Cogswell
c 1618/9-1700
Susanna Hawkes
1633-*a* 1696

Plate 10   Thomas Jefferson

THOMAS JEFFERSON

1743-1826
3RD PRESIDENT OF THE UNITED STATES OF AMERICA
1801-09

Genius is easier to recognize than define, but no one would deny that Thomas Jefferson had it, alone of American Presidents. Whatever he attempted, he mastered, except the art of public oratory. Writer, architect, scientist, musician, inventor; in everything he showed outstanding ability, and more crucially, in everything had an individual touch. But his master-art was politics.

Like Washington, he was Virginian to the bone, and his political philosophy cannot be understood without reference to the society in which he grew up: a society of free speaking, self-governing gentleman farmers, who acknowledged many equals but no superiors. He came from the Virginia hill country (Washington was a son of the tidewater), where social rank was less settled than in the east, and where it was easy to rise in the social scale, from the yeomanry or even lower to the status of planter, with broad acres and public honour in proportion. Jefferson clung to this belief in social mobility all his life; it made him an egalitarian and a democrat, as well as a stout defender of liberty; and he was intellectually tortured by the inconsistency that this republican dream was only made possible, at any rate in Virginia, by the labour of African slaves. Washington had the robust and simple belief that slavery was an evil whose day was passing, and freed his slaves in his will. Jefferson was sure it was an evil, but he did not see how white and black Americans could live together in freedom (he was the exponent of a most unfortunate racial prejudice), he did not want to offend his fellow planters by leading a crusade for the abolition of slavery, and by the end of his life he was in such desperate financial straits that he was not able to free more than a handful of his own slaves; they really belonged to his creditors. In all this Jefferson incarnated the best and the worst of the South, and his inconsistencies, between liberty and slavery, between equality and racial prejudice, were precisely those which would eventually bring a civil war upon America.

But in his youth liberty was a simple matter of self-assertion against the oppressions of the King of England, and Jefferson first came to public notice by his brilliant pamphlet, *A Summary View of the Rights of British America* (1774). He sat in the Continental Congress and in 1776 was on the small committee appointed to draft the Declaration of Independence. The other members (among them Franklin and John Adams) left the work almost entirely to him; thus at the early age of 33 Jefferson won immortality as the author of the greatest public document in American history.

In the years that followed he was ceaselessly active both in public and in private, but the road that took him to the presidency may be said to have opened when he agreed to lead the party of anti-Hamiltonians (or Republicans, as they quickly came to call themselves) while he was Secretary of State. He came a close second to John Adams in the 1796 election and in 1801 he assumed the presidency, the first man to do so as the avowed head of a party, after a thoroughly partisan election.

Jefferson liked to think that his victory had saved America from some dreadful peril of monarchism or oligarchy — he called it 'the revolution of 1800' (conveniently forgetting the part played in his elevation by his arch-foe, Hamilton); but the really important thing about the election was that it showed that in America it was possible to change governments without violence. In an age which was witnessing the endless civil strife of revolutionary France this was an important achievement, as Jefferson explicitly recognized when, in his Inaugural Address, he emphasized all that Americans had in common; echoing many of the themes of Washington's Farewell Address, and declaring "We are all Republicans, we are all Federalists." Having beaten the enemy in fair fight, he made it his business to win them over by fair words. And during his first term in office he was amazingly successful.

The Adamses had camped out, so to speak, in the Executive Mansion (not yet the White House); Jefferson, though a widower, found it easy to play the affable host there. Every notability in Washington was regularly invited to dine, and what with the President's fine French wines and French cook, and enchanting conversation and delightful modesty, it is no wonder that almost everyone succumbed to his charm, particularly when contrasting the pleasures of such parties with the mud, noise and ramshackle boarding-houses of which most of the rest of Washington consisted. Jefferson was soon the complete master of Congress, and remained so till his retirement. He was less successful in winning control of the Supreme Court, though he tried hard enough; he engineered an unsuccessful impeachment of the Federalist Justice Samuel Chase, and in other matters was frustrated by Chief Justice Marshall (who by an irony was his distant cousin). He never had any trouble with the minuscule Federal bureaucracy.

Foreign affairs continued to dominate the scene, but they took a very lucky turn for Jefferson during his first term. Peace was made between France and all her enemies, and though it did not last long, it gave the United States a breathing space. Then, as war drew near again, the question of Louisiana arose and was settled with astonishing speed. Control of the Mississippi and of New Orleans was essential, in the long run, for the development of the West, but the United States could afford to wait while it was in the languid hands of Spain. Then word arrived that Napoleon had bullied the Spanish into ceding Louisiana to France. The idea of having such an active neighbour was appalling to the Americans; worse, if war broke out, the British would certainly attack Louisiana and probably conquer it, and the American drive westward might be checked for good. Jefferson sent James Monroe to Paris to see what might be done and Monroe discovered that Napoleon was willing to sell the whole of Louisiana to the United States for 60,000,000 francs. The Americans lost no time; the purchase was made; the way to the West was clear and Jefferson characteristically exploited the fact by sending out the celebrated Lewis and Clark expedition to explore the new domain. This expedition (led by his former secretary, Meriwether Lewis, and William Clark) had various aims, but Jefferson made sure that it was scientific as well as political, reporting on the flora and fauna of the West as well as on its economic possibilities.

Jefferson's second term was much less fortunate. He had to survive an embarrassing scandal, when his former Vice-President, Aaron Burr, who had shot Hamilton in a duel in 1804, seemed to be plotting to detach the Mississippi Valley from the Union; and the renewal of war between Britain and France brought with it all the old difficulties, only much intensified. American shipping was intercepted; American sailors were kidnapped (by both sides, but especially by the dominant British); endless provocation seemed to show that the United States was powerless. Jefferson had always been something of a pacifist; he had largely dismantled the strong navy that President Adams had been building up; now all he could propose was to halt trade with the outer world. He was following precedents of the American Revolution, only far more rigorously. In effect, America blockaded herself. This did nothing to intimidate the belligerents, but it wrecked the American economy, especially that of Virginia. Jefferson could set against this the bright light of the law forbidding the importation of slaves (1807), but it was not enough. In 1809, a few days before he left office, he admitted defeat by repealing the Embargo Act and substituting for it the less harsh Non-Intercourse Act.

He enjoyed his retirement at Monticello, except for the ceaseless financial difficulties that his lavish building there had brought upon him. He continued, discreetly, to play a part in the affairs of the

Republican party, which he had founded; enjoyed his celebrated correspondence with John Adams; laboured long and lovingly over the University of Virginia, which he founded, and for which he designed the buildings and chose the teachers; and never lost the eager intellectual curiosity which was, in the last analysis, his outstanding personal characteristic.

THOMAS JEFFERSON'S FAMILY

In old age Jefferson wrote a family memoir in which he recorded the belief among his father's family that they had originated in the Snowdon area of North Wales. He did not say he shared in the belief himself and he pointed out the relative rarity of the name Jefferson in Wales. Actually, he said, he could only go back with certainty to his paternal grandfather. The most thorough modern research has not managed much better — a single further generation back in the male line is all. One can therefore only record without comment that a man called Jefferson was among the burgesses who attended North America's first representative assembly of colonists at Jamestown in Virginia in 1619.

The male Jeffersons were new arrivals among the ruling class. Thomas Jefferson's father, Peter, a younger son and surveyor like George Washington, owned about 1,650 acres at Thomas's birth in 1743 (including a tract of 200 acres acquired from his wife Jane's first cousin William Randolph in return for a bowl of arrack punch, the American equivalent of the mess of pottage Esau traded his birthright with Jacob for). It was a respectable estate in European terms. But not all of it was cultivable and to begin with at any rate Peter was of yeoman stock rather than gentry, although hard-and-fast rulings about what class a man belonged to are particularly dangerous in America at this date, even in Virginia with a class structure similar to England's.

Peter acquired more land in his lifetime, however, ending with about 7,500 acres. He became a member of the Virginia House of Burgesses and one of Albemarle County's three Justices of the Peace as well as county surveyor and County Lieutenant, in charge of defending the frontier against Indians. This last position made him the chief military man at county level and was regarded as the most prestigious provincial honour obtainable. Both in official and political weight he had assumed the leadership of the county by the time of his death and in so doing had become one of the gentry.

With the distant origins of Thomas Jefferson's mother's family we are on surer ground. In marrying a Randolph, Peter did decidedly well, thereby following something of a Jefferson tradition whereby males married above themselves: Peter's grandfather, the first Thomas Jefferson we have definite knowledge of, had done much the same thing with Mary Branch in 1677. The Randolphs are one of the most 'aristocratic' of American families. Jane Jefferson's father Isham Randolph commemorated in his Christian name a descent from the Ishams of Northamptonshire in England. Their present head is Sir Ian Isham, 13th Bart, but Jefferson's Isham ancestors, some of whom were confidential men of business to more than one Plantagenet monarch in late-medieval England, stem from before the conferring of the baronetcy.

From the point of view of Thomas Jefferson's career as a revolutionary and statesman, a still more interesting family link, again through his mother, is with the Lilburnes, of the splendidly named Thickley Puncherdon in Co Durham in northern England. Throughout the period of the English Civil War in the mid-17th century few families had played a more important part. Thomas Lilburne, whose brother William was grandfather of Jane Rogers, herself grandmother of the 3rd President, was a staunch supporter of Cromwell, although in 1660, after Cromwell's death, he helped George Washington's kinsman-by-marriage Lord Fairfax pave the way for the Restoration. William and Thomas Lilburne's two cousins were even more prominent. Robert Lilburne, the elder, was one of the regicides who signed Charles I's death warrant. Later he opposed the scheme to make Cromwell king. His younger

Plate 11   Martha (Patsy) Jefferson Randolph,
Jefferson's daughter and hostess in the President's House

brother John was one of the most celebrated and effective political agitators of the day, persistently up before Parliament for sedition. He was a genuine promoter of civil liberties, though often with an eye to the main chance, whereas Parliament was more or less content to keep to itself the power won from the king. John Lilburne's cantankerousness apart, he and his near relations stood for a number of things Thomas Jefferson would have had no difficulty supporting a little over a century later. (In contrast, one of Thomas Jefferson's Randolph ancestors fought for Charles I at Edgehill in 1642.)

Jefferson in his memoirs is famous for saying of his mother's ancestry "They trace their pedigree far back in England and Scotland, to which let everyone ascribe the faith and merit he chooses." The words are usually assumed to mean he set small store by it himself. But the wording is ambiguous, and in the early 1770s he asked his agent in London to search the Heralds' College for any record of a grant of arms to his family. He had, he said, what he had been told were the family arms, though he was not sure how great the authority was for this statement. If it turned out that there had been no official grant, he continued, let the agent arrange to purchase one. Unfortunately under the regrettable system that has operated there any correspondence between an officer of the College of Arms and Jefferson's man of business would have become the personal property of the herald with the result that it has proved impossible to trace.

The apparent contradiction between radicalism and desire for a coat of arms is resolvable. The fact is, Jefferson was perfectly genuine in his hostility toward monarchy. But he did have a very considerable reverence for the institution of the family. Not only is there plenty of evidence for that in his addressing his daughter when he felt obliged to write down a defence of his religious beliefs, or his mortification when one of the ringleaders in a student revolt at his own foundation the University of Virginia — pet project of his life — turned out to be a nephew. It exists especially in his despair just before dying at having so little to leave his children and grandchildren. On the other hand he would not countenance nepotism. When President he wrote to his kinsman George Jefferson that the public would never believe any presidential appointment of a relative to a public office was made on merit alone, "uninfluenced by family views." He added "It is true . . . this places the relations of the President in a worse situation than if he were a stranger; but the public good . . . requires this sacrifice." As Rector of the University of Virginia he opposed the appointment of a nephew as professor, though the man was perfectly well-qualified for the post. Unexceptionable sentiments nowadays, but singular in the 19th century.

The Randolph connection benefitted Thomas Jefferson from an early date. When at college one of his three chief influences for good was Peyton Randolph, a relative on his mother's side. There were many marriages between Jeffersons and Randolphs over the next few generations. One of Jefferson's sisters married a man who was her first cousin through his Randolph mother. Jefferson's only surviving brother did the same thing. Jefferson's daughter Patsy also married a Randolph and his 700 or so living descendants through her — roughly half the total — therefore have additional Randolph blood. There were further cousinly marriages with Randolphs, at least two among the third generation, two among the fourth and five among the great-great-grandchildren. In addition there were several marriages among cousins which did not involve a Randolph infusion directly. Not only has Jefferson the greatest number of descendants of any president but they are as interbred as the Washingtons and much more so than the Roosevelts.

Jefferson married well himself, his wife's nett inheritance being about equal to his own patrimony. By 1774 he owned 5,000 acres and with the economic decline of the old landed gentry families of Virginia from mid-18th century on, which meant land could be bought cheaply, he was able as a successful lawyer to increase his existing holdings substantially. He doubled his acreage in his first seven years of professional practice and by 1809 his property included 10,000 acres and 200 slaves and was worth about $200,000. Yet by his death he was in financial difficulties, partly because of debts he had inherited from his father-in-law but not least because of his building activities and the way he neglected business for politics. Added to this was the amount of entertaining he undertook, sometimes providing for as many as 50 guests at table. He fed them with choice French cooking and fine European wines, moreover.

He was not alone among Virginia squires in seeing his wealth melt away in his own lifetime. In the opening session of the revolutionary Virginia assembly he completed the destruction of the old landed order by bringing in a bill to abolish entail, thus allowing estates to be divided among a landowner's offspring. His son-in-law Thomas Randolph proved to be one of the chief sufferers from this measure. Jefferson's own marriage was singularly happy. His wife's death in 1782 was very painful but it made him change his mind about accepting Congress's invitation to serve as a peace commissioner in Europe. The death in 1804 of his daughter Polly hit him hard too but it did at least start the long process of reconciliation with the Adamses, for Polly had stayed with them when a girl. Abigail Adams was readier to bury the hatchet than her husband, however, and only in 1811 did Jefferson make it up with John Adams.

Jefferson's son-in-law John Eppes was a member of Congress and chairman of the Finance Committee in 1813 when Madison's administration was undergoing an economic crisis. Jefferson wrote to Eppes at that time giving general financial advice. His favourite grandson Jefferson Randolph represented Albemarle County in the Virginia state legislature and in 1832 introduced a bill to bring about gradual emancipation of the slaves, despite Albemarle County's being one of the principal slave-holding regions of Virginia, itself the major slave state. The bill was debated but never put to a vote. It is of interest as perhaps the last time when southern slave-holders at an official level called in question the 'peculiar institution'. By 1816 Jefferson Randolph had taken on the entire financial responsibility for his grandfather's already embarrassed estate. Within 10 years he had had to sell off Jefferson's library to clear debts. He only saved Monticello by paying up $40,000 out of his own pocket.

Jefferson Randolph's brother James has the distinction of being the first child born in the White House. Another brother, George (1818-67), was the first military official to serve as Confederate Secretary of War and was allegedly the ablest. He was one of the first advocates of strict conscription in the South during the Civil War and among the most vigorous Confederate legislators in pushing through the measure. In the field he served as chief of artillery under Magruder. Tuberculosis ended his career prematurely.

Ellen Wayles Randolph, sister of Jefferson and George Randolph and a favourite granddaughter of Jefferson's, married in 1825 a member of the Coolidge family of Boston and since she had lost her writing desk at sea Jefferson sent her husband his, on which the Declaration of Independence had been composed. Ellen wrote some recollections of her grandfather which are valuable as counteracting a somewhat inaccurate picture drawn by Daniel Webster. Her niece Sarah N. Randolph, a girls' school headmistress, wrote *The Domestic Life of Thomas Jefferson* (1871), a compilation of family letters and reminiscences. It purports to give a verbatim account of the celebrated confrontation on the evening of 3 March 1801 between Levi Lincoln, Jefferson's incoming Attorney-General, and Judge Marshall, Adams's acting Secretary of State, in which Adams's attempt to commission a host of Adamsite judges in the dying hours of his administration was partially frustrated.

Other notable descendants of Thomas Jefferson divide broadly into soldiers, members of learned professions, diplomats and financiers, reflecting Jefferson's own multifarious skills (even finance, for despite his money worries in old age he did after all create the United States' currency). They include Jefferson Randolph Anderson (1861-1950), a great-great-great-grandson, who was both historian and Georgia state senator; General Jefferson Randolph Kean of the US Army Medical Corps (1860-1950), a great-great-grandson who served against the Sioux Indians and in the Spanish-American War and World War I; another great-great-grandson, Archibald Cary Coolidge (1866-1928), who served in US diplomatic missions in St Petersburg, Vienna and Paris and as a Red Cross negotiator with Soviet Russia in an attempt to alleviate famine there, who also as professor of history at Harvard wrote *The United States as a World Power* (1908), a classic of its kind and an important influence against American isolationism; and a great-grandson, Thomas Jefferson Coolidge (1831-1920), who was US Minister to France from 1892 to 1896, during which time his nephew Archibald acted as his private secretary, and a member of several commissions resolving international disputes. Savants include the research biologist Martha Jefferson Taylor Stedman (1910-87), great-granddaughter of Patsy Randolph, Jefferson's granddaughter; Robert Hill Kean (the above-mentioned General Kean's son), a noted chemical engineer; and Julian Lowell Coolidge, brother of the above-mentioned Archibald Coolidge and a Harvard professor of mathematics.

Lastly, it must not be thought that Jefferson's descendants married only among themselves. There were alliances with the British peerage and its collaterals, with descendants of the Indian princess Pocahontas, with connections of Presidents Madison and Jackson — even on two occasions with relatives of Paul Revere, whose legendary ride to warn of the coming of the British during the Revolutionary War became as famous for physical boldness as Jefferson was for the intellectual variety.

BIOGRAPHICAL DETAILS AND DESCENDANTS

JEFFERSON, THOMAS, *b* Shadwell, Goochland (later Albemarle) Co, Va., 13 April 1743 (2 April according to Julian Calendar); *educ* William and Mary Coll; JP and Vestryman Goochland Co 1764, admitted Virginia Bar 1767, Memb Virginia House of Burgesses for Albermarle Co 1769-75, County-Lt Albemarle Co 1775, Memb 1st Virginia Provincial Convention 1774 and 1775 (attended Virginia Assembly 1776 and 1781, memb ctee revising Virginia laws 1776), Chm Albemarle Co Ctee of Safety 1776, Govr Virginia 1779-81, Delegate to 2nd Continental Congress 1775-76 (Memb Ctee drafting Declaration of Independence 1776) and Congress 1781 and 1783 (Chm 1784), Congress's Commissioner to France 1784 (Minister to France 1785-89), 1st US Secretary of State (office which at that time had combined with it that of Post-Master Gen) 1790-93, 2nd V-Pres USA 1797-1801, 3rd President (Anti-Hamilton Republican) of the USA 1801-09, fndr first chair of law in America at William and Mary Coll 1779, fndr U of Virginia 1819 (Rector 1819), LLD Yale 1786, LLD Harvard 1788, Pres American Philosophical Soc 1797-1814, awarded gold medal of Soc of Agriculture at Paris for his improved model of plough 1807, foreign assoc of Soc of Agriculture at Paris 1807, author: *A Summary View of the Rights of British America* (1774), *Notes on the State of Virginia* (1785), *Kentucky Resolutions* (1798), *Manual of Parliamentary Practice* (1801), *An Essay Towards Facilitating Instruction in the Anglo-Saxon and Modern Dialects of the English Language* (1851); *m* The Forest, Charles City Co., Va., 1 Jan 1772, as her 2nd husb, Martha (*b* Charles City Co 19 Oct 1748; *m* 1st 20 Nov 1766 Bathurst Skelton (*b* June 1744; *d* 30 Sept 1768) and with him had issue one s, John Skelton, *b* 7 Nov 1767, *d* 10 June 1771; Mrs Thomas Jefferson *d* Monticello 6 Sept 1782, *bur* there); Mrs Thomas Jefferson was the only child by his 1st w of John Wayles (*m* 2nd ——— Cocke, with whom he had 1 dau, *d* young; *m* 3rd Jan 1760 Elizabeth Lomax, widow of Reuben Skelton, er bro of Bathurst Skelton, with whom he had three daus Elizabeth, Tabitha and Anne, and *d* 28 May 1773), of The Forest, Charles City Co, barrister, and his 1st w Martha Eppes, and *d* Monticello 4 July 1826, having had issue:

President Jefferson's daughter
I Martha (Patsy) Jefferson, *b* Monticello 27 Sept 1772; *m* there 23 Feb 1790 her cousin Thomas Mann RANDOLPH, Jr, of Edgehill, Albemarle Co (*b* Tuckahoe, Goochland Co, 17 May 1769; Govr Virginia 1819-22; *d* Monticello 20 June 1829, *bur* there), 2nd s of Col Thomas Mann Randolph, of Tuckahoe, and his 1st w Anne, dau of Archibald Cary, and *d* Edgehill 10 Oct 1836 (*bur* Monticello), having had issue:

Grandchildren
1 Anne (name chosen by her gf President JEFFERSON after her parents had asked him to select one) Cary Randolph, *b* Monticello 23 Jan 1791; *m* there 19 Sept 1808 Charles Lewis BANKHEAD (*b* 3 May 1788; *d* Albemarle Co 1835), s of Dr John Randolph Bankhead, of Caroline Co, Va., and his w Mary Warner Lewis, and *d* Monticello 11 Feb 1826 (*bur* there), leaving issue:

Great-grandchildren
(1) John Warner BANKHEAD, of Missouri, *b* Monticello 1 Dec 1809 or 1810; *m* 3 Nov 1832 Elizabeth Poindexter (*b* 9 March 1814; *d* Prairieville, Mo., 23 Dec 1895), dau of Archibald Christian and his w Fanny Warren, and *d* 21 Nov 1896, having had issue:

Great-great-grandchildren
1a Archer Christian BANKHEAD, *b* Va. 15 Sept 1833; *m* 10 June 1857 Mary Graves (*b* St Louis, Mo., 3 Sept 1840; *d* Pike Co, Mo., 2 April 1906), dau of Col A. B. Chambers, and *d* 14 Nov 1911, leaving issue:

Great-great-grandchildren's children
1b John Warren BANKHEAD, *b* Pike Co 25 Feb 1859; *m* there 4 Nov 1886 Selma Presca (*b* Ashburne, Mo., 12 May 1870; *d* Hannibal, Mo., 19 June 1956), dau of Charles William Purgahn and his w Pauline Waggoner, and *d* Pike Co 19 Oct 1916, leaving issue:

Great-great-grandchildren's grandchildren
1c Charles Archie BANKHEAD, *b* Pike Co 28 April 1887; *m* 1st St Louis 5 Jan 1909 Vera (*b* New Hartford, Mo., 17 Feb 1886; *d* New London, Mo., 5 May 1924), dau of Eli Hugh Rees and his w Mary Elizabeth Johnson, and left issue:

Great-great-grandchildren's great-grandchildren
1d Lowell Cary BANKHEAD, *b* Cyrene, Mo., 14 Oct 1909; *m* Hannibal, Mo., 30 Jan 1937 *Erma Lee [Box 38, Higbee, MO 65257, USA] (*b* Hannibal 4 Nov 1913), dau of Claude Green and his w Erma Lee Lillard, and *d* 11 May 1979, having had issue:

Great-great-grandchildren's great-great-grandchildren
1e Warren Lee BANKHEAD, *b* and *d* Hannibal 23 Feb 1943
2e *Lowell Cary BANKHEAD, Jr [PO Box 179, Jefferson City, MO 65102, USA], *b* Hannibal 14 Oct 1947; *m* Higbee, Mo., 15 Sept 1968 *Charla Marie (*b* 7 July 1950), dau of Charles J. Rockett, and has issue:

Great-great-grandchildren's great-great-grandchildren's children
1f *Lowell Cary BANKHEAD III, *b* Adana, Turkey, 15 Sept 1972
2f *Chanda Rose Lee BANKHEAD, *b* Moberly, Mo., 30 April 1976

Great-great-grandchildren's great-grandchildren
2d *Audrey Louise Bankhead [Mrs Joseph E Howard, 2735 W Las Encinas Rd, Santa Barbara, CA 93105, USA], *b* Cyrene, Mo., 16 May 1913; *m* Hannibal 21 April 1935 *Joseph Eugene HOWARD (*b* Hannibal 8 July 1912), s of Orin William Howard and his w Nettie Rachel Rubison, and has issue:

Great-great-grandchildren's great-great-grandchildren
1e *Sharon Jo Ann Howard [Mrs Steven G Stockwell, 1723 Mission Ridge, Santa Barbara, CA 93103, USA], *b* Santa Barbara 31 Oct 1939; *m* Riverside, Calif., 14 July 1962 *Steven George STOCKWELL (*b* 1939), s of John F. Stockwell and his w Beatrice Gurlich, and has issue:

Great-great-grandchildren's great-great-grandchildren's children
1f *Todd Howard STOCKWELL [19 Latimer Rd, Santa Monica, CA 90402, USA], *b* Los Angeles 1 Jan 1966
2f *Charlton Howard STOCKWELL, *b* Los Angeles 29 May 1967

Great-great-grandchildren's great-great-grandchildren
2e *Kristen Audell Howard [Mrs David Druker, 157 10th St, Del Mar, CA 92014, USA], *b* Santa Monica 4 July 1947; *m* there 4 April 1971 *David Samuelson DRUKER (*b* St Paul, Minn.), s of Leonard Druker, and has issue:

Great-great-grandchildren's great-great-grandchildren's children
1f *Michael David DRUKER, *b* 8 Oct 1977
2f *Mara Bankhead DRUKER, *b* 22 May 1981

Great-great-grandchildren's great-grandchildren
3d *Iris Jean Bankhead [Mrs Wilford Caldwell, 777 North 15th Street, San Jose, CA 95112, USA], *b* Cyrene 5 May 1916; *educ* San Jose State U; *m* Macon, Mo., 14 March 1936 Wilford Cameron CALDWELL (*b* New London, Mo., 29 July 1914; *d* Hannibal, Mo., 29 June 1976), s of Greenville Caldwell and his w Dollie Flowerree Smith, and has had issue:

Great-great-grandchildren's great-great-grandchildren
1e Stanley Terrill CALDWELL, *b* Hannibal 1 April 1942; *d* San Jose 20 May 1958
2e *Randolph Cameron CALDWELL [1134 Rickenbacker Street, San Jose, CA 95128, USA], *b* Hannibal 23 Aug 1945; *educ* Lincoln High Sch and SJ State U; pest-control operator; *m* San Jose 10 March 1972, as her 2nd husb, *Roxanne Kay (*b* San Jose 1946), dau of Wilbur Garlick and his w Mildred Laviena Hershey, and has issue:

Great-great-grandchildren's great-great-grandchildren's children
1f *Terrill Cameron CALDWELL, *b* Mountain View, Calif., 27 Sept 1973
2f *Cary Randolph CALDWELL, *b* Mountain View 14 Feb 1977

Great-great-grandchildren's great-grandchildren
4d Selma Elizabeth Bankhead, *b* Cyrene 10 May 1918; *m* Ventura, Calif., 26 Nov 1938 *Richard Philip WEST [4280 Calle Real #6c, Santa Barbara, CA 93110, USA] (*b* Cicero, Ill., 14 Sept 1914), s of Maxwell Walter West and his w Gulborg Ruud, and *d* 5 Sept 1987, leaving issue:

Great-great-grandchildren's great-great-grandchildren
1e *Stephen Matthew WEST, *b* Santa Barbara 30 Oct 1939; *m* 1st Montecito, Calif., 1963 (divorce 1967) Lois Ione (*b* Detroit, Mich., 1939; *m* 2nd 19—— —— Grouda), dau of Walter Harold Kleiber, Jr, and his w Augusta Adams, and has issue:

Great-great-grandchildren's great-great-grandchildren's children
1f *Jeffrey Stephen GROUDA (*b* West but adopted by his stepfather, whose name he assumed), *b* Detroit May 1964

Great-great-grandchildren's great-great-grandchildren
1e (cont.) Stephen M. West *m* 2nd Roseville, Mich., 1968 *Linda (*b* Springfield, Tenn., 1942), dau of George Gregory and his w Lena, and has further issue:

Great-great-grandchildren's great-great-grandchildren's children
2f *Richard Austin WEST, *b* Alpena, Mich., 22 May 1971; *m* Traverse City, Mich., 23 June 1991 *Laura Brazee and has issue:

Great-great-grandchildren's great-great-grandchildren's grandchildren
1g *Rachael Nancy WEST, *b* 10 Dec 1991

Great-great-grandchildren's great-great-grandchildren's children
3f *Ruth Ann WEST, *b* Santa Barbara 23 June 1972

Great-great-grandchildren's great-great-grandchildren
2e *Penny Jeanne West, *b* Santa Barbara 11 March 1946; *m* 1st Santa Barbara 1966 (divorce 1967) Duane Raymond LAMOUREAUX (*b* Corona, Calif.), s of 'Frenchie' LaMoureaux and his w Viola Stratton; *m* 2nd Ventura, Calif., 1968 (divorce 1972) Erich Kurt HUTZLER (*b* Boston 1944), s of Albert Hutzler and his w Ruth Harpel, and has issue:

Great-great-grandchildren's great-great-grandchildren's children
1f *Megan Wayles HUTZLER, *b* Santa Barbara 20 Nov 1969

Great-great-grandchildren's grandchildren
1c (cont.) Charles A. Bankhead *m* 2nd 14 March 1928 Nora Belle Ogden and *d* 1 Jan 1976
2c John Warren BANKHEAD, Jr, *b* Cyrene, Mo., 23 Dec 1888; *m* 29 May 1909 Minnie Kirk and *d* Cyrene 28 Dec 1918, leaving issue:

Great-great-grandchildren's great-grandchildren
1d Robert Eugene BANKHEAD, *b* Cyrene 22 April 1913; *m* Hannibal, Mo., 2 July 1938 *Eva Lena James (*b* there 19—) and *d* there 28 April 1968, leaving issue:

Great-great-grandchildren's great-great-grandchildren
1e *Deanna Marlene Bankhead, *b* Hannibal 29 Nov 1942; *m* there 11 Nov 1961 *Kenneth Wayne TAYLOR and has issue:

Great-great-grandchildren's great-great-grandchildren's children
1f *Matthew Brent TAYLOR, *b* 20 June 1964
2f *James Kirk TAYLOR, *b* 6 Sept 1968

Great-great-grandchildren's great-grandchildren
2d *Pauline Bankhead [Mrs Paul Bramblett, 1845 Ninth Avenue, Yuma, AZ 85364, USA], *b* Cyrene 29 April 1918; *m* Hannibal 23 Oct 1937 *Paul Edward BRAMBLETT (*b* Frankford, Mo.) and has issue:

Great-great-grandchildren's great-great-grandchildren
1e *Sherrilee Bramblett, *b* Hannibal 10 Oct 1940; *m* 31 Aug 1968 *Del(bert) M. BERRY, of Detroit, and has issue:

Great-great-grandchildren's great-great-grandchildren's children
1f *Paul Edward BERRY, *b* San Diego, Calif., 20 July 1971
2f *Robert Lee BERRY, *b* Santa Monica, Calif., 6 Aug 1973

Great-great-grandchildren's grandchildren
3c Selma Pauline Bankhead, *b* Cyrene 29 Aug 1893; *m* Bowling Green, Mo., 8 Oct 1909 Ansel SANDERSON (*b* Edgewood, Mo., 31 Oct 1892; *d* Jonesboro, Ark., 7 June 1963), s of Samuel M. Sanderson and his w Cora Williams, and *d* Cyrene 24 Dec 1916, leaving issue:

Great-great-grandchildren's great-grandchildren
1d *Genevie Sanderson [Mrs Lewis Erickson, 3636 North Olive, Kansas City, MO 64116, USA], *b* Cyrene 5 Jan 1913; *m* Maywood, Mo., 9 Aug 1934 Lewis Olie ERICKSON (*b* Bowling Green 21 Nov 1911; *d* 6 May 1993), s of Emil Erickson and his w Fannie Moore, and has issue:

Great-great-grandchildren's great-great-grandchildren
1e *Charles Ansel ERICKSON [4507 NE Carolane, Kansas City, MO 64116, USA], *b* Maryville, Mo., 8 Jan 1939; *m* 1st North Kansas City, Mo., 20 July 1960 (divorce 19—) Barbara Jean O'Connor; *m* 2nd North Kansas City 26 Dec 1964 *Kathryn Mae (*b* Valeo, Calif., 19 Jan 1944), dau of Henry Joseph Hoon and his w Mary Sanders, and with her has issue:

Great-great-grandchildren's great-great-grandchildren's children
1f *Kristina Marie Erickson [Mrs Dan P Davis, N2 Box 12, CNFJ, FPO, Seattle, WA 98762, USA], *b* Kansas City 2 Aug 1965; *m* 16 April 1988 *Dan Patrick DAVIS
2f *Karin Maria ERICKSON [4507 NE Carolane, Kansas City, MO 64116, USA], *b* Kansas City 10 Nov 1966

Great-great-grandchildren's great-great-grandchildren
2e *John Lewis ERICKSON [1046 Chippenham Dve, Baton Rouge, LA 70808, USA], *b* Smithville, Mo., 8 Nov 1942; *educ* U of Kansas; scout executive Boy Scouts of America, Baton Rouge; *m* Liberty, Mo., 6 June 1970 *Sarah Kathleen (*b* Kansas City 20 May 1945), dau of John P. Turner and his w Marjorie E. Anstrand, and has issue:

Great-great-grandchildren's great-great-grandchildren's children
1f *Thomas Jeffrey ERICKSON, *b* Kansas City 20 Sept 1973
2f *Michael John ERICKSON, *b* Kansas City 17 Oct 1976

Great-great-grandchildren's great-grandchildren
2d *Marjorie Sanderson [Mrs Clifford Orcutt, 1520 Kingston Road, Lincoln, NE 68506 USA], *b* Cyrene 18 Jan 1916; *m* Lawrence, Kans., 27 Oct 1945 *Clifford A. ORCUTT (*b* Seminole, Okla., 24 Sept 1920), s of Clifford O. Orcutt and his w Ina Charnick, and has issue:

Great-great-grandchildren's great-great-grandchildren
1e *Pamela Sue Orcutt [Mrs Edward Trehearn, 2200 S 37, Lincoln, NE 68506, USA], *b* Lincoln 8 June 1952; *m* there 28 Dec 1973 *Edward Lee TREHEARN (*b* Colorado Springs, Colo., 24 Jan 1952), s of Art Trehearn and his w Edna, and has issue:

Great-great-grandchildren's great-great-grandchildren's children
1f *Tamara TREHEARN, *b* 30 June 1984
2f *Clifford Allen TREHEARN, *b* 1 June 1988

Great-great-grandchildren's grandchildren
4c Jay Houchins BANKHEAD, *b* Pike County, Mo., 28 Oct 1899; *d* Louisiana, Mo., 17 Dec 1926
5c Mary Clara Bankhead, *b* Pike County 31 Oct 1901; *m* 1st St Louis, Mo., 19— Samuel OWENS; *m* 2nd 19— Edwin CONRAD and *d* 19 Sept 1945

Great-great-grandchildren's children
2b Thomas Randolph BANKHEAD, *b* 1863; *m* 1891 Elizabeth Haynie and *d* 1936, leaving issue:

Great-great-grandchildren's grandchildren
1c William Chambers BANKHEAD, *b* 1894; *m* 1914 *Agnes Temple (*b* 1898) and *d* 1956, leaving issue:

Great-great-grandchildren's great-grandchildren
1d Marie Elizabeth Bankhead, *b* 1923; *m* 1946 *Lloyd MILLER and *d* 1991, leaving issue:

Great-great-grandchildren's great-great-grandchildren
1e *Warren Randolph MILLER, *b* 1947
2e *Michael Reginald MILLER, *b* 29 June 1956; *m* 9 Aug 1980 *Valda Ray Shaw

Great-great-grandchildren's grandchildren
2c Thomas Jefferson BANKHEAD, *b* 1897; *m* 1920 *Blanche Kerr and *d* 1975, having had issue:

Great-great-grandchildren's great-grandchildren
1d Robert Wayne BANKHEAD, *b* 1925; *d* Louisiana, Mo., 1942

Great-great-grandchildren's grandchildren
3c Katherine Bankhead Bankhead, *b* 1901; *m* 1920 *Karl Emil ZUBER and *d* 3 Oct 1986, leaving issue:

Great-great-grandchildren's great-grandchildren
1d Frieda Bell Zuber, *b* 1925; *m* Prairieville, Mo., 1950 *Obed HALL, Jr [PO Box 31, Bowling Green, MO 63334, USA], and *d* 21 Dec 1990, leaving issue:

Great-great-grandchildren's great-great-grandchildren
1e *Jeannine Bankhead Hall [Mrs David M Osborn, 14 Lemp Rd, Kirkwood, MO 63122, USA], *b* 1953; *m* 12 Aug 1978 *David Martin OSBORN and has issue:

Great-great-grandchildren's great-great-grandchildren's children
1f *Kathrene Hall OSBORN, *b* 23 Sept 1982
2f *Sarah Bankhead OSBORN, *b* 7 July 1986

Great-great-grandchildren's great-great-grandchildren
2e *Karl Obed HALL [1609 Rathford Dve, St Louis; MO 63146, USA], *b* 4 July 1955; *m* 18 April 1987 *Terri Lee DePrender and has issue:

Great-great-grandchildren's great-great-grandchildren's children
1f *Kory Zuber HALL, *b* 9 Feb 1992

Great-great-grandchildren's children
3b Elizabeth Chambers Bankhead, *b* 1865; *m* 1886 William Everett BELL and *d* 12 June 1958, leaving issue:

Great-great-grandchildren's grandchildren
1c Mary Elizabeth Bell, *b* 3 Dec 1886; *m* 19— Horace Leonard HUTCHISON (*b* Bunceton, Mo., 1885; *d* Pueblo, Colo., 2 March 1952), s of Edward Chilton Hutchison and his w Lacy Anderson Mann, and *d* 29 Nov 1969 leaving issue:

Great-great-grandchildren's great-grandchildren
1d Lucy Elizabeth Hutchison, *b* 1912; *m* 1941 Frank HUMBEUTEL (*d* 1989) and *d* 1978
2d *(Horace) Leonard HUTCHISON, Jr [8 Little Drive, Lake Charles, LA 70605, USA], *b* Cassville, Mo., 9 Feb 1915; *m* Lake Charles 2 Nov 1946 *Alice Elizabeth (*b* Columbus, Miss., 10 Oct 1923), dau of Ira Clinton Dimmick, Sr, and his w Mary Ella Evans, and has issue:

Great-great-grandchildren's great-great-grandchildren
1e *Janet Elizabeth Hutchison [Mrs Robert Glenn Jr, 808 Cambridge, Round Rock, TX 78664, USA], *b* Lake Charles 1 Jan 1949; *m* there 12 June 1971 *Robert Carson GLENN, Jr (*b* Charleston, S Carolina, 22 Nov 1946), s of Robert Carson Glenn and his w Ethel Emeline McIver, and has issue:

Great-great-grandchildren's great-great-grandchildren's children
1f *Roger Christopher GLENN, *b* Harlingen, Tex., 14 Feb 1974
2f *Robin Casey GLENN (dau), *b* Round Rock, Tex., 19 May 1984

Great-great-grandchildren's great-great-grandchildren
2e *Revd Hal Thomas HUTCHISON [Rt1 PO Box 228 B, Hendersonville, NC 28792, USA], *b* Orange, Tex., 10 May 1950; *m* West Monroe, La., 2 Sept 1984 *Sandy Gail Curry Self and has three adopted s:

a *Roger Wayne HUTCHISON
b *Jeremy Michael HUTCHISON
c *Luke Thomas HUTCHISON

Great-great-grandchildren's great-great-grandchildren
3e *Mary Lynn Hutchison [Mrs Richard C Ogus, PO Box 313, Beaufort, NC 28516, USA], *b* Lake Charles 12 March 1954; *m* there 2 Dec 1989 *Richard Charles OGUS and has issue:

Great-great-grandchildren's great-great-grandchildren's children
1f *Rebecca Elizabeth OGUS, *b* 12 Nov 1991

Great-great-grandchildren's great-great-grandchildren
4e *Susan Frances HUTCHISON [124 29th Ave E, Seattle, WA 98112, USA], *b* Lake Charles 19 Oct 1957

Great-great-grandchildren's great-grandchildren
3d Everett Bell HUTCHISON, *b* Cassville, Mo., 4 May 1918; owner Hutchison Pest Control Co; *m* Raton, N. Mex., 15 May 1951 *Virginia Agnes [Mrs Everett *b* Hutchison, 3202 Northridge Dve, Pueblo, CO 81008, USA] (*b* Joliet, Ill., 8 Nov 1924), dau of Earl C. Casey and his w Elizabeth Agnes Kirkham, and *d* 5 Dec 1981, leaving issue:

Great-great-grandchildren's great-great-grandchildren
1e *Thomas Casey HUTCHISON [3068 Deliverance Drive, Colorado Springs, CO 80918, USA], *b* Pueblo 13 Aug 1952; *educ* U of Southern Colorado; *m* there 11 Oct 1972 *Mary Elizabeth (*b* Pueblo 22 May 1954), dau of Mearl Brooks and his w Annabelle, and has issue:

Great-great-grandchildren's great-great-grandchildren's children
1f *Keri Lee HUTCHISON, *b* Pueblo 11 Aug 1974
2f *Thomas Casey HUTCHISON, Jr, *b* Pueblo 26 Jan 1977

Great-great-grandchildren's great-great-grandchildren
2e *Holly Elizabeth Hutchison [Mrs Frank J Vigil, 2796 S Fenton St, Denver, CO 80227, USA], *b* Pueblo 4 Jan 1956; *educ* U of Southern Colorado; *m* Colorado Springs 29 July 1978 *Frank Joseph VIGIL, Jr (*b* Pueblo 8 Oct 1951), s of Frank Joseph Vigil, Sr, and his w Florene Claudia
3e *Patricia Anne Hutchison [Mrs Neil C Ramhorst, PO Box 4424, Bozeman, MT 59772-4424, USA], *b* Pueblo 24 July 1957; *educ* Colorado Mountain Coll; dispatcher Montana State U facilities serv 1990-; *m* Pueblo 4 Aug 1973 *Neil Charles RAMHORST (*b* Colorado Springs 12 Nov 1952), s of Cleo Willard Ramhorst and his w Myrtle M.
4e *Kenneth Todd HUTCHISON [4832 Baldwin Place, Boulder, CO, USA], *b* Pueblo 25 Feb 1962; *educ* Colorado Mountain Coll; *m* Spring Lake, Mich., 17 Oct 1987 *Tonya Lynn (*b* Benton Harbor, Mich., 12 Sept 1962), dau of Robert Emory Morrow and his w Karen Jeanne

Great-great-grandchildren's grandchildren
2c William Everett BELL III, *b* 1887; *m* 19— Alma Arnaldy and has issue:

Great-great-grandchildren's great-grandchildren
1d *William Everett BELL IV [4208 Cobblers Lane, Dallas, TX 75252, USA], *b* 1927; *m* 19— and has two daus

Great-great-grandchildren's grandchildren
3c Emily Carr Bell, *b* 25 Jan 1891; *m* 23 Nov 1910 Frank F. MARR (*b* 1888; *d* 1948) and *d* 2 June 1972, leaving issue:

Great-great-grandchildren's great-grandchildren
1d *William Lee MARR, *b* 3 Sept 1911; *m* 25 Sept 1931 *Thelma Morrison and has issue:

Great-great-grandchildren's great-great-grandchildren
1e *Nancy Lee Marr, *b* 4 Dec 1932; *m* 16 April 1952 *Richard Louis URBINA and has issue:

Great-great-grandchildren's great-great-grandchildren's children
1f *Laura Lee URBINA, *b* 26 April 1953
2f *William Nicholas URBINA, *b* 11 Jan 1955

Great-great-grandchildren's great-great-grandchildren
2e *John Randolph MARR, *b* 18 May 1938

Great-great-grandchildren's great-grandchildren
2d *Helen Elizabeth Marr [Mrs A Townsend, 225 East Plymouth, Long Beach, CA 90805, USA], *b* 24 Feb 1914; *m* 21 Nov 1943 *Arthur A. TOWNSEND and has issue:

Great-great-grandchildren's great-great-grandchildren
1e *John David TOWNSEND, *b* 6 May 1955; *m* 1st 21 May 1977 Raelynn Carol Pratt; *m* 2nd 21 Nov 1981 *Jane Cole Abbott

Great-great-grandchildren's grandchildren
4c Helen Catherine Bell, *b* Nelson, Mo., 2 April 1893; *m* Cassville, Mo., 14 May 1912 (Ulysus) Earl MITCHELL (*b* Iowa 10 July 1891; *d* St Louis, Mo., 1934), s of John Mitchell, and *d* Miami 26 Aug 1978, leaving issue:

Great-great-grandchildren's great-grandchildren
1d *(John) William (Bill) MITCHELL [26920 South West 157th Avenue, Homestead, FL 33031, USA], *b* Cassville, Mo., 1 June 1914; *m* Nashville, Tenn., 3 Dec 1943 *Margaret (*b* Quirigna, Guatemala, 18 May 1917), dau of Earl Ames and his w Marjorie, and has issue:

Great-great-grandchildren's great-great-grandchildren
1e *John William MITCHELL, Jr [15885 SW 272 Street, Homestead, FL 33031, USA], b Miami Beach 30 May 1944; m Homestead 22 March 1968 *Aletha Sue (b Homestead 20 Feb 1948), dau of Clinton James Bishop and his w Suzy Jane Leggett, and has issue:

Great-great-grandchildren's great-great-grandchildren's children
1f *John William MITCHELL III, b Coral Gables, Fla., 27 June 1972
2f *Amy Aletha MITCHELL, b South Miami 2 Feb 1977

Great-great-grandchildren's great-great-grandchildren
2e *Robert Ames MITCHELL [26920 SW 157th Avenue, Homestead, FL 33031, USA], b Miami Beach 16 Dec 1948; m Tallahassee, Fla., 30 Sept 1972 *Frances (b Jamestown, New York, 15 Sept 1950), dau of Dr John Lincoln and his w Martha

Great-great-grandchildren's great-grandchildren
2d *Leonard Bell MITCHELL [1301 SW 94 Court, Miami, FL 33100, USA], b Cassville, Mo., 30 Sept 1916; m 19— *Louise, dau of W. G. Quisenberry, and has issue:

Great-great-grandchildren's great-great-grandchildren
1e *Leonard Bell MITCHELL, Jr, b Shelbyville, Mo., 5 Sept 1945
2e *Earl Spencer MITCHELL, b Miami Beach 15 Oct 1946

Great-great-grandchildren's great-grandchildren
3d Betty Jane Mitchell, b St Louis, Mo., 10 Feb 1928; m Coral Gables, Fla., 23 Nov 1949 George SOLBERG (b Coral Gables 31 Aug 1928; d 9 May 1988), s of Harry Solberg and his w Bernice, and d 25 Sept 1981, leaving issue:

Great-great-grandchildren's great-great-grandchildren
1e *Robert M. SOLBERG [Route 2, 121 Hideaway Dve, Chapel Hill, NC 27514, USA], b Miami 26 April 1951; m Fayetteville, N Carolina, 22 Dec 1972 *Marion Patrice (b Va. 11 May 1951), dau of Marion Walker and his w Patricia, and has issue:

Great-great-grandchildren's great-great-grandchildren's children
1f *Jennifer Leigh SOLBERG, b 19 Aug 1976
2f *Michael Paul SOLBERG, b 7 Nov 1978
3f *Nathaniel James SOLBERG, b 2 Feb 1982

Great-great-grandchildren's great-great-grandchildren
2e *Janet Gail Solberg [Mrs Peter W Hampton, 1301 Galilean Trail, Chapel Hill, NC 27516, USA], b Coral Gables, Fla., 3 March 1954; m 28 June 1987 *Peter William HAMPTON and has issue:

Great-great-grandchildren's great-great-grandchildren's children
1f *Andrew Solberg HAMPTON, b 10 July 1988
2f *Sarah Elizabeth HAMPTON, b Durham, N Carolina, 31 Jan 1993

Great-great-grandchildren's grandchildren
5c *Robert Griffith BELL, Sr [1012 North Ocean Boulevard, Pompano Beach, FL 33062, USA], b Nelson, Mo., 8 March 1902; m 1st St Louis, Mo., 1931 Hortense (b St Louis 1906; d there Nov 1950), dau of Theo Lucks and his w Anna, and has issue:

Great-great-grandchildren's great-grandchildren
1d *Robert Griffith BELL, Jr [140E Reading Way, Winter Park, FL 32789, USA], b St Louis 26 May 1936; m 1st St Louis 7 May 1960 (divorce 19—) Donna Dorothy (b St Louis 1932), dau of William Dewitt and his w Margaret, and has issue:

Great-great-grandchildren's great-great-grandchildren
1e *William BELL, b 1961
2e *Robert BELL, b 1964

Great-great-grandchildren's great-grandchildren
1d (cont.) Robert G. Bell, Jr, m 2nd *Peggy Conway and has further issue:

Great-great-grandchildren's great-great-grandchildren
3e *Michael BELL, b 1970
4e *Matthew BELL, b 1972

Great-great-grandchildren's great-grandchildren
2d *Randolph Bankhead BELL [432 Seale Ave, Palo Alto, CA 94301, USA], b St Louis, Mo., 26 April 1945

Great-great-grandchildren's grandchildren
5c (cont.) Robert Griffith Bell, Sr, m 2nd 21 May 1952, as her 2nd husb, *Kathleen (b Marion, Kans., 10 April 1910), widow of —— Bair and dau of Albert H. Wheeler and his w Naomi Malone
6c Kenneth Cary BELL, b Nelson, Mo., 12 Aug 1904; m 3 July 1937 Martha Jane Brown (b Duluth, Minn., 3 April 1899; d Amarillo, Tex., 22 Aug 1983) and d Coral Gables, Fla., 25 Nov 1986, leaving issue:

Great-great-grandchildren's great-grandchildren
1d *Kenneth Cary BELL, Jr [5716 Berget Drive, Amarillo, TX 79106, USA], *b* Miami 5 Feb 1942; *educ* Kemper Mily Sch and Purdue U; Ch Exec Offr Bell Pest Control Inc 1970-; *m* 1st 6 June 1969 Bette Jon Fitzpatrick (*d* 1972); *m* 2nd 27 Nov 1976 *Sue Anne, dau of Edward K. Wiens and his w Grace Jane Roth, and has issue:

Great-great-grandchildren's great-great-grandchildren
1e *Cary Jane Anne BELL, *b* Amarillo 11 Feb 1978
2e *Kenneth Cary BELL III, *b* Amarillo 15 Jan 1981

Great-great-grandchildren's children
4b Benjamin Chambers BANKHEAD, *b* 1867; *m* Kate Smith (*b* 1865; *d* 1951) and *d* 1928
5b Archie Cary BANKHEAD, *b* 1874; *m* 1901 Grace Major and *d* 1921, leaving issue:

Great-great-grandchildren's grandchildren
1c Mary Clio BANKHEAD, *b* 1901; *d* 1984
2c Benjamin Nelson BANKHEAD, *b* 1907; *m* 19— Betty Varweek and *d* 1985, having had issue:

Great-great-grandchildren's great-grandchildren
1d Judith Ann BANKHEAD, *b* 1937; *d* 1942
2d *Mary Elizabeth BANKHEAD, *b* 1940
3d *Thomas Randolph BANKHEAD, *b* 1942
4d *Jeanne BANKHEAD, *b* 1945

Great-great-grandchildren
2a Dr Cary Randolph BANKHEAD, *b* 5 March 1835; *m* 1860 Amanda Ellen Errett (*b* 1839; *d* 1895) and *d* 12 March 1907, having had issue:

Great-great-grandchildren's children
1b Elizabeth BANKHEAD, *b* 27 Dec 1860; *d* 5 June 1863
2b Martha BANKHEAD, *b* 20 Nov 1862; *d* 28 Oct 1930
3b Dr Joseph Errett BANKHEAD, *b* 21 Sept 1864; *m* 1st 18— Laura Hughes (*d* 1900); *m* 2nd 19— Elizabeth Cake and *d* Dec 1941, having with her had issue:

Great-great-grandchildren's grandchildren
1c Ellen Cary Bankhead, *b* 12 Feb 1905; *m* 1st 19— Robert Benton MACKEY and had issue:

Great-great-grandchildren's great-grandchildren
1d *Joseph Benton MACKEY [2994 North Penstemon Court, Wichita, KS 67226, USA], *b* 1928; *m* 1949 *Jean Smith and has issue:

Great-great-grandchildren's great-great-grandchildren
1e *Joellen MACKEY, *b* 20 June 1952

Great-great-grandchildren's great-grandchildren
2d *Betsy Cake MACKEY [9530 Parklane, St Louis, MO 63124, USA], *b* 1934

Great-great-grandchildren's grandchildren
1c (cont.) Ellen Bankhead Mackey *m* 2nd *William B. WEAKLEY and *d* 25 Jan 1977

Great-great-grandchildren's children
4b Mary Archer Bankhead, *b* 12 Feb 1867; *m* 1887 Mark Miller GILLUM (*d* 1950) and *d* 27 July 1944, having had issue:

Great-great-grandchildren's grandchildren
1c Cary Randolph Bankhead GILLUM, *b* 1889; *m* 19— Ruth Stark and *d* 1953, having had issue:

Great-great-grandchildren's great-grandchildren
1d *Mildred Gillum, *b* 1913; *m* 19— *Ross ELGIN
2d *Rachel Errett Gillum [Mrs Gordon Haskell, 664 37th Ave, Santa Cruz, CA 95062, USA], *b* 1917, *m* 1st 19— ——— FATHMAN and has issue:

Great-great-grandchildren's great-great-grandchildren
1e *Dr Charles Garrison FATHMAN [177 Grove Dve, Portola, CA 94025, USA], *b* 19—; *m* 19— *Ann Kohlmoos and has issue:

Great-great-grandchildren's great-great-grandchildren's children
1f *Christopher Erritt FATHMAN, *b* 15 April 1975
2f *Carrie Ann FATHMAN, *b* 29 July 1977
3f *John Warner FATHMAN, *b* 1 March 1979

Great-great-grandchildren's great-great-grandchildren
2e *Dr Anthony E. FATHMAN [4967 Pershing Place, St Louis, MO 63108, USA], *b* 19—; *m* 19— *——— and has issue:

Great-great-grandchildren's great-great-grandchildren's children
1f *Elizabeth FATHMAN, b 19—
2f *Melissa G. FATHMAN, b 19—

Great-great-grandchildren's great-great-grandchildren
3e *Mary B. Fathman [Ms Mary B Thomas, 733 St Claire, Grosse Pointe, MI 48230, USA], b 19—; m 19— *—— THOMAS

Great-great-grandchildren's great-grandchildren
2d (cont.) Rachel Gillum Fathman m 2nd 19— *Gordon HASKELL

Great-great-grandchildren's grandchildren
2c Rachel Errett Gillum, b 1891; m 19— Clinton Talbert YATES and d 1917, leaving issue:

Great-great-grandchildren's great-grandchildren
1d Mark Milton YATES, b 8 Jan 1913; m 16 Oct 1937 Rose Cecilia Conrard (d 6 Nov 1988) and d 24 Nov 1969, leaving issue:

Great-great-grandchildren's great-great-grandchildren
1e *Kathryn Cecilia Yates [Mrs Joe H Walker, 2077 Pershing Rd, New London, WI 54961, USA], b 12 Jan 1939; m 1st 2 Feb 1957 Lalo A. SERRANO and has issue:

Great-great-grandchildren's great-great-grandchildren's children
1f *Michael Jesus SERRANO, b 29 March 1958; m 31 July 1976 (divorce 19—) Carmen Kay Bland and has issue:

Great-great-grandchildren's great-great-grandchildren's grandchildren
1g *Heather Michelle SERRANO, b 10 Jan 1978
2g *Candice Anne SERRANO, b 4 Aug 1980
3g *Christopher Michael SERRANO, b 4 Dec 1981

Great-great-grandchildren's great-great-grandchildren's children
2f *Rose Anne Serrano, b 26 April 1959; m 4 Oct 1980 *Thomas James RYFF and has issue:

Great-great-grandchildren's great-great-grandchildren's grandchildren
1g *Brandon James RYFF, b 29 April 1985
2g *Kristen Nichole RYFF, b 30 Sept 1988

Great-great-grandchildren's great-great-grandchildren's children
3f *Daniel Mark SERRANO, b 21 Dec 1962; m 17 July 1992 *Cynthia R. Thompson
4f *Anthony David SERRANO, b 12 Dec 1965; m 20 Aug 1988 (divorce 19—) Diana Lara and has issue:

Great-great-grandchildren's great-great-grandchildren's grandchildren
1g *Eric Anthony SERRANO, b 30 Jan 1989

Great-great-grandchildren's great-great-grandchildren's children
5f *Timothy Martin SERRANO, b 2 Nov 1966; m 23 Aug 1986 (divorce 19—) Monique Salcido and has issue:

Great-great-grandchildren's great-great-grandchildren's grandchildren
1g *Tiffany Loren SERRANO, b 14 Oct 1985
2g *Chantelle Rose SERRANO, b 4 July 1990

Great-great-grandchildren's great-great-grandchildren
1e (cont.) Kathryn Yates Serrano m 2nd 3 June 1983 *Joe Henry WALKER

Great-great-grandchildren's children
5b Dr Charles Lewis BANKHEAD, b 15 Nov 1869; m 1915 Margaret Cheatwood (d 1954) and d 29 Nov 1949, leaving issue:

Great-great-grandchildren's grandchildren
1c Charles Lewis BANKHEAD III, b 21 Jan 1925; m 1946 *Marion Clark Omohundro and d 19 Feb 1985, having had issue:

Great-great-grandchildren's great-grandchildren
1d *Michael Errett BANKHEAD [RR1 Box 23 A, Clarksville, MO 63336, USA], b 31 July 1947; m 16 Sept 1972 *Janet Elaine Lovell and has issue:

Great-great-grandchildren's great-great-grandchildren
1e *Shelley Marie BANKHEAD, b 28 July 1974
2e *Reid Hamilton BANKHEAD, b 22 June 1978

Great-great-grandchildren's great-grandchildren
2d *Margaret Elaine Bankhead [Mrs Benjamin F Jeans, 19 E 11th, Washington, MO 63090, USA], b Louisiana, Mo., 6 July 1949; educ Culver Stockton Coll; teacher; m 27 May 1972 *Benjamin Franklin JEANS, Jr, s of Benjamin Franklin Jeans and his w Genevieve Dreon, and has issue:

Great-great-grandchildren's great-great-grandchildren
1e *Matthew Seth JEANS, *b* Marshal, Mo., 29 April 1974
2e *Carey Elizabeth JEANS, *b* Marshall 11 Oct 1975

Great-great-grandchildren's great-grandchildren
3d *Mary Leigh Bankhead [Mrs Douglas M Burns, 2310 Plum Court, Pembroke Pines, FL 33026, USA], *b* Clarksville, Mo., 2 Aug 1954; *educ* South West Missouri State Coll; *m* 18 May 1974 *Dr Douglas Mackey BURNS, s of Mackey Douglas Burns and his w Betty Ann, and has issue:

Great-great-grandchildren's great-great-grandchildren
1e *Jessica Leigh BURNS, *b* Nashville, Tenn., 30 July 1980
2e *Jeffrey Douglas BURNS, *b* Cleveland, Ohio, 13 Dec 1983

Great-great-grandchildren's children
6b Ellen Cary Bankhead, *b* 26 Sept 1871; *m* 1892 Dr Clemence Griffith SMITH and *d* 29 April 1962, having had issue:

Great-great-grandchildren's grandchildren
1c Katheryn Smith, *b* 7 Sept 1893; *m* 1916 Willard MOYER and *d* 21 May 1957, leaving issue:

Great-great-grandchildren's great-grandchildren
1d *William Bankhead MOYER, *b* 1919; *m* 1944 *Atha Bell Peacock
2d *Anne Cary Moyer, *b* 1926; *m* 1st 1944 Billie WAERS and has issue:

Great-great-grandchildren's great-great-grandchildren
1e *Anne Randolph WAERS, *b* 27 Oct 1946
2e *David Moyer WAERS, *b* 12 May 1951
3e *Jeff WAERS, *b* 19—

Great-great-grandchildren's great-grandchildren
2d (cont.) Anne Moyer Waers *m* 2nd 19— *Bob DAVIS
3d *Jane Randolph Moyer [2540 Clairmont Dve Unit #107, San Diego, CA 92117, USA]; *b* 30 April 1931; *m* 14 Jan 1952 *William Emmett BANKS IV, s of William Emmett Banks III, and has issue:

Great-great-grandchildren's great-great-grandchildren
1e *Kathryn Emily Banks, *b* 19—; *m* 18 June 1987 *Alfred Michael MEDRANO and has issue:

Great-great-grandchildren's great-great-grandchildren's children
1f *Gregory Michael MEDRANO, *b* 20 Feb 1989

Great-great-grandchildren's great-great-grandchildren
2e *Scott BANKS, *b* 19—

Great-great-grandchildren's grandchildren
2c Ellen Clemence Smith, *b* 1895; *m* 19— Dr Paul Edgar HAMILTON and *d* 6 April 1946, leaving issue:

Great-great-grandchildren's great-grandchildren
1d *Richard Edgar HAMILTON [1613 Fairgreen Dve, Fullerton, CA 92633, USA], *b* 10 April 1923; *m* 19— Ima Jean Tiffin (*d* 14 April 1984) and has issue:

Great-great-grandchildren's great-great-grandchildren
1e *Gary Paul HAMILTON, *b* 15 April 1952
2e *Mark Roger HAMILTON, *b* 10 Nov 1957
3e *Scott Lester HAMILTON, *b* 19 Feb 1960

Great-great-grandchildren's great-grandchildren
2d *Anne Hamilton [2404 Boothbay, Raleigh, NC 27613, USA], *b* 16 Dec 1929; *m* 1947 Thomas Mett BEAUCHAMP (*d* 23 Feb 1988) and has issue:

Great-great-grandchildren's great-great-grandchildren
1e *Lynne Beauchamp [Mrs William E Woods, R1 Box 206A, Louisiana, MO 63353, USA], *b* Louisiana, Mo., 23 March 1949; *educ* Clopton High School; telemarketing operative; *m* 30 June 1967 *William Eugene WOODS, s of William M. Woods and his w Alma R., and has issue:

Great-great-grandchildren's great-great-grandchildren's children
1f *Troy Paul WOODS, *b* St Louis, Mo., 4 March 1975
2f *Todd Michael WOODS, *b* Quincy, Ill., 13 Aug 1980

Great-great-grandchildren's great-great-grandchildren
2c *Thomas Lawrence BEAUCHAMP [RR #1 Box 14, Stone Bridge Rd, Annada, MO 63330, USA], *b* Pike Co, Missouri, 27 March 1951; *educ* U of Missouri; Capt Chesterfield Fire Protection District 1975-; *m* 5 June 1971 *Susan Elizabeth, dau of Herman Wayne Smoker and his w Chaume Elizabeth, and has issue:

Great-great-grandchildren's great-great-grandchildren's children
1f *Thomas Lawrence BEAUCHAMP, Jr, *b* Kentucky 25 June 1974

2f *Ted Michael BEAUCHAMP, *b* Missouri 4 June 1982
3f *Tyler Randolph BEAUCHAMP, *b* Missouri 8 Sept 1984

Great-great-grandchildren's great-great-grandchildren
3e *Lori Hamilton Beauchamp [Mrs Douglas J Tarwater, 3817 Woodland Dve, Columbia, MO 65202, USA], *b* 7 May 1959; *m* 14 Feb 1981 *Douglas Jay TARWATER and has issue:

Great-great-grandchildren's great-great-grandchildren's children
1f *Andrew Ross TARWATER, *b* 31 July 1981
2f *Rachel Randolph TARWATER, *b* 10 May 1987

Great-great-grandchildren's grandchildren
3c Mary Emily Smith, *b* 1901; *m* 1925 Frank Wirt MINOR and *d* 1 July 1975
4c A child; *d* in infancy

Great-great-grandchildren's children
7b Henry Russell BANKHEAD, of Bowling Green, Mo., *b* 9 Sept 1873; *m* 1901 Edythe Kemble and *d* 9 Jan 1946, leaving issue:

Great-great-grandchildren's grandchildren
1c *Martha Lu Bankhead, *b* 13 Jan 1906 [Mrs Earnest B Crosley, 110 East Manhattan Dve, Tempe, AZ 85282, USA]; *m* 1st 11 Jan 1926 Charles Lester STOUFFER and has issue:

Great-great-grandchildren's great-grandchildren
1d *Martha Jane Stouffer [Mrs Winston P Jaskowiak, 110 East Manhattan Dve, Tempe, AZ 85282, USA], *b* 4 Dec 1926; *m* 1st 30 June 1946 Edward Henry SMITH and has issue:

Great-great-grandchildren's great-great-grandchildren
1e *Edythe (Dee) Lu(cretia) Smith [Mrs Thomas H Turner III, 14027 E Williamsfield Rd, Gilbert, AZ 85234, USA], *b* Phoenix, Ariz., 25 Sept 1947; *educ* Arizona State U; respiratory therapist; *m* 1st 4 July 1969 Carter Charles GAFFNEY and has issue:

Great-great-grandchildren's great-great-grandchildren's children
1f *Michael Charles GAFFNEY, *b* 12 Jan 1970; *m* 15 June 1991 *Catherine Theresa Miedowicz

Great-great-grandchildren's great-great-grandchildren
1e (cont.) Edythe Smith Gaffney *m* 2nd 26 April 1974 *Thomas Howard Anderfore TURNER III, *s* of Thomas H. A. Turner II and his *w* Beatrice El, and has issue:

Great-great-grandchildren's great-great-grandchildren's children
2f *Thomas Howard Anderfore TURNER IV, *b* Arizona 25 Sept 1976

Great-great-grandchildren's great-great-grandchildren
2e *Katherine Jayne Smith [Mrs Fred W Neff, 8701 S Kenwood Lane, Tempe, AZ 85284, USA], *b* 26 March 1950; *m* 12 April 1970 *Fred Willis NEFF and has issue:

Great-great-grandchildren's great-great-grandchildren's children
1f *Kenneth Edward NEFF, *b* 7 Dec 1971
2f *Andrea Katherine NEFF, *b* 22 Aug 1978

Great-great-grandchildren's great-great-grandchildren
3e *Edward Henry SMITH, Jr, *b* 30 Oct 1953; *m* 1st 19 Jan 1973 Pamela Anita Carey and has issue:

Great-great-grandchildren's great-great-grandchildren's children
1f *Katherine Nedra Michelle SMITH, *b* 25 June 1973

Great-great-grandchildren's great-great-grandchildren
3e (cont.) Edward H. Smith, Jr, *m* 2nd 8 July 1978 *Geraldine Kay Sands and has further issue:

Great-great-grandchildren's great-great-grandchildren's children
2f *Edra Jayne SMITH, *b* 2 Aug 1980
3f *Spring April SMITH, *b* 6 April 1983

Great-great-grandchildren's great-great-grandchildren
4e *Mary Elizabeth Smith [Mrs Frank Ruiz, 110 East Manhattan Dve, Tempe, AZ 85283, USA], *b* 12 March 1957; *m* 1st 22 Feb 1976 Ralph Michael DESTRINI and has issue:

Great-great-grandchildren's great-great-grandchildren's children
1f *Nicholas Ralph DESTRINI, *b* 23 Aug 1983

Great-great-grandchildren's great-great-grandchildren
4e (cont.) Mary Smith Destrini *m* 2nd 28 Feb 1988 *Frank RUIZ and has further issue:

Great-great-grandchildren's great-great-grandchildren's children
2f *Frank Vincent RUIZ, *b* 18 Aug 1988
3f *Anthony Kemble RUIZ, *b* 3 Aug 1989

Great-great-grandchildren's great-great-grandchildren
5e *Carl Kemble SMITH, *b* 12 May 1960

Great-great-grandchildren's great-grandchildren
1d (cont.) Martha Stouffer Smith *m* 2nd 1 July 1972 *Winston Peter JASKOWIAK

Great-great-grandchildren's grandchildren
1c (cont.) Martha Bankhead Stouffer *m* 2nd 7 Oct 1968 *Earnest Benjurman CROSLEY
2c Charles Kemble BANKHEAD, *b* 1908; *m* 1936 *Billie Bradshaw and *d* 3 July 1989

Great-great-grandchildren's children
8b Fannie Warren BANKHEAD, *b* 16 Aug 1875; *d* 10 Nov 1879
9b Dr Cary Randolph BANKHEAD, Jr, *b* 2 Jan 1878; *m* 1905 Mary Lucilla Miller (*d* 1935) and *d* 21 Nov 1935, having had issue:

Great-great-grandchildren's grandchildren
1c Henry Miller BANKHEAD, *b* 21 Sept 1906; *m* 1931 *Annette Louise Gasser (*b* 1910) and *d* Aug 1959, leaving issue:

Great-great-grandchildren's great-grandchildren
1d *Barbara Bankhead [Mrs Frank E Booker 23726 North Shore Dve, Edwardsburg, MI 49112, USA], *b* St Louis, Mo., 21 Sept 1932; *educ* Washington U, St Louis; research assist 1954-60, Montessori dir 1980-88; *m* 2 Feb 1957 *Frank Edwin BOOKER, s of Ernest Booker and his w Eula Sherman, and has issue:

Great-great-grandchildren's great-great-grandchildren
1e *Thomas Randolph BOOKER [5200 Holston Dve, Knoxville, TN 37914, USA], *b* Missouri 21 Feb 1958; *m* Indiana 21 Oct 1989 *Carolyn Lee Gray
2e *Elizabeth Lenore Booker [Mrs John J Lyon, 3391 North Hillsdale Rd, Hillsdale, MI 49242, USA], *b* Missouri 25 Jan 1960; *m* Wisconsin 19— *John Joseph LYON and has issue:

Great-great-grandchildren's great-great-grandchildren's children
1f *Jean Marie LYON, *b* 25 May 1984
2f *Christopher LYON, *b* 25 June 1986
3f *Brendon Andrew LYON, *b* 3 June 1989
4f *Sheilagh Maureen LYON, *b* 19 July 1992

Great-great-grandchildren's great-great-grandchildren
3e *Leigh Ann Booker [Mrs Fred A Shaul, 1417 Valley Dve, Westchester, PA 19382, USA] *b* Florida 8 March 1961; *m* Indiana 27 Sept 1992 *Fred(erick) Armstrong SHAUL
4e *Suzanne Melinda BOOKER [23726 North Shore Dve, Edwardsburg, MI 49112, USA], *b* Florida 22 May 1962
5e *Robert Frank BOOKER, *b* Indiana 3 March 1969
6e *Rachel Eleanor BOOKER, *b* Florida 31 Aug 1971

Great-great-grandchildren's great-grandchildren
2d *Malvern Miller Bankhead, *b* 15 Aug 1933; *m* 26 Dec 1955 *Sheila Jo-Ann Walsh and has issue:

Great-great-grandchildren's great-great-grandchildren:
1e *Henry Miller BANKHEAD, *b* 13 Oct 1964
2e *Joseph Randolph BANKHEAD, *b* 5 Feb 1969
3e *Benjamin Lewis BANKHEAD, *b* 24 July 1971
Mr and Mrs Malvern M. Bankhead have also adopted a daughter:
à *Jennifer Ann BANKHEAD, *b* 24 Jan 1963

Great-great-grandchildren's great-grandchildren
3d *William Marion BANKHEAD [11445 5th St E, Treasure Island, FL 33706, USA], *b* 14 June 19—; *m* 15 July 1957 *Verna Ruth Page and has issue:

Great-great-grandchildren's great-great-grandchildren
1e *Jodie Marie Bankhead, *b* 13 June 1959; *m* 19— *David Paul TOMCZAK and has issue:

Great-great-grandchildren's great-great-grandchildren's children
1f *Krista Marie TOMCZAK, *b* 22 Aug 1979
2f *David Paul TOMCZAK, Jr, *b* 18 July 1980
3f *Jeremy Paul TOMCZAK, *b* 9 March 1987

Great-great-grandchildren's great-great-grandchildren
2e *Ruth Annette Bankhead, *b* 11 April 1961; *m* 18 Nov 1983 *Robert Allen BAKULA and has issue:

Great-great-grandchildren's great-great-grandchildren's children
1f *Cassandra Marie BAKULA, *b* 24 Sept 1987
2f *Randall Robert BAKULA, *b* 24 Feb 1989

Great-great-grandchildren's great-great-grandchildren
3e *William Page BANKHEAD, *b* 16 Oct 1963

Great-great-grandchildren's great-grandchildren
4d *Bettie Bankhead [Mrs James H Branson, 23465 Harborview #1029, Charlotte Harbor, FL 33980-2170, USA], *b* 30 Sept 1939; *m* 9 May 1958 *James Hoyle BRANSON and has issue:

Great-great-grandchildren's great-great-grandchildren
1e *Deborah Marie BRANSON [Rt3 Box 156, Live Oak, FL 32060, USA], *b* St Louis, Mo., 7 Feb 1959; *educ* Lake City Community Coll; forest technologist 1993-; has issue:

Great-nephew's great-great-grandchildren's grandchildren
1f *Timothy Lowell BRANSON, *b* St Petersburg, Fla., 16 March 1980
2f *Jessica Lynn RYLKO, *b* St Petersburg 31 May 1985

Great-great-grandchildren's great-great-grandchildren
2e *Denise Lynn Branson [Mrs Stephen M Thompson, 3695 Lakeview St, House Springs, MO 63051, USA], *b* St Louis, Mo., 17 June 1960; served USN 1979-91; *m* 5 Oct 1990, as his 2nd w, *Stephen Michael THOMPSON, s of Carl Delond Thompson and his w Hazel Marie
3e *Kevin Matthew BRANSON [3031 Willow Wood, St Charles, MO 63303, USA], *b* 17 June 1960; *m* 28 Nov 1992 *Lisa Michele Thompson

Great-great-grandchildren's grandchildren
2c *Cary Randolph BANKHEAD III [Route 1 Box 145, Fayette, MO 65248, USA], *b* 20 Oct 1910; *m* 25 Oct 1941 *Katherine Bernice Lubke and has issue:

Great-great-grandchildren's great-grandchildren
1d *Robert Randolph BANKHEAD, *b* 29 Oct 1942; *m* 22 July 1972 *Martha C. Harrold and has issue:

Great-great-grandchildren's great-great-grandchildren
1e *William Randolph BANKHEAD, *b* 9 April 1977
2e *Mary McFarland BANKHEAD, *b* 1 June 1980

Great-great-grandchildren's great-grandchildren
2d *Thomas Alfred BANKHEAD, *b* 2 June 1945; *m* 20 March 1976 *Judith K. Lemon and has issue:

Great-great-grandchildren's great-great-grandchildren
1e *Laura Kay BANKHEAD, *b* 2 Oct 1977
2e *Sarah Anne Cary BANKHEAD, *b* 26 Oct 1979

Great-great-grandchildren's grandchildren
3c Marion Swain BANKHEAD, *b* 12 Dec 1912; *d* 14 Nov 1915
4c *Joseph Russell BANKHEAD [109 S Everett, Kennett, MO 63857, USA], *b* 2 Nov 1917; *m* 11 July 1941 *Katherine G. Jones (*b* 1917) and has issue:

Great-great-grandchildren's great-grandchildren
1d *Terry Jo Bankhead [Mrs Norman A Garrison, 9419 Winfield Place, Montgomery, AL 36117, USA], *b* Fulton, Mo., 24 Jan 1943; *educ* U of Mississippi; sec/receptionist for husb 1975-; *m* 1st 6 Aug 1961 (divorce 1974) Byron Keith MITCHELL and has issue:

Great-great-grandchildren's great-great-grandchildren
1e *Brian Keith MITCHELL [PO Box 791, Kennett, MO 63857, USA], *b* Kennett 9 Nov 1962; PhD pharmacy, pharmacist 1987-
2e *Dr Joseph Blake MITCHELL [6811 Old Canton Rd #803, Ridgeland, MS 39157, USA], *b* 17 March 1964; *m* 27 Dec 1991, as her 2nd husb, *Dr Elizabeth Wyatt
3e *Kerri Renée MITCHELL, *b* 20 March 1967

Great-great-grandchildren's great-grandchildren
1d (cont.) Terry Jo Bankhead Mitchell *m* 2nd 11 Feb 1975 *Dr Norman Asa GARRISON, Jr
2d *James Lewis BANKHEAD [2132 Lynbridge Dve, Charlotte, NC 28270-7767, USA], *b* Kennett, Mo., 4 April 1945; *educ* Southern Methodist U, Dallas, Tex.; salesman with Glaxo Pharmaceuticals 1985-; *m* 1st 12 Dec 1967 (divorce May 1977) Kay E. Collier and has issue:

Great-great-grandchildren's great-great-grandchildren
1e *Noel Keith BANKHEAD [9606A Vinca Circle, Charlote, NC 28213, USA], *b* 5 July 1968
2e *Nicholas (Nick) Andrew BANKHEAD [820 Francis Pl, St Louis, MO 63105, USA], *b* 16 Oct 1973

Great-great-grandchildren's great-grandchildren
2d (cont.) James L. Bankhead *m* 2nd 4 Oct 1989 *Rebecca, dau of Percy R. Ashby and his w Rebecca W.

Great-great-grandchildren's children
10b Katie Clyde BANKHEAD, *b* 11 Feb 1880; *d* 28 July 1960
11b Bessie Guy BANKHEAD, *b* 23 Oct 1883; *d* 12 Dec 1962

Great-great-grandchildren
3a Martha Jefferson Bankhead, *b* 1837; *m* 1858 Kinzea Howard NORRIS and *d* 1891, leaving issue:

Great-great-grandchildren's children
1b Elizabeth Bankhead Norris, *b* 1858; *m* Peter NORTON and *d* 1898, leaving issue:

Great-great-grandchildren's grandchildren
1c Natalie Norton, *b* 18—; *m* 1st Eugene SCHMIERLE; *m* 2nd William DALLET

Great-great-grandchildren's children
2b Mollie Norris, *b* 1860; *m* 1st Eugene WELLS and had issue:

Great-great-grandchildren's grandchildren
1c Howard Custis WELLS, *b* 1881; *m* Meta Fragstein and *d* 1950
2c Dixie Annette Wells; *m* Alfred LUND

Great-great-grandchildren's children
2b (cont.) Mollie Norris Wells *m* 2nd James Augustus SUBLETTE
3b Ellen B. Norris, *b* 1862; *m* Emmanuel DANIELS
4b Charles A. NORRIS, *b* 1866; *m* 1st Harriet Amos; *m* 2nd his cousin Anne Carter Clark and *d* 1921
5b John Bankhead NORRIS, *b* 1868; *d* 1901

Great-great-grandchildren
4a Thomas Jefferson BANKHEAD, *b* 1839; *d* 1863 in a Federal prison camp during Civil War

Great-grandchildren
(2) Thomas Mann Randolph BANKHEAD, of Arkansas, *b* 30 Dec 1811; *educ* U of Virginia; Memb Arkansas State Legislature, Charter Memb Bd Tstees Spring Hill Acad, Ark.; *m* betwen 1844 and 1846 (Anne) Elizabeth, dau of Maj Richard Pryor and his w Virginia, and *d* La Vaca, Tex., 1 July 1851
(3) Ellen Wayles Randolph Bankhead, also known as Ellen Monroe Bankhead, *b* 3 Sept 1812; *m* 7 July 1832, as his 1st w, John Coles CARTER (*b* 1800; lawyer, magistrate; *d* Pike Co., Mo., 1876), est s of Robert Hill Carter (ggs of Robert 'King' Carter, ancestor also of Presidents WILLIAM H. and BENJAMIN HARRISON, also possibly of President CARTER) and his w Mary Eliza (Polly) Coles, and *d* 6 Jan 1838, leaving issue:

Great-great-grandchildren
1a Anne Carter, *b* 1833; *m* 1852 Henry PRESTON and *d* 1895, leaving issue:

Great-great-grandchildren's children
1b Mary Coles PRESTON, *b* 1854; *d* 1914
2b Margaret B. PRESTON, *b* 1855; *d* 1926
3b Ellen Preston, *b* 1857; *m* Otway Giles BAILEY and *d* 1923, having had issue:

Great-great-grandchildren's grandchildren
1c Preston H. BAILEY, *b* 25 May 1891; *m* 19 June 1917 Elizabeth Marie Leftwich and *d* 11 Oct 1918, leaving issue:

Great-great-grandchildren's great-grandchildren
1d *Margaret Preston Bailey, *b* 1918; *m* 1941 *Robert JACOBSON and has issue:

Great-great-grandchildren's great-great-grandchildren
1e *Betty Rae JACOBSON, *b* 1942

Great-great-grandchildren's grandchildren
2c *Otway Giles BAILEY, Jr, *b* 1895; *m* 1923 *Ellen Verena DeFord and has issue:

Great-great-grandchildren's great-grandchildren
1d *Otway Giles BAILEY III, *b* 1924; *m* 1948 *Elsie Watson and has issue:

Great-great-grandchildren's great-great-grandchildren
1e *Anne Lynne BAILEY, *b* 1950
2e *Barbara Leigh BAILEY, *b* 1955

Great-great-grandchildren's great-grandchildren
2d *Ellen Olivia Bailey, *b* 1926; *m* 1950 *Curtis GEANNINI and has issue:

Great-great-grandchildren's great-great-grandchildren
1e *David Curtis GEANNINI, *b* 19—
2e *Stephen Philip GEANNINI, *b* 19—
3e *Giles Anderson GEANNINI *b* 19—

Great-great-grandchildren's great-grandchildren
3d *Jeanne Bailey, *b* 1928; *m* 1952 *Robert Pierce WHITMAN and has issue:

Great-great-grandchildren's great-great-grandchildren
1e *Robert Pierce WHITMAN, Jr, *b* 1953

Great-great-grandchildren's children
4b Elizabeth Preston, *b* 1858; *m* 1900 Dr James White CUMMINGS and *d* 1906
5b Henry PRESTON, Jr, *b* 1861; *m* 1890 Mary Helen (Nellie) Carson and *d* 1921, leaving issue:

Great-great-grandchildren's grandchildren
1c Sidney PRESTON, *b* 1891; *d* 1938
2c *Henley PRESTON, *b* 1891 (twin with Sidney)
3c *Anne Carter PRESTON, *b* 1893
4c *Henry PRESTON III, *b* 1895; *m* 1930 *Leta P. Wilson and has issue:

Great-great-grandchildren's great-grandchildren
1d *Henry Donald PRESTON, *b* 1933; *m* 1952 *Nancy Neal

Great-great-grandchildren's grandchildren
5c Robert Carson PRESTON, *b* 1902; *d* 1941

Great-great-grandchildren's children
6b Anne Cary Preston, *b* 1863; *m* 1899 Albert Pendleton KILLINGER and *d* 1931
7b Jane PRESTON, *b* 1863; *d* 1907
8b Isaetta R. PRESTON, *b* 1865; *d* 1916
9b Eugenia F. Preston, *b* 1868; *m* 1889 Charles Cummings GIBSON and *d* 1913
10b Percy Thomas PRESTON, *b* 1875; *m* 1905 Corinne Roane Wills and *d* 1941, leaving issue:

Great-great-grandchildren's grandchildren
1c *Virginia Wills Preston, *b* 1906; *m* 1928 *Albert Basil WILSON, Jr, s of Albert Basil Wilson, and has issue:

Great-great-grandchildren's great-grandchildren
1d *Elizabeth Ann Wilson, *b* 23 June 1931; *m* 27 Aug 1951 *Dwight Eugene BOGLE and has issue:

Great-great-grandchildren's great-great-grandchildren
1e *Keith Eugene BOGLE, *b* 9 Aug 1952
2e *Barbara Ann BOGLE, *b* 10 Oct 1953
3e *Jerry Wayne BOGLE, *b* 11 Dec 1954

Great-great-grandchildren's great-grandchildren
2d *Albert Percy WILSON, *b* 5 July 1933; *m* 8 July 1956 *Betty Lou Umbarger
3d *Charlotte Louise WILSON, *b* 13 Dec 1937

Great-great-grandchildren's grandchildren
2c *Percy Thomas PRESTON, Jr, *b* 1909; *m* 1933 *Mary Marguerite Carter
3c *Elizabeth Madison Preston, *b* 1913; *m* 1940 *Kyle Roosevelt FERRIS

Great-great-grandchildren
2a Robert Hill CARTER, *b* 1835; *d* 1854
3a John Coles CARTER, Jr, *b* 1837; *m* Sarah E. Calvert and *d* 1902, having had issue:

Great-great-grandchildren's children
1b Anne C. P. Carter, *b* 1865; *m* 1st Edward J. CLARK and had issue:

Great-great-grandchildren's grandchildren
1c Carter Bankhead CLARK, *b* 1903; *m* Merlie King and *d* 1963

Great-great-grandchildren's children
1b (cont.) Anne Carter Clark *m* 2nd her cousin Charles Bankhead NORRIS
2b Mary Bankhead CARTER, *b* 186?; *d* 1939

Great-grandchildren
(4) William Stuart BANKHEAD, of Albemarle, nr Courtland, Ala., *b* Monticello 30 Jan 1826; *educ* U of Virginia; planter, Capt Co I 16th Alabama Regt Confederate States Army Civil War; *m* 1st 1850 Martha Jane Watkins (*d* 1851 in a carriage accident) and had issue:

Great-great-grandchildren
1a —— BANKHEAD; *d* shortly after birth as a result of the same accident which brought about the death of his mother

Great-grandchildren▸
(4) (cont.) William Stuart Bankhead *m* 2nd 1854 Barbara Elizabeth (*d* 1867), dau of William Garth, of Birdwood, Albemarle Co, Va., and his w Elizabeth Lewis Woods Martin, and with her had issue:

Great-great-grandchildren
2a Anne Cary (Nannie) Randolph Bankhead, *b* 1856; *m* 1873 J. Harvey GILCHRIST and *d* 1900, leaving issue:

Great-great-grandchildren's children
1b Katie Frank Gilchrist, *b* 19 Oct 1876; *m* 29 Sept 1896 Lawson SYKES and *d* 10 Feb 1968, having had issue:

Great-great-grandchildren's grandchildren

1c A dau; *d* in infancy

2c *Leila Scaife Sykes, *b* 7 Oct 1905; *m* 16 Feb 1934 *David Lawson MARTIN and has issue:

Great-great-grandchildren's great-grandchildren

1d *Lawson Sykes MARTIN [PO Box 356, Courtland, AL 35618, USA], *b* 18 July 1936; *m* 24 Nov 1962 *Donie De Bardeleben Neal and has issue:

Great-great-grandchildren's great-great-grandchildren

1e *Virginia Larkin MARTIN, *b* 2 Sept 1963

2e *Anne Randolph Martin, *b* 19 Jan 1965; *m* 15 April 1989 *Maj Joseph FLYNN

3e *Ellen Pratt MARTIN, *b* 19 Jan 1965

4e *Donie Neal MARTIN, *b* 4 Jan 1970

Great-great-grandchildren

3a William Stuart BANKHEAD, Jr, *b* 10 May 1858; *d* 6 Sept 1862

4a A dau, *b* 1860; *d* in infancy

5a Elizabeth Garth Bankhead, *b* 28 Aug 1865; *m* 1886 William Edgar HOTCHKISS (*b* 1855; *d* 1932) and *d* nr Courtland, Ala., 19 Aug 1932, leaving issue:

Great-great-grandchildren's children

1b Cary Randolph HOTCHKISS, *b* 18 May 1887; *d* 3 March 1978

2b Anna Frances Hotchkiss, *b* 18 Nov 1889; *m* 5 Sept 1911 Campbell Houston GILLESPIE, of Sherman, Tex., and *d* 26 Nov 1943, leaving issue:

Great-great-grandchildren's grandchildren

1c Campbell Houston GILLESPIE, Jr, *b* 7 Aug 1913; *m* 1937 his 5th cousin *Mary Ruffin [Mrs Campbell H Gillespie Jr, 1313 East Richards St, Sherman, TX, 75090, USA] (*b* 14 Oct 1913), yst dau of Robert Montagu McMurdo and his w Caryanne Randolph Ruffin (for whom *see* below under issue of William Ruffin, 3rd s of (4) Caryanne Nicholas Randolph, 4th child of Jefferson Randolph, President JEFFERSON's eldest gs), and *d* 3 Sept 1986, leaving issue:

Great-great-grandchildren's great-grandchildren

1d *Campbell Houston GILLESPIE III [1710 Shields Drive, Sherman, TX 75090], *b* 21 Aug 1938; *m* 1 Sept 1962 *Mary Bert Patillo and has issue:

Great-great-grandchildren's great-great-grandchildren

1e *Maryanna Keeval GILLESPIE, *b* 1 May 1968

2e *Cary Ruffin GILLESPIE, *b* 14 April 1970

Great-great-grandchildren's great-grandchildren

2d *Robert McMurdo GILLESPIE [5112 Evelyn Byrd Rd, Richmond, VA 23225, USA], *b* 29 July 1945; *m* 7 Nov 1981 *Dr Susan Estes Robinson and has issue:

Great-great-grandchildren's great-great-grandchildren

1e *William Bennett GILLESPIE, *b* 8 June 1984

2e *James Campbell GILLESPIE, *b* 23 Feb 1990

Great-great-grandchildren's grandchildren

2c *Stuart Edgar GILLESPIE, *b* 13 Sept 1919; *m* 1st 1942 Layle Church and has issue:

Great-great-grandchildren's great-grandchildren

1d *Clark Patton GILLESPIE, *b* 13 April 1944; *m* 2 Aug 1972 *Anne Marie Varn and has issue:

Great-great-grandchildren's great-great-grandchildren

1e *Kelly Elizabeth GILLESPIE, *b* 23 Aug 1973

2e *Patricia DeAnne GILLESPIE, *b* 24 Feb 1975

3e *Adam Stuart GILLESPIE, *b* 18 Sept 1980

Mr and Mrs Clark P. Gillespie have also adopted a dau:

a *Teresa Marie GILLESPIE, *b* 6 Feb 1961

Great-great-grandchildren's great-grandchildren

2d *Layle Christine GILLESPIE, *b* 7 Feb 1946

3d *William Stuart GILLESPIE, *b* 6 Sept 1950

Great-great-grandchildren's grandchildren

2c (cont.) Stuart E. Gillespie *m* 2nd 7 Aug 1958 *Dorothy, *née* Hastings, formerly w of —— Wellman, and adopted her daughters by him:

a *Julia Elizabeth Gillespie, *née* Wellman, *b* 18 Jan 1947; *m* 30 June 1973 *James Henderson COLLINS and has issue:

i *James Henderson COLLINS, Jr, *b* 6 Jan 1977

ii *Kimberleigh Pamela COLLINS, *b* 21 Oct 1979

b *Anna Kate Gillespie, *née* Wellman, *b* 25 March 1950; *m* 19— *——— AYERS

Great-great-grandchildren's children

3b Elizabeth Bankhead Hotchkiss, *b* 29 July 1891; *m* 1929 Virgil JAMES and *d* 27 Feb 1944

4b Revd David Stuart HOTCHKISS, *b* 28 June 1894; *m* 22 Dec 1919 Martha Maddox Smith and *d* 23 Aug 1935, leaving issue:

Great-great-grandchildren's grandchildren

1c *David Stuart HOTCHKISS, Jr, *b* 5 Oct 1920; *m* 19— *Beryl ———

2c Martha Jane Hotchkiss, *b* 28 May 1924; *m* 19 Dec 1942 *Robert Tweedy McWHORTER (*b* 20 July 1918) and *d* 15 April 1973, leaving issue:

Great-great-grandchildren's great-grandchildren

1d *Robert Tweedy McWHORTER, Jr, *b* 28 Sept 1943; *m* 27 Oct 1967 *Kathleen Marie Morrison and has issue:

Great-great-grandchildren's great-great-grandchildren

1e *Cary Bankhead McWHORTER, *b* 3 April 1973

Great-great-grandchildren's great-grandchildren

2d *Roger Barton McWHORTER II, *b* 9 Sept 1945; *m* 6 July 1969 *Barbara Hudson and has issue:

Great-great-grandchildren's great-great-grandchildren

1e *Elizabeth Randolph McWHORTER, *b* 14 Dec 1971

2e *Roger Barton McWHORTER III, *b* 28 Sept 1973

Great-great-grandchildren's great-grandchildren

3d *Martha Stuart McWhorter, *b* 25 June 1947; *m* 7 March 1970 *John Thomas TERRY and has issue:

Great-great-grandchildren's great-great-grandchildren

1e *Katherine Stuart TERRY, *b* 17 Aug 1976

2e *Virginia Garth TERRY, *b* 30 Aug 1980

3e *Ellen Wayles TERRY, *b* 30 Aug 1980

Great-great-grandchildren's grandchildren

3c *Revd William Edgar HOTCHKISS III, *b* Dunedin, Fla., 24 Aug 1926; *m* 8 Sept 1951 *Jean Downes Hinson and has issue:

Great-great-grandchildren's great-grandchildren

1d *Jean Randolph Hotchkiss, *b* 6 Sept 1952; *m* 23 June 1973 *Gene Ray HARRIS and has issue:

Great-great-grandchildren's great-great-grandchildren

1e *William Randolph HARRIS, *b* 28 April 1975

Great-great-grandchildren's great-grandchildren

2d *David William HOTCHKISS, *b* 9 Dec 1953; *m* 23 June 1978 *Elizabeth Ann Stophel

3d *Thomas Odus Hinson HOTCHKISS, *b* 12 Nov 1955; *m* 12 May 1979 *Edna Kathleen Schell and has issue:

Great-great-grandchildren's great-great-grandchildren

1e *Shelley Louise HOTCHKISS, *b* 29 June 1981

Great-great-grandchildren's great-grandchildren

4d *William Edgar HOTCHKISS IV, *b* 20 Nov 1958

5d *Stuart Andrew HOTCHKISS, *b* 13 Feb 1961

6d *Mae Stone HOTCHKISS, *b* 1 May 1963

Great-great-grandchildren's children

5b William Edgar HOTCHKISS, Jr, *b* 26 Jan 1899; *m* 18 May 1922 *Mary Beard Walker and *d* 4 July 1959, leaving issue:

Great-great-grandchildren's grandchildren

1c *William Bankhead HOTCHKISS, *b* 19 Dec 1923; *m* 31 Aug 1947 *Jo Vaughn Paulus and has issue:

Great-great-grandchildren's great-grandchildren

1d *Nancy Vaughn Hotchkiss [Mrs Jimmy B Aston Jr, 912 Emily Dve, Goodlettsville, TN 37072, USA], *b* 25 Oct 1949; *m* 20 March 1970 *Jimmy Burch ASTON, Jr, and has issue:

Great-great-grandchildren's great-great-grandchildren

1e *Jennifer Elizabeth ASTON, *b* 21 Jan 1972

2e *Amy Gail ASTON, *b* 30 Sept 1974

Great-great-grandchildren's great-grandchildren

2d *Charles William HOTCHKISS, *b* 31 July 1951

Great-great-grandchildren's grandchildren

2c *Cary Randolph HOTCHKISS II [Bonnie Doon, PO Box 276, Courtland, AL 35618, USA], *b* 23 Aug 1931; *m* 26 Feb 1953 *Charlotte Taylor Shackelford and has issue:

Great-great-grandchildren's great-grandchildren
1d *Ellen Garth Hotchkiss [Mrs Theodore Straub, 436 Sherman Ave SE, Decatur, AL 35601, USA], *b* 29 Sept 1954; *m* 1st 10 Sept 1976 John Claude MORRIS III and has issue:

Great-great-grandchildren's great-great-grandchildren
1e *John Bankhead Morris STRAUB, *b* 20 June 1977 and named John Claude Morris IV but took stepf's name

Great-great-grandchildren's great-grandchildren
1d (cont.) Ellen Hotchkiss Morris *m* 2nd 18 July 1981 *Theodore STRAUB
2d *Michael Cary HOTCHKISS [2659 Flamingo Court S, West Palm Beach, FL 33406, USA], *b* Decatur, Ala., 22 July 1957; *educ* Auburn and Maryland Colls; civil engr in nuclear power industry 1981-
3d *Elizabeth Bankhead Hotchkiss [Mrs David E McCraine, 9c Oppenheimer 333 Clay, Suite 4700, Houston, TX 77002, USA], *b* 27 Feb 1963; *m* 1st 23 Feb 1982 John Daniel WYKER III; *m* 2nd 4 Jan 1986 *David Ewel McCRAINE and has issue:

Great-great-grandchildren's great-great-grandchildren
1e *Daniel Cary McCRAINE, *b* 2 June 1990

Great-great-grandchildren's children
6b Charles Wilcox HOTCHKISS, *b* 22 July 1903; *m* 3 July 1929 Gene Marie Fennel (*d* 28 July 1963) and *d* 12 Dec 1951, leaving issue:

Great-great-grandchildren's grandchildren
1c *Gene Bankhead Hotchkiss [Mrs Wilbur Craft Jr, Rt1 Box 585, Leighton, AL 35646, USA], *b* Sheffield, Ala., 6 Oct 1930; owner C & H Farms (cotton, soy beans and timber), Colbert and Lawrence Cos, Ala.; *m* 19 May 1953 *Wilburn CRAFT, Jr (*b* 1928), s of James Lee Wilburn Craft and his w Novella Gilbert, and has issue:

Great-great-grandchildren's great-grandchildren
1d *Rebecca Lecky Craft, *b* 30 July 1954; *m* Sheffield, Ala., 23 Nov 1981 *William Neal GRAY (*b* Mitchell but took stepf's name) and has issue:

Great-great-grandchildren's great-great-grandchildren
1e *William Craft Mitchell GRAY, *b* 20 Feb 1983

Great-great-grandchildren's grandchildren
2c *John Fennel HOTCHKISS [PO Box 143, Courtland, AL, USA], *b* 20 March 1939

Great-great-grandchildren
6a Stuart Gibbons BANKHEAD, *b* 1869; *d* in infancy

Great-grandchildren
(4) William Stuart Bankhead *m* 3rd 1868 Catherine, *née* Gilchrist, widow of his 2nd w's bro George Garth, and *d* 19 Nov 1898, having with her had issue:

Great-great-grandchildren
7a Stuart Gibbons BANKHEAD, *b* 1869; *d* in infancy

Grandchildren
2 (Thomas) Jefferson RANDOLPH, of Edgehill, King George Co, Va., *b* Monticello 12 Sept 1792; *educ* U of Pennsylvania; Col Virginia Militia, Memb Virginia Legislature, Rector U of Virginia, Pres Democratic Nat Convention at Baltimore 1872, financier; *m* Mount Warren, Albemarle Co, Va. (his bride's father's house) 10 March 1815 Jane Hollins (*b* 16 Jan 1798; *d* Edgehill 18 Jan 1871, *bur* Monticello), dau of Wilson Cary Nicholas, Govr Virginia 1814-16, and his w Margaret Smith, and *d* Edgehill 18 Oct 1875 (*bur* Monticello), having had issue:

Great-grandchildren
(1) Margaret Smith Randolph, *b* the Governor's House, Richmond, Va., 17 Feb or 7 March 1816; *m* 2 Sept 1839 her 2nd cousin once-removed William Mann RANDOLPH (*b* 1811; *educ* U of Virginia; Judge Probate Court Port Gibson, Miss., 1842-50; *d* Pass Christian, Miss., 1850), est s of Dr John Randolph and his w Judith Lewis, and *d* Edgehill 20 Dec 1842 probably of tuberculosis, leaving issue:

Great-great-grandchildren
1a Jane Margaret Randolph, *b* 1 May 1840; *m* 8 Nov 1860 Edward Clifford ANDERSON, Jr, of Savannah, Ga. (*b* 17 Jan 1839; Col 7th Georgia Cavalry Confederate States Army; *d* 27 Sept 1876), s of George Wayne Anderson and his w Eliza Clifford Stites, and *d* 27 June 1914, having had issue:

Great-great-grandchildren's children
1b Jefferson Randolph ANDERSON, *b* Savannah 4 Sept 1861; *educ* Chatham Acad, Va., U of Virginia (BL 1885) and Göttingen U, Germany; Hon DCL U of the South (1931), lawyer, Memb: Georgia House of Reps 1905-06 and 1909-12, Georgia State Senate 1913-14 (Pres) and Democratic Nat Convention 1912, Pres Monticello Assoc 1933-35 (Historian Monticello Assoc 1937-38); *m* 27 Nov 1895 Anne Page (*b* 15 April 1873), dau of Joseph John Wilder, of Savannah, and his w Georgia Page King, and *d* Savannah 17 July 1950, having had issue:

Great-great-grandchildren's grandchildren
1c Page Randolph Anderson, b Oakton, Cobb Co, Ga., 27 Aug 1899; m 2 April 1921 *Henry Norris PLATT, s of Charles Platt, of Philadelphia, and his w Elizabeth Norris, and d 27 Dec 1984, leaving issue:

Great-great-grandchildren's great-grandchildren
1d *Henry Norris PLATT, Jr [520 N 15th St, Philadelphia, PA 19130, USA], b Philadelphia 23 March 1922; m 26 June 1953 *Lenore Guest MacLeish and has issue:

Great-great-grandchildren's great-great-grandchildren
1e *Henry Norris PLATT III, b 12 June 1954
2e *Lenore McCall PLATT, b 17 May 1956
3e *Martha Hillard PLATT, b 29 April 1959
4e *Caroline Anderson PLATT, b 23 Nov 1961

Great-great-grandchildren's great-grandchildren
2d *Ann Page Platt, b Philadelphia 22 Nov 1924; m 1 July 1950 *Thomas Elliott ALLEN and has issue:

Great-great-grandchildren's great-great-grandchildren
1e *Page Randolph Allen, b 6 Sept 1951; m 1st 19 June 1970 William Scott MORRIS; m 2nd 19— *Nathaniel OWINGS
2e *James Elliot ALLEN, b 26 July 1953
3e *Samuel Wilder ALLEN, b 9 Nov 1956
4e *Abigail Brewster ALLEN, b 14 Feb 1960
5e *Mary Davis ALLEN, b 11 April 1963

Great-great-grandchildren's great-grandchildren
3d *Jefferson Davis PLATT, b Philadelphia 13 May 1929; m 22 Aug 1971 *Veronica Chisholm

Great-great-grandchildren's grandchildren
2c Jefferson Randolph ANDERSON, Jr, b 3 Sept 1900; d 30 Nov 1903
3c *Joseph Randolph ANDERSON, b Savannah 22 March 1905; m 15 Nov 1930 *Edith O'Driscoll Hunter, of Savannah, and has issue:

Great-great-grandchildren's great-grandchildren
1d *Page O'Driscoll Anderson [Mrs James Hungerpiller, 12730 Rockwell Avenue, Savannah, GA 31405, USA], b 7 Nov 1932; m 26 April 1953 *James Eggleston HUNGERPILLER and has issue:

Great-great-grandchildren's great-great-grandchildren
1e *Susan Page Hungerpiller [Mrs George H Oelschig Jr, 455 Old Creek Rd, Atlanta, GA 30342, USA], b 23 Feb 1954; m 12 May 1979 *George Henry OELSCHIG, Jr, and has issue:

Great-great-grandchildren's great-great-grandchildren's children
1f *Edith Page OELSCHIG, b 29 Nov 1982
2f *Katherine Leland OELSCHIG, b 3 Sept 1986

Great-great-grandchildren's great-great-grandchildren
2e *James Randolph HUNGERPILLER [130 E 50th Street, Savannah, GA 31405, USA], b 24 Nov 1955; educ U of the South, Sewanee, Tenn.; shipping exec 1979-89, investment broker 1989-; m 11 June 1988 *Andrea Elaine, dau of Earle M. Craig, Jr, and his w Dorothy Meyer, and has issue:

Great-great-grandchildren's great-great-grandchildren's children
1f *Audrey Randolph HUNGERPILLER, b Savannah 26 July 1990

Great-great-grandchildren's great-great-grandchildren
3e *Dr John Colin HUNGERPILLER [125 E 49th Street, Savannah, GA 31405, USA], b 18 March 1959; m 1st 16 July 1983 Mary Jennifer Hardin; m 2nd 13 April 1991 *Dr Jeanne Moratta

Great-great-grandchildren's children
2b George Wayne ANDERSON, of Richmond, Va., b Edgehill 10 July 1863; educ Hanover Acad, Va., and U of Virginia (BL 1888); Richmond City Attorney 1921, Col 1st Virginia Regt, Historian Monticello Assoc 1916-18; m Charlottesville 21 Dec 1889 Estelle Marguerite, dau of Frederick George Burthe, of New Orleans, and his w Mary, dau of Senator Robert Carter Nicholas and gdau of Govr Wilson Cary Nicholas, and d Richmond 30 Dec 1922, having had issue:

Great-great-grandchildren's grandchildren
1c *Edward Clifford ANDERSON [20 E 74th St, Apt 8G, New York, NY 10021, USA], b Richmond 26 Nov 1893; educ U of Virginia; Lt 5th Field Artillery 1st Div American Expeditionary Force World War I (Croix de Guerre with silver star); m 12 Jan 1922 *Isabel Scott [Mrs Edward C Anderson, 1234 Rothesay Road, Richmond, VA 23221, USA], of Richmond, and has issue:

Great-great-grandchildren's great-grandchildren
1d *George Wayne ANDERSON III [1108 E Main Street, Richmond, VA 23219, USA], b 1 May 1927; m 4 Oct 1952 *Virginia Lee Richardson and has issue:

Great-great-grandchildren's great-great-grandchildren
1e *Cary Randolph ANDERSON [Mrs Thomas E Trainor, RR 1 Box 530, Sanbornville, NH 03872, USA], 30 June 1953; *m* 22 Jan 1983 *Thomas Edward TRAINOR and has issue:

    Great-great-grandchildren's great-great-grandchildren's children
    1f *Thomas Clifford TRAINOR, *b* 23 July 1983
    2f *Cary Richardson TRAINOR, *b* 18 April 1985

Great-great-grandchildren's great-great-grandchildren
2e Edward Clifford ANDERSON II, *b* 2 Dec 1958; *d* 25 July 1985

Great-great-grandchildren's great-grandchildren
2d Elizabeth Strother Anderson, *b* 11 April 1929; *m* 6 Dec 1952 *Jonathan BRYAN III, s of Jonathan Bryan, Jr, and *d* 7 July 1992, leaving issue:

    Great-great-grandchildren's great-great-grandchildren
    1e *Robert Carter BRYAN, *b* 31 Jan 1954; *m* 15 Aug 1986 *Judy Lynn Blackwell and has issue:

        Great-great-grandchildren's great-great-grandchildren's children
        1f *Robert Coalter BRYAN, *b* 26 Dec 1987
        2f *Will Hamilton BRYAN, *b* 4 Sept 1992

    Great-great-grandchildren's great-great-grandchildren
    2e *Isabel Scott Bryan, *b* 5 April 1955; *m* 9 May 1985 (divorce 19—) Stephen MILLER and has issue:

        Great-great-grandchildren's great-great-grandchildren's children
        1f *David Bryan MILLER II, *b* 19 July 1987

    Great-great-grandchildren's great-great-grandchildren
    3e *John Randolph BRYAN, *b* 8 March 1959; *m* 12 Dec 1986 *Susan Carter Agnor and has issue:

        Great-great-grandchildren's great-great-grandchildren's children
        1f *John Edward BRYAN, *b* 2 Oct 1988
        2f *Catherine Augusta BRYAN, *b* 21 Nov 1989
        3f *Elizabeth Walker BRYAN, *b* 7 Feb 1991

Great-great-grandchildren's great-grandchildren
3d *Isabel Scott Anderson [Mrs Harry Fitzgerald, 4106 Cambridge Rd, Richmond, VA 23221, USA], *b* 27 Sept 1932; *m* 1st 29 Dec 1962 James Turner SLOAN, Jr (*d* 18 April 1965), s of James Turner Sloan, and has issue:

    Great-great-grandchildren's great-great-grandchildren
    1e *Louise Williams SLOAN, *b* 24 June 1963
    2e *Edward Anderson SLOAN, *b* 16 July 1965

Great-great-grandchildren's great-grandchildren
3d (cont.) Isabel Anderson Sloan *m* 2nd 24 May 1968 *Harry Wilkinson FITZGERALD and has further issue:

    Great-great-grandchildren's great-great-grandchildren
    3e *Isabel Scott FITZGERALD, *b* 28 June 1969
    4e *Caroline Harris FITZGERALD, *b* 1970

Great-great-grandchildren's grandchildren
2c George Wayne ANDERSON, Jr, *b* Richmond, Va., 20 June 1896; *educ* U of Virginia; Capt 313th Field Artillery 80th Div American Expeditionary Force World War I; *ka* Le Grand Carré Farm, Meuse-Argonne, France, 1 Nov 1918
3c *Cary Nicholas Anderson, *b* Richmond 4 Feb 1903; *m* 10 April 1926 Manfred KELLER (*b* Zurich, Switzerland, 1904; *d* Wilmington, Del., 19 June 1959) and has issue:

    Great-great-grandchildren's great-grandchildren
    1d *Estelle Wayne KELLER, *b* 7 June 1927
    2d *Ursula Sophie Keller, *b* 26 Sept 1928; *m* 8 Sept 1951 *Irénée DuPont MAY, of Wilmington, Delaware, and has issue:

        Great-great-grandchildren's great-great-grandchildren
        1e *Sophie Christine May [Mrs Peter Gerard, 1824 Circle Rd, Baltimore, MD 21204, USA], *b* 2 Aug 1953; *m* 16 June 1973 *Peter Charles Rupert GERARD (*b* 27 Sept 1951; film actor), yr s of Major Rupert Charles Frederick Gerard, MBE (*b* 1916; served Grenadier Guards; *d* 1978, see BURKE'S PEERAGE & BARONETAGE), and his w Huguette Reiss-Brian, of Brazil
        2e *Irénée DuPont MAY, *b* 6 Aug 1954
        3e *Wilson Cary Nicholas MAY, *b* 21 April 1965

Great-great-grandchildren's children
3b Eliza Clifford ANDERSON, *b* 24 Oct 1864; *d* 11 Sept 1876
4b Margaret Randolph Anderson, *b* Savannah 21 Aug 1866; *m* 1st 24 Nov 1893 Abbott Lawrence ROTCH (*b* Boston

6 Jan 1861; meteorologist; *d* 7 April 1912), s of Benjamin Smith Rotch and his w Annie Bigelow Lawrence, and had issue:

Great-great-grandchildren's grandchildren
1c Elizabeth ROTCH, *b* 1895; *d* 29 June 1895
2c Margaret Randolph Rotch, *b* Boston 14 June 1896; *m* 1 June 1916 James Jackson STORROW, Jr, s of James Jackson Storrow, and *d* 19 March 1945, leaving issue:

Great-great-grandchildren's great-grandchildren
1d James Jackson STORROW, *b* 17 May 1917; *m* 1st 26 June 1940 Patricia Blake (*b* 13 April 1917) and had issue:

Great-great-grandchildren's great-great-grandchildren
1e *Gerald Blake STORROW, *b* 15 July 1944
2e *Peter STORROW, *b* 26 Sept 1946; *m* 19— *Nancy ——
3e *James Jackson (changed name from Arthur Rotch) STORROW III, *b* 7 June 1948
4e *Margaret Randolph STORROW, *b* 4 Jan 1955

Great-great-grandchildren's great-grandchildren
1d (cont.) James J. Storrow *m* 2nd 15 Dec 1962 *Linda Eder and *d* 13 Jan 1984

Great-great-grandchildren's grandchildren
3c Arthur ROTCH, *b* Boston 1 Feb 1899; *m* Dedham, Mass., 30 April 1935 Alice Gedney (*b* Milton, Mass., 21 Nov 1900; *d* there 8 Dec 1971), dau of Edward Cabot Storrow and his w Caroline, and *d* Boston 6 Feb 1973, leaving issue:

Great-great-grandchildren's great-grandchildren
1d *Ann Storrow Rotch [Mrs Henry Magendantz, Rte 164, Old Louisquisset Pike, Lincoln, RI 02865, USA], *b* Boston 28 Jan 1937; *m* Milton, Mass., 16 July 1960 *Henry G. MAGENDANTZ (*b* 20 Aug 1936), s of Heinz Magendantz and his w Marianna, and has issue:

Great-great-grandchildren's great-great-grandchildren
1e *Nicholas Alexander MAGENDANTZ, *b* 28 Nov 1973
2e *Elisa Margaret MAGENDANTZ, *b* 11 Oct 1976
Mr and Mrs Henry Magendantz have also adopted two sons:
a *Eric Ashley MAGENDANTZ, *b* 1 April 1967
b *Christopher Lawrence MAGENDANTZ, *b* 12 Dec 1968

Great-great-grandchildren's great-grandchildren
2d *Abbott Lawrence ROTCH [RFD #1 Box 2275, Liberty, ME 04949, USA], *b* Boston 8 March 1939; *educ* Harvard; self-employed electrical engr; *m* N Edgecomb, Maine, 31 Aug 1963 *Emily Beaumelle (*b* Berkeley, Calif., 1943), dau of Robert Roe and his w Mary Elizabeth, and has issue:

Great-great-grandchildren's great-great-grandchildren
1e *Elizabeth Ann Rotch [Mrs Rocha, 40 Woodbury, Arlington, MA 02174, USA], *b* Boston 23 Oct 1964; *m* there 26 June 1989 *Jairo ROCHA and has issue:

Great-great-grandchildren's great-great-grandchildren's children
1f *Julia Mary ROCHA, *b* 30 Jan 1990

Great-great-grandchildren's great-great-grandchildren
2e *Arthur Randolph ROTCH [1205 Second St, Douglas, AK 99824, USA], *b* Boston 11 Aug 1966; *educ* Harvard; theatre designer and technician; *m* Maine 21 Nov 1991 *Kathryn Laura, dau of Lloyd Sherer Kurtz, Jr, and his w Patricia Jean
3e *Andrew Lawrence ROTCH, *b* Boston 6 Feb 1970

Great-great-grandchildren's great-grandchildren
3d *Edward Cabot ROTCH [PO Box 255, Washington, ME 04574, USA], *b* Boston 9 July 1941

Great-great-grandchildren's grandchildren
4c Katherine Lawrence Rotch, *b* Boston 26 May 1906; *m* 17 June 1925 Malcolm Whelan GREENOUGH (*b* Jan 1904; *d* 7 Feb 1948), s of Malcolm Scollay Greenough and his w Violet Whelan, and *d* 31 March 1966, having had issue:

Great-great-grandchildren's great-grandchildren
1d *Malcolm Whelan GREENOUGH, Jr [Paine Ave, Prides Crossing, MA 01965, USA], *b* 11 June 1926; *m* 1st 7 Feb 1948 Sarah Eden Browne and has issue:

Great-great-grandchildren's great-great-grandchildren
1e *Katherine Lawrence GREENOUGH, *b* 16 Nov 1949
2e *Sarah Eden Greenough, *b* 25 May 1951; *m* 17 June 1978 *Nicolai CIKOVSKY
3e *Margaret Randolph Greenough, *b* 19 July 1954; *m* 13 Sept 1985 *Joel Frederick JOHNSON
4e *Malcolm Whelan GREENOUGH III, *b* 16 Sept 1957

Great-great-grandchildren's great-grandchildren

1d (cont.) Malcolm W. Greenough *m* 2nd 29 Nov 1969 *Catherine Royce McKenna and has further issue:

Great-great-grandchildren's great-great-grandchildren
5e *Charles William GREENOUGH, *b* 12 March 1971
6e *Andrew Scollay GREENOUGH, *b* 26 June 1973
7e *George Pelham GREENOUGH, *b* 6 May 1976

Great-great-grandchildren's great-grandchildren

2d Lawrence Rotch GREENOUGH, *b* 16 Dec 1930; *m* 14 April 1956 *Pamela Antoinette Marguerite Seddon [Hill Ash Farm, West Harting, nr Petersfield, Hants, UK] and *d* 17 April 1964, leaving issue:

Great-great-grandchildren's great-great-grandchildren
1e *Elizabeth Tiffany Greenough [Mrs Richard Mullings, Caudle Green House, Caudle Green, Cheltenham, Glos GL53 9PR, UK], *b* 31 May 1957; *m* Hill Ash Farm 11 Oct 1986 *Richard Randolph MULLINGS (*b* 16 July 1953), slr, of Pinbury Park, Cirencester, Glos, UK, and has issue:

Great-great-grandchildren's great-great-grandchildren's children
1f *John Lawrence Randolph MULLINGS, *b* England 14 May 1987
2f *Eleanor Violett MULLINGS, *b* England 25 Nov 1988
3f *Josephine Beatrice Livingstone MULLINGS, *b* England 31 March 1992

Great-great-grandchildren's great-great-grandchildren
2e *Lawrence Rotch GREENOUGH, Jr [17 Ladbroke Gdns, London W11 2PT, UK], *b* 2 June 1959; *m* 27 Nov 1987 *Thekla Helene Howell (*b* 6 Sept 1960) and has issue:

Great-great-grandchildren's great-great-grandchildren's children
1f *Georgina Rosamond GREENOUGH, *b* 25 Oct 1989
2f *Horatio William Wurlitzer GREENOUGH, 1 May 1991

Great-great-grandchildren's children

4b (cont.) Margaret Anderson Rotch *m* 2nd 1 Nov 1919 Henry PARKMAN, Jr, and *d* Milton, Mass., 3 May 1941
5b Sarah Randolph ANDERSON, *b* 21 May 1872; *d* 17 Jan 1960

Great-great-grandchildren

2a William Lewis RANDOLPH, *b* 20 Dec 1841; Ordnance Offr Armistead's Bde, Pickett's Div, Confederate States Army; *m* 1st 1866 Agnes (*b* 23 Jan 1846; *d* 8 May 1880, *bur* Monticello), dau of Michael Dillon, of Savannah, formerly of Ireland, and his w Margaret Riley, and had issue:

Great-great-grandchildren's children

1b Margaret Gibson RANDOLPH, *b* 19 Nov 1866; *d* 13 Sept 1872 (*bur* Monticello)
2b Thomas Jefferson RANDOLPH IV, *b* 21 July 1868; *m* 1st 14 Nov 1895 Laura Lester and had issue:

Great-great-grandchildren's grandchildren

1c Laura Lester Randolph, *b* 9 Feb 1899; *m* 18 Dec 1920 *Alfred Wright THOMPSON [1723 South Edgewood Avenue, Jacksonville 5, FL 32205, USA] and *d* 19 March 1969, leaving issue:

Great-great-grandchildren's great-grandchildren

1d *Randolph Hines THOMPSON, *b* 13 July 1924; *m* 30 June 1951 *Sarah Beauvois L'Engle (*b* 6 Sept 1929) and has issue:

Great-great-grandchildren's great-great-grandchildren
1e *Michael L'Engle THOMPSON, *b* 26 June 1955
2e *Sara THOMPSON, *b* 19—

Great-great-grandchildren's grandchildren

2c Martha Jefferson Randolph, *b* 23 Sept 1900; *m* 9 June 1920 John Porter STEVENS, of Savannah (*d* 10 May 1969), and *d* 23 Aug 1969, leaving issue:

Great-great-grandchildren's great-grandchildren

1d Martha Randolph STEVENS, *b* 23 July 1921; *d* 29 July 1935
2d *Laura Randolph Stevens [Mrs Donald A Devendorf, Springfield Plantation, RFD 1 Box 206 E, Midway, GA 31320, USA], *b* 23 Nov 1931; *educ* U of Wisconsin; artist, writer, course-designer international horseshow jumping, Pres Seabrook Sch Fndn; *m* 1st 14 Oct 1950 (divorce 1960) Frank Kohler PEEPLES and has issue:

Great-great-grandchildren's great-great-grandchildren
1e *Marla Randolph STEVENS (born PEEPLES but name legally changed 1989), *b* 10 Dec 1951
2e *Daryn Stewart Peeples [Mrs Stuart S Beringer, 64 Highland Rd, Rye, NY 10580, USA], *b* 15 April 1954; *m* 20 Oct 1984 *Stuart Stratton BERINGER and has issue:

Great-great-grandchildren's great-great-grandchildren's children
1f *Taylor Randolph BERINGER, *b* 18 Aug 1986
2f *Stuart Marshall BERINGER, *b* 13 April 1988

Great-great-grandchildren's great-grandchildren
2d (cont.) Mrs Laura Stevens Peeples *m* 2nd 3 Aug 1961 *Donald Allan DEVENDORF and has issue:

Great-great-grandchildren's great-great-grandchildren
3e *Meredith Randolph DEVENDORF, *b* 11 Oct 1970

Great-great-grandchildren's children
2b (cont.) Thomas Jefferson Randolph IV *m* 2nd Nancy Clifton de Marclay and *d* 18 Feb 1926 (*bur* Monticello)
3b Dr William Mann RANDOLPH, *b* Albemarle Co, Va., 14 Jan 1870; *educ* Virginia U (MD 1900); *m* 20 Oct 1894 his 1st cousin once-removed Mary Walker (*b* Albemarle Co 14 June 1866; *d* Wild Acres, Charlottesville, 9 Dec 1957, *bur* Monticello), yst dau of Thomas Jefferson Randolph, Jr (for whom *see below*), and *d* 25 Jan 1944 (*bur* Monticello), having had issue:

Great-great-grandchildren's grandchildren
1c Carolina Ramsay RANDOLPH, *b* Charlottesville 23 Sept 1895; *educ* Agnes Scott Coll, Atlanta, and Johns Hopkins (MS); author: *School Health Services* (1941) and other works, Sec-Treasurer Monticello Assoc 1951-56; *d* Wild Acres 1 March 1958 (*bur* Monticello)
2c Sarah Nicholas Randolph, *b* 8 Dec 1896; *m* 29 March 1919 Gen Lucian King TRUSCOTT, Jr, US Army (*b* Chatfield, Tex., 9 Jan 1895; *d* Washington, DC, 12 Sept 1965), s of Lucian King Truscott and his w Maria Temple Tully, and *d* 17 Aug 1974, leaving issue:

Great-great-grandchildren's great-grandchildren
1d Mary Randolph Truscott, *b* 3 May 1920; *m* 1st 28 April 1942 (divorce 19—) Robert WILBOURN; *m* 2nd 14 Dec 1957 *Graeme Grant BRUCE and *d* 19 July 1991 (*bur* Monticello)
2d *Col Lucian King TRUSCOTT III [5508 Lakeview Drive NE, Apt E, Kirkland, WA 98033-7373, USA], *b* Hawaii 17 Sept 1921; served US Army; *m* 16 April 1946 *Anne Harloe and has issue:

Great-great-grandchildren's great-great-grandchildren
1e *Lucian King TRUSCOTT IV [431 W Roscoe Apt 12A, Chicago, IL 60657, USA], *b* 12 April 1947; *m* 17 March 1979 *Carol Troy
2e *Francis (Frank) Meriwether TRUSCOTT [206 Fathom Cove, Stafford, VA 22554, USA], *b* San Antonio, Tex., 28 Jan 1949; *educ* U of Kansas; fiscal analyst with Smithsonian Inst; *m* 3 Jan 1970 *Deborah Newell, dau of William Van Sloan Jackson and his w Barbara Newell Doan, and has issue:

Great-great-grandchildren's great-great-grandchildren's children
1f *Christopher Harloe TRUSCOTT, *b* Prince William Co, Va., 8 Aug 1978
2f *Lucas Randolph TRUSCOTT, *b* Prince William Co 28 Oct 1981

Great-great-grandchildren's great-great-grandchildren
3e *Susan Harloe Truscott [14918 Linden Ave NE, Seattle, WA 98133, USA], *b* 19 Jan 1953; *m* 1st 5 June 1971 (divorce *c* 1974) Allan MOSKOWITZ, chiropractor, and has issue:

Great-great-grandchildren's great-great-grandchildren's children
1f *Rachel MOSKOWITZ, *b* 1971
2f *Sara MOSKOWITZ, *b* 25 June 1972

Great-great-grandchildren's great-great-grandchildren
3e (cont.) Mrs Susan Moskowitz *m* 2nd 18 Sept 1987 *Christopher Lance WREDE
4e *Mary Randolph Truscott [9061 E Shorewood Dve #687, Mercer Island, WA 98040, USA], *b* Kansas 7 Aug 1959; advertising retail manager, author: *Brats* (1990); *m* 11 April 1981 *Robert Frank SPICKNALL and has issue:

Great-great-grandchildren's great-great-grandchildren's children
1f *Ian Harloe SPICKNALL, *b* Seattle 7 Aug 1981

Great-great-grandchildren's great-great-grandchildren
5e *Virginia (Ginny) Anne Truscott [Mrs Kevin E Butcher, 19248 SE 49th St, Issaquah, WA 98027, USA], *b* Kansas 12 May 1961; *educ* U of New Mexico; computer analyst Gen Dynamics 1984-91 and Boeing 1991-; *m* 16 Aug 1980 *Kevin Edward Roland BUTCHER, s of Glen E. Butcher and his w Rolande Anguiano, and has issue:

Great-great-grandchildren's great-great-grandchildren's children
1f *Thomas Randolph BUTCHER, *b* Texas 5 Sept 1986
2f *Nicholas Truscott BUTCHER, *b* Texas 29 Dec 1988

Great-great-grandchildren's great-grandchildren
3d *Lt-Col James Joseph TRUSCOTT [469 New Castle St, Slippery Rock, PA 16057-1012, USA], *b* 26 Dec 1930; served USAF; *m* 31 Aug 1957 *Helen Kelly Haydock and has issue:

Great-great-grandchildren's great-great-grandchildren
1e *James Joseph TRUSCOTT, Jr, *b* 1 Aug 1958
2e *S/Sgt Thomas Haydock TRUSCOTT [4153 Lee Village Apt B, Fort Campbell, KY 42223, USA], *b* 30 Nov

1959
 3e *Patrick Moore TRUSCOTT [2232 Brier Ave, Los Angeles, CA 90039, USA], *b* 16 July 1962
 4e *Sarah Randolph TRUSCOTT, *b* 6 Jan 1968

Great-great-grandchildren's grandchildren

3c Agnes Dillon Randolph, *b* 13 April 1898; *m* 1st 25 May 1925 George MARVIN; *m* 2nd 28 Dec 1934 Edward Buffam HILL (*b* Brooklyn, New York, 1879; *d* Woodside, Calif., 14 Oct 1957) and *d* Jan 1977

4c William Lewis RANDOLPH, *b* 10 July 1899; *d* 7 Jan 1906

5c Col Thomas Jefferson RANDOLPH V, *b* Charlottesville 7 Oct 1900; served US Army, Pres Monticello Assoc 1953-55 (V-Pres 1951-53); *m* 24 April 1930 Augusta Lyell Blue (*d* 8 March 1981) and *d* 22 Oct 1984 (*bur* Monticello), leaving issue:

 Great-great-grandchildren's great-grandchildren

 1d *Virginia Hyland Randolph [Mrs Landry T Slade, 250 George Rd #7D, Cliffside Park, NJ 07010, USA], *b* 10 May 1931; *m* 28 Dec 1957 *Landry Thomas SLADE and has issue:

  Great-great-grandchildren's great-great-grandchildren

  1e *Lyell Landry SLADE, *b* 19 Sept 1959
  2e *Lawrence Randolph SLADE, *b* 9 Aug 1964; *m* 19— *———
  3e *William Learned SLADE, *b* 10 Feb 1967

 Great-great-grandchildren's great-grandchildren

 2d *Lt-Col William Mann RANDOLPH III [124 Creekstone Dve, Newport News, VA 23603, USA], *b* 20 April 1933; *m* 28 Jan 1956 *Maria Teresa Osma (*b* 7 May 1934) and has had issue:

  Great-great-grandchildren's great-great-grandchildren

  1e *Helen Augusta Randolph [1417 Key Blvd #407, Arlington, VA 22209, USA], *b* 14 March 1958; *m* 27 Oct 1992 *Carl Francis CANAVAN
  2e *Elizabeth Virginia RANDOLPH [285-34 Merrimac Trail, Williamsburg, VA 23185-4662, USA], *b* Darmstadt, W Germany, 15 Sept 1959; *educ* MUW and CNC; medical technologist Veterans Admin, Hampton, Va., 1982-87, kindergarten teacher, Williamsburg, Va., 1990-
  3e Peter Jefferson RANDOLPH, *b* 5 March, *d* 9 March 1961
  4e *(Susan) Carolina Randolph [Mrs Matthias Steup, 813 13th Ave S, St Cloud, MN 56301, USA], *b* Cheyenne, Wyo., 4 Feb 1964; *educ* Wells Coll and SUNY, Buffalo; *m* 24 Nov 1989 *Matthias Peter STEUP, s of Hans Steup and his w Fanny
  5e *Thomas Joseph RANDOLPH [814 N Daniel St, Arlington, VA 22201, USA], *b* 30 July 1965

Great-great-grandchildren's grandchildren

6c Mary Walker RANDOLPH, *b* 30 April 1903; Pres Monticello Assoc 1948-49 (V-Pres 1946-48, Sec-Treasurer 1970-73, Treasurer 1975-76, Historian 1975-76); *d* 20 June 1988

7c Hollins Nicholas RANDOLPH, Jr, *b* Charlottesville 14 June 1904; *m* 22 Aug 1933 Mary Virginia (*b* Wheeling 1908; *d* 14 April 1986), dau of William Hoge and his w Virginia Blue, and *d* 21 Nov 1976, leaving issue:

 Great-great-grandchildren's great-grandchildren

 1d *Hollins Nicholas RANDOLPH III [Rt1, Box 263-513, Charles Town, WV 25414, USA], *b* Wheeling 2 June 1934; *m* Oklahoma City, Okla., 18 July 1957 (divorce 1978) Nancy Lee (*b* Winchester, Va., 26 July 1939), dau of Sewell Walter Wilson and his w Hilda Walford, and has issue:

  Great-great-grandchildren's great-great-grandchildren

  1e *Bonnnie Sue Randolph, *b* Oklahoma City, 8 Jan 1958; *m* 26 Oct 1979 *Henry Harrison SMITH III
  2e *Martha Christine RANDOLPH, *b* Winchester, Va., 31 Dec 1959
  3e *Hollins Nicholas RANDOLPH IV, *b* Winchester 28 Sept 1961; semi-truck driver; *m* 16 July 1983 *Nancy Louise, dau of William Kraft and his w Ruth, and has issue:

   Great-great-grandchildren's great-great-grandchildren's children

   1f *Nicole Crystal RANDOLPH, *b* Oxnard, Calif., 31 March 1985
   2f *Nira Christine RANDOLPH, *b* Laporte, Ind., 29 March 1990

  Great-great-grandchildren's great-great-grandchildren
  4e *Angela Marie RANDOLPH, *b* Winchester 16 March 1971

 Great-great-grandchildren's great-grandchildren

 2d *Thomas Jefferson RANDOLPH VI [114 Bedford Dve, Winchester, VA 22602, USA], *b* Wheeling, W. Va., 8 Oct 1936; personnel superintendent West Virginia Air Guard; *m* 20 Dec 1958 *Mary Marie, dau of Melvin Franklin Spitler and his w Pauline Huffman Beydler, and has issue:

  Great-great-grandchildren's great-great-grandchildren

  1e *Thomas Jefferson RANDOLPH VII [1620 Rockwood Rd, Richmond, VA 23226, USA], *b* Warrensburg, Mo., 11 Feb 1960; *m* Richmond, Va., 19 Sept 1987 *Mary Susan Oliver and has issue:

   Great-great-grandchildren's great-great-grandchildren's children
   1f *Thomas Jefferson RANDOLPH VIII, *b* Richmond 30 March 1991

Great-great-grandchildren's great-great-grandchildren

2e *William Franklin RANDOLPH [PO Box 684, Woodstock, VA 22664, USA], *b* Winchester, Va., 8 July 1963; served US Army 1981-85, mechanic 1985-, with Virginia Nat Gd 1989-; *m* Woodstock 20 Oct 1990 *Janice Lee, dau of Milford Grover Parker

3e *John Michael RANDOLPH [114 Bedford Dve, Winchester, VA 22602, USA], *b* Winchester 23 April 1972

Great-great-grandchildren's grandchildren

8c Francis Meriwether RANDOLPH, *b* 22 April 1906; *m* 21 Dec 1935 *Leonne Gouaux and *d* 19 Oct 1978, leaving issue:

Great-great-grandchildren's great-grandchildren

1d *Thomas Mann RANDOLPH [757 Castle Kirk Dve, Baton Rouge, LA 70808, USA], *b* 24 Sept 1936; *m* 24 Nov 1960 *Evelyn Adele Morash and has issue:

Great-great-grandchildren's great-great-grandchildren

1e *Margaret Elizabeth Randolph [3728 Hermitage, Chicago, IL 60613, USA], *b* 26 Aug 1961; *m* 7 Sept 1991 *David A. GLOCKNER

2e *Hugh Jefferson RANDOLPH [2000 Burton St Apt 286, Austin, TX 78741, USA], *b* 16 Oct 1962

3e *Aileen Ann RANDOLPH [4236 River Rd NW, Washington, DC 20016, USA], *b* 17 March 1964

4e *Timothy Lawrence RANDOLPH [426 Packard St #2, Ann Arbor, MI 48104, USA], *b* 23 Sept 1966; *m* 3 June 1990 *Jessica Reed

5e *Matthew Thomas RANDOLPH [2201 Rocky Lane #1810, Odessa, TX 79762, USA], *b* 8 Feb 1969

Great-great-grandchildren's great-grandchildren

2d *(William) Lew(is) RANDOLPH [345 Bridgewater Dve, Newport News, VA 23603, USA], *b* 28 Sept 1940; *m* 1st Dec 1961 Brenda Theresa Cherami and has issue:

Great-great-grandchildren's great-great-grandchildren

1e *Katherine (Kay) Anne RANDOLPH [1055 W Yosemite Ave #7, Merced, CA 95348, USA], *b* 30 Oct 1962; *educ* California State U, Fresno; manager with Big 5 Sporting Goods 1987-90, personnel analyst City of Merced 1991-93, training coordinator McClane Pacific June 1993-

2e *Joseph Adam RANDOLPH [4068 Rio Rd, Carmel, CA 93923, USA], *b* 28 Nov 1963

3e *Frances Margaret Randolph [Mrs Kerry Rollins, 5739 N Cedar #216, Fresno, CA 93710, USA], *b* 8 Sept 1966; *m* 5 Oct 1991 *Kerry ROLLINS

Great-great-grandchildren's great-grandchildren

2d (cont.) Lew Randolph *m* 2nd 3 July 1976 (divorce 19—) Dana Grafton Kroyer

3d *Michael Joseph RANDOLPH [213 Edgewood Dve, Wilmington, DE 19809, USA], *b* 19 Feb 1942; *m* 15 Aug 1965 *(Marie) Eliska (Licky) Moore and has issue:

Great-great-grandchildren's great-great-grandchildren

1e *Paul Raymond RANDOLPH [108 W Central Ave, Moorestown, NJ 08057, USA], *b* Wilmington, Del., 12 Sept 1966; *educ* U of Delaware; sr research assist Ecogen Inc 1990-; *m* 13 Jan 1990 *Linda Susan, dau of William Edwin Bird and his w Mary Louise Trivetts

2e *Deborah (Debbie) Ann Randolph [Mrs Walter D Wildman, 819 Montgomery St, Blacksburg, VA 24060, USA], *b* 3 June 1968; *m* 5 Oct 1991 *Walter Davis WILDMAN

3e *Jennifer Marie RANDOLPH, *b* 6 Dec 1971

Great-great-grandchildren's children

4b Hollins Nicholas RANDOLPH, *b* 25 Feb 1872; *educ* U of Virginia (BL 1895); attorney at Atlanta, Ga., Pres Monticello Assoc 1926-29; *m* 17 Oct 1899 Caroline Tyson (*b* 1875; *d* 1960), dau of George Walter, of Savannah, and *d* Washington, DC, 29 April 1938 (*bur* Monticello)

5b Arthur Dillon RANDOLPH, *b* 9 Feb, *d* 6 Nov 1874 (*bur* Monticello)

6b Agnes Dillon RANDOLPH, *b* 12 July 1875; *d* 3 Dec 1930 (*bur* Monticello)

Great-great-grandchildren

2a (cont.) William Lewis Randolph *m* 2nd 9 Nov 1887 his 1st cousin Margaret Randolph (*b* 14 Nov 1843; *d* 12 Feb 1898, *bur* Monticello), 3rd dau of John Charles Randolph Taylor, of Lego, Albemarle Co, Va. (for whom *see below*), and *d* 7 June 1892 (*bur* Monticello)

Great-grandchildren

(2) Martha (Patsy) Jefferson Randolph, *b* Mount Warren 20 July 1817; *m* Edgehill 22 Dec 1834 her cousin John Charles Randolph TAYLOR, of Elmington, Clarke Co, Va. (*b* there 30 May 1812; *educ* U of Virginia; *d* Lego, Albemarle Co, Va., 6 Jan 1875, *bur* Monticello), s of Bennett Taylor and his w Susan Beverley, dau of Edmund Randolph, Govr Virginia 1786-88, and *d* Midway, Albemarle Co, 16 July 1857 (*bur* Monticello), having had issue:

Great-great-grandchildren

1a Bennett TAYLOR, *b* Edgehill 15 Aug 1836; *educ* U of Virginia; Lt-Col 19th Virginia Regt Confederate States Army; *m* Albemarle Co 1866 Lucy (*b* 9 March 1842; *d* Page, W. Va., 4 March 1928), dau of Edward Colston and his w Sarah Jane Brockenbrough, and *d* Bedford, Va., 9 April 1898 (*bur* Monticello), leaving issue:

Great-great-grandchildren's children
1b Patsy Jefferson TAYLOR, *b* 24 March 1867; *d* Ansted, W. Va., 20 Nov 1903 (*bur* Monticello)
2b Raleigh Colston TAYLOR, of Lego and Charlottesville, *b* Albemarle Co 22 June 1869; Pres Monticello Assoc 1929-31; *m* 1907 Mary Tayloe (*b* 1875; *d* Charlottesville, Va., 1949, *bur* Monticello) and *d* Charlottesville 11 April 1952 (*bur* Monticello), leaving issue:

Great-great-grandchildren's grandchildren
1c Raleigh Colston TAYLOR, Jr, *b* Ansted, W. Va., 13 Feb 1909; *m* Richmond, Va., 1940 Margaret (*b* 22 July 1904; *d* Richmond, Va., 6 Aug 1978, *bur* Monticello), dau of Paul Howard Lamb and his w Margaret, and *d* Tuscaloosa, Ala., 19 April 1959 (*bur* Monticello), leaving issue:

Great-great-grandchildren's great-grandchildren
1d *Dr Jane Colston TAYLOR [Dr Jane Taylor Gaede, PO Box 747, Hillsborough, NC 27278, USA], *b* Washington, DC, 8 July 1941; *m* Winston-Salem, N Carolina, 12 Feb 1966 *William Hanks GAEDE (*b* Pittsburg, Pa., 6 Feb 1922), s of William Adolf Gaede and his w Lucy Lucas

Great-great-grandchildren's children
3b Lewis Randolph TAYLOR, *b* 22 Sept 1871; *m* 10 Sept 1901 Natalie Dorsey Sefton (*d* Martinsburg, W. Va., 5 July 1969) and *d* Martinsburg, W. Va., 12 April 1945 (*bur* Monticello), leaving issue:

Great-great-grandchildren's grandchildren
1c *Bennett TAYLOR III [300 N Georgia Avenue, Martinsburg, WV 25401, USA], *b* 14 May 1904; *m* 8 June 1935 *Anne Spottswood Harrison
2c Lewis Randolph TAYLOR, Jr, *b* Roanoke, Va., 11 March 1909; *m* Bluefield, W. Va., 7 June 1941 *Carolyn [Mrs Lewis R Taylor Jr, 55 W 11th St, New York, NY 10011, USA], dau of Harry Douthat and his w Anna, and *d* 3 May 1976, leaving issue:

Great-great-grandchildren's great-grandchildren
1d *Susan Randolph Taylor [1312 51st Ave NE, St Petersburg, FL 33703, USA], *b* New York 3 Aug 1949; *educ* Duke U; *m* 15 Nov 1975 *James Addison MARTIN, Jr, and has issue:

Great-great-grandchildren's great-great-grandchildren
1e *Steven Randolph MARTIN, *b* 16 May 1979

Great-great-grandchildren's grandchildren
3c *Walter Dorsey TAYLOR [1004 Abingdon Road, Virginia Beach, VA 23451, USA], *b* 5 Dec 1916; *m* Norfolk, Va., 19— *Emily Rawlings and has issue:

Great-great-grandchildren's great-grandchildren
1d *Emily Hume Taylor [Mrs Bradford W Gile, 6 Hopewell Point Rd, Wolfeboro, NH 03894, USA], *b* Norfolk, Va., 6 July 1942; *m* 16 April 1966 *Bradford Willis GILE and has issue:

Great-great-grandchildren's great-great-grandchildren
1e *Bradford Willis GILE, Jr, *b* 20 Jan 1969
2e *Emily Hume GILE, *b* 23 March 1973

Great-great-grandchildren's great-grandchildren
2d *Walter Dorsey TAYLOR, Jr [5914 Sunnycrest Rd, Roanoke, VA 24018, USA], *b* Norfolk, Va., 23 Dec 1945; *m* 8 June 1968 *Linda Sue Bohon and has issue:

Great-great-grandchildren's great-great-grandchildren
1e *Linda Bohon Taylor, *b* 2 Aug 1971; *m* 5 Oct 1991 *Lionel Page EWELL
2e *Martha Randolph TAYLOR, *b* 16 Oct 1975
3e *Lucy Colston TAYLOR, *b* 21 Jan 1981

Great-great-grandchildren's children
4b John Charles Randolph TAYLOR III, *b* Lego, Albemarle Co, Va., 21 Aug 1874; *m* Halifax, Va., 18 June 1907 Mary Grammer (*b* Leigholm, Va., 7 Sept 1881; *d* Halifax, Va., 1 Aug 1959), dau of Thomas Watkins Leigh and his w Mary Elizabeth Faulkner, and *d* Salem, Va., 27 Jan 1962, leaving issue:

Great-great-grandchildren's grandchildren
1c Martha Jefferson Taylor, *b* Page, W. Va., 10 Dec 1910; research biologist 1931-71 (leukaemia in mice, resistance to anthrax in rats, bacterial genetics), Sec Monticello Assoc 1973-83; *m* Edinburgh, Scotland, 8 Sept 1964 Edgar STEDMAN, DSc, PhD, FRS (*b* Guildford, Surrey, UK, 12 July 1890; *d* May 1975), s of Albert Stedman and his w Ellen Eagle, and *d* 29 June 1987
2c John Charles Randolph TAYLOR IV, *b* Page, W. Va., 22 Sept 1914; *m* Norfolk, Va., 9 Dec 1944 *Mary Farrant (*b* there 7 Nov 1922), dau of George E. Ferebee and his w Mary Farrant, and *d* 29 April 1988, leaving issue:

Great-great-grandchildren's great-grandchildren
1d *John Charles Randolph TAYLOR V [4212 Ave F, Austin, TX 78751, USA], *b* Norfolk, Va., 26 March 1946
2d *Randolph Emory TAYLOR, *b* Norfolk, Va., 1 Oct 1947; *m* 26 or 27 Nov 1988 *Duane Lougee

Great-great-grandchildren's grandchildren
3c *William Leigh TAYLOR [310 Townes Street, Danville, VA 24541 USA], b Page, W. Va., 7 May 1919; Pres Monticello Assoc 1975-77 (V-Pres 1973-75, Treasurer 1982-); m Norfolk, Va., 24 Jan 1942 *Norma (b Hamilton, Ontario, Canada, 8 Oct 1918), dau of Stanley C. Pamplin and his 1st w Mae Roberts, and has issue:

Great-great-grandchildren's great-grandchildren
1d *Mary Leigh Taylor [Mrs Philip Shepard, 3609 Whispering Lane, Falls Church, VA 22041, USA], b Savannah, Ga., 9 Dec 1942; m Danville, Va., 10 July 1965 *Philip Wilson'SHEPARD (b Haverhill, Mass., 20 Oct 1938), s of Paul W. Shepard and his w Helen Carey, and has issue:

Great-great-grandchildren's great-great-grandchildren
1e *Jennifer Leigh SHEPARD, b Washington, DC, 29 April 1969
2e *Douglas Carey SHEPARD, b Washington 16 May 1972

Great-great-grandchildren's great-grandchildren
2d *William Leigh TAYLOR, Jr [1403 Banks St, Houston, TX 77006, USA], b Norfolk, Va., 26 Feb 1947
3d *Charles MacLellan TAYLOR [612 Richmond St, El Cerrito, CA 94530, USA], b Staunton, Va., 2 Sept 1949; m Madison, Wis., 11 Sept 1977 *Alice Whitcomb Clark and has issue:

Great-great-grandchildren's great-great-grandchildren
1e *Alice Theresa TAYLOR, b Madison 24 Oct 1977
2e *Joanna Leigh TAYLOR, b Madison 8 Feb 1983

Great-great-grandchildren's great-grandchildren
4d *Martha Jefferson Taylor [Mrs Mark I Raper, 3911 Seminary Ave, Richmond, VA 23227, USA], b Danville, Va., 9 Jan 1954; Sec Monticello Assoc 1973-83; m Danville 17 Sept 1977 *Mark Irvin RAPER (b Greensboro, NC, 26 Aug 1954) and has issue:

Great-great-grandchildren's great-great-grandchildren
1e *Carter Jefferson RAPER, b Norfolk, Va., 27 Oct 1983
2e *Martha Stuart RAPER, b Richmond, Va., 3 July 1986
3e *Lucy Colston RAPER, b Richmond 20 April 1989

Great-great-grandchildren's grandchildren
4c *Mary Leigh Taylor [Mrs Martin Shaw, 33 Woodvale Avenue, Asheville, NC 28804, USA], b Page, W. Va., 1 Aug 1922; m Halifax, Va., 13 Jan 1951 *Martin Nisbet SHAW, Jr (b Leaksville, N Carolina, 17 April 1925), s of Martin Shaw and his w Jane Nelson Marr, and has issue:

Great-great-grandchildren's great-grandchildren
1d *Christopher Gordon SHAW [34 Eola Ave, Asheville, NC 28806, USA], b Elizabeth City, N Carolina, 28 Feb 1953; m Asheville, N Carolina, 15 April 1989 *Susan Ruth Wolter (b there 28 Feb 1952) and has issue:

Great-great-grandchildren's great-great-grandchildren
1e *Rebecca Ruth SHAW, b Asheville 10 May 1990

Great-great-grandchildren's great-grandchildren
2d *Margaret Hope SHAW [4831A Tower Rd, Greensboro, NC 27410, USA], b Asheville, N Carolina, 19 Jan 1956; V-Pres Monticello Assoc 1991-93

Great-great-grandchildren's children
5b Edward Colston TAYLOR, Sr, b 22 Feb 1877; m Jessie Alwine (d Charleston, W. Va., 6 Dec 1973, bur Monticello) and d Charleston 23 June 1940 (bur Monticello), leaving issue:

Great-great-grandchildren's grandchildren
1c *Edward Colston TAYLOR, Jr [561 Asharoken Ave, Northport, Long Island, NY 11768, USA], b Salemville, Pa., 21 March 1911; educ U of Virginia; architect, Pres Monticello Assoc 1955-57 (V-Pres 1953-55); m 9 Sept 1972 Alis Emily (d 11 Sept 1988), dau of Harry Shanks and his w Leafy Nalle and widow of Edward Andrew Cremer

Great-great-grandchildren's children
6b Jane Brockenbrough TAYLOR, b 29 Jan 1881; d 11 Nov 1955 (bur Monticello)

Great-great-grandchildren
2a Jane Randolph TAYLOR, b Avonwood 2 April 1838; d Lego 12 Jan 1917 (bur Monticello)
3a Susan Beverley Taylor, b Avonwood 8 Feb 1840; m John Sinclair BLACKBURN, of Alexandria, Va., and d Alexandria 22 Sept 1900, having had issue:

Great-great-grandchildren's children
1b Dr Richard Scott BLACKBURN, of Orange Grove, Fresno County, Calif., b 29 April 1875; m Ruth Darwin (b 1884; d 1948, bur Monticello) and d 4 April 1946 (bur Monticello), having had issue:

Great-great-grandchildren's grandchildren
1c John Sinclair BLACKBURN, b 31 March 1916; d 27 May 1935 (bur Monticello)
2c Gertrude Blackburn, b 10 June 1918; m 19— *George F. FOWLER and d 1977
3c *Ruth Blackburn, b 17 May 1920; m 19— *Walter Thomas NOBLES and has issue:

Great-great-grandchildren's great-grandchildren
1d *Charlotte Ruth NOBLES, *b* 3 Nov 1949

Great-great-grandchildren's children
2b Charlotte Moncure Blackburn, *b* 1881; *m* 23 Dec 1909 Thomas SHEPHERD and *d* 27 July 1917, leaving issue:

Great-great-grandchildren's grandchildren
1c *John Blackburn SHEPHERD, *b* 19—; *m* 19— *——* and has issue:

Great-great-grandchildren's great-grandchildren
1d *James SHEPHERD

Great-great-grandchildren's grandchildren
2c *Arnold Page SHEPHERD, *b* 19—; *m* 19— *——* and has issue:

Great-great-grandchildren's great-grandchildren
1d *Richard SHEPHERD

Great-great-grandchildren's grandchildren
3c *Blackburn Edward WILLIAMS (born Shepherd but adopted by a Mr and Mrs Eustace Williams following his mother's death), *b* 22 July 1917
4c Moncure SHEPHERD, *b* 22 July, *d* 9 Sept 1917

Great-great-grandchildren's children
3b John Sinclair BLACKBURN, Jr, *b* 1881; *d* 1900

Great-great-grandchildren
4a Revd Jefferson Randolph TAYLOR, *b* 27 Dec 1842; *m* Accomac, Va., Mary Hubard (*b* 20 Nov 1857; *d* 18 Feb 1909, *bur* Monticello), dau of Edward C. Bruce and his w Eliza Thompson Hubard, and *d* 15 April 1919 (*bur* Monticello), leaving issue:

Great-great-grandchildren's children
1b Martha Randolph Taylor, *b* 31 May 1892; *m* 6 April 1935, as his 2nd w, her brother-in-law, George Hyndman ESSER, Sr (*b* 5 May 1880; *d* Norton, Va., 28 March 1956, *bur* Monticello), s of John Alfred Esser and his w Esther Hyndman, and *d* 11 Jan 1968
2b Mary Cary Taylor, *b* 10 Aug 1894; *m* 4 Sept 1920, as his 1st w, George Hyndman ESSER, Sr (*see above*), and *d* 2 Jan 1923 (*bur* Monticello), leaving issue:

Great-great-grandchildren's grandchildren
1c *George Hyndman ESSER, Jr [211 North Elliott Rd, Chapel Hill, NC 27514, USA], *b* 6 Aug 1921; Pres Monticello Assoc 1961-63 (Recording Sec 1950-54, V-Pres 1959-61); *m* 20 June 1953 *Mary Parker and has issue:

Great-great-grandchildren's great-grandchildren
1d *Mary Cary ESSER [301-A Hillsboro St, Chapel Hill, NC 27514, USA], *b* 16 Sept 1955
2d *John Parker ESSER [211 North Elliott Rd, Chapel Hill, NC 27514, USA], *b* 1 Nov 1957
3d *G(eorge) Randolph ESSER [211 North Elliott Rd, Chapel Hill, NC 27514, USA], *b* 8 Sept 1960; *m* 2 Jan 1993 *Sarah Elizabeth Durant

Great-great-grandchildren's grandchildren
2c *Jefferson Randolph Cary ESSER [29 Black Horse Drive, Acton, MA 01720, USA], *b* Norton, Va., 28 Dec 1922; *m* Waukegan, Ill., 18 July 1953 *Kathryn (*b* there 29 Aug 1927), dau of B. C. Swanson and his w Jessie, and has issue:

Great-great-grandchildren's great-grandchildren
1d *Jefferson Randolph ESSER, *b* Berwyn, Ill., 26 April 1954; *m* 4 Oct 1980 *Carolyn Patricia Smith and has issue:

Great-great-grandchildren's great-great-grandchildren
1e *Katie Lynn ESSER, *b* 19 Jan 1985
2e *David Randolph ESSER, *b* 27 Dec 1988

Great-great-grandchildren's great-grandchildren
2d *Karyn Ann ESSER [Children's Medical Research Foundation, PO Box 61, Camperdown, NSW, Australia], *b* Milwaukee, Wis., 16 April 1957
3d *Douglas Swanson ESSER [3346 S Wakefield St Apt B-2, Arlington, VA 22206, USA], *b* Hinsdale, Ill., 1 April 1963

Great-great-grandchildren
5a Margaret Randolph Taylor, *b* Avonwood 14 Nov 1843; *m* 9 Nov 1887, as his 2nd w, her 1st cousin William Lewis RANDOLPH (*b* 20 Dec 1841; *d* 7 June 1892), s of Judge William Mann Randolph and his 1st w Margaret Smith, est dau of Thomas Jefferson Randolph (for whom *see above*) and *d* Lego 12 Feb 1898 (*bur* Monticello)
6a Charlotte TAYLOR, *b* 17 Dec 1845; *d* 17 May 1846
7a Stevens Mason TAYLOR, *b* Avonwood 6 July 1847; *m* Staunton, Va., 7 Feb 1882 Mary Mann (*b* Locust Grove 24

Feb 1852; *d* Lochlyn, Va., 3 March 1954, *bur* Monticello), dau of Edwin Randolph Page and his w Olivia Alexander, and *d* Lego 10 Jan 1917 (*bur* Monticello), having had issue:

Great-great-grandchildren's children
1b Page Taylor, *b* Ansted, W. Va., 25 Jan 1885; *m* Lego 26 June 1913 Edwin Kirk (*b* Richland, S. Dak., 6 Dec 1884; *d* Washington, DC, 17 Nov 1955, *bur* Monticello), s of Nathan Allen Kirk and his w Caroline Freeman, and *d* 1 May 1983, leaving issue:

Great-great-grandchildren's grandchildren
1c *Mary Ann Page Kirk [Mrs James Moyer, 141 White Springs Road, Geneva, NY 14456, USA], *b* Washington, DC, 9 Sept 1915; *m* there 6 June 1942 *James Charles MOYER (*b* Guelph, Ontario, Canada, 24 Feb 1914), s of Joseph B. Moyer and his w Emma Keleher, and has issue:

Great-great-grandchildren's great-grandchildren
1d *Margaret Randolph MOYER, *b* Geneva, New York, 16 Sept 1944
2d *Stevens Mason MOYER [751 Seneca Parkway, Rochester, NY 14613, USA], *b* Geneva, New York, 6 June 1947
3d *Elizabeth Duncan Moyer [Mrs Michael C Powanda, 435 Marin Ave, Mill Valley, CA 94941, USA], *b* Geneva, New York, 23 Oct 1952; *m* 30 April 1982 *Michael Christopher POWANDA

Great-great-grandchildren's grandchildren
2c E(dwin) Roger KIRK, *b* Washington, DC, 27 June 1917; *m* Toledo 21 Sept 1946 *Charlotte Louise Homrighaus and *d* 14 Dec 1986, leaving issue:

Great-great-grandchildren's great-grandchildren
1d *C(harlotte) Louise KIRK [4156 Jamesway Dve, Toledo, OH 43606, USA], *b* Raleigh, N Carolina, 26 July 1949
2d *Elizabeth Page Kirk [Mrs Alfred D Land III, 2697 Euclid Heights Bldg 6, Cleveland, OH 44106, USA], *b* Toledo, Ohio, 24 July 1953; *m* 21 Dec 1984 *Alfred Davis LAND III

Great-great-grandchildren's children
2b Mary Randolph TAYLOR, *b* 1886; *d* 1887
3b Margaret Randolph TAYLOR, *b* Ansted, W. Va., 9 June 1888; *d* 1 April 1985 (*bur* Monticello)
4b Olivia Alexander TAYLOR, *b* Lexington, Va., 31 Oct 1890; Pres Monticello Assoc 1971-73 (Sec-Treasurer 1941-51, Historian 1953-64); *d* 3 April 1985 (*bur* Monticello)

Great-great-grandchildren
8a Cornelia Jefferson TAYLOR, *b* Avonwood, Jefferson Co, Va., 29 March 1849; Co-Fndr Monticello Assoc (V-Pres 1913-37); *d* Washington, DC, 3 March 1937 (*bur* Monticello)
9a Moncure Robinson TAYLOR, *b* Avonwood 23 Feb 1851; *m* Gordonsville, Va., 1901 Lucie Madison (*b* Orange County, Va., 29 Sept 1871; *d* New York 11 Aug 1944, *bur* Monticello), dau of John Willis, Jr (est s of John Willis, Sr, whose mother Nelly Conway Madison was niece of President MADISON), and his w Mary Elizabeth Lupton, and *d* Gordonsville 7 Dec 1915 (*bur* Charlottesville), leaving issue:

Great-great-grandchildren's children
1b *John Byrd TAYLOR [16 North Lancaster Avenue, Margate City, NJ 08402, USA], *b* Lego 4 March 1903; Pres Monticello Assoc 1951-53 (Recording Sec 1938-41, V-Pres 1949-51); *m* 1st Northport, Long Island, New York, 4 Oct 1930 Mildred Powell (*b* Norfolk, Va., 9 July 1906), dau of Minor Bronaugh and his w Mildred Lee Drewry, and has issue:

Great-great-grandchildren's grandchildren
1c *Moncure Robinson TAYLOR II [826 Westham Parkway, Richmond, VA 23229, USA], *b* Lynchburg, Va., 8 Nov 1932; Pres Monticello Assoc 1981-83 (V-Pres 1979-81); *m* Pasadena, Tex., 22 March 1957 *Patsy Harline (*b* Abilene, Tex., 30 Oct 1933), dau of Harper Williams and his w Pauline Evans, and has issue:

Great-great-grandchildren's great-grandchildren
1d *Moncure Robinson TAYLOR III [826 Westham Parkway, Richmond, VA 23229, USA], *b* Wareham, Mass., 6 Nov 1957
2d *John Harper TAYLOR [5021 Sycamore Ave, Pasadena, TX 77503, USA], *b* Raleigh, N Carolina, 7 Nov 1959
3d *Minor Bronaugh TAYLOR, *b* Winter Park, Fla., 4 June 1961; *m* 11 May 1990 *Cynthia Michelle Bobbitt
4d *Lawrence Colston TAYLOR, *b* Winter Park 27 May 1969

Great-great-grandchildren's grandchildren
2c *Mildred Lee Drewry Taylor [Mrs Claude Farmer Jr, 6003 Morningside Drive, Richmond, VA 24541, USA; 119 W Williamsburg Rd, Richmond, VA 23231, USA], *b* Lynchburg, Va., 17 July 1936; *m* Margate, New Jersey, 7 Sept 1963 *Claude Crisp FARMER, Jr (*b* Richmond, Va., 10 Dec 1937), s of Claude Crisp Farmer and his w Eliza Ragland, and has had issue:

Great-great-grandchildren's great-grandchildren
1d Claude Crisp FARMER III, *b* Carlisle, Pa., 28 March, *d* 1 April 1965

2d *Taylor Bronaugh FARMER, *b* Richmond, Va., 3 Jan 1968
3d *Paul Crisp FARMER, *b* Richmond 3 June 1971

Great-great-grandchildren's grandchildren
3c *Lucie Bronaugh Taylor [Mrs Louis Carnesale, 6060 La Goleta Road, Goleta, CA 93117, USA], *b* Lynchburg, Va., 14 Dec 1938; *m* Middlesex, New Jersey, 21 Sept 1958 *Louis John CARNESALE (*b* Pleasantville, New Jersey, 15 June 1934), s of Peter L. Carnesale and his w Mary Saviano, and has issue:

Great-great-grandchildren's great-grandchildren
1d *Louis Vincent CARNESALE [2212 Bermuda Dunes Dve, Oxnard, CA 93035, USA], *b* Santa Barbara, Calif., 16 Jan 1963
2d *John Lawrence CARNESALE [1375 Kelton Ave, #109, Los Angeles, CA 90024, USA], *b* Santa Barbara 16 Jan 1963
3d *Carrie Lee CARNESALE, *b* Santa Barbara 28 April 1969
4d *Virginia Powell CARNESALE, *b* 1 June 1975

Great-great-grandchildren's children
1b (cont.) John B. Taylor *m* 2nd 8 June 1985 *Grace Douglas Reid Ambler

Great-great-grandchildren
10a Edmund Randolph TAYLOR, *b* Avonwood, Va., 12 July 1853; *m* 7 July 1892 Julia Paca Kennedy and *d* 16 June 1919, leaving issue:

Great-great-grandchildren's children
1b Juliana Paca TAYLOR, *b* 31 Jan 1894; *d* 17 Jan 1986
2b Elizabeth Gray TAYLOR, *b* 10 June 1895; *d* 19 Jan 1978
3b *Edmund Randolph TAYLOR [131 East Third St, Ranson, WV 25438, USA], *b* 5 Oct 1898; *m* 26 Dec 1924 Alice Hunt (*d* 28 June 1963) and has issue:

Great-great-grandchildren's grandchildren
1c *Edmund Randolph TAYLOR, Jr [556 Bedford Rd, N Tarrytown, NY 10591, USA], *b* 21 Oct 1925; Electronic Supervisor Physics Dept Columbia U 1955-90; *m* 29 May 1954 *Patricia Ann, dau of Michael J. Kilmartin and his w Susan M. Smith, and has issue:

Great-great-grandchildren's great-grandchildren
1d *Patricia Ann Taylor [Mrs Antonio Salazar, 10240 Little Brick House Court, Ellicot City, MD 21042, USA], *b* New York 1 Aug 1959; *m* New York 7 Nov 1987 *Antonio Patrick SALAZAR and has issue:

Great-great-grandchildren's great-great-grandchildren
1e *Rebecca Leigh SALAZAR, *b* 23 July 1989

Great-great-grandchildren's children
4b Margaret Beverley TAYLOR, *b* 1 Sept 1904; *d* 2 Feb 1988

Great-great-grandchildren
11a Sidney Wales TAYLOR, *b* Midway, Charlottesville, Va., 27 Nov 1854; *d* there 4 Aug 1856 (*bur* Monticello)
12a John Charles Randolph TAYLOR, *b* Midway 8 May 1857; *d* Edgehill 8 June 1863 (*bur* Monticello)

Great-grandchildren
(3) Mary Buchanan RANDOLPH, *b* Tufton, nr Monticello, Va., 23 Nov 1818; *d* 21 or 24 Oct 1821
(4) Caryanne Nicholas Randolph, *b* Tufton 22 April 1820; *m* Edgehill 28 Dec 1840 Francis (Frank) Gildart RUFFIN, of Valley Farm, Chesterfield Co, Va. (*b* 1816; Sec Virginia Agricultural Soc, Lt-Col Confederate States Army, Assist Head Confederate States Bureau of Subsistence, an Auditor of Virginia 1877-92; *d* 1892), s of William Ruffin and his w Frances Gildart, and *d* 24 July 1857 (*bur* Monticello), having had issue:

Great-great-grandchildren
1a Spencer Roane RUFFIN, *b* 1841; *d* in infancy
2a Jefferson Randolph RUFFIN, *b* 16 Nov 1842; *d* 9 Dec 1907 (*bur* Monticello)
3a William Roane RUFFIN, *b* Valley Farm, Chesterfield Co, Va., 3 July 1845; *m* Petersburg, Va., 7 April 1870 Sally Walthall (*b* Petersburg, Va., 30 Aug 1851; *d* there 12 Feb 1932), dau of James McIlwaine, of Petersburg, and his w Fannie Susan Dunn, and *d* Valley Farm, Chesterfield Co, 27 May 1899, having had issue:

Great-great-grandchildren's children
1b James McIlwaine RUFFIN, of Petersburg, *b* Charles City 22 Feb 1871; *m* Petersburg, Va., 31 Oct 1901 Anne Lillian (*b* there 17 Jan 1878; *d* Hilton Village, Va., 21 Feb 1941), dau of William Robert Nichols and his w Nora Preot, and *d* Chesterfield Co, Va., 21 Nov 1936, leaving issue:

Great-great-grandchildren's grandchildren
1c James McIlwaine RUFFIN, Jr, *b* Petersburg, Va., 3 Aug 1902; *m* Cincinnati, Ohio, 27 July 1929 Jean Fairfax (*b* Portsmouth, Ohio, 18 March 1908; *d* Augusta, Ga., 19 June 1980), dau of F. H. Dickey and his w Charlotte Lewis, and *d* Atlanta, Ga., 8 Aug 1961, leaving issue:

Great-great-grandchildren's great-grandchildren

1d *Page Dickey Ruffin [Mrs Harry L Martin, 2304 Lakeview Drive, Melbourne, FL 32935, USA], *b* Cincinnati, Ohio, 27 July 1930; *m* 1st Cincinnati 14 Oct 1950 Richard Anthony MEYERS (*b* there 15 Oct 1928; *d* May 1963), s of Charles H. Meyers and his w Lucy Campbell; *m* 2nd Belvedere, S Carolina, 16 July 1964 Dean Hale CASE (*b* Estherville, Iowa, 26 Oct 1932; *d* 8 April 1975), s of Charles Edward Case and his w Lola Hale, and has issue:

Great-great-grandchildren's great-great-grandchildren

1e *Michael Dean CASE [526 Mackenzie Pl, Appling, GA 30802, USA], *b* Augusta, Ga., 2 Aug 1966

2e *Toni Page CASE, *b* Augusta 16 May 1968

Great-great-grandchildren's great-grandchildren

1d (cont.) Page Ruffin Meyers Case *m* 3rd 15 Jan 1977 (divorce 2 July 1980) William Haig ROWE; *m* 4th 11 Sept 1982 Ronald L. McFALL (*d* 1 Sept 1983); *m* 5th 16 Aug 1984 Harry LeRoy MARTIN (*d* 22 Nov 1990)

2d Jean Fairfax Ruffin, *b* Richmond, Ind., 26 Jan 1946; *m* Augusta, Ga., 6 March 1971 (divorce 1978) Louis Ruben WEGNER (*b* Elgin, N Dak., 2 Feb 1941), s of Ruben Samuel Wegner and his w Phyllis Hunkle, and *d* Augusta 28 Aug 1992, leaving issue:

Great-great-grandchildren's great-great-grandchildren

1e *Wendi Charlotte WEGNER, *b* Augusta 28 Sept 1975

Great-great-grandchildren's great-grandchildren

3d *Jane McIlwaine Ruffin [Mrs Clayton Hartzell, 917 Yardley Drive, North Augusta, SC 29841, USA; 139 New Castle St, N Augusta, SC, USA], *b* Richmond, Ind., 26 Jan 1946; *m* 1st North Augusta 16 April 1966 (divorce 1971) James R. KNAPP (*b* Toronto, Canada, 31 May 1946), s of Frank I. Knapp and his w Erna; *m* 2nd North Augusta 14 June 1973 *Clayton HARTZELL (*b* Augusta, Ga., 24 Aug 1946), s of William McKinley Hartzell and his w Myrtice Lee Kirkendohl, and has issue:

Great-great-grandchildren's great-great-grandchildren

1e *David McKinley HARTZELL, *b* Augusta 21 Nov 1975

Great-great-grandchildren's grandchildren

2c William Nichols RUFFIN, *b* Petersburg, Va., 9 Oct 1905; *m* Las Vegas, Nev., 10 Aug 1936 Naomi (*b* Petersburg, Va., 22 April 1912; *d* 16 Sept 1986), dau of James Fulford and his w Alice Walker, and *d* 26 Oct 1979, leaving issue:

Great-great-grandchildren's great-grandchildren

1d *William Nichols RUFFIN, Jr [Gowrie House, Mobjack, VA 23118, USA], *b* Los Angeles 9 March 1938; *m* Petersburg, Va., 10 Sept 1960 *Dorothy Leonard (*b* there 10 Sept 1938), dau of Marvin Winfree Gill, Jr, and his w Dorothy Field Leonard, and has issue:

Great-great-grandchildren's great-great-grandchildren

1e *Anna Sutherland RUFFIN, *b* Petersburg, Va., 22 Sept 1962

2e *Robert Nichols RUFFIN [292 8th Ave Apt 2, New York, NY 10001, USA], *b* Shelby, N Carolina, 21 May 1964; *educ* E Carolina U; actor, teacher and producer

Great-great-grandchildren's great-grandchildren

2d *Thomas Randolph RUFFIN [20 Pinehurst Dve, Shalimar, FL 32579, USA], *b* Los Angeles 22 July 1947; V-Pres Monticello Assoc 1983-85 and Pres 1985-87; *m* Petersburg, Va., 10 Aug 1969 *Bonnie Susan (*b* there 25 June 1947), dau of Clyde L. Bowman and his w Martha Worsham, and has issue:

Great-great-grandchildren's great-great-grandchildren

1e *Susan Randolph RUFFIN, *b* Petersburg, Va., 5 April 1970

2e *Robin Gayle RUFFIN, *b* 25 June 1974

Great-great-grandchildren's children

2b Francis Gildart RUFFIN, *b* Valley Farm, Chesterfield Co, Va., 21 Aug 1874; *d* there 12 Feb 1898

3b Caryanne Randolph Ruffin, *b* Valley Farm 31 May 1876; Custodian of the Monticello Graveyard 1922-38; *m* Petersburg, Va., 3 Dec 1901 Robert Montagu McMURDO (*b* Roorkee, NW Provinces, India, 8 May 1867; *d* Richmond, Va., 1 Jan 1952), s of Charles Edward McMurdo and his w Madeline Susan Baxter, and *d* Petersburg, Va., 5 Nov 1945 (*bur* Monticello), leaving issue:

Great-great-grandchildren's grandchildren

1c *Sally Roane McMurdo [Mrs William Williston, Oak Ridge Retirement Center, Laboratory Rd, Oak Ridge, TN 37830, USA], *b* Petersburg, Va., 5 Dec 1904; *m* Edgehill Chapel, Albemarle Co, Va., 8 June 1929 William Wardlaw WILLISTON (*b* Northampton, Mass., 9 Oct 1904; *d* Oak Ridge, Tenn., 8 Aug 1983), s of Robert Lyman Williston and his w Margaret Randolph Bryan, and has issue:

Great-great-grandchildren's great-grandchildren

1d *Anne Cary Williston [Mrs Charles Nowlin, 117 Malvern Road, Oak Ridge, TN 37830, USA], *b* Northampton, Mass., 24 April 1934; *m* there 16 June 1956 *Charles Henry NOWLIN (*b* Wilmington, Del., 1 Feb 1932), s of Charles Mackey Nowlin and his w Gertrude Agnes Craig, and has had issue:

Great-great-grandchildren's great-great-grandchildren
1e Elizabeth Anne NOWLIN, *b* Oak Ridge, Tenn., 15 May, *d* there 16 June 1963
2e *William Charles NOWLIN [2149 Junction Ave Apt 5, Mountain View, CA 94043, USA], *b* Oak Ridge 1 Oct 1964; *m* 15 Aug 1987 *Sara Elizabeth Ginnings
3e *Margaret Anne NOWLIN [3115 Morningside Dve, Raleigh, NC 27607, USA], *b* Oak Ridge 4 Nov 1966

Great-great-grandchildren's great-grandchildren
2d *Margaret Randolph Williston [Mrs Ernest J Laidlaw, 307 Yonge Boulevard, Toronto, Ontario M5M 3J4, Canada], *b* Northampton, Mass., 10 Sept 1937; *m* there 14 Sept 1957 *Ernest John LAIDLAW (*b* Toronto 28 July 1927), s of Ernest John Laidlaw and his w Hilda Clara Brown, and has issue:

Great-great-grandchildren's great-great-grandchildren
1e *Gillian Randolph LAIDLAW, *b* Toronto 10 April 1979

Great-great-grandchildren's grandchildren
2c *Madeline Montagu McMurdo [Mrs H Bruce Whitmore, The Colonnades, 2600 Barracks Rd Apt 247, Charlottesville, VA 22901, USA], *b* Petersburg, Va., 8 Sept 1906; *educ* U of Virginia; teacher Greenvale Country Day Sch 1953-68, Historian Monticello Assoc 1971-75 (Custodian 1975-76); *m* Charlottesville, Va., 3 Sept 1932 H(erbert) Bruce WHITMORE (*b* Brooklyn, New York, 3 Jan 1906; *d* 1976), s of Walter Gray Whitmore and his w Kathryn Marcellus Bruttick, and has issue:

Great-great-grandchildren's great-grandchildren
1d *Caryanne Randolph Whitmore [Mrs William L Ericson, 933 Westbrook Drive, Herkimer, NY 13350, USA], *b* East Orange, New Jersey, 24 May 1937; *m* Boston 17 Sept 1977 *William Lars ERICSON
2d *Bruce Gray WHITMORE [350 Pond View, Devon, PA 19333-1732, USA], *b* Glencove, New York, 7 May 1944; *educ* Tufts and Harvard; V-Pres and Gen Counsel Arco Chemical Co; *m* New York City 18 Nov 1972 *Carol Elizabeth (*b* Pittsburgh, Pa., 7 Aug 1949), dau of Daniel M. Rugg, Jr, and his w Carol Van Zandt, and has issue:

Great-great-grandchildren's great-great-grandchildren
1e *Robert Gray WHITMORE, *b* Pasadena, Calif., 7 July 1978
2e *Daniel Bruce WHITMORE, *b* Bryn Mawr, Pa., 8 Jan 1981
3e *Martha Elizabeth WHITMORE, *b* Bryn Mawr 14 April 1985

Great-great-grandchildren's grandchildren
3c Robert Montagu McMURDO, Jr, *b* Charlottesville, Va., 31 Oct 1911; Treasurer Monticello Assoc 1977-83; *m* 1st Petersburg, Va., 6 June 1942 Bettie W. (*b* there 14 Dec 1911; *d* 19—), dau of Robert Hamilton Seabury and his w Janie McIlwaine Vaughan and had issue:

Great-great-grandchildren's great-grandchildren
1d *Jane Vaughan McMurdo [Mrs William Bagwell, 704 East 5th St, Chillicothe, OH 45601, USA], *b* Washington, DC, 31 Oct 1944; *m* Camden, S Carolina, 22 July 1967 *William Demord BAGWELL (*b* Savannah, Ga., 10 Aug 1940), s of Jesse Greenbury Bagwell and his w Thealia Salyer, and has issue:

Great-great-grandchildren's great-great-grandchildren
1e *Keith Montagu BAGWELL [342 5th St NE, Atlanta, GA 30308, USA], *b* Birmingham, Ala., 19 May 1972; *m* 19— *——
2e *Kirk Seabury BAGWELL, *b* 24 April 1975

Great-great-grandchildren's great-grandchildren
2d *Martha Seabury McMurdo [Mrs John A Diffey, 12 Balsam Court, Chapel Hill, NC 27514, USA], *b* Petersburg, Va., 4 Feb 1948; *m* 17 Sept 1983 *John Alexander DIFFEY and has issue:

Great-great-grandchildren's great-great-grandchildren
1e *Matthew DIFFEY, *b* 19—

Great-great-grandchildren's great-grandchildren
3d *Sally Ruffin McMurdo [Mrs Peter J Minnich, PO Box 801, Glenn, NH 03838, USA], *b* Camden 4 Sept 1951; *m* 11 July 1981 *Peter J. MINNICH and has issue:

Great-great-grandchildren's great-great-grandchildren
1e *Joseph Robert McMurdo MINNICH, *b* 25 Feb 1983
2e *Caitlin Vaughn McMurdo MINNICH, *b* 22 May 1986

Great-great-grandchildren's grandchildren
3c (cont.) Robert M. McMurdo, Jr, *m* 2nd 20 Nov 1982 *Frances Elizabeth Driver Jennings, and *d* 25 March 1984
4c *Mary Ruffin McMurdo, *b* Petersburg, Va., 14 Oct 1913; *m* Charlottesville, Va., 1937 Campbell Houston GILLESPIE, Jr (*see above* under descendants of William Stuart Bankhead, 3rd s of President JEFFERSON's est gchild Anne)

Great-great-grandchildren's children
4b William Roane RUFFIN, Jr, *b* Valley Farm, Chesterfield Co, Va., 8 March 1878; *m* Amelia Co, Va., 1919 Martha

Cocke (b Amelia Co; d there), dau of Harvey Taylor, and d 26 June 1943

5b John Francis Walthall RUFFIN, b Chesterfield Co., Va., 17 May 1880; m Gordonsville 19 Oct 1910 Sara McElroy (b Pittsburgh, Pa., 19 April 1882; d Pottstown, Philadelphia, 31 July 1971), dau of John M. Osborne and his w Virginia McElroy, and d Pottstown, Pa., 22 May 1952, leaving issue:

Great-great-grandchildren's grandchildren

1c John Francis Walthall RUFFIN, Jr, b Gordonsville, Va., 2 Sept 1911; m Pottstown, Pa., 5 June 1937 *Jane [Mrs John F Ruffin Jr, 1713-C Northfield Sq, Northfield, Winnetka, IL 60093, USA] (b Perkasie, Pa., 1913), dau of St Clair Barnes and his w Edith Morgan, and d 30 Oct 1987, leaving issue:

Great-great-grandchildren's great-grandchildren

1d *Sara Jane Ruffin [Mrs Michael Kennerley, 196 Bedford Park Avenue, Toronto, Ontario M5M 1J3, Canada], b Pottstown 5 June 1939; m Christ Church, Winnetka, Ill., 1 Feb 1964 *Michael KENNERLEY (b Paris, France, 2 Nov 1934), s of John Kennerley and his w Jane Atkinson, and has issue:

Great-great-grandchildren's great-great-grandchldren
1e *Elizabeth Anne KENNERLEY, b Toronto 28 Nov 1970
2e *Michael Andrew Ruffin KENNERLEY, b Toronto 26 April 1972

Great-great-grandchildren's great-grandchildren
2d *Elizabeth Anne Ruffin [Mrs Ivor Balyeat, 580 Orchard Lane, Winnetka, IL 60093, USA], b Pottstown, Pa., 12 June 1941; m Christ Church, Winnetka, Ill., 30 June 1962 *Ivor Lee BALYEAT (b Mansfield, Ohio, 1938), s of Ivor A. Balyeat and his w Hildegarde Weinert, and has issue:

Great-great-grandchildren's great-great-grandchildren
1e *Jonathan Lee BALYEAT, b Chicago 13 April 1970
2e *Nicholas Barnes BALYEAT, b Chicago 20 Dec 1974
3e *Peter Randolph BALYEAT, b Chicago 20 Feb 1979

Great-great-grandchildren's grandchildren

2c William Roane RUFFIN III, b Gordonsville, Va., 13 Nov 1912; V-Pres Monticello Assoc 1977-79 and Pres 1979-81; m Harrisburg, Pa., 30 June 1945 *Jane [Mrs William R Ruffin III, 1215 Sylvan Avenue, Latrobe, PA 15650, USA] (b Ligonier, Pa., 18 Nov 1919), dau of W. Boyd Evans and his w Elizabeth Fillion, and d 3 Dec 1986, leaving issue:

Great-great-grandchildren's great-grandchildren
1d *William Roane RUFFIN IV [3 Bridlewood Dve, New Hope, PA 18938, USA], b Latrobe, Pa., 6 Feb 1948; m 10 Aug 1974 *Mary Lou Neurohr and has issue:

Great-great-grandchildren's great-great-grandchildren
1e *Jane Best RUFFIN, b 7 Aug 1980
2e *Elizabeth Kathleen RUFFIN, b 21 Oct 1981

Great-great-grandchildren's great-grandchildren
2d *Elizabeth Evans Ruffin [1215 Sylvan Ave, Latrobe, PA 15650, USA], b Latrobe 5 April 1953; m 27 Aug 1977 *Howard Lynn DOUGLAS and has issue:

Great-great-grandchildren's great-great-grandchildren
1e *William Howard DOUGLAS, b 28 Nov 1980

Great-great-grandchildren's grandchildren

3c *Sidney Mathews RUFFIN [600 Grant, Pittsburgh, PA 15219, USA; 107 Westchester Drive, Pittsburgh, PA 15215, USA], b Gordonsville, Va., 5 June 1915; V-Pres Monticello Assoc 1963-65 and Pres 1965-67; m Roxborough, Pa., 26 June 1943 Harriet (b Ogontz, Pa., 30 May 1920; d 23 Jan 1991), dau of Sydney E. Martin and his w Margaret Fox, and has issue:

Great-great-grandchildren's great-grandchildren
1d *Nicholas Cary RUFFIN [2022 Columbia Rd NW Apt 210, Washington, DC 20009, USA], b Philadelphia, Pa., 20 Aug 1944; m 1 July 1992 *Shauna Spencer
2d *Martha Martin Ruffin, b Pittsburgh 11 March 1947; m there 8 April 1972 *Bruce Lawrence ACKERMAN (b Philadelphia 30 Nov 1945), s of Samuel Ackerman and his w Wilma, and has issue:

Great-great-grandchildren's great-great-grandchildren
1e *John Wolfe ACKERMAN, b 31 May 1977
2e *Robin Cary ACKERMAN (dau), b 15 June 1980

Great-great-grandchildren's great-grandchildren
3d *Caryanne Randolph Ruffin [394 Langley Rd, Newton, MA 02159, USA], b Pittsburgh 9 Aug 1951; m 5 April 1991 *Samuel Allen GOLDBERG and has issue:

Great-great-grandchildren's great-great-grandchildren
1e *Raleigh Fox GOLDBERG, b 1 Jan 1992

Great-great-grandchildren's great-grandchildren
4d *Harriet Fox RUFFIN [112 W Graves Lane, Philadelphia, PA 19118, USA], b Pittsburgh 12 July 1954

Great-great-grandchildren's grandchildren
4c *Virginius Osborne RUFFIN [Box 207, Worcester, PA 19490, USA], b Gordonsville, Va., 12 March 1918; m Pottstown, Pa., 16 June 1951 *Nancy (b there 28 May 1921), dau of Harry J. Diefenbeck and his w Frances Healy

Great-great-grandchildren's children
6b Mary McIlwaine RUFFIN, b Valley Farm, Chesterfield Co, Va., 17 Dec 1883; d Petersburg, Va., 5 May 1951
7b Sally Walthall RUFFIN, b Valley Farm 17 Feb 1886; d Petersburg 21 Jan 1966
8b Wilson Cary Nicholas RUFFIN, b Valley Farm 5 July 1888; d there 17 Dec 1892

Great-great-grandchildren
4a Wilson Nicholas RUFFIN, of Danville, Va., b 19 March 1848; m 20 April 1875 Mary Winston (d 6 Jan 1939), dau of John Harvie and his w Mary Blair, and d 22 Feb 1919, having had issue:

Great-great-grandchildren's children
1b John Harvie RUFFIN, b Richmond, Va., 15 Jan 1876; executive with British American Tobacco Co., Pres Monticello Assoc 1946-48; m 7 April 1907 Laura Virginia Walters (d April 1958) and d Charlottesville 3 May 1961, leaving issue:

Great-great-grandchildren's grandchildren
1c *Nelson Randolph RUFFIN, of Charlottesville, b 3 April 1910

Great-great-grandchildren's children
2b Ellen Harvie Ruffin, b 24 Sept 1877; m 27 June 1906 James M. FEATHERSTON and d 3 Nov 1977, leaving issue:

Great-great-grandchildren's grandchildren
1c Ellen Ruffin Featherston, b 26 May 1907; m 7 July 1932 *Revd William Franklin TAYLOR (b Johnson City, Tenn., 17 July 1906), s of William Franklin Taylor and his w Ada Lee Wood, and d 10 July 1941, leaving issue:

Great-great-grandchildren's great-grandchildren
1d *Ellen Ruffin Taylor [Mrs John Stevens, 8509 Fairburn Drive, Springfield, VA 22150, USA], b 24 Dec 1933; m 23 Nov 1954 *John Rodney STEVENS and has issue:

Great-great-grandchildren's great-great-grandchildren
1e *Laura Lynn STEVENS, b 3 Aug 1957
2e *Ellen Elizabeth STEVENS, b 5 May 1959
3e *John Rodney STEVENS, Jr, b 16 Dec 1961

Great-great-grandchildren's great-grandchildren
2d *Ada Lee Taylor, b 30 April 1940; m 18 Nov 1972 *Richard J. THOMAS

Great-great-grandchildren's children
3b Wilson Nicholas RUFFIN, b 15 Sept 1879; m 18 Aug 1910 Martha Pearl Woods and d 2 June 1951
4b Francis Gildart RUFFIN, b 1881; d 1883
5b Lewis Rutherford RUFFIN, b 29 Oct 1884; d 18 Aug 1907
6b Cary Randolph RUFFIN, b 22 Dec 1886; d 19 Aug 1914
7b William Pickett RUFFIN, b 19 April 1889; d 24 April 1915
8b Mary Blair Harvie RUFFIN, b 13 June 1892; d 23 April 1985

Great-great-grandchildren
5a George Randolph RUFFIN, of Texas, b 1849; m 1883 Amarilla Gholson (b 1861; d 1888), dau of William Bell and his w Mary, and d 1915, having had issue:

Great-great-grandchildren's children
1b William Ragsdale RUFFIN, b 1884; d in infancy
2b Mary Helen Ruffin, b Hope, Ark., 9 April 1886; m Marshall, Tex., 5 March 1913 Fred MARSHALL (b Terry, Miss., 1880; d Texarkana, Ark., 20 Dec 1940), s of Bishop McKendre Marshall and his w Caroline Barnes, and d Urbana, Ill., 22 Sept 1972, having had issue:

Great-great-grandchildren's grandchildren
1c Mary Bell Marshall II, b 26 March 1914; m Sept 1942 *Robert D. SARD and d 25 Dec 1981, leaving issue:

Great-great-grandchildren's great-grandchildren
1d *David Paul SARD [434 West 120th Street, New York, NY 10027, USA], b 10 Nov 1943; m 19— *Sarah Dooley and has issue:

Great-great-grandchildren's great-great-grandchildren
1e *Kristen Anna SARD, b 2 April 1966

Great-great-grandchildren's great-grandchildren
2d *Frederick Marshall SARD, b 27 Feb 1946
3d *Hannah Belloch SARD, b 31 May 1951

Great-great-grandchildren's grandchildren
2c George Randolph Ruffin MARSHALL, *b* 7 July 1915; *m* 21 Aug 1954 *Olga di Nicola [Mrs George Marshall, 70 Brookside Place, New Rochelle, NY 10801, USA] and *d* 20 March 1964, leaving issue:

Great-great-grandchildren's great-grandchildren
1d *Mary Helen Ruffin Marshall [Mrs Joseph Fragola, 178 Bon Air Ave, New Rochelle, NY 10804, USA], *b* 25 Dec 1955; *m* 23 Oct 1977 *Joseph FRAGOLA and has issue:

Great-great-grandchildren's great-great-grandchildren
1e *Gregory FRAGOLA, *b* 6 Feb 1991

Great-great-grandchildren's great-grandchildren
2d *George Ruffin Randolph MARSHALL, Jr [4 Fairview Place, New Rochelle, NY 10805, USA], *b* 25 March 1957; *m* 15 1983 *Barbara Daughtery and has issue:

Great-great-grandchildren's great-great-grandchildren
1e *George Ruffin Randolph MARSHALL III, *b* 15 Sept 1987

Great-great-grandchildren's great-grandchildren
3d *Clara Ann MARSHALL (retains maiden name) [116 Loring Ave, Pelham, NY 10803, USA], *b* 13 Jan 1959; *m* 9 March 1989 *Thomas R. EICH and has issue:

Great-great-grandchildren's great-great-grandchildren
1e *Jonathan Marshall EICH, *b* 8 Feb 1991
2e *Douglas EICH, *b* 16 March 1992

Great-great-grandchildren's grandchildren
3c *(Caroline) Margaret Marshall [Mrs Armand W Kitto, 601 Mendelssohn, Kirkwood, MO 63122-2543, USA], *b* Texarkana, Ark., 24 April 1927; *educ* Chicago Musical Coll; piano teacher and church organist 1948-; *m* Hope, Ark., 14 July 1950 *Armand William KITTO, Jr (*b* New Orleans 15 April 1929), s of Armand William Kitto and his w Cornelia P. Bridger, and has issue:

Great-great-grandchildren's great-grandchildren
1d *Katherine Babette Kitto [Mrs Joseph Kott III, 68 Conant Ave, Auburn, ME 04210, USA], *b* New Orleans 30 July 1951; *educ* Wayne State U; librarian Bates Coll 1988-; *m* Detroit 28 Sept 1973 *Joseph KOTT III (*b* there 15 July 1947), s of Joseph Kott II and his w Catherine Szydloska, and has issue:

Great-great-grandchildren's great-great-grandchildren
1e *Paul Thomas KOTT, *b* Detroit 18 July 1975
2e *Andrew Joseph KOTT, *b* Durham, N Carolina, 5 March 1980
3e *Amy Elizabeth KOTT, *b* Springfield, Ill., 7 July 1985

Great-great-grandchildren's great-grandchildren
2d *Laurence Bridger KITTO [5757 N Washington Blvd, Indianapolis, IN 46220, USA], *b* New Orleans 7 July 1953; *m* 1st 21 May 1977 (divorce Jan 1981) Elizabeth Elliot; *m* 2nd Indiana 27 Oct 1987 *Jody Stanley
3d *Robert Marshall KITTO [5966 Waterworks Rd, Saline, MI 48176, USA], *b* New Orleans 31 Jan 1955; *m* Indianapolis 31 Aug 1984 *Beverly Eppler and has issue:

Great-great-grandchildren's great-great-grandchildren
1e *Benjamin Robert KITTO, *b* 4 June 1987
2e *Elizabeth Eppler KITTO, *b* 26 Jan 1989

Great-great-grandchildren's great-grandchildren
4d *Jonathan Bell KITTO [162 Flood, San Francisco, CA 94131, USA], *b* St Louis, Mo., 23 Aug 1958

Great-great-grandchildren
6a Francis (Frank) Gildart RUFFIN, Jr, of Mobile, Ala., *b* 6 Jan 1852; *m* 1887 Margaret Ellen (*b* 26 Aug 1861; author (as M. E. Henry): *Drifting Leaves* (1884) and (as M. E. Henry-Ruffin) *John Gildart, an heroic poem* (1901), *The North Star, a tale of Norway in the tenth century* (1904) and *The Shield of Silence* (1914); *d* 1941), dau of Thomas Henry, and *d* 12 Jan 1902, leaving issue:

Great-great-grandchildren's children
1b Frances Ruffin, *b* 27 Feb 1889; *m* 8 Jan 1914 Joseph Francis DURHAM and *d* 23 June 1972, leaving issue:

Great-great-grandchildren's grandchildren
1c *Mary Frances Durham, *b* 4 Nov 1914; *m* 1st 3 Sept 1938 Paul de Vendal CHAUDRON, Jr, s of Paul de Vendal Chaudron, and has issue:

Great-great-grandchildren's great-grandchildren
1d *Lucia Marie Chaudron, *b* 24 June 1939; *m* 21 March 1963 *Heino KRISTALL

Great-great-grandchildren's grandchildren
1c (cont.) Mary Durham Chaudron *m* 2nd 19— *Simon Peter MILITANO and with him has issue:

Great-great-grandchildren's great-grandchildren

2d *Michael Francis MILITANO, *b* 29 Sept 1944; *m* 1st 29 Sept 1965 *Nancy Helen Hiler and has issue:

Great-great-grandchildren's great-great-grandchildren

1e *Angela Marie Militano, *b* 16 Dec 1966; *m* 8 Dec 1989 *Glenn Allen BENNINGHOFF

2e *Anthony Joseph MILITANO, *b* 27 March 1970; *m* 8 Sept 1990 *Jennifer Louise Whire

Great-great-grandchildren's great-grandchildren

2d (cont.) Michael F. Militano *m* 2nd 29 Nov 1980 *Patricia Ann Costa and has further issue:

Great-great-grandchildren's great-great-grandchildren

3e *Kristan Marie MILITANO, *b* 12 April 1982

Great-great-grandchildren's children

2b Mary Henry RUFFIN, *b* 5 May 1890; became a Sister of Charity and was known as Sister Miriam; *d* 18 March 1980

3b Ellen Randolph RUFFIN, *b* 10 July 1892; also became a Sister of Charity, being known as Sister Rita; *d* 28 June 1990

4b Thomas Henry RUFFIN, *b* 31 Oct 1894; *m* 1924 Anna Cecilia Kelly and *d* 18 Aug 1964, leaving issue:

Great-great-grandchildren's grandchildren

1c *Joseph Henry RUFFIN, *b* 10 April 1926; *m* 1st 4 Sept 1948 Waurine Bradley and has issue:

Great-great-grandchildren's great-grandchildren

1d *Joan Charlene Ruffin, *b* 7 June 1949; *m* 23 April 1977 *Michael Woodrow SHARP and has issue:

Great-great-grandchildren's great-great-grandchildren

1e *Jennifer Elizabeth SHARP, *b* 24 Jan 1979

Great-great-grandchildren's great-grandchildren

2d *Margaret Cecilia Ruffin, *b* 4 July 1950; *m* 3 June 1972 *Kerry Bruce MILLER and has issue:

Great-great-grandchildren's great-great-grandchildren

1e *Justin Thomas MILLER, *b* 11 Dec 1972

2e *Graham Ryan MILLER, *b* 22 Jan 1975

Great-great-grandchildren's grandchildren

1c (cont.) Joseph H. Ruffin *m* 2nd 16 July 1988 *Eva Marie Rihn

Great-great-grandchildren's children

5b Thomas Jefferson RUFFIN, *b* 31 Oct 1894; *d* 12 Sept 1975

6b Caroline Randolph RUFFIN, *b* 27 April 1897; *d* Oct 1919

7b Elizabeth de l'Esprit RUFFIN, *b* June 1901; *d* March 1903

Great-great-grandchildren

7a Benjamin Randolph RUFFIN; *d* in infancy

8a Eliza McDonald RUFFIN, *b* 26 July 1853; *d* 20 April 1904 (*bur* Monticello)

9a Cary Randolph RUFFIN, *b* 24 July 1857; changed name to Cary Ruffin RANDOLPH; *m* 18— or 19— Ethel Patterson (*d* 1910) and *d* 27 Aug 1910 (*bur* Monticello)

Great-grandchildren

(5) Mary Buchanan RANDOLPH, *b* Tufton 17 Dec 1821; Principal Edgehill Sch for Girls; *d* Edgehill 23 June 1884 (*bur* Monticello)

(6) Eleanor (Ellen) Wayles Randolph, *b* Tufton 1 Dec 1823; *m* Edgehill 1 May 1859, as his 2nd w, William Byrd HARRISON, of Upper Brandon, Va. (*b* Brandon 1800; *educ* U of Virginia; plantation-owner; *d* Ampthill, Cumberland Co, 22 Sept 1870), and *d* 15 Aug 1896 (*bur* Monticello), having had issue:

Great-great-grandchildren

1a Evelyn Byrd HARRISON, *b* Upper Brandon 14 March, *d* 16 March 1860

2a Jane Nicholas Randolph Harrison, *b* Ampthill 26 June 1862; Historian Monticello Assoc 1913-16 and 1918-20; *m* 31 Dec 1892 Alexander Burton RANDALL, of Annapolis, Md. (*b* 1856; *d* 23 March 1938), s of Col Burton Randall and his w Virginia Taylor, and *d* Waterbury, Conn., 16 Aug 1926 (*bur* Monticello), leaving issue:

Great-great-grandchildren's children

1b Burton Harrison Randolph RANDALL, *b* 13 Oct 1893; Lt Field Artillery American Expeditionary Force World War I, Pres Monticello Assoc 1949-51 (V-Pres 1948-49); *m* 1st 25 Aug 1919 Louise Florentine (Florence) Monganaste (*b* 1896) and had issue:

Great-great-grandchildren's grandchildren

1c Edith Richards Randall, *b* 3 Aug 1920; *m* 3 March 1946 *John K. KOTZ [116 Laurel Lane, Broomall, PA 19008, USA] and *d* 14 Oct 1990 (*bur* Monticello), leaving issue:

Great-great-grandchildren's great-grandchildren

1d *Randall Michael KOTZ [5122 Rochelle St, Philadelphia, PA 19128, USA], *b* 15 Nov 1952; *m* 19— *——

2d *Nancy Margaret Kotz [Ms Nancy Kotz Shore, 220 West Rittenhouse Sq Unit 2E, Philadelphia, PA 19103, USA], *b* 10 Dec 1958; *m* 9 May 1978 *Kenneth Harris SHORE and has issue:

Great-great-grandchildren's great-great-grandchildren
1e *Janice Lynn SHORE, *b* 9 July 1981
2e *Elisa Suzanne SHORE, *b* 25 May 1984

Great-great-grandchildren's grandchildren
2c A boy, stillborn June 1924 (*bur* Monticello)

Great-great-grandchildren's children
1b (cont.) Burton Harrison Randolph Randall *m* 2nd 31 Aug 1935 Anne Holloway (*b* 17 Aug 1902; *d* 13 June 1986) and *d* 29 Sept 1971

Great-great-grandchildren
3a Jefferson Randolph HARRISON, *b* Ampthill 9 Dec 1863; *d* 11 May 1931 (*bur* Monticello)

Great-grandchildren
(7) Maria Jefferson Carr Randolph, *b* Tufton 2 Feb 1826; *m* 1848 Charles MASON, of King George Co, Va., and *d* 12 July 1902, having had issue:

Great-great-grandchildren
1a Jefferson Randolph MASON, of Texas, *b* 12 July 1850; *d* 29 July 1888
2a Lucy Wiley Mason, *b* 4 March 1852; *m* 26 April 1881 Edward Jaquelin SMITH and *d* 18 July 1922, leaving issue:

Great-great-grandchildren's children
1b Dr Charles Mason SMITH, *b* 29 July 1882; *m* 10 Nov 1914 Emma Copeland Lawless and *d* 2 Jan 1933, leaving issue:

Great-great-grandchildren's grandchildren
1c *Jaquelin Randolph Smith [Mrs Angus Lamond, 7509 Fort Hunt Road, Alexandria, VA 22307, USA], *b* 21 Oct 1915; *m* 10 Nov 1939 Angus Slater LAMOND (*d* 19——) and has issue:

Great-great-grandchildren's great-grandchildren
1d *Cary Randolph Lamond [Mrs Joseph A Lynch, 32-14 214th Place, Bayside, NY 11361, USA], *b* 1 Aug 1940; *m* 1st 10 Nov 1962 Francis Patrick DILLON and has issue:

Great-great-grandchildren's great-great-grandchildren
1e *Cary Randolph DILLON, *b* 23 April 1963
2e *Francis Patrick DILLON, Jr, *b* 10 May 1966

Great-great-grandchildren's great-grandchildren
1d (cont.) Cary Lamond Dillon *m* 2nd 31 March 1977 *Joseph Antony Michael LYNCH
2d *Jaquelin Ambler Lamond, *b* 22 Sept 1942; *m* 18 April 1970 *Peter Mueller SCHLUTER and has issue:

Great-great-grandchildren's great-great-grandchildren
1e *Jane Randolph SCHLUTER, *b* 25 March 1972
2e *Charlotte Mueller SCHLUTER, *b* 19 June 1973
3e *Anne Ambler SCHLUTER, *b* 12 Aug 1976

Great-great-grandchildren's great-grandchildren
3d *Angus Slater LAMOND, Jr [501 Slaters Lane, Alexandria, VA 22314, USA], *b* 17 April 1946; *m* 1st 6 Nov 1970 Sandra Delayne Taylor; *m* 2nd 1 June 1974 June Hollis Altman and has issue:

Great-great-grandchildren's great-great-grandchildren
1e *Ann Randolph LAMOND, *b* 23 Aug 1978
2e *Angus Slater LAMOND III, *b* 19 Feb 1981

Great-great-grandchildren's great-grandchildren
3d (cont.) Angus S. Lamond *m* 3rd 5 Aug 1989 *CiCi Williamson
4d *Lucy Mason Lamond [Mrs Donald B Falkenberg, 2969 Treadwell Lane, Herndon, VA 22071, USA], *b* 28 July 1947; *m* 7 Dec 1978 *Donald Bruce FALKENBERG

Great-great-grandchildren's grandchildren
2c *Cary Ambler Smith [Mrs Addison G Billingsley Jr, c/o Mrs R C Shomo, 11106 Ingalston Rd, Richmond, VA 23223, USA], *b* 28 July 1917; *m* 15 Aug 1935 *Addison Gordon BILLINGSLEY, Jr; Mr and Mrs Addison Billingsley have adopted a dau:

a *Cary Copeland Billingsley, *b* 27 Sept 1948; *m* Oct 1974 *Richard Charles SHOMO

Great-great-grandchildren's children
2b William Taylor SMITH, *b* 24 Aug 1885; *m* 10 Sept 1915 Ellen Dickinson Wallace (*b* 1884; *d* 19——) and *d* 1951, leaving issue:

Great-great-grandchildren's grandchildren
1c Lucy Randolph Smith, *b* 6 Nov 1916; *m* 1st 23 Aug 1934 Stiles Morrow DECKER, Jr, s of Stiles Morrow Decker, and had issue:

Great-great-grandchildren's great-grandchildren
1d *Cary Randolph Morrow DECKER, *b* 28 Feb 1936
2d *Joel Porter Wallace DECKER, *b* 5 April 1937; *m* 3 Feb 1960 *Carole Jean Meyers and has issue:

Great-great-grandchildren's great-great-grandchildren
1e *Ellen Marie Decker, *b* 2 Sept 1960; *m* 1st June 1982 Michael Everett WEST; *m* 2nd 29 June 1986 *Mark Randolph DEHNBOSTEL and has issue:

Great-great-grandchildren's great-great-grandchildren's children
1f *Sarah Christine DEHNBOSTEL, *b* 21 Jan 1992

Great-great-grandchildren's great-great-grandchildren
2e *Cary Wallace DECKER, *b* 29 July 1962; *m* 19 Nov 1984 *Gigi Marie Zacharias and has issue:

Great-great-grandchildren's great-great-grandchildren's children
1f *Anna Lee DECKER, *b* 25 June 1990
2f *Taylor Van DECKER, *b* 6 March 1992

Great-great-grandchildren's great-grandchildren
3d *Diane Lewis Hammond (*b* Decker 15 March 1944, but adopted by her stepf Douglas T. Hammond); *m* 28 Aug 1965 *George Roger GIELOW and has issue:

Great-great-grandchildren's great-great-grandchildren
1e *Mary Elizabeth (Molly) GIELOW, *b* 17 Feb 1969
2e *James Randolph GIELOW, *b* 9 Oct 1975

Great-great-grandchildren's great-great-grandchildren
4d *Christine Cary Hammond (*b* Decker 15 March 1952, but adopted by her stepf Douglas T. Hammond); *m* 23 Aug 1975 (divorce 19—) James AGUILLARD

Great-great-grandchildren's grandchildren
1c (cont.) Lucy Smith Decker *m* 2nd 27 Dec 1954 *Douglas T. HAMMOND and *d* 21 Sept 1991

Great-great-grandchildren
3a John Enoch MASON, *b* 11 July 1854; *m* 24 Nov 1885 Kate Kearney Henry and *d* 10 Dec 1910, having had issue:

Great-great-grandchildren's children
1b Flora Randolph Mason, *b* 16 April 1887; *m* 1st 2 April 1917 George B. NICHOLSON; *m* 2nd 24 Oct 1931 Joseph Parkes CROCKETT (*b* 1901) and *d* 29 April 1972
2b Charles T. MASON, *b* 7 Feb 1893; *d* 6 Nov 1896
3b Thomas Jefferson MASON, *b* 14 April 1896; *d* 21 Oct 1918

Great-great-grandchildren
4a Wilson Cary Nicholas MASON, *b* 1856; *d* 1866

Great-grandchildren
(8) Carolina Ramsay RANDOLPH, *b* Edgehill 15 Jan 1828; *d* there 28 June 1902
(9) Thomas Jefferson RANDOLPH, Jr, *b* Edgehill 29 Aug 1829; *m* 1st 20 July 1853 Mary Walker Meriwether (*b* 29 April 1833; *d* 4 Oct 1863) and had issue:

Great-great-grandchildren
1a Francis (Frank) Meriwether RANDOLPH, *b* 22 Oct 1854; *m* 1883 his 1st cousin Charlotte Nelson (*d* 24 May 1935), dau of George W. Macon and his w Mildred Nelson Meriwether, and *d* Albermarle Co., Va., 8 Sept 1922, having had issue:

Great-great-grandchildren's children
1b Margaret Douglas RANDOLPH, *b* Cloverfields, Albemarle Co, Va., 17 March 1884; V-Pres Monticello Assoc 1937-45; *d* Cloverfields 15 Feb 1955 (*bur* Grace Episcopal Church, Cismont, Va.)
2b Mildred Nelson RANDOLPH, *b* 27 Oct 1885; *d* 16 Jan 1886
3b Carolina Ramsay Randolph, *b* 28 Oct 1886; *m* 1 Aug 1906 Edward H. JOSLIN and *d* 16 Aug 1971
4b Charlotte Nelson Randolph, *b* 5 May 1888; *m* 25 Jan 1919 Gilbert T. RAFFERTY, Jr (*d* 12 Aug 1929), s of Gilbert T. Rafferty, and *d* 7 Feb 1987, leaving issue:

Great-great-grandchildren's grandchildren
1c *Caroline Randolph Rafferty [Mrs Richard Hall, Keswick, VA 22947, USA], *b* 23 July 1919; *m* 1941 *Richard White HALL
2c *Anne Rafferty [Mrs Silas W Barnes, Rt1 Box 318, Cloverfields, Keswick, VA 22947, USA], *b* 16 Sept 1920; *m* 9 June 1947 *Silas Wright BARNES and has issue:

Great-great-grandchildren's great-grandchildren
1d *Charlotte Randolph Barnes [Mrs Ralph K Dammann, Rte 7 Box 248, Charlottesville, VA 22901, USA], b 13 Nov 1949; m 2 Sept 1972 *Ralph Kellogg DAMMANN and has issue:

Great-great-grandchildren's great-great-grandchildren
1e *Christopher Randolph DAMMANN, b 17 July 1984

Great-great-grandchildren's great-grandchildren
2d *Sara Lee Barnes, b 4 Aug 1952; m 13 Sept 1975 *John Reeves FRIZZELL III

Great-great-grandchildren's grandchildren
3c Frances Douglas RAFFERTY, b 13 April 1922; d 7 Jan 1982
4c *Doris Rafferty [Mrs Roberts Coles Jr, Cloverfields, Keswick, VA 22947, USA], b 9 June 1925; m 27 March 1951 *Roberts COLES, Jr, s of Roberts Coles, and has issue:

Great-great-grandchildren's great-grandchildren
1d *Roberts COLES III [PO Box 385, Charlottesville, VA 22902, USA], b 7 May 1952
2d *John COLES [PO Box 267, Whitewood Farm, The Plains, VA 22171, USA], b 26 Nov 1953
3d *Margaret Douglas Coles [Mrs William J Anderson, 136 Judd Falls Rd, Ithaca, NY 14850, USA], b 19 April 1955; m 21 June 1980 *William J. ANDERSON and has issue:

Great-great-grandchildren's great-great-grandchildren
1e *Charlotte Randolph ANDERSON, b 3 Nov 1982
2e *William Seth ANDERSON, b 3 Sept 1985

Great-great-grandchildren's great-grandchildren
4d *Edward Joslin COLES [PO Box 135, Keswick, VA 22947, USA], b 3 May 1956; m 30 June 1984 *Anne Eliza Willis
5d *Caroline COLES, b 15 June 1959

Great-great-grandchildren
2a Thomas Jefferson RANDOLPH III, b 23 Oct 1855; d 30 Sept 1884
3a Margaret Douglas RANDOLPH, b 6 Aug 1857; d 17 Dec 1880
4a Francis Nelson RANDOLPH, b 4 Oct 1858; d 15 Dec 1880
5a Jane Hollins RANDOLPH, b 1 Aug 1861; d 30 Nov 1862
6a George Geiger RANDOLPH, b 15 Aug 1863; d 23 Dec 1893

Great-grandchildren
(9) (cont.) Thomas Jefferson Randolph m 2nd 1865 Charlotte Nelson Meriwether (d 1876), and d nr Hawk's Nest, W. Va., 8 Aug 1872, having with her had issue:

Great-great-grandchildren
7a Mary Walker Randolph, b Albemarle Co, Va., 14 June 1866; m 20 Oct 1894 her 1st cousin once-removed Dr William Mann RANDOLPH (see above under children of William Lewis Randolph, himself s of Margaret Smith Randolph, dau of Thomas Jefferson Randolph, gs of President JEFFERSON) and d Charlottesville 9 Dec 1957, leaving issue
8a Charlotte Nelson RANDOLPH, b 28 Dec 1868; d 1 Nov 1870

Great-grandchildren
(10) Jane Nicholas Randolph, b Edgehill 11 Oct 1831; m 24 April 1854, as his 1st w, Robert Garlick Hill KEAN, of Lynchburg, Va. (b 1828; educ U of Virginia; Ch Bureau of War Confederate States War Dept, Pres Virginia State Bar, Visitor and Rector U of Virginia; d 1898), s of John Vaughan Kean and his w Caroline Hill, and d 26 Aug 1868, leaving issue:

Great-great-grandchildren
1a Lancelot Minor KEAN, of New Orleans, b Edgehill 11 Jan 1856; educ U of Virginia (BL 1877); m 1st Lynchburg 25 May 1880 Elizabeth Tucker (b Magnolia Plantation, Washington, La., 5 June 1854; d Washington, La., 17 Jan 1902), dau of William Marshall Prescott, of Washington, La., and his w Evalina Moore, and had issue:

Great-great-grandchildren's children
1b Jane Randolph Kean, b Lynchburg 19 May 1881; m Alexandria, La., 21 Dec 1903 John Samuel BUTLER, Jr (b Opelousas, La., 1861; d Baton Rouge, La., 6 Oct 1916), s of John Samuel Butler, and d 18 Oct 1948, leaving issue:

Great-great-grandchildren's grandchildren
1c John Samuel BUTLER III, b Chenneyville, La., 26 Jan 1905; m Abbeville, La., 9 June 1934 *Miriam Elizabeth [Mrs John S Butler, 2724 Palmer Ave, New Orleans, LA 70118, USA] (b Abbeville 12 May 1907), dau of Francis Marie Leguenec and his w Maybelle Thompson, and d 9 March 1973, leaving issue:

Great-great-grandchildren's great-grandchildren
1d *Miriam Elizabeth Butler [Mrs Richard Moore, Route 9, 20482 Johnsen Rd, Covington, LA 70433, USA], b Abbeville 21 May 1938; educ Acad of the Sacred Heart, New Orleans, and Sophie Newcomb Coll; newspaper columnist ('Covington Town Talk' and the society column 'Northshore Notables') for New Orleans Times Picayune, author: Louisiana Indian Tales (1990) and Mimi's First Mardi Gras (1992); m New Orleans 19 March 1960 *Lt-Cdr

Richard Joseph MOORE, USN (*b* Denver, Colo., 6 Oct 1936), s of Edward William Moore and his w Frances Isabel Nolan, and has issue:

Great-great-grandchildren's great-great-grandchildren
1e *(Richard) Joseph MOORE, Jr [1727 South West 24th Ave, Fort Lauderdale, FL 33312, USA], *b* New Orleans 21 Aug 1961; *educ* The Hill Sch and Tulane U; advertising sales manager *Saltwater Fly Fishing* magazine 1992-; *m* Fort Lauderdale, Fla., 3 Aug 1991 *Lynda Rene, dau of Clifford G. Talley and his w Susan Carol Vogt, and has issue:

Great-great-grandchildren's great-great-grandchildren's children
1f *Elizabeth Carol MOORE, *b* Florida 30 Dec 1992

Great-great-grandchildren's great-great-grandchildren
2e *Sean Samuel Butler MOORE [195 Bank Street Extension, Lebanon, NH 03766, USA], *b* New Orleans 9 Sept 1962; *m* 18 May 1985 *Tracy Louise Mizell
3e *Patrick Edward MOORE [20482 Johnsen Rd Rte 9, Covington, LA 70433, USA], *b* Charleston, S Carolina, 16 Aug 1964; *m* 1st 19— Randalle ——; *m* 2nd Covington, La., 14 March 1992 *Mary Kelli Paige Stuart
4e *Jefferson Randolph Kean MOORE [4610 Prytania St, New Orleans, LA 70115, USA], *b* Charleston 16 Aug 1964
5e *Miriam Elizabeth MOORE, *b* Ceiba, Puerto Rico, 6 Sept 1977
6e *Sarah Archer Leigh MOORE, *b* New Orleans 18 Dec 1979

Great-great-grandchildren's grandchildren
2c Lancelot Kean BUTLER, *b* 16 July 1906; *m* 25 Dec 1939 *Eddy Louise Hood and *d* 23 May 1957
3c Jane Kean Randolph Butler, *b* New Orleans 26 Oct 1908; *m* Alexandria, La., 15 March 1941 Wesley Cleo LANCASTER (*d* 27 Nov 1963) and *d* New Orleans 26 Jan 1963, having had issue:

Great-great-grandchildren's great-grandchildren
1d Wesley Cary LANCASTER, *b* Baton Rouge, La., 19 March, *d* there 20 March 1943
2d *Susan Jane Lancaster [Mrs Thomas Burgess, 2619 Decatur St, Kenner, LA 70062-5023, USA], *b* Vicksburg, Miss., 15 June 1944; *m* New Orleans 16 Dec 1962 *Thomas BURGESS, s of Walter Lee Burgess and his w Grace Williams, and has issue:

Great-great-grandchildren's great-great-grandchildren
1e *Evelyn Joyce BURGESS [4117 Trenton St, Metairie, LA 70002, USA], *b* New Orleans 8 Nov 1962 and has issue:

Great-great-grandchildren's great-great-grandchildren's children
1f *Sharon Nicole BURGESS, *b* 26 Jan 1988

Great-great-grandchildren's great-great-grandchildren
2e *Marilyn Rene Burgess [Mrs Anthony James, 233 West Loyola, Kenner, LA 70065, USA], *b* New Orleans 23 March 1964; *m* Kenner, La., 15 July 1984 *Anthony O'Dell JAMES and has issue:

Great-great-grandchildren's great-great-grandchildren's children
1f *Amanda Rene JAMES, *b* New Orleans 20 Dec 1982
2f *Suzzane [*sic*] Joyce JAMES, *b* New Orleans 18 Feb 1984
3f *Anthony O'Dell JAMES, Jr, *b* Metairie, La., 27 Jan 1986

Great-great-grandchildren's great-great-grandchildren
3e Kathleen Rochelle Burgess [Mrs Leon J Russo, 3009 Melville Dewey, Metairie, LA 70002, USA], *b* New Orleans 12 May 1965; *m* Metairie 10 Aug 1985 *Leon Joseph RUSSO III and has issue:

Great-great-grandchildren's great-great-grandchildren's children
1f *Vickie Lynn RUSSO, *b* Metairie 3 March 1986

Great-great-grandchildren's great-great-grandchildren
4e *Susan Jane BURGESS, *b* New Orleans 24 July 1966 and has issue:

Great-great-grandchildren's great-great-grandchildren's children
1f *Thomas Walter BURGESS, *b* New Orleans 16 Sept 1984
2f *Angel Marie BURGESS, *b* Metairie 26 May 1986
3f *Susan Jane BURGESS, *b* New Orleans 15 Jan 1988

Great-great-grandchildren's great-great-grandchildren
5e *Thomas BURGESS, Jr [2619 Decatur, Kenneer, LA 70062, USA], *b* Jackson, Miss., 22 Sept 1967; volunteer firefighter 1991-; has issue:

Great-great-grandchildren's great-great-grandchildren's children
1f *Christina Rachelle BURGESS, *b* New Orleans 1 Sept 1991

Great-great-grandchildren's great-great-grandchildren
6e *Larisa Jane BURGESS, *b* Jackson 18 Feb 1973
7 *Lisa Grace BURGESS, *b* Jackson 18 Feb 1973

Great-great-grandchildren's great-grandchildren

3d *William Joseph LANCASTER [416 Oak St, St Rose, LA 70087, USA], b Vicksburg, Miss., 29 Oct 1945

Great-great-grandchildren's grandchildren

4c Joseph Edmund BUTLER, b 29 Jan 1912; m 25 April 1937 *Boyd Evelyn Phillips [Mrs Joseph E Butler, 9323 St Tampa, Baton Rouge, LA 70815, USA] and d 19—

Great-great-grandchildren's children

2b Lancelot Minor KEAN, Jr, b 9 Sept 1884; d 23 June 1885
3b Lancelot Minor KEAN, b March, d April 1886
4b A son, b 1886; d 1891
5b (Mary) Evalina Sanfrosa Prescott Kean, b Sioux City, Iowa, 30 July 1891; m Washington, DC, 15 Jan 1927 Constant SOUTHWORTH (b Duluth, Minn., 12 Aug 1894; d Oct 1984, bur Monticello), s of D. D. Franklin Chester Southworth and his w Alice Berry, and d 3 April 1988
6b Elizabeth Caroline Hill Kean, b Sioux City 12 Jan 1896; m 3 June 1920 Raymond H. CAMPBELL (d New Orleans 21 Oct 1969) and d New Orleans 25 April 1969, leaving issue:

Great-great-grandchildren's grandchildren

1c *Elizabeth Eva CAMPBELL [345 Bonnabel Blvd, Metairie, LA 70005, USA], b 6 Jan 1921
2c Althée Marion Campbell, b 21 Sept 1922; m 25 March 1942 *Francis Thomas MOORE [4609 Alexander Drive, Metairie, LA 70003, USA] and d 10 Feb 1992, leaving issue:

Great-great-grandchildren's great-grandchildren

1d *Francis Thomas MOORE, Jr [1201 Massachusetts Ave, Metairie, LA 70003, USA; 3217 Florida Avenue, Kenner, LA 70065, USA], b 15 March 1947; atty
2d *Roy Victor MOORE [329 Little Farms Ave, River Ridge, LA 70123, USA], b 26 May 1948; m 19— *Karen Cooper and has issue:

Great-great-grandchildren's great-great-grandchildren

1e *Heather Estelle MOORE, b 7 June 1974
2e *Eric James MOORE, b 5 Sept 1976
3e *Kathleen Ann MOORE, b 14 Aug 1984

Great-great-grandchildren's great-grandchildren

3d *Terry Carol Moore, b 7 Nov 1952; m 24 Jan 1973 *Chris Joseph BODE and has issue:

Great-great-grandchildren's great-great-grandchildren

1e *Christopher Joseph BODE, Jr, b 3 Oct 1973
2e *Sean Patrick BODE, b 25 March 1975
3e *Kyle Michael BODE, b 31 March 1980

Great-great-grandchildren's great-grandchildren

4d *Patricia Ellen Moore [Mrs Andrew A Frost, PO Box 127 Dept 03, Kingshill, St Croix, US Virgin Islands 00851, USA], b 22 Nov 1955; m 6 June 1980 *Andrew Albert FROST
5d *Renée Erseld MOORE, b 23 Aug 1961; m Nov 1982 *Steve McWHARTER and has issue:

Great-great-grandchildren's great-great-grandchildren

1e *Rebecca Lynne McWHARTER, b 18 June 1983

Great-great-grandchildren's grandchildren

3c *Raymond Henry CAMPBELL, Jr [335 Harding St, Jefferson, LA 70121, USA], b 27 May 1924; m 18 June 1948 *Betty Cantelli and has issue:

Great-great-grandchildren's great-grandchildren

1d *Kristen Marie CAMPBELL, b 13 July 1949
2d *Michael Raymond CAMPBELL, b 14 Jan 1955

Great-great-grandchildren's grandchildren

4c *Ruth Virginia Campbell [Mrs Claude B Walker, 5012 Bennington Dve, Marrero, LA 70072, USA], b 7 July 1925; m 30 June 1960 *Claude Benoit WALKER and has issue:

Great-great-grandchildren's great-grandchildren

1d *Jacques Doak WALKER, b 18 March 1962; m 17 Nov 1990 *Jean L.Pinney
2d *Dantin Kean WALKER, b 11 Nov 1963

Great-great-grandchildren's grandchildren

5c *Martin Bradburn CAMPBELL [PO Box 15556, New Orleans, LA 70175, USA], b 26 Oct 1928

Great-great-grandchildren

1a (cont.) Lancelot Minor Kean m 2nd 3 Oct 1911 Martha Foster (b Jeanerette, La., 10 June 1879), dau of James Crow Murphy, of St Mary Parish, La., and d 8 Jan 1931, having with her had issue:

Great-great-grandchildren's children

7b James Louis Randolph KEAN, *b* New Orleans 17 May 1913; *m* 16 Nov 1940 *Mary Louise McCarter (*b* 8 Dec 1914) and *d* 21 Jan 1988, leaving issue:

Great-great-grandchildren's grandchildren

1c *James Louis Randolph KEAN, Jr, *b* 18 June 1942
2c *Susan Foster KEAN, *b* 1 Oct 1949
3c *John Michael KEAN, *b* 28 Jan 1952
4c *Thomas Jefferson KEAN, *b* 8 Jan 1954

Great-great-grandchildren

2a Martha (Pattie) Cary Kean, *b* Lynchburg 11 April 1858; *m* there 27 April 1882 John Speed MORRIS (*b* Lynchburg 1 April 1855; *d* Ancon, Panama Canal Zone, 24 Oct 1928), yst s of Dr William Sylvanus Morris and his w Laura Page Waller, and *d* Annapolis, Md., 5 March 1939 (*bur* Monticello), leaving issue:

Great-great-grandchildren's children

1b Robert Kean MORRIS, Sr, *b* Lynchburg 12 April 1883; *m* 1st Ancon, Panama Canal Zone, 30 Aug 1906 Meta Elaine (*b* Brainerd, Minn., 20 July 1888; *d* Santa Barbara, Calif., 1963), dau of Frank B. Thomas, of Faribault, Minn., and his w Ella Eliza Brown, and had issue:

Great-great-grandchildren's grandchildren

1c *Dorothy Elaine Morris, *b* Gorgona, Panama Canal Zone, 14 July 1907; *m* 1st Washington, DC, 3 Nov 1930 Janvier L. LAMAR and has issue:

Great-great-grandchildren's great-grandchildren

1d *Dorothy Elaine Lamar, *b* Washington, DC, 20 Aug 1932; *m* 19— *Fred Rogers SAUNDERS and has issue:

Great-great-grandchildren's great-great-grandchildren

1e *Daniel Price SAUNDERS, *b* 15 Feb 1963
2e *Patricia Morris SAUNDERS, *b* 29 Oct 1966

Great-great-grandchildren's grandchildren

1c (cont.) Dorothy Morris Lamar *m* 2nd 19— Daniel W. SMITH, s of Fred H. Smith, and with him has issue:

Great-great-grandchildren's great-grandchildren

2d *Bonnycastle SMITH, *b* Fort Benning, Ga., 1940; *m* 19— *—— McCABE and has issue three children
3d *Daniel SMITH, Jr, *b* Tex. 15 Feb 1942; *m* 1st 20 Aug 1964 Joyce Ann Reynolds and has issue:

Great-great-grandchildren's great-great-grandchildren

1e *Leslie Jeanne SMITH, *b* 30 April 1968

Great-great-grandchildren's great-grandchildren

3d (cont.) Daniel Smith, Jr, *m* 2nd 30 Nov 1974 *Nancy Jean Smith

Great-great-grandchildren's grandchildren

1c (cont.) Dorothy Morris Lamar Smith *m* 3rd Panama Canal Zone 19— *Raymond PRICE
2c *Robert Kean MORRIS, Jr [3670 31st Street Apt B, San Diego, CA 92104, USA], *b* Balboa, Panama Canal Zone, 24 Dec 1917; *m* Pueblo, Colo., 14 Feb 1946 *Muriel Ellen (*b* there 9 Dec 1917), dau of Edward R. Walker and his w Anne Frances Leonard, and has issue:

Great-great-grandchildren's great-grandchildren

1d *Robert Kean MORRIS III, *b* San Diego 12 Dec 1946
2d *Cynthia Anne MORRIS, *b* San Diego 13 June 1949

Great-great-grandchildren's children

1b (cont.) Robert Kean Morris, Sr, *m* 2nd Balboa 18 April 1925, as her 2nd husb, Louise Newcom (*d* 16 Aug 1989), *née* Richards, formerly w of William E. Baughman, and *d* Mexico City 14 Dec 1961 (*bur* Monticello)
2b Mary Randolph Morris, *b* Lynchburg 5 Feb 1885; *m* Washington, DC, 12 May 1909 Lt Allen Melancthon SUMNER, US Marine Corps (*b* Boston 4 Oct 1883; *ka* France 19 July 1918), and *d* 2 Aug 1955, leaving issue:

Great-great-grandchildren's grandchildren

1c Margaret Page Sumner, *b* 21 Feb 1910; *m* 24 Sept 1932 Burton Francis MILLER (*d* 19 Aug 1992, *bur* Monticello) and *d* 12 Aug 1991 (*bur* Monticello), leaving issue:

Great-great-grandchildren's great-grandchildren

1d *Margaret Page Miller [Mrs Robert S Hinton Jr, 7605 Wheat Fall Court, Derwood, MD 20855, USA], *b* 13 Sept 1933; *m* 12 Nov 1955 *Robert Sanders HINTON, Jr, s of Robert Sanders Hinton, and has issue:

Great-great-grandchildren's great-great-grandchildren

1e *Robert Sanders HINTON III [6301 Reafield Dve, Charlotte, NC 28226, USA], *b* 6 Jan 1959; *m* 10 Nov 1990 *Melissa Roberson Holt
2e Jeffrey Brady HINTON, *b* 7 April 1963; *d* 26 July 1989
3e *Richard Francis HINTON, *b* 26 Jan 1966; *m* 26 Oct 1991 *Anastasia Martha Ryon

Great-great-grandchildren's great-grandchildren
2d *Adelaide Randolph Miller, *b* 4 Feb 1935; *m* 1st 31 March 1956 Gordon Conrad COINER and has issue:

Great-great-grandchildren's great-great-grandchildren
1e *Patricia Jane Coiner, *b* 10 Jan 1958; *m* 15 Oct 1982 *Richard Frank WILLIAMS and has issue:

Great-great-grandchildren's great-great-grandchildren's children
1f *Timothy Allen Coiner WILLIAMS, *b* 2 June 1982
2f *Melissa Jane Coiner WILLIAMS, *b* 27 July 1984

Great-great-grandchildren's great-great-grandchildren
2e *Gordon Conrad COINER, Jr, *b* 13 June 1963
3e *Elizabeth Randolph COINER, *b* 22 Dec 1969
4e *Burton Grayson COINER, *b* 22 Dec 1969
5e *Margaret Page COINER, *b* 22 Dec 1969

Great-great-grandchildren's great-grandchildren
2d (cont.) Adelaide Miller Coiner *m* 2nd 15 Nov 1980 *Kitchel LUDY

Great-great-grandchildren's children
3b Page Waller Morris, *b* Edgehill 1 July 1886; *m* 20 June 1910 Frederick Campbell Stuart HUNTER II (*d* 1930) and *d* 19 Sept 1956 (*bur* Monticello), leaving issue:

Great-great-grandchildren's grandchildren
1c *Frederick Campbell Stuart HUNTER III, *b* 14 March 1911; *m* 1 Jan 1939 (divorce 19—) Dorothy Dulany and has issue:

Great-great-grandchildren's great-grandchildren
1d *Grace Page HUNTER, *b* 15 Jan 1941

Great-great-grandchildren's grandchildren
2c John Morris HUNTER, *b* 17 Jan 1916; *m* 23 Jan 1943 *Juliet King Lehmann (*b* 1911) and *d* 10 Jan 1984

Great-great-grandchildren's children
4b William Sylvanus MORRIS, *b* Campbell Co, Va., 5 May 1888; *m* 2 Aug 1923 Pearl Lenore Oberg and *d* Duluth, Minn., 6 Sept 1947, leaving issue:

Great-great-grandchildren's grandchildren
1c Mary Elizabeth MORRIS, *b* 28 March 1924; *d* 14 April 1962

Great-great-grandchildren's children
5b Pattie Nicholas Morris, *b* Indian Territory 9 April 1893; *m* Washington, DC, 28 April 1920 Horace King HUTCHENS (*b* Pulaski, New York; *d* Euclid, Ohio, 1972, *bur* Monticello), s of James Lovell Hutchens and his w Katherine Douglas King, and *d* 18 Oct 1980, leaving issue:

Great-great-grandchildren's grandchildren
1c *Katherine King Hutchens [Mrs William J Ermisch, 1981 Powers Ferry Rd #F, Marietta, GA 30067, USA], *b* New York 25 Feb 1921; *m* 1st New Rochelle, New York, 6 June 1942 George William WILEY (*b* Oak Park, Ill., 13 July 1913; *d* Cleveland, Ohio, 1 April 1970, *bur* Monticello), s of William Joseph Wiley and his w Helen Gettle, and has issue:

Great-great-grandchildren's great-grandchildren
1d *John Hutchens WILEY [2009-I Powers Ferry Rd, Marietta, GA 30067, USA], *b* New York 30 Nov 1948

Great-great-grandchildren's grandchildren
1c (cont.) Katherine Hutchens Wiley *m* 2nd Cleveland, Ohio, 12 Oct 1973 William Joseph ERMISCH (*d* 7 July 1990)

Great-great-grandchildren's children
6b Adelaide Prescott Morris, *b* Indian Territory 28 April 1896; *m* Washington, DC, 21 April 1919 V-Adml Thomas Ross COOLEY, USN (*b* Grass Valley, Calif., 26 June 1893; *d* Quantico, Va., 29 Nov 1959, *bur* Monticello), s of Thomas Ross Cooley and his w Mary Adelaide Cota, and *d* 23 Nov 1958 (*bur* Monticello), having had issue:

Great-great-grandchildren's grandchildren
1c Adelaide Morris Cooley, *b* 6 March 1920; *m* 1st 8 May 1943 Dr Hal Waugh SMITH and had issue:

Great-great-grandchildren's great-grandchildren
1d *Ross Emerson SMITH (later took stepfather's name of GADEBERG) [719 G St, Petaluma, CA 94952, USA], *b* 10 May 1949; *m* 1st 5 Jan 1974 Deborah Lynn McBride; *m* 2nd 12 Feb 1978 (divorce 19—) Margaret Rose Andresen and has issue:

Great-great-grandchildren's great-great-grandchildren
1e *Michael Emerson GADEBERG, *b* 27 June 1980

Great-great-grandchildren's great-grandchildren
2d *Margaret Waugh Smith (later took stepfather's name of Gadeberg) [Mrs Margaret Smith Morrow, c/o

Everything Sews, 9353 Greenback Lane #2, Orangevale, CA 95662, USA], *b* San Francisco 3 June 1950; *educ* Deanza Coll, Calif.; tailor 1976- ; *m* 15 Feb 1969 (divorce 19—) Michael Anthony MORROW, s of Loren Rosie, and has issue:

Great-great-grandchildren's great-great-grandchildren

1e *Adelaide Leigh Morrow [Mrs Rodney Brown, 210 N Marion #2, Ottumwa, IA 52561, USA], *b* Calif. 24 May 1969; *m* Iowa 30 June 1990 *Rodney BROWN

Great-great-grandchildren's great-grandchildren

3d *Adelaide Leigh Smith (later took stepfather's name of Gadeberg) [Mrs William J Cleere, 910 Rockerfellow Dve #18A, Sunnyvale, CA 94087, USA], *b* California 15 Feb 1952; *educ* San Jose State U; performing arts specialist; *m* 30 June 1972 *William James CLEERE, s of William Paul Cleere and his w Freida Quass, and has issue:

Great-great-grandchildren's great-great-grandchildren

1e *William Burnett CLEERE, *b* California 15 Nov 1974

2e *(Lawrence) Ryan CLEERE, *b* California 8 Aug 1978

Great-great-grandchildren's grandchildren

1c (cont.) Adelaide Cooley Smith *m* 2nd 31 March 1955 *Burnett Laurence GADEBERG and *d* 9 Feb 1974

2c *Mary Lawrence Cooley [Mary Cooley Aitken, 8569 Richmond Highway #303, Alexandria, VA 22309, USA], *b* Panama City, Panama, 21 May 1930; *educ* Georgetown Visitation Sch; child care assist; *m* Treasure Island, Calif., 8 Jan 1951 (divorce 13 March 1981) Brig-Gen Hugh Sommerville AITKEN, US Marine Corps, s of Hugh Aitken and his w Elizabeth Douglas, and has issue:

Great-great-grandchildren's great-grandchildren

1d *Mary Lawrence Aitken [8569 Richmond Highway, Alexandria, VA 22309, USA], *b* Pensacola, Fla., 28 Oct 1951; *m* 14 April 1974 (divorce 19—) Michael A. YANNIELLO and has issue:

Great-great-grandchildren's great-great-grandchildren

1e *Christina Marie YANNIELLO, *b* 19 Sept 1974

Great-great-grandchildren's great-grandchildren

2d *Elizabeth Sommerville Aitken, *b* Camp Pendleton, Calif., 11 Nov 1952; *m* 1st 28 April 1971 (divorce 19—) Peter F(rank) CRUIKSHANK and has issue:

Great-great-grandchildren's great-great-grandchildren

1e *Elizabeth Marie CRUIKSHANK, *b* Sumter, S Carolina, 26 July 1972

2e *William Francis CRUIKSHANK, *b* Sumter 5 April 1974

Great-great-grandchildren's great-grandchildren

2d (cont.) Mrs Elizabeth Aitken Cruikshank *m* 2nd Fairfax Co, Va., 1 Jan 1982 *Daniel Cleveland PIERCE (*b* Alexandria, Va., 10 Dec 1954), s of Walter Cleveland Pierce and his w Betty Louise Braumback, and has issue:

Great-great-grandchildren's great-great-grandchildren

1e *Daniel Cleveland PIERCE, Jr, *b* Alexandria 16 Sept 1982

Great-great-grandchildren's great-grandchildren

3d *Hugh Wylie AITKEN, *b* Pittsburgh 25 June 1955

4d *William Ormond AITKEN, *b* Newport, Rhode Island, 25 April 1961; *m* 1st 19— Mary Bernadette Love (*d* Alexandria, Va., 30 Dec 1984); *m* 2nd 19— (divorce 19—) ——

5d *Thomas Ross-Cooley AITKEN, *b* Oakland, Calif., 28 Oct 1964

6d *Margaret Randolph Aitken, *b* Bethesda, Md., 18 Jan 1966; *m* 16 Dec 1989 *Timothy Hagood SAMS (*b* S Carolina 19 May 1965)

Great-great-grandchildren's grandchildren

3c Margaret Ross COOLEY, *b* 14 Dec 1931; *d* 24 Aug 1940 (*bur* Monticello)

Great-great-grandchildren

3a Dr Jefferson Randolph KEAN, *b* Lynchburg 27 June 1860; *educ* U of Virginia (MD); served US Army Medical Corps 1884-1924 (Far West against Sioux 1890-91, Spanish-American War of 1898 with 7th Army, Corps Area Ch Surgeon Cuba 1898-1902, Advsr Dept of Sanitation Provisional Govt of Cuba 1906-09, World War I as Dir-Gen American Red Cross 1916-17, Ch US Ambulance Service and Depy Ch Surgeon American Expeditionary Force Western Front 1917-19), Memb Commission for Nat Expansion Memorial, St Louis, 1934 and Thomas Jefferson Memorial, Washington, DC, 1938, Pres: Monticello Assoc 1913-20 (Historian 1920-37 and 1938-48) and Assoc Military Surgeons 1914-15 (sec and ed AMS journal 1924-34), awarded DSM, Légion d' Honneur (France), Grand Cross Order of Merit, Carlos J. Finley (Cuba) and Gorgas Medal of Assoc of Military Surgeons (1942); *m* 1st St Augustine, Fla., 10 Oct 1894 Louise Hurlbut (*b* 1 Sept 1877; *d* Fort Leavenworth, Kans., 5 Dec 1915, *bur* Monticello), dau of Mason Young, of New York, and his w Louisa M. Hurlbut, and had issue:

Great-great-grandchildren's children

1b Martha Jefferson Kean, *b* Key West, Fla., 7 Aug 1895; *m* Washington, DC, 5 Dec 1917 (divorce 1932) William CHASON and *d* 1 Nov 1978, leaving issue:

Great-great-grandchildren's grandchildren

1c *William Randolph CHASON, *b* 8 April 1919

2c *Louise Young CHASON, *b* Hopewell, Va., 11 Sept 1921

3c *Col Robert Leonard CHASON [104 Janeway, Greenwood, SC 29646, USA], *b* Hopewell, Va., 30 Oct 1923; USAF ret; *m* 1st 7 March 1945 Shirley Lucille Flynn (*d* Greenwood, S Carolina, 15 March 1989) and has issue:

Great-great-grandchildren's great-grandchildren

1d *Patricia Lucille Chason, *b* 11 Aug 1955; *m* 8 June 1974 *Timothy L. BLADON and has issue:

Great-great-grandchildren's great-great-grandchildren

1e *Sara Elizabeth BLADON, *b* 16 Sept 1976

Great-great-grandchildren's great-grandchildren

2d *Carol Randolph CHASON [4228 Spruce St, Philadelphia, PA 19104, USA], *b* 18 Jan 1962

Great-great-grandchildren's grandchildren

3c (cont.) Col Robert L. Chason *m* 2nd 28 Sept 1991 *Sarah Katherine Safford Rowland

4c *Helen Borodell Chason [Mrs John Crump, 4838 Broad Brook Drive, Bethesda, MD 20814, USA], *b* Miami 16 July 1928; *m* Alexandria, Va., 21 Nov 1945 *John Wesley CRUMP (*b* Philadelphia, Pa., 24 Aug 1923), s of James E. Crump and his w Hazel Everett, and has issue:

Great-great-grandchildren's great-grandchildren

1d *Sheila Kean Crump [Mrs Dennis J Hartzell, 32 Casilli Ave, San Francisco, CA 94114, USA], *b* Alexandria, Va., 13 Sept 1946; *m* 1st 22 June 1968 Carson Lee FIFER, Jr; *m* 2nd 3 Dec 1988 *Dennis Jeffrey HARTZELL

Great-great-grandchildren's children

2b Robert Hill KEAN, *b* Morristown, New Jersey, 5 July 1900; *educ* U of Virginia (PhD) and MIT (BS, MS); chemical engineer, Chm Virginia Section Chemical Soc 1945-46 and Chemistry Section of Virginia Acad of Science 1946-47, Tstee Virginia Inst for Scientific Research 1949-68, Research Assoc U of Virginia 1956-62, Sec-Treasurer Monticello Assoc 1927-39, Pres 1939-41 and Recording Sec 1941-50, AICE (Emeritus) (1972); *m* New Orleans 26 Dec 1927 Sarah Rice (*b* Albemarle Co, Va., 19 June 1905; *d* 11 Feb 1993, *bur* Monticello), dau of John Barnwell Elliott and his w Noel Forsyth, and *d* 16 Jan 1985 (*bur* Monticello), leaving issue:

Great-great-grandchildren's grandchildren

1c Jefferson Randolph KEAN, *b* New Orleans 18 Feb 1930; *m* 1st Evanston, Ill., 13 July 1957 (divorce 1968) Barbara (*b* 4 May 1932), adopted dau of Lewis Miller and his wife Helen Mathews; Mr and the first Mrs Jefferson Kean adopted a s:

a *Robert Hill KEAN II, *b* Prince George's Co, Md., 5 July 1961

Mr and Mrs Jefferson R. Kean also have issue:

Great-great-grandchildren's great-grandchildren

1d *Evelina Southworth KEAN [410 15th St SE Apt B, Washington, DC 20033, USA], *b* Washington, DC, 5 Nov 1964

Great-great-grandchildren's grandchildren

1c (cont.) Jefferson Randolph Kean *m* 2nd Alexandria, Va., 24 April 1971 *Leah Jones [Mrs Jefferson R Kean, Cliftwood Circle, Mounted Route 8, Clifton Forge, VA 2442, USA] (*b* West Point, New York, 30 June 1943), dau of Brig-Gen John DuVal Stevens and his w Frances Cramer, and *d* 16 Jan 1990

2c *Margaret Young Kean [Mrs Edward Rubel, 55 Balsam Drive, East Greenwich, RI 02818, USA], *b* Charlotteville, Va., 24 Sept 1938; *m* there 17 June 1961 *Edward Alexander RUBEL, s of Adrian Rubel and his w Elizabeth Smith, and has issue:

Great-great-grandchildren's great-grandchildren

1d *Daniel Martin RUBEL [2013 Pembroke Dve, Glenshaw, PA 15116, USA], *b* Providence, Rhode Island, 16 March 1965; *m* 8 Aug 1987 *Katherine Rissel

2d *Stephen Elliott RUBEL, *b* Providence 12 Dec 1966

3d *Sarah Rice Rubel, *b* Providence 13 Sept 1968; *m* 12 Oct 1991 *Stefan Charles MATZEL

Great-great-grandchildren

3a (cont.) Gen Jefferson Randolph Kean *m* 2nd Tours, France, 24 March 1919 Cornelia Butler (*b* 1 March 1875; *d* Washington, DC, April 1954), dau of Col Thomas T. Knox, US Army, and *d* Washington, DC, 4 Sept 1950 (*bur* Monticello)

4a Robert Garlick Hill KEAN, Jr, *b* 26 Dec 1862; *d* after 1883

5a Lewis Randolph KEAN, *b* and *d* 17 Aug 1864

6a George Randolph KEAN, *b* 6 April 1866; *d* 27 Aug 1869 (*bur* Monticello)

Great-grandchildren

(11) Dr Wilson Cary Nicholas RANDOLPH, of Charlottesville, *b* Edgehill 26 Oct 1834; Col Confederate States Army

Medical Corps, Rector U of Virginia 1889-1904; *m* 1st 11 Nov 1858 Anne (Nannie) Elizabeth (*b* Sunning Hill, Louisa Co, Va., 19 July 1839; *d* Charlottesville 9 Oct 1888), dau of John Zachary Holladay, of Louisa Co, lawyer and Memb Virginia House of Delegates 1841-42, and his w Julia Ann Minor, and had issue:

Great-great-grandchildren

1a Virginia Minor Randolph, *b* Underhill, Albemarle Co, 28 Nov 1859; *m* Charlottesville 1 July 1884 George Scott SHACKELFORD, of Orange, Va. (*b* Warrenton, Va., 12 Dec 1856; Judge 9th Virginia Judicial Circuit, Memb: Virginia House of Delegates 1889-92, Virginia State Senate 1901-06 and Bd Visitors U of Virginia; *d* Orange 29 Dec 1918), s of Benjamin Howard Shackelford and his w Rebecca Beverley Green, and *d* Orange 28 Jan 1937, leaving issue:

Great-great-grandchildren's children

1b Virginius Randolph SHACKELFORD, *b* Orange, Va., 15 April 1885; *educ* Woodberry Forest Sch and U of Virginia (BA, LLB 1907); lawyer, Memb Virginia House of Delegates 1918, Pres: Virginia State Bar Assoc 1931-32 and Orange County Chamber Commerce, Monticello Assoc 1937-39 (Sec-Treasurer 1913-20, Treasurer 1920-23), Dir Nat Bank Orange and Kentucky Flooring Corp of Virginia; *m* Orange 10 Nov 1910 *Peachy Gascoigne [Mrs Virginius Shackelford, Willow Grove, RD1, Box 6, Orange, VA 22960, USA] (*b* Fairview, Orange Co, Va., 16 July 1887), dau of William Henry Lyne, of Richmond, Va., memb 3rd Richmond Howitzers Confederate States Army, and his w Cassandra Oliver Moncure, and *d* Willow Grove 19 Jan 1949 (*bur* Graham Cemetery, Orange), having had issue:

Great-great-grandchildren's grandchildren

1c Virginius Randolph SHACKELFORD, *b* Orange 24 Aug 1911; *d* 25 July 1912

2c Lyne Moncure SHACKELFORD, *b* Orange 22 May 1914; *educ* Woodberry Forest Sch and U of Virginia (BA); banker, Maj US Army World War II; *m* Orange 2 Oct 1948 *Elizabeth (*b* Greenbriar Co, W. Va., 25 Oct 1911), dau of John Devereux Burrow and his w Jeraldine Dixon, and *d* 4 Nov 1991, leaving issue:

Great-great-grandchildren's great-grandchildren

1d *Lyne Moncure SHACKELFORD, Jr [PO Box 65, Orange, VA 22960, USA], *b* Charlottesville 17 Nov 1952; *educ* Blue Ridge Sch and St Andrew's Presbyterian Coll (BA 1971); *m* 1st 13 Nov 1974 Marguerite Lynn Simpson and has issue:

Great-great-grandchildren's great-great-grandchildren

1e *Mary Elizabeth SHACKELFORD, *b* 1 June 1979

Great-great-grandchildren's great-grandchildren

1d (cont.) Lyne M. Shackelford *m* 2nd 15 June 1985 *Terry Jo Devers and has further issue:

Great-great-grandchildren's great-great-grandchildren

2e *Alan Lyne SHACKELFORD, *b* 3 Nov 1989

3e *Robert Hunter SHACKELFORD, *b* 21 March 1992

Great-great-grandchildren's grandchildren

3c *Virginius Randolph SHACKELFORD, Jr [1 Perry Plaza, Orange, VA 22960, USA; PO Box 871 Brampton, Orange, VA 22960, USA], *b* Orange 15 Jan 1916; *educ* Woodberry Forest Sch and U of Virginia (BA, LLB 1937); Maj US Army World War II, lawyer, Pres: Monticello Assoc 1957-59 (V-Pres 1955-57) and Virginia State Bar Assoc 1964-65, Memb Bd Visitors Medical Coll of Virginia; *m* Kansas City, Mo., 7 Aug 1943 *Carroll (*b* Newcastle, Wyo., 31 Oct 1920), dau of Senator James Preston Kem, of Missouri, and his w Mary Elizabeth Carroll, and has issue:

Great-great-grandchildren's great-grandchildren

1d *Virginius Randolph SHACKELFORD III [147 W Davis Street, Culpeper, VA 22701, USA; PO Box 871 Brampton, Orange, VA 22960, USA], *b* Charlottesville 27 July 1946; *educ* Woodberry Forest Sch, Princeton (AB 1968) and U of Virginia (JD 1974); lawyer; *m* 27 Sept 1975 *Jane Lee Schwartzschild and has issue:

Great-great-grandchildren's great-great-grandchildren

1e *Virginius Randolph SHACKELFORD IV, *b* 17 Jan 1979

Great-great-grandchildren's great-grandchildren

2d *Carroll Preston Shackelford [Mrs John B Todd, St Helena, CA 94574, USA; c/o Coombs & Dunlap, attorneys, 1211 Division, Napa, CA, USA], *b* Charlottesville 30 Jan 1948; *educ* Chatham Hall, Smith Coll, State U of New York (BA 1970) and U of California at Berkeley (JD 1973); *m* 1st 24 Oct 1980 James Richard GEISLER; *m* 2nd 4 July 1987 *John Barry TODD

3d *Mary Gascoigne Lyne Shackelford, *b* Charlottesville 19 May 1953; *educ* Chatham Hall, Woodberry Forest Sch and U of Colorado; *m* 22 April 1978 *James Stuart Chaffee BURKE and has issue:

Great-great-grandchildren's great-great-grandchildren

1e *Chaffee Kem Shackelford BURKE, *b* 12 Sept 1983

2e *Margot Stuart Shackelford BURKE, *b* 12 March 1987

Great-great-grandchildren's great-grandchildren

4d *Kem Moncure Shackelford [4612 N 24th St, Arlington, VA 22207, USA], *b* Charlottesville 22 Oct 1954; *educ* Chatham Hall, U of Virginia (BSLA), Harvard (MLA) and U of California, Berekeley (MBA); real estate consultant; *m* 5 June 1983 *Roger Guy COURTENAY, *s* of Terence Henry Courtenay and his *w* Carroll Irene, and has issue:

Great-great-grandchildren's great-great-grandchildren
1e *Carroll Irene COURTENAY, *b* Virginia 19 Feb 1990

Great-great-grandchildren's grandchildren
4c *George Green SHACKELFORD [Box 219, 301 Wall Street, Blacksburg, VA 24063, USA], *b* Orange 17 Dec 1920; *educ* Woodberry Forest Sch, U of Virginia (BA 1943, MA 1948, PhD 1955) and Columbia U; Lt US Naval Reserve World War II, Prof History Virginia Polytechnic Inst and State U 1968-90, Memb Bd Advsrs Nat Trust for Historic Preservation, Pres Monticello Assoc 1969-71 (V-Pres 1967-69); *m* Blacksburg 9 June 1962 *Grace Howard (*b* Marion, Va., 3 Dec 1925), dau of Earle Lambert McConnell and his *w* Ruby Winston Dickinson

Great-great-grandchildren's children
2b Nannie Holladay Shackelford, *b* Orange, Va., 23 Feb 1887; *m* 1 Oct 1913 Rt Revd Karl Morgan BLOCK, DD, Episcopal Bishop of California (*b* Washington, DC, 27 Sept 1886; *d* San Francisco 20 Sept 1958), s of Sigismund Joseph Block and his *w* Joanna Christine Linden, and·*d* San Francisco 15 Feb 1945, leaving issue:

Great-great-grandchildren's grandchildren
1c *Virginia Randolph Block [Mrs Wayne Snowden, 1761 Scott St, St Helena, CA 94574, USA], *b* 5 May 1915; *m* 3 Jan 1941 *Wayne Horton SNOWDEN, *s* of Raymond Fort Snowden and his *w* Elsie Horton, and has issue:

Great-great-grandchildren's great-grandchildren
1d *Wayne Scott SNOWDEN [1735 Spring St, St Helena, CA 94574, USA], *b* 6 April 1946; *educ* Washington and Lee (BA) and U of California, Berkeley (JD); Superior Court Judge, Napa Co, Calif.; *m* 17 Oct 1969 *Nancy Helen Jones and has issue:

Great-great-grandchildren's great-great-grandchildren
1e *Diana Styles SNOWDEN, *b* 3 March 1978
2e *Susanne Maria SNOWDEN, *b* 22 March 1980

Great-great-grandchildren's great-grandchildren
2d *Randolph Fort SNOWDEN [2033 Lone Oak Ave, Napa, CA 94558, USA], *b* 12 Sept 1949; *educ* U of California at Davis (AB and JD); *m* 19 Sept 1970 *Janet Fake and has issue:

Great-great-grandchildren's great-great-grandchildren
1e *Christian Randolph SNOWDEN, *b* 18 March 1979
2e *Carey Holladay SNOWDEN, *b* 3 Dec 1981

Great-great-grandchildren's grandchildren
2c Karl Morgan BLOCK, Jr, *b* 16 Jan 1921; *m* 2 June 1945 Marion Lambert Niedringhaus (*d* 14 May 1991) and *d* 29 Aug 1979, leaving issue:

Great-great-grandchildren's great-grandchildren
1d *Karl Morgan BLOCK III, *b* 6 April 1946; *m* 15 Feb 1975 *Priscilla Beleveau and has issue:

Great-great-grandchildren's great-great-grandchildren
1e *Sally Southerland BLOCK, *b* 28 April 1976
2e *Brian BLOCK, *b* 20 July 1979
3e *Karl Morgan BLOCK IV, *b* 19 April 1984

Great-great-grandchildren's great-grandchildren
2d *Lambert Stafford BLOCK, *b* 26 Jan 1948; *m* 24 Aug 1970 *Lucille Lanning and has issue:

Great-great-grandchildren's great-great-grandchildren
1e *Gerald Lambert BLOCK, *b* 5 Oct 1981
2e *Katrina Aurora BLOCK, *b* 14 July 1985

Great-great-grandchildren's great-grandchildren
3d *Nancy Holladay Block, *b* 17 Oct 1949; *m* 27 Nov 1979 *Miodrag Zeibert CVITKOVIC and has issue:

Great-great-grandchildren's great-great-grandchildren
1e *Anna Linden CVITKOVIC, *b* 3 Oct 1980
2e *Adrian Birch CVITKOVICH, *b* 28 Feb 1985

Great-great-grandchildren's great-grandchildren
4d *Florence Parker Block, *b* 25 April 1951; *m* 12 June 1971 *John Henry LLOYD and has issue:

Great-great-grandchildren's great-great-grandchildren
1e *Jessica May LLOYD, *b* 12 March 1973
2e *Joseph Marion LLOYD, *b* 4 Nov 1975
3e *Phillip Block LLOYD, *b* 20 Oct 1981

Great-great-grandchildren's great-grandchildren
5d *Warne Niedringhaus BLOCK [44 Countryside Lane, St Louis, MO 63131, USA], b 8 June 1955; m 24 April 1982 *Lisa A. Koch and has issue:

Great-great-grandchildren's great-great-grandchildren
1e *Clare Taylor BLOCK, b 23 Oct 1986
2e *Audrey Lambert BLOCK, b 27 July 1989

Great-great-grandchildren's great-grandchildren
6d *Anne Randolph Block, b 11 Feb 1959; m 24 July 1981 *Earl GERFEN and has issue:

Great-great-grandchildren's great-great-grandchildren
1e *Grace Virginia GERFEN, b 28 Oct 1985
2e *Peter Morson GERFEN, b 18 March 1989

Great-great-grandchildren's great-grandchildren
7d *Marion Lambert Block, b 11 Feb 1959; m 9 June 1984 *John Aloysius REARDON and has issue:

Great-great-grandchildren's great-great-grandchildren
1e *John Aloysius REARDON, Jr, b 13 Jan 1990
2e *Marion Lee REARDON, b 21 Sept 1992

Great-great-grandchildren's great-grandchildren
8d *Amy Carter BLOCK, b 25 April 1963
9d *Andrew Minor BLOCK [683Å W Wrightwood Apt # 2 S, Chicago, IL 60614, USA], b St Louis, Mo., 29 July 1966; educ DePaul U

Great-great-grandchildren's children
3b George Scott SHACKELFORD, Jr, b Orange 27 Jan 1897; m Roanoake, Va., 26 Feb 1927 *Mary Evelyn (b Roanoke, Va., 6 March 1898), dau of Junius Blair Fishburn and his w Grace Parker, and d Roanoke 31 July 1965, leaving issue:

Great-great-grandchildren's grandchildren
1c *Mary Parker Shackelford [Mrs John Crosland, 2440 Lemon Tree Lane, Charlotte, NC 28211, USA], b Roanoke 19 Jan 1929; educ Chatham Hall and Hollins Coll; m Roanoke 8 Dec 1951 (divorce Nov 1974) John CROSLAND, Jr (b Charlotte 20 Sept 1928), s of John Crosland and his w Lillian Mason Floyd, and has issue:

Great-great-grandchildren's great-grandchildren
1d *Mary Parker Crosland [6 Ancrum Rd, Camden, SC 29020, USA], b Roanoke, Va., 4 Jan 1954; m 1st 21 July 1979 William Oliver TANKARD; m 2nd 24 March 1988 *Calvin McCaskill MOSIER
2d *John CROSLAND III [4501 Oglukian Rd, Charlotte, NC 28226, USA], b Charlotte, N Carolina, 30 Jan 1957

Great-great-grandchildren's grandchildren
2c *George Scott SHACKELFORD III [2919 Wycliffe Avenue SW, Roanoke, VA 24014, USA], b Roanoke 20 Sept 1933; m there 10 Sept 1960 *Virginia Ria (b El Paso, Tex., 4 Jan 1940), dau of William Stephenson Thomas and his w Virginia Armistead Hardy, and has issue:

Great-great-grandchildren's great-grandchildren
1d *William Scott SHACKELFORD [1344 29th St NW, Washington, DC 20007, USA], b Roanoke 12 May 1962
2d *George Randolph SHACKELFORD [212 Miller St, Lexington, VA 24450, USA], b Roanoke 7 Nov 1964
3d *Virginia Travis SHACKELFORD [2919 Wycliffe Avenue SW, Roanoke, VA 24014, USA], b Roanoke 17 March 1967

Great-great-grandchildren's children
4b Margaret Wilson Shackelford, b Orange, Va., 28 Oct 1898; m St Thomas's Church, Orange, 5 Dec 1923 Frank Stringfellow WALKER (b Woodberry Forest, Va., 2 Jan 1883; d Gordonsville, Va., 10 June 1971), s of Robert Stringfellow Walker and his w Anne Goss, and d Charlottesville, Va., 13 July 1963, leaving issue:

Great-great-grandchildren's grandchildren
1c *Anne Carter Walker [Mrs Atwell Somerville, PO Box 1218 358 E Main Street, Orange, VA 22960, USA], b Charlottesville 4 April 1925; m St Thomas's Church, Orange, 14 Oct 1948 *Atwell Wilson SOMERVILLE (b Hillsville, Va., 19 Nov 1921), s of Revd Walter Gray Somerville and his w Hattie Nottingham, and has issue:

Great-great-grandchildren's great-grandchildren
1d *Atwell Wilson SOMERVILLE, Jr [4604D Mercury Drive, Greensboro, NC 27410, USA], b Charlottesville 24 Nov 1949; m N Carolina 31 Dec 1987 *Rebecca Houren Shields and has issue:

Great-great-grandchildren's great great grandchildren
1e *Margaret Houren SOMERVILLE, b Asheville, N Carolina, 20 June 1984

Great-great-grandchildren's great-grandchildren
2d *Frank Walker SOMERVILLE [PO Box 26, 236 Blue Ridge Dve, Orange, VA 22960, USA], b Charlottesville 21 Feb 1952; educ Davidson Coll and U of Virginia; atty; m 4 June 1977 *Laura Adair, dau of William and Margie Farmer, and has issue:

Great-great-grandchildren's great-great-grandchildren
1e *Laura Adair SOMERVILLE, *b* Charlottesville 25 Oct 1983
2e *John Walker SOMERVILLE, *b* Charlottesville 23 Oct 1986

Great-great-grandchildren's great-grandchildren
3d *Anne Carter SOMERVILLE [PO Box 1218, Orange, VA 22960, USA], *b* Charlottesville 3 Jan 1954

Great-great-grandchildren's grandchildren
2c *Virginia Randolph Walker [Mrs Andrew Christian, 106 Penshurst, Richmond, VA 23231, USA], *b* Orange, Va., 23 April 1927; *educ* St Margaret's and Sweetbriar Coll; bd memb Jefferson's, Poplar Forest (the 3rd President's second home); *m* St Thomas's Church, Orange, 10 Sept 1947 *Andrew Henry CHRISTIAN (*b* Richmond, Va., 26 Jan 1921), s of Andrew Dunscomb Christian and his w Eleanor (Nellie) Addison Rennolds, and has issue:

Great-great-grandchildren's great-grandchildren
1d *Andrew Henry CHRISTIAN, Jr [5000 San Jose Blvd #198, Jacksonville, FL 32207, USA], *b* Richmond, Va., 19 Sept 1950; *m* 10 Sept 1977 *Jennifer Jenkins
2d *Scott Shackelford CHRISTIAN [Rte 5 Box 358, Martinsville, VA 24112, USA], *b* Richmond 3 Sept 1953; *m* Virginia 27 Aug 1981 *Sharon Marie Martin
3d *Virginia Randolph Christian [Mrs Edward D Beach, 6890 Maybank Highway, Wadmalaw Island, SC 29487, USA], *b* Richmond 19 May 1957; *m* there 17 Sept 1983 *Edward Dana BEACH (*b* 20 Aug 1955) and has issue:

Great-great-grandchildren's great-great-grandchildren
1e *Nellie Christian BEACH, *b* 16 Sept 1990

Great-great-grandchildren's grandchildren
3c *Margot Shackelford Walker [Mrs Cary Humphries, 4512 Moorland Avenue, Edina, MN 55424, USA], *b* Madison Co., Va., 8 Aug 1931; *m* St Thomas's Church, Orange, Va., 18 Dec 1954 *Cary Hill HUMPHRIES (*b* Culpeper, Va., 17 Oct 1929), s of Kemper Hill Humphries and his w Anne Green, and has issue:

Great-great-grandchildren's great-grandchildren
1d *Raleigh Green HUMPHRIES [3023 Lake Forest Dve, Greensboro, NC 27408-3824, USA], *b* Baltimore, Md., 6 Feb 1956; *m* 6 Sept 1981 *Betty Scott Whitlow and has issue:

Great-great-grandchildren's great-great-grandchildren
1e *Margot Walker HUMPHRIES, *b* 17 Oct 1983
2e *Nancy Barrier HUMPHRIES, *b* 3 July 1986

Great-great-grandchildren's great-grandchildren
2d *Cary Hill HUMPHRIES, Jr [8915 Clubside Circle, Wichita, KS 67206, USA], *b* Bryn Mawr, Pa., 6 Feb 1958; *m* 21 June 1980 *Susan Lynn Murphy and has issue:

Great-great-grandchildren's great-great-grandchildren
1e *Kiley Elizabeth HUMPHRIES, *b* 30 Sept 1985
2e *Luke Walker HUMPHRIES, *b* 6 April 1987
Mr and Mrs Cary H. Humphries also have two adopted children:
a *Grace Anne HUMPHRIES, *b* 24 Oct 1988
b *Nathanael Hill HUMPHRIES, *b* 7 Dec 1989

Great-great-grandchildren's great-grandchildren
3d *Robert Walker HUMPHRIES [1306 Goodview Ave, Fayetteville, NC 28305, USA], *b* Memphis, Tenn., 30 July 1960; *m* 5 Nov 1988 *Jane Gray Hanlon and has issue:

Great-great-grandchildren's great-great-grandchildren
1e *Turner Gray HUMPHRIES, *b* 14 Sept 1989

Great-great-grandchildren's grandchildren
4c *Frank Stringfellow WALKER, Jr [10199 Little Skyline Drive, Orange, VA 22960, USA], *b* Madison Co, Va., 11 Oct 1935; atty; *m* St Paul's Church, Richmond, Va., 3 Dec 1960 *Bernice, dau of Stamo Spathey and his w Eunice Wilson, and has issue:

Great-great-grandchildren's great-grandchildren
1d *Susan Stringfellow WALKER, *b* Charlottesville, Va., 22 Jan 1964
2d *Margaret Austin Walker [Mrs James W St Clair, 1111 12th Ave, Huntington, WV 25701, USA], *b* Charlottesville 27 Feb 1967; *m* St Thomas's Church, Orange, Va., 20 May 1989 *James William St CLAIR and has issue:

Great-great-grandchildren's great-great-grandchildren
1e *Virginia Randolph St CLAIR, *b* Huntington, W. Va., 17 May 1991

Great-great grandchildren
2a Wilson Cary Nicholas RANDOLPH, Jr, of Lynchburg, Va., *b* 1 Aug 1861; *m* 2 Jan 1890 Margaret Henderson Hager (*b* 27 Dec 1861; *d* 29 March 1946) and *d* 1 March 1923, leaving issue:

Great-great grandchildren's children
1b John Hager RANDOLPH, *b* 16 July 1893; Sec-Treasurer 1939-41 and Pres Monticello Assoc 1941-43; *m* 15 Aug 1917 Grace Lee (*b* 15 April 1892; *d* 19——) and *d* 12 June 1981, having had issue:

Great-great-grandchildren's grandchildren
1c Margaret Lee Randolph, *b* 15 Sept 1919; *m* 2 Jan 1946 *William Moreau PLATT, Jr (*b* 2 March 1912), and *d* 24 Nov 1976, leaving issue:

Great-great-grandchildren's great-grandchildren
1d *William Moreau PLATT III [Rte2 Box 1B, Providence Forge, Richmond, VA 23140, USA], *b* 4 Jan 1955; *m* 7 July 1979 *Rebecca Ann Hylton and has issue:

Great-great-grandchildren's great-great-grandchildren
1e *Andrew Moreau PLATT, *b* 31 Jan 1989

Great-great-grandchildren's grandchildren
2c *John Hager RANDOLPH, Jr [Flyaway, Box 104A, Topping, VA 23169, USA], *b* Fredericksburg, Va., 27 July 1921; Tstee Monticello Assoc Endowment Fund 1974-87; *m* 7 Sept 1946 *Rebecca Holmes Meem (*b* 15 March 1920) and has issue:

Great-great-grandchildren's great-grandchildren
1d *Beverly Langhorne RANDOLPH [6813 Porcher Dve, Unit 23, Myrtle Beach, SC 29572, USA], *b* Richmond, Va., 25 April 1948; *educ* St Mary's Coll; banker
2d *Rebecca Hutter Randolph [Mrs Scott W Boyers, 209 Melwood Lane, Richmond, VA 23229, USA], *b* 22 July 1949; *m* 28 Jan 1984 *Scott William BOYERS and has issue:

Great-great-grandchildren's great-great-grandchildren
1e Phillip Randolph BOYERS, *b* 18 May, *d* 7 June 1985
2e *Grace Bliss BOYERS, *b* 12 Feb 1987
3e *Randoph Scott BOYERS, *b* 22 May 1990

Great-great-grandchildren's grandchildren
3c Cary Ann Randolph, *b* 12 April 1925; *m* 23 April 1949 *Carroll Marcus COOPER (*b* 4 July 1926) and *d* 10 Jan 1983, leaving issue:

Great-great-grandchildren's great-grandchildren
1d *Carroll Marcus COOPER, Jr [3 Douglas Drive, Newport News, VA 23601, USA], *b* Memphis, Tenn., 17 July 1950; *educ* U of Virginia; financial advisor; *m* 28 Sept 1979 *Jane Bordon, dau of George Emmett Hazelwood, Jr, and his w Regina Adams, and has issue:

Great-great-grandchildren's great-great-grandchildren
1e *John Randolph COOPER, *b* Va. 22 Aug 1983
2e *Nathalie McCann COOPER, *b* Va. 29 July 1985
3e *Carroll Marcus COOPER III, *b* 6 June 1989

Great-great-grandchildren's grandchildren
2d *Margaret Lee Cooper [Mrs Stephen W Fuller, 3822 Chelsea Dve, Webb City, MO 64870, USA], *b* 24 Feb 1953; *m* 18 June 1983 *Stephen Washington FULLER and has issue:

Great-great-grandchildren's great-great-grandchildren
1e *Cary Randolph FULLER, *b* 7 July 1985
2e *Jane Brewster FULLER, *b* 11 April 1987

Great-great grandchildren
3a Mary Buchanan RANDOLPH, *b* 1865; *d* 1900
4a Julia Minor Randolph, *b* 19 Feb 1866; *m* 26 Sept 1891 William PORTERFIELD and *d* 10 July 1946, having had issue:

Great-great grandchildren's children
1b Mary Elizabeth PORTERFIELD, *b* 17 July 1893; *d* Staunton, Va., 8 May 1965
2b Virginia Randolph PORTERFIELD, *b* 23 Aug 1897; *d* 22 July 1898
3b John PORTERFIELD, *b* 7 March 1900; *d* Orange, Va., 5 July 1916
4b Wilson Randolph PORTERFIELD, *b* 17 Feb 1903; *m* 30 July 1931 Mary Hamilton Cook (*d* 19——) and *d* April 1977

Great-grandchildren
(11) (cont.) Dr Wilson Cary Nicholas Randolph *m* 2nd 10 June 1891 Mary McIntire (*b* 1855; *d* 1937), of Charlottesville, and *d* Charlottesville 26 April 1907 (*bur* Maplewood Cemetery, Charlottesville), leaving further issue:

Great-great grandchildren
5a Elizabeth McIntire Randolph, *b* 9 Jan 1893; *m* 19 Aug 1917 Gen Thomas Jeffries BETTS, US Army (*d* 23 May 1977), and *d* 28 Feb 1966, leaving issue:

Great-great grandchildren's children

1b *Mary McIntire Betts [Mrs Walter S Anderson Jr, 5310 Albemarle Street, Bethesda, MD 20816, USA], *b* Richmond, Va., 29 May 1920; *educ* George Washington U (BA), Corcoran Sch of Art, Art Inst and Art League Workshop; artist; *m* Washington, DC, 30 Sept 1944 Walter Stratton ANDERSON, Jr (*b* New York 1912; *educ* Harvard (BS); US Foreign Service Offr 1937-62, V-Pres GTE Internat; *d* May 1977), s of Walter Stratton Anderson and his w Virginia Miller Ewing, and has issue:

Great-great-grandchildren's grandchildren

1c *Virginia Randolph Anderson [Mrs Mats Samuelsson, 277 Washington St, Arlington, MA 02174, USA], *b* London, UK, 20 Dec 1947; *educ* Bryn Mawr, Reed Coll and London Business Sch; training consultant 1985-; *m* 19 Feb 1983 *Mats Ake Sigvard SAMUELSSON

2c *Thomas Stratton ANDERSON [45 Park Place, Brooklyn, NY 11217, USA], *b* Washington, DC, 27 July 1951; *m* Bethesda, Md., 5 Sept 1981 *Mina Roustayi

Great-great grandchildren's children

2b *Elizabeth Hill BETTS [Bethesda Retirement Center, 8700 Jones Mill Rd, Chevy Chase, MD 20815, USA], *b* 29 March 1923

Great-grandchildren

(12) (Meriwether) Lewis RANDOLPH, *b* Edgehill 17 July 1837; *educ* Franklin Minor's Ridgeway Sch and U of Virginia; ptnr August & Randolph, attys, 1858, served Confederate States Army Civil War (Pte Co F 21st Virginia Infy, Lt Co C 1st Virginia Infy Bn, Provost-Marshal Frederick, Md., Sept 1862, Capt Signal Corps, Capt Infy, cited six times for gallantry in action), civil engr with Chesapeake and Ohio Railroad; *m* 1869 his 2nd cousin once-removed Anna (*b* 1851; *d* July 1873, *bur* Monticello), dau of John Daniel, of Broomfield, Cumberland Co, Va., and his w Anna Page (ggdau of Archibald and Mary Randolph), and *d* Aiken, S Carolina, 1 Feb 1871 of tuberculosis (*bur* Monticello), leaving issue:

Great-great grandchildren

1a Meriwether Lewis RANDOLPH, Jr, *b* 1870; *d* March 1877 (*bur* Monticello)

Great-grandchildren

(13) Sarah Nicholas RANDOLPH, *b* Edgehill 10 Oct 1839; Principal Patapsco Inst, Ellicott City, Md., 1884 and Miss Randolph's Sch for Girls, Eutaw Place, Baltimore, author: *The Domestic Life of Thomas Jefferson* (1871) and *Life of General Thomas J. Jackson* (1876); *d* Baltimore 25 April 1892 or 1895 (*bur* Monticello)

Grandchildren

3 Ellen Wayles RANDOLPH, *b* Monticello 30 Aug 1794; *d* and *bur* there 26 July 1795

4 Ellen Wayles Randolph, *b* Monticello 13 Oct 1796; *m* there 27 May 1825 Joseph COOLIDGE IV, of Boston (*b* there Oct 1798; *d* there 15 Dec 1879), s of Joseph Coolidge III (himself gggs of Jonathan Coolidge (1647-1724), whose er bro Simon was gggf of President COOLIDGE's gggf) and his w Elizabeth Bulfinch, and *d* Boston 21 April 1876, having had issue:

Great-grandchildren

(1) Ellen Randolph Coolidge, *b* Boston 30 March 1826; *m* 24 Jan 1855 Edmund DWIGHT (*b* 30 Sept 1824; *educ* Harvard; *d* 6 June 1900) and *d* 9 May 1894

(2) Elizabeth Bulfinch COOLIDGE, *b* Boston 1827; *d* there 9 June 1932

(3) Joseph Randolph COOLIDGE, *b* Boston 29 Jan 1828; *m* there 18 Dec 1860 Julia (*b* Boston 4 Aug 1841; *d* there 6 Jan 1921, *bur* Mount Auburn Cemetery, Cambridge, Mass.), dau of John Lowell Gardner, of Boston, and his w Catherine Elizabeth, dau of Capt Joseph Peabody, of Salem, and *d* Boston 9 Feb 1925 (*bur* Mount Auburn Cemetery), having had issue:

Great-great grandchildren

1a Joseph Randolph COOLIDGE, Jr, of Center Harbor, New Hampshire, *b* Boston 17 May 1862; *educ* Harvard (AB 1883, AM 1884), Dresden Polytechnic, Berlin U, MIT and Ecole des Beaux Arts, Paris; architect; *m* King's Chapel, Boston, 28 Oct 1886 Mary Hamilton (*b* Boston 16 Oct 1862; *d* Groton, Mass., 6 Oct 1952), dau of Hamilton Alonzo Hill, of Boston, and his w Mary Eliza Robbins, and *d* Center Sandwich, New Hampshire, 8 Aug 1928, having had issue:

Great-great grandchildren's children

1b Joseph Randolph COOLIDGE III, *b* Boston 13 Dec 1887; *educ* Harvard; Capt Engineers US Expeditionary Force France World War I; *m* Emmanuel Church, Boston, 30 July 1913 *Anna Lyman [Far Pastures, Center Sandwich 27, NH, USA], dau of William Brooks Cabot and his w Elizabeth Lyman Parker, and *d* Sandwich, New Hampshire, 22 Sept 1936, leaving issue:

Great-great-grandchildren's grandchildren

1c *Julia COOLIDGE, *b* Brookline, Mass., 8 March 1914

2c *Joseph Randolph COOLIDGE IV [Rte 1 Box 23, Center Sandwich, NH 03227, USA; 200 E 66th St C-702, New York, NY 10021, USA], *b* Brookline 17 Feb 1916; *educ* Groton and Harvard; freelance editor in New York City 1947-75; *m* Emmanuel Church, Boston, 8 Nov 1952 Peggy (*b* Swampscott, Mass., 19 July 1913; *d* 7 May 1981), dau of Willoughby Herbert Stuart, Jr, and his w Claire Ingalls

Great-great grandchildren's children
2b Julia Gardner Coolidge, *b* Brookline 6 Sept 1889; *m* King's Chapel, Boston, 10 June 1910 Henry Howe RICHARDS (*b* Boston 23 Feb 1876; *d* Groton, Mass., 16 Nov 1968), s of Henry Richards and his w Laura Elizabeth Howe, and *d* Center Harbor, New Hampshire, 22 June 1961, leaving issue:

Great-great-grandchildren's grandchildren
1c Henry Howe RICHARDS, Jr, *b* Groton, Mass., 15 March 1911; *m* St John's Chapel, Groton, 21 June 1952 Mary Pauline (*b* Lawrence, Mass., 17 July 1918; *d* 19——), dau of Charles Henry Choate and his w Mary Pauline Culver, and *d* Meredith, New Hampshire, 1 Nov 1986
2c *Hamilton RICHARDS [14 Old Farm Rd, Dover, MA 02030, USA], *b* Groton 15 Sept 1913; *m* First Parish Church, Brookline, Mass., 8 Oct 1937 *Edith (*b* Cohasset, Mass., 22 April 1917), dau of Geoffrey Whitney Lewis and his w Edith Louise Lincoln, and has issue:

Great-great-grandchildren's great-grandchildren
1d *Hamilton RICHARDS, Jr, *b* Boston 14 Feb 1939; *m* Ethiopia 4 July 1968 *Joanne, dau of Jack Feldman and his w Evelyn Waitsman, and has issue:

Great-great-grandchildren's great-great-grandchildren
1e *Benjamin Lewis RICHARDS, *b* 13 March 1976

Great-great-grandchildren's great-grandchildren
2d *James Lincoln RICHARDS, *b* Glen Cove, New York, 22 Oct 1942; *m* 12 June 1965 *Deborah Ann Davis and has issue:

Great-great-grandchildren's great-great-grandchildren
1e *Christine RICHARDS, *b* 22 Dec 1969

Great-great-grandchildren's great-grandchildren
3d *Anne Hallowell Richards [Mrs John H Coolidge, 640 Homer Ave, Palo Alto, CA 94301, USA], *b* 7 Nov 1946; *m* 6 June 1981 her 2nd cousin *John Hamilton COOLIDGE and has issue:

Great-great-grandchildren's great-great-grandchildren
1e *Nathan Richards COOLIDGE, *b* 23 Feb 1984

Great-great-grandchildren's grandchildren
3c *Tudor RICHARDS [112 Old Henniker Rd, Hopkinton, NH 03229, USA], *b* Groton 15 Feb 1915; *m* Wolverton Parish Church, Oxford, UK, 10 Aug 1949 *Barbara (*b* Oxford 1 Jan 1929), dau of William Robert Day and his w Ida Levick, and has issue:

Great-great-grandchildren's great-grandchildren
1d *Francis Tudor RICHARDS, *b* Ann Arbor, Mich., 15 Feb 1952; *m* 31 May 1980 *Amy Corinne Goble
2d *Victoria Day Richards, *b* Keene, New Hampshire, 18 Nov 1956; *m* 10 June 1979 *Peter Alan HINGSTON and has issue:

Great-great-grandchildren's great-great-grandchildren
1e *Honor Christine HINGSTON, *b* 27 Oct 1981
2e *Josephine Laura HINGSTON, *b* 16 April 1984
3e *James Robert Tudor HINGSTON, *b* 11 May 1987

Great-great-grandchildren's great-grandchildren
3d *Robert Gardner RICHARDS, *b* Keene 7 Nov 1960; *m* 17 Aug 1991 *Kierstyn Leigh Crawford

Great-great-grandchildren's grandchildren
4c *Anne Hallowell Richards [Mrs John Preedy, 9 Steam Gun Place, Port Royal Plantation, Hilton Head Is, SC 29928, USA], *b* Groton 13 Sept 1917; *m* 3 April 1966 *Dr John Robert Knowlton PREEDY, Prof Medicine, Emory U, Atlanta
5c *John RICHARDS II [21 Hidden Field Rd, Andover, MA 01810, USA], *b* Groton 15 March 1932; *m* Old Lyme Congregational Church, Conn., 14 June 1955 *Carol Meredith (*b* New York 10 Oct 1936), dau of David Pierre Guyot Cameron and his w Carol Moore Dunbar, and has issue:

Great-great-grandchildren's great-grandchildren
1d *Laura Elizabeth Richards, *b* Harlingen, Tex., 2 Nov 1956; *m* 1st 19 June 1976 Harvey Milton MILLIER; *m* 2nd 21 June 1980 John Joseph McWILLIAMS III; *m* 3rd 19 Sept 1985 *Stephen A. JAMES and has issue:

Great-great-grandchildren's great-great-grandchildren
1e *Taylor Veronica JAMES, *b* 7 April 1989
2e *Carter Isabella JAMES, *b* 10 Nov 1990

Great-great-grandchildren's great-grandchildren
2d *Pamela Moore Richards, *b* Methuen, Mass., 3 June 1958; *m* 16 Aug 1984 *Stephen A. COHAN and has issue:

Great-great-grandchildren's great-great-grandchildren
1e *Julia Cameron COHAN, *b* 4 May 1989
2e *Emily Jeanne COHAN, *b* 3 Feb 1991

Great-great-grandchildren's great-grandchildren
3d *Christopher Cameron RICHARDS, *b* 4 May 1963; *m* 15 June 1991 *Elisabeth Johnson Wilder
4d *John Timothy RICHARDS, *b* 4 May 1963; *m* 2 Aug 1989 *Anne Cecilia Kiely and has issue:

Great-great-grandchildren's great-great-grandchildren
1e *Maxwell Kiely RICHARDS, *b* 9 Feb 1992

Great-great-grandchildren's great-grandchildren
5d *Catherine Coolidge Richards, *b* 11 June 1964; *m* 24 Aug 1991 *Ayres STOCKLY

Great-great grandchildren's children
3b Mary Eliza COOLIDGE, *b* Paris, France 10 Dec 1890; *d* Brookline, Mass., 21 Aug 1935
4b Hamilton COOLIDGE, *b* Brookline 1 Sept 1895; *educ* Harvard; Capt Air Service US Army World War I (French Croix de Guerre and DSC); *ka* France 27 Oct 1918
5b John Gardner COOLIDGE II, *b* Boston 12 Dec 1897; *educ* Harvard; *m* Boston 12 June 1918 Mary Louise (*b* Boston 1 May 1899; *d* 3 Aug 1978), dau of Arthur Debon Hill and his w Henriette McLean, and *d* 5 March 1984, having had issue:

Great-great-grandchildren's grandchildren
1c Natalie McClean Coolidge, *b* Boston 30 April 1919; *m* Boston 23 Nov 1941 *John Wilbur KELLER (*b* Newton, Mass., 9 Sept 1919), s of Capt Harold Russell Keller, USN, and his w Edith B. Wilbur, and *d* 24 March 1965, leaving issue:

Great-great-grandchildren's great-grandchildren
1d *Jeremy KELLER [Box 7732, Washington, DC 20044, USA], *b* Boston 23 Aug 1942; *m* 1st 1969 Justin Hartman; *m* 2nd 23 Aug 1978 *Giuliana Reed
2d *Natalie Russell Keller [Mrs Milford H Sprecher, 24 Pine Ave, Takoma Park, MD 20912, USA], *b* Boston 17 May 1945; *educ* Rhode Island Sch of Design; software engr Xerox Corp; *m* 30 May 1981 *Milford Harsh SPRECHER and has issue:

Great-great-grandchildren's great-great-grandchildren
1e *Eliza McLean Keller SPRECHER, *b* Boston 9 Aug 1978
2e *William Harsh SPRECHER, *b* Washington, DC, 2 Feb 1987

Great-great-grandchildren's great-grandchildren
3d *Peter Gardner KELLER [190 Harvard St, Brookline, MA 02146, USA], *b* Laconia, New Hampshire, 17 July 1949
4d *Mary Hill Keller [Mrs Philip Westra, 1100 NE 181st St N, Miami Beach, FL 33162, USA], *b* Laconia 30 Aug 1955; *m* 1st 19— George EBANKS and has issue:

Great-great-grandchildren's great-great-grandchildren
1e *Marissa Keller EBANKS, *b* 5 June 1980
2e *John Myrick EBANKS, *b* 11 May 1982

Great-great-grandchildren's great-grandchildren
4d (cont.) Mary Keller Ebanks *m* 2nd 26 July 1987 *Philip John WESTRA and has further issue:

Great-great-grandchildren's great-great-grandchildren
3e *Cathryn Rose WESTRA, *b* 7 April 1988

Great-great-grandchildren's grandchildren
2c *Mary Hamilton Coolidge [Mrs Donald S Pitkin, 72 Islington St Unit 4, Portsmouth, NH 03801, USA], *b* Boston 8 July 1921; *m* 1st Boston 4 June 1942 (divorce 19—) Albert Lamb LINCOLN, Jr (*b* Boston 27 Oct 1920), s of Albert Lamb Lincoln and his w North Winnett, and has issue:

Great-great-grandchildren's great-grandchildren
1d *Albert Lamb LINCOLN III, *b* Lake City, Fla., 16 March 1945; *m* 23 March 1968 *Joan Millar and has issue:

Great-great-grandchildren's great-great-grandchildren
1e *Joshua LINCOLN, *b* 29 April 1970
2e *Daniel LINCOLN, *b* 10 Jan 1972
3e *Jessica LINCOLN, *b* 14 April 1976

Great-great-grandchildren's great-grandchildren
2d *Christine Lincoln [Mrs James Danneskiold, PO Box 132, Tierra Amarilla, NM 87575, USA], *b* Laconia 16 Sept 1947; *m* 4 Sept 1971 *James DANNESKIOLD
3d *Matthew Dehon LINCOLN [26 Stacey Circle, Concord, MA 01742, USA], *b* Boston 30 Nov 1948; *m* 29 Sept 1984 *Leanne M. George and has issue:

Great-great-grandchildren's great-great-grandchildren
1e *Talia George LINCOLN, *b* 3 Aug 1985
2e *Benjamin Albert George LINCOLN, *b* 21 April 1988

Great-great-grandchildren's grandchildren
2c (cont.) Mrs Mary Coolidge Lincoln *m* 2nd 18 Feb 1968 Dr George NICHOLS, Jr, s of George Nichols; *m* 3rd 30 Aug 1975 *Donald S. PITKIN
3c *Olivia Hill Coolidge [Mrs Harry Dworkin, 8 Rose Way, Jamaica Plain, Boston, MA 02130, USA], *b* Brookline, Mass., 8 April 1923; *m* Rye, New York, 17 June 1950 *Harry William DWORKIN (*b* New York 13 June 1919), s of Isidore Dworkin and his w Molly Gotthelf, and has issue:

Great-great-grandchildren's great-grandchildren
1d *Michael Hill DWORKIN [Box 745, Calais Stage, Montpelier, VT 05602, USA], *b* Philadelphia 28 May 1953; *m* 10 Oct 1983 *Loring Starr and has issue:

Great-great-grandchildren's great-great-grandchildren
1e *Samuel McLean DWORKIN, *b* 21 Aug 1984
2e *Alice Starr DWORKIN, *b* 27 Nov 1986

Great-great-grandchildren's great-grandchildren
2d *Victoria Gail Dworkin [1486 Ulupuni St, Kailua, HI 96734, USA], *b* Philadelphia 29 April 1955; *m* 8 Aug 1986 *John WENDELL
3d *Thomas Adam DWORKIN [877 Bay Rd, Amherst, MA 01002, USA], *b* Harrisburg, Pa., 11 June 1959; *m* 19— *Motoka Maeda and has issue:

Great-great-grandchildren's great-great-grandchildren
1e *Charles Kiyoshi DWORKIN, *b* 28 March 1987

Great-great-grandchildren's grandchildren
4c *Hamilton COOLIDGE II [235 Goddard Avenue, Brookline, MA 02146, USA; 98 High Rock Lane, Westwood, MA 02090, USA], *b* Boston 11 Nov 1924; *educ* Groton and Harvard; with New England Mutual Life Insur Co 1947-89; *m* New York 16 Oct 1948 *Barbara Fiske (*b* Springfield, Mass., 27 Aug 1927), dau of Chester Bowles and his w Julia Fiske Winchester, and has issue:

Great-great-grandchildren's great-grandchildren
1d *John Hamilton COOLIDGE [203 Pond St, Hopkinton, MA 01748, USA], *b* Boston 21 Feb 1950; *m* Hopkinton 6 June 1981 *Anne Hallowell Richards (*see above*)
2d *Linda Bowles Coolidge [Mrs Lawrence W Berndt, Box 211, Cornish, NH 03746, USA], *b* Boston 7 March 1952; *m* Cornish, New Hampshire, 17 July 1982 *Lawrence William BERNDT and has issue:

Great-great-grandchildren's great-great-grandchildren
1e *Julia Gardner Coolidge BERNDT, *b* 20 Feb 1986
2e *Laura McLean Coolidge BERNDT, *b* 19 April 1988

Great-great-grandchildren's great-grandchildren
3d *Hope McLean Coolidge [Mrs Mark A Brown, 5 Maverick Place, Dedham, MA 02026, USA], *b* Boston 20 Aug 1953; *m* Brookline, Mass., 25 June 1983 *Mark Alan BROWN and has issue:

Great-great-grandchildren's great-great-grandchildren
1e *Emily Coolidge BROWN, *b* 25 July 1985
2e *Clayton McLean BROWN, *b* 3 Oct 1987

Great-great-grandchildren's great-grandchildren
4d *Malcolm Hill COOLIDGE [1821 Summit Place NW, Washington, DC 20009, USA], *b* Boston 20 April 1956

Great-great-grandchildren's children
6b Eleonora Randolph Coolidge, *b* Boston 31 Jan 1899; *m* King's Chapel, Boston, 20 June 1921 *Charles Enoch WORKS [127 Lafayette Street, Denver, CO 80218, USA] (*b* Rockford, Ill., 18 Jan 1897), s of Charles Augustus Works and his w Eva Panthea Enoch, and *d* 2 Feb 1984, leaving issue:

Great-great-grandchildren's grandchildren
1c *Charles Chandler WORKS, *b* Denver 25 March 1923
2c *John Hamilton WORKS [315 Marion St, Denver, CO 80218, USA], *b* Denver 29 March 1925; *m* 1st Emmanuel Baptist Church, Ridgewood, New Jersey, 27 Aug 1950 Ellen Linnea (*b* Melcher, Iowa, 20 July 1924), dau of Edwin Nikolas Johnson and his w Lillian Olson, and has issue:

Great-great-grandchildren's great-grandchildren
1d *Linnaca Coolidge Works [Mrs T Gilbert Bowles, 1951 N 600 East, Orem, UT 84057, USA], *b* Philadelphia 17 Aug 1952; *educ* Brigham Young U (BS 1974); social worker for State of Utah, currently craft business proprietor; *m* Salt Lake City, Utah, 30 June 1976 *T(heron) Gilbert BOWLES, s of Theron Arlynn Bowles and his w Sherry LaDean Lloyd, and has issue:

Great-great-grandchildren's great-great-grandchildren
1e *Valerie Linnaea BOWLES, *b* Salt Lake City, Utah, 17 May 1978
2e *Andrea Lillian BOWLES, *b* Colorado Springs, Colo., 15 Oct 1980
3e *Meredith LaDean BOWLES, *b* Colorado Springs 12 March 1983
4e *Todd Gilbert BOWLES, *b* Colorado Springs 15 April 1986

Great-great-grandchildren's great-grandchildren
2d *John Hamilton WORKS, Jr [25 Underhill Rd, Locust Valley, NY 11560, USA], *b* Kansas City, Mo., 13 July 1954; *educ* U of Kansas (BA 1977), Sorbonne and U of Denver Coll of Law (JD 1982); assoc Cahill, Gordon & Reindel 1985-90, V-Pres & Assist Gen Counsel J. P. Morgan & Co Inc 1990-, Chllr Episcopal Diocese of Long Island 1990-, Ed-in-Ch *Denver Journal of International Law and Policy*, Memb: Exec Ctee Monticello Assoc 1983- (Pres 1987-89) and Bd Govrs Descendants of Signers of Declaration of Independence 1987-, Assist Sec Sons of the Revolution 1986-; *m* 15 Oct 1983 *Angela, dau of Angelo Demeo and his w Mary, and has issue:

Great-great-grandchildren's great-great-grandchildren
1e *Christian Coolidge WORKS, *b* New York 9 Aug 1989
2e *Miles Jefferson WORKS, *b* New York 22 April 1992

Great-great-grandchildren's great-grandchildren
3d *David Aaron WORKS [PO Box 4118, Whitefish, MT 59927, USA], *b* Kansas City 3 Sept 1956; *educ* U of Colorado (BA 1982); owner David Works & Co 1980-89 and Grand Universal 1991-; *m* 2 May 1987 *Marie Elaine Scharpe and has isue:

Great-great-grandchildren's great-great-grandchildren
1e *Stephanie Pauline WORKS, *b* Whitefish 28 Jan 1989
2e *Laurie Anne WORKS, *b* Whitefish 28 Jan 1989
3e *Rachel Elizabeth WORKS, *b* Denver, Colo., 26 Jan 1991

Great-great-grandchildren's grandchildren
2c (cont.) John H. Works, Sr, *m* 2nd 13 Aug 1983 *Ursula Ronnebeck Moore
3c *Josephine Randolph Works [Mrs Willis L Turner, 140 Broadbent Dve, Riverside, CA 92507, USA], *b* Denver 28 April 1929; *m* St Martin's Chapel, St John's Episcopal Cathedral, Denver 20 Dec 1949 *Willis Lloyd TURNER (*b* Loveland, Colo., 9 Sept 1927), s of Gerald Simpson Turner and his w Edith Christina Johnson, and has two adopted children:

a *Michael Gerald TURNER, *b* 25 Sept 1958
b *Erika Edith Turner [Mrs Britton 2925 Stockton Ct, Riverside, CA 92503, USA], *b* 10 Aug 1960; *m* 19—
*——— BRITTON

Great-great-grandchildren's children
7b Oliver Hill COOLIDGE, *b* Manchester, Mass., 5 Aug 1900; *educ* Harvard; *m* St Peter's Church, Cazenovia, New York, 31 Aug 1925 Elizabeth Ten Eyck (*b* Boston 2 Nov 1903; *d* 7 May 1987), dau of John Arthur Brooks and his w Mary Ten Eyck Oakley, and *d* 17 Jan 1992, having had issue:

Great-great-grandchildren's grandchildren
1c *Oliver Hill COOLIDGE, Jr [1 Meetinghouse Green, Ipswich, MA 01938, USA], *b* New York City 13 March 1927; *m* Shadwell, Bedford Hills, New York, 29 Dec 1956 *Lee (*b* Cleveland, Ohio, 21 June 1924 and originally named Leonarda), dau of James P. McGrath and his w Sylvia Slovak, and has issue:

Great-great-grandchildren's great-grandchildren
1d *Peter Brian COOLIDGE, *b* New York 3 Oct 1957; *m* 25 Sept 1983 *Susan Burney and has issue:

Great-great-grandchildren's great-great-grandchildren
1e *Brian Patrick COOLIDGE, *b* 6 Feb 1985

Great-great-grandchildren's great-grandchildren
2d *Liza Hill Coolidge, *b* New York 27 May 1959; *m* 24 June 1978 *Donald Green NEAFSEY and has issue:

Great-great-grandchildren's great-great-grandchildren
1e *Daniel Glenn NEAFSEY, *b* 6 Nov 1978

Great-great-grandchildren's grandchildren
2c Peter Jefferson COOLIDGE, *b* New York 24 Aug 1928; *d* Bedford Hills, New York, 14 Feb 1934
3c *Henry Ten Eyck COOLIDGE [7 Irene Street, Burlington, MA 01803, USA], *b* Mount Kisco, New York, 14 May 1935; *m* Gulfport, Miss., 9 Jan 1959 *Camilla Starnes (*b* Birmingham, Ala., 28 Dec 1935), dau of Vincent H. Tedford and his w Camilla Johnson, and has issue:

Great-great-grandchildren's great-grandchildren
1d *Henry Ten Eyck COOLIDGE, Jr [370 11th St, Gulfport, MS 39501, USA], *b* Gulfport 4 Oct 1959; *m* 10 April 1982 *Julie Jennifer Frank and has issue:

Great-great-grandchildren's great-great-grandchildren
1e *David Ten Eyck COOLIDGE, *b* 30 Jan 1988

Great-great-grandchildren's great-grandchildren
2d *John Vincent COOLIDGE [370 11th St, Gulfport, MS 39501, USA], *b* Camden, New Jersey, 20 Feb 1962;
m 17 Dec 1984 *Tamara Renee Spitzke and has issue:

    Great-great-grandchildren's great-great-grandchildren
    1e *Nathaniel John COOLIDGE, *b* 30 June 1985
    2e *Brittany Jennae COOLIDGE, *b* 27 May 1987

Great-great-grandchildren's children
8b *Roger Sherman COOLIDGE [PO Box 123, Epsom, NH 03234, USA], *b* Brookline, Mass., 30 Sept 1904; *educ*
Groton and Harvard (BA 1927); *m* Cantitoe Farm, Katonah, New York, 1 July 1950, as her 2nd husb, *Barbara V.
(*b* Greenwich, Conn., 10 Aug 1910), formerly w of Warren Milne and dau of Bayard S. Litchfield and his w Marguerite
V. Berg, and has issue:

    Great-great-grandchildren's grandchildren
    1c *Bayard Randolph COOLIDGE [Box 385, Bedford, NY 10506, USA], *b* New York 16 Aug 1951, *educ* Brooks
    Sch and U of Miami (BSEE 1974); *m* 5 July 1980 *Kathleen Maureen Parker and has issue:

        Great-great-grandchildren's great-grandchildren
        1d *Elizabeth Anne COOLIDGE, *b* 11 Dec 1981
        2d *Charles Randolph COOLIDGE, *b* 27 March 1983

Great-great-grandchildren
2a John Gardner COOLIDGE *b* Boston 4 July 1863; *educ* Harvard (AB 1884); diplomat; *m* Stevens Estate, North
Andover, Mass., 29 April 1909 Helen Granger (*b* North Andover 3 April 1876; *d* Boston 19 April 1962), dau of Henry
James Stevens and his w Helen Granger, and *d* Boston 28 Feb 1936
3a Archibald Cary COOLIDGE, *b* Boston 6 March 1866; *educ* Harvard (AB 1887, LLD 1916), Berlin U and Freiburg
U (PhD 1892); Acting Sec of Legation St Petersburg 1890-91, Private Sec (1892) to his uncle Thomas Jefferson Coolidge
(for whom *see below*) when latter US Minister to France, Sec of Legation Vienna 1893, Prof History Harvard, Harvard
Exchange Prof to France 1906-07 and Berlin 1913-14, Harvard and US Delegate Pan-American Scientific Congress at
Santiago, Chile, 1908-09, Dir Harvard U Library 1913-28, Special Agent of US in Sweden and North Russia 1918, Ch
US Mission in Paris and Vienna during Paris Peace Conference 1919, Pres Monticello Assoc 1920-25, Ed-in-Ch Cncl
on For Rels-sponsored journal *Foreign Affairs* 1922-27, selected by President HOOVER to negotiate with USSR to
arrange supplies to alleviate Russian famine 1931, author: *The United States as a World Power* (1908), *Origins of the Triple
Alliance* (1917) and *Ten Years of War and Peace* (1927); *d* Boston 14 Jan 1928
4a Charles Apthorp COOLIDGE, *b* Boston 10 Jan, *d* 11 Jan 1868
5a Harold Jefferson COOLIDGE, *b* Nice, France, 22 Jan 1870; *educ* Hopkinson's Sch, Boston, and Harvard (AB 1892,
LLB 1896); lawyer, Dir Nat Shawmut Bank of Boston, Pres Monticello Assoc 1931-33, author: (with Robert H. Lord)
The Life and Letters of Archibald Cary Coolidge and *Thoughts on Thomas Jefferson or What Thomas Jefferson Was Not* (1936); *m*
the Church of our Saviour, Longwood, Brookline, Mass., 19 Feb 1903, as her 1st husb, Edith (*b* Boston 10 Nov 1879;
m 2nd Boston 30 June 1936 (divorce 1953) James Amory Sullivan; *m* 3rd Beverly, Mass., 28 May 1954 Gen Sherman
Miles; *d* 7 Oct 1966), dau of Amory Appleton Lawrence, of Boston, and his w Emily Fairfax Silsbee, and *d* Squam
Lake, New Hampshire, 31 July 1934 (*bur* Mount Auburn Cemetery), leaving issue:

    Great-great-grandchildren's children
    1b Harold Jefferson COOLIDGE, Jr, *b* Boston 15 Jan 1904; *educ* Arizona U, Harvard and Cambridge (UK); *m* 1st
    Westminster Presbyterian Church, Scranton, Pa., 25 Jan 1931 (divorce 1972) Helen (*b* Scranton 5 Nov 1907), dau
    of Albert George Isaacs and his w Anne Carpenter Richards, and had issue:

        Great-great-grandchildren's grandchildren
        1c *Nicholas Jefferson COOLIDGE [c/o Coolidge Securities Corp, 800 5th Ave, New York, NY 10021, USA], *b*
        Brookline, Mass., 12 Feb 1932; *m* 1st St John's Church, Fisher's Island, New York, 11 July 1959 (divorce 1977)
        Sarah Flanagan (*b* New York 6 Nov 1939; *m* 2nd George Bickler), dau of Albert Hamilton Gordon and his w Mary
        Rousmaniere, and has issue:

            Great-great-grandchildren's great-grandchildren
            1d *Nicole Rousmanière Coolidge [Mrs Daniel R Finamore, 2 Ware St Apt 306, Cambridge, MA 02138, USA],
            b New York 29 May 1961; *m* 31 Oct 1987 *Daniel Robert FINAMORE
            2d *Peter Jefferson Coolidge [c/o A. H. Gordon, 10 Gracie Sq, New York, NY 10028, USA], *b* New York
            17 April 1963; *educ* Hunter Coll and Harvard (MBA 1992); equity trader with Kidder Peabody
            3d *Alexandra Randolph COOLIDGE [3200 Scott Place, Washington, DC 20007, USA], *b* 15 May 19—

        Great-great-grandchildren's grandchildren
        1c (cont.) Nicholas J. Coolidge *m* 2nd 26 June 1977 *Eliska Hasek
        2c *Thomas Richards COOLIDGE [Red Fox Farm, Falls Village, CT 06031, USA], *b* Boston 29 Jan 1934; *m*
        Greenwich, Conn., 8 May 1965 *Susan Lane (*b* 6 Nov 1940), dau of Albert Freiberg and his w Harriet Hall, and
        has issue:

            Great-great-grandchildren's great-grandchildren
            1d *Laura Jefferson COOLIDGE, *b* New York 27 June 1967

2d *Anne Richards COOLIDGE, *b* New York 10 Feb 1969
3d *Thomas Lawrence COOLIDGE, *b* New York 6 July 1973

Great-great-grandchildren's grandchildren
3c *Isabella Gardner COOLIDGE [700 New Hampshire Ave NW Apt 514, Washington, DC 20037, USA], *b* Boston 1 June 1939

Great-great-grandchildren's children
1b (cont.) Harold Jefferson Coolidge, Jr, *m* 2nd West Medway, Mass., 26 May 1972 *Martha Thayer (*b* Cambridge, Mass., 26 Jan 1925), dau of Robert Graham Henderson and his w Lucy Gregory, and *d* 14 Feb 1985
2b Lawrence COOLIDGE, *b* Boston 17 Jan 1905; *educ* Groton, Arizona U and Harvard (AB 1927, LLB 1931); *m* Bethlehem Chapel, Washington Cathedral, 16 Jan 1932, as her 1st husb, *Victoria Stuart [Mrs Gilbert L Steward, Windy River, Topsfield, MA, USA] (*b* Tyringham, Mass., 23 Oct 1909; *m* 2nd Hamilton, Mass., 1952 Gilbert L. Steward), dau of Robb De Peyster Tytus and his w Grace S. Henop, and *d* Beverly, Mass., 3 Jan 1950 (*bur* Hamilton Cemetery), leaving issue:

Great-great-grandchildren's grandchildren
1c *Robert Tytus COOLIDGE [PO Box 4070, Westmount PQ, Canada H3Z 2X3], *b* Boston 30 March 1933; *m* the Church of the Resurrection, New York, 10 Sept 1960 (divorce *c* 1978) Ellen Leonard (*b* New York 8 Dec 1936), dau of Edmund Burke Osborne and his w Anne Louise Loeb, and has issue:

Great-great-grandchildren's great-grandchildren
1d *Christopher Randolph COOLIDGE, *b* Oxford, UK, 4 April 1962
2d *Miles Cary COOLIDGE, *b* Montreal, Canada, 22 Dec 1963
3d *Matthew Perkins COOLIDGE, *b* Montreal 31 Dec 1966

Great-great-grandchildren's grandchildren
2c *Lawrence COOLIDGE, Jr [230 Conress St, Boston, MA 02110, USA], *b* Boston 2 March 1936; *m* 1st Lexington, Mass., 22 June 1963 (divorce 19—) Nancy Winslow Rich and has issue:

Great-great-grandchildren's great-grandchildren
1d *David Stewart COOLIDGE [149 Warren Avenue, Boston, MA 02136, USA], *b* Boston 7 Aug 1964
2d *Edward Winslow COOLIDGE, *b* Boston 30 June 1967
3d *Elizabeth Appleton COOLIDGE, *b* Boston 12 Oct 1969

Great-great-grandchildren's grandchildren
2c (cont.) Lawrence Coolidge Jr *m* 2nd 19—, as her 2nd husb, *Nancy Myers
3c *Nathaniel Silsbee COOLIDGE [Still Pond, Topsfield Road, Boxford, MA 01921, USA], *b* Boston 24 Jan 1939; *educ* Harvard (AB 1961); US Naval Reserve 1961-67, Assist V-Pres Bank of New England 1964-73, Sr V-Pres John Hancock Mutual Life 1973-; *m* St John's Chapel, Groton, 14 June 1961 *Camilla (*b* Boston 17 June 1940), dau of Robert Bradley Cutler and his w Marion Lawrence Osborn, and has issue:

Great-great-grandchildren's great-grandchildren
1d *Richard Lawrence COOLIDGE, *b* Beverly, Mass., 6 April 1965
2d *Hilary COOLIDGE, *b* Boston 7 Sept 1966
3d *Joanna COOLIDGE, *b* Boston 19 April 1970

Great-great-grandchildren's children
3b Emily Fairfax Coolidge, *b* Boston 13 Oct 1907; *m* 1st the Chapel of the Isabella Stewart Gardner Museum, Boston, 3 Oct 1927 Harry Adsit WOODRUFF (*b* Fort Wright, Wash., 29 Jan 1903; *d* Brooklyn, New York, 12 Jan 1952), s of Harry Adsit Woodruff and his w Regina Dravo, and had issue:

Great-great-grandchildren's grandchildren
1c *Edith Lawrence Woodruff, *b* Paris, France, 25 April 1932; *m* St Matthew's Church, Bedford Village, New York, 2 July 1952 (divorce 1970) Kenneth Bradish KUNHARDT (*b* New York 6 Jan 1930), s of Philip Kunhardt and his w Dorothy Meserve, and has issue:

Great-great-grandchildren's great-grandchildren
1d *Kenneth Bradish KUNHARDT, Jr, *b* New York 1 March 1954; *m* 8 May 1982 *Denise Daria Williams and has issue:

Great-great-grandchildren's great-great-grandchildren
1e *Edward David KUNHARDT, *b* 1 April 1985
2e *Emily Coolidge KUNHARDT, *b* 19 Aug 1987
3e *Katherine Bradish KUNHARDT, *b* 2 March 1991

Great-great-grandchildren's great-grandchildren
2d *Linda Lawrence Kunhardt [Mrs William H Lehmann Jr, Box 289 Schoolhouse Rd, Sandwich, NH 03227, USA], *b* New York 27 Dec 1955; *m* 9 July 1988 *William Hugh Campbell LEHMANN, Jr, and has issue:

Great-great-grandchildren's great-great-grandchildren
1e *Elizabeth Lawrence LEHMANN, *b* 23 Aug 1989
2e *Thomas Woodruff LEHMANN, *b* 11 Aug 1991

Great-great-grandchildren's great-grandchildren
3d *Christopher Calvé KUNHARDT, *b* New York 1 July 1959
4d *Timothy Woodruff KUNHARDT, *b* 2 Oct 1964

Great-great-grandchildren's grandchildren
2c John WOODRUFF, *b* New York City 9 Nov 1935; *d* there 22 June 1947

Great-great-grandchildren's children
3b (cont.) Emily Coolidge Woodruff *m* 2nd 17 Nov 1962 Thomas Archibald STONE (*b* Chatham, Ontario, Canada 1901; with Canadian foreign service; *d* Fontainebleau, France, 26 July 1965), s of Spencer Stone, and *d* 5 June 1991

Great-great-grandchildren
6a Julian Lowell COOLIDGE, *b* Brookline, Mass., 28 Sept 1873; *educ* Harvard (AB 1895, LLD 1940), Balliol Coll, Oxford, UK (BSc 1897), and Bonn U, Germany (PhD 1904); Prof Mathematics Harvard and Master of Lowell House 1930-40; *m* St Paul's Church, Boston, 17 Jan 1901 Theresa (*b* Nahant, Mass., 26 Sept 1874; *d* Cambridge, Mass., 16 Jan 1972), dau of John Phillips Reynolds, of Boston, and his w Jane Minot Revere, sister of Mrs Nicholas Philip Trist Burke (for whom *see below* under the eldest grandchild of Virginia Jefferson Randolph, herself 6th child of Patsy Jefferson, President JEFFERSON's est dau) and ggdau of Paul Revere, the Revolutionary War soldier whose celebrated midnight ride of some 10 miles from Charlestown to Lexington in 1775 gave warning to disaffected New England colonists of the approach of British troops from Boston; Prof Julian Coolidge *d* Cambridge, Mass., 5 March 1954, having had issue:

Great-great-grandchildren's children
1b *Jane Revere Coolidge [Mrs Walter Whitehill, 44 Andover Street, North Andover, Massachusetts 01845, USA], *b* Lynn, Mass., 17 July 1902; *educ* Vassar (AB 1923) and Radcliffe (AM 1926); *m* Cambridge, Mass., 5 June 1930 *Walter Muir WHITEHILL, PhD (Lond), FSA (*b* Cambridge, Mass., 28 Sept 1905; Dir and Librarian Boston Athenaeum 1946-73, Pres Thomas Jefferson Memorial Foundation), s of Revd Walter Muir Whitehill and his w Florence Marion Williams, and has issue:

Great-great-grandchildren's grandchildren
1c *Jane Coolidge Whitehill [Mrs William Rotch, 808 Fendall Terrace, Charlottesville, VA 22903, USA], *b* Barcelona, Spain, 2 Dec 1931; *educ* Radcliffe (AB 1953, AM 1957); *m* Boston 20 Dec 1952 *William ROTCH (*b* Cambridge, Mass., 19 Nov 1929), s of Charles Morgan Rotch and his w Helen Bradley, and has issue:

Great-great-grandchildren's great-grandchildren
1d *Jane Revere Rotch [Mrs Frederick H Boissevain, Rt #6 Box 136 A, Esmont, VA 22937, USA], *b* Charlottesville, Va., 31 Oct 1959; *m* 7 Feb 1990 *Frederick Hartley BOISSEVAIN
2d *William ROTCH, Jr [124 Appleton St, Boston, MA 02116, USA], *b* Charlottesville 2 May 1962; *m* 27 July 1991 *Caroline Elizabeth Sedelmeyer
3d *Sarah Aldis ROTCH [808 Frendall Terrace, Charlottesville, VA 22903, USA], *b* Charlottesville 20 Dec 1965

Great-great-grandchildren's grandchildren
2c *Diana Whitehill [Mrs Christopher Laing, 12 Mulberry Way, The Beeches, Prickwillow Rd, Ely, Cambs CB7 4TH, UK], *b* London, UK, 1 Aug 1934; *educ* Bryn Mawr; *m* the Memorial Church, Harvard U, 30 Oct 1954 *C(harles) Christopher LAING (*b* Nurawa Eliya, Ceylon, 10 Feb 1930), s of Charles Arthur John Laing and his w Jessie Anderson, and has issue:

Great-great-grandchildren's great-grandchildren
1d *Diana Randolph Laing [Mrs Charles A Thierry, 26 Heusted Dve, Old Greenwich, CT 06870, USA], *b* Chelsea, Mass., 3 Aug 1957; *m* 20 Aug 1988 *Charles Adams THIERRY and has issue:

Great-great-grandchildren's great-great-grandchildren
1e *Elizabeth Lowell THIERRY, 15 May 1989
2e *Mary Coolidge THIERRY, *b* 24 June 1990
3e *Thomas Jefferson THIERRY, *b* 26 Dec 1992

Great-great-grandchildren's great-grandchildren
2d *Julia Gardner Laing, *b* Cambridge, Mass., 4 Oct 1958; *m* 25 June 1979 *Jonathan PEEVERS and has issue:

Great-great-grandchildren's great-great-grandchildren
1e *Charlotte Emma PEEVERS, *b* 11 Dec 1979
2e *Camilla PEEVERS, *b* 7 Jan 1982

Great-great-grandchildren's great-grandchildren
3d *Christopher Stephens LAING, *b* Cambridge, Mass., 8 March 1961

Great-great-grandchildren's children
2b Julian Gardner COOLIDGE, *b* Turin, Italy, 30 Sept 1903; *d* Cambridge, Mass., 18 Feb 1907
3b *Archibald Cary COOLIDGE II [RD3, Cambridge, MD 21613, USA], *b* Cambridge, Mass., 10 Dec 1905; *educ*

Harvard, Balliol Coll, Oxford, UK, and Trin Coll Dublin; *m* 1st the Chapel of the Holy Cross, Holderness, New Hampshire, 27 June 1927 (divorce 1946) Susan Thistle (*b* Brooklyn, New York, 22 Feb 1905), dau of John Edward Jennings and his w Florence Isabel Thistle, and has had issue:

Great-great-grandchildren's grandchildren

1c *Archibald Cary COOLIDGE, Jr [304 Brown Street, Iowa City, IA 52245, USA], *b* Oxford, UK, 9 June 1928; Prof English U of Iowa; *m* All Souls' Unitarian Church, Washington, DC, 21 June 1951 *Lillian Dobbell (*b* Washington, DC, 26 Aug 1929), dau of Charles White Merrill and his w Lillian May Dobbell, and has issue:

Great-great-grandchildren's great-grandchildren

1d *Lillian Merrill Coolidge, *b* Providence, Rhode Island, 21 May 1953; *m* 26 Oct 1974 *Kimberly Bryan BOYER and has had issue:

Great-great-grandchildren's great-great-grandchildren

1e Eliza BOYER; *d* in infancy

Great-great-grandchildren's great-grandchildren

2d *Emily White Coolidge, *b* Providence 5 Aug 1955; *m* 23 Dec 1976 *Stephen (Steve) CONWAY and has issue:

Great-great-grandchildren's great-great-grandchildren

1e *Kathleen Brehany CONWAY, *b* 9 Sept 1984
2e *Ryan David Coolidge CONWAY, *b* 7 July 1986

Great-great-grandchildren's great-grandchildren

3d *Sarah Revere Coolidge, *b* Iowa City 16 April 1957; *m* 2 Sept 1978 *David COLEMAN and has issue:

Great-great-grandchildren's great-great-grandchildren

1e *Jonathan COLEMAN, *b* 2 July 1983
2e *Jeremy COLEMAN, *b* 12 April 1985

Great-great-grandchildren's great-grandchildren

4d *Archibald Cary COOLIDGE III, *b* Iowa City 4 Nov 1959
5d *Anne Edwards COOLIDGE, *b* Iowa City 14 March 1963
6d *John Jennings COOLIDGE, *b* Iowa City 24 June 1967
7d *Alexander Reynolds COOLIDGE, *b* Iowa City 3 Aug 1969; *m* 5 July 1990 *Michelle Murr

Great-great-grandchildren's grandchildren

2c Joel COOLIDGE, *b* and *d* Brooklyn, New York, 21 Nov 1929
3c *Susan Thistle Coolidge [Mrs Malcolm R Battle, 10102 Daphne Avenue, Palm Beach Gardens, FL 33404, USA], *b* Sharon, Conn., 3 April 1931; *m* 1st Trinity Church, Westport, Conn., 8 May 1954 Henry Hammond BARNES (*b* Pittsfield, Mass., 15 Jan 1929), s of Hammond Barnes and his w Gladys Wright, and has issue:

Great-great-grandchildren's great-grandchildren

1d *Henry Hammond BARNES, Jr, *b* Providence, Rhode Island, 11 March 1955; *m* 11 July 1981 *Debi Jones and has issue:

Great-great-grandchildren's great-great-grandchildren

1e *Kimberley BARNES, *b* 24 Oct 1982

Great-great-grandchildren's great-grandchildren

2d *Nancy Susan Barnes, *b* Providence 27 Aug 1957; *m* 6 Aug 1988 *Anthony Gerard PATRIARCO
3d *Deborah Coolidge Barnes, *b* Berwyn, Pa., 12 June 1961; *m* 21 April 1984 *Mark Burleigh LEACH and has issue:

Great-great-grandchildren's great-great-grandchildren

1e *Melissa LEACH, *b* 8 June 1985
2e *Rachel LEACH, *b* 9 Aug 1988

Great-great-grandchildren's grandchildren

3c (cont.) Susan Coolidge Barnes *m* 2nd 2 April 1982 *Malcolm Rudolph BATTLE
4c *Julian Lowell COOLIDGE II, *b* Sharon, Conn., 1 Sept 1933; *educ* US Naval Acad; *m* City Court, Yonkers, New York 13 Sept 1958 *Gail (*b* Honolulu, Hawaii, 30 Dec 1937), dau of Albert Lilly Becker and his w Marjorie Emily Tarr, and has issue:

Great-great-grandchildren's great-grandchildren

1d *Margaret Olivia Coolidge, *b* New London, Conn., 9 May 1959; *m* 21 Aug 1982 *Ronald FRY
2d *David Andrew COOLIDGE, *b* New London 30 Aug 1961; *m* 9 Sept 1989 *Caroline Cameron

Great-great-grandchildren's grandchildren

5c *Elizabeth Crane Coolidge, *b* Sharon, Conn., 29 Nov 1939; *m* St Matthew's Church, Wilton, Conn., 17 June 1960 *Lewis Holmes MILLER, Jr (*b* New York 24 Sept 1937), s of Lewis Holmes Miller and his w Alice Levy, and has issue:

Great-great-grandchildren's great-grandchildren
1d *Susan Thistle Miller, *b* Ithaca, New York, 12 July 1962; *m* 17 June 1989 *William C. BARTOW
2d *Lewis Holmes MILLER III, *b* 10 Nov 1964

Great-great-grandchildren's children
3b (cont.) Archibald Cary Coolidge *m* 2nd Lakeville, Conn., 14 June 1946 *Margaret Olivia (*b* London, UK, 16 Oct 1908), dau of Sir Robert Charles Kirkwood Ensor, ch leader-writer *Daily Chronicle* 1912-30 and fellow of Corpus Christi and Nuffield Colls, Oxford, UK, and his w Helen Fisher
4b Margaret Wendell Coolidge, *b* Cambridge, Mass., 17 Oct 1907; *m* the Memorial Church, Harvard U, 10 Dec 1938 *C(harles) Stacy FRENCH [11970 Rhus Ridge Dve, Los Altos Hills, CA 94022-4412, USA] (*b* Lowell, Mass., 3 Oct 1907), s of Charles Ephraim French and his w Helena Stacy, and *d* Los Altos Hills 6 Jan 1992, leaving issue:

Great-great-grandchildren's grandchildren
1c *Helena Stacy French [Mrs Bertrand Halperin, 11 Gray St, Arlington, MA 02174, USA], *b* Minneapolis, Minn., 16 Nov 1941; *m* Hidden Ranch Villa, Los Altos Hills, Calif., 23 Sept 1962 *Bertrand Israel HALPERIN (*b* New York 6 Dec 1941), s of Morris Halperin and his w Eva Teplitsky, and has issue:

Great-great-grandchildren's great-grandchildren
1d *Jeffery Arnold HALPERIN, *b* Berkeley, Calif., 5 May 1963
2d *Julia Stacy HALPERIN, *b* Summit 17 March 1967

Mr and Mrs C. Stacy French also adopted a boy:
a *Charles Ephraim FRENCH [1601 Gillespie St, Santa Barbara, CA 93101, USA], *b* 30 Oct 1943; *m* 1st 19— Mary Dwight and has issue:

i *Ghala FRENCH, *b c* 1967

a (cont.) Charles E. French *m* 2nd Santa Barbara June 1989 *Chrise Mehlig and has further issue:

ii *Emma Mehlig FRENCH, *b* Santa Barbara 23 June 1990

Great-great-grandchildren's children
5b *Elizabeth Peabody Coolidge [Mrs Charles Moizeau, 5 Concord Avenue, Cambridge, MA 02138, USA], *b* Vinal Haven, Maine, 30 Aug 1909; *m* Paris, France, 27 Feb 1933 Charles Joseph MOIZEAU (*b* Noirmoutiers, Vendée, France, 31 Dec 1901; *d* 19—), s of Charles Moizeau and his w Aline Victorine Gautier, and has issue:

Great-great-grandchildren's grandchildren
1c *Charles Julian MOIZEAU [33 Old Forge Road, Millington, NJ 07946, USA], *b* Paris, France, 7 Feb 1934; *m* Western Presbyterian Church, Elmira, New York, 27 Aug 1960 *Gail Stark (*b* Rochester, New York, 19 Jan 1936), dau of Edward William Fisher and his w Sidonia Ender, and has issue:

Great-great-grandchildren's great-grandchildren
1d *Catherine Elizabeth MOIZEAU, *b* New York 22 Nov 1961
2d *Margaret Theresa MOIZEAU, *b* 1966

Great-great-grandchildren's grandchildren
2c *Elizabeth Peabody Moizeau, *b* St Cloud, Seine, France, 14 Sept 1937; *m* 1st Berkeley, Calif., 9 June 1957 (divorce 19—) Sylvain MERENLENDER (*b* Paris, France, 1932), s of Z. Merenlender, and has issue:

Great-great-grandchildren's great-grandchildren
1d *Havazalet Merenlender, *b* Dec 1957; *m* 31 Oct 1982 *Larry FIELD and has issue:

Great-great-grandchildren's great-great-grandchildren
1e *Wesley Aaron FIELD, *b* 20 May 1990

Great-great-grandchildren's grandchildren
2c (cont.) Mrs Elizabeth Moizeau Merenlender *m* 2nd 22 Oct 1972 *Frederick SHIMA

Great-great-grandchildren's children
6b *Rachel Revere Coolidge [Mrs Frederick Kimball, 66 Bartlet Street, Andover, MA 01810, USA], *b* Cambridge, Mass., 21 Feb 1911; *m* there 3 Oct 1936 Frederick Milton KIMBALL (*b* Lawrence, Mass., 15 Feb 1911; *d* 2 Dec 1986), s of Walter Milton Kimball and his w Jessie Fifield, and has issue:

Great-great-grandchildren's grandchildren
1c *Rachel Revere Kimball, *b* New York 20 Oct 1938; *m* 16 Sept 1980 *John E. ALLEN and has issue:

Great-great-grandchildren's great-grandchildren
1d *Sarah Revere ALLEN, *b* 5 June 1980

Great-great-grandchildren's grandchildren
2c *Carolyn Coolidge Kimball [Mrs Bryant F Tolles Jr, 1002 Kent Rd, Westover Hills, Wilmington, DE 19807, USA], *b* New York 7 Sept 1940; *m* Christ Church, Andover, Mass., 15 Sept 1962 *Bryant Franklin TOLLES, Jr (*b* Hartford, Conn., 14 March 1939), s of Bryant Franklin Tolles and his w Grace Frances Ludden, and has issue:

Great-great-grandchildren's great-grandchildren
1d *Thayer Coolidge Tolles, *b* 7 Aug 1965; *m* 9 Nov 1991 *Paul Jonathan MICKEL
2d *Bryant Franklin TOLLES III, *b* 11 July 1968

Great-great-grandchildren's grandchildren
3c *Margaret Revelle Kimball [Mrs Chalmers M Hardenbergh, PO Box 941, Yarmouth, ME 04096, USA], *b* New York 2 Sept 1945; *m* Boston 7 June 1986 *Chalmers Morgan HARDENBERGH (*b* New York 5 Dec 1944), s of Collis Morgan Hardenbergh and his w Nancy Chalmers, and has an adopted s and dau:

a *Cyrus Coolidge Morgan HARDENBERGH, *b* 6 Feb 1989
b *Chloe Christina Hardenbergh KIMBALL, *b* 16 Dec 1992

Great-great-grandchildren's grandchildren
4c *Cynthia Fifield Kimball [Mrs Cynthia Merriam, 7 Thoreau Rd, Lexington, MA 02173, USA], *b* New York 2 Sept 1945; *m* Andover, Mass., 26 Aug 1972 (divorce 19—) Richard Lloyd MERRIAM and has issue:

Great-great-grandchildren's great-grandchildren
1d *Priscilla Anne Fifield MERRIAM, *b* 2 Dec 1975
2d *Scott Roger Kimball MERRIAM, *b* 17 June 1978
3d *Lillian Cynthia Coolidge MERRIAM, *b* 4 Oct 1981

Great-great-grandchildren's children
7b *John Phillips COOLIDGE [24 Gray Gardens West, Cambridge, MA 02138, USA], *b* Cambridge, Mass., 16 Dec 1913; *educ* Harvard and New York U; *m* Cambridge, Mass., 25 May 1935 *Mary Elizabeth (*b* Boston 14 Jan 1912), dau of Ralph Waldo Welch and his w Mary Elizabeth Bruce, and has issue:

Great-great-grandchildren's grandchildren
1c *Mary Elizabeth Coolidge [Mrs Mary Coolidge Warren, 520 East 86th Street, New York, NY 10028, USA], *b* New York 19 March 1936; *m* St James's Protestant Episcopal Church, Florence, Italy, 6 Aug 1955 (divorce 19—) William Bradford WARREN (*b* Boston 25th July 1934), s of Minton Machado Warren and his w Sarah Ripley Robbins, and has issue:

Great-great-grandchildren's great-grandchildren
1d *John Coolidge WARREN [170 Center St, Milton, MA 02186, USA], *b* Boston 16 May 1956; *m* 18 June 1983 *Laura Parker Appell and has issue:

Great-great-grandchildren's great-great-grandchildren
1e *Ethan Reynolds Appell WARREN, *b* 2 May 1986
2e *Amanda Pfaltzgraff Appell WARREN, *b* 23 July 1989

Great-great-grandchildren's great-grandchildren
2d *Sarah Robbins WARREN, *b* Boston 4 Jan 1958

Great-great-grandchildren's children
8b *Theresa Reynolds Coolidge [Mrs Theresa Coolidge Ceruti, 52 East 72nd Street, New York, NY 10021, USA], *b* Cambridge, Mass., 21 May 1915; *m* New York 2 Dec 1967 (divorce 19—), as his 3rd w, William Tracy CERUTI

Great-grandchildren
(4) (Philip) Sidney COOLIDGE, *b* Boston 22 Aug 1830; *educ* Sillig Sch, Vevey, Switzerland, and Royal Mily Acad, Dresden, Kingdom of Saxony; surveyor, assist to the astronomer George Bond at Harvard Observatory (Hon MA Harvard 1858), assist astronomer Japan Exploring Expedition, served US Civil War as Maj 16th Infy US Army; *ka* Chickamauga 19 Sept 1863
(5) Dr Algernon Sidney COOLIDGE, *b* Boston 22 Aug 1830; *educ* Sillig Sch, Kadetenhaus, Dresden, Lawrence Scientific Sch and Harvard (MD 1854); Inspector Sanitary Commission 1862, Visiting Surgeon Massachusetts Gen Hosp; *m* 15 July 1856 Mary Lowell (*b* 1833; *d* 1915), gdau of Francis Cabot Lowell, fndr of the cotton-manufacturing industry in the USA and the person after whom the town of Lowell, Mass., is named, and *d* 4 Jan 1912, leaving issue:

Great-great-grandchildren
1a Dr Algernon COOLIDGE, *b* Boston 24 Jan 1860; *educ* Harvard (AB 1881, MD 1886); Prof of Laryngology Harvard; *m* 15 Dec 1896 Amy Peabody, dau of Thornton Kirkland Lothrop, and *d* 16 Aug 1939, having had issue:

Great-great-grandchildren's children
1b *Anne Coolidge, *b* Boston 4 Nov 1897; *educ* Bryn Mawr; *m* 1946 *Edward W. MOORE
2b Algernon Lothrop COOLIDGE, *b* Boston 24 May 1900; *d* 16 Nov 1927
3b *Thornton Kirkland COOLIDGE, *b* Boston 11 Oct 1906

Great-great-grandchildren
2a Francis Lowell COOLIDGE, *b* Boston 20 Nov 1861; *m* 19 Nov 1901 Alice Brackett White (*b* 2 April 1864; *d* 22 Dec 1927) and *d* Milton, Mass., 2 Sept 1942
3a Sidney COOLIDGE, *b* Boston 8 March 1864; *educ* Harvard (AB 1911); *m* 18 Aug 1890 Mary Laura (*b* St Joseph, Mo., 17 Dec 1866), dau of B. F. Colt, of St Joseph, and *d* 6 June 1939, having had issue:

Great-great-grandchildren's children
1b Mary Lowell COOLIDGE, *b* La Grange, Ill., 9 Dec 1891; *d* Wellesley, Mass., 8 Oct 1958
2b Sidney COOLIDGE, Jr, *b* La Grange 9 Nov 1894; *educ* Harvard (SB 1915); *m* 19 Aug 1917 Lucy Kent Richardson and *d* 17 Feb 1958, leaving issue:

Great-great-grandchildren's grandchildren
1c *Sidney COOLIDGE III, *b* 20 May 1919; *m* 22 May 1954 *Adele Chevillat
2c *Mary Elizabeth Coolidge, *b* 16 April 1923; *m* 1948 *Raymond L. BARNETT and has issue:

Great-great-grandchildren's great-grandchildren
1d *Patricia Elizabeth BARNETT, *b* 15 Aug 1949
2d *Sidney Louis BARNETT, *b* 19 Aug 1952

Great-great-grandchildren's children
3b Edmund Jefferson COOLIDGE, *b* Concord, Mass., 13 April 1899; *educ* Harvard (AB 1921); served World War I (DSC and Croix de Guerre); *m* 1940 *Elizabeth Francesca Bender and *d* 11 Aug 1974, leaving issue:

Great-great-grandchildren's grandchildren
1c *Edmund Dwight COOLIDGE, *b* 22 Jan 1943
2c *Katherine TenBrinck Coolidge, *b* 7 Sept 1946; *m* 1st 19— Elwood LENNY; *m* 2nd 19— *———
3c *Marta Elizabeth COOLIDGE, *b* 29 Oct 1948

Great-great-grandchildren's children
4b Thomas Buckingham COOLIDGE, *b* Concord, Mass., 2 July 1901; *m* 1st 24 June 1924 (divorce 19—) Ellen Whitney Watson and had issue:

Great-great-grandchildren's grandchildren
1c *Thomas Buckingham COOLIDGE, Jr, *b* 20 Feb 1926
2c *John Lowell COOLIDGE, *b* 24 July 1927
3c *Richard Warren COOLIDGE, *b* 11 Aug 1930; *m* 19— *Norma Tucker and has issue:

Great-great-grandchildren's great-grandchildren
1d *Dolleen Grace Coolidge, *b* 19—; *m* 13 Aug 1988 *Eric TARGIN

Great-great-grandchildren's children
4b (cont.) Thomas Buckingham Coolidge *m* 2nd 15 Feb 1944 *Helen Knight and *d* 6 March 1990, having had further issue:

Great-great-grandchildren's grandchildren
4c *Algernon Knight COOLIDGE, *b* 30 Sept 1945
5c *Robert Buckingham COOLIDGE, *b* 6 April 1947

Great-great-grandchildren's children
5b John Lowell COOLIDGE, *b* 19 Dec 1902; *d* 11 Dec 1918
6b Helen Coolidge, *b* Concord, Mass., 24 May 1904; *m* 19— *Arthur Maxwell STEVENS and *d* Sept 1976, leaving issue:

Great-great-grandchildren's grandchildren
1c *Amy Stevens [Amy Wexler, 1599 W 71st Ave, Suite 401, Vancouver VCP 3C3, BC, Canada], *b* 9 July 1942; lawyer; *m* 20 April 1968 *Stephen Martin WEXLER and has issue:

Great-great-grandchildren's great-grandchildren
1d *Jeremy WEXLER, *b* 20 Jan 1970

Mr and Mrs Arthur M. Stevens also have an adopted s:
a *Timothy STEVENS, *b* 19—

Great-great-grandchildren's children
7b Francis Lowell COOLIDGE, *b* Concord, Mass., 4 Dec 1906; *m* 17 May 1940 *Helen Read Curtis and *d* 15 Jan 1972, leaving issue:

Great-great-grandchildren's grandchildren
1c *Mary Coolidge, *b* 21 May 1942; *m* 1st 26 June 1965 Thomas Benham HELLIAR and has issue:

Great-great-grandchildren's great-grandchildren
1d *Trevor Lowell HELLIAR, *b* 21 Oct 1970

Great-great-grandchildren's grandchildren
1c (cont.) Mary Coolidge Helliar *m* 2nd 28 Dec 1975 *Salvatore PACE and has issue:

Great-great-grandchildren's great-grandchildren
2d *Salvatore PACE, Jr, *b* Dec 1976

Great-great-grandchildren's grandchildren
2c *Georgina Lowell Coolidge, *b* 5 Oct 1943; *m* July 1970 *Philip BOGETTO and has issue:

Great-great-grandchildren's great-grandchildren
1d *Christina Randolph BOGETTO, b 1971
2d *Curtis Lowell BOGETTO, b 17 March 1973

Great-great-grandchildren's grandchildren
3c *Francis Lowell COOLIDGE, Jr, b 4 Aug 1945; m 7 July 1984 *Mary Louise Redmond and has issue:

Great-great-grandchildren's great-grandchildren
1d *Georgina Lowell COOLIDGE, b 10 Dec 1985
2d *Lucy Read COOLIDGE, b 8 Jan 1987

Great-great-grandchildren's grandchildren
4c *Ellen Randolph Coolidge, b 4 Aug 1945; m 13 June 1970 *Stephen Bradner BURBANK and has issue:

Great-great-grandchildren's great-grandchildren
1d *Peter Jefferson BURBANK, b 19 April 1981

Great-great-grandchildren's children
8b Philip COOLIDGE, b Concord, Mass., 25 Aug 1908; d Los Angeles 23 May 1967

Great-great-grandchildren
4a Ellen Wayles COOLIDGE, b 24 Jan 1866; d 29 April 1953
5a Mary Lowell Coolidge, b 24 Aug 1868; m 14 June 1898 Frederick Otis BARTON (d 14 Feb 1904) and d 3 May 1957, having had issue:

Great-great-grandchildren's children
1b *Frederick Otis BARTON, b 5 Jan 1899
2b Ellen Randolph BARTON, b 21 Aug 1900; d 5 Feb 1922
3b Mary Lowell Barton, b 5 Dec 1901; m 7 July 1927 Dr Edward Delos CHURCHILL (b Chenoa, Ill., 25 Dec 1895; d 19—), s of Ebenezer Delos Churchill and his w Marion A. Farnsworth, and d 11 Sept 1991, leaving issue:

Great-great-grandchildren's grandchildren
1c *Mary Lowell Churchill [Mrs Robert Fischelis, 43 Livingston Street, New Haven, CT 06605, USA], b 15 Oct 1930; m 1st 25 June 1955 (divorce 19—) John Herd HART; m 2nd 11 March 1960 *Robert Lynn FISCHELIS and has issue:

Great-great-grandchildren's great-grandchildren
1d *Peter Conway FISCHELIS, b 20 April 1962
2d *William Churchill FISCHELIS, b 21 April 1964
3d *Mary Lowell FISCHELIS, b 29 May 1968

Great-great-grandchildren's grandchildren
2c *Frederic Barton CHURCHILL, b 14 Dec 1932; m 23 May 1981 *Sandra Riddle
3c *Edward Delos CHURCHILL, Jr [119 Mountwell Ave, Haddonfield, NJ 08033, USA], b 5 May 1934; m 18 June 1971 *Ellen Buntzie Ellis and has issue:

Great-great-grandchildren's great-grandchildren
1d *Eric Coolidge CHURCHILL, b 20 Dec 1974
2d *Eva Lowell CHURCHILL, b 7 Feb 1977

Great-great-grandchildren's grandchildren
4c *Algernon Coolidge CHURCHILL, b 15 Aug 1937; m 31 Oct 1959 *Ann Marshall Chapman and has issue:

Great-great-grandchildren's great-grandchildren
1d *Susan Lowell CHURCHILL, b 22 May 1960
2d *David Lawrence CHURCHILL, b 14 Nov 1962

Great-great-grandchildren's children
4b *Francis Lowell BARTON, b 4 June 1903; m 1st 24 Feb 1930 Elizabeth Harris and has issue:

Great-great-grandchildren's grandchildren
1c *James Harris BARTON [130 Appleton Street, Cambridge, MA 02138, USA], b 10 April 1934; m 12 June 1957 *Alberta Vaughan Castellanos and has issue:

Great-great-grandchildren's great-grandchildren
1d *Matthew Vaughan BARTON, b 16 May 1961
2d *Patrick Lowell BARTON, b 19 Feb 1964

Great-great-grandchildren's grandchildren
2c *Elizabeth Lowell Barton, b 13 May 1937; m 1 Sept 1962 *Garrett Gregory GILLESPIE; Mr and Mrs Garrett G. Gillespie have adopted a dau:

a *Melanie L. GILLESPIE, b 18 Jan 1968
Mr and Mrs Garrett G. Gillespie also have issue:

Great-nephew's great-great-grandchildren
1d *Garrett Gregory GILLESPIE, Jr, *b* 29 June 1971

Great-great-grandchildren's children
4b (cont.) Francis L. Barton *m* 2nd 19— *Phyllis M. Saunders Simpson

Great-grandchildren
(6) T(homas) Jefferson COOLIDGE, *b* Boston 26 Aug 1831; *educ* Geneva, Switzerland, Dr Blochman's Gymnasium, Dresden, and Harvard; US Minister to France 1892-96, Memb: Massachusetts Taxation Commission 1896, Jt Internat Commission (USA, Great Britain, Canada and Newfoundland) on Alaskan fisheries and furs 1898, Pan-American Congress 1898 and Bd of Overseers of Harvard, Treasurer Boott Mills (New England cotton spinners) and Dir: Merchants Nat Bank of Boston, New England Tst Co and Bay State Tst Co, Massachusetts Hosp Life Insur Co 1878-1920 and Chicago, Burlington & Quincy Railroad 1876-80, an original incorporator of Old Colony Tst Co (Boston) 1890, Pres: Atchison, Topeka and Santa Fe Railroad 1880-81, Oregon Railroad, Boston & Lowell Railroad and the Navigation Co, memb first park commission to lay out public park in Boston, donated Jefferson Physical Laboratory to Harvard (of which he was Overseer 1896-97) and funds for research in physics, author: *Autobiography of T. Jefferson Coolidge* (1923); *m* 4 Nov 1852 Mehitable (Hetty) Sullivan (*b* 29 May 1831), dau of William Appleton, of Boston, US Congressman, and his w Mary Ann Cutler, and *d* Boston 17 Nov 1920, having had issue:

Great-great-grandchildren
1a Marian Appleton Coolidge, *b* 7 Sept 1853; *m* 16 Nov 1876 Lucius Manilius SARGENT (*b* 5 July 1848; *d* 14 Nov 1893) and *d* 15 Feb 1924, having had issue:

Great-great-grandchildren's children
1b Hetty Appleton Sargent, *b* 28 Oct 1877; *m* 7 June 1905 Francis Lee HIGGINSON (*b* Boston 29 Nov 1877; *d* July 1969), s of Francis Lee Higginson and his w Julia Borland, and *d* 27 June 1921, leaving issue:

Great-great-grandchildren's grandchildren
1c Francis Lee HIGGINSON, *b* 5 June 1906; *m* 1st 10 Oct 1927 (divorce 19—) Dorothy Lucas; *m* 2nd 1935 (divorce 19—) Harriet Beecher Scoville and with her had issue:

Great-great-grandchildren's great-grandchildren
1d *Francis Lee HIGGINSON [5766 Matautu uta, Apia, Western Samoa], *b* 12 Aug 1937; *m* 22 July 1961 *Cornelia Parker Wilson and has issue:

Great-great-grandchildren's great-great-grandchildren
1e *Francis Lee HIGGINSON, Jr [20 Stratham Green, Stratham, NH, USA], *b* 3 May 1962; *m* 19— Rosalina Maeli and has issue:

Great-great-grandchildren's great-great-grandchildren's children
1f *Puanoa Alieta HIGGINSON, *b* 1 Dec 1990

Great-great-grandchildren's great-great-grandchildren
2e *James Samuel HIGGINSON [58 Tracy Cir, Amherst, MA 01002, USA], *b* 26 Sept 1965

Great-great-grandchildren's great-grandchildren
2d *John HIGGINSON [Rte 1 Box 19A, White Post, VA 22663, USA], *b* 2 May 1939; *m* 8 July 1967 *Lida Windover Reismeyer and has issue:

Great-great-grandchildren's great-great-grandchildren
1e *Hadley Scoville HIGGINSON, *b* 16 March 1969

Great-great-grandchildren's grandchildren
1c (cont.) Francis Lee Higginson *m* 3rd 30 Jan 1959 *Katherine Dues Hobson and *d* 1 May 1991
2c *Joan Higginson, *b* London, UK, 7 March 1908; *m* 1st Boston, Mass., 16 June 1928 (divorce 1948) Alexander MACKAY-SMITH (*b* New York 31 Jan 1903), s of Clarence Bishop Smith and his w Catharine Cook, and has had issue:

Great-great-grandchildren's great-grandchildren
1d *Alexander MACKAY-SMITH, Jr [The Meadows, Rte 1 Box 19, White Post, VA 22663, USA], *b* New York 31 March 1929; *m* Deming, N. Mex., 6 Feb 1949 *Virginia Leigh (*b* White Post, Va., 29 Jan 1930), dau of Arthur Le Baron Ribble and his w Helen Mae Simpson, and has issue:

Great-great-grandchildren's great-great-grandchildren
1e *Mark Sargent MACKAY-SMITH (later changed name to Alexander MACKAY-SMITH IV), *b* Miami 5 Dec 1949
2e *Francis Higginson MACKAY-SMITH [13 Brownville Avenue, Ipswich, MA 01938, USA], *b* Alexandria, La., 7 Oct 1951; *m* Ipswich, Mass., 23 Jan 1971 *Janet Leslie (*b* Salem, Mass., 15 Feb 1951), dau of Lester I. Hills and his w Phyllis Guerette, and has issue:

Great-great-grandchildren's great-great-grandchildren's children
1f *Gillian Frances MACKAY-SMITH, *b* 15 Sept 1982
2f *Hillary Page MACKAY-SMITH, *b* 4 July 1985

Great-great-grandchildren's great-great-grandchildren
3e *Catherine Cook Mackay-Smith [Mrs Kenneth E Kempson, 4825 N 24th Rd, Arlington, VA 22207, USA, *b* Wiesbaden, West Germany, 15 July 1954; *m* 10 Sept 1983 *Kenneth Earl KEMPSON and has issue:

Great-great-grandchildren's great-great-grandchildren's children
1f *Emily Sumner KEMPSON, *b* 27 Feb 1985
2f *Alexander Mackay-Smith KEMPSON, *b* 27 Feb 1985
3f *Peter Randolph KEMPSON, *b* 21 Oct 1987
4f *Abigail Leigh KEMPSON, *b* 22 May 1991

Great-great-grandchildren's great-great-grandchildren
4e *Virginia Leigh MACKAY-SMITH, *b* Charlottesville, Va., 14 April 1956
5e *Anne Carter Mackay-Smith, *b* Charlottesville 19 Oct 1957; *m* 27 April 1985 *Terry Clarke VANCE and has issue:

Great-great-grandchildren's great-great-grandchildren's children
1f *Elizabeth Leigh VANCE, *b* 13 March 1991

Great-great-grandchildren's great-great-grandchildren
6e *(Mary) Alexandra Mackay-Smith [Mrs James Mackay-Smith-Keirstead, 156G Park Fairfax Dve, Charlotte, NC 28208, USA], *b* Cincinnati, Ohio, 10 Sept 1960; *m* 21 May 1989 *James Mackay-Smith KEIRSTEAD
7e *Helen Susanne Mackay-Smith [Mrs Thanassis G Mazarakis, 34 Plaza St Apt 409, Brooklyn, NY 11238, USA], *b* Ipswich, Mass., 17 Nov 1962; *m* 20 May 1988 *Thanassis George MAZARAKIS and has issue:

Great-great-grandchildren's great-great-grandchildren's children
1f *George Alexander MAZARAKIS, *b* 20 Jan 1992

Great-great-grandchildren's great-great-grandchildren
8e *Barbara Joan MACKAY-SMITH [The Meadows, Rte 1 Box 19, White Post, VA 22663, USA], *b* Ipswich 9 Oct 1964

Great-great-grandchildren's great-grandchildren
2d *Mehitable Mackay-Smith [Mrs Charles Abeles, 4531 Dexter Street NW, Washington, DC 20007, USA], *b* 22 Aug 1931; *m* 29 Sept 1961 *Charles Calvert ABELES and has issue:

Great-great-grandchildren's great-great-grandchildren
1e *Nathaniel Calvert ABELES [4531 Dexter St NW, Washington, DC 20007, USA], *b* 26 June 1962
2e *Damaris Sargent ABELES [2819 28th St NW, Washington, DC, USA], *b* 28 March 1964
3e *Jessica Appleton Kay ABELES [4531 Dexter St NW, Washington, DC 20007, USA], *b* 17 May 1969

Great-great-grandchildren's great-grandchildren
3d *Matthew Page MACKAY-SMITH [Greenwood, Route 1 Box 31, White Post, VA 22663, USA], *b* Washington, DC, 15 Sept 1932; *educ* St Paul's, Harvard and Us of Georgia and Pennsylvania; veterinarian and ed *Equus* magazine, DVM and MSciMed; *m* Annapolis, Md., 16 June 1958 *Wingate (*b* Annapolis 1939), dau of Rear-Adml Ian Crawford Eddy and his w Emily Austin, and has issue:

Great-great-grandchildren's great-great-grandchildren
1e *Wingate Joan Mackay-Smith [Mrs John C Dalton, 8 Bedford Rd, Carlisle, MA 01741, USA], *b* West Chester, Pa., 10 March 1960; *m* Virginia 7 May 1988 *John C. DALTON and has issue:

Great-great-grandchildren's great-great-grandchildren's children
1f *Schuyler Campbell DALTON, *b* 2 May 1990
2f *Juliet Sargent DALTON, *b* 10 Feb 1993

Great-great-grandchildren's great-great-grandchildren
2e *Juliet Higginson Mackay-Smith [Mrs George S McCagg, Box 183, White Post, VA 22663, USA], *b* Philadelphia 15 March 1962; *m* 16 June 1985 *George S. Winslow McCAGG and has issue:

Great-great-grandchildren's great-great-grandchildren's children
1f *Isabel Townsend McCAGG, *b* 30 Oct 1990
2f *Eleanor Austin McCAGG, *b* 5 Feb 1993

Great-great-grandchildren's great-great-grandchildren
3e *Emily Austin Mackay-Smith, *b* Philadelphia 19 Feb 1968; *m* 4 June 1989 *James Michael DAY and has issue:

Great-great-grandchildren's great-great-grandchildren's children
1f *Ian Michael DAY, *b* 16 March 1990
2f *William Page DAY, *b* 18 April 1992

Great-great-grandchildren's great-grandchildren
4d Frances Lee MACKAY-SMITH, *b* 23 Sept 1934; *d* 15 April 1935
5d *Amanda Joan Mackay SMITH [*sic*] [1900 Winkler Rd, Durham, NC 27712, USA], *b* White Post, Va., 25 Jan 1940; *educ* Radcliffe, Harvard and Columbia; writer on gender issues; *m* 1st 19 Aug 1961 (divorce 1968) Jacobus

Egbert deVRIES; *m* 2nd 25 Nov 1972 *James David BARBER, s of Dr Daniel Newman Barber and his w Edith Naismith, registered nurse, and with him has adopted two s:

a *Luke David BARBER, *b* Durham, N Carolina, 9 Nov 1976
b *Silas Higginson BARBER, *b* Honolulu, Hawaii, 21 July 1980

Great-great-grandchildren's great-grandchildren
6d *Justin MACKAY-SMITH [Farnley Farm, White Post, VA 22663, USA], *b* Washington, DC, 24 Sept 1945; *m* Malden, Mass., 23 Nov 1964 *Meredith Mason (*b* New York 1947), dau of Frederick M. Stone and his w Jane, and has issue:

Great-great-grandchildren's great-great-grandchildren
1e *Joshua Dabney MACKAY-SMITH, *b* Wilmington, Del., 6 Feb 1969
2e *Seth Wentworth MACKAY-SMITH, *b* Cambridge, Mass., 15 Aug 1972

Great-great-grandchildren's grandchildren
2c (cont.) Joan Higginson Mackay-Smith *m* 2nd 19 Sept 1971 *Sigourney Bond ROMAINE
3c *Griselda Higginson [Mrs J Lawrence Williams, Montana Hall, White Post, VA 22663, USA], *b* Boston 6 Jan 1915; *m* 1st 16 Jan 1935 (divorce 1949) Abram Stevens HEWITT (*b* Hampstead, Long Island, 27 Jan 1902), s of Edward Ringwood Hewitt and his w Mary E. Ashley, and has issue:

Great-great-grandchildren's great-grandchildren
1d *Camilla C. HEWITT [305 Lexington Avenue, Apt 4B, New York, NY 10016, USA], *b* 26 March 1936

Great-great-grandchildren's grandchildren
3c (cont.) Mrs Griselda Hewitt *m* 2nd Dec 1954 (divorce 1969) Robert N. CUNNINGHAM; *m* 3rd 27 Aug 1977 *J(ames) Lawrence Basil WILLIAMS, s of H. Walter B. Williams and his w Clara Denmead

Great-great-grandchildren
2a Eleonora Randolph Coolidge, *b* 21 Sept 1856; *m* 18 June 1879 Frederick Richard SEARS, Jr (*b* 1 March 1855; *d* 31 Dec 1939), s of Frederick Richard Sears and his w Marian Shaw, and *d* 19 Dec 1912, leaving issue:

Great-great-grandchildren's children
1b Frederick Richard SEARS III, *b* Boston 30 March 1881; *m* 1925 Norma Fontaine and *d* New York Jan 1948
2b Eleonora Randolph SEARS, *b* Boston 28 Sept 1882; *d* Palm Beach, Fla., 26 March 1968

Great-great-grandchildren
3a Sarah Lawrence Coolidge, *b* Boston 2 Jan 1858; *m* there 2 June 1880 Thomas NEWBOLD (*b* New York 19 May 1849; *d* there 21 Nov 1929), s of Thomas Haines Newbold and his w Mary Elizabeth Rhinelander, and *d* New York 27 Dec 1922, leaving issue:

Great-great-grandchildren's children
1b Mary Edith Newbold, *b* New York 19 Feb 1883; *m* Hyde Park, New York, 3 June 1916 Gerald MORGAN (*b* New York 1879; *d* there 14 Oct 1948), s of William Dare Morgan and his w Angelica, and *d* Hyde Park, New York, 28 Oct 1969, leaving issue:

Great-great-grandchildren's grandchildren
1c *Gerald MORGAN, Jr [3701 Old Gun Road East, Midlothian, VA 23113, USA], *b* New York 2 June 1923; Sec Monticello Assoc 1988- (Sec-Treasurer 1956-61, V-Pres 1961-63, Pres 1963-64); *m* Rochester, New York, 19 Sept 1953 *Mary Emily Dalton and has issue:

Great-great-grandchildren's great-grandchildren
1d *David Gerald MORGAN [9206 Tunemaker Terrace, Columbia, MD 21045, USA], *b* Richmond, Va., 7 Oct 1956; *educ* William and Mary U and U of Maryland; mechanical engr 1987-; *m* 17 Sept 1983 *Karen Ann, dau of Nelson Glasgow Richards and his w Sally Jean, and has issue:

Great-great-grandchildren's great-great-grandchildren
1e *Peter Gerald MORGAN, *b* Maryland 25 June 1986
2e *Eric Richards MORGAN, *b* Maryland 14 Sept 1988

Great-great-grandchildren's great-grandchildren
2d *John Dalton MORGAN [2710 Windingdale Dve, Richmond, VA 23233, USA], *b* Richmond 11 March 1959; *educ* James Madison U; sales representative; *m* 24 Sept 1988 *Cheryl Anne, dau of Robert P. Smith and his w Martha Jordan, and has issue:

Great-great-grandchildren's great-great-grandchildren
1e *Shelley Dalton MORGAN (dau), *b* Richmond 6 April 1990
2e *Andrew John MORGAN, *b* Richmond 19 June 1992

Great-great-grandchildren's great-grandchildren
3d *Nancy MORGAN [3332 Lassiter St, Durham, NC 27707, USA], *b* Richmond, Va., 15 Aug 1961; teacher

Great-great-grandchildren's grandchildren
2c *Thomas Newbold MORGAN [14 East 93rd Street, New York, NY 10028, USA], *b* New York 6 May 1928

Great-great-grandchildren's children
2b Thomas Jefferson NEWBOLD, b New York 26 March 1886; m 21 Jan 1914 Katherine Hubbard (d Dec 1978) and d nr Saranac Lake, New York, 4 July 1939, leaving issue:

Great-great-grandchildren's grandchildren
1c Thomas Jefferson NEWBOLD, b 2 Nov 1914; m 29 Aug 1942 *Mary Dell Mathis and d 3 March 1960, having had issue:

Great-great-grandchildren's great-grandchildren
1d *Thomas Jefferson NEWBOLD III, b 7 Oct 1943; m 22 June 1974 *Donna Clare Marshall and has issue:

Great-great-grandchildren's great-great-grandchildren
1e *Amanda Lucille NEWBOLD, b 2 May 1976

Great-great-grandchildren's great-grandchildren
2d Peter Mathis NEWBOLD, b 29 April 1948; d 4 July 1953

Great-great-grandchildren's grandchildren
2c *Thomas NEWBOLD [PO Box 186 58 Todd Pond Rd, Lincoln, MA 01773, USA], b 4 Jan 1916; m 19 Oct 1945 *Mary Noreen Maxwell and has issue:

Great-great-grandchildren's great-grandchildren
1d *Thomas NEWBOLD, Jr [RFD 1 Box 143, Curtis Farm Rd, Wilton, NH 03086, USA], b 7 June 1947; m 4 Aug 1979 *Mary Louise St Onge
2d *John Cunningham NEWBOLD [2165 S Nucla Way, Aurora, CO 80013, USA], b 1 June 1950
3d *Peter Jefferson NEWBOLD [1513 E Fremont Circle S, Littleton, CO 80122, USA], b 1 June 1950; m 12 June 1985 *Rhonda Goodman and has issue:

Great-great-grandchildren's great-great-grandchildren
1e *Thomas Jefferson NEWBOLD, b 11 Aug 1990

Great-great-grandchildren's great-grandchildren
4d *Alexander Maxwell NEWBOLD [31 Brookview Rd, Holliston, MA 01746, USA], b 1 Aug 1954; m 12 June 1983 *Carrie Wilson and has issue:

Great-great-grandchildren's great-great-grandchildren
1e *Christine Maxwell NEWBOLD, b 20 July 1988

Great-great-grandchildren's great-grandchildren
5d *Richard Coolidge NEWBOLD [2306 Union St #2, San Francisco, CA 94123-3924, USA], b 1 Aug 1954; m 4 April 1992 *Julie Ann Schaefer
6d *Robert Hubbard NEWBOLD [3461 16th St, San Francisco, CA 94114, USA], b 24 Aug 1960

Great-great-grandchildren's grandchildren
3c *Katherine Newbold [Mrs George H Lowe III, 212 Powder Point Ave, Duxbury, MA 02332, USA], b 6 March 1918; m 12 March 1955 *George Hale LOWE III, s of George Hale Lowe, Jr, and has issue:

Great-great-grandchildren's great-grandchildren
1d *Jonathan Newbold LOWE [212 Powder Point Ave, Duxbury, MA 02332, USA], b 4 Jan 1960

Great-great-grandchildren's grandchildren
4c Sarah Hubbard Newbold, b 23 March 1922; m 27 April 1957 *Charles Alan KRAHMER and d 6 Oct 1962, leaving issue:

Great-great-grandchildren's great-grandchildren
1d *Frances Penelope KRAHMER [18 Fort Hill Lane, Duxbury, MA 02332, USA], b 19 Feb 1960

Great-great-grandchildren's grandchildren
5c *Herman LeRoy NEWBOLD [625 Lowell Road, Concord, MA 01742, USA], b Beverly, Mass., 8 July 1924; educ Brooks Sch and Harvard; engineer; m 1st 12 June 1948 Mary Cheney Crocker (d 4 June 1978) and with her has issue:

Great-great-grandchildren's great-grandchildren
1d *Beth Weyman NEWBOLD [1430 G SE, Washington, DC 20003, USA], b 16 Jan 1955
2d *David LeRoy NEWBOLD [47 Vermont St, W Roxbury, MA 02132, USA], b 22 Aug 1956; m 30 June 1984 *Maxine Hunter and has issue:

Great-great-grandchildren's great-great-grandchildren
1e *Bryan LeRoy NEWBOLD, b 24 Sept 1985
2e *Jane Hunter NEWBOLD, b 29 Oct 1988

Great-great-grandchildren's great-grandchildren
3d *Stephen Randolph NEWBOLD [160 West End Ave #28-S, New York, NY 10023, USA], b Concord, Mass., 15 Feb 1959; educ Ithaca Coll; architect; m 3 July 1982 *Christine Marie, dau of Mario Nigro and his w Louise

4d *Susan Crocker NEWBOLD [625 Lowell Rd, Concord, MA 01742, USA], *b* 8 April 1961

5d *Wendy Jefferson NEWBOLD [1722 Beacon St, Brookline, MA 02146, USA], *b* 8 April 1961

Great-great-grandchildren's grandchildren

5c (cont.) Herman Newbold *m* 2nd 18 May 1980 *Cynthia Bingaman, dau of Lester L. Burdick and his *w* Esta

Great-great-grandchildren's children

3b Julia Appleton Newbold, *b* New York 1 Nov 1891; *m* 19 April 1913 William Redmond CROSS, of New York City (*b* Orange, New Jersey, 8 June 1874; *d* Princeton, New Jersey, 16 Nov 1940), s of Richard James Cross and his *w* Matilda Redmond, and *d* New York 10 May 1972, leaving issue:

Great-great-grandchildren's grandchildren

1c *Emily Redmond CROSS [The Rt Hon The Lady Reigate, 36 Eaton Sq, London SW1W 9DH, UK], *b* New York 10 Feb 1914; *m* there 13 March 1940 *Rt Hon Sir John Kenyon Vaughan-Morgan, 1st Bart (*cr* a life peer as Baron Reigate 1970 — *see also* BURKE'S PEERAGE & BARONETAGE, Vaughan-Morgan) (*b* London 2 Feb 1905; Conservative MP for Reigate 1950-70, Parly-Sec Ministry of Health 1957, Min of State Bd of Trade 1957-59, sometime Dir Morgan Crucible), yr s of Sir Kenyon Pascoe Vaughan-Morgan, OBE, DL, Unionist MP for Fulham East 1922-23, and his *w* Muriel Marie Collett, and has issue:

Great-great-grandchildren's great-grandchildren

1d *Hon Julia Redmond Vaughan-Morgan [Hon Mrs King, 132 Caroline St, Fredericksburg, VA 22401, USA], *b* London 14 Jan 1943; *educ* Courtauld Inst of Art, London U, UK (BA 1965), and Oxford (Dip Pub 1979), UK; lecturer Newport (Wales) Coll of Art 1966-68, archivist and bibliographer Griffith Inst, Oxford U, UK, 1980-83, teacher of art history St Helen's Sch, Abingdon, Oxon, UK, 1983-84, with Soc for Protection of Ancient Buildings 1985-87, author: *The Flowering of Art Nouveau Graphics* (1990); *m* 1st St Margaret's, Westminster, London, UK, 3 April 1962 (divorce 1978), as his 1st *w*, Henry Walter WIGGIN (*b* Worcester, UK, 12 Aug 1939; *educ* Eton and Trin Cambridge; solicitor; yr s of late Col Sir William Henry Wiggin, KCB, DSO, TD, JP, DL (*see* BURKE'S PEERAGE & BARONETAGE) and his *w* Elizabeth (Betty) Ethelston Power, and has issue:

Great-great-grandchildren's great-great-grandchildren

1e *Lucy Redmond Wiggin [Mrs Joel P Ford, 1401 Narrow Lane #4, Johnson City, TN 37604, USA], *b* London 25 Aug 1965; *m* Kingsport, Tenn., 20 Oct 1990 *Joel Patrick FORD (*b* Bonham, Tex., 12 Nov 1958), s of Roy Ford and his *w* Elizabeth Sorrell

2e *Caroline Julia WIGGIN [1212 Radcliffe Ave, Kingsport, TN 37664, USA], *b* London 25 Nov 1970

Great-great-grandchildren's great-grandchildren

1d (cont.) Hon Mrs Julia Wiggin *m* 2nd Warsaw, Va., 1 Nov 1986 *Dr Joseph Austin KING (*b* Hopkinsville, Ky., 12 Nov 1932), s of William Thayer King and his *w* Mary Elizabeth Griffith

2d *Hon Deborah Vaughan-Morgan [Hon Mrs Whitfeld, Querns, Goring Heath, Reading, Berks RG8 7RH, UK], *b* Paignton, Devon, UK, 1 Sept 1944; *m* St Margaret's, Westminster, 3 May 1966 *Michael Whitfeld (*b* London 3 March 1939), yr s of Lt-Col Ernest Hamilton Whitfeld, MC, and his *w* Iris Esmé Scully, and has issue:

Great-great-grandchildren's great-great-grandchildren

1e *Nicholas John WHITFELD, *b* 31 Jan 1968

2e *Mark David WHITFELD, *b* 27 Aug 1971

3e *Melanie Katherine WHITFELD, *b* 24 Feb 1976

Great-great-grandchildren's grandchildren

2c *Dr Richard James CROSS [210 Elm Road, Princeton, NJ 08540, USA], *b* New York 31 March 1915; *m* Bryn Mawr, Pa., 28 June 1939 *Margaret Whittemore (*b* there 14 Jan 1916), dau of John Kidd Lee and his *w* Margaret Whittemore, and has issue:

Great-great-grandchildren's great-grandchildren

1d *Richard James CROSS, Jr [120 Forest Hill Road, North Haven, CT 06473, USA; Yale Dept of Chemistry, 225 Prospect St, PO Box 6666, New Haven, CT 06511, USA], *b* New York 28 June 1940; *educ* Groton, Yale and Harvard; Prof of Chemistry Yale 1978-; *m* Newport, Rhode Island, 29 Oct 1969 *Ann Marie, dau of John D. Dyman and his *w* Catherine Kolassa Oxman, and has issue:

Great-great-grandchildren's great-great-grandchildren

1e *Donna Louise CROSS, *b* New Haven, Conn., 16 Dec 1971

2e *John Dyman CROSS, *b* New Haven 24 Dec 1974

Great-great-grandchildren's great-grandchildren

2d *(Margaret) Lee Cross [Ms Lee Cross, 31 Schermerhorn St, Brooklyn, NY 11201, USA], *b* New York 8 March 1942; *educ* Swarthmore and Harvard Law Sch; Judge New York City Criminal Court 1990-; *m* Nairobi, Kenya, ? Jan 1976 *William Martin BRODSKY (*b* 3 April 1941), s of Aaron D. Brodsky and his *w* Sylvia Yanow, and has issue:

Great-great-grandchildren's great-great-grandchildren

1e *Sarah Newbold CROSS, *b* New York 28 Oct 1977

2e *Rachel Lee BRODSKY, *b* New York 20 April 1979

Great-great-grandchildren's great-grandchildren

3d *Alan Whittemore CROSS [238 Knollwood Drive, Chapel Hill, NC 27514, USA], *b* New York 11 July 1944; *m* Stamford, Conn., 31 Aug 1968 *Marion Morgan, dau of Bernhard Johnson, and has issue:

Great-great-grandchildren's great-great-grandchildren

1e *Julia Marion CROSS, *b* Columbus, Ga., 4 April 1972
2e *Katherine Lee CROSS, *b* 23 Oct 1974
3e *Susanna Hunt CROSS, *b* 22 Feb 1979
4e *Caroline Whittemore CROSS, *b* 22 Feb 1979

Great-great-grandchildren's great-grandchildren

4d *Anne Redmond CROSS [4313 Glenrose St, Kensington, MD 20895, USA], *b* New York 10 March 1948
5d *Jane Randolph Cross [Mrs Paul D Spector, 39 Goodrich St, Hamden, CT 06514, USA], *b* New York 18 Feb 1953; *educ* Brown and Yale Us; paediatrician; *m* 14 Sept 1985 *Paul David SPECTOR, s of Richard Spector and his w Helen, and has issue:

Great-great-grandchildren's great-great-grandchildren

1e *Jessie Cross SPECTOR, *b* New Haven, Conn., 22 Sept 1986
2e *Abby Cross SPECTOR, *b* New Haven 1 Sept 1989

Great-great-grandchildren's grandchildren

3c *William Redmond CROSS, Jr [701 South Bedford Road, Mount Kisco, NY 10549, USA; 1 E 42nd Street, New York, NY 10017, USA], *b* New York 26 April 1917; *educ* Groton and Yale (BS 1941); banker, Exec V-Pres Morgan Guaranty Trust Co 1973-79, Exec Pres Jacob & Valeria Langeloth Foundation; *m* New York 14 June 1958 *Sally Curtiss (*b* New York 21 Feb 1929), dau of F. Harold Smith and his w Pauline Curtiss, and has issue:

Great-great-grandchildren's great-grandchildren

1d *William Redmond CROSS III [4740 N Paulina St, Chicago, IL 60640, USA], *b* New York 21 July 1959; *educ* Groton, Yale (BA 1981) and Harvard (MBA 1986); salesman then shift foreman Corning Glass Works 1981-83, business devpt analyst 1983-84, journalist 1984, Sr Assoc Alan Patricof Assocs 1986-89, Pres Corinthian Capital Corp, Chicago, 1989-, Dir Preservation League of Evanston, Ill., 1990-; *m* 23 Dec 1989 *Ellen Patricia, dau of Daniel Alphonsus Healy and his w Dorothy Rita Connolly
2d *Pauline Curtiss Cross [Mrs Brock Reeve, 161 Cambridge St, Winchester, MA 01890, USA], *b* New York 19 Oct 1960; *educ* Harvard; *m* 5 July 1985 *Brock REEVE and has issue:

Great-great-grandchildren's great-great-grandchildren

1e *Nathaniel Cross REEVE, *b* 24 Oct 1988
2e *Adam Cross REEVE, *b* 25 Nov 1990
3e *Hannah Cross REEVE, *b* 2 Feb 1993

Great-great-grandchildren's great-grandchildren

3d *Frederic Newbold CROSS, *b* New York 3 Dec 1962; *m* 28 Sept 1991 *Jane Frances Gillern

Great-great-grandchildren's grandchildren

4c *Dr Thomas Newbold CROSS [310 Corrie Road, Ann Arbor, MI 48105, USA; 308-A S State, Ann Arbor, MI 48105, USA], *b* New York 19 Feb 1920; *m* there 22 March 1946 *Patricia Geer (*b* New York 21 May 1920), dau of Harold Townsend and his w Grace Carpenter, and has with her adopted a s and dau:

a *John Townsend CROSS, *b* Evanston, Ill., 28 May 1951
b *Katherine Newbold Cross, *b* Evanston 23 Sept 1954; *m* 12 May 1984 *David Clark REECE
Dr and Mrs Thomas Cross also have issue:
Great-great-grandchildren's great-grandchildren
1d *Peter Redmond CROSS, *b* Ann Arbor, Mich., 19 Aug 1955

Great-great-grandchildren's grandchildren

5c *Mary Newbold Cross [Mrs Donald Spence, 9 Haslet Avenue, Princeton, NJ 08540, USA], *b* Manchester, Mass., 5 Aug 1925; *educ* St Timothy's Sch and Bryn Mawr; *m* Bernardsville, New Jersey, 2 June 1951 *Donald Pond SPENCE (*b* New York 8 Feb 1926), s of Ralph Beckett Spence and his w Rita Pond, and has issue:

Great-great-grandchildren's great-grandchildren

1d *Alan Keith SPENCE [1052 Glen Echo Drive, Jacksonville, FL 32211, USA], *b* New York 10 June 1952; *m* 1st 26 Aug 1978 Pamela W. Hughes; *m* 2nd Jacksonville, Fla., 4 July 1992 *Bonnie Joseph Carey
2d *Sarah Coolidge Spence [Mrs James H McGregor, 778 Hill St, Athens, GA 30606, USA], *b* New York 14 Aug 1954; *m* Princeton, New Jersey, 25 May 1985 *James Harvey McGREGOR and has issue:

Great-great-grandchildren's great-great-grandchildren

1e *Edward Isham Spence McGREGOR, *b* Boston 18 Nov 1992

Great-great-grandchildren's great-grandchildren

3d *Laura Newbold Spence [Mrs Adam M Spence-Ash, 1038 Bloomfield St, Hoboken, NJ 07030, USA], *b* New York 5 Oct 1959; *m* Princeton, New Jersey, 16 Oct 1982 *Adam Miller ASH
4d *Katherine Beckett SPENCE [9 Haslet Av, Princeton, NJ 08540, USA], *b* New York 22 Aug 1961

Great-great-grandchildren

4a Thomas Jefferson COOLIDGE, Jr, *b* Boston 6 March 1863; banker; *m* 30 Sept 1891 Clara, dau of Charles W. Amory, of Boston, and *d* Manchester, Mass., 4 April 1912, leaving issue:

Great-great-grandchildren's children

1b Thomas Jefferson COOLIDGE III, *b* Manchester, Mass., 17 Sept 1893; *educ* St Mark's Sch and Harvard (AB 1915); V-Pres First Nat Bank, Boston, Chm Old Colony Trust Co, Pres Boston Museum of Fine Art 1917-19, Pres Monticello Assoc 1943-46, author: *Why Centralized Government?* (1941); *m* 20 Aug 1927 Katherine Hill (*d* 3 Nov 1984), dau of William Spear Kuhn, of Pittsburgh, Pa., and *d* Beverly, Mass., 6 Aug 1959, having had issue:

Great-great-grandchildren's grandchildren

1c A son, *b* 1 Sept, *d* 4 Sept 1928

2c *Dr Catherine Coolidge [Dr Catherine Lastavica, Box 1443, Manchester, MA 01944, USA], *b* 26 Sept 1930; *m* 1st 29 May 1965 (divorce 1970) John Winthrop SEARS; *m* 2nd 4 Oct 1978 *John LASTAVICA

3c *Thomas Jefferson COOLIDGE, Jr [7 Brown Street, Marblehead 01945, MA, USA; 131 State Street, 01209 Boston, MA, USA; Ninth Floor, 100 Charles River Plaza, Boston, MA 02114, USA], *b* 6 Oct 1932; *m* 30 June 1978 *Gloria A. Geary Dyett

4c *John Linzee COOLIDGE [44 Beacon Street, Boston, MA 02108, USA], *b* Boston 10 Dec 1937; *educ* St Mark's and Harvard; real estate manager and investor 1965-; *m* 5 Jan 1973, as her 2nd husb, *Mrs Elizabeth O'Donahoe, dau of Donald Graham and his w Elizabeth

Great-great-grandchildren's children

2b Amory COOLIDGE, *b* Boston 23 March 1895; *educ* Harvard; *d* 2 April 1952

3b William Appleton COOLIDGE, *b* Boston 22 Oct 1901; *educ* Balliol Coll, Oxford, UK; established Pathfinders' Scheme 1955, whereby eight Balliol students a year visit America, later financed scheme to send MIT students to Balliol; *d* Massachusetts 24 May 1992

4b John Linzee COOLIDGE, *b* 21 March 1905; *d* 22 May 1917

Grandchildren

5 Cornelia Jefferson RANDOLPH, *b* Edgehill, Va., 26 July 1799; *d* Alexandria, Va., 24 Feb 1871 (*bur* Monticello)

6 Virginia Jefferson Randolph, *b* Monticello 22 Aug 1801; teacher; *m* there 11 Sept 1824 Nicolas Philip TRIST (*b* Charlottesville 2 June 1800; clerk US State Dept 1828-32, Private Sec to President JACKSON 1832, US Consul to Cuba 1833, later Ch Clerk State Dept to 1848, lawyer thereafter; *d* Alexandria 11 Feb 1874), est s of Hore Browse Trist, Port Collector for lower Mississippi River, and his w Mary Louise Brown, and *d* Alexandria 26 April 1882, leaving issue:

Great-grandchildren

(1) Martha Jefferson Trist, *b* Monticello 8 May 1826; *m* 12 Oct 1858, as his 2nd w, John Woolfolk BURKE, of Ivy Mount, Caroline Co, Va., (*b* there 21 Jan 1824; banker; *d* Alexandria 1907), s of John Muse Burke and his w Sophia F. Woolfolk, and *d* Alexandria 8 Aug 1915, having had issue:

Great-great-grandchildren

1a Nicholas Philip Trist BURKE, *b* Philadelphia 16 July 1859; *m* Boston 18 Jan 1901 Jane Revere (*b* Boston 3 June 1871; *d* Bryn Mawr, Pa., 24 April 1965), sister of Mrs Julian Lowell Coolidge (for whom and whose parentage *see above*), and *d* Alexandria 12 Feb 1907, leaving issue:

Great-great-grandchildren's children

1b Jane Revere BURKE, *b* Alexandria 14 Nov 1904; *d* Milton, Mass., 15 April 1920

2b John Randolph BURKE, *b* Alexandria 19 April 1906; *m* 1st New York 22 March 1941 Phyllis (*b* New York 4 April 1914), dau of Robert S. Brewster and his w Mabel Tremaine, and had issue:

Great-great-grandchildren's grandchildren

1c *Nicholas Randolph BURKE [4701 Woodway Lane, Washington, DC 20016, USA], *b* New York 6 Oct 1942; *m* 8 Nov 1975 *Claire Juliette Geszty Gardiner

Great-great-grandchildren's children

2b (cont.) John R. Burke *m* 2nd 6 Oct 1965 *Agnes Hayes Honeycutt and *d* 12 Oct 1984

Great-great-grandchildren

2a Frances (Fanny) Maury BURKE, *b* Alexandria 25 March 1861; *d* there 18 Jan 1933

3a John Woolfolk BURKE, *b* 9 Feb 1863; *d* 1 Aug 1865

4a Harry Randolph BURKE, *b* Alexandria 14 Oct 1864; *m* New Orleans 19 April 1898 Rosella Gordon (*b* New Orleans 26 May 1869; *d* Alexandria 3 March 1945), dau of Nicholas Browse Trist, of New Orleans, and his w Augustine Gordon, and *d* Alexandria 21 Nov 1947, having had issue:

Great-great-grandchildren's children

1b Nicholas Browse Trist BURKE, *b* Alexandria 28 Feb 1899; *m* 1 Sept 1928 *Mary Weeden (*b* Matunuck, Rhode Island), dau of Nathanael Smith, and *d* 28 Jan 1930

2b Ellen Coolidge BURKE, *b* Alexandria 10 May 1901; *d* 29 Dec 1975

3b Rosella Trist Burke, *b* Fairfax Co, Va., 30 Nov 1903; *m* Alexandria 3 Nov 1924 *Robert Edwin GRAHAM (*b* 24 July 1899), s of Robert Montrose Graham and his w Alice Henderson, and *d* 3 April 1986, leaving issue:

Great-great-grandchildren's grandchildren
1c *Robert Montrose GRAHAM II [7701 Greenview Terrace, Baltimore, MD 27204, USA], *b* 6 Feb 1926; *m* 1st Charlottesville, Va., 27 Nov 1950 (divorce 19—) Hazel Delmer and has issue:

Great-great-grandchildren's great-grandchildren
1d *Martina Trist Graham [Mrs James H Creger II, 10716 Warren Rd, Glen Allen, VA 23060, USA], *b* Washington, DC, 19 May 1958; *educ* Mary Baldwin Coll; referral coordinator Bon Secours St Mary's Hosp 1988-; *m* 27 Oct 1984 *James H. CREGER II, s of James H. Creger and his w Alma G., and has issue:

Great-great-grandchildren's great-great-grandchildren
1e *Adrienne Trist CREGER, *b* Richmond, Va., 30 March 1987

Great-great-grandchildren's grandchildren
1c (cont.) Robert Montrose Graham II *m* 2nd 26 Oct 1969 *Patricia, dau of Dr Laurence Shemonek and his w Bernice Weldon
2c *Rosella Trist Graham [Mrs Walter G Schendel, 210A 69th St, Virginia Beach, VA 23451, USA], *b* Alexandria 13 Jan 1930; *m* 1st there 3 Feb 1915 (divorce 19—) Richard Charles LAMB (*d* 20 Dec 1987) and has issue:

Great-great-grandchildren's great-grandchildren
1d *John Graham LAMB [Cleveland Express Trucking Co, 3091 Broadway Ave, Cleveland, OH 44115, USA], *b* Cleveland, Ohio, 23 Nov 1951
2d *Elizabeth Randolph Lamb [Mrs Michael C Roach, 4060 Wakefield Rd, Richmond, VA 23235, USA], *b* Cleveland 7 Dec 1953; *educ* Virginia Commonwealth U; organization devpt consultant 1976-; *m* 1st 25 Oct 1980 Martin Francis CASEY; *m* 2nd 28 Feb 1986 *Michael C. ROACH, s of Jean Paul Roach and his w Virginia B. Kemp

Great-great-grandchildren's grandchildren
2c (cont.) Mrs Rosella Graham Lamb *m* 2nd 1 Aug 1963 *Walter Gerald SCHENDEL, Jr, s of Walter Gerald Schendel, and has further issue:

Great-great-grandchildren's great-grandchildren
3d *Walter Gerald SCHENDEL III [9 Keets Rd, Short Hills, NJ 07078, USA], *b* 24 May 1964; *m* 31 Aug 1991 *Sharon Melody Klein

Great-great-grandchildren's children
4b Gordon Trist BURKE, *b* Alexandria 6 Jan 1907; *m* Omaha, Nebr., 19 April 1926 *Cornelia Lee (*b* 21 Dec 1904), dau of Daniel Baum and his w Harriet H. Hackett, and *d* 7 Nov 1964, leaving issue:

Great-great-grandchildren's grandchildren
1c *Nicholas Gordon Trist BURKE [7101 57 Cypress Lake Dve, Fort Myers, FL 33907, USA], *b* Omaha 20 Oct 1930; *m* there 1st 19 April 1954 Betty Ann Clayton and has issue:

Great-great-grandchildren's great-grandchildren
1d *Jane Randolph BURKE, *b* 15 May 1963

Great-great-grandchildren's grandchildren
1c (cont.) Nicholas G. Burke *m* 2nd 17 Jan 1975 *Joan Ruth Arnold
Mr and Mrs Gordon T. Burke also adopted a dau:
a *Harriet Holland Hackett BURKE, *b* 26 March 1940

Great-great-grandchildren
5a Virginia Randolph BURKE, *b* Alexandria 20 Oct 1866; *d* there 29 Dec 1953
6a Ellen Coolidge Burke, *b* Alexandria 11 Oct 1868; *m* Alexandria 7 June 1902 Charles Brown EDDY, of West Hartford, Conn. (*b* New Britain, Conn., 29 Nov 1872; lawyer; *d* Hartford, Conn., 9 Jan 1951), s of James Henry Eddy and his w Maria Nancy Brown, and *d* Plainfield, New Jersey, 30 Sept 1941, having had issue:

Great-great-grandchildren's children
1b Martha Jefferson EDDY, *b* Plainfield, New Jersey, 28 June 1903; *d* in infancy
2b James Henry EDDY, *b* Plainfield 28 Jan 1907; *m* Wallingford, Conn., 28 Oct 1939 *Phyllis Audrey [Mrs James Eddy, 210 Southport Woods Drive, Southport, CT 06490, USA] (*b* Port Chester, New York, 9 Dec 1916), dau of Philip Ambrose Merian and his w Bessie Strobridge, and *d* Port Chester, New York, 29 March 1971; Mr and Mrs James H. Eddy adopted a dau and s:

a *Phyllis Merian Eddy, *b* Chicago 13 Dec 1944; *m* 24 June 1967 *Nicholas Radcliffe OREM
b *James Henry EDDY, Jr, *b* Chicago 14 Sept 1946; *m* 15 March 1969 *Terry West James and has issue:

i *James Henry EDDY III, *b* 18 June 1971

Great-great-grandchildren's children
3b Charles Brown EDDY, Jr, *b* Plainfield, New Jersey, 19 Oct 1908; *m* New York 23 Nov 1946 *Mary Elizabeth (*b* Teaneck, New Jersey, 1923), dau of Charles Hillard and his w Rose Boyer, and *d* 19—, leaving issue:

Great-great-grandchildren's grandchildren
1c *Ellen Hillard Eddy [Mrs Alan Thorndike, 1864 Taber Hill Rd, Stowe, VT 05672, USA], *b* Morristown, New

Jersey, 8 Sept 1947; *m* Scarborough, Maine, 13 July 1974 *Alan THORNDIKE (*b* New York 14 March 1946), s of Joseph Thorndike and his *w* Virginia Lemont, and has issue:

Great-great-grandchildren's great-grandchildren
1d *Nicholas Peter THORNDIKE, *b* 1 June 1978
2d *Edward Hillard THORNDIKE, *b* 12 Dec 1981

Great-great-grandchildren's grandchildren
2c *Charles Brown EDDY III [18045 Reed Knoll, Los Gatos, CA 95030, USA], *b* Morristown 1 June 1950; *m* 6 Aug 1983 *Melissa Crane White

Great-great-grandchildren's children
4b John Burke EDDY, *b* 15 Nov 1910; *m* 6 Jan 1945 *Elizabeth Westcott and *d* 20 Aug 1974, leaving issue:

Great-great-grandchildren's grandchildren
1c *Stephen Burke EDDY [667 Midvale Avenue Apt 3, Los Angeles, CA 90024, USA], *b* 28 Oct 1945; *m* 29 Aug 1970 *Susan Lorraine Osborn
2c *Susan Westcott Eddy [Mrs Raymond Parker, 1250 Upper Happy Valley Rd, Lafayette, CA 94549, USA], *b* 30 Aug 1948; *m* 1st 27 Aug 1971 Thomas Richard FULLER; *m* 2nd 21 July 1979 *Raymond PARKER and has issue:

Great-great-grandchildren's great-grandchildren
1d *John Robert PARKER, *b* 4 Feb 1981
2d *Lauren Elizabeth PARKER, *b* 11 Feb 1984

Great-great-grandchildren
7a Edmund Jefferson BURKE, *b* Alexandria 10 Dec 1870; *m* 13 April 1903 Gertrude Lucy Storey and *d* 14 Nov 1942, having had issue:

Great-great-grandchildren's children
1b John Woolfolk BURKE, *b* 20 May 1904; *d* 29 March 1905
2b Martha Jefferson BURKE, *b* 18 March 1907; *d* 14 Oct 1957

Great-grandchildren
(2) (Thomas) Jeff(erson) TRIST, *b* Monticello 1828; *educ* Pennsylvania Iinstitution for the Deaf and Dumb and New York Institution for the Deaf and Dumb; teacher Pennsylvania Inst for Deaf and Dumb 1856-90; *m* 1st New Brighton, Staten Island, New York, 5 Oct 1858, as her 2nd husb, Ellen Dorothea, dau of J. H. Lyman, of Northampton, Mass., and formerly *w* of —— Strong; *m* 2nd Sophia, dau of Valentine Wilhelm Ludwig Knabe, of Baltimore, piano-manufacturer, and *d* 1890
(3) (Hore) Browse TRIST, *b* Washington, DC, 20 Feb 1832; *educ* in Switzerland, the UK, U of Virginia and Jefferson Medical Coll, Philadelphia; surgeon USN; *m* 1861 Anna Mary Waring, of Savannah, Ga., and *d* 1896, having had issue:

Great-great-grandchildren
1a Nicholas Browse TRIST, *b* 1 April 1862; *m* 1st 18— Delia Porter; *m* 2nd 18— Alice Cook and with her had issue:

Great-great-grandchildren's children
1b Mary Cook Trist, *b* 24 Feb 1888; *m* 1st 23 Sept 1908 Albert R. KENNY and had issue:

Great-great-grandchildren's grandchildren
1c Katherine Mary Kenny, *b* 2 June 1909; *m* 23 Aug 1934 *John William FULTON and *d* 2 Oct 1966, leaving issue:

Great-great-grandchildren's great-grandchildren
1d *John William FULTON, Jr [16551 Las Casas Pl, Pacific Palisades, CA 90272, USA], *b* 15 May 1936; *m* 19— *Lotus Pua Keonaona and has issue:

Great-great-grandchildren's great-great-grandchildren
1e *Lilianaikiwai FULTON, *b* 11 April 1975
2e *Maile Katherine FULTON, *b* 8 Nov 1977

Great-great-grandchildren's grandchildren
2c Virginia Jefferson Kenny, *b* 11 Feb 1911; *m* 8 June 1935 Seward DAVIS, Jr (*d* 2 Sept 1974), and *d* 30 May 1960, leaving issue:

Great-great-grandchildren's great-grandchildren
1d *Virginia Jefferson Davis [Mrs Richard D Irwin, 95 Grumman Hill Rd, Wilton, CT 06897, USA], *b* Chicago 17 May 1936; *educ* Middlebury Coll; stage dir; *m* 29 April 1966 *Richard Duckworth IRWIN, s of Harry Whetstone Irwin and his *w* Helen Hagemann Duckworth, and has issue:

Great-great-grandchildren's great-great-grandchildren
1e *Katherine Seward IRWIN, *b* La Jolla, Calif., 24 May 1970
2e *Christopher Jefferson IRWIN, *b* La Jolla 5 April 1972

Great-great-grandchildren's great-grandchildren
2d *Katherine Roy Davis [Mrs J William Flynn Jr, 63 Pinckney St, Boston, MA 02114, USA], *b* 3 July 1939; *m* 13 Oct 1962 *J(ames) William FLYNN, Jr, s of James William Flynn, and has issue:

Great-great-grandchildren's great-great-grandchildren
1e *Virginia Kenny Flynn [Mrs Gary R Koops Jr, Apt 444 3000 S Randolph St, Arlington, VA 22206, USA], *b* 16 Oct 1964; *m* 11 Nov 1992 *Gary Ross KOOPS, Jr
Mr and Mrs J. William Flynn, Jr, have also adopted a s:

a James William FLYNN III, *b* 28 June 1970

Great-great-grandchildren's children
1b (cont.) Mary Trist Kenny *m* 2nd Oct 1949 *Edward Joseph RUDEL and *d* 19—

Great-great-grandchildren
1a (cont.) Nicholas Browse Trist *m* 3rd 19 June 1920 Kathleen B. Watts and *d* 1928
2a George Waring TRIST, *b* 16 Nov 1863; *d* 1884
3a Hore Browse TRIST, *b* 12 Sept 1865; *d* in infancy
4a Mary Helen TRIST, *b* 12 Sept 1872; *d* 6 March 1959

Grandchildren
7 Mary Jefferson RANDOLPH, *b* Edgehill, Va., 2 Nov 1803; *d* Alexandria, Va., 29 March 1876
8 James Madison RANDOLPH, *b* The President's (now White) House, Washington, DC, 17 Jan 1806; *d* Tufton 23 Jan 1834 (*bur* Monticello)
9 Dr Benjamin Franklin RANDOLPH, of Round Top, Albemarle Co, Va., *b* Edgehill 14 July 1808; *educ* U of Virginia; *m* Redlands 13 Nov 1834 Sarah Champe (*b* 1810; *d* Round Top 20 May 1896), dau of Robert Hill Carter, of Redlands, and his w Polly Coles, and *d* Round Top 18 Feb 1871, leaving issue:

Great-grandchildren
(1) Isaetta (Etta) Carter Randolph, *b* Redlands 24 March 1836; *m* Round Top 13 Nov 1860 James Lenaeus HUBARD (*b* 1835; *educ* Virginia Mily Inst and U of Virginia; Lt-Col 44th Infy Regt Virginia Volunteers and Pte 4th Virginia Cavalry Civil War, lawyer; *d* 1913), s of Robert Thruston Hubard, of Chellowe, Buckingham Co, Va., and his w Susan Pocahontas Bolling, and *d* 9 Dec 1888 of tuberculosis, having had issue:

Great-great-grandchildren
1a Benjamin Randolph HUBARD, *b* 2 Feb 1862; *m* 18— Mary Neil Grub and *d* 7 March 1942, leaving issue:

Great-great-grandchildren's children
1b Thomas James HUBARD, *b* 15 Nov 1892; *m* 8 Sept 1924 Lora Stella Letsinger and *d* 3 June 1968, leaving issue:

Great-great-grandchildren's grandchildren
1c *Wiley Nelson HUBARD, *b* 29 June 1925; *m* 1st 3 July 1947 Grace Jeanette Cupp and has issue:

Great-great-grandchildren's great-grandchildren
1d *Sherry Lorraine Hubard, *b* 10 Dec 1948; *m* 5 Aug 1964 *Jack MILES and has issue:

Great-great-grandchildren's great-great-grandchildren
1e *Samuel Christopher MILES, *b* 2 May 1965
2e *Timi Lanay MILES, *b* 27 July 1967
3e *Amber Marie MILES, *b* 13 Nov 1970

Great-great-grandchildren's great-grandchildren
2d *Wiley Dan HUBARD, *b* 17 July 1952
3d *Deborah Gail Hubard, *b* 25 Aug 1955; *m* 28 Aug 1971 *Steve CARNES and has issue:

Great-great-grandchildren's great-great-grandchildren
1e *Nicole Rochelle CARNES, *b* 3 April 1978

Great-great-grandchildren's grandchildren
1c (cont.) Wiley N. Hubard *m* 2nd 19 June 1964 *Annie Renie Kemp
2c *Mary Crissie Hubard [Mrs Raymond E Tillery, 8728 Conner Rd, Powell, TN 37849, USA], *b* 21 July 1927; *m* 1st 18 Aug 1945 Elmo E. WILLIAMS and has issue:

Great-great-grandchildren's great-grandchildren
1d *Jean Kay Williams, *b* 21 Nov 1946; *m* 11 June 1966 *Turner Louis JONES III and has issue:

Great-great-grandchildren's great-great-grandchildren
1e *Amanda Kay JONES, *b* 15 Jan 1969
2e *Anita Melanie JONES, *b* 1 Aug 1971

Great-great-grandchildren's great-grandchildren
2d Larry Dean WILLIAMS, *b* 29 Dec 1948; *d* 23 Jan 1961

Great-great-grandchildren's grandchildren
2c (cont.) Mary Hubard Williams *m* 2nd 24 June 1972 *Raymond Earl TILLERY
3c *Lora Stella Hubard, *b* 10 Feb 1933; *m* 1st 1 Nov 1950 James FRENCH and has issue:

Great-great-grandchildren's great-grandchildren
1d *Thomas James FRENCH, *b* 12 Dec 1951
2d *Gary Steven FRENCH, *b* 22 May 1953; *m* 23 Sept 1972 *Christine Tillery and has issue:

Great-great-grandchildren's great-great-grandchildren
1e *Jonathon Steven FRENCH, *b* 7 June 1979

Great-great-grandchildren's grandchildren
3c (cont.) Lora Hubard French *m* 2nd 19— *Don HAIR and has issue:

Great-great-grandchildren's great-grandchildren
3d *Cindy Janice Hair, *b* 14 Oct 1957; *m* 19— *Theodore Clinton MORSE II and has issue:

Great-great-grandchildren's great-great-grandchildren
1e *Theodore Clinton MORSE III, *b* July 1975
2e *Kenny Allen Eugene MORSE, *b* Aug 1977
3e *Christopher Lee MORSE, *b* Sept 1978

Great-great-grandchildren's children
2b Robert Thruston HUBARD, *b* 2 Oct 1902; *m* 1st 19— Emily Bolen and with her had issue:

Great-great-grandchildren's grandchildren
1c Benjamin Randolph HUBARD II, *b* 2 Aug 1923; *m* 7 Feb 1946 *Margaret Hellard and *d* 4 Aug 1952, leaving issue:

Great-great-grandchildren's great-grandchildren
1d *John Robert HUBARD, *b* 19 Nov 1946; *m* 25 Jan 1967 *Carolyn Caldwell and has issue:

Great-great-grandchildren's great-great-grandchildren
1e *John Robert HUBARD, Jr, *b* 3 June 1968
2e *Angela Kay HUBARD, *b* 13 May 1970
3e *Jason Robert HUBARD, *b* 10 April 1976

Great-great-grandchildren's great-grandchildren
2d *Benjamin Randolph HUBARD III, *b* 4 Oct 1947; *m* 17 June 1966 *Norma Lee Beall and has issue:

Great-great-grandchildren's great-grandchildren
1e *Benjamin Randolph HUBARD IV, *b* 20 Sept 1967

Great-great-grandchildren's grandchildren
2c *Robert King HUBARD [116 Glider Dve, Baltimore, MD 21220, USA], *b* 18 Jan 1925; *m* 1st 3 March 1958 Irene Stumpf and has issue:

Great-great-grandchildren's great-grandchildren
1d *Robert Kule HUBARD, *b* 18 Sept 1958
2d *Terry Keith HUBARD, *b* 2 March 1964

Great-great-grandchildren's grandchildren
2c (cont.) Robert K. Hubard *m* 2nd 17 March 1978 *Frances Ruth Riehenberger and has further issue:

Great-great-grandchildren's great-grandchildren
3d *Nicole Lee HUBARD, *b* 19 Oct 1979

Great-great-grandchildren's.grandchildren
3c *Ramona Jean Hubard, *b* 3 July 1927; *m* 1st 10 March 1946 Alonzo STOKES and has issue:

Great-great-grandchildren's great-grandchildren
1d *Wesley Ann Stokes, *b* 28 Jan 1947; *m* 10 Oct 1967 *Rodney SCHILZ and has issue:

Great-great-grandchildren's great-great-grandchildren
1e *Karen Elizabeth SCHILZ, *b* 24 June 1968
2e *Matthew SCHILZ, *b* 12 March 1971

Great-great-grandchildren's great-grandchildren
2d *Barbara Jean Stokes, *b* 14 Sept 1950; *m* 19— *Bobby McCOY and has issue:

Great-great-grandchildren's great-great-grandchildren
1e *Carrie Ann McCOY, *b* 3 Sept 1973
2e *Erin Keiley McCOY, *b* 3 April 1975

Great-great-grandchildren's great-grandchildren
3d *Robert Alonzo STOKES, Jr, *b* 195-; *m* 14 Aug 1976 *Mary Vasquez and has issue:

Great-great-grandchildren's great-great-grandchildren
1e *Desideria Cloe STOKES, *b* 7 Jan 1978

Great-great-grandchildren's grandchildren
3c (cont.) Ramona Hubard Stokes *m* 2nd 14 Aug 1969 *Robert SHARP

Great-great-grandchildren's children
2b (cont.) Robert T. Hubard *m* 2nd 19— Alice Hensley and *d* 4 Nov 1952, having had further issue:

Great-great-grandchildren's grandchildren
4c Thomas Carr Jefferson HUBARD, *b* 6 Nov 1945; *d* 7 Dec 1967

Great-great-grandchildren
2a Susan Bolling Hubard, *b* 5 Oct 1863; *m* 1888 John SLAUGHTER and *d* 20 Feb 1894, leaving issue:

Great-great-grandchildren's children
1b Charles Hubard SLAUGHTER, *b* 16 April 1889; *m* 8 Sept 1914 Evelyn Morman Meech and *d* 4 May 1977
2b Isaetta Randolph Slaughter, *b* 12 Oct 1892; *m* 15 April 1912 Harry Benjamin MUNDAY and *d* 4 Nov 1979, leaving issue:

Great-great-grandchildren's grandchildren
1c Harry Benjamin MUNDAY, *b* 1 Feb 1913; *m* 19— *Pauline Vaughn and *d* 9 Dec 1979
2c *Mary Frances Munday, *b* 23 Jan 1930; *m* 25 Oct 1952 *Robert Lawrence WARWICK and has issue:

Great-great-grandchildren's great-grandchildren
1d *Stephen Lawrence WARWICK [317 Yorktown Dve, Colonial Heights, VA 23834, USA], *b* 8 Sept 1965

Great-great-grandchildren
3a James Thruston HUBARD, *b* 17 April 1865; *d* 17 June 1882
4a Robert Thruston HUBARD, *b* 31 Oct 1866; *m* 1st 1897 Leila C. Moss and had issue:

Great-great-grandchildren's children
1b Robert Thruston HUBARD, Jr, *b* 1898; *d* 1899
2b Martha Randolph Hubard, *b* 29 April 1900; *m* 6 Jan 1920 Louis ELSINGER and *d* 19—, leaving issue:

Great-great-grandchildren's grandchildren
1c *James Hubard ELSINGER, *b* 1 May 1924; *m* 6 Aug 1949 *Jo Ann Fossett and has issue:

Great-great-grandchildren's great-grandchildren
1d *Patricia Ann ELSINGER, *b* 2 July 1953

Great-great-grandchildren
4a (cont.) Robert T. Hubard *m* 2nd 19— Mary Brennan Swift and *d* 3 Jan 1923, having had further issue:

Great-great-grandchildren's children
3b Stephen Swift HUBARD, *b* 14 April 1914; *d* 6 March 1956

Great-great-grandchildren
5a Sarah Champe HUBARD, *b* 18 Aug 1868; *d* 1 Jan 1903
6a Mary Randolph Hubard, *b* 7 May 1870; *m* 28 Oct 1896 Edward Miles MATHEWES (*b* 8 Oct 1868; *d* Dec 1952) and *d* 25 Aug 1930, having had issue:

Great-great-grandchildren's children
1b Eliza Peronneau MATHEWES, *b* 15 Sept 1897; *d* 15 April 1898
2b Edward Miles MATHEWES, *b* 19 Dec 1898; *d* 4 March 1906
3b Mary Randolph Hubard MATHEWES, *b* 16 Aug 1902; *d* 12 March 1943
4b Celia Peronneau Mathewes, *b* 2 Aug 1906; *m* 23 Sept 1933 *Thomas Richard WARING [48 Murray Blvd, Charleston, SC 29401, USA] (*b* Charleston, S Carolina, 10 May 1907), *s* of Thomas Richard Waring and his *w* Laura Campbell Witte, and *d* Charleston 3 July 1967, leaving issue:

Great-great-grandchildren's grandchildren
1c *Mary Randolph Waring [Mrs Robert Berretta, 1305 New Castle St, Charleston, SC 29407, USA], *b* 20 June 1939; *m* 1st 15 March 1958 Kenneth J. ELDER and has issue:

Great-great-grandchildren's great-grandchildren
1d *Thomas Waring ELDER BERRETTA (added stepf's name to his own) [2803 Ranchwood Dve, Anderson, SC 29621, USA], *b* 9 Dec 1960

Great-great-grandchildren's grandchildren
1c (cont.) Mary Waring Elder *m* 2nd 22 Sept 1962 *Robert Eugene BERRETTA and has further issue:

Great-great-grandchildren's great-grandchildren
2d *Mary Randolph Berretta [Mrs Louis M Montgomery, 148 Darby Way, W Columbia, SC 29170, USA], *b* Charleston, S Carolina, 7 Dec 1964; *educ* Winthrop Coll; teacher of mentally handicapped 1986-; *m* 8 Aug 1987 *Louis Miles MONTGOMERY, *s* of Charles Edward Montgomery and his *w* Louisa Miles, and has issue:

Great-great-grandchildren's great-great-grandchildren
1e *Eliza Peronneau MONTGOMERY, *b* W Columbia 28 July 1991

Great-great-grandchildren's grandchildren
2c *Thomas WARING [10 Atlantic Street, Charleston, SC 29401, USA], *b* 5 March 1944; *m* 29 Nov 1975 *Janice Virginia Duffie and has issue:

Great-great-grandchildren's great-grandchildren
1d *Joseph Ioor WARING, *b* 20 Oct 1979
2d *Katherine Peronneau WARING, *b* 5 May 1981
3d *Thomas Richard WARING II, *b* 12 July 1983

Great-great-grandchildren's children
5b James Hubard MATHEWES, *b* 16 June 1908; *m* 25 Nov 1939 *Elizabeth Gaillard Lowndes [Mrs James H Mathewes, 1029 Glendalyn Circle, Spartanburg, SC 29302, USA] and *d* 16 Feb 1975

Great-great-grandchildren
7a Isaetta Carter Hubard, *b* 18 April 1872; *m* 28 Jan 1916 Beverley Landon AMBLER (*d* 23 Oct 1940) and *d* 3 March 1952
8a Bernard Markham HUBARD, *b* 187-
9a Ellen Wayles Hubard, *b* 187-; *m* 18— or 19— ——— ROBINSON and *d* 18— or 19—
10a Jefferson Randolph HUBARD, *b* 14 March 1877; *m* 18 Nov 1908 Louise Moore and *d* 1925, having had issue:

Great-great-grandchildren's children
1b Agnes Moore HUBARD, *b* 2 Aug 1909; *d* 10 Oct 1910

Great-great-grandchildren
11a Archibald Blair HUBARD, *b* Nelson Co, Va., 21 July 1879; Pres Monticello Assoc 1925-26; *m* 28 Oct 1905 Carlotta D. (*b* 2 May 1885; *d* Doylestown, Pa., 4 Jan 1954), dau of Charles D. Barney and his w Laura E. Cooke, and *d* Doylestown 26 May 1952, leaving issue:

Great-great-grandchildren's children
1b Lt-Col Randolph Bolling HUBARD, *b* 15 June 1906; served US Army, Pres Monticello Assoc 1967-69 (V-Pres 1965-67, Treasurer 1975-77); *m* 2 May 1936 *Ina Walker Cochran (*b* 22 Sept 1910) and *d* 28 Aug 1991 (*bur* Monticello), leaving issue:

Great-great-grandchildren's grandchildren
1c *Lt-Col John Bolling HUBARD [4827 N 27th Place, Arlington, VA 22207, USA], *b* Wyoming 20 April 1937; *educ* US Mily Acad and U of Kentucky; served US Army 1960-83, physics master Georgetown Visit Preparatory Sch 1984-; *m* 29 May 1970 *Margaret Bate, dau of Howard L. Cobb and his w Peggy Barnes, and has issue:

Great-great-grandchildren's great-grandchildren
1d Randolph Bolling HUBARD II, *b* Kentucky 3 Oct 1971; *d* 24 July 1980
2d *Robin Mitchell HUBARD, *b* Kentucky 28 July 1974
3d *John Randolph HUBARD, *b* Washington, DC, 7 May 1981

Great-great-grandchildren's grandchildren
2c *Cynthia Ann Hubard [Mrs Ferdinand J Spangler, 267 South Windover Grove, Memphis, TN 38111, USA], *b* 17 March 1942; *m* 1st 14 March 1964 Samuel Bartow STRANG III, s of Samuel Bartow Strang, Jr, and has issue:

Great-great-grandchildren's great-grandchildren
1d *Samuel Bartow STRANG IV [Apt 324, 2855 Peachtree Rd NE, Atlanta, GA 30305, USA], *b* 22 Sept 1964

Great-great-grandchildren's grandchildren
2c (cont.) Cynthia Hubard Strang *m* 2nd 15 June 1972 James Craig ZIEGLER; *m* 3rd 16 Feb 1985 *Ferdinand J. SPANGLER

Great-grandchildren
(2) Lewis Carter RANDOLPH, *b* Round Top 13 June 1838; *educ* U of Virginia, Jefferson Sch of Medicine, Philadelphia, and Virginia Mily Inst; 1st Lt Green Mountain Grays (vol infy co, later incorporated into 1st Infy Regt in Brig-Gen Henry A. Wise's Legion), transferred to Confederate States Army Medical Corps as assist then full surgeon attached to Maj-Gen Howell Cobb's Georgia Legion; *m* 29 Jan 1867 Louisa (*b* Chellowe, Buckingham Co, Va., 1 May 1845), his sister Isaetta's husband's sister and only dau of Robert Thruston Hubard and his w Susan Pocahontas Bolling (*see above*), and *d* Markham, Nelson Co, Va., 29 May 1887, leaving issue:

Great-great-grandchildren
1a Robert Carter RANDOLPH, *b* 11 Dec 1867; *m* 31 Oct 1906 Letitia Lawrence and *d* 9 July 1939
2a Louise Hubard RANDOLPH, *b* 22 May 1869, *d* 23 Aug 1951
3a Sarah Champe Randolph, *b* 1 July 1871; *m* 24 June 1908 Randolph Warren HAMMERSLOUGH and *d* 1 Jan 1959
4a Susan Bolling RANDOLPH, *b* 28 Aug 1874; *d* 19 April 1929
5a Benjamin Franklin RANDOLPH, *b* 9 Sept 1876; *d* 31 March 1951
6a Lewis Carter RANDOLPH, *b* 28 July 1877; *m* 6 Sept 1906 Dorothy Atkins and *d* 29 Aug 1934, leaving issue:

Great-great-grandchildren's children
1b *John RANDOLPH, b 23 April 1915

Great-great-grandchildren
7a Eugene Jefferson RANDOLPH, b 19 March 1880; m 28 Feb 1902 Anne Elizabeth Carrier and d 6 Oct 1950, having had issue:

Great-great-grandchildren's children
1b Hubard Carrier RANDOLPH, b 21 Dec 1902; d 28 Oct 1929
2b Catharine Carrier Randolph, b 22 July 1904; m 3 Oct 1931 E(dgar) Reid RUSSELL (b 1898; d 8 July 1978) and d 26 July 1988, leaving issue:

Great-great-grandchildren's grandchildren
1c *Catharine Randolph Russell [Mrs Catharine Russell Little, 5 Lone Pine Road, Biltmore Forest, Asheville, NC 28803, USA], b 25 June 1933; m 27 June 1957 (divorce 1962) James Leake LITTLE (d 8 July 1978) and has issue:

Great-great-grandchildren's great-grandchildren
1d *Catharine Randolph Little [Mrs Mehran Nazemi, 5 Lone Pine Rd, Asheville, NC 28803, USA], b 17 May 1958; m 2 July 1988 *Mehran NAZEMI

Great-great-grandchildren's children
3b *Elizabeth Carrier Randolph, b 10 Nov 1905; m 1st 28 Oct 1927 (divorce 19—) William Lord RIVERS (b 1900) and has issue:

Great-great-grandchildren's grandchildren
1c *William Lord RIVERS [3815 Hidden Acres Circle, N Fort Myers, FL 33903, USA], b 10 Aug 1933; m 1st 11 July 1959 Gayle Musick (d 5 Aug 1973) and has issue:

Great-great-grandchildren's great-grandchildren
1d *Laura Blake Rivers [Mrs John J Morse, 1444 Dubonnet Court, Fort Myers, FL 33919, USA], b Fort Myers 15 Feb 1961; educ U of S Florida; m 31 Dec 1983 *John James MORSE, s of Frank B. Morse and his w Carol K., and has issue:

Great-great-grandchildren's great-great-grandchildren
1e *Bradley James MORSE, b Fort Myers 30 Dec 1988
2e *Rachel Elizabeth MORSE, b Fort Myers 30 April 1992

Great-great-grandchildren's grandchildren
1c (cont.) William L. Rivers m 2nd 10 Oct 1973 *Silvia Willis Griffin

Great-great-grandchildren's children
3b (cont.) Mrs Elizabeth Rivers m 2nd 9 March 1946 *Monroe Stanley BOBST

Great-great-grandchildren
8a Janet Thruston RANDOLPH, b 27 Jan 1884; d 19 April 1951

Great-grandchildren
(3) Robert Mann RANDOLPH, b Round Top 15 April 1851; m 1885 Margaret Calhoun Harris (d 1927) and d 1927

Grandchildren
10 Meriwether Lewis RANDOLPH, b Monticello 31 Jan 1810; educ U of Virginia; clerk US State Dept, Sec of the Territory of Arkansas 1835-36; m Clifton, nr Nashville, Tenn., 9 April 1835, as her 1st husb, Elizabeth (who m 2nd 1841, as his 2nd w, her 1st cousin once-removed Andrew Jackson Donelson, nephew of Rachel Donelson, w of President JACKSON, and the adopted son of President JACKSON), dau of James Glasgow Martin, of Clifton, nr Nashville, Tenn., and his w Catherine Donelson, dau of John Donelson (himself er bro of Rachel Donelson) and his w Mary Purnell, and d Terre Noire, Ark., 24 Sept 1837 of measles complicated by malaria, leaving issue:

Great-grandchildren
(1) Lewis Jackson RANDOLPH, b nr Nashville 31 Jan 1836; d Nashville 1840

Grandchildren
11 Septimia Anne Randolph, b Monticello 3 Jan 1814; m Havana, Cuba, 13 Aug 1838 Dr David Scott MEIKLEHAM (b Glasgow, Scotland, 6 Jan 1804; educ Glasgow and Oxford Us; physician; d New York 20 Nov 1849), s of William Meikleham, LLD, Prof of Natural Philosophy Glasgow U, and d Washington, DC, 14 Sept 1887, having had issue:

Great-grandchildren
(1) William Moreland MEIKLEHAM, b Havana 11 Dec 1839; educ Fordham U (AB 1868); V-Pres New York Life Insur & Trust Co 1878-89; m 1st 25 April 1865 Fanny Cassidy (b 9 Oct 1845; d 1 Jan 1885) and had issue:

Great-great-grandchildren
1a William Arabin MEIKLEHAM, b 1 March 1866; educ Columbia U; m 28 Jan 1903 Margaret Breckenridge (d 31 July 1950) and d Short Hills, New Jersey, 12 Nov 1942
2a (Thomas Mann) Randolph MEIKLEHAM, of Edgartown, Mass., b Fordham, New York, 14 Feb 1869; educ Columbia

U (CE 1890); engineer; *m* 7 Oct 1896 Agnes (*b* New York 31 Oct 1868), dau of Bowie Dash, of New York, and *d* 10 April 1954, having had issue:

Great-great-grandchildren's children
1b Frances Louise MEIKLEHAM, *b* New York 4 Aug 1902; *d* 20 July 1977
2b Martha Randolph MEIKLEHAM, *b* 8 May 1905; *d* 15 Sept 1919

Great-great-grandchildren
3a Frank Sydney MEIKLEHAM, *b* Westchester Co, New York, 28 May, *d* 14 Sept 1872
4a Henry Parish MEIKLEHAM, *b* Westchester Co 28 May 1872; *educ* Columbia U; Pres Monticello Assoc 1935-37; *m* 1st 9 June 1897 (divorce 1912) Virginia Grafton; *m* 2nd 16 Jan 1926, as her 2nd husb, Juliet Graves, *née* Howell, and *d* 23 July 1937

Great-grandchildren
(1) (cont.) William M. Meikleham *m* 2nd 8 June 1887 Isabella Parlby Cuthbert and *d* 27 July 1889
(2) Thomas Mann Randolph MEIKLEHAM, *b* Havana 30 Dec 1840; *d* 7 April 1922
(3) Esther Alice MEIKLEHAM, *b* Havana 12 Nov 1842; *d* Glasgow, Scotland, 4 Sept 1843
(4) Esther Alice MEIKLEHAM, *b* Glasgow, Scotland, 28 Dec 1843; *d* 6 Feb 1927
(5) Ellen Wayles MEIKLEHAM, *b* New York 29 Aug 1846; *d* 22 Feb 1913

Grandchildren
12 George Wythe RANDOLPH, *b* Monticello 10 March 1818; *educ* U of Virginia (LLB 1840); served US Navy, Memb Virginia Secession Convention, Brig-Gen Confederate Army, Confederate Sec of War 1862-64; *m* New Orleans 10 April 1852, as her 2nd husb, Mary Elizabeth (*b* 1830; *d* Edgehill 1871), *née* Adams, widow of William Pope and *d* Edgehill 3 April 1867 (*bur* Monticello)

President Jefferson's daughters and son
II Jane Randolph JEFFERSON, *b* Monticello 3 April 1774; *d* there Sept 1775
III A son, *b* Monticello 28 May, *d* there 14 June 1777
IV Mary (Maria, also called Poll or Polly by her father) Jefferson, *b* Monticello 1 Aug 1778; *m* there 13 Oct 1797, as his 1st w, her half-1st cousin John Wayles EPPES (*b* City Point, Va., 7 April 1773; Senator and Congressman; *m* 2nd 1809 Martha Burke Jones, of Halifax, North Carolina, and had issue by her; *d* Millbrook, Buckingham Co, Va., 5 Sept 1823), est s of Francis Eppes, of Eppington, Chesterfield Co, Va., and his 1st w Elizabeth Wayles (half-sister of Mrs Thomas Jefferson), and *d* Monticello 17 April 1804 (*bur* there), having had issue:

Grandchildren
1 A dau, *b* 31 Dec 1799; *d* Jan 1800
2 Francis Wayles EPPES, *b* Monticello 20 Sept 1801; moved to Leon Co, Fla., 1828, Intendant (Mayor) Tallahassee, Fla., 1841-44, 1856-57 and 1865-66, surrendered that city to Federal troops 10 May 1865; *m* 1st Ashton, Albemarle Co, Va., 28 Nov 1822 his 4th cousin Mary Elizabeth Cleland (*b* 16 Jan 1801; *d* L'Eau Noir April 1835), est dau of Thomas Eston Randolph, of Ashton, and his w Jane Cary Randolph (sister of Thomas Mann Randolph, Jr, who *m* President JEFFERSON's est dau Patsy, *see above*), and had issue:

Great-grandchildren
(1) Jane Cary EPPES, *b* Ashton 9 Nov 1823; *d* 12 Feb 1893
(2) Dr John Wayles EPPES, *b* Bedford Co, Va., 4 July 1825; *educ* U of Virginia; physician; *m* 10 Nov 1854 Josephine H., dau of Col John Bellamy, and *d* 1908, having had issue:

Great-great-grandchildren
1a Francis EPPES; *d* in infancy
2a Elizabeth Wayles Eppes, *b* 1857; *m* 1878 Alexander KENNEDY and *d* 1898, leaving issue:

Great-great-grandchildren's children
1b Margaret Kennedy; *b* 1878; *m* 1915 Alberto HERNANDEZ BLANC, s of —— Hernandez and his w —— Blanc, and *d* 1918
2b Josephine Bellamy Kennedy, *b* 6 May 1879; *m* 1908 Marion Howard BRADLEY (*b* 1871; *d* 21 Feb 1920) and *d* 7 May 1961, having had issue:

Great-great-grandchildren's grandchildren
1c Annie Ward BRADLEY, *b* and *d* 1911
2c Marion Howard BRADLEY, Jr, *b* 11 Dec 1914; *m* 30 Dec 1941 *Joyce Patricia Clark [Mrs Marion H Bradley, 23 Rolling Hills Court, Valdosta, GA 31602, USA] (*b* 23 March 1919) and *d* 10 Sept 1987, leaving issue:

Great-great-grandchildren's great-grandchildren
1d *Ann Randolph Bradley [Mrs R Bradford Burnette, 3326 Bellmeade Dve, Valdosta, GA 31602, USA], *b* 28 Jan 1944; *m* 1 Dec 1962 *R(obert) Bradford BURNETTE and has issue:

Great-great-grandchildren's great-great-grandchildren
1e Elizabeth Ann BURNETTE, *b* 7 Jan 1964; *d* 4 April 1981
2e *Catherine Randolph Burnette [Mrs Jeffery E Hanson, 1036 E Lakeshore Dve, Dalton, GA 30720, USA], *b*

Winston-Salem, N Carolina, 20 April 1966; *educ* U of Georgia; bank assist manager 1989-92; *m* 24 Sept 1988 *Jeffery Ely HANSON, s of James Ely Hanson and his w Joyce Etheridge, and has issue:

Great-great-grandchildren's great-great-grandchildren's children
1f *Margaret Elizabeth HANSON, *b* Illinois 17 May 1992

Great-great-grandchildren's great-grandchildren
2d *Josephine Eppes Bradley [703 Maplewood Dve, Valdosta, GA 31602, USA], *b* Atlanta, Ga., 10 Sept 1947; *educ* Emory U (BA 1969) and Tulane U (MSW 1972); social worker; *m* 9 Feb 1976 *Robert Benedict CHURCH, s of King Benedict Church and his w Carmella LaRocca, and has issue:

Great-great-grandchildren's great-great-grandchildren
1e *Laura Maria CHURCH, *b* Thomasville, Ga., 6 Feb 1976
2e *Robert Bradley CHURCH, *b* Valdosta 21 Jan 1980

Great-great-grandchildren's great-grandchildren
3d *Marion Howard BRADLEY III [1729 Monteagle Dve, Birmingham, AL 35244, USA], *b* 18 Sept 1951; *m* 26 June 1982 *Terri Lee Adams and has issue:

Great-great-grandchildren's great-great-grandchildren
1e *John Wayles BRADLEY, *b* 30 June 1986
2e *Harrison Adams BRADLEY, *b* 17 March 1992

Great-great-grandchildren's children
3b Agnes Kennedy, *b* 1882; *m* 1917 James Washington HERBERT and *d* 19—, having had issue:

Great-great-grandchildren's grandchildren
1c *Eliza Eppes Herbert, *b* 23 March 1921; *m* 24 April 1943 *Joseph Byron DAVIS (*b* 10 March 1914) and has issue:

Great-great-grandchildren's great-grandchildren
1d *Joseph Byron DAVIS, Jr, *b* 10 March 1944
2d *Ann Lynwood DAVIS, *b* 7 Aug 1945
3d *James Kennedy DAVIS, *b* 18 Sept 1947
4d *William Lewis DAVIS, *b* 1 Feb 1950

Great-great-grandchildren's grandchildren
2c *Julia Francis Herbert, *b* 15 June 1922; *m* Sept 1943 *Robert Edward Lee Hall FORBES and has issue:

Great-great-grandchildren's great-grandchildren
1d *Julia Lee FORBES, *b* 25 June 1945
2d *Florence Patty Kennedy FORBES, *b* 8 Oct 1946
3d *Robert Edward Lee Hall FORBES, Jr, *b* 29 Sept 1948
4d *George Joseph FORBES, *b* 7 May 1951
5d *Clarence Aloysius Hall FORBES, *b* 18 July 1952

Great-great-grandchildren's grandchildren
3c Agnes Kennedy HERBERT; *d* in infancy

Great-great-grandchildren's children
4b Alexander KENNEDY, Jr, *b* 1885; *d* 1903
5b John Wayles KENNEDY, *b* 15 June 1889; *m* 19 Nov 1921 Laura Cecilia Hebb (*d* 21 July 1968) and *d* 4 July 1932, leaving issue:

Great-great-grandchildren's grandchildren
1c *John Wayles KENNEDY, Jr [950 Holly Lane, Boca Raton, FL 33486, USA], *b* St Mary's City, Md., 24 Feb 1923; *educ* Georgetown U; US Foreign Serv 1950-75; *m* 1 June 1949 *Dina Morelli and has issue:

Great-great-grandchildren's great-grandchildren
1d *Lisa Morelli Kennedy, *b* Germany 21 Feb 1952; *m* Seattle, Wash., 22 April 1983 *Stewart JAY and has issue:

Great-great-grandchildren's great-great-grandchildren
1e *Alexa KENNEDY-JAY, *b* 13 Dec 1985
2e *Chloë KENNEDY-JAY, *b* 1 July 1988

Great-great-granchildren's great-grandchildren
2d *John Wayles KENNEDY, *b* France 28 July 1960

Great-great-grandchildren's grandchildren
2c *Margaret Combs Kennedy [Mrs Eugene Johnstone, Wickes House, 102 High St, Chestertown, MD 21620, USA], *b* St Mary's Co, Md., 29 Sept 1924; *educ* Georgetown U; *m* 14 Aug 1954 *Eugene Hall JOHNSTONE, s of Eugene Donald Johnstone and his w Mary Esther Hall, and has issue:

Great-great-grandchildren's great-grandchildren
1d *Eugene Hall JOHNSTONE, Jr [4016 62nd St, Bethesda, MD 20816, USA], *b* Charlotte, N Carolina, 19 July

1955; *educ* U of N Carolina; building contractor 1978-; *m* 15 May 1976 *Elizabeth Moore, dau of Joseph Scott Harrell and his *w* Beverley Moore, and has issue:

Great-great-grandchildren's great-great-grandchildren
1e *Joseph Nicholas JOHNSTONE, *b* Easton, Md., 14 Dec 1983
2e *Alexander Hall JOHNSTONE, *b* Edenton, N Carolina, 26 Nov 1985

Great-great-grandchildren's great-grandchildren
2d *Laura Hebb Johnstone [Mrs John F Wilson, PO Box 25, Kennedysville, MD 21645, USA], *b* 19 Dec 1956; *m* 4 Oct 1980 *John Frederick WILSON and has issue:

Great-great-grandchildren's great-great-grandchildren
1e *Laura Wayles WILSON, *b* 22 June 1981
2e *Nathaniel Hall WILSON, *b* 22 July 1983
3e *Garth Johnstone WILSON, *b* 24 June 1987

Great-great-grandchildren's great-grandchildren
3d *Virginia Coad Johnstone [Mrs Peter Allen, 536 High St, Chestertown, MD 21620, USA], *b* 30 Nov 1958; *m* 30 May 1981 *Peter Dewitt ALLEN and has issue:

Great-great-grandchildren's great-great-grandchildren
1e *Peter Michael ALLEN, *b* 27 Feb 1984
2e *Thomas Randolph ALLEN, *b* 19 Oct 1985
3e *Katherine Johnstone ALLEN, *b* 15 June 1990
4e *Margaret Kennedy ALLEN, *b* 15 June 1990

Great-great-grandchildren's great-grandchildren
4d *Margaret Kennedy Johnstone [Mrs Patrick A Wilson, 5883 Soledad Rd, La Jolla, CA 92037, USA], *b* Washington, DC, 29 March 1961; *educ* San Diego State U; *m* 12 Feb 1982 *Patrick Alexander WILSON, s of Charles Alexander Wilson and his *w* Katherine Farquhar, and has issue:

Great-great-grandchildren's great-great-grandchildren
1e *Charles Alexander WILSON, *b* La Jolla 27 Nov 1989

Great-great-grandchildren's great-grandchildren
5d *Jane Randolph JOHNSTONE [77 Beaver St, San Francisco, CA 94114, USA], *b* 30 Sept 1962
6d *Ann Katherine Johnstone [Mrs William H Norris III, 8110 Brices Mill Rd, Chestertown, MD 21620, USA], *b* 22 Dec 1964; *m* 15 Dec 1990 *William Henry NORRIS III
7d *Rebecca Chisholm Johnstone, *b* 21 May 1966; *m* 27 July 1991 *Brady Robert APPLETON

Great-great-grandchildren's grandchildren
3c *Alexander KENNEDY, *b* 15 April 1926; *m* 25 March 1957 *Mary Colette Barrett and has issue (with two other children):

Great-great-grandchildren's great-grandchildren
1d *Mary Grace KENNEDY, *b* 23 Dec 1957
2d *John Wayles KENNEDY, *b* 24 Aug 1959
3d *Colette Kennedy, *b* 19—; *m* 9 Sept 1989 *Stephen Chandler SHOEMAKER

Great-great-grandchildren's grandchildren
4c *Patricia Hebb Kennedy [Mrs Samuel R Garrabrant, 5406 Spangler Ave, Bethesda, MD 20816, USA], *b* 28 June 1928; *m* 22 Oct 1955 *Samuel Robert GARRABRANT and has issue:

Great-great-grandchildren's great-grandchildren
1d *Laura Wayles GARRABRANT [145 Copeland Rd NW Apt B10, Atlanta, GA 30342, USA], *b* Washington, DC, 31 Aug 1956; *educ* Atlanta Coll od Art; graphic designer, painter and jewellery-designer 1980-
2d *Robert Bayard GARRABRANT [1 Cathedral St, Annapolis, MD 21401, USA], *b* 24 Feb 1957
3d *Peter Buckley GARRABRANT [906 19th Ave E, Seattle, WA 98112, USA], *b* 15 April 1963

Great-great-grandchildren's grandchildren
5c *Anne Katherine Kennedy [Mrs Owen W Hendon, 1100 Shipman Lane, McLean, VA 22101, USA], *b* St Mary's City, Md., 4 Nov 1929; *educ* Georgetown Visitation Preparatory Sch and Jr Coll; *m* 17 Jan 1953 *Owen William HENDON, s of Col Robert Randall Hendon and his *w* Kathleen Grubaugh, and has issue:

Great-great-grandchildren's great-grandchildren
1d *Nicole Noel Hendon [Mrs Mark Pearl, 3325 Hemlock Dve, Falls Church, VA 22042, USA], *b* Chateauroux, France, 9 Nov 1955; *educ* Virginia Polytechnical U; admin offr and computer specialist US Dept of State; *m* Maryland 7 Sept 1984 *Mark Allen PEARL, s of Charles Pearl and his *w* Mabel, and has issue:

Great-great-grandchildren's great-great-grandchildren
1e *Kristin Noel PEARL, *b* Fairfax, Va., 7 April 1986
2e *Molly Hendon PEARL, *b* Fairfax 5 June 1988
3e *Michael Tyler PEARL, *b* Fairfax 5 May 1992

Great-great-grandchildren's great-grandchildren
2d *Kim Kennedy HENDON [1260 Lamplighter Way, Reston, VA 22094, USA], b Paris, France, 18 March 1958; gen manager; m Virginia 21 March 1987 *Elizabeth Jo, dau of James Ahlberg and his w Suzanne L., and has issue:

Great-great-grandchildren's great-great-grandchildren
1e *Christopher Robert HENDON, b Washington, DC, 21 April 1988
2e *Nicholas Owen HENDON, b Washington, DC, 21 May 1990

Great-great-grandchildren's great-grandchildren
3d *Derek Robert HENDON [5902 Ramsgate Rd, Bethesda, MD 20816, USA], b Paris, France, 24 Aug 1959; educ James Madison U; commercial real estate asset manager; m 31 March 1984 *Elizabeth Bieber, dau of William Biscoe Wallace and his w Sallie Bennett
4d *Danielle HENDON [1524 Spring Vale Ave, McLean, VA 22101, USA], b Washington, DC, 6 Jan 1962

Great-great-grandchildren's children
6b Florence Patti KENNEDY, b 1891; d 29 Dec 1981

Great-grandchildren
(3) Thomas Jefferson EPPES, b Poplar Forest 29 June 1827; educ U of Georgia; atty, Florida State Senator and Pres State Senate to 1861, Memb Florida Delegn Democratic Nat Convention 1860, Speaker Florida House of Reps 1864; m Lyndhurst Plantation, Jefferson Co, Fla., 28 April 1859 Theodosia Burr Bellamy (d 11 Aug 1872), sister of his er bro's w (see above) and d 4 Aug 1869, having had issue:

Great-great-grandchildren
1a Thomas Jefferson EPPES, Jr, b 22 Feb 1861; m 1st 1883 Kate Edna Shaler and had issue:

Great-great-grandchildren's children
1b Thomas Jefferson EPPES III, b 6 Sept 1884; m 1912 Katherine Davis and d 1 Feb 1944

Great-great-grandchildren
1a (cont.) Thomas J. Eppes, Jr, m 2nd 1891 Mamie Jeanette Gones, née Shoemaker (b 18 Oct 1868; d 21 April 1923), and d 2 Nov 1910, having had further issue:

Great-great-grandchildren's children
2b Edna Bellamy Eppes, b 12 Dec 1892; m 1 Sept 1915 Dr Ralston LATTIMORE (b 1871; d 1938) and d 24 Oct 1979, leaving issue:

Great-great-grandchildren's grandchildren
1c *Edna Eppes Lattimore [Mrs Jack S Clancy, 553 Marjorie Place, Macon, GA 31204, USA], b 9 Sept 1916; m 12 July 1941 Jack Stacey CLANCY (d 18 March 1992) and has issue:

Great-great-grandchildren's great-grandchildren
1d Helen Lattimore Clancy, b 6 March 1943; m 1st 26 Dec 1962 William Dowin HEIMBROOK and had issue:

Great-great-grandchildren's great-great-grandchildren
1e *William Dowin BARNETTE (b Heimbrook but took stepf's name) [1011 Ashbrook Court, Marietta, GA 30068, USA], b Japan 9 Nov 1963; educ U of Alabama; V-Pres and Finance Dir American-European Corp; m 16 March 1990 *Bertha Maria, dau of Remberto Junquera and his w Maria Diez, and has issue:

Great-great-grandchildren's great-great-grandchildren's children
1f *Lauren Clancy BARNETTE, b Georgia 13 Nov 1990
2f *Patrick William BARNETTE, b Georgia 5 Sept 1992

Great-great-grandchildren's great-grandchildren
1d (cont.) Helen Clancy Heimbrook m 2nd 6 Sept 1967 *Thomas Jackson BARNETTE [690 Atlanta Country Club Dve, Marietta, GA 30067, USA] and d 13 March 1981
2d *Jack Stacey CLANCY [2423 Covington Creek, Circle West, Jacksonville, FL 32224, USA], b 14 June 1947; m 22 Feb 1971 *Lorraine Glenys Lawson and has issue:

Great-great-grandchildren's great-great-grandchildren
1e *Elizabeth Grace CLANCY, b 6 Oct 1976

Great-great-grandchildren's great-grandchildren
3d *Carolyn Eppes Clancy, b 2 July 1949; m 30 Aug 1969 *Philip Jewett MARKERT and has issue:

Great-great-grandchildren's great-great-grandchildren
1e *Philip Jewett MARKERT, Jr, b 29 March 1976
2e *Jennifer Winter MARKERT, b 11 Nov 1977

Great-great-grandchildren's grandchildren
2c *William LATTIMORE [2 Crazy Possum Lane, Savannah, GA 31411, USA], b Savannah 8 June 1918; educ US Naval Acad, Wharton Postgraduate Sch, U of Pennsylvania; offr USN 1940-52, real estate developer; m 20 Dec 1943 *Helen Mable, dau of James Edgar Clancy and his w Anna Mable Stacy, and has issue:

Great-great-grandchildren's great-grandchildren
1d *Anne Eppes Lattimore [2 Crazy Possum Lane, Savannah, GA 31411, USA], *b* Savannah 19 Feb 1947; *m* 1st Savannah 1966 Henry M. EASON, Jr, s of Henry M. Eason, and has issue:

Great-great-grandchildren's great-great-grandchildren
1e *Sterling Fennel EASON, *b* 20 March 1968

Great-great-grandchildren's great-grandchildren
1d (cont.) Anne Lattimore Eason *m* 2nd 7 July 1982 *John Albert JANAS
2d *Elizabeth Bellamy Lattimore [Elizabeth Sparks Rousakis, 1905 Colonial Dve, Savannah, GA 31406, USA], *b* Savannah 24 Nov 1949; *m* 1st Savannah June 1971 William Earle SPARKS and has issue:

Great-great-grandchildren's great-great-grandchildren
1e *Catherine Ashley SPARKS [c/o Mrs John P Rousakis, 1905 Colonial Dve, Savannah, GA 31406, USA], *b* 26 Sept 1972
2e *William Earl SPARKS, Jr, *b* 22 Jan 1975
3e *Robert Lattimore SPARKS, *b* 21 June 1977

Great-great-grandchildren's great-grandchildren
2d (cont.) Elizabeth Lattimore Sparks *m* 2nd 19— *John P. Rousakis
3d *William LATTIMORE, Jr [14 Middleton Rd, GA 31411, USA], *b* 25 May 1954; *m* 25 Aug 1973 *Elizabeth Landon DeVaughn and has issue:

Great-great-grandchildren's great-great-grandchildren
1e *Elizabeth Landon LATTIMORE, *b* 2 July 1976
2e *Catherine Eppes LATTIMORE, *b* 16 May 1979
3e *Mary Ralston LATTIMORE, *b* 28 May 1981
4e *William LATTIMORE III, *b* 12 Nov 1982

Great-great-grandchildren's grandchildren
3c *Harry Hays LATTIMORE [334 E 53rd St, Savannah, GA 31405, USA], *b* 18 March 1924

Great-great-grandchildren
2a Victoria Eppes, *b* 1862; *m* 1st Carlton M. MARSHALL; *m* 2nd Arthur B. HARRISON
3a Mary Eppes, *b* 1864; *m* 18— George MORRISON and had issue:

Great-great-grandchildren's children
1b Theodosia Bellamy Morrison, *b* 18—; *m* 1st 29 Dec 1909 her 1st cousin once-removed Dudley Shepard SHINE, Jr (*see below* under issue of (13) Caroline Matilda Eppes, 13th child of Francis Wayles Eppes, himself 2nd s of Mary/Maria/Poll/Polly Jefferson, 4th dau of President JEFFERSON), and had issue:

Great-great-grandchildren's grandchildren
1c *Dudley Shepard SHINE, Jr, *b* 17 July 1914; *m* 4 March 1936 *Margaret Pinkham and has issue:

Great-great-grandchildren's great-grandchildren
1d *Dudley Shepard SHINE III, *b* 22 Feb 1938
2d *Randolph SHINE, *b* 3 April 1942

Great-great-grandchildren's grandchildren
2c *Theodosia Morrison Shine, *b* 5 June 1916; *m* 19— *Dean RADER and has issue:

Great-great-grandchildren's great-grandchildren
1d *Randolph RADER, *b* 22 Oct 1945

Great-great-grandchildren's children
1b (cont.) Theodosia Morrison Shine *m* 2nd 19— Cyril Norman BOLAND

Great-great-grandchildren
4a Francis EPPES, *b* 11 Sept 1865; *m* 1890 Alberta R. Wharton and *d* 23 Feb 19—, having had issue:

Great-great-grandchildren's children
1b Francis EPPES, Jr, *b* 28 July 1891; *m* 14 Sept 1921 Willie Lois Meek (*b* 5 June 1899) and *d* 8 April 1931, leaving issue:

Great-great-grandchildren's grandchildren
1c *Alberta Lee Eppes [Mrs William T Carroll, 125 Bankhead Ave, Carrollton, GA 30117, USA], *b* Alma, Ga., 8 Nov 1923; *educ* Fitzgerald Business Sch; typist with Soil Conservation Serv of Fedl Govt to 1985; *m* 10 Aug 1947 William Thomas CARROLL (*b* 28 Feb 1913; *d* 5 March 1965) and has issue:

Great-great-grandchildren's great-grandchildren
1d *Donnie Mac Carroll [Mrs Harvel B Hamm, 110 Lost Lake Rd, Carrollton, GA 30117, USA], *b* Carrollton 28 Jan 1950; *educ* West Georgia Coll; elementary sch teacher 1972-; *m* 4 Sept 1971 *Harvel Burns HAMM (*b* 21 Jan 1947), s of Lewis Howard Hamm and his w Miriam, and has issue (both girls):

Great-great-grandchildren's great-great-grandchildren
1e *Lori Lee HAMM, *b* Carrollton 19 Aug 1975
2e *Leigh Carroll HAMM, *b* Carrollton 27 Feb 1981

Great-great-grandchildren's great-grandchildren
2d *William Thomas CARROLL, Jr [109 Mountain Brook Dve, Carrollton, GA 30117, USA], *b* Carrollton 20 Dec 1955; *m* Georgia 26 June 1981 *Teresa Willa Hornsby (*b* 10 Nov 1961) and has issue:

Great-great-grandchildren's great-great-grandchildren
1e *Allison LeAnne CARROLL, *b* 7 June 1983
2e *William Thomas CARROLL III, *b* 17 Aug 1987

Great-great-grandchildren's grandchildren
2c *Francis EPPES III [Rte 3 Box 750, Fitzgerald, GA 31750, USA], *b* 15 Jan 1925; *m* 9 July 1950 *Lois Myrtle McBryant and has issue:

Great-great-grandchildren's great-grandchildren
1d *Susan Beverly Eppes, *b* 24 June 1954; *m* 1st 30 June 1973 Billy Jerome COBB and has issue:

Great-great-grandchildren's great-great-grandchildren
1e *Melissa Deanne COBB, *b* 26 March 1979

Great-great-grandchildren's great-grandchildren
1d (cont.) Susan Eppes Cobb *m* 2nd 23 Nov 1984 *Robert Douglas HINTON
2d *Francis Keith EPPES, *b* 18 June 1957
3d *Jan Ellen EPPES, *b* 21 Sept 1963

Great-great-grandchildren's children
2b Mamie Loula Eppes, *b* 8 June 1897; *m* 24 March 1933 Charles Everett FLEMING and *d* 1975

Great-great-grandchildren
5a Paul EPPES, *b* 1866; *d* 1868
6a Randolph EPPES, *b* 21 Oct 1868; *m* 15 Dec 1898 Sarah Josephine Mays and *d* 5 Dec 1941, leaving issue:

Great-great-grandchildren's children
1b *Edith Bellamy Eppes, *b* 26 Dec 1899; *m* 16 Nov 1920 Haskell Harris BASS (*b* 18 Sept 1893; *d* 1 Aug 1988) and has issue:

Great-great-grandchildren's grandchildren
1c *Edith Eppes Bass [Mrs William E Thompson, 11019 Gainsborough Rd, Potomac, MD 20854, USA], *b* 19 Dec 1921; *m* 18 Nov 1944 William Ellison THOMPSON, Jr (*b* 3 Dec 1923; *d* 13 Oct 1992), s of William Ellison Thompson, and has issue:

Great-great-grandchildren's great-grandchildren
1d *William Ellison THOMPSON III, *b* 29 Aug 1945; *m* 2 Feb 1980 *Teresa Francinerose Silva
2d *David Craig THOMPSON, *b* 22 March 1947; *m* 14 Aug 1971 *Patricia Ann Bearden
3d *Mark Randolph THOMPSON, *b* 29 March 1952; *m* 17 June 1975 *Joyce Ragsdale and has issue:

Great-great-grandchildren's great-great-grandchildren
1e *Julie Elizabeth THOMPSON, *b* 30 Aug 1982
2e *Anne Marie THOMPSON, *b* 13 March 1984

Great-great-grandchildren's great-grandchildren
4d *Sarah (Sally) Ann Thompson, *b* 6 Nov 1953; *m* 19 Oct 1974 *William Nathaniel SHIPLEY, Jr, and has issue:

Great-great-grandchildren's great-great-grandchildren
1e *William Ellison SHIPLEY, *b* 19 Sept 1980
2e *Lisa Ann SHIPLEY, *b* 17 March 1982

Great-great-grandchildren's great-grandchildren
5d *Randall Harris THOMPSON, *b* 19—; *m* 12 May 1984 *Deborah Lee Carestia

Great-great-grandchildren's grandchildren
2c *Eleanor Mays Bass [Mrs Joseph Ganey, 5060 Riverview Blvd W, Bradenton, FL 34209, USA], *b* 3 Jan 1924; *m* 19 Oct 1946 *Dr Joseph Brannen GANEY (*b* 28 May 1921) and has issue:

Great-great-grandchildren's great-grandchildren
1d *Dr Joseph Brannen GANEY, Jr [6208 Shore Acres Dve NW, Bradenton, FL 34209, USA], *b* 25 July 1949; MD; *m* 3 Oct 1987 *Kimberley Anne DeVice and has issue:

Great-great-grandchildren's great-great-grandchildren
1e *Brannen Joseph GANEY, *b* 16 July 1989
2e *Jordan Allen GANEY, *b* March 1991

Great-great-grandchildren's great-grandchildren
2d *Dr James Nowell GANEY [4506 Riverview Blvd, Bradenton, FL 34209, USA], b 16 July 1950; MD; m 22 Jan 1983 *Mary Jo Anne Simmons and has issue:

Great-great-grandchildren's great-great-grandchildren
1e *Nowell James GANEY, b 23 April 1984
2e *Christopher Bellamy GANEY, b 19 March 1986

Great-great-grandchildren's great-grandchildren
3d *Dr Thomas Harris GANEY [2383 Landings Circle, Bradenton, FL 34209, USA], b 15 Nov 1954; m 24 July 1982 *Susan Allison Boyd and has issue:

Great-great-grandchildren's great-great-grandchildren
1e *Ellen Brannen GANEY, b 6 July 1984
2e *Thomas Harris GANEY, Jr, b 25 May 1989

Great-great-grandchildren's great-grandchildren
4d *Anne Eppes Ganey [Mrs Robert J Beasley, 4119 24th Ave W, Bradenton, FL 34205, USA], b Bradenton 10 Feb 1962; educ U of Alabama; m 26 March 1988 *Robert Joseph (Joe) BEASLEY and has issue:

Great-great-grandchildren's great-great-grandchildren
1e *Robert Joseph BEASLEY, Jr, b Bradenton 16 Nov 1989
2e *Kathryn Eppes BEASLEY, b Bradenton 12 Oct 1992
3e *William Randolph BEASLEY, b Bradenton 12 Oct 1992

Great-great-grandchildren's great-grandchildren
5d *Susan Randolph Ganey [Mrs Jeffrey A Conley, 408 51st St NW, Bradenton, FL 34209, USA], b Bradenton 1 Aug 1957; educ U of Alabama (BA 1979, MEd 1980); schoolteacher 1980-85; m 26 June 1982 *Jeffrey Alan CONLEY, s of Iley Conley and his w Bertha, and has issue:

Great-great-grandchildren's great-great-grandchildren
1e *Jeffrey Alan CONLEY, Jr, b Bradenton 27 Sept 1985
2e *Courtney Randolph CONLEY, b Bradenton 5 June 1987
3e *Christopher Bennett CONLEY, b 4 April 1991

Great-great-grandchildren's grandchildren
3c *Dr Haskell Harris BASS, Jr [6823 S Florence Ave, Tulsa, OK 74136, USA], b 6 June 1930; m 16 Aug 1958 *Patricia Elizabeth, dau of Charles E. Smith and his w Beatrice P. Messner, and has issue:

Great-great-grandchildren's great-grandchildren
1d *Haskell Harris BASS III [5511 E 91st St South, Tulsa, OK 74137, USA], b Bradenton, Fla., 9 Dec 1961
2d *Patricia Randolph Bass [Mrs Brant A. Schneider, 4302 E 106th St, Tulsa, OK 74137, USA], b Bradenton 13 April 1963; m 6 Oct 1990 *Dr Brant Alan SCHNEIDER
3d *Elizabeth Andrews BASS, b Bradenton 25 June 1964
4d *Robert Jefferson BASS, b Bradenton 3 June 1968

Great-great-grandchildren's children
2b Martha Simpkins (Patty) Eppes, b 30 June 1903; m 1st 1923 Edward Baldwin YOUNG and had issue:

Great-great-grandchildren's grandchildren
1c *Meta Baldwin Young [Mrs Richard E Crane Jr, 2841 E Sherran Lane, Phoenix, AZ 85016, USA], b Albany, Ga., 6 Nov 1924; educ Florida S U; librarian USAF 1968-84; m 1st 12 April 1947 (divorce July 1976) William Dyer SHACKELFORD and has issue:

Great-great-grandchildren's great-grandchildren
1d *Martha Eppes Shackelford, b 9 June 1954; m 1st 1 Nov 1972 (divorce 1978) Craig Lee ROBINSON and has issue:

Great-great-grandchildren's great-great-grandchildren
1e *William Dyer ROBINSON, b 20 Aug 1973
2e *Meta Baldwin ROBINSON, b 28 May 1975

Great-great-grandchildren's great-grandchildren
1d (cont.) Mrs Martha Robinson m 2nd 1979 *Jack V. NELSON and has further issue:

Great-great-grandchildren's great-great-grandchildren
3e *Sylvie Randolph NELSON, b 20 Feb 1980

Great-great-grandchildren's great-grandchildren
2d *Theresa Dyer SHACKELFORD [PO Box 99, Monteagle, TN 37356, USA], b 8 May 1956
3d *Meta Baldwin SHACKELFORD, b 22 Feb 1961
4d *Maria Eppes SHACKELFORD [PO Box 55350, Atlanta, GA 30308, USA], b Birmingham, Ala., 27 March 1962

Great-great-grandchildren's grandchildren
1c (cont.) Meta Young Shackelford *m* 2nd 6 May 1984 *Richard Edwin Creighton CRANE, Jr, s of Richard E. C. Crane and his w Beatrice Nardini

Great-great-grandchildren's children
2b (cont.) Martha Eppes Young *m* 2nd 26 April 1934 Francis Putney WETHERBEE (*d* Oct 1978) and *d* 21 Nov 1991, having had further issue:

Great-great-grandchildren's grandchildren
2c *Francis Putney WETHERBEE, Jr [PO Box 3610, Albany, GA 31706, USA], *b* Albany 3 April 1935; *educ* Woodberry Forest U, Ga.; *m* 1st 17 March 1959 Nancy Elizabeth Butts and with her has issue:

Great-great-grandchildren's great-grandchildren
1d *Wallace Butts WETHERBEE, *b* 11 Oct 1960; *m* 19— (divorce 19—) Liz Pomphery and has issue:

Great-great-grandchildren's great-great-grandchildren
1e *Taylor WETHERBEE, *b* 2 April 1987

Mr and the 1st Mrs Francis P. Wetherbee also have an adopted dau:
a Diane Michelle WETHERBEE, *b* 4 Feb 1961
They have further issue:
Great-great-grandchildren's great-grandchildren
2d *Harold Berkeley WETHERBEE II [PO Box 8, Albany, GA 31703-5301, USA], *b* 23 Dec 1961

Great-great-grandchildren's grandchildren
2c (cont.) Francis P. Wetherbee, Jr, *m* 2nd 18 Sept 1965 Rosemary Bligh Rhyne and has further issue:

Great-great-grandchildren's great-grandchildren
3d *Francis Putney WETHERBEE III, *b* 1 Sept 1968

Great-great-grandchildren's grandchildren
2c (cont.) Francis P. Wetherbee, Jr, *m* 3rd 10 May 1985 *Edith Catellaos Gomez
3c *(James) Roland WETHERBEE [205 Byron Plantation Rd, Albany, GA, USA], *b* 4 Jan 1940; *m* 3 May 1965 *Diane Whitney Weller and has issue:

Great-great-grandchildren's great-grandchildren
1d *Dawn Weller WETHERBEE, *b* 18 May 1966
2d *Daniel James WETHERBEE, *b* 6 March 1970

Great-great-grandchildren's grandchildren
4c *Sally Eppes Wetherbee [Mrs Hunt, 1207 Palmyra Rd, Albany, GA 31701, USA], *b* 23 Jan 1943; *m* 19— *——— HUNT

Great-grandchildren
(4) Revd William Eston EPPES, *b* nr Tallahassee, Fla., 5 July 1830; *educ* Ravenscroft Coll, Columbia, Tenn., and U of Georgia; Episcopalian clergyman, chaplain Confederate States Army Civil War; *m* 1st Athens, Ga., 1 Aug 1854 Emily (*d* 1873), dau of James Bancroft, of Baltimore, and had issue:

Great-great-grandchildren
1a Matilda Bancroft EPPES, *b* 1855; *d* 26 Jan 1929
2a Elizabeth Cleland EPPES, *b* 1857; *d* 1881
3a Francis EPPES, *b* 1859; *m* 1881 his 1st cousin Mary Margaret Bancroft (*b* 1861; *d* 27 March 1950) and *d* 1921, having had issue:

Great-great-grandchildren's children
1b Fred EPPES, *b* 1882
2b William Eston EPPES, *b* 10 June 1885; *d* 1918
3b James Bancroft EPPES, *b* 1888; *m* 1st 1908 Elizabeth Williford (*b* 1890; *d* 17 Oct 1945) and *d* 9 Nov 1977, having had issue:

Great-great-grandchildren's grandchildren
1c Elizabeth EPPES, *b* and *d* 1910
2c Caroline Frances Eppes, *b* 1911; *m* 1st 1929 Stanford Ivan HOFF and had issue:

Great-great-grandchildren's great-grandchildren
1d Stanford Ivan HOFF, Jr, *b* 1930; *d* on active service in Korea 4 Nov 1950

Great-great-grandchildren's grandchildren
2c (cont.) Caroline Eppes Hoff *m* 2nd 1934 *William Bernard LOVING and *d* 14 Feb 1987 or 5 Feb 1988, having had further issue:

Great-great-grandchildren's great-grandchildren
2d *William Bernard LOVING, Jr [2704 Vermont NE, Albuquerque, NM 87110, USA], *b* 1936; *m* 1st 7 Jan 1959 (divorce 19—) Myrna Joyce Burner and has issue:

Great-great-grandchildren's great-great-grandchildren
1e *William Bernard LOVING III [2704 Vermont St NE, Albuquerque, NM 87110, USA], b 14 Aug 1959; m 1st 12 Aug 1978 Cynthia Kay Hulen; m 2nd 31 Dec 1982 Donna Brnovich; m 3rd 13 June 1987 *Deborah Jean Simerdla and has issue:

Great-great-grandchildren's great-great-grandchildren's children
1f *Skyler Aaron LOVING (dau), b 1 Nov 1987

Great-great-grandchildren's great-great-grandchildren
2e *Theron Lindsey LOVING [2704 Vermont St NE, Albuquerque, NM 87110, USA], b 29 April 1965; m 17 April 1985 *Julie Foster and has issue:

Great-great-grandchildren's great-great-grandchildren's children
1f *Kyle Ryan LOVING, b 30 June 1986
2f *Chelsea Lynd LOVING, b 28 Feb 1988
3f *Tory Theron LOVING, b 9 May 1989

Great-great-grandchildren's great-grandchildren
2d (cont.) William B. Loving, Jr, m 2nd 7 Aug 1976 *Janice Kay Perry
3d *Claire Bancroft Loving [Mrs Albert Dworkin, 721 Greenwood Rd, Wilmington, DE 19807, USA], b Washington, DC, 22 Oct 1938; educ Wilmington Gen Hosp; registered nurse; m 1st 2 March 1959 (divorce 1959) Dr Merrill Eugene SPEELMAN; m 2nd 23 Nov 1964 *Dr Albert DWORKIN (b 1926), s of Isidore Dworkin and his w Alice, and has issue:

Great-great-grandchildren's great-great-grandchildren
1e *Carolyn Elizabeth DWORKIN, b Delaware 15 July 1966
2e *Kathryn Bancroft DWORKIN, b Wilmington 18 Nov 1969
3e *Paul Joseph DWORKIN, b Wilmington 8 Feb 1972

Great-great-grandchildren's grandchildren
3c *James Bancroft EPPES, Jr [Rte2 Box 165, Hiawassee, GA 30546, USA], b Washington, DC, 29 Jan 1913; educ Johns Hopkins; telephone engr with C & P Telephone Co, US Patent Office, Navy Dept Bureau of Ships World War II, Rural Electrification Admin US Dept of Agriculture 1950-75 and Standard Telephone Co; m 18 May 1940 *Elizabeth Claude (b Annapolis, Md., 18 April 1919), dau of Henry Grafton Fuller and his w Lucy Claude, and has issue:

Great-great-grandchildren's great-grandchildren
1d *John Williford EPPES [1369 Pasadena Ave NE, Atlanta, GA 30306, USA], b Annapolis, Md., 21 June 1941; educ Emory U (PhD); psychologist
2d *James Bancroft EPPES III [543 N Livingston St, Arlington, VA 22203, USA], b Washington, DC, 1 Nov 1942; m S. Dak. Nov 1968 *Carol Lynne Pritchard and has issue:

Great-great-grandchildren's great-great-grandchildren
1e *Thomas Edward EPPES, b 31 Jan 1976
2e *Marie Elizabeth EPPES, b 28 May 1980

Great-great-grandchildren's great-grandchildren
3d *Thomas Jefferson EPPES [Box 1487 101 Rainbow Dve, Livingston, TX 77351, USA], b Washington, DC, 21 May 1946; m 24 March 1973 *Susan Louise, dau of Lee Campbell and his w Louise, of McLean, Va., and has issue:

Great-great-grandchildren's great-great-grandchildren
1e *Samantha Lee EPPES, b Annapolis, Md., 25 Sept 1988

Great-great-grandchildren's great-grandchildren
4d *Lucy Elizabeth Eppes [Mrs Kenneth Swanson, 3040-C Boxer Rd, Ewa Beach, HI 96707, USA], b Washington, DC, 16 June 1956; educ Mary Washington Coll; travel agent 1979-90; m 15 June 1985 *Kenneth Linné SWANSON, s of Ralph K. Swanson and his w Dorothy S. Livengood, of Florida, and has issue:

Great-great-grandchildren's great-great-grandchildren
1e *Brandon Scott SWANSON, b Bethesda, Md., 21 June 1987

Great-great-grandchildren's grandchildren
4c Emily EPPES, b 1914; d 1921
5c *Mary Eppes [Mrs Remus Turner, 111 Battle Road, Greensboro, NC 27410, USA], b 1921; m 1943 *Dr Remus Strother TURNER (b 1921) and has issue:

Great-great-grandchildren's great-grandchildren
1d *Remus Strother TURNER, Jr [842 Ashmead Rd, Charlotte, NC 28211, USA], b 4 Feb 1945; m 16 June 1968 *Diane Elizabeth Morris and has issue:

Great-great-grandchildren's great-great-grandchildren
1e *Adam Morris TURNER, b 7 Dec 1973

2e *Christine Lynn TURNER, *b* 7 March 1977
3e *Ryan William TURNER, *b* 17 Jan 1979

Great-great-grandchildren's great-grandchildren
2d *Janet Elizabeth Turner, *b* 6 April 1947; *m* 1st 21 Dec 1968 William Carroll CHEWNING and has issue:

Great-great-grandchildren's great-great-grandchildren
1e *Page Louise CHEWNING, *b* 18 April 1973

Great-great-grandchildren's great-grandchildren
2d (cont.) Janet Turner Chewning *m* 2nd 12 June 1977 *Robert S. BARROWS
3d *Joseph Eppes TURNER, *b* 11 June 1950; *m* 4 Aug 1973 *Paula Ellen Scott and has issue:

Great-great-grandchildren's great-great-grandchildren
1e *Benjamin Scott TURNER, *b* 24 Nov 1981
2e *David Eppes TURNER, *b* 24 April 1984
3e *Sarah Ellen TURNER, *b* 12 Dec 1985

Great-great-grandchildren's great-grandchildren
4d *Paul Alan TURNER [76 Marlowe Dve, Asheville, NC 28801, USA], *b* 26 April 1954; *m* 1st 10 Aug 1977 Elizabeth Lee Ausley and has issue:

Great-great-grandchildren's great-great-grandchildren
1e *Bradley Eppes TURNER, *b* 8 June 1983

Great-great-grandchildren's great-grandchildren
4d (cont.) Paul A. Turner *m* 2nd 31 May 1991 *Susan Hense

Great-great-grandchildren's grandchildren
6c *Dr Williford EPPES [19 Bridle Bridge Road, Covered Bridge Lane, Newark, DE 19711, USA], *b* 1923; *m* 1st 9 Oct 1948 Emily Mulligan and has issue:

Great-great-grandchildren's great-grandchildren
1d *Emily Elizabeth Eppes, *b* 27 July 1949; *m* 19— *James Lester McDONOUGH and has issue:

Great-great-grandchildren's great-great-grandchildren
1e *James Lester McDONOUGH, Jr, *b* 10 Dec 1981

Great-great-grandchildren's great-grandchildren
2d Douglas Williford EPPES, *b* 26 June 1950; *d* 7 Aug 1991
3d *Thomas Wayne EPPES [109 W 36th St, Wilmington, DE 19801, USA], *b* 24 Sept 1952
4d *Barbara Carolyn Eppes, *b* 30 July 1955; *m* 16 Dec 1978 *Michael John PLEVA
5d *David Charles EPPES, *b* 3 June 1957; *m* 22 Sept 1990 *Sharon Marie Lister and has issue:

Great-great-grandchildren's great-great-grandchildren
1e *Marisa Lee EPPES, *b* 3 Jan 1992

Great-great-grandchildren's great-grandchildren
6d *Robert Francis EPPES [2 Allandale Dve Apt B-7, Newark, DE 19713, USA], *b* 26 March 1964

Great-great-grandchildren's grandchildren
6c (cont.) Dr Williford Eppes *m* 2nd 19— *Nancy Jane Litzenberg

Great-great-grandchildren's children
3b (cont.) James Bancroft Eppes *m* 2nd 1945 *Carrie Frances Williford (*b* 1893) and *d c* 1975
4b Lillie Jeanerette EPPES, *b* 1890; *d* 1892
5b John Wayles EPPES, *b* 1892; *m* 1915 Mary Lou Lemon and *d* 6 Nov 1961, leaving issue:

Great-great-grandchildren's grandchildren
1c *John Francis EPPES, *b* 4 April 1921; *m* 1st 27 Aug 1944 Margaret Temple and has issue:

Great-great-grandchildren's great-grandchildren
1d *Constance Bancroft EPPES, *b* 27 Nov 1953

Great-great-grandchildren's grandchildren
1c (cont.) John F. Eppes *m* 2nd 25 Jan 1957 *Doris Lipscomb

Great-great-grandchildren
4a James Bancroft EPPES, *b* 1860; *d* 1861
5a Lucy Bancroft Eppes, *b* 1861; *m* 1881 her 1st cousin Edward BANCROFT and *d* 1896, having had issue:

Great-great-grandchildren's children
1b Lucy Eppes BANCROFT, *b* 1882; *d* 1883
2b Irene Scott BANCROFT, *b* 1883; *d* 28 Oct 1935
3b Dr Edward BANCROFT, Jr, *b* 1886; *d* 1924

4b Emily Cleland BANCROFT, *b* 1888; *d* 22 June 1956
5b Matilda Eppes Bancroft, *b* 10 Oct 1893; *m* 27 Sept 1929 Thomas Wetzell RICHARDS and had issue:

Great-great-grandchildren's grandchildren
1c *Thomas Edward RICHARDS [1230 Phimarga Lane, Athens, GA 30606, USA], *b* 26 Feb 1932; *m* 6 Sept 1953 *Charlene Jeannette Ruark (*b* 4 Nov 1935) and has issue:

Great-great-grandchildren's great-grandchildren
1d *Keith Randolph RICHARDS [8979 Palos Verde, Orlando, FL 32825, USA], *b* 26 Jan 1955; *m* 2 Nov 1985 *Kathy Lynn Crosby and has issue:

Great-great-grandchildren's great-great-grandchildren
1e *Michelle Renee RICHARDS, *b* 24 July 1988
2e *David Bancroft RICHARDS, *b* 20 Nov 1989

Great-great-grandchildren's great-grandchildren
2d *Thomas Jeffrey RICHARDS, *b* 18 Oct 1958; *m* 19— *——
3d *Dr Bartley Ruark RICHARDS [4350 Jimmy Carter Blvd Apt 1805, Norcross, GA 30093, USA], *b* 29 Dec 1961; *m* 13 July 1985 *Suzanna Lynn Tompkins and has issue:

Great-great-grandchildren's great-great-grandchildren
1e *Caleb Dane RICHARDS, *b* 6 Dec 1988
2e *Clayton Forrest RICHARDS, *b* 28 Jan 1992

Great-great-grandchildren
6a Jane Cary EPPES, *b* 1863; *d* in infancy
7a William Eston EPPES, Jr, *b* 24 Dec 1864; *m* 2 Jan 1889 Irene Ada Bancroft and *d* 22 Feb 1945, leaving issue:

Great-great-grandchildren's children
1b Adella Evelyn Eppes, *b* 6 June 1890; *m* 19 April 1913 James William LOCKETT and *d* 17 April 1966, having had issue:

Great-great-grandchildren's grandchildren
1c *Martha Anne Lockett [Mrs Emory McNeil, 110 Holcomb Street, Isle of Hope, Savannah, GA 31406, USA], *b* Albany, Ga., 26 April 1914; *educ* Draughn's Business Coll; secretary; *m* 1st 1935 William Ewell LEWIS (deceased); *m* 2nd 30 Aug 1957 Emory H. McNEIL (*d* 23 Jan 1978)
2c Adella Evelyn LOCKETT, *b* 11 Oct 1915; *d* in infancy
3c *Frances Hunter Lockett, *b* 25 Dec 1917; *m* 1938 *Alton A. ROGERS and has issue:

Great-great-grandchildren's great-grandchildren
1d *Jane Elizabeth Rogers, *b* 1939; *m* 23 Aug 1958 *Carl William QUANTE, Jr, and has issue:

Great-great-grandchildren's great-great-grandchildren
1e *Carl William QUANTE III, *b* 17 May 1959; *m* 7 Aug 1982 *Sandra Lynn Birch and has issue:

Great-great-grandchildren's great-great-grandchildren's children
1f *Anna Elizabeth QUANTE, *b* 19 April 1989
2f *Victoria Jane QUANTE, *b* 15 Sept 1991

Great-great-grandchildren's great-great-grandchildren
2e *Timothy Alton QUANTE, *b* 26 April 1961; *m* 1st 19— Carrie Lynn Kay and has issue:

Great-great-grandchildren's great-great-grandchildren's children
1f *Christopher Thompson QUANTE, *b* 12 Oct 1985

Great-great-grandchildren's great-great-grandchildren
2e (cont.) Timothy A. Quante *m* 2nd 28 Oct 1989 *Deborah Darnell Roberts
3e *Albert John QUANTE, *b* 16 Feb 1963; *m* 16 Dec 1989 *Alicia Longwater

Great-great-grandchildren's great-grandchildren
2d *Joyce Hunter Rogers, *b* 1940; *m* 10 Aug 1963 *David Roy TYLER and has issue:

Great-great-grandchildren's great-great-grandchildren
1e *David Roy TYLER, Jr, *b* 19 Sept 1964
2e *Michael Edward TYLER, *b* 14 Jan 1967

Great-great-grandchildren's grandchildren
4c James William LOCKETT, Jr, *b* 20 Nov 1920; *m* 1941 *Madie Sapp and *d* 3 April 1978, leaving issue:

Great-great-grandchildren's great-grandchildren
1d *Evelyn Mae Lockett, *b* 1943; *m* 19— *Marion Russell PIERCE and has issue:

Great-great-grandchildren's great-great-grandchildren
1e *Gary Russell PIERCE, *b* 18 March 1965; *m* 7 Nov 1987 *Robin Speegel and has issue:

Great-great-grandchildren's great-great-grandchildren's children
1f *Kristen Lorraine PIERCE, *b* 3 July 1989

Great-great-grandchildren's great-great-grandchildren
2e *Deborah Lynn Pierce, *b* 21 May 1966; *m* 19 Sept 1987 *John Joseph WISE and has issue:

Great-great-grandchildren's great-great-grandchildren's children
1f *John Benjamin WISE, *b* 23 Aug 1989

Great-great-grandchildren's great-grandchildren
2d *Patricia Fay Lockett, *b* 1945; *m* 24 Nov 1965 *Terry James WOODS and has issue:

Great-great-grandchildren's great-great-grandchildren
1e *Alicia Faye Woods, *b* 3 Sept 1966; *m* 11 Feb 1984 *David CARTEE and has issue:

Great-great-grandchildren's great-great-grandchildren's children
1f *Christopher CARTEE, *b* 9 Feb 1985

Great-great-grandchildren's great-great-grandchildren
2e *Terry James WOODS, Jr, *b* 18 Feb 1973

Great-great-grandchildren's great-grandchildren
3d *Martha Anne Lockett, *b* 1950; *m* 16 Aug 1969 *Richard Allen STOOPS and has issue:

Great-great-grandchildren's great-great-grandchildren
1e *Richard Allen STOOPS, Jr, *b* 30 July 1970
2e *Tammy Lynn STOOPS, *b* 22 July 1973
3e *James Patrick STOOPS, *b* 25 July 1981
4e *Jonathan Curtis STOOPS, *b* 25 July 1981

Great-great-grandchildren's great-grandchildren
4d *James William LOCKETT III, *b* 24 June 1956; *m* 1st 29 March 1982 Janice Coleman; *m* 2nd 9 Sept 1989
*Karen Denise Cooper

Great-great-grandchildren's grandchildren
5c *Randolph Eppes LOCKETT, *b* 11 May 1922; *m* 1st 1942 Catherine Roberts; *m* 2nd 4 Sept 1951 *Betty Ruth
Reynolds and with her has issue:

Great-great-grandchildren's great-grandchildren
1d *Randolph Eppes LOCKETT, Jr, *b* 3 Jan 1956; *m* 19— *Raja Mousa Sammor and has issue:

Great-great-grandchildren's great-great-grandchildren
1e *Randolph Sharif LOCKETT, *b* 26 Feb 1992

Great-great-grandchildren's grandchildren
6c *Frederick Buckner LOCKETT, *b* 1930; *m* 19— *Josephine Rodewolt and has issue:

Great-great-grandchildren's great-grandchildren
1d *Cynthia Diane Lockett [Mrs Robert H Herndon, Rte4 Box 5295, Fitzgerald, GA 31750, USA], *b* June 1952;
m 24 May 1975 *Robert Holman HERNDON and has issue:

Great-great-grandchildren's great-great-grandchildren
1e *Lori Kathryn HERNDON, *b* 11 Sept 1980
2e *Kristin Leigh HERNDON, *b* 23 May 1982

Great-great-grandchildren's great-grandchildren
2d *Frederick Buckner LOCKETT, Jr, *b* 18 Jan 1955
3d *David Michael LOCKETT, *b* 29 Jan 1964
4d *Allen John LOCKETT, *b* 10 Aug 1965

Great-great-grandchildren's children
2b William Randolph EPPES, *b* 20 Aug 1892; *m* 2 Jan 1918 Marion Grey McCorkle and *d* 13 Jan 1919, leaving issue:

Great-great-grandchildren's grandchildren
1c William Randolph EPPES, Jr, *b* 25 April, *d* 26 April 1919

Great-great-grandchildren's children
3b Arthur Beverley EPPES, *b* 22 Oct 1893; *m* 1st 1921 Nora Nedra Reddick; *m* 2nd 9 June 1927 *Klara Elizabeth
Schmitt and *d* 8 Aug 1959, having with her had issue:

Great-great-grandchildren's grandchildren
1c *Clara Elizabeth Eppes [Mrs James Evans, 114 Majestic Oaks, Savannah, GA 31406, USA], *b* 20 May 1928; *m*
21 Aug 1948 *James Patrick EVANS and has issue:

Great-great-grandchildren's great-grandchildren
1d *Lynn Carol Evans [Mrs Gary W Moses, 616 Wheeler St, Savannah, GA 31405, USA], *b* 12 Dec 1952; *m* 25
Aug 1973 *Gary W. MOSES and has issue:

Great-great-grandchildren's great-great-grandchildren
1e *Karen Lynn MOSES, *b* 27 March 1978
2e *Leslie Ann MOSES, *b* 11 Feb 1980

Great-great-grandchildren's great-grandchildren
2d *Randolph James EVANS [2980 Pennsylvania St, Melbourne, FL 32904, USA], *b* Frankfurt, Germany, 13 Feb 1955; *educ* Us of Oklahoma and Georgia; scientist/meteorologist with Ensco Inc; *m* 27 Dec 1979 *Adrienne Eloise, dau of Robert Eugene Wolfard and his w Mildred Eloise Carr and formerly w of —— Evans, and has issue:

Great-great-grandchildren's great-great-grandchildren
1e *Mason Randolph EVANS, *b* Melbourne, Fla., 29 Aug 1985
2e *Jordan Thomas EVANS, *b* Melbourne 7 July 1988

Great-great-grandchildren's great-grandchildren
3d *David Arthur EVANS [Rte 3 Box 314-C, Winder, GA 30680, USA], *b* 12 July 1957; *m* 1 April 1989 *Catherine Clayton and has issue:

Great-great-grandchildren's great-great-grandchildren
1e *Erin Michelle EVANS, *b* 27 Aug 1991

Great-great-grandchildren's great-grandchildren
4d *Nancy Elizabeth EVANS, *b* 12 July 1957
5d *Robert Patrick EVANS [1234 Druid Knoll Dve, Atlanta, GA 30319, USA], *b* 1 March 1962

Great-great-grandchildren's children
4b Irene Ada Eppes, *b* 23 Oct 1895; *m* 10 July 1939 *Thomas Maloney HALLAM and *d* 19 Sept 1980
5b *Catherine Eppes, *b* 21 May 1897; *m* 1st 20 May 1925 Joseph Forrester BUCKNER and has had issue:

Great-great-grandchildren's grandchildren
1c *Emily Bancroft Buckner [Mrs William Ratcliffe, 409 East 49th Street, Savannah, GA 31405, USA], *b* 16 April 1926; *m* May 1948 *Arthur CODY, Jr, and has issue:

Great-great-grandchildren's great-grandchildren
1d *Craig Stephens CODY, *b* 29 July 1949; *m* 1st 28 May 1977 *Lynn Mydell Leggett and has issue:

Great-great-grandchildren's great-great-grandchildren
1e *Catharine Courtenay CODY, *b* 18 Aug 1981

Great-great-grandchildren's great-grandchildren
1d (cont.) Craig S. Cody *m* 2nd 13 Feb 1988 *Leigh O'Connor
2d *Donald Alan CODY, *b* 23 Aug 1951; *m* 23 April 1978 *Hulda Lynn Tillman and has issue:

Great-great-grandchildren's great-great-grandchildren
1e *Robert Arthur CODY, *b* 21 Feb 1981
2e *Emily Grace CODY, *b* 19 Jan 1984
3e *William Allen Gaston CODY, *b* 10 Feb 1986

Great-great-grandchildren's great-grandchildren
3d *Arthur Gary CODY, *b* 6 Dec 1954

Great-great-grandchildren's grandchildren
2c Joseph Forrester BUCKNER, Jr, *b* 16 April 1928; *d* 30 May 1941

Great-great-grandchildren's children
5b (cont.) Catherine Eppes Buckner *m* 2nd Dec 1952 *William E. RATCLIFFE
6b Thomas Jefferson EPPES, *b* Athens, Ga., 7 Feb 1899; *m* 1st Augusta, Ga., 11 Oct 1919 (divorce 19—) Lilla Camille (*b* Thompson, Ga., 15 Sept 1895; *d* Athens, Ga., Sept 1976), dau of Thomas Bowdre Hamilton and his w Lilla Lee Hunt, and had issue:

Great-great-grandchildren's grandchildren
1c *Gloria Camille Eppes [Mrs Joseph McDavid, 10219 Scout Drive, Fairfax, VA 22030, USA], *b* Orlando, Fla., 13 Nov 1926; *m* 1st Valdosta, Ga., 29 July 1947 (divorce 19—) Francis Xavier MULHERRIN, Jr (*b* Augusta, Ga., 13 March 1913), s of Francis Xavier Mulherrin and his w Eulalia, and has issue:

Great-great-grandchildren's great-grandchildren
1d *Linda Anne McDavid (*b* Mulherrin but took stepf's name 1966), *b* Augusta, Ga., 21 April 1948; *m* 1st Athens, Ga., 30 Dec 1976 (divorce 19—) Arthur Eugene STURGILL, Jr (*b* El Paso, Tex., 6 Jan 1947), s of Arthur Eugene Sturgill and his w Curtis Strain, and has issue:

Great-great-grandchildren's great-great-grandchildren
1e *Christine Camille STURGILL, *b* Athens, Ga., 14 May 1969

Great-great-grandchildren's great-grandchildren
1d (cont.) Mrs Linda McDavid Sturgill *m* 2nd Fairfax, Va., 25 Nov 1978 *Donald Conard EARMAN (*b* 17 June 1939), s of Randolph N. Earman and his w Dorothy A. Conard

Great-great-grandchildren's grandchildren
1c (cont.) Mrs Gloria Eppes Mulherrin *m* 2nd Athens, Ga., 16 Sept 1949 *Joseph Terrell McDAVID (*b* Lowell, Mass., 12 Oct 1926), s of Hubert H. McDavid and his w Laura Henderson, and has further issue:

Great-great-grandchildren's great-grandchildren
2d *Gloria Elizabeth McDavid, *b* Memphis, Tenn., 15 Aug 1953; *m* Dallas 23 Sept 1973 *Gene Craig STEPHENS (*b* Dallas 12 Nov 1949), s of David H. Stephens, Sr, and his w Alice, and has issue:

Great-great-grandchildren's great-great-grandchildren
1e *Katie Marie STEPHENS, *b* Dallas 7 Dec 1979

Great-great-grandchildren's great-grandchildren
3d *Carole Hamilton McDAVID, *b* Memphis, Tenn., 5 Nov 1954

Great-great-grandchildren's children
6b (cont.) Thomas J. Eppes *m* 2nd, as her 2nd husb, Eunice Burrell, *née* Treadwell, and *d* Atlanta, Ga., Oct 1962
7b William Eston EPPES III, *b* 3 Oct 1901; *d* 11 Jan 1919
8b *Marion Theresa Eppes [Mrs William Moss, 6603 Vernon Street, La Grange, GA 30240, USA], *b* 20 Oct 1904; *m* 16 May 1928 *William Byrd MOSS and has issue:

Great-great-grandchildren's grandchildren
1c *William Lee MOSS, *b* 14 Feb 1929; *m* 24 Dec 1950 *Betty Ann Rieber and has issue:

Great-great-grandchildren's great-grandchildren
1d *John Michael MOSS, *b* 6 Oct 1951
2d *Theresa Anne MOSS, *b* 25 April 1954
3d *William Scott MOSS, *b* 5 Nov 1959
4d *Judith Marie MOSS, *b* 25 Jan 1962

Great-great-grandchildren's grandchildren
2c *Mary Catharine Moss, *b* 3 June 1931; *m* 26 Feb 1949 *Thomas James WOODS and has issue:

Great-great-grandchildren's great-grandchildren
1d *James Anthony WOODS, *b* 14 Dec 1949; *m* 9 June 1969 *Cynthia Margaret Johnson and has issue:

Great-great-grandchildren's great-great-grandchildren
1e *Stephen Lance WOODS, *b* 12 Jan 1970

Great-great-grandchildren's great-grandchildren
2d *David William WOODS, *b* 19 Nov 1954
3d *Richard Lee WOODS, *b* 4 Dec 1955

Great-great-grandchildren's grandchildren
3c *John Hill MOSS [3112 Quimby Road, Virginia Beach, VA 23452, USA], *b* 17 July 1937; *m* 13 June 1959 *Joy Louise Pickler and has issue:

Great-great-grandchildren's great-grandchildren
1d *Daniel Lee MOSS, *b* 1 Sept 1960
2d *John Eric MOSS, *b* 21 Jan 1962
3d *Steven Patrick MOSS, *b* 2 July 1964
4d *Julia Elizabeth MOSS, *b* 12 July 1969

Great-great-grandchildren's children
9b Revd Benjamin Scott EPPES, *b* 5 Aug 1906; *m* 28 June 1932 *Frances Watkins Crane and *d* 1 Jan 1989, leaving issue:

Great-great-grandchildren's grandchildren
1c *Frances Crane Eppes, *b* 21 Dec 1933; *m* 4 June 1954 *Albert Whitman BRAME and has issue:

Great-great-grandchildren's great-grandchildren
1d *Anne Catherine Brame, *b* 11 Nov 1954; *m* 10 Sept 1988 *David Sheldon BAKER
2d *Albert Whitman BRAME, Jr, *b* 8 April 1956; *m* 1st 15 Sept 1979 Teri Louise Lee and has issue:

Great-great-grandchildren's great-great-grandchildren
1e *Caroline Lee BRAME, *b* 31 Aug 1981
2e *Catherine Ward BRAME, *b* 15 Oct 1984

Great-great-grandchildren's great-grandchildren
2d (cont.) Albert W. Brame, Jr, *m* 2nd 13 April 1991 *Ruthanne Kohler
3d *Scott Eppes BRAME, *b* 8 Dec 1958; *m* 15 Oct 1988 *Melissa Ionta

Great-great-grandchildren's grandchildren
2c *Amalia Scott Eppes, *b* 29 Jan 1937; *m* 17 Aug 1960 *Howard Griffin ROGERS and has issue:

Great-great-grandchildren's great-grandchildren
1d *Katherine Rogers, *b* 30 Aug 1962; *m* 1st 19— ——; *m* 2nd 14 April 1990 *Donnie Pierre DEVALCOURT
2d *Howard Griffin ROGERS, Jr, 15 Sept 1966; *m* 17 Aug 1991 *Ana Gloria Basas Borbolla
3d *William Scott ROGERS, *b* 15 July 1969

Great-great-grandchildren's grandchildren
3c *Benjamin Scott EPPES, Jr, *b* 17 April 1943; *m* 24 July 1964 *Sandra Lee Amerson and has issue:

Great-great-grandchildren's great-grandchildren
1d *Denesse Irene Eppes [Mrs Todd R Iocco, 2311 Creek Meadows Dve, Missouri City, TX 77459, USA], *b* Jasper, Ala., 29 April 1965; *educ* Texas Women's U; registered nurse; *m* 8 Oct 1988 *Todd Robert IOCCO, s of Georgia L. Iocco, and has issue:

Great-great-grandchildren's great-great-grandchildren
1e *April Lee IOCCO, *b* Houston, Tex., 8 April 1992

Great-great-grandchildren's great-grandchildren
2d *Benjamin Scott EPPES III [1250 Hillside Lane, Lumberton, TX 77656, USA], *b* 14 Nov 1972
3d *Christopher Lee EPPES, *b* 31 July 1977

Great-great-grandchildren
8a John Wayles EPPES, *b* 1866; *d* 1874
9a Emily Bancroft EPPES, *b* Clarksville, Ga., 1868; *d* 1873
10a Edward Bancroft EPPES, *b* Clarksville 1868 (twin with Emily); *m* Spartanburg, S Carolina, 1 July 1908 Jennie (*b* Eufaula, Ala., 10 Feb 1886; *d* there 27 Sept 1965), dau of John Marshall Kendall and his w Sally Jennings, and *d* Augusta, Ga., 1918, leaving issue:

Great-great-grandchildren's children
1b Dr John Kendall EPPES, *b* Augusta 13 Sept 1916; *m* Salt Lake City, Utah, 16 July 1943 *Nell Richardson [Mrs John Eppes, 210 East Broad Street, Box 557, Eufaula, AL 36027, USA] (*b* Baton Rouge, La., 1919), dau of Edward Carroll Reilly and his w Hilda Richardson, and *d* Birmingham, Ala., 7 May 1974, leaving issue:

Great-great-grandchildren's grandchildren
1c *(John) Kendall EPPES, Jr [5440 Woodford Dve, Birmingham, AL 35242, USA; 534 W Broad St, Eufaula, AL, USA], *b* Eufaula 9 Dec 1944; *m* 1st Abbeville, Ala., 26 Jan 1965 *Carol (*b* Fort Wayne, Ind., 4 Oct 1944), dau of Donald I. Reaves and his w Joanne Gunter, and has issue:

Great-great-grandchildren's great-grandchildren
1d *John Kendall EPPES III [Route 1 Box 135, Fairhope, AL 36532, USA], *b* Opelika, Ala., 6 Dec 1966
2d *David Marshall EPPES, *b* Baton Rouge, La., 29 July 1969; *m* 8 Jan 1993 *Carol Louise Vick and has issue:

Great-great-grandchildren's great-great-grandchildren
1e *Clayton Ivy EPPES (s), *b* 14 Dec 1990

Great-great-grandchildren's grandchildren
1c (cont.) Kendall Eppes, Jr, *m* 2nd 14 Feb 1982 *Sunny Ann Rainey Clowdus

Great-great-grandchildren
11a Maria Jefferson EPPES, *b* 1871; *d* 1916

Great-grandchildren
(4) (cont.) Revd William Eston Eppes *m* 2nd 1877 Augusta Jones Kollock (*d* 1896) and *d* in his 2nd w's mother's house nr Clarksville, Ga., 25 April 1896
(5) Mary Elizabeth Cleland EPPES, *b* L'Eau Noir 5 July 1832; *d* 1903
(6) Francis EPPES, *b* L'Eau Noir April 1835; *d* in infancy

Grandchildren
2 Francis Wayles Eppes *m* 2nd 15 March 1837, as her 2nd husb, Susan Margaret, dau of Nicholas Ware (*b* 1769; Memb Georgia House of Reps 1808-11 and 1814-15, Mayor of Augusta 1819-21, US Senator from Georgia 1821-24; *d* 7 Sept 1824) and his w Susan Brooks Carr and widow of —— Couch or Crouch, and *d* 30 May 1881, having with her had issue:

Great-grandchildren
(7) Susan Frances Eppes, *b* Tallahassee, Fla., 15 March 1839; *m* St John's Episcopal Church, Tallahassee (her bro Revd William Eppes officiating), 25 April 1861 John Armstrong CRAIG (*d* 1885), s of Dr John Adam Craig, of Baltimore, and *d* Tallahassee 21 Jan 1908, leaving issue:

Great-great-grandchildren
1a John Armstrong CRAIG, Jr, *b* 8 Dec 1862; *d* 17 Sept 1927
2a Frances Maude Craig, *b* 28 Jan 1870; *m* 27 Oct 1906 Albert George GOODBODY and *d* 30 Sept 1952, leaving issue:

Great-great-grandchildren's children

1b Amy Goodbody, *b* 14 Dec 1907; *m* 30 Sept 1947 Dr George Lester PATTERSON (*d* 19 April 1985) and *d* 23 April 1988; Dr and Mrs George L. Patterson adopted a dau:

a *Margaret Ann Patterson, *b* 2 March 1951; *m* 1st 17 Dec 1971 William Shannon PHILIPS and has issue:

i *William Shane PHILIPS, *b* 13 Aug 1974

a (cont.) Margaret Patterson Philips *m* 2nd 13 April 1978 *Terry Newton GAMBLE

Great-great-grandchildren

3a Francis Eppes CRAIG, *b* 25 Feb 1872; *m* 7 Sept 1921 his 1st cousin Mary Armstrong Forbes, *née* Craig, a widow, and *d* 22 Aug 1927

Great-grandchildren

(8) Maria Jefferson Eppes, *b* 12 April 1840; *m* 1868 Dr William Francis SHINE (*educ* Tallahassee Seminary and U of Georgia (MD), Surgeon in Gen Beauregard's Div Confederate States Army; *d* St Augustine, Fla., 21 Oct 1910), s of Capt R. A. Shine, Memb Tallahassee City Cncl, and *d* 1897, leaving issue:

Great-great-grandchildren

1a Dr Francis Eppes SHINE, *b* St Augustine, Fla., 13 Jan 1871; *m* 2 Aug 1904 Ann Barker (*b* Toronto, Canada, 1874; *d* Los Angeles 29 April 1955, *bur* Monticello) and *d* Paris, France, 8 Sept 1922 (*bur* Monticello), leaving issue:

Great-great-grandchildren's children

1b Francis Eppes SHINE, Jr, *b* 13 May 1906; *m* 19— *Elinor Goodrich and *d* 29 May 1985 (*bur* Monticello), leaving issue:

Great-great-grandchildren's grandchildren

1c *Cdr Francis Eppes SHINE III, USN (ret) [5567 Cameo Dve N, Boca Raton, FL 33433, USA], *b* 16 Jan 1933; *educ* Cate Sch, Stanford U and Stanford Law Sch; USN 1955-57 (active reserve 1957-75), lawyer 1960-89; *m* 1st 26 July 1958 Alice C., dau of Samuel Graff Miller and his w Christine Brandt, and has issue:

Great-great-grandchildren's great-grandchildren

1d *Christine Eppes SHINE [812 S Arlington Mill Dve, Arlington, VA 22204, USA], *b* 2 Oct 1960
2d *Ann Wayles Shine [Mrs Glenn A Craig, Rte7 Box 774, Harpers Ferry, WV 25425, USA], *b* 27 March 1962; *m* 17 May 1991 *Glenn Alexander CRAIG
3d *John Randolph SHINE [11 Robinhood Lane, Northfield, IL 60093, USA], *b* 9 Sept 1966

Great-great-grandchildren's grandchildren

1c (cont.) Cdr Francis E. Shine III *m* 2nd 1 Feb 1985 *Janet Dale, dau of Oliver B. Jaynes and his w Frankie Dale

Great-great-grandchildren's children

2b Randolph Eppes SHINE, *b* 9 July 1907; *m* 29 April 1950 *Bernice Johnson Reed and *d* 7 Jan 1982
3b *Elizabeth Shine [Mrs Semler Shine, 942 Valencia Mesa Drive, Fullerton, CA 92632, USA], *b* 7 Nov 1912; *m* 19— (divorce 1938) Adolf SEMLER and has issue:

Great-great-grandchildren's grandchildren

1c *Anne Leys Semler [Mrs Francisco Muñoz, 1824 Sun Crest, El Cajon, CA 92021, USA], *b* Los Angeles 29 Sept 1935; *educ* Bishops Sch and U of S California; music teacher; *m* 11 Oct 1969 *Francisco MUNOZ

Great-grandchildren

(9) Nicholas Ware EPPES, *b* Tallahassee 1 Nov 1843; *educ* West Florida Seminary; Lt Confederate States Army, Superintendent Public Instruction, Leon Co, Fla., 1884-1900 (re-elected 1904 but did not live to reassume office); *m* 1 Nov 1866 Susan Branch (*b* 3 March 1846; author: *The Negro of the Old South* and *Through Some Eventful Years*; *d* 2 July 1942), dau of Dr Edward Bradford and his w Martha Lewis Henry, and *d* 3 Sept 1904 after being shot in the street by a person or persons unknown, having had issue:

Great-great-grandchildren

1a Edward Bradford EPPES, *b* 15 March 1868; *d* 25 Jan 1934
2a Susan Ware EPPES, *b* 8 May 1871; *d* 30 Dec 1965
3a Francis EPPES, *b* 25 March 1874; *d* 28 July 1875
4a Martha Branch Eppes, *b* 18 Aug 1876; *m* 24 June 1903 Richard H. BRADFORD and *d* 17 April 1964
5a Elizabeth Cleland EPPES, *b* 15 Feb 1882; *d* 20 Feb 1950
6a Alice Bradford EPPES, *b* 24 Jan 1886; *d* 13 Oct 1962

Great-grandchildren

(10) Mary EPPES, *b* 1845; *d* in infancy
(11) (Martha) Virginia Eppes, *b* Tallahassee 14 Nov 1847; *m* 1st 1867 Thomas Jabez SHINE (*b* 14 Oct 1842; Capt Co F 1st Florida Cavalry Confederate States Army Civil War, Clerk Circuit Court Orange Co, Fla., Dir First Nat Bank, Orlando, fndr and commander Orlando Gds (after his death renamed Shine Guards in his honour); collapsed and *d* 20 April 1899 after exercising the guards on a day of extreme heat), s of Capt R. A. Shine and bro of Dr William F. Shine (*see above* against (8)), and had issue:

Great-great-grandchildren

1a Lillias Eleanor Shine, *b* 5 May 1867; *m* 14 April 1914 Frank Bryant STONEMAN (*b* Indianapolis, Ind., 26 June 1857; *d* Miami 1 Feb 1941), s of Dr Mark D. Stoneman and his w Áletha White, and *d* 6 March 1956

2a Dr Francis Wayles SHINE, *b* 25 June 1874; *m* 14 May 1938 Edna Bedell, *née* Wood, a widow, and *d* 24 Sept 1941 (*bur* Monticello)

3a Richard Alexander SHINE, *b* 28 May 1876; *m* 1907 Rose Boyd and *d* 1931, having had issue:

Great-great-grandchildren's children

1b *Richard Alexander SHINE, Jr, *b* 29 July 1910; *m* 1932 *Gladys ———

2b Virginia Elizabeth SHINE, *b* 18 April 1913; *d* 1946

3b *William Boyd SHINE, *b* 30 Sept 1924

Great-great-grandchildren

4a Thomas Jefferson SHINE, *b* 1881; *d* 1884

5a William Eston SHINE, *b* 18 May 1885; *m* 19 April 1911 Florence Dunn Howard and *d* 8 Jan 1913

Great-grandchildren

(11) (cont.) Martha Virginia Eppes Shine *m* 2nd 1891 Revd Henry Williston GREATHAM, Episcopalian clergyman, and *d* 9 Sept 1920

(12) Robert Francis EPPES, *b* Tallahassee 19 May 1851; *m* 15 Nov 1881 Martha Rebecca Whitehead and *d* 12 Feb 1894 of fever, having had issue:

Great-great-grandchildren

1a Amos Whitehead EPPES, *b* 1883; *d* 1890

2a Susan Margaret Eppes, *b* 12 Jan 1886; *m* 22 May 1907 Hugh Moultrie GRIFFIN (*b* 8 July 1880; *d* 14 May 1958) and *d* 21 Dec 1971, having had issue:

Great-great-grandchildren's children

1b *Susan Ola Griffin [Mrs Thomas McRorie, 620 South East Fourth Avenue, Gainesville, FL 32601, USA], *b* Tallahassee, Fla., 24 June 1908; *m* 24 May 1935 *Thomas H. McRORIE, Jr (*b* 8 Dec 1913), s of Thomas Henry McRorie and his w Emma, and has issue:

Great-great-grandchildren's grandchildren

1c *Thomas Henry McRORIE, Jr [9642 Bay Meadow Drive, Huntington Beach, CA 92646, USA], *b* Raleigh, N Carolina, 28 Oct 1936; *m* Gainesville, Fla., 30 Jan 1958 *Joyce, dau of Harold Monck and his w Eleanor, and has issue:

Great-great-grandchildren's great-grandchildren

1d *Thomas Hugh McRORIE, *b* Gainesville 7 Sept 1962

2d *James Michael McRORIE, *b* Gainesville 6 Oct 1964

3d *Devon Lynn McRORIE, *b* Scotland, UK, 27 Nov 1967

Great-great-grandchildren's grandchildren

2c *Hugh Larry McRORIE [PO Box 1413, Lakeland, FL 33802, USA], *b* Jacksonville, Fla., 19 Dec 1938; *m* Lakeland, Fla., 19 July 1972 *Camie McClelland

Great-great-grandchildren's children

2b Hugh Moultrie GRIFFIN, Jr, *b* Waldo, Fla., 18 Sept 1911; *d* Gainesville 3 June 1951

3b Helen Martha Griffin, *b* Waldo 21 May 1914; *m* 1st Marcus DAUGHTRY; *m* 2nd 16 July 1945 (divorce 1973) Horace L. MOCK and *d* Aug 1982

4b Richard Eppes GRIFFIN, *b* Waldo 5 June 1921; *m* Clayton, Ga., 30 March 1946 *Eva Ruth (*b* Abbeville, S Carolina, 16 March 1925), dau of Bennett G. Campbell and his w Essie, and *d* 2 Sept 1987, leaving issue:

Great-great-grandchildren's grandchildren

1c *Margaret Jeanette Griffin [Mrs Kenneth L Bostwick, PO Box 297, Waldo, FL 32694, USA], *b* Gainesville 12 March 1947; *m* 1st Waldo 2 Sept 1967 (divorce 1973) Martin FRYAR; *m* 2nd 14 Aug 1979 *Kenneth L. BOSTWICK (*b* Dayton, Ohio, 31 Jan 1942), s of Kenneth L. Bostwick and his w Elizabeth

2c *Evelyn Anne Griffin [Mrs Sammy Walden, 2020 Old Grantham Rd, Goldsboro, NC 27530, USA], *b* Jacksonville, Fla., 21 Jan 1949; *educ* Us of Florida and East Carolina; elementary teacher 1971-; *m* Waldo, Fla., 22 Jan 1970 *Samuel (Sammy) Carelock WALDEN (*b* Paris Island, S Carolina, 20 Jan 1948), s of William L. Walden and his w Genevieve, and has issue:

Great-great-grandchildren's great-grandchildren

1d *Samuel Carelock WALDEN, Jr, *b* Goldsboro 24 May 1976

2d *Susan Margaret WALDEN, *b* Goldsboro 24 Aug 1977

Great-great-grandchildren's grandchildren

3c *Sherry Lee Griffin [Mrs David A Edwards, 210 Smythe Dve, Summerville, SC 29483, USA], *b* Gainesville 16 Aug 1950; *m* 28 Jan 1972 *David A. EDWARDS and has issue:

Great-great-grandchildren's great-grandchildren
1d *Renee Lynn EDWARDS, b Goldsboro, N Carolina, 5 Jan 1974
2d *Wesley David EDWARDS, b England 14 June 1977

Great-great-grandchildren's children
5b *Cladie Ruth Griffin [Mrs William Dees, PO Box 626, Waldo, FL 32694, USA], b Waldo 5 June 1923; m there 13 Feb 1943 *William Clyde DEES (b Fla. 21 Sept 1923), s of Marvin C. Dees and his w Minnie, and has issue:

Great-great-grandchildren's grandchildren
1c *Margaret Elizabeth Dees [Mrs John F Peters, 4326 NW 115th Street, Gainesville, FL 32606, USA], b Jacksonville, Fla., 25 Nov 1943; m 1st 2 June 1962 (divorce 1972) Clayton Averitte JONES and has issue:

Great-great-grandchildren's great-grandchildren
1d *Clayton Averitte JONES, Jr [c/o Mrs J F Peters, 4326 NW 15th St, Gainesville, FL 32606, USA], b 31 Jan 1963; m 19— *Theresa —— and has issue:

Great-great-grandchildren's great-great-grandchildren
1e *Leah Lynn JONES, b 20 Jan 1986
2e *Courtney Amanda JONES, b 30 Oct 1987

Great-great-grandchildren's great-grandchildren
2d *James Edward JONES [c/o Mrs J F Peters, 4326 NW 15th St, Gainesville, FL 32606, USA], b 1 Jan 1964; m 19— *Beth Van Nostrum and has issue:

Great-great-grandchildren's great-great-grandchildren
1e *Jayson Alexander JONES, b 29 April 1987

Great-great-grandchildren's grandchildren
1c (cont.) Mrs Margaret Jones m 2nd 1972 Horace De Wayne BRUCE (b 11 June 1941); m 3rd 16 Sept 1983 *John Franklin PETERS
2c *William Clyde DEES, b Gainesville 28 Feb 1947; m 1st 1 Dec 1966 (divorce 1968) Sharon Ann Kennedy and has issue:

Great-great-grandchildren's great-grandchildren
1d *Louie Ann DEES, b 12 July 1967

Great-great-grandchildren's grandchildren
2c (cont.) William Clyde Dees m 2nd 1968 *Carolyn J. Beazlie and with her has issue:

Great-great-grandchildren's great-grandchildren
2d *Brenda Renée DEES, b 8 Sept 1969

Great-great-grandchildren
3a Francis EPPES, b 1887; d 18— or 19—
4a Thomas Jefferson EPPES, b 1890; m 29 March 1914 Nannie Edrie Bowen and d 13 Nov 1972, leaving issue:

Great-great-grandchildren's children
1b *Thomas Jefferson EPPES, Jr [2630 Riverhead Drive, Ruskin, FL 33570, USA], b 24 Aug 1916; m 1944 *Kathleen Newton and has issue:

Great-great-grandchildren's grandchildren
1c *Rosemary Edrie EPPES, b 19—
2c *Rebecca Diane EPPES, b 19—

Great-great-grandchildren's children
2b *Revd Jack (Francis Edward) EPPES [219 W 7th Ave, Tallahassee, FL 32303, USA], b 17 Oct 1917
3b *Richard Llewellyn EPPES [714 Tuscarora Trail, Maitland, FL 32751, USA], b 27 Jan 1919; m 15 July 1944 *Estelle Brewer and has issue:

Great-great-grandchildren's grandchildren
1c *Wanda EPPES, b 11 Oct 1945

Great-great-grandchildren's children
4b *James Alfred EPPES [219 West 7th Ave, Tallahassee, FL 32751, USA], b 24 Jan 1921; m 19— *Martha Ann Stelts (b 1927) and has issue:

Great-great-grandchildren's grandchildren
1c *Marguerite Eppes, b 9 Sept 1945; m 7 March 1964 *Arthur Charles GLASGOW, Jr, and has issue:

Great-great-grandchildren's great-grandchildren
1d *Virginia Anne GLASGOW, b 13 June 1979

Great-great-grandchildren's grandchildren
2c *Susan Bradford Eppes, b 23 Feb 1947; m 1st 1964 Billy McLAIN and has issue:

Great-great-grandchildren's great-grandchildren
1d *Susan Page McLAIN, *b* 4 May 1966

Great-great-grandchildren's grandchildren
2c (cont.) Susan Eppes McLain *m* 2nd 19— *Wilton L. REDDICK and has issue:

Great-great-grandchildren's great-grandchildren
2d *Philip Causey REDDICK, *b* 7 Feb 1970
3d *Richard Thomas REDDICK, *b* 3 Nov 1972

Great-great-grandchildren's grandchildren
3c *Martha Lucille Eppes, *b* 18 Jan 1950; *m* 19— *John DuBOSE and has issue:

Great-great-grandchildren's great-grandchildren
1d *John Paul DuBOSE, *b* 7 July 1969

Great-great-grandchildren's grandchildren
4c *James Alfred EPPES, Jr, *b* 2 Aug 1956

Great-great-grandchildren's children
5b *Nicholas Ware EPPES, *b* 4 Nov 1923; *m* 4 Oct 1952 *Betty Fletcher and has issue:

Great-great-grandchildren's grandchildren
1c *Nicholas Ware EPPES, Jr [1409 Ferzon Way, Tallahassee, FL, USA], *b* 17 May 1955; *m* 20 Oct 1980 *Rebecca Sizemore and has issue:

Great-great-grandchildren's great-grandchildren
1d *Nicholas Ware EPPES III, *b* 1 June 1982
2d *Lindsey Rebecca EPPES, *b* 13 July 1984
3d *Megan Elizabeth EPPES, *b* 31 Oct 1989

Great-great-grandchildren's grandchildren
2c *Jeffery Fletcher EPPES [7404 Candle Wood, Tallahassee, FL, USA], *b* 27 May 1960; *m* 3 Nov 1978 *Charlotte Joyce Robinson and has issue:

Great-great-grandchildren's great-grandchildren
1d *Bradford Jeffery EPPES, *b* 10 Feb 1980
2d *Christopher Fletcher EPPES, *b* 27 April 1983
3d *Andrew Ryan EPPES, *b* 30 May 1987
4d *Candace Elizabeth EPPES, *b* 11 Sept 1990

Great-great-grandchildren's grandchildren
3c *Scott Patrick EPPES [2465 Talpeco Hills Dve, Tallahassee, FL 32303, USA], *b* 6 May 1967

Great-great-grandchildren
5a Sarah Ruth EPPES, *b* 1894; *d* 13 Feb 1981

Great-grandchildren
(13) Caroline Matilda Eppes, *b* Tallahassee 26 July 1857; *m* Athens, Ga., 30 Oct 1882 David Shepard SHINE (*educ* U of Georgia; Depy Clerk of Courts Orlando, Fla., Postmaster Orlando; *d* 12 Oct 1939), s of Capt R. A. Shine and bro of Dr William F. Shine and Thomas J. Shine (*see above* against (8) and (11)) and *d* 20 Jan 1940, having had issue:

Great-great-grandchildren
1a Dudley Shepard SHINE, *b* 19 Dec 1886; *m* 29 Dec 1909 Theodosia Bellamy (who *m* 2nd Cyril Norman Boland), only dau of George Morrison and his w Mary Eppes, and *d* June 1933, leaving issue (for whom *see above*)
2a Wharton Hume SHINE, *b* 1887; *d* 1888
3a Dr Cecil Eppes SHINE, *b* 28 Sept 1888; *m* 13 Dec 1917 Alice Munnerlyn (*b* 21 July 1889; *d* 29 June 1953) and *d* 7 Dec 1963, leaving issue:

Great-great-grandchildren's children
1b *Cecil Eppes SHINE, Jr, *b* 11 June 1919; *m* 2 June 1943 *Jessie Jones and has issue:

Great-great-grandchildren's grandchildren
1c *Elizabeth Eppes SHINE, *b* 27 Oct 1946
2c *Cecil Eppes SHINE III, *b* 11 Nov 1948
3c *Marilyn SHINE, *b* 23 July 1951

Great-great-grandchildren's children
2b *Sarah Coachman Shine [12827 Eileen Lane, Jacksonville, FL 32258, USA], *b* Jacksonville 13 Jan 1921; *m* 7 Sept 1946 *Jesse Wayne MILLER, s of Daniel Helt Miller and his w Julia Logan, and has issue:

Great-great-grandchildren's grandchildren
1c *Daniel Wayne MILLER [1126 Hutch Lane, Snellville, GA 30278, USA], *b* Jacksonville 22 Aug 1947; *m* Toccoa, Ga., 2 June 1973 *Wanda Joanne Holland and has issue:

Great-great-grandchildren's great-grandchildren
1d *Leigh Ann MILLER, b 13 Aug 1975
2d *Daniel Wayne MILLER, Jr, b 26 Oct 1977

Great-great-grandchildren's grandchildren
2c *Jane Miller [Mrs Raymond Wallace, 3034 Kellogg Creek Rd, Acworth, GA 30102, USA], b Patuxent, Md., 27 Oct 1950; m Ga. 14 Nov 1976 *Raymond WALLACE and has issue:

Great-great-grandchildren's great-grandchildren
1d *Julie Christine WALLACE, b 30 Nov 1982
2d *Jessica Rae WALLACE, b 23 Aug 1985

Great-great-grandchildren's grandchildren
3c *David Wendell MILLER [9915 Beauclerc Terrace, Jacksonville, FL 32217, USA], b Jacksonville 18 Aug 1954; m there 17 Jan 1981 *Jerry Barlow
4c *Ann MILLER [12827 Eileen Lane, Jacksonville, FL 32258, USA], b Bethesda, Md., 23 March 1957

Great-great-grandchildren's children
3b *Caroline Eppes Shine, b 9 Feb 1926; m 6 May 1950 *Judson MARSHALL and has issue:

Great-great-grandchildren's grandchildren
1c *Sarah Alice MARSHALL, b 11 July 1955

Great-great-grandchildren's children
4b *James Munnerlyn SHINE [Switzerland Route, 1984 Eventide Rd, Green Cove Springs, FL 32259, USA], b 14 Jan 1928; m 12 March 1955 *Mary Julia Tonnisen and has issue:

Great-great-grandchildren's grandchildren
1c *James Munnerlyn SHINE, Jr [216 Northwest Ave I, Belle Glade, FL 33430, USA], b 8 April 1958; m 13 June 1987 *Dr Margaret Bly Hoover Lindrose and has issue:

Great-great-grandchildren's great-grandchildren
1d *Sarah Elizabeth SHINE, b 6 April 1991

Great-great-grandchildren's grandchildren
2c *Wallace Tonnisen SHINE, b 28 Dec 1959

Great-great-grandchildren
3a *Margaret Virginia Shine, b 15 Jan 1890; m 15 July 1917 Harold W. WILSON (d 1955) and has had issue:

Great-great-grandchildren's children
1b Margaret Shine WILSON, b and d 10 Feb 1920
2b *Margaret Virginia Wilson, b 17 Sept 1921; m 19— *Guy BAILEY and has issue:

Great-great-grandchildren's grandchildren
1c *Susan Ware BAILEY, b 1953

Great-great-grandchildren
4a Lillias Eleanor SHINE, b 1894; d 1895

Grandchildren
3 Maria Jefferson EPPES, b Edgehill 15 Feb 1804; d July 1807

President Jefferson's daughters
V Lucy Elizabeth JEFFERSON, b Monticello 3 Nov 1780; d there 15 April 1781
VI Lucy Elizabeth JEFFERSON, b Monticello 8 May 1782; d Eppington c 13 Oct 1784 of whooping cough

MALE LINE ANCESTRY AND COLLATERAL DESCENDANTS

Thomas JEFFERSON, b 16—; farmer, wolf-hunter and surveyor, settled in Virginia, owning plantation in Henrico Co by 1677, did jury duty; m c 1678/9, as her 1st husb, Mary (sometimes called Martha; she m 2nd on or after 16/17 Nov 1700 Joseph Mattocks or Mattox, of Charles City Co), dau of Christopher Branch, Jr, and gdau of Christopher Branch, of Kingsland, Chesterfield Co, Virginia, and his w Mary Addie, and d before 7 Dec 1697, leaving issue:

I Martha Jefferson; m —— WINN
II Capt Thomas JEFFERSON, Jr

The s,
    Capt Thomas JEFFERSON, Jr, of Jefferson's landing (later known as Osborne's), Chesterfield Co, Virginia, b probably

Henrico Co *c* 1679; a 'gentleman justice' of Henrico Co 1706-24, High Sheriff Henrico Co 1718-19, Capt of Militia; *m* 1st (?) Henrico Co on or after 20 Oct 1697 Mary (*b* 3 Feb 1679/80; *d* 13 Aug 1715), er dau of Maj Peter Field, of Henrico and New Kent Counties, and his 2nd w Judith, widow of Capt Henry Randolph, of Henrico County, and dau of Henry Soane, of James City County, Speaker Virginia House of Burgesses, and had issue:

I Judith Jefferson, *b* 30 Aug 1698; *m* —— FARRAR
II Thomas JEFFERSON III, *b* 24 Sept 1700; *d* at sea (aboard a ship commanded by his bro Peter's future father-in-law Isham Randolph) 14 Feb 1723
III Field JEFFERSON, *b* 6 March 1702; settled on the banks of the Roanoke River, was a JP in Lunenburg Co; *m* and has many descendants; *d* 10 Feb 1765
IV Col Peter JEFFERSON, for whom *see below*
V Mary Jefferson, *b* in or after 1709; *m* Thomas TURPIN, engaged in surveying expeditions with Peter Jefferson and one of the first magistrates of Cumberland Co, Va., and with him had issue:

1 Dr Philip TURPIN, *b c* 1743; *educ* Edinburgh U, Scotland (MD 1774); claimed to be an American patriot in Revolutionary War but was refused permission to return to Virginia by patriot elements as late as 1778, afterward surgeon on a British transport and was with Cornwallis's army at the time of the surrender at Yorktown 1781, subsequently permitted to reside in Virginia with status of prisoner-of-war on parole, readmitted to citizenship 22 Dec 1781, later lived at Salisbury, his estate in Chesterfield Co, Va., and *d* 1828

VI Martha JEFFERSON, *b* after 1709

Capt Thomas Jefferson, Jr, may have *m* between 1715 and 1725, as his 2nd w, Ailce (error for Alice?) —— (*d* by 1725) and himself *d* in or before April 1731

The 4th child and 3rd s,
Col Peter JEFFERSON, of Shadwell, Goochland (later Albemarle) Co, Va., *b* probably at Osborne's, Chesterfield County, 29 Feb 1707/8; Justice of Goochland County Court 1734, High Sheriff 1737-39, County Surveyor of Goochland 1751, JP Albemarle County (part of the old Goochland Co) 1744/45, Lt-Col 1745, Col and County Lt 1754, Burgess 1755; *m* (bond dated 3 Oct) 1739 Jane (baptized St Paul's Church, Shadwell, London, Great Britain, 20 Feb 1720; *d* Monticello 31 March 1776 and *bur* there), est child of Col Isham Randolph, of Dungeness, Goochland Co, and his w Jane Rogers; Col Peter Jefferson *d* Shadwell (which estate was named after his wife's place of baptism in London) 17 Aug 1757, having had issue:

I Jane JEFFERSON, *b* Shadwell 27 June 1740; *d* 1 Oct 1765
II Mary Jefferson, *b* Shadwell 1 Oct 1741; *m* 24 Jan 1760 Col John BOLLING, of Chestnut Grove, Chesterfield Co, Va., sometime representative for Goochland Co in Virginia House of Burgesses and Sheriff of Goochland Co, s of John Bolling and his w Elizabeth Blair and gs of John Bolling and his w Mary Kennon (from whose sister Martha descends President BUSH), and *d* 1817, leaving issue:

1 Archibald BOLLING, *b* 17—; *m* Catherine Payne and had issue:

(1) Archibald BOLLING, Jr; *m* Anne E. Wigginton and had issue:

1a William Holcombe BOLLING; *m* Sallie Spiers White and had issue:

1b Edith Bolling, *b* Wytheville, Va., 15 Oct 1872; *m* 1st Norman GALT (*d* 19—); *m* 2nd The White House, Washington, DC, 18 Dec 1915, as his 2nd w, President WILSON

III THOMAS JEFFERSON, 3rd President of the UNITED STATES of AMERICA
IV Elizabeth JEFFERSON, *b* Shadwell 4 Nov 1744; *d* Feb or March 1774
V Martha Jefferson, *b* Tuckahoe 29 May 1746; *m* 20 July 1765 Dabney CARR (*b* 26 Oct 1743; *d* Charlottesville, Va., 16 May 1773; *bur* Monticello), s of John Carr, of Louisa Co, Va., and his w Barbara, and *d* 3 Sept 1811 (*bur* Monticello), having had issue (along with three daus):

1 Peter CARR
2 Sam CARR
3 Dabney CARR, Jr, *b* 1773; Judge Virginia Court of Appeals; *m* —— and *d* 1837, having had (with other issue):

(1) Jane Cary Carr (his yst dau), *b* 1809; *m* 18— Revd Peyton Randolph HARRISON, of Clifton, Cumberland Co, Va., s of Randolph Harrison, himself 1st cousin of President WILLIAM H. HARRISON, and *d* 1858

VI Peter Field JEFFERSON, *b* Tuckahoe 16 Oct, *d* there 29 Nov 1748
VII A son, *b* and *d* Tuckahoe 9 March 1750
VIII Lucy Jefferson, *b* Shadwell 10 Oct 1752; *m* 12 Sept 1769 her 1st cousin Col Charles Lilburne LEWIS, Jr, of Buck Island, Va., s of Charles Lilburne Lewis and his w Mary Randolph, and had one s and five daus
IX Anna Scott Jefferson, *b* Shadwell 1 Oct 1755; *m* Oct 1788 Hastings MARKS (*d c* 1813), s of Peter Marks, and *d* 1828
X Randolph JEFFERSON, of Snowden, Buckingham Co, Va., *b* Shadwell 1 Oct 1755; *m* 1st 30 July 1780 his 1st cousin Anne Jefferson, dau of Charles Lilburne Lewis and his w Mary Randolph, and had issue (along with three s):

1 Anna Scott Jefferson; *m* Col Zachariah NEVIL (Memb House of Reps for Nelson Co; *d* 1830), and had issue

X (cont.) Randolph Jefferson *m* 2nd Mitchie B. Pryor, sister of Nicholas B. Pryor, and *d* Snowden 7 March 1815, having had a 4th s

Robert Randolph

— —
William Randolph
d ?1657

Richard Lane
Dorothy Lane
b c 1589

Elizabeth Vincent

John Ryland/Riland

— —

Lionel Branch
c 1566-*c* 1605

Sir Euseby Isham
1552/3-1626

Valentia Sparkes
Christopher Branch
c 1602/3—78-81/2

Anne Borlase
d 1627
William Isham
b c 1587/8

Francis Addie
Mary Addie

William Brett
c 1562-1624
Mary Brett
c 1604-*c* 1682

— —
Mary —
d p 1624

John Lilburne

Henry Soane
d 1632

Isabel Wortley
George Lilburne
c 1585-*p* 1681

Elizabeth Worger
d p 1632

Revd John Hicks
d in/p 1631
Eleanor Hicks
d 1677

Alice Blaikston

Alan Nicholson
d 1616

Susan Hechstetter
d 1642
Christopher Nicholson
c 1602-70

John Butler
d 1643
Jane Butler
b 1611

Jane Huntley

THOMAS JEFFERSON
FAMILY TREE

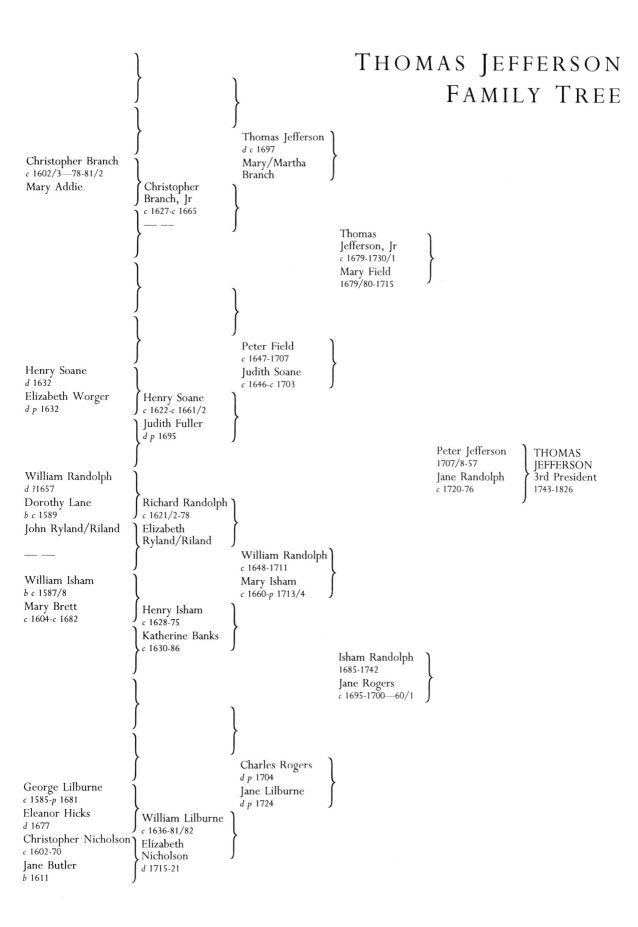

Christopher Branch
c 1602/3—78-81/2
Mary Addie

Christopher
Branch, Jr
c 1627-*c* 1665
— ——

Thomas Jefferson
d c 1697
Mary/Martha
Branch

Thomas
Jefferson, Jr
c 1679-1730/1
Mary Field
1679/80-1715

Peter Field
c 1647-1707
Judith Soane
c 1646-*c* 1703

Henry Soane
d 1632
Elizabeth Worger
d p 1632

Henry Soane
c 1622-*c* 1661/2
Judith Fuller
d p 1695

Peter Jefferson
1707/8-57
Jane Randolph
c 1720-76

THOMAS
JEFFERSON
3rd President
1743-1826

William Randolph
d ?1657
Dorothy Lane
b c 1589
John Ryland/Riland

Richard Randolph
c 1621/2-78
Elizabeth
Ryland/Riland

— ——

William Randolph
c 1648-1711
Mary Isham
c 1660-*p* 1713/4

William Isham
b c 1587/8
Mary Brett
c 1604-*c* 1682

Henry Isham
c 1628-75
Katherine Banks
c 1630-86

Isham Randolph
1685-1742
Jane Rogers
c 1695-1700—60/1

Charles Rogers
d p 1704
Jane Lilburne
d p 1724

George Lilburne
c 1585-*p* 1681
Eleanor Hicks
d 1677
Christopher Nicholson
c 1602-70
Jane Butler
b 1611

William Lilburne
c 1636-81/82
Elizabeth
Nicholson
d 1715-21

Plate 12   James Madison

JAMES MADISON

1750-1836
4TH PRESIDENT OF THE UNITED STATES OF AMERICA
1809-17

The Father of the Constitution, also a Virginian, who had served as Jefferson's Secretary of State and was with him co-founder of the Republican party, was Jefferson's chosen successor, and won a comfortable victory over the Federalist candidate in 1808. But he was not destined to enjoy a very happy presidency.

Partly this was a matter of his own limitations. Like Jefferson, Madison was extremely studious and at his best in small, select gatherings. His learning, practical political sense and extreme reasonableness had enabled him to play a leading part in shaping the Constitution at the Philadelphia Convention in 1787 and in inducing the Virginian convention to ratify the document in the following year. He soon came to enjoy comparable influence in the US House of Representatives, where he sat throughout Washington's presidency, and from which he mounted the first effective challenge to Alexander Hamilton. He proved an extremely competent Secretary of State. But the presidency seemed to demand gifts of leadership which he did not possess. Jefferson was extremely fond of getting his own way, and usually found the means to do it, however underhand. Madison was much more circumspect. And if he did not have Washington's commanding presence or Jefferson's friendly charm, nor did he have Adams's undignified but rocklike character. It was difficult for him to give a lead and impossible for him to outshine some of the new stars that were rising in Congress, such as young Henry Clay of Kentucky or John C. Calhoun of South Carolina. Nor was he a man of action: in the worst crisis of his administration, when the British attacked Washington, he had to leave it to Monroe, his Secretary of State and War, to do what could be done.

Yet his worst misfortunes were not of his making. The Anglo-American War of 1812 broke out chiefly because of British folly. In spite of Saratoga and Yorktown the British seem to have found it impossible to accept the real independence of their former colonies, and humiliated them in every possible way from 1783 onward. The last straw was the Orders in Council of 1807 which in effect forbade all trade between the United States and Napoleonic Europe; Napoleon in retaliation forbade all trade between the United States and Britain. It was not merely the economic injury that the Americans resented, or even the practice of kidnapping American sailors to serve on French and British ships; it was the unscrupulous, systematic policy of disregarding American rights and interests. Negotiations dragged on until 1812; voices in the West rose in a great clamour demanding that Canada be seized from the national enemy, who was also fomenting trouble among the Indians; it was clear that war in the name of national honour was imminent. The Orders in Council also being intensely unpopular in Britain itself, the government there prepared to repeal them; but then the Prime Minister was assassinated, and in the confusion that followed the last opportunity for peace was let slip. On 1 June 1812 Madison recommended war to Congress; and war was declared in July. It is still hard to see what alternative the Americans had, given British behaviour, and Madison's actions were not those of a weak President.

The war that followed brought little glory to either side. The Americans beat on the door of Canada, and might actually have conquered that country if the war had lasted a year longer; the British swept down the east coast, conquering Maine and laying New England under tribute. They were rebuffed at Baltimore (where a young witness, Francis Scott Key, seeing the Stars and Stripes waving defiantly aloft, conceived the words for "The Star-Spangled Banner"), but captured Washington, and in perhaps the most humiliating episode in American history burned the President's house and the Capitol, including (what upset Mr Jefferson most) the Library of Congress (as a result Jefferson sold his vast collection of books to the nation for $24,000, much less than its true worth). Negotiations were begun, and eventually peace was agreed at Ghent in December 1814. A month later, before news of the treaty had crossed the Atlantic, the British tried to take New Orleans by storm; they were crushingly defeated by an American army under General Andrew Jackson.

Historians usually speak of Madison's luck: the peace restored the status quo; the battle of New Orleans restored America's self-respect; the whole experience taught the British, as a first principle of foreign policy, never, if it could be avoided, to fight the United States in future — it was too much trouble. But Madison deserves more credit for the outcome than he is usually given. His record as a war President for two and a half years is not much worse than that of Abraham Lincoln over the same period; if Lincoln is given credit for Gettysburg, why should not Madison be given credit for New Orleans? Organizing an unprepared young country such as the United States for war was a gigantic task; the Madison Administration did not fail, though it took its time about succeeding. Finally, 'Mr Madison's War' taught the British a lesson, as we have seen, and gave a sharp stimulus to the growth of American industry. Even if Madison fumbled in the execution of his policy, the policy itself was correct.

So Madison may be reckoned a worthy member of the 'Virginia Dynasty'. He carried on Jefferson's economic and domestic policies, on the principle "that government is best which governs least", but when the war convinced him that, contrary to Jefferson's dogma, the country needed a national bank, he was ready (with many misgivings) to assist in founding the Second Bank of the United States to replace the First, whose charter he had allowed to lapse in 1811. He got the credit of resisting treason and sedition when, during the war, the Federalists of New England talked of seceding from the Union if peace was not instantly made on their terms. And his enchanting wife, Dolley, kept up the social reputation of the President's House by her brilliant receptions.

The British arson of 1814 necessitated wholesale reconstruction of the mansion and in the next 10 years substantial additions were made. The stone walls had always been painted, but it was apparently the contrast between their blackened state, after the fire, and their shining appearance when refurbished, which induced people to talk of 'the White House', as they have been doing ever since.

JAMES MADISON'S FAMILY

James Madison enjoys a magnificent reputation as the great theorist of republican government as it might best be practised in the United States. But he became President under an early 19th-century and essentially monarchical convention. This said that whoever held a certain post — that of Secretary of State, as Madison did under Jefferson — was the President's heir apparent. Madison turned out to be less successful at running a government than theorizing about it. Perhaps this was because his character was fundamentally academic. He acted as tutor to his brothers and sisters after returning home from his studies at what is now Princeton (where his room-mate was Philip Freneau, America's leading 18th-century poet). In short, he was the first of two professorial Presidents who lacked the human touch, the other being Woodrow Wilson a century later.

Plate 13   Dolley Payne Todd Madison

His lack of the sort of back-slapping good fellowship necessary in a successful politician matches the curious nullity in his private life. It is hard to find out much about his relations with his kin, even though his vivacious wife Dolley is one of the most memorable of First Ladies. He did, however, while a member of the Virginia Council of State during the Revolutionary period, correspond regularly with a second cousin, the Revd James Madison (1749-1812). (When Edmund Randolph corresponded with Madison at the same time he proposed they follow a code whose key would be Cupid, the Revd James's black attendant.) Even then the two Madisons were not particularly close and the letters deal almost entirely with public matters. One gets from them an impression that the parson cousin is chiefly interested in what he can glean in the way of war news from a politically active bigwig.

Madison does not come to mind as a particularly martial character, but in the years leading up to the Revolution he served as second in command to his father, who commanded the Orange County Militia. So nepotistic was Virginia at the time that the second-in-command's post was automatically assigned to the son if the father held the lieutenancy proper. Madison did not in the event do any substantial amount of fighting, partly because he was prone to seizures. Nevertheless he used in later years to be addressed as 'Colonel'. And by a quirk of history he is one of two Presidents to assume active combat command while in office (the other being Lincoln during the Civil War). During the War of 1812 a British force landed at Benedict, Maryland, and started to march on Washington. A few days later they had got to Bladensburg, scarcely six miles from the heart of the capital, and put an opposing American force to flight. Madison went out to take command of an artillery post just north of Bladensburg, but the British sacked Washington anyway.

The other Madisons were not particularly active in politics, though one of the future president's brothers may have sat in on proceedings of the Virginia General Assembly as spectator. Certainly another second cousin, Thomas Madison (1746-98), was a delegate to the Assembly from Botetourt County just before the peace with Britain was signed. But that is all. Among remoter kin there was an exception in Madison's second cousin on his paternal grandmother's side, President Zachary Taylor. Francis Taylor (1747-99), another second cousin, never rose higher than clerk of the Orange County (Virginia) Committee of Safety in 1775.

Madison looked after his private papers in moderately scholarly fashion, preparing them for the use of future historians in the period of over half a century that followed the Revolution. Those that survived were almost entirely to do with public affairs, however. Yet though he put aside much family material, he used as copyists for the important papers Dolley and her son by her first husband Payne Todd, and as chief scribe his brother-in-law John Coles Payne. He also used Dolley as something like an editor. If she thought anybody's feelings might be hurt she was at liberty, her husband said, to make emendations. Though not as drastic a censor as Lady Burton, wife of the great traveller and translator of the *Arabian Nights*, she was nevertheless wholly unqualified for the job. In 1837 Dolley sold her husband's papers to the US Department of State for $30,000, though she had hoped for $100,000. By 1840 Dolley needed money again and the profligate Payne Todd still more so. Todd sold some of his stepfather's papers without Dolley's knowledge but she too was ready enough to make money from them. In 1848 President Polk authorized the US Treasury to pay her $25,000 for what remained and a few months later Dolley delivered four trunks-full to the future President James Buchanan, then Secretary of State.

Dolley Madison is the only person to have been in effect First Lady for two Presidents. While Jefferson, a widower, was in office, his daughters Patsy and Polly sometimes acted as hostess. But neither cared to expose their children to Washington's pestilential fevers and Dolley often presided instead, her position as the Secretary of State's wife providing her with, as it were, the reversion of First Lady status. In the War of 1812 she played a more spectacular part than her husband, rescuing George Washington's portrait and sundry cabinet papers from the executive mansion shortly before it was burnt.

She was said to have been called Dorothea after Patrick Henry's second wife, Dorothea Dandridge, but seems to have been known by the shortened version Dolley or Dolly from an early age, possibly after a younger brother started calling her by it. Her parents were Quakers, but originally lived in Virginia, where they owned slaves. The Quakers disapproved of slavery and her father freed his slaves then moved to Philadelphia, where unfortunately he failed in business. She was introduced to her future husband by Aaron Burr. On closer examination her legendary brilliance as a hostess seems to have amounted to little more than an excellent memory for people's names and what interested them, backed up by great friendliness, though such gifts are never to be despised, particularly in a President's wife and least of all when the President in question was as reserved in large gatherings as James Madison. Again, her tact was a greater blessing than any amount of wit; she was said to have been "brilliant in the things she did not say and do".

In 1837 she returned to Washington accompanied by her niece Anna Payne, whom she adopted. Late in life she was granted the unusual privilege of a seat within the House of Representatives, rather than having to observe proceedings from the strangers' gallery.

BIOGRAPHICAL DETAILS

MADISON, JAMES, *b* Port Conway, King George Co, Va., 16 March 1751; *educ* Donald Robertson's Sch, Innes Plantation, King and Queen County, Va., privately by Revd Thomas Martin and Coll of New Jersey (subsequently Princeton) (baccalaureate 1771), fndr there of literary soc called The American Whig Society; Memb Orange County Ctee of Safety 1772 (Chm 1775), Col Orange County Militia 1775, Orange County Delegate Virginia Convention 1776-77 (Memb Ctee drafting State Constitution) and Memb: Virginia Cncl of State 1778-79, Virginia Legislature 1784-86 (Memb Ctee on Religion) and 1799-1801, Virginia Convention on ratification of Constitution 1788, Virginia Constitutional Convention 1829-34, Virginia Delegate 2nd Continental Congress 1780-83 and 1786-88, Memb US House of Representatives 1789-97, US Sec of State 1801-09, 4th President (Democratic-Republican) of the United States 1809-17, Pres Agricultural Soc of Albemarle, Memb Bd of Rectors U of Virginia 1826, author: (with John Jay and Alexander Hamilton) of many papers (20 certainly, nine others probably) collected in the 85 comprising *The Federalist, An Examination of the British Doctrine which subjects to Capture a Neutral Trade not open in Time of Peace* (1806), his writings being posthumously gathered together and published as *Writings*, ed Gaillard Hunt, 9 vols (1900-10) and *Papers*, ed William Hutchinson and William M.E. Rachal (1962-); *m* Harewood (house belonging to his bride's sister Mrs George Steptoe Washington, *qv*), nr Charles Town, Jefferson Co, Va., 15 Sept 1794 Dolley (*b* Guilford County, N Carolina, 20 May 1768; *m* 1st 7 Jan 1790 John Todd, Jr (*d* before 1794), and with him had issue 2 s, (John) Payne Todd, *b* Philadelphia 29 Feb 1792; *d* 1852; and an unnamed boy who was *b* Oct and *d* Nov 1793), est dau of John Payne, of Scotchtown, Hanover Co, Va., and his w Mary, dau of William Coles, of Coles Hill, Hanover Co; President James Madison *d* and was *bur* Montpelier 28 June 1836, leaving no issue

MALE LINE ANCESTRY AND COLLATERAL DESCENDANTS

John MADISON, Sr, *b c* 1630, Gloucester, England; ship's carpenter; acquired grants of land in Virginia from 1653, where he settled in St Stephen's parish, New Kent Co, and *d* before 16 April 1683, leaving issue:

John MADISON, Jr, fl 1683-1717; Sheriff King and Queen Co, Va., 1714; *m* Isabella Minor Todd (*d* after 1706) and had at least two children, sons, one of whom *m* and had issue a s, who *m* and had issue:

I Thomas MADISON, *b* 1746; sometime delegate from Botetourt Co, to Virginia Legislative Assembly; *d* 1798
II Revd James MADISON, *b* 1749; Pres Coll of William and Mary (Prof Natural Philosophy and Mathematics, one of his students being the future President TYLER) and 1st Bishop (consecrated in England 19 Sept 1790) of the Protestant Episcopal Church in Virginia, being one of the three bishops through whom the Church of England Episcopate's ecclesiastical organization continued in the newly independent USA; *m* 28 April 1779 Sarah Taite (*d* 1815), of Williamsburg, and *d* 1812, leaving issue:

  1 James Catesby MADISON, *b* before 18 Sept 1782; *d c* 1844

Another of John Madison, Jr's sons,

  Ambrose MADISON, *b c* 1700; *m* probably in Orange Co, Va., 24 Aug 1721 Frances (*b c* 1700; *d* 25 Nov 1761), dau of James Taylor, of Hare Forest, Orange Co, Va., and his w Martha Thompson and sister of Zachary Taylor (President TAYLOR's gf), and *d* probably Spotsylvania Co, Va., 27 Aug 1732, leaving (with other issue):

James MADISON, *b* probably Orange Co 27 March 1723; plantation-owner, Lt Orange Co; *m* probably Orange Co 13 Sept 1749 Eleanor (Nelly) Rose (*b* Caroline Co, Va., 9 Jan 1731; *d* Montpelier, Orange Co, 11 Feb 1829), dau of Francis Conway and his w Rebecca Catlett, and *d* Montpelier 27 Feb 1801, leaving issue:

I JAMES MADISON, 4th PRESIDENT of the UNITED STATES of AMERICA
II Francis MADISON, *b* 1753; *m* 1772 Susanna Bell and *d* 1800, having had three s (though President Madison himself compiled a pedigree stating that his brother Francis had five s) and five daus
III Ambrose MADISON, *b* 1755; Capt 3rd Virginia Regt; *m c* 1780 Mary Willis Lee (*d* 1798), dau of Hancock Lee, Jr (whose sister Elizabeth *m* Zachary Taylor and was gmother of President TAYLOR) and *d* 1793, leaving issue:

  President Madison's niece
  1 Nelly Conway Madison; *m* Dr John WILLIS (*d* 1812) and *d* 1865, leaving issue:

Great-nephew
(1) John WILLIS; *m* 1838 his 2nd cousin Lucy Taliaferro (*b* 1820; *d* 1868), eldest dau of Maj Ambrose Madison, of Woodbury Forest, Va., and his w Jane Bankhead Willis (for whom *see below*), and *d* 1885, leaving issue:

Great-nephew's children
1a Mary Lee WILLIS, *b* 1840; *d* 1908
2a Jane Champe Willis, *b* 18—; *m* 18— Major John D. RICHARDSON and had issue:

Great-nephew's grandchildren
1b Maria Jane Richardson, *b* 1877; *m* 1907 George Lauman POLLOCK, of Chicago, and *d* 19—, having had issue:

Great-nephew's great-grandchildren
1c Janie Willis POLLOCK, *b* 1909; *d* 1912
2c *Margaret Lee POLLOCK, *b* 1914

Great-nephew's grandchildren
2b Lucy Lee Richardson, *b* 1878; *m* 1918 her 1st cousin Lewis Byrd WILLIS (*b* 1884), only s of William Byrd Willis and his w Nelly Conway Willis (for whom *see below*)
3b Ambrose Madison RICHARDSON, *b* 1880; *m* 1912 Louise McDonald and *d* 19—, having had issue:

Great-nephew's great-grandchildren
1c *Irving RICHARDSON, *b* 1914
2c *Ambrose Madison RICHARDSON, *b* 1916
3c *Louise RICHARDSON, *b* 1919

Great-nephew's grandchildren
4b Alice Balmaine Richardson, *b* 1882; *m* 1909 Philip Brown SHILLITO and *d* 19—, having had issue:

Great-nephew's great-grandchildren
1c *Jane Champe SHILLITO, *b* 1917

Great-nephew's children
3a John WILLIS, *b* 18—; *m* 1st 1866 Lucie Robinson and had issue:

Great-nephew's grandchildren
1b James Shephard WILLIS, *b* 1867; *m* 1891 Evelyn McDonald and *d* 1908, leaving issue:

Great-nephew's great-grandchildren
1c George WILLIS

Great-nephew's children
3a (cont.) John Willis *m* 2nd 1870 Mary Elizabeth Lupton and with her had issue:

Great-nephew's grandchildren
2b Lucie Madison Willis, *b* 1871; *m* 1901 Moncure Robinson TAYLOR (*b* 23 Feb 1851; *d* 7 Dec 1915), s of John Charles Randolph Taylor and his w Martha Jefferson Randolph (herself gdau of Thomas Mann Randolph by his w Patsy Jefferson, dau of President JEFFERSON), and had issue (*see* President JEFFERSON's descendants)
3b Bessie Milton WILLIS, *b* 1873; *d* 1926
4b Nellie Ross WILLIS, *b* 1875; *d* 1892
5b John Byrd WILLIS, *b* 1877; *m* 1908 Verna Gabbert and had issue:

Great-nephew's great-grandchildren
1c *Mary Francis Willis, *b* 1909; *m* 19— *Frederick K. KEISKER

Great-nephew's grandchildren
6b Annie Scott WILLIS, *b* 1879
7b Revd William Taylor WILLIS, *b* 1885; Rector St Luke's Church, Norfolk, Va.; *m* 1917 Gertrude Scott Hendrix and *d* 1971, leaving issue:

Great-nephew's great-grandchildren
1c *Lt-Gen William Taylor WILLIS, USAF (ret) [PO Box 52, USAF Regional Hospital, Minot, ND 58701, USA], *b* 1920

Great-nephew's children
4a Claudia Marshall Willis, *b* 18—; *m* 1869 William Wallace SCOTT and had issue:

Great-nephew's grandchildren
1b Philip Henshaw SCOTT, *b* 18—; *m* Martha M. Leitch and had issue:

Great-nephew's great-grandchildren
1c Philip Henshaw SCOTT, Jr, *d* aged 11   2c Martha M. Scott; *m* William S. BELFIELD
3c William Wallace SCOTT, *d* aged 25   4c Meredith SCOTT   5c John SCOTT

Great-nephew's grandchildren
2b Claudia Dennis Scott, *b* 18—; *m* 1st Dr Robert Sylvester BLAKEMAN; *m* 2nd Thomas Edwin GRIMSLEY

3b Robert Lewis Madison SCOTT, *b* 18—; *d* 1918

4b Ellen Ritchie Scott, *b* 18—; *m* 1901 Revd James Jeffries CHAPMAN and *d* 19—, having had issue:

> Great-nephew's great-grandchildren
> 1c *Claudia Marshall Willis Chapman, *b* 19—; *m* 19— *Hugh Wood ROGER and has issue:
>
> > Great-nephew's great-great-grandchildren
> > 1d *Edwin Dennis ROGER
> > 2d *Robin D. ROGER
>
> Great-nephew's great-grandchildren
> 2c *Dennis Scott CHAPMAN
> 3c *James Jeffries CHAPMAN, Jr
> 4c *Ellen Ritchie Chapman; *m* 1933 *John I. WOODRIFF
> 5c *Marijane Stewart CHAPMAN
> 6c *Josephine J. CHAPMAN
> 7c *William Wallace Scott CHAPMAN

Great-nephew's grandchildren
5b Garrett Willis SCOTT; *m* Alice S. Shields and *d* 1927, leaving issue:

> Great-nephew's great-grandchildren
> 1c *Wyklif SCOTT
> 2c *Willis Shields SCOTT
> 3c *Garrett SCOTT
> 4c *Harriet S. SCOTT

Great-nephew's grandchildren
6b Wyklif SCOTT; *d* 1906

7b Caroline Barbour Scott; *m* Joseph Hayward STRATTON and *d* 1918, leaving issue:

> Great-nephew's great-grandchildren
> 1c *Caroline Barbour STRATTON
> 2c *Joseph Hayward STRATTON, Jr

Great-nephew's grandchildren
8b John SCOTT, *d* 1933

Great-nephew's children
5a Nelly Conway Willis, *b* 18—; *m* 1877 William Byrd WILLIS and had issue:

> Great-nephew's grandchildren
> 1b Jane Bailey Willis, *b* 1879; *m* 1906 Norbert Edward MULICK and *d* 19—, having had issue:
>
> > Great-nephew's great-grandchildren
> > 1c *Norbert Edward MULICK, Jr, *b* 1907
> > 2c *Margaret Lee MULICK, *b* 1909
> > 3c *Dorothy Madison Mulick, *b* 1909 (twin with Margaret); *m* 1930 Nicholas K. LYONS and has issue:
> >
> > > Great-nephew's great-great-grandchildren
> > > 1d *Florence Lee LYONS, *b* 1931
>
> Great-nephew's grandchildren
> 2b Lewis Byrd WILLIS, *b* 1884; *m* 1918 his 1st cousin Lucy Lee (*b* 1879; *d* 19—), 2nd dau of Maj John D. Richardson and his w Jane Champe Willis (for whom *see above*), and *d* 19—
> 3b Mary Lee Willis, *b* 1886; *m* 1911 John William BROWNING

Great-nephew's children
6a Lucy Cornelia Willis, *b* 1851; *m* 1880 Charles NORRIS (*d* 1910) and *d* 19—

7a Ambrose Madison WILLIS, *b* 18—; *m* Maude Bagley and *d* 18— or 19—, having had issue:

> Great-nephew's grandchildren
> 1b David Madison WILLIS; *m* Clothoe Newcomb and had issue:
>
> > Great-nephew's great-grandchildren
> > 1c *Newcomb WILLIS, *b* 1914
> > 2c *Maj David Madison WILLIS, Jr, US Army
> > 3c *Barbara WILLIS

Great-nephew's children
8a Revd Andrew Johnson WILLIS, *b* 18—; *m* 1st Margaret Mitchell and had issue:

> Great-nephew's grandchildren
> 1b John Mitchell WILLIS; *m* Anne Gibson and had issue:

Great-nephew's great-grandchildren
1c *John Mitchell WILLIS, Jr, b 1916

Great-nephew's grandchildren
2b Andrew Hunter WILLIS; m Elizabeth Sheldon and had issue:

Great-nephew's great-grandchildren
1c *Andrew Hunter WILLIS, Jr, b 1916
2c *Mary Elizabeth WILLIS, b 1919
3c *Edward WILLIS, b 1921

Great-nephew's grandchildren
3b Margaret Willis; m Floyd BLIVEN and had issue:

Great-nephew's great-grandchildren
1c *Floyd BLIVEN, Jr, b 1921
2c *Andrew BLIVEN
3c *Margaret BLIVEN

Great-nephew's children
8a (cont.) Revd Andrew Johnson Willis m 2nd Georgette Strider

Great-niece
(2) Mary Lee Willis; m Col John Hancock LEE, of Orange, Va., and had issue:

Great-niece's children
1a Nelly LEE   2a Lucy LEE   3a Letitia Ramolino Lee; m Dr Robert MADISON and had issue:

Great-niece's grandchildren
1b Mary MADISON   2b Letitia MADISON

IV Catlett MADISON b and d 1758
V Nelly Conway Madison, b 1760; m 1783 Major Isaac HITE, Jr, of Belle Grove, Va. (b 1758; d 1836), s of Isaac Hite, and d 1802, having had issue:

President Madison's nephew and niece
1 James Madison HITE, b 1788; d 1791
2 Nelly Conway Hite, b 1789; m 1809 Dr Cornelius BALDWIN (b 1791; d 1849) and d 18—, having had issue:

Great-niece
(1) Eleanor Conway Baldwin; m 1835 Edward Jacquelin DAVISON (b 1805) and had issue:

Great-niece's children
1a Eleanor Cornelia Davison, b 1836; m 1855 John H. PEDIGO (b 1823) and had issue:

Great-niece's grandchildren
1b Eleanor Conway Pedigo, b 1857; m 1880 John Warren EDWARDS (b 1842) and had issue:

Great-niece's great-grandchildren
1c Ann Eleanor Edwards, b 1881; m 1898 Herbert Martin GRANDON and had issue:

Great-niece's great-great-grandchildren
1d *Herbert Martin GRANDON, b 1899
2d *Eleanor Katherine GRANDON, b 1901

Great-niece's great-grandchildren
2c Mabel Pedigo EDWARDS, b 1885; d 1893   3c John Cummins EDWARDS, b 1892   4c Maury EDWARDS, b 1896
.

Great-niece's grandchildren
2b Lallie Louis PEDIGO, b 1859   3b Jenny Grey PEDIGO, b 1861   4b Robert Edward PEDIGO, b 1863
5b Norborne Elijah PEDIGO, b 1865   6b Mack Henry PEDIGO, b 1867   7b Mary Louisa PEDIGO, b 1870
8b John Hardin PEDIGO, b 1871   9b Ann Maury PEDIGO, b 1878   10b Jessie Davison PEDIGO, b 1880

Great-niece's children
2a Mary Baldwin DAVISON, b 1837; d 1846
3a Edward Jacquelin DAVISON, Jr, b 1842; d 1844
4a Judge William Smith DAVISON, b 1845; m 1876 Anna Maria Davison (b 1848) and d 1904, having had issue:

Great-niece's grandchildren
1b Edmonia Louisa DAVISON, b 1881   2b Cecil Armstrong DAVISON, b 1883; d 1888
3b Fontaine Hite DAVISON, b 1884   4b Joseph William DAVISON, b 1888   5b Anna DAVISON, b and d 1894

Great-niece's children
5a Edmonia Louise DAVISON, b 1848; d 1856

Great-nieces and -nephew

(2) Mary Briscoe BALDWIN, *b* 1811; Episcopalian missionary; *d* 1877

(3) Dr Isaac Hite BALDWIN, *b* 1813; Assist Surg US Army; *m* 18— and *d* 1882

(4) Ann Maury Baldwin, *b* 1817; *m* 1844 Isaac Hite HAY, lawyer, US Consul at Jaffa, Ottoman Empire, and had issue:

Great-niece's children

1a John Baldwin HAY, *b* 1845; US Consul-Gen Constantinople; *m* 18— Cornelia Badger (*d* 1879) and had issue (with three other children):

Great-niece's grandchildren

1b Alice Hay, *b* 18—; *m* John LEEDS   2b Errol HAY

Great-nephew

(5) James Madison BALDWIN, *b* 18—; *m* 18— —— and had issue:

Great-nephew's children

1a Hite BALDWIN   2a Mary BALDWIN   3a Briscoe BALDWIN   4a Ann BALDWIN   5a Eleanor BALDWIN

Great-nephew

(6) Dr Robert Stuart BALDWIN, *b* 1824; Surg Confederate States Army; *m* 18— Letitia Jane Speck (*b* 1824) and had issue:

Great-nephew's children

1a Cornelius Hite BALDWIN, *b* 1846; *d* 1864   2a Robert Stuart BALDWIN, Jr, *b* 1848; lawyer
3a Frederica Briscoe BALDWIN, *b* 1850; *d* 1883
4a Augusta Madison Baldwin, *b* 1852; *m* 1875 Thomas L. WATTS and had issue:

Great-nephew's grandchildren

1b Mary Baldwin WATTS, *b* 1879

Great-nephew's children

5a William Daniel BALDWIN, *b* 1856; *d* young   6a Martha Daniel BALDWIN, *b* 1865; *d* 1883

President Madison's nephew

3 James Madison HITE, *b* 1793; *m* 1815 Matilda Irvine and *d* 1860, leaving issue:

Great-niece

(1) Caroline Matilda Hite, *b* 18—; *m* 18— Alexander BAKER and had issue (with six other children):

Great-niece's children

1a Alexander BAKER   2a Lillian BAKER

Great-nephew

(2) Isaac Irvine HITE, *b* 1820; *m* 1st 1838 Susan Meade and had issue (with two other children):

Great-nephew's children

1a William Meade HITE   2a Isaac Irvine HITE, Jr   3a Susan Hite, *b* 18—; *m* 18— —— BAKER
4a Mary Meade Hite, *b* 18—; *m* 18— —— BAKER

Great-nephews

(2) (cont.) Isaac Irvine Hite *m* 2nd Ann Maria, *née* Hopkins, widow of —— Cutler

(3) James Madison HITE, Jr, *b* 18—; *m* 1849 Harriet Green Meade and had issue:

Great-nephew's children

1a Drayton Meade HITE   2a Mattie HITE; *d* 1886

Great-niece

(4) Ann Eliza Hite, *b* 1831; *m* 1848 Thomas Julian SKINKER and had issue:

Great-niece's children

1a Thomas Julian SKINKER, Jr, *b* 1849; *m* 1872 Nannie Brown Rose
2a Hampson SKINKER, *b* 18—; *m* 1st Maria Carr; *m* 2nd Annie Mai Kennerley and had issue:

Great-niece's grandchildren

1b Mary Clothilde SKINKER   2b Dorothy Ann SKINKER

Great-niece's children

3a Cornelius Hite SKINKER, *b* 18—; *m* 1888 Minnie Lee Gravey and had issue:

Great-niece's grandchildren

1b Howard SKINKER   2b Cornelius Hite SKINKER, Jr   3b Lois Evelyn SKINKER

Great-niece's children

4a Hugh Garland SKINKER, *b* 18—; *m* Annie Lee Rucker and had issue:

Great-niece's grandchildren

1b Hugh Garland SKINKER, Jr   2b Julian Hampson SKINKER   3b Susan Hite SKINKER

President Madison's niece
4 Frances Madison Hite; *m* 18— James Lackland RANSOM and had issue:

Great-niece
(1) Georgianna Hite Ransom, *b* Jefferson Co, Va., *c* 1822; *m* Charlestown, Va., 22 Oct 1845 Benjamin Franklin WASHINGTON (for whom *see* President WASHINGTON's brothers' and sisters' descendants), 3rd s of John Thornton Augustine Washington and his w Elizabeth, and *d* San Francisco 3 Dec 1860, having had issue

VI Gen William MADISON, of Woodbury Forest, Va., *b* 1762; *educ* Coll of New Jersey (subsequently Princeton) and Hampden-Sydney Acad; Artillery Lt Revolutionary War; *m* 1783 Frances (*b* 1765; *d* 1831), dau of Robert Throckmorton and his cousin Lucy (*see* BURKE's PEERAGE & BARONETAGE) and *d* 1843, having had issue:

President Madison's niece
1 Rebecca Conway Madison, *b* 1795; *m* 1803 Reynolds CHAPMAN, of Berry Hill, Orange Co, Va. (*b* 1778; *d* 1844), and *d* 1860, leaving issue:

Great-nephews
(1) William Madison CHAPMAN
(2) Judge John Madison CHAPMAN, *b* 1810; *m* 1842 Susan Digges Cole, of Effingham, Prince William Co, Va., and *d* 1879, leaving issue:

Great-nephew's children
1a Mary Ella Chapman, *b* 18—; *m* Dr Nathaniel CHAPMAN, of Charles Co, Md., Lt Confederate States Army, and had issue:

Great-nephew's grandchildren
1b Ridgely CHAPMAN   2b Mary Sigismunda CHAPMAN   3b Emma Boykin Chapman; *m* Mitchell SMOOT
4b John Madison CHAPMAN   5b Nathaniel CHAPMAN   6b Cora CHAPMAN   7b Helen CHAPMAN
8b Minnie Thomas CHAPMAN   9b John Webb CHAPMAN

Great-nephew's children
2a Emma Chapman, *b* 18—; *m* 1st Capt Robert V. BOYKIN, Hampton Legion, Confederate States Army, and had issue:

Great-nephew's grandchildren
1b Virginia Young Boykin; *m* —— GRANT, of Norfolk, Va.   2b Mary Madison Boykin; *m* —— POWERS, of Washington, DC   3b Robert V. BOYKIN, Jr, of Glymont, Charles Co, Md.

Great-nephew's children
2a (cont.) Emma Chapman Boykin *m* 2nd Samuel CULVER
3a Constance CHAPMAN (twin with Emma); *d* in infancy
4a Susie Ashton Chapman, *b* 18—; *m* 1878 Calvin PERKINS, lawyer, of Memphis, Tenn., and had issue:

Great-nephew's grandchildren
1b Blakeney PERKINS, *b* 1880   2b Belle Moncure PERKINS, *b* 1881   3b Ashton Chapman PERKINS, *b* 1883
4b Mary Anderson PERKINS, *b* 1884   5b Louis Allen PERKINS, *b* 1885   6b William Alexander PERKINS, *b* 1886

Great-nephew's children
5a Sallie Foote Alexander CHAPMAN
6a Belle Chapman, *b* 1858; *m* 1878 William MONCURE, of Richmond, Va. (*b* 1851), and had issue:

Great-nephew's grandchildren
1b Dr William MONCURE, *b* 1880   2b Belle Perkins MONCURE, *b* 1882
3b Vivienne Daniel MONCURE, *b* 1885

Great-nephew's children
7a Ashton Alexander CHAPMAN, *b* 1867; *m* 1895 Nannie Eaton Gregory, of Oxford, N Carolina

Great-niece
(3) Jane Chapman; *m* Dr Thomas Towles SLAUGHTER (*b* 1804; *d* 1890) and had issue:

Great-niece's children
1a Thomas Towles SLAUGHTER, Jr; *d* young   2a Larkin SLAUGHTER; *d* young   3a A s; *d* in infancy
4a Reynolds Chapman SLAUGHTER; Capt of Engrs Confederate States Army; *m* Louise Lake, of Vicksburg, Miss.
5a Philip Peyton SLAUGHTER; Lt-Col Confederate States Army; *m* Emma Thompson and had issue:

Great-niece's grandchildren
1b Elizabeth Pendleton Slaughter; *m* Lucien SMITH and had issue:

Great-niece's great-grandchildren
1c Katherine Mercer SMITH

Great-niece's children
6a Thomas Towles SLAUGHTER; *k* in the Seven Days Battle, Civil War, which took place in the region of Richmond, Va., 26 June-2 July 1862

7a Dr Alfred Edwin SLAUGHTER, *b* 1839; Surg 17th Virginia Regt, Stonewall Bde, Confederate States Army; *m* 1869 Eugenia Taylor (*b* 1842) and *d* 1893, leaving issue:

Great-niece's grandchildren
1b Robert Carroll SLAUGHTER; *m* Lucy Lawrence Lyne and had issue:

Great-niece's great-grandchildren
1c *Lucy Lawrence SLAUGHTER, *b* 1923
2c *Jane Madison SLAUGHTER, *b* 1924
3c *Robert Carroll SLAUGHTER, Jr, *b* 1925

Great-niece's grandchildren
2b Jane Chapman Slaughter; *m* Charles Forest MOORE and had issue:

Great-niece's great-grandchildren
1c Donna Moore; *m* John MATTHEWS

Great-niece's grandchildren
3b Sadie Patton Slaughter; *m* 1905 William Bane SNIDOW (*b* 1877) and had issue:

Great-niece's great-grandchildren
1c *William Bane SNIDOW, Jr, *b* 1906
2c *Eugenia Tilghman SNIDOW, *b* 1907
3c *John Temple SNIDOW, *b* 1909
4c *Carroll SNIDOW, *b* 1916

Great-niece's grandchildren
4b Alfred Edwin SLAUGHTER, Jr

Great-niece's children
8a Mercer SLAUGHTER, *b* 1844; Lt Fry's Battery, Stonewall Bde, Confederate States Army; *m* 18— Mary Shepherd Bull and *d* 1897, having had issue:

Great-niece's grandchildren
1b Mary SLAUGHTER; *d* in infancy
2b Vivian SLAUGHTER, *b* 1880; Lt 23rd London (Queen's) Regt World War I; *k* Flanders 1918

Great-niece's children
9a James Shepherd SLAUGHTER; served 17th Virginia Regt (Montpelier Guards), Stonewall Bde, Confederate States Army; *d* Mississippi of yellow fever
10a Richard Chapman SLAUGHTER; Midshipman Confederate States Navy

Great-nephew
(4) James Alfred CHAPMAN, *b* 1813; *m* 1837 Mary Edmonds Kinney (*b* 1817; *d* 1886) and *d* 1876, leaving issue:

Great-nephew's children
1a Anna Madison Chapman, *b* 1844; *m* 1866 Joseph D. McGUIRE (*b* 1842; *d* 1914) and *d* 1904, leaving issue:

Great-nephew's grandchildren
1b Major James Clark McGUIRE, of New York City, *b* 1867   2b Mary Madison McGUIRE

Great-niece and -nephew
(5) Ella Chapman; *m* —— MEYERS, of Richmond, Va.   (6) Richard Conway CHAPMAN

President Madison's nephews
2 John MADISON, *b* 1787; *d* 16 Sept 1819   3 William MADISON, *b* 1789; *d* 1812
4 Alfred MADISON, *b* 1791; *d* 1811   5 Robert Lewis MADISON, *b* 1794; *d* 1828
6 Maj Ambrose MADISON, of Woodbury Forest, Va., *b* 1796; *m* 18— Jane Bankhead Willis (*b* 1803; *d* 1862), sister of Lewis Willis (for whom *see below*), and had issue:

Great-nieces
(1) Lucy Taliaferro Madison, *b* 1820; *m* 1838 Col John WILLIS (*d* 1885), her second cousin and s of Dr John Willis and his w Nelly Conway Madison (for whom *see above*)
(2) Mary Frances Madison, *b* 1823; *m* Col Robert B. MARYE, of Fredericksburg, Va., and had issue:

Great-niece's children
1a Alfred J. MARYE; *m* Nancy C. Anderson and had issue:

Great-niece's grandchildren
1b Robert B. MARYE   2b Ambrose Madison MARYE   3b Janey Colquhoun MARYE   4b William Gordon MARYE

Great-niece's children
2a Ambrose MARYE

Great-nephews
(3) William Willis MADISON, *b* 1826; *m* 18— Roberta Willis Taliaferro, sister of Col Thomas Dorsey Taliaferro,

Confederate States Army (himself husb of William Willis Madison's sister Eliza), and *d* 1888, leaving a child (*d* unmarried)
(4) James Ambrose MADISON, *b* 1828; *m* 1850 Lucy Hiden and had issue:

Great-nephew's children
1a Ambrose Gilmer MADISON, *b* 1851; *m* Margaret McGary and had issue:

Great-nephew's grandchildren
1b Margaret MADISON   2b Kate MADISON   3b William MADISON   4b Ambrose MADISON
5b Annie MADISON

Great-nephew's children
2a Fanny Throckmorton Madison; *m* Revd J. A. FRENCH   3a Susan Daniel MADISON   4a James MADISON
5a Edward Cooper MADISON, *b* 1857; *m* 1886 Elizabeth Fox Stagg (*b* 1864) and had issue:

Great-nephew's grandchildren
1b Ida Renshaw Madison, *b* 1887; *m* Thomas PATRICK   2b Susan Daniel Madison, *b* 1891; *m* Dr C. C. RICHARDS
3b Lucy Hiden Madison, *b* 1893; *m* Chesley A. HADEN
4b James Gordon MADISON, of Tuscaloosa, Ala., *b* 1900; lawyer; *m* 1924 Mabel Curtis Campbell (*b* 1903) and had issue:

Great-nephew's great-grandchildren
1c *James Gordon MADISON, Jr, *b* 1926
2c *Richard Fleetwood MADISON, *b* 1930

Great-nephew's children
6a Alfred MADISON   7a Joseph Hiden MADISON, *b* 1868

Great-niece
(5) Eliza Lewis Madison, *b* 1834; *m* 1854 Col Thomas Dorsey TALIAFERRO (*see above*) and had issue (with three other children):

Great-niece's children
1a Fanny Lewis TALIAFERRO   2a Jane Taliaferro; *m* and had two children   3a Edmonia TALIAFERRO

Great-niece
(6) Leila Bankhead Madison, *b* 1837; *m* Judge William Pope DABNEY, of Powhatan Co, Va., and had issue:

Great-niece's children
1a Robert Kelso DABNEY, *b* 1858; *m*   2a Leila Dabney; *m* Marshall TAYLOR, of Richmond, Va.
3a Julia Byrd DABNEY   4a Percy DABNEY; *m* Ethel Crane   5a Champe DABNEY
6a James Madison DABNEY   7a Ruby Bailey DABNEY

President Madison's nephew and nieces
8 James Edwin MADISON, *b* 1798; *d* 1821   9 Lucy Frances MADISON, *b* 1800; *d* 28 Dec 1813
10 Elizabeth Madison, *b* 1802; *m* Lewis WILLIS, bro of Jane Bankhead Willis, Mrs Ambrose Madison (for whom *see above*), and had issue:

Great-niece
(1) Frances Willis; *m* Col John Hancock LEE, of Litchfield, Orange Co, Va., and had issue:

Great-niece's children
1a Mary Willis LEE, *b* 1845; *d* young
2a Lizzie Madison Lee, *b* 1848; *m* 1872 William A. BRAGG (*b* 1840; *d* 1901) and *d* 1907, leaving issue:

Great-niece's grandchildren
1b Hancock Lee BRAGG, *b* 1874
2b Elise Calvin Bragg, *b* 1876; *m* 1904 Granville Gray VALENTINE, of Richmond, Va., and had issue:

Great-niece's great-grandchildren
1c *Elizabeth Lee Valentine, *b* 1907; *m* 1931 *Wilfred Lacy GOODWYN, Jr, s of Wilfred Lacy Goodwyn
2c *Maria Gray VALENTINE, *b* 1914
3c *Granville Gray VALENTINE, *b* 1920

Great-niece's grandchildren
3b Frances Madison Bragg, *b* 1878; *m* 1901 George SMALL, of York, Pa., and had issue:

Great-niece's great-grandchildren
1c *Elizabeth Lee Small, *b* 1902; *m* 1926 *Revd Richard Henry BAKER, DD, and has issue:

Great-niece's great-great-grandchildren
1d *Frances Lee BAKER, *b* 1928

Great-niece's great-grandchildren
2c *Katharine Moore Small, *b* 1904; *m* 1929 *Laurence TALBOT   3c *Anna Maria SMALL, *b* 1907
4c *Frances Madison SMALL, *b* 1919

Great-niece's children
3a Lewis Herman LEE, *b* 1849; *m* 1876 Georgia G. Hansbrough and *d* 1878, leaving issue:

Great-niece's grandchildren
1b Mary Madison LEE

President Madison's niece
10 Letitia Madison, *b* 1804; *m* 18— Daniel French SLAUGHTER and had issue:

Great-nephews
(1) Brig-Gen James Edwin SLAUGHTER, Confederate States Army
(2) Maj Philip Madison SLAUGHTER, Confederate States Army; *m* Clementine Luzenburg and had issue:

Great-nephew's children
1a Edward Luzenburg SLAUGHTER; *m* Lucy Williams
2a Mary Clementine Slaughter; *m* Hugh Mercer HAMILTON and had issue:

Great-nephew's grandchildren
1b Cornelia Long HAMILTON   2b Edwin Slaughter HAMILTON   3b Kathryn HAMILTON   4b Philip HAMILTON

VII Sarah Catlett Madison, *b* 1764; *m* 1790 Thomas MACON (*b* 1765; *d* 1838) and *d* 1843, having had (with seven s (the yst *b* 1808) and one other dau (*b* 1803; *d* 1805)):

President Madison's niece
1 Lucie H. Macon, *b* 1794; *m* 18— Reuben CONWAY (*b* 1788; *d* 1838) and *d* 1871

VIII A boy, *b* and *d* the same day 1766
IX Elizabeth MADISON, *b* 1768; *d* of dysentery 17 May 1775
X A stillborn child 1770
XI Reuben MADISON, *b* 19 Sept 1771; *d* of dysentery 5 June 1775
XII Frances Taylor Madison, *b* 1774; *m* 1800 Dr Robert Henry ROSE (*d* 1833), est s of Col Hugh Rose, of Amherst Co, Va., and his w Caroline Matilda Jordan, and *d* 1823, having had issue:

President Madison's nephew
1 Dr Hugh Francis ROSE, of Tenn., *b* 1801; *m* 18— Emma Taliaferro Newman and *d* 1856, having had issue:

Great-nieces and -nephews
(1) Ellen Conway Rose; *m* R. J. JONES   (2) Frances Madison ROSE   (3) Eliza Camilla Rose; *m* H. A. ROGERS
(4) Octavia ROSE   (5) Emma Newman Rose; *m* T. A. MOORE   (6) Robert ROSE
(7) Samuel Patrick ROSE; *m* 1st, Celeste Coombs; *m* 2nd Mildred L. Cage and with her had issue:

Great-nephew's children
1a Harriet Howard ROSE   2a Telisflora ROSE   3a Hugh Francis ROSE

Great-niece and -nephew
(8) Anne Fitzhugh Rose; *m* Dr W. L. BELL   (9) Hugh Francis ROSE

President Madison's nephew
2 Ambrose James ROSE, *b* 1802; *m* —— Kelly, of Miss., and had issue:

Great-nieces
(1) Jennie ROSE   (2) Frances Rose; *m* William WINSTON

President Madison's nephews
3 James Madison ROSE; *d* in infancy
4 Henry ROSE, *b* 1804; *m* Sarah Smith, of Rushville, Ill., and had issue:

Great-nephew
(1) Robert Henry ROSE; *m* Maggie M. Fisher and had issue:

Great-nephew's children
1a Nellie Madison ROSE   2a Belle ROSE   3a Hugh Francis ROSE   4a Sadie Madison ROSE

Great-nephew and -nieces
(2) Samuel Jordan ROSE, of Macon, Tenn.   (3) Margaret Ellen Rose; *m* Hugh Francis ROSE
(4) Nannie T. Rose; *m* 1st Dr —— BELLE; *m* 2nd —— McCARTY

President Madison's nephew
5 Samuel Jordan ROSE, of Randolph Co, Tenn., *b* 1805; *m* 1st Prudence W. Jones and had five children, all of whom *d* young; *m* 2nd Dorothy W. Jones and *d* 1868, having with her had issue:

Great-nieces and nephew
(1) Maria Jones ROSE   (2) Poll Ward Rose; *m* John G. HALL
(3) Bronson Baylis ROSE, of Texas; *m* Mrs Alice T. Lytle

President Madison's nephew
6 Dr Erasmus Taylor ROSE, of Tenn., *b* 1806; *m* Mary Louise Rose, of Macon, Ga., and *d* 1874, leaving issue:

Great-niece and -nephews
(1) Mary Ella ROSE   (2) Hugh James ROSE   (3) John Nicholas ROSE   (4) Robert ROSE; *m* Mrs Matilda W. Christian

President Madison's nieces
7 Ann Fitzhugh ROSE; *d* young
8 Nelly Conway Rose; *m* Capt John Francis NEWMAN and had issue:

Great-niece
(1) Ellen Rose Newman; *m* Revd John Ambrose WHEELOCK (*d* 1866) and *d* 1869, leaving issue:

Great-niece's children
1a Elizabeth Josephine WHEELOCK

Great-niece
(2) Mary Frances Newman; *m* James ROSE and had issue:

Great-niece's children
1a William Arthur ROSE; *m* Ella Baggett
2a Dr Francis Newman ROSE; *m* Mary E. Clements
3a Nelly Conway Rose; *m* William T. BAGGETT, lawyer, of Calif., and had issue:

Great-niece's grandchildren
1b Nelly Rose BAGGETT

President Madison's nieces and nephew
9 Frances ROSE; *d* young   10 Mary ROSE; *d* young   11 Robert H. ROSE, of Ill.; *m* and had issue

JAMES MADISON
FAMILY TREE

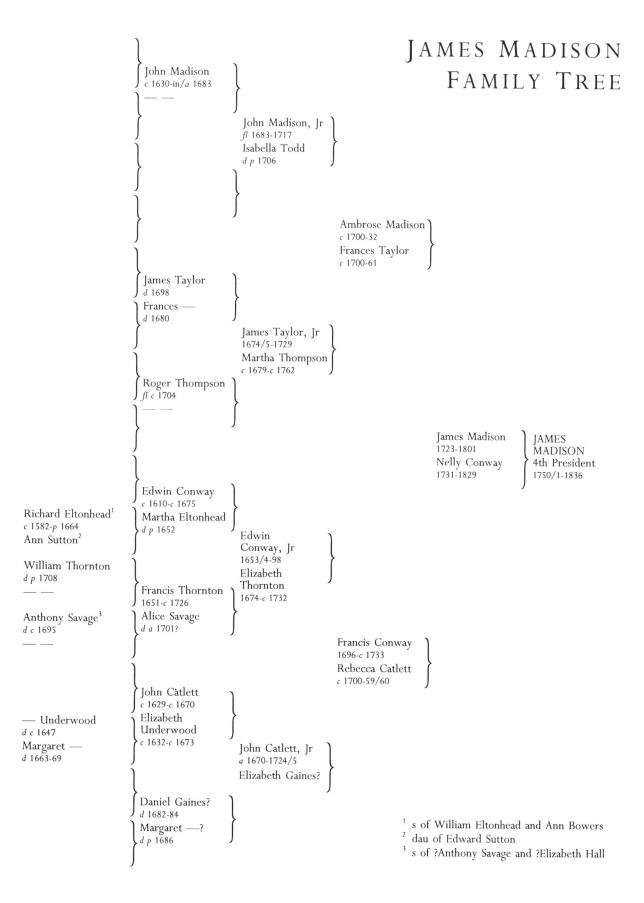

John Madison
c 1630-in/*a* 1683
— —

John Madison, Jr
fl 1683-1717
Isabella Todd
d p 1706

Ambrose Madison
c 1700-32
Frances Taylor
c 1700-61

James Taylor
d 1698
Frances —
d 1680

James Taylor, Jr
1674/5-1729
Martha Thompson
c 1679-*c* 1762

Roger Thompson
fl c 1704
— —

James Madison
1723-1801
Nelly Conway
1731-1829

JAMES
MADISON
4th President
1750/1-1836

Edwin Conway
c 1610-*c* 1675
Martha Eltonhead
d p 1652

Richard Eltonhead[1]
c 1582-*p* 1664
Ann Sutton[2]

Edwin
Conway, Jr
1653/4-98
Elizabeth
Thornton
1674-*c* 1732

William Thornton
d p 1708
— —

Francis Thornton
1651-*c* 1726
Alice Savage
d a 1701?

Anthony Savage[3]
d c 1695
— —

Francis Conway
1696-*c* 1733
Rebecca Catlett
c 1700-59/60

John Catlett
c 1629-*c* 1670
Elizabeth
Underwood
c 1632-*c* 1673

— Underwood
d c 1647
Margaret —
d 1663-69

John Catlett, Jr
a 1670-1724/5
Elizabeth Gaines?

Daniel Gaines?
d 1682-84
Margaret —?
d p 1686

[1] s of William Eltonhead and Ann Bowers
[2] dau of Edward Sutton
[3] s of ?Anthony Savage and ?Elizabeth Hall

Plate 14   James Monroe

JAMES MONROE

1758-1831
5TH PRESIDENT OF THE UNITED STATES OF AMERICA
1817-25

It is difficult to bring the last and least of the Virginia Dynasty to life. He had been an officer under Washington during the War of the Revolution, serving both at the battle of Trenton and at Valley Forge; he had subsequently served as US Senator, as Governor of Virginia, and as a US emissary abroad (under both Washington and Jefferson); he had been a useful Secretary of State to Madison, and an indispensable acting Secretary of War. He was, in short, a decent, blameless, seasoned statesman, of unimpeachable Jeffersonian antecedents; the senior man in the Republican party on Madison's retirement; and as such was rather unenthusiastically given the party's nomination by the Congressional caucus in 1816. He did little during his first term as President, but no obvious successor emerged, so he was renominated and re-elected for a second term, during which he did even less. He does not seem to have felt that the times called for any dramatic action on his part, and regarded the presidency as an honour he had earned, which he enjoyed as a sort of antechamber to retirement. At least he did not make any money out of it. Like his immediate predecessors, he was much poorer at the end of his life than at the beginning, and before his death had been forced to sell his plantation and retire to New York City.

If Monroe was dull, the period of his presidency was not, and it is a measure of his worthy mediocrity that he left so little mark. The War of 1812 had generated a great economic boom, which lasted for a year or two after peace; then came the first of the great crashes which were to punctuate American history for the next century and more. The question of whether and how Missouri might be admitted as a slave state to the Union erupted into a major political crisis, foreshadowing worse to come. Jefferson said that it awoke him like a firebell in the night, but it did not awaken Monroe; it was Henry Clay who found the formula by which the Missouri Compromise was agreed. General Andrew Jackson invaded Spanish Florida on his own impulsive initiative; it was Secretary of State John Quincy Adams who conducted the subsequent negotiations with Spain that resulted in the cession of Florida to the United States in 1819 and the recognition of the US claim, to stretch all the way to the Pacific.

Even the great message which has kept Monroe's name alive, that which incorporates the Monroe Doctrine (1823), owes at least as much to Secretary John Quincy Adams as to the President who signed it. But it was Monroe, after all, who approved and sent to Congress the statement that the United States would henceforth recognize no new colonial ventures anywhere in the Americas; reaffirmed the disinclination of the US government to interfere in European politics; and by the same token warned European governments not to interfere in the Americas, for example by trying to reimpose Spanish rule on the colonies which had just thrown it off. So he deserves the credit, although it is clear he did not foresee what swollen claims future administrations would base on the Doctrine, thereby vastly increasing its importance. He had no thought of establishing an hegemony, or informal empire, over Latin America, which is much to his credit.

His administration was weakened by the rivalries of the politicians who wanted to succeed him: Clay, Calhoun, Adams, Jackson and Crawford of Georgia. Monroe's attempts to call his cabinet ministers to order were unavailing. On one occasion he had a furious row with Crawford, his Secretary of the Treasury, who threatened him with his walking stick, shouting "You damned infernal old scoundrel". The President of the United States seized the tongs from the fireplace for self-defence, and with strong language ordered Crawford out of the house. Crawford half apologized, but the two men never met again. One cannot imagine such an incident occurring under earlier Presidents.

JAMES MONROE'S FAMILY

Spence Monroe, the 5th President's father, was a planter, not on a big scale yet on terms of social equality with much richer men who sent their sons to be educated at the two ancient universities in England. In his youth, however, he had been apprenticed to a joiner to learn carpentry. In Europe such a course of action might have raised eyebrows as being infra dig, even though during the Enlightenment manual labour had a certain vogue among the landowning classes. (Louis XVI put up walls and mended locks as a pastime and readers of *War and Peace* may recall the character Prince Bolkonski, who we are told was a portrait of Tolstoy's grandfather, turning snuff boxes on a lathe.) In Virginia it was a reminder that the gentry were not purely a leisured class, for the frontier had still to be pacified, trained and trimmed.

Spence's education was not confined to wood-working and he was later able to instruct his son James in the classics. But he died in James Monroe's first year at William and Mary College and for the rest of Monroe's time there his mother's brother Judge Joseph Jones of the Virginia General Court paid for his education. Jones became something of a surrogate father and Monroe corresponded with him regularly. In a letter he wrote to Jones in 1794 we learn how he regularly gave his sister Elizabeth money to help bring up her son, although her irresponsible husband was rich enough to do it himself. In another letter to the Judge Monroe mentions his youngest brother Joseph, a sponger who squandered his patrimony and looked to Monroe to put him in the way of making money. Monroe's daughter Eliza claimed her father's money troubles arose partly from his having to pay for Joseph's extravagance in London when Monroe himself was the US representative there in the years 1805 to 1807. Joseph's hopes for advancement through his brother's influence were realised. When Monroe was President he at one point employed Joseph as his private secretary. Presumably this was at least partly to keep him under his eye, though a sponger does not necessarily make a bad secretary and Joseph must have had some ability since he was not only a lawyer but had held down a minor state appointment in Virginia. At another point during his presidency Monroe employed Samuel L. Gouverneur, a nephew of his wife's, as his private secretary. Gouverneur eventually married Monroe's younger daughter Maria.

As well as being a moral and educational support to his nephew Judge Jones was on friendly terms with the other three members of the Virginia Dynasty, Washington, Jefferson and Madison. It was through Jones that Monroe was able to choose between two advantageous springboards to success. There were two men in whose office he could study law. Both would guide him. It depended whether he wanted to be principally a lawyer or politician. On the one hand there was George Wythe, Chancellor of the Virginia High Court; on the other, Thomas Jefferson. Wythe's was reckoned the better legal brain but on Jones's recommendation Monroe chose Jefferson, with the result that he benefited from Jefferson's patronage throughout his career. Another educational influence on Monroe may well have been his mother. According to Monroe's great-granddaughter Rose Gouverneur Hoes, Elizabeth Monroe was particularly well educated for her time.

Plate 15   Elizabeth Kortright Monroe

*Plate 16   Eliza Monroe Hay, Monroe's daughter
and hostess in the White House*

Monroe's wife, Elizabeth Kortright, came from a New York family of Dutch and English descent. (Through her mother, an Aspinwall, she was related to President Franklin D. Roosevelt.) In contrast to Monroe's Revolutionary record the Kortrights were pro-British, Elizabeth's father having actually served as an officer in the British army. Quite apart from whatever doubts the Kortrights may have had about their son-in-law politically, he could not have seemed a spectacular catch when he and Elizabeth got married in 1786. He quitted Congress soon after marrying and was about to settle in Virginia to practise law. At Uncle Joseph Jones's prompting Monroe moved into a house the Judge owned at Fredericksburg while he got established. But then he was made Minister to France and his career took off. Sad to say, Elizabeth failed to keep pace. By all accounts she was gracious, comely and statuesque but she nevertheless seems to have been something of a nullity — splendidly null in fact. The French called her "the beautiful American woman" but thought she could have done more to help her husband in his diplomatic post. Her one memorable action during her time in France, in her entire life indeed, was rescuing the wife of the Marquis de Lafayette from the guillotine. Even this was at the prompting of her husband.

She suffered from increasing ill health as she got older and by the time her husband became President, when she was nearly 50, she felt unable to entertain on the scale thought appropriate for the First Lady hitherto. She discontinued the custom of First Ladies paying calls on diplomats' and politicians' wives. This caused offence but may have had some justification since Washington had grown, with more foreign representatives, to say nothing of Senators and Congressmen as new states became admitted to the Union. Most of her ailments are mysterious but she is said to have developed rheumatism after attending Napoleon's coronation, which must indeed have been a chilly ceremony as it took place in the gigantic cathedral of Notre Dame in the month of December when snow lay on the ground and the three-and-a-half-hour ceremony was prolonged at either end by the necessity of the onlookers being seated beforehand and by the late arrival of the Emperor himself. Given his wife's bad health it is surprising that Monroe should have started the custom of Presidents giving their Inaugural addresses al fresco. (It was to kill President William Harrison and the wife of President Fillmore.) During her time in the White House Elizabeth Monroe seems to have been fit for little more than superintending the slaves as they prepared wax candles for public functions, a process that lasted weeks on end.

The Monroes' elder daughter Eliza tried to repair the damage done by her mother's aloofness, paying calls all over Washington and explaining about her mother's ill health. She had something of her mother's attractiveness but less of her charm and tact, for Elizabeth Monroe, whatever her other failings, was evidently not as stiff in manner as in limb. Indeed one gets the distinct impression that Eliza was difficult, for she fell out with her sister Maria after the latter's marriage and was prone to social feuding. She unselfishly (or perhaps not so unselfishly) gave up living at Richmond and moved into the White House to substitute for her mother. She nevertheless maintained her mother's ban on paying the first call where foreign representatives' wives were concerned and introduced a personal element into America's external relations by persuading her father to keep the foreign representatives themselves at bay. The resultant web of jealousy and bad feeling threatened to entangle civilized intercourse generally, and the question of how best to receive the diplomatic corps came up for discussion in the Cabinet.

Like other Americans of their generation the Monroes had absorbed a great deal of French influence. Eliza was educated at St Germain, staying on after her father left France in 1796 at the end of his first posting there. One of her best school friends was Hortense de Beauharnais, Napoleon's stepdaughter and later wife of his brother Louis, King of Holland. Eliza Monroe christened her daughter after Hortense. In addition, Hortense's brother Eugène had been educated with Monroe's cousin, his uncle Joseph's son. Monroe's autobiography, in which, like Julius Caesar, he narrates his adventures in the third person as if they had hapened to somebody else, hints that the Beauharnais connection may have influenced Napoleon to oblige the father of his stepdaughter's old school chum in the matter of the Louisiana Purchase.

The Monroes had built up a collection of French furniture while abroad and adorned the newly restored White House with it. Their silver was in use there too, both collections being purchased by the nation. (The furniture later became scattered throughout the White House and various official repositories until reassembled in one room of the White House a century later by Lou Hoover.)

Monroe and his wife were in such poor health his last year in office that they did no entertaining at the White House at all. After his presidency they gladly retired to Oak Hill, which had been designed by Jefferson and erected by James Hoban, the architect of the White House. As with so many Presidents, Monroe got into money difficulties. He had to sell Oak Hill and had moved in with his daughter Maria in New York when he died. He does not seem to have been very methodical either in his accounts or — doubtless partly a result of the muddle — in extracting compensation from the US government for his expenditure while representing his country abroad. Which makes it ironic that through the Monroes the US acquired one of the greatest bargains of all time in the Louisiana Purchase.

BIOGRAPHICAL DETAILS AND DESCENDANTS

JAMES MONROE, *b* Monroe's Creek, Westmoreland Co., Va., 28 April 1758; *educ* privately and William and Mary Coll; 2nd Lt 3rd Virginia Regt 1775, 1st Lt 1776, saw action under Washington at Battles of Harlem Heights (wounded), White Plains and Trenton (wounded), Capt Dec 1776, ADC to Maj-Gen William Alexander, self-styled Earl of Stirling, 1777, seeing action at Battles of Brandywine and Germantown, Maj Nov 1777, saw action at Battle of Monmouth 1778, Mily Commissioner to Southern Revolutionary Army with rank of Lt-Col 1780, Memb from King George Co of Virginia House of Delegates and Memb Exec Cncl 1782, Virginia Delegate to Continental Congress 1783-86, admitted to Virginia Bar 1786, Memb Virginia Assembly 1787-88 and 1810-11, Memb Virginia Convention ratifying US Constitution 1788, unsuccessful candidate (being defeated by the future President MADISON) for US House of Reps 1788, US Senator from Virginia 1790-94 (Memb Ctee investigating Alexander Hamilton's use of public money 1792), Memb Commission revising laws of Virginia 1791, US Minister to France 1794-96, Govr Virginia 1799-1802 and Jan-March 1811, US Envoy Extraordinary to France to negotiate Louisiana Purchase Jan 1803, US Minister to Britain April 1803-07, also US Envoy Extraordinary to Spain 1803-07, Commissioner settling differences between US and Britain 1806, unsuccessful presidential candidate 1808, US Sec State 1811-14 and Feb-March 1815, US Sec War ad interim Jan-Feb 1814 and 3-27 Sept 1814, full Sec War Sept 1814-15, 5th President (Democratic-Republican) of the USA 1817-25, Regent U of Virginia 1826, Chm Virginia Constitutional Convention 1829, author: *Observations Upon the Proposed Plan of Federal Government* (1788), *A View of the Conduct of the Executive in the Foreign Affairs of the United States* (1797), *The Writings of James Monroe*, seven vols (1898-1903), *Papers of James Monroe*, ed S. M. Hamilton (1904) and *The Autobiography of James Monroe*, ed Stuart G. Brown with Donald G. Baker (1959); *m* Trinity Episcopal Church New York, 16 Feb 1786 Elizabeth (*b* New York 30 June 1768; *d* Oak Hill, Loudoun Co., Va. 23 Sept 1830, *bur* first Oak Hill, reinterred beside her husband Hollywood, Richmond, Va., 1903), eldest dau of Capt Laurence or Lawrence Kortright, of New York, merchant and former British army officer, and his *w* Hannah Aspinwall, and *d* New York 4 July 1831 (initially *bur* Marble Hill Cemetery there, re-interred Hollywood Cemetery alongside his *w* 1858), having had issue:

President Monroe's daughter
I Eliza Kortright MONROE, *b* Fredericksburg, Va., 5 Dec 1787; *educ* France; *m* 17 Oct 1808, as his 2nd *w*, Judge George Hay, of Richmond, Va. (*b* Williamsburg, Va., 15 Dec 1765; *d* Richmond, Va., 21 Sept 1830), *s* of Anthony Hay and his *w* Elizabeth Davenport, and *d* Paris, France, 27 Jan 1840 (*bur* Père Lachaise Cemetery), leaving issue:

Grandchildren
1 Hortensia (Hortense) Monroe Hay, *b c* 1809; *m* 5 July 1829, as his 2nd *w*, Nicholas Lloyd ROGERS, of Druid Hill, Baltimore (*b c* 1787; *d* Baltimore 12 Nov 1860), *s* of Nicholas Rogers and his *w* Eleanor Buchanan, and *d* 10 Dec 1854, leaving issue:

Great-grandchildren
(1) Harriet Rogers, *b* 18—; *m* as his 1st *w* Charles WILMER
(2) Mary Custis Rogers, *b* 18—; *m* 1st —— HARRIS and had issue:

Great-great-grandchildren
1a Barton Chapin HARRIS, *d* young

Great-grandchildren
(2) (cont.) Mary Rogers Harris *m* 2nd Richard HARDESTY (*d* 1871) and *d* 1869, leaving further issue:

Great-great-grandchildren
2a Hortense Hay Hardesty, *b* 24 Oct 1865; *m* William Watson McINTIRE (*b* Chambersburg, Pa., 30 June 1850; US Congressman; *d* Baltimore Co, Md., 30 March 1912) and *d* 1933, having had issue:

Great-great-grandchildren's children
1b Mary Custis McINTIRE, *b* 24 Aug 1887; *d* 10 April 1897
2b Hortense Rogers McIntire, *b* Baltimore 3 Jan 1889; *m* there 23 Jan 1907 John William STORK, of Roland Park, Md. (*b* Baltimore 26 Jan 1871; *d* there 13 Nov 1958), s of William L. Stork and his w Clintonia, and *d* 27 Sept 1951, having had issue:

Great-great-grandchildren's grandchildren
1c Anne Monroe STORK, *b* Baltimore 20 June 1909; *d* 8 Oct 1936
2c Lloyd Rogers STORK, *b* Baltimore 5 Aug 1911; *d* there 29 Jan 1929
3c *Jean Monroe Stork [Mrs Bernard Kamtman, 14 St Martin's Road, Baltimore, MD 21218, USA], *b* Baltimore 24 Dec 1913; *m* there 17 June 1938 *Bernard S. KAMTMAN (*b* Baltimore 16 March 1907), s of George Kamtman and his w Helen Kaufman, and has issue:

Great-great-grandchildren's great-grandchildren
1d *Sandra Monroe Kamtman [Mrs Robert Patterson Jr, 5605 Enderly Road, Baltimore, MD 21212, USA; 33 Faraday Drive, Timonium, MD, USA; 11843 Sherbourne Road, Timonium, MD, USA], *b* Baltimore 8 Jan 1943; *m* there Sept 1966 *Robert Urie PATTERSON, Jr (*b* Washington DC), s of Robert Urie Patterson and his w Eleanor Reeve, and has issue:

Great-great-grandchildren's great-great-grandchildren
1e *Robert Baden PATTERSON, *b* Baltimore 20 Dec 1968
2e *Lloyd Reeve PATTERSON, *b* Baltimore 11 April 1970

Great-great-grandchildren
3a Elizabeth Kortright Hardesty, *b* 1867; *m* John S. RICHARDSON, of Bel Air, Md. (*b* 1864; *d* 1927), and *d* 26 May 1955, having had issue:

Great-great-grandchildren's children
1b John Monroe RICHARDSON, of Denver, Colorado, *b* 1890; *m* 1st 19— Evelyn Davis; *m* 2nd 19— Marguerite McIntire and *d* 1954
2b Lloyd Nicholas RICHARDSON, *b* 1891; *m* 19— Mary Geneva Dean
3b Elizabeth Hardesty RICHARDSON, *b* 1893; *d* aged 8 months
4b *Richard Hardesty RICHARDSON, *b* 1894; *m* 19— *Margaret Hoffman and has issue:

Great-great-grandchildren's grandchildren
1c *Richard Hardesty RICHARDSON, Jr, *b* 1941
2c *Nancy RICHARDSON, *b* 1947

Great-great-grandchildren's children
5b *Eleanor Agnes Richardson, *b* 1896; *m* 1923 *Dr Charles B. CANTON and has issue:

Great-great-grandchildren's grandchildren
1c *Eleanor Agnes Canton, *b* 1927; *m* 1952 *John ZINK
2c *Geraldine CANTON, *b* 1928

Great-great-grandchildren's children
6b *James Jerome RICHARDSON, *b* 1901; *m* 1927 *Martha Evans and has issue:

Great-great-grandchildren's grandchildren
1c *James Jerome RICHARDSON, Jr, *b* 1931; *m* 1953 *Sally Brown Thomas and has issue:

Great-great-grandchildren's great-grandchildren
1d *John David RICHARDSON, *b* April 1955

Great-great-grandchildren's children
7b *Frances Kortright Monroe Richardson [Mrs Aloysius Valentine, 610 North Carolina Avenue, SE, Washington, DC 20003, USA], *b* 1904; *m* 1935 Dr Aloysius William VALENTINE (*b* 1875; *d* 1951)

Great-grandchildren
(3) Hortense Rogers, *b* 18—; *m* —— COZENS/COUSINS

President Monroe's children
II James (?) Spence (?) MONROE, *b* May 1799; *d* Richmond, Va., 28 Sept 1800
III Maria Hester Monroe, *b* Paris, France, 1803; *m* the White House, Washington, DC, 9 March 1820 her 1st cousin Samuel Laurence GOUVERNEUR, of New York (*b* 1799; Memb New York State Legislature, priv sec to his f-in-law President MONROE, Postmaster of New York City 1828-36; *d* 1867), s of Nicholas Gouverneur, of New York, and his w Hester Kortright, and *d* Oak Hill, Loudoun Co, Va., 1850, leaving issue:

Grandchildren

1 James Monroe GOUVERNEUR, b 18—

2 Elizabeth Kortright Gouverneur, b Washington, DC; m 1st Washington 9 June 1842 Dr Henry Lee HEISKELL (b Winchester, Va., 1799; Maj and Surg US Army; d Meechwood 12 Aug 1855, bur Washington, DC), s of John Heiskell and his w Ann Sowers, and had issue:

Great-grandchildren

(1) James Monroe HEISKELL, b Washington, DC, 5 June 1844; lawyer, one of "Mosby's Men" in Confederate States Army, ran for election as mayor of Baltimore; m 1st Leesburg, Va., 26 Feb 1867 Esther Fairfax (b 1847; d Baltimore 18 July 1873), dau of Col John West Minor and his w Louisa Fairfax, and had issue:

Great-great-grandchildren

1a Teakle Wallace HEISKELL, b Leesburg, Va., 29 Jan 1868; d c 1873

2a Minor Fairfax Heiskell GOUVERNEUR (took grandmother's maiden name of Gouverneur), b Baltimore 15 Dec 1869; inventor and banker; m Wilmington, N Carolina, 2 Dec 1896 his 3rd cousin Mary Fairfax (b Wilmington 30 Sept 1874; d Alexandria, Va., 27 May 1956), er dau of George Davis, Atty-Gen of the Confederacy, and his w Monimia (herself 3rd dau of Dr Orlando Fairfax (see BURKE'S PEERAGE & BARONETAGE) and his w Mary Randolph, 2nd dau of Wilson Jefferson Cary, of Carysbrook, great-nephew of President JEFFERSON), and d Baltimore 8 June 1933, leaving issue:

Great-great-grandchildren's children

1b Fairfax Heiskell GOUVERNEUR, OBE, b Yonkers, New York, 5 Sept 1897; educ Phillips Exeter Acad; offr with US Army Air Corps in World Wars I and II, investment banker; m Rochester, New York, 6 June 1922 *Caroline Erickson, dau of Thornton Jeffress and his w Carolyn Erickson Perkins, and d Clearwater Beach, Fla., 15 April 1967, having had issue:

Great-great-grandchildren's grandchildren

1c *Minor Fairfax Heiskell GOUVERNEUR II [PO Box 105, Goshen, CT 06756, USA; Route 63, Goshen, CT 06756, USA], b Rochester, New York, 9 Sept 1923; educ Rensselaer Polytechnic Inst, Troy, New York; m Maplewood, New Jersey, 21 May 1949 *Carolyn Marie, dau of Reynier Jacob Wortendyke, Jr, and has issue:

Great-great-grandchildren's great-grandchildren

1d *Elizabeth Rogers Gouverneur, b Rochester 17 May 1950; educ U of Rochester (BA); m Litchfield, Conn., 23 May 1976 *Richard Arnold COHEN and has issue:

Great-great-grandchildren's great-great-grandchildren

1c *Aaron Erickson COHEN, b Wilmington, Del., 27 Feb 1979

Great-great-grandchildren's great-grandchildren

2d *Sallie Thornton GOUVERNEUR, b St Charles, Ill., 3 Nov 1951; educ Harvard (BA)

3d *Jeffress GOUVERNEUR, b Geneva, Ill., 30 Oct 1955; educ Boston U (BA)

4d *Abigail Josephine GOUVERNEUR, b Wheaton, Ill., 29 Dec 1960

5d *Jacob Reynier GOUVERNEUR, b Torrington, Conn., 3 Feb 1968

Great-great-grandchildren's grandchildren

2c Sallie Thornton GOUVERNEUR, b 192-; d in infancy

3c *Caroline Erickson Gouverneur [Mrs Daniel Dillon III, 855 Penny Royal Lane, San Rafael, CA 94903, USA], b Rochester, New York, 23 March 1927; educ Bennett Coll; m San Francisco 9 Sept 1978 *Daniel DILLON III

4c *Jane Fairfax Gouverneur, b Rochester, New York, 29 April 1931; m there 21 Dec 1954 *Benjamin Lansing Boyd TEN EYCK IV, s of Benjamin Lansing Boyd Ten Eyck III, and has issue:

Great-great-grandchildren's great-grandchildren

1d *Benjamin Boyd TEN EYCK, b Rochester 8 April 1956

2d *Thomas Jeffress TEN EYCK, b Rochester 18 Sept 1959

3d *Peter Fairfax TEN EYCK, b Rochester 7 Nov 1960

Great-great-grandchildren's children

2b Esther Gouverneur, b Wilmington, N Carolina, 21 Feb 1905; m Bastia, Corsica, France, 22 Dec 1944 Harris Elliott KIRK (b Nashville, Tenn., 4 May 1898; d 14 April 1988), s of Revd Dr Harris Elliott Kirk, of Baltimore, Moderator of Gen Assembly US Presbyterian Church 1928, and his w Helen O. McCormick, and d 24 March 1991, leaving issue:

Great-great-grandchildren's grandchildren

1c *Mary Fairfax Kirk [Mrs Robert W Wright, 306 Brooks Avenue, Raleigh, NC 27607, USA], b Baltimore 16 Feb 1950; educ Roanoke Coll (AB 1972); advertising manager with The News & Observer newspaper; m Alexandria, Va., 30 Sept 1972 (divorce 19—) Robert Webb WRIGHT (b Richmond, Va., 5 May 1950) and has issue:

Great-great-grandchildren's great-grandchildren

1d *Katherine Fairfax WRIGHT, b Morehead City, N Carolina, 2 Oct 1976

Great-great-grandchildren
3a (James) Monroe HEISKELL, *b* 20 May 1872; *d* 20 Oct 1873

Great-grandchildren
(1) (cont.) James Monroe Heiskell *m* 2nd Philadelphia 2 July 1882, as her 1st husb, Mary (*m* 2nd J. Herman Ireland and *d* Baltimore 1941), dau of Bronaugh Derringer and his w Estalena Woodland, and *d* 1899, having with her had issue:

Great-great-grandchildren
4a Marian Gouverneur Heiskell, *b* Baltimore 27 June 1886; *m* 1st Baltimore 1905 Richard EMORY (*b* Inverness, Baltimore Co., Md., 1870; *d* San Jose, Calif., Nov 1906), s of Thomas Lane Emory and his w Griselda Holmes, and had issue:

Great-great-grandchildren's children
1b *Elizabeth Kortright Monroe Emory [Mrs G Gordon Gatchell, Blakehurst Retirement Home, W Joppa Rd, Baltimore, MD 21204, USA], *b* Baltimore 11 Feb 1907; Memb James Monroe Museum, Fredericksburg, Va.; *m* Baltimore 1929 G. Gordon GATCHELL (*b* Baltimore 1898; *d* there 1983), s of Skipwith Gordon Gatchell and his w Gertrude Gantz, and has issue:

Great-great-grandchildren's grandchildren
1c *G. Gordon GATCHELL, Jr [127 Bedford Road, Lincoln, MA 01773, USA], *b* Baltimore 26 Feb 1930; *educ* Boston Inst; formerly with Boston office of Merrill Lynch (now ret), Memb Soc of Cincinnati and James Monroe Museum, Fredericksburg, Va.; *m* Philadelphia Oct 1953 *Esther Allen (*b* Philadelphia 23 Jan 1932), dau of Donald MacLea and his w Catherine Miskey, and has issue:

Great-great-grandchildren's great-grandchildren
1d *Catharine Allen GATCHELL [47 Eliphamets Lane, Chatham, MA 02633, USA], *b* Bryn Mawr, Pa., 8 July 1954
2d *Elizabeth Emory GATCHELL [47 Eliphamets Lane, Chatham, MA 02633, USA], *b* Concord, Mass., 11 April 1956
3d *William Hugh GATCHELL [47 Eliphamets Lane, Chatham, MA 02633, USA], *b* Concord 14 Aug 1962

Great-great-grandchildren's grandchildren
2c *Richard Emory GATCHELL [1411 Walnut Hill Lane, Baltimore, MD 21204, USA], *b* Baltimore 20 March 1933; *educ* Calvert Sch, Gilman Sch for Boys, and Johns Hopkins U; real estate broker, partner in firm Hill & Co, Tstee Peale Museum, Bd Memb Soc for Preservation of Maryland Antiquities, Baltimore Heritage and Soc for Preservation of Fells Point and Federal Hill, Memb James Monroe Museum, Fredericksburg, Va.; *m* the Church of the Redeemer, Baltimore, Oct 1960 Margaret Brian (divorce 19—) (*b* Pittsburg, Pa., 2 Sept 1935), dau of Thomas Brian Parsons and his w Fanny Glenn Whitman, and has issue:

Great-great-grandchildren's great-grandchildren
1d *Margaret Parsons GATCHELL, *b* Baltimore 7 July 1963
2d *Richard Emory GATCHELL, Jr, *b* Baltimore 8 March 1965

Great-great-grandchildren's grandchildren
3c *Monroe Tyler GATCHELL [1402 Ruxton Road, Baltimore, MD 21204, USA], *b* Baltimore 16 Dec 1940; *educ* Gilman Sch and Johns Hopkins; Memb James Monroe Museum, Fredericksburg, Va.; *m* Baltimore 19 June 1965 *Susan Miller (*b* there 1942), dau of Joseph Eugene Rowe, Jr, and his w Gene Claire Miller

Great-great-grandchildren
4a (cont.) Marian Heiskell Emory *m* 2nd Baltimore 1915 E. Griswold THELIN (*b* Baltimore 1872; *d* there April 1924), s of William T. Thelin and his w Elizabeth Griswold, and *d* Baltimore 5 Oct 1931

Great-grandchildren
(2) Henry Lee Heiskell, *b* Washington, DC, 17 Oct 1850; *educ* Rock Hill Coll, Ellicott City, Md., and US Naval Acad; businessman in St Louis and Yazoo City, Miss., 1869-76, Sgt US Signal Corps 1876 (service transferred to Ag Dept as US Weather Bureau 1888), Prof Meteorology US Weather Bureau 1913; *m* 1st 16 Oct 1878 Emma Leona Heiskell (*d* DC 19 April 1890) and had issue:

Great-great-grandchildren
1a Esther Hill Heiskell, *b* Oxon Hill, Md., 16 Sept 1879; *m* 1900 Edward/Edwin SEFTON (*b* 1876; lawyer; *d* Mill Neck, Long Island, New York, 28 June 1943) and *d* 2 July 1954, leaving issue:

Great-great-grandchildren's children
1b *Elizabeth Monroe Sefton, *b* 1901; *m* 19— *Charles Wayne KERWOOD (*b* 1 Aug 1897) and has issue:

Great-great-grandchildren's grandchildren
1c *Wayne Sefton KERWOOD, *b* 20 Feb 1929

Great-great-grandchildren
2a Elizabeth Kortright Gouverneur Heiskell, *b* 1884; *m* 1905 Harry Freeman CLARK, of Washington, DC (*b* 23 Sept 1871; Sec and Treasurer Washington Steel & Ordnance Co; *d* 11 Dec 1944) and *d* 25 Feb 1978, having had issue:

Great-great-grandchildren's children
1b James Monroe CLARK, *b* and *d* 2 July 1912
2b *James Monroe CLARK, *b* 19 July 1913; *m* Sept 1936 Sarah Williams (*d* 1972) and has issue:

Great-great-grandchildren's grandchildren
1c *Elise Clark [Mrs Philip Heald, 771 Sandalwood Drive, El Centro, CA 92243, USA], *b* 21 Oct 1941; *m* 19— *Philip P. HEALD and has issue:

Great-great-grandchildren's great-grandchildren
1d *Frederick HEALD, *b* 1966
2d *Amy HEALD, *b* 1968

Great-great-grandchildren's grandchildren
2c *Harry Freeman CLARK, *b* 14 April 1948; *m* 1975 *Denise —— and has issue:

Great-great-grandchildren's great-grandchildren
1d *Brian Williams CLARK, *b* 24 Dec 1976

Great-great-grandchildren's children
3b *Henry Lee CLARK [3806 Leland Street, Chevy Chase, MD 20015, USA], *b* 22 Aug 1915; *m* 27 June 1942 *Nancy Lewis Heiskell (*b* 8 July 1920) and has issue:

Great-great-grandchildren's grandchildren
1c *Nancy Lewis CLARK, *b* 18 July 1944
2c *Susan Hill CLARK, *b* Oct 1946
3c *Henry Lee CLARK, Jr, *b* 20 Oct 1947; *m* 24 Jan 1970 *Mary Lou Johnson, of Sidney, Nebr., and has issue:

Great-great-grandchildren's great-grandchildren
1d *Christopher Lee CLARK, *b* 11 Jan 1972
2d *Jeffrey Johnson CLARK, *b* 8 Jan 1974
3d *Ashley Lewis CLARK, *b* 9 March 1977

Great-great-grandchildren's grandchildren
4c *Mary Fitzhugh Clark, *b* 3 Oct 1954; *m* 24 Nov 1978 *William Borden AYERS

Great-grandchildren
(2) (cont.) Henry Lee Heiskell *m* 2nd 12 Oct 1892 Henrietta Brent and *d* 28 Jan 1914, having with her had issue:

Great-great-grandchildren
3a John Carroll Brent HEISKELL, *b* Washington, DC, 1 Aug, *d* 3 Aug 1893
4a John Carroll Brent HEISKELL, *b* 13 July 1896; *d* 1980

Great-grandchildren
(3) Dr Sydney Otho HEISKELL, *b* Washington, DC, 12 Jan 1853; *m* 1st 1882 Abbie (*d* 1884), dau of —— Townsend, of Baltimore; *m* 2nd Doralyn, dau of —— Miller, of Philadelphia, and *d* 1906

Grandchildren
2 (cont.) Elizabeth Kortright Gouverneur Heiskell *m* 2nd 27 Oct 1856 (James) Monroe BIBBY (*d* 3 March 1860) and had further issue:

Great-grandchildren
(4) Elizabeth (Lilly) Monroe BIBBY, *b* Baltimore 14 June 1859; *d* 10 May 1860

Grandchildren
2 (cont.) Elizabeth Kortright Gouverneur Heiskell Bibby *m* 3rd 186- Dr Grafton D. SPURRIER, Col US Army Medical Corps, and *d* Needwood, Md., 2 April 1868, having had further issue:

Great-grandchildren
(5) Grafton D. SPURRIER, Jr; *d* 1930

Grandchildren
3 Samuel Laurence GOUVERNEUR, Jr, *b* 1820; Lt 4th US Artillery Mexican War, first US Consul Foo Chow, China, Maryland Delegate Liberal Republicans Convention 1872, publisher *Maryland Herald*; *m* 5 March 1855 Marian (*b* Jamaica, Long Island, New York, 1821; author: *As I Remember — Recollections of American Society During the 19th Century* (1911); *d* Washington, DC, 12 March 1914), dau of Judge James Campbell and his *w* Mary Ann Hazard, and *d* Washington, DC, 1880, leaving issue:

Great-grandchildren
(1) Maud Campbell GOUVERNEUR, *b* Washington, DC, 8 April 1856; *d* there 29 March 1947
(2) Ruth Monroe Gouverneur, *b* Washington, DC, 27 Nov 1858; *m* there 6 Dec 1882 Dr William Crawford JOHNSON (*b* Frederick, Md., 17 July 1856; *d* there 28 Dec 1943), s of George Johnson and his *w* Emily Ann Crawford, and *d* Frederick 28 Feb 1949, leaving issue:

Great-great-grandchildren
1a Marian Campbell Johnson, *b* 19 June 1885; *m* Washington, DC, 1913 Brig-Gen Green Clay GOODLOE (*b* Lexington,

Ky., 1845; Paymaster US Medical Corps; *d* Washington, DC, 1917), s of ——— Goodloe and his w Sally Ann Smith, and *d* Washington, DC, leaving issue:

Great-great-grandchildren's children

1b Green Clay GOODLOE, Jr, *b* 1914; *educ* US Mil Acad, Annapolis, Md.; Lt-Cdr USN World War II; *d* 1945

Great-great-grandchildren

2a Emily Crawford JOHNSON [112 North Bentz Street, Frederick, MD 21701, USA], *b* Frederick 1 Aug 1887

3a *William Monroe JOHNSON [PO Box 66, Woodston, Kansas 67675, USA], *b* Frederick 19 Feb 1895; *educ* George Washington U (LLB); attorney (ret), Sgt 127th Infy American Expeditionary Force World War I, Memb Soc of the Cincinnati, author of numerous historical articles; *m* Downs, Kans., 25 Dec 1921 *Lillian Elizabeth (*b* Whitehall, Ill., 14 Aug 1897), dau of Thomas Bryant Smith and his w Eva Lonella Bentley, and has issue:

Great-great-grandchildren's children

1b *Elizabeth Gouverneur Johnson, *b* Washington, DC, 1 Sept 1923; *m* 1st 19— Harvey PARKER, Jr, and has issue:

Great-great-grandchildren's grandchildren

1c *Carroll Elizabeth Parker, *b* 1947; *m* 19— *Robert HAWBAKER and has issue:

Great-great-grandchildren's great-grandchildren

1d *Margaret HAWBAKER, *b* 4 March 1968

Great-great-grandchildren's grandchildren

2c *Margaret Monroe Parker, *b* 1952; *m* 19— *Thomas SNOOK and has issue:

Great-great-grandchildren's great-grandchildren

1d *Elizabeth Ann SNOOK, *b* 24 Jan 1971

Great-great-grandchildren's children

1b (cont.) Elizabeth Gouverneur Johnson Parker *m* 2nd *Thomas A. LIVELY and has further issue:

Great-great-grandchildren's grandchildren

3c *Ann Kortright LIVELY, *b* 1957

4c *Thomas A. LIVELY, Jr, *b* 1959

Great-great-grandchildren's children

2b *Monroe JOHNSON [3221 Bristolhall Drive, Bridgeton, MO 63044, USA], *b* Savannah, Ga., 7 July 1930; *educ* Washburn U; Maj USAF, personnel administrator, historian; *m* Joplin, Mo., 6 Oct 1956 *June Edith (*b* Joplin 12 July 1935), dau of Elmer Franklin Mitchell and his w Edith Laura Snyder, and has issue:

Great-great-grandchildren's grandchildren

1c *Bradley Monroe JOHNSON, *b* Wichita, Kans., 25 Sept 1958

2c *Elizabeth June JOHNSON, *b* Wichita 3 May 1961

Great-grandchildren

(3) Rose de Chine Gouverneur, *b* Foo Chow, China, 1860; *m* Washington, DC, 5 Dec 1888 Revd Roswell Randall HOES (*b* 1850; Capt and Chaplain USN; *d* 1921) and *d* Washington, DC, 26 May 1933, having had issue:

Great-great-grandchildren

1a Gouverneur HOES, *b* 1889; Capt US Army; *m* 19— *Gourley Edwards [2204 Q Street, NW, Washington, DC, USA] and *d* 1943

2a Roswell Randall HOES, Jr, *b* 1891; *d* 1901

3a Laurence Gouverneur HOES, *b* 8 Jan 1900; *educ* St Alban's Sch, Washington, DC; investment banker, lecturer, historian and writer, owner and founder James Monroe Nat Shrine, Fredericksburg, Va., Pres Monroe Memorial Fndn, Memb Sons of Revolution; *m* 1st 24 Nov 1928 (divorce 1969) Ingrid, dau of Dr Joseph per Ludwig Westesson, of Philadelphia, and had issue:

Great-great-grandchildren's children

1b *Monroe Randall HOES [19 Happy Hollow Road, Wayland, MA 01778, USA], *b* Washington, DC, 26 Sept 1931; *educ* William and Mary Coll (BS 1953), MIT (BSEE 1958) and Northeastern U, Boston (MSEE 1964); Lt USN 1953-56, consultant engineer; *m* 2 June 1956 *Mary Alice, dau of Arthur Abraham Regier and his w Dorothy Grace White, of Newport News, Va., and has issue:

Great-great-grandchildren's grandchildren

1c *Randall Monroe HOES [54 Barrows St, Dedham, MA 02026, USA], *b* Boston 7 Jan 1959; *educ* Tufts U (BS/MS Chemistry 1983) and U of Rochester Simon Sch of Business (MBA 1989); product manager; *m* 27 June 1992 *Christine Anne Foro, of Rochester

2c *Kathryn Westesson HOES, *b* Boston 21 Oct 1960; *educ* Dartmouth Coll, Hanover, New Hampshire (BA 1983); television producer

Great-great-grandchildren

3a (cont.) Laurence Hoes *m* 2nd 19— ——— and *d* 11 Nov 1978

MALE LINE ANCESTRY AND COLLATERAL DESCENDANTS

It has been claimed with some plausibility (and was implied by Monroe himself in his autobiography) that the 5th President's male line ancestors stem from a younger branch of the Munros of Foulis, whose lands lay along the north shore of the Cromarty Firth (a sea inlet) in northeast Scotland. However, even the most modern research in America is unable to trace Monroe's lineage back definitely beyond an Andrew Monroe, who had emigrated from Scotland to St Mary's Co, Maryland, by 1642 (the President in his autobiography says "about the year 1645"). Be that as it may, the early history of the Munros of Foulis is as follows:

The Munros were in early times vassals of the Earls of Ross, who held sway in the eastern part of what later became Ross and Cromarty and is now part of the Highland Region of Scotland. Their possession of Foulis dates to a time beyond written record. According to the genealogist and heraldic writer Alexander Nisbet (1657-1725) William Earl of Sutherland granted a charter "to my dearest and most faithful relative, George Munro of Foulis" in the reign of King ALEXANDER II (1214-49). DONALD, Baron (a territorial designation, with no suggestion of its conferring the status of a Lord of Parliament or peerage) of Foulis, *fl* 1025. His successor:

GEORGE, Baron of Foulis, *fl* 1101 and was succeeded by HUGH, Baron of Foulis, *fl c* 1120; he was succeeded by ROBERT, Baron of Foulis, who *d* 1164 and was succeeded by DONALD, Baron of Foulis, who *d* 1192 and was succeeded by ROBERT, Baron of Foulis, who *d* 1239 and was succeeded by GEORGE, Baron of Foulis, who *d* 1282 and was succeeded by ROBERT, Baron of Foulis, who *d* 12— or 13— and was succeeded by GEORGE, Baron of Foulis, who *d* 1333 and was succeeded by ROBERT, Baron of Foulis, representative of the family 1341 to his death, *k* 1369 together with a large number of his clan, apparently in a feud, and was succeeded by

HUGH, Baron of Foulis, fought at the Battle of Harlaw, in Aberdeenshire, 24 July 1411, one of the bloodiest fights in Scottish history, where Donald Lord of the Isles attempted unsuccessfully to assert his title to the earldom of Ross against the forces of the crown, and *d* 1424, leaving a yr s, one of whose descendants had a baronetcy conferred on him in 1825 (*see* BURKE'S PEERAGE & BARONETAGE, Munro of Lindertis); Hugh was succeeded by

GEORGE, Baron of Foulis, who was *k* 1454 and was succeeded by JOHN, Baron of Foulis, who *d* 14— or 15— and was succeeded by WILLIAM, Baron of Foulis, who was *k* 1505 and was succeeded by

Hector MUNRO of Foulis; *m* 1st Katherine, dau of Sir Kenneth Mackenzie of Kintail; *m* 2nd Katherine, widow of Donald Macdonald of Slate and dau of Roderick Macleod of Lewis, and *d* 1541, leaving issue by his 1st w:

Robert MUNRO of Foulis; *m* Margaret, dau of Sir Alexander Dunbar of Westfield, Sheriff of Moray, and was *k* at the Battle of Pinkie (a little to the east of Edinburgh) 10 Sept 1547, in which the Duke of Somerset, Protector of England, routed a Scots army; Robert left issue:

I Robert MUNRO of Foulis; *m* 1st Margaret, dau of James Ogilvy of Cardell and aunt of 1st Lord Ogilvy of Deskford (*see* BURKE'S PEERAGE & BARONETAGE, Seafield), and had issue (with two daus):

1 Robert MUNRO of Foulis; *m* four times and *d* leaving only female issue:

(1) Margaret Munro; *m* Robert MUNRO of Assynt

2 Hector MUNRO of Foulis; *m* 1st Anne Fraser, dau of 5th Lord Lovat (*see* BURKE'S PEERAGE & BARONETAGE), and *d* 14 Nov 1603, having had issue:

(1) Col Robert MUNRO of Foulis ('The Black Baron'), a minor on 8 Jan 1608; served in the Swedish armies in the Thirty Years War in Germany as a volunteer Capt in the Scottish corps raised by Sir Donald Mackay, 1st Lord Reay (*see* BURKE'S PEERAGE & BARONETAGE), and was later Col of a Dutch regt of horse and foot under King GUSTAVUS ADOLPHUS of Sweden; *m* 1st Margaret, dau of William Sutherland of Duffus; *m* 2nd Mary Haynes and *d* Ulm, Germany, 1633 after being shot in the foot by a musket, leaving issue:

1a Margaret Munro; *m* 1634 Kenneth MACKENZIE of Scatwell   2a Florence MUNRO

(2) Col Sir Hector MUNRO, 1st Bart (*see* BURKE'S PEERAGE & BARONETAGE, Munro of Foulis-Obsdale)

I (cont.) Robert Munro of Foulis *m* 2nd Katherine, dau of Alexander Ross of Balnagowan, and with her had issue (together with two other offspring):

3 George MUNRO of Obsdale; *m* Catherine, dau of Andrew Munro of Milnton and Newmore, and *d* 1589, having had (with other issue):

(1) John MUNRO of Obsdale; *m* Catherine, dau of John Gordon of Embo, and *d* 1623, having had (with other issue):

1a Sir Robert MUNRO, 3rd Bart (*see also* BURKE'S PEERAGE & BARONETAGE, Munro of Foulis-Obsdale)
2a A son
3a Sir George MUNRO or MONRO of Newmore; served Thirty Years War in Germany under his kinsman Col Robert Munro, The Black Baron (*see above*), also in Ireland with rank of Col under another uncle, also called Robert Munro

(*see below*), joined Scottish expedition into England to relieve CHARLES I 1648, seems to have commanded a unit in which his putative kinsman Andrew Monroe (great-great-grandfather of President MONROE) served at the time of the Battle of Preston 1648, MP Ross-shire 1661-63, 1680-86 and 1689-93 and Sutherland 1669-74, *cr* Knight of the Bath by CHARLES II; *m* 16— Margaret (also referred to as Christian), dau of Sir Frederick Hamilton and sister of 1st Viscount Boyne (*see* BURKE'S PEERAGE & BARONETAGE), and *d* 11 Jan 1693, leaving issue (*see* BURKE'S PEERAGE & BARONETAGE, Munro of Foulis-Obsdale)

(2) Robert MUNRO or MONRO; served in Thirty Years War 1627-34, ending with rank of Col, and Scottish War 1639-40, Burgess of Aberdeen 1640, 2nd-in-Command in Ireland then Commander as Maj-Gen 1642; *m* before 12 Sept 1648 Lady Jean Alexander (*d* 1670), er dau of 1st Earl of Stirling and widow of 2nd Viscount Montgomery of the Great Ardes, and *d* 1680?

II A son   III A son   IV A son

V George MUNRO or MONROE of Katewell; *k* 10 Sept 1547 with his father at the Battle of Pinkie, leaving issue:

George MONROE of Katewell; *m* 1st Katherine, dau of Hector Mackenzie of Fairburn; *m* 2nd Euphemia, dau of John Monroe of Pittonachy, and with her had issue; *m* 3rd Agnes, only dau of Hugh Monroe of Coul and Balconie; his 3rd *s* by his 2nd w:

David MONROE; *m* Agnes, dau of Revd Alexander Monroe or Munro, of Durness, and his w Janet Cumming, and had (with other issue) a 3rd son, who may be identical with:

Andrew MONROE; described by his gggs President MONROE in a letter of 17 Nov 1817 to Sir John Sinclair, 1st Bart (first President of the Board of Agriculture in Britain and a man with enormously wide interests, including antiquarianism; *see* BURKE'S PEERAGE & BARONETAGE, Thurso) as an adherent to the house of Stuart, having arrived in St Mary's Co, Md., was assessed there July 1642 as liable to 50lbs of tobacco in tax to defray expenses of the war against the Susquehanna Indians, appointed Memb of local Assembly 22 Aug 1642, joined Col William Claiborne, Maryland's arch-enemy throughout his life, and the pirate Richard Ingle in a rebellion against Govr Leonard Calvert 1644-45, later had his property confiscated when the rebels were put down and fled across the Potomac into Virginia, returned to Scotland 1648, served under Gen Sir George Monro (*see above*) at the time of the Battle of Preston between the Scots and Oliver Cromwell on 17 Aug the same year, was taken prisoner and banished to Virginia, but escaped and settled in Northumberland Co, Va., where he received several grants of land amounting to 200 ac in all 8 June 1650, later (29 Nov 1652) obtained title to other and more extensive lands (440 ac) in Westmoreland Co, Va., situated on a creek still known as Monroe Creek or Monroe Bay, Vestryman Appamattocks (modern Appomattox) Parish 1661; *m c* 1652, as her 1st husb, Elizabeth (*b* 16—; *m* 2nd before 30 July 1679 George Horner; *m* 3rd before 23 Feb 1686 Edward Mountjoy), thought to have been dau of John Alexander, and *d* at this plantation 1668 (*bur* near Doctors Point, Westmoreland Co), leaving issue (not necessarily in the order given):

I Andrew MONROE; *m* Eleanor Spence and had issue:

1 Andrew MONROE

2 Spence MONROE; *m* 1st Margaret, dau of Nathaniel Gray; *m* 2nd, as her 1st husb, Christian (she *m* 2nd her deceased husb's cousin Andrew Monroe, for whom *see below*), dau of Charles Tyler (settled Westmoreland Co by 1690; *d* before 1723) and his w Jane (*m* 2nd William Woffendall and *d* probably before 1737/8); Spence Monroe *d* 1726

II William MONROE, Sr, *b* Westmoreland Co *c* 1666; *m c* 1689 Margaret, dau of Thomas Bowcock, of Westmoreland Co, and *d* 1737 (will dated 13 March), leaving issue (with five other children):

1 William MONROE, Jr; *m* 1st 17— ——; *m* 2nd 17— Rachael (*d* 1859), dau of John Piper, and *d* 1775, leaving issue:

(1) Andrew MONROE, of Virginia and Kentucky, *b* 1749; *m* 1789 Anne, dau of Thomas Bell, and *d* 1815, leaving (with other issue):

1a Thomas Bell MONROE, *b* 1791; Fedl Judge Dist of Kentucky 1834; *m* 1812 Eliza Palmer (*b* 1790; *d* 1871), dau of Gen John Adair (1759-1840), and *d* Mississippi 1865, leaving issue:

1b Victor MONROE, *b* 1813; Fedl Judge Washington Territory; *m* 1840 Mary Townsend (*b* 1822; *d* 1883), dau of William Winder Polk, US Navy, and *d* 1856, leaving issue:

1c Frank Adair MONROE, *b* Maryland 1844; Ch Justice Louisiana; *m* 1878 Alice (*b* 1857; *d* 1935), dau of Jules Arnaud Blanc (1819-1904), and *d* 1927, having had issue:

1d Frank Adair MONROE, of Cortley, Rye, New York, *b* 26 Nov 1878; *educ* Tulane U, La., (BE 1897, ME 1909); Pres and Dir The Cuba Co, New York City, and Compania Cubana, Cuba; *m* 12 June 1912 Elizabeth, dau of Amos Bush McNairy, of Cleveland, Ohio, and his w Mary Pack, and *d* 19—, having had issue:

1e *Allyn Adair MONROE, *b* 18 June 1916
2e Willis Lathrop MONROE, *b* 17 Aug 1917; *d* 15 March 1920
3e *Elizabeth MONROE, *b* 5 April 1913

2d Jules Blanc MONROE, *b* 1880; *m* 1908 Mabel Overton Logan
3d Alice Monroe, *b* 1882; *m* 1908 Samuel Stanhope LABOUISSE (*d* 1918)
4d Kate Adair Monroe, *b* 1883; *m* 1909 Gustaf Rhinehold WESTFELDT
5d Gertrude Monroe, *b* 1885; *m* 1908 Thomas Mudrup LOGAN (*d* 1928)

6d Winder Polk MONROE, *b* 1887; *d* 1915   7d Adele Monroe, *b* 1888; *m* 1911 George Elliott WILLIAMS
8d Marion Monroe, *b* 1890; *m* 1921 John Taylor CHAMBERS
9d William Blanc MONROE, *b* 1895; *m* 1918 Arthemise Vairin   10d James Hill MONROE, *b* 1899

2 Andrew MONROE, for whom *see* next para.

William Monroe, Sr's yr s,
   Andrew MONROE, *b* 16— or 17—; Sheriff Westmoreland Co, Va., 1731; *m* 17—, as her 2nd husb, Christian Tyler (*see above*), widow of his cousin Spence Monroe (she *m* 3rd Richard Fry), and *d* 1735, leaving issue:

I Andrew MONROE; *d* Caroline Co, Va., 1775
II Spence MONROE, for whom *see below*
III Jane Monroe; *m* John CHANCELLOR (*b* 1726; *d* 1815)

The yr s,
   Spence MONROE, *b c* 1727; farmer and circuit judge, Westmoreland Co, signed that part of the Virginia Resolutions outlawing enforcement of the Stamp Act in Westmoreland Co; *m c* 1752 Elizabeth (*b* probably King George Co, Va.), dau of James Jones (*d* on or before 1 June 1744), architect, and his w Hester Davis (herself dau of Joshua Davis, of Richmond Co, Va., lawyer), and *d* 1774 (will dated 14 Feb), leaving issue:

I Elizabeth Monroe, *b* 1758; *m* William BUCKNER (*b* 1753), of Mill Hill, and had issue:

President Monroe's nephews and niece
1 A son; *d* young   2 A son; *d* young   3 A son; *m* and had issue one s, who *d* without issue
4 Elizabeth Bankhead Buckner; *m* Norborne TALIAFERRO and had issue:

Great-nephew
(1) A son; *m* and had issue:

Great-nephew's children
1a Thomas Dorsey TALIAFERRO; Col Confederate States Army; *m* 1854 Eliza Lewis Madison, a great-niece of President MADISON
2a Roberta Willis Taliaferro; *m* William Willis MADISON (*b* 1826; *d* 1888), great-nephew of President MADISON and bro of Mrs Thomas D. Taliaferro

President Monroe's nieces
5 A dau; *m* but left no issue   6 A dau; *m* but left no issue   7 A dau; *m* but left no issue

III JAMES MONROE, 5th PRESIDENT of the UNITED STATES of AMERICA
IV Spence MONROE, *b* 1759?; said to have *d* in early manhood
V Andrew MONROE, *b* 17—; *m* 1789 Ann Bell and/or Frances Garnett, of Essex Co, Va., and *d* 1826 or 1836, leaving issue:

President Monroe's nephews
1 A son
2 James MONROE, *b* 1799; Colonel, Congressman; *m* 18— Elizabeth Mary Douglas and had issue (with an er s, who *d* in infancy):

Great-niece
(1) Fannie Monroe, *b* 1826; *m* 18— Douglas ROBINSON, of New York, and *d* 1906, leaving issue:

Great-niece's children
1a Douglas Robinson, *b* 3 Jan 1855; *m* 29 April 1882 Corinne (*b* New York 27 Sept 1861; authoress; Memb Presidents COOLIDGE's and HOOVER's Advsy Ctees, also Exec Cncl Republican Nat Ctee, Fndr First Red Cross War Chapter 1914; *d* 17 Feb 1933), yr dau of Cornelius Roosevelt and sister of President THEODORE ROOSEVELT, and *d* 12 Sept 1918, having had issue (*see* under that President)

VI Joseph Jones MONROE, *b* 1764; Commonwealth Attorney, Albemarle Co, Va., priv sec to his brother President MONROE, Clerk District and Circuit Courts, Northumberland Co, Va., 1804-10; *m* 1st 1790 Elizabeth Kerr and had issue:

President Monroe's niece
1 A dau; *m* and had issue

VI (cont.) Joseph J. Monroe *m* 2nd 1801 Sarah (Sally) Gordon, of Northumberland Co, Va.; *m* 3rd 1808 Elizabeth Glasscock and *d* Franklin, Mo., 5 Aug 1824

JAMES MONROE
FAMILY TREE

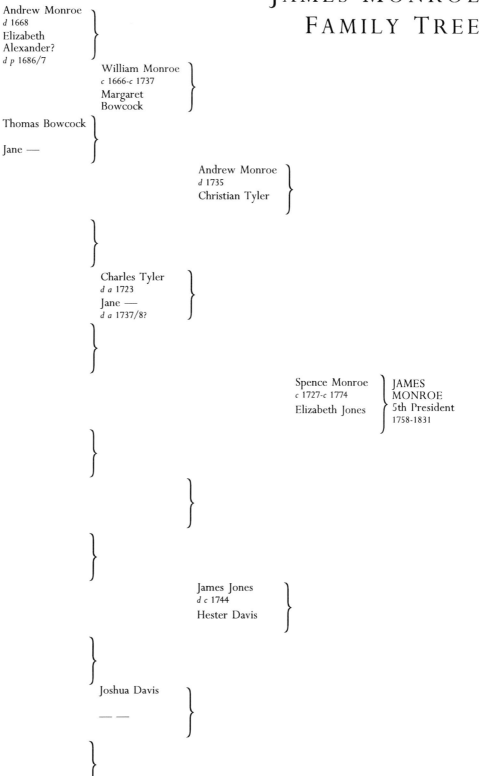

Andrew Monroe
d 1668
Elizabeth
Alexander?
d p 1686/7

William Monroe
c 1666-c 1737
Margaret
Bowcock

Thomas Bowcock

Jane —

Andrew Monroe
d 1735
Christian Tyler

Charles Tyler
d a 1723
Jane —
d a 1737/8?

Spence Monroe
c 1727-c 1774
Elizabeth Jones

JAMES
MONROE
5th President
1758-1831

James Jones
d c 1744
Hester Davis

Joshua Davis

— —

Plate 17   John Quincy Adams

JOHN QUINCY ADAMS

1767-1848
6TH PRESIDENT OF THE UNITED STATES OF AMERICA
1824-29

John Quincy Adams came to the presidency through muddle and left it after the worst political defeat thus far endured by any President. The muddle was not his doing; the defeat largely was.

By 1820 or thereabouts the so-called 'first party system' had largely disappeared. The Federalists, disabled by their conservatism, their successive defeats in presidential elections and their apparent defeatism in the War of 1812, had ceased to exist as an effective national political force. Everyone was a Republican, including the son and heir of John Adams, yet for that very reason it might be said that no one was. There was no party programme, no party discipline, no dominant party leader, above all no party organization; only a number of personal followings. The only remnant of the old Republican party with any sign of life was the Congressional caucus, and it was increasingly felt that the choice of presidential candidates was too important a matter to be left to Congressmen and Senators. When the Congressional favourite, Crawford, suffered a disabling stroke, 'King Caucus' to all intents and purposes ceased to exist and a scramble began to win the necessary majority of electoral votes by other means. This proved impossible. There were too many candidates. Andrew Jackson and Henry Clay neutralized each other in the West, Adams held New England, Calhoun and Crawford split the South and the mid-Atlantic states were divided. In these circumstances it is not surprising that the election was thrown into the House of Representatives.

Henry Clay, Speaker of the House, was not among the three candidates with most electoral votes, so he was out of the running. He threw his great influence behind Adams, who was apparently the best qualified of the candidates and the nearest in views to Clay; on the first ballot Adams was elected. He showed his appreciation of Clay's services by making him Secretary of State.

This was a mistake. The followers of Jackson and Crawford were already bitterly disappointed in the outcome of the election and they now raised a cry of corrupt bargain. Henry Clay was said to be the Judas of the West, and Andrew Jackson vowed vengeance. He soon found effective allies in Martin Van Buren, the master of New York State politics, and in John C. Calhoun, the dominant statesman of the South. The election campaign of 1828 began almost before that of 1824 was finished.

This did not disturb Clay, a vigorous fighter in the new mode of democratic politics, but he was cruelly hampered by his leader. Adams was a strong nationalist, and had Hamiltonian views about the role the national government might play in fostering the economy and culture of America. But his life had bred in him a fatal fastidiousness. He was much less approachable than his father. A less likely man for a corrupt bargain cannot be imagined. He undertook the presidency with a grim conscientiousness which surpassed that of Washington; he carried out his duties without looking to left or right; he refused to use the powers of presidential patronage to build up a political machine, and he disdained any trick which might make him more popular. The opposition made up fantastic stories about him (for example, that while American minister to Russia he had acted as a pander for the Tsar) which he did not bother to notice. Congress rejected his ambitious programmes; he did nothing. His followers went into the election of 1828 with despair in their hearts and were handsomely beaten; yet the margin was sufficiently close in the popular vote to suggest that if Adams had been willing to change with the times he could at least have given Jackson a run for his money. But no Adams ever bent with the wind; he boycotted Jackson's Inauguration as his father had boycotted Jefferson's, and went home to Boston. He did not stay there long; he soon came back to Washington as a member of the House of Representatives, the only President to do so, and there began perhaps the greatest part of his career, as an antislavery leader. Eventually his long career of public service met a fitting end: he had a stroke on the floor of the House on 21 February 1848, and died in the Speaker's Room two days later.

JOHN QUINCY ADAMS'S FAMILY

If John Quincy Adams thought he deserved the presidency it was not so much because he was John Adams's son as because he had the necessary native abilities plus experience of high politics. Although as a child he got his formal education from his mother while his father was away in Europe, he then joined John Adams there and became his travelling companion. His first-hand knowledge of his father's career even led him to consider writing his father's biography, which induced John Adams to put his papers in order. Secondly, he had served as US envoy to most of the courts of Europe, being recalled from Prussia in 1801 by President John Adams only because the latter feared the next President, Thomas Jefferson, would sack him. Finally, he had been Monroe's Secretary of State and at that time, as has already been mentioned in Madison's case, whoever held the post was seen as more or less heir apparent to the President.

However, he had undeniably enjoyed such early promotion because of his family background. And he was a robust supporter of what would nowadays be called elitism. In the debate of the 1790s between the Federalists, who were thought to favour centralized government to the point of restoring the monarchy, and Republicans, who were thought to favour rugged republican simplicity and decentralization, John Quincy was not only a leading Federalist but wrote a series of articles signed 'Publicola' which attacked Thomas Jefferson.

When he became President, suspicion in the public mind that his career had depended too much on pull may have been reinforced by the fuss over the 'corrupt bargain'. Also, America by now was undergoing one of its periodic reactions against the supposedly corrupt manners and tastes of the great cosmopolitan world. Here John Quincy's early immersion in Europe's high society became a handicap, and if it came about through family connections, so much the worse. In fact few Presidents have found the purely social duties of the job so irksome. But he and his wife Louisa made the mistake of refusing to visit new members of Congress on their arrival in Washington; the first call had to be made on themselves. And his reputation for aristocratic ways more suited to Europe was compounded by his wife's improved catering in the White House, where fine wines and a sophisticated cuisine replaced the plain fare of the Madison and Monroe administrations. One has to admit that Louisa was distressingly Un-American, using the term to describe cultural background rather than moral turpitude. Her mother was English; her father, though American-born, lived in England before and after the Revolutionary War and in France during it. As a result Louisa, who had been educated at a convent in Nantes, was completely gallicized in dress, language and manners — so much so that she had to relearn English after her father's return from France. On the other hand she was extremely active socially in the period leading up to the 1824 election, entertaining the many political figures whose support would be vital to John Quincy. This was all the more important since he made no effort to mix and be affable. Later, when her husband

Plate 18   Louisa Catherine Johnson Adams

was a Member of the House of Representatives, she helped him co-ordinate his campaign to have the gag rule against petitions (mostly anti-slavery ones) rescinded.

But in many ways John Quincy and Louisa Adams were ill-suited. He was stern, she more easy-going, though given to invalidism. Both had preferred somebody else early in life and the realization that she was not her husband's ideal choice seems to have embittered Louisa Adams permanently. Moreover, her father failed in business shortly before their wedding and Louisa always feared John Quincy might think he had been tricked into marrying her. Where she might have established herself in an activity practised also by her husband was literature. Compared with his solid output her verse and stories look a bit meagre. She did manage to produce a "Story of My Life", though it never got very far. It was subsequently pruned of embarrassing passages by a genuine literary talent — John Quincy and Louisa's grandson Henry Adams. The result he called "Biographical Notes on Louisa Johnson Adams".

The Adamses eldest son, George, was unsatisfactory. Although brilliant — at Harvard he won the Boylston Prize, beating Ralph Waldo Emerson — he was erratic, careless and prone to what would now probably be diagnosed as manic-depression. He studied law in Daniel Webster's office but was unsuited to a profession where accuracy is vital. His father thought him run-down by his late twenties but could come up with no better solution than to advise him to keep a diary and send him extracts. Subsequently George slid into increasing money difficulties, got a Boston girl pregnant and began to suffer from hallucinations. On the boat from Providence to New York in late April 1829 (he was travelling to Washington to collect his mother) he complained of headaches, was very restless and finally demanded to be put ashore as he said the other passengers were laughing at him. Shortly afterward his hat was seen floating on the water near the ship's stern. The body was found above the East River at the western end of Long Island Sound. It is uncertain whether he fell overboard or jumped.

John Quincy's second son, John Adams II, was private secretary to his father when President but his health was not good and he died two years after his father left office. During those two years John Quincy Adams urged him to leave Washington, with its unhealthy climate, and come up to Boston to manage the family's affairs. But John II may have been too far gone by then for a change of residence to do much good. During President John Quincy Adams's time in the White House other members of the family living there included his youngest son Charles Francis and three orphaned children of Louisa Adams's dead sister Nancy — Mary, Johnson and Thomas Hellen (their father Walter Hellen subsequently married his wife's younger sister Adelaide). Mary, described by contemporaries as a coquette, was at first engaged to the eldest Adams son George but he only wrote to her from Boston once a month and she transferred her attention to John II, marrying him just over a year before his father left the White House. In that era — as the example of Fanny Price and her cousin Edmund Bertram in Jane Austen's *Mansfield Park* shows most famously — bringing young people up in the same household was likely to lead to sexual complications rather than the indifference bred of familiarity one would expect today. John Quincy Adams had objected to Mary and John II's marriage on the grounds that his son could not yet support a wife. In consequence their White House wedding was a very quiet one. But after John Adams II's death the senior Adamses took Mary and her two daughters to live with them at 1333-5 F Street, Quincy. Once again the upshot was a marriage within the family circle, when the younger Mary took her second cousin William Johnson as husband. In contrast, her uncle Johnson Hellen had had the decency while living at the White House to run away with one of the housemaids rather than carry on intrigues under the presidential roof.

Charles Francis Adams, President John Quincy's youngest son, is the most interesting of the children. For a start he was more astringent about his formidable parents. He wrote of his rejoicing at becoming independent of them, adding "A more pitiable set I do not think I know than my father and mother." He disapproved of his father's decision to enter the House of Representatives after leaving the White House and relations between father and son were strained for a while. He is also of importance in American political history. True, he did not get far in elective politics — his nomination as the Barnburners' or Free Soil (Democratic) Party's vice-presidential contender in the 1848 election is hardly a major event. But he was a leading Republican moderate in the fatal months before the Civil War, being asked by Thomas Corwin, chairman of the Congressional Committee of Thirty-three (*i.e.*, those states which had not, or not yet, seceded) to put to the whole committee a policy of concession toward the South on non-essentials which had been agreed by two-thirds of them. Lincoln's appointing him US minister to London in 1861 was crucial in hamstringing British support for the South in the Civil War.

(He had been suggested as Secretary of the Treasury but the London post was considered more important, as indeed it proved to be.) Charles Francis Adams had been educated for a time in England, which helped. Better still, he got on well with Lord John Russell, the British Foreign Secretary, and this may have been instrumental in persuading Russell to stop the Confederate warship *Alexandra* and two ironclad rams from leaving British ports.

After the war Charles Francis Adams was appointed a member of the arbitration commission settling US claims against Britain as the country of manufacture of Confederate warships. He insisted on considering only direct damage to US shipping, knowing that claims for indirect damage, impossibly high, would never be met. Following this the Liberal Republicans for a time considered him as a presidential candidate; indeed he led in the first ballot at their convention in 1872. A man of scholarly and literary inclinations as well as public affairs, just like his father, he edited his father's diary, producing 12 massive volumes. His son Henry Brooks Adams reckoned he had the only perfectly balanced mind — presumably in the sense of not being neurotic — of the whole family. Against that Henry reckoned that he suffered from the New England Puritan conscience of his ancestors without having their firm Puritan theology. Henry implied that was a flaw. Nowadays we would think it, if not a plus, at any rate better than the other way round.

Charles Francis Adams's eldest son achieved little. But his second son, Charles Francis Adams Jr (1835-1915), was president of the Union Pacific Railroad and served as head of the Massachusetts railroad commission. This latter body had been set up to deal with the abuses practiced at the time by the railroad corporations and under Adams's enlightened leadership it influenced those many other states which favoured a conservative approach to such matters.

The third son Henry Brooks Adams, already mentioned briefly above, served as his father's secretary in London. He is better known as the author of *The Education of Henry Adams*, one of the classic autobiographies and a critical examination of his milieu to boot. His history of the Jefferson and Madison administrations is usually considered a masterpiece too, though latterly his *Mont-Saint-Michel and Chartres* has come in for praise as one of his two major works (the other being *The Education*). It is certainly a competent cultural study of the 12th century. He also wrote a couple of political novels. The first, *Democracy* (1880), he published anonymously, although the public was quick to attribute authorship to him — also to Lincoln's former secretary John Hay and the geologist Clarence King (now remembered only for his investigations into the Comstock lode in Nevada). The former British Home Secretary and Chancellor Roy Jenkins — that rarest of late 20th-century specimens, a leading politician who both writes well and reads widely — recently praised *Democracy* as the novel that shows the best grasp of political life. Henry Adams wrote another political novel, *Esther* (1884), under the pseudonym Frances Snow Compton. The heroine is said to have been based on his wife Marian, whose suicide in 1885 was not just devastating in itself but the culmination of a process in which Adams had been feeling discontented with life in America for some time already. It was now that he started travelling, both in the East and in the American Sierras, his companion in the latter region being Clarence King.

Academic leanings in the Adamses were perfectly normal, creative ones less so. It is true that President John Quincy Adams's epic poem on the 12th-century Norman invasion of Ireland ran to four editions, but one suspects this was because its author had been a President. It is virtually unknown in Ireland, a country usually enthusiastic about poets, especially those treating Irish themes.

As with so many presidential families, the achievements of later generations were relatively tame. The trouble was, the Adamses hitherto had been so successful in so many fields that almost anything afterward was likely to be anticlimactic. Charles Francis Adams III, a grandson of the Charles Francis who was Minister to Britain, was Secretary of the Navy under President Hoover. His only son, Charles Francis Adams IV, was a member of the Fine Arts Committee set up by Jacqueline Kennedy during her husband's administration to make the White House less of a working executive mansion and more a repository of American memorabilia. He was also a great friend of Bill Patten and his wife Susan Mary, *née* Jay, later Susan Mary Alsop (*see* under President THEODORE ROOSEVELT, Male Line Ancestry). In Mrs Alsop's fascinating book on life in Paris just after World War II — which reveals *inter alia* that Nancy Mitford drew on her to create the character of Mildred Jungfleisch in *Don't Tell Alfred* — she records Charles Francis Adams IV as remarking often what complexes being a presidential descendant can cause one in youth.

BIOGRAPHICAL DETAILS AND DESCENDANTS

JOHN QUINCY ADAMS, *b* Braintree (now Quincy), Mass., 11 July 1867; *educ* in France and The Netherlands (including Leyden U), also Harvard; Sec and Interpreter to Francis Dana, American representative at St Petersburg, Russia, 1781-83, admitted to Massachusetts Bar 1790, US Minister: The Netherlands 1794-96, Portugal 1797-98 and Prussia 1797-1801, Memb Massachusetts Senate 1802-03, US Senator from Massachusetts 1803-08, Boylston Prof of Rhetoric and Oratory Harvard 1805, US Minister to Russia 1809-15, apptd Assoc Justice Supreme Court but refused to serve 1811, a Peace Commissioner negotiating end to War of 1812 with Great Britain 1814, US Minister to Britain 1815-17, US Sec of State 1817, unsuccessful presidential candidate 1820, 6th President (ran as representative of western faction of Democratic-Republican Party but elected by House of Reps) of the USA 1825-29, Memb Bd Overseers Harvard 1830, Memb US House of Reps 1831-48 (Memb Special Ctee investigating Bank of US 1832, Chm House Foreign Affrs Ctee 1841-43), unsuccessful Anti-Masonic gubernatorial candidate Massachusetts 1833, unsuccessful candidate US Senate 1836, Hon LLD Coll of New Jersey (now Princeton) 1806, author: numerous polemical articles as 'Publicola' (particularly against Thomas Paine), 'Menander', 'Marcellus' and 'Columbus', also *A Journal by John Quincy Adams 1779-1845*, *Letters from Silesia* (1804), *Lectures on Rhetoric and Oratory*, 2 vols (1810), *A Letter to the Hon Harrison Gray Otis* (1808), *Report on Weights and Measures* (1821), *The Duplicate Letters, the Fisheries and the Mississippi* (1822), *Eulogy on James Monroe* (1831), *Dermot McMorrogh, or The Conquest of Ireland: an historical tale of the twelfth century in four cantos* (epic poem) (1832), *Oration on Lafayette* (1835), *Eulogy on James Madison* (1836), *Speech of John Quincy Adams, of Massachusetts, upon the Right of the People, Men and Women, to Petition; on the Freedom of Speech and of Debate in the House of Representatives* (1831), *Poems of Religion and Society* (1848), *Memoirs*, ed Charles Francis Adams, 12 vols (1874-77), and *Writings of John Quincy Adams*, ed W. C. Ford (1913); *m* All Hallows, Barking-by-the-Tower, London, Great Britain, 26 or 27 July 1797 Louisa Catherine (*b* London 12 Feb 1775; *d* Washington, DC, 15 May 1852, *bur* the Congressional Cemetery, Washington, later removed to Quincy, Mass., with her husband), 2nd dau of Hon Joshua Johnson, of Baltimore, American Consul-Gen London 1785-99, and his *w* Catherine Nuth, and *d* in the Speaker's Room at the Capitol, Washington, DC, 23 Feb 1848 after a stroke, having had issue:

President John Q. Adams's sons
I George Washington ADAMS, *b* Berlin, Prussia, 12 April 1801; *educ* Harvard; Capt US Army, admitted Massachusetts Bar 1824, Memb Massachusetts Legislature 1826; drowned Long Island Sound 30 April 1829
II John ADAMS II, *b* Washington, DC, 4 July 1803; *educ* Harvard (expelled for unruliness 1823 but awarded degree posthumously 1873, along with other senior student rioters, by Harvard Corporation); private sec to his father when the latter President; *m* the White House 25 Feb 1828 his 1st cousin Mary Catherine (*b c* 1806; *d* 1870), dau of Walter Hellen and his 1st *w* Nancy/Ann, est dau of Hon Joshua Johnson, and *d* Washington, DC, 23 Oct 1834, leaving issue:

Grandchildren
1 Mary Louisa Adams, *b* the White House, Washington, DC, 2 Dec 1828; *m* 30 June 1853, as his 2nd *w*, her 2nd cousin William Clarkson JOHNSON (*b* Utica, New York, 16 Aug 1823; *d* New York 28 Jan 1893), 4th s of Alexander Bryan Johnson, of Utica, and his *w* Abigail Louisa Smith Adams, and *d* Far Rockaway, Long Island, New York, 16 July 1859, leaving issue (for which *see under* President JOHN ADAMS)
2 Georgeanna Frances (Fanny or Fannie) ADAMS, *b* Quincy, Mass., 1830; *d* there 2 Oct or 20 Nov 1839

President John Q. Adams's son
III Charles Francis ADAMS, *b* Boston 18 Aug 1807; *educ* Boston Latin Sch, Harvard (AB 1825) and in the UK; Memb: Massachusetts House of Reps 1840-43 and Massachusetts Senate 1843-45, ed *Boston Whig* 1846-48, nominated by Free Soil (Democratic) Party ('Barnburners' and 'Conscience Whigs') as v-presdtl candidate 1848, Memb (R) 36th US Congress from Massachusetts 1859-61, US Minister to UK 1861-68, Memb Geneva Arbitration Tribunal Discussing *Alabama* Claims 1871-72, author: *An Appeal from the New to the Old Whigs* (1835), *John Adams* (ed), 10 vols (1850-56) and *Memoirs of John Quincy Adams*, 12 vols (1874-77); *m* Medford, Mass., 3 Sept 1829 Abigail Brown (*b* there 25 April 1808; *d* 6 June 1889), 3rd and yst dau of Peter Chardon Brooks and his *w* Ann Gorham, and *d* Boston 21 Nov 1886, having had issue:

Grandchildren
1 Louisa Catherine Adams, *b* Boston 13 Aug 1831; *m* 13 April 1854 Charles KUHN, of Philadelphia (*b* 1821; *d* 31 Oct

1899), and d Bagni di Lucca, Italy, 13 July 1870

2 John Quincy ADAMS II, of Mount Wollaston Farm, Mass., b Boston 22 Sept 1833; educ Harvard (AB 1853); lawyer, Memb (D) Massachusetts General Court, staff offr (Col) under Govr Andrew in Civil War, v-presdtl candidate Democratic Party anti-Horace Greeley faction ('Straight-Out Democrats') 1872; m 29 April 1861 Fanny Cadwallader (b 15 Oct 1839; d 16 May 1911), dau of George Caspar Crowninshield and his w Harriet Sears, and d Quincy, Mass., 14 Aug 1894, having had issue:

Great-grandchildren

(1) John Quincy ADAMS III; b Boston 23 Feb 1862; d 12 April 1876

(2) George Caspar ADAMS; b Boston 24 April 1863; educ Harvard (AB 1886); d Quincy 13 July 1900

(3) Charles Francis ADAMS III, b Quincy 2 Aug 1866; educ Harvard (AB 1888); Treasurer of Harvard, Mayor of Quincy, Sec of the Navy 1929-33; m 3 April 1899 Frances, dau of Hon William Croade Lovering, of Taunton, Mass., Memb of Congress from Massachusetts 1897-1910, and d Boston 19 June 1954, leaving issue:

Great-great-grandchildren

1a *Catherine Adams [Mrs Henry Morgan, 120 East End Avenue, New York, NY, USA], b 13 Jan 1902; m 26 June 1923 *Henry Sturgis MORGAN (b London, UK, 24 Oct 1900), yr s of the financier John Pierpont Morgan, of Wall Hall, Watford, Herts, UK, and Matinicock Point, Glen Cove, Long Island, New York, and his w Jane Norton Grew, and has issue:

Great-great-grandchildren's children

1b* Rear-Adml Henry Sturgis MORGAN, Jr, USN [Brookvale, Stonington, CT, USA], b 10 Aug 1924; educ Harvard; m 28 March 1945 *Fanny Gray (b 30 Sept 1925), dau of Leon M. Little, and has issue:

Great-great-grandchildren's grandchildren

1c *Catherine Adams Morgan, b 2 Oct 1946; m Aug 1967 *Alec Mitchell PELTIER and has issue:

Great-great-grandchildren's great-grandchildren
1d *Patricia Gray PELTIER, b 6 May 1972

Great-great-grandchildren's grandchildren
2c *Henry MORGAN, b 20 Oct 1948
3c *Polly MORGAN, b 11 July 1951
4c *Joan Morgan, b 4 Dec 1953; m Northport, Long Island, New York, 22 Sept 1973 *Peter Lincoln FOLSOM

Great-great-grandchildren's children
2b *Charles Francis MORGAN, b 16 April 1926; m Feb 1960 *Sarah Baldwin Lambert (b 17 July 1934) and has issue:

Great-great-grandchildren's grandchildren
1c *Charles Francis MORGAN, Jr, b 4 March 1961
2c *Maria Baldwin MORGAN, b 7 June 1963
3c *Samuel Lambert MORGAN, b 15 March 1965

Great-great-grandchildren's children
3b *Miles MORGAN, b 1 Nov 1928
4b *John Adams MORGAN, b 17 Sept 1930; m 1st 6 June 1953 (divorce 19—) Elizabeth Robbins Choate (b 13 Dec 1933) and has issue:

Great-great-grandchildren's grandchildren
1c *John Adams MORGAN, Jr, b 13 Aug 1954

Great-great-grandchildren's children
4b (cont.) John Adams Morgan m 2nd Feb 1961 *Tania Goss (b 17 Nov 1935) and with her has issue:

Great-great-grandchildren's grandchildren
2c *Chauncey Goss MORGAN, b 19 April 1963

Great-great-grandchildren's children
5b *Peter Angus MORGAN [15 Lafayette Road, Schenectady, NY, USA], b 23 Oct 1938

Great-great-grandchildren
2a *Charles Francis ADAMS IV [195 Dedham Street, Dover, MA 02030, USA], b Boston 2 May 1910; educ St Mark's Sch, Southboro, Mass., and Harvard (AB 1932); with USNR World War II, Chm Raytheon Co (electronics corp), Lexington, Mass., 1964, Hon DBA Suffolk U 1953 and Northeastern U 1959, LLD Bates Coll 1960; m 16 June 1934 Margaret (b 22 April 1915; d 11 July 1972), dau of Philip Stockton, banker, of Boston, and has issue:

Great-great-grandchildren's children
1b *Abigail Adams [Mrs James C Manny, 530 East 86th Street, New York, NY, USA], b 29 April 1935; m 11 June 1955 *James Craven MANNY and has issue:

Great-great-grandchildren's grandchildren
1c *Alison Adams MANNY, b 16 March 1956
2c *Walter R. MANNY II, b 11 June 1957

3c *Alix MANNY, *b* 12 Nov 1960
4c *Timothy MANNY, *b* 5 Nov 1970

Great-great-grandchildren's children
2b *Alison Adams, *b* 18 March 1937; *m* 19— (divorce 19—) Beverley ROBINSON and has issue:

Great-great-grandchildren's grandchildren
1c *S. Philippse ROBINSON II
2c *John ROBINSON
3c *Stephen ROBINSON

Great-great-grandchildren's children
3b *Timothy ADAMS, *b* 7 Oct 1947

Great-grandchildren
(4) Fanny Crowninshield ADAMS, *b* Quincy 19 Aug 1873; *d* there 11 April 1876
(5) Arthur G. ADAMS, of Dover, Mass., *b* Quincy 20 May 1877; *educ* Harvard (AB 1899); sometime V-Pres Adams Tst Co and City Tst Co, Lt USN World War I; *m* 5 Oct 1921 *Margery (*b* Brookline, Mass., 2 May 1893), widow of Francis Williams Sargent and dau of George Lee and his w Eva Ballerina, and *d* 19 May 1943, leaving issue:

Great-great-grandchildren
1a *John Quincy ADAMS V [200 Berkeley Street, Boston, MA 02116, USA], *b* Dover, Mass., 24 Dec 1922; *educ* St Paul's Sch and Harvard (AB 1945); insur exec; *m* 1 Feb 1947 *Nancy Motley (*b* 4 April 1926) and has issue:

Great-great-grandchildren's children
1b *Nancy Barton ADAMS, *b* 1 Oct 1948
2b *John Quincy ADAMS VI [Wilsondale Road, Dover, MA 02023, USA], *b* 2 Nov 1950
3b *Margery Lee ADAMS, *b* 13 April 1954
4b *Benjamin Crowninshield ADAMS, *b* 13 Dec 1964

Great-great-grandchildren
2a *Arthur ADAMS, Jr [Dover, MA 02023, USA; 2 Crest Drive, W Dover, MA, USA], *b* 5 Nov 1926

Great-grandchildren
(6) Abigail Adams, *b* Quincy 6 Sept 1879; *m* there 10 June 1907 Robert HOMANS (*b* Boston 3 Oct 1873; *d* there 23 April 1934), s of John Homans and his w Helen Amory Perkins, and *d* Boston 4 Feb 1974, having had issue:

Great-great-grandchildren
1a *George Caspar HOMANS [11 Francis Avenue, Cambridge, MA 02138, USA], *b* Boston 11 Aug 1910; *educ* St Paul's Sch, Harvard (AB 1932) and Cambridge (UK) (MA 1955); Lt-Cdr USNR World War II, Prof Sociology Harvard 1953, Ford Foundation Visiting Prof Graduate Sch Business Admin 1961, Simon Visiting Prof Manchester U (UK) 1953, Prof Social Theory Cambridge (UK) 1955-56, Visiting Prof Kent U (UK) 1967, Memb: American Academy of Arts and Sciences, American Sociologial Assoc (Pres 1963-64) and American Philosophical Soc, author: *Marriage, Authority and Final Causes* (1955) and *Coming to my Senses: the autobiography of a sociologist* (1984); *m* Hyde Park, New York, 27 June 1941 *Nancy Parshall (*b* Keokula 28 Nov 1913), dau of Dexter Cooper and his w Gertrude Sturgis, and has issue:

Great-great-grandchildren's children
1b *Elizabeth Cooper HOMANS, *b* Boston 6 Oct 1942
2b *Susan Welles Homans, *b* Boston 11 July 1944; *m* 16 Dec 1972 *Cameron ELIAS and has issue:

Great-great-grandchildren's grandchildren
1c *Abigail Homans ELIAS, *b* 7 March 1975
2c *Margaret Ward ELIAS, *b* 29 Sept 1979

Great-great-grandchildren's children
3b *Peter Chardon Brooks HOMANS, *b* Boston 6 Aug 1955

Great-great-grandchildren
2a *Fanny Crowninshield Homans, *b* Boston 21 Aug 1911; *educ* Radcliffe; *m* 1st Howland Shaw WARREN (*b* 2 Feb 1910); *m* 2nd 15 Aug 1939 *Henry Lowell MASON, Jr (*b* 17 Feb 1910), and with him has issue:

Great-great-grandchildren's children
1b *Henry Lowell MASON III, *b* 10 Feb 1941; *m* June 1969 *Elaine Brobcowicz
2b *Abigail Adams Mason, *b* 17 Dec 1943; *m* 9 Aug 1967 *Alfred L. BROWNE, Jr (*b* 7 July 1937), and has issue:

Great-great-grandchildren's grandchildren
1c *Alfred L. BROWNE III, *b* 18 Oct 1968
2c *Priscilla Crowninshield BROWNE, *b* 5 Aug 1970

Great-great-grandchildren's children
3b *John Homans MASON, *b* 24 Oct 1945

Great-great-grandchildren

3a *Helen Amory Homans, *b* Boston 29 Oct 1913; *educ* Radcliffe; *m* 27 June 1936 *Carl Joyce GILBERT (*b* Bloomfield, New Jersey, 3 April 1906), s of Seymour Parker Gilbert and his w Carrie Jennings Cooper, and has issue:

Great-great-grandchildren's children

1b *Thomas Tibbots GILBERT, *b* 8 Jan 1947; *m* 28 June 1968 *Margaret Helen Bay (*b* 28 Nov 1946)

Great-great-grandchildren

4a Robert HOMANS, Jr, *b* Boston 25 Oct 1918; *educ* Harvard; *m* 12 Jan 1946 *Mary Aldrich (*b* 25 Jan 1921) and *d* Hillsboro, New Hampshire, 18 Dec 1964, leaving issue:

Great-great-grandchildren's children

1b *Robert HOMANS III, *b* 12 Oct 1946
2b *Lucy Aldrich HOMANS, *b* 18 Feb 1948
3b *Abigail HOMANS, *b* 25 Oct 1955

Grandchildren

3 Charles Francis ADAMS, Jr, *b* Boston 27 May 1835; *educ* Harvard (AB 1856, LittD, LLD); served Union Cavalry Civil War (Brevet Brig-Gen Volunteers 1865), Pres: Union Pacific Railroad 1884-90, Massachusetts Historical Soc 1895-1915 and American Historical Assoc 1900-1, author: *Railroads, Their Origins and Problems* (1878), *Three Episodes of Massachusetts History* (1892), *Charles Francis Adams* (biography of his father) (1900), *Lee at Appomattox and Other Papers* (1902), *Theodore Lyman and Robert Charles Winthrop, Jr, Two Memoirs* (1906) and *Three Phi Beta Kappa Addresses* (1907); *m* Newport, Rhode Island, 8 Nov 1865 Mary Hone (*b* New York 23 Feb 1843; *d* Concord, Mass., 23 March 1935), dau of Edward Ogden, of New York City and Newport, Rhode Island, and his w Caroline Hone Callender, and *d* Washington, DC, 20 March 1915, leaving issue:

Great-grandchildren

(1) Mary Ogden Adams, *b* Quincy 27 July 1867; *m* 30 Sept 1890 Grafton St Loe ABBOTT, of Concord, Mass. (*b* Lowell, Mass., 14 Nov 1856; *d* Concord 27 Feb 1915), s of Hon Josiah Gardiner Abbott, Memb Congress from Massachusetts, and his w Caroline Livermore, and *d* Concord 21 Aug 1933, leaving issue:

Great-great-grandchildren

1a Henry Livermore ABBOTT, *b* Lewiston, Maine, 12 April 1892; *educ* Groton and US Naval Acad; Capt USN World Wars I and II, Sr Naval Memb Jt and Combined Intelligence Staff Jt Chiefs of Staff 1943-46, awarded Naval Cross (1918) and Green Commendation Ribbon (1946); *m* 1st Washington, DC, 24 April 1920 Elizabeth Lee (*d* 19—), dau of William Morton Grinnell and his w Elizabeth Lee Ernst, and had issue:

Great-great-grandchildren's children

1b *Mary Lee Abbott, *b* 27 July 1921; artist; *m* 1st 2 March 1943 (divorce 19—) R. Lewis TEAGUE; *m* 2nd 17 May 1950 (divorce) Thomas Hill CLYDE
2b *William Henry Grafton ABBOTT, *b* 19 March 1923

Great-great-grandchildren

1a (cont.) Capt Henry L. Abbott *m* 2nd Englewood, New Jersey, 2 Jan 1932 Marie Farnsworth (*b* 18 Oct 1900; *d* 3 Aug 1991), dau of Orlando Blodget Willcox and his w Jessie Cooke, and *d* Washington, DC, 2 April 1969, having with her had issue:

Great-great-grandchildren's children

1b *Elizabeth Marsden Abbott [Mrs Michael de Mowbray, 135c Holland Park Ave, London W11 4UT, UK], *b* New York 14 Sept 1942; *educ* Madeira Sch and New York U; social worker and puppeteer; *m* Delray Beach, Fla., 31 Dec 1982 *Dr Michael Stuart de MOWBRAY (*b* 1 Oct 1921; *educ* Oxford, UK), s of Dr Ralph de Mowbray and his w Evelyn Mary Miles, and has issue:

Great-great-grandchildren's grandchildren

1c *Stuart Henry de MOWBRAY, *b* London, UK, 19 July 1989

Great-great-grandchildren

2a Mary Ogden ABBOTT, *b* 12 Oct 1894; *educ* Sch of Boston Mus of Fine Arts; *d* 11 May 1981
3a *John Adams ABBOTT [58 Beaver Pond Road, Lincoln, MA 01773, USA], *b* Concord 9 July 1902; *educ* Groton, Harvard (BA 1925) and Harvard Medical Sch (MD 1931); Memb Massachusetts Gen Hosp Consultation Bd and Sr Consulting Staff McLean Hosp, US Amb Extraordinary to Republic of Niger 1970; *m* Concord 9 Aug 1945 *Diana Asken (*b* Calcutta, India, 4 Aug 1913; BS, MA, MPH, Chm Dept and Assoc Prof Nutrition Simmons Coll, Boston), dau of Herbert Ballin and his w Esther Raleigh Michael, and has issue:

Great-great-grandchildren's children

1b *Peter Michael ABBOTT [857 Union St N, Marshfield, MA 02059, USA], *b* Burlington, Vt., 9 Oct 1952; *educ* Lincoln Public Schs, Cardigan Mountain Sch and Hoosac Sch; arborist; *m* 28 Aug 1982 *Patricia Anne, dau of Francis Garrity and his w Winifred, of Boston, and has issue:

Great-great-grandchildren's grandchildren
1c *Sarah Elizabeth ABBOTT, *b* Weymouth, Mass., 24 July 1984
2c *Peter Michael ABBOTT, Jr, *b* Weymouth 20 Oct 1986

Great-great-grandchildren's children
2b *Rosemarie Livermore ABBOTT [Mrs Thomas M Abbott-Dallamora, 2 Barnes Rd, Newton, MA 02158, USA], *b* Patras, Greece, 24 Oct 1953; *educ* Lincoln Public Schs, House in the Pines and Cambridge Sch; *m* Massachusetts 24 July 1974 *Thomas Michael DALLAMORA and has issue:

Great-great-grandchildren's grandchildren
1c *Jesse ABBOTT-DALLAMORA, *b* Massachusetts 5 Nov 1978
2c *Jason ABBOTT-DALLAMORA, *b* Massachusetts 10 Feb 1985

Great-grandchildren
(2) Louisa Catherine Adams, *b* 28 Dec 1871; *m* 6 June 1900 Thomas Nelson PERKINS, of Westwood, Mass. (*b* Milton, Mass., 6 May 1870; lawyer; *d* 7 Oct 1937), s of Edward Cranch Perkins and his w Jane Sedgwick Watson, and *d* 19—, having had issue:

Great-great-grandchildren
1a *Elliott PERKINS [18 Hawthorn Street, Cambridge, MA 02138, USA], *b* Westwood, Mass., 17 March 1901; *educ* Harvard; Prof History Harvard and former master of Lowell House, Harvard; *m* 1 April 1937 *Mary Frances (*b* 19 Aug 1904), 2nd dau of late Sir Philip Wilbraham Baker Wilbraham, 6th Bart, KBE (see BURKE'S PEERAGE & BARONETAGE)
2a *James Handasyd PERKINS, *b* Westwood 7 Nov 1903; *m* 28 June 1930 *Marion H. Gibbs (*b* 17 May 1904) and has issue:

Great-great-grandchildren's children
1b *Louisa Catherine Perkins, *b* 14 April 1934; *m* 10 July 1961 *Henry H. PORTER (*b* 13 Nov 1934) and has issue:

Great-great-grandchildren's grandchildren
1c *Mary K. PORTER, *b* 2 June 1963
2c *Louisa Catherine PORTER, *b* 16 Oct 1966

Great-great-grandchildren's children
2b *James Handasyd PERKINS, Jr, *b* 29 Jan 1936; *m* Dec 1966 *Judith O'Connel (*b* 25 March 1939) and has issue:

Great-great-grandchildren's grandchildren
1c *Elliott K. PERKINS, *b* 30 Oct 1968
2c *Edith PERKINS, *b* 1 Nov 1970

Great-great-grandchildren's children
3b *Rufus Gibbs PERKINS, *b* 14 Oct 1939

Great-great-grandchildren
3a Thomas Nelson PERKINS, Jr, *b* Westwood, Mass., 30 April 1907; *m* 2 June 1938 *Annie Bissell Houghton (*b* 4 Nov 1910) and *d* 3 May 1965, leaving issue:

Great-great-grandchildren's children
1b *Mary Perkins, *b* 21 May 1940; *m* 12 Sept 1964 *John H. BAUGHAN (*b* 22 Jan 1932) and has issue:

Great-great-grandchildren's grandchildren
1c *Hobart Perkins BAUGHAN, *b* 20 Aug 1965
2c *John H. BAUGHAN, *b* 26 Dec 1966
3c *Anne Laughlin BAUGHAN, *b* 5 Sept 1969

Great-great-grandchildren's children
2b *Anne Perkins, *b* 15 July 1941; *m* 3 June 1967 *William McDOWELL (*b* 7 Nov 1936) and has issue:

Great-great-grandchildren's grandchildren
1c *Stewart Laughlin McDOWELL, *b* 17 Sept 1969
2c *Susan Houghton McDOWELL, *b* 16 Jan 1972

Great-great-grandchildren's children
3b *Thomas Nelson PERKINS III, *b* 2 Aug 1944; *m* 3 June 1968 *Laura Kerrin (*b* 23 Sept 1945) and has issue:

Great-great-grandchildren's grandchildren
1c *Thomas Nelson PERKINS IV, *b* 27 Oct 1968
2c *Samuel Houghton PERKINS, *b* March 1971

Great-grandchildren
(3) Elizabeth Ogden ADAMS, *b* 3 Dec 1873; *d* Oct 1945
(4) John ADAMS III, of Lincoln, Mass., *b* Quincy 17 July 1875; *educ* Harvard (AB 1898); *m* 3 Oct 1905 Marian (*b* Topeka, Kans., 9 March 1878; *d* 25 June 1959), dau of Charles F. Morse and his w Ellen Holdredge, and *d* Concord, Mass., 30 Aug 1964, leaving issue:

Great-great-grandchildren

1a Mary Ogden Adams, *b* 13 Aug 1906; *m* 14 June 1941 *James Barr AMES (*b* 20 April 1911) and *d* 23 July 1967, leaving issue:

Great-great-grandchildren's children

1b Elizabeth Bigelow Ames, *b* 1 May 1942; *m* 24 Aug 1968 Michael Joseph WOLLAN (*d* 28 Aug 1968) and *d* 30 Aug 1968

2b *Richard AMES, *b* 23 April 1944; *m* 26 April 1967 *Heather Ann Woods (*b* 13 July 1945) and has issue:

Great-great-grandchildren's grandchildren

1c *Michael Wollan AMES, *b* 24 Oct 1970

Great-great-grandchildren's children

3b *Charles Cabell AMES, *b* 3 April 1947; *m* 30 June 1968 *Kathleen Lawrence Fisk (*b* 19 April 1947) and has issue:

Great-great-grandchildren's grandchildren

1c *Brooks Averill AMES, *b* 20 Jan 1971

Great-great-grandchildren

2a *John Quincy ADAMS IV, *b* 15 July 1907; *m* 12 Oct 1937 *Lucy Dodge Rice (*b* 21 Dec 1907) and has issue:

Great-great-grandchildren's children

1b *Benjamin Dodge ADAMS, *b* 23 June 1938; *m* 19— *Serita Babson (*b* 26 Feb 1937) and has issue:

Great-great-grandchildren's grandchildren

1c *Benjamin Dodge ADAMS, Jr, *b* 29 April 1959

Great-great-grandchildren's children

2b *Elizabeth Ogden Adams, *b* 27 Aug 1939; *m* 19— *Samuel D. WEAVER (*b* 31 May 1939) and has issue:

Great-great-grandchildren's grandchildren

1c *Marian Adams WEAVER, *b* 1 June 1962
2c *Samuel D. WEAVER, Jr, *b* 16 July 1963
3c *Timothy WEAVER, *b* 2 Dec 1968

Great-great-grandchildren's children

3b *Susanna Boylston Adams, *b* 1 May 1944; *educ* Colorado U; *m* 1 Nov 1969 *Nicholas WHITTEMORE, s of John Howard Whittemore
4b *Lydia Staniford ADAMS, *b* 5 June 1951

Great-great-grandchildren

3a *Thomas Boylston ADAMS [Baker Farm, Lincoln, MA 01773, USA], *b* 25 July 1910; *educ* Harvard; Capt USAF World War II; *m* 5 June 1940 *Ramelle Frost Cochrane (*b* 14 Aug 1916) and has issue:

Great-great-grandchildren's children

1b *John ADAMS, *b* 13 April 1941; *m* 3 June 1967 *Patricia Jones (*b* 17 March 1943) and has issue:

Great-great-grandchildren's grandchildren

1c *Samuel ADAMS, *b* 25 Aug 1972

Great-great-grandchildren's children

2b *Peter Boylston ADAMS, *b* 27 Aug 1942; *m* 16 Feb 1969 *Sharon Kaye Pruett (*b* 19 May 1948)
3b *Francis Douglas ADAMS, *b* 12 Feb 1945; *m* 17 Aug 1968 *Patricia Ingersoll (*b* 2 Nov 1944)
4b *Henry Bigelow ADAMS, *b* 12 May 1949; *educ* Harvard; *m* 12 June 1971 *Ann Louise Jensen (*b* 3 July 1949)
5b *Ramelle Frost ADAMS, *b* 16 Feb 1953

Great-great-grandchildren

4a *Frederick Ogden ADAMS [Old Concord Road, Lincoln, MA 01773, USA], *b* 13 Sept 1912
5a *Abigail Adams, *b* 3 June 1915; *m* 14 June 1940 *Gilbert W. KING (*b* 13 Jan 1914) and has issue:

Great-great-grandchildren's children

1b *Helen Elizabeth King, *b* 29 May 1942; *m* 12 March 1971 *Theodore CORONGES
2b *James Anthony KING, *b* 3 April 1947; *m* 21 June 1970 *Dione Read Christensen (*b* 5 July 1948)

Great-grandchildren

(5) Henry ADAMS, of Lincoln, Mass., *b* Quincy 17 July 1875; *educ* Harvard (AB 1898); with Red Cross France and Russia World War I; *d* 26 April 1951

Grandchildren

4 Henry (Brooks) ADAMS, *b* Boston 16 Feb 1838; *educ* Harvard (AB 1858); private sec to his father Charles Francis Adams while latter US Minister to UK 1861-68, Assist Prof History Harvard 1870-77, ed *North American Review* 1870-76, author: (with his er bro Charles Francis Adams, Jr) *Chapters of Erie and Other Essays* (1871), (with H. C. Lodge, Ernest Young and J. L. Laughlin) *Essays in Anglo-Saxon Law* (1876), *Documents Relating to New England Federalism*, ed (1877), *Life of Albert Gallatin* (1879), *Writings of Albert Gallatin*, ed, 3 vols (1879), *Democracy* (1880), *John Randolph* (1882), *Esther* (1884), *Memoirs of Marau Taaroa, Last Queen of Tahiti* (1893), *History of the United States under the Administration of Jefferson and Madison*, 9 vols (1889-1901),

Mont-Saint-Michel and Chartres (privately printed 1904, published 1913) and *The Education of Henry Adams* (privately printed 1907, published 1918); *m* 27 June 1872 Marian (*b* Boston 13 Sept 1843; committed suicide Washington, DC, 6 Dec 1885, *bur* Rock Creek Cemetery, Washington), dau of Dr Robert William Hooper and his *w* Ellen Sturgis, and *d* Washington, DC, 27 March 1918

5 Arthur ADAMS, *b* Boston 23 July 1841; *d* 9 Feb 1846

6 Mary Adams, *b* Boston 19 Feb 1846; *m* 20 June 1877 Dr Henry Parker QUINCY and *d* 1928, leaving issue:

Great-grandchildren

(1) Dorothy Adams Quincy, *b* Dedham, Mass., 14 Dec 1885; *m* 7 Feb 1906 Frederick Russell NOURSE (*b* 24 May 1877; *d* 3 April 1952) and had issue:

Great-great-grandchildren

1a *Dorothy Quincy Nourse, *b* 6 July 1907; *m* 1st 20 Oct 1928 (divorce 19—) Edwin Lawrence BECKWITH (*b* 25 July 1905; *d* April 1968) and has issue:

Great-great-grandchildren's children

1b *Dorothy Quincy Beckwith, *b* 2 Jan 1930; *m* 23 June 1956 *Warren G. NELSON (*b* 7 Oct 1931) and has issue:

Great-great-grandchildren's grandchildren

1c *George Adams NELSON, *b* 8 Jan 1957

2c *Dorothy Quincy NELSON, *b* 18 Feb 1959

3c *Brooks Endicott NELSON, *b* 13 April 1962

4c *Abigail Thorndike NELSON, *b* 17 Aug 1968

Great-great-grandchildren's children

2b *Harry Lawrence BECKWITH, *b* 10 May 1933; *m* 2 Oct 1964 *Kristina Adelle Landall (*b* 14 Aug 1942) and has issue:

Great-great-grandchildren's grandchildren

1c *Daniele Barteau BECKWITH, *b* 6 Dec 1965

2c *Stephanie Adams BECKWITH, *b* 24 July 1967

3c *David Lincoln BECKWITH, *b* 3 Feb 1970

Great-great-grandchildren's children

3b *Richard Adams BECKWITH, *b* 6 May 1936; *m* 28 Dec 1957 *Virginia Churchill Dangelmayer and has issue:

Great-great-grandchildren's grandchildren

1c *Jacqueline Churchill BECKWITH, *b* 14 May 1961

2c *Scott Adams BECKWITH, *b* 14 April 1964

3c *Russell Lawrence BECKWITH, *b* 4 April 1968

Great-great-grandchildren

1a (cont.) Dorothy Quincy Nourse Beckwith *m* 2nd 2 Jan 1944 *Henry V. POPE (*b* Sept 1907)

2a Frederic Russell NOURSE, Jr, *b* 5 Feb 1910; *m* 26 Jan 1935 *Margaret Dunn (*b* 21 Aug 1916) and *d* 5 June 1943, leaving issue:

Great-great-grandchildren's children

1b *Frederic Russell NOURSE III, *b* 9 Feb 1936; *m* 19— *Jane Buxton and has issue:

Great-great-grandchildren's grandchildren

1c *Frederic Russell NOURSE IV, *b* 22 March 1958

Great-great-grandchildren's children

2b *George Dunn NOURSE, *b* 16 June 1938

3b *Martha Elsie Nourse, *b* 23 July 1941; *m* 24 April 1971 *Stephen Dalrymple REYNOLDS, Jr

Great-grandchildren

(2) Eleanor Adams Quincy, *b* Dedham, Mass., 11 March 1888; *m* Oct 1920 Claude SIMPSON

Grandchildren

7 Brooks ADAMS, *b* Quincy 24 June 1848; *educ* Harvard (AB 1870); lawyer 1870-81, lecturer Boston U Law Sch 1904-11, author: *The Emancipation of Massachusetts* (1887), *The Law of Civilization and Decay* (1895), *America's Economic Superiority* (1900) and *The New Empire* (1902); *m* 7 Sept 1889 Evelyn (*b* Cambridge, Mass., 4 Jan 1853; *d* 14 Dec 1926), dau of Rear-Adml Charles Henry Davis and his *w* Harriette Blake Mills, and *d* Boston 13 Feb 1927

President John Q. Adams's daughter

IV Louise Catherine ADAMS, *b* St Petersburg, Russia, 12 Aug 1811; *d* there 15 Sept 1812

MALE LINE ANCESTRY AND COLLATERAL DESCENDANTS

See Ancestry of President JOHN ADAMS

Edward Boylston
(a) *see* J Adams tree
Anne Bastian
(b) *see* J Adams tree

Thomas Boylston
(c) *see* J Adams tree
Sarah ——
(d) *see* J Adams tree

Myles Fowle?
c 1562-1620
Iden Thorlton?
c 1577-1611

George Fowle
c 1610-82
Mary ——
c 1613-76/7

Henry Bright
c 1560-1609
Mary ——
d p 1618
Henry Goldstone
c 1591-1638
Anne ——
c 1591-1670

Henry Bright
c 1602-86
Anna Goldstone
b c 1615

Edmund Quincy
c 1602-*c* 1637
Judith Pares
d 1654
Charles Hoar
d 1638
Joanna Hincksman
d 1661

Edmund Quincy, Jr
1627/8-97/8
Joanna Hoar
c 1624-80

Revd Thomas Shepard
1605-49
Margaret Touteville
c 1606-35/6
William Tyng
c 1605-52/3
Elizabeth Coytmore
c 1617——42/43-48/9

Revd Thomas Shepard
1635-77
Anna Tyng
1639/40-1709

William Norton
b c 1575
Alice Bownest/Bonus

William Norton
d 1694

Emanuel Downing
c 1585-*c* 1660
Lucy Winthrop
1600/1-79

Lucy Downing
d 1697/8

Arthur Mason
c 1630-1707/8

Nicholas Parker
d p 1655
Ann ——

Joanna Parker
1635-1704/5

JOHN QUINCY ADAMS
FAMILY TREE

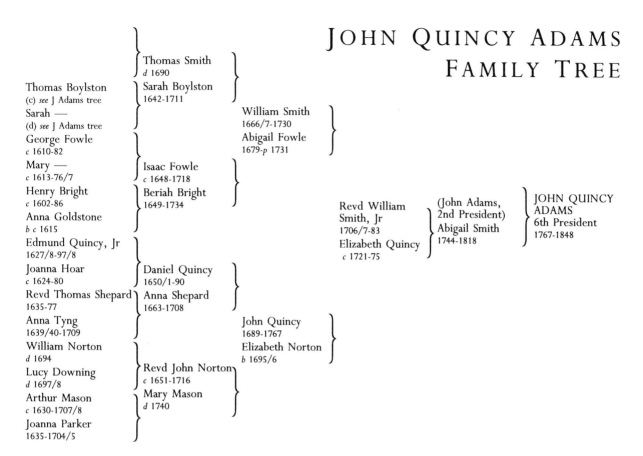

Thomas Smith
d 1690

Thomas Boylston
(c) *see* J Adams tree

Sarah ——
(d) *see* J Adams tree

Sarah Boylston
1642-1711

George Fowle
c 1610-82

Mary ——
c 1613-76/7

Isaac Fowle
c 1648-1718

William Smith
1666/7-1730

Abigail Fowle
1679-*p* 1731

Henry Bright
c 1602-86

Anna Goldstone
b c 1615

Beriah Bright
1649-1734

Edmund Quincy, Jr
1627/8-97/8

Joanna Hoar
c 1624-80

Daniel Quincy
1650/1-90

Revd William
Smith, Jr
1706/7-83

Elizabeth Quincy
  c 1721-75

(John Adams,
2nd President)

Abigail Smith
1744-1818

JOHN QUINCY
ADAMS
6th President
1767-1848

Revd Thomas Shepard
1635-77

Anna Shepard
1663-1708

Anna Tyng
1639/40-1709

John Quincy
1689-1767

William Norton
d 1694

Elizabeth Norton
b 1695/6

Lucy Downing
d 1697/8

Revd John Norton
c 1651-1716

Arthur Mason
c 1630-1707/8

Mary Mason
d 1740

Joanna Parker
1635-1704/5

Plate 19   Andrew Jackson

ANDREW JACKSON

1767-1845
7TH PRESIDENT OF THE UNITED STATES OF AMERICA
1829-37

Andrew Jackson decisively transformed the presidency. In this respect he ranks with Washington, Lincoln and very few others. Yet his overall achievement is shot through with ambiguities and contradictions, making his rank as a statesman exceptionally hard to judge. At least there can be no doubt that he was an outstandingly gifted politician, and one of the most colourful figures in American history.

He was not what he seemed. To his numerous enemies he was a demagogue, a military chieftain, 'King Andrew the First', who would overthrow all the rights and liberties of Americans, a wilful, illiterate backswoodsman. To his even more numerous admirers he was a Washington for valour, a Jefferson for his love of freedom and equality, a hero who beat the British and then came from the West to overthrow the oligarchy of the East, champion of the Union, foe of privilege, tribune of the people. It was a simpler age than ours; people took the parade and hyperbole of presidential elections more seriously than they do today, for they had had much less experience of them.

In cold fact Andrew Jackson, born in a log cabin, was the heir of a respectable Scots-Irish family, and had made his way to eminence by his close association with influential circles in South Carolina, his native state, and Tennessee, where he settled as a young man. It makes no sense to talk of his early life in terms of aristocracy or democracy; everyone on the frontier shared the same values and wanted to get ahead in the same way. Jackson became a planter quite young, and though his financial position was shaky for most of his life he maintained his status as a gentleman lawyer, militia officer and politician quite easily. What was unique about him was his indomitable will and his military talent. He displayed both amply during his campaigns against the Creek Indians (when his great powers of endurance won him the nickname 'Old Hickory') and of course against the British. His military reputation made him an extremely valuable political property. Lots of people stood to gain if Jackson could be induced to run for the presidency, and still more if he could get elected. He was long reluctant ("I am not fit to be President"), but eventually his competitive spirit was aroused, and after a long struggle he won the White House, as we have seen.

He was welcomed to Washington by something like a carnival. Thousands of enthusiastic supporters crowded the streets on Inauguration Day and invaded the White House. Jackson had to retreat from the crush to a boarding house, and the only way the mob could be got out of the mansion was by putting out large tubs of punch for them on the lawn. The Jacksonians were convinced that a new day had dawned; their opponents feared that the destruction of society was at hand.

Jackson himself, mourning the recent death of his wife (the victim, he was sure, of campaign slanders) and beset by officeseekers, seemed little disposed to gratify expectation. His Secretary of State, Martin Van Buren, on arriving in Washington, found him weary and melancholy. If Jackson was a volcano, he was apparently going to be a dormant one.

But the old hero proved very easy to stir into eruption. It only needed someone to challenge his will. Did Congress propose to pay for a national road across the state of Kentucky? He vetoed it. Did the Senate refuse to confirm Van Buren's appointment as American minister to London? "By the Eternal", he said, "I'll smash them", and made Van Buren Vice-President. Did Nicholas Biddle, the President of the Second Bank of the United States, ally himself with Henry Clay? Jackson vetoed the bill to renew the Bank's charter, denouncing 'the Monster' as a conspiracy of the rich against the poor, and unconstitutional into the bargain. Was the King of the French withholding compensation due to US citizens because of incidents during the Napoleonic Wars? Jackson took the country to the brink of war to compel France to climb down. Did Chief Justice Marshall, speaking for the Supreme Court, try to put a stop to the process by which Indian tribes were being driven from their lands in Alabama, Mississippi and Georgia? The President defied him ("John Marshall has made his law, now let him enforce it"). Was South Carolina, led by Calhoun, trying to nullify the US tariff and threatening secession? Jackson would march at the head of an army into the state, and was only restrained from doing so by the swift negotiation of a compromise. Whatever else may be said of Jackson's presidency, it was never for a moment dull.

Jackson enunciated and enacted a new theory of the presidency: that, as the electoral college was little more than a fiction, and the real choice was made by ordinary voters (universal white male suffrage was by then more or less the rule) the President, more than any other organ of government, represented the whole people, and spoke for them. In effect he claimed for the presidency the first place in American government, and popular support made the claim good. It has never been forgotten since, even during eras of weak Presidents. But paradoxically, Jackson, while strengthening the presidency within the federal government, weakened the federal government within the nation. He was a better Jeffersonian than Jefferson, genuinely believing that Washington should interfere as little as possible in the lives of the people, whose state governments were their truest representatives. Not for him the 'American Programme' of a Henry Clay or John Quincy Adams. In this respect Jackson was a true son of the South. But unlike many Southerners he was an unqualified supporter of the Union. One of the most dramatic incidents of his presidency was the Jefferson Day banquet in Washington, which Calhoun wanted to turn into a demonstration in favour of states' rights, but which Jackson, present as the guest of honour, turned into a demonstration of a very different kind by the simple device of proposing the toast "Our Federal Union; It Must Be Preserved". In the eyes of many Southerners, Jackson was being wildly inconsistent, but anyone who tried to tell him so would have got a stormy reception indeed.

Undoubtedly Jackson's most important legacy was the Democratic Party that he and Van Buren together founded. Jackson, was an admirer of the mediaeval Scottish chieftain William Wallace, especially in the matter of rewarding his followers, but he was well aware that rewarding followers with jobs in the Federal government was a matter of securing zealous election workers, as well as of patriarchal generosity. Even the great battles of the Jacksonian period had a party purpose. By splitting the party they exposed the discontented and the weak; they bound the loyal more tightly together; and since Jackson was a very shrewd judge of the attitudes that would attract maximum popular support, they attracted new hordes of voters to the Democratic standard. Thus the cry of 'corrupt bargain' helped to win the battle in 1828; the declaration of war on 'the Monster' won re-election in 1832; and so much happened in the next four years that the opposition (now beginning to call itself the Whig party) decided in despair not to nominate a single candidate for the presidency in 1836, but to let anyone run under the Whig banner who thought he might win. As a result, Van Buren, Jackson's chosen heir, had an easy ride into office. Jackson himself respected the two-term tradition laid down by Washington and reinforced by the rest of the Virginia Dynasty and retired to Tennessee, saying his only regret was that he had not hanged Calhoun and shot Henry Clay. As a last gesture to the gallery, he made part of the journey by railroad, the first, but by no means the last, President to exhibit himself from the rear platform of a train. The immense crowd that assembled for his departure watched him go in a total silence more impressive than any applause.

He left Van Buren a strong but not impregnable political position. Two weaknesses were soon to show themselves. First, Jacksonism had no weapons with which to deal with economic crisis; second, and in the long run more important, it had made party discipline so strong that Presidents in the future, less dynamic and authoritative than Jackson, would find that the party, brought into being to serve them, was now their master, or at best their rival for power.

ANDREW JACKSON'S FAMILY

Andrew Jackson could have been called a man of no family in two senses. He was the first President of indisputably humble birth and not only was he born posthumously but by the time he was 15 his mother and both brothers had died too. He begot no children and in later life, after he had become famous, discouraged approaches from a numerous body of cousins scattered throughout the Carolinas. Even his wife was somebody else's at the time he married her.

Such observations tend to the glib of course. Andrew and Elizabeth Jackson, his father and mother, were simply typical settlers, dying young because that is what most settlers did. They seem to have worked their way down from Pennsylvania to the Waxhaw settlement, where like them most of the other settlers were from Northern Ireland. They brought with them from Ireland both their elder sons Hugh and Robert. Andrew had been a poor tenant farmer, Elizabeth a weaver. Several close relatives of hers had already settled in the Waxhaw area: one sister, Jane, was married to a man called James Crawford or Crafford, another, Margaret, to a man called George McKemy or McCamie and two others to men by the name of Leslie. On her husband's death Elizabeth abandoned the family smallholding of some 200 acres — the Jacksons probably had barely a squatters' right to it and title to it was disputed — and went to live with her relatively prosperous sister Mrs Crawford, keeping house for her as the latter was in poor health. On her way to the Crawfords' she stopped off at her brother-in-law McKemy's cabin, where she may have given birth to the future President. He was born either there or at the Crawfords'.

Jackson's mother was a pious woman who is said to have wanted her son Andrew to take holy orders. He was not parson timber, however, although as he grew older he put up less resistance to religious feeling. The first brick building he put up on his 1,000-acre Tennessee plantation, long after he was married, was a Presbyterian church intended specially for his wife Rachel, who had just joined the Presbyterians. And when Governor of Florida — a position he had wanted to refuse as Rachael loathed the thought of living there — he acquiesced in her promptings to him to crack down on Sunday opening for shops, gaming houses and dancing. The result was to make the Spanish *Domingo* as dreary as the Sabbath in northern Protestant countries. It seems to have been at her prompting also that he became a Presbyterian, though it took him till 10 years after her death.

Instead of the church he chose war. His mother may not have succeeded in imbuing him with religious feeling but she certainly did with her strong anti-British sentiments. She is said to have told her young sons stories of the siege of Carrickfergus, back in Ireland, where their grandfather had suffered at William III's hands. That was back in 1690, however, which would have made Andrew's grandfather Hugh Jackson very young at the time since he is known to have died in 1782.

Andrew Jackson was little more than 13 when he joined the Revolutionary Army in the summer of 1780. The next year he and his elder brother Robert were captured by the British. He only spent two weeks as a prisoner-of-war, being included in an exchange of prisoners after his mother pleaded for him with his British captors, but the experience did nothing to lessen his anti-British attitude. Robert died

Plate 20   Rachel Donelson Robards Jackson aged 52,
from a miniature painted in 1819

of the small-pox that was so prevalent during the Revolutionary War shortly after his younger brother was released, though his death may also have been brought on by a sabre wound a British officer inflicted on him during his captivity. The eldest Jackson boy Hugh had died near the beginning of the war following the battle of Stono Ferry. Only a few months after Robert's death their mother died. She had volunteered to go and nurse American prisoners aboard British ships in the harbour at Charleston (they included her nephews William and James Crawford) and succumbed to what was then called prison or ship fever, more specifically either cholera or yellow fever. And so Andrew Jackson became an orphan aged 14. His was not an unusual case; only because this particular orphan became President does it stand out.

He seems as the surviving son to have inherited money from his grandfather Hugh Jackson. This supports the argument that his father was an eldest son. A nest-egg would have been useful when at the age of 17 he started reading for the bar. In fact it seems he had already spent his inheritance from his grandfather by then. After qualifying as a lawyer he moved to Nashville (at that time still part of North Carolina) and found lodgings with a Mrs Donelson, a widow. His relations with Rachel Robards, *née* Donelson, his landlady's daughter, were for the next few years part melodrama part sentimental comedy. They became increasingly attracted to each other, but unfortunately she had a husband already in Lewis Robards. Jackson was involved in several altercations with him — and with others, for he was a quarrelsome man. Andrew Jackson and the society he lived in were undoubtedly crude and violent, but his frequent duels were conducted according to a gentlemanly code that had its counterpart in the very highest of aristocratic circles in Europe (for instance Canning, a future British Prime Minister, fought a duel with Lord Castlereagh, a future Foreign Secretary). Jackson was capable of a certain delicacy when not fighting duels. He moved out of Mrs Donelson's boarding house rather than compromise Rachel; Lewis Robards was a nasty, jealous and brutal man anyway so that paying court to her could be represented as doing her a good turn, provided his ultimate intentions were honourable (which they proved to be);

Plate 21 Emily Tennessee Donelson, Andrew Jackson's niece and hostess in the White House

Plate 22 Sarah Yorke Jackson, Andrew Jackson's daughter-in-law and hostess in the White House

and there was a certain chivalrous touch about his stepping forward to escort Rachel to Natchez, in what was still then Spanish-held territory, when she determined to travel to a foreign jurisdiction so that she might escape Robards.

One could look at it another way. Duelling was a fatuous way of settling quarrels, whether indulged in by titled European personages or frontiersmen; Jackson had no business interfering between husband and wife, particularly when he was the cause of much of Robards's jealousy; it looks suspiciously as if he began living with Rachel before Robards even applied for legal permission to initiate divorce proceedings, let alone start the proceedings themselves, not least because there is no record of a marriage in Natchez; and he showed a very poor grasp of the law, particularly for a lawyer, when he married Rachel (if he did marry her that first time in Natchez) after grabbing at the flimsiest hearsay evidence that she had obtained a divorce — hearsay which proved false. It stands in Jackson's favour that he made Rachel a good husband. His Byronic, almost Celliniesque escapades were confined to the period before his marriage. He went through a proper marriage with her (the Justice of the Peace who performed the ceremony being Rachel's brother-in-law Robert Hays) as soon as she became indisputably free.

It is perhaps a mercy that Rachel died a few months before her husband was inaugurated President. As early as 1815, after years of outdoor life managing the Tennessee plantation while her husband was away at war, she had grown fat and dumpy; she smoked a pipe (it was said Jackson's mother had done so too), though Rachel did so on doctor's orders to counteract her pthisis; she was ill-educated and provincial. It is possible that the back-biting prevalent throughout Jackson's tenure of the White House would have killed her even if the scurrility of the 1828 campaign had not (she died two weeks after reading for the first time some of the appalling things said about her during the election, and though no direct cause and effect can be proved, it is not implausible given her weak heart toward the end). Yet she was an asset to Jackson. She was from a highly distinguished family in western Tennessee, perhaps the second most prominent in the entire area. She was a good mother to their adoptive son Andrew Jackson Jr. In marrying Rachel, Jackson took on a whole family, an agreeable replacement of the family he had lost as a child. Her sister Jane's husband Col Robert Hays, the Justice mentioned above, was a friend and adviser to Jackson throughout his life; her niece Rachel married John Coffee, Jackson's best cavalry commander in the War of 1812 and one of his most competent comrades in arms generally.

The Donelson connection helped him rebuild his finances when after some unfortunate land specualtions he went into business with two of Rachel's nephews.

Even after Rachel's death Jackson continued to derive pleasure in having his wife's family revolve about him. He and Rachel had adopted a nephew of hers, one of the twin sons of Severn and Elizabeth Donelson, the boy's natural mother being too weak in health to look after both children. The boy was christened Andrew Jackson Jr, and although he spent too much money on clothes and was inept in business, Jackson cheerfully paid his debts, even though not legally obliged to, advising him meanwhile to steer clear of banks. Andrew Jr managed the Hermitage plantation while the President was away in Washington but made rather a hash of it. He left the place to look after itself for lengthy periods and inevitably the plantation failed to prosper. On one occasion while he was away the house burnt down. Nothing seemed to put the President off. He even bought a plantation on the Mississippi and turned that over to Andrew Jr's management. The President also felt obliged to sort out the young man's entanglements with prospective brides. On at least one occasion he wrote to the girl's father to clarify the situation. He was just as fond of his adoptive son's wife Sarah York, with rather more justification since she obligingly acted as hostess in the White House during part of his time there, for all that her Quaker background might have been thought to sit uneasily with such an aggressive man.

As well as adopting a son the Jacksons had numerous wards. They included John Samuel Donelson and Daniel Smith Donelson, sons of Rachel's dead brother Samuel, and Mary Eastin, Rachel's great-niece. There may have been an element of atonement with John S. and Daniel S., for Jackson had encouraged their father to elope with their mother Mary against the wishes of her father Daniel Smith, Jackson's successor as US Senator from Tennessee. When President, Jackson employed yet another nephew of his wife's, a man called Andrew Jackson Donelson, as his private secretary. Jackson had had Donelson educated at Transylvania University and nursed a high regard for him. Donelson's real position was more than that of a secretary, for his genuine ability and the favour in which he was held by Jackson elevated him to the President's kitchen cabinet. Donelson's wife Emily, whom Rachel Jackson had asked to accompany her when she went to Washington as First Lady and help out as hostess at the White House, took on the responsibility single-handed when her patroness died. She was not quite 21 when she became substitute First Lady but grew (literally perhaps as well as metaphorically) in the job. She and Donelson left the White House for a time at the height of the Eaton Affair, an episode that revolved around the wife of John H. Eaton, Jackson's Secretary of War. Margaret Eaton, who had already had one husband (he committed suicide), was thought to have had sexual relations with her second husband before their marriage. The wives of the other Cabinet members ostracized her. Jackson stood by Eaton, however, as with his marital history he was almost bound to do (he also knew that Rachel had not objected to her). Eventually he grew so irritated with the grundyism of his Cabinet members' womenfolk that he replaced most of the Cabinet, though he could well have been going to do something of the sort anyway. In particular he now transferred his support to Martin Van Buren as heir apparent away from John C. Calhon, who had been his Vice-President during his first term but whose wife strongly disapproved of Margaret Eaton.

Emily's attitude certainly seems to have bordered on the petty. She agreed to receive Mrs Eaton on her uncle-in-law's behalf but she drew the line at visiting the woman. Her scruples caused her to stay away from the White House from May 1830 to September 1831 after the President had given her and her husband the choice either of staying and extending the ordinary courtesies to the Eatons or of surrendering to their prejudices and going elsewhere. Andrew Donelson moved back into the White House at the end of the summer of 1830 but Emily remained obdurate for another year. Jackson evidently fretted at the loss, for despite his pugnacity in the political field the old warrior was a bit of a softy at heart, even attending to Andrew and Emily Donelson's children when they cried at night. The fire-eating victor of New Orleans had turned into Colonel Newcome, and all because he had become mellowed by a teeming family, in the best 19th-century novel tradition.

BIOGRAPHICAL DETAILS AND DESCENDANTS

JACKSON, ANDREW, *b* Waxhaw (Warsaw) settlement, Lancaster Co, S or N Carolina (there is some doubt as to which state, though Jackson himself believed it was S Carolina; Waxhaw is now in Union Co, N Carolina), 15 March 1767; saddler's assist 1781, schoolteacher 1783-84, studied law Salisbury, N Carolina, 1784-87; admitted to N Carolina Bar 1787, Constable and Depy Sheriff McLeansville, N Carolina, Prosecuting Atty Western Dist N Carolina (which later became Tennessee) 1788, Atty-Gen Mero District, N Carolina, 1791-92, Judge Advocate Davidson Co Militia 1792, Tstee Davidson Acad, Nashville, 1794, Delegate Tennessee Constitutional Convention 1795-96, Memb from Tennessee US House of Reps 1796-97, US Senator from Tennessee 1797-1798 and 1823-1825 (Chm Ctee on Mily Affrs, Memb For Rels Ctee), Judge Tennessee Superior Court 1798-1804, Maj-Gen Tennessee Militia 1802, Tennessee State Senator 1807, Maj-Gen US Volunteers 1812-14 in Georgia and Alabama, defeating the Creek Indians at Tallushatchee 3 Nov 1813, Talladega, Ala., 9 Nov 1813 and Tohopeka (Horeshoe Bend) 27 March 1814, Maj-Gen US Army May 1814 (captured Pensacola, Fla., 7 Nov 1814, defeated British at New Orleans 8 Jan 1815), US Cdr Seminole War 1818, Military Govr Florida April-Dec 1821, 7th President (D/Democratic-Republican) of the USA 1829-1837, Hon LLD Harvard 1833; author: *Correspondence*, ed John S. Bassett, 7 vols (1926-35), *Papers*, ed Sam S. Smith and Harriet C. Owsley (1980); went through a form of marriage in Natchez, Spanish Territory (subsequently Miss.), Aug 1791 (or conceivably as early as Oct 1790) with, *m* legally Nashville, Tenn., 18 Jan 1794, as her 2nd husb, Rachel (*b* Pittsylvania or Halifax Co, Va., 15 June 1767; *m* 1st Harrodsburg, Ky., 1 March 1785 or 1787 (divorce 27 Sept 1793, mistakenly believed by her to have been granted Dec 1790) Capt Lewis Robards; *d* The Hermitage, nr Nashville, 22 Dec 1828, *bur* in The Hermitage garden), 4th dau of Col John Donelson, Memb Virginia House of Burgesses, and his *w* Rachel Stockley, and *d* Nashville 8 June 1845 of consumption and dropsy, leaving a nephew-by-marriage (*s* of Mrs Jackson's brother Severn Donelson and his *w* Elizabeth Rucker), whom he had adopted:

President Jackson's adopted son:

a Andrew JACKSON, Jr, of The Hermitage, Nashville, Tennessee, *b* nr Nashville 4 Dec 1808, adopted 1809; *educ* Cumberland Coll, Nashville, and Nashville U; *m* Philadelphia 24 Nov 1831 Sarah (*b* Philadelphia July 1805; *d* The Hermitage 23 Aug 1887), dau of Peter Yorke, of Philadelphia, and was accidentally *k* 17 April 1865, having had issue:

Adoptive grandchildren

i Rachel Jackson, *b* The Hermitage 1 Nov 1832; *m* 25 Jan 1853 Dr John Marshall LAWRENCE (*b* 6 Sept 1823; *d* 30 Nov 1882) and *d* 3 Feb 1923, having had issue:

Adoptive great-grandchildren

(i) Sarah Yorke Lawrence, *b* The Hermitage 15 March 1854; *m* 18 May 1880 Dr Charles W. WINN and *d* Maury Co, Tenn., 6 May 1882, leaving issue:

Adoptive great-great-grandchildren

i *a* (Charles) Lawrence WINN, *b* 17 March 1882; *m* 1st 31 Oct 1907 Minnie Henderson (*b* 8 June 1882; *d* 3 July 1951) and had issue:

Adoptive great-great-grandchildren's children

i *b* *Marian Henderson Winn, *b* 9 July 1912; *m* 6 Oct 1932 *Charles G. FULLER, Jr, *s* of Charles G. Fuller, and has issue:

Adoptive great-great-grandchildren's grandchildren

i *c* *Jean Winn Fuller, *b* 25 Dec 1934; *m* 2 Sept 1955 *Charles Brandon GUY and has issue:

Adoptive great-great-grandchildren's great-grandchildren

i *d* *Karen GUY, *b* 1957

ii *d* *Charles Brandon GUY, Jr, *b* 1958

iii *d* *Judith Fuller GUY, *b* 1960

Adoptive great-great-grandchildren

i *a* (cont.) Lawrence Winn *m* 2nd *Grace M. McKibbon and *d* 1967

Adoptive great-grandchildren

(ii) Annie Laurie Lawrence, *b* 3 April 1855; *m* 18— Joshua Wright SMITH and *d* 4 Feb 1937, leaving issue:

Adoptive great-great-grandchildren

i *a* Revd Walton Lawrence SMITH, *b* Nashville 1 July 1891; Presbyterian Minister of Woodbury, Tenn., (ret 1962); *m* 18 Oct 1921 Lucinda Mayfield Alexander (*d* 1970) and had issue:

Adoptive great-great-grandchildren's children

i *b* Martha Ann SMITH, *b* 19—; *d* 19—

Adoptive great-great-grandchildren
ii *a* *Rachel Jackson Smith [Mrs Leonard Donelson, 3335 Harrison Street, Kansas City, MO 64109, USA], *b* 1893; *m* 19— Leonard H. DONELSON

Adoptive great-grandchildren
(iii) Dr Andrew Jackson LAWRENCE, *b* 9 July 1857; *m* 1st Emma H. George (*b* 16 Oct 1867; *d* 3 March 1894) and had issue:

Adoptive great-great-grandchildren
i *a* Dr Andrew Jackson LAWRENCE, Jr, *b* 26 Sept 1888; *m* 19— Sarah Foster Schell (*b* 18 Oct 1889) and *d* 1971, leaving issue:

  Adoptive great-great-grandchildren's children
  i *b* *Andrew Jackson LAWRENCE III, *b* 22 May 1923; *m* 19— *Mary L. Humphrey (*b* 16 Oct 1924) and has issue:

    Adoptive great-great-grandchildren's grandchildren
    i *c* *Sarah Louise LAWRENCE, *b* 23 Sept 1948
    ii *c* *Deborah Anne LAWRENCE, *b* 30 July 1950
    iii *c* *Rachel Jackson LAWRENCE, *b* 21 Sept 1955
    iv *c* *Andrew Jackson LAWRENCE IV, *b* 19—

Adoptive great-great-grandchildren
ii *a* Marie Guerrant LAWRENCE, *b* 19 Sept 1891

Adoptive great-grandchildren
(iii) (cont.) Dr Andrew Jackson Lawrence *m* 2nd Julia E. Millican (*b* 30 June 1878; *d* 11 June 1938) and *d* 24 June 1935, having with her had issue:

Adoptive great-great-grandchildren
iii *a* *Mary Louise Lawrence, *b* 26 Aug 1903; *m* *Cecil H. GRAHAM (*b* 23 Oct 1896) and has issue:

  Adoptive great-great-grandchildren's children
  i *b* *Mary Lu Graham, *b* 30 July 1926; *m* 19— *James Hay PAGE (*b* 17 April 1924) and has issue:

    Adoptive great-great-grandchildren's grandchildren
    i *c* *Ellen Marie PAGE, *b* 31 March 1949
    ii *c* *Lucille PAGE, *b* 25 June 1951
    iii *c* *Jane Louise PAGE, *b* 28 Feb 1955

  Adoptive great-great-grandchildren's children
  ii *b* *Julia Ann Graham, *b* 16 June 1932; *m* 19— *Richard Dwight KANAKANUI (*b* 6 July 1929) and has issue:

    Adoptive great-great-grandchildren's grandchildren
    i *c* *Karen Ann KANAKANUI, *b* 8 Aug 1955

Adoptive great-great-grandchildren
iv *a* *Dr James Walton LAWRENCE, *b* 1 Aug 1907; *m* 19— Lillie Mae Dinkins (*b* 26 Aug 1911; *d* 1971) and has issue:

  Adoptive great-great-grandchildren's children
  i *b* *Barbara Josephine LAWRENCE, *b* 29 Aug 1932
  ii *b* *James Walton LAWRENCE, Jr, *b* 29 June 1938
  iii *b* *Pamela Ann LAWRENCE, *b* 16 May 1946

Adoptive great-great-grandchildren
v *a* *Edward Montgomery LAWRENCE, *b* 1 Aug 1914; *m* 19— *Barbara Decker (*b* 8 July 1916) and has issue:

  Adoptive great-great-grandchildren's children
  i *b* *Linda Marie LAWRENCE, *b* 21 Feb 1939
  Mr and Mrs Edward M. Lawrence also have an adopted s:
  a *Robert Decker LAWRENCE

Adoptive great-grandchildren
(iv) John Marshall LAWRENCE, Jr, *b* 5 July 1859; *d* 26 June 1926
(v) Carrie Minerva Lawrence, *b* 29 April 1861; *m* Revd Dr William D. BRADFIELD and *d* before 1953, having had issue:

  Adoptive great-great-grandchildren
  i *a* Florence BRADFIELD, *b* 16 June 1893; *d* young
  ii *a* *(William) Landon BRADFIELD, *b* 23 June 1895; *m* 19— *Nell E. Walling (*b* 12 Sept 1895) and has issue:

    Adoptive great-great-grandchildren's children
    i *b* *Thomas Walling BRADFIELD, *b* 12 Oct 1921; *m* 19— *Mary Ann Latham (*b* 13 Sept 1926) and has issue:

Adoptive great-great-grandchildren's grandchildren
i *c* *Rebecca Ruth BRADFIELD, *b* 5 Dec 1952
ii *c* *Melinda Nell BRADFIELD, *b* 18 July 1954

Adoptive great-great-grandchildren's children
ii *b* *Elizabeth Ann Bradfield, *b* 12 May 1929; *m* 19— *Donald Hugh CUMMINS (*b* 9 Oct 1928) and has issue:

Adoptive great-great-grandchildren's grandchildren
i *c* *William Bradfield CUMMINS, *b* 1 Oct 1952
ii *c* *Thomas Walling CUMMINS, *b* 7 June 1955

Adoptive great-great-grandchildren
iii *a* James Lee BRADFIELD, *b* 18— or 19—; *d* young
iv *a* *Dr John Lawrence BRADFIELD, *b* 8 Dec 1901; *educ* Baylor U; *m* 1969

Adoptive great-grandchildren
(vi) Dr Samuel Jackson LAWRENCE, *b* 22 June 1863; *m* 18— Maude V. Johnson (*b* 18 Sept 1866; *d* 8 Oct 1937) and *d* 1 March 1935, having had issue:

Adoptive great-great-grandchildren
i *a* Samuel Jackson LAWRENCE, *b* 18— ; *d* young
ii *a* *John Marshall LAWRENCE III, *b* 5 Nov 1895; *m* 19— *Helen G. Barton (*b* 3 Dec 1900) and has issue:

Adoptive great-great-grandchildren's children
i *b* *Helen Virginia Lawrence, *b* 20 July 1923; *m* 19— *Henry C. TRUSSEL (*b* 17 May 1923)
ii *b* *Dorothy Ann Lawrence, *b* 15 Nov 1925; *m* 19— *Collins MASON (*b* 5 March 1924) and has issue:

Adoptive great-great-grandchildren's grandchildren
i *c* *Lawrence Collins MASON, *b* 19 Jan 1948
ii *c* *Dorothy Ann MASON, *b* 13 Jan 1949
iii *c* *Robert Ralph MASON, *b* 10 June 1953
iv *c* *—— MASON, *b* 1955 (?)

Adoptive great-great-grandchildren
iii *a* *Maude Wanda Lawrence, *b* 4 May 1897; *m* 19— *William Horace BARSE, Jr, *s* of William Horace Barse
iv *a* *Dr Clifton Hyde LAWRENCE, *b* 9 Nov 1900; *m* 19— *Kathleen Goodman (*b* 3 May 1907) and has issue:

Adoptive great-great-grandchildren's children
i *b* *Thomas N. LAWRENCE, *b* 7 May 1934
ii *b* *Kay LAWRENCE, *b* 2 March 1936
iii *b* *Samuel Jackson LAWRENCE II, *b* 12 March 1941

Adoptive great-grandchildren
(vii) William Walton LAWRENCE, of Nashville, Tenn., *b* 1866; *m* 18— or 19— Mary Fisher and *d* 1924, leaving issue:

Adoptive great-great-grandchildren
i *a* *Edith Eudora Lawrence, *b* 18— or 19—; *m* 2 June 1920 *Charles Murphey CANDLER, Jr (*b* Decatur, Ga., 5 Feb 1898), *s* of Charles Murphey Candler and his *w* Mary Hannah Scott and *bro* of Milton A. Candler (for whom *see below*), and has issue:

Adoptive great-great-grandchildren's children
i *b* *Edith Lawrence Candler, *b* 19—; *m* 1st 19— Philip SHAW and has issue:

Adoptive great-great-grandchildren's grandchildren
i *c* *Murphey Candler SHAW, *b* 19—
ii *c* *Pattie SHAW, *b* 19—

Adoptive great-great-grandchildren's children
i *b* (cont.) Edith Candler Shaw *m* 2nd *Lon C. THOMAS and has further issue:

Adoptive great-great-grandchildren's grandchildren
iii *c* *Lon C. THOMAS, Jr, *b* 19—

Adoptive great-grandchildren
(viii) Marion Yorke Lawrence, *b* 15 Nov 1869; *m* 18— or 19— John Cleves SYMMES (*b* 27 Jan 1868; *d* 1918), a great-nephew of the wife of President WILLIAM H. HARRISON, and *d* Philadelphia 1 Feb 1971, having had issue·

Adoptive great-great-grandchildren
i *a* John Cleves SYMMES, Jr, *b* 15 Jan 1891; *m* 19— Catherine Crichton and had issue:

Adoptive great-great-grandchildren's children
i *b* *John Cleves SYMMES III, *b* 19—; *m* 1st 19— (divorce 19—) Gwendolyn Jefferson and has issue:

Adoptive great-great-grandchildren's grandchildren
i *c* *Carol Symmes, *b* 12 Nov 1944; *m* 15 March 1967 *Louis J MITCHELL (*b* 24 Nov 1944) and has issue:

Adoptive great-great-grandchildren's great-grandchildren
i d *John P. MITCHELL, b 14 Jan 1969

Adoptive great-great-grandchildren's grandchildren
ii c *Holly Sue Symmes, b 4 April 1947; m 5 Dec 1970 *Ernest MONTFORD

Adoptive great-great-grandchildren's children
i b (cont.) John Cleves Symmes III m 2nd 1956 *Jane H. Campbell and has further issue:

Adoptive great-great-grandchildren's grandchildren
iii c *Jeanne Campbell SYMMES, b 9 Nov 1959
iv c *Anne Cleves SYMMES, b 15 Jan 1962

Adoptive great-great-grandchildren
ii a Sue Rae Symmes, b 12 Aug 1893; m 13 Oct 1920 James J McCUTCHEON, Jr (b 17 Nov 1891), s of James J. McCutcheon, and had issue:

Adoptive great-great-grandchildren's children
i b *Sue Symmes McCutcheon [Mrs William Pass Jr, 6375 Sherman Street, Philadelphia, PA 19144, USA], b 3 Oct 1924; m 19— *William Nice Wilmerton PASS, Jr (b Sept 1930), s of William Nice Wilmerton Pass, and has issue:

Adoptive great-great-grandchildren's grandchildren
i c *Suzanne Lee Pass, b 25 Dec 1946; m 26 Dec 1970 *Gordon LASH
ii c *William Nice Wilmerton PASS III, b 26 July 1948
iii c *(John) Mark PASS, b 3 Sept 1950
iv c *Barbara Jean PASS, b 26 April 1952

Adoptive great-great-grandchildren's children
ii b Essy McCUTCHEON, b 29 July 1926; d 9 July 1935
iii b *Sarah Yorke McCutcheon, b 7 April 1928; m 1st 1949 (divorce 19—) James ADAMS and has issue:

Adoptive great-great-grandchildren's grandchildren
i c *James Edward ADAMS, b 22 Nov 1950
ii c *Dorothy Lee ADAMS, b 22 Jan 1952
iii c *Robert Benjamin ADAMS, b 22 Oct 1953

Adoptive great-great-grandchildren's children
iii b (cont.) Mrs Sarah Adams m 2nd 1962 *James O. STEVENSON (b 17 Oct 1930) and has further issue:

Adoptive great-great-grandchildren's grandchildren
iv c *David Andrew STEVENSON, b 30 April 1965
v c *Linda Sue STEVENSON, b 20 July 1966

Adoptive great-great-grandchildren's children
iv b *James S. J. McCUTCHEON [7836 Old North Court, Charlotte, NC, USA; 6419 Prett Ct, Charlotte, NC, USA], b 20 April 1934; m 20 Dec 1958 *Linda Weis and has two adopted children:

a *Kelly Elizabeth McCUTCHEON, b 25 March 1963
b *James Christopher McCUTCHEON, b 5 March 1967

Adoptive great-great-grandchildren
iii a Marion Yorke Symmes, b 8 Aug 1895; m 1916 Milton Anthony CANDLER (b Decatur, Ga., 19 Nov 1892), s of Charles Murphey Candler, of Atlanta, Ga., and his w Mary Hannah Scott and bro of Charles Murphey Candler, Jr (for whom see above), and d June 1965, leaving issue:

Adoptive great-great-grandchildren's children
i b *Marion Lawrence Candler, b 26 Oct 1920; m 19— *William Gordon EMREY and has issue:

Adoptive great-great-grandchildren's grandchildren
i c *William Gordon EMREY, Jr, b 19—
ii c *Milton Candler EMREY, b 19—

Adoptive great-great-grandchildren's children
ii b *Rebekah Scott Candler, b 7 Aug 1922; m 14 June 1945 *(Henderson) Crawford WARD and has issue:

Adoptive great-great-grandchildren's grandchildren
i c *Henderson Crawford WARD, Jr, b 6 Aug 1947; m 1969 *Barbara Pond and has issue:

Adoptive great-great-grandchildren's great-grandchildren
i d *Catherine Lawrence WARD, b 28 April 1971

Adoptive great-great-grandchildren's grandchildren
ii c *Candler Symmes WARD, b 9 Sept 1949
iii c *Charles Scott WARD, b 1 Sept 1955

Adoptive great-grandchildren
(ix) Thomas Donelson LAWRENCE, *b* 1870 (?); *d* before 1953

Adoptive grandchildren
ii Andrew JACKSON III, *b* The Hermitage, Nashville, 4 April 1834; *educ* West Point; Col Confederate States Army; *m* 15 Oct 1877 Amy A. Rich (*b* Ohio 31 Aug 1851; *d* 9 Jan 1921) and *d* 17 Dec 1906, leaving issue:

Adoptive great-grandchildren
(i) Andrew JACKSON IV, *b* The Hermitage 1887; *educ* S California and Paris; high sch teacher and actor; *m* 4 Jan 1913 (divorce 19—) Marion Caulkins and *d* Los Angeles 23 May 1953, leaving issue:

Adoptive great-great-grandchildren
i *a* *Amy Lee JACKSON, *b* 19—
ii *a* *Andrew JACKSON V, *b* 19—; *m* 19— 1st (divorce 19—) Lola Kapps; *m* 2nd 1955 Carolyn ——
iii *a* *Edith Jackson, *b* 19—; *m* 19— *West MORELAND and has issue:

Adoptive great-great-grandchildren's children
i *b* *Sharon MORELAND, *b* 19—
ii *b* *Diane MORELAND, *b* 19—
iii *b* *Robin MORELAND, *b* 19—

Adoptive great-great-grandchildren
iv *a* *Douglas JACKSON, *b* 1923; *m* 19— *Violet Lower (*b* 1925) and has issue:

Adoptive great-great-grandchildren's children
i *b* *Barbara JACKSON, *b* 1947
ii *b* *Cynthia JACKSON, *b* 1950
iii *b* *Douglas William JACKSON, *b* 1953

Adoptive great-grandchildren
(ii) Albert Marble JACKSON, *b* 18—; *m* 18— or 19— and disappeared 1919

Adoptive grandchildren
iii Thomas Jefferson JACKSON, *b* 1836; *d* 1840
iv Samuel JACKSON, *b* The Hermitage 9 June 1837; Capt Confederate States Army; *d* 27 Sept 1863
v Robert Armstrong JACKSON, *b* 18 June; *d* 11 Nov 1843

MALE LINE ANCESTRY AND COLLATERAL DESCENDANTS

Thomas JACKSON inherited a paternal estate of the great part of the Townland of Ballyregan (an area about 1 sq mile in extent situated about a mile east of what is now the former Parliament Building in Belfast), in the parish of Dundonald, Co Down, Ireland, and was witness to a will 31 Jan 1761; *m* —— and had issue:

I Revd James JACKSON; was a clergyman 40 years at Ballybay, Co Monaghan, Ireland; *m* and *d* at the 'mansion house' of Ballyregan, leaving issue:

1 Thomas JACKSON; MD, of Ballybay; *m* and had issue:

(1) Thompson JACKSON, of Dublin; inherited *c* 1821 the property at Ballyregan, then reckoned worth *c* £300 a year; *d* unmarried

2 Martha Jackson; *m* Robert BRADFORD, of 'near Ballybay' and had issue one *s* and one dau (*m* twice and left issue)
3 Elizabeth Jackson; *m* James McCULLY, of Dundonald, and had issue (together with three daus):

(1) William McCULLY, of Ballymisca, Dundonald, formerly Kirkdonald, Co Down; travelled to America where he delivered a letter of 8 Jan 1822 to the future President Gen Andrew Jackson, then stationed in Pensacola, Fla., catalogued among the Jackson Papers in the Library of Congress as *Wm. McCully to Genl Jackson relating to the Genls parentage*

4 Mary Jackson; *m* David DALZELL and *d* by 1821, having had issue seven *s* and three daus
5 Jane Jackson, of 'near Fivemiletown, Co Tyrone'; *m* James BURNSIDE and had issue one *s* and two daus

II Hugh JACKSON, for whom *see below*
III A son; received his 'diploma' as a clergyman and *d* shortly thereafter

The 2nd *s*,

Hugh JACKSON, of Carrickfergus, Co Antrim, weaver and merchant; *m* and *d c* 1782, having had issue (but *see* Robert V. Remini, *Andrew Jackson and the Course of American Empire, 1767-1821* (1977), p. 427, note 2, for reasons why he accepts the I Andrew Jackson mentioned immediately below as the youngest of four brothers, not the eldest):

I Andrew JACKSON, for whom *see below*

II James JACKSON; *m* and had issue:

1 James Andrew JACKSON; emigrated to USA *c* 1798; *m* —— McCreary, sis of Thomas McCreary, banker, and had issue (with two er s):

1a Thomas JACKSON, *b* Beaver Co 1826; *m* Malinda (*b* Moon Township, Beaver Co, 1831; *d* 1911), dau of William Alcorn and his w Sarah Hultz, and had issue (with other children):

1b Sarah M. Jackson; *m* Dr J. M. DOUDS, of Beaver Falls
2b Dr J. O. JACKSON, of Corrie, Pa.
3b Thomas Sharpe JACKSON; schoolmaster, farmer and businessman

III Hugh JACKSON; soldier; *m* and had issue(?):

1 James JACKSON, *b c* 1780; living in Beaver Township 1802, owned real estate assessed at $3,000 1850; *m* Jane, said to have been dau of his uncle Robert Jackson (but that Jane was *b* 1804, making her 24 years yr than her husb, whereas this Jane is said to have been *b c* 1780) and had (with other issue):

(1) John JACKSON, *b* 1801
(2) Agnes Jackson, *b* 1809; *m* 1829 John Hartman WHISLER, boat-builder, and had issue (with seven other children):

1a Leander WHISLER, *b* 1833; boat-builder
2a Charles F. WHISLER; co-publisher of *The Star* newspaper, his half share in which he sold 1885

IV Robert JACKSON, *b c* 1750; emigrated to the USA *c* 1798, settling in Brighton Township, Beaver Co, Pa.; *m* and had issue:

1 James JACKSON; a ruling elder of the Presbyterian Church, Beaver Co, 1823
2 Andrew JACKSON, *b c* 1780; emigrated to the USA with his parents 1798, farmer at North Sewickley Township 1808, memb Presbyterian Church 1823 and Methodist Church 1838; *m c* 1800 Agnes Robison (*b* Newark, New Jersey, before 1790) and had issue:

(1) Martha JACKSON
(2) Robinson JACKSON, *b* 1803; bucket-maker, owned real estate assessed at $2,800 in 1850; *m* Ann —— (*b* 1810) and had issue:

1a Kirby C, JACKSON, *b* 1832   2a Andrew JACKSON, *b* 1834   3a Robert JACKSON, *b* 1836   4a William Henry JACKSON, *b* 1838   5a Alice JACKSON, 1840   6a Cornelius JACKSON, *b* 1843   7a Addison JACKSON, *b* 1846   8a Cardine JACKSON, *b* 1849

(3) Jane JACKSON, *b* 1804; living Indianapolis 1888
(4) Mary JACKSON, *b* 1808; living Indianapolis 1888
(5) Robert JACKSON; farmer in North Sewickley Township in 1850; *m* Elizabeth —— (*b* 1815) and had issue:

1a Sarah JACKSON, *b* 1839   2a Andrew JACKSON, *b* 1840   3a Mary A. JACKSON, *b* 1842   4a Thompson JACKSON, *b* 1844   5a William JACKSON, *b* 1845   6a Eliza JACKSON, *b* 1849

(6) Ann JACKSON, *b* 1810; living Alleghany City 1888
(7) James JACKSON; stonecutter, bought a farm 1849 and later the adjacent 200 ac, memb Methodist Episcopal Church; *m* 1838 Esther Akin and had issue:

1a Kate Agnes JACKSON   2a Jane JACKSON; *d* by 1888   3a James A. JACKSON   4a Andrew JACKSON; *d* by 1888   5a Sarah Ann Jackson; *m* Harry POTTER, of Franklin Township, Beaver Co, Pa.   6a Henderson JACKSON   7a John JACKSON   8a Robert JACKSON

(8) Agnes JACKSON
(9) Andrew JACKSON, *b* Beaver Co 1812; *m* Belinda Hays (*b* there *c* 1818) and had issue:

1a Martha Jackson, *b* 1844; *m* —— SMITH
2a William Henderson JACKSON, of Beaver Falls, *b* 1847
3a John Andrew JACKSON; founded clothiers called Butler & Jackson 1885 and *d* Fallston 3 Nov 1911

Hugh Jackson's est (?) s,
Andrew JACKSON, *b* Carrickfergus *c* 1730: emigrated to America, settling in Waxhaw, S Carolina, where he farmed, by 1760; *m* Carrickfergus before 1760 Elizabeth (*b* Carrickfergus *c* 1740; *d* Charleston, S Carolina, Nov 1781 of cholera or yellow fever), dau of —— Hutchinson and his w —— Leslie, and *d* Waxhaw *c* 1 March 1767 (*bur* Waxhaw Churchyard), leaving issue:

I Hugh JACKSON, *b* Ireland 1762 or 1763; served in Col William R. Davie's Regt (on the patriot side) Revolutionary War; *d* of exhaustion following his participation in Battle of Stono Ferry, S Carolina, 20 June 1779
II Robert JACKSON, *b* Ireland 1764 or 1765; *d* 27 April 1781 of smallpox and/or the effect of a sabre wound inflicted on him while a prisoner of war by a British officer
III ANDREW JACKSON, 7th PRESIDENT of the UNITED STATES of AMERICA

ANDREW JACKSON
FAMILY TREE

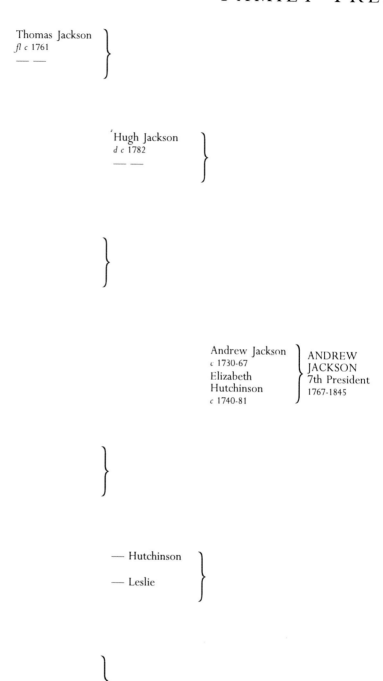

Thomas Jackson
fl c 1761
— —

'Hugh Jackson
d c 1782
— —

Andrew Jackson
c 1730-67
Elizabeth
Hutchinson
c 1740-81

ANDREW
JACKSON
7th President
1767-1845

— Hutchinson

— Leslie

Plate 23   Martin Van Buren

MARTIN VAN BUREN

1782-1862
8TH PRESIDENT OF THE UNITED STATES OF AMERICA
1837-41

Van Buren was an unlucky President. Jackson had scarcely got back to Nashville before the Panic of 1837 announced itself in a rash of bank failures. The Democrats did badly in the elections that year. Things recovered somewhat in 1838, and so did the Democracy, but in 1839 the real economic collapse occurred. The electorate looked in vain to their government for help. The dogmas of Van Buren's party were impotent to deal with a crisis that was world-wide in its causes and effects. The utmost he could do was to save the credit of the US government by setting up an independent Treasury for the deposit of tax receipts (previously kept in banks which now seemed unreliable); a wise precaution, for the credit of various states, notably Pennsylvania which had grossly over-invested in canals, was tottering; but it did not help the merchant forced into bankruptcy, or the workman thrust into unemployment. Van Buren was also the victim of rising hostility between sections of the Union. He was suspect as a Northerner in the South, and as a polished cosmopolitan in the West. The abolitionist agitation was mounting to its height, with John Quincy Adams in his new role of 'Old Man Eloquent' thundering in the House of Representatives; anything which Van Buren did, or neglected to do on this issue, was bound to affect some important group. The Whigs plucked up courage and began to look round for a winning candidate for 1840.

Van Buren deserved a better fate. The age was a scurrilous one, and every President in turn was a victim of spiteful rumour. Every leader was denounced, either as a corrupt demagogue or a corrupt aristocrat. Van Buren was denounced as both. In reality he was an honest, good-natured professional politician, who grasped before anyone else the importance of a permanent party organization and permanent party principles if democracy in America was to work. Without the evolution of parties which could transcend individual ambitions and state or sectional loyalties, the United States might split up, or political control might fall into the hands of the rich and their allies, who had dominated American society and politics completely until the Revolution, and in some ways for long after it. Van Buren had several reasons for standing out against such tendencies. He was of Dutch descent (Dutch was the language of his boyhood) and was the first person of non-British stock to reach the presidency. He was the son of an innkeeper, who had worked his way upward to gentility and prosperity by his own abilities, notably as a lawyer. To get to the top he had had to fight and break the ascendancy of the old aristocracy of New York state, and in that fight had found a party machine indispensable; only such a machine could rouse up the voters on election day in sufficient numbers. He was, in short, a worthy partner and successor of Andrew Jackson, and in happier times his presidency might have been one of substantial achievement. As it was, he managed to damp down some of the wilder animosities of Jackson's day. Nicholas Biddle came to dinner at the White House and Van Buren unswervingly followed the principle he had adopted in his youth, of never making an enemy on personal grounds.

The 1840 election proved to be one of the greatest in American history. The Democrats went into battle with the confidence of veterans and indeed managed to win more votes for Van Buren than they ever had for Jackson. Unfortunately the Whigs had learned their lesson; they doubled and redoubled their efforts against Democratic ones, and always there was the depression to encourage them. When the votes were counted it was found they had swept Van Buren away: William Henry Harrison, the Whig candidate, got 234 electoral votes, Van Buren only 60.

Van Buren behaved with his usual good manners, but he had no intention of retiring. The story of the presidency in the next eight years was to be substantially affected by his continuing activity.

MARTIN VAN BUREN'S FAMILY

Martin Van Buren is the first and so far only President whose every known ancestor comes from outside the British Isles. He was the first President to have been born a US citizen and the first to be groomed for the post by his immediate predecessor and patron, in this case Andrew Jackson. He was the first presidential candidate to be unfairly labelled aristocratic, for although John Quincy Adams had the same slur flung at him his background was at least patrician, whereas Van Buren was entirely self-made. The notion that a 'Van' in front of one's name denotes riches and lofty social position persists in America to this day.

To begin with Van Buren kept to the small enclosed world of Dutch Americans he had grown up in. He studied law under a celebrated lawyer called William Van Ness, who was Aaron Burr's second in his duel with Alexander Hamilton. He may conceivably have been a distant cousin, for Van Buren through his maternal grandmother's own maternal grandmother had Van Ness ancestors although on the other hand the name is a common Dutch one. At any rate, when Van Buren retired from the presidency in 1841 he bought a Van Ness property in New York state which he rechristened Lindenwald ('Lime Tree Wood' in English), a name suggested by a member of his family, possibly his son John. On completing his studies he became a law partner with his elder half-brother James Van Alen in Kinderhook, where James had worked up a solid practice among local farmers. When Van Buren became Surrogate for Columbia County it was in succession to James, who himself had succeeded his stepfather Abraham (Van Buren's father) as Kinderhook's town clerk. The Dutch element was most pronounced in his domestic life. He spoke Dutch with his wife Hannah when they were at home. After Hannah's death his sister Maria looked after the children, later settling on a farm Van Buren owned near his brother Laurence's house.

Hannah Hoes (or Jannetje as her husband called her) was the first President's wife born a US citizen. She was also born in the same small town as her future husband (she and he were first cousins once-removed) and educated at the same school. She is said to have been a tranquil person. One is inclined to interpret that as colourless, since Van Buren makes no mention of her in his autobiography. After her relatively early death at the age of 36 Van Buren seems to have rejected any idea of getting married again, although there was a rumour in 1822 that he was keen on Jefferson's granddaughter Ellen Wayles Randolph, then aged 25. It is interesting that although he enjoyed female company he thought mixed gatherings gave wives a chance of influencing their husbands. One cannot imagine his own wife doing so if she had lived to see him President. He must have had another example in mind.

With Van Buren's sons a definite move away from exclusively Dutch society becomes detectable, although Dutch family names were bestowed on two of them, Abraham and Martin Jr. It is John Van Buren, with his wholly English first name, who seems to have been his father's favourite, however. He accompanied Van Buren on the latter's brief mission to England and it was partly Van Buren's hopes of a political career for John that led him to get involved with the Barnburners (Free Soil Party or antislavery

Plate 24   Hannah Hoes Van Buren

Plate 25   Angelica Singleton Van Buren, Martin Van Buren's daughter-in-law and hostess in the White House

Democrats), a disastrous episode in terms of winning votes. John, who drank, gambled and had a series of love affairs, was a worry to his father. He was hard-working, though, and intelligent as well. His father sent him to London in 1838 with a private message of conciliation for the British Foreign Secretary Lord Palmerston after an incident on the Canadian-American border threatened to upset relations with Britain and had so incensed the American public that the President was obliged to tick the British off in a stiff official protest. John also helped his father prepare campaign literature when running on the Free Soil ticket in 1848.

When Van Buren became President he took all four of his surviving sons to work for him at the White House and they became known as his 'privy counsellors'. His eldest son Abraham had been the go-between with Andrew Jackson for years and Smith, his youngest son, later liaised between his father and Polk during the latter's presidency. But the line between an official position as presidential adviser and a more informal one as go-between was not easy to draw. When Van Buren was about to be inaugurated he arranged for Abraham to resign his commission as an army officer and take up a civil service job, ensuring that he would be paid a salary while acting as his father's secretary. Later Martin Jr was found a snug berth in the land office, which paid his salary while he too worked for his father. The family remained just as close-knit after Van Buren stepped down from the presidency. He retired to Lindenwald and Martin Jr and Smith Van Buren moved in with him, Smith's task being to manage the property. Smith's second wife Henrietta was a niece of the writer Washington Irving, who had been American chargé d'affaires in London when Van Buren was nominated as the new Minister there and with whom Van Buren toured England, stopping among other places at Stratford-on-Avon to pay homage to Shakespeare's birthplace.

Another of Van Buren's daughters-in-law had family links with political figures rather than with literary ones. Abraham's wife Angelica, the daughter of a prosperous southern planter, acted as Van Buren's hostess in the White House. She was from South Carolina and was connected with many of the best families in that part of the world, including the Cabells, which would make her kin to Van Buren's successor William H. Harrison. She was also a cousin of Dolley Madison. The Dutch might be one of the lesser minorities in America but they made up for it with their capture of the presidency: both Roosevelts were distant cousins of Van Buren. No other non-Anglo-Saxon group apart from the Celts has done so conspicuously well at capturing the very summit of the American political pyramid.

BIOGRAPHICAL DETAILS AND DESCENDANTS

VAN BUREN, MARTIN, *b* Kinderhook, Columbia Co, New York, 5 Dec 1782; *educ* Kinderhook Acad; admitted New York Bar 1803, Counsellor New York Supreme Court 1807, Surrogate of Columbia Co, New York, 1808-13, New York State Atty-Gen 1815-19; Memb: New York Court for the Correction of Errors (then highest court in the state) 1812, New York State Senate 1813-20, New York State Constitutional Convention 1821, US Senate 1821-28 (Chm Judiciary Ctee), Govr New York Jan-March 1829, US Sec of State March-May 1829, apptd US Minister to Britain 1831 but rejected by Senate 1832, V-Pres USA 1833-37, 8th President (D/Democratic-Republican) of the USA 1837-41, Democratic presidential candidate 1840, candidate for nomination as Democratic presidential candidate 1844, Barnburners' and Free Soil Party's presidential candidate 1848, author: *Inquiry into the Origin and Course of Political Parties in the United States* (compiled from his memoirs by his sons) (1867) and *Autobiography* (1920); *m* the Haxtun House, Catskill, New York, 21 Feb 1807 Hannah (*b* Kinderhook 8 March 1783; *d* Albany, New York, 5 Feb 1819, of tuberculosis, *bur* first in the cemetery of the Second Presbyterian Church, Albany, later (1855) removed to Kinderhook), dau of his 1st cousin John Dircksen Hoes and his w Maria Quackenboss, and *d* Kinderhook 24 July 1862, having had issue:

President Van Buren's son
I Abraham VAN BUREN, *b* Kinderhook 27 Nov 1807; *educ* West Point; Lt US Army 1827, Capt 1st Dragoons under Gen Winfield Scott against Seminole Indians 1836, private sec to his father 1837, Maj and Paymaster Mexican War 1846, breveted

Lt-Col 1847 for gallant and meritorious conduct following the US victories at Contreras and Churubusco, ret 1854; *m* Nov 1838 Angelica (*b* Sumpter District, S Carolina, 1816; *d* New York 29 Dec 1878), dau of Richard Singleton and his w, dau of John Coles and cousin of Mrs James Madison) and *d* New York 15 March 1873, having had issue:

Grandchildren
1 Rebecca VAN BUREN, *b* the White House March 1840; *d* autumn 1840
2 Singleton VAN BUREN, *b* 1840; *educ* Columbia Law Sch; *d* New York 9 June 1879
3 Travis C. VAN BUREN
4 Martin VAN BUREN, engineer

President Van Buren's son
II John VAN BUREN, *b* Hudson, New York, 10 or 18 Feb 1810; *educ* Yale; admitted New York Bar 1830, ptnr Van Buren & McKean, attys, attaché US Legation to UK 1831-33, Atty-Gen New York State 1845-46; *m* 22 June 1841 Elizabeth Vanderpoel (*b* 22 May 1810; *d* 19 Nov 1844), dau of Judge Vanderpoel, and *d* at sea 13 Oct 1866, leaving issue:

Grandchildren
1 (Sarah) Anna Vanderpoel Van Buren, *b* 30 July 1842; *m* 26 March 1870 Edward Alexander DUER (*b* 8 March 1840; *d* 1906), s of William Denning Duer and his w Caroline King, and *d* Oct 1923, having had issue:

Great-grandchildren
(1) Edward Alexander DUER, *b* New York 28 June 1871; *educ* Columbia (AB 1893); *m* 29 April 1916 Dorothea (*b* North Wales, Pa., 6 April 1886; *d* 1951), dau of Edward Harrison King and his w Elizabeth Whitall Atkinson, and *d* Camden, New Jersey, 29 March 1944
(2) Elizabeth Vanderpoel Duer, *b* Poultney, Vt., 21 Aug 1874; *m* Hoboken, New Jersey, 5 Oct 1898 Daniel Carroll HARVEY (*b* Jenkintown, Pa., 25 Sept 1867; *d* New York 6 May 1939), s of Dr Samuel Dawes Harvey and his w Mary Beatty, and *d* 28 Jan 1952, leaving issue:

Great-great-grandchildren
1a Alexander Duer HARVEY, *b* 5 Sept 1899; *educ* MIT; *m* Black Point, Conn., 8 Sept 1928 *Anna Maricka [Mrs Alexander Harvey, 139 E 66th St, New York, NY 10021, USA] (*b* 19 June 1900), 2nd dau of Pierre Jay (gggs of John Jay (1745-1829), Pres Congress 1778, Min to Spain 1779-82, negotiator with John Adams and Benjamin Franklin of peace with Britain 1783, Sec For Affrs 1784-89, 1st US Ch Justice 1789-95 and Min Plenipotentiary to Britain 1794-95) and his w Louisa Shaw Barlow, and *d* New York 9 Jan 1968, leaving issue:

Great-great-grandchildren's children
1b *Dereke Jay HARVEY [139 E 66th St, New York, NY 10021], *b* Norwalk, Conn., 3 Aug 1929
2b *Phoebe Duer Harvey [Mrs Robert Frackman, Baptist Church Rd, Yorktown Heights, NY 105987, USA], *b* Norwalk 27 Dec 1932; *m* 1st New York 19 June 1952 Bertrand Faugeres BELL III (*b* Mount Kisco, New York, 15 April 1931), s of Bertrand F. Bell, Jr, and his w Helen Runkle, and has issue:

Great-great-grandchildren's grandchildren
1c *Daphne Jay BELL, *b* Philadelphia 20 Jan 1953
2c *Alexandra Duer BELL, *b* Bryn Mawr, Pa., 29 Jan 1956
3c *Frederick Talmadge BELL, *b* Chestnut Hill, Pa., 2 April 1958

Great-great-grandchildren's children
2b (cont.) Phoebe Harvey Bell *m* 2nd New York 27 Dec 1963 *Robert J. FRACKMAN (*b* 25 Sept 1926 New York), s of H. David Frackman and his w Ruth Warren, and with him has issue:

Great-great-grandchildren's grandchildren
4c *David Alexander FRACKMAN, *b* New York 2 Aug 1970

Great-grandchildren
(3) Sarah Gracie DUER, *b* Poultney, Vt., 1876; *d* New York 7 June 1946
(4) Angelica Singleton Duer, *b* 1878; *m* 1st 1901 Lucius Tuckerman GIBBS (*d* 1909) and had issue:

Great-great-grandchildren
1a (Oliver) Wolcott GIBBS, *b* New York 15 March 1902; drama critic *New Yorker*; *m* 1st 1929 Ada Elizabeth Crawford (*d* 1930); *m* 2nd 14 Oct 1933 Elinor Mead Sherwin and *d* Fire Island, New York, 16 Aug 1958, having with her had issue:

Great-great-grandchildren's children
1b *Janet Sherwin GIBBS, *b* 19—
2b *(Oliver) Wolcott GIBBS, Jr, *b* 19—

Great-great-grandchildren
2a Angelica Singleton Gibbs, *b* 1908; *educ* Vassar; assoc ed *McCall's Magazine*; *m* 1932 (divorce 19—) Robert Elliott CANFIELD and *d* New York 10 Jan 1955, leaving issue:

Great-great-grandchildren's children
1b *Sarah Duer CANFIELD, *b* 19—
2b *David E. CANFIELD, *b* 19—

Great-grandchildren

(4) (cont.) Angelica Duer Gibbs *m* 2nd in or after 1909 Ewing SPEED and *d* before 1944

(5) Denning DUER, *b* Weehawken, New Jersey, 1880; *d* there in infancy

(6) John Van Buren DUER, *b* Poultney, Vt., 9 April 1882; *educ* Stevens Inst of Technology (ME 1903); *m* 7 Sept 1911 Mary Aline Sabine (*b* March 1881; *d* 1956), dau of Charles Davis Haines and his *w* Mary Taunton Sabine, and *d* Essex, Conn., Dec 1967, leaving issue:

Great-great-grandchildren

1a *Rufus King DUER [18 Parker Terrace, Essex, CT 06426, USA], *b* New York 30 June 1912; *educ* Yale; *m* 1940 *Rosella Barry (*b* 1915) and has issue:

Great-great-grandchildren's children

1b *Susan Barry Duer, *b* 1941; *m* 10 July 1965 *Richard WATROUS and has issue:

Great-great-grandchildren's grandchildren

1c *Marc WATROUS, *b* 13 June 1968

Geat-great-grandchildren's children

2b *Ann Van Buren Duer, *b* 1945; *m* 21 Sept 1968 *William Sharp EVANS

Great-grandchildren

(7) James Gore King DUER, *b* Poultney, Vt., 5 May 1885; *d* West Chester, Pa., Jan 1961

(8) William Alexander DUER, *b* 1886; *d* Weehawken, New Jersey, 1909

President Van Buren's children

III Martin VAN BUREN, Jr, *b* Hudson, New York, 20 Dec 1812; assistant to his father when latter President, clerk US Land Office; *d* Paris, France, 19 March 1855 of tuberculosis

IV Winfield Scott VAN BUREN, *b* 1814; *d* after a few weeks

V Smith Thompson VAN BUREN, *b* Hudson 16 Jan 1817; admitted to New York Bar 1841; *m* 1st 18 June 1842 Ellen King (*b* 20 Jan 1813; *d* 3 Oct 1849), dau of William James, of Albany, New York, and his *w* Catharine Barber, and had issue:

Grandchildren

1 Ellen James Van Buren, *b* Albany, New York, 10 June 1844; *m* St Mark's Church, New York, 10 Dec 1868 Dr Stuyvesant Fish MORRIS (*b* New York 3 Aug 1843; *d* there 10 May 1928), yst *s* of Dr Richard Lewis Morris and his *w* Elizabeth Sarah Stuyvesant Fish, and *d* 1929, having had issue:

Great-grandchildren

(1) Elizabeth Marshall Morris, *b* New York 1869; *m* B. Woolsey ROGERS and *d* 10 Jan 1919

(2) Ellen Van Buren Morris, *b* New York 10 June 1873; *m* there 9 Oct 1899 Francis Livingston PELL (*b* New York 23 Sept 1873; architect; *d* New York 7 Sept 1945), 2nd *s* of Walden Pell and his *w* Melissa Augusta Hyatt, and *d* New York 10 March 1954, having had issue:

Great-great-grandchildren

1a Revd Walden PELL, Jr, *b* Quogue, Long Island, New York, 3 July 1902; *educ* St Mark's, Princeton and Ch Ch Oxford (MA); sometime headmaster St Andrew's Sch, Middletown, Del.; *m* Lenox, Mass., 25 Aug 1928 Edith Minturn (*b* Newport, Rhode Island, 1902; *d* 20 Dec 1973), dau of W. Roscoe Bonsal and his *w* Mary Minturn Potter, and *d* 23 March 1983, leaving issue:

Great-great-grandchildren's children

1b Melissa Pell, *b* Lenox, Mass., 17 Dec 1929; *educ* Sarah Lawrence; *m* Middletown, Del., 18 Dec 1948 *John Schuyler THOMSON [636 S Britain Rd, South Britain, CT 06487, USA] (*b* 1926), *s* of Alexander Thomson, and *d* 30 March 1992, leaving issue:

Great-great-grandchildren's grandchildren

1c *Ellen Van Buren Thomson [Mrs Paul Burlinson, Ye Olde Gate Inne, Well St, Brassington, Derbyshire DE4 4HJ, UK], *b* New Haven, Conn., 12 Aug 1950; *educ* St Margaret's, Foxhollow; innkeeper; *m* 21 June 1975 *Paul Scott BURLINSON, *s* of Thomas Scott Burlinson and his *w* Joan Alice, and has issue:

Great-great-grandchildren's great-grandchildren

1d *Alice Pell BURLINSON, *b* England 26 March 1980

2d *Lucy Ellen BURLINSON, *b* England 20 April 1982

Great-great-grandchildren's grandchildren

2c *Abbie Hotchkiss Thomson [Mrs Ian Spires, Limpsfield Lodge Farm, Limpsfield, Surrey RH8 0SA, UK], *b* New Haven 1953; *m* Oct 1972 *Ian Christian SPIRES and has issue:

Great-great-grandchildren's great-grandchildren

1d *Katherine SPIRES, *b* 28 June 1979

2d *Andrew John SPIRES, *b* 8 Feb 1982

Great-great-grandchildren's grandchildren

3c *Melissa Pell THOMSON [636 South Britain Rd, South Britain, CT 06487, USA], *b* New Haven 16 March 1957

Great-great-grandchildren's children
2b *Stuyvesant Bonsal PELL [697 Rosedale Rd, Princeton, NJ, USA], b Pittsfield, Mass., 9 Aug 1931; educ St Mark's Sch and Princeton; underwriter Chubb and Son, Inc, of New York, 1957-89; m Wilmington, Del., 21 April 1956 *Patricia Chancellor, dau of Ira Flaven Doom and his w Marian Bradford, and has issue:

Great-great-grandchildren's grandchildren
1c *Alison Chancellor Pell [Mrs James M Helms, 11715 Ingraham Rd, Snohomish, WA 98290, USA], b Bronxville, New York, 13 May 1960; educ St Andrews Sch, Evergreen State Coll, Olympia, Wash., and U of Washington; paramedic 1986- and physician's assist 1993-; m Snohomish 11 April 1991 *James Michael HELMS, s of James Arthur Helms and his w Loretta Nance, and has issue:

Great-great-grandchildren's great-grandchildren
1d *James Stuyvesant HELMS, b Kirkland, Wash., 26 Jan 1992

Great-great-grandchildren's grandchildren
2c *Sarah Bonsal PELL [906 Eagles Chase Drive, Lawrenceville, NJ 08648, USA], b Seattle, Wash., 1964

Great-great-grandchildren's children
3b *Mary Leigh Pell [99 Old Barn Rd, Fairfield, CT 06430, USA], b Middletown, Del., 29 April 1934; m there 27 April 1957 *Robert Foster WHITMER III, s of Robert Foster Whitmer, Jr, and his w Laura Taylor, and has issue:

Great-great-grandchildren's grandchildren
1c *Robert Foster WHITMER IV, b Hartford, Conn., 2 Sept 1961
2c *Walden Pell WHITMER, b Hartford 8 Dec 1963
3c *John Love WHITMER, b Hartford 23 Feb 1965

Great-great-grandchildren
2a Stuyvesant Morris PELL, b New York 12 March 1905; educ Princeton and Cornell (MS 1939); m 1933 Katherine Pomeroy (who m 2nd Winthrop M. Crane, of Dalton, Mass., and d 1986), dau of Philip Weston, of Pittsfield, Mass., and d Pittsfield 30 Aug 1943, leaving issue:

Great-great-grandchildren's children
1b Brenton Pomeroy PELL CRANE (added stepf's name to his own), b 1938; m 19— *Nancy —— and d 1988, leaving issue:

Great-great-grandchildren's grandchildren
1c *Katherine Pell Crane [Mrs James Francis, 72 Harrington Rd, Broad Brook, CT 06016, USA], b 19—; m 19— *James FRANCIS and has issue a child

Great-great grandchildren
3a Francis Livingston PELL, Jr, b New York 26 Nov 1906; m 1932 *Clarissa Wardwell [Mrs Francis L Pell Jr, Apt C-304 551 E Evergreen Ave, Wyndmoor, PA 19118, USA] and d 1987, leaving issue:

Great-great-grandchildren's children
1b *Robert L. PELL [Box 728, Keene Valley, NY 12943, USA], b 1933; educ Princeton
2b *Revd Lewis Morris PELL [933 Hudson St, Hoboken, NJ 07030, USA], b New York 5 April 1936; educ Yale and Pacific Sch of Religion; m 28 Feb 1970 *Christiana Ruth, dau of Guido Giacomasso and his w Ruth Perch, and has issue:

Great-great-grandchildren's grandchildren
1c *Jason Trail PELL [72 W 69th St, New York, NY 10021, USA], b New York 22 July 1972; educ Juilliard Sch of Music; violinist (recital debut Carnegie Hall 17 Jan 1993)
2c *Salim Ti PELL, b Pune, India, 22 Dec 1975

Great-great-grandchildren's children
3b *Edward W. PELL [1709 Lombard St, Philadelphia, PA 19146, USA], b 1938; educ Princeton, Oxford U, UK, and New York U Law Sch; m 19— *Farizee —— and has issue:

Great-great-grandchildren's grandchildren
1c *Harry PELL
2c *Olivia PELL

Great-grandchildren
(3) Richard Lewis MORRIS, b New York 26 Nov 1875; educ St Mark's and Columbia U (AB 1896); investment banker; m 9 June 1908 Carolyn Whitney (b New York 24 April 1882), dau of Cornelius Fellowes, of New York, and d 19—, having had issue:

Great-great-grandchildren
1a *Cornelia Fellowes Morris [Mrs Malcolm Field, 82 Eagle Valley Rd, Sloatsburg, NY, USA], b Wave Crest, Long Island, New York, 24 June 1909; m 1933 *Malcolm Graham FIELD and has issue:

Great-great-grandchildren's children
1b *Eileen Morris Field, b 1940; m 19— *John W. LONSDALE

311

Great-great-grandchildren
2a Eileen James MORRIS, *b* 22 Aug 1913; *d* 19 April 1916
3a Richard Lewis MORRIS, Jr, New York *b* 22 Aug 1917; *d* 1944

Great-grandchildren
(4) Stuyvesant Fish MORRIS, Jr, *b* New York 22 May 1877; *educ* Columbia U (AB 1898); *m* 27 Dec 1900 Elizabeth Hilles (*b* 1878; *d* 19——), dau of Dr Gerardus Hilles Wynkoop and his w Ann Eliza Woodbury, and *d* Hewlett, Long Island, 9 April 1925, leaving issue:

Great-great-grandchildren
1a Stuyvesant Fish MORRIS III, *b* New York 19 Feb 1902; *m* 29 April 1925 *Madeleine Marie, dau of —— White and widow of Spencer Kennard, and *d* New York 22 March 1948, leaving issue:

Great-great-grandchildren's children
1b *Stuyvesant Fish MORRIS IV, *b* 1926; *m* 1952 *Katherine Renée Cassitt and has issue:

Great-great-grandchildren's grandchildren
1c *Stuyvesant Fish MORRIS V, *b* 1953
2c *Charles Cassitt MORRIS, *b* 8 Sept 1954

Great-great-grandchildren's children
2b *Livingston Van Buren MORRIS, *b* 1930; *m* 19—— Ann Chapman (divorce 19——) and has three children
3b *Peter McKinney MORRIS, *b* 1931; *m* 1953 *Audrey Watts and has issue:

Great-great-grandchildren's grandchildren
1c *Peter McKinney MORRIS, Jr, *b* 1 Sept 1954
2c *Cameron MORRIS (dau), *b c* 1959

Great-great-grandchildren
2a Martin Van Buren MORRIS, *b* 23 Sept 1904; *m* 1937 *Helen de Russy Sloan (*b* 21 Oct 1910) and *d* 2 Jan 1951, leaving issue:

Great-great-grandchildren's children
1b *Martin Van Buren MORRIS, Jr [1021 Matanzas Ave, Coral Gables, FL 33134, USA], *b* 11 May 1938; *educ* Brown U; *m* 31 Dec 1964 Sara E. Layman and has issue:

Great-great-grandchildren's grandchildren
1c *Martin Van Buren MORRIS III, *b* 7 Sept 1967
2c *Heather de Russy MORRIS, *b* 20 May 1971

Great-great-grandchildren's children
2b *Helen de Russy MORRIS [4131 Park Ave, Coconut Grove, FL 33133, USA], *b* 15 Sept 1942

Great-great-grandchildren
3a *Hilles Morris [Mrs Robert Timpson, Maizeland, 12 Insala Rd, Kloof, Natal 3600, South Africa; Box 1241, Southampton, Long Island, NY 11968, USA; Milestone Brook Rd, Southampton, Long Island, NY 11101, USA], *b* Quogue, Long Island, 28 June 1907; *m* 1st Grace Church, New York, 1 Nov 1926 Louis Gordon HAMERSLEY (*b* Newport, Rhode Island, 20 July 1892; *d* Southampton, Long Island, 2 June 1942), only s of James Hooker Hamersley and his w Margaret Willing Chisholm, and has issue:

Great-great-grandchildren's children
1b *Louis Gordon HAMERSLEY, Jr [Box 302, Poughkeepsie, NY 12602, USA], *b* New York 14 Jan 1928; *educ* Harvard; *m* Poughkeepsie 27 Aug 1949 *Elsey de Riemer (*b* Pouhgkeepsie 18 Jun 1929), dau of Baltus Barentsen Van Kleeck and his w Ethelyn Hinkley, and has issue:

Great-great-grandchildren's grandchildren
1c *Louis Gordon HAMERSLEY III [267 Allston St, Cambridge, MA 02138, USA], *b* Boston 23 Feb 1951; *educ* Boston U
2c *Andrew Carré HAMERSLEY, *b* New York 8 Oct 1954; *educ* Boston U
3c *Nicholas Bayard HAMERSLEY, *b* New York 15 May 1959
4c *Katherine Van Kleeck HAMERSLEY, *b* New York 4 June 1962

Great-great-grandchildren's children
2b *Stuyvesant Morris HAMERSLEY [Box 147, Sorrento, British Columbia, Canada], *b* New York 11 June 1932; *m* Tuxedo, New York, 9 Jan 1960 *Irmy (*b* Hamadan, Iran, Oct 1930), dau of Eduard Borowski and his w Elinor Kuhn, and has issue:

Great-great-grandchildren's grandchildren
1c *Linda Hilles HAMERSLEY, *b* New York 17 Feb 1961
2c *Leslie Carrée HAMERSLEY, *b* New York 13 Jan 1963

Great-great-grandchildren's children
3b *Hilles Elizabeth Hamersley [Mrs Terence Martin, 47 Station Rd, Irvington, NY, USA], b New York 7 April 1935; m Southampton, New York, 6 Oct 1956 Terence Michael MARTIN (d 29 Jan 1970) and has issue:

Great-great-grandchildren's grandchildren
1c *Terence Michael MARTIN, b New York 25 Sept 1957
2c *Tracy Hamersley MARTIN, b New York 24 Nov 1958
3c *Elizabeth Hilles MARTIN, b Ridgewood, New Jersey, 8 Feb 1963

Great-great-grandchildren's children
4b *James Hooker HAMERSLEY [112 E 91st St, New York, NY 10028, USA], b New York 16 Nov 1937; educ Washington and Lee; m 24 April 1970 (divorce 1972) Joanne Fitzgerald

Great-great-grandchildren
3a (cont.) Hilles Morris Hamersley m 2nd Quogue, Long Island, 17 June 1947 (divorce 1965) George Leslie BARTLETT (b New York 22 Nov 1908), s of Horace Edward Bartlett and his w Camille Harriet Levieux; m 3rd Tuxedo, New York, 15 Jan 1966, as his 3rd w, *Robert Clermont Livingston TIMPSON (b Hampshire, UK, 14 May 1908; sometime Maj USAAC and banker), 2nd s of Lawrence Timpson, of Appleton Manor, Berks, UK, memb New York bar, and his w Katharine Livingston

Grandchildren
2 Hannah VAN BUREN; d in infancy
3 Edward Singleton VAN BUREN, b 1848; d 1873
4 Katherine Barber Van Buren, b 1849; m 1st Peyton F. MILLER; m 2nd —— WILSON and d before 1942

President Van Buren's children
V (cont.) Smith Thompson VAN BUREN m 2nd 1 Feb 1855 Henrietta Eckford Irving (b 18—; d Bournemouth, UK, 13 April 1921), niece of the writer Washington Irving, and d 1876, having with her had issue:

Grandchildren
5 Martin VAN BUREN, b Kinderhook 4 March 1856; educ Harvard; d New York 28 Dec 1942
6 Eliza Eckford VAN BUREN, b 1858; d before 1942
7 Marion Irving Van Buren, b 1860; m 1893 Hamilton EMMONS (b Hamble, Southampton, UK, 1863; d 1933) and d 1927, leaving issue:

Great-grandchildren
(1) Robert Van Buren EMMONS, b 1894; m 1st 1919 Sally Robinson (b 18—; d 1926); m 2nd 1928 Anita Mazzini (b 1894) and d 13 May 1963, leaving issue:

Great-great-grandchildren
1a *Giulietta Elizabeth Emmons, b 1929; m 1948 *Geoffrey VERDON-ROE and has issue:

Great-great-grandchildren's children
1b *Vivienne VERDON-ROE, b 1949
2b *Eric Alliott VERDON-ROE, b 1952

Great-great-grandchildren
2a *Hamilton EMMONS, b 1931

Great-grandchildren
(2) Marion Van Buren Emmons, b 10 April 1900; m 19— Richard Sears HUMPHREY (b 4 May 1898) and d 17 March 1939, leaving issue:

Great-great-grandchildren
1a *Joan Van Buren Humphrey, b 1924; m 19— *Tedrowe WATKINS and has issue:

Great-great-grandchildren's children
1b *Marion Van Buren WATKINS, b 1 June 1948
2b *Tedrowe WATKINS, Jr, b 17 Feb 1950

Great-great-grandchildren
2a *Richard Sears HUMPHREY, Jr [450 Essex St, Beverly, MA, USA], b 1925; m 31 Jan 1948 *Katherine, formerly w of —— Downey and dau of —— Van Ingen, and has issue:

Great-great-grandchildren's children
1b *Joan Faber HUMPHREY, b 22 Nov 1948
2b *Katherine Van Ingen HUMPHREY, b 17 March 1950

Great-great-grandchildren
3a *Marion Irving Humphrey, b 1927; m 12 Jan 1952 *Allen JACOBSON

MALE LINE ANCESTRY AND COLLATERAL DESCENDANTS

Cornelis MAESSEN (VAN BUREN), emigrated to America from Buurmalsen, Gelderland Province, in the Dutch Republic, 1631, settling at Papsknee, nr Greenbush (since 1897 called Rensselaer), New York; *m c* 1635/6 Catalyntje Martense (*d* Papsknee *c* 1648) and *d* Papsknee *c* 1648 also, leaving (with three other s, the descendants of one of whom took the surname BLOEMENDAAL, and one dau):

Marten CORNELISZ (VAN BUREN), *b* Houten, Utrecht Province, Dutch Republic, *c* 1638; settled at Albany, New York, Capt in Col Pieter Schuyler's Regt 1700; *m* 1st *c* 1662 Marritje (*b* probably Oestgeest, nr Leyden, South Holland Province, Dutch Republic, *c* 1646), probably dau of Pieter Quackenbush or Quackenbosch, alias Pieter Bont (*fl* Albany 1650-80), and his w Marritje; *m* 2nd 7 May 1693 Tanneke Adams, widow of Pieter Pieterson Winne, and *d* 13 Nov 1703, leaving at least one s by his 1st w:

Pieter MARTENSE (VAN BUREN), of Albany, *b c* 1670; *m* Albany 15 Jan 1693 Adriaantje, dau of Barent Meynders (*d* Albany *c* 1679), shoemaker, and his w Eytie, and *d* probably before 1743, leaving (with other issue):

Martin VAN BUREN, *bapt* Albany 28 Sept 1701; *m* 7 Nov 1729 Dirkje (bapt 30 April 1710), dau of Abraham Janse Van Alstyne (*d* in or after 1742), of Kinderhook, New York, and his w Marritje, dau of Teuwis/Matheeus/Matthew Abrahamse Van Deusen (*b c* 1631), of Albany and Claverack, Columbia Co, New York, and his w Helen Robberts and sister of Tryntje Van Deusen, an ancestor of President FRANKLIN D. ROOSEVELT, and *d* 17—, having had (with other issue):

Abraham VAN BUREN, *bapt* Albany 27 Feb 1737; farmer and tavern keeper, Town Clerk Kinderhook 1787-97 (his successor being his step-s James, for whom *see below*); *m c* 1776, as her 2nd husb, Maria (*b* Claverack 16 Jan 1747/8, dau of Johannes Dircksen Hoes and his w Jannetje Laurense Van Schaick (herself gdau of Claas Gerritse Van Schaik, whose gggdau Maria Van Schaack *m* James J. Roosevelt; they were great-great-grandparents of President THEODORE ROOSEVELT); Maria *m* 1st Linlithgo, New York, 31 Dec 1767 Johannes Van Alen (1744-c 1773) and had issue:

Half-siblings of President Van Buren
I Marytje Van Alen, *bapt* Kinderhook 20 Aug 1768; *m c* 1787 John GOES (bapt Kinderhook 25 May 1766; *d* 23 Dec 1838), s of Laurens Goes or Hoes and his w Maria Van Alstyne, and *d* Adolphustown, Upper Canada (now Ontario, Canada), 1 Sept 1829, having had two daus
II Johannes VAN ALEN, *bapt* Kinderhook 15 July 1770; *d* 13 April 1805 (*bur* Kinderhook)
III Jacobus or James Isaac VAN ALEN, either *bapt* Kinderhook 1 Jan 1773; ptnr with his half-bro, the future 8th President, in law firm at Kinderhook, Town Clerk Kinderhook 1797-1801, Justice of the Peace 1801-4, Surrogate (probate judge) Columbia Co 1804-08 (his successor being his half-bro, the future 8th President) and 1815-22, Memb: New York State Assembly 1804 and US House of Reps 1807-09; *d* 18 May 1822

Maria Van Alen Van Buren, *née* Hoes, *d* Kinderhook 16 Feb 1817, having had with her 2nd husb, Abraham Van Buren (*d* Kinderhook 8 April 1817), further issue:

IV Derike or Dirckie VAN BUREN, *b* 1777; *m* 1806 Barent Hoes and *d* 1865, leaving four s and four daus
V Hannah or Jannetje VAN BUREN, *bapt* 16 Jan 1780
VI MARTIN VAN BUREN, 8th PRESIDENT of the UNITED STATES of AMERICA
VII Lawrence VAN BUREN, *bapt* 8 Jan 1786; *m* Harriet Vosburgh and *d* 1 July 1868, leaving two s and three daus
VIII Abraham VAN BUREN, *bapt* 11 May 1788; *m* 1816 Catherine Hogeboom and *d* 30 Oct 1836

MARTIN VAN BUREN
FAMILY TREE

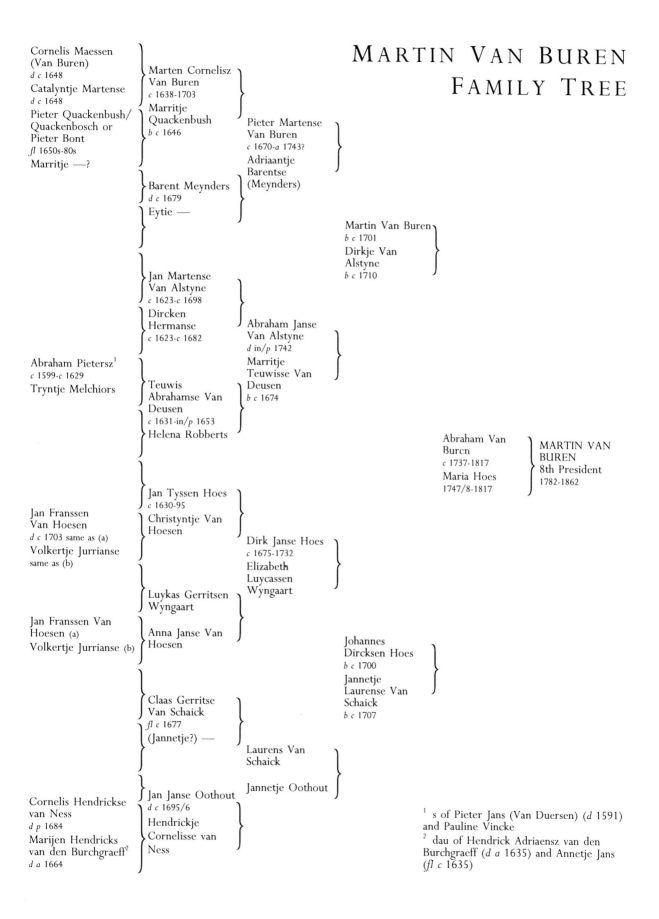

Cornelis Maessen
(Van Buren)
d c 1648
Catalyntje Martense
d c 1648
Pieter Quackenbush/
Quackenbosch or
Pieter Bont
fl 1650s-80s
Marritje —?

Marten Cornelisz
Van Buren
c 1638-1703
Marritje
Quackenbush
b c 1646

Pieter Martense
Van Buren
c 1670-*a* 1743?
Adriaantje
Barentse
(Meynders)

Barent Meynders
d c 1679
Eytie —

Martin Van Buren
b c 1701
Dirkje Van
Alstyne
b c 1710

Jan Martense
Van Alstyne
c 1623-*c* 1698
Dircken
Hermanse
c 1623-*c* 1682

Abraham Janse
Van Alstyne
d in/*p* 1742
Marritje
Teuwisse Van
Deusen
b c 1674

Abraham Pietersz[1]
c 1599-*c* 1629
Tryntje Melchiors

Teuwis
Abrahamse Van
Deusen
c 1631-in/*p* 1653
Helena Robberts

Abraham Van
Buren
c 1737-1817
Maria Hoes
1747/8-1817

MARTIN VAN
BUREN
8th President
1782-1862

Jan Tyssen Hoes
c 1630-95
Christyntje Van
Hoesen

Dirk Janse Hoes
c 1675-1732
Elizabeth
Luycassen
Wyngaart

Jan Franssen
Van Hoesen
d c 1703 same as (a)
Volkertje Jurrianse
same as (b)

Luykas Gerritsen
Wyngaart

Jan Franssen Van
Hoesen (a)
Volkertje Jurrianse (b)

Anna Janse Van
Hoesen

Johannes
Dircksen Hoes
b c 1700
Jannetje
Laurense Van
Schaick
b c 1707

Claas Gerritse
Van Schaick
fl c 1677
(Jannetje?) —

Laurens Van
Schaick

Cornelis Hendrickse
van Ness
d p 1684
Marijen Hendricks
van den Burchgraeff[2]
d a 1664

Jan Janse Oothout
d c 1695/6
Hendrickje
Cornelisse van
Ness

Jannetje Oothout

[1] s of Pieter Jans (Van Duersen) (*d* 1591)
and Pauline Vincke
[2] dau of Hendrick Adriaensz van den
Burchgraeff (*d a* 1635) and Annetje Jans
(*fl c* 1635)

Plate 26   William H. Harrison

WILLIAM H. HARRISON

1773-1841
9TH PRESIDENT OF THE UNITED STATES OF AMERICA
1841

'Tippecanoe and Tyler Too'; 'A Log Cabin And Hard Cider'. It is poor Harrison's fate to be remembered chiefly for the rumbustious campaign which brought him to the presidency and for the fact that his was, and is likely to remain, the shortest administration of all; he died exactly a month after his Inauguration.

The campaign of 1840 proved that the Democrats had grown stale in office and that the Whigs had all the vigour of a new party — the sort of party that the Jacksonians had been in the 1820s. They had learned all that their opponents had to teach in the way of organization and clap-trap. They had found a candidate: General Harrison was a very passable counterfeit of General Jackson. An indiscreet Democratic journalist, sneering at the Whig candidate as the sort of backwoodsman who lived in a log cabin with a gallon of hard cider ready for any riff-raff who pulled on his door string, gave the opposition party a heavensent chance to puff their candidate as a man of the people, unlike the gilded aristocrat in the White House. From now on every Whig parade exhibited a log cabin, and no doubt many honest Whigs got conscientiously drunk on hard cider too.

This triumph was all the more remarkable when it is remembered that Van Buren's father was only a tavern-keeper, as we have seen, while Harrison's father was one of Virginia's most conspicuous leaders, having actually signed the Declaration of Independence, and that William Henry, his third son, had been born in the family mansion.

True he had made up for it since. He had left Virginia as a young man, and had spent the rest of his life in the old North-West, either as a young soldier, as Governor of Indiana Territory, as the conqueror of the Indian patriot Tecumseh or as Congressman and Senator from Ohio. In fact it was Harrison's identification with his region, and the friendly attention he had always lavished on the rising city of Cincinnati, which gave him his basic political strength. He was a popular local figure, and had never been prominent enough on the national scene to make enemies as his rival Henry Clay (or for that matter President Van Buren) had done. He was also (a fact frequently overlooked) a shrewd old thing, who by the time he came to Washington had deftly taken the real as well as the titular leadership of the Whigs away from Clay. His administration bade fair to be a successful one.

Only he would insist on displaying his meagre oratorical powers. His nominee for the Secretaryship of State, Daniel Webster, did his best to abridge the proposed Inaugural Address, but to little avail. It went on for an hour and three-quarters; the weather was very cold; the President was not wearing a coat. He caught a chill, ignored it (there was a lot of work to be done), the chill turned to pneumonia and he died even before his wife could get to Washington. It was all very sad and, alas, slightly ludicrous too.

WILLIAM H. HARRISON'S FAMILY

Through his Harrison ancestors' numerous marriage alliances stretching back to the 17th century William H. Harrison was related to almost everybody of note in Virginia: Washington, Jefferson, the Randolphs, the Lees, the Carters, the Pages, Claibornes, Cabells. He was capable of using these ties when it suited him — he got his army commission through the influence of his kinsman, Governor Richard H. Lee of Virginia — but they lost a good deal of potency in the Northwest Territory where he settled. (And to a certain extent in Virginia too, once he had moved away: he failed to carry that state when he ran against Van Buren for President in 1836.) Privilege had its limits. All the family pull in the world could not have secured Harrison the military success which made his name: first at Tippecanoe on the river of the same name in 1811 over a confederation of Indians living between the Ohio River and the Great Lakes, then over the British and Indians at the Battle of the Thames River in 1813. The latter, though almost lightning swift, has been portrayed as the more important, but in 1840 the cry 'Tippecanoe and Tyler too' had the merit of rhyme and alliteration. Besides, Harrison had been a national figure since the earlier battle.

Family pressures shaped his life all the same. When in the year 1787-88 evangelical fervour gripped Hampden-Sidney College, where Harrison was being educated, principally in the classics, he was removed before his schooling was complete. Lack of money could hardly have been the reason; it has been suggested that his Episcopalian family disliked the religious atmosphere at Hampden-Sidney — what the 18th century stigmatized as 'enthusiam'. Next he started first one, then another, course in medicine. The first was curtailed, possibly because his hidebound slave-holder father disapproved of his involvement in an abolitionist society. The second was curtailed too, by his father's death.

Harrison became an elaborate and long-winded public speaker (for an example of his style *see* the Introduction to this book). Long-winded elaboration was very much the fashion then, of course. But since in his case it led to his death, one may reasonably speculate whether he would have lived longer had he specialized in a terser language such as French rather than Ciceronian Latin. And surely, if he had completed his medical studies, he would have been more aware of the likely consequences of delivering an Inaugural address in freezing weather without a coat.

In 1799 Harrison temporarily left the Northwest Territory, where he was Secretary, and paid a visit with his wife to the capital (then Philadelphia). The name of his father Benjamin still meant a lot there, even though the 'Signer' had been dead nearly 10 years. Both Federalists and Republicans who had known the Harrisons in Virginia or were William H.'s relatives joined in feting him. He first met his wife Anna Symmes through a family connection. Anna was staying with her sister Mrs Peyton Short in Lexington, Ky., where William Harrison's cousin Carter Henry Harrison (one of the Clifton branch) had settled. The Harrisons and Shorts may even have known each other in Virginia, for Peyton Short's father had lived there at one time. Harrison married Anna while her father Judge Symmes was away from home. One version has it that Judge Symmes, after initially welcoming the match, broke it off because he had heard disquieting stories about Harrison. Whatever the truth of that, the Judge seems to have stayed away from the wedding. He eventually became reconciled to his son-in-law, however, and made him a co-executor of his will.

Anna became ill shortly after her husband was promoted to be Governor of the Northwest Territory, so that although he had been appointed to his post in 1800 he lingered on in Richmond, Va., where he seems initially to have gone to visit his brother Benjamin, until early the next year. A Governor of a Territory at that time had enormous power — everything was in his hands except the judiciary — and corresponding opportunities to dispense patronage. Yet the only nepotism he seems to have been guilty

Plate 27   Anna Tuthill Symmes Harrison

Plate 28   Jane Findlay Irwin Harrison, William H. Harrison's daughter-in-law and hostess in the White House

of was awarding the Attorney-Generalship to a Randolph family connection and working to get his sister Anne's husband David Coupland a judgeship. Harrison could have echoed Clive of India, that he was astounded at his own moderation.

In a purely personal way Harrison's landed gentry Virginia background stood him in good stead out in the North-West. As Governor he combined authority with affability and ease of manner, together with lavish hospitality, in the traditional manner of the 'Old Dominion'. Whether the Virginia ancestral tradition of farming was as useful is open to doubt. Harrison was constantly striving to make his landed property more productive but nearly always needed other sources of income and did not give up seeking public office. Here his family connections did him harm. When in 1822 he ran for Congress as representative from Ohio he was accused of having illegally acquired land from the huge tract patented by his dead father-in-law Judge Symmes many years before. The charge was never proved, but it was indisputable that he had procured a post as receiver of public moneys at Vincennes (now in Indiana) for his son John. In 1822 the public was indignant at the alleged corruption of the Monroe administration and Harrison was defeated. Another of Harrison's sons, William Henry Jr, stated 12 years later that his father had known he would be beaten but had stood to please party leaders. This has an air of special pleading.

When Harrison went to Bogotá as US Minister his son Carter Bassett Harrison travelled with him as attaché — a common device of the time for sharing out as much public money as possible between members of the same family. It was to a certain extent acceptable to regard public office as a sinecure. When Harrison was made Clerk of the Court of Common Pleas of Hamilton Co, Ohio, a son-in-law undertook the duties, leaving Harrison free to pocket the stipend and concentrate on working his land. The election of Benjamin Harrison 50 years later, partly on the grounds that he was William H.'s grandson, shows that the public still looked indulgently on office as a family business.

BIOGRAPHICAL DETAILS AND DESCENDANTS

WILLIAM HENRY HARRISON, *b* the Berkeley Plantation, Charles City Co, Va., 9 Feb 1773; *educ* Hampden-Sidney Coll, Va., and Pennsylvania U; Ensign 1st Infy Regt 1791, 2nd Lt and ADC to Gen Anthony Wayne 1792, participated in Battle of Fallen Timbers against the Indian Chief Little Turtle's men (mentioned in despatches) 1794, Actg Capt 1795, Cdr Fort Washington 1796, Full Capt 1797, resigned commission 1798, Sec Northwest Territory 1798-99, Delegate from Northwest Territory to US House of Reps 1799-1800, Govr New Indiana Territory 1801-13, Govr Louisiana Territory 1804, a Fndr Vincennes U Jr Coll 1806 (later Tstee Vincennes U), defeated Chief Tecumseh at Battle of Tippecanoe 1811, Maj-Gen Kentucky Militia and Brig-Gen US Army 1812, Maj-Gen US Army 1813, defeated British and Indians at Battle of the Thames 1813, resigned from army and apptd Ch Commissioner to negotiate with Indians 1814, Memb from Ohio US House of Reps 1816-19 (Chm Ctee on Militia and Memb Ctee on Public Lands), Memb Ohio State Senate 1819-21 (chm two ctees investigating canal devpt), Ohio Presidential Elector 1820 and 1824, unsuccessful gubernatorial candidate Ohio 1820, unsuccessful candidate for US Senate 1821 and 1822, Memb US Senate 1825-28 (Chm Ctee on Mily Affrs and Memb Ctee on Militia), US Minister to Colombia 1828-29, unsuccessful candidate for US Senate 1831, Memb Bd of Visitors West Point 1832, Clerk Court of Common Pleas, Hamilton Co, Ohio, 1834, Whig presidential candidate 1836, 9th President (Whig) of the USA 4 March-4 April 1841, author: *Remarks of General Harrison, late envoy extraordinary of* [sic] *Colombia, on certain charges made against him by that government*, pamphlet (1830), and *Messages and Letters*, ed Logan Esarey, 2 vols (1922); *m* at her father's house in North Bend, Ohio, 22 Nov 1795 Anna Tuthill (*b* Flatbrook, Sussex Co, New Jersey, 25 July 1775; *educ* Clinton Acad and Mrs Graham's Boarding Sch, New York; *d* North Bend 25 Feb 1864, *bur* with her husband), yr dau of Col John Cleves Symmes, Congressman and Chief Justice New Jersey Supreme Court, and his 1st w Anna, dau of Henry Tuthill III, of Southold, Long Island, New York, and *d* the White House 4 April 1841 of pneumonia, having had issue:

President William H. Harrison's daughter
I Elizabeth Bassett Harrison, *b* Fort Washington 29 Sept 1796; *m* 29 June 1814 her 1st cousin Judge John Cleves SHORT (*b* 1792; *d* 1864), s of Peyton Short and his w Maria (herself dau of Col John Cleves Symmes and sister of Mrs William H. Harrison) and *d* 27 Sept 1846, having had issue:

Grandchildren
1 Mary SHORT, *b* 1815; *d* 1816

President William H. Harrison's son
II John Cleves Symmes HARRISON, *b* Fort Washington 28 Oct 1798; Receiver Vincennes (Indiana) Land Office 1819; *m* 29 Sept 1819 Clarissa (*b* 24 Feb 1803; *d* 1 Feb 1837), dau of Gen Zebulon Montgomery Pike and his *w* Clarissa Brown, and *d* 30 Oct 1830, leaving issue:

Grandchildren
1 Rebecca (also called Zebuline Adelaide) Pike Harrison, *b* 29 Aug 1821; *m* John HUNT and *d* 14 June 1849, leaving issue:

  Great-grandchildren
  (1) Symmes Harrison HUNT, *b* 18—; *m* 18— Josephine Albertine Cheek and had issue:

    Great-great-grandchildren
    1a Zebuline Adelaide Pike Harrison Hunt, *b* 18—; *m* 1889 Paul Joseph SCHAEFER and had issue:

      Great-great-grandchildren's children
      1b Josephine Symmes SCHAEFER
      2b Paul Joseph SCHAEFER, Jr

  Great-grandchildren
  (2) Clara Pike Hunt, *b* 18—; *m* James VAUGHN and *d* in a fire six weeks later
  (3) Mary Susan Hunt, *b* 18—; *m* 1st George SOUTER and had issue:

    Great-great-grandchildren
    1a Clara Hunt Souter, *b* 1868; *m* William H. WHITEMAN and had issue:

      Great-great-grandchildren's children
      1b William John WHITEMAN; *m* Jessie Waterman
      2b Lee G. WHITEMAN; *m* Myrtle Clark
      3b Nellie Whiteman; *m* Edward SCHROEDER
      4b Harry WHITEMAN; *m* 1st Helen Mackie; *m* 2nd Myrtle Schwab and with her had issue:

        Great-great-grandchildren's grandchildren
        1c *Cleo Whiteman; *m* *Rudolph PETERSON and has issue:

          Great-great-grandchildren's great-grandchildren
          1d *Wayne PETERSON, *b* 1943

        Great-great-grandchildren's grandchildren
        2c *Gerald WHITEMAN; *m* *Ann Knight and has issue:

          Great-great-grandchildren's great-grandchildren
          1d *Cherlyn WHITEMAN
          2d *Carol Ann WHITEMAN

    Great-great-grandchildren
    2a Brenhilda Harrison SOUTER
    3a Nellie Pike SOUTER

  Great-grandchildren
  (3) (cont.) Mary Hunt Souter *m* 2nd William J. McGEE

Grandchildren
2 Anna Maria Symmes Harrison, *b* 1822; *m* Dr James Madison ROBERTS, s of John L. Roberts and his *w* Martha Zane, and *d* 1849, having had issue:

  Great-grandchildren
  (1) Gabriella ROBERTS, *b* 1840; *d* 1846
  (2) James Montgomery ROBERTS, *b* 1844; *m* Elizabeth Allen (*b* 1849; *d* 1934) and *d* 1930, having had issue:

    Great-great-grandchildren
    1a Anna Maria ROBERTS, *b* 1867; *d* 1868

Grandchildren
3 Clarissa Louisa Harrison, *b* 1824; *m* 1st Dr Tomlin Miller BANKS, s of Jedediah Banks and his *w* Elizabeth, and had issue:

  Great-grandchildren
  (1) Symmes Harrison BANKS, *b* 8 Jan 1841; *d* 8 Aug 1842
  (2) Mary Florer BANKS; *d* young
  (3) Tomlin Pike BANKS; *d* young

Grandchildren
3 (cont.) Clarissa Harrison Banks *m* 2nd Oliver Perry MORGAN and *d* 1883, having had further issue:

Great-grandchildren
(4) William Henry Harrison MORGAN; *d* young
(5) Oliver Perry MORGAN, Jr; *d* 1900
(6) Montogomery Pike MORGAN; *d* young

Grandchildren
4 William Henry HARRISON II, *b* 1828; *m* 1st Elvira (*b* 19 March 1833; *d* 13 Sept 1875), dau of Benjamin Rogers, and had issue:

Great-grandchildren
(1) Montogomery Pike HARRISON, *b* 1850; *m* Allah Etta Scott (*b* 1858; *d* 1887) and *d* 1932, having had issue:

  Great-great-grandchildren
  1a William Scott HARRISON, *b* 1876; *d* 1896
  2a (Margaret) Elvira Willis Harrison, *b* 1879; *m* Charles Bronston HUGHES (*b* 1879; *d* 19—) and *d* 19—, having had issue:

    Great-great-grandchildren's children
    1b *Harrison Bronston HUGHES, *b* 1903; *m* 19— *Lorena Evelyn Lloyd (*b* 1905)
    2b *Irene Esther Hughes, *b* 1905; *m* 1st 19— (divorce 19—) Grant SINCLAIR (*b* 1899) and has issue:

      Great-great-grandchildren's grandchildren
      1c *Stanley Grant SINCLAIR, *b* 1924; *m* 19— *Durene Heed (*b* 1926) and has issue:

        Great-great-grandchildren's great-grandchildren
        1d *David Stanley SINCLAIR, *b* 1952

    Great-great-grandchildren's children
    2b (cont.) Mrs Irene Sinclair *m* 2nd 1949 *Ray HORN
    3b *Charles Algin Pike HUGHES, *b* 1911; *m* 19— *Wilhelmina Jane Figurel (*b* 1916) and adopted two children:

      a *Deborah Bronston HUGHES
      b *Montgomery August HUGHES

  Great-great-grandchildren
  3a Oliver Pike HARRISON, *b* 1880; *m* Rose Stearley (*b* 1886) and *d* 19—, having had issue:

    Great-great-grandchildren's children
    1b *Dr Stearley Pike HARRISON [1031 Scenic Drive, Ada, OK 74820], *b* 1913; *educ* Northwestern U Med Sch (MD 1942); *m* 19— *Martha Nell Hitchcock (*b* 1917) and has issue:

      Great-great-grandchildren's grandchildren
      1c *Terry Pike HARRISON, *b* 1945
      2c *Sandra Lynn HARRISON, *b* 1946
      3c *Cynthia Ann HARRISON, *b* 1948

    Great-great-grandchildren's children
    2b *Rebecca Louise Harrison, *b* 1917; *m* 19— *Darrell MILLER (*b* 1915) and has issue:

      Great-great-grandchildren's grandchildren
      1c *Lee Oliver MILLER, *b* 1946
      2c *Kent Harrison MILLER, *b* 1948
      3c *Melvin Darrell MILLER, *b* 1951
      4c *Kristina Louise MILLER, *b* 1953

  Great-great-grandchildren
  4a Revd Clarence Willis HARRISON, *b* 1882; *m* Anna Katherine Oliver (*b* 1877) and *d* 1952, leaving issue:

    Great-great-grandchildren's children
    1b *Revd William Henry Oliver HARRISON, *b* 1911; *m* 19— *Nell Betty Anderson (*b* 1913) and has issue:

      Great-great-grandchildren's grandchildren
      1c *Michael Anderson HARRISON, *b* 1942
      2c *William Henry HARRISON, *b* 1945
      3c *Katherine HARRISON, *b* 1947

  Great-great-grandchildren
  5a Earl Leslie HARRISON, *b* 1886; *m* 19— Bertha Jane Ake (*b* 1887) and *d* 19—, having had issue:

    Great-great-grandchildren's children
    1b *Allah Mae Harrison, *b* 1913; *m* 19— Clarence AVANT (*b* 1910; *d* 1951) and has issue:

      Great-great-grandchildren's grandchildren
      1c *Jerry AVANT, *b* 1937
      2c *Barbara Jean AVANT, *b* 1938

Great-great-grandchildren's children
2b *Clara Ellen Harrison, *b* 1915; *m* 19— *Paul BARKER (*b* 1908)
3b *Earl Leslie HARRISON, Jr, *b* 1920; *m* 19— *Mina Singleton (*b* 1924) and has issue:

Great-great-grandchildren's grandchildren
1c *Sandy Earl HARRISON, *b* 1947
2c *Rebba Jane HARRISON, *b* 1950

Great-grandchildren
(2) William Taylor HARRISON, *b* and *d* 1852
(3) John Cleves Symmes HARRISON III, *b* 1855; *d* 12 Feb 1945
(4) Clara Elvira HARRISON, *b* 1856; *d* 1937
(5) Henry Leslie HARRISON, *b* 1867; *m* Margaret Pearl Moore (*b* 1875; *d* 9 Nov 1954) and *d* 1928, leaving issue:

Great-great-grandchildren
1a *Clara Irene Harrison, *b* 1897; *m* 1st 19— (divorce 19—) Elwood TANNER and has issue:

Great-great-grandchildren's children
1b *(Iona) Pearl Tanner, *b* 19—; *m* *Bruce STEPHENS and has issue:

Great-great-grandchildren's grandchildren
1c *Joan STEPHENS
2c *Lois STEPHENS

Great-great-grandchildren
1a (cont.) Mrs Clara Tanner *m* 2nd *William BRYANT
2a *Raymond Leslie HARRISON, *b* 15 Nov 1906; *m* 19— *Mildred Markel (*b* 1910)

Grandchildren
4 (cont.) William Henry Harrison II *m* 2nd 18— Mary Ann MacIntyre (*d* 1907) and *d* 1900
5 Montgomery Pike HARRISON, *b* 1829; *ka* 1848 Mexican War
6 John Cleves Symmes HARRISON, Jr; *d* young

President William H. Harrison's daughter
III Lucy Singleton Harrison, *b* Richmond, Va., 5 Sept 1800; *m* 30 Sept 1819 David K. ESTES (*b* Morristown, New Jersey, 1786; Judge Ohio Supreme Court; *d* Cincinnati 1 April 1876) and *d* Cincinnati 7 April 1826, having had issue:

Grandchildren
1 William Harrison ESTES; *d* young
2 Lucy Anne Harrison Estes, *b* 1822; *m* 18– Joseph F. REYNOLDS (*b* 1815; *d* 1895), s of Isaac Reynolds, of Baltimore, and *d* 1868, leaving issue:

Great-grandchildren
(1) Anna Harrison Reynolds, *b* 1844; *m* 18— John Law CRAWFORD and *d* 1875, having had issue:

Great-great-grandchildren
1a Lucy Estes Crawford, *b* Baltimore 1867; *m* George Catlin WOODRUFF (*b* 18—; ed Litchfield (Conn.) *Enquirer*; *d* before 1944) and *d* New York 7 Jan 1944
2a Alexander Grisbrooke CRAWFORD; *d* young

Great-grandchildren
(2) John Estes REYNOLDS, *b* 1846; *m* 18— Lydia Davis, *née* Presstman, and *d* 1888, having had issue:

Great-great-grandchildren
1a Joseph Graeme REYNOLDS; *m* Eleanor Addison Gittings Brogden (*d* 1940) and *d* 1936
2a Minna Davis REYNOLDS, *b* 1873
3a Isaac Trimble REYNOLDS, *b* and *d* 1873
4a Lydia Presstman Reynolds, *b* 18—; *m* Revd Horace Wood STOWELL (*d* 1931)

Great-grandchildren
(3) David Estes REYNOLDS, *b* 1849; *m* 18— Mary Stuart Davidson and *d* 1887, leaving issue:

Great-great-grandchildren
1a Henrietta Davidson REYNOLDS, *b* 18—

Great-grandchildren
(4) Revd Joseph F. REYNOLDS, Jr, *b* Baltimore 12 Jan 1854; *educ* U of Virginia and Gen Theological Seminary; *m* 10 Oct 1894 Louise Moller (*b* New York 19 May 1870), dau of Samuel Clark Smith, and *d* 1938, leaving issue:

Great-great-grandchildren
1a Louise Harrison REYNOLDS, *b* New York 8 Sept 1895; *d* 24 April 1972
2a Dorothea Estes REYNOLDS, *b* New York 14 July 1896; *d* 1944

Great-grandchildren
(5) Lucy Singleton REYNOLDS, *b* 1858; *d* 1912

(6) William Henry Harrison REYNOLDS, *b* 1861; *d* 1904

(7) Mary REYNOLDS, *b* 1864; *d* 1917

Grandchildren

3 William Henry Harrison ESTES; *d* young

4 Davis ESTES; *d* young

President William H. Harrison's son

IV William Henry HARRISON, Jr, *b* Vincennes, Ind., 3 Sept 1802; *educ* Transylvania Coll; lawyer and farmer; *m* 18 Feb 1824 Jane Findlay (*b* 1804; appointed to act as hostess at the White House by her mother-in-law Mrs William H. Harrison; *d* 1846), dau of Archibald Irwin and his w Mary Ramsey, and *d* North Bend, Ohio, 6 Feb 1838, leaving issue:

Grandchildren

1 James Findlay HARRISON, *b* Cincinnati, Ohio, 9 March 1825; *educ* West Point; admitted Indiana Bar, Lt Mexican War, Col Union Army Civil War; *m* 1st 1848 Caroline M. Alston (*d* 1863), of S Carolina, and had issue:

Great-grandchildren

(1) James Findlay HARRISON, Jr, *b* 1848; *d* 1870

(2) William Alston HARRISON, *b* 1850; *d* 1851

(3) William Henry HARRISON, *b* 1852; *d* 1861

Grandchildren

1 (cont.) Col James F. Harrison *m* 2nd 24 Dec 1864 Alice Merriam (*b* Natchez, Miss., 28 Oct 1842; *d* Kansas City, Mo., 6 June 1911), dau of John Kennedy, formerly of Belfast, Ireland, and *d* Mound City, Kans., 14 Feb 1907, having with her had issue:

Great-grandchildren

(4) Jane Alice HARRISON, *b* 1865; *d* 1866

(5) John Scott HARRISON, of Helena, Mont., *b* Mound City 30 April 1867; civil engr; *m* Helena 24 March 1903 Mary Sophie (*b* Sun River, Mont., 10 Jan 1875; *d* Helena May 1938), dau of Joseph Smith Hill and his w Augusta Ford, and *d* Calico Rock, Ark., 29 April 1949, having had issue:

Great-great-grandchildren

1a James Findlay Hill HARRISON, *b* Helena 28 June, *d* 5 July 1905

2a *William Henry HARRISON [43 East Street, Carlisle, MA 01741, USA], *b* 4 Aug 1906; *educ* George Washington U; lecturer and museum official; *m* 1st Washington, DC, 1935 (divorce 1958) Margaret Ann Linforth Willgoose; *m* 2nd London, UK, 1958 *Eleni Clio Marie, former w of John Graham Apostolides and dau of Revd Charles Dobson, MC, and his w Eleni Georgoulopoulos, and with her has issue:

Great-great-grandchildren's children

1b *Anthea Io HARRISON, *b* Boston 25 Feb 1961; *educ* Harvard; with Acquisitions Dept Boston Athenaeum

Great-great-grandchildren

3a Scott Hill HARRISON, *b* Helena 30 Sept 1907; *educ* Montana State U; oil industry engr; *m* Boulder, Mont., 5 Sept 1931 Elizabeth (*b* Helena 14 Dec 1910; *d* 6 Jan 1988), dau of Hiram E. Bower and his w Rose Runyan, and *d* Minneapolis, Minn., 18 Aug 1971, leaving issue:

Great-great-grandchildren's children

1b *Sylvia Hill Harrison, *b* Helena 12 Nov 1933; *m* Portland, Oreg., 29 Dec 1953 *John Palmer EGAN (*b* Portland 5 Sept 1930) [c/o Arabian American Oil Co, Box 1815, Dhahran, Saudi Arabia], s of John Egan and his w Beatrice Palmer, and has issue:

Great-great-grandchildren's grandchildren

1c *John Harrison EGAN, *b* Dhahran 4 Sept 1956; *educ* Oregon Episcopal Schs, Portland

2c *Scott Edward EGAN, *b* Portland 6 Sept 1958

3c *Michael Patrick EGAN, *b* Portland 24 Nov 1963

Great-great-grandchildren's children

2b *Sheila Elizabeth Harrison [Mrs David Dougherty, 6720 SW King Boulevard, Beaverton, OR, USA], *b* Helena 25 March 1938; *m* Portland 20 March 1965 *David M. DOUGHERTY (*b* 8 Dec 1930), s of David Dougherty

3b *John Scott HARRISON [812 Hill St, Shelby, MT 59474, USA], *b* Helena 17 May 1941; *educ* U of Montana U; elementary counsellor 1976-93; *m* Long Island, New York, 11 Aug 1971 *Maria Alma (*b* New York 20 March 1944), dau of Albin Cibeu and his w Antoinette Marinig, and has issue:

Great-great-grandchildren's grandchildren

1c *Erika Nicole HARRISON [1005 Gerald, Missoula, MT, USA], *b* Dhahran 21 Oct 1972

2c *Rebecca Cibeu HARRISON, *b* Shelby, Montana, 24 Jan 1979

Great-grandchildren

(6) William Henry HARRISON, *b* La Cygne, Kans., 27 March 1869; ptnr Harrison & Harrison (real estate) with his cousin John S. Harrison (bro of President BENJAMIN HARRISON); *m* 1st Mound City, Kans., 6 Nov 1893 Lura Myrtle

(*b* Detroit, Mich., 28 Sept 1869; *d* Kansas City, Mo., 9 Feb 1922), dau of Charles Newton Adams and his *w* Amelia Dawes, and had issue:

Great-great-grandchildren

1a Alice Amelia Harrison, *b* Kansas City 19 Oct 1896; *m* 1st Kansas City Sept 1915 Reuben Nathan FREDLUND (*b* 1893; *d* Iola, Kans., 5 Aug 1916); *m* 2nd Glendale, Calif., 16 March 1925 Joseph Lawrence GREEN (*d* Glendale 1948) and *d* Feb 1946

2a *Virginia Harrison [Mrs Albert Ware, 7548 Wandotte Street, Kansas City, MO 64114, USA], *b* Kansas City 31 Dec 1899; *m* there 23 Sept 1922 Albert Randolph WARE (*b* Chicago 2 Nov 1897; *d* Oakland, Calif., 1969), s of Albert R. Ware and his *w* Marcia, and has had issue:

Great-great-grandchildren's children

1b *Virginia Louise Ware [Mrs Charles Dreyer, 3808 Van Demen Drive, Forth Worth, TX 76116, USA], *b* Kansas City 22 Aug 1923; *m* Hemet, Calif., 13 Nov 1943 *Charles W. DREYER (*b* Kansas City 10 Dec 1921), s of Albert F. Dreyer and his *w* Laura, and has issue:

Great-great-grandchildren's grandchildren

1c *Constance Louise Dreyer [Mrs Dale Bell, 1252 North 78th East Avenue, Tulsa, OK 74115, USA], *b* Dayton, Ohio, 6 July 1949; *m* Prairie Village, Kans., 12 Aug 1970 *Dale Edward BELL, s of L. M. Bell and his *w* Mary

2c *Lawrence Harrison DREYER, *b* Minneapolis, Minn., 15 Oct 1954; with US Army

3c *Lori Diane DREYER, *b* Minneapolis 28 March 1962

Great-great-grandchildren's children

2b William Randolph WARE, *b* Kansas City 9 March 1927; *d* Independence, Mo., 23 Feb 1938

Great-grandchildren

(6) (cont.) William H. HARRISON *m* 2nd Edwardsville, Kans., 1 March 1923 Ethel Etzenhouser (*b* 1889; *d* Independence 2 May 1970) and *d* Independence 15 April 1945

(7) Mary Randolph Harrison, *b* Mound City 28 Oct 1871; *m* Kansas City 16 Jan 1896 John Walter FARRAR (*b* Chicago 1872; *d* Kansas City 3 Feb 1960), s of Samuel Henry Farrar and his *w* Winnie Scott Harrison, and *d* Kansas City 1938, leaving issue:

Great-great-grandchildren

1a *James Harrison FARRAR [Haines, OR 97833, USA], *b* Kansas City 7 Sept 1907; *m* Yuma, Ariz., 5 June 1935 *Dorothy (*b* Santa Barbara, Calif., 22 July 1898), dau of Carl Stoddard and his *w* Linda Romero

2a *Alice Elizabeth Farrar [Mrs Norman Quay, 7609 Conser, Overland Park, KS 66204, USA], *b* Kansas City 8 Oct 1908; *m* there 14 June 1947 *Norman Stanley QUAY (*b* Fort Lauderdale, Fla., 1914) and has issue:

Great-great-grandchildren's children

1b *Mary Katherine Quay [Mrs Richard Wray, 7609 Conser, Overland Park, KS 66204, USA], *b* Kansas City 5 May 1948; *m* Chillicothe, Mo., 1979 *Richard M. WRAY (*b* Kansas City Aug 1949) and has issue:

Great-great-grandchildren's grandchildren

1c *Robert Harrison WRAY, *b* Kansas City 4 April 1971

Great-great-grandchildren

3a *Agnes Winifred Farrar [Mrs Rex Black, 673 Orchard Avenue, Santa Barbara, CA 93108, USA], *b* Kansas City 23 Nov 1911; *m* Olatha, Kans., 8 Jan 1938 Rex Clifford Black (*b* Hurley, S. Dak., 9 Aug 1905; *d* Denver, Colo., 26 Dec 1946)

Great-grandchildren

(8) James Findlay HARRISON, *b* La Cygne, Kans., 28 Dec 1876; served 3rd Missouri Regt Spanish-American War 1898; *d* Calico Rock, Ark., 25 Feb 1958

(9) Archibald Irwin HARRISON, *b* 7 April 1881; Sgt 3rd US Engrs World War I; *d* 7 March 1920

Grandchildren

2 William Henry HARRISON; *d* 1849

President William H. Harrison's son

V (John) Scott HARRISON, *b* Vincennes, Ind., 4 Oct 1804; Memb (Whig) House of Reps for 2nd Ohio Dist 1853-57; *m* 1st 1824 Lucretia Knapp Johnson (*b* Boone Co, Ky., 16 Sept 1804; *d* 6 Feb 1830) and had issue:

Grandchildren

1 Elizabeth (Betsey) Short Harrison, *b* 1825; *m* Dr George Coleman EATON, of Cincinnati, Ohio (*b* 1820; *d* 1866), s of William Eaton and his *w* Mary Keyes, and *d* North Bend, Ohio, 12 May 1904, having had issue:

Great-grandchildren

(1) Scott Harrison EATON, *b* 1848; *d* 1878

(2) Mary Goodrich EATON, *b* 1851; *d* 1877

(3) George Coleman EATON, Jr, *b* 1853; *m* 1880 Lillian Antoinette Storch (*b* 1854; *d* 1932) and *d* 1889, having had issue:

Great-great-grandchildren
1a Robert Brown EATON; *d* young
2a Scott Harrison EATON, *b* 1883; *m* 1942 Jenny Bennett
3a George Coleman EATON III; *d* young

Great-grandchildren
(4) Anna Harrison EATON, *b* 8 Sept 1856; *d* 8 Nov 1857
(5) Archibald Irwin EATON, *b* 1859; *d* 1895

Grandchildren
2 William Henry HARRISON, *b* 9 March 1827; *d* 15 Sept 1829
3 Sarah (Sallie) Lucretia Harrison, *b* 1829; *m* 18— Thomas Jefferson DEVIN, of Ottumwa, Iowa, s of Thomas Devin, of McConnelsville, and had issue:

Great-grandchildren
(1) Ann Harrison DEVIN, *b* 18—
(2) Scott Harrison DEVIN, *b* 18—; *m* Lucretia Griffith and had issue:

Great-great-grandchildren
1a John Scott Harrison DEVIN, *b* 1892; *m* 19— Virgil McLaughland
2a Harry E. DEVIN, *b* 1894; *m* 1st 19— Dorothy Barto and had issue:

Great-great-grandchildren's children
1b *Dorothy Lou Devin, *b* 1918; *m* 19— *Paul B. McCANN

Great-great-grandchildren
2a (cont.) Harry E. Devin *m* 2nd Wanda Findley (*d* 1950); *m* 3rd 1950, as her 2nd husb, Julia, *née* Sandres (*b* 1896), widow of his f's 2nd cousin Benjamin Harrison (for whom *see below*)

President William H. Harrison's son
V (cont.) Scott Harrison *m* 2nd 12 Aug 1831 Elizabeth Ramsey (*b* Mercersburg, Pa., 18 July 1810; *d* North Bend, Ohio, 15 Aug 1850), dau of Archibald Irwin and his w Mary Ramsey and sister of Jane (w of Scott Harrison's er bro William H. Harrison), and *d* Point Farm, nr North Bend, Ohio, 25 May 1878 (*bur* Harrison Tomb), having with her had issue:

Grandchildren
4 (Archibald) Irwin HARRISON, *b* North Bend 9 June 1832; Lt-Col US Vols; *m* 18— Elizabeth Lawrence, dau of William Sheets and his w Mary Skipwith Randolph, and *d* Indianapolis 16 Dec 1870 of tuberculosis, leaving issue:

Great-grandchildren
(1) Mary Randolph Harrison, *b* 18—; *m* 18— Frank Campbell NICKELS (*b* 4 Aug 1857; *d* 1923) and *d* 1896, leaving issue:

Great-great-grandchildren
1a Harrison Campbell NICKELS, *b* 20 Dec 1892; *d* 6 Jan 1912
2a Irwin Harrison NICKELS, *b* 15 June 1894; *m* 19— Jeanette Gilbert and had issue:

Great-great-grandchildren's children
1b Jean G. Nickels, *b* 6 May 1916; *m* 19— *John W. BEATIE and *d* 26 March 1954, leaving issue:

Great-great-grandchildren's grandchildren
1c *Susan Nickels BEATIE, *b* 1944
2c *Carolyn Nickels BEATIE, *b* 1949

Great-grandchildren
(2) William Sheets HARRISON, *b* 18—; *d* 17 Dec 1890
(3) Elizabeth Irwin Harrison, *b* 18—; *m* 1889 her 2nd cousin Thornton LEWIS, est s of John Calvin Lewis and his w Alice Fitzhugh Thornton (4th child of Mary Symmes Harrison, herself 7th child of President WILLIAM H. HARRISON, and her husb Dr John Thornton), and *d* Richmond, Va., 6 May 1946, leaving issue:

Great-great-grandchildren
1a William Sheets Harrison LEWIS, *b* 1890; *m* 1917 Rema Doris and had issue:

Great-great-grandchildren's children
1b Thornton LEWIS II, *b* 1919; *d* 1942
2b *William Harrison LEWIS, *b* 1925

Great-great-grandchildren
2a Alice Thornton Lewis, *b* 1894; *m* 19— Franklin Attilla BOTTS (*b* 1889; *d* 1937) and had issue:

Great-great-grandchildren's children
1b *Elizabeth Thornton Botts, *b* 1916; *m* 1940 *William Ledwith PAUL (*b* 1907) and has issue:

Great-great-grandchildren's grandchildren
1c *Elizabeth Thornton PAUL, *b* 1941

2c *Mary Ledwith PAUL, *b* 1945
3c *William Ledwith PAUL, Jr, *b* 1953

Great-great-grandchildren's children
2b Franklin Attilla BOTTS, Jr, *b* 1918; *d* 1921

Great-great-grandchildren
3a Lawrence LEWIS, *b* 1895; *m* 1st 1917 (div 192-) M. Louise Wise (*b* 1895; *d* 1937) and had issue:

Great-great-grandchildren's children
1b *Lawrence LEWIS, Jr, *b* 1918; *m* 1940 *Janet Kean Patton (*b* 1920) and has issue:

Great-great-grandchildren's grandchildren
1c *Louise Wise LEWIS, *b* 1941
2c *Janet Patton LEWIS, *b* 1953

Great-great-grandchildren's children
2b *Mary Lily Flagler Lewis, *b* 1920; *m* 1946 *Frederick Gresham POLLARD (*b* 1918) and has adopted two s:

a *Lewis Butler POLLARD
b *Nelson Carter POLLARD

Great-great-grandchildren
3a (cont.) Lawrence Lewis *m* 2nd 1926 *Ruby Bigger (*b* 1903) and *d* Nov 1954

Great-grandchildren
(4) Jean Carter Harrison; *m* George Evans DAVIS and had issue:

Great-great-grandchildren
1a Bettie Harrison Davis; *m* 1st George Edward DARLING; *m* 2nd Hugh FLEMING, Jr, and with him had issue:

Great-great-grandchildren's children
1b *Carter FLEMING

Grandchildren
5 BENJAMIN HARRISON, 23rd PRESIDENT of the UNITED STATES of AMERICA
6 Mary Jane Irwin Harrison, *b* 5 July 1835; *m* 14 April 1859 Samuel Vance MORRIS (*b* 1833; *d* 1913), s of Bethnel Franklin Morris and his w Margaret E. Vance, and *d* 14 Sept 1867, having had issue:

Great-grandchildren
(1) Scott Harrison MORRIS, *b* 1860; *m* 18— Laura Ann Pease (*b* 1862; *d* 1947) and *d* 1913, having had issue:

Great-great-grandchildren
1a Mabel Mary Morris, *b* 18—; *m* 18—or 19— George Duffield SLAYMAKER and had issue:

Great-great-grandchildren's children
1b Clara Morris SLAYMAKER, *b* 18— or 19—; *d* young

Great-great-grandchildren
2a Jane Elizabeth Morris, *b* 1884; *m* 18— or 19— Russell McDANIEL
3a Louis Parker MORRIS, *b* 18—; *d* young
4a Anna Harrison Morris, *b* 1893; *m* 1913 Marcus WALKER (*b* 1890) and had issue:

Great-great-grandchildren's children
1b *Scott Harrison Morris WALKER, *b* 21 Oct 1917; *m* 1940 *Nancy Colleen Murray (*b* 1919) and has issue:

Great-great-grandchildren's grandchildren
1c *Joann Colden WALKER, *b* 1943
2c *Nancy Jane WALKER, *b* 1945

Great-great-grandchildren's children
2b *Nancy Annette Walker, *b* 11 Aug 1924; *m* 1947 *William Herbert TEESDALE and has issue:

Great-great-grandchildren's grandchildren
1c *Ann Harrison TEESDALE, *b* 1951
2c *Sally Jane TEESDALE, *b* 1954

Great-grandchildren
(2) Frank MORRIS, *b* 18—; *d* 1863
(3) Elizabeth Irwin Morris, *b* 1863; *m* 1903 Edmund Gordon REEL and *d* 1940

Grandchildren
7 Anna Symmes HARRISON, *b* 23 Aug 1837; *d* 26 Aug 1838
8 John Irwin Harrison, *b* 25 June, 25 Oct 1839
9 Carter Bassett HARRISON II, of Tenn., *b* 26 Sept 1840; *m* 1863 Sophie Ridgely (*b* 10 Sept 1826; *d* 1926), widow of William Lytle and dau of Alfred H. Dashiell, of Elk Ridge, Md., and his w Ann Ridgely, and *d* 6 Dec 1905, having had issue:

Great-grandchildren
(1) John Scott HARRISON, *b* 25 Feb 1864; *m* 19 Aug 1886 Margaret Willis (*b* May 1868; *d* 1 Nov 1960) and *d* 1 April 1928, leaving issue:

Great-great-grandchildren
1a Alyn HARRISON, *b* 16 Dec 1887; *m* 2 July 1921 Mary Frances Matheny (*b* 13 July 1897; *d* 18 July 1969) and had issue:

Great-great-grandchildren's children
1b *Alyn HARRISON, Jr, *b* 3 April 1922; *m* 5 June 1961 *Jayne McHugh Harrison (*b* 18 Nov 1925) and has issue:

Great-great-grandchildren's grandchildren
1c *Cynthia Louise HARRISON, *b* 1 March 1962
2c *Scott Alyn HARRISON, *b* 7 Dec 1963

Great-great-grandchildren
2a Margaret Harrison, *b* 21 July 1889; *m* 23 Oct 1909 Seward Harvey KINNEY (*b* 1884; *d* 1950) and *d* 21 May 1968, leaving issue;

Great-great-grandchildren's children
1b *Pamela Kinney, *b* 27 Oct 1927; *m* 26 April 1942 *David William NEWCOMER III (*b* 19 March 1911) and has issue:

Great-great-grandchildren's grandchildren
1c *David William NEWCOMER IV, *b* 19 Nov 1942; *m* 6 June 1964 *Sharon Rogers and has issue:

Great-great grandchildren's great-grandchildren
1d *David William NEWCOMER V, *b* 11 Oct 1967
2d *Marissa NEWCOMER, *b* 18 Aug 1971

Great-great-grandchildren's grandchildren
2c *Douglas Barry NEWCOMER, *b* 25 March 1947

Great-great-grandchildren's children
2b *Harrison KINNEY, *b* 17 Feb 1921; *m* 12 March 1949 *Caroline Roberts (*b* 27 July 1923) and has issue:

Great-great-grandchildren's grandchildren
1c *Harrison KINNEY, Jr, *b* 27 Feb 1951; *m* 30 May 1970 *Kathleen Ann La Croix (*b* 5 April 1951) and has issue:

Great-great-grandchildren's great-grandchildren
1d *Mari Kathleen KINNEY, *b* 10 Jan 1973

Great-great-grandchildren's grandchildren
2c *Julie Ann KINNEY, *b* 2 July 1954

Great-grandchildren
(2) Carter Bassett HARRISON III, *b* 1868; *d* 1892
(3) Elizabeth Irwin Harrison, *b* 1874; *m* 1893 William Thornton Taliaferro BUCKNER, of Cincinnati, Ohio, and *d* 1966, leaving issue:

Great-great-grandchildren
1a Sophia Harrison Buckner, *b* 1894; *m* 1927 *William Proctor BELL, of Cincinnati, and has issue:

Great-great-grandchildren's children
1b *Elizabeth Buckner Bell, *b* 1928; *m* 8 March 1953 *Frank Donald DRAKE

Great-great-grandchildren
2a *Elizabeth Harrison Buckner [Mrs Daniel McCarthy, 200 West Galbreth Road, Cincinnati, OH, USA], *b* 1902; *m* 1921 *Daniel W. McCARTHY

Grandchildren
10 Anna Symmes Harrison, *b* 4 Nov 1842; *m* 12 Oct 1869, as his 2nd w, her brother-in-law Samuel Vance MORRIS (*b* 1833; *d* 1913) and *d* 26 March 1926, having had issue:

Great-grandchildren
(1) Samuel Vance MORRIS, Jr, *b* 1870; *m* 1897 Nellie Prouse (*d* 1949) and *d* 1928, leaving issue:

Great-great-grandchildren
1a *Margaret Morris, *b* 1898; *m* 19— *Cecil BRADY

Great-grandchildren
(2) Margaret Vance Morris, *b* 1872; *m* 1891 William H. CURTISS (*d* 1923) and *d* 1952, leaving issue:

Great-great-grandchildren
1a *Ray Harrison CURTISS, *b* 1893; *m* 19— *Janet Hood and has issue:

Great-great-grandchildren's children
1b *Jean Eleanor Curtiss, *b* 1919; *m* 1940 *Pettus B. WILLIAMS and has issue:

Great-great-grandchildren's grandchildren
1c *Scott Harrison WILLIAMS, *b* 1945
2c *Ann Elizabeth WILLIAMS, *b* 1948

Great-great-grandchildren's children
2b *Nancy Harrison Curtiss [Mrs Howard Baugman, 29 Winding Glen, Danville, CA 94526, USA], *b* 1922; *m* 1st 1943 William H. FOLLMER (*d* 1949) and has issue:

Great-great-grandchildren's grandchildren
1c *Sharon Ann FOLLMER, *b* 1943
2c *William Curtiss FOLLMER, *b* 1946

Great-great-grandchildren's children
2b (cont.) Nancy Curtiss Follmer *m* 2nd California 19— *Howard BAUGMAN

Great-grandchildren
(3) Allen Harrison MORRIS, *b* 1874; *d* 1913
(4) Clara Vaughn MORRIS, *b* 1877; *d* 1889
(5) Anna Thornton Morris, *b* Indianapolis, Ind., 1879; *m* Minneapolis, Minn., 1903 Charles Thompson STEVENSON (*b* Edinburgh, Scotland, 1877; *d* Minneapolis 25 July 1958), s of William Stevenson and his w Mary Ann Howie, and *d* Minneapolis 24 Nov 1968, leaving issue:

Great-great-grandchildren
1a Mary Stevenson, *b* Minneapolis 1905; *m* there 1928 George F. WILLIAMSON (*d* Minneapolis 22 Sept 1978), s of James F. Williamson and his w Emma Elmore, and *d* Winchester, Mass., 4 June 1988, leaving issue:

Great-great-grandchildren's children
1b *Ann Felice Williamson [Mrs Lane McGovern, 12 Dartmouth, Winchester, MA 01890, USA], *b* Minneapolis 7 Sept 1930; *educ* Wellesley; *m* Minneapolis 26 Nov 1952 *(Addison) Lane McGOVERN (*b* Boston 1924), s of James Joseph McGovern and his w Marion Stritzinger, and has issue:

Great-great-grandchildren's grandchildren
1c *Susan Ann McGOVERN [10 Perth Rd, Arlington, MA 02174, USA], *b* Boston 6 Dec 1954; *educ* Vassar and Boston U; communications and marketing exec, v-pres advertising and public rels firm
2c *Sara Williamson McGovern [Mrs Paul J Morrissey, 540 Poe Ave, Worthington, OH, USA], *b* Boston 21 Sept 1956; *m* Winchester, Mass., 21 June 1980 *Paul Joseph MORRISSEY (*b* Boston 3 Jan 1957) and has issue:

Great-great-grandchildren's great-grandchildren
1d *Paul Joseph MORRISSEY III, *b* Maine 10 May 1981
2d *James McGovern MORRISSEY, *b* Maine 29 July 1983
3d *Brian Patrick MORRISSEY, *b* 30 Sept 1986

Great-great-grandchildren's grandchildren
3c *Lisa Stevenson McGovern [Mrs Jonathan R Wallace, 15 Branch Lane PO Box 257, Prides Crossing, MA 01965, USA], *b* Boston 22 April 1959; *educ* Princeton and Harvard Law Sch; prosecutor; *m* Winchester, Mass., 16 Sept 1989 *Jonathan (Jay) Raymond WALLACE (*b* Boston 19 Sept 1960), s of Neil W. Wallace and his w Elise R., and has issue:

Great-great-grandchildren's great-grandchildren
1d *Marlana Ann WALLACE, *b* Boston 8 May 1990
2d *Jacqueline Grace WALLACE, *b* Boston 24 Dec 1991

Great-great-grandchildren's grandchildren
4c *Laura Stritzinger McGOVERN [12 Dartmouth St, Winchester, MA 01890, USA], *b* Boston 9 Aug 1962

Great-great-grandchildren
2a *Nancy Morris Stevenson [Mrs James Lane, 4625 Highland Road, Minnetonka, MN 55345, USA], *b* Minneapolis 6 Oct 1907; *educ* Northrop Pine Manor Coll; secretary to school headmaster 1947-72, seller of advertising for Minnesota Horse Show; *m* Minneapolis 26 Oct 1933 James Sargent LANE (*b* Minneapolis 1902; *d* 7 Jan 1947), s of Mark Dormer Lane and his w Corabelle Ryan, and has issue:

Great-great-grandchildren's children
1b *James Sargent LANE III [2605 Hamel Rd, Medina, MN 55340, USA], *b* Minneapolis 8 July 1939; *educ* Princeton and William Mitchell Coll of Law; atty; *m* Minneapolis 14 July 1961 *Joan, dau of Jack D. Lee and his w Helen H., and has issue:

Great-great-grandchildren's grandchildren
1c *Anne Stevenson Lane [Mrs Lawrence Martinez, 4727 Spring Creek Drive, Deephaven, MN 55331, USA], *b* Honolulu, Hawaii, 26 Feb 1962; *m* Minnetonka Beach, Minn., 8 Aug 1986 *Lawrence T. MARTINEZ and has issue:

Great-great-grandchildren's great-grandchildren
1d *Joseph Alexander MARTINEZ, *b* Minneapolis 4 Nov 1961
2c *Joan Harrison LANE [175 Prospect St Apt #2, Cambridge, MA 02139, USA], *b* St Paul, Minn., 21 Jan 1964
3c *Jacqueline Lee LANE, *b* Washington, DC, 29 June 1968
4c *Linda Wells LANE, *b* Washington, DC, 8 May 1970

Great-great-grandchildren's children
2b *Charles (Chuck) Stevenson LANE [5253 Edgewater Beach Rd, Green Bay, WI 54311, USA], *b* Minneapolis 18 March 1942; *educ* Washington and Lee U; Assist V-Pres Public Rels Employers Health Insur, Green Bay, Wis.

Great-grandchildren
(6) Eleanor Morris, *b* 1882; *m* 1908 Albert Lewis BUTLER and *d* 19—, leaving issue:

Great-great-grandchildren
1a *Vance BUTLER, *b* 1912; *m* 1940 *Beverley Johnson

Grandchildren
11 John Scott HARRISON II, of Kansas City, Mo., *b* 12 Nov 1844; *m* 7 Oct 1872 (Marie) Sophia Elizabeth (*b* 1854; *d* 1932), dau of William Lytle and his w Sophia Ridgely, and *d* 9 Jan 1926, having had issue:

Great-grandchildren
(1) Archibald Irwin HARRISON, *b* Kansas City 27 Nov 1874; *m* Portland, Oreg., 6 Oct 1902 Louise Irene Mount (*b* 1871; *d* 1949) and *d* 19 Oct 1912, having had issue:

Great-great-grandchildren
1a Archibald Irwin HARRISON, *b* Fort Snelling, Minn., 9 July, *d* 18 July 1903
2a *Katherine Louise Harrison [Mrs David Caldwell, 4600 J C Nichols Parkway, Kansas City, MO 64112, USA], *b* San Francisco, Calif., 1904; *m* Kansas City 6 Oct 1927 David Pollard CALDWELL (*b* Union City, Tenn., 1888; *d* Kansas City 25 Sept 1942), s of David Caldwell and his w Maude Bostar, and has issue:

Great-great-grandchildren's children
1b *Katherine Louise Caldwell, *b* Topeka, Kans., 22 July 1936; *m* Kansas City 21 Aug 1965 *James Hannon CONELY, Jr, USAF (*b* New Smyrna Beach, Fla., 9 July 1938), s of James Hannon Conely and his w Euda, and has issue:

Great-great-grandchildren's grandchildren
1c *Karen Louise CONELY, *b* New York 15 May 1966
2c *David Hannon CONELY, *b* Colorado Springs, Colo., 27 Nov 1968
3c *Anne Katherine CONELY, *b* Colorado Springs 27 Nov 1968

Great-great-grandchildren's children
2b *David Pollard CALDWELL, Jr, *b* Chattanooga, Tenn., 27 Feb 1940; *m* Kansas City 8 Jan 1972 *Sue Etrick

Great-grandchildren
(2) Lytle HARRISON, of Los Angeles, *b* Kansas City 22 Feb 1876; Paymr USN Spanish-American War, rancher and developer; *m* Kansas City 4 Feb 1904 Esther Allen (*b* there 10 Oct 1878; *d* San Bernadino, Calif., 28 March 1952), dau of Steven Davis Thatcher and his w Esther Allen, and *d* Los Angeles 23 March 1956, leaving issue:

Great-great-grandchildren
1a *Lytle HARRISON, Jr [11970 Montana Avenue, Los Angeles, CA 90049, USA], *b* Mercedes, Tex., 29 Sept 1908; with Armoured Command US Army World War II, subsequently exec; *m* Los Angeles 25 Aug 1926 *Antoinette (*b* Los Angeles 29 Sept 1905), dau of John Munro and his w Ella Mae Heinzeman, and has issue:

Great-great-grandchildren's children
1b *William Lytle HARRISON [Belle Vue/Cascade Box 3353, Mahé, Seychelle Islands, Indian Ocean, East Africa], *b* Cameron, Tex., 20 May 1927; USN (ret), fought World War II, Korea and Vietnam, logistics engr; *m* Auckland, New Zealand 29 May 1945 *Edith Elizabeth (*b* Dunedin, New Zealand, 29 June 1926), dau of Alexander Bell and his w Jesse Bethune Duncan, and has issue:

Great-great-grandchildren's grandchildren
1c *Loretta Elizabeth Harrison [Mrs Leonard Nunes, 46 Huggins Drive, Orland, CA 95963, USA], *b* San Francisco 14 Jan 1947; *educ* Anokia Sch and St Mary's Acad; *m* Reno, Nev., 7 July 1968 *Leonard Laverne NUNES (*b* Chico, Calif., 23 July 1947), s of William Robert Nunes and his w Velma Louise Landingham, and has issue:

Great-great-grandchildren's great-grandchildren
1d *Ainsley Mari NUNES, *b* Paradise, Calif., 12 April 1969
2d *Marcia Louise NUNES, *b* Paradise 12 Aug 1971

Great-grandchildren
(3) James Ridgely HARRISON, *b* 1880; *d* young
(4) John Scott HARRISON III, of Kansas City, *b* 22 April 1882; *m* 5 Feb 1910 Norma Freyschlag (*b* 1887; *d* 1964) and *d* 1952, leaving issue:

Great-great-grandchildren
1a E(dward) Webb HARRISON, *b* 1910; *m* 1935 *Elizabeth (Betty) Nash (*b* 1909) and *d* 3 Dec 1986, leaving issue:

Great-great-grandchildren's children
1b *Anne Carter Harrison [Anne Harrison-Clark, 7200 Denton Rd, Bethesda, MD 20814, USA], *b* New York 24 Oct 1938; *educ* Miss Fine's Sch and Smith (AB, MA); assist dir volunteers Museum of Science, Boston, 1960-62, English teacher Pakistan 1966-68, project dir and consultant women, health and housing issues 1974-78, consultant HEW Dept 1978, Legislative Dir Nat Consumers' League, Washington, DC, 1977-78, Washington Rep Populations Resource Center/Population Assoc of America 1978-83, Dir Constituency Devpt John Glenn Presdtl Ctee Inc 1983-84, Consultant/Fundraiser Population/Environment Balance 1984-85, V-Pres Public Affrs March of Dimes Birth Defects Fndn 1985-90, Dir Public Policy American Fndn AIDS Research 1991-92, Public Affairs Specialist Population Assoc of American Assoc of Population Centers 1992-; *m* 21 June 1963 *Edwin Hill CLARK II, s of Robert Ober Clarke and his w Martha White, and has issue:

Great-great-grandchildren's grandchildren
1c *(Elisa)Beth Bayley CLARK, *b* Princeton, New Jersey, 4 Sept 1964
2c *Carter Harrison CLARK, *b* Princeton 25 Aug 1967; *m* Minneapolis, Minn., 28 Aug 1992 *Laura Whitmore

Great-great-grandchildren's children
2b Edward Webb HARRISON, Jr, *b* 22 Jan 1942; *d* 6 Oct 1975
3b A girl; *d* in infancy

Great-great-grandchildren
2a *John Scott HARRISON IV, *b* 1913; *m* 1st 1940 Lucie Howe Dix (*b* 1918; *d* 1947) and has issue:

Great-great-grandchildren's children
1b *Lucie Howe Harrison, *b* 1941; *m* 1964 *Dennis DeWITT (*b* 1942) and has issue:

Great-great-grandchildren's grandchildren
1c *John DeWITT, *b* 1966
2c *Dennis DeWITT, *b* 1968
3c *Andrew DeWITT, *b* 1971

Great-great-grandchildren's children
2b *Sallie Dix Harrison, *b* 1945; *m* 1966 *Thomas BRODHAY (*b* 1944) and has issue:

Great-great-grandchildren's grandchildren
1c *Alisa Jean BRODHAY, *b* 1971
2c *Cynthia BRODHAY, 1973

Great-great-grandchildren
2a (cont.) John S. Harrison IV *m* 2nd 1949 Janice Hoyt (*b* 1918; *d* 1988) and with her has issue:

Great-great-grandchildren's children
3b *Iley Harrison, *b* 1952; *m* 1974 *David BROCKETT (*b* 1949) and has issue:

Great-great-grandchildren's grandchildren
1c *Kyle BROCKETT, *b* 1975
2c *Curtis BROCKETT, *b* 1977
3c *Phillip BROCKETT, *b* 1982

Great-great-grandchildren
3a *Carter Ridgely HARRISON [7231 Booth St, Prairie Village, KS 66208-3352, USA], *b* Kansas City, Mo., 7 June 1918; *educ* Williams Coll; *m* 1st 22 July 1944 Joan Cuper Fitts (*b* 1925; *d* 1985), sis of Jean Marie Fitts (*see below*), and has issue:

Great-great-grandchildren's children
1b *Carter Ridgely HARRISON, Jr, *b* 1946; *m* 1st 1971 Betty Jean Lorance (*d* 1977); *m* 2nd 1978 *Day Hoxie (*b* 1948) and has issue:

Great-great-grandchildren's grandchildren
1c *Ridgely H. HARRISON, *b* 1980
2c *Catherine H. HARRISON, *b* 1982

Great-great-grandchildren's children
2b *Susan Marie Harrison, *b* 1947; *m* 1978 *Stephen PETERSEN (*b* 1943) and has issue:

Great-great-grandchildren's grandchildren
1c *Ryan PETERSEN, *b* 1979
2c *Katherine PETERSEN, *b* 1982

Great-great-grandchildren's children
3b *Cynthia Norma Harrison, *b* 1952; *m* 19— *John DAVIS (*b* 1944) and has issue:

Great-great-grandchildren's grandchildren
1c *Bret DAVIS, *b* 1969
2c *Kara DAVIS, *b* 1971

Great-great-grandchildren's children
4b *John Scott HARRISON V, *b* 18 Sept 1954; *m* 19— *Mary Levesque (*b* 1956) and has issue:

Great-great-grandchildren's grandchildren
1c *Melissa HARRISON, *b* 1981
2c *Rebecca HARRISON, *b* 1983
3c *John Scott HARRISON VI, *b* 19—

Great-great-grandchildren
3a (cont.) Carter R. Harrison *m* 2nd 1986 *Jean Fitts (*b* 1929), sister of his 1st w and widow of his 1st cousin Benjamin Harrison (*see below*)

Great-grandchildren
(5) Marguerita Harrison, *b* 9 Dec 1884; *m* 1st 4 June 1905 Simpson ROBINSON; *m* 2nd 1927 William F. SAEGER; *m* 3rd Henry COFFELT and *d* 19—
(6) Benjamin HARRISON, of Kansas City *b* 1892; *m* 1916 Julia Sandres (*b* 1896; *m* 2nd 1950 Harry E. DEVIN (for whom *see above*)) and *d* 1937, leaving issue:

Great-great-grandchildren
1a *Julia Margaretta Harrison, *b* 1920; *m* 1947 *David Heaton WILSON (*b* 1913) and has issue:

Great-great-grandchildren's children
1b *David Heaton WILSON, Jr, *b* 1948; *m* 19— *———
2b *Robert Scott WILSON, *b* 1952

Great-great-grandchildren
2a Benjamin HARRISON, Jr, *b* 1922; *m* 1947, as her 1st husb, *Jean Marie Fitts (*b* 1929), sister of Joan Cooper Fitts (for whom *see above*), and *d* 1968, leaving issue:

Great-great-grandchildren's children
1b *Patricia Ann Harrison, *b* 1947; *m* 1971 *Trevor MULRONEY (*b* 1950) and has issue:

Great-great-grandchildren's grandchildren
1c *Adam MULRONEY, *b* 1972
2c *Rebekka MULRONEY, *b* 1974
3c *David MULRONEY, *b* 1976
4c *Malcolm MULRONEY, *b* 1984

Great-great-grandchildren's children
2b *John Russell HARRISON, *b* 1950; *m* 1972 *Barbara Rush and has issue:

Great-great-grandchildren's grandchildren
1c *Christopher HARRISON, *b* 1972
2c *Benjamin HARRISON, *b* 1975
3c *Rebecca HARRISON, *b* 1979

Grandchildren
12 James Findlay HARRISON, *b* 1847; *d* 1848
13 James Irwin HARRISON, *b* 1849; *d* 1850
Mr and the 2nd Mrs (John) Scott Harrison also adopted 1848 their nephews Benjamin and William Henry (*see below* under 2nd and 3rd children of Dr Benjamin Harrison)

President William H. Harrison's son
VI Dr Benjamin HARRISON, *b* Vincennes, Ind., 5 May 1806; *m* 1st 18— Louisa Smith Bonner and had issue:

Grandchildren
1 John Cleves Short HARRISON, *b* Vincennes 7 May 1829; banker; *m* 1st 9 April 1851 Mary Frances Harris and had issue:

Great-grandchildren
(1) Dr Frank Hanson HARRISON, *b* 18—; *m* 18— or 19— Adella Elvira Young and had issue:

Great-great-grandchildren
1a *Ella HARRISON, *b* 18— or 19—
2a *Margaret HARRISON, *b* 18— or 19—

Great-grandchildren
(2) Benjamin HARRISON, of Indianapolis, *b* 18—; *m* 2 Oct 1883 Marion (*b* 8 Jan 1863), dau of Buwell Smith Goode, of Cincinnati, Ohio, and his w Hannah Inghram Rinehart, and *d* 18— or 19—
(3) George Washington HARRISON, *b* 18—; *m* 18— or 19— Julia Talbott and *d* 18— or 19—
(4) Julia Callus HARRISON, *b* 18—

Grandchildren
1 (cont.) John Cleves Short Harrison *m* 2nd Margaret Ruth McCarty and *d* Los Angeles April 1904, having with her had issue:

Great-grandchildren
(5) Nicholas McCarty HARRISON, *b* 18—; *m* 18— or 19— Nancy Elston and *d* 1920, leaving issue:

Great-great-grandchildren
1a Nicholas McCarty HARRISON, Jr, *b* 18— or 19—; *m* 19— *Virginia Seeley and *d* 1934, leaving issue:

Great-great-grandchildren's children
1b *Nicholas McCarty HARRISON III, *b* 1930

Great-great-grandchildren
2a Elston Mills HARRISON, *b* 1910; *d* 1942

Great-grandchildren
(6) Cleves HARRISON, *b* 18— or 19—

President William H. Harrison's son
VI (cont.) Dr Benjamin Harrison *m* 2nd Mary Raney, of Point Coupee, La., and *d* 9 June 1840, having with her had issue:

Grandchildren
2 Benjamin HARRISON, *b* 18—, adopted together with his yr bro 1848 by his unc and aunt Mr and the 2nd Mrs (John) Scott Harrison
3 William Henry HARRISON, *b* March 1839; *d* 7 Aug 1850

President William H. Harrison's daughter
VII Mary Symmes Harrison, *b* Ellettsville or Vincennes 22 or 28 Jan 1809; *m* 5 March 1829 Dr John Henry Fitzhugh THORNTON (*b* 8 June 1798; *d* 6 Dec 1871), s of Capt Charles Thornton and his w Sarah Fitzhugh and *d* 16 Nov 1842, having had issue:

Grandchildren
1 William Henry Harrison THORNTON, *b* 21 Feb 1830; *d* 10 July 1903
2 Dr Charles THORNTON, *b* 28 July 1832; *d* 22 June 1868
3 Anna Harrison Thornton, *b* 1835; *m* 23 April 1863 Lee Mason FITZHUGH (*b* nr Madison, Ind., 27 Nov 1838; *d* Los Angeles 12 March 1906), s of George Dulany Fitzhugh and his w Elizabeth Yellott Worthington, and *d* 17 Jan 1883, having had issue:

Great-grandchildren
(1) Thornton FITZHUGH, *b* 4 Dec 1864; *m* 1st 1888 Anna Harrison (*b* 1867; *d* 1908), dau of David W McClung and his w Anna Carter Harrison (*see below*), and had issue:

Great-great-grandchildren
1a James McClung FITZHUGH, *b* 1890; *m* 19— Gladys Rowley (*b* Downey, Calif., 29 May 1888; *d* Long Beach, Calif., 22 Oct 1975) and *d* 1930, leaving issue:

Great-great-grandchildren's children
1b James McClung FITZHUGH, Jr, *b* Los Angeles 12 Jan 1916; *m* 25 March 1944 *Virginia Glover (*b* Chicago, Ill., 26 Aug 1917) and *d* 23 Nov 1989, leaving issue:

Great-great-grandchildren's grandchildren
1c *Carol Lee Fitzhugh, *b* San Diego, Calif., 18 Nov 1945; *m* July 1982 *Carl BOGUCKI
2c *James McClung FITZHUGH III, *b* San Diego 25 April 1948; *m* 28 May 1977 *Sue Ann McNeil

Great-great-grandchildren's children
2b Jean Remick FITZHUGH, *b* Los Angeles 11 July 1917; *d* 24 May 1987
3b Quintin Rowley FITZHUGH, *b* Los Angeles 21 Oct 1923; *m* 19 Oct 1946 *Viola Mae ('Sue') French (*b* S Bridgeton, Maine, 2 Jan 1923) and *d* June 1990, leaving issue:

Great-great-grandchildren's grandchildren
1c *Susan French Fitzhugh, *b* Portland, Oreg., 9 Jan 1949; *m* 8 May 1976 *Timothy GALVIN and has issue:

Great-great-grandchildren's great-grandchildren
1d *Kathryn Jennings GALVIN, *b* Long Beach, Calif., 31 Jan 1980

Great-great-grandchildren's grandchildren
2c *Rachel Rowley Fitzhugh, *b* Long Beach 27 May 1954; *m* 26 July 1975 *Steven PROCTOR and has issue:

Great-great-grandchildren's great-grandchildren
1d Allison Meredith PROCTOR, *b* 24 April, *d* 27 April 1984
2d *Samuel Benjamin PROCTOR, *b* 6 May 1985
3d *Nathaniel Quintin PROCTOR, *b* 31 March 1987

Great-great-grandchildren's grandchildren
3c *Quintin Rowley FITZHUGH, Jr, *b* Long Beach 1 Jan 1958

Great-great-grandchildren
2a Lee Mason FITZHUGH III, *b* 17 Sept 1894; *m* 1 Aug 1921 Barbara Lillingston (*b* 3 May 1896; *d* 1 March 1984) and *d* 10 Jan 1954, leaving issue:

Great-great-grandchildren's children
1b *Laura Elizabeth Fitzhugh [Mrs Wayne Taggart, 23320 Los Encinos Way, Woodland Hills, CA 91367, USA], *b* Glendale, Calif., 18 July 1925; *educ* Van Nuys High Sch and UCLA; elementary teacher 1947-51 and 1970-93; *m* 14 Oct 1949 Wayne Albert TAGGART (*b* 26 Aug 1923; *d* 16 Dec 1989), s of James William Taggart and his w Edith Emily Johnson, and has issue:

Great-great-grandchildren's grandchildren
1c *James Lee TAGGART [320 Bellevue Ct, Los Altos, CA 94024, USA], *b* Van Nuys, Calif., 11 April 1952; *m* California 14 Sept 1974 *Pamela Anne Melton and has issue:

Great-great-grandchildren's great-grandchildren
1d *Eric James TAGGART, *b* 30 May 1981
2d *Kent Corson TAGGART, *b* 17 March 1986
3d *Anna Patricia TAGGART, *b* 27 Jan 1989

Great-great-grandchildren's grandchildren
2c *Thomas Albert TAGGART [6818 El Carmen, Long Beach, CA 90815, USA], *b* Fresno, Calif., 19 Aug 1953; *m* California 10 Oct 1987 *Jennifer Ann Matthias and has issue:

Great-great-grandchildren's great-grandchildren
1d *Lauren Elizabeth TAGGART, *b* 6 March 1988
2d *Matthew Thomas TAGGART, *b* 28 May 1990

Great-great-grandchildren's grandchildren
3c *Kenneth Robert TAGGART [318 Hawthorne, Los Altos, CA 94022, USA], *b* Fresno, Calif., 3 May 1955; *m* California 15 Oct 1983 *Cheryl Lee York (*b* 25 Feb 1954) and has issue:

Great-great-grandchildren's great-grandchildren
1d *Kenneth Ryan TAGGART, *b* 13 Feb 1984
2d *Tyler Wayne TAGGART, *b* 20 Feb 1987

Great-great-grandchildren's grandchildren
4c *Teri Elizabeth Taggart, *b* Northridge, Calif., 14 June 1960; *m* California 14 Oct 1989 *Glenn WOYTHALER
5c *Tracy Anne TAGGART, *b* Canoga Park, Calif., 5 May 1964

Great-great-grandchildren's children
2b *Anna Grace Fitzhugh, *b* Santa Monica, Calif., 26 Nov 1927; *m* 1947 *Thomas E. DUGAN (*b* Santa Monica 11 April 1926) and has had issue:

Great-great-grandchildren's grandchildren
1c *Jill Ann Dugan, *b* Pomona, Calif., 8 Nov 1949; *m* 1st Sept 1967 (divorce 1969) Scott BAKER and has issue:

Great-great-grandchildren's great-grandchildren
1d *Scott Thomas BAKER, *b* 29 March 1968
2d *Shannon Anne BAKER, *b* 1 Aug 1969

Great-great-grandchildren's grandchildren
1c (cont.) Mrs Jill Baker *m* 2nd 24 July 1971 *David CHESTNUT and has further issue:

Great-great-grandchildren's great-grandchildren
3d *Amy Diane CHESTNUT, *b* 29 Sept 1973
4d *Todd Wesley CHESTNUT, *b* 24 Oct 1975

Great-great-grandchildren's grandchildren
2c Kenton Thomas DUGAN, *b* 10 Dec 1951; *d* 8 July 1976

Great-great-grandchildren
3a Anna Thornton Fitzhugh, *b* North Hollywood 1903; *m* 1929 Alexander Cyril BELL (*b* Vancouver, BC, Canada 1889; *d* San Francisco 1959) and *d* 1957, leaving issue:

Great-great-grandchildren's children
1b *Alexander Peter BELL, *b* San Francisco 4 Oct 1930
2b *Robert Fitzhugh BELL, *b* San Francisco 7 July 1936; *m* Portola Valley, Calif., 1973 *Rose Ann Merker (*b* Quincy, Ill., 1943)

Great-grandchildren
(1) (cont.) Thornton Fitzhugh *m* 2nd Mabel Hawley Lum (*d* 1964) and *d* 1933, having with her had issue:

Great-great-grandchildren
4a William Thornton FITZHUGH, *b* 1924; *d* 1971

Great-grandchildren
(2) George Lee FITZHUGH, *b* 1866; *m* 1st 1891 Mary Phipps (*d* 1897); *m* 2nd Indianapolis 6 May 1897 Mary Timmons Hawkins (*b* Austin, Minn., 12 Nov 1873; *d* Los Angeles 30 May 1958) and *d* Coronado, Calif., 1902, having with her had issue:

Great-great-grandchildren
1a Margaret Prior FITZHUGH, *b* 18––; *d* in infancy
2a George Dulany FITZHUGH, *b* 16 Sept 1900; *m* 26 July 1924 Louise Whitaker (*b* Indianapolis 11 June 1900; *d* Los Angeles 17 April 1988) and *d* 16 Dec 1965, leaving issue:

Great-great-grandchildren's children
1b *Nancy Lee Fitzhugh [Ms Nancy Brown, 22 Duke Dve, Rancho Mirage, CA 92270, USA], *b* Los Angeles 28 Aug 1927; *educ* U of Oregon; *m* 27 Dec 1947 (divorce 19—) Mercer Groman BROWN (*d* 19—) and has an adopted dau:

a *Karen Louise Brown [Mrs Kinsey L Carpenter, 26901 Sand Canyon Rd, Santa Clarita, CA 91351, USA], *b* Los Angeles 26 Jan 1954; *m* there 26 April 1978 *Kinsey Leas CARPENTER and has issue:

i *Kinsey L. CARPENTER, Jr, *b* 1980
ii *Kary Louise CARPENTER, *b* 1982

Great-grandchildren
(3) Charles Harris FITZHUGH, *b* 1868; *d* 1869
(4) Anna Thornton FITZHUGH, *b* 1873; *d* 1957
(5) Lee Mason FITZHUGH, Jr, *b* Indianapolis 11 Oct 1876; *m* Phoenix, Ariz., 18 Feb 1912 Grace (*b* Ontario, Canada 18 Nov 1872; *d* Agawam, Mass., 25 May 1958), dau of Richard Fyfe and his w Agnes Crawford (both natives of Ediburgh, Scotland), and *d* Phoenix 12 Jan 1937, leaving issue:

Great-great-grandchildren
1a *Lt-Col Andrew Fyfe FITZHUGH [99 Arlington Road, Longmeadow, MA 01106, USA], *b* Phoenix 29 Dec 1912; *educ* Stanford (BA) and U of Arizona (MS); served US Army Ordnance 1940-46, Sr Research Specialist Monsanto Polymer Research 1946-77; *m* 1st 29 Dec 1945 Louise Marian (*b* New York City 8 Sept 1918; *d* Springfield, Mass., 14 Oct 1972), dau of Irving Charles Fox and his w Katherine Celia Young, and has had issue:

Great-great-grandchildren's children
1b Katherine Grace FITZHUGH, *b* Springfield 25 Dec 1946; *d* 7 April 1953
2b *Richard Henry Lee FITZHUGH, *b* Springfield 27 July 1948
3b *Mary Louise FITZHUGH, *b* Springfield 14 Feb 1950
4b *Charles Andrew FITZHUGH, *b* Springfield 11 Aug 1952; *m* 25 June 1983 *Maryann Cathleen Iwanicki (*b* 4 Feb 1954) and has issue:

Great-great-grandchildren's grandchildren
1c *Rebecca Ann FITZHUGH, *b* Pittsfield, Mass., 2 Sept 1989

Great-great-grandchildren's children
5b *William Henry Harrison FITZHUGH, *b* Springfield 14 Nov 1955

Great-great-grandchildren
1a (cont.) Lt-Col Andrew Fitzhugh *m* 2nd 30 Oct 1977, as her 2nd husb, *Betty Felicia Roberts (*b* Colorado Springs, Colorado, 29 May 1914), widow of —— Holley

Grandchildren
4 Alice Elizabeth Fitzhugh Thornton, *b* 1838; *m* 1863 John Calvin LEWIS (*b* 1836; *d* 1919), s of Joseph Lewis and his w Mary Wakefield, and *d* Chicago 28 April 1920, having had issue:

Great-grandchildren
(1) Thornton Lewis, for whom *see above*
(2) Joseph Dixon LEWIS, *b* 1867; *m* 1890 Sarah Melcher (*b* 1871) and *d* 1940, leaving issue:

Great-great-grandchildren
1a *Raymond LEWIS, *b* 1891

Great-grandchildren
(3) Charles Rea LEWIS, *b* 1874; *m* 1st 1899 Alice McCullough (*b* 1876; *d* 1902) and had issue:

Great-great-grandchildren
1a *Mary Wakefield LEWIS, *b* 1900

Great-grandchildren
(3) (cont.) Charles R. Lewis *m* 2nd 1905 Jane Wheaton (*b* 1874)
(4) Mary Wakefield Lewis, *b* 1876; *m* 1897 George Ely Van HAGEN (*b* 1873; Pres Standing Forging Corp, Chicago; *d* Miami Beach, Fla, 6 April 1946) and had issue:

Great-great-grandchildren
1a George Ely Van HAGEN, Jr, b 1898; m 19— *Ardetta Ford (b 1900) and d 1931, leaving issue:

Great-great-grandchildren's children
1b *George Ely Van HAGEN III, b 1922; m 1951 *Barbara Krancz (b 1932)
2b *Mary Claire Van Hagen, b 1924; m 19— *Rodney Goddard ALLER (b 1914) and has issue:

Great-great-grandchildren's grandchildren
1c *Catherine ALLER, b 1947
2c *Goddard ALLER, b 1949
3c *Constance ALLER, b 1951

Great-great-grandchildren's children
3b *Ford Lawrence Van HAGEN, b 1928; m 1952 *Jane Fulton (b 1932) and has issue:

Great-great-grandchildren's grandchildren
1c *Ford Lawrence Van HAGEN, Jr, b 1953
2c *Fulton Van HAGEN, b 1954

Great-great-grandchildren
2a *Elizabeth Van HAGEN, b 1905

Great-grandchildren
(5) Frank Edwin LEWIS, b 1880; m 1st 1904 Ethel Cornell (b 1883) and had issue:

Great-great-grandchildren
1a *Catherine LEWIS, b 1907

Great-grandchildren
(5) (cont.) Frank Edwin Lewis m 2nd Virginia Houston (b 1895; d 1942) and with her had issue:

Great-great-grandchildren
2a John Calvin LEWIS II, b 1921; d 1941

Great-grandchildren
(6) Harry LEWIS, b 1882; d in infancy

Grandchildren
5 Lucy Harris THORNTON, b 6 Feb, d Dec 1840
6 John Fitzhugh THORNTON, b 1842; m 18— Leila Morgan, dau of Daniel West and his w Martha Griffith Morgan, and had issue:

Great-grandchildren
(1) Charles West THORNTON, b 18—; d young

President Wiliiam H. Harrison's son
VIII Carter Bassett HARRISON, b Vincennes, Ind., 26 Oct 1811; attaché American Legation, Bogotá, Colombia, 1829; m 16 June 1836 Mary Anne Sutherland (b 1814; d 1893) and d 12 Aug 1839, leaving issue:

Grandchildren
1 Anna Carter Sutherland Harrison, b 1837; m 18 March 1862 David Weddle McCLUNG (b 18 Dec 1831; d after 1904) and had issue:

Great-grandchildren
(1) Anna Harrison McClung, b 1867; m 1888 her 2nd cousin Thornton FITZHUGH (b 1864; d 1933) and d 1908, leaving issue (for whom *see above*)

President William H. Harrison's daughter
IX Anna Tuthill Harrison, b North Bend, Ohio, 28 Oct 1813; m 16 June 1836 her 1st cousin once-removed William Henry Harrison TAYLOR (b 1813; Col of Cavalry Union Army Civil War, Postmaster Cincinnati, State Librarian Minnesota; d 1894), est s of Thomas Taylor and his w Lucy Harrison, dau of Capt Anthony Singleton and his w Lucy, sis of President WILLIAM H. HARRISON, and d 5 July 1865, having had issue:

Grandchildren
1 William Henry Harrison TAYLOR, Jr, b 1837; m 1st 18— Mary King and had issue:

Great-grandchildren
(1) William Rennick TAYLOR, b 18—
(2) Henry Serrill TAYLOR, b 18—
(3) Myra TAYLOR, b 18—

Grandchildren
1 (cont.) William Henry Harrison Taylor, Jr, m 2nd 18— or 19— Clara Jenkins and d 1906, having with her had issue:

Great-grandchildren
(4) Mattie Fullerton TAYLOR, *b* 18— or 19—; *m* 18— or 19— ——
(5) John Thomas TAYLOR II, *b* 18— or 19—; *d* 1906

Grandchildren
2 Lucy Singleton Taylor, *b* 1839; *m* 18— Harrison Scott HOWELL (*d* 1907) and *d* 1906, having had issue:

  Great-grandchildren
  (1) Harrison Taylor HOWELL, *b* 18—; *d* young
  (2) Jean Lyall HOWELL, *b* 18—; *d* young
  (3) Scott Singleton HOWELL, *b* 18—; *d* young
  (4) Bessie HOWELL, *b* 18—; *d* young
  (5) Cleves Harrison HOWELL, *b* 13 Aug 1880; *m* 18— or 19— Sara May Hill and had issue:

    Great-great-grandchildren
    1a *Cleves Harrison HOWELL, Jr, *b* 25 July 1911; *m* 19— *Edith Shallenberger and has issue:

      Great-great-grandchildren's children
      1b *Cleves Harrison HOWELL III

Grandchildren
3 Anna Harrison TAYLOR, *b* 7 April, *d* 7 Nov 1840
4 John Thomas TAYLOR, *b* 1841; *m* 1st 18— Agnes Kennedy and had issue:

  Great-grandchildren
  (1) Alice Kennedy TAYLOR, *b* 18—; *d* young
  (2) Anna Harrison TAYLOR, *b* 18—; *d* young

Grandchildren
4 (cont.) John T. Taylor *m* 2nd Amelia Martha Wilson and *d* 1906
5 Mary Thornton Taylor, *b* 1843; *m* 1870 George Albert PLUMMER (*d* 1914) and *d* 1905, leaving issue:

  Great-grandchildren
  (1) Virginia Berkeley Plummer, *b* 1872; *m* 1st 1893 Silas DECKER (*d* 1894); *m* 2nd 1900 William A. BADGER (*d* 1909) and *d* 1929, leaving issue:

    Great-great-grandchildren
    1a *Virginia Berkeley Badger, *b* 1903; *m* 1934 Corwin GIBSON (*b* 1890) and has issue:

      Great-great-grandchildren's children
      1b *Mary Virginia GIBSON, *b* 1935
      2b *Corwin Henry GIBSON, *b* 1941

  Great-grandchildren
  (2) Scott Howell PLUMMER, *b* 1874; *m* 1904 Lucy Towler (*b* 1878) and *d* 1927, leaving issue:

    Great-great-grandchildren
    1a *William Howell PLUMMER, *b* 1905; *m* 1931 *Margaret Gale Merrick and has issue:

      Great-great-grandchildren's children
      1b *William Howell PLUMMER, Jr, *b* 1932
      2b *Joanne PLUMMER, *b* 1935

    Great-great-grandchildren
    2a *Robert Kinsman PLUMMER, *b* 1910

  Great-grandchildren
  (3) Harriet Putnam Plummer, *b* 1878; *m* 1902 Arthur L. HELLIWELL, of Chelan, Washington, DC (*b* 1870; *d* 1941), and *d* 1946, leaving issue:

    Great-great-grandchildren
    1a *Revd George Albert Plummer HELLIWELL, *b* 1903; *m* 19— *Eleanor McAfree and has issue:

      Great-great-grandchildren's children
      1b *Thomas HELLIWELL, *b* 1936
      2b *Sally Sue HELLIWELL, *b* 1936

    Great-great-grandchildren
    2a *Elizabeth Helliwell, *b* 1906; *m* 1934 *George SYLLING (*b* 1904) and has issue:

      Great-great-grandchildren's children
      1b *Patricia SYLLING, *b* 1936
      2b *David SYLLING, *b* 1942

  Great-grandchildren
  (4) Bess Taylor PLUMMER, *b* 1881

Grandchildren

6 Anna Cleves Taylor, *b* 1844; *m* Keokuk, Iowa, 1873 George Henry COMSTOCK (*b* Lee, Mass., 1838; *d* Minneapolis 1903), s of William H. Comstock and his w Phebe Bassett Spellman, and *d* Minneapolis 1937, leaving issue:

Great-grandchildren

(1) Anna Harrison Comstock, *b* Keokuk 3 June 1874; *m* St Paul, Minn., 15 Oct 1895 Charles MANN (*b* New Albany, New York, 9 July 1870; *d* Minneapolis 1952), s of Walter Mann and his w Elizabeth Butler, and *d* Minneapolis 25 June 1946, having had issue:

Great-great-grandchildren

1a Charles Edward MANN, Jr, *b* St Paul, Minn., 15 Feb 1898; *d* there 2 Feb 1902

2a Stewart Harrison MANN, *b* St Paul 26 Dec 1903; *educ* Macalester Coll, St Paul, Minn., and Parsons Coll, Iowa; radio and television script writer and sports writer; *m* 1st Minneapolis 27 July 1934 (divorce 19—) Alice M., dau of Marcus Gilbertson and his w Mattie; *m* 2nd Minneapolis 12 Sept 1947 (divorce 1951) Vivian Leona (*b* Truman, Minn., 16 May 1918), dau of Hans Albert Hansen and his w Anna Marie Nielsen, and with her had issue:

Great-great-grandchildren's children

1b *Gina Laurin Catherine Mann [Mrs Raymond L Salisbury, 3104 Edgewood Av S, St Louis Pk, MN 55426-3423, USA], *b* Minneapolis 11 Feb 1949; *educ* U of Minnesota (BSc 1971); *m* Minneapolis 17 July 1971 *Raymond Lea SALISBURY (*b* Buffalo, New York, 28 June 1949), s of Donald Leroy Salisbury and his w Joan Edna Barber, and has issue:

Great-great-grandchildren's grandchildren

1c *Emily Anna-Marie SALISBURY, *b* Boone, Iowa, 7 Feb 1973

2c *Nicholas Michael Mann SALISBURY, *b* Minneapolis 3 Dec 1975

3c *Anna-Marie Alexandra Harrison SALISBURY, *b* Minneapolis 16 Sept 1981

Great-great-grandchildren

2a (cont.) Stewart H. Mann *m* 3rd Minneapolis 1 Oct 1956 *Mrs Delores Lola Dutton, author (as Dee Mann): *Minnesota Outdoors Vacation and Travel Guides*, Pres Prestige Publication Series Inc, dau of Frederick Dutton and his w Ruth M. Briggs, and *d* 19 Feb 1981, having adopted her two children:

a *Marcia Ruth Stanley Mann [Mrs Evan Robbins, Jr, Los Gatos, CA, USA], *b* St Paul 24 Oct 1940; *m* 19— *Evan Spencer ROBBINS, Jr, s of Evan Spencer Robbins, of Omaha, Nebr., and has issue:

i *Evan Spencer ROBBINS III, *b* 19—

ii *Dike Baker ROBBINS, *b* 19—

iii *Dee Malia ROBBINS, *b* 19—

b *Marshall Bruce MANN [Providence, Rhode Island, USA], *b* Chicago 18 Jan 1947; *m* 1st 19— (divorce 19—) Susan Eileen Grimley, of Massachusetts, and has issue:

i *Christopher Noel MANN, *b* 19—

b (cont.) Marshall B. MANN *m* 2nd 1972 *Doreen Giles, of Cranston, Rhode Island, and with her has issue:

ii *—— MANN, *b* May 1975

Great-great-grandchildren

3a George Comstock MANN, *b* St Paul, Minn., 30 Aug 1906; owner of women's shoe store; *m* Bartlesville, Okla., 8 Aug 1929 *Erma Edna (*b* Gans, Okla., 17 Nov 1910), dau of Sidney Jackson Toney and his w Lula Waco Reed, and *d* Oceanside, Calif., 2 Aug 1983, leaving issue:

Great-great-grandchildren's children

1b *Erma Dean Mann [Mrs Dale Yeager, 6440 S Dorsey Lane, Tempe, AZ 85283, USA], *b* Minneapolis 22 Oct 1934; *m* Chandler, Ariz., 1 July 1952 *Dale Albert YEAGER (*b* Coolidge, Ariz., 14 April 1932), s of David Anderson Yeager and his w Hattie Ellen Brock, and has issue:

Great-great-grandchildren's grandchildren

1c *Dana Allen YEAGER, *b* Phoenix, Ariz., 4 Jan 1956; *m* Tempe 8 Feb 1980 *Betty Jane (*b* Edmonton, Alberta, Canada, 8 May 1960), dau of Ralph Jon Hobe and his w Corrie Verhoog, and has issue:

Great-great-grandchildren's great-grandchildren

1d *Dale Albert YEAGER, *b* Mesa, Ariz., 18 April 1981

2d *Elyse Emily YEAGER, *b* Mesa 28 July 1984

Great-great-grandchildren's grandchildren

2c *Karen Ann Yeager [Mrs Ealick, 3026 East Brookwood Court, Phoenix, AZ 85044, USA], *b* Mesa 27 Oct 1959; *m* Tempe 11 Feb 1984 *Troy Raymond EALICK (*b* Phoenix 23 May 1960), s of Lloyd Raymond Ealick and his w Judith Elaine Wasley, and has issue:

Great-great-grandchildren's great-grandchildren
1d *Adam Christopher EALICK, *b* Mesa 10 Nov 1985
2d *Brandon Alexander EALICK, *b* Mesa 29 June 1988

Great-great-grandchildren's children
2b *Charles Eugene MANN, *b* Shreveport, La., 18 Aug 1939; *m* 1st Mesa 15 Sept 1958 (divorce 1973) Mary Diann (*b* Phoenix 18 Aug 1939), dau of Gerald Stapley and his w Mary Elizabeth Pitts, and has issue:

Great-great-grandchildren's grandchildren
1c *Carrie Diann Mann, *b* Mesa 19 Jan 1960; *m* 1st Palos Verdes, Calif., 6 Jan 1979 (divorce 1989) Donald James SCHECTER (*b* Ohio 1 July 1943), s of Albert J. Schecter and his w Lucille, and has issue:

Great-great-grandchildren's great-grandchildren
1d *Casie Diann SCHECTER, *b* Torrance, Calif., 12 Feb 1981
2d *Ryan James SCHECTER, *b* Torrance 4 Aug 1982

Great-great-grandchildren's grandchildren
1c (cont.) Mrs Carrie Schecter *m* 2nd Phoenix 11 Sept 1992 *Mark Sigler HOMAN (*b* Phoenix 15 Feb 1962), s of James Howard Homan and his w Mildred Adele Sigler, and has issue:

Great-great-grandchildren's great-grandchildren
3d *Michael James HOMAN, *b* Chandler, Ariz., 24 Feb 1993

Great-great-grandchildren's grandchildren
2c *Kelli Charleen MANN, *b* Phoenix 20 Nov 1963; has issue:

Great-great-grandchildren's great-grandchildren
1d *Jacob Charles MANN, *b* Chandler 24 Sept 1992

Great-great-grandchildren's children
2b (cont.) Charles E. Mann *m* 2nd Ottawa, Kans., 9 April 1988 *Phyllis Maxine (*b* Chanute, Kans., 22 June 1952), dau of Leon Adair Spence and his w Fern Eunice Goff

Great-great-grandchildren
4a *Anna Elizabeth (Betty) Mann [Mrs Richard Stein, 5004 Chicago Avenue, Minneapolis, MN 55417, USA; 7717 Chicago Avenue, S Richfield, MN, USA], *b* Minneapolis 23 Nov 1910; *m* there 10 Aug 1940 *Richard Warren STEIN (*b* Cass Lake, Minn., 1904), s of George Stein and his w Minnie McMullen

Great-grandchildren
(2) Lucy Bassett Comstock, *b* 18—; *m* 18— or 19— George McKAY and *d* 18— or 19—

Grandchildren
7 Bessie Short Taylor, *b* 1846; *m* 18— or 19— John OGDEN and *d* 1940
8 Fanny Gault Taylor, *b* 1848; *m* 1876 Charles Fitch HENDRYX (*b* 1847; *d* 1935) and *d* 1932, leaving issue:

Great-grandchildren
(1) James Beardsley HENDRYX, *b* Sank Center, Minn., 9 Dec 1880; *m* 1915 Hermione Flagler (*b* Boston, Mass., 24 Oct 1888; *d* Traverse City, Mich., 17 Feb 1967) and *d* Traverse City 1 March 1963, leaving issue:

Great-great-grandchildren
1a *Hermione Flagler Hendryx [Mrs Fred Swartz Jr, 1137 Balfour Road, Grosse Point, MI 48230, USA], *b* Cincinnati 17 Jan 1918; *m* Traverse City 2 Sept 1942 *Dr Fred George SWARTZ, Jr (*b* Boulder, Colo., 8 July 1916), s of Dr George Swartz and his w Edith Morgan, and has issue:

Great-great-grandchildren's children
1b *Fred George SWARTZ III [1260 Astor, Ann Arbor, MI 48104, USA; 515 W Hoover, Ann Arbor, MI, USA], *b* Corvallis, Oreg., 10 Aug 1943; *m* 19— (divorce 19—) Christine Ann Wendt (*b* Benton Harbor, Mich., 14 Feb 1945)
2b *Mary Ann SWARTZ [2030 Spruce Street, Philadelphia, PA 19103, USA], *b* Ann Arbor 5 June 1946
3b *Edit Myra SWARTZ, *b* Grosse Point, Mich., 10 Sept 1952

Great-great-grandchildren
2a James Beardsley HENDRYX, Jr, *b* Cincinnati 30 Aug 1919; *m* 19— *Hilda ('Terri') Lang (*b* New York 16 Feb 1918) and *d* 3 July 1992, leaving issue:

Great-great-grandchildren's children
1b *Patricia Hendryx [Mrs John Kennedy, Amackassin Road, Blairstown, NJ 07825, USA], *b* Brooklyn, New York, 28 Aug 1945; *educ* Michigan State U; Pres Cornet Inc 1986-; *m* 26 June 1971 *John Bernard KENNEDY (*b* Mayfield, Pa., 26 Nov 1940), s of Bernard Kennedy and his w Esther, and has issue:

Great-great-grandchildren's grandchildren
1c *Sean Hendryx KENNEDY, *b* Englewood, New Jersey, 1 Sept 1972
2c *Kevin Bernard KENNEDY, *b* Hackettstown, New Jersey, 28 Sept 1979

Great-great-grandchildren's children
2b *Susan Harrison Hendryx [Mrs Sabry Joseph, 305 E 72nd Street, New York, NY, USA], b Brooklyn, New York, 17 March 1948; m 19— *Sabry JOSEPH (b Palestine 19—)

Great-great-grandchildren
3a *Betty Harrison Hendryx [Mrs Robert Loomis, Route 2, Box 345, Lee Point Road, Sutton's Bay, MI 49682, USA], b Cincinnati 4 May 1921; m Annapolis, Md., 9 June 1943 *Capt Robert James LOOMIS, USN (ret) (b Big Rapids, Mich., 30 March 1921) and has issue:

Great-great-grandchildren's children
1b *Robert James LOOMIS, Jr [42 Dogwood Lake Drive, Texarkana, TX 75503, USA], b Portland, Maine, 23 Aug 1946; m Detroit, Mich., 29 Nov 1969 *Elaine Marie Babiarz (b Dearborn 15 July 1950) and has issue:

Great-great-grandchildren's grandchildren
1c *Kristina Elaine LOOMIS, b Newton, New Jersey, 26 Sept 1976
2c *Robert James LOOMIS III, b Newton 28 Dec 1978

Great-great-grandchildren's children
2b *Stephen Hendryx LOOMIS [103 Sandlewood Drive, Madison, MS 39110, USA], b Norfolk, Va., 23 Feb 1949; m 1st Arlington, Va., 22 Jan 1972 (divorce 19—) Ruth Staley; m 2nd 19— *Janet Schabacker (b Houston, Tex., 4 Jan 1949) and with her has issue:

Great-great-grandchildren's grandchildren
1c *Jennifer Lee LOOMIS, b Cleveland 10 Oct 1977

Great-great-grandchildren's children
3b *Barbara Anne Loomis [Mrs James Altis, 2764 Williamswood Road, Richmond, VA, USA; 13450 Torrington Drive, Midlothian, VA, USA], b Bethesda, Md., 19 Sept 1950; m Fairfax, Va., 4 Dec 1971 *James Michael ALTIS (b Roanoke, Va., 6 Nov 1948) and has issue:

Great-great-grandchildren's grandchildren
1c *Kelley Anne ALTIS, b Richmond 3 Dec 1974

Great-great-grandchildren's children
4b *Betty Jo Loomis [Mrs Reginald Early Jr, 324 Albany Street, Fredericksburg, VA 22401, USA], b Bethesda, Md., 19 Sept 1950 (twin); m Fairfax 2 Oct 1971 *Reginald Saunders EARLY, Jr (b Norfolk, Va., 11 Aug 1950), and has issue:

Great-great-grandchildren's grandchildren
1c *Ryan Saunders EARLY, b Alexandria, Va., 21 March 1972
2c *Carrie Tae EARLY, b Alexandria 25 Feb 1973
3c *Travis James EARLY, b Alexandria 27 March 1977
4c *Tracey Elizabeth EARLY, b Alexandria 2 June 1979

Great-great-grandchildren's children
5b *Timothy Glenn LOOMIS [5270 Victoria Lane, Apartment 104, North Olmstead, OH 44070, USA; 1192 Commonwealth Av, Cleveland, OH, USA], b Traverse City 19 Oct 1954; m 19— *Cheryl Holland (b Alexandria 22 July 1956) and has issue:

Great-great-grandchildren's grandchildren
1c *Kyle Beardsley LOOMIS, b Elyria, Ohio, 6 April 1980

Great-great-grandchildren's children
6b *Cynthia Sue LOOMIS, b Newport, Rhode Island, 19 Feb 1958

Great-grandchildren
(2) Anna Harrison Hendryx, b 1883; m 1st 1914 William Sinclair BACOT (b 1860; d 1917); m 2nd 1919 Revd Frederick Lincoln FLINCHBAUGH (b 1874) and d 1930, leaving issue:

Great-great-grandchildren
1a *Anne Harrison Flinchbaugh, b 19—; m 19— *Job TAYLOR

Great-grandchildren
(3) Myra Bingham Hendryx, b 1885; m 1912 John C. OAKES and d 1947

Grandchildren
9 Virginia Berkeley Taylor, b 1851; m 18— or 19— Frank W. STRATTON and d 1928
10 Jane Harrison Taylor, b 1852; m 1875 Edward Jason DAVENPORT (b 1852; d 1930) and d 1939, having had issue:

Great-grandchildren
(1) Lee Butler DAVENPORT, b 1876; m 1904 Evita Clara Rait and had issue:

Great-great-grandchildren
1a *Donald Murray DAVENPORT, b 1910; m 1933 *Helga Clarkson Andenberg and has issue:

Great-great-grandchildren's children
1b *Donald McKinnon DAVENPORT, *b* 1940
2b *Anne Melissa DAVENPORT, *b* 1943
3b *Bret Carstairs DAVENPORT, *b* 1947

Great-great-grandchildren
2a *Lee Butler DAVENPORT, Jr, *b* 1915

Great-grandchildren
(2) Cleves Harrison DAVENPORT, *b* and *d* 1881
(3) Murray Taylor DAVENPORT, *b* 1882; Capt US Army; *m* 1920 Ethel Margaret (*b* 1898; *d* 1952), widow of —— Wilson and dau of —— Douglas, and *d* 19—

Grandchildren
11 Nellie Bassett TAYLOR, *b* 1853; *d* 5 Jan 1864
12 Edward Everett TAYLOR, *b* 1856; *m* 1st 18— or 19— Belle Bradley; *m* 2nd 18— or 19— Mrs Harriet Chapman

President William H. Harrison's son
X James Findlay HARRISON, *b* North Bend, Ohio 15 May 1814; *d* 6 April 1819

MALE LINE ANCESTRY AND COLLATERAL DESCENDANTS

Thomas Harrison, of Gobion's Manor, Northamptonshire, England, *m c* 1581, as her 1st husb, Elizabeth Bernard (she *m* 2nd Henry Travel, of Coventry, Warwickshire, England), aunt of Richard Bernard and William Bernard, first cousins who emigrated to Virginia, and either great-great-aunt or great-great-great-aunt of Sir Francis Bernard, 1st Bart (*c* 1712-79), Govr of New Jersey and Massachusetts in the Colonial Period. Sir Francis's firmness in the latter post is said to have won him his baronetcy, although it contributed to the very considerable ill-feeling among Americans which precipitated the Revolution. Thomas (who *d* before 1616) and Elizabeth Harrison may have been parents of:

Benjamin HARRISON, possibly *bapt* St Giles, Northants, Dec 1594; had emigrated to Virginia by 15 March 1633/4, when he was Clerk of the Virginia Council, acquired grants of land on the James River and resided at a plantation called Wakefield, in Surry Co, Memb Virginia House of Burgesses 1642; *m* Mary —— (who *m* 2nd Benjamin Sidway and *d* between 1 March 1687/8 and 29 May 1688, leaving further issue), and *d* probably Wakefield, Surry Co, Va., or Jamestown between 1643 and 1649, leaving (with a yr s, who is thought to have had no issue):

Benjamin HARRISON, Jr, *b* Southwark, Surry Co, 20 Sept 1645; Justice of Surry Co 1671, Sheriff 1679, Memb Virginia House of Burgesses for Surry Co 1680, 1682, 1692, 1696 and 1698, Memb Cncl 1698-1713, one of original govrs William and Mary Coll; *m* Hannah —— (*b* 13 Feb 1651/2; *d* Surry Co 16 Feb 1698/9) and *d* Wakefield 30 Jan 1712/3 (*bur* Cabin Point), having had issue (with another dau):

I Sarah Harrison; *m* June 1687 Revd James BLAIR, of Henrico Parish, a fndr William and Mary Coll, apptd Commissary (officer representing the bishop and executing his functions in a large diocese) by Bishop of London
II Benjamin HARRISON III, for whom *see below*
III Nathaniel HARRISON; was bequeathed plantation of Martin's Brandon, Prince George Co, Va., and was ancestor of the Harrisons of Brandon
IV Hannah Harrison, *b c* 1678; *m* 11 Nov 1697 Philip LUDWELL, of Greenspring (an estate which had originally belonged to Sir William Berkeley, Govr of Virginia 1641-*c* 1651 and *c* 1660-77, and which passed to the Ludwells by the marriage of the widowed Lady Berkeley with Philip Ludwell I), Memb Virginia Cncl, and had (with other issue):

1 Hannah Ludwell, *b* Rich Neck, nr Jamestown, Va., 5 Dec 1701; *m* between 23 and 30 May 1722 Thomas LEE (1690-1750), fourth s of Richard Lee and his w Laetitia Corbin, and was ancestor of the Lees of Stratford; Thomas and Hannah Lee's ggs was the Confederate commander Robert E. Lee

V Henry HARRISON, resided at Wakefield, Memb Virginia Cncl

The est s,
Benjamin HARRISON III, *b c* 1673; *educ* in England; first of his family to reside at Berkeley, Charles City Co, Va. (one of the oldest plantations in Virginia, although the mansion does not seem to have been built till 1706), lawyer, Clerk of William and Mary Coll, Clerk Charles City 1702, Memb Virginia House of Burgesses 1704 and 1705 (when Speaker), sometime Atty-Gen Virginia, Treasurer of Virginia 1705-10; *m* Elizabeth (*b c* 1678; *d* probably Berkeley 30 Dec 1734), 2nd dau of Col Lewis Burwell, Jr (*c* 1647-1710), of Carter's Creek, Gloucester Co, and King's Creek, York Co, Va., Memb of the Cncl, and his 1st w Abigail Smith (1656-92), and *d* Berkeley 10 April 1710 (*bur* Westover Churchyard), leaving issue (with a dau, Elizabeth):

Colonel Benjamin HARRISON IV, of Berkeley, *b c* 1695; *educ* William and Mary Coll; Memb Virginia House of Burgesses for Charles City Co 1736, 1738, 1740, 1742 and 1744, Maj Charles City Co Militia, sometime Sheriff; *m c* 1722 Anne (*b* probably Corotoman, Lancaster Co, Va., *c* 1702; *d* probably Berkeley between 17 Oct 1743 and Aug 1945), dau of Col Robert ('King') Carter, of Corotoman, Pres of the Cncl, and his w Elizabeth Landon (according to Gary B. Roberts, *Ancestors of American Presidents*, 1989) or Judith Armistead (*b* before 1666; *d* 1699) (according to Stella P. Hardy, *Colonial Families of the Southern States of America*, 1968, according to which daughter Anne would have been *b* 1696 not *c* 1702), and was *k* (with his 2 yst daus Lucy and Hannah) 12 July 1745 when his house was struck by lightning, having had issue (not necessarily in the order given apart from the first two):

I A son; *d* young

II Benjamin HARRISON V, for whom *see below*

III Carter Henry HARRISON; resided at Clifton, Cumberland Co, Va., Memb: Cumberland Co Ctee of Safety 1774-76 and Virginia House of Delegates from 1784; *m* Susanna, dau of Isham Randolph, of Dungeness, Goochland Co, Va., and sister of President JEFFERSON's mother Jane

IV Henry HARRISON, resided at Hunting Quarters, Sussex Co, Va.; *d* 28 July 1772

V Robert HARRISON; had issue:

  1 Collier HARRISON, of Kittewan, Charles City Co 2 Braxton HARRISON, of Farmer's Rest

VI Nathaniel HARRISON; Memb Virginia Senate and Sheriff Prince George Co 1779-80

VII Charles HARRISON; Col of Artillery Continental Army; *m* Mary Herbert, dau of Col Augustine Claiborne, of Sussex Co

VIII Elizabeth (Betty) Harrison; *m* Peyton RANDOLPH, Pres 1st Continental Congress

IX Anne Harrison; *m* William RANDOLPH, of Wilton

The est surviving s,

  Benjamin HARRISON V, *b* Berkeley *c* April 1726; *educ* William and Mary Coll; Memb Virginia House of Burgesses for Charles City Co 1749-75, memb ctee draughting petition to King GEORGE III protesting against the Stamp Act 1765, represented Charles City Co in Revolutionary Conventions 1775, a 'Signer' of Declaration of Independence, Delegate 1st and 2nd Continetal Congresses 1774-June 1776 and Oct 1776-78 (Pres Bd of War, Chm Ctee on Resolution for Independence of American Colonies 1776, Memb Ctees on Foreign Correspondence, also Treaties), Memb Virginia House of Delegates for Charles City Co 1776-81 (Speaker 1778-81), Govr Virginia 1781-84, Memb Virginia Convention 1788 (where he opposed ratification of the Fedl Constitution); *m c* 1748 his 2nd cousin Elizabeth (*b* Eltham, New Kent Co, Va., 13 Dec 1730; *d* Berkeley *c* 1792), dau of Col William Bassett IV (1709-*a* 1752) and his w Elizabeth Churchill, and *d* Berkeley 24 April 1791, leaving issue:

I Elizabeth Harrison, *b* 1751; *m* 1st Dr William RICKMAN, Dir-Gen Continental Hosp at Richmond, Va., during Revolution; *m* 2nd —— EDMONDSON

II Anne Harrison, *b* Berkeley 21 May 1753; *m* there 9 March 1775, as his 2nd w, David COUPLAND, of Springfield, Buckingham Co, Va., Justice Cumberland Co (*b* Nansemond Co, Va., 3 Aug 1749; *d* 1821), 2nd s of William Coupland and his w Alice Apsley O'Sheals, and *d* 1821, having had four s and six daus

III Benjamin HARRISON VI, of Berkeley, *b* 1755; Richmond merchant, Deputy Paymaster-Gen of Virginia for Continental Army in Revolutionary War; *m* 1st 1785 Anna (*b* 9 Sept 1760; *d* 28 Aug 1787), dau of Judge James Mercer, of the Virginia Court of Appeals, and had one s (whose descendants are still living); *m* 2nd before 16 Nov 1787 Susan, dau of Richard Randolph, Jr, of Curles Neck, and *d* 1799

IV Lucy Harrison, *b* 17—; *m* 1st Maj Peyton RANDOLPH, of Wilton, Henrico County, Va., ADC to Marquis de Lafayette, and had three s and one dau; *m* 2nd on or shortly after 8 Oct 1788 Anthony SINGLETON, of Williamsburg and Richmond, Capt Artillery in Revolutionary War (*d* 1795), and *d* 1809, having had (together with a further two s) a yr dau:

President William H Harrison's niece

  1 Lucy Harrison Singleton, *b* 1789; *m* Thomas TAYLOR (1767-1832) and had (with other issue):

  Great-nephew

  (1) William Henry Harrison Taylor, *m* his 1st cousin once removed Anna Tuthill, yst dau of President WILLIAM H. HARRISON

V Carter Bassett HARRISON, *b* 17—; *educ* William and Mary Coll; Memb Virginia House of Delegates from Surry Co 1784-85 and 1785-86 and from Prince George Co 1805-06, 1806-07 and 1807-08, Memb Congress 1793-99; *m* 1st Mary Howell, dau of William Allen, of Claremont, Surry Co, and had two s and one dau; *m* 2nd Jane Byrd

VI Sarah Harrison, *b* 1770; *m* John MINGE, of Weyanoke, Charles City Co, and *d* 1812, leaving seven s and two daus

VII WILLIAM HENRY HARRISON, 9th PRESIDENT of the UNITED STATES of AMERICA

?Thomas Harrison
d a 1616
?Elizabeth Bernard

Benjamin Harrison
c 1594—1643-49
Mary —
d 1687/8

William Bassett
d 1646
Anne —
fl c 1671

John Cary
c 1583-1661
Alice Hobson

Miles Cary
c 1622-67

Thomas Taylor
fl 1626-43
— —

Anne Taylor

Edward Burwell
c 1579-1626 same as (a)
Dorothy Bedell
d p 1635/6 same as (b)
Robert Higginson
d 1649 same as (c)
Joanna Tokesy
same as (d)

Lewis Burwell
c 1621-53 same as (g)
Lucy Higginson
c 1626-75 same as (h)

Edward Burwell
(a)
Dorothy Bedell
(b)
Robert Higginson
(c)
Joanna Tokesy
(d)

Lewis Burwell
(g)
Lucy Higginson
(h)

Anthony Smith
d c 1662-67 same as (i)
Martha Bacon
same as (j)

Anthony Smith
(i)
Martha Bacon
(j)

Revd James Bacon
b 1649 same as (e)
Martha Woodward
same as (f)
?Thomas Carter
b c 1528
— —

?John Carter
c 1574-1630
?Bridget Benion
d a 1630

Revd James Bacon
(e)
Martha Woodward
(f)
Richard Churchill
1524-92
— —

Henry Churchill
1565-1628
Bridget —
1565-1625

Thomas Ludlow
c 1555-*c* 1607
Jane Pyle/Pile
d p 1607

Gabriel Ludlow
c 1587—1639-46
Phyllis —
d 1657

John Landon?

— —

Sylvanus Landon
d 1681
Anne —

Anthony Armistead
b c 1587
Frances Thompson

William Armistead
c 1610-*a* 1666
Ann Ellis

WILLIAM H. HARRISON
FAMILY TREE

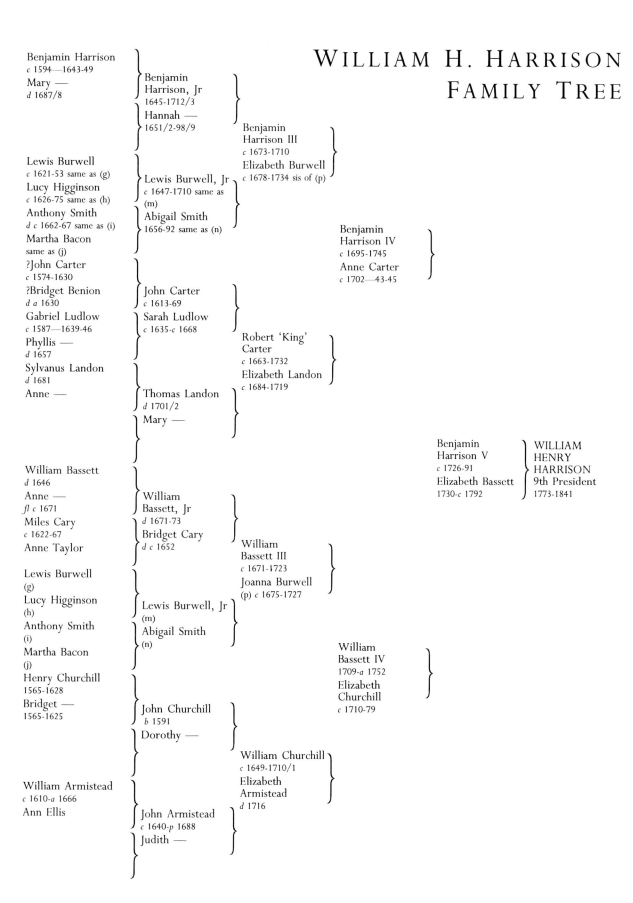

Benjamin Harrison
c 1594—1643-49
Mary —
d 1687/8

Benjamin
Harrison, Jr
1645-1712/3
Hannah —
1651/2-98/9

Benjamin
Harrison III
c 1673-1710
Elizabeth Burwell
1678-1734 sis of (p)

Lewis Burwell
c 1621-53 same as (g)
Lucy Higginson
c 1626-75 same as (h)
Anthony Smith
d c 1662-67 same as (i)
Martha Bacon
same as (j)

Lewis Burwell, Jr
c 1647-1710 same as
(m)
Abigail Smith
1656-92 same as (n)

Benjamin
Harrison IV
c 1695-1745
Anne Carter
c 1702—43-45

?John Carter
c 1574-1630
?Bridget Benion
d a 1630
Gabriel Ludlow
c 1587—1639-46
Phyllis —
d 1657

John Carter
c 1613-69
Sarah Ludlow
c 1635-c 1668

Sylvanus Landon
d 1681
Anne —

Robert 'King'
Carter
c 1663-1732
Elizabeth Landon
c 1684-1719

Thomas Landon
d 1701/2
Mary —

Benjamin
Harrison V
c 1726-91
Elizabeth Bassett
1730-c 1792

WILLIAM
HENRY
HARRISON
9th President
1773-1841

William Bassett
d 1646
Anne —
fl c 1671
Miles Cary
c 1622-67
Anne Taylor

William
Bassett, Jr
d 1671-73
Bridget Cary
d c 1652

William
Bassett III
c 1671-1723
Joanna Burwell
(p) c 1675-1727

Lewis Burwell
(g)
Lucy Higginson
(h)
Anthony Smith
(i)
Martha Bacon
(j)

Lewis Burwell, Jr
(m)
Abigail Smith
(n)

William
Bassett IV
1709-a 1752
Elizabeth
Churchill
c 1710-79

Henry Churchill
1565-1628
Bridget —
1565-1625

John Churchill
b 1591
Dorothy —

William Churchill
c 1649-1710/1
Elizabeth
Armistead
d 1716

William Armistead
c 1610-a 1666
Ann Ellis

John Armistead
c 1640-p 1688
Judith —

Plate 29   John Tyler

JOHN TYLER

1790-1862
10TH PRESIDENT OF THE UNITED STATES OF AMERICA
1841-45

Tyler, as it happened, was born not merely in the same state (Virginia) but in the same county (Charles City) as Harrison. Unlike his predecessor he had stayed at home, doing his best to carry into a later age the gentlemanly politics of his childhood. He failed. The times defeated him. In spite of his best efforts he came to resemble John C. Calhoun, or even Jefferson Davis, much more than Washington, Jefferson or Madison.

He had been put on the Whig ticket as a Southern balance for the Northern and Western Harrison. Nobody cared, at the time, that he was a thorough anomaly in the Whig party, and had only joined it because he greatly disliked Andrew Jackson. He had been Governor of his state and US Senator, he was amiable, able, dignified (unlike the Democratic Vice-President, the very undignified Richard Johnson); he would do. Then suddenly he was President.

Or was he? The point had never been settled; did a Vice-President inherit the office or merely its powers? Tyler behaved as if there was no problem and his precedent has been followed ever since; when a President dies in office the Vice-President succeeds him in the fullest sense.

The point dealt with, Tyler could turn to the business of governing. Clay, he found, had seized back the leadership of the Whigs, and not only meant to be the party nominee in 1844, but meanwhile to dictate the President's policies. Tyler moved quickly to disillusion him. He remained a strict Jeffersonian and had no sympathy for Clay's belief in a strong national government. When the two men were unable to reach agreement on such things as a law setting up yet another national bank (Van Buren's independent treasury was immediately abolished) and Clay started pushing bills through Congress and sending them up to the White House, Tyler took to the veto. Clay in turn tried to terrify the President into docility by ordering the members of the Cabinet to resign. They all did, with one exception. That exception was Daniel Webster, who had no wish to clear a path for Clay and anyway thought the whole quarrel unnecessary. He stayed in office, to Tyler's deep gratification, and negotiated the Webster-Ashburton Treaty with Britain, which settled the boundary between Maine and Canada and gave the administration its first great success.

Tyler was something of a success all round. He was a capable administrator, courteous, kindly and humorous, whom men liked to work for. He had clear policies and knew how to impose them. The trouble was they were clearly not Whig policies, as was shown by his repeated vetoes of what he thought, as a Southerner, were unduly high tariff bills. Even Webster eventually resigned; his successor was John C. Calhoun.

From that moment on it was clear that Tyler, though a decently patriotic American, was a Southerner before anything else. He had broken the Whig party for the sake of his Southern principles; now he pressed on toward the annexation of Texas.

There were good nationalistic reasons for this, to be sure, but the fact remained that it was a project that both Jackson and Van Buren had left strictly alone, being so clearly one that could split the Union, as well as the parties, along sectional lines. Tyler and Calhoun did not care. As a result the Texas question dominated the election of 1844. When Van Buren, the leading Democratic candidate, came out against immediate annexation he was denied his party's nomination; he could not get the two-thirds majority at the convention which was required under a rule that ironically had been imposed on the party by Andrew Jackson in 1832 to ensure that his chosen Vice-Presidential candidate — Martin Van Buren — should get a thoroughly convincing endorsement. This rule was to cause the Democrats infinite trouble until Franklin Roosevelt abolished it. When Henry Clay, the Whig candidate, equivocated over annexation he lost the election. Tyler renounced his chance to run on a third-party ticket and backed the Democrats. They carried New York by a narrow margin and their man, James K. Polk, was declared elected.

Tyler was not finished. Just before he left office on 1 March 1845 he was able to sign a joint resolution of both houses of Congress by which Texas became part of the Union. He had achieved his ambition and in doing so gave perhaps the decisive push toward civil war, for the quarrels arising out of the Texas question were not to be finally settled until Lee surrendered to Grant.

Tyler went off to gracious retirement with the new wife he had married in the White House. He had had eight children by his first wife; he now had seven by his second, the last of whom was born when he was 70, two years before his death. "His eye was not dim, nor his natural force abated." In 1861 Tyler was an early advocate of the view that Virginia should secede from the Union and he was elected to the Confederate Congress (thus becoming the only President of the United States to commit treason). He died before he could take his seat or watch the terrible destruction that the creed which he supported all his life brought on his beloved Virginia.

JOHN TYLER'S FAMILY

It was strange the way the Tylers were so insistent that they descended from Wat Tyler, the leader of the Peasants' Revolt in England in 1381. Tyler the peasant leader wanted an end to serfdom; the Virginia Tylers were slave-owners. Tyler the peasant leader is said to have been anxious to put an end to traitors; President Tyler committed treason against the United States. Yet the 10th President's elder brother was christened Wat and he himself always insisted he was related to the 14th-century Wat. Actually no connection can be established at all. About the only thing President and peasant had in common was a distaste for ordinances in restraint of trade: Wat the peasant presented Richard II with demands for their abolition and John Tyler the President persistently vetoed high tariff bills sent up to him by Congress.

It would have been more appropriate for President Tyler to dwell on his mother's family, the Armisteads. Through her he was a fourth cousin of his predecessor as President, William H. Harrison. His fifth cousin through her, General Lewis Armistead, was a Confederate brigade commander at Gettysburg, where he died of wounds received in the advance by Pickett's division of Virginians (part of Longstreet's corps) on the strongly entrenched Union lines. The general's wife was a great-granddaughter of Richard H. Lee, the Signer. Their son married a granddaughter of Daniel Webster, who turned down the vice-presidential nomination on William H. Harrison's ticket; had he accepted he would have become President instead of Tyler.

In his origins, if not ultimate career, Tyler was very much in the mould of the Virginia Dynasty Presidents of an earlier generation. Tyler's father Judge John Tyler had roomed with Jefferson when studying law and Jefferson in later life was a guest in Judge John's house, where the adolescent Tyler

Plate 30   Letitia Christian, John Tyler's 1st wife

Plate 31   Julia Gardiner, John Tyler's 2nd wife

Plate 32   Letitia Tyler Semple, John Tyler's
daughter and hostess in the White House

Plate 33   Priscilla Cooper Tyler, John Tyler's
daughter-in-law and hostess in the White House

met him. Judge John was as ardent a republican as Jefferson, to the embarrassment of his own father, who held office under the Crown. The Judge also hero-worshipped Patrick Henry and gave the name Henry to two of his children, Maria and Wat. He was a most conscientious paterfamilias, acting as guardian to 21 children in addition to the eight he fathered by his wife. He owned over 1,900 acres in Virginia, as well as mineral rights in Kentucky, so that John Tyler, despite being a younger son, had rosy expectations.

Like most of the young gentry of Virginia John Tyler was educated at William and Mary College, where his father the judge and grandfather, yet another John Tyler, had gone and where two of his sons were to go (another son, Lyon G. Tyler, became President of the College). Two of his aunts married members of the teaching staff there. Judge John died opportunely as far as his son was concerned, leaving him a plantation in his will. Tyler, who would otherwise have needed to find somewhere of his own to live on taking a wife, got married a few weeks later. After two years he sold the place, called rather pretentiously Mons Sacer (Latin for the Sacred Mountain or Holy Hill), and moved to another plantation nearby, where he built a house he called Woodburn. A few years later still he exchanged Woodburn for another house, Greenway.

This restlessness does not seem to have been shared by Tyler's first wife, Letitia, although she is so shadowy a figure (none of her letters survive) it is hard to be certain. One might think her self-effacing except that she is said to have had a strong mind and character. She declined to join Tyler in Washington when he became a senator. She was a good housekeeper, as she would have needed to be on a large plantation with seven surviving children to look after. She brought influential connections and money to the marriage, and it has been suggested that without her sensible housekeeping Tyler would not have been able to take up a political career and run his property at the same time. Although they were virtually the same age he regarded himself as having much the more mature character, indeed he spoke of himself as old for his age at the time of their marriage, which took place on his 23rd birthday. She cannot have been much of a companion for him intellectually since according to her daughter-in-law Priscilla her reading was confined to the Bible and prayer book. Her religion was narrowly Protestant (she objected to the Tylers' daughter Mary being educated at a convent). One wonders what she would have said had she known the second Mrs Tyler would convert to Catholicism.

On acceding to the presidency Tyler is said to have delivered a little homily to his children. It is not very original in its sentiments, but at least he spelled out what the rules should be; moreover the children seem by and large to have obeyed them: "My children, by a deplored event I am unexpectedly elevated to the presidency of the United States. You, as my children, of course rise with me . . . this promotion is only temporary and if, at any moment, you should forget to sustain it with humility and meekness, the error of such a moment will be visited on you bitterly . . . my sons and daughters, act with reference to the day . . . when I must return to plain John Tyler again; and may you never, as the President's family, either in thought, or word or deed, do aught which you will regret hereafter, when you shall be nothing higher than plain John Tyler's children." His son Robert committed a mild breach of his father's commandments when in the late summer of 1841 he denounced the bank bill to a New York representative. A few days later his father vetoed it. Press suggestions at the time that Robert and his brother John had been indiscreet were never substantiated. It was no worse than that. Some of the children of other Presidents could have observed the Tyler rules with advantage.

From the above it may already have been guessed that Tyler was an old-fashioned man. He thought the waltz improper when he first came across it in the late 1820s and wrote to his eldest daughter Mary saying so. In fairness one must remember that this was a widespread reaction to a dance in which for the first time in generations men and women held each other closely. By the 1840s, when Tyler had succeeded as President, the waltz had established itself across the civilized world and he allowed it to be performed in the White House, perhaps in part because his second wife Julia was commemorated in the 'Julia Waltzes' composed by a contemporary New York musician. On the whole he lived in the White House at a relatively informal pitch. He rode out in an old carriage acquired from Van Buren's Secretary of the Navy and at state dinners the attendants wore second-hand liveries purchased at the sale of effects of a foreign diplomat who had been recalled.

Tyler's deportment was far from casual, however. The former President John Quincy Adams in his *Memoirs* recorded that Tyler and his daughter-in-law Priscilla (standing in for Letitia Tyler, who was slowly dying upstairs from the effects of a stroke) rivalled European royalty in their courtesy to guests, particularly during the huge reception given for Washington Irving and Charles Dickens in 1842. And Adams, who had visited most European courts, knew what he was talking about. Tyler's old-fashioned courtesy as a southern gentleman of the traditional school was almost complete; press comment claimed there had been nothing like it since the Madisons, an appropriate parallel since the aged Dolley Madison was now acting as Priscilla's consultant on social matters. But he was not above following Van Buren's practice in securing a post for his son Robert in the Land Office. Robert's younger brother John, who acted as his father's secretary, slid smoothly into the post when Robert left Washington in 1844.

Tyler's second wife Julia Gardiner, like his first, had money. In 1844 the future President James Buchanan wrote in a letter to a friend "The President is the most lucky man that ever lived. Both a belle and a fortune to crown and close his Presidential career." And Buchanan alluded, in a letter to Mrs James Roosevelt (probably the lady of that name who was the third wife of FDR's great-grandfather) a month before the wedding, to "the divine Julia". He added "with all her follies and foibles, she is a lady, and this implies much." Julia had hesitated about marrying Tyler till the awful accident in February 1844 when her father (together with four other people, two of them Cabinet members) were killed after a gun exploded on board a warship carrying the President and a party of guests. Quite why this should have changed Julia's mind is hard to say, though since Tyler was old enough to be her father it may simply be that she thought he would do as a substitute. She was one of those girls who idolize their fathers and once said "Papa was the only handsome man (except the President) I have ever seen." Her money came in useful for refurbishing the White House, although she was only mistress of it for a few months, having married in the summer of 1844 and being obliged to leave it in March 1845. She behaved a shade too grandly to suit some Washingtonians, and didn't hesitate to interfere in policy, particularly the annexation of Texas.

Like many people who marry out of their accustomed milieu — she was born in New York of New England stock — Julia became more passionate a supporter of the society to which her husband belonged, in this case the Old South, than if she had been bred to it. She supported outright secession, whereas Tyler put up a short struggle to avert it before accepting his and the South's fate. She defended slavery in articles for the press. She became alienated from her family over the North-South conflict and refused to take the oath of allegiance to the Union when she returned to live in the North after Tyler's death. She nevertheless managed to settle in New York, but once there she spent the last year of the war agitating on behalf of the Confederacy. Tyler is sometimes called lucky in dying when he did, for he did not survive to see the South ruined. Even if he had he would have been luckier than most Southerners, for despite their uniform adherence to the Confederacy all his huge brood survived the bloody battles bar a single grandson. He was every bit as lucky in not surviving to see his wife make a fool of herself, for it is unlikely that he would have been able to curb what was clearly a headstrong personality.

BIOGRAPHICAL DETAILS AND DESCENDANTS

TYLER, JOHN, *b* Greenway, Charles City Co, Va., 29 March 1790; *educ* William and Mary Coll; admitted to Virginia Bar 1809, Memb Virginia House of Delegates from Charles City Co 1811-15 (Memb Virginia State Cncl 1815-16), 1823-24 and 1838-41 (Speaker), Capt Militia 1813, Memb US House of Reps from Virginia 1816-21, Govr Virginia 1825-27, US Senator from Virginia 1827-36 (Pres Senate pro tempore 1835-36), Memb Virginia Convention revising State Constitution 1829-30, unsuccessful Whig V-Presdtl candidate 1836, Pres Virginia African Colonization Soc 1838, V-Pres (Whig) USA 4 March-4 April 1841, 10th President of the USA 4 April 1841-1845, Nat Democratic Tyler Convention presdtl candidate 1844, Chllr William and Mary Coll 1859, apptd by Virginia Gen Assembly a Commissioner to President BUCHANAN to preserve peace 19 Jan 1861, Chm Peace Convention, Washington, DC, 4-27 Feb 1861, Memb Virginia Convention on Policy 1 March 1861, Memb Provisional Congress of Confederation 5 May 1861, elected Memb House of Reps of permanent Confed Congress 7 Nov 1861 (never took seat); *m* 1st Cedar Grove, New Kent Co, Va., 29 March 1813 Letitia (*b* there 12 Nov 1790; *d* the White House 10 Sept 1842 of a paralytic stroke sustained almost four years earlier), 3rd dau of Col Robert Christian, of Cedar Grove, planter, and his w Mary Brown, and had issue:

President Tyler's daughter
I Mary Tyler, *b* Charles City Co, Va., 15 April 1815; *m* 14 Dec 1835 Henry Lightfoot JONES, of Woodham, Va. (*b* N Carolina 1813), and *d* New Kent Co, Va., 17 June 1848, having had issue:

Grandchildren
1 John JONES, *b* 18—
2 Henry JONES, *d c* 1890
3 Robert Tyler JONES, *b* Washington, DC, 24 Jan 1843; *educ* William and Mary Coll; Capt Confederate States Army; *m* 10 Nov 1891 Sally Breedon Gresham (*b* Petersburg, Va., 2 Aug 1868; *d* Washington, DC, 25 Feb 1951) and *d* Washington, DC, 18 May 1895, leaving issue:

Great-grandchildren
(1) Louis Armistead JONES, of Herndon, Va., *b* Washington, DC, 22 June 1893; *m* 2 Oct 1922 Frances Strother (*b* Dranesville, Fairfax Co, Va., 5 Feb 1894; *d* Herndon 9 Feb 1960), dau of Richard McMillen, and *d* Washington, DC, 1 Dec 1961, leaving issue:

Great-great-grandchildren
1a *Margaret McMillen Jones, *b* Alexandria, Va., 10 Oct 1923; *m* 10 June 1961 *George Frederick COOMBER, of Herndon, Va. (*b* London, UK, 15 Nov 1925), s of Alfred H. Coomber, and has issue:

Great-great-grandchildren's children
1b *Virginia COOMBER, *b* Washington 5 May 1964
2b *A dau

Grandchildren
4 A dau; *d* in infancy 1847

President Tyler's son
II Robert TYLER, *b* Charles City Co, Va., 9 Sept 1816; Col Volunteer Regt Mexican War, priv sec to his father when latter President, Registrar Confederate States Treasury, Ed *Montgomery Mail and Advertiser*, Ala.; *m* St James's Episcopal Church, Bristol, Pa., 12 Sept 1839 (Elizabeth) Priscilla (*b* New York 14 June 1816; *d* Montgomery, Ala., 29 Dec 1889), 2nd dau of Thomas Abthorpe Cooper, actor, and his 2nd w Mary Fairlie, and *d* Montgomery 3 Dec 1877, having had issue:

Grandchildren
1 Mary Fairlie TYLER, *b* Dec 1840; *d* Philadelphia June 1845
2 Letitia Christian TYLER, *b* the White House 1842; *d* Montgomery 1927
3 John TYLER IV, *b* July 1844; *d* Philadelphia July 1846
4 Grace Rae Tyler, *b* Philadelphia May 1845; *m* Mount Meigs, Ala., Nov 1863 John Baytop SCOTT (*b* Lowndesboro, Ala., 16 Oct 1831; *d* Montgomery 1894), s of Thomas Baytop Scott and his w Martha Gaines Marks (and gs of John Baytop Scott, one of Montgomery's founders), and *d* Montgomery 1919, leaving issue:

Great-grandchildren
(1) James Mark SCOTT, *b* 17 May 1866; *m* 8 Oct 1888 Adelaide Bauerlein (*b* 29 March 1869; *d* 5 May 1957) and *d* 13 Oct 1932, having had issue:

Great-great-grandchildren
1a Grace Fairlie SCOTT, *b* Montgomery; *d* 1894
2a *John Baytop SCOTT, *b* Montgomery 23 March 1906; *m* 19— *Ellie Dreyspring and has issue:

Great-great-grandchildren's children

1b *John Baytop SCOTT, Jr, b Montgomery 21 July 1934; m 23 Nov 1956 *Elizabeth Bowers Hill (b 23 April 1934) and has issue:

Great-great-grandchildren's grandchildren
1c *Elliott Dreyspring SCOTT, b Montgomery 22 Sept 1957
2c *Laura Hill SCOTT, b Montgomery 5 June 1960
3c *Amelie Katherine SCOTT, b Montgomery 17 July 1964

Great-great-grandchildren's children

2b *James Marks SCOTT, b Montgomery 23 July 1936; m 31 May 1960 *Vivian McLean Butler (b Montgomery 13 May 1937) and has issue:

Great-great-grandchildren's grandchildren
1c *Anderson Butler SCOTT, b Montgomery 26 Sept 1961
2c *Virginia Fairlie SCOTT, b Montgomery 31 Dec 1969

Great-great-grandchildren

3a Louise Stewart Scott, b Montgomery 19 Jan 1908; m 19— *Clifton FONVILLE and d 20 Nov 1945

4a *Mary Virginia Scott, b Montgomery 1 Jan 1910; m 19 June 1937 *Emory Malcolm MARTIN (b 22 Sept 1910) and has issue:

Great-great-grandchildren's children

1b *Louise Scott Martin, b Montgomery 7 June 1939; m 19— *John Calvin HUNT (b 16 Sept 1936) and has issue:

Great-great-grandchildren's grandchildren
1c *John Emory HUNT, b 11 May 1964

Great-great-grandchildren's children
2b *Mary Virginia MARTIN, b Montgomery 7 Aug 1940
3b *William Kelly MARTIN, b Montgomery 27 Jan 1946; m 28 Sept 1973 *Dorothy Molly Dunn

Great-grandchildren

(2) Mary Virginia Scott, b 1868; m 18— or 19— Charles A. COLEMAN and had issue:

Great-great-grandchildren

1a *Elizabeth COLEMAN [34 Guild's Wood, Tuscaloosa, AL 35401, USA]

Great-grandchildren

(3) Robert Tyler SCOTT, b 18—

(4) Julia Campbell Scott, b Mount Miegs, Ala., 3 June 1876; m 6 Sept 1899 William Adams GUNTER II (b Rembert Hills, Marengo Co, Ala., 9 Oct 1872; sometime Mayor Montgomery; d Montgomery 4 Dec 1940), s of William Adams Gunter and his w Ellen Poellnitz, and d Montgomery 23 Oct 1955, leaving issue:

Great-great-grandchildren

1a *Grace Scott Gunter, b Montgomery 13 April 1901; m 1 July 1925 Colquitt Hill LANE (b Auburn, Lee Co, Ala., 22 Sept 1899; d Montgomery 1 Nov 1957) and has issue:

Great-great-grandchildren's children

1b *Virginia Fairlie Lane, b Montgomery 24 Jan 1933; m 28 July 1951 *Oliver Lynn HAYNES (b Montgomery 11 June 1927) and has issue:

Great-great-grandchildren's grandchildren
1c *Fairlie Gunter HAYNES, b Montgomery 26 Oct 1954
2c *Oliver Lynn HAYNES III, b Montgomery 22 May 1959
3c *William Sidney HAYNES, b Montgomery 11 Jan 1962

Great-great-grandchildren's children

2b *Elizabeth Tyler Lane, b Montgomery 18 Aug 1935; m 24 Aug 1960 *Paul Geoffrey FISCHER (b Douglaston, Nassau Co, Long Island, NY, 13 Feb 1937) and has issue:

Great-great-grandchildren's grandchildren
1c *Jason Chase FISCHER, b Santa Monica, Calif., 13 March 1974

Great-great-grandchildren

2a *Dr William Adams GUNTER III [66 Haardt Drive, Montgomery, AL 36105, USA], b Montgomery 3 Nov 1902; educ Alabama U (BS 1922), Johns Hopkins Sch of Medicine (MD 1926) and New York Hosp; Fell American Coll of Surgs, practised gen surg Montgomery, Ala., 1930-63, Col USAF Medical Corps 1942-46; m 14 Oct 1946 *Annie Laurie (b Tarheel, Bladen Co, N Carolina, 23 June 1919), dau of —— Cain, of Lake Wales, Fla., and has issue:

Great-great-grandchildren's children

1b *William Adams GUNTER IV [Mount Zion Road, Ramer, Montgomery, AL 36096, USA; Rt 2, Ramer, Montgomery, AL 36096, USA; c/o William A. Gunter Investments, 272 Commerce Street, Montgomery, AL 36104, USA], b Montgomery 23 Nov 1952; m 26 April 1980 *Alice Ross Davis (b Montgomery 24 May 1958)

Great-great-grandchildren
3a *Ellen Von Poellnitz Gunter, b Montgomery 7 Feb 1904; m 29 Sept 1925 Charles Platt ROGERS (b Madison, Morris Co, New Jersey, 18 July 1898; d Montgomery 8 Nov 1970) and has issue:

Great-great-grandchildren's children
1b *Ellen Von Poellnitz Rogers, b Montgomery 14 April 1933; m 1st 18 Dec 1951 (divorce 19——) Frank RANDOLPH (b Montgomery 11 March 1931) and has issue:

Great-great-grandchildren's grandchildren
1c *Frank Gunter TROTMAN, b (as Randolph) Montgomery 18 Sept 1952; later took stepf's name

Great-great-grandchildren's children
1b (cont.) Mrs Ellen Randolph m 2nd 14 Oct 1955 *John McNeill TROTMAN (b Troy, Pike Co, Ala., 12 March 1927) and has further issue:

Great-great-grandchildren's grandchildren
2c *John McNeill TROTMAN II, b Montgomery 5 Aug 1956; m 7 Aug 1978 *Terri Ashmore (b Montgomery 17 May 1958) and has issue:

Great-great-grandchildren's great-grandchildren
1d *John McNeill TROTMAN III, b Montgomery 11 Oct 1977

Great-great-grandchildren's grandchildren
3c *Charles Rogers TROTMAN, b Montgomery 15 March 1958
4c *Robert Tyler TROTMAN, b Montgomery 10 Feb 1962

Great-great-grandchildren
4a *Mary Virginia Gunter [Mrs Homer Orvis, 1656 Gilmer Avenue, Montgomery, AL 36104, USA], b Montgomery 2 Aug 1906; m 1st 7 Sept 1927 (divorce 19——) Robert Henry HAAS (b Pittsburgh, Pa., 17 Dec 1905; d there 14 Sept 1972) and has issue:

Great-great-grandchildren's children
1b *Henry Paul HAAS, b Montgomery 14 Sept 1928; m 11 April 1953 *Dora Pratt Smith (b Montgomery 6 Jan 1930) and has issue:

Great-great-grandchildren's grandchildren
1c *Robert Gunter HAAS, b Montgomery 13 April 1963
2c *Josephine Pratt HAAS, b Montgomery 3 Oct 1968

Great-great-grandchildren
4a (cont.) Mrs Mary Haas m 2nd Homer Waitstill ORVIS (b S Orange, New Jersey, 23 Aug 1890; d Montgomery 17 June 1972)
5a Rose Darrington Gunter, b Montgomery 22 Feb 1908; m 30 Nov 1932 *Thomas Seay LAWSON [4000 Fieldcrest Drive, Montgomery, AL 36111, USA] (b Greensboro, Ala., 3 May 1907; Justice Alabama Supreme Court) and d 23 March 1963, leaving issue:

Great-great-grandchildren's children
1b *Thomas Seay LAWSON, Jr [1262 Glen Grattan Avenue, Montgomery, AL 36111, USA; 57 Adams Avenue, Montgomery, AL 36104, USA], b Montgomery 10 Oct 1935; attorney; m 27 May 1961 *Sarah Hunter Clayton (b Clayton, Ala., 23 July 1937) and has issue:

Great-great-grandchildren's grandchildren
1c *Rose Gunter LAWSON, b Montgomery 23 Nov 1963
2c *Gladys Robinson LAWSON, b Montgomery 22 Oct 1966
3c *Thomas Seay LAWSON III, b Montgomery 9 Nov 1971

Great-great-grandchildren's children
2b *Jule Gunter Lawson, b Montgomery 15 Dec 1939; m 6 Dec 1963 *Clifford Anderson LANIER, Jr (b Montgomery 22 Jan 1936), s of Clifford Anderson Lanier, and has issue:

Great-great-grandchildren's grandchildren
1c *Jule Gunter LANIER, b Montgomery 13 Dec 1964
2c *Clifford Anderson LANIER III, b Montgomery 8 April 1968

Great-great-grandchildren
6a *Julia Fairlie Gunter, b Montgomery 11 April 1914; m 28 Nov 1934 *Ethelbert Henry EVANS (b Montgomery 5 March 1910) and has issue:

Great-great-grandchildren's children
1b *Florence Phillips Evans, b Montgomery 11 Oct 1939; m 27 April 1962 *George Edmund JORDAN (b Montgomery 28 Jan 1933) and has issue:

Great-great-grandchildren's grandchildren
1c *Julia Fairlie JORDAN, b Montgomery 1 Feb 1963

2c *George Edmund JORDAN, Jr, *b* Montgomery 16 May 1965
3c *Ethelbert Evans JORDAN, *b* Montgomery 25 June 1970

Great-great-grandchildren
7a *Elizabeth Tyler Gunter, *b* Montgomery 29 Aug 1916; *m* 1 Aug 1942 *Bruce Johnson DOWNEY, Jr (*b* Nashville, N Carolina, 23 Feb 1918), s of Bruce Johnson Downey, and has issue:

Great-great-grandchildren's children
1b *Bruce Johnson DOWNEY III, *b* Montgomery 10 Oct 1943; *m* 13 June 1970 *Victoria Ann Stewart (*b* Great Lakes, Ill., 22 April 1947) and has issue:

Great-great-grandchildren's grandchildren
1c *Victoria Tyler DOWNEY, *b* Montgomery 13 May 1974
2c *Bruce Johnson DOWNEY IV, *b* Montgomery 19 Oct 1978

Great-great-grandchildren's children
2b *Elizabeth Tyler Gunter Downey, *b* Montgomery 23 May 1947; *m* 24 Aug 1968 *Mat Constantine RAYMOND, Jr (*b* Durham, N Carolina, 2 April 1945), s of Mat Constantine Raymond, and has issue:

Great-great-grandchildren's grandchildren
1c *Mat Constantine RAYMOND III, *b* Jacksonville, N Carolina, 18 June 1972
2c *Elizabeth Tyler RAYMOND, *b* Jacksonville 21 Oct 1976

Great-grandchildren
(5) Thomas Baytop SCOTT, *b* Mount Meigs, Montgomery, Ala., 17 May 1881; *m* Savannah, Ga., 15 Aug 1910 Kathleen Ann Swain (*b* Altamaha, Tattnall Co, Ga., 10 Nov 1891; *d* Atlanta, Ga., 1 March 1972) and *d* Montgomery 3 Jan 1946, having had issue:

Great-great-grandchildren
1a Kathleen Mozelle Scott, *b* Savannah 27 June 1911; *m* Montgomery 5 June 1935 *Charles Hannon POINTER (*b* Montgomery 1908) and *d* Montgomery 10 Aug 1937
2a *Grace Tyler Scott, *b* Savannah 8 April 1913; *m* Montgomery 29 Sept 1937 *Benjamin Watkins LACY IV (*b* Louisville, Ky., 23 Oct 1912) and has issue:

Great-great-grandchildren's children
1b *Benjamin Watkins LACY V, *b* Montgomery 22 Oct 1941; *m* Pensacola, Fla., 10 Sept 1966 *Judith Ann Vucovich (*b* there 30 July 1944) and has issue:

Great-great-grandchildren's grandchildren
1c *Judith Ann LACY, *b* Bunnell, Fla., 4 Feb 1970
2c *Benjamin Walker LACY VI, *b* Bunnell 8 Sept 1974

Great-great-grandchildren's children
2b *Thomas Scott LACY, *b* Montgomery 11 Aug 1942; *m* Atlanta, Ga., 1 Sept 1965 *Martha Elizabeth Dodd (*b* Atlanta 24 March 1947) and has issue:

Great-great-grandchildren's grandchildren
1c *Thomas Scott LACY, Jr, *b* Atlanta 11 July 1966
2c *Joseph Arthur LACY, *b* Tallahassee, Fla., 8 May 1969

Great-great-grandchildren's children
3b *Kathleen Medora LACY, *b* Montgomery 22 Sept 1949

Great-great-grandchildren
3a *Mary Helen Scott, *b* Savannah, Ga., 22 Aug 1915; *m* Bessemer, Ala., 29 Dec 1936 *George Hails FOSTER (*b* Montgomery 26 Dec 1914) and has issue:

Great-great-grandchildren's children
1b *George Hails FOSTER, Jr, *b* Montgomery 15 Dec 1937; *m* Mobile, Ala., 31 July 1965 *Alice Vivian Mighell (*b* New Orleans 19 March 1943) and has issue:

Great-great-grandchildren's grandchildren
1c *George Hails FOSTER III, *b* Winston Salem, N Carolina, 28 Dec 1968
2c *Ashley Mighell FOSTER, *b* Winston Salem 26 Dec 1971

Great-great-grandchildren's children
2b *Robert Scott FOSTER, *b* Alhambra, Calif., 3 April 1944; *m* 1st San Diego, Calif., 2 July 1966 (divorce 19—) Lucy Ann Olsen (*b* 11 Aug 1944) and has issue:

Great-great-grandchildren's grandchildren
1c *Robert Scott FOSTER, Jr, *b* Waukegan, Ill., 17 May 1969

Great-great-grandchildren's children
2b (cont.) Robert S. Foster *m* 2nd Houma, La., 2 Jan 1972 *Charlene Gayle Crawley (*b* New Orleans 30 April 1948)

3b *Kathleen Ann Foster, *b* Long Beach, Calif., 23 Dec 1947; *m* Montgomery 11 July 1968 *Michael Elmore HAVEY (*b* Howard Air Force Base, Panama Canal Zone, 14 Dec 1946) and has issue:

Great-great-grandchildren's grandchildren
1c *Kathleen Scott HAVEY, *b* Fairborn, Ohio, 28 April 1970

Great-great-grandchildren's children
4b *Mary Fairlie FOSTER, *b* Taft, Calif., 26 Dec 1951

Great-great-grandchildren
4a *Priscilla Cooper Scott, *b* Savannah, Ga., 21 Dec 1919; *m* Montgomery 5 May 1943 *Quentin Claiborne CROMMELIN (*b* Montgomery 26 Sept 1918) and has issue:

Great-great-grandchildren's children
1b *Quentin Claiborne CROMMELIN, Jr, *b* Montgomery 11 Oct 1944
2b *Priscilla Tyler CROMMELIN, *b* Baltimore, Md., 21 Aug 1947

Great-great-grandchildren
5a *Robert Tyler SCOTT, *b* Savannah, Ga., 23 Sept 1922; *m* Mansfield, Ohio, 17 March 1951 *Margaret Van Tilbury (*b* there 11 Oct 1928) and has issue:

Great-great-grandchildren's children
1b *Susan Finlay SCOTT, *b* Cleveland, Ohio, 25 Aug 1952
2b *Kathleen Mozelle SCOTT, *b* New Orleans 27 Aug 1957
3b *Joann SCOTT, *b* New Orleans 9 Aug 1959

Great-great-grandchildren
6a *Ann Linwood Scott [Mrs Milton Wood III, R+I, Box 26, Sandersville, GA 31082, USA], *b* Montgomery 23 April 1926; *m* there 3 May 1949 *Milton LeGrand WOOD III (*b* Selma, Ala., 21 Aug 1922) and has issue:

Great-great-grandchildren's children
1b *Elizabeth Leigh Wood, *b* Mobile, Ala., 24 Oct 1950; *m* Atlanta, Ga., 16 June 1973 *Charles Bealer PATE (*b* Darlington, S Carolina, 30 Aug 1944)
2b *Kathleen Anne WOOD, *b* Mobile 15 Nov 1951
3b *Milton LeGrand WOOD IV, *b* Atlanta 24 June 1954
4b *Roberta Owen WOOD, *b* Atlanta 11 Jan 1960

Great-grandchildren
(6) Priscilla Cooper Scott, *b* Mount Meigs, Ala., 1 Nov 1883; *m* Savannah 3 July 1902 Dr Charles Lewis MARKS (*b* Montgomery 31 March 1882; *d* there 30 April 1943), s of Samuel B. Marks and his w Laura Lewis James, and *d* Perdido Beach, Baldwin Co, Ala., 29 June 1957, leaving issue:

Great-great-grandchildren
1a Katherine Crain Marks, *b* Montgomery 17 Feb 1904; *m* 7 Sept 1923 Zachary Taylor TRAWICK (*b* Opelika, Lee Co, Ala., 27 Sept 1901; *d* 18 March 1991) and *d* 28 Dec 1982, leaving issue:

Great-great-grandchildren's children
1b *Dr Zachary Taylor TRAWICK, Jr [3137 Southview Ave, Montgomery, AL, USA], *b* Montgomery 9 Feb 1926; *m* 1st 3 June 1951 (divorce 19—) Jeanne Carolyn Rogers (*b* Montgomery 20 Nov 1925) and has issue:

Great-great-grandchildren's grandchildren
1c *Zachary Taylor TRAWICK III, *b* 19 Nov 1952
2c *James Rogers TRAWICK, *b* 3 June 1954
3c *Charles Leonard TRAWICK, *b* 30 June 1956
4c *Michael Kelley TRAWICK, *b* 7 May 1959
5c *Robert Scott TRAWICK, *b* 3 Sept 1961

Great-great-grandchildren's children
1b (cont.) Dr Zachary T. Trawick, Jr, *m* 2nd 19— *Patricia Brannon Little (*b* Hendersonville, Henderson Co, N Carolina, 29 June 1931)
2b *Katherine Marks Trawick [Mrs Allyn M Thames, 1829 Fairlee Court, Montgomery, AL 36106, USA], *b* Montgomery 5 Nov 1933; *educ* Mary Baldwin Coll; owner Career Personnel Consultants 1959-93; *m* 1st 5 Sept 1953 (divorce 1965) Hugh Browning THORNTON (*b* 19 Nov 1928) and has issue:

Great-great-grandchildren's grandchildren
1c *Hugh Browning THORNTON, Jr, *b* 16 Aug 1954; *m* 19— *Cecelia Vow and has issue:

Great-great-grandchildren's great-grandchildren
1d *Tere Trawick THORNTON, *b* 19—
2d *Hugh Browning THORNTON III, *b* 19—

Great-great-grandchildren's grandchildren
2c *Katherine Trawick Thornton, *b* 30 July 1957; *m* 19— *Dr Gary Hampton BEACHUM and has issue:

Great-great-grandchildren's great-grandchildren
1d *Hugh Hampton BEACHUM, *b* 19—
2d *Hunter SCott BEACHUM, *b* 19—

Great-great-grandchildren's children
2b (cont.) Mrs Katherine Thornton *m* 2nd 7 April 1967 *Allyn Mabson THAMES (*b* Montgomery 8 May 1920), s of William Thames and his w Llyde Allyn Ray

Great-great-grandchildren
2a Revd John Scott MARKS, *b* Montgomery 2 Sept 1905; LLB, BD, a priest of the Protestant Episcopal Church; *m* 1st Ellen Norwood Allison (*b* Montgomery 14 Oct 1904; *d* Mobile, Ala., 26 Dec 1958) and had issue:

Great-great-grandchildren's children
1b *Dr John Scott MARKS, Jr [PO Box 1003, Point Clear, AL 36564, USA], *b* Montgomery 7 March 1931; *educ* U of Alabama; physician specializing in neurosurgery, ret 1993; *m* 1st 1 June 1954 (divorce 1963), as her 1st husb, Jan McDonald (*b* 14 Feb 1935; *m* 2nd May 1965 Peter S. Reinthaler; *d* 17 Oct 1987), of Knoxville, Tenn., and has issue:

Great-great-grandchildren
1c *(Ellen) Allison Reinthaler [Mrs Harry Olsson, 659 Partridge Circle, Golden, CO 80403, USA], *b* (as Marks) Birmingham. Ala., 2 June 1956; adopted by stepf 1965; *educ* Houston Baptist U and U of Colorado; musician Calvary Episcopal Church 1984- and freelance 1980-; *m* 1st 1 Sept 1973 (divorce 10 Nov 1975) Robert Bruce GIBBONS (*b* 6 July 1955); *m* 2nd 24 Nov 1979 *Harry Robertson OLSSON (*b* 3 Nov 1953), s of Harry Rudolph Olsson and his w Mildred Campbell, and has issue:

Great-great-grandchildren's children
1d *Rebecca Anne OLSSON, *b* Jefferson City, Colo., 4 July 1980
2d *Harry Robertson OLSSON, Jr, *b* Jefferson Co, Colo., 5 Jan 1982
3d *John Randall OLSSON, *b* 6 May 1984

Great-great-grandchildren
2c John Scott REINTHALER, *b* (as Marks) 22 April 1959; adopted by stepf 1965; *d* 13 April 1992

Great-great-grandchildren's children
1b (cont.) Dr John S. Marks, Jr, *m* 2nd 2 April 1964 *Julia Rhinehart (*b* Louisville, Ky., 20 Sept 1942), dau of David Mclain and his w Harriet, and with her has issue:

Great-great-grandchildren's grandchildren
3c *Ellen Caroline MARKS [501 Cedar Chase Circle, Atlanta, GA 30324, USA], *b* Louisville, Ky., 10 Dec 1964; *educ* Smith (BA 1984) and Northwestern (MA 1991); in public relations
4c *Anna Meriwether MARKS, *b* 29 Indianapolis May 1968
5c *Juliet Scott MARKS, *b* 23 July 1970

Great-great-grandchildren's children
2b *William Byron MARKS [1615 Manchester Lane NW, Washington, DC 20011, USA], *b* Montgomery 30 July 1933; biophysicist; *m* 1958 (divorce 19—) Anne Pattillo Foerster (*b* San Antonio, Tex., 4 Dec 1933) and has issue:

Great-great-grandchildren's grandchildren
1c *Matthew Pattillo MARKS [2346R Camden Dve, Houston, TX 77021, USA], *b* Baltimore 12 May 1959; *educ* U of Texas at Houston (BBA 1993); *m* 18 Oct 1989 *Paula Ellen (*b* Washington, DC, 1960), dau of Richard Theodore Burch and his w Janis Diane Derry, and has issue:

Great-great-grandchildren's great-grandchildren
1d *William Wolfe Burch MARKS, *b* Houston 23 April 1992

Great-great-grandchildren's grandchildren
2c *Michael Meriwether MARKS [141 Flora Ave #26, Walnut Creek, CA 94595, USA], *b* 2 March 1961; *educ* Stanford U; software engr; *m* 17 Sept 1989 *Caryl Jane, dau of Jack Morton and his w Elizabeth
3c *Laura Underhill MARKS [66 Ft Hill Terr No 5, Rochester, NY 14620, USA; 40 Priem St, Rochester, NY 14607, USA], *b* 14 Sept 1963; *m* and has issue

Great-great-grandchildren's children
3b *Charles Lewis MARKS III [611 Constitution Ave NE, Washington, DC 20002, USA], *b* Montgomery 2 Sept 1935; *m* 1980 *Barbara Cleaves (*b* Washington, DC, 28 April 1943) and has issue:

Great-great-grandchildren's grandchildren
1c *Barbara C. MARKS, *b* Washington, DC, 18 May 1982

Great-great-grandchildren
2a (cont.) Revd John S. Marks *m* 2nd 19— *Lillian Davis and *d* Fairhope, Ala., Sept 1976
3a Samuel Blackburn MARKS, *b* Montgomery 9 Dec 1907; *m* 10 June 1939 *Regina Worthington [Mrs Sam B Marks, 3535 Carter Hill Rd, Montgomery, AL, USA] (*b* Petrey, Crenshaw Co, Ala., 6 Dec 1914) and *d* 19—, having had issue:

Great-great-grandchildren's children
1b Samuel Blackburn MARKS, Jr, *b* 26 July 1945; *d* 15 Nov 1948
2b *Scott Chesser MARKS, *b* 27 Jan 1951; *m* 196- *Donna Jean Donaldson (*b* 25 Feb 1950) and has issue:

Great-great-grandchildren's grandchildren
1c *Megan Gwynneth MARKS, *b* Houston, Tex., 21 Oct 1969

Great-great-grandchildren
4a *Charles Lewis MARKS, Jr, *b* Montgomery 27 Aug 1912; *m* 16 Nov 1938 *Mary Jeanne Saunders (*b* Montgomery 14 July 1919) and has issue:

Great-great-grandchildren's children
1b *Fairlie Marks, *b* Montgomery 29 July 1939; *m* 6 Oct 1960 *Charles Homer ODELL and has issue:

Great-great-grandchildren's grandchildren
1c *Kevin Scott ODELL, *b* Atlanta, Ga., 31 July 1961
2c *Charles Marks ODELL, *b* 1 July 1963

Great-great-grandchildren's children
2b *Jeanne Saunders Marks, *b* Montgomery 5 July 1946; *m* 22 July 1967 *Steven Huddart SWINGENSTEIN and has issue:

Great-great-grandchildren's grandchildren
1c *Allison SWINGENSTEIN, *b* 14 Oct 1971

Great-great-grandchildren
5a *Priscilla Fairlee Marks [Mrs Priscilla Thornton, 3610 Thomas Avenue, Montgomery, AL 36111, USA], *b* Montgomery 13 May 1916; *m* 1st 13 Sept 1942 Jonathan Mills THORNTON, Jr (*b* Montgomery 10 April 1915; *d* Rochester, Minn., 21 Aug 1960), s of Jonathan Mills Thornton and his w Katherine Hailes, and has had issue:

Great-great-grandchildren's children
1b *Prof Jonathan Mills THORNTON III, PhD [804 Berkshire Rd, Ann Arbor, MI 48104, USA], *b* Montgomery 27 Oct 1943; *educ* Princeton (AB) and Yale (PhD); Prof of History U of Michigan 1982- (Assist Prof 1974-77, Assoc Prof 1977-82); *m* 5 Jan 1985 *Brenda, dau of George Donald Booth and his w Virginia Simmons
2b *Priscilla Fairlie Thornton, *b* Montgomery 8 May 1946; *m* 15 July 1967 *Col John Ledbetter CONDON, Jr, US Army (ret) (*b* Birmingham, Ala., 29 Aug 1940), s of John Ledbetter Condon, and has issue:

Great-great-grandchildren's grandchildren
1c *Priscilla Tyler CONDON, *b* Montgomery 24 July 1970
2c *Catherine Hails CONDON, *b* Pinehurst, N Carolina, 7 Dec 1975
3c *Elizabeth Broun CONDON, *b* Alexandria, Va., 6 Sept 1981

Great-great-grandchildren's children
3b Charles Marks THORNTON, *b* Montgomery 21 Jan 1959; *d* there 2 May 1961

Great-great-grandchildren
5a (cont.) Priscilla Marks Thornton *m* 2nd 19— (div 19—) Thomas Seay LAWSON, her cousin Rose D. Gunter's former husb (for whom *see above*)
6a *Henry Churchill MARKS [3591 Bankhead Ave, Montgomery, AL, USA], *b* Montgomery 4 Oct 1920; *m* 30 July 1943 *Emily Keyton (*b* Montgomery 25 Aug 1921) and has issue:

Great-great-grandchildren's children
1b *Emily Keyton Marks [Mrs Peter W Curtis, 8118 Wynlakes Blvd, Montgomery, AL 36117, USA], *b* Montgomery 6 Nov 1948; *m* 22 Sept 1973 *Peter William CURTIS (*b* Woking, Surrey, UK, 29 Aug 1945) and has issue:

Great-great-grandchildren's grandchildren
1c *William Churchill CURTIS, *b* Memphis, Tenn., 13 Feb 1977
2c *Andrew Marks CURTIS, *b* New Orleans 22 May 1980
3c *Spencer Bush CURTIS, *b* Montgomery, Ala., 22 Feb 1990

Great-great-grandchildren's children
2b *Catherine Churchill Marks, *b* Montgomery 17 May 1955; *m* 21 Sept 1991 *Michael John MAGINNIS (*b* New Orleans 25 Oct 1946)
3b *Lucille Watkins Marks, *b* Montgomery 16 June 1959; *m* 16 Jan 1982 *Leo Hanson LUQUIRE (*b* Montgomery 28 April 1958) and has issue:

Great-great-grandchildren's grandchildren
1c *Lewis Hanson LUQUIRE, *b* Montgomery 27 June 1985
2c *Frances Keyton LUQUIRE, *b* Montgomery 11 June 1988

Grandchildren
5 Thomas Cooper TYLER, *b* 1848; *d* July 1849
6 Elizabeth (Lizzie) Tyler, *b* Philadelphia Jan 1852; *m* Montgomery April 1871 Thomas Gardner FOSTER (*b* Elberton, Ga.,

1845; *d* Montgomery 1915), s of Thomas Flournoy Foster and his w Elizabeth Gardner, and *d* Montgomery 1915, leaving issue:

Great-grandchildren

(1) James Henry FOSTER, *b* Montgomery 1871; *m* there 1913 Alice Borgfeldt (*b* Montgomery 1880), dau of James Lahey and his w Lucy Winter, and *d* 1938, leaving issue:

Great-great-grandchildren

1a Lyra Nickerson Foster, *b* 1915; *m* 19— *George Ware SMITH (*b* 1909) and *d* May 1968, leaving issue:

Great-great-grandchildren's children

1b *Alice Lahey Smith [Mrs Robert Nyberg, 201 Huntley Drive, Montgomery, AL 36105, USA], *b* Montgomery 1940; *m* there 1971 *Robert NYBERG and has issue:

Great-great-grandchildren's grandchildren

1c *Robert Kel NYBERG, *b* Montgomery 1973

Great-great-grandchildren

2a *Elizabeth Gindrat Foster [Mrs D F Stakeley Jr, 2353 College Street, Montgomery, AL 36106, USA; 3139 Lebron Avenue, Montgomery, AL 36106, USA], *b* 1919; *m* 19— *Davis Fouville STAKELEY, Jr (*b* Montgomery 1917), s of Davis Fouville Stakeley and his w LeGrand Smith

Great-grandchildren

(2) Priscilla Tyler Foster, *b* Montgomery 1873; *m* there 1899 Dr Forney Caldwell STEVENSON (*b* Jacksonville, Ala., 1873; *d* Montgomery 1951), s of Horace Lee Stevenson and his w Mary Abernathy, and *d* Montgomery 1951, leaving issue:

Great-great-grandchildren

1a Elizabeth Tyler Stevenson, *b* Montgomery 1900; *m* there 1926 Sparta FRITZ, Jr (*b* Philadelphia 1902; *d* Oct 1954), s of Sparta Fritz and his w Emily Weiss, and *d* Tucson, Ariz., 18 Feb 1986, leaving issue:

Great-great-grandchildren's children

1b *Susan Dunlap Fritz [Mrs John Blye III, 8130 E Cloud Road, Tucson, AZ 85715, USA], *b* Philadelphia 1928; *educ* Vassar; *m* Philadelphia 24 Oct 1959 *John Henry BLYE III (*b* there 1926), s of John H. Blye, Jr, and his w Eleanore Trenchard Wurts, and has issue:

Great-great-grandchildren's grandchildren

1c *Eleanore Wurts Blye [Mrs Mark A Holloway, 1059 Cn Perry Ave, Calexico, CA 92231, USA], *b* Andrews Air Force Base, Md., 1961; *m* 10 April 1987 *Mark Allen HOLLOWAY and has issue:

Great-great-grandchildren's great-grandchildren

1d *Craig Samuel HOLLOWAY, *b* Brawley, Calif., 8 May 1989
2d *Katherine Anne HOLLOWAY, *b* Brawley 10 May 1991

Great-great-grandchildren's grandchildren

2c *John H. BLYE IV [8130 E Cloud Rd, Tucson, AZ 85715, USA], *b* Andrews Air Force Base 16 Nov 1962

Great-great-grandchildren's children

2b *Priscilla Tyler Fritz [Mrs John E Henderson, 7126 East Sabino Vista Circle, Tucson, AZ 85715, USA], *b* Philadelphia 1932; *m* Indian Head, Md., 1962 John E. HENDERSON (*b* Waco, Tex., 1922; *d* 1989) and has issue:

Great-great-grandchildren's grandchildren

1c *Elizabeth Tyler HENDERSON, *b* Alexandria, Va., 1968

Great-great-grandchildren

2a *Frances Abernathy Stevenson [Mrs Francis S Pruyn, Portland, OR, USA], *b* Montgomery 1905; *m* Philadelphia 1938 *Francis Nott PRUYN (*b* New York 1902), s of Francis N. Pruyn and his w Adelaide Mills, and has an adopted dau:

a *Priscilla Thusber PRUYN, *b* 1944

Great-grandchildren

(3) Dr Thomas Gardner FOSTER, *b* Montgomery 1875; *educ* U of Virginia; Lt-Cdr USN Medical Corps; *m* New York 1945 Evelyn Stitchell (*b* Cortland, New York) and *d* Buenos Aires, Argentina, 1964

Grandchildren

7 Priscilla Cooper Tyler, *b* Bristol, Pa., 15 Oct 1848; *m* St John's Episcopal Church, Montgomery, Ala., 22 Dec 1869 Albert Taylor GOODWYN (*b* Robinson Springs, Ala., 17 Dec 1842; *d* Birmingham, Ala., 1 July 1931), s of Dr Albert Gallatin Goodwyn and his w Harriet Bibb, and *d* Birmingham, Ala., 24 Feb 1936, leaving issue:

Great-grandchildren

(1) Robert Taylor GOODWYN, *b* Montgomery Alabama 4 Nov 1870; attorney; *m* Wetumpka, Ala., 21 Nov 1895 Jessie Dora (*b* there 27 July 1875; *d* Robinson Springs 16 Sept 1941), 2nd dau of Judge John Lancaster and his w Aldora Lett, and *d* Montgomery 10 May 1949, leaving issue:

Great-great-grandchildren

1a Elizabeth Aldor GOODWYN, *b* Wetumpka 22 Oct 1896; *m* Montgomery 22 Jan 1921 James Francis HEGENWALD (*b* Albany (now Decatur), Ala., 13 Feb 1896; *d* Montgomery 6 April 1966), 4th s of John George Hegenwald and his w Belle Roberts, and *d* 11 Feb 1982, leaving issue:

Great-great-grandchildren's children

1b *James Francis HEGENWALD, Jr [225 South Rio Vista, Apt 54, Anaheim, CA 92806, USA], *b* Albany, Ga., 6 Feb 1922;, *educ* Alabama U; aircraft design manager with N America, Rockwell, Englewood, Calif.; *m* Los Angeles 16 Feb 1945 *Rebecca Elizabeth (*b* 13 April 1924), dau of Russell Porter Coleman and his w Frances Deason, and has issue:

Great-great-grandchildren's grandchildren

1c *Elizabeth Rebecca HEGENWALD, *b* Los Angeles 12 Dec 1951; *educ* U of California at Riverside
2c *James Francis HEGENWALD III, *b* Los Angeles 25 April 1954, *educ* UCLA

Great-great-grandchildren's children

2b *Tyler Goodwyn HEGENWALD [445 Pennsylvania Avenue, Shreveport, LA 71105, USA], *b* Albany, Ga., 24 Jan 1924; *educ* Alabama U; former Assist V-Pres E. F. Hutton, stockbrokers, ret; *m* Coushatta, La., 1 Nov 1952 *Shirley Ann (*b* there 4 Sept 1927), dau of Henry William Bethard, Jr, and his w Shirley Edgerton, and has issue:

Great-great-grandchildren's grandchildren

1c *Ann Hegenwald [Mrs Frank W Harrison III, 6615 Sewanee, Houston, TX 77005, USA], *b* New Orleans 21 Sept 1954; *educ* Louisiana State U; *m* Shreveport, La., 4 Feb 1978 *Frank William HARRISON III, s of Frank William Harrison, Jr, and his w (Mary) Patricia McCoy, and has issue:

Great-great-grandchildren's great-grandchildren

1d *(Frank) Will(iam) HARRISON IV, *b* Houston 13 May 1982
2d *Andrew Tyler HARRISON, *b* Houston 27 Dec 1984

Great-great-grandchildren's grandchildren

2c *Janet Hegenwald, *b* Shreveport 8 April 1956; *educ* Louisiana State U; *m* Shreveport 14 May 1988 *Mark Wade TAYLOR (*b* 12 April 1955), s of Robert Lamar Taylor, Jr, and his w June Wade, and has issue:

Great-great-grandchildren's great-grandchildren

1d *Mark Wade TAYLOR, Jr, *b* Shreveport 10 Feb 1991

Great-great-grandchildren

2a *Priscilla Cooper Goodwyn [Mrs James Fowler, 2533 Montevallo Drive, Birmingham, AL 35223, USA], *b* Wetumpka, Ala., 15 Jan 1898; *m* Montgomery Jan 1923 *James Thomas FOWLER, Jr (*b* 21 Dec 1897), s of Dr James Thomas Fowler, and has issue:

Great-great-grandchildren's children

1b James Thomas FOWLER III, *b* 10 Sept 1923; *m* 19— *Lila Jean Hodges (*b* 26 Jan 1927) and *d* 6 Dec 1980, leaving issue:

Great-great-grandchildren's grandchildren

1c *James Thomas FOWLER IV [2068 Lakewood Drive, Birmingham, AL 35216, USA], *b* Tuscaloosa, Ala., 29 May 1948; *educ* U of Alabama; investment banker 1972-93; *m* 19— (divorce 19—)
2c *Jean Hodges FOWLER, *b* 1955; *educ* Alabama U

Great-great-grandchildren's children

2b *William Goodwyn FOWLER, *b* 4 Dec 1925; *educ* Alabama U; attorney; *m* 1st Birmingham, Ala., 19— (divorce 19—) Jane Steele Darnall (*b* 17 Dec 1927) and has issue:

Great-great-grandchildren's grandchildren

1c *William Goodwyn FOWLER, Jr, *b* Birmingham, Ala., 19 Jan 1951
2c *Gertrude Browning FOWLER, *b* Birmingham 26 March 1952
3c *John Darnall FOWLER, *b* Birmingham 1954

Great-great-grandchildren's children

2b (cont.) William G. Fowler *m* 2nd Birmingham, Ala., 19— *Dawn —— and with her has issue:

Great-great-grandchildren's grandchildren

4c *Priscilla Goodwyn FOWLER, *b* Birmingham, Ala., 1971

Great-great-grandchildren

3a Robert Tyler GOODWYN, Jr, *b* Wetumpka, Ala., 10 Aug 1900; *educ* Alabama U; attorney, Clerk of the Alabama House of Reps; *m* Montgomery 9 July 1932 *Alice McGehee (*b* 18 May 1909), dau of George A. Thomas and his w Mildred Spencer McGehee, and *d* Montgomery 13 April 1957, leaving issue:

Great-great-grandchildren's children

1b *Robert Tyler GOODWYN III [4202 Pickering Place, Alexandria, VA 22309, USA], *b* Montgomery 18 July 1933; *educ* US Mily Acad, Georgia Inst of Technology and Marymount U; Lt-Col USAF (ret), Dept Manager Computer

Systems 1981-93; *m* Leonia, New Jersey, 9 June 1956 *Judith (*b* 2 Jan 1935), dau of Edward Millar and his w Erma, and has issue:

Great-great-grandchildren's grandchildren
1c *Leslie Goodwyn [Mrs Mark Anstey, 24 Ballon St, Hampton, VA 23669, USA], *b* Columbus, Ga., 13 Nov 1957; *m* Alexandria, Va., 22 June 1985 *Mark ANSTEY and has issue:

Great-great-grandchildren's great-grandchildren
1d *Elizabeth Millar ANSTEY, *b* 27 April 1991

Great-great-grandchildren's grandchildren
2c *Robert Tyler GOODWYN IV [5310 Adean Ct, Williamsburg, VA 23188, USA], *b* Würzburg, Germany, 3 March 1960
3c *Reid Millar GOODWYN, *b* Atlanta, Ga., 25 July 1962

Great-great-grandchildren's children
2b *George Thomas GOODWYN [3368 Southview Avenue, Montgomery, AL 36111, USA], *b* Montgomery 8 March 1937; *educ* Alabama U and ROTC; sometime engr with US Army, subsequently civil engr in Montgomery; *m* Tuskegee, Ala., 19— *Winifred Hutchison (*b* there 17 June 1940), dau of Phillip Lightfoot and his w Winifred Hutchison, and has issue:

Great-great-grandchildren's grandchildren
1c *George Thomas GOODWYN, Jr [2467 Wildwood Drive, Montgomery, AL 36111, USA], *b* Bad Hersfeld, Germany, 18 July 1960; owner of McGehee Construction Co 1985-; *m* 4 Sept 1986 *Leslie Alison (*b* Montgomery 28 June 1963), dau of William Craig Coats and his w Binnie Pulliam, and has issue:

Great-great-grandchildren's great-grandchildren
1d *Alison Coats GOODWYN, *b* Montgomery 14 Nov 1987
2d *George Thomas GOODWYN III, *b* Montgomery 8 Sept 1989

Great-great-grandchildren's grandchildren
2c *Philip Lightfoot GOODWYN [710 Cloverdale Rd, Montgomery, AL 36106, USA], *b* Bad Hersfeld 18 Dec 1961
3c *Winifred Lightfoot GOODWYN, *b* Montgomery 14 July 1967

Great-great-grandchildren
4a William Bibb GOODWYN, *b* Wetumpka, Ala., 4 Feb 1902; *educ* Auburn U (BS); Lt-Cdr Civil Engrg Corps USN World War II; *m* Brundidge, Ala., 4 Oct 1928 *Foy Glen [Mrs William B. Goodwyn, 1302 Augusta Avenue, Montgomery, AL 36111, USA] (*b* Brundidge 8 Oct 1905), dau of Willis Glen Gilmore and his w Julia Wilkerson, and *d* Montgomery 20 Sept 1973, leaving issue:

Great-great-grandchildren's children
1b *William Bibb GOODWYN, Jr [3119 Pinehurst Drive, Montgomery, AL 36111, USA], *b* Montgomery 13 Aug 1930; *educ* Auburn U; bridge-constructor; *m* Montgomery 8 May 1954 *Jean Elizabeth, dau of Aubrey Harris Fleming and his w Elizabeth McKibbon, and has issue:

Great-great-grandchildren's grandchildren
1c *Elizabeth McKibbon Goodwyn [Mrs Robert T Thetford, 3370 Narrow Lane Rd, Montgomery, AL 36111, USA], *b* Montgomery 25 April 1955; *educ* Auburn U; *m* 8 April 1978 *Robert Teague THETFORD, s of William Fletcher Thetford and his w Dorothy Teague, and has issue:

Great-grat-grandchildren's great-grandchildren
1d *Foy Goodwyn THETFORD, *b* Macon, Ga., 5 Feb 1979
2d *Dorothy Teague THETFORD, *b* Macon 16 Feb 1982
3d *Robert Teague THETFORD, Jr, *b* Montgomery 28 Aug 1987

Great-great-grandchildren's grandchildren
2c *William Bibb GOODWYN III [2342 Tankersley Road, Montgomery, AL 36106, USA], *b* Montgomery 11 April 1957; *m* Montgomery 14 June 1980 *Mary Jeanette Johnson and has issue:

Great-great-grandchildren's great-grandchildren
1d *William Bibb GOODWYN IV, *b* 11 Dec 1982
2d *John Fleming GOODWYN, *b* 21 Sept 1984
3d *Mary Lindsey GOODWYN, *b* 10 July 1987

Great-great-grandchildren's grandchildren
3c *Foy Gilmore Goodwyn [Mrs Samuel B McGowin Jr, 275 Park Terrace, Mobile, AL 36604, USA], *b* Montgomery 12 May 1962; *educ* Auburn U; television stage manager and assist film location manager; *m* 12 Sept 1992 *Samuel Bernard McGOWIN, Jr

Great-great-grandchildren
5a John Lancaster GOODWYN, *b* Montgomery 13 Oct 1903; *educ* Alabama U; attorney, sometime Mayor Montgomery and Justice Alabama Supreme Court; *m* Montgomery 16 April 1931 *Elizabeth Hudson [Mrs John L Goodwyn, 1567

Gilmer Avenue, Montgomery, AL 36104, USA], dau of Dr R. S. Hill and his w Elizabeth Hudson, and *d* Montgomery April 1968, leaving issue:

Great-great-grandchildren's children
1b *Warren Hudson GOODWYN, *b* 1934
2b *Elizabeth Lancaster GOODWYN, *b* 1946

Great-great-grandchildren
6a *Louise Tyson Goodwyn [Mrs James M Faircloth, 220 Fox Run, Tuscaloosa, AL 35406, USA], *b* Montgomery, Ala., 13 June 1906; *m* 1st Robinson Springs, Ala., 21 Aug 1935 James William MUSTIN, Jr (*d* Tuscaloosa, Ala., 16 May 1954), s of James William Mustin and his w Lucile Noble, and has issue:

Great-great-grandchildren's children
1b *Priscilla Goodwyn Mustin, *b* 9 Feb 1938; *m* 19— (divorce 19—) James Mason PLEDGE and has issue:

Great-great-grandchildren's grandchildren
1c *Marcus Shaw PLEDGE, *b* 1 Oct 1959
2c *Grace PLEDGE, *b* 8 Sept 1961

Great-great-grandchildren's children
2b *James William MUSTIN III, *b* 25 May 1943; *m* 1st 1962 (divorce 1971) Peggy Grant; *m* 2nd 1974 (divorce 1981) —— and with her has issue:

Great-great-grandchildren's grandchildren
1c *Kasha MUSTIN, *b* 1975
2c *Joshua MUSTIN, *b* 1977

Great-great-grandchildren's children
3b *Lucile Noble Mustin, *b* 18 Jan 1950; *m* 1st 1967 (divorce 1970) William Walden BOOTHE and has issue:

Great-great-grandchildren's grandchildren
1c *Louise Tyson BOOTHE, *b* 1969

Great-great-grandchildren's children
3b (cont.) Mrs Lucile Boothe *m* 2nd 1975 *Keith MARTIN and has issue:

Great-great-grandchildren's grandchildren
1c *Brooks MARTIN, *b* 1978

Great-great-grandchildren
6a (cont.) Louise Goodwyn Mustin *m* 2nd Tuscaloosa, Ala., James M. FAIRCLOTH (*d* 19—)
7a Albert Taylor GOODWYN, Jr, *b* 19 June 1911; *educ* Alabama U; Lt-Col US Army Engrs; *m* Miami Dec 1944 (divorce 1972) Mary Spears (*b* 18 April 1914) and *d* Montgomery, Ala., 8 April 1973, leaving issue:

Great-great-grandchildren's children
1b *Albert Taylor GOODWYN III [Albuquerque, NM 87101, USA], *b* 28 Dec 1945

Great-grandchildren
(2) Adele Goodwyn, *b* 6 Nov 1873; *m* 18— John Davidson McNEEL (*b* 13 Oct 1872; *d* 8 March 1940) and *d* 28 April 1939, leaving issue:

Great-great-grandchildren
1a *Letitia Tyler McNeel [Mrs William D Arant, 2815 Argyle Road, Birmingham, AL 35213, USA], *b* 7 Nov 1898; *m* 19— *William Douglas ARANT (*b* 19 May 1897) and has issue:

Great-great-grandchildren's children
1b *Adele Goodwyn Arant [Mrs Richard J Stockham, 9 Office Park Cir, Mountain Brook, Birmingham, AL 35203, USA; 19 Glen Iris Park South, Birmingham, AL 35205, USA], *b* 26 June 1931; *m* Sept 1951 *Richard James STOCKHAM
2b *Letitia Christian ARANT, *b* 14 March 1935
3b *Frances Fairlie ARANT, *b* 25 Sept 1936

Great-great-grandchildren
2a *Hulda McNeel, *b* 5 Nov 1906; *m* 19— *Peyton Dandridge BIBB (*b* 3 Oct 1904) and has issue:

Great-great-grandchildren's children
1b *Adele Goodwyn BIBB, *b* 23 Aug 1940
2b *Peyton Dandridge BIBB, Jr, *b* 15 Nov 1941

Great-grandchildren
(3) Albert Gallatin GOODWYN, *b* Robinson Springs, Ala., 1 Oct 1875; Col US Army; *m* Nashville, Tenn., 30 Aug 1902 Charlie (*b* Huntsville, Ala., 9 Jan 1878; *d* Summerville, S Carolina, 29 Jan 1955), dau of Hector David Lane and his w Margaret Mason, and *d* Summerville, S Carolina, 28 Jan 1956, leaving issue:

Great-great-grandchildren
1a *Marion Ely Goodwyn [Mrs Milton Shattuck, Gray Craig, Paradise Avenue, Middletown, RI 02840, USA], b Guimeras, Philippines, 25 June 1903; m 1929 *Milton Cogswell SHATTUCK (b Manila, Philippines, 23 March 1901), s of Amos Blanchard Shattuck and his w Susan, and has issue:

Great-great-grandchildren's children
1b *Margaret Lane Shattuck [Mrs John C Rahmann, 599 Greenleaf Avenue, Glencoe, IL 60022, USA; 199 Hazel Avenue, Glencoe, IL 60022, USA], b Washington, DC, 12 Dec 1929; m Fort Benning, Ga., 27 July 1954 *John Charles RAHMANN (b Tarentum, Pa., 11 Aug 1927), s of Carl Antone Rahmann and his w Dorothy Lucille, and has issue:

Great-great-grandchildren's grandchildren
1c *John Charles RAHMANN, Jr, b Fort Benning, Ga., 17 Oct 1955
2c *Pamela Lane RAHMANN, b Natrona Heights, Pa., 28 Sept 1957
3c *Susan Marion RAHMANN, b Syracuse, New York, 8 May 1962

Great-great-grandchildren's children
2b *(Marion) Pamela Shattuck [Mrs John M Burleigh, 43 Oak Ridge Lane, West Hartford, CT 06107, USA], b Honolulu, Hawaii, 17 Sept 1931; m St James's Episcopal Church, Augusta, Maine, 7 July 1951 *John Medlicott BURLEIGH (b Springfield, Mass., 25 Jan 1928), s of Lewis Albert Burleigh and his w Harriet Medlicott, and has issue:

Great-great-grandchildren's grandchildren
1c *Christopher Medlicott BURLEIGH, b Hartford, Connecticut 10 Aug 1955
Mr and Mrs John M. Burleigh also adopted a child:
a *Lane Shattuck BURLEIGH, b Boston, Mass., 15 May 1958

Great-great-grandchildren's children
3b *Milton Cogswell SHATTUCK [Box 132, Fort Gulick, Panama Canal Zone], b 193-; m 19— *Susan Shattuck
4b *Susan Lane Shattuck [Mrs William Benson, 618 Constitution Avenue NE, Washington, DC 20002, USA], b Missoula, Mont., 12 April 1939; m Newport, Rhode Island, 6 Sept 1968 *William M. BENSON

Great-great-grandchildren
2a *Margaret Lane Goodwyn [Mrs J Blake Middleton, 42 Society St, Charleston, SC 29401, USA; 5 Legare Street, Charleston, SC 29401, USA], b Fort Douglas, Utah, 17 Oct 1904; m Deland, Fla., 13 Feb 1926 *Julius Blake MIDDLETON (b Charleston 9 Nov 1900), s of William Dehon Middleton and his w Julia Blake, and has issue:

Great-great-grandchildren's children
1b *Julius Blake MIDDLETON, Jr [19745 Lakeview Avenue, Excelsior, MN 55331, USA], b Cleveland, Ohio 15 Aug 1932; educ Williams Coll., Mass.; m Milwaukee, Wis., 15 Sept 1954 *Nancy [Nancy Middleton, 20245 Lakeview Avenue, Deephaven, MN, USA] (b Milwaukee), dau of Harold Daniels and his w Grace King, and has issue:

Great-great-grandchildren's grandchildren
1c *Julius Blake MIDDLETON III, b Milwaukee 12 Feb 1959
2c *(Mark) Tyler MIDDLETON [17705 Susan Drive, Minnetonka, MN 55345, USA], b Milwaukee 15 Sept 1960; m 19— *Kimberley ——
3c *Gardner King MIDDLETON, b Milwaukee 10 May 1962
4c *Lane Goodwyn MIDDLETON, b Milwaukee 16 Sept 1964

Great-great-grandchildren's children
2b *Charlie Lane Middleton [Mrs Francis Kinsman, The Mossings, Great Maplestead, Halstead, Essex, UK], b Toledo, Ohio, 9 May 1938; educ Heathfield Sch, Ascot, UK, and the Sorbonne, Paris; m London 7 Aug 1959 *Francis John Morland KINSMAN (b London 28 Aug 1934), s of Harold John Alfred Kinsman and his w Barbara Moncaster, and has issue:

Great-great-grandchildren's grandchildren
1c *Blake Middleton KINSMAN, b London 10 Dec 1960
2c *Emmeline Hilbery KINSMAN, b London 28 March 1962
3c *Francis John KINSMAN, b Dacca, East Pakistan, 29 Sept 1964

Great-grandchildren
(4) Gardner F. GOODWYN, b 1880; m Lora Williams (d 6 July 1942) and d 11 Jan 1962, leaving issue:

Great-great-grandchildren
1a *Judge Gardner F. GOODWYN, Jr [3 Meadow Lane, Lakewood, Bessemer, AL 35020, USA], b Bessemer, Ala., 27 April 1914; educ Virginia Mily Inst, U of Alabama and Harvard; with US Army World War II 1941-46, Assist Atty Genevea, Ala., 1946-50, Circuit Judge Alabama 1950-81; m 11 Dec 1955 *Margaret Myrtle, dau of Jacob Bart Williams and his w Myrtle Geneva Durbin, and has issue:

Great-great-grandchildren's children
1b *Gardner F. GOODWYN III [PO Box 2855, Gulf Shores, AL 36547, USA], b Birmingham, Ala., 26 Oct 1958

2b *Margaret Priscilla GOODWYN [5442 Martel, Dallas, TX 75206, USA], *b* Birmingham 25 March 1962

3b *Tyler W. GOODWYN [3 Meadow Lane, Lakewood, Bessemer, AL 35020, USA], *b* Birmingham 22 Sept 1963

Great-great-grandchildren

2a Marvin William GOODWYN, *b* Bessemer, Ala., 29 March 1917; *educ* Alabama U (LLD 1940); Col USAF (ret 1964), served World War II (20 decorations); *m* Montgomery, Ala., 22 Jan 1954 (divorce 19—) Lilla Davenport (*b* Birmingham, Ala., 1923), dau of Charles Frederick Anderson and his w Lilla Davenport, and *d* 20 Dec 1991, leaving issue:

Great-great-grandchildren's children

1b *Marvin William GOODWYN, Jr [2220 Park Newport, Newport Beach, CA 92660, USA; 2080 Park Newport, Newport Beach, CA 92660, USA], *b* Macon, Ga., 7 Feb 1955; *educ* Vanderbilt U, Nashville, Tenn.

Great-grandchildren

(5) Priscilla Cooper Goodwyn, *b* 25 Feb 1887; *m* 1 April 1913 Frank Hastings GRIFFIN (*b* 16 July 1886) and *d* 3 July 1965, leaving issue:

Great-great-grandchildren

1a *Adele Goodwyn Griffin [Mrs James Sands, Sunnyside, Wawa, PA 18660, USA], *b* Swarthmore, Pa., 25 June 1920; *m* 1st 1941 William Logan McCOY, Jr (*b* April 1920; *d* 19 June 1943), s of William Logan McCoy, and has issue:

Great-great-grandchildren's children

1b *Marguerite Logan McCoy, *b* 5 Oct 1943; *m* 19— *James Pickney BORDEN, V-Pres Chase Manhattan Bank, London, s of Richard Borden, and has issue:

Great-great-grandchildren's grandchildren
1c *Elizabeth Evans BORDEN, *b* 23 May 1969
2c *William McCoy BORDEN, *b* 29 April 1971

Great-great-grandchildren

1a (cont.) Adele Griffin McCoy *m* 2nd 18 Jan 1947 *James A. SANDS and has further issue:

Great-great-grandchildren's children

2b *Priscilla Goodwyn Sands, *b* 10 Oct 1947; *m* 19— *Robert E. WATSON III, s of Robert E. Watson, Jr, and has issue:

Great-great-grandchildren's grandchildren
1c *Adele Griffin WATSON, *b* 29 July 1970
2c *Robert Sands WATSON, *b* 15 March 1972

Great-great-grandchildren's children
3b *James A. SANDS, Jr, *b* 12 Sept 1949
4b *William Franklin SANDS III, *b* 25 July 1951
5b *Elizabeth Keating SANDS, *b* 6 April 1953
6b *Adele Griffin SANDS, *b* 21 April 1961
7b *Geoffrey Keating SANDS, *b* 14 Aug 1962

Great-great-grandchildren

2a *Frank Hastings GRIFFIN, Jr [Old Orchard, Wawa, PA 18660, USA], *b* Swarthmore, Pa., 26 Aug 1921; *m* 10 June 1943 *Mary Dercum Mifflin (*b* 25 Feb 1925) and has issue:

Great-great-grandchildren's children

1b *Frank Hastings GRIFFIN III [1000 Conestoga Road, Rosehill, PA, USA], *b* 31 May 1946; *m* 16 Nov 1968 *Jeffory Anne Horning (*b* Jacksonville, Fla., 27 May 1947)

2b *Elizabeth Dercum Griffin, *b* 21 July 1948; *m* 10 Aug 1968 *Charles Davis BELCHER, Jr (*b* 27 Jan 1947), s of Charles Davis Belcher

3b *Mary Lloyd GRIFFIN, *b* 27 Feb 1951

4b *Samuel Wright Mifflin GRIFFIN, *b* 28 May 1953

Great-great-grandchildren

3a *J(ohn) Tyler GRIFFIN [624 Dorset Road, Devon, PA 19333, USA], *b* Wawa, Pa., 30 Aug 1923; *m* 21 Sept 1944 *Sophronia Marguerite Worrell (*b* 18 Nov 1925) and has issue:

Great-great-grandchildren's children

1b *Marguerite Worrell Griffin, *b* 17 Nov 1945; *m* 18 Oct 1969 *Larry Wayne CHARTIER and has issue:

Great-great-grandchildren's grandchildren
1c *Priscilla Marguerite CHARTIER, *b* 28 Sept 1974
2c *Tyler Wayne CHARTIER, *b* 3 Aug 1976
3c *Samual Homer CHARTIER, *b* 21 June 1978

Great-great-grandchildren's children

2b *John Tyler GRIFFIN, Jr, *b* 24 Sept 1949; *m* 18 May 1974 *Mary C. Barili and has issue:

Great-great-grandchildren's grandchildren
1c *John Tyler GRIFFIN III, *b* 10 May 1983

Great-great-grandchildren's children
3b *Priscilla Goodwyn Griffin [Mrs Erik Tank-Nielsen, 201 Church Rd, Devon, PA 19333, USA], *b* Philadelphia 4 Oct 1952; *educ* Agnes Irwin and Bates Coll; administrator for non-profit fund-raising; *m* 28 Aug 1971 *Erik TANK-NIELSEN, *s* of Reidar and Marie Tank-Nielsen, and has issue:

Great-great-grandchildren's grandchildren
1c *Kari TANK-NIELSEN, *b* Philadelphia 28 Oct 1975
2c *Sonia Marie TANK-NIELSEN, *b* Philadelphia 18 April 1977
3c *Lise TANK-NIELSEN, *b* 10 Aug 1981

Great-great-grandchildren
4a *Priscilla Tyler Griffin, *b* Wawa, Pa., 6 Dec 1927; *m* 15 March 1952 *Herman Albert SCHAEFER (*b* 14 March 1921) and has issue:

Great-great-grandchildren's children
1b *Nancy Griffin SCHAEFER, *b* 14 July 1953
2b *Priscilla Goodwyn SCHAEFER, *b* 25 Jan 1956
3b *Herman Albert SCHAEFER, Jr, *b* 18 July 1958

Grandchildren
8 Julia Campbell Tyler, *b* Philadelphia 6 Dec 1854; *m* Montgomery, Ala., 15 April 1874 Henry Hewlings TYSON (*b* 5 Dec 1845; *d* 7 Sept 1887) and *d* 5 July 1884, leaving issue:

Great-grandchildren
(1) Marie Louise TYSON, *b* 26 Jan 1875; *d* Upperville, Va., *c* 1950
(2) Grace Tyson, *b* 20 June 1878; *m* 5 Dec 1901 Eugene Cameron GATEWOOD (*b* 27 Aug 1877; *d* 30 Nov 1926) and *d* Upperville 1962, leaving issue:

Great-great-grandchildren
1a Julia Campbell GATEWOOD, *b* Rectortown, Va., 19 Sept 1903; *d* 1966

Great-grandchildren
(3) Alan Campbell TYSON, *b* 14 Aug 1877; *m* 1st (divorce) Gabriella Smythe and had one child (*d* at birth); *m* 2nd Sophie von Riesner; *m* 3rd Cora Barnhart

Grandchildren
9 Robert TYLER, *b* Philadelphia Dec 1857; *d* Montgomery, Ala., 1937

President Tyler's son
III John TYLER, *b* 27 April 1819; Assist Sec of War of the Confederacy; *m* 25 Oct 1838 Martha Rochelle (*b* 23 Jan 1820; *d* 11 Jan 1867) and *d* 26 Jan 1896, leaving issue:

Grandchildren
1 James Rochelle TYLER, *b* 9 Sept 1839
2 Letitia Christian Tyler, *b* 27 April 1844; *m* 13 Sept 1860 Gen William Briggs SHANDS (*b* 7 Feb 1820; *d* 1906) and *d* 23 Jan 1863, leaving issue:

Great-grandchildren
(1) William SHANDS, *b* 6 Sept 1861; State Senator; *m* 1st 18— Nancy Pretlow; *m* 2nd 5 Nov 1895 Annie Byrum Ridley (*b* 27 Feb 1877) and with her had issue:

Great-great-grandchildren
1a *William Ridley SHANDS, *b* 17 Aug 1896; *m* June 1922 *Josephine Winston and has issue:

Great-great-grandchildren's children
1b *Martha Jane Shands, *b* 20 Feb 1924; *m* 19— *John W. ALBUS
2b *William Ridley SHANDS, Jr, *h* 23 Nov 1932

Great-great-grandchildren
2a *Letitia Christian SHANDS, *b* 19 Aug 1898
3a *Bessie Thomas SHANDS, *b* 20 June 1900

Grandchildren
3 Mattie Rochelle TYLER, *b* 1 March 1844; *d* Jan 1928

President Tyler's daughters
IV Letitia Tyler, *b* 11 May 1821; *m* Feb 1839 James A. SEMPLE and *d* Baltimore 28 Dec 1907
V Elizabeth (Lizzie) Tyler, *b* 11 July 1823; *m* the White House 31 Jan 1842, as his 1st w, William Nevison WALLER, of Williamsburg, Va., *s* of William Waller and his w Mary Berkely Griffin, and *d* 1 June 1850, leaving issue:

Grandchildren
1 William Griffin WALLER, *b* 184-; served with Confederate States Army, Assist Ed *Savannah News* and Managing Ed

Richmond Times; *m* 1st the Confederate White House, Richmond, Va., Nov 1863 Jenny Kent, dau of William Burr Howell, of The Briers, Natchez, Miss., and his w Margaret Louise Kempe, and sister of the second w of Jefferson F. Davis, President of the Confederate States of America, and had issue:

Great-grandchildren
(1) Elizabeth Tyler WALLER, *b* 18—
(2) William Griffin WALLER, *b* 18—
(3) Maggie Howell WALLER, *b* 18—; *d* in infancy

Grandchildren
1 (cont.) William G. Waller *m* 2nd Elizabeth Hale Austin and with her had issue:

Great-grandchildren
(4) Mary Austin Waller, *b* 1879; *m* 1908 John DE SAUSSURE (*d* 1945) and had issue:

Great-great-grandchildren
1a *Elizabeth Waller De Saussure, *b* 1909; *m* 19— *R. H. KNAPP and has issue:

Great-great-grandchildren's children
1b *Dana M. KNAPP
2b *R. H. KNAPP, Jr

Great-great-grandchildren
2a *Mary C. De Saussure, *b* 1916; *m* 19— *C. G. MORTENSON and has issue:

Great-great-grandchildren's children
1b *Karel MORTENSON, *b* 19—
2b *Ellen MORTENSON, *b* 19—

Great-grandchildren
(5) John Tyler WALLER, *b* 1881; *m* Lucy Bacon
(6) Clara WALLER; *d* in infancy

Grandchildren
2 John WALLER, *b* 18—; one of the irregular troops under the command of John S. Mosby during the Civil War; ka
3 Letitia WALLER; *d* in infancy
4 Mary Stuart Waller; *m* 1867 Gen Louis G. YOUNG, of Savannah, Ga.
5 Robert WALLER; *m* Emily Johnstone and had issue:

Great-grandchildren
(1) Robert Tyler WALLER, *b* 1879; *d* 1943

President Tyler's daughters
VI Ann Contesse TYLER, *b* 5 April 1825; *d* July 1825
VII Alice Tyler, *b* 23 March 1827; *m* Sherwood Forest, Charles City Co., Va., 11 July 1850 Revd Henry Mandeville DENISON, Rector of Bruton Parish, Williamsburg, of St Paul's, Louisville, and St Peter's, Charleston (*b* Wyoming, Pa., 1822; *d* 1858), and *d* 8 June 1854, leaving issue:

Grandchildren
1 Elizabeth Russell Denison, *b* 1852; *m* 1st 18— William Gaston ALLEN (*b* 1849; served US Consular Service; *d* 1891) and had issue:

Great-grandchildren
(1) Alice Denison Allen, *b* 1887; *m* 1st 1910 William BACHOFEN and had issue:

Great-great-grandchildren
1a William Henry BACHOFEN, *b* 1913; *d* 1915

Great-grandchildren
(1) (cont.) Alice Allen Bachofen *m* 2nd 1919 Raymond Pierson NICHOLSON (*b* 1892)
(2) William Gaston ALLEN, *b* 1890; *m* 1st 1914 Edna Knowles and had issue:

Great-great-grandchildren
1a *Louise ALLEN, *b* 1915
2a *Elizabeth Denison ALLEN, *b* 1917
3a *Edna ALLEN, *b* 1921

Great-grandchildren
(2) (cont.) William G. Allen *m* 2nd 1926 Megan Jones (*d* 1928) and with her had issue:

Great-great-grandchildren
4a *Megan ALLEN, *b* 1928

Great-grandchildren
(2) (cont.) William G. Allen *m* 3rd 1929 *Nanie Jones

Grandchildren
1 (cont.) Elizabeth Denison Allen *m* 2nd Revd —— WILLIAMSON and *d* 1928

President Tyler's son
VIII Dr Tazewell TYLER, *b* 6 Dec 1830; Surgeon Confederate States Army; *m* 1857 (divorce 1873) Nannie Bridges, and *d* Calif. 8 Jan 1874, leaving issue:

Grandchildren
1 James TYLER; *m* May ——
2 Martha TYLER; *d* 1943

President TYLER *m* 2nd New York 26 June 1844 Julia (*b* Gardiner's Island, New York, 4 May 1820; *d* Richmond, Va., 10 July 1889, *bur* with her husb), dau of David Gardiner, sometime New York Senator (*k* in the explosion aboard the USS *Princeton* 28 Feb 1844 which also killed President TYLER'S Secs of State and of the Navy), and his *w* Juliana, dau of Michael McLachlan, merchant (whose own father was *k* 1746 at the Battle of Culloden, in Scotland, between the Jacobites, on whose side it is likely the elder McLachlan fought, and the forces of the Hanoverian GEORGE II), and *d* Richmond, Va., 18 Jan 1862 of bilious fever, having with her had further issue:

President Tyler's son
IX (David) Gardiner (Gardie) TYLER, of Sherwood Forest, Charles City Co, Va., *b* East Hampton, New York, 12 July 1846; *educ* Washington Coll (now Washington and Lee U); served Confederate States Army 1863-65, Memb Virginia Senate 1891-92 and 1900-04, Memb US Congress 1893-97, Judge Virginia 14th Judicial Circuit 1904; *m* Richmond, Va., 6 June 1894 Mary Morris (*b* there 1 June 1865; *d* Sherwood Forest 30 Aug 1931), dau of James Alfred Jones, of Richmond, and his *w* Mary Henry Lyon, and *d* Sherwood Forest 1 or 5 Sept 1927, having had issue:

Grandchildren
1 Mary Lyon Tyler, *b* Washington, DC, 31 March 1895; *m* Sherwood Forest 25 Sept 1926 George Peterkin GAMBLE (*b* Richmond 20 Sept 1899; *d* Solana Beach, Calif., 14 Aug 1986), s of Cary Gamble and his *w* Elizabeth Hanson Peterkin, and *d* La Jolla, Calif., 25 Jan 1975, leaving issue:

Great-grandchildren
(1) *Mary Morris Gamble [Mrs Lea Booth, 208 Rowland Drive, Lynchburg, VA 24503, USA], *b* Richmond 31 Dec 1927; *educ* Sweet Briar Coll, Va. (BA); *m* Kirkwood, Mo., 29 Dec 1951 *(Augustus) Lea BOOTH (*b* Danville, Va., 28 Sept 1917), s of Augustus Arsell Booth and his *w* Emma Lea, and has issue:

Great-great-grandchildren
1a *Mary Lyon Booth [Mrs Thomas P Verlin, 1290 Edgewood Ave S, Jacksonville, FL 32205, USA], *b* Lynchburg, Va., 23 June 1954; *educ* Davidson Coll; *m* Lynchburg 30 Dec 1978 *Thomas Patrick VERLIN (*b* New York 22 May 1954), s of Ambrose Verlin and his *w* Angela Popovich, and has issue:

Great-great-grandchildren's children
1b *Mary Morris VERLIN, *b* Jacksonville 17 Jan 1989

Great-great-grandchildren
2a *George Lea BOOTH [4706 Bromley Lane, Richmond, VA 23226, USA], *b* Lynchburg 8 Oct 1957
3a *Cary Gamble BOOTH [1408 Trouville Ave, Norfolk, VA 23505, USA], *b* Lynchburg 8 Oct 1957; *educ* Washington and Lee U and U of Virginia; Market Devpt Manager Norfolk Southern Corp; *m* Lexington, Va., 17 Aug 1985 *Jane Wallace, dau of Thomas Vance McClure and his *w* Betty Jordan, and has issue:

Great-great-grandchildren's children
1b *Richard Whitaker BOOTH, *b* Norfolk, Va., 8 June 1988
2b *Alexander Tyler BOOTH, *b* Norfolk 5 June 1991

Grandchildren
2 Margaret Gardiner Tyler, *b* Washington, DC, 3 Feb 1897; *m* Sherwood Forest 2 July 1919 Stephen Fowler CHADWICK (*b* Colfax, Wash., 14 Aug 1894; *d* Seattle 28 Aug 1975), s of Stephen James Chadwick and his *w* Emma Plummer, and *d* Seattle 6 Sept 1981, leaving issue:

Great-grandchildren
(1) *Mary Tyler Chadwick [Mrs W Chave McCracken, Box 173 Turner Mountain, Ivy, VA 22945, USA], *b* Seattle 5 May 1921; *m* Webster Groves, Mo., 11 May 1949 *W(illiam) Chave McCRACKEN (*b* New York 21 June 1920), s of Frederick Beekman McCracken and his *w* Mildred Chave, and has issue:

Great-great-grandchildren
1a *Adelaide Tyler McCracken [Ms Adelaide McCracken, RFD 2, Bethel, VT 05032, USA], *b* Oberlin, Ohio, 13 May 1950; *m* Mexico City 23 Feb 1979 (divorce 19—) (William) David POWELL (*b* Albany, Ga., 2 Sept 1947), s of Jason Powell and his *w* Bertha Hall, and has issue:

Great-great-grandchildren's children
1b *Jason Chave POWELL, *b* Randolph, Vt., 13 Jan 1983
2b *Margaret Chloe POWELL, *b* Randolph 12 Jan 1985

Great-great-grandchildren
2a *Margaret Chadwick McCracken [Mrs Theodore Turner, Box 9, Bridgwater, VT 05034, USA], *b* Oberlin 17 Nov 1952; *educ* Pine Manor Junior Coll and Boston U; *m* Woodstock, Vt., 4 June 1978 *Theodore Smith TURNER, Jr (*b* New York City 7 Aug 1947), s of Theodore Smith Turner and his w Jane White, and has issue:

Great-great-grandchildren's children
1b *Caleb McCracken TURNER, *b* Randolph, Vt., 31 Jan 1981
2b *Frederick Lion TURNER, *b* Randolph 3 Aug 1983

Great-great-grandchildren
3a *Sara Chave McCracken [Mrs Kenneth L Norcross, RFD1 Box 84, Reading, VT, USA], *b* Oberlin 4 Oct 1954; *m* South Woodstock, Vt., 12 July 1980 *Kenneth Lee NORCROSS (*b* 18 Dec 1950), s of Theodore Norcross and his w Lois Davis, and has issue:

Great-great-grandchildren's children
1b *Julia Tyler NORCROSS, *b* Springfield, Vt., 6 July 1986

Great-grandchildren
(2) *Stephen Fowler CHADWICK, Jr [Arrow Point, Bainbridge Island, WA 98140, USA], *b* Seattle 20 Oct 1924; *educ* Yale (BA) and U of Washington (JD); *m* 1st Seattle 25 Nov 1953 (divorce 19—) Diane (*b* Berkeley, Calif., 25 Aug 1928), dau of Roy Halsey and his w Catalena Sedgwick, and has issue:

Great-great-grandchildren
1a *Ann Tyler CHADWICK [16118 NE 15th, Bellevue, WA 98008, USA], *b* Seattle 24 Aug 1955
2a *Paul Halsey CHADWICK [5733 Benner Street No 7, Los Angeles, CA 90042, USA], *b* Seattle 3 Sept 1957

Great-grandchildren
(2) (cont.) Stephen F. Chadwick, Jr, *m* 2nd Seattle 28 May 1965 *Annice Buckner Ciszek (*b* Worcester, Mass., 25 April 1927), dau of Orello S. Buckner and his w Virginia Siler

Grandchildren
3 David Gardiner TYLER, Jr, *b* Sherwood Forest, Va., April 1899; *educ* William and Mary Coll; *m* 19— *Anne Shelton [Mrs David G Tyler, Creek Plantation, Charles City County, VA 23030, USA] and *d* Williamsburg, Va., 29 March 1983 (his gf President TYLER's 203rd birthday), leaving issue:

Great-grandchildren
(1) *David Gardiner TYLER III [14201 John Tyler Memorial Highway, Charles City, VA 23030, USA], *b* 19—; *m* 19— *Dolores —— and has issue:

Great-great-grandchildren
1a *David TYLER
2a *William TYLER

Great-grandchildren
(2) *Ann Shelton TYLER
(3) *George Keesee TYLER

Grandchildren
4 James Alfred Jones TYLER, *b* Sherwood Forest 16 Aug 1902; *educ* U of Virginia; Commonwealth's Attorney for Charles City County, Va., 1927-51 and 1955-63; *m* Richmond, Va., 1938 Katherine Thomason (*b* Richmond 1909; *d* 1967) and *d* Richmond 27 July 1972, leaving issue:

Great-grandchildren
(1) *Emily Thomason TYLER [6201 Bard's Lane, Browns Summit, Greensboro, NC 27420, USA], *b* 1941
(2) *Mary Gardiner Tyler [Mrs Garnett Stover, 813 Horsepen Road, Richmond, VA 23229, USA], *b* 19 April 1943; *m* 4 May 1968 *Garnett Edward STOVER, Jr (*b* 27 June 1942), s of Garnett Edward Stover, and has issue:

Great-great-grandchildren
1a *Garnett Edward STOVER III, *b* 22 May 1970
2a *Katherine Thomason STOVER, *b* 14 April 1972

Great-grandchildren
(3) *James Alfred Jones TYLER, Jr [11400 Goose Pond Lane, Charles City, VA 23030, USA; c/o Scott & Stringfellow Investment Corp, PO Box 1575, Richmond, VA 23213-1575, USA], *b* Richmond 9 June 1945; *educ* Washington and Lee U (BS 1967) and Emory U (MBA 1968); stockbroker; *m* Greenville, S Carolina, 1966 *Alice (*b* there 25 June 1947), dau of W. E. Watt and his w Alice Sharp, and has issue:

Great-great-grandchildren
1a *James Alfred Jones TYLER III, *b* Staunton, Va., 3 March 1967; *educ* Washington and Lee U
2a *Benjamin Alexander TYLER, *b* Richmond 24 March 1970

Grandchildren
5 John TYLER; *d* in infancy

President Tyler's son

X (John) Alexander TYLER, *b* Sherwood Forest, Va., 7 April 1848; served Confederate States Army 1864-65, mining engineer, fought in Franco-Prussion War 1870-71, US Surveyor for Dept of Interior in New Mexico 1879-83; *m* East Hampton 5 Aug 1875 Sarah Griswold, dau of Samuel Bell Gardiner, New York State Assemblyman, and *d* Santa Fe, N. Mex., 1 Sept 1883, having had issue:

Grandchildren

1 A child; *d* at birth June 1876
2 Samuel Gardiner TYLER, *b* Jan 1878; *d* March 1892
3 Lilian Horsford Tyler, *b* 1879; *m* Aug 1910 (divorce 19—) Alben N. MARGRAF, German Naval Offr, and *d* May 1918, leaving issue:

Great-grandchildren
(1) *Margaret TYLER (*née* Margraf but changed to mother's maiden name), *b* March 1912

President Tyler's daughter

XI Julia Gardiner Tyler, *b* Sherwood Forest, Va., 25 Dec 1849; *educ* Sacred Heart Convent, Halifax; *m* New York 26 June 1869 William H. SPENCER and *d* 8 May 1871, leaving issue:

Grandchildren

1 Julia Tyler Spencer, *b* May 1871; *m* 1st 18— George FLEUROT and had issue:

Great-grandchildren
(1) Fanny FLEUROT, *b* 1893; *d* 1921

Grandchildren

1 (cont.) Julia Spencer Fleurot *m* 2nd W. Durant CHEEVER

President Tyler's sons

XII Dr Lachlan TYLER, *b* Sherwood Forest, Va., 2 Dec 1851; *m* 1876 Georgia Powell and *d* New York 26 Jan 1902
XIII Lyon (formerly Lion) Gardiner (Lonie) TYLER, *b* Sherwood Forest 24 Aug 1853; *educ* U of Virginia (AB 1874, AM 1875); Pres William and Mary Coll 1888-1919 (Pres Emeritus from 1919), publisher and ed *William and Mary College Quarterly Historical Magazine*, author: *Letters and Times of the Tylers*, 3 vols (1884-96), *Parties and Patronage in the United States* (1890), *Cradle of the Republic* (1900), *England in America* (1906) and *Williamsburg, the Old Colonial Capital* (1908), LLD: Trinity 1895, Pittsburgh U 1911, Brown 1914 and William and Mary Coll 1919; *m* 1st 14 Nov 1878 Annie Baker (*b* Charlottesville, Va., 8 April 1855; *d* Richmond 2 Nov 1921), dau of Lt-Col St George Tucker, Confederate States Army, of Ashland, Va., and his *w* Elizabeth Anderson Gilmer, and had issue:

Grandchildren

1 Julia Gardiner Tyler, *b* Memphis, Tenn., 7 Dec 1881; *m* Williamsburg, Va., 17 April 1911 James Southall WILSON (*b* Bacon's Castle, Surry Co, Va., 12 Nov 1880; PhD, Poe Prof of Literature U of Virginia; *d* Charlottesville 26 June 1963), s of John S. Wilson and his *w* Mary Eliza Jordan, and *d* Charlottesville 29 Nov 1967, leaving issue:

Great-grandchildren
(1) *Nancy Tucker Wilson [Mrs James Mann Jr, 214 66th Street, Virginia Beach, VA 23451, USA], *b* Williamsburg 24 Feb 1912; *educ* St Anne's, Sweet Briar, Va. (BA), and U of Virginia (ME 1969); legal sec, French teacher to deaf, artist and writer; *m* 1st 1938 (divorce 1951) John Metcalf DREWRY (*d* 18 Jan 1978) and has issue:

Great-great-grandchildren
1a *Patricia Metcalf Drewry [Patricia D Sanger, 2623 East Lake Drive, Virginia Beach, VA 23454, USA], *b* 20 Sept 1940; *m* 6 June 1963 *Cdr Kenneth Tisdale SANGER, USN (ret), and has issue:

Great-great-grandchildren's children
1b *(Kenneth) Scott SANGER [Virginia Beach, VA 23451, USA], *b* 20 Oct 1967
2b *Derek John SANGER, *b* 10 Dec 1973; *educ* Middleburg Coll, Va.
3b *Stephanie Ann SANGER, *b* 25 March 1975

Great-great-grandchildren
2a *John Tyler DREWRY [110 Commonage Drive, Southdown Farm, Great Falls, VA 22066, USA], *b* 3 July 1942; *m* Baltimore 2 July 1966 *Diane Patricia Robinson and has issue:

Great-great-grandchildren's children
1b *Laura Katherine DREWRY, *b* 15 Aug 1969
2b *Alison Tucker DREWRY, *b* 10 May 1971

Great-great-grandchildren
3a *James Southall Wilson DREWRY [3317 Wessynton Way, Alexandria, VA 22309, USA], *b* Alexandria 9 April 1944; *educ* Randolph-Macon Coll, U of Virginia Law Sch and LSE; lawyer: Trial Atty USN 1969-74, and with Nat Oceanic & Atmospheric Admin 1975-80 and US Senate 1980-93; *m* Alexandria 25 April 1981 *Maria Teresinha (*b* Florianopolis, Brazil, 5 Jan 1955), dau of Agenor Machado and his *w* Elvira De Oliveira, of Brazil, and has issue:

Great-great-grandchildren's children
1b *John Wilson DREWRY, b Washington, DC, 27 Aug 1981
2b *Patrick James Tyler DREWRY, b Washington 21 March 1983

Great-grandchildren
(1) (cont.) Mrs Nancy Drewry m 2nd Norfolk, Va., 2 May 1970 James MANN, Jr (b 2 Dec 1911; d 25 June 1977), s of James Mann
(2) *Alida Wilson [Mrs Charles Davison, 1856 Edgewood Lane, Charlottesville, VA 22903-1603, USA], b Williamsburg 27 Nov 1913; educ Wellesley; teacher 1935-38; m Charlottesville 10 Sept 1938 *Charles Marshall DAVISON, Jr (b Richmond 19 June 1914; former Prof Law U of Virginia), s of Charles Marshall Davison and his w Katherine Stonestreet, and has had issue:

Great-great-grandchildren
1a *Katherine Stonestreet DAVISON [302 Hickory Dve, Manakin Sabot, VA 23103, USA], b Charlottesville 9 May 1942; Assist Librarian U of Richmond, Va.
2a Julia Tyler DAVISON, b 16, d 18 April 1945

Grandchildren
2 Elizabeth Gilmer Tyler, b Richmond 13 March 1885; m Williamsburg 16 Oct 1907 Capt Alfred Hart MILES, USN (b Norfolk, Va., 2 Nov 1883; author song Anchors Aweigh; d Norfolk 6 Oct 1956), s of Lt Charles Richard Miles, USN, and his w Evelyn Wayne Wilson, and d 11 June 1976, having had issue:

Great-grandchildren
(1) Lion Tyler MILES, b Williamsburg 4 March 1910; educ US Naval Acad; Lt USN; m Yuma, Ariz., 23 June 1932 *Elizabeth Innes (b Minneapolis 19 June 1914), dau of John Holwill Lighthipe and his w Alice Innes Graves, and d in action at sea off Java 2 March 1942, leaving issue:

Great-great-grandchildren
1a *Lion Gardiner MILES [RFD #1, West Stockbridge, MA 01269, USA], b Pensacola, Fla., 17 March 1934; educ Yale, William and Mary Coll (AB 1961) and Columbia U (AM 1964); Capt with American Airlines; m 1st Williamsburg 1 Dec 1956 (divorce 1970) Patricia Lee (b Pittsburgh, Pa., 5 Nov 1933), dau of Edward Hubert Rouen and his w Helene Violette Affolter, and has issue:

Great-great-grandchildren's children
1b *Julia Gardiner MILES, b Okinawa 26 Nov 1958
2b *Margaret Rouen MILES, b New York 22 June 1963
3b *Elizabeth Tyler MILES, b N Tarrytown, New York, 28 May 1966

Great-great-grandchildren
1a (cont.) Lion G. MILES m 2nd New York 22 May 1971 *Susanna (b Pittsburgh 6 Nov 1939), dau of Edwin Wilhard Laatu and his w Charlotte Irwin Caum

Grandchildren
3 John TYLER, b Richmond 1 Feb 1887; educ William and Mary Coll, MIT and Ohio State U; Assoc Prof US Naval Acad; m Virginia Beach 18 Sept 1916 Elizabeth (b there 1894; d Little Rock, Ark., 31 July 1992), dau of William George Parker, of Portsmouth, Va., and his w May Isabel Godwin, and d Annapolis, Md., 14 June 1969, leaving issue:

Great-grandchildren
(1) Elizabeth Parker TYLER, b Annapolis 3 Feb 1918; d 19—
(2) *Anne Gardiner Tyler [Mrs Clay Raney, 801 Pleasant Valley Drive No 1, Little Rock, AR 72207, USA], b Annapolis 29 Oct 1920; educ Georgetown Visitation Convent, Washington, DC; m Honolulu, Hawaii, 12 June 1941 *Capt Clay Hayes RANEY, USN (ret) (b Newark, Ark., 1915), s of Thomas Jefferson Raney and his w Inez Brannan, and has issue:

Great-great-grandchildren
1a *John Tyler RANEY [1137 Simon Rd, Endicott, NY 13760, USA], b Annapolis, Md., 22 Oct 1942; educ St Louis U, Mo.; m St Louis Oct 1963 *Catherine Frances (b Nov 1942), dau of Firmin Desloge Fusz and his w Catherine Cowey, and has issue:

Great-great-grandchildren's children
1b *Ann Desloge RANEY, b 18 Feb 1964
2b *Catherine Hayes RANEY, b 18 March 1965
3b *Julia Fusz RANEY, b 3 July 1970
4b *Mary Elizabeth Tyler RANEY, b 19 Sept 1978

Great-great-grandchildren
2a *Mary Brannan Raney [4820 Stonewall Rd, Little Rock, AR 72207, USA], b Bremerton, Wash., 16 Feb 1946; educ St Louis U; physical therapist; m Little Rock 16 Aug 1969 *Frank Stephen HIEGEL (b 3 Aug 1946), s of Theodore Joseph Hiegel and his w Frances Enderlin, and has issue:

Great-great-grandchildren's children

1b *Francis Stephen HIEGEL, Jr, *b* Little Rock 25 Oct 1970

2b *Theodore Joseph HIEGEL II, *b* Little Rock 27 Dec 1972

Great-great-grandchildren

3a *Teresa (Terry) Gardiner Raney [Mrs Earl R Ball, 6408 Pontiac Rd, North Little Rock, AR 72116, USA], *b* Annapolis 7 June 1949; *educ* U of Arkansas; Depy Prosecuting Atty Pulaski Co, Ark., 1986-91, atty with Gill, Wallace, Clayton 1991-93, law clerk to Circuit Judge Chris Piazza 1991-93; *m* 29 June' 1973 *Earl Ray BALL (*b* 4 May 1945), *s* of Charles Ray Ball and his *w* Edna Earl, and has issue:

Great-great-grandchildren's children

1b *Charles Clay BALL, *b* Little Rock 24 Nov 1974

2b *John Tyler BALL, *b* Mountain Home, Ark., 19 Feb 1979

Great-great-grandchildren

4a *Anne St George Tucker Raney [Ms Anne Raney, 4222 Pitt St, New Orleans, LA 70115, USA], *b* Charleston, S Carolina, 26 March 1952; *educ* St Louis U and UALR Sch of Law; assoc counsel legal servs and coordinator Energy Servs Inc; *m* 19— (divorce 19—) Lewis MATHIS

5a *Elizabeth (Lisa) Gilmer Raney [Mrs Terry Bowen, 4015 N Old Wire Rd, Fayetteville, AR 72703, USA], *b* Annapolis 5 June 1958; *educ* NE Louisiana U, UAMS Coll of Pharmacy (BSph, DP); retail pharmacist 1983-85, hosp pharmacist 1985-91, clinical consultant 1991-; *m* 21 June 1975 *Terry Dean BOWEN (*b* 21 Dec 1954), *s* of Melvin Doyle Bowen and his *w* Juanita Belle Rookard, and has issue:

Great-great-grandchildren's children

1b *Melissa Anne BOWEN, *b* Fayetteville 2 Dec 1975

2b *Olivia Tucker BOWEN, *b* Hot Springs, Ark., 22 July 1982

President Tyler's son

XIII (cont.) Dr Lyon Tyler *m* 2nd 12 Sept 1923 Sue (*b* Charles City Co, Va., 5 May 1889; *d* 2 May 1953), dau of John Ruffin, of Charles City Co, and his *w* Jane Cary Harrison, and *d* Charles City Co 12 Feb 1935, having with her had issue:

Grandchildren

4 *Lyon Gardiner TYLER, Jr [49 Church Street, Charleston, SC 29401, USA], *b* Richmond 3 Jan 1925; *educ* William and Mary Coll (AB), U of Virginia (JD 1951) and Duke U (MA and PhD); law clerk to Judge Armisted Dobie, US Court of Appeals 4th Circuit, 1949-50, assoc atty Christian, Baxton, Parker & Boyd and ptnr White & Roberts, Richmond, Va., 1950-63, Commonwealth's Attorney Charles City Co, Va., 1951-55, Assist Dir Virginia Civil War Commission 1959-63, Prof History Virginia Mily Inst and Professor Emeritus The Citadel; *m* 18 Jan 1958 *Lucy Jane (*b* 10 April 1924), dau of Barton Pope and his *w* Selina Dorricott, and has issue:

Great-grandchildren

(1) *Susan Selina Pope TYLER, *b* 27 March 1964

Grandchildren

5 *Harrison Ruffin TYLER [5416 Tuckahoe Ave, Richmond, VA 23226, USA], *b* Lions Den, Charles City, Va., 9 Nov 1928; *educ* William and Mary Coll (BS) and Virginia Polytech Inst (BS); Pres ChemTreat Inc; *m* Mulberry Hill Plantation, Johnston, S Carolina, 1957 *Frances Payne (*b* there 11 March 1933), dau of William Miller Bouknight and his *w* Frances Payne Turner, and has issue:

Great-grandchildren

(1) *Julia Gardiner Tyler, *b* 30 Dec 1958; *m* 24 Nov 1990 *Daniel SAMANIEGO and has issue:

Great-great-grandchildren

1a *David Tyler SAMANIEGO, *b* 18 Jan 1992

Great-grandchildren

(2) *Harrison Ruffin TYLER, Jr, *b* 17 Sept 1960; *m* 26 Sept 1987 *Catherine M. Smith

(3) *William Bouknight TYLER, *b* 3 Jan 1962

Grandchildren

6 Henry TYLER, *b* Richmond, Va., 18 Jan, *d* 26 Jan 1931

President Tyler's children

XIV Robert FitzWalter TYLER, *b* Sherwood Forest 12 March 1856; *educ* Georgetown Coll; farmer in Hanover Co, Va.; *m* Fannie Glinn and *d* Richmond, Va., 30 Dec 1927

XV Pearl Tyler, *b* Sherwood Forest 13 or 20 June 1860; *m* 1894 Maj William Mumford ELLIS (*b* 1846; *d* 1921) and *d* Elliston, Va., 30 June 1947, leaving issue:

Grandchildren

1 Pearl Tyler ELLIS, *b* 1885

2 John Tyler ELLIS, *b* 1887; *m* 19— Helen R. Watson

3 Leila McLachlan Ellis, *b* 1888; *m* 1920 Ambrose Madison MARYE (*b* 1887) and *d* 19—, having had issue:

Great-grandchildren
(1) *Madison Ellis MARYE, b 1925; m 1950 *Charlotte Urbas and has issue:

Great-great-grandchildren
1a *Charlotte Madison MARYE, b 1951
2a *Juliana Madison MARYE, b 1953

Grandchildren
4 Cornelia Horsford Ellis; m 1916 Yelverton E. BOOKER
5 Gardiner Tyler ELLIS, b 1893
6 Mumford ELLIS, b 1895; m 19— Ruth Woods
7 Julia Fleurot Ellis, b 1898; m 1924 *William ROBINSON and d 19—, leaving issue:

Great-grandchildren
(1) *Pearl Tyler ROBINSON, b 1927
(2) *Elizabeth B. ROBINSON, b 1930

Grandchildren
8 Lyon Alexander ELLIS, b 1900; m 19— Margaret Northcross and d 1954

MALE LINE ANCESTRY AND
COLLATERAL DESCENDANTS

Henry TYLER, b possibly in Shropshire, England, c 1604; emigrated to America and settled at Middle Plantation, nr Williamsburg, Va.; m 1st Mary ——; m 2nd shortly after 1655, as her 2nd husb, Ann (m 1st John Orchard, who d before c 1655; m 3rd Martin Gardner; d York Co, Va., 2 April 1679) and d Middle Plantation 13 April 1672, having with his 2nd w had issue (with two other s):

Henry TYLER, b probably York Co c 1660; Justice, Coroner and High Sheriff York Co; m c 1683 Elizabeth (d Williamsburg 19 Jan 1702/3), dau of Walter Chiles (d in or before 1671, s of Col Walter Chiles, Memb Cncl of State 1652) and his w Mary (dau of Col John Page, who emigrated from England to Virginia 1650), and d between 2 July and 15 Dec 1729, having had issue (with an er and yr s and one dau):

John TYLER, b probably York Co c 1685; educ William and Mary Coll; Justice of James City, Va.; m Elizabeth, dau of John Jarrett (d probably between 1697 and 1704) and his w Joanna Lowe (housekeeper at Westover, the plantation belonging to William Byrd II), and d probably Williamsburg c 1727, leaving issue (with two other s):

John TYLER, Jr, b probably Williamsburg between c 1710 and 1715; educ William and Mary Coll; Marshal to Vice-Admiralty Court of Virginia; m Anne, dau of Louis Contesse (a Huguenot who emigrated c 1715 from France to Williamsburg, where he practiced as a doctor and d 11 Sept 1729) and his w Mary Morris, and d probably Williamsburg between 24 July and 20 Sept 1773, leaving (with other issue):

John ('Judge John') TYLER III, of Greenway, Charles City Co, Va., b Yarmouth, Va., 28 Feb 1747; educ William and Mary Coll; Memb Virginia House of Delegates 1778-86 (Speaker 1782-86), Judge Admiralty Court, proposed resolution drafted by James Madison (afterward 4th President) calling the Annapolis Convention which led to the Constitutional Convention of 1787 in Philadelphia, V-Pres Virginia Constitutional Convention 1788, Judge Gen Court 1788-1808, Govr Virginia 1808-11, Judge US Dist Court of Virginia 1812-13; m Weryanoke, Va., c 1776 Mary Marot (b probably York Co c 1761; d Greenway 5 April 1797), dau of Robert Booth Armistead (in or before 1737-before 21 July 1766) and his w Anne Shields, and d Greenway 6 Jan 1813, having had issue:

I Anne Contesse Tyler, b 1778; m 1795 James SEMPLE (b 1768; Judge Gen Court of Virginia and Prof Law William and Mary Coll; d 1834) and d 12 June 1803, leaving two s and three daus
II Elizabeth Armistead Tyler, b 1780; m 1798 John Clayton PRYOR (b 1780; d 1846) and d 1824, having had two s (both d young) and five daus
III Martha Jefferson Tyler, b 1782; m 1805 Thomas Ennalls WAGGAMAN (b 1782; d 1832) and d 1855, having had three s and five daus
IV Maria Henry Tyler, b 1784; m 1800 John Boswell SEAWELL, of Gloucester, Va. (b 1780), and d 1843, leaving six s and one dau
V Wat Henry TYLER, b 1788; doctor; m 1st 18— Elizabeth Warren Walker and had three s and one dau; m 2nd 18— Margaret Govan and d July 1862, having with her had one s and one dau
VI JOHN TYLER, 10th PRESIDENT of the UNITED STATES of AMERICA
VII William TYLER, b 179-; Memb Virginia House of Delegates; m 18— Susan Harrison Walker and d 1856, leaving five s and three daus

VIII Christiana Booth Tyler, *b* 1795; *m* 1813 Dr Henry CURTIS (*b* 1793; *d* 1862) and *d* 1842, having had six s and three daus

Great-great-great-great grandparents on the father's side

Henry Tyler
c 1604-72
Ann —
d 1679

Walter Chiles
c 1608/9-*c* 1653
Elizabeth —

Walter Chiles, Jr
d in/*a* 1671
Mary Page

John Page
c 1626-91/2
Alice Lukin
c 1625-98

Michael Lowe
— —

Great-great-great-great grandparents on the mother's side

William Armistead
c 1610-66
Ann Ellis

Anthony Armistead
d a 1726
Hannah Ellyson
d 1726-28

Robert Ellyson
d a 1688
— —

Robert Booth
d c 1657
Frances —
b c 1609

Robert Booth, Jr
d 1695
Ann Bray
d 1692

James Bray
d 1691
Angelica —

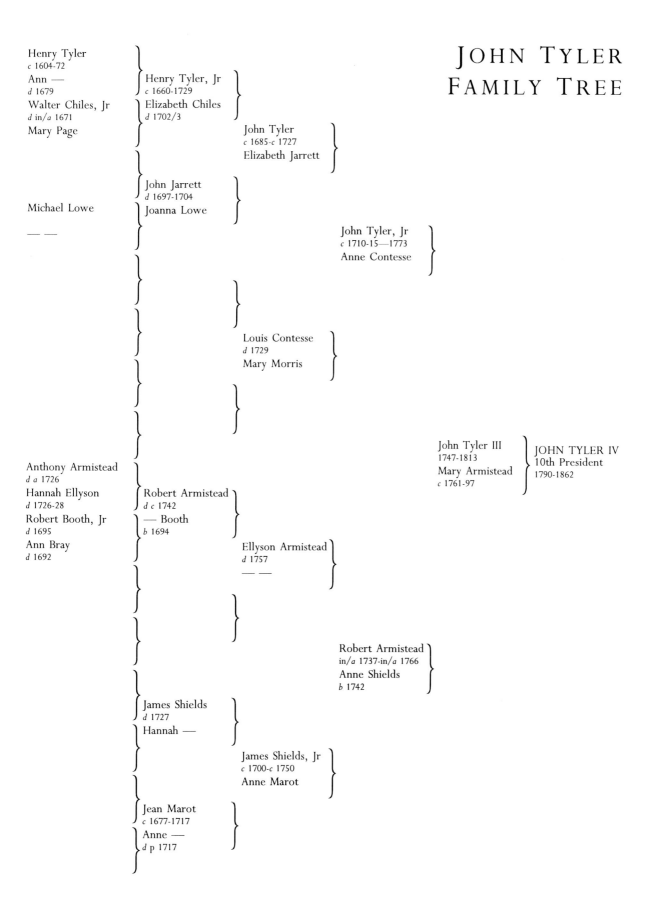

JOHN TYLER
FAMILY TREE

Henry Tyler
c 1604-72

Ann —
d 1679

Walter Chiles, Jr
d in/a 1671

Mary Page

Henry Tyler, Jr
c 1660-1729

Elizabeth Chiles
d 1702/3

John Tyler
c 1685-c 1727

Elizabeth Jarrett

Michael Lowe

— —

John Jarrett
d 1697-1704

Joanna Lowe

John Tyler, Jr
c 1710-15—1773

Anne Contesse

Louis Contesse
d 1729

Mary Morris

John Tyler III
1747-1813

Mary Armistead
c 1761-97

JOHN TYLER IV
10th President
1790-1862

Anthony Armistead
d a 1726

Hannah Ellyson
d 1726-28

Robert Booth, Jr
d 1695

Ann Bray
d 1692

Robert Armistead
d c 1742

— Booth
b 1694

Ellyson Armistead
d 1757

— —

Robert Armistead
in/a 1737-in/a 1766

Anne Shields
b 1742

James Shields
d 1727

Hannah —

James Shields, Jr
c 1700-c 1750

Anne Marot

Jean Marot
c 1677-1717

Anne —
d p 1717

Plate 34   James Knox Polk

JAMES KNOX POLK

1795-1849
11TH PRESIDENT OF THE UNITED STATES OF AMERICA
1845-49

"There are four great measures which are to be the measures of my administration," said President Polk, hitting his thigh for emphasis. "One; a reduction of the tariff, another the independent treasury, a third the settlement of the Oregon boundary question and, lastly, the acquisition of California". It shows the ability of the man that he achieved every one of these aims; it shows his limitations that in spite of his success the United States was in greater danger when he retired than when he took office. He is a very difficult man to judge.

The Whigs pretended that he was a nonentity ('Who is James K. Polk?') and he has a reputation as the first of the dark horse candidates. At the time of his nomination he was in fact a well-established politician of the second rank; he had been both Speaker of the House of Representatives and Governor of Tennessee. Andrew Jackson had tried hard to get him the Democratic nomination for Vice-President in 1840 and in 1844, as a veteran party leader from the West, strongly backed by Jackson, he was a natural compromise candidate when the convention deadlocked between Van Buren and Calhoun. Thanks in part to President Tyler the cry was up for territorial expansion and Polk, following Jackson's advice, made 'Manifest Destiny' the theme of his campaign. In this way he seized the initiative from Clay and came into office determined not merely to carry out his campaign promises to expand, but also to restore the Jacksonian verities that had been overthrown by Van Buren's defeat four years previously.

He kept a diary while he was President and in its pages one can follow his dismally triumphant progress. Polk was morbidly suspicious of everyone and saw only one way of circumventing the intriguers: ceaseless hard work. He toiled away for four years with scarcely a moment's rest; no wonder he dropped dead three months after leaving office. He delegated nothing and he quarrelled with far too many of his collaborators, including both the generals (Zachary Taylor and Winfield Scott) who were fighting the Mexican War for him (they happened to be Whigs). By sheer doggedness and great political professionalism he had his way, in spite of formidable obstacles.

In the process, as many historians reckon, he plunged the United States into war. Perhaps this is unfair. There is little indication that Mexico was ready to acquiesce peacefully in the final loss of Texas. Nor was Polk altogether in command of events. US citizens had been moving into the Mexican state of Upper California for some time and were just about ripe for revolt on the model of the Texans in 1835 (1846 was also the 'year of decision' which saw the Mormons moving toward Utah and large numbers of American settlers heading for the Columbia River basin). Even a less abrasive President than Polk could probably not have avoided war. As it was the war came and the United States was smashingly victorious in battle after battle. The climax was Winfield Scott's capture of Mexico City. Then, after some extremely delicate negotiations, conducted by an emissary whom Polk had officially superseded, peace was made and the United States gained new territory almost as extensive as that brought in by the Louisiana purchase: Utah, Colorado, New Mexico, Nevada, Arizona, California. At the same time

Polk successfully negotiated a partition of the Oregon Territory with the British that left the boundary between British Columbia and the United States where it lies today. He might well feel modestly proud of an enormous achievement.

But his very success created frightful problems for his country. Here were these vast new lands; should they be open to slavery or not? Polk took the view that the question had already been settled by geography and that therefore those who professed concern about slavery, whether for or against, were mere factious agitators, putting the Union at risk for their own selfish advantage. There was something to be said for his view but too few to say it. In August 1846 Congressman David Wilmot of Pennsylvania moved his celebrated Proviso that slavery should be excluded forever from any lands acquired from Mexico; the United States moved another stage nearer disaster. Impassioned controversy about the question of slavery and the territories was to rage for years to come, was indeed to continue until the outbreak of the Civil War.

These events were shaped under, rather than by, President Polk. He is remembered for what he was, a narrowly able man who did better in the White House than most people had ever expected and whose wife's idea of making the place cheerful for him was to forbid all dancing, card-playing and alcohol.

JAMES KNOX POLK'S FAMILY

Polk's family circumstances resembled Washington's. He was childless himself but came from a large family. Six of his brothers and sisters had children (and three died young), just as with Washington. His still more numerous cousins, some of whose letters to and from each other are a useful source of information on Polk's family life, tended to be just as fecund as Washington's.

Polk was thought to resemble his maternal grandfather, James Knox, who had been a Militia Captain in the Revolution and later earned his living as a blacksmith and farmer, but it was from his father's family he got his material start in life. Samuel Polk, his father, had moved in 1806 to the upper reaches of the Duck River, in central Tennessee, where several members of Samuel's family were already settled, including his father Ezekiel. The Polks became leaders among the settlers roundabout and were responsible for the successful petition which resulted in the area being formed into a county. Samuel Polk and his brother-in-law John Campbell were among the first jurors to serve on the Maury County Court. Through successful real estate deals Samuel became the richest Polk. He had not started empty-handed, however, for his father Ezekiel had presented him and his brother Thomas on their respective marriages with a 250-acre farm each, the two farms lying side by side on Sugar Creek not far from Ezekiel's own plantation.

Like most settlers in the Southern states, Samuel Polk was staunchly Protestant. It is true that he quarrelled with the minister at what was to have been his eldest son's christening, so that the 11th President was never baptized in childhood at all and only got round to it in the last days of his life, like the Emperor Constantine. (Constantine, who legislated to make Sunday a public holiday, was evidently also a soul mate of the fervent Sabbatarian Sarah Polk.) But Samuel took to religion again before he died. He had never been robust after contracting in 1821 a bad case of rheumatism, which kept him at home for several months. Some idea of his vigour in his heyday can be grasped from his becoming his eldest son the future President's client the latter's first day in practice as a lawyer, when Samuel was indicted for a breach of the peace.

Samuel Polk left land amounting to several thousand acres together with 50 slaves. The will was disputed by several members of the family, notably Polk's sister Lydia and her husband, Dr Silas W. Caldwell. Another sister, Jane Maria, had independent financial links with the deceased as well as being

Plate 35   Sarah Childress Polk

a beneficiary since she had married one of her father's business partners. A third sister, Ophelia, seems to have resembled her Shakespearian namesake in having a rather unstable temperament. At any rate she made her husband's life such hell that Polk often had to intervene. He was obliged early on to assume the headship of the family in any case. His brother Franklin was an alcoholic and died in 1831 at the age of 28. The year 1831 cut quite a swathe through the Polk family since in addition both John and another brother Marshall died then. Marshall left debts and two young children for his eldest brother to look after. At least John had been unmarried. Polk continued to look to the welfare of his nieces and nephews well into middle age, his and Sarah's childlessness making this relatively easy. When President he followed custom and appointed as his private secretary his nephew James Knox Walker, whose father had been involved with him in various business projects.

Polk developed a special sense of responsibility toward Marshall's son Marshall Polk Jr. In his diary he records that Marshall Jr was so idle and inattentive at college that he, Polk, feared he would have to take him away. Polk slaved away himself so inexorably it is difficult to know if Marshall Jr was really idle or just less industrious than his uncle. And anyway Polk's diary is one of those documents that are more interesting for what they don't say than what they do. He hardly ever mentions his wife; he notes that watching an innocent entertainment such as a juggler is a waste of time, besides lacking in edification. This suggests his wife's ban on cards, dancing and drink in the White House, like the similar ban on drink supposedly imposed by Lucy Hayes 30 years later, reflected the husband's wishes more than has been generally recognised. Polk's diary also reflects his relief when a social function is over, a grim passage lightened by unconsciously comical detail on how to avoid injury when shaking hands with thousands of visitors. (According to Polk, the trick is to take a firm grip and squeeze the other man's hand rather than let him squeeze yours; there is an extra significance to presidential handshakes in that most Chief Executives have been freemasons.)

The diary's longwindedness and redundancies suggest Polk worked himself harder than necessary, unless one agrees with Pascal that short literary compositions take more time to create than long ones. He need not have kept a diary at all. But then the diary is the Protestant confessional, and Polk was nothing if not a Protestant. Not that he is always above being a bit disingenuous. He rather pathetically records that in late August 1846 he took his first excursion outside Washington since becoming President — bar a single day in the spring immediately after his Inauguration — with a jaunt aboard a steamboat accompanied by his wife and a niece of hers, a Miss Rucker. An equally pathetic revelation might on the face of it be that he spent Christmas Day of that year working in his office while the family attended church. But that may have been less of a sacrifice than he implied since his wife Sarah kept the Lord's Day so scrupulously she on one occasion had the Austrian envoy turned away when he called to present his credentials on a Sunday.

Sarah Childress Polk may have been a Puritan, but she was relatively well educated for a woman of her time and had a lively mind with a particular interest in politics. When Polk proposed marriage to her she is said to have given him a conditional acceptance, the condition being that he run for the Tennessee legislature first. Just so might Lady Macbeth have denied her husband hot dinners till he had procured the thaneship of Cawdor. Sarah acted as her husband's communications director during his Tennessee gubernatorial bid in 1839, overseeing his correspondence, supervising distribution of his campaign literature and scheduling his public appearances. In the White House she kept him up-to-date on the latest books and what the newspapers were saying, not to mention the latest political gossip in town when he was on business elsewhere. No doubt his suspicious attitude toward his colleagues while President boosted her importance as a confidante. She had known him from an early age, having been privately tutored by one Samuel Black, the same man who taught Polk, while her brother Anderson Childress was at school with Polk. She was said to be at her best in social gatherings — provided there was no card-playing, drinking or dancing of course. (She never went to the races or the theatre either.) When in 1845 she and Polk attended an inaugural ball for two hours, all dancing ceased during that time. Since alcohol, dancing and gambling were the 19th-century equivalents of modern-day wickednesses such as smoking and reverence for dead white European males, she is surely of all 19th-century First Ladies the most like Hillary Clinton.

After she became a widow in 1849 she anticipated Queen Victoria's posthumous relationship with Prince Albert by making the rooms her husband had lived in at Nashville into a shrine to the cult of the dead. She also erected a mausoleum outside in front of the house. Otherwise she was more active than Queen Victoria: she ran a 1,000-acre plantation in Mississippi which Polk had bought shortly before he died. She did not live on it, however, which in a way makes the fact she ran it at a profit and without undue cruelty to the slaves more remarkable, since absentee landlords were one of the great curses of the 19th century.

There are interesting qualifications to this picture of a tough-minded but intelligent woman. She was not too austere to spend $600 on the latest Paris modes shortly after becoming First Lady. And she had a vindictive streak: Van Buren's son John called several times on President Polk but omitted to pay his respects to Mrs Polk, so every time her husband invited him to dinner she had his name expunged from the guest list. On one occasion, when her husband's desire to foster good relations with the Van Burens had initially outrun her vigilance, she got hold of John Van Buren's invitation card before it could be despatched and burnt it. Clearly her religion, though strong, was short on charity. Her husband, too, exhibited both the strengths and weaknesses of that iron Presbyterianism he had inherited from his mother.

BIOGRAPHICAL DETAILS

POLK, JAMES KNOX, *b* nr Pineville, Mecklenburg Co, N Carolina, 2 Nov 1795; *educ* U of N Carolina (AB 1818); admitted to Tennessee Bar 1820, Ch Clerk Tennessee Senate 1821-23, Memb: Tennessee House of Reps 1823-25, US House of Reps from Tennessee 1825-39 (Speaker 1835-39), Govr Tennessee 1839-1841, 11th President (D) of the USA 1845-1849; author: *The Diary of James K. Polk*, ed Milo M. Quaife, 4 vols (1910), *Correspondence*, ed Herbert Weaver and Kermit L. Hall (1969); *m* Murfreesboro, Rutherford Co, Tenn., 1 Jan 1824 Sarah (*b* nr Murfreesboro 4 Sept 1803; *d* Nashville, Tenn., 14 Aug 1891, *bur* Nashville with her husband), dau of Joel Childress, merchant and farmer, and his *w* Elizabeth Whitsitt, and *d* Nashville 15 June 1849

MALE LINE ANCESTRY AND COLLATERAL DESCENDANTS

Sir John POLLOK, of Renfrewshire, Scotland, *b* 15—; *m* Janet Mure and was *k* 1593 at the Battle of Lockerbie (strictly speaking at Dryfe Sands, 2 miles west of the town itself, which is in Dumfriesshire, southwestern Scotland); in this battle two local families, the Maxwells and the Johnstones, met in a bloody clash, the Maxwells being chased into Lockerbie and so nearly exterminated that the term 'Lockerbie Lick' came to signify an overwhelming defeat; Sir John left issue:

Robert POLLOK; by grant acquired land in Coleraine, Co Derry, Ireland 1605/8; *m* and had issue:

Robert POLLOK, of Coleraine, *b c* 1595/8; Covenanter (follower of the Scottish league, predominantly Presbyterian, organized against anglicanizing tendencies in the Church in Scotland, especially bishops); *m* 16— and *d c* 1640, leaving as his probable issue:

Robert POLLOK or POLK, *b* 16—; fought against Charles I in Col Porter's Regt during the civil strife in the British Isles that lasted from the late 1630s to the late 1640s, later emigrated from Co Donegal, Ireland, to Maryland and acquired from the Catholic Lord Baltimore a land grant known as 'Polke's Lott' and 'Polke's Folly' 7 March 1687; *m* Magdalen (*b* 16—; *d* on or after 7 April 1726), widow of —— Porter and dau of —— Tasker, of Moneen (an estate inherited by his dau Magdalen), nr Strabane, Co Tyrone, Ireland, and *d* between 1699 and 1704, leaving (with other issue):

William POLK, of White Hall, Md., *b* probably in Co Donegal *c* 1664; *m* 1st Nancy, widow of —— Owens and dau of —— Knox; *m* 2nd —— Gray, a widow, and *d c* 1739 (will proved 24 Feb 1739/40), leaving issue by his 1st *w*:

William POLK, Jr, *b* White Hall *c* 1700; settled first in Hopewell Township, Cumberland Co, Pa., later moved to N Carolina; *m c* 1730 Margaret Taylor (*d* after her husb) and *d* N Carolina *c* 1753, leaving (with other issue):

I William Polk, *b* Cumberland Co, Pa.; moved with his father to N Carolina; *m* 1st ——; *m* 2nd —— and d, leaving issue (whether by his 1st or 2nd *w* is unknown; there may have been other children too):

  1 Thomas POLK, *b* probably N Carolina; settled at Little Mountain, afterward known as Polk's Mountain and now as Gibraltar, N Carolina; *m* 1842 Mary, sister of Reese and Thomas Shelby, of Chesterfield, S Carolina, and *d* Little Mountain 1842, leaving issue:

    (1) Shelby POLK, moved to Tennessee 1813; *m* Winifred Colburn and *d* 1847, leaving seven children
    (2) Andrew POLK (3) Thomas POLK (4) Job POLK (5) Hannah POLK (6) Dicy POLK
    (7) Patsy POLK (8) Mary POLK (9) Elizabeth POLK

  2 John POLK; moved to S Carolina 3 Ezekiel POLK; Ensign US Infy Regt 1790; *d* 1791

II Thomas POLK, *b* Cumberland Co, Pa., *c* 1730; surveyor, Memb N Carolina Assembly 1766-76, Tstee Queen's Coll, Charlotte, N Carolina, Col Continental Line Regt 1776, later Brig-Gen, delegate to Continental Congress; *m* 1755 Susanna, dau of Thomas Spratt, of Mecklenburg Co, N Carolina, and *d* Charlotte 26 June 1794, leaving issue at least one s:

  1 William POLK, *b* 1758; Colonel; *m* 1st Grizelda Gilchrist and had issue:

    (1) Dr William Julius POLK, *b* 1793; *m* 18— Mary Rebecca Long and *d* 1860, having had issue:

      1a Capt Rufus POLK, *b* 1843; *m* Cynthia Martin and *d* 1912, having had issue:

      1b William Julius POLK, *b* 1874; *m* Sarah Eliza Chambers and *d* 1953

  1 (cont.) Col William Polk *m* 2nd Sarah Hawkins and *d* 1834, having with her had further issue:

    (2) Hon Lucius Junius POLK, *b* 1802; *m* Mary Ann, dau of William Eastin and his *w* Rachel Donelson (herself dau of Mary Purnell and her husb John Donelson, er bro of Rachel Donelson, *w* of President JACKSON) and *d* 1870, having had issue:

      1a Sarah Polk, *b* 1833; *m* 18— Cadwallader JONES and *d* 1905, having had issue:

1b Sarah Polk Jones, b 1860; m James C. BRADFORD (b his f's plantation, Jefferson Co, Miss., 16 Sept 1852; d 1914), Judge, of Nashville, Tenn., and had issue:

1c Thomas BRADFORD, b 1890; served with Artillery, US Army, Western Front World War I; financier in New York; d c 1940

2c Sarah Polk Bradford, b Woodstock, Nashville, 5 March 1891; m 1st Nashville 30 April 1912 Hon Alfred Thomas SHAUGHNESSY (b 18 Oct 1887; educ McGill U; stockbroker, served with Canadian Militia and as Capt Canadian 60th Bn World War I; ka 31 March 1916), yr s of 1st Baron Shaughnessy, KCVO (see BURKE'S PEERAGE & BARONETAGE), and had issue:

1d *Elizabeth (Betty) Sarah Polk Shaughnessy [Mrs Derek Lawson, Flat 3, 36 Sloane Court West, London SW3 4TB, UK], b Montreal 23 Jan 1913; m 1st 25 July 1932 (divorce 1946) 2nd Baron GRENFELL (see BURKE'S PEERAGE & BARONETAGE) and had issue; m 2nd 26 Jan 1946 Maj Berkeley Buckingham Howard STAFFORD, KRRC (d 30 Oct 1966), er s of late Berkeley Howard Stafford, of Sway Place, Hants, UK; m 3rd 2 May 1969 (divorce 1975) Trevor Walton (Rex) KING, s of late William Samuel King, MBE; m 4th 1983 Cdr (Arnold) Derek Arthur LAWSON, RN (d 1984)

2d *Thomas Bradford Shaughnessy [Apt 10, 3621 University St, Montreal H3A 2B3, Canada], b 14 Jan 1915; educ Eton, Oxford U, UK (BA 1937), and McGill (BCL 1947); served Welsh Gds and SAS World War II, called to Montreal Bar 1947, slr Canadian Industs Ltd; m 18 June 1949 *Margot, only dau of late William Daney Chambers, of Westmount, Montreal, and has issue:

1e *Amanda Marguerite Polk SHAUGHNESSY, b 14 Feb 1951

2e *Roxane Elizabeth Shaughnessy, b 30 Sept 1952; m 1984 *Thomas Herbert McGREEVY, s of John McGreevy, of Quebec City, Canada, and has issue:

1f *Sarah Paige McGREEVY, b 1986
2f *Julian Thomas Gray McGREEVY, b 1989
3f *Madelein Claire Elizabeth McGRREEVY, b 1989

3e *Tara Evelyn Shaughnessy, b 15 Nov 1954; m 1983 *Alain DU BOIS, s of Leopold Du Bois, of Magog, Quebec, Canada, and has issue:

1f *Louis Shaughnessy DU BOIS, b 1985
2f *Chella Eveleyn DU BOIS, b 1988

3d *Alfred James SHAUGHNESSY [The Grange, Yattendon, Newbury, Berks RG16 0UE, UK], b 19 May 1916; educ Eton and RMC Sandhurst; served Gds Armoured Div World War II, film and television screenwriter, producer and dir, playwright: Release, The Heat of the Moment, Double Cut and Old Herbaceous, author: Dearest Enemy (novel), Both Ends of the Candle (autobiography), (ed) Sarah: the letters and diaries of a courtier's wife 1906-1936 (1989); m 18 Sept 1948 Jean Margaret, dau of late George Lodge, of Kirkella, Yorks, UK, and has issue:

1e *Charles George Patrick SHAUGHNESSY, b London 9 Feb 1955; educ Eton; m in the USA 21 May 1983 *Susan, dau of Sydney Fallender, of Los Angeles

2e *David James Bradford SHAUGHNESSY, b London 3 March 1957; m in the USA 25 Oct 1986 *Anne-Marie, dau of Henry Schoettler, of Indianapolis

2c (cont.) The Hon Mrs Alfred Shaughnessy m 2nd 15 Nov 1920 Lt-Col Hon Sir Piers ('Joey') Walter LEGH, GCVO, KCB, CMG, CIE, OBE, JP (Berks and County of London), Gren Gds (b 12 Dec 1890; educ Eton; Mily Sec World War I (mentioned in despatches, Croix de Guerre (France), Order of St Maurice and St Lazarus (Italy)), Equerry to HRH The Prince of Wales 1919-36, HM King EDWARD VIII 1936 and HM King GEORGE VI 1937-46 (Extra Equerry 1946-55), Master of the Household to HM King GEORGE VI 1941-52 and HM Queen ELIZABETH II 1952-53; d 16 Oct 1955), yr s of 2nd Baron Newton (see BURKE'S PEERAGE & BARONETAGE) and his w Evelyn, dau of William Bromley Davenport, MP, and d 17 Oct 1955, having with her 2nd husb had further issue:

4d *Diana Evelyn Legh [Mrs Norman Colville, Penheale Barton, Launceston, Cornwall PL1 8RX; 11 Kensington Sq, London W8, UK], b London 28 March 1924; High Sheriff of Cornwall 1988-89; m 1st 27 Oct 1945 (divorce 1948), as his 1st w, 4th Earl of KIMBERLEY (see BURKE'S PEERAGE & BARONETAGE); m 2nd 1 June 1951 Col Norman Robert COLVILLE, MC (d 1974) (see BURKE'S PEERAGE & BARONETAGE, Clydesmuir), only surviving s of late David Colville, JP, of Jerviston House, Lanarks, UK, and his w Katherine, and with him has issue:

1e *James Charles David COLVILLE, b Plymouth, UK, 16 April 1952; educ Eton; Page of Honour to HM Queen ELIZABETH II 1966-68; m Bromley, Kent, UK, 16 April 1983 *Fiona, dau of John Gaylor, of Bromley, Kent, UK, and has issue:

1f *Robert John James COLVILLE, b 1984
2f *Sarah Elizabeth Rose COLVILLE, b 1986
3f *Lucy Isabel Amy COLVILLE, b 1988

2a Rachel POLK   3a Robin POLK

(3) Leonidas POLK, *b* Raleigh, N Carolina, 10 April 1806; *educ* West Point; ordained in Protestant Episcopal Church 1831, consecrated misssionary Bishop of Southwest, Arkansas Indian Territory, Louisiana, Alabama and Mississippi 1838, Bp of Louisiana 1841 (resigned bishopric 1861), Maj-Gen Confederate States Army Civil War (Corps-Cdr at Battle of Shiloh 1862, Lt-Gen Oct 1862, Corps-Cdr Army of Tennessee, offr commanding Dept of Alabama, Mississippi and E Louisiana); *ka* Marietta, nr Pine Mountain, Ga., 14 June 1864

III Ezekiel POLK, *b* nr what is now Carlisle, Cumberland Co, Pa., 7 Dec 1747; fought Revolutionary War, acquired substantial amounts of land in Tennessee Territory (in what was then N Carolina), Clerk Tryon Co, N Carolina, 1770-72, Lt-Col 12th Regt S Carolina Militia 1775; *m* 1st Mecklenburg Co, N Carolina, *c* 1769 Mary (*d* nr Pineville, N Carolina, 1791, *bur* Polk Cemetery), dau of Samuel Wilson, of Mecklenburg Co, and his w Mary Winslow, and had (with perhaps other issue):

1 Thomas POLK, *b* probably Tryon Co, N Carolina, 5 Dec 1770; *m* Mecklenburg Co (in a double wedding with his yr bro Samuel) 25 Dec 1794 ——

2 Matilda Golden Polk, *b* 5 Dec 1770; moved to Missouri 1835; *m* 1st 3 May 1792 John CAMPBELL (*d* between 21 April and 21 June 1816), Lt Artillery, 2nd N Carolina Regt, Revolutionary War, and had issue; *m* 2nd Maury Co, Tenn., Dec 1821 Philip JENKINS

3 Samuel POLK, for whom *see below*

III (cont.) Col Ezekiel Polk *m* 2nd N Carolina *c* 1792 Bessie Davis or Polly Campbell; *m* 3rd Maury Co, Tenn., *c* 1812/3 Sophia, widow of —— Leonard and dau of James Neely, and *d* nr Bolivar, Tenn., 31 Aug 1824

Col Ezekiel Polk's 3rd s by his 1st marriage:

Samuel POLK, *b* probably Tryon Co, N Carolina, 5 July 1772; moved to Maury Co 1806, Maj War of 1812, planter and farmer; *m* Mecklenburg Co 25 Dec 1794 Jane (also known as Jean Gracy, *b* probably Iredell Co, N Carolina, 13 Nov 1776; *d* Columbia, Maury Co, 11 Jan 1852, *bur* Greenwood Cemetery, Columbia), dau of Capt James Knox (*b c* 1752; *d* 10 Oct 1794), of Iredell Co, and his w Lydia Gillespie, and *d* Columbia 5 Nov 1827 (*bur* Greenwood Cemetery), leaving issue:

I JAMES KNOX POLK, 11th PRESIDENT of the UNITED STATES of AMERICA

II Jane Maria Polk, *b* Mecklenburg Co 14 Jan 1798; *m* Maury Co 24 Feb 1813 James WALKER and *d* Columbia, Tenn., 11 Oct 1876, having had (with other issue):

1 Samuel Polk WALKER, *b* 26 Jan 1814; *m* Maury Co, Tenn., 22 Oct 1834 Eleanor T. Wormley and *d* Memphis, Tenn., 5 Nov 1870, having had issue at least 11 children, of whom one s James served with the Confederate States Army and was *ka* Battle of Belmont

2 James Hayes WALKER, *b* 4 May 1816; *m* Corinth, Miss., 18 May 1869 Sophy Davis and *d* Columbia 27 May 1902

3 Joseph Knox WALKER, *b* 19 July 1818; private sec to his uncle President POLK 1845-49, Col 2nd Tennessee Infy Confederate States Army; *m* Lynchburg, Va., 2 Dec 1841 Augusta T. Tabb and *d* Memphis, Tenn., 21 Dec 1963, having had nine children

4 Jane Clarissa Walker, *b* 7 Oct 1820; *m* Columbia 21 June 1842 Isaac Newton BARNETT and *d* Columbia 27 Nov 1899, having had five children

5 Mary Eliza Walker, *b* 8 March 1823; *m* Columbia 12 July 1842 William Sanford PICKETT and *d* Memphis 2 Nov 1900, having had eight children

6 Sarah Naomi Walker, *b* 20 Feb 1825; *m* Columbia 7 Jan 1847 John Burton GREEN and *d* Nashville, Tenn., 5 March 1916, having had six children

7 Annie Maria Walker, *b* 8 April 1827; *m* Columbia 26 Dec 1854 Lemuel M. PHILLIPS and had one child, who *d* in infancy

8 Lucius Marshall WALKER

III Lydia Eliza Polk, *b* Mecklenburg Co 17 Feb 1800; *m* 1st Maury Co 5 Aug 1817 Silas William CALDWELL and had two s; *m* 2nd Edward RICHMOND and *d* Haywood Co, Tenn., 29 May 1864

IV Franklin Ezekiel POLK, *b* Mecklenburg Co 23 Aug 1802; *d* Columbia 21 Jan 1831

V Marshall Tate POLK, *b* Mecklenburg Co 17 Jan 1805; *m* Charlotte, N Carolina, 25 Oct 1827, as her 1st husb, Laura Teresa (she *m* 2nd 18— Dr Tate), dau of Judge Joseph Wilson and his w Mary Wood, and *d* Charlotte 12 April 1831, leaving issue:

President Polk's nephews and nieces

1 Roxana (Eunice Ophelia) POLK, *b* 1828; *d* 1842

2 Marshal Tate POLK, Jr, *b* Charlotte 15 May 1831; *educ* Georgetown U and US Mily Acad; Capt Artillery Confederate States Army, Tennessee State Treasurer; *m* Bolivar 10 Jan 1856 Evelina McNeal (*b* 26 March 1836; *d* Nashville 8 March 1926), dau of Major John Houston Bills and his w Prudence Tate McNeal, and *d* Nashville 29 Feb 1884 (*bur* Polk Cemetery, Bolivar), having had issue:

Great-nephews

(1) Edward McNeal POLK, *b* Bolivar 18 Nov 1856; *d* 19 Sept 1858

(2) James Knox POLK, *b* Bolivar 26 Jan 1859; Capt 1st Tennessee Vol Infy Spanish-American War of 1898; *m* Bolivar 27 Jan 1880 Mary Frances (*d* 26 Oct 1920), dau of Robert Hibbler and his w Ann Kelsey, and *d* 30 April 1932, leaving issue:

Great-nephew's children

1a James Knox POLK, Jr, *b* Nashville 3 March 1881; with 1st Tennesse Volunteer Infantry Spanish-American War of 1898; *m* Nashville 27 Jan 1915 Virginia Galtney (*d* June 1980), dau of W. G. Prichard and his w Mary Gibson, and *d* 7 Nov 1960, leaving issue:

Great-nephew's grandchildren

1b *Mary Polk [Mrs John Kirby-Smith, 2416 K St NW, Washington, DC 20037, USA], *b* Nashville 26 Oct 1915; *educ* Peabody Sch, Nashville; served Canadian Div Munitions Supply, Washington, DC, World War II; *m* 17 April 1942 John Selden KIRBY-SMITH (*d* May 1990), s of Reynold Marvin Kirby-Smith (himself s of Gen Edward Kirby-Smith, the last Confederate commander to surrender at the end of the Civil War, doing so nearly two months after Appomattox, and the last living full general of either the Union or Confederate Army) and his w Maud Tompkins, and has had issue:

Great-nephew's great-grandchildren

1c *Marshall Selden Kirby-Smith [331-B West Hamilton Ave, State College, PA 16801, USA], *b* Sewanee, Tenn., 5 Nov 1945; *educ* State Coll of Pa.; *m* Colorado 4 Aug 1981 (divorce 19——) Denis Dane GRAY and has issue:

Great-nephew's great-great-grandchildren

1d *Jonathan James Selden GRAY, *b* Colo. 4 July 1982

Great-nephew's great-grandchildren

2c *Laurance Polk Kirby-Smith [Mrs Alexis I du Pont, 2054 Veteran Ave, Los Angeles, CA 90025, USA], *b* Oak Ridge, Tenn., 5 Aug 1951; *educ* U of the South; *m* 1st Washington, DC, 1973 (divorce 19——) Thomas GIBSON; *m* 2nd New York 12 March 1982 *Alexis Irénée du PONT, Jr, s of Alexis Irénée du Pont and his w Anne Smith, and has issue:

Great-nephew's great-great-grandchildren

1d *Fairfax Polk du PONT, *b* Calif. 11 May 1988
2d *Sophie Kane du PONT, *b* Calif. 27 July 1992

Great-nephew's great-grandchildren

3c John Selden KIRBY-SMITH, Jr, *b* 1 Feb 1953; *d* Switzerland 10 July 1968

Great-nephew's grandchildren

2b *Virginia Knox Polk, *b* Nashville 31 May 1918; *m* 22 March 1947 *Thomas Kelly VAN ZANDT and has issue:

Great-nephew's great-grandchildren

1c *Mary Gibson VAN ZANDT, *b* Nashville 31 May 1949
2c *Effie Morgan Van Zandt, *b* Nashville 29 March 1951; *m* 10 June 1972 *Dr Walter MERRILL and has issue:

Great-nephew's great-great-grandchildren

1d *Virginia Kelly MERRILL, *b* Baltimore, Md., 27 Nov 1974
2d *Gibson MERRILL, *b* Baltimore 12 Oct 1977

Great-nephew's great-grandchildren

3c *James Knox Polk VAN ZANDT, *b* Greenville, Miss., 29 Nov 1952; *m* 31 May 1975 *Mary Josephine Pratt and has issue:

Great-nephew's great-great-grandchildren

1d *Mary Balfour VAN ZANDT, *b* 4 Aug 1977

Great-nephew's children

2a Kelsey Hibbler POLK, *b* Nashville 30 Dec 1884; *m* Mount Pleasant, Tenn., 18 Oct 1910 Eleanor Frances, dau of Edward Gregory, and *d* 19——, having had issue:

Great-nephew's grandchildren

1b *Mary Elizabeth POLK, *b* 3 April 1912
2b *Kelsey Hibbler POLK, Jr, *b* 3 Feb 1919

Great-nephew's children

3a Albert McNeal POLK, *b* 12 Aug 1888; with 50th Infantry US Army World War I; *m* Lawrenceville, Ga., 26 Nov 1924 Rubye Oliver (*b* 4 Jan 1902), dau of Lemuel Carol Mauldin and his w Margaret Oliver, of Dacula, Ga., and *d* 19——, having had issue:

Great-nephew's grandchildren

1b James Knox POLK, *b* Lincolnton, Ga., 13 June 1929; *d* 1930

Great-nephew's children

4a Edward Marshall POLK, *b* Chattanooga, Tenn., 1 June 1891; *m* Nashville 8 Dec 1912 Olivia Winston, dau of Charles F. Sharpe and his w Olivia Winston Scott, and *d* 19——, having had issue:

Great-nephew's grandchildren

1b *Olivia Sharpe POLK, *b* 21 June 1914
2b *Elizabeth McNeal POLK, *b* 18 May 1918

Great-nephew's children

5a Laurence Norton POLK, b Nashville 17 Feb 1896; Lt 25th Aero Sqdn in France World War I; m St Paul, Minn., 19 June 1926 *Marjorie Lee Shapard and d Chattanooga, Tenn., 1966, having adopted two children:

a *Laurence Norton POLK, b 31 May 1929
b *Marjorie Shapard POLK, b 1930

Great-niece

(3) Mary Wilson Polk, b Bolivar 24 Aug 1861; m Nashville 27 Nov 1884 Alexander Humphreys KORTRECHT (b Memphis 14 Aug 1859), of Memphis, Tenn., s of Judge Charles Kortrecht and his w Augusta Betts, and d April 1932, having had issue:

Great-niece's children

1a Charles Murray KORTRECHT, b Bolivar 13 Aug 1886; m Birmingham, Ala., 6 June 1919 Mary Lee Skeggs and d 19—

2a Humphreys KORTRECHT, b Memphis 15 May 1888; d 19—

3a Evelyn Marshall Kortrecht, b Memphis 30 Jan 1890; m Nashville 6 June 1914 Edgar Morrison RICHARDSON, s of Edgar Morrison Richardson and his w Anna B. Price, and d 19—, leaving issue:

Great-niece's grandchildren

1b *Mary (Mamie) Polk Richardson [Mrs Gordon Thacker, 366 South Highland Apt 304, Memphis, TN 32795-47, USA], b 27 Jan 1916; m 19— *Gordon THACKER

Great-niece's children

4a Eunice Polk Kortrecht, b Memphis 13 Jan 1892; m Norfolk, Va., 13 April 1918 Wylie Stegar DOLLAR and d 19—, leaving issue:

Great-niece's grandchildren

1b Eunice Adair Dollar, b 11 May 1919 } one of these m —— SCALLAN
2b Evelyn Polk Dollar, b 23 June 1923 } and d 19—, leaving issue:

Great-niece's great-grandchildren

1c *Joseph Andrew SCALLAN [3018 44th Place NW, Washington, DC 20016, USA]

Great-niece's children

5a Augustus KORTRECHT, b Memphis 30 Jan 1897

Great-nieces

(4) Laura Prudence POLK, b Bolivar 4 Feb 1865; d Nashville, Tenn., 1951 or 1952

(5) Eunice Ophelia Polk, b Bolivar 2 Aug 1867; m 1st Nashville 15 Nov 1894 Jesse Rowland NORTON (d June 1901), of Nashville, and had issue:

Great-niece's children

1a Evelyn Polk NORTON, b Chicago 25 Aug 1895; d Nashville 1969

2a Frederic Rowland NORTON, b Chicago 6 Aug 1897; m Nashville 14 June 1923 Louise Cooper and had issue:

Great-niece's grandchildren

1b *Eunice Polk Norton, b Nashville 4 Aug 1924; m 19— *—— PARDON
2b *Ann Frederic Norton, b Nashville 4 June 1928; m 19— *—— HARRINGTON

Great-niece's children

3a Rowland Polk (changed name from Jesse Rowland) NORTON, b Nashville 29 Oct 1900; m Zanesville, Ohio, 2 July 1927 *Gertrude Wolters [Mrs Rowland P Norton, 1501 Portola Rd, Portola Valley, CA 94028, USA] and d Menlo Park, Calif., Nov 1968, leaving issue:

Great-niece's grandchildren

1b *George Hillman NORTON [Star Route 2 Box 404, La Honda, CA 94020, USA], b Marietta, Ohio, 21 Nov 1930; educ Brown U (AB 1951) and Stanford U (JD 1957); jr grade Lt USN Korean War 1951-54, lawyer 1957-; m 25 June 1955 *Adele, dau of Edward Keim Woods and his w Adele Lund, and has issue:

Great-niece's great-grandchildren

1c Edward Polk NORTON, b San Francisco 26 March 1959; d 1984
2c *Carol Lund Norton [Mrs Glen Banks, 50 Quail Meadow Rd, Placitas, NM 87043, USA], b San Francisco 16 Feb 1961; educ Brown U (AB 1982); with Claris Corp 1988-92, gen contractor 1992-; m New Mexico 27 May 1990 *Glen BANKS, s of Ed Banks and his w Geneva
3c *Neil Wolters NORTON [1626 St Rose Ave, Baton Rouge, LA 70808, USA], b Redwood City, Calif., 12 Nov 1963; educ Pitzer Coll and Tulane U (MBA 1991)

Great-niece and -nephew

(5) (cont.) Eunice Polk Norton m 2nd Sewanee, Tenn., 10 Aug 1918 George H. HELLMAN and d 1964

(6) Clara Allison POLK, b Bolivar 16 Nov 1870; d 21 March 1872

(7) Marshall Tate POLK III, of Nashville, b Bolivar 8 March 1873; m Nashville 17 April 1902 Annie Sperry, dau of Robert Hill and his w Ann Patterson, and d 19—, having had issue:

Great-nephew's children
1a *Robert Hill POLK, *b* Nashville 28 April 1903
2a *Marshall Tate POLK IV, *b* Nashville 1 Nov 1904; *m* 19—— —— and has issue:

Great-nephew's grandchildren
1b *Marshall Tate POLK V [101 Jocelyn Hills Rd, Nashville, TN 37205, USA]

Great-nephew's children
3a *Prudence McNeal Polk [Mrs W Bryson Scott, Route 1 Box 140-B, Lovingston, VA 22949, USA], *b* Nashville 8 Sept 1906; *m* 1st 19—— William F. McGOWAN and has issue:

Great-nephew's grandchildren
1b *William F. McGOWAN, Jr [1004 Siwany St, Tampa, FL 33629, USA]

Great-nephew's children
3a (cont.) Prudence Polk McGowan *m* 2nd 19—— *W. Bryson SCOTT
4a *Thomas Wilson POLK, *b* Nashville 13 Dec 1908
5a *Anne Patterson Polk [Mrs Carmack Armisted, 4487 Post Place, Nashville, TN 37203, USA], *b* Nashville 5 April 1911; *m* 19—— *Carmack ARMISTED
6a *John Houston POLK, *b* Nashville 14 June 1913
7a *Evalina McNeal Polk [Mrs Pierce Ross, 713 Mt Carmel Place, Nashville, TN 37203, USA], *b* Nashville 14 March 1916; *m* 19—— *Pierce ROSS
8a *Richard Bradford POLK, *b* 11 Sept 1917

Great-niece
(8) Evelina McNeal Polk, *b* Bolivar 9 Dec 1875; *m* Nashville 12 Jan 1904 Dique ELDRED (*b* 5 Dec 1874), of Princeton, Ky., *s* of Orson P. Eldred and his *w* Susan Delia Harpending, and *d* Princeton 28 Jan 1963, leaving issue:

Great-niece's children
1a George Orson ELDRED, *b* Princeton 14 Sept 1904; *educ* Vanderbilt U and Coll of Law, U of Kentucky U; lawyer Princeton 1933-89; *m* Washington, DC, 9 Oct 1943 *Olive [Mrs George O Eldred, 702 W Locust St, Princeton, KY 42445, USA], dau of Eugene Forrest Seaton and his *w* Flora Crutcher, and *d* Princeton 26 Sept 1989, leaving issue:

Great-niece's grandchildren
1b *John Shelley ELDRED [2939 Albemarle St, Washington, DC 20008, USA], *b* Paducah, Ky., 21 Jan 1945; *educ* Vanderbilt U, Ky., (BA, JD); ptnr Keller & Heckman, Washington, DC, 1978-; *m* 1st Owensboro, Ky., 30 Sept 1969 Ann Stanton Macdonald; *m* 2nd 24 May 1980 *Kathryn Elder, dau of Edwin Findlay Pauli and his *w* Mary Elder, and with his 2nd *w* has issue:

Great-niece's great-grandchildren
1c *Alexander Stratton ELDRED, *b* Washington, DC, 25 Sept 1984
2c *Christopher Pauli ELDRED, *b* Washington 1 Aug 1988

Great-niece's grandchildren
2b *George Orson ELDRED, Jr [715 W Main St, Princeton, KY, USA], *b* Princeton 13 Jan 1954; *educ* U of The South, Sewanee, Tenn., and U of Kansas; musician, photographer

Great-niece's children
2a *Marshall Polk ELDRED [110 Travois Rd, Louisville, KY, USA; Citizens Plaza, Louisville, KY, USA], *b* Princeton 14 Sept 1904; *educ* Vanderbilt U and Coll of Law, U of Kentucky; lawyer; *m* Princeton 10 July 1935 *Laura Hale and has issue:

Great-niece's grandchildren
1b *Marshall Polk ELDRED, Jr [515 Club Lane, Louisville, KY 40207, USA; Citizens Plaza, Louisville, KY 40202, USA], *b* Princeton 27 Nov 1938; *educ* Vanderbilt U and Coll of Law, U of Kentucky; lawyer; *m* 1st Louisville 15 June 1962 Penelope Harrison and has issue:

Great-niece's great-grandchildren
1c *Marshall Polk ELDRED III, *b* 15 June 1965
2c *Katherine Owen ELDRED, *b* 15 March 1967

Great-niece's grandchild
1b (cont.) Marshall P. Eldred *m* 2nd 19—— *Andrée Mondor

Great-niece's children
3a Mary Wilson ELDRED, *b* Princeton 7 Aug 1907; *educ* Mary Baldwin Coll, Ohio State U and Sch of Library Science, U of Kentucky; regional librarian; *d* Princeton 7 Oct 1983

Great-nephew
(9) Leonidas POLK, of Toledo, Ohio, *b* Nashville 27 March 1878; with 1st Tennessee Vol Infy Spanish-American War of 1898; *m* Toledo 28 March 1908 Rachel Marie Scott and *d* 1948, having had issue:

Great-nephew's children
1a *Elmer Scott POLK, *b* Toledo 24 May 1909

2a *Dora Marie POLK, *b* Toledo 12 Jan 1911

3a *Leonidas POLK (subsequently known as Judd Knox Polk), *b* Toledo 3 July 1912; *m* 1946 *Sally E. Ritzmann and has issue:

Great-nephew's grandchildren
1b *Julie Polk, *b* 19——; *m* 19—— and has one s and one dau
2b *Benjamin POLK *b* 19——
3b *Mimi Polk, *b* 19——; *m* 19——

Great-nephew's children
4a *William McNeal POLK, *b* Toledo 1 Aug 1915
5a *Evelina Bills Polk [Mrs Otto Bird, 17835 Ponader Drive, South Bend, IN 46635, USA], *b* Toledo 7 Nov 1916; *m* 19—— *Otto BIRD

Great-nephew
(10) Thomas Allison POLK, *b* Nashville 13 June 1879; *d* there 14 Sept 1884

VI John Lee POLK, *b* Maury Co 23 March 1807; *d* Columbia 28 Sept 1831

VII Naomi Tate Polk, *b* Maury Co 2 July 1809; *m* Columbia 18 Aug 1825 Adlai O. HARRIS and *d* Memphis 6 Aug 1836, leaving four daus

VIII Ophelia Clarissa Polk, *b* Maury Co 6 Sept 1812; *m* Columbia 24 Sept 1829 John B. HAYS and *d* Columbia 18 April 1851, leaving two daus

IX Hon William Hawkins POLK, *b* Maury Co 24 May 1815; Memb Tennessee Legislature, US Chargé d'Affaires Kingdom of the Two Sicilies, Maj 3rd Tennessee Dragoons, Memb US House of Reps; *m* 1st 18—— Belinda G. Dickins; *m* 2nd 1847 Mary L. Corse and with her had issue:

President Polk's nephew
1 James Knox POLK, *b* 1849; *m* 1885 Louise von Isenberg and *d* 1912

IX (cont.) William H. Polk *m* 3rd 1854 Lucy Eugenia Williams and *d* 16 Dec 1862, having with her had issue:

President Polk's nephews
2 William Hawkins POLK, *b* 1856; *m* 1885 Adelaide Marabel and *d* 1886
3 Tasker POLK, *b* 1861; Lt 3rd N Carolina Infantry, lawyer, Mayor Warrenton, N Carolina, Memb N Carolina Senate; *m* 1895 Eliza Tannahill Jones and *d* 19——, having had issue:

Great-nephews and -nieces
(1) *William Tannahill POLK, *b* 1896
(2) *Mary Tasker POLK, *b* 1898
(3) *(Lucy) Fairfax Polk [Mrs Fairfax Polk Mitchell, 200 Trade St, Tarboro, NC 27886, USA], *b* 1901; *m* 19—— —— MITCHELL
(4) *James Knox POLK, *b* 1904

X Samuel Wilson POLK, *b* Maury Co 17 Oct 1817; *d* Columbia 24 Feb 1839

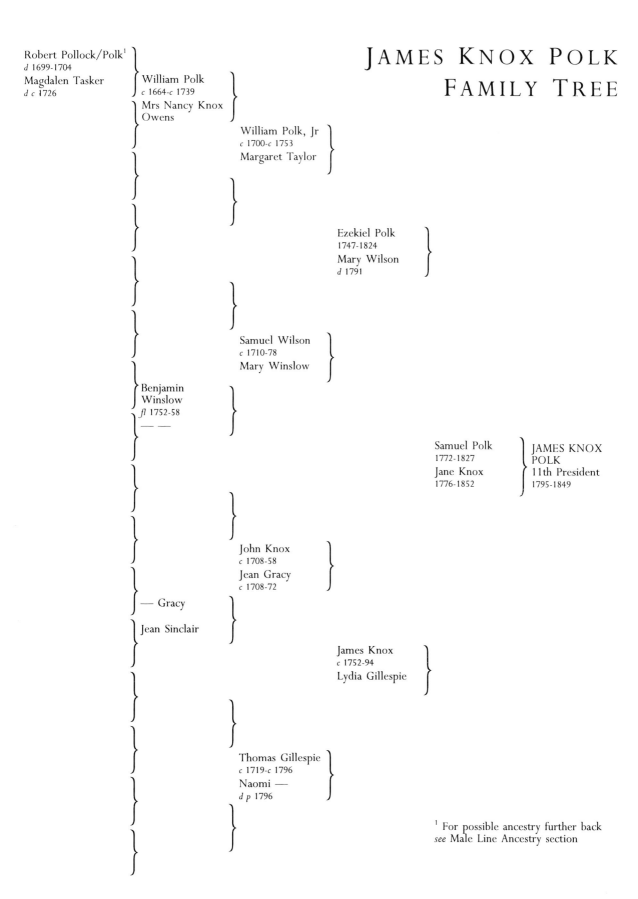

JAMES KNOX POLK
FAMILY TREE

Robert Pollock/Polk[1]
d 1699-1704
Magdalen Tasker
d c 1726

William Polk
c 1664-*c* 1739
Mrs Nancy Knox
Owens

William Polk, Jr
c 1700-*c* 1753
Margaret Taylor

Ezekiel Polk
1747-1824
Mary Wilson
d 1791

Samuel Wilson
c 1710-78
Mary Winslow

Benjamin
Winslow
fl 1752-58
— —

Samuel Polk
1772-1827
Jane Knox
1776-1852

JAMES KNOX
POLK
11th President
1795-1849

John Knox
c 1708-58
Jean Gracy
c 1708-72

— Gracy

Jean Sinclair

James Knox
c 1752-94
Lydia Gillespie

Thomas Gillespie
c 1719-*c* 1796
Naomi —
d p 1796

[1] For possible ancestry further back
see Male Line Ancestry section

Plate 36 Zachary Taylor

ZACHARY TAYLOR

1784-1850
12TH PRESIDENT OF THE UNITED STATES OF AMERICA
1849-50

Decidedly the Whigs were an unlucky party. In Henry Clay and Daniel Webster they had two of the most remarkable leaders of the age, but they only won presidential elections when they nominated famous generals and on each occasion the wretch died on them.

The case of Zachary Taylor was particularly hard. He had never voted in an election in his life and the party had thoughtfully spared his embarrassment by failing to issue a platform. He was a Southern slaveholder (the last such to be elected President) and a good many Northern antislavery Whigs had walked out of the party to support Martin Van Buren who was making his last appearance in a presidential election as candidate for the Free Soil party; those that remained seemed quite willing to accept Taylor. His appeal to the voters was nationalistic; he was the hero of Buena Vista, 'Old Rough and Ready', who had thrashed the Mexican foe. It was expected that he would be a conservative, docile President content to do as little as possible until the party managers had filled all the offices and worked out some sort of compromise on the great slavery issues. Instead he showed himself truly rough-and-ready: reckless as Tyler (only not so suave), obstinate as Polk. He liked to see himself as a second Washington but his real model was Andrew Jackson. At any rate he was determined to impose his will on all comers. As a result he brought the United States nearer to the brink of civil war than it was to come again for 10 years. Then a meal of cherries and iced milk during a typically oppressive Washington summer brought on an illness which in turn brought on a fatal heart attack; the Union gained a breathing space and the Whig party had a last chance to pull itself together.

Taylor's presidency is thus a curiosity, an ambiguous, contradictory, dangerous episode in an ambiguous, dangerous period. Explanations of the President's course vary. Some see him as a simpleton, a Southern man who let himself be bamboozled by the antislavery Northerner Senator William H. Seward of New York. Certainly Seward, who had helped Taylor to win the presidential nomination, had immense influence over him. But it seems likely that Taylor, who knew the Western territories far better than did the Congressional leaders, was of Polk's opinion that slavery could not expand into them and therefore should not be supported there. If slavery was ever seriously attacked it would have to be defended in the old Southern states of the Atlantic seaboard and the Mississippi valley, not in the West. Furthermore, Taylor had been in the army all his life and was a sturdy patriot. He saw the proslavery agitators as potential secessionists (which indeed they were) and determined to resist them. He would settle the question, in fact, by excluding slavery from the territories and crushing, by force if need be, any resistance. He relied on Seward to guide him safely through the politics of all this; an unwise choice, for Seward at this period was as rash as any hothead from the South. He and Taylor convinced each other that the South was merely bluffing and challenged its spokesman at every point.

Meanwhile, in Congress, Henry Clay, with Webster's powerful assistance, was struggling to get his great compromise proposal passed. It was disheartening to think that even if he succeeded his bill might suffer a presidential veto and was likely to fail anyway for lack of presidential assistance. It must have been with very mixed feelings indeed that the greatest of the Whigs heard the news that once more a Whig President had died prematurely.

ZACHARY TAYLOR'S FAMILY

Taylor was a soldier rather than politician, so it is of interest that his father's mother was one of the Lees of Virginia. This made him a third cousin once-removed of Robert E. Lee — twice over, since Lee's parents were cousins — and Lee is one of the greatest generals in American history. Taylor was not in that class, though his 1847 victory of Buena Vista over Santa Anna against odds of four-to-one in the Mexican War was undeniably brilliant. But as well as Robert E. Lee the family produced 'Light Horse Harry' Lee, who during the Revolutionary War took the garrison at Paulus Hook, New Jersey, under the very guns of the British fleet; Admiral Samuel P. Lee, USN; the Confederate General George B. Crittenden (a relatively unsuccessful soldier admittedly) and his brother General Thomas L. Crittenden, a Union man who served with distinction at Shiloh (and had earlier been made US Consul in Liverool by his cousin President Taylor). So there is a strong case for attributing Zachary Taylor's most important achievements — his military ones — to his Lee ancestry.

Even on Taylor's mother's side there was a modest degree of soldierly activity. And it was as an indirect result of military service in the Revolutionary War that Taylor's father Richard took up life as a planter, in which he was a success. Richard Taylor in 1783 received a bonus grant of 6,000 acres in what was then the West (it later became incorporated in Kentucky). Inevitably he had to battle against Indians, and his reputation as a fighter was such that Charles Scott, Kentucky's Governor from 1808 to 1812, said that if he had to storm the gates of Hell he would want Dick Taylor to lead the column. Richard Taylor was not just a fighting man and landowner. He helped draw up the state constitution when in 1790 Kentucky was admitted to the Union and also took part in amending it seven years later. Meanwhile he prospered materially: he owned a mere seven slaves in 1790, but these had increased to 19 in 1795, 26 in 1800 and 37 in 1810. By 1797 he was cultivating 1,650 acres of his original 6,000-acre wilderness grant.

The disadvantage of frontier life was lack of educational opportunity. Richard Taylor may have gone to William and Mary College; Sarah, his wife, had certainly had the benefit of tutors from Europe. But their son Zachary's education was nothing much to boast of. He did not go to West Point, but was commissioned directly into the army. And even when he had become President one Congressman, the Free Soiler George W. Julian, called him uncultivated and uninformed, adding that he couldn't carry on a proper conversation, mispronounced words and was incapable of writing a decent letter. Julian published a biography of his father-in-law the anti-slavery Congressman Joshua R. Giddings as well as collections of his own speeches so perhaps attached excessive importance to literary skills. Certainly those letters of Taylor's which survive (the bulk do not) are scarcely models of spelling or linguistic felicity. And since many documents bearing his signature were composed by his son-in-law and assistant William Bliss it is reasonable to assume the genuine, unghosted article would have been even worse. That didn't mean Zachary Taylor was unappreciative of education. He gave his children as much of it as possible, sending his son Richard to both Harvard and Yale. And he never made the mistake of thinking an army could get by with uneducated officers. In a letter to his son-in-law Robert C. Wood he wrote "There is nothing more important to insure [sic] a young man a high standing either in the army or navy than literary attainments and a taste for study if he has books etc. which will be a source of amusement as well as education." He would undoubtedly have approved of his two great successors, Grant and Eisenhower, who were nearly as mighty with the pen as with the sword (Eisenhower may

Plate 37   Mary Elizabeth Taylor Bliss Dandridge,
Zachary Taylor's daughter and hostess in the White House

not have written as well as Grant, but he sold superlatively well; *see* his biographical details). And there is some evidence that Taylor made up for his lack of formal education by private study, at any rate in his professional field. His one-time son-in-law Jefferson Davis reckoned Taylor was one of the best-read and most learned men as regards military history he had ever known.

Of Zachary Taylor's brothers and sisters only Joseph and Sarah lived to see him become President. Joseph, whom contemporaries such as Senators Salmon P. Chase and William H. Seward thought remarkably similar to his elder brother Zachary in manner as well as appearance, followed Zachary into the army. When after the War of 1812 Joseph was first let go then reinstated at a lower rank his father complained to their cousin President Madison, but it was fruitless. Joseph served with his elder brother in the Mexican campaign and the letters from Zachary to Joseph are some of the few by Zachary that survive. Seward thought it worth cultivating Joseph to ingratiate himself with Taylor, so the brothers must have been close.

Zachary Taylor's wife came from the same sort of background as her husband, being the daughter of a well-off southern planter. She met him when visiting her sister, who was married to a Kentucky man, Samuel Chews. Margaret Taylor became a good army wife, accompanying her husband to the various outposts he was sent to, though she usually returned to Louisville, Ky., to give birth to their children. The one exception was their second daughter Sarah Knox Taylor, whom they always called Knox because she had been born at the Fort of that name. By 1820 Taylor, newly promoted to Lieutenant-Colonel, intended to settle in the South and when he was assigned to the 4th Infantry in the lower Mississippi Valley he took with him his wife and children (at that stage just four daughters, his son not yet having been born). He settled them with his wife's sister at Bayou Sara, near Baton Rouge, where the two youngest girls died that summer. Margaret Taylor was already delicate and the loss further debilitated her.

She was hardly ever to act as official hostess at the White House, though she did preside at family gatherings. The presidential side of entertaining she left to her daughter Betty Bliss. The Democrats in the 1848 election portrayed her as a boorish frontierswoman drawing on a long-stemmed corncob pipe, a ploy resorted to the more readily because Zachary Taylor's war hero status made it impossible to go for him. The caricature was completely unfair but was made possible because almost nothing was known about Margaret Taylor before her arrival in Washington. And even that she managed in self-effacing style, travelling separately from her husband and by a different route — almost furtively. She could be perfectly pleasant in small, intimate family gatherings. Varina Davis, the second wife of the Taylors' former son-in-law Jefferson Davis, found the time spent with her hostess when visiting the White House the pleasantest part of the whole experience. Possibly Margaret Taylor was reluctant to put herself forward in a wider milieu as part of her bargain with the Almighty, for during her husband's long military career she had been so afraid he would be killed that she had vowed to abandon the world of fashion and society provided he was spared death. She never liked his plunge into politics and in 1848 prayed every night that someone else should succeed Polk. Nine days after her husband's death she left Washington and settled with her son Richard in New Orleans. She never went near the capital again.

The Taylors' eldest daughter Ann had less of a pull to the South than other members of the family. She stayed in the North when her husband Richard Wood, a New Englander, accompanied his father-in-law to Mexico and when the Taylors were installed in the White House lived at Baltimore, which though a Southern city is nevertheless on a slightly higher latitude than Washington. Wood was on very close terms with Zachary Taylor and supplied him with titbits of political information. In return the President was probably more confidential with him than any other of his associates. Wood, an army surgeon, attended Taylor professionally on an 1849 presidential tour of northeastern states which had to be cut short when Taylor fell ill. Wood also attended him during his last fatal illness in the summer of 1850. The Woods' second son Robert Jr was a favourite of his Taylor grandparents and at one stage was brought up by them in their own house.

The marriage of the Taylors' second daughter Knox to Jefferson Davis, later President of the Confederacy, took place with the grudging consent rather than outright approval of her parents. The reason for Taylor's opposition to Davis as a son-in-law is unclear. Taylor said he'd be damned if another of his daughters married into the army (Davis was then on Taylor's staff), with its long separation of father and children. But he got on well with his other son-in-law, another army officer, and there is no evidence that he opposed his daughter Betty's marriage 13 years later to Colonel Bliss, yet a third army officer. In any case Davis resigned his commission two weeks after the wedding. The real story is supposed to be that Taylor and Davis had fallen out while in the army together, with Davis becoming so enraged he is said to have wanted to challenge Taylor to a duel (an impossibility certainly in the British army, where no officer was allowed to challenge a superior since it would have tempted men of junior rank to create vacancies in higher ranks by calling out their seniors). Later Davis and Taylor became reconciled, which is the more remarkable because Davis's removal with Knox to his Mississippi plantation resulted in her dying of fever less than three months after the wedding. Davis claimed that his quarrel with Taylor arose because he had been slandered to Taylor by a third party and Taylor had imputed to him "motives the reverse of those by which I was actuated". What motives, though? And what action did Davis take that involved motives being imputed at all? In the event Davis decided not to demand satisfaction. Literal satisafction, however, sprang up on both sides eventually, for Taylor employed Davis to help him draft peace proposals in 1846 during the Mexican War and Davis supplied Taylor with items of political gossip when the latter entered public life.

Davis's ties with Taylor helped swing the South behind the latter in the 1848 election, and Davis himself, though a Democrat who supported Lewis Cass, his party's presidential nominee, spoke so flatteringly of his former father-in-law that some Democrats claimed he was working for Taylor's election. Taylor and his third son-in-law William Bliss (known to his in-laws as 'Perfect' Bliss) had a more straightforward relationship. Bliss acted as a secretary to Taylor in the army and the White House. Well educated, well read, a linguist and gallant soldier, he was like a son to Taylor. West Point thought him a prodigy and he may even have been one. The Washington *Union* used to thunder against his strong hold on the President, but as with every such relationship one can never say precisely how strong it really was.

Bliss was the more welcome to his father-in-law because Richard, Taylor's only son, was a mild disappointment. Partly it was his poor health. As early as 20 he suffered from rheumatism and felt obliged to attend spas. Although Richard set off for the Mexican War in which his father won the glory that made him President, he had to turn back when struck down by rheumatism. But his indecision about his future was more his own fault. Perhaps he had been overeducated: he knew the classics, French and Spanish and was a great reader. Had he been as supple of limb as a comic book hero, these do not sound the accomplishments of a man of action. Taylor suggested he go and manage Cypress Grove, a cotton plantation of 2,100 acres in Mississippi that Taylor had bought for $95,000 in 1841 against the day he retired. Initially he was satisfied with Richard's progress but the price of cotton fell to rock bottom in 1850 and anyway Cypress Grove was subject to floods. Richard was authorized by his father to buy a sugar plantation instead and chose a 1,000-acre property with 64 slaves some 20 miles from New Orleans. This cost $115,000, payable in five tranches, and Taylor was intending to finance it when he died. Richard's sisters were not interested in helping him run it so he operated it singlehandedly, with some success until it was captured and laid waste in the Civil War. He seems to have been more unlucky than inept, but since luck is the prerequisite in a general its lack in a general's son tends to stand out all the more.

BIOGRAPHICAL DETAILS AND DESCENDANTS

ZACHARY TAYLOR, *b* Montebello, Orange Co, Va., 24 Nov 1784; 1st Lt 7th Infy Regt 1808, Capt 1810, Cdr Fort Knox, Vincennes, Indian Territory, 1811, Brevet Maj 26th Infy 1812, full Maj as of 1814, resigned commission 1815, re-commissioned Maj 3rd Infy 1816, Lt-Col 4th Infy 1819, assigned to 4th Infy 1820, Cdr Fort Snelling, Northwest Territory (now Minnesota), 1828, Col and Cdr Fort Crawford, Michigan Territory (now Wisconsin) 1829, Col 1st Regt 1832, served Black Hawk War (Black Hawk surrendered to Taylor in person after his victory of Bad Axe 2 Aug) 1832, Cdr Jefferson Barracks, Mo., 1836, won victory against Seminole Indians nr Lake Okeechobee, Fla., in Second Seminole War 1837, Brevet Brig-Gen 1838 and Cdr all Florida forces 1838-40, Cdr 2nd Dept Western Div of US Army 1841, Cdr 1st Dept Western Div US Army 1844, won victory over Mexicans at Palo Alto and Resaca de la Palma 1846, Maj-Gen 1846, Cdr US Forces Northern Mexico 1847, 12th President (Whig) of the USA 1849-50, Hon Memb Soc of Cincinnati 1847, author: *Letters of Zachary Taylor from the Battlefields of the Mexican War* (1908); *m* Jefferson Co, Ky., 21 June 1810 Margaret Mackall (*b* Calvert Co, Md., 21 Sept 1788; *d* East Pascagoula, Miss., 14 Aug 1852, *bur* with her husband in the Zachary Taylor National Cemetery, Jefferson Co, Ky.), dau of Walter Smith, planter, of Md., and his *w* Ann Mackall, and *d* the White House 9 July 1850 (*bur* temporarily Washington, DC, subsequently reinterred Zachary Taylor Nat Cemetery), having had issue:

President Taylor's daughter
I Ann Margaret Mackall Taylor, *b* Jefferson Co, Ky., 9 April 1811; *m* Fort Crawford, Prairie du Chien, Michigan Territory (now Wisconsin), 20 Sept 1829 Dr Robert Crooke WOOD, Actg Surg-Gen Union Army Civil War (*b* Rhode Island 23 Sept 1801; *d* 28 March 1869), and *d* Freiburg, Germany, 2 Dec 1875, leaving issue:

Grandchildren
1 John Taylor WOOD, *b* Fort Snelling, Minn., 13 Aug 1830; served USN and Confederate States Navy Civil War (commanded CSS *Tallahassee*), Col on staff of Confederate Pres Jefferson Davis (his unc by marriage); *m* 25 Nov 1856 Lola

(b 1834; d 1909), dau of George Mackubin, of Annapolis, Md., and his w Eleanor MacCubbin, and d Halifax, Nova Scotia, 19 July 1904, having had issue:

Great-grandchildren
(1) Anne Mackall WOOD, b 1858; d in infancy
(2) Zachary Taylor WOOD, CMG (1913), of Dawson City, Yukon, Canada, b 27 Nov 1860; educ RMC Kingston, Ontario; with Roy NW Mounted Police (served NW Frontier Rebellion 1885, Insp 1885, Lt-Col and Assist Commissioner 1892), Memb Cncl Yukon Territory 1900; m 9 April 1888 Frances Augusta, dau of Joseph Daly, of Kingston, Ontario, and d Ashville, N Carolina, 15 Jan 1915, leaving issue:

Great-great-grandchildren
1a Stuart Zachary Taylor WOOD, of Vancouver, BC, Canada, b 1889; Maj RCMP; m 1918 *Gertrude Peterson (b 1900) and d 19——, having had issue:

Great-great-grandchildren's children
1b Donald Zachary Taylor WOOD, b 1918; m 1941 *Mignonne Castonguay and was ka World War II 1944, leaving issue:

Great-great-grandchildren's grandchildren
1c *Sheryl Ann Taylor WOOD, b 1943

Great-great-grandchildren's children
2b Herschel Theodore Taylor WOOD, b 1924; with RCMP; d 1950
3b *John Taylor WOOD III, b 1931; with RCMP
4b *Frances Helen Taylor WOOD, b 1937
5b *Marjorie Lola Taylor WOOD, b 1941

Great-great-grandchildren
2a John Taylor WOOD II, b 1901; d 1930

Great-grandchildren
(3) Elizabeth Simms WOOD, b 1862; d in infancy
(4) Lola Mackubin WOOD, b 1864
(5) Robert Crooke WOOD, b 1867; d 1884
(6) Eleanor Mackubin Wood, b 1869; m 1894 John Duncan D'Urban CAMPBELL, of Montreal, Canada (b 1856; d 1920), and d 26 Jan 1953, having had issue:

Great-great-grandchildren
1a Duncan John MacLeod CAMPBELL, b 1895; with Canadian Expeditionary Force World War I; ka Western Front 1916
2a *Archibald Bruce Duchesnay CAMPBELL, b 1899; with RCAF World War I; m 1930 *Miriam Alberta Harrop (b 1904), of Regina, Saskatchewan, Canada, and has issue:

Great-great-grandchildren's children
1b *Duncan Archibald Edmund CAMPBELL, b 1931; m 1954 *Isabel Jean MacKay (b 1931)
2b *Bruce John Charles CAMPBELL, b 1932; m 1952 *Jacqueline Louise Ennette Katherina Burns (b 1933) and has issue:

Great-great-grandchildren's grandchildren
1c *Karen Louise CAMPBELL, b 1953

Great-great-grandchildren
3a *Charles Carroll Wood CAMPBELL, b 1903; m 1933 *Nellie Kate Robbins (b 1905) and has issue:

Great-great-grandchildren's children
1b *Charles Colin Robin CAMPBELL, b 1935
2b *Carol Ann Eleanor CAMPBELL, b 1937

Great-great-grandchildren
4a *Lola Henrietta CAMPBELL, b 1908

Great-grandchildren
(7) John Taylor WOOD, b 1871
(8) Geoge Mackubin WOOD, of Halifax, Nova Scotia, Canada, b 1872; civil engr; m 1923 Mary Muriel Buss, of Victoria, BC, Canada, and d 1927
(9) Blandina von Grabow ('Nina') WOOD, b 1873
(10) Mary Catherine Hammond WOOD, b 1875; d 1898
(11) Charles Carroll WOOD, b 1876; served N Lancs Regt Boer War; ka Kimberley, S Africa, 1899

Grandchildren
2 Robert Crooke WOOD, Jr, b Fort Snelling 4 April 1832; educ West Point; Cavalry Lt US Army 1855-58, Cavalry Col Confederate States Army; m 18—— Mary Wilhelmine, dau of Hore Browse Trist, of Ascension Parish, La., and his w Rosella Bringier, and d New Orleans 4 Dec 1900, having had issue:

Great-grandchildren
(1) John Burke Trist WOOD, of New Orleans, d 1953
(2) Mary Wilhelmine Trist WOOD
(3) Richard Taylor WOOD (twin with Mary Wilhelmine); d young
(4) Nina Sarah WOOD; d young
(5) Marie Rosella Wood; m William Edwin BRICKELL, Jr, s of William Edwin Brickell, and had issue:

  Great-great-grandchildren
  1a William Edwin BRICKELL III

Great-grandchildren
(6) Robert Crooke WOOD; d young
(7) Zachary Taylor WOOD; Lt US Army; m 1st Helen McGlon and had issue:

  Great-great-grandchildren
  1a *Helen WOOD

Great-grandchildren
(7) (cont.) Zachary T. Wood m 2nd Beatrice Thomas

Grandchildren
3 Blandina Dudley Wood, b Fort Crawford, Wis., 9 Jan 1835; m 1st 18— Maj Edward BOYCE, Paymaster US Army (d 28 Feb 1862) and had issue:

  Great-grandchildren
  (1) William VON GRABOW (b Boyce but assumed stepf's name), b 18—

Grandchildren
3 (cont.) Blandina Wood Boyce m 2nd 4 Jan 1866 Baron Guido VON GRABOW, Prussian Min to Venezuela, and d 7 Sept 1892, leaving further issue:

  Great-grandchildren
  (2) Baron Ernst Romanus Guido VON GRABOW
  (3) Baron —— VON GRABOW; d young

Grandchildren
4 Sarah Knox WOOD, b Prairie du Chien, Wis., 21 Nov 1839; d 28 Feb 1915

President Taylor's children
II (Sarah) Knox Taylor, b Fort Knox, Missouri Territory, 6 March 1814; m Louisville, Ky., 17 June 1835, as his 1st w, Jefferson DAVIS (b Fairview, Christian (later Todd) Co, Ky., 3 June 1808; Memb (D) US House of Reps 1845-46, US Senator 1847-51 and 1857-61, US Sec of War 1853-57, President Confederate States of America 1861-65, author: *Rise and Fall of the Confederate Government*, 2 vols (1881), and *A Short History of the Confederate States of America* (1890); d New Orleans 6 Dec 1889), s of Samuel Emory Davis and his w Jane Cook, and d Locust Grove, La., 15 Sept 1835 of malarial fever
III Octavia Pannill TAYLOR, b Jefferson Co, Ky., 16 Aug 1816; d Bayou Sara, La., 8 July 1820 of fever
IV Margaret Smith TAYLOR, b Jefferson Co, Ky., 27 July 1819; d Bayou Sara, La., 22 Oct 1820 of fever
V Mary Elizabeth (Betty) Taylor, b Jefferson Co, Ky., 20 April 1824; acted as her father's hostess in the White House; m 1st 5 Dec 1848 Lt-Col William Wallace Smith BLISS (b 17 Aug 1815; educ West Point; Adj-Gen to his f-in-law Gen Taylor and priv sec when f-in-law President; d 4 Aug 1853), s of Capt John Bliss, US Army, and his w Olive Hall Simonds; m 2nd 11 Feb 1858, as his 2nd w, Philip Pendleton DANDRIDGE, 2nd s of Adam Stephen Dandridge, of The Bower, Jefferson Co, Va., and his w Sarah Pendleton, and d Winchester, Va., 25 or 26 July 1909
VI Richard ('General Dick') TAYLOR, b nr Louisville, Ky., 27 Jan 1826; educ Harvard and Yale; Lt-Gen Confederate States Army (Commandg Offr Louisiana, helped administer western Confederacy after fall of Vicksburg, won victory of Sabine Cross Roads over Union forces under Gen N. P. Banks 8 April 1864, succeeded John B. Hood as Gen Commandg Confederate Army of Tennessee 22 Jan 1865), author: *Destruction and Reconstruction* (1879); m 10 Feb 1851 Louise Marie Myrthé (b Hermitage Plantation, St James Parish, La.; d 1875), dau of Michel Doradon Bringier and his w Aglaé du Bourg de St Colombe, and d New York 12 April 1879, having had issue:

Grandchildren
1 Louise Margaret TAYLOR, b 6 Jan 1852; d 2 Sept 1901
2 Betty Taylor, b 1854; m 1881 Walter Robinson STAUFFER, s of Isaac Hull Stauffer and his w Marie Céleste Bonford, and had issue:

  Great-grandchildren
  (1) Myrthé Stauffer; m Albert SCHWARTZ (d 1922) and d 1963, leaving issue:

    Great-great-grandchildren
    1a Wilhelmina SCHWARTZ, b 1907; d 19—
    2a Marie Louise Schwartz, b 1908; m Bernard J. McCLOSKEY and d 1965, leaving issue:

      Great-great-grandchildren's children
      1b *Patrick McCLOSKEY [509 Mesa Road, Santa Monica, CA 90402, USA], b 1936

2b *Walter Stauffer McCLOSKEY [226 Centre St, Milton, MA 02186, USA], b New Orleans 26 Aug 1938; educ Harvard (AB, PhD); teacher of literature Milton Coll 1971-; m 1965 *Josephine Grace and has issue:

Great-great-grandchildren's grandchildren
1c *Walter Robinson McCLOSKEY, b 28 Sept 1972
2c *Caroline Grace McCLOSKEY, b Brookline, Mass., 28 Aug 1978

Great-great-grandchildren
3a Harry P. SCHWARTZ [730 Esplanade Avenue, New Orleans, LA 70116, USA], b 1912; m 1944 *Eugenie Chavanne and d 19—, leaving issue:

Great-great-grandchildren's children
1b *Eugenie Chavanne SCHWARTZ, b 1951

Great-grandchildren
(2) Alice B. Stauffer; m Lewis HARDIE and d 1960, leaving issue:

Great-great-grandchildren
1a *Walter S. HARDIE [1521 Eighth Street, New Orleans, LA 70115, USA], b 1907; m 1st Shirley Baehr and has issue:

Great-great-grandchildren's children
1b *Eve HARDIE

Great-great-grandchildren
1a (cont.) Walter S. Hardie m 2nd *Dorothy Thomas [4206 Danneel, New Orleans, LA 70115, USA] and with her has had issue:

Great-great-grandchildren's children
2b *Alice HARDIE [6315 Fontainebleau Drive, New Orleans, LA 70125, USA], b 1946
3b Walter S. HARDIE, Jr; d 1969

Great-great-grandchildren
2a Betty Hardie, b New Orleans 1908; m there 1939 Marchese Benedetto CAPOMAZZA DI CAMPOLATTARO (b Naples, Italy, 1903; d Rome 15 July 1991), s of Marchese Carlo Emilio Capomazza di Campolattaro (creation of 1681 by King CHARLES V of the Two Sicilies (CHARLES II of Spain)), and d Rome 26 July 1990, leaving issue:

Great-great-grandchildren's children
1b *Simonetta Capomazza di Campolattaro [Sga Corigliano, Lungotevere Sanzio 9, Rome, Italy 00153], b Copenhagen, Denmark, 6 Aug 1942; educ Liceo Belle Arti; m Rome 14 Dec 1968 *Gino CORIGLIANO, s of Placido Corigliano and his w Olga de Vita, and has issue:

Great-great-grandchildren's grandchildren
1c *Piero CORIGLIANO, b Rome 29 Jan 1973

Great-great-grandchildren's children
2b *Carlo CAPOMAZZA DI CAMPOLATTARO [1614 State Street, New Orleans, LA 70118, USA], b Stockholm, Sweden, 21 Dec 1943; educ Montana Internat Sch, Zug, Switzerland; with Lykes Bros Steamship Co 1972-82, formed tour company 1984 and currently operates same; m New Orleans 27 Nov 1970 *Rosemonde (b New Orleans 1942), dau of Emile N. Kuntz and his w Julia Hardin, and has issue:

Great-great-grandchildren's grandchildren
1c *Carlo-Emilio CAPOMAZZA DI CAMPOLATTARO, b New Orleans 22 Feb 1972
2c *Stefano CAPOMAZZA DI CAMPOLATTARO, b New Orleans 24 Nov 1975

Great-grandchildren
(3) Anita Vincent Stauffer, b 1887; m 30 Nov 1907 John Avery McILHENNY (b Iberia Parish, La., 29 Oct 1867; served with the future President Theodore Roosevelt's 'Rough Riders' Spanish-American War of 1898, seeing action at San Juan Hill, subsequently US Minister to Haiti; d c 1937), s of Edmund McIlhenny (fndr Tabasco Sauce Co) and his w Mary Eliza Avery, and d 1969, leaving issue:

Great-great-grandchildren
1a *John Avery McILHENNY, Jr [8337 Jefferson Highway, Baton Rouge, LA 70809, USA], b 1909
2a Walter Stauffer McILHENNY, b 22 Oct 1910; educ U of Virginia; served Citizens Mily Training Corps pre-World War II and 1st Bn 5th Regt US Marine Corps World War II (Navy Cross and Silver Star for valour at Guadalcanal 1942, later Brig-Gen Marine Corps Reserve to 1968), Memb President's Hundred (list of 100 best marksmen in US) 1931 and several times subsequently (winner Leach Cup for marksmanship), head of McIlhenny Co (manufacturers of Tabasco Sauce) 1949-85, Dir Nat Wildlife Fedn, a Fndr and Tstee Marine Mily Acad, Harlingen, Tex.; d 22 June 1985

Great-grandchildren
(4) Walter J STAUFFER; m Elizabeth White
(5) Richard STAUFFER
(6) Celeste Stauffer; m Harry BURNETT and had issue:

Great-great-grandchildren
1a *Peter BURNETT [25 Juniper Lane, Framingham, MA 01701, USA], b 1918; Col US Army; m 19— *Norma ——— and has issue:

Great-great-grandchildren's children
1b *Medora BURNETT
2b *Celeste BURNETT

Great-grandchildren
(7) William STAUFFER

Grandchildren
3 Zachary TAYLOR, b 1857; d young
4 Richard TAYLOR, b 1860; d young
5 Myrthé Bianca Taylor, b Nachitoches, La., Nov 1864; m New Orleans 1884 Isaac Hull STAUFFER, Jr (b New Orleans 1861; d Haverford, Pa., 1897), s of Isaac Hull Stauffer and his w Marie Celeste Bonford and bro of Walter Robinson Stauffer (for whom see above), and d New Orleans 1942, leaving issue:

Great-grandchildren
(1) Isaac Hull STAUFFER III, b New Orleans 30 March 1885; m there 1 June 1910 Helene (b Paris, France, 8 May 1887; d New Orleans May 1957), dau of James Henry Maury and his w Helen Deas Ross, and d New Orleans 9 May 1967, having had issue:

Great-great-grandchildren
1a Marie Myrthé Stauffer, b New Orleans 19 April 1911; m there 12 May 1937 *Eugene TRUAX and d 9 Jan 1946
2a Marie Helene Alice Stauffer, b New Orleans 22 May 1913; m there 28 March 1936 Alvin Anthony HERO (b New Orleans 14 Oct 1908; d July 1977), s of George Alfred Hero and his w Anna Olivier, and d New Orleans 21 April 1965, leaving issue:

Great-great-grandchildren's children
1b *Hélène Claire Hero [Mrs Alfred Rufty, 639 Arbor Road, Winston-Salem, NC 27104, USA], b New Orleans 30 Sept 1938; educ Newman-Randolph Sch, Macon, Ga., and U of N Carolina; m New Orleans 21 Dec 1960 *Dr Alfred Jackson RUFTY, Jr (b Atlanta, Ga., 8 Feb 1936), s of Alfred Jackson Rufty and his w Anne Graham, and has issue:

Great-great-grandchildren's grandchildren
1c *Helene Stauffer RUFTY, b New Orleans 10 May 1962
2c *Alfred Jackson RUFTY III, b New Orleans 22 June 1963; m Myrtle Beach, S Carolina, 19 Oct 1991 *Melissa Marsh Miles (b there 30 July 1965)

Great-great-grandchildren's children
2b *Myrthé (Mimi) Taylor Hero [Mrs John Le Bourgeois, Axis Chofu 1003, 1-40-2 FUDA, Chofu-Shi Tokyo 182, Japan], b New Orleans 1 Feb 1940; educ Newman Sch and Smith; m New Orleans 2 April 1962 *John Young LE BOURGEOIS (b New Orleans 25 April 1938), s of Joseph C. Le Bourgeois and his w Astrid Johannessen, and has issue:

Great-great-grandchildren's grandchildren
1c *Marie Louise Stauffer LE BOURGEOIS [1436 W Thorndale St #2B, Chicago, IL 60660, USA], b New Orleans 13 Jan 1964; educ U of Wisconsin, Madison (BS 1985), Sch of the Art Inst of Chicago (BFA 1990) and Northwestern
2c *Anne Charless Hero LE BOURGEOIS [435 E 70th St, New York, NY 10021, USA], b New Orleans 13 April 1965; educ U of Chicago; depy manager Bloomingdale's 1988-90, store manager Ann Taylor 1990-92, merchandising assist J. Crew 1992-

Great-great-grandchildren's children
3b *Céleste Bringier Hero [Mrs Benjamin F King, 2769 NW 27th Ave, Boca Raton, FL 33434, USA], b New Orleans 12 June 1942; educ Smith and Johns Hopkins; research consultant public affairs 1970-77; m 1st New Orleans 20 April 1968 (divorce 1977) Richard Warren MARTIN (b Ireland 1930); m 2nd Seattle, Wash., 15 June 1978 *Benjamin Francis KING III (b Chicago 25 Feb 1933), s of Benjamin F. King, Jr, and his w Esther Valentine, and with him has issue:

Great-great-grandchildren's grandchildren
1c *Alexandra Taylor KING, b Seattle 26 Oct 1979

Great-great-grandchildren's children
4b Ann Oliver Hero, b New Orleans 14 Nov 1947; m there 1 Feb 1969 *Dr William Irving J. JOHNSON, s of Lee Johnson and his w Eulalie McKay, and d 10 Aug 1975, leaving issue:

Great-great-grandchildren's grandchildren
1c *Emily Taylor JOHNSON [5950 Harbord Drive, Oakland, CA 94611, USA], b Oakland 14 Dec 1974

Great-great-grandchildren's children
5b *Caroline Gray Hero [Mrs Charles L Ephraim, 2130 Sheridan Rd, Highland Park, IL 60035, USA], b New Orleans 29 June 1952; educ Lawrence U, Wis.; m New Orleans 29 June 1974 *Charles Lamont EPHRAIM (b Washington,

DC, 3 June 1952; *educ* U of Chicago Law Sch; atty with Neal, Gerber & Elsenberg, Chicago), s of Herbert Charles Ephraim and his w Marguerite Lamont, and has issue:

Great-great-grandchildren's grandchildren
1c *Sara Olivier EPHRAIM, *b* Evanston, Ill., 30 Nov 1979
2c *Alexander Lamont EPHRAIM, *b* Chicago 20 June 1984

Great-great-grandchildren
3a Marie Louise Stauffer, *b* New Orleans 14 May 1916; *m* there 26 May 1939 Warren Gabriel POSEY (*b* there 24 Jan 1910; *d* there March 1976), s of John Francis Posey and his w Lillian Songy, and *d* there April 1990, leaving issue:

Great-great-grandchildren's children
1b *Warren Maury POSEY [1040 Buchanan Avenue, Lancaster, PA 17603, USA], *b* New Orleans 16 Sept 1940; *educ* California U (BA) and Wharton Sch of Finance, Pennsylvania U (MBA); with Internat Finance Dept Armstrong Cork Co, Lancaster, Pa.; *m* Shenandoah, Pa., 18 Sept 1965 *Alexandra Jane, dau of Edward Peter Wowak and his w Mary Dorothy Nadzon, and has issue:

Great-great-grandchildren's grandchildren
1c *Melissa Fontaine POSEY, *b* Alexandria, Va., 21 April 1968
2c *Matthew Tyler POSEY, *b* Lancaster, Pa., 1 Feb 1974

Great-grandchildren
(2) Marie Louise STAUFFER, *b* New Orleans 27 Sept 1886; *d* there June 1964

MALE LINE ANCESTRY AND COLLATERAL DESCENDANTS

JAMES TAYLOR, allegedly a native of Carlisle, Cumberland, England, emigrated to America *c* 1635, settling in Tidewater (subsequently renamed Caroline) Co, Va., where he acquired substantial landed property on the Mattaponi River; *m* 1st Frances —— (*d* probably New Kent Co 23 Sept 1680); *m* 2nd 1682 Mary Gregory and *d* King and Queen Co 30 April 1698, having had issue by both wives

His son by his 1st w,
James TAYLOR, *b* probably King and Queen Co 14 March 1674/5; held land in Caroline, Orange and King and Queen Cos, Col of Militia, Memb Virginia House of Burgesses, Surveyor-Gen of Virginia; *m* probably New Kent or King and Queen Co 23 Feb 1699 Martha (*b c* 1679; *d* probably Orange Co 19 Nov 1762), almost certainly dau of Roger Thompson (*d* in or after 1704), of New Kent Co, and *d* probably Orange Co 23 June 1729, leaving issue (with one er s, two yr s and four other daus):

I Frances Taylor, *b c* 1700; *m* probably Orange Co 24 Aug 1721 Ambrose MADISON and was grandmother of President MADISON
II Zachary TAYLOR, for whom *see below*

The s,
Zachary TAYLOR, b 17 April 1707; *m* probably Northumberland Co, Va., before 23 Feb 1737/8 Elizabeth, dau of Hancock Lee (1652/3-1709, great-great-great-uncle of Gen Robert E. Lee) and his 2nd w Sarah Allerton (c 1671-1731, gdau of Isaac Allerton and his 2nd w, he being an ancestor of President FRANKLIN ROOSEVELT through his first w, as also was his sister Sarah Allerton) and aunt of Mrs Ambrose Madison, sister-in-law of President MADISON, and *d* Orange Co before 29 March 1768, leaving issue:

Richard (Dick) TAYLOR, *b* Orange County 3 April 1744; fought in the Revolutionary War, ret from army Feb 1781 with rank of Lt-Col, moved to Beargrass Creek, nr Louisville, Va. (Ky. from 1792), 1785, Collector Internal Revenues Louisville, Memb Kentucky State Legislature, Presidential Elector 1812-24; *m* probably Orange Co 20 Aug 1779 Sarah Dabney (*b* probably Orange Co 14 Dec 1760; *d* 13 Dec 1822), dau of William Strother (*c* 1725-*c* 1808), and *d* nr Lexington, Ky., 19 Jan 1829, having had issue:

I Hancock TAYLOR, of Springfield, nr Louisville, *b* 29 Jan 1781; *m* 1st 1806 Sophia Elizabeth Hoard and had one s (who *m* and had issue); *m* 2nd 1814 Annah Hornsby Lewis (*b* 1796; *d* 1882) and *d* 20 March 1841, having with her had six other s and four daus (of whom several *m* and had issue)
II William Dabney Strother TAYLOR, *b* 1782; Surg US Army, 2nd Lt Artillery 1807; *d* 3 June 1808
III ZACHARY TAYLOR, 12th PRESIDENT of the UNITED STATES of AMERICA
IV George TAYLOR, *b* 1790; *d* Sept 1829
V Elizabeth Lee Taylor, *b* 14 Jan 1792; *m* 1812 John Gibson TAYLOR (*b* 1786; *d* 1828) and *d* 22 April 1845, leaving two s (both *d* unmarried) and seven daus (five of whom *m* and had issue)
VI Joseph Pannill TAYLOR, *b* 4 May 1796; joined US Army in War of 1812, 1st Lt 1814, honourable discharge 1815 on

signing of peace with Britain, enlisted again as 2nd Lt Artillery 1816, Col 1847, later Brig-Gen and Commissary Gen of Subsistence, also served Indian, Mexican and Civil Wars; *m* 18— Evelyn McLean (*d* 1887) and *d* 29 June 1864, having had five s and four daus (several of whom *m* and had issue)

VII Strother Taylor; *d* in infancy

VIII Sarah Bailey or Strother TAYLOR, *b* 11 June 1799; *m* 18— French Strother GREY and *d* 6 Sept 1851

IX Emily Richard Taylor, *b* 30 June 1801; *m* John S. ALLISON and *d* 30 Nov 1842, having had two s and two daus (who both *d* in infancy)

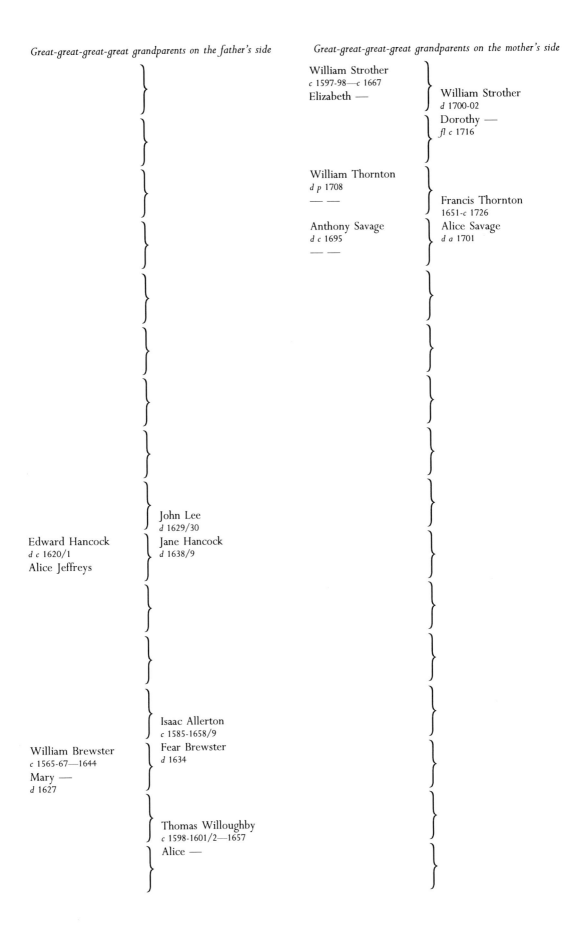

Great-great-great-great grandparents on the father's side

Great-great-great-great grandparents on the mother's side

William Strother
c 1597-98—*c* 1667
Elizabeth —

William Strother
d 1700-02
Dorothy —
fl c 1716

William Thornton
d p 1708
— —

Francis Thornton
1651-*c* 1726
Alice Savage
d a 1701

Anthony Savage
d c 1695
— —

John Lee
d 1629/30
Jane Hancock
d 1638/9

Edward Hancock
d c 1620/1
Alice Jeffreys

Isaac Allerton
c 1585-1658/9
Fear Brewster
d 1634

William Brewster
c 1565-67—1644
Mary —
d 1627

Thomas Willoughby
c 1598-1601/2—1657
Alice —

ZACHARY TAYLOR
FAMILY TREE

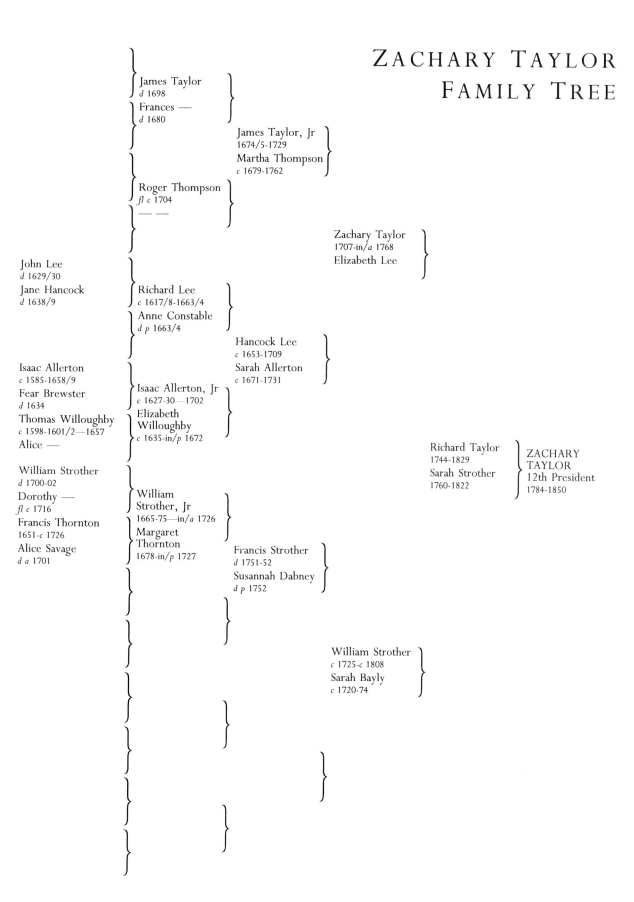

James Taylor
d 1698

Frances ——
d 1680

James Taylor, Jr
1674/5-1729

Martha Thompson
c 1679-1762

Roger Thompson
fl c 1704

—— ——

Zachary Taylor
1707-in/*a* 1768

Elizabeth Lee

John Lee
d 1629/30

Jane Hancock
d 1638/9

Richard Lee
c 1617/8-1663/4

Anne Constable
d p 1663/4

Hancock Lee
c 1653-1709

Sarah Allerton
c 1671-1731

Isaac Allerton
c 1585-1658/9

Fear Brewster
d 1634

Thomas Willoughby
c 1598-1601/2—1657

Alice ——

Isaac Allerton, Jr
c 1627-30—1702

Elizabeth
Willoughby
c 1635-in/*p* 1672

Richard Taylor
1744-1829

Sarah Strother
1760-1822

ZACHARY
TAYLOR
12th President
1784-1850

William Strother
d 1700-02

Dorothy ——
fl c 1716

Francis Thornton
1651-*c* 1726

Alice Savage
d a 1701

William
Strother, Jr
1665-75—in/*a* 1726

Margaret
Thornton
1678-in/*p* 1727

Francis Strother
d 1751-52

Susannah Dabney
d p 1752

William Strother
c 1725-*c* 1808

Sarah Bayly
c 1720-74

Plate 38　Millard Fillmore

MILLARD FILLMORE

1800-74
13TH PRESIDENT OF THE UNITED STATES OF AMERICA
1850-53

America has on the whole been fortunate in the men who have succeeded to the presidency on the death or resignation of incumbents. Considering that Vice-Presidents have usually been chosen to balance a ticket, or for any reason rather than their fitness for the top job, one may even say that America has been luckier than it deserved. Never was this truer than in the case of Millard Fillmore.

He had been put on the ticket in 1848 because it was necessary to have a Northerner to balance the Southern Taylor, and because Fillmore was a New York Whig who was a strong opponent of Thurlow Weed, who had been largely responsible for nominating Taylor. It was calculated that if the Fillmore faction got the Vice-Presidential nomination it would be more enthusiastic than if it were merely confronted with the Weed candidate and a running mate from another state. This calculation may be said to have paid off; at any rate the Whigs narrowly carried New York against a Democratic party deeply divided between Barnburners (supporters of Van Buren) and Hunkers (party regulars). So far as Fillmore was concerned the result of the election was that he had to sit in the Senate listening to the great debates of 1850, in which his rival Seward played a divisive role with his antislavery talk of 'a higher law' than the Constitution, while most of the other influential voices proclaimed the dangers of the crisis and the necessity of compromise. Fillmore came to share these views and when he so unexpectedly became President he acted upon them.

He accepted the resignation of Taylor's entire Cabinet and appointed Daniel Webster Secretary of State — a clear sign that the Administration was now wholly behind Clay's proposals and one confirmed by the use of patronage. He moved quickly to resolve a violent quarrel about the border between Texas and New Mexico into which Taylor had needlessly plunged, and when as a result of Stephen A. Douglas's skilled management the bills of the compromise began to reach his desk he signed them as promptly as possible. In a word, Fillmore not merely removed the obstacles that Taylor had placed in the way, he actively furthered the cause of compromise.

How creditable to him this seems will depend on whether it is thought that civil war was or was not likely, should or should not have been avoided in 1850. But at least the incident shows that Fillmore was no weakling, on the contrary a man of clear judgement and firm principle. Of the three Whig Presidents (Tyler not counting) he is easily the most impressive.

Unfortunately for him and itself his party did not see it that way. Many Northern Whigs — Seward's following — were bitterly opposed to the 1850 Compromise and especially to the Fugitive Slave Law which was part of it. They wanted to dump Fillmore in 1852. Southern Whigs wanted to stick to him. Daniel Webster, though within a few weeks of his death, still dreamed of getting the presidential nomination which had so long eluded him and took enough votes away from Fillmore to throw the nomination to Winfield Scott, another Southern general who seemed to be in Seward's pocket. It was too much for the Southern Whigs; they deserted the party and Scott went down to a shattering defeat.

Fillmore retired gracefully enough. He was a hero to his fellow citizens of Buffalo. He was quite well off and still young enough to enjoy life. He had another fling at the presidency in 1856, when the disintegration of party politics had reached a critical stage. He got the nomination of the dying rump of the Whigs and of the new American, or 'Know-Nothing' party, the central belief of which was that too many foreigners, especially Irishmen, were settling in the United States. Fillmore held this belief very tepidly if at all; his real appeal was still to the South, where he was remembered as the sympathetic President of the Compromise and where he got a very respectable number of votes. He was swamped in the North by the votes for the Democrat Buchanan and the nominee of the new Republican party, Fremont.

Perhaps this defeat explains his attitude to the Civil War. Although a strong Union man he never ceased to criticize the Lincoln administration, going so far as to back McClellan for the presidency in 1864. He was also a strong supporter of Andrew Johnson during Reconstruction, but by then it mattered only to Buffalo what Millard Fillmore thought.

MILLARD FILLMORE'S FAMILY

Fillmore was not the first President to come from a very poor background. Jackson and Van Buren had had similar origins. Nonetheless his family was quite poor enough. His parents had moved from New England to upper New York State a couple of years before their eldest son's birth. His father Nathaniel foolishly acquired a farm without inspecting it first. The soil turned out to be heavy clay. Moreover there had been inadequate surveying of the terrain and considerable legal confusion existed over land titles. So the Fillmores moved a few miles north to another farm. This too proved to be on clay soil and after 17 years Nathaniel gave up the struggle to make a living from such unpromising material, moved a dozen miles southwest and began working the land of a county judge called Walter Wood as a tenant. Not surprisingly he was unenthusiastic about any of his sons becoming farmers. Clearly he should not have tried it himself.

For a President with such a low-key reputation — it was once said of him that he was famous for being obscure — Fillmore was remarkably quarrelsome as a youth. He was apprenticed at the age of 14 to a wool-carder and cloth-dresser but they had a dispute and when his master threatened to beat him Fillmore picked up an axe and dared the man to do his worst. He then decamped and trudged the 100 miles back to his parents on foot. He said afterward that the episode gave him sympathy for the weak and oppressed. Not in every case it didn't: as President, Fillmore signed into law a Fugitive Slave Act which featured such gems of jurisprudence as no trial by jury, no testifying by fugitives on their own behalf and fees twice as high for the commissioner trying a dispute when he favoured the slave-owner as when he favoured the slave.

His son's wool-carding days over, Nathaniel asked his landlord Judge Wood to take the boy on as a clerk in his law office. The judge agreed but Fillmore quarrelled with this new master too and again returned home. Whatever the reason for these disputes, it could not have been laziness, for Fillmore worked extremely hard when he was a lawyer. It is just conceivable that the fault was on the master's side in both quarrels. Certainly Fillmore was anxious to learn; in fact he had an admirable enthusiasm for education and taught for a while himself; he also supported education in a broader context and helped found the Buffalo High School Association. He met his first wife through the educational process, being her pupil for a few months in 1818. She was almost two years older than he but neither the age gap nor the gap between teacher and pupil nor the social gap (she was the daughter of a clergyman of old Massachusetts family and her brother was a judge) seems to have inhibited them. There is a hint or two in various biographical sources that she took the initiative in making it clear she was attracted to

Plate 39   Abigail Powers, Millard Fillmore's 1st wife

Plate 40   Mary Abigail Fillmore, Millard Fillmore's
daughter and hostess in the White House

Plate 41   Caroline Carmichael McIntosh,
Millard Fillmore's 2nd wife

him. According to contemporary accounts he possessed considerable good looks, something his surviving photographs fail to do full justice to. Many years later in 1866, when Fillmore and his second wife were on a European tour, he was presented to Queen Victoria and a legend grew up back in the States that Her Majesty thought him the handsomest man she had ever seen. Victoria was a connoisseur of male beauty, so her opinion (if it was her opinion) carries what one might almost call professional weight as well as royal authority.

Fillmore established himself as a lawyer within two years of being admitted to the bar. He had got engaged to Abigail not long after their first meeting, however, so that they were fiancés eight long years till their marriage, often being obliged to live far from one another while Fillmore first studied then built up a law practice. They were well suited as husband and wife, with similar interests such as books and education. Even religion, for whereas Fillmore for one had not been much of a churchgoer when a bachelor, after he was married he and Abigail became Unitarians. Unitarians do not reject baptism but they rarely administer it to adults and it is possible that Fillmore and Abigail outdid even Polk, whose deathbed reception into full membership of the Christian faith has already been mentioned, in never being baptized at all. There seems to have been no particular family tradition of Unitarianism among the Fillmores. A cousin, the Revd Glezen Fillmore, was a Methodist minister who organized the first Methodist congregation in Buffalo and was presiding over its when the Fillmores moved there in 1830. Abigail's father was a Baptist. She and Fillmore were married according to Episcopalian rites. Perhaps their choosing a form of Christianity which rejected the Trinity was simply a way of affirming their oneness of outlook.

Being great readers the Fillmores built up a library of 4,000 books. When Fillmore went down to New York he always returned with a few books for his wife. When they went to live in the White House Abigail Fillmore was shocked to find there were no books there, not even a Bible. Presumably the procession of pious First Ladies before her had taken their copies away with them. She had started up libraries before, having instituted a circulating one in Sempronius, New York, before her marriage. She now turned the oval saloon on the second floor of the White House into a library and persuaded her husband to wring $250 out of Congress to stock it (he managed to get additional sums later). Not much is known in detail of this bookworm first couple's literary tastes, except that Fillmore admired Pope's *Essay on Man* and thought Shakespeare overrated. His attitude to the latter may have been along the lines of Jack Kennedy's remark to Gore Vidal after the latter had suggested Kennedy read *Coriolanus* following his defeat for the Democratic Vice-Presidential nomination in 1956, namely that Shakespeare's knowledge of the democratic process was, to say the least, limited.

Abigail Fillmore developed some interest in politics and was consulted by her husband on the issues of the day. She has been credited with persuading him to abolish flogging in the Navy, though no evidence for this exists. She correctly forsaw that his endorsing the Fugitive Slave Law would damage him, and said so. She was happier reading or making music than politicking, however. She was a competent pianist and accompanied her daughter Abby when the latter sang. The two women breached the custom which laid down that First Ladies should not go anywhere unattended by the President and went on their own to hear Jenny Lind sing. Abigail faded away gradually, her death of pneumonia shortly after Pierce's Inauguration being simply the culmination of a long deterioration during which Abby acted as the White House's hostess. Unlike her mother, Abby died very suddenly indeed. A year after her father had left office she was on a visit to her grandfather Nathaniel Fillmore in East Aurora. Less than 24 hours after being in perfect health she was dead. It has been suggested that the loss was one of the factors determining Fillmore to return to politics and become the Know Nothing presidential candidate in 1856. It cannot have been the sole cause, for he seems to have shared some of the Know Nothings' bigotry, joining the secret anti-Catholic organization the Order of the Star Spangled Banner in 1855.

The Fillmores' son Millard Powers Fillmore became a lawyer, like his father. The latter took him into his office as a student at the age of 16 and into the White House as a secretary at the age of 22, by which time Millard Powers had qualified professionally. Perhaps it was lawyer's caution that led him to make a will in which he ordered most of his father's letters destroyed. Whatever the reason, it looks as if President Fillmore's obscurity is largely his son's fault, for it would surely have been less pronounced had his letters survived. Fillmore himself refused to practise law again after leaving office on the grounds that it was undignified in an ex-President. Had he not married in Caroline McIntosh a second wife of means he would have continued hard up. As it was she turned over her considerable estate to her husband to manage. Indeed it could be said that although Fillmore had no regular profession after leaving office he was in effect a fund manager. With her money they bought an imposing house in Niagara Square in Buffalo. Although Buffalo was proud of Fillmore she became rather a figure of fun among its citizens for filling the house with numerous portraits and busts of her husband. As she grew older she suffered from ill health and it was chiefly because they hoped foreign travel would alleviate it that the Fillmores went to Europe in 1866. Yet she outlived her husband by more than seven years. When some years later still the last of the direct line of Fillmores, Millard Powers, died he left over a quarter of a million dollars. It was thought the bulk of the sum had been inherited from his stepmother, which does not say much for his earning power. At least his father had managed to marry money. Millard Powers did not marry at all.

BIOGRAPHICAL DETAILS AND DESCENDANTS

FILLMORE, MILLARD, *b* Locke (now Summerhill), Cayuga Co, New York, 7 Jan 1800; apprenticed as wool carder and cloth dresser 1815, schoolmaster at Scott, New York, 1818-19, studied law at Montville and Moravia, New York 1819-21, law clerk with firm of Rice & Clay in Buffalo, New York, 1822-23, admitted to New York Bar at Court of Common Pleas of Erie Co 1823, admitted as Attorney of New York Supreme Court 1827, Representative (Anti-Masonic Party) from Erie Co, New York State Assembly, 1829-31, Memb (Anti-Jacksonian) US House of Reps 1833-35 and (Whig) 1837-43 (Chm Ways and Means Ctee 1841-43), Whig gubernatorial candidate New York State 1844, Chllr Buffalo U from 1846 to his death, first elected Comptroller New York State 1848-49, V-Pres USA (Whig) 1849-9 July 1850, 13th President of USA 9 July 1850-53, unsuccessful candidate for Whig presidential nomination 1852, American National (Know-Nothing) Party presidential candidate 1856 (also endorsed by Whigs), organized Union Continentals (company of old militiamen in home guard) 1861 and granted rank of Maj (resigned 1862), Bd Memb Buffalo Fine Arts Acad, Chm Buffalo Ctee Public Defense 1862, Pres: Buffalo Hist Soc 1862-67 (first holder of the honour), Buffalo Club 1867, Buffalo Gen Hospital 1870, Co-Fndr and Dir Buffalo Mutual Fire Insur Co, V-Pres: Buffalo Lyceum (educational and cultural institute) and Buffalo chapter Soc Prevention Cruelty to Animals from 1867 to his death; author of *Is it Right to Require any Religious Test as a Qualification to be a Witness in a Court of Justice?* (1832), *Millard Fillmore Papers*, 2 vols, ed Frank H. Severance (1907); *m* 1st in her father's house at Moravia, New York, 5 Feb 1826 Abigail (*b* Stillwater, Saratoga Co, New York, 13 March 1798; *d* Willard Hotel, Washington, DC, 30 March 1853 of pneumonia developing out of a chill contracted at President PIERCE's Inauguration, *bur* Forest Lawn Cemetery, Buffalo), yst dau of Revd Lemuel Powers, Baptist Minister, and his w Abigail Newland, and had issue:

President Fillmore's children
I (Millard) Powers FILLMORE, *b* East Aurora, New York, 25 April 1828; *educ* Harvard; lawyer; *d* Buffalo 15 Nov 1889
II Mary Abigail FILLMORE, *b* Buffalo 27 March 1832; *d* East Aurora 26 July 1854

President FILLMORE *m* 2nd Albany, New York, 10 Feb 1858, as her 2nd husb, Caroline (*b* Morristown, New Jersey, 21 Oct 1813; *d* Buffalo 11 Aug 1881, *bur* Forest Lawn Cemetery, Buffalo), widow of Ezekiel C. McIntosh, of Troy, New York, merchant, and dau of Charles Carmichael and his w Temperance Blachley, and *d* Buffalo 8 March 1874 of a stroke

MALE LINE ANCESTRY AND
COLLATERAL DESCENDANTS

John FILLMORE, of Ipswich, Mass., *b c* 1676; mariner, bought an estate at Beverly, Mass., 1704; *m* either Ipswich or Hampton Falls, New Hampshire, 19 June 1701 Abigail (*b* 1 April 1679; *m* 2nd 7 Nov 1717 Robert Bell, of Norwich, Conn. (*d* 23 Aug 1727), and *d* 13 Nov 1727), dau of Abraham Tilton, of Ipswich, and his w Deliverance Littlefield (whose uncle Anthony Littlefield was ancestor of President COOLIDGE), and *d c* 1708-11, having had issue (with a yr son and dau):

John FILLMORE, of Norwich (now Franklin), Conn., *b* Ipswich 18 March 1702; sea capt and later Capt 7th Military Co in Norwich, author: *A Narrative of John Fillmore on Board the Noted Pirate Vessel Commanded by Captain John Phillips*; *m* 1st 28 Nov 1724 Mary Spiller, of Ipswich, and had two s and two daus; *m* 2nd 26 June 1735 Dorcas Day, of Pomfret, Conn. (*b* 2 Feb 1714/5; *d* 22 March 1759), and with her had five s and seven daus; *m* 3rd Mary Roach, widow (*d* after 22 Feb 1777), and *d* Norwich 22 Feb 1777 (*bur* there). His est s by his 2nd w:

Nathaniel FILLMORE, of Bennington, Vt., *b* Franklin, Conn., 20 March 1739/40; fought Revolutionary War; *m* 28 Oct 1767 Hepzibah (*b* 14 April 1747; *d* Bennington 11 May 1783), dau of Ebenezer Wood (whose great-aunt Ruth Wood was ancestor of Presidents HOOVER and FORD) and his w Philippa Storey (whose mother Mary Emerson was great-niece of Joseph Emerson, ancestor of President TAFT), and *d* Bennington 7 Sept 1814, leaving (with four other s and one dau) a 2nd s:

Nathaniel FILLMORE, *b* Bennington 19 April 1771; bought farm in Locke township, Cayuga Co, New York, with his brother Calvin Fillmore 1797, later moved with his brother to Sempronius, Cayuga Co, taking a perpetual lease on a 130-ac farm, 17 years later exchanged tenancy there for one at Montville, nearby, then moved to Aurora, New York, 1822, civil magistrate; *m* 1st *c* 1796-97 Phoebe (*b* Pittsfield, Mass., 12 Aug 1781; *d* 2 April 1831), dau of Dr Abiathar Millard (whose great-uncle Nathaniel Millard was ancestor of President BUSH), of Bennington, and his w Tabitha Hopkins, and had issue:

I Olive Armstrong Fillmore, *b* Bennington 16 Dec 1797; *m* 7 March 1816 Henry S. JOHNSON, of Sempronius, farmer, and had five s and one dau
II MILLARD FILLMORE, 13th PRESIDENT of the UNITED STATES of AMERICA
III Cyrus FILLMORE, *b* 22 Dec 1801; *m* 19 May 1825 Laura Morey and *d* 18—, having had three s and three daus
IV Almon Hopkins FILLMORE, *b* 13 April 1806; *d* 17 Jan 1830
V Calvin Turner FILLMORE, *b* 9 July 1810; *m* 1830 Miranda Waldo and *d* 18—
VI Julia Fillmore, *b* 29 Aug 1812; *m* 27 Oct 1840 A. C. HARRIS, lawyer, of Toledo, Ohio, and *d* 18—
VII Darius Ingraham FILLMORE, *b* 16 Nov 1814; *d* 9 March 1837
VIII Charles De Witt FILLMORE, *b* Sempronius 23 Sept 1817; *m* 11 Feb 1840 Julia Etta Green (*b* Buffalo, New York; *m* 2nd Daniel Cady; *d* Washington, DC, 2 June 1869) and *d* St Paul, Minnesota Territory, 27 July 1854, leaving issue:

President Fillmore's niece and nephew
1 Phoebe Mary FILLMORE, *b* East Aurora, New York, March 1841; *d* Aug 1842
2 George Millard FILLMORE, *b* East Aurora, 28 May 1842; *m* Washington, DC, 1 June 1869 Lottie Anne Norfleet (*b* 22 Nov 1851; *d* 27 April 1915) and *d* Suffolk, Va., 12 Feb 1910, having had issue:

Great-nephews and -niece
(1) Millard Norfleet FILLMORE, *b* Washington, DC, 8 July 18— ; *d* 19 Sept 1870
(2) George Thomas FILLMORE, *b* Washington, DC, Nov 1871; *d* 27 June 1872
(3) Susie Juliette Fillmore, *b* Washington, DC, 27 July 1873; *m* there 10 Oct 1894 Guy William Arthur CAMP and *d* 6 Oct 1914, leaving issue:

Great-niece's children
1a *Vaille Louise Camp, *b* 22 Feb 1896; *m* 19— Elwood Kempton PIERCE, of Elizabeth, New Jersey, and has issue:

Great-niece's grandchildren
1b *Elizabeth PIERCE, *b* 19—
2b *Elwood Kempton PIERCE, Jr, *b* 19—
3b *Carol PIERCE, *b* 19—

Great-niece's children
2a *Millard Fillmore CAMP, *b* 28 Jan 1904; *m* 19— *Helen Blakemore, of New York, and has issue:

Great-niece's grandchildren
1b *David Sumner CAMP, *b* 19—
2b *Helen Elizabeth CAMP, *b* 19—

Great-niece's children
3a *Guy William Arthur CAMP, Jr, *b* 28 Jan 1904; *m* 19— *Ruth Roth, of Boonerville, Ind., and has issue:

Great-niece's grandchildren
1b *Guy William Arthur CAMP III, *b* 19—

Great-niece

(4) Lottie Norfleet Fillmore, *b* Washington, DC, 21 Dec 1875; *m* there 28 Aug 1901 Robert Jethro NORFLEET, of Suffolk, Va. (*b* 1866; *d* 1945), and *d* Atlanta, Ga., 23 March 1945, leaving issue:

Great-niece's children

1a *Robert Fillmore NORFLEET, *b* Suffolk, Va., 3 Sept 1903; *m* Charlottesville, Va., 19 Nov 1938 *Elizabeth Randolph Copeland (*b* Richmond, Va., 3 May 1908) and has issue:

Great-niece's grandchildren

1b *Robert Fillmore NORFLEET, Jr, *b* Richmond 9 Feb 1942; regnl manager Crestar Bank, Richmond, Va.; *m* there 8 June 1968 *Virginia June Seymour Elliot and has issue:

Great-niece's great-grandchildren

1c *Robert Fillmore NORFLEET III, *b* Richmond 9 Sept 1970

2c *Bryan Randolph NORFLEET, *b* Richmond 10 July 1972

Great-niece's grandchildren

2b *Mary Abigail Fillmore Norfleet, *b* Richmond 4 Dec 1947; *m* Charlottesville 29 Aug 1970 *John Frederick JAMES

Great-nephews

(5) Charles De Witt FILLMORE, *b* Washington, DC, 14 May 1880; *d* in infancy

(6) Edward Valentine FILLMORE, *b* Washington, DC, 14 June 1883; *m* 1st Myrtle McDonald, of Anderson, S Carolina; *m* 2nd 11 April 1925 Ina Griffin (*d* 5 May 1970), of Springvale, Ga., and *d* Atlanta 25 Feb 1964, having with her had issue:

Great-nephew's children

1a *Ina Laurelle Fillmore [Mrs John Neel, 2711 Birchwood Drive, Monroe, LA 71201-2338, USA], *b* Atlanta 2 Feb 1926; *educ* Newcomb Coll, Tulane U; *m* New Orleans 20 Nov 1948 *John Irwin NEEL (*b* 7 Aug 1924), *s* of Walter Irwin Neel and his *w* Roberta Parker, and has issue:

Great-nephew's grandchildren

1b *Laurelle Fillmore Neel, *b* Monroe, La., 23 Jan 1951; *m* 1st Monroe 20 May 1970 (divorce 197-) David Elmore VERLANDER III (*b* New Orleans 3 March 1950, attorney); *m* 2nd Monroe 30 June 1978 *James Irvin Moody WILLIAMS (*b* Jasper, Ala., 20 Nov 1949) and with him has issue:

Great-nephew's great-grandchildren

1c *James Fillmore Neel WILLIAMS, *b* Monroe 18 March 1981

Great-nephew's grandchildren

2b *John Edward NEEL, *b* 15 Nov 1954; *m* Monroe 1 April 1978 (divorce June 1983) Mary Candyce Ellis (*b* Lake Providence, La., 28 March 1949) and has issue:

Great-nephew's great-grandchildren

1c *Candyce Laurelle NEEL, *b* Monroe 6 Nov 1978

2c *John Thomas NEEL, *b* Monroe 31 July 1980

Great-nephew's grandchildren

2b (cont.) John E. Neel *m* 2nd Shreveport, La., 11 Jan 1992 *Statia Lynn Calhoun (*b* Monroe 22 Sept 1959)

IX Phoebe Maria Fillmore, *b* 23 Nov 1819; *d* 2 July 1843

Nathaniel Fillmore *m* 2nd May 1834 Eunice Love, widow, and *d* Aurora, New York, 28 March 1863

John Millard
d 1684-89

}
Robert Millard
c 1632-99

}
Elizabeth Sabin
c 1642-43—1717/8

William Sabin
d 1686/7
— Wright
d c 1661

}

William Tilton
c 1589-1653
Susannah —
d 1654/55

}
Abraham Tilton
c 1638-42—1728

Francis Littlefield
c 1619-1712/3
Rebecca —
1630-in/*p* 1683

}
Deliverance Littlefield
d 1730-33

Sampson Shore
fl 1641-79
Abigail Purchase
b c 1624

}
Jonathan Shore
1649-1668/9

John Hathorne
c 1621-76
Sarah —
d p 1676

}
Priscilla Hathorne
b c 1649

}

}
Anthony Day
c 1624-27—1707
Susannah Matchett
c 1623-1717

}

}
John Eddy
d 1695
Deliverance Owen
1654/5-1726

}

William Owen
d 1702
Elizabeth Davis
c 1634-1702

}

John Rowe
d 1661/2
Bridget ?Jeggles
d 1680

}
Hugh Rowe
c 1645-96

Joseph Langton

Rachel Parsons/Varney
d 1707

}
Rachel Langton
d c 1673/4

?William Randall
c 1615-93
?Elizabeth Barstow
d p 1692

}
?Joseph Randall
c 1645-1723

?William Macomber
c 1610-*a* 1670
?Ursula Cooper
d p 1670

}
?Hannah Macomber

}

Thomas Wood
c 1633-87
Ann —
c 1637-1714

}
John Wood
1656-*p* 1738/9

Edward Hazen
c 1614-83
Hannah Grant
c 1631-1715/6

}
Isabel Hazen
1662-*p* 1726

John Hopkins
d a 1654
Jane —
d c 1679

}
Stephen Hopkins
c 1635/6-89

John Bro(w)nson
c 1602-80
Frances Hills
d p 1680

}
Dorcas Bronson
c 1633-97

}

Jonathan Rudd
d 1658
— —

}
Nathaniel Rudd
c 1652-1727

John Post
c 1626/7-1710/1
Hester/Esther Hyde
d 1703

}
Mary Post
1662-1705

Richard Butler
d 1684
Elizabeth —
d 1691

}
Samuel Butler
c 1641-92

Nicholas Olmstead
c 1612-84
Sarah Loomis
c 1617/8-67

}
Elizabeth Olmstead
d 1681

}

William Story
c 1614-*a* 1702/3
Sarah Foster
b c 1620

}
Samuel Story
c 1658-60—1726
Elizabeth —

Andrew Messenger
d a 1681
— —
d p 1681

}
Samuel Messenger
a 1650-85
Susannah —

}

}

Nathaniel Emerson
c 1631-1712
Sarah —
d 1670

}
Thomas Emerson
c 1671-1738

Jacob Perkins
c 1646-1719
Sarah Wainwright
d 1688

}
Philippa Perkins
1670-1738

Robert Royce
d 1676
Mary —
d 1696

}
Nehemiah Royce
c 1636-1706

James Morgan
c 1607-85
Margery Hill

}
Hannah Morgan
1642-1706

}

MILLARD FILLMORE
FAMILY TREE

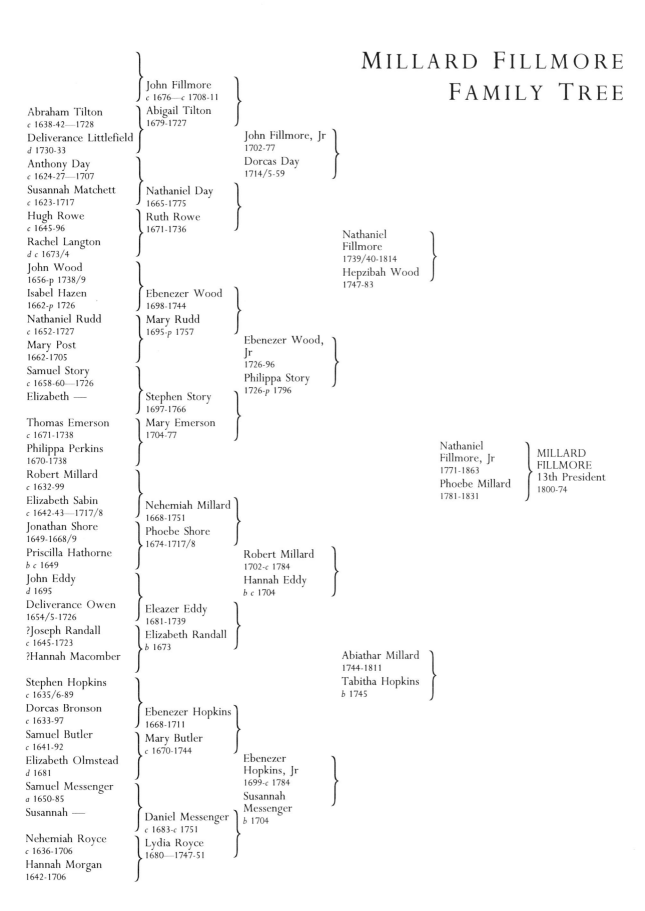

Abraham Tilton
c 1638-42—1728

Deliverance Littlefield
d 1730-33

John Fillmore
c 1676—c 1708-11

Abigail Tilton
1679-1727

John Fillmore, Jr
1702-77

Dorcas Day
1714/5-59

Anthony Day
c 1624-27—1707

Susannah Matchett
c 1623-1717

Nathaniel Day
1665-1775

Ruth Rowe
1671-1736

Hugh Rowe
c 1645-96

Rachel Langton
d c 1673/4

Nathaniel
Fillmore
1739/40-1814

Hepzibah Wood
1747-83

John Wood
1656-p 1738/9

Isabel Hazen
1662-p 1726

Ebenezer Wood
1698-1744

Mary Rudd
1695-p 1757

Nathaniel Rudd
c 1652-1727

Mary Post
1662-1705

Ebenezer Wood,
Jr
1726-96

Philippa Story
1726-p 1796

Samuel Story
c 1658-60—1726

Elizabeth —

Stephen Story
1697-1766

Mary Emerson
1704-77

Thomas Emerson
c 1671-1738

Philippa Perkins
1670-1738

Nathaniel
Fillmore, Jr
1771-1863

Phoebe Millard
1781-1831

MILLARD
FILLMORE
13th President
1800-74

Robert Millard
c 1632-99

Elizabeth Sabin
c 1642-43—1717/8

Nehemiah Millard
1668-1751

Phoebe Shore
1674-1717/8

Jonathan Shore
1649-1668/9

Priscilla Hathorne
b c 1649

Robert Millard
1702-c 1784

Hannah Eddy
b c 1704

John Eddy
d 1695

Deliverance Owen
1654/5-1726

Eleazer Eddy
1681-1739

Elizabeth Randall
b 1673

?Joseph Randall
c 1645-1723

?Hannah Macomber

Abiathar Millard
1744-1811

Tabitha Hopkins
b 1745

Stephen Hopkins
c 1635/6-89

Dorcas Bronson
c 1633-97

Ebenezer Hopkins
1668-1711

Mary Butler
c 1670-1744

Samuel Butler
c 1641-92

Elizabeth Olmstead
d 1681

Ebenezer
Hopkins, Jr
1699-c 1784

Susannah
Messenger
b 1704

Samuel Messenger
a 1650-85

Susannah —

Daniel Messenger
c 1683-c 1751

Lydia Royce
1680—1747-51

Nehemiah Royce
c 1636-1706

Hannah Morgan
1642-1706

Plate 42   Franklin Pierce

FRANKLIN PIERCE

1804-69
14TH PRESIDENT OF THE UNITED STATES OF AMERICA
1853-57

Pierce is the dimmest of the Presidents. He was elected with a huge majority; his party, the Democrats, controlled both Houses of Congress; the Compromise of 1850 seemed to have settled the dangerous issue of slavery and the territories for good. Pierce's watchword on the matter was 'finality'; the country was prosperous. He had, in short, as fair an opportunity as a man could want. He squandered it helplessly and left office with only one solid achievement to his name, the Gadsden Purchase from Mexico, which bought what is now southern Arizona. Against that is to be set the fact that once more, largely by his own fault, the United States was on the brink of tearing itself to pieces.

Like Fillmore, he had an opportunity to do his country a great service. In January 1854 a group of Democratic Senators led by Douglas came to the White House and informed him of their intention of repealing the Missouri Compromise as part of the proposed law for organizing the territories of Kansas and Nebraska. As a Northerner (he came from New Hampshire) Pierce should have known that this proposal was impossibly dangerous. Douglas himself who seems to have undertaken the whole operation as a means of furthering his cherished dream of a transcontinental railroad starting from Chicago, had said earlier that the business would raise a "hell of a storm". Pierce should have told his visitors that he would veto their proposal if it ever came before him. Instead he let himself be overborne by them (except for Douglas they were all Southerners, like his Secretary of War Jefferson Davis, the only Cabinet member present at the meeting) and agreed that the Missouri Compromise was "inoperative and void". In May he kept his word and signed the Kansas-Nebraska bill into law. By so doing he helped to wreck the Democratic party as a national institution and stirred up a storm of free soil rage that was hardly to subside until after the Civil War.

Pierce was a weakling and his career proves the folly of relying on 'dark horses' and compromise candidates. All his record had to show before 1852 was one undistinguished term as US Senator and a scarcely more distinguished period of service as brigadier-general during the Mexican War. The Democratic party had a dozen leaders of greater capacity than Pierce but they all stood rigidly in each other's way and had by their actions at various times alienated various groups. So Pierce was nominated because he had no enemies. By the end of his presidency he had no friends.

He was unlucky in his personal life. All his three children died in infancy, the last just before he took office. His wife buried herself in her grief and refused to come to Washington. It is no wonder that in Pierce's time the White House was an extremely gloomy mansion.

FRANKLIN PIERCE'S FAMILY

A generation after Franklin Pierce's male line ancestors first came to America they moved five or so miles north from Charlestown, Mass., to Woburn, which had been co-founded in 1642 as a township (the first one separate from Charlestown) by another of Pierce's ancestors, Ezekiel Richardson. Ezekiel's granddaughter Sarah Richardson had a daughter Esther who married Pierce's great-grandfather Stephen Pierce Jr. Apart from Stephen Jr's son, Benjamin Pierce Sr, the Pierces were a long-lived family until Franklin Pierce's generation, where he outlived all his brothers and sisters except one.

Not that his father, General Benjamin Pierce Jr, was very robust toward the end; by the time his son entered the Senate in 1837 he was partly paralyzed. Still, he did live to be 82. He was born on a Christmas Day and died on an April Fool's Day and his life too touched now on episodes of high aspiration, now on the stuff of low comedy. He had been one of the chief early settlers in Hillsborough (now Hillsboro), where his son the 14th President was born; he had not only been a long-serving soldier in the Revolutionary War but became a local militia commander thereafter; during the War of 1812 he was instrumental in preventing New Hampshire's participation in the Hartford Convention, whereby anti-war New Englanders whose trade had been disrupted proposed changes in the Constitution (possibly as a precursor to secession, though the war ended before things went any further). Yet he was so convivial he several times took out a licence so he could run his home as a tavern. And his wife, though loving, was volatile and tended to hit the bottle.

Perhaps it was she who introduced a weak strain into the Pierce family. She was senile in her last years, although she not only lived to be 70 but for a while during the last decade of her life joined her husband in bringing up two orphaned grandchildren after the deaths first of their son Sullivan in 1824 then of his widow Marietta five years later. Nevertheless Franklin Pierce had an exceptionally weak head for alcohol all his life and believed he had got it from his mother. From that point of view he could hardly have chosen a worse career than politics, and it must undoubtedly have been in part because politics more or less obliged a man to spend evening after evening drinking with cronies if he wanted to get ahead that his wife Jane came to dislike politics and Washington so much. Nevertheless she had been determined to marry him at a time when his predilection for politics was already plain, and it was her family who were chiefly opposed to him both on that count and because of the drinking. (They may even have known him better than she did because his teacher at Bowdoin College was Jane's brother, Packard Appleton.) Moreover she was at the relatively advanced age of 28 when she married, hence hardly subject to the giddy enthusiasms of youth. For his part Pierce enjoyed socializing, was interested in politics and started out with useful connections through his father's two terms as Governor plus experience in the state legislature, especially since New Hampshire was such a small state. That went for other professional matters too. It was through Benjamin Pierce's friendship with the father of Judge Woodbury that Franklin went to study law in the judge's chambers.

As if to underline the new short-lived tendency of the Pierces, Franklin Pierce, known to his many friends as 'Frank', attained most rungs of the political ladder unusually young: speaker of his state legislature aged 26 and in the House of Representatives at 29, the Senate at 33 (being at that time its youngest member) and the White House at 47. He was in 1852 the youngest man ever elected President and as the first one to be born in the 19th century would have had something of the novelty of Bill Clinton in 1992 as the first President born after World War II. There even seems to have been a mild youth cult at the time, though nothing like as intense as in 1960, when Kennedy succeeded Eisenhower. A movement called 'Young America' existed, made up of people enthusiastic about intervening with arms in the 1848 revolutions in Europe, particularly Hungary; it also favoured free trade and US

Plate 43   Jane Appleton Pierce

expansion to the south. It had little in common apart from its title with contemporary movements in Europe such as 'Young England', 'Young Ireland' or 'Young Italy' but it caused Pierce, who was seen as representative of youth, to arouse in the future President James Buchanan this typically wishy-washy judgement: "Should he fall into proper hands, he will administer the Government wisely and well. Heaven save us from the mad schemes of 'Young America'!"

There was a certain weakness of character in Pierce which he may also have got from his mother. Pierce himself mentions that his mother was weak in the way she always came up with excuses and justifying remarks in circumstances when others used reproaches. It is interesting that Julian Hawthorne, son of Pierce's old college friend the writer Nathaniel Hawthorne, described Pierce as gentle and tender as a woman. Pierce was certainly kind to Julian, having him educated at his own expense (as also his nephew Frank Pierce, son of his dead brother Henry.) For all Pierce's charm one gets an impression of unsteadiness at times. Whether Pierce inherited a sense of guilt is unclear. But his morbid acceptance, even justification, of the loss of his children certainly suggests guilt, even if in the early days that guilt existed wholly in his mind rather than deriving from some concrete act he had committed. When his son Frank died aged three he expressed himself in warped theological terms that even Job might have considered self-condemnatory, saying for instance that the "chastisement . . . was doubtless needed." He went on to confess that he and his wife Jane had lived too much for their children, whereas they should have lived for God.

His religion was an odd one in formal terms. He claimed to be an orthodox believer but lacked his wife's profound and instinctive faith. Jane was a Congregationalist, following her minister father in this, but Pierce, who seems to have conformed to his wife's creed when they first got married, became restless when Congregationalist ministers attacked slavery and moved over to Episcopalianism. Yet he only got himself baptized in 1865, a couple of years after Jane's death. He had affirmed rather than sworn his inaugural oath as President, which no other President has felt obliged to do even when from Protestant sects every bit as opposed to oath-taking as Congregationalism.

Jane's faith was a much more solid affair. Even her neurotic brooding over Bennie, the son they lost in a railway accident two months before her husband's Inauguration, had a certain consistency about it.

The pencilled notes she composed to the dead Bennie while in the White House stood well within the high Victorian custom of communing with the dear departed. On the two-year European tour she and Pierce made after he left the presidency she hauled everywhere a casket containing locks not only of Bennie's hair but of hair from her other "precious dead" — her two earlier sons, her mother and her sister. But in mid-19th-century terms this was no more bizarre than Sarah Polk's behaviour as a mourning widow. Jane Pierce's failure to preside over the White House was by the early 1850s almost standard behaviour for a First Lady. A slightly unusual touch was the way the role of hostess fell not to a daughter, niece or daughter-in-law but to her aunt, Mrs Abby Means, although Abby was actually a childhood friend of Jane's who had married as his second wife Jane's uncle, a man much older than herself. Not surprisingly considering the morgue-like atmosphere in the White House, Pierce liked to get out and about and attended every dedication and commencement he could. He even preferred attending other people's funerals to staying at home where his wife, the 'shadow in the White House' as she was known, made it home only for the living dead and the death-obsessed living.

Pierce cited his wife's frail health and dislike of Washington as a reason for turning down the Attorney-Generalship when offered it by President Polk in 1846. Yet he felt able to leave his wife behind and go to war against Mexico a year later. Jane seems never to have trusted her husband again after discovering from a cousin of hers, Senator Atherton, shortly before her husband's Inauguration that he had been working to win the Democratic nomination when he had told her he was against the idea. Just two days before his Inauguration Pierce went to see his wife in Baltimore, where she had holed up instead of completing the journey from New Hampshire down to Washington. He returned to Washington early the next morning without waiting to hear everything in the way of reproaches she had prepared to heap on him and — worse — without even the locket containing Bennie's hair that Jane had prepared for him to wear next his heart. Here at last was an episode he could decently feel guilty about ever after. Jane now persuaded herself that God had taken Bennie to prevent her husband being distracted while President. It constituted her final and most abject surrender to morbidity, for she had neither wanted Bennie taken away nor the end for which he was supposedly taken. McKinley and Lincoln win praise for coping with wives no more difficult than Jane Pierce. Lincoln was a great man, however, and even McKinley was a better President than Pierce. But Pierce was at least a competent husband. It seems hard that because he failed as a President he has failed to win credit for coping with his wife too. She sounds the sort of wet blanket who would have blighted the life of men much stronger.

BIOGRAPHICAL DETAILS AND DESCENDANTS

PIERCE, FRANKLIN, *b* Hillsborough (now Hillsboro), New Hampshire, 23 Nov 1804; *educ* Hancock Acad, Francestown Acad, Bowdoin Coll, Brunswick, Maine (AB 1824), and law sch in Northampton, Mass.; admitted to New Hampshire Bar 1827, Memb New Hampshire State Legislature for Hillsborough 1829-33 (Speaker 1831 and 1832), Justice of the Peace Hillsborough 1829, Memb US House of Reps from New Hampshire 1833-37, US Senator from New Hampshire 1837-42, DA New Hampshire 1844, enlisted as Pte Concord Vols 1846 (Col 9th Infy Regt 1847, Brig-Gen 1847) Mexican War, resigned commission 1848, Pres 5th New Hampshire Constitutional Convention 1850, 14th President (D) of the USA 1853-57, unsuccessful candidate for Democratic presidential nomination 1856, author: *Some Papers of Franklin Pierce 1852-62*, ed P. O. Ray (1905); *m* Amherst, New Hampshire, 19 Nov 1834 Jane Means (*b* Hampton, New Hampshire, 12 March 1806; *d* Andover, Mass., 2 Dec 1863, *bur* Concord, New Hampshire), 3rd of the six children of Revd Jesse Appleton, Congregational Minister and Pres of Bowdoin Coll, and his *w* Elizabeth, dau of Robert Means, and *d* Concord 8 Oct 1869 of inflammation of the stomach, having had issue:

President Pierce's sons
I Franklin PIERCE, *b* Hillsborough 2 Feb, *d* 5 Feb 1836
II Frank Robert PIERCE, *b* Concord 27 Aug 1839; *d* there 14 Nov 1843 of typhus
III Benjamin (Bennie) PIERCE, *b* Concord 13 April 1841; *k* nr Andover, Mass., 6 Jan 1853 in a train accident

MALE LINE ANCESTRY AND COLLATERAL DESCENDANTS

Thomas PIERCE, *b* England *c* 1583/4; emigrated to Charlestown, Mass., 1633/4; *m* Elizabeth (*b* probably *c* 1595/6; *d* after 1666/7) and *d* Charlestown 7 Oct 1666, leaving (with other issue):

Thomas PIERCE, *b* England between *c* 1608 and 1618?; *m* Charlestown 6 May 1635 Elizabeth (*d* Woburn, Mass., 5 March 1688), dau of Rice or Ryce Cole and his w Arrold —, and *d* Woburn 6 Nov 1683, leaving issue (with allegedly another son, who the family of President BUSH's wife Barbara claim was her father Marvin Pierce's great-grandfather's great-great-grand-father):

Stephen PIERCE, *b* Woburn 16 July 1651; *m* Chelmsford 18 Nov 1676 Tabitha (*b* there 28 Feb 1658/9; *d* there 31 Jan 1741/2,) dau of Jacob Parker and his w Sarah, and *d* Chelmsford 10 June 1733, leaving issue:

Stephen PIERCE, Jr, *b* Chelmsford *c* 1679; *m* there 5 Jan 1707 Esther (*b* there *c* 1681; *d* probably there 21 Sept 1767), dau of William Fletcher, Jr, of Chelmsford, and his w Sarah Richardson (whose great-uncle Thomas Richardson was ancestor of President COOLIDGE and whose great-aunt Elizabeth Richardson was ancestor of President HOOVER), and *d* there 9 Sept 1749, leaving (with other issue):

Benjamin PIERCE, *b* Chelmsford 25 Nov 1726; *m* Methuen, Mass., 2 Aug 1746, as her 1st husb, Elizabeth (*b* there 22 Feb 1727/8; *m* 2nd Oliver Bowers), dau of Abel Merrill, of Methuen, and his w Sarah Bodwell, and *d* Chelmsford 16 June 1764, leaving issue (with nine other children):

General Benjamin PIERCE, Jr, *b* Chelmsford 25 Dec 1757; fought Revolutionary War, Memb (D) New Hampshire Legislature 1789-1803, Govr New Hampshire 1827-30, V-Pres Soc of Cincinnati, Massachusetts; *m* 1st 24 May 1787 Elizabeth Andrews (*b* probably Hillsborough 1768; *d* 13 Aug 1788) and had issue:

 I Elizabeth Pierce, *b* 9 or 13 Aug 1788; *m* 1811 Brig-Gen John McNEIL (*d* 1850) and *d* 27 March 1855, having had two s and two daus

Gen Benjamin Pierce, Jr, *m* 2nd 1 Feb 1790 Anna (*b* Amherst 30 Oct 1768; *d* probably Hillsboro 7 Dec 1838), dau of Benjamin Kendrick and his w Sarah Harris, and *d* Hillsboro 1 April 1839, having with her had issue:

 II Benjamin Kendrick PIERCE, *b* 29 Aug 1790; Lt-Col 1st US Artillery, Col Creek Mounted Volunteers, served War of 1812; *m* 1st 18— Josephine La Framboise (*d* 1820) and had issue:

  President Pierce's nephew and niece
  1 Langdon PIERCE, *b* 18—
  2 Harriet Josephine Pierce, *b* 1817; *m* 1840 Maj-Gen James Brewerton RICKETTS, US Army (*b* 1817; *d* 1887), and *d* 1850, leaving a dau who *m* and left issue

 II (cont.) Col Benjamin Kendrick Pierce *m* 2nd 18— ——; *m* 3rd 18— —— Reed, of Newcastle, Del., and *d* 1 Aug 1850
 III Nancy Pierce, *b* 2 Nov 1792; *m* 1815 Gen Solomon McNEIL and *d* 27 Aug 1837, leaving two s and one dau
 IV (John) Sullivan PIERCE, *b* 5 Nov 1796; served War of 1812; *m* 1818 Marietta O. (*b* 1802; *d* Detroit, Mich., 1829), dau of —— Putthoff, Indian agent at Mackinac Island, on Lake Michigan, and *d* 13 March 1824, leaving issue:

  President Pierce's nieces
  1 Mary O. Pierce, *b* 1820; *m* 18— A. B. WARBAUGH
  2 Anne Kendrick Pierce, *b* 1824; *m* 18— Dr C. E. PARKER, of Springfield, Ill.

 V Harriet B. Pierce, *b* 1800; *m* 1822 Hugh JAMESON and *d* 24 Nov 1837
 VI Charles Grandison PIERCE, *b* 1803; *d* 15 June 1828
 VII FRANKLIN PIERCE, 14th PRESIDENT of the UNITED STATES of AMERICA
 VIII Charlotte PIERCE; *d* in infancy
 IX Henry Dearborn PIERCE, *b* 19 Sept 1812; *m* 1841 Susan Tuttle (*b* 1815; *d* 1874) and *d* 1880, leaving issue:

  President Pierce's nephew
  1 Kirk Dearborn PIERCE, *b* 1846; *m* 1879 Mary Ann Collins (*b* 1845) and had issue:

   Great-nieces
   (1) Susan H. PIERCE, *b* 18— or 19—; *d* 1974
   (2) Mary Kirk PIERCE, *b* 18— or 19—; *d* 1972

  President Pierce's nephew
  2 Frank H. PIERCE, *b* 1848; *d* 18— or 19—

Thomas Pierce
c 1583/4-1666
Elizabeth —
c 1595/6?-*p* 1666/7
Rice/Ryce Cole
d 1646
Arrold —
d 1661

Thomas Pierce, Jr
c 1608-18?—83
Elizabeth Cole
d 1688

John Kendrick
c 1604-86
Anna Smith
d 1656

Jacob Parker
d a 1669
Sarah —
c 1626-1707/8

John Green

Elizabeth —

Robert Fletcher
c 1592-1677
— ?Hartwell

?Richard Fairbanks

— —

William Fletcher
c 1622-77
Lydia ?Fairbanks
c ?1622-1704

Griffith Bowen
c 1600-*c* 1675/6
Margaret Fleming

Isaac Johnson
d 1675
Elizabeth Porter
d 1683

Henry Bowen
c 1633/4-1724
Elizabeth Johnson
1637-83

Ezekiel Richardson
c 1604-47
Susanna —
d 1681
William Underwood
c 1615-97
Sarah —
d 1684
Nathaniel Merrill
c 1601-54/5
Susanna —
d 1672

Josiah Richardson
c 1635-95
Remembrance
Underwood
1639/40-1718/9

Nathaniel Merrill, Jr
c 1634-1682/3
Joanna Ninian/Ninny/
Nanny/Kenney/Kinney
c 1627-1717/8

Daniel Brewer
d 1646
Joanna —
c 1602-88/9
Isaac Morrill
c 1588-1661
Sarah —
c 1600-72
Thomas
Williams/Harris
d a 1634
Elizabeth —
c 1577/8-1670
Edmund Angier
d 1677/8
Bridget Rogers
fl c 1678

Daniel Brewer, Jr
c 1624-1708
Hannah Morrill
1636-1717

John Harris
c 1607-94/5
Bridget Angier
c 1607-72

John Webster
c 1605-*c* 1645/6
Mary Shatswell
c 1610-94
Nicholas Batt
d 1679
Lucy —
d 1678/9

John Webster, Jr
c 1632-*p* 1716
Ann Batt
1635-53

John Pearson
d 1693
Dorcas —
d 1702/3

John Emery
1598-1683
?Mary —

John Emery, Jr
c 1629-*p* 1693
Mary —
d 1709

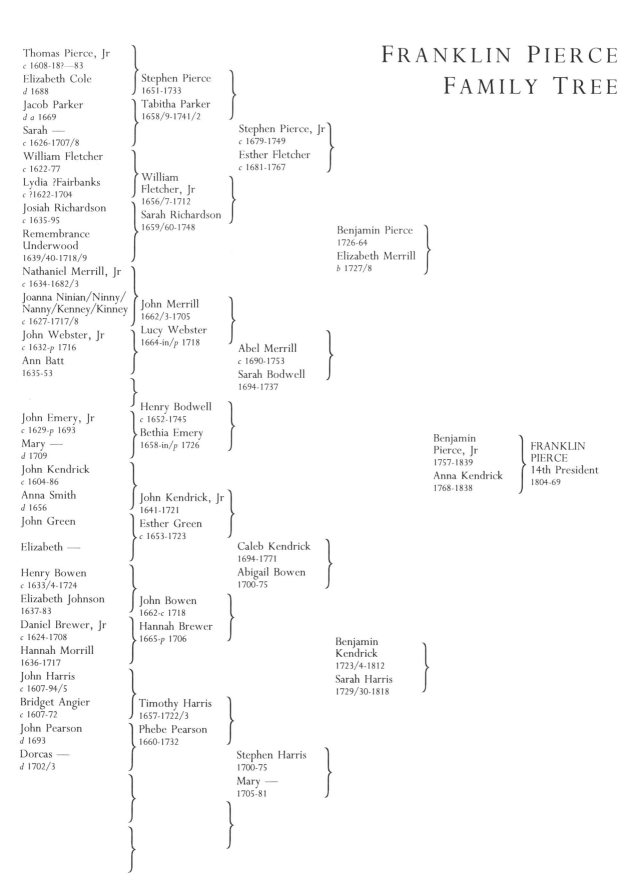

FRANKLIN PIERCE
FAMILY TREE

Thomas Pierce, Jr
c 1608-18?—83

Elizabeth Cole
d 1688

Stephen Pierce
1651-1733

Jacob Parker
d a 1669

Tabitha Parker
1658/9-1741/2

Sarah —
c 1626-1707/8

Stephen Pierce, Jr
c 1679-1749

William Fletcher
c 1622-77

Esther Fletcher
c 1681-1767

Lydia ?Fairbanks
c ?1622-1704

William
Fletcher, Jr
1656/7-1712

Josiah Richardson
c 1635-95

Sarah Richardson
1659/60-1748

Remembrance
Underwood
1639/40-1718/9

Benjamin Pierce
1726-64

Elizabeth Merrill
b 1727/8

Nathaniel Merrill, Jr
c 1634-1682/3

Joanna Ninian/Ninny/
Nanny/Kenney/Kinney
c 1627-1717/8

John Merrill
1662/3-1705

John Webster, Jr
c 1632-p 1716

Lucy Webster
1664-in/p 1718

Ann Batt
1635-53

Abel Merrill
c 1690-1753

Sarah Bodwell
1694-1737

John Emery, Jr
c 1629-p 1693

Henry Bodwell
c 1652-1745

Mary —
d 1709

Bethia Emery
1658-in/p 1726

John Kendrick
c 1604-86

Anna Smith
d 1656

John Kendrick, Jr
1641-1721

John Green

Esther Green
c 1653-1723

Benjamin
Pierce, Jr
1757-1839

Anna Kendrick
1768-1838

FRANKLIN
PIERCE
14th President
1804-69

Elizabeth —

Caleb Kendrick
1694-1771

Henry Bowen
c 1633/4-1724

Abigail Bowen
1700-75

Elizabeth Johnson
1637-83

John Bowen
1662-c 1718

Daniel Brewer, Jr
c 1624-1708

Hannah Brewer
1665-p 1706

Hannah Morrill
1636-1717

Benjamin
Kendrick
1723/4-1812

John Harris
c 1607-94/5

Sarah Harris
1729/30-1818

Bridget Angier
c 1607-72

Timothy Harris
1657-1722/3

John Pearson
d 1693

Phebe Pearson
1660-1732

Dorcas —
d 1702/3

Stephen Harris
1700-75

Mary —
1705-81

Plate 44   James Buchanan

JAMES BUCHANAN

1791-1868
15TH PRESIDENT OF THE UNITED STATES OF AMERICA
1857-61

By 1856 the dangers which had begun to threaten the United States because of slavery were plain to all. The slaveholding leaders of the South, sensing that the tide of history was running deep and fast against their 'peculiar institution', could think of no better way of defending it than by making every dispute that arose between the sections a test-case for the survival of the Union; if they did not get their way, they said, the Southern states would secede. This habit of inflating every trivial occurrence (from the point of view of the survival of slavery) into a major test of wills and of political power infuriated the North, from whose point of view the issue (say, the question of whether Kansas should be admitted as a legally slave state or not) was often not trivial at all. It created a wonderful opportunity for the abolitionist leaders, who stuck at nothing in their propaganda, depicting all Southerners and their friends as bloodthirsty, sex-crazed, cowardly villains, who needed to be resisted in the name of God, liberty and America. Their threats of disunion should be disregarded; they were mere bluff.

It is not certain how serious the 1856 threats of disunion really were. Even if they were bluff the general atmosphere of violence and crisis made the election especially important. Pierce had failed and in ordinary times this would have ensured victory for the opposition party. But the times were not ordinary. The Whig party had broken up into fragments (insofar as there was a regular Whig candidate in 1856, it was Millard Fillmore). The largest of the fragments provided the nucleus of a new anti-slavery party, which called itself 'Republican' in fond memory of Thomas Jefferson; it would win no votes in the South. Yet so large was the population growing in the North and West that the Republicans might nevertheless win the election, which might bring on Southern rebellion. So all good unionists rallied to the Democrats and, allied 'with Southern sectionalists, carried the day. Once more the Democrats had a majority in Congress as well as control of the White House and for the last time they had the chance to settle the issues which were tearing the Union apart. But once more they had chosen the wrong man for the job.

Like Pierce, James Buchanan of Pennsylvania was a Doughface, "a Northern man of Southern principles". He was a veteran Democratic politician, the best trained President since John Quincy Adams (he called himself "The Old Public Functionary"); unfortunately, like Adams he demonstrated that training is not necessarily any use. Blind to the real nature of the emergency, he failed in his attempt to end it; instead he unintentionally smashed the Democratic party and with it the last support of the Union.

Nobody has ever described Buchanan as a strong man, but his real failing was lack of imagination. He had been trained as a lawyer and he had been a party regular for 30 years. He thought that a combination of legalism and practical politics would solve a difficulty that transcended both. Take the case of Kansas. He seems to have thought that a law, any law, would settle the matter. He did not wish to upset his Southern political allies (whose friendly support was the more necessary to him as, being a bachelor, he felt lonely in the White House). So he accepted the fraudulent Lecompton

Constitution which the pro-slavery men had foisted on that territory in preparation for statehood and tried to ram it through Congress as Pierce had rammed through the Kansas-Nebraska Act. He failed because the Northern Democrats were outraged at the chicanery involved and anyway could not support the President and survive politically. All Northerners knew that the vast majority of the people of Kansas wanted a free-soil constitution or, failing that, were prepared to postpone statehood; they suspected a great conspiracy between the President and the South; they fought successfully to give the people of Kansas what they wanted. By the late summer of 1858 Buchanan's administration was a spent force.

Thereafter everything else went wrong. The mad abolitionist John Brown tried to launch a slave revolt in Virginia; he was caught and hanged but his exploit had terrified the South while his execution outraged the North. At their convention in April 1860 the Democrats split hopelessly; the South would not have Stephen A. Douglas as the candidate (he had led the fight against the Lecompton Constitution), while the Northern Democrats would not have anyone else. This split guaranteed victory to the Republicans. The South, having made Republican victory inevitable, declared as before that the event would bring about secession and proved its point. The Republicans won and the Southern states began to troop out of the Union, beginning with South Carolina in December 1860. Suddenly it was clear the United States faced a large-scale rebellion which could probably not be suppressed without civil war. Perhaps prompt action would save the day; none was forthcoming.

Buchanan was to blame. His administration would hold office until March 1861; if anything was to be done before then it would have to be done by him. That would mean decisively breaking with his friends and the habits of a lifetime. He could not bring himself to do it, even though the Southern members of his Cabinet had resigned when their states seceded. The fact was, he understood Southern views far too well to dream of coercing Southern states. Besides, although he thought it unconstitutional to secede, he also thought it was unconstitutional to coerce secessionists. He thought the President had no constitutional power to act. He was full of reasons for doing nothing. He could not bring himself to act even when bullied by his new Secretary of State, Jeremiah S. Black, and his new Attorney-General Edwin Stanton, both Northern men of Northern principles. It was all they could do to make sure that the Federal forts in Charleston harbour were not handed over immediately to the secessionists. Buchanan sat in the White House miserably waiting for the end of his term of office, terrified war might break out before his retirement. He dared not, for fear of precipitating war, do anything to prepare his countrymen for it or try to stop it. He left office more utterly defeated by events than any President in American history. He had allowed even the decision for war or peace to slip out of the hands of the United States government into those of the Southern rebels and of Major Anderson in Fort Sumter. Nothing redeems his name. It is impossible even to be sorry for him; his limitations cost too much of other men's blood.

JAMES BUCHANAN'S FAMILY

Rathmelton, the home town of James Buchanan's putative great-great-grandfather Thomas Buchanan, lies on the western shores of Lough Swilly in the present Republic of Ireland. The town had been built for settlers from England as well as Scotland and in its heyday was full of prosperous merchants. But by the time of Buchanan's grandfather the Buchanan family were farmers. They were also Presbyterian, a brand of Protestantism they had probably followed since migrating from Scotland. Buchanan's father emigrated to America just before America and Britain signed their peace treaty in 1783. He had already in America an uncle on his mother's side called Joshua Russel. This man lived in York County and put up James Buchanan Sr till he could find his feet. James soon did so, establishing a thriving business as a merchant and serving twice as a Justice of the Peace.

*Plate 45 Harrier Lane Johnston, Buchanan's
niece and hostess in the White House*

Buchanan's mother was an important educational influence on him, particularly in passing on the desirability of hard work and a taste for the great English poets. Her father was of Scots-Irish Presbyterian origin too, so Buchanan was justified in proclaiming his Irish ancestry — and himself proud of it — in a speech attacking General Winfield Scott during the 1852 presidential campaign. This, however, was when Scott had proclaimed his love for the Irish brogue. Buchanan thereupon referred to the Irish love of blarney in a way that misleadingly implied he was one of the boys himself rather than a Protestant from the north.

Two of his nephews acted as his secretaries while he was in the White House: James Buchanan Henry, his sister Harriet's boy, and James Buchanan, his brother Edward's eldest son by a sister of Stephen Foster, the celebrated American song-writer. Along with so many other 19th-century Presidents, Buchanan had to do without a wife in the White House who would entertain on the scale thought desirable in a head of state. In his case, however, this arose not from the startlingly common problem of the President's wife's nervous or physical debility but from lack of any wife at all. Much was written during his life about the sudden breaking off in 1819 of his engagement. The fiancée, Anne Coleman, initiated the breach and died suddenly some three or four months later. There is every reason to believe Buchanan himself was heartbroken. All his papers on the matter bar one were destroyed unread after his death. The exception is a letter from Buchanan to Miss Coleman's father which suggests she broke with him because of spiteful misrepresentation by others. Certainly this is the explanation accepted by his earliest biographer, G. Ticknor Curtis. On the other hand Curtis was a close personal friend of Buchanan and is reckoned biased. Others hint at an innate coldness in Buchanan's character that put the fiancée off independently of any tale-bearing. The chief historical significance is that according to Buchanan himself it impelled him into public life, whereas if he had married Miss Coleman he would, he claimed, have been content with domestic obscurity.

Buchanan's niece Harriet Lane acted as hostess both in the White House and before that in London, where her uncle was Minister during Pierce's administration. She was evidently a charming one. Indeed Washington in Buchanan's time seems to have been jollier than under most 19th-century presidents, though the appalling gloom of the White House under Buchanan's immediate predecessor Pierce and the grim Civil War years that followed may lend a false bloom. Miss Lane undoubtedly deserves much of the credit for the successful visit of the Prince of Wales in 1860, even though her uncle forbade any dancing in the White House — something the Prince pleaded for. She could probably have done equally well when in London, but had been handicapped there through not being able to share the rank of her uncle in the way a wife would have done.

There was something distinctly patrician about Buchanan's appearance. Partly this was due to his height, bulk and dignity. Possibly his spell as American minister at the Tsarist court in St Petersburg, or again at the Court of St James's, imparted an aristocratic tinge. He once when a senator made a speech in which he called the Senate "the most aristocratic branch of our government". Not many other American politicians would have used that description, even if they agreed with the sentiment. When envoy to Britain, however, he got into the same sort of scrape about court dress as Joseph Kennedy was to do a century later. The Secretary of State in Washington had decreed that US ministers in Europe should wear the simple dress of an American citizen. Queen Victoria's Master of Ceremonies wanted him to follow the court's elaborate dress code. Buchanan observed that British court etiquette was even stricter than Russia's. It was subsequently suggested to him that he might wear civil dress as worn by Washington, but Buchanan realised how absurd the fashion of 70 years earlier would look, not to say how presumptuous it would be in him to ape the Father of his Country, and turned the suggestion down. He finally compromised by attaching a plain black sword to his ordinary costume and the British court succumbed.

At the personal level Buchanan hit it off well with Queen Victoria and Prince Albert. It was Buchanan who first raised the idea of the Prince of Wales extending his visit from Canada to the USA in 1860. The Queen responded warmly. It was the first visit by British royalty (apart from the Duke of Kent in transit from Canada to military service in the West Indies in 1794) since the former colonies had broken away from the mother country. The danger to an American politician of seeming too thick with European royalty became apparent when in the bitterly partisan climate of the Civil War Buchanan was accused of taking pictures of Queen Victoria and Prince Albert away from the White House when he left office. Buchanan's defenders retorted that the Prince of Wales had presented Miss Lane in her private capacity with engravings of himself, his father and mother. An even more ludicrous charge was that Buchanan had sent Harriet's picture to the *Almanach de Gotha* arguing that Republican rulers had as much right to be listed in the famous reference book on European royalty and nobility as the monarchs of Europe. The episode is a fitting note to end on, for despite his dignified mien and personal probity there is often a note of inadequacy and pomposity about Buchanan.

BIOGRAPHICAL DETAILS

BUCHANAN, JAMES, *b* Cove Gap, nr Foltz, Franklin Co, Pa., 23 April 1791; *educ* Old Stone Acad, Mercersburg, Pa., and Dickinson Coll, Carlisle, Pa. (BA 1809); admitted to Pennsylvania Bar 1812, Assist Prosecutor Lebanon Co, Pa., 1813-14, served War of 1812, Memb (Fedlst) Pennsylvania State Assembly 1814-15, unsuccessful candidate for US House of Reps 1816, ptnr Buchanan & Rogers, attys, 1816-21, Memb (Fedlst) US House of Reps 1821-31 (Dep Chm Judiciary Ctee 1829-31, conducting impeachment of Judge James H. Peck 1830), US Minister to Russia 1831-33, apptd a Pennsylvania state commissioner to resolve with New Jersey state commission use by riparian states of Delaware River 1834, Memb US Senate from Pennsylvania 1834-45 (Chm For Affrs Ctee 1837), unsuccessful candidate for Democratic presidential nomination 1844, 1848 and 1852, US Sec of State 1845-49, 1st Pres Bd Tstees Franklin & Marshall Coll, Lancaster, Pa., 1853, US Minister to UK 1853-56, Hon DCL Oxford (UK) 1855, 15th President (D) of the USA 1857-61, author: *Mr Buchanan's Administration on the Eve of the Rebellion* (1866) and *Works of James Buchanan*, ed John B. Moore, 12 vols (1908-1911); *d* at his mansion of Wheatland, Lancaster, Pa., 1 June 1868 of rheumatic gout

MALE LINE ANCESTRY AND COLLATERAL DESCENDANTS

Gilbert BUCHANAN, 8th Laird of Buchanan, a place on the southeastern shore of Loch Lomond, in what used to be Stirlingshire but is now the Central Region of Scotland, was steward to the Earls of Lennox and the first of his family to assume the surname Buchanan; his s:

Sir Maurice BUCHANAN, 9th Laird of Buchanan, fl in the 13th century and had issue:

I Sir Maurice BUCHANAN, 10th Laird of Buchanan, for whom *see below*
II Allan BUCHANAN; *m* ——, dau and heiress of —— Leny or Lany of that Ilk (a Scottish term in fairly frequent use meaning 'the same', and denoting a family whose surname is identical to that of their lands or estate, so that Leny of that Ilk could equally well be called Leny of Leny), and had issue; the fourth in descent from Allan Buchanan was John Buchanan of Leny, whose dau Janet *m* her cousin John Buchanan, 12th Laird of Buchanan (for whom *see below*)
III John BUCHANAN, from whom descend the Buchanans of Aucheiven

The est s,

Sir Maurice BUCHANAN, 10th Laird of Buchanan, held the castle of Buchanan in which King ROBERT I the BRUCE allegedly sought refuge after his followers were put to flight at the skirmish of Dalry (11 Aug 1306) by Macdougall, Lord Lorne; Sir Maurice's s:

Sir Walter BUCHANAN, 11th Laird of Buchanan; *m* and had issue:

John BUCHANAN, 12th Laird of Buchanan; *m* Janet, dau of John Buchanan of Leny (*see above*), and had issue:

I Sir Alexander BUCHANAN; killed King HENRY V's brother Thomas, Duke of Clarence, at the Battle of Beaugé, France, 22 March 1421 while fighting on the French side against the English during the Hundred Years War; *ka* Battle of Verneuil 1424, where the English and Burgundian troops under John, Duke of Bedford, crushed the French forces under King CHARLES VII
II Sir Walter BUCHANAN, 13th Laird of Buchanan, for whom *see below*
III John BUCHANAN, inherited the lands of Leny; 5th in descent from him was Alexander BUCHANAN, who had two s:

1 John BUCHANAN of Mochastel
2 Walter BUCHANAN, Laird of Glenny; *m* and had issue:

(1) A son; *m* and had issue Capt James BUCHANAN, Laird of Glenny, who *d* without issue, whereupon Glenny was inherited by his uncle
(2) Alexander BUCHANAN, Laird of Glenny, succeeded his nephew; *m* and had issue:

1a Andrew BUCHANAN; bought from 3rd Lord Napier of Merchistoun (*see* BURKE'S PEERAGE & BARONETAGE, Napier and Ettrick) 1 Oct 1673 the estate of Gartocharan and had issue:

1b Alexander BUCHANAN, ancestor of the Buchanans of Gartocharan
2b George BUCHANAN, of Buchanan House, Glasgow; maltster and JP (Glasgow), one of the Covenanters (Scottish Protestants hostile to the episcopacy) who were defeated at the Battle of Bothwell Bridge 2 July 1679 by royalist forces under King CHARLES II's illegitimate son the Duke of Monmouth; *m* 22 July 1685, as her 2nd husb, Mary, widow of John Scott and dau of Gabriel Maxwell, merchant, and had issue:

1c George BUCHANAN, *b* 3 June 1686; merchant, Treasurer of Glasgow 1726 and Baillie (local magistrate elected by town council) of Glasgow 1732, 1735 and 1738, Co-Fndr 1725 with his three brothers of the Buchanan Soc (for the assistance of apprentices and support of widows called Buchanan); *m* 1st ——; *m* 2nd ——; *m* 3rd ——, dau of Sir John Forbes, 3rd Bart (*see* BURKE'S PEERAGE & BARONETAGE, Stuart-Forbes), and his 2nd w Barbara Dalmahoy, and *d* 12 Sept 1773, having with his 3rd w had four s and four daus

2c Andrew BUCHANAN, *b* 1690; Dean of Guild of Glasgow (a municipal official with authority over building and alteration of houses) 1728-29, Lord Provost (Ch Magistrate) of Glasgow 1740-41, merchant trading with Virginia (where he had a tobacco plantation), whereby he became one of the richest Glaswegians of the day (he drove a road through some of his extensive Glasgow property on which he erected 'gentlemen's houses' and which he called Virginia Street; he also planned a town residence which he intended calling Virginia Mansion, but did not live to see it completed), one of a five-man commission selected to negotiate with the Young Pretender's representative during the initially successful Jacobite Uprising of 1745, whereby he succeeded in lowering an initial demand for a loan of £15,000 to £5,500, a founding ptnr in the Ship Bank 1750; *m* 1st 1723 Marion Montgomerie, of Bourtrehill, and *d* 20 Dec 1759, having had issue (with five other s and two daus):

1d James BUCHANAN, *b* 17—; *m* 17— Margaret, dau of Hon John Hamilton, advocate, 2nd s of 6th Earl of Haddington (*see* BURKE'S PEERAGE & BARONETAGE), and the Hon John's w Margaret, herself dau of Sir John Home, 3rd Bart, of Blackadder (*see* BURKE'S PEERAGE & BARONETAGE), and *d* 17— or 18—, having had one s and several daus

2d George BUCHANAN, *b* 1728; bought property in Shettleston (now a suburb of Glasgow), Lanarkshire, Scotland, which was (or came to be) called Mount Vernon (possibly — given the Buchanans' Virginia connections — in commemoration or emulation of President WASHINGTON's family estate) 1758; *m* 1750 Lilias, dau of James Dunlop of Garnkirk, and *d* 1762, having had (with other issue):

1e Andrew BUCHANAN, of Mount Vernon, *b* 1755; *d* 1795

2e David CARRICK-BUCHANAN, *b* 1760; added name of Carrick on being left property by a Glaswegian banker, Robert Carrick; *m* 29 May 1788 Marion (*d* 1800), dau of James Gilliam, of Mount Alta, Virginia, North America, and *d* 20 May 1827, leaving two s and two daus; the yr son's great-granddaughter Joanna Carrick-Buchanan *m* 1931 Donovan Macomb CHANCE, great-grandson of George Chance, of Birmingham, UK, and New York, USA, and his w Cornelia Maria, herself dau of Arent Schuyler de Peyster, also of New York

3c Neil BUCHANAN, of Hillington, Renfrewshire, MP for the burghs district of Glasgow; *m* and left one s and three daus

4c Archibald BUCHANAN, of Auchintorlie, Dunbartonshire

5c Mary (was not necessarily the youngest child) Buchanan; *m* her cousin George BUCHANAN, of Auchintoshan, Dunbartonshire

John Buchanan, 12th Laird of Buchanan's 2nd (but er surviving) s,

Sir Walter BUCHANAN, 13th Laird of Buchanan, *b* in or before 1398; *m* 1st ——; *m* 2nd Isobel or Isabella (*b* probably in or up to *c* 20 years after 1392), dau of Murdoch Stewart, 2nd Duke of Albany (beheaded for treason against the Scottish crown 1425), and his w Isabel, Countess of Lennox in her own right; through the Duke of Albany Sir Walter's 2nd w was great granddaughter of ROBERT II, King of Scots; by his 1st w Sir Walter had issue:

Thomas BUCHANAN, of Gartincaber and Drumikill, Stirlingshire; had issue:

Thomas BUCHANAN, of Carbeth, Stirlingshire; *d* before 1493, leaving a yr s:

John BUCHANAN, of Camoquhill, Stirlingshire; had issue:

Thomas BUCHANAN, of Carbeth, *fl c* 1555; *m* 1st ——; *m* 2nd Janet Buchanan and had issue:

John BUCHANAN, *fl* in Gartincaber *c* 1591; had issue:

George BUCHANAN, *fl* in Gartincaber *c* 1629; *m* Elizabeth, dau of Walter Leckie, of Disheour, Stirlingshire, and had issue:

John BUCHANAN, of Blairlusk, *m* 1st ——; *m* 2nd —— and *d* 1662; his issue by his 1st w:

George BUCHANAN, of Blairlusk, *b c* 1648; declared his father's heir 1 Aug 1662, emigrated to Deroran, Co Tyrone, Ireland, 1674; *m* Ireland 1675 Elizabeth Mayne and had issue:

Thomas BUCHANAN, of Ramelton (or Rathmelton), Co Donegal, Ireland, *b c* 1685; *m* and had issue a son, who is said to have been the father of:

John BUCHANAN, of The Cairn, Ramelton, *b* 17—; *m c* 1751 Jane, dau of Samuel Russell, of The Ards, nr Ramelton, and his w Mary Watt, and had issue:

James BUCHANAN, *b* Ramelton *c* 1761; emigrated to Pennsylvania 1783; *m* 16 April 1788 Elizabeth (*b* Lancaster Co, Pa., *c* 1767; *d* Greensburg, Pa., 14 May 1833), dau of James Speer (*b* Ireland but emigrated to Lancaster Co, Pa.) and his w Mary Patterson (*d* before 1788), and *d* Mercersburg, Pa., 11 June 1821, having had issue:

I Mary BUCHANAN, *b* 1789; *d* 1791

II JAMES BUCHANAN, 15th PRESIDENT of the UNITED STATES of AMERICA

III Jane Buchanan, *b* 1793; *m* Mercersburg, Pa., 1813 Elliott Tole LANE (*b* 1784; *d* 1840) and *d* Mercersburg 1839, having had issue:

President Buchanan's nephews and nieces
1 James Buchanan LANE, of Lancaster, Pa., *b* 1814; *m* 1845 Martha Armor (*b* 1820), dau of William Jenkins and his w —— Hubley, and *d* 1863, having had five s (three of whom *d* young) and four daus (all *d* young)
2 Thomas Newton LANE, *b* 1817; *d* 1835
3 Joseph Stark LANE, *b* 1820; *d* 1822
4 Elliott Eskridge LANE, *b* 1823; *d* Washington, DC, April 1857
5 Mary Elizabeth Speer Lane, *b* 1826; *m* 1848 George Washington BAKER and *d* 1855
6 Harriet Rebecca LANE, *b* 1830; hostess at the White House for her uncle during latter's presidency, Fndr: Choir Sch of Cathedral of SS Peter and Paul, Washington, DC, and Harriet Lane Home for Invalid Children, Johns Hopkins Hosp, Baltimore, Md.; *m* Wheatland, Lancaster, Pa., 11 Jan 1866 Henry Elliott JOHNSTON, of Baltimore, banker, and *d* 1906, having had issue:

Great-nephews
(1) James Buchanan JOHNSTON, *b* 1866 or 1867; *d* 25 March 1881
(2) Henry JOHNSTON, *d* Nice, France, 30 Oct 1882

President Buchanan's nephew
7 William Edward LANE, *b* 1833; *d* 1834

IV Maria Buchanan, *b* 1795; *m* 1st Dr Jesse MAGAW and had one dau; *m* 2nd Thomas Samuel JOHNSON; *m* 3rd Dr Charles M. YATES and *d* 1849, leaving two further daus and three s, of which one was

President Buchanan's nephew
1 James Buchanan YATES; Midshipman, USN; living mid-1843

V Sarah Buchanan, *b* 1798; *m* James J. HUSTON and *d* 1825, leaving one dau
VI Elizabeth BUCHANAN, *b* 1800; *d* 1801
VII Harriet Buchanan, *b* Mercersburg 5 Aug 1802; *m* there 21 May 1832 Revd Robert HENRY (*b* Allegheny Co, Pa., 9 June 1801; Min Greensburg Presbyterian Church, Pa.; *d* Greensburg 1838), s of John Henry, of Allegheny Co, and his w Margaret McMillan, and *d* Greensburg 23 Jan 1840, having had issue:

President Buchanan's nephew
1 James Buchanan HENRY, *b* Greensburg 1 March 1833; priv sec to his uncle during latter's presidency, later Assist US Atty S Dist New York; *m* 1st 1860 Mary Hagner (*b* 1837; *d* 1863), dau of Joseph H. Nicholson, of Annapolis, Md., and had issue:

Great-nephews
(1) Buchanan HENRY, *b* 1860; *d* 1862
(2) Dr Joseph Nicholson HENRY, *b* 1862; Maj and Surg US Vols; *m* 1890 Alice Truehart, widow, dau of Revd Thomas A. Hoyt, DD, of Philadelphia, and *d* 1904

President Buchanan's nephew
1 (cont.) James B. Henry *m* 2nd 18 Dec 1872 Louisa (*b* 3 June 1848; *d* 10 March 1886), dau of Dr William Astley Cooper Anderson, of Staten Island, New York, and his w Louisa Morgan, and with her had issue:

Great-nephew
(3) William Cooper Anderson HENRY, *b* Staten Island 1873; railroad engr, gen supt motive power, Pennsylvania System SW Regn; *m* Atlanta, Ga., 16 Oct 1906 Mary Lamar (*b* Woodville Plantation, Milledgeville, Ga., 1881; *d* Atlanta 19 Feb 1972), dau of Fleming Grantland du Bignon, of Savannah, Ga., and his w Caro Nicoll Lamar, and *d* Tryon, N Carolina, 8 Dec 1943, leaving issue:

Great-nephew's children
1a *William Anderson HENRY [2401 Penna Ave, Wilmington, DE 19806, USA; 22 Caro Sound Rd, Key Largo, FL 33037, USA], *b* Columbus, Ohio, 17 April 1908; *m* 1st 24 Sept 1937 Bessie Agens (*b* Louviers, Colo., 9 June 1910; *d* Miami 10 April 1982), dau of Edward Washburn Maynard and his w Harriet Ledair Harrington, and has issue:

Great-nephew's grandchildren
1b *Mary du Bignon Henry [Mrs Stephen R Lyne, 25 Carlton St, Brookline, MA 02146, USA], *b* Wilmington 7 Nov 1938; *educ* Mt Holyoke Coll; *m* there 20 June 1959 *Stephen Richard LYNE (*b* Fall River, Mass., 20 May 1935), s of Horace James Lyne and his w Anne Bromley, and has issue:

Great-nephew's great-grandchildren
1c *Deborah Elizabeth Lyne [Mrs David H Simon, 2310 Ashboro Drive, Chevy Chase, MD 02815, USA], *b* Alexandria, Va., 13 Sept 1961; *educ* Bucknell U; environmental consultant; *m* Vienna, Va., 7 Sept 1992 *David Herman SIMON, s of Herman Reichwyin Simon and his w Mary Ella
2c *Richard James LYNE [40300 Washington St Apt Z 202, Bermuda Dunes, CA 92201, USA], *b* Bangkok, Thailand, 20 Aug 1963; *m* Calif. 6 April 1991 *Charlotte Lynn Cano

Great-nephew's grandchildren
2b *Elizabeth Maynard Henry [Mrs Lafayette H Caldwell Jr, 411 East Brow Rd, Lookout Mountain, TN 37350, USA], *b* Wilmington 2 June 1940; *m* 1st Wilmington 20 Aug 1966 (divorce 19——) David Zachariah WALLEY, Jr (*b* Chattanooga, Tenn., 24 May 1938), and has issue:

Great-nephew's great-grandchildren
1c *David Zachariah WALLEY III, b Chattanooga 15 Sept 1969
2c *Edward Harrington WALLEY, b Chattanooga 1 March 1971

Great-nephew's grandchildren
2b (cont.) Mrs Elizabeth Walley m 2nd Tennessee 23 June 1990 *Lafayette Hardwick CALDWELL, Jr (b Chattanooga 3 March 1923)

Great-nephew's children
1a (cont.) William A. Henry m 2nd 19— *Janet M. Jordan
2a *Caro du Bignon Henry, b Columbus, Ohio, 8 Nov 1909; m 1st Atlanta, Ga., 23 Oct 1930 Albert HOWELL (b Atlanta 27 Sept 1904; architect), s of Clark Howell and his w Annie Comer, and has issue:

Great-nephew's grandchildren
1b *Henry Lamar HOWELL [2492 Habersham Road NW, Atlanta, GA 30305, USA], b Atlanta 11 Feb 1938; banker; m New Haven, Conn., 29 June 1963 *Stephanie Southgate (b New Haven 2 March 1939), dau of William Huse Dunham and his w Helen Garrison, and has issue:

Great-nephew's great-grandchildren
1c *Helen Garrison Howell, b Atlanta 9 Nov 1966; m 19— *Christopher WRAY
2c *Catherine Caro HOWELL, b Atlanta 24 July 1970
3c *Evan Huse HOWELL, b Atlanta 21 Dec 1975

Great-nephew's children
2a (cont.) Caro Henry Howell m 2nd Atlanta 25 Sept 1979 *Michael A. McDOWELL (b Fla. 3 Feb 1910; Prof of Music and Piano), s of Michael A. McDowell and his w Enlalee Greer

Great-nephew
(4) James Buchanan HENRY, Jr, b 1875; Lt-Col 12th US Cavalry; m 1904 Mary Catherine, dau of Major R. W. McClaughry, of Leavenworth, Kans., and d 1948, leaving issue:

Great-nephew's children
1a *Elizabeth McClaughry Henry [Mrs Henry H Bruhn, 5925 E 5th St, Tucson, AZ 85711, USA], b 1905; m 1st 1939 Paul GAD; m 2nd 1956 Henry H. BRUHN (d 30 July 1988), mining engr
2a James Buchanan HENRY III, b 1919; Capt and Adj 93rd Engrs World War II; m 1945 *Eleanor McNeill, née Nixon [55 Myrtle Ave, Montclair, NJ 07042, USA], and d 24 Aug 1981, leaving issue:

Great-nephew's grandchildren
1b *James Buchanan HENRY IV [1402B Southport Dve, Austin, TX 78704, USA], b Manhattan 14 March 1949; educ U of Arizona; musician; m 1st 1975 Susan Henn; m 2nd 1985 Leslee Burton
2b *Mary Catherine Henry [Mrs James Yuenger, 3530 N Lakeshore Dve #7A, Chicago, IL 60657, USA], b 1949 (twin with James); educ Yale (BA 1972) and U of Chicago (MA 1979); publications manager Northwestern U 1990-; m 5 Oct 1985 *James Laury YUENGER, s of David Anthony Yuenger and his w Carol Jeanette Haines
3b *Elizabeth Eleanor HENRY [1402A Southport Dve, Austin, TX 78704, USA], b 1952

Great-nephew
(5) Robert Edward HENRY, b Stapleton, Staten Island, New York, 12 June 1877; Pres Associated Industrials Corp, ptnr Hallowell & Henry, New York City; m Brooklyn 26 Oct 1904 Virginia Bell (b there 17 Aug 1877; d Lake George, New York, 8 July 1956), dau of John R. Tolar, of Fayetteville, N Carolina, and his w Ella Bell, and d 22 Feb 1943, leaving issue:

Great-nephew's children
1a Robert Edward HENRY, Jr, b 28 Feb 1906; educ Yale (AB) and Harvard Business Sch (MBA); securities analyst with Foster & Adams, New York City; m 1st Lake George, New York, 25 June 1930 Hester Makepeace (b New York 12 Dec 1911), dau of Sidney Homer and his w Louise Beatty, and had issue:

Great-nephew's grandchildren
1b *Virginia Tolar Henry, b New York 11 Jan 1932; m 1st 1957 Jon VAN WINKLE, s of John R. Van Winkle and his w Margaret, and has issue:

Great-nephew's great-grandchildren
1c *Geoffrey VAN WINKLE, b Schenectady, New York, 4 Nov 1958

Great-nephew's grandchildren
1b (cont.) Virginia Henry Van Winkle m 2nd 1960 *John Aldrich ACHEY (b Santa Ana, Calif., 21 July 1928), s of Arthur C. Achey and his w Linda Cox, and has further issue:

Great-nephew's great-grandchildren
2c *John Stephen ACHEY, b Berkeley, Calif., 9 Nov 1960
3c *Linda Katherine ACHEY, b New York 15 Jan 1963
4c *James Sidney ACHEY, b Princeton, New Jersey, 29 Feb 1964

Great-nephew's grandchildren
2b *Louise Homer Henry [Mrs John Beekley Jr, 208 Sorrel Drive, Surrey Park, Wilmington, DE, USA], *b* New York 27 April 1934; *m* Ticonderoga, New York, 7 Dec 1958 *John Sherman BEEKLEY, Jr (*b* Charleston, W. Va., 31 Aug 1931), s of John Sherman Beekley and his w Louise Tatnall, and has issue:

  Great-nephew's great-grandchildren
  1c *Louise Homer BEEKLEY, *b* Wilmington 27 Sept 1959
  2c *John Sherman BEEKLEY III, *b* Hagerstown, Md., 10 March 1961
  3c *Robert Edward Henry BEEKLEY, *b* Hagerstown 27 July 1963

  Great-nephew's grandchildren
  3b *Hester Makepeace HENRY, *b* New York 26 April 1938
  4b *Julia Morgan Henry, *b* New York 9 Jan 1948; *m* Hague, New York, 28 June 1969 *Kenneth Joseph McPARTLIN (*b* Joliet, Ill., 21 May 1947), s of Arthur Robert McPartlin and his w Helen Jean Garrett
Great-nephew's children
1a Robert E. Henry, Jr, *m* 2nd Cashiers, N Carolina, 10 Sept 1968 *Elizabeth Radeker (*b* Middletown, New York, 7 April 1916) and *d* 1973
2a *John Tolar HENRY [Viewpoint, Hague, NY 12836, USA], *b* New York 6 Oct 1913; *educ* U of Virginia; V-Pres and Gen Manager Tolar Hart & Holt Mills, Fayetteville, N Carolina, Analyst CIA, Washington, DC; *m* 1st Rye, New York, 29 June 1937 Priscilla Adele, dau of Henry C. Steers and his w Lillian Palmer; *m* 2nd Ticonderoga, New York, 30 June 1945 *Dorothy Jane, dau of Ernest Wilbur Byer and his w Mary Elizabeth Dickson, and with her has issue:

  Great-nephew's grandchildren
  1b *John Robert HENRY [Calle 9 #148, Santa Isidra, Fajardo, Puerto Rico 00648], *b* Ticonderoga 4 Dec 1947; Manager Alcon Laboratories, Humacao, Puerto Rico; *m* 1st Detroit, Mich., 27 Oct 1967 (divorce 197-) Geraldine McCabe (*b* 2 Nov 1946) and has issue:

    Great-nephew's great-grandchildren
    1c *Lisa Jane HENRY, *b* Port Deposit, Md., 10 Sept 1968
    2c *Jennifer Lynn HENRY, *b* Ceba, Puerto Rico, 2 Oct 1971

  Great-nephew's grandchildren
  1b (cont.) John R. Henry *m* 2nd Ceba, Puerto Rico, 17 March 1974 *Nelida Tòmas Sanchez-Ramirez (*b* Luquillo, Puerto Rico, 19 March 1947) and with her has issue:

    Great-nephew's great-grandchildren
    3c *Vivienne Nelida HENRY, *b* Fajardo, Puerto Rico, 23 April 1975
    4c *Juan Tòmas HENRY, *b* Fajardo 8 March 1977

  Great-nephew's grandchildren
  2b *Mary Virginia Henry, *b* Ticonderoga 6 Feb 1949; *m* Munich, Germany, 197- *Werner Andreas KÜNZEL (*b* Hof, Germany, 17 Nov 1941) and has issue:

    Great-nephew's great-grandchildren
    1c *Stefan Alexander Wilhelm KÜNZEL, *b* Munich 27 June 1977
    1c *Tobias Sebastian Edward KÜNZEL, *b* Munich 22 Sept 1979

  Great-nephew's grandchildren
  3b *Edward Anderson HENRY [Box 852, Afton, WY 83110, USA], *b* Arlington, Va., 13 June 1952; drilling supt, Loffland Bros, Caspar, Wyo.
Great-nephew
(6) Sidney Morgan HENRY, *b* Staten Island, New York, 2 Dec 1878; *educ* Georgetown U, US Naval Acad Annapolis, and MIT; Capt Construction Corps USN, V-Pres: Balto Dry Docks and Shipbuilding Co, US Shipping Bd EFC and Munson Steam Ship Line; *m* Mare Island, Calif., 11 Sept 1907 Julia Barnett (*b* Opelika, Ala., 15 March 1888; *d* Lake George, New York, 24 Sept 1933), dau of Cdre Remus Charles Persons, Medical Dir USN, and his w Susan Barnett, and *d* Tucson, Ariz., 16 March 1959, having had issue:

  Great-nephew's children
  1a Sidney Morgan HENRY, Jr, *b* San Francisco 13 Aug 1908; *educ* St Albans Sch, Yale (BA 1930) and Harvard (MBA 1932); Assist to ·Financial V-Pres American-Hawaiian Steam Ship Co 1935-41 (Assist Tresr, Tresr and Assist Sec 1945-55), Assist Tresr and Assist Sec Transport, Trading & Terminal Corp 1945-55 (Dir 1954-55), investment management Brown Bros, Harriman & Co, New York, 1955-61, ptnr Farley Assocs, New York, 1960, V Pres & Dir E. I. Farley & Co, New York, 1960, Memb Maritime Assocs (Pres 1939-41); *m* New York 19 June 1948 *Mrs Olivia Ames Pool [520 E 86th, New York, NY, USA] (*b* Milton, Mass., 26 Nov 1917), dau of R. Dudley Peters and his w Ruth Sumner Draper, and *d* 20 May 1978, leaving issue:

    Great-nephew's grandchildren
    1b *Olivia Peters HENRY, *b* New York 29 June 1950
    2b *S(idney) Morgan HENRY III [4656 S 36th St, Arlington, VA 22206, USA], *b* New York 30 Jan 1953; *educ* Avon Old Farms Sch and U of Virginia (BA 1977); Manager Music and Arts 1978, computer salesman with CWS 1980

and BASICFOUR 1982, joined Zenith 1984 (Manager 1986), salesman Sybase 1989, consultant 1991; *m* 28 May 1982 *Melanie Kay, dau of Royce Hansen and his w Joy Buckendorf, and has issue:

Great-nephew's great-grandchildren
1c *Emily Joy HENRY, *b* Arlington 8 April 1987
2c *S(idney) Morgan HENRY IV, *b* Arlington 1 Sept 1990

Great-nephew's children
2a Julia Persons HENRY, *b* 24 Nov 1909; *d* 26 June 1911

Great-nephew
(7) Dr Reginald Buchanan HENRY, *b* Staten Island, New York, 1881; Capt USN Medical Corps, compiler *Genealogies of the Families of the Presidents* (1935); *m* Norfolk, Va., 1918 Jane Byrd (*d* 2 Sept 1991), dau of Edmund Sumter Ruffin, of Norfolk, and his w Cordelia Byrd, and *d* Feb 1969, leaving issue:

Great-nephew's children
1a *Evelyn Byrd Henry [Mrs George Sargeant, 616 Redgate Ave, Norfolk, VA 23507, USA], *b* 1919; *m* 1946 *George Harris SARGEANT, Jr, s of George Harris Sargeant and his w Evelyn Byrd Trigg, and has issue:

Great-nephew's grandchildren
1b *Evelyn Byrd Sargeant [Mrs Paul C Hutton, 4216 Holborn Ave, Annandale, VA 22003, USA], *b* 1 Aug 1948; *educ* Mary Washington Coll; *m* 28 April 1973 *Col Paul Churchill HUTTON III, US Army (ret), s of Paul Churchill Hutton, Jr, and his w Frances Stearns, and has issue:

Great-nephew's great-grandchildren
1c *Paul Churchill HUTTON IV, *b* Germany 8 Sept 1977
2c *George Sargeant HUTTON, *b* Pa. 28 Nov 1978
3c *Richard Willing Byrd HUTTON, *b* Portsmouth, Va., 11 Dec 1982
4c *Cuthbert Powell Stearns HUTTON, *b* Bad Tölz, Germany, 10 June 1985

Great-nephew's grandchildren
2b *Jane Byrd Sargeant [Mrs Ian McCurdy, 5 Seawanhaka Pl, Oyster Bay, Long Island, NY 11771, USA], *b* Newport News, Va., 17 Sept 1949; *educ* Longwood Coll; *m* 6 Jan 1973 *Ian Arrison McCURDY, s of James Arrison McCurdy and his w Faith Trumbull Higgins, and has issue:

Great-nephew's great-grandchildren
1c *Peter Johnston McCURDY, *b* Michigan 4 April 1974
2c *James Morgan McCURDY, *b* New York 17 April 1979

Great-nephew's grandchildren
3b *Louisa Morgan SARGEANT [312 Cherokee Rd, Hampton, VA 23661, USA], *b* Newport News, Va., 8 April 1954; *educ* Old Dominion U; curator 1986-88, Dir Devpt Planned Parenthood 1988-

Great-nephew's children
2a *Dr Reginald Buchanan HENRY, Jr [1350 W Princess Anne Road, Norfolk, VA 23507, USA], *b* Norfolk, Va., 18 July 1926; *educ* U of Virginia (MD 1950); Lt USNR Medical Corps 1951-54, in private medical practice 1957-92; *m* 1st 19— Ruth McAfee, of Cincinnati, Ohio (*d* 29 Sept 1966), and has issue:

Great-nephew's grandchildren
1b *Dr Reginald Buchanan HENRY III [5373 Lake Lawson Rd, Virginia Beach, VA 23455, USA], *b* 18 June 1956; *educ* Duke U; dermatologist; *m* 27 Oct 1986 *Deborah Anne (*b* 1956), dau of William McCauley and his w Audrey, and has issue:

Great-nephew's great-grandchildren
1c *Richard Buchanan HENRY, *b* Virginia Beach 2 Nov 1992

Great-nephew's grandchildren
2b *Elizabeth Davidson Henry [Mrs Barto L Lehman, 2232 Bee Ridge Rd, Columbia, SC, USA], *b* Norfolk, Va., 27 Sept 1958; *educ* Guilford Coll; *m* 13 June 1987 *Barto Leon LEHMAN, s of Paul Harold Lehman and his w Esther Ellen, and has issue:

Great-nephew's great-grandchildren
1c *Rebecca Ruffin LEHMAN, *b* Va. 24 May 1990

Great-nephew's children
2a (cont.) Dr Reginald B. Henry, Jr, *m* 2nd 2 Nov 1968 *Barbara Anne (*b* 1932), dau of Stonewall Jackson Dix and his w Pattie Montgomery Beaman, and with her has issue:

Great-nephew's grandchildren
3b *Edmund Ruffin HENRY, *b* Norfolk, Va., 26 Oct 1969
4b *Thomas Dix HENRY, *b* Norfolk 15 Sept 1971

Great-nephew
(8) Frank Anderson HENRY, *b* Garden City, Long Island, New York, 1883; US Consul Valparaiso, Chile, Nassau,

Bahamas, Melbourne, Australia, Malta and Port Elizabeth, S. Africa; *m* Tenerife, Canary Islands, 1921 Gladys (*b* Cork, Ireland, 1882; *d* Nutley, Sussex, UK, 1959), widow of Richard Martin and dau of Robert Allen, of Jersey, Channel Islands, and his *w* Alica Townsend, and *d* Nutley 1967, leaving issue:

Great-nephew's children
1a *Pamela Joan HENRY [The Laurels, Nutley, Uckfield, Sussex, UK], *b* Barcelona, Spain, June 1923

President Buchanan's nephew and niece
1 (cont.) James Buchanan Henry *m* 3rd 1904 Margaret Grote, dau of Henry B. Elliman, of New York, and *d* Coconut Grove, Fla., 17 Feb 1915
2 Jane Elliott HENRY, *b* and *d* 1836

VIII John BUCHANAN, *b* and *d* 1804
IX William Speer BUCHANAN, *b* 14 Nov 1805; *educ* Princeton and Litchfield Law Sch, Conn.; *d* 19 Dec 1826 or 1827
X George Washington BUCHANAN, *b* 1808; *educ* Dickinson Coll.; apptd US Atty for W Dist of Pennsylvania 1830; *d* 13 Nov 1832
XI Revd Edward Young BUCHANAN, *b* 30 May 1811; DD, Episcopalian Rector of Trinity Church, Oxford, Philadelphia; *m* 1833 Ann Eliza Foster, dau of William Barclay Foster, Memb Pennsylvania State Legislature, and er sis of Stephen Collins Foster, the lyricist and composer, and *d* 20 Jan 1895, having had issue:

President Buchanan's nephews and nieces
1 James BUCHANAN, *b* 1834; priv sec to his uncle during latter's presidency; *m* 1868 Florence Myers and *d* 1871
2 Charlotte Foster BUCHANAN, *b* 1836; *d* 1850
3 Ann Elizabeth Speer BUCHANAN, *b* 1838; *d* 1927
4 Harriet BUCHANAN, *b* 1841; *d* 1912
5 Edward Young BUCHANAN, Jr, of San Francisco, *b* 1843; civil engr; *m* 1870 Agnes Scott and *d* 1927, leaving issue:

Great-nephew and -nieces
(1) James BUCHANAN, *b* 18—
(2) Agnes Foster Buchanan, *b* 18—; *m* 1908 Dr Daniel CROSBY and *d* 1924
(3) Henrietta Jane BUCHANAN, *b* 18—; *d* 1894

President Buchanan's nieces
6 Henrietta Jane BUCHANAN, *b* 1844; *d* 1906
7 Maria Lois Buchanan, *b* 1847; *m* Alexander Johnston CASSATT (*b* 1839; Pres Pennsylvania Railroad Co; *d* 1906), brother of the impressionist painter Mary Cassatt (1845-1926), and *d* 1920, having had issue:

Great-nephew
(1) Edward Buchanan CASSATT, *b* 1869; Lt-Col US Army (13th US Cavalry) and US Mily Attaché London; *m* 1st Emily Louise Phillips and had issue:

Great-nephew's children
1a Lois Buchanan Cassatt; *m* 1917 John Borland THAYER III, s of John Borland Thayer, Jr, and had issue:

Great-nephew's grandchildren
1b *John Thorland BAYER IV, *b* 1918; *m* 1942 *Charlotte Rush Toland and has issue:

Great-nephew's great-grandchildren
1c *Lois Cassatt THAYER, *b* 1943
2c *John Borland THAYER V, *b* 1946
3c *Emily B. THAYER, *b* 1953
4c *Edward Dale THAYER, *b* 1955

Great-nephew's grandchildren
2b Alexander Johnson Cassatt THAYER, *b* and *d* 1919
3b Edward Cassatt THAYER, *b* 1920; Lt USAF, missing in action over the Pacific 1943
4b *Lois Thayer, *b* 1923; *m* 1945 *William West FRAZIER, Jr, s of William West Frazier, and has issue:

Great-nephew's great-grandchildren
1c *Lois FRAZIER, *b* 1946
2c *William West FRAZIER III, *b* 1949

Great-nephew's grandchildren
5b *Julie Thayer [Mrs C Oliver Iselin III, Fiddlers Green Farm, Unison, VA, USA; Wolver Hill Farm, Middleburg, VA 22117, USA], *b* 1928; *m* 1953 *C. Oliver ISELIN III, s of C. Oliver Iselin, Jr, and has issue:

Great-nephew's great-grandchildren
1c *Julie ISELIN, *b* 1958

Great-nephew's grandchildren
6b *Pauline Thayer, *b* 1930; *m* 1954 *James Robert MAGUIRE, lawyer, and has issue:

Great-nephew's great-grandchildren
1c *James Robert MAGUIRE, *b* 1955

2c *Pauline Thayer MAGUIRE, *b* 1956
3c *George E. B. MAGUIRE, *b* 1958

Great-nephew
(1) Col Edward B. Cassatt *m* 2nd Eleanor Blackford Smith, of Virginia, and *d* 1922, having with her had issue:

Great-nephew's children
2a Edward Buchanan CASSATT, *b* 1910; *d* 1911

Great-niece and -nephew
(2) Katherine Kelso Johnston Cassatt, *b* 1871; *m* 1903 Dr James Pemberton HUTCHINSON, of Philadelphia, and *d* 1905
(3) Robert Kelso CASSATT, *b* 1873; ptnr Cassatt & Co, Philadelphia (bank); *m* 1900 Minnie Drexel Fell (*d* 1955) and *d* 1944, having had issue:

Great-nephew's children
1a Sarah D. CASSATT; *d* in infancy
2a Alexander Johnston CASSATT, *b* 1904; *m* 1st 1928 Cassandra Morris (*d* July 1977), dau of —— Stewart, of Baltimore, and had issue:

Great-nephew's grandchildren
1b *Robert Kelso CASSATT [Box 234 RR1, Brooksville, ME 04617, USA], *b* Philadelphia 3 March 1929; *educ* St Marks and Harvard; engr, USAF pilot 1950-64; *m* 1st 4 Jan 1954 Sheila (*d* 1985), dau of James Simpson and his w Ella Carter, and has issue:

Great-nephew's great-grandchildren
1c *Lydia S. Cassatt, *b* Baltimore 30 June 1955; *m* Maine 1985 *Philip OSGOOD
2c *Sheila S. Cassatt, *b* Baltimore 30 Nov 1957; *m* *—— ISSENBERG

Great-nephew's grandchildren
1b (cont.) Robert K. Cassatt *m* 2nd 1988 (divorce 1991) Anne Gaunt Bussey
2b *Alexander Johnston CASSATT, *b* 1933
3b *Cassandra CASSATT, *b* 1929

Great-nephew's children
2a (cont.) Alexander J. Cassatt *m* 2nd *Leona E. Burns and *d* April 1985
3a Anthony Drexel CASSATT [c/o Guaranty Trading Co, 14 Place Vendôme, Paris, France], *b* 19—; *m* 1930 *Madeleine Randolph, *née* Cochrane, widow, and has issue:

Great-nephew's grandchildren
1b Minnie Fell Cassatt, *b* 1931; *m* 1953 *Daniel Willis JAMES

Great-niece
(4) Eliza Foster Cassatt, *b* 1875; *m* 1902 William Plunket STEWART, of Baltimore, and *d* 1931, having had issue:

Great-niece's children
1a Alexander Johnston Cassatt STEWART, *b* 1903; *d* 1912
2a *Katherine Kelso Stewart, *b* Bar Harbor, Maine, 13 July 1905; *m* 1932 Vicomte Eric Antoine Ghislain Joseph DE SPOELBERCH (*b* Brussels, Belgium, 15 Feb 1903; *d* Nivelles, Belgium 27 Jan 1939), yr son of Vicomte Guillaume de Spoelberch (title *cr* 1816 by King WILLIAM I of The Netherlands in consideration of the family's long-standing nobility of blood) and his w Colienne de Neufforge, and has issue:

Great-niece's grandchildren
1b *Vicomte Guillaume DE SPOELBERCH, *b* Brussels 28 March 1933
2b *Vicomte Jacques DE SPOELBERCH, *b* Brussels 8 June 1936

Great-niece's children
3a *Doris Lurman Stewart [Mrs William P Wear, Enterprise, Cecilton, MD 21913, USA], *b* 1910; *m* 1931 *William Potter WEAR and has had issue:

Great-niece's grandchildren
1b *Elsie Cassatt Wear, *b* 1933; *m* 1952 *James STOCKWELL
2b *Joseph WEAR, *b* 1935
3b *Nancy Holliday Wear, *b* 1937; *m* 1960 *Frank Lyon POLK, Jr
4b A son, *b* and *d* 1939
5b *Priscilla Stewart WEAR, *b* 1940
6b *Adeline Potter WEAR [1720 Pine Street, Philadelphia, PA 19103, USA], *b* 1942

Great-niece's children
4a *Elsie Cassatt Stewart, *b* 1915; *m* 1944 *Thomas F. SIMMONS

President Buchanan's nephews and niece
8 William Foster BUCHANAN, *b* 1849; *d* 1875
9 Ridley BUCHANAN, *b* and *d* 1851

10 Alice Conyngham Buchanan, *b* 1853; *m* 1876 Maskell EWING, of Philadelphia (*b* 1847; *d* 1931) and *d* 1931, having had issue:

Great-niece

(1) Cornelia Lansdale Ewing, *b* 1877; *m* 1898 Robert E. BROOKE, of Brooke Manor, Birdsboro, Pa. (*d* 1942), and had issue:

Great-niece's children

1a Robert Clymer BROOKE, *b* 1898; *m* 1st 1925 Virginia Lafayette, dau of —— Blair, of Washington, DC, and had issue:

Great-niece's grandchildren

1b *Virginia Blair Brooke [Mrs Nathaniel Pennypacker, 916 Sorrel Lane, Bryn Mawr, PA 19010, USA], *b* 1927; *m* 1949 *Nathaniel Ramsay PENNYPACKER and has issue:

Great-niece's great-grandchildren
1c *D. Ramsay PENNYPACKER

Great-niece's grandchildren

2b *Robert Clymer BROOKE, Jr, *b* 1929; *m* 19— *Ellen —— and has issue

Great-niece's children

1a (cont.) Robert C. Brooke *m* 2nd 19— *Miriam Clymer
2a *Maskell Ewing BROOKE, *b* 1903
3a *John Louis Barde BROOKE [83 Main Street, Lenox, MA 01240, USA], *b* 1906; *m* 1946 *Louisa Geary Ludlow and has issue:

Great-niece's grandchildren

1b *Louisa G. BROOKE [235 West 76th Street, New York, NY 10023, USA]
2b *Cornelia E. BROOKE [71 Old Niskayuna Road, Loudonville, NY 12211, USA]
3b *John L. BROOKE; *educ* Cornell
4b *James B. BROOKE; *educ* St Paul's Sch

Great-niece's children

4a *Cornelia Lansdale Brooke [Mrs Charles D Marshall, Laurel Locks Farm, Pottstown, PA 19464, USA], *b* 1912; *m* 1940 *Charles Donnell MARSHALL, Jr, s of Charles Donnell Marshall, and has issue:

Great-niece's grandchildren

1b *Charles Noble MARSHALL [1040 West Schuylkill Rd, Pottstown, PA 19464, USA], *b* 1942
2b *Alice Brooke MARSHALL, *b* 1944
3b *Eliza Phipps MARSHALL [500 East 86th Street, New York, NY 10028, USA]

Great-nieces and -nephews

(2) Alice Buchanan EWING, *b* 1879; artist
(3) Anne Foster EWING, *b* 1880; *d* 1909
(4) Lois Buchanan EWING, *b* and *d* 1884
(5) Maskell EWING, Jr, of Philadelphia, *b* 1885; lawyer, Lt US Army World War I; *d* 1938
(6) Buchanan EWING, *b* 1887; civil engr; *m* 1915 Belinda Meeks and *d* 1930, leaving issue:

Great-nephew's children

1a *Helen Ewing, *b* 1916; *m* 1938 *Richard Rundle PLEASANTS and has issue:

Great-nephew's grandchildren
1b *Belinda PLEASANTS, *b* 1941
2b *Elizabeth PLEASANTS, *b* 19—

Great-nephew's children

2a *Buchanan EWING, Jr, *b* 1917; *m* 1941 *Gretchen Winifred Wunder and has had issue:

Great-nephew's grandchildren
1b *Buchanan EWING III, *b* 1942
2b Timothy Wunder EWING; *d* in infancy

Great-nephew's children

3a *James Hunter EWING, *b* 1920
4a *Edward Buchanan EWING, *b* 1921

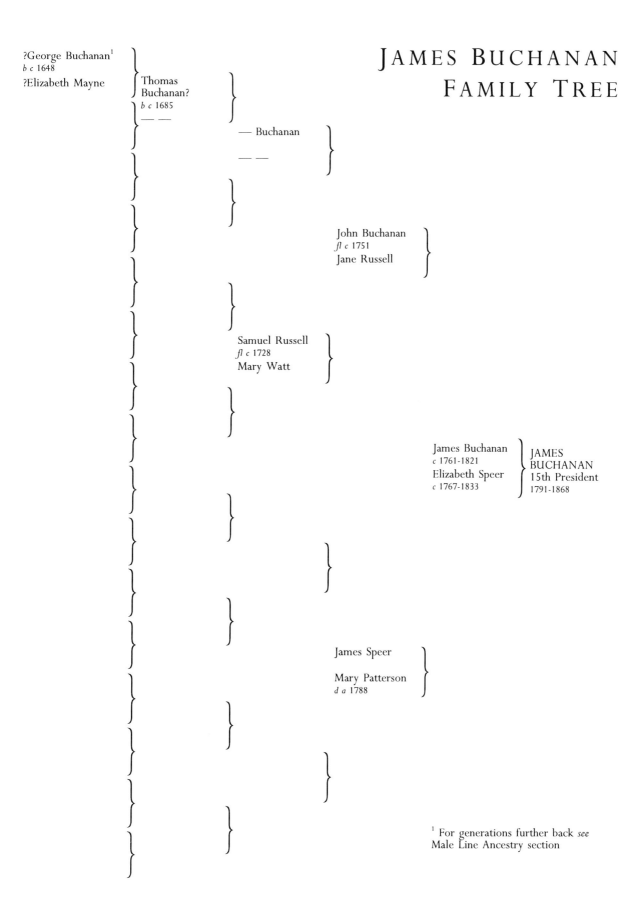

?George Buchanan[1]
b c 1648

?Elizabeth Mayne

Thomas
Buchanan?
b c 1685

— Buchanan

JAMES BUCHANAN
FAMILY TREE

John Buchanan
fl c 1751
Jane Russell

Samuel Russell
fl c 1728
Mary Watt

James Buchanan
c 1761-1821
Elizabeth Speer
c 1767-1833

JAMES
BUCHANAN
15th President
1791-1868

James Speer

Mary Patterson
d a 1788

[1] For generations further back *see*
Male Line Ancestry section

Plate 46   Abraham Lincoln

ABRAHAM LINCOLN

1809-65
16TH PRESIDENT OF THE UNITED STATES OF AMERICA
1861-65

God, they say, looks after idiots, drunkards and the United States of America. This saying never seems more plausible than when applied to the election of the 16th President. The political system was collapsing in ruins and not only that, it was burying in its fall the one man who, on his record, might have been able to restore it — Stephen A. Douglas. As a result civil war was impending. Power was won by a party which contained many able veterans but had never formed an administration. The successful candidate for the presidency, if not exactly a compromise candidate (the Republicans were too united in their views and interests to need one), was certainly the darkest of dark horses: a country lawyer from Illinois who had once served a single term in the House of Representatives. Yet, by a stroke of good fortune that nobody foresaw, not even himself, Abraham Lincoln turned out to be not only the right man for the crisis but the greatest of all the Presidents. If this was not a miracle it was at least very like one, and certainly, given the facts, a vindication of democracy.

For Lincoln embodied the myth of America. Other Presidents had been born in log cabins, but none to quite such poor, illiterate parents. He had very little schooling and as a young man earned his living as an axeman, splitting logs to make into fences — when he became a Presidential candidate they called him 'the Railsplitter'. By his own efforts and a fluid social system he had risen steadily to modest affluence and fame in Illinois as a good lawyer and finally to the presidency of his country. No wonder that he believed so fervently in that country and what it stood for, so that one of the most deeply felt sentences he ever uttered asserted that America was a nation "conceived in Liberty, and dedicated to the proposition that all men are created equal". No wonder he was to devote his life to saving it from destruction.

Lincoln's view of the Civil War was complex, but may be summarized as the belief that only if the Union of all the states was saved could democracy, with all its blessings for the world, be preserved; that breaking up the Union by secession for any cause was therefore wrong; and that secession for the sake of slavery was hellish. So when the South opened fire on Fort Sumter and the US flag, he accepted the challenge. As the years of war went on he saw ever more clearly that a democracy which had for so long tolerated slavery deserved the terrible judgement which had come upon it; and for that reason as well as the undeniable fact that slavery was ultimately the cause of Southern rebellion, the 'peculiar institution' would have to be destroyed. He also came to see that slavery was of military value to the Confederacy. So on 1 January 1863 he issued the Emancipation Proclamation, by which all slaves in the states then in rebellion were declared "now, henceforward and forever free". He subsequently devoted a large part of his time and energy to forwarding the 13th Amendment to the Constitution, which abolished slavery throughout the United States. This was his noblest achievement, but he also managed to put together a team of soldiers and statesmen who were able to hold off the South long enough, and organize the North effectively enough, to win total victory in the field after four years of hideous and all too often apparently indecisive struggle. Over the years he was able to find the ideas and words which would give the North the resolution and courage to sustain the struggle, and in the hour of victory, struck down by a fatuous neurotic (the usual type of assassin), he crowned his mission with the supreme sacrifice. In death as in life he vindicated his cause: "government of the people, by the people, for the people".

He was no story-book hero like George Washington, no polymath like Jefferson (although his judgement of Shakespeare's works was deeper than that of the people who tittered at him for his lack of formal education). He was tall, strong and awkward, never quite sure what to do with his large hands and feet, or how to arrange his lanky frame comfortably. At the same time he was personally unselfconscious to a marvellous degree, and deeply provincial; he had little experience of life away from the prairies and it showed. He would sometimes be found padding around the White House in his nightshirt, his long shanks showing, in search of someone to tell a joke to; he opened the Cabinet meeting that was to consider the Emancipation Proclamation by reading out a humorous article that had caught his fancy. He tended to make his points in homely anecdotes and his clothes almost always looked ill-fitting. This sort of thing made superior persons look down their noses at him and they were encouraged to do so by his humility, his patience, his refusal to make great decisions in a hurry. So they all made the same mistake: Edwin Stanton, who became his Secretary of War; William H. Seward, his Secretary of State; George McClellan, the most tiresome of his generals; and of course the leaders of the South. At one time or another they all wrote off Lincoln as a fool and they all lived to recognize their error.

For though he was humble, knowing that there is always something which a wise man needs to learn, he was at the same time supremely and rightly confident of his own abilities. He was patient because he saw things in proportion and did not sacrifice prime objectives, such as saving the Union, to secondary matters, such as his irritation with a general's bad manners. If he refused to be hurried it was not because he was indecisive; on the contrary, once he had made up his mind it stayed made up and he had a way of imposing his decisions on everybody else, since he was an excellent judge of the right moment to act. His sense of humour gave him a huge advantage over the pomposities who looked down on him and a long training at the grassroots had given him complete mastery of the techniques of American politics. Lincoln was fully as intelligent as anyone he ever met and so proved the master of his able but quarrelling Cabinet, of his job lot of generals, of a thoroughly restive Congress and of a country in the agonies of war.

The personal price he paid for greatness was exorbitant. Long before, he had made an unfortunate marriage to a pretty, silly, neurotic, Mary Ann Todd. He was too kind, too just, too sorry for her to do less than his best to make her happy, but she was no companion for him and her irrational jealousy, her compulsive extravagance, her nervous anxiety made life in the White House very difficult for him. They had four sons to whom Lincoln was devoted. The eldest, Robert, was a young man at the time of the Civil War and anxious to fight for his country, but his mother's distress was such that Lincoln had to keep Robert in relatively safe occupations (at one time he was on General Grant's staff) to the embarrassment of both of them. The second boy, Edward, died in Springfield at the age of four, to Lincoln's great sorrow, but the subsequent births of Willy and Tad gave him joy again. The boys were 10 and 8 respectively when the family came to Washington; they brought the only light into their father's grim life during the first and worst years of the war; and then Willy, the most promising of them all, died, a blow from which Lincoln never really recovered. At least his own death spared him the knowledge that Tad too would die before reaching manhood. Poor Mrs Lincoln, on the other hand, had to endure not only that blow but also the horrible experience of her husband's murder in the box at Ford's Theater beside her on Good Friday 1865. He was shot in the head by the actor John Wilkes Booth, whom a negligent sentry had allowed to get to the President. Lincoln was carried to a little house across the road from the theatre and there, at six in the morning, he died. Secretary Stanton was there. "Now he belongs to the ages," he said.

Lincoln had died fulfilled. Only a week previously, Robert E. Lee, commander of the Army of Northern Virginia, had surrendered to Ulysses S. Grant at Appomattox Court House. The Civil War was nearly over and the President had lived long enough to be sure of it.

ABRAHAM LINCOLN'S FAMILY

Abraham Lincoln is said to have been named after his grandfather, Captain Abraham Lincoln, although the name Abraham had been introduced into the family as far back as the late 17th century. Lincoln was sufficiently interested in his father's family to write, when a member of Congress in 1848, to the Hon Solomon Lincoln, of Hingham, Mass., presumably a remote connection, and mention a vague tradition that his grandfather had migrated from Pennsylvania to Virginia.

As for his mother's origins, even today genealogists do not agree on who her parents were, let alone the identity of Lincoln's remoter ancestors through her. Lincoln himself was reticent about his mother and it has been suggested he thought she was illegitimate. Certainly he called both his parents products of "undistinguished families". Yet family connections through his mother were to play a crucial role in Lincoln's life on at least two occasions. It was a cousin of his mother's who, by writing enthusiastically about Illinois, persuaded his father Thomas to move there from Indiana in 1830. And in 1860 a cousin of Lincoln's on his mother's side, John Hanks, helped Lincoln by a piece of showmanship to sew up the Illinois Republican delegation for the forthcoming national convention, held that year in Chicago. It was the state of Illinois that presented his name to the convention, so this proved crucial. The convention was the liveliest since the one that had nominated William H. Harrison 20 years earlier. Moreover, although Lincoln had won national fame recently through his debates with Stephen Douglas (not only a political rival but a former suitor of Mrs Lincoln), William H. Seward had been a national figure for much longer and by most betting men would have been reckoned a likelier nominee. Salmon P. Chase, Lincoln's fourth cousin once removed and the man who was to be his Secretary of the Treasury for most of his time in the White House, was also more prominent nationally and hoped for the nomination but was too anti-slavery to be thought a likely winner of waverer states. Seward even drew ahead of Lincoln on the first ballot. But Lincoln supporters had occupied most of the seats in 'The Wigwam' on Lake Street, the venue for the convention and the first building specifically constructed to house one, and he soon ran ahead of his rival.

Much has been made of Lincoln's obscurity in national terms till just before 1860. It is true that as late as 1860 most Americans knew very little about him. But curiosity was intense and a pamphlet biography sold over a million copies. In any case Lincoln, like Clinton shaking hands with Kennedy a century later, had already come into contact with a personification of his country's leadership. In 1832 he had served in the war against the Black Hawk Indians under the future President, Zachary Taylor, whom he was to support in the Whig national convention in 1848 and campaign for in that year's presidential election. In 1833 he had benefited from Andrew Jackson's powers of patronage when he was appointed postmaster of New Salem, Illinois. His supposed lack of enthusiasm for military exploits was later flung in his teeth by political opponents and Lincoln himself was self-deprecatory about his early soldiering experience. The fact remains that as Commander-in-Chief he won the first modern war. The Civil War was modern not just in its horrific casualty figures but in the way it required propaganda skills to rally opinion and keep up civilian morale on the home front. Lincoln was superb there. Moreover, Lincoln is one of only two Presidents to command troops in the field when in office — in May 1862 he personally took over from John Wool and mounted the successful amphibious assault by Union troops on Norfolk, Virginia.

In 1840, when Lincoln began courting his future wife Mary Todd, he was very much the social inferior. Mary came from Lexington, Kentucky, where her father, a banker, was on close terms with leading national politicians. Her ancestry was distinguished: her great-grandfather Andrew Porter had played an important role in the Revolutionary War, reaching the rank of General, and was offered the post of Secretary of War by Madison in 1813, though he refused on grounds of age. Two great-uncles, David Rittenhouse Porter and James Madison Porter, were respectively governor of Pennsylvania and a member of the Pennsylvania state legislature who was nominated Secretary of War by President Tyler in 1843, though the Senate refused to confirm the appointment. In early 1841 it was the social gulf between Mary Todd and Lincoln that is thought to have contributed to Lincoln's breaking off their engagement. Perhaps it was because of his wife's exalted connections that in 1843, when he ran for Congress unsuccessfully, he was labelled the "candidate of pride, wealth and aristocratic distinction". It could hardly have been any personal qualities. To stress these difficulties nowadays might seem excessively class conscious. That was not how Lincoln and his contemporaries saw it. The future President was always prone to depression, but particularly so in the early 1840s over his plebeian background. Later he was able to see things more calmly and cite his own advance from humble origins as an argument for free labour over slavery.

During his presidency Mary was simultaneously a furious partisan of her husband and something of an anxiety to him — a combination not unusual in First Ladies. One reason she aroused criticism was because her character was in such contrast to those of the last few Presidents' wives. She was vivacious where they had been retiring. Vivacity can come awkwardly close to frivolity in wartime, however, and with Mary Todd Lincoln it may well have seemed to acute observers to verge on hysteria. Charles Francis Adams, an acute observer if ever there was one, said of her "she wanted to do the right thing but, not knowing how, was too weak and proud to ask." She overspent both on personal shopping and in doing up the White House, but at least the effect of the latter was impressive. Her choice of cronies was similarly mixed in outcome. Her black sewing woman Lizzie Keckley, who had been born a slave and at one time had worked for Jefferson Davis, played roughly the role of Susanna to Mary's Countess Almaviva — confidante and booster of her employer's none too robust confidence. But her close friend Henry Wikoff surreptitiously fed the press stories about the Lincolns. After the death in 1862 of her third son Willie, Mary had a nervous breakdown and stayed in her room for three months. She then took to spiritualist seances and acted as official hostess only when utterly obliged to. In 1875 she was judged insane — after the question of her mental stability had been raised by her son Robert — and spent some months in an asylum. Although the premature death of three of her four sons undoubtedly contributed to this, a 20th-century study of her and her family conducted from a medical and scientific point of view has stated that three of her five brothers and sisters had abnormal personalities, so a family leaning toward instability would seem to be a strong contributing factor.

But the greatest embarrassment Mary involved Lincoln in was her family's Confederate sympathies. Mary's mother and half-sisters supported the South. One of them, Emilie, came to stay in the White House after her husband the Confederate General Ben H. Helm was killed at Chickamauga. Mary's brother George Todd was a surgeon in the Confederate army and of her four half-brothers Samuel, a soldier, was among the Confederate dead at Shiloh; David, a Confederate officer, died of wounds after Vicksburg; and Alexander, a Confederate Captain on the staff of his brother-in-law General Helm, was killed by a stray shot fired by Confederate irregulars who had mistaken the column he was in for a Union formation. This was on 5 August 1862, shortly before the Battle of Baton Rouge on 20 August. That Lincoln at one point voluntarily appeared before the Senate Committee on the Conduct of the

Plate 47   Mary Todd Lincoln in mourning 1865

Plate 48   Robert Todd Lincoln, Lincoln's
eldest son, US Secretary of War 1881-85
and Minister to Britain 1889-93

War and testified that none of his family held treasonable relations with the enemy is, however, no more than a legend.

The eldest and only surviving member of the Lincoln offspring, Robert, was reluctant to exploit his name politically, but others gave him no choice. In 1880 he headed a delegation to the Illinois state convention in Chicago; it initially supported Ulysses S. Grant, but then swung to James Garfield. After the latter became President he made Robert Lincoln Secretary of War. Robert's tenure of office was unenthusiastic but on the whole trouble-free. In 1884 and 1888 he won a handful of delegates at the Republican conventions but was never a serious contender for the presidential nomination against the party's heavyweights, the current President, Chester Arthur, or James G. Blaine in 1884 and Benjamin Harrison in 1888. He was one of two founders of the Little Mothers, an informal club of senators and other senior political figures who met to discuss politics in convivial surroundings (Warren G. Harding was later a member). In 1889 President Benjamin Harrison made him Minister to London, where he proved unusually immune to the social wiles of the natives. Theodore Roosevelt cited him as the only US envoy to the Court of St James's who was not pro-British. It is an interesting reminder of how much the contemporary Henry James theme of Americans ensnared by European duplicity mirrored a diplomatic reality, not just a social one.

BIOGRAPHICAL DETAILS AND DESCENDANTS

LINCOLN, ABRAHAM, *b* Rock or Sinking Spring Farm, nr Hodgenville, Hardin (now Larue) Co, Ky., 12 Feb 1809; ferryman 1827, flatboat operator 1830, clerk 1831-32, unsuccessful candidate for Illinois House of Reps 1832, enlisted, becoming Capt of his company, for service in Black Hawk War 1832, storekeeper 1832-33, Postmaster New Salem, Ill., 1833-36, Depy Surveyor Sangamon Co, Ill., 1833, Memb Illinois State Legislature 1834-42 and 1854-55, admitted to Illinois Bar 1836, Whig floor leader 10th Illinois Gen Assembly 1835-36, Ptnr: Stuart & Lincoln, attys, 1837-41, Logan & Lincoln, attys, 1841-43 and Lincoln & Herndon, attys, 1844-65, unsuccessful candidate for Whig nomination for US Congressional election 1842, Memb (Whig) US House of Reps from Illinois 1847-49, unsuccessful Whig candidate for US Senate 1855, unsuccessful candidate for Whig V-Presdtl nomination 1856, unsuccessful candidate (R) from Illinois for US Senate 1858, 16th President (R) of the USA 1861-15 April 1865, author: *Collected Works of Abraham Lincoln*, ed Roy P. Basler, 8 vols (1953-55) and *Supplement* (1974); *m* Springfield, Ill., 4 Nov 1842 Mary Ann (*b* Lexington, Ky., 13 Dec 1818; *d* Springfield 16 July 1882 of a stroke, *bur* there), dau of Robert Smith Todd, banker, manufacturer, merchant and farmer, and his w Ann Eliza Parker, and *d* William Peterson's boarding house, 453 Tenth Street, Washington, DC, 15 April 1865 of a bullet wound to the head after being shot by John Wilkes Booth at Ford's Theater, Washington, DC, 14 April 1865 (*bur* Oak Ridge Cemetery, Springfield), having had issue:

President Lincoln's son
I Robert (Bob) Todd LINCOLN, *b* Springfield 1 Aug 1843; *educ* Phillips Exeter Acad, Harvard and Harvard Law Sch; staff offr (Capt) under Gen (later Pres) ULYSSES S. GRANT during Civil War, lawyer in Chicago from 1867 (when admitted to Illinois Bar), Charter Memb Chicago Bar Assoc 1874, US Sec of War 1881-85, US Minister to UK 1889-93, Pres The Pullman Co 1897-1911 (Chm Bd Dirs thereafter); *m* 24 Sept 1868 Mary Eunice (*b* 25 Sept 1846; *d* 31 March 1937), dau of Senator James Harlan, of Iowa, Sec of the Interior 1865-66, and his w Ann Eliza Peck, and *d* Manchester, Vt., 25 July 1926, having had issue:

Grandchildren
1 Mary Todd Lincoln, *b* Chicago 15 Oct 1869; *m* 2 Sept 1891 Charles ISHAM, of Chicago (*b* 20 July 1853; lawyer; *d* 8 June 1919), and *d* 21 Nov 1938, leaving issue:

Great-grandchildren
(1) Lincoln ISHAM, *b* Chicago 8 June 1892; *m* 30 Aug 1919 Leahalma Correa and *d* Bennington, Vt., 1 Sept 1971

Grandchildren
2 Abraham LINCOLN, *b* Chicago 14 Aug 1873; *d* London, UK, 5 March 1890
3 Jessie Harlan Lincoln, *b* Chicago 6 Nov 1875; *m* 1st 10 Nov 1897 (divorce 1907) Warren BECKWITH (*b* 8 Aug 1873) and had issue:

Great-grandchildren
(1) *Mary Lincoln BECKWITH [Hildene, Manchester, VT 05254, USA], *b* 22 Aug 1898
(2) *Robert Todd Lincoln BECKWITH [Hildene, Manchester, VT 05254, USA], *b* 19 July 1904; *m* 1st 14 March 1937

Mrs Hazel Holland Wilson (*b* 29 March 1898); *m* 2nd 6 Nov 1967 *Annemarie Hoffman (*b* Germany) and with her has issue:

Great-great-grandchildren

1a *Timothy Lincoln BECKWITH, *b* Williamsburg, Va., 14 Oct 1968

Grandchildren

3 (cont.) Mrs Jessie Beckwith *m* 2nd 22 June 1915 (divorce 1925) Frank Edward JOHNSON (*b* 5 July 1873); *m* 3rd 28 Dec 1926 Robert J. RANDOLPH (*b* April 1875; electrical engr) and *d* Bennington, Vt., 5 Jan 1948

President Lincoln's sons

II Edward Baker LINCOLN, *b* Springfield 10 March 1846; *d* there 1 Feb 1850

III William (Willie) Wallace LINCOLN, *b* Springfield 21 Dec 1850; *d* the White House, Washington, DC, 20 Feb 1862 of typhoid

IV Thomas ('Tad') LINCOLN, *b* Springfield 4 April 1853; *d* Chicago 15 July 1871

MALE LINE ANCESTRY AND COLLATERAL DESCENDANTS

Robert LINCOLN, of Hingham, Norfolk, England, claimed Sir Thomas Lincoln (*fl* 1298) as ancestor; *m* Johanna Bawdiven and *d* 1543, leaving issue:

Robert LINCOLN, of Hingham; *m* Margaret Alberye or Abell and *d* on or shortly after 14 Jan 1556, leaving issue:

I John LINCOLN, of Hingham, *b c* 1554; *d c* 1622, leaving issue:

1 Thomas LINCOLN, of Hingham, *bapt* 27 June 1576 and had issue:

(1) Thomas LINCOLN, *b* 28 Dec 1600; emigrated to Massachusetts, where he was co-fndr of Hingham, Mass.; *m* 1st 16— ———; *m* 2nd 10 Dec 1665 Elizabeth Harvey, widow of Francis Streete, and *d c* 1683; his s by his 1st w:

1a Thomas LINCOLN, *b c* 1628; *m* 1st Mary, dau of Jonah Austin, of Kent, England; *m* 2nd Susanna Smith and *d* 1720, having had a s (whether by his 1st or 2nd w is unknown):

1b Samuel LINCOLN, *b* 16 March 1658; settled first in Norwich, Conn., then in Windham, Conn.; *m* 2 June 1692 Elizabeth Jacobs and *d* 1704, leaving issue:

1c Samuel LINCOLN, of Windham, *b* 29 Nov 1693; *m* 23 Aug 1723 Ruth, dau of Thomas Huntington, of Conn., and *d* 1794, leaving issue:

1d John LINCOLN, of North Windham, Conn., *b* 28 July 1726; fought in Revolutionary War; *m* 30 May 1758, as her 2nd husb, Anna, widow of Ebenezer Stowell and dau of George Martin, and *d* 1810, leaving issue:

1e Jonah LINCOLN, of Windham, *b* 15 Nov 1760; *m* 1 May 1783 Lucy, dau of John Webb, of Scotland, and *d* 14 May 1845, leaving issue:

1f Elisha LINCOLN, of Windham, *b* 12 Jan 1795; *m* 22 May 1817 Elizabeth Pray, dau of Benjamin Aplin, and *d* 7 Aug 1850, leaving issue:

1g Benjamin Aplin LINCOLN, *b* 12 Aug 1821; settled Ohio; *m* 16 Dec 1849 Harriet Newell, dau of John Wright, of Ohio, and *d* 18 May 1900, leaving issue:

1h Charles Sanford LINCOLN, *b* 2 Feb 1863; *m* 23 March 1885 Christiana, dau of Samuel Bayless, of Ohio, and with her had issue:

1i Harold Dwight LINCOLN, *b* 25 June 1886; *d* Jan 1905

2i Edmond Earl LINCOLN, *b* 5 Feb 1888; educ Ohio Wesleyan U (BA 1909), Lincoln Coll, Oxford (UK, Rhodes Scholar, BA 1910, MA 1914), and Harvard (PhD 1917); Prof of English Mount Union Coll, Ohio, and of History and Economics St John's Coll, Md., 1911-14, Memb Economics and Business Sch Faculties Harvard 1914-22, Ch Statistician and Economist Western Electric, New York, 1922-27, Economist with IT&T, New York, 1927-31, Economic Advsr to E I Du Pont De Nemours & Co from 1931; *m* 14 Aug 1915 Edith, dau of Edward C. Walker, of Ohio, and his w Ella Logan, and *d* 19—, having had issue:

1j *Elinore LINCOLN, *b* 25 Oct 1918

2j *Robert Edmond LINCOLN, *b* 18 Aug 1921

II Richard LINCOLN, of Hingham, *b* 15—; *m* Elizabeth, dau of Richard Remching and his w Elizabeth, and *d* 1620, leaving issue:

Edward LINCOLN, *b* Hingham *c* 1575; gentleman; *m c* 1600 Bridget Gilman, dau of Edward Gilman (*bapt* 1557), of Caston, Norfolk, and Hingham, and sister of Edward Gilman (ancestor of President FORD) also of Mary Gilman (who with her 1st husb Nicholas Jacob was an ancestor of President BUSH); Edward Lincoln *d* 1639/40, leaving issue (with two er sons, names unknown):

I Samuel LINCOLN, *b c* 1619 (*bapt* Hingham, England, 24 Aug 1622); emigrated to Salem, Mass., as a weaver's apprentice 1635 and settled at Hingham, Mass., with his two er brothers 1637, owned property there by 1649; *m* Martha (*b* probably Ireland before 1624; *d* Hingham, Mass., 10 April 1693), dau of Revd John Lyford and his w Sarah, and *d* Hingham, Mass., 26 May 1690, leaving issue:

 1 Samuel LINCOLN, *b* 1650; soldier; *m* 1687 Deborah, dau of William Hersey, of Hingham, Mass., and *d* 1721, leaving issue:

   (1) Jedediah LINCOLN, *b* 1692; *m* 1716 Bethia, dau of Enoch Whiton, of Hingham, Mass., and *d* 1783, leaving issue:

    1a Henry LINCOLN, *b* 1765; clergyman in Hingham, subsequently settled at Falmouth, Mass., and later Nantucket, Mass.; *m* 1790 Susannah, dau of Timothy Crocker, of Falmouth, and *d* 1857, leaving issue:

     1b Henry LINCOLN, Jr, *b* 1798; settled in Boston then Brookline; *m* 1832 Charlotte A. Lewis, dau of Leonard French, of Boston, and *d* 1882, leaving issue:

      1c William Henry LINCOLN, *b* 1835; shipping merchant; *m* 1863 Cecelia Frances (*b* 1838; *d* 1925), dau of James Wiggin Smith, and *d* 1925, leaving issue:

       1d Henry LINCOLN, *b* 1864; *m* 1910 Anna Mae, dau of Jacob Billette, of Newport, Ky.
       2d Helen Frances Lincoln, *b* 1866; *m* 1916 Holger J. SORENSON, of Boston, and *d* 1929
       3d Alexander LINCOLN, *b* 31 Oct 1873; *educ* Harvard (AB 1895, AM 1896), U of Göttingen, Germany, and Harvard Law Sch (LLB 1902); Assist Atty-Gen Massachusetts 1920-27, Memb Massachusetts Bd of Tax Appeals 1930-36; *m* 22 June 1909 Eleanor, dau of Oliver Ames, and *d* 19—, leaving issue:

        1e *Alexander LINCOLN, Jr, *b* 25 May 1910; *educ* Harvard (AB 1932, AM 1938); *m* 17 May 1937 Elizabeth, dau of Cornelius P. Kitchel, of Englewood, New Jersey
        2e *William A. LINCOLN, *b* 22 March 1912
        3e *Emily A. LINCOLN, *b* 9 Dec 1913

       4d Elsie Lincoln, *b* 1875; *m* 1899 Samuel C. PAYSON

 2 Mordecai LINCOLN, *bapt* Hingham, Mass., 14 June 1657; foot soldier in Hingham 1679, moved to Hull *c* 1680 where worked as a blacksmith, later moved to Cohasset then to N Scituate, where he became a prosperous miller as well as blacksmith; *m* 1st probably Hull, Mass., *c* 1680-85 Sarah (probably *b* there 1660-65; *d* probably Scituate before 17 Feb 1701/2), dau of Abraham Jones (from whom the name Abraham came into the Lincoln family) and Sarah Whitman, and had issue:

   (1) Mordecai LINCOLN, for whom *see below*
   (2) Abraham LINCOLN, *b* probably Hingham 13 Jan 1688/9; settled first in New Jersey then Pennsylvania; *m* Rebecca
   _____
   (3) Isaac LINCOLN, *b* 24 Oct 1691; inherited the family homestead at Cohasset; *m* 1st Sarah Cummings; *m* 2nd Jael Garrett
   (4) Sarah Lincoln, *b* 29 July 1694; *m* Hingham 25 Feb 1715/6 Daniel TOWER

 2 (cont.) Mordecai Lincoln *m* 2nd Braintree, Mass., 17 Feb 1701/2, as her 2nd husb, Mary (*b* there 12 Jan 1663/4; *m* 1st Samuel Chapin; *d* Scituate 19 April 1743), dau of Caleb Hobart and his w Mary Eliot, and *d* Scituate, Mass., 12 or 28 Nov 1727 of apoplexy, leaving further issue:

   (5) Elizabeth Lincoln, *b* 1703; *m* Scituate 29 Dec 1720 Ambrose COLE and *d* there 14 Sept 1724
   (6) Jacob LINCOLN, *bapt* Hingham 23 May 1708; inherited Mordecai's Scituate property; *m* 1st Mary Holbrook; *m* 2nd Susanna Marble

Mordecai Lincoln's est s,
  Mordecai LINCOLN, Jr, *b* Hingham 24 April 1686; iron founder, moved to Chester Co, Pa.; *m* 1st probably Monmouth Co, New Jersey, before 14 Sept 1714 Hannah (*d c* 1727), dau of Richard Salter (lawyer, judge and colonial legislator, *d* after 1728) and his w Sarah, dau of Maj John Bowne, and *d* Amity, Pa., 12 May 1736, leaving issue:

John LINCOLN, *b* Freehold, New Jersey, 3 May 1716; weaver, settled Rockingham Co, Va., *c* 1750; *m* probably Berks Co, Pa., 5 July 1743 Rebecca (*b* 30 March 1720; *d* probably Linville's Creek, Rockingham Co, 20 July 1806), dau of Enoch Flowers and his w Rebecca Barnard, and *d* Linville's Creek Nov 1788, having had issue:

I John LINCOLN, *b* 17—; *m* Mary Yarnell and had issue:

 1 Mordecai LINCOLN; *m* Sophia Williams Heiskell and had issue:

   (1) Mary Sophia Lincoln; *m* 18—, as his 1st w, William Ramsay BROWN (*b* 18—; *m* 2nd, as her 2nd husb, 20 April 1869 (divorce 1876) Mary, widow of Col Daniel Stover and yr dau of President ANDREW JOHNSON)

II Capt Abraham LINCOLN, *b* Berks Co, Pa., 13 May 1744; settled in Kentucky *c* 1780; *m* 1st Mary Shipley; *m* 2nd Augusta Co, Va., 9 July 1770 Bathsheba, allegedly dau of Alexander Herring or Herron and his w Abigail Harrison, and was *k* Jefferson Co, Ky., by Indians probably May 1786, having with his 2nd w had issue:

Thomas LINCOLN, *b* Rockingham Co 6 Jan 1778; farmer and carpenter in Kentucky, Indiana and Illinois; *m* 1st Beech Creek, Washington Co, Ky., 12 June 1806 Nancy (*b* Campbell Co, Va., 5 Feb 1784; *d* nr Gentryville, Ind., 5 Oct 1818), dau of James/Abraham/Thomas Hanks and his w Lucy Shipley/Sarah Harper/Mary Berry, and had issue:

I Nancy (Sarah) LINCOLN, *b* Hardin Co, Ky., 10 Feb 1807; *d* Spencer Co, Ind., 20 Jan 1828
II ABRAHAM LINCOLN, 16th PRESIDENT of the UNITED STATES of AMERICA
III Thomas LINCOLN, *b* Knob Creek, Ky., 1811 or 1812; *d* 1813

Thomas Lincoln *m* 2nd 2 Dec 1819 Sarah (*b* probably Hardin Co 12 Dec 1788; *d* probably Charleston, Ill., 10 April 1869), widow of Daniel Johnston (with whom she had issue) and dau of —— Bush, and *d* nr Farmington, Ill., 17 Jan 1851

Samuel Lincoln[1]
?1619-90
Martha Lyford
a 1624-93
Abraham Jones
c 1630-1718
Sarah Whitman
d 1718

Mordecai Lincoln
1657-1727
Sarah Jones
1660-65—in/*a* 1701/2

?Thomas Hanks
d p 1674
?Elizabeth —

William Hanks?
c 1650-in/*a* 1704
Sarah —?

Richard Salter
d p 1728
Sarah Bowne
1669-*p* 1714

John Bowne
c 1630-84
Lydia Holmes
d p 1693

William Flower
d 1692
Elizabeth Moris

Richard Barnard
d c 1698
Frances Lambe

Richard Lambe

Lucy Baillie

Adam Shipley?
fl 1668-87
Lois? ?Howard
c 1655-*c* 1725

Charles Stevens?
c 1615-*c* 1658
Susannah (Norwood?)
b c 1620

Charles Stevens, Jr?
c 1645-*c* 1703
Elizabeth —?

Robert Shipley
c 1678-*c* 1763 same as (a)
Elizabeth Stevens?
same as (b)

[1] For earlier
generations *see*
Male Line
Ancestry section

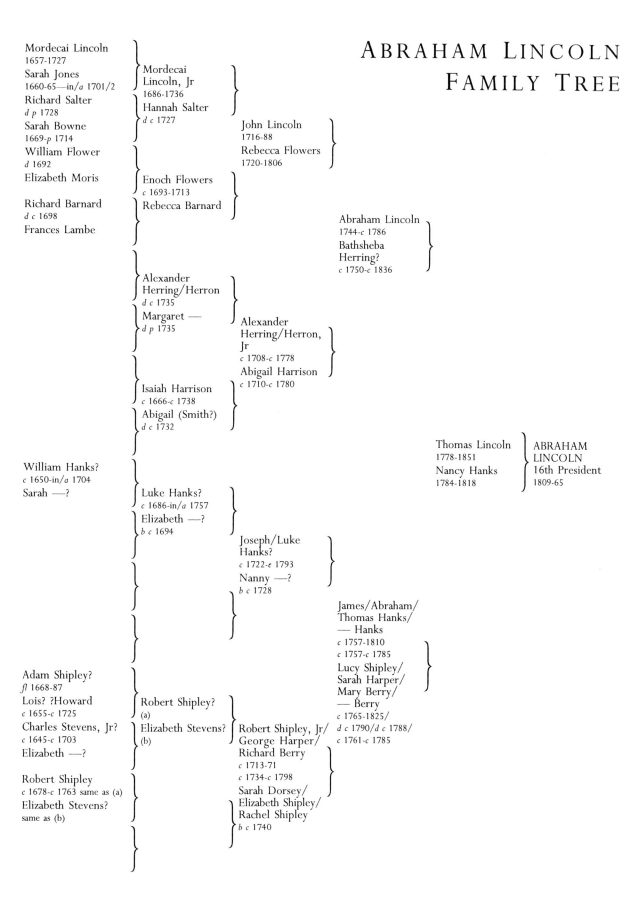

ABRAHAM LINCOLN
FAMILY TREE

Mordecai Lincoln
1657-1727
Sarah Jones
1660-65—in/a 1701/2
Richard Salter
d p 1728
Sarah Bowne
1669-p 1714

Mordecai
Lincoln, Jr
1686-1736
Hannah Salter
d c 1727

John Lincoln
1716-88
Rebecca Flowers
1720-1806

William Flower
d 1692
Elizabeth Moris

Richard Barnard
d c 1698
Frances Lambe

Enoch Flowers
c 1693-1713
Rebecca Barnard

Abraham Lincoln
1744-c 1786
Bathsheba
Herring?
c 1750-c 1836

Alexander
Herring/Herron
d c 1735
Margaret —
d p 1735

Alexander
Herring/Herron,
Jr
c 1708-c 1778
Abigail Harrison
c 1710-c 1780

Isaiah Harrison
c 1666-c 1738
Abigail (Smith?)
d c 1732

Thomas Lincoln
1778-1851
Nancy Hanks
1784-1818

ABRAHAM
LINCOLN
16th President
1809-65

William Hanks?
c 1650-in/a 1704
Sarah —?

Luke Hanks?
c 1686-in/a 1757
Elizabeth —?
b c 1694

Joseph/Luke
Hanks?
c 1722-e 1793
Nanny —?
b c 1728

James/Abraham/
Thomas Hanks/
— Hanks
c 1757-1810
c 1757-c 1785
Lucy Shipley/
Sarah Harper/
Mary Berry/
— Berry
c 1765-1825/
d c 1790/d c 1788/
c 1761-c 1785

Adam Shipley?
fl 1668-87
Lois? ?Howard
c 1655-c 1725
Charles Stevens, Jr?
c 1645-c 1703
Elizabeth —?

Robert Shipley?
(a)
Elizabeth Stevens?
(b)

Robert Shipley, Jr/
George Harper/
Richard Berry
c 1713-71
c 1734-c 1798
Sarah Dorsey/
Elizabeth Shipley/
Rachel Shipley
b c 1740

Robert Shipley
c 1678-c 1763 same as (a)
Elizabeth Stevens?
same as (b)

Plate 49   Andrew Johnson

ANDREW JOHNSON

1808-75
17TH PRESIDENT OF THE UNITED STATES OF AMERICA
1865-69

Andrew Johnson is chiefly remembered as one of only two Presidents against whom serious impeachment proceedings have been launched. But his trial (he was narrowly acquitted and no one today would argue that there was any merit in the case against him) was in most respects a mere appendage to his presidency, the result of bad temper on the part of his adversaries rather than anything more serious. The real significance of Johnson's administration lay elsewhere.

He had been chosen to be Lincoln's second Vice-President because the election of 1864 looked like being a close one (in the event Lincoln won handsomely); Johnson, as a Democrat and Southerner who was loyal to the Union (he had been the only Southern Senator to remain in the Senate after his state seceded) would widen the appeal of the ticket and confirm its claim to represent the nation, rather than just the Republicans. Unfortunately the very qualities which made Johnson a good Vice-Presidential candidate made him a weak President, for it was the Republican party which controlled Congress, a party that was strictly Northern. After Lincoln's death, it desperately wanted a leader and would have accepted Johnson, but only if he accepted the Republican programme. This he would not do.

He refused partly because that programme was incoherent and fluid. Still, at the very least the Republicans wanted, reasonably enough, some guarantee that secession would not revive; that the ex-rebels would not be allowed to come easily back to Congress and resume the political control they had thrown away in 1860-61; that help and hope would continue to be given to the ex-slaves. There was ample room for argument about achieving these objectives and Lincoln was deeply involved in such argument at the time of his death. There was, and is, too much reason to think that some of them (especially anything trying to ensure decent treatment to the freedmen) were unattainable. But the real difficulty between the Republicans and the new President was that he had a quite different set of aims.

This fact had been obscured by the freedom with which both Johnson and his opponents claimed that they were acting according to the wishes of the martyred Lincoln. Johnson had at least this justice on his side, that Lincoln's Second Inaugural, a deeply moving meditation on the causes of Civil War, had included a reference to a healing peace, to binding the nation's wounds. Lincoln also tried repeatedly to find a basis for magnanimous collaboration with the rebels — once they had surrendered. But there is no reason to think that he would have given up the Republican programme merely to satisfy the South. This was what Johnson did. He offered immensely liberal terms: let the seceded states only accept the 13th Amendment, accept the restoration of the Union and repudiate the Confederate war debt and they could get back all their political privileges and rights. He made no stipulation about the freedmen and did nothing to secure the political interests of the Republicans. This they could not forgive. A full-scale political battle broke out which culminated in the Congressional elections of 1866. These resulted in overwhelming victory for the Republicans; thereafter, though the President vetoed one bill after another, every one was re-passed by the requisite two-thirds majority in each house. It was only the President's continuing obstinacy (which of course he was convinced was righteousness) that provoked Congress at last to impeach him.

It is a sad story because in many ways both sides were right. The tragedy was that the President and Congress could not understand each other. Johnson came from Eastern Tennessee, a hilly, poor region. He was born among poor folk himself. His rise to political eminence paralleled Lincoln's; indeed he and his predecessor had much in common. But he lacked Lincoln's insight into men's motives. Hot-tempered like Andrew Jackson (after whom he was named), ignorant of the North, and too unimaginative to see how deeply he was affronting the cause for which hundreds of thousands had died, he only knew that a golden opportunity was being missed. The generous terms he was offering to the South were being enthusiastically accepted (no wonder); a true peace of reconciliation was at hand; what did it matter if it was at the expense of the blacks? He himself had swallowed his ancient dislike of the planter class in the cause of peace; why could not radical Republicans swallow their abolitionism? Why, because they were greedy only for power. So he blundered persistently forward, never suspecting that he, quite as much as the radicals, the unregenerate South (still set on keeping the blacks in subjection) quite as much as the victorious North, were responsible for creating conditions that would curse America almost as disastrously as slavery itself for nearly another century.

ANDREW JOHNSON'S FAMILY

For a long time the obscurity of Andrew Johnson's pedigree was so impenetrable that it was easy to assume his family had always been poor. A recent study suggests the family had held a respectable amount of land only two generations back, but that the 17th President's grandfather had got into difficulties and had had to part with his holding in a forced sheriff's sale.

Whether in consequence of this or not, Jacob and Polly Johnson, Andrew Johnson's parents, were illiterate servants in a tavern. When Joseph died, it is thought from the after-effects of plunging into an icy stream to save the lives of two men, he was buried in an unmarked grave. The two men he had rescued, who were both rich, seem to have given him no substantial reward. Nor his widow, for Polly had to work as a washerwoman and seamstress to keep herself and her two sons, Andrew the future President and William, becoming known as 'Polly the weaver'. It is reasonable to blame this prime example of the ingratitude of wealth for Andrew Johnson's later detestation of 'aristocrats'. The future President Grant, for instance, thought Johnson's attitude to the South in the early days after the Civil War smacked of a desire to get his revenge on men of higher social standing while simultaneously craving their acknowledgement of him as an equal — and Grant was not the sort of man to clutter up his assessment of another person's character with highfalutin amateur psychology. Another possibility, though much slighter, is that the rumours which circulated when Andrew Johnson became famous, namely that he was not the son of his legal father but either of Judge John Haywood or William Ruffin, a lawyer, were known to him. If so they must have piqued him. His mother had worked in Haywood's house as a washerwoman and Johnson bore some resemblance to him. The bastard's celebrated sense of injustice may have worked on a nature already rough and sympathetic to the underdog to produce a positively Jacobinical viewpoint. It must be said that there is no real evidence for either theory, however.

Johnson's birth-place is now thought not to have been a back room at Casso's Inn, Fayetteville Street, Raleigh, North Carolina, despite the statements of various reference books, for the legend only grew up this century. Instead, he seems to have been born in a two-and-a half-storey house built of logs — not even a log cabin really, since the phrase usually suggests a one-storey structure. Andrew Johnson's latest biographer suggests that Abraham Jobe, a Post Office official who lived in Raleigh in the 1860s, knew the real birth place and so successfully made a showplace of it to so many visitors that it was

Plate 50   *Eliza McCardle Johnson*   Plate 51   *Martha Johnson Patterson, Andrew Johnson's
elder daughter and hostess in the White House*

pulled apart by souvenir-hunters. Jobe, however, was in Raleigh 60 years after Andrew Johnson's birth and perhaps had a financial interest in displaying an alternative site.

Johnson and his brother William were apprenticed to a Raleigh tailor, James Selby, in 1822. They were 14 and 18 respectively. Two years later, when Johnson was still only a youth, he and his elder brother, together with a couple of other apprentices, threw stones at the house of a neighbouring old woman. Fearing arrest, the two Johnsons fled to South Carolina. In 1825 Andrew returned to his master, who in the meantime had offered a reward for his capture, and offered to complete the term of apprenticeship. Selby refused either to take him back or to release him, so he left town again, this time for Rutledge, Tennessee, settling at Greeneville soon afterward. The Selby episode was the second time Andrew had enjoyed a spot of local notoriety as a member of a gang involving another member of his family. After his father's death, when it seems likely his mother boarded him out with his uncle Jesse, he ran with some cousins, the gang being known as 'Jesse Johnson's Boys'. Mary's second marriage some time between 1812 and 1825 (the exact date is not known) compounded the family's difficulties. Her new husband was a wastrel. He was also easily led, for he and his wife were persuaded to move out to Tennessee by his stepson Andrew, a mere 17 years old, after that stepson had settled as an independent journeyman tailor in Tennessee.

Another conflicting story about Andrew Johnson is the extent to which his wife Eliza taught him to read and/or write. Older biographies used to say she taught him to do both. One of the more recent ones asserts that he could read already but that she taught him to write. The position is complicated by the very latest biographer's statement that he wrote to Eliza when courting her, though it is always possible that over a long courtship she instructed him in the means by which he brought that courtship to a successful conclusion. On the other hand many illiterates in the 19th century had someone else write their love letters for them. Then again, it is said that Andrew Johnson arranged for people to read to him while he worked away at tailoring (he claims to have been a good one, none of his work ever ripping or giving at the seams), as if this proved he was unable to read himself. But it proves nothing either way as no tailor could keep one eye on the printed page and the other on his needle and thread. When Johnson was President he kept six secretaries, an unusually high number for the mid-19th century, and he rarely wrote anything himself. This was supposedly because he had hurt his right arm in a railroad accident in 1857, but it is not being unnecessarily cynical to surmise that it was more because he was unhappy about his spelling and grammar. Whatever his skills or lack of them he was at least conscious of them. (He is even said to have written poetry, which argues some feeling for language.) He was no Harding, Eisenhower or Bush then, with their sublime disregard for the rhythms, cadences and even meaning of the English language. Whether he learned reading and writing from his fiancée or men met casually through his trade, he exhibited a ferocious and praiseworthy determination to educate himself. Doubtless this entailed his wife tutoring him to bring him up to the general standard.

Unfortunately Eliza, whatever her attainments as an instructress in two of the three Rs, was suffering by the time her husband entered the White House from the ill health that dogged virtually all 19th-century First Ladies. She had developed tuberculosis (a disease her youngest son Frank also suffered from) and now retired to a second-storey bedroom, seldom emerging thereafter. Johnson was thrown back on the company of his children and grandchildren. Fortunately he seems to have been happy in the company of most of them, particularly when he could go on picnics with the grandchildren. Martha, the Johnsons' eldest child, was the first of the family to move into the White House after her father took over from Lincoln. Her husband David T. Patterson, US Senator from Tennessee, was an old friend and supporter of Johnson, to whom Martha was "my oldest and favorite child". She took over the hostess's role from her mother and performed capably if not particularly brilliantly, the White House allegedly acquiring an atmosphere of simple, if somewhat sombre, dignity. Where she did do a superb job was in utilizing to the best effect the niggardly $30,000 Congress voted for refurbishing the White House. In the wake of Lincoln's assassination the place had been invaded by a horde of souvenir-hunters, who stripped the building almost as effectively as others of their breed had Johnson's birthplace.

Charles and Robert, the two elder boys, worked as aides to their father in his scramble up the greasy pole of national politics, attending the Charleston, S Carolina, Democratic convention in 1860 as his representatives (aspirants to the presidential nomination, as Johnson was that year, stayed away from conventions in those days). Next year Tennessee seceded and Johnson was left not only high and dry as the sole southern Senator supporting the Union, but in some personal danger as well, so that he was obliged to escape northward over the border to Kentucky. Charles and Robert meanwhile retired eastward to the mountain country where their father had started his career over 30 years earlier and attempted to get up a resistance movement against Confederate rule. Charles worked for a time as editor of a newspaper, the *Spy*, which his father had got going. When studying to be a pharmacist he developed a taste for alcohol. It cannot be said for certain that alcohol caused his fatal fall from a horse in 1863. What is certain is that he showed promise in several fields — finance, music and medicine — which makes his death all the more a shame.

Robert was an out-and-out case of drunkenness, being obliged because of it to resign his Union Army commission as a Colonel. In 1866 he so dragged the presidency into disrespect as a result of drinking while on duty as his father's aide, in addition bringing prostitutes into the White House in broad daylight, that his father found it advisable to send him on a world tour disguised as a diplomatic mission, paying for it out of his own pocket. Robert's drinking eventually led to his suicide in 1869, exactly seven weeks after his father left office. He left debts which worried Johnson mightily but when Johnson himself died he left over $100,000, a respectable fortune by the standards of the time.

The younger daughter Mary, unlike her biblical namesake, pitched in to help Martha over domestic chores such as entertaining. Her first husband having died a few months before Lincoln's assassination, she took as her second husband a cousin-by-marriage of Lincoln's. It was an unhappy choice but because Johnson disapproved of divorce the couple waited until after his death to dissolve it. Misfortune dogged nearly all the Johnsons; only Andrew Johnson managed to rise above it.

BIOGRAPHICAL DETAILS AND DESCENDANTS

JOHNSON, ANDREW, *b* Raleigh, N Carolina, 29 Dec 1808; tailor's apprentice 1822-24, independent tailor 1824-28, leader of a workingmen's party he organized 1828, Alderman Greeneville, Tenn., 1828-30, Mayor Greeneville 1830-33, Tstee Rhea Acad 1833, Memb (D) Tennessee State Legislature for Greene and Washington Cos 1835-37 and 1839-41, Memb (D) Tennessee State Senate 1841-43, Memb (D) US House of Reps from Tennessee 1843-53, Govr Tennessee 1853-57, Memb (D) US Senate from Tennessee 1857-62 (Tennessee seceded 1861, leaving Johnson as sole Southerner in US Senate) and 5-24 March 1875, Mily Govr Tennessee 1862-65, Brig-Gen Volunteers 1862-65, V-Pres (R, or National Union Party) USA 4 March-15 April 1865, 17th President (R) of the USA 15 April 1865-69, unsuccessful candidate: presidency (D) 1868, US Senate 1871 and US House of Reps 1872, author: *Speeches* (1865) and *Papers*, ed Leroy P. Graf and Ralph W. Haskins (1967); *m* Warrensburg (?), Greene Co, Tenn., 17 May 1827 Eliza (*b* Greeneville 4 Oct 1810; *d* Carter Co, Tenn., 15 Jan 1876, *bur* Andrew Johnson National Cemetery, Greeneville, with her husb), dau of John McCardle, of Warrensburg, cobbler (later innkeeper), originally from Washington Co, Tenn., and his w Sara(h) Phillips, and *d* Carter's Station, Tenn., 31 July 1875 of a stroke, having had issue:

President Andrew Johnson's daughter

I Martha Johnson, *b* Greeneville 25 Oct 1828; *educ* Miss S. L. English's Female Seminary, Georgetown, DC; *m* Georgetown 13 Dec 1855 David Trotter PATTERSON (*b* Cedar Creek, Tenn., 28 Feb 1818; Judge Tennessee Circuit Court 1854-63, US Senator 1866-69; *d* Afton, Tenn., 3 Nov 1891), s of Andrew Patterson and his w Susanna Trotter, and *d* Greeneville 10 July 1901, having had issue:

Grandchildren

1 Mary Belle Patterson, *b* Greeneville 11 Nov 1857; *m* there 17 Feb 1886 John LANDSTREET, of Loudoun Co, Va. (*b* there 25 April 1853; *d* Richmond, Va., 1 Aug 1927), s of Revd John Landstreet and his w Mary, and *d* Auburn, Calif., 9 July 1891, leaving issue:

Great-grandchildren

(1) Martha Belle Patterson Landstreet, *b* Port Richmond, Staten Island, New York, 6 Aug 1887; *m* Richmond, Va., 1907 Robert Josiah WILLINGHAM, Jr (*b* Athens, Ga., 27 June 1875; *d* Washington, DC, 10 Oct 1953), s of Robert Josiah Willingham and his w Corneille Bacon, and *d* Richmond 26 Dec 1969, having had issue:

Great-great-grandchildren

1a *Martha Belle Willingham [Mrs Martha Willingham Colt, 215 Park Street, Hanover, NH 03755, USA], *b* Richmond 20 Dec 1908; *m* there 17 June 1933 (divorce 1951) Thomas Clyde COLT, Jr (*b* East Orange, New Jersey, 20 Feb 1905), s of Thomas Clyde Colt and his w Florence Clery, and has issue:

Great-great-grandchildren's children

1b *Thomas Clyde COLT III [440 Westview Place, Fort Lee, NJ 07024, USA], *b* Richmond 1 March 1935; *educ* Oregon U (BS 1959); journalist

2b *Jon Landstreet COLT [1109 Marion Street, Denver, CO 80218, USA], *b* Richmond 21 July 1938; *educ* Dartmouth Coll, Hanover, New Hampshire (BA 1959)

3b *Corinne Patterson COLT [2122 Vista del Mar, Hollywood, CA 90068, USA], *b* Richmond 28 Oct 1946; *educ* George Washington U

Great-great-grandchildren

2a Elizabeth Landstreet Willingham, *b* Richmond 19 Nov 1910; *m* there 1931 *James Taylor Ellyson CRUMP (*b* Richmond 1903), s of Frank T. Crump and his w Nancy Ellyson, and *d* 1968, leaving issue:

Great-great-grandchildren's children

1b *Taylor Nicholas CRUMP [3020 Scarsborough Drive, Richmond, VA 23235, USA], *b* Richmond 16 Sept 1935; *m* there 4 Aug 1956 *Katherine Morris and has issue:

Great-great-grandchildren's grandchildren

1c *Kevin L. CRUMP, *b* Richmond 30 April 1958

2c *Taylor Nicholas CRUMP, Jr [1513 Winbury Drive, Midlothian, VA, USA], *b* Richmond 17 Aug 1959

Grandchildren

2 Andrew Johnson PATTERSON, *b* Greeneville, Tenn., 25 Feb 1859; mfr, Memb Tennessee Legislature, US Consul British Guiana; *m* Limestone, Tenn., 19 Dec 1889 Martha Ellen (*b* Washington Co, Tenn., 28 May 1864; *d* Greeneville 13 March 1948), dau of John Henry Barkley and his w Margaret Susanna Nelson, and *d* Greeneville 25 June 1932, leaving issue:

Great-grandchildren

(1) *Margaret Johnson Patterson [Mrs William Bartlett, 107 West McKee Street, Greeneville, TN 37743, USA], *b* Greeneville 29 Sept 1903; *m* there 15 June 1949 William Thaw BARTLETT, of Maryville, Tenn. (*b* 20 Sept 1876; *d* 27

Nov 1954), s of Peter Mason Bartlett and his w Florence Alden
(2) *Martha Barkley PATTERSON, b 19—

President Andrew Johnson's children
II Charles JOHNSON, b Greeneville 19 Feb 1830; doctor, newspaper ed and pharmacist, Col (surgeon) Union Army Civil War; k Nashville, Tenn., 4 April 1863 in a fall from his horse
III Mary Johnson, b Greeneville 8 May 1832; educ Rogersville (Tenn.) Female Acad; m 1st Greeneville 27 April 1852 Col Daniel STOVER, of Carter Co, Tenn. (b there 14 Nov 1826; ka Nashville 18 Dec 1864), s of William Stover and his w Sarah Murray Drake, and had issue:

Grandchildren
1 Lily Stover, b Carter Co 11 May 1855; m Greeneville 14 Oct 1874 Thomas Fleming MALONEY (b Warrensburg, Tenn., 6 Dec 1846; d Ogden, Utah, 17 March 1904), s of William Conway Maloney and his w Louisa Cureton, and d Knoxville, Tenn., 5 Nov 1892
2 Sarah Drake Stover, b Carter Co 27 June 1857; m Bluff City, Tenn., 7 June 1881, as his 1st w, William Bruce BACHMAN (b Kingsport, Tenn., 24 Nov 1852; d Bluff City 9 Sept 1922), s of Samuel Bachman and his w Sarah Kitzmiller, and d Bluff City 22 March 1886, leaving issue:

Great-grandchildren
(1) (Andrew) Johnson BACHMAN, b Bluff City 13 June 1882; City Judge Elizabethton, Tenn.; m Nashville 8 Sept 1920 *Ethel Crockett (b 15 Aug 1892), dau of James Irwin and his w Emma Johnson, and d Elizabethton, Tenn., 25 Jan 1955
(2) Samuel Bernard BACHMAN, b Carter Co 13 May 1884; d Bluff City 3 April 1914

Grandchildren
3 Andrew Johnson STOVER, b Carter Co 6 March 1860; d there 25 Jan 1923

President Andrew Johnson's children
III (cont.) Mrs Mary Stover m 2nd 20 April 1869 (divorce 1876), as his 2nd w, William Ramsay BROWN and d Bluff City 19 April 1883
IV Robert JOHNSON, b Greeneville 22 Feb 1834; Col 1st Tennessee Cavalry Civil War, lawyer; committed suicide Greeneville 22 April 1869
V Andrew (Frank) JOHNSON, Jr, b Greeneville 5 Aug 1852; educ Georgetowsn Coll, DC; newspaper-publisher Greeneville; m Rutland, Hot Springs, N Carolina, 25 Nov 1875 Kate May (Bessie), dau of James H. Rumbough and his w Caroline Powell, and d Elizabethton 12 March 1879

MALE LINE ANCESTRY AND COLLATERAL DESCENDANTS

The late Mr Hugh B. Johnston, Jr, a N Carolina genealogist who specialized in the ancestries of both Andrew and Lyndon B. Johnson, claimed to have researched that of Andrew Johnson back to:

Silvanus JOHNSON; farmed 934 acres of his own land in Amelia Co, Va.; m Elizabeth —— and had issue:

Richard JOHNSON; settled in N Carolina 1754, where he farmed beside the Neuse River and acquired two slaves; had issue:

William JOHNSON; acquired a land grant of 700 acres near Wake City, N Carolina; had issue:

William JOHNSON, Jr (other authorities have argued that Andrew JOHNSON, of Augusta Co, Va., was the father of the Jacob Johnson mentioned below) had issue:

I Jesse JOHNSON (not necessarily older than Jacob); had several children
II Jacob JOHNSON

William Johnson's yr(?) s,
Jacob JOHNSON, b 17 April 1778; resident of Raleigh, N Carolina, constable, janitor and servant in a tavern; m Raleigh 9 Sept 1801 Mary ('Polly') (b probably Beaufort Co, N Carolina, 17 July 1782; m 2nd Turner Daughtrey or Dougherty (d 1852); d Greene Co, Tenn., 13 Feb 1856), dau of Andrew McDonough, Jr, of Bledsoe Co, Tenn., and Tyrrell and Wake Cos, N Carolina, soldier in Revolutionary War, and his 1st w, and d Raleigh 4 Jan 1812, having had issue:

I William JOHNSON, b 10 Oct 1803 or 1804; tailor's apprentice, moved to Texas 1857, apptd to minor Federal post June 1865; d Oct 1865, having accidentally shot himself while hunting
II Elizabeth JOHNSON, b 14 March 1806; d in infancy
III ANDREW JOHNSON, 17th PRESIDENT of the UNITED STATES of AMERICA

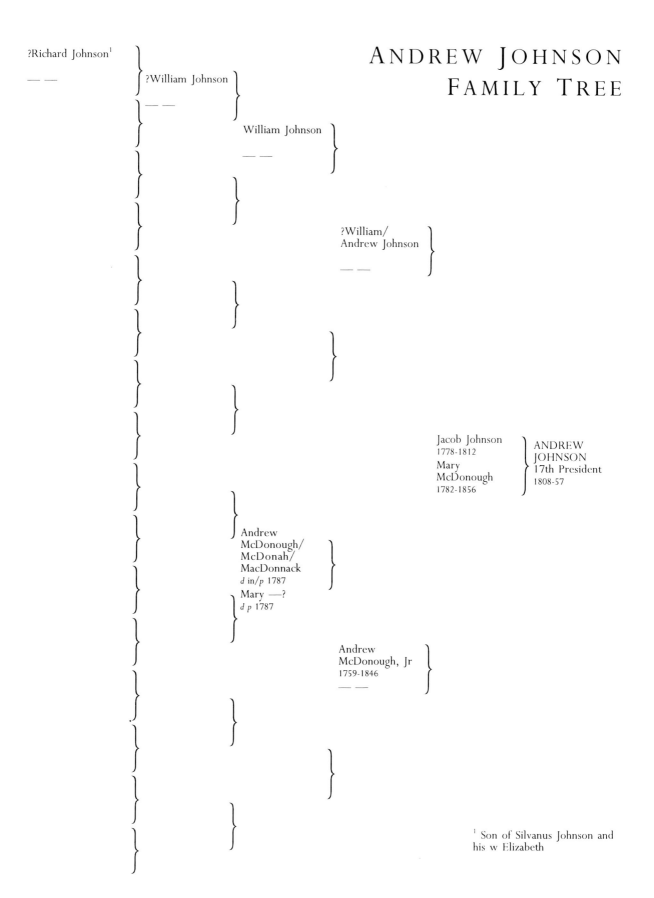

ANDREW JOHNSON
FAMILY TREE

?Richard Johnson[1]

?William Johnson

William Johnson

?William/
Andrew Johnson

Jacob Johnson
1778-1812

Mary
McDonough
1782-1856

ANDREW
JOHNSON
17th President
1808-57

Andrew
McDonough/
McDonah/
MacDonnack
d in/p 1787

Mary —?
d p 1787

Andrew
McDonough, Jr
1759-1846

[1] Son of Silvanus Johnson and
his w Elizabeth

Plate 52   Ulysses S. Grant

ULYSSES S. GRANT

1822-85
18TH PRESIDENT OF THE UNITED STATES OF AMERICA
1869-77

Grant was Lincoln's favourite general. In the early days of the war, after Grant's hideously bloody victory of Shiloh, in which the Union forces lost more men than the defeated Confederates, the President refused to dismiss the general, saying "I can't spare this man: he fights". He had other traits to commend him. When he fought he usually won. He never allowed himself to be disheartened ("I propose to fight it out on this line if it takes all summer" he said after the particularly disheartening slaughter of Spotsylvania in 1864). He had a sound strategic grasp, perceiving and never losing sight of the fact that the one sure way to defeat the South was by attrition, by bludgeoning it until it was forced to recognize that it could fight no more. Above all he knew how to obey orders. It may be presumed that Lincoln also liked Grant's personal modesty, his shabbiness, his poor beginnings — in all of which the two men resembled each other. Certainly the public warmed to this unpretentious, incessantly cigar-smoking general, who loved animals, hated war and eventually forced the great Lee to surrender. The war threw up more gifted generals — Lee and Jackson in the South, Sherman in the North — but none whose gifts (and Grant was highly talented) were more appropriate to the job that needed to be done. He ended the war on a pinnacle of glory and in 1866 Congress revived for him the rank of full general, borne by no one since the death of George Washington.

It was probably inevitable that Grant would become President. Lincoln being dead he was the outstanding national hero; the Republicans in 1868 badly needed a certain winner; he had quarrelled with Andrew Johnson and though he was not exactly ambitious, he certainly felt that the presidency was an honour that he had earned. That it was a responsibility beyond his ability does not seem to have occurred to him.

He and his family enjoyed life in the White House, which sets them apart; occupants have usually hated it. Unfortunately far too many other people enjoyed having him there. The clearness of vision which had characterized his generalship seems to have deserted him, leaving behind simply a groping feeling — perhaps the legacy of the loyalty he felt for his staff — that he must stand by his friends at all costs. Unhappily the cost was usually borne by the American taxpayer. These were the years of greed, known as the 'Gilded Age'. Congress doubled the President's salary and raised its own members salaries by 50% plus two years' back pay at the same rate. This 'Salary Grab' produced a storm of criticism, but Grant had signed the bill without a tremor. Nor had he been much disturbed when it came out that the Union Pacific Railroad, in pursuit of a murky financial swindle, had dealt out large blocks of lucrative stock to the Vice-President, Schuyler Colefax, and to several Congressmen, including James Garfield, a future President. Grant's private secretary Babcock was discovered to have involved the President's good name in several unsavoury deals, including the bold attempt of two Wall Street buccaneers, Jim Fisk and Jay Gould, to get control of the gold supply, and had helped the St Louis 'Whiskey Ring' to cheat the government of millions of dollars. "Let no guilty man escape" said Grant

— but he helped Babcock to evade justice. His Secretary of War was impeached for selling favours and avoided conviction only by resignation; his Secretary of the Navy amassed an enormous fortune, no one knew how, while holding office; the minister to England and the minister to Brazil were both involved in swindles; Grant's own family was not above suspicion, although the President himself left office rather poorer than he had entered it. Coupled with nearly universal ineptitude in all other matters of government it amounted to a sorry record. Grant did not exactly betray his trust, but he proved that he was quite unfit for it; the common verdict is probably correct, that he was one of the very worst American Presidents.

His greatness showed again during his last years. Thanks to bad investments, the fund presented to him by private admirers was gone and he had no pension, either as a former President or as a former general. He found that he was dying from cancer of the throat. To provide for his wife and family he set out to write his war memoirs, disregarding pain with the same grit he had shown when battling Lee. He finished the book four days before his death; on publication it earned nearly half a million dollars and is universally agreed to be a classic autobiography, lucid, truthful and wise. His granite tomb is one of the most famous sights of New York, but his book is his true memorial.

ULYSSES S. GRANT'S FAMILY

Grant had through the male line a number of ancestors with military experience, but on no very great scale. Through the same ancestors he was connected with his Civil War brother-general Don Carlos Buell, but by marriage not blood. In any case this ancestral involvement in military operations can be exaggerated. Any able-bodied New England male with little in the way of property at the time of the Revolutionary War, as Grant's grandfather Noah was, had more or less to fight either for the Americans or the British or flee to some loyalist territory such as Canada. And Lexington, one of only two engagements he is known to have been in, is only called a battle out of courtesy to American patriotism. (Bunker Hill, on the other hand, which Noah also fought at, was of major importance.) The French and Indian War, in which the 18th President's great-grandfather Captain Noah Grant took part, also involved chiefly skirmishes. One might as well argue that Grant was readier than other Union generals to wage a war of bloody attrition against the South because his father had run a slaughterhouse as point to his supposed military ancestry.

Moreover the genealogist-historian who focusses on the undoubted bravery and leadership powers of Grant's ancestors — for instance, his grandfather Noah was a principal mover in organizing the frontiersmen of his time against Indians — must explain away the lack of tenacity which made Grant resign his commission in 1854 and take to subsistence farming and real estate broking. Grant himself claimed he left the army because he could not support his wife and children on service pay, but he found things just as difficult in civilian life. His lack of tenacity as a career officer in peace is all the odder in that he was able to draw on such vast reserves of it in the Civil War. And what of the drinking? For all the cant about 'a drink problem' it is more a problem to the historian than Grant himself since, however much alcohol he may have swallowed, he proved one of the most successful commanders in American history. (A point made obliquely by Lincoln when he enquired what brand of whiskey Grant liked so he could send a barrel to his other generals — a variation on the remark of George II who, when told that General Wolfe was mad, said he hoped Wolfe would bite his other generals.) The historian must also explain how Grant came to take refuge in drink to begin with. Frustration did not arise entirely from lack of a war in which to win glory, for all that Grant later complained how slow promotion was. The truth is that as early as West Point, Grant later recalled, "a military life had no

Plate 53   Julia Dent Grant

charms for me, and I had not the faintest idea of staying in the army even if I should be graduated." In addition he disliked uniform.

The clue probably lies in the advantages a West Point education offered a poor country boy — in this case one who had exchanged farm work for an even more detestable job in his father's tannery. West Point had lifted up Zachary Taylor, after all; it was to do the same with Eisenhower. (Another thing Grant had in common with Eisenhower was an apolitical outlook till just before adoption as the Republican presidential candidate; indeed the only vote Grant cast for President before 1868 was for Buchanan, and as late as the start of that year the Democrats had hopes of making him their presidential candidate.)

As with Andrew Johnson, the Grant family seem to have become poor in the last two generations. Grant's grandfather Noah was "not thrifty in 'laying up stores on earth'", Grant tells us. When Noah's wife died the family split up and their son Jesse, Grant's father, who was only 11, was brought up by a Supreme Court judge. He later worked for and lived with the family of John Brown, of Harper's Ferry fame, but in boyhood had worked as an agricultural labourer. Grant went out to the fields at much the same age and just before the Civil War was reduced to taking a clerical job in the leather goods retail section of his father's tannery. At West Point Grant proved a very good horseman and competent mathematician. How much pleasanter to utilize these skills in cavalry manoeuvres and artillery calculations — though Grant records that what he would really have liked was to use his mathematics in academic life — than tending a pack animal and working out what x pecks of barley would fetch at market.

Grant's initials, U. S., so apt for the defender of the Union, were an afterthought. His original first name, 'Hiram', was that of a remote ancestor on his mother's side, the Simpsons. But the Simpsons were not much interested in family history, though they may have been aware they came from Northern Ireland (and possibly before that from Scotland). At any rate, 'Ulysses' soon elbowed 'Hiram' aside. In some ways that could not have been more inappropriate. The Ulysses of legend is wiliness itself; his 19th-century namesake was blunt, straightforward and so naive about his fellow men that his presidency was one of the most corrupt ever. The Ulysses of legend left his wife and son Telemachus behind when going off to the Trojan War. His 19th-century namesake fought with an 11-year old son in tow and often had Julia with him in camp when besieging a Confederate stronghold. (This was partly because she did not get on with one of Grant's sisters, so could not be left at his father's house.) On the other hand the exotic 'Ulysses' allegedly found favour with the Grant and Simpson families because Jesse Grant and his mother-in-law Rebecca Simpson had been reading the 17th-century French cleric François Fénelon's *Télémaque* (in translation, one imagines). *Télémaque* was virtually a didactic political novel, written to form the mind of the young Duc de Bourgogne, Louis XIV of France's grandson, who at the time was expected to be the next King of France but one. It inculcated the notion that kings exist for the sake of their subjects, not the other way round. It denounced war. It upheld institutions. Grant, substituting only 'Presidents' for 'kings' and specifying the Union (or possibly the Union Army) as the ultimate institution, would have agreed with all that. And Fénelon praised, even if in writing *Télémaque* he failed to practise, what he called Homer's "amiable simplicity". It was Ulysses Grant's salient characteristic too.

Just as with Lincoln's family, embarrassing Confederate connections cropped up. Grant's Simpson aunts were anti-Union and after Lee's surrender Grant was confronted by a Confederate cousin, one of his aunt Rachel's sons. He was luckier than Lincoln in his wife. Julia Boggs Dent, the sister of a fellow officer in the Mexican War and daughter of a slave-owning Missouri planter, was as fond of horses as her husband and both were good riders. Horace Porter, Grant's aide-de-camp during the Civil War and the man who, by then a general, chaired the appeal to raise funds for Grant's tomb, recalled how the Grants used to sit in a corner of his campaign headquarters hand-in-hand of an evening, "a perfect Darby and Joan". She was very popular with Grant's staff as she put the General in a good humour.

Julia was unusual among First Ladies of the time in enjoying the White House. She was lucky in that ostentation was becoming the fashion and she enjoyed dressing up and entertaining. Her parties were not unduly exclusive, except as regards southerners, of whom Washington was still very largely composed, and they stayed away voluntarily out of dislike for the victorious Yankees in general and probably Grant in particular, referring waspishly to the White House as 'Dent's Retreat'. Julia Grant invited the wives of Cabinet officials to join with her in receiving guests, which breached precedent even more than her political interference. At least the interference was frivolous: she urged Hamilton Fish, Secretary of State, to reconsider his resignation so that his wife could continue to help her receive guests. Grant's secretary thought her judgement of people sometimes superior to the President's. It was not difficult to be that, however. It is perhaps more shocking that she should have interfered in his running of the War, demanding for instance that he sack General William S. Rosecrans on one occasion, or that he mount a massed frontal assault on Vicksburg.

She would have loved a third term for her husband and Grant had to work behind her back when scotching an embryonic movement in the Republican Party to secure him one. It may seem odd that it was she who urged her husband to keep their son Fred with him when campaigning during the Civil War, whereas he wanted to send the lad home. She cited the example of Philip of Macedon, who took the future Alexander the Great with him to war. Her grasp of ancient history was better than that of ancient literature, for when the Grants were cruising in the Mediterranean during their European tour after he had stepped down from the presidency, she confused the Isle of Calypso, which an equally ignorant ship's officer claimed to have identified, with that of the Sirens and launched on a whimsical speech about not having to stuff her husband's ears with cotton wool.

Plate 54   Ida Honoré, Mrs Frederick Dent Grant, Ulysses S. Grant's daughter-in-law

Plate 55   Frederick Dent Grant, Ulysses S. Grant's eldest son, Minister to Austria-Hungary 1889-93 and Maj-Gen US Army

Plate 56   Nellie Grant Sartoris Jones, Ulysses S. Grant's only daughter

Plate 57   Ulysses S. Grant Jr, Presidential Elector-at-Large 1904 and 1908

Plate 58   Jesse Grant, Grant's youngest son, author of memoirs about his father, and his 1st wife, Elizabeth Chapman

The Grants were a happy family and it showed. It boosted Grant's enormous personal popularity as President. It may even have saved his life, for the Grants had been invited to the theatre with the Lincolns the night Lincoln was killed but had begged off to visit their children at school in Burlington, New Jersey, though it is also said that Mary Todd Lincoln, jealous as ever, had picked a quarrel with Julia. John A. Creswell, the Post-Master General, noted: "Relations with his family were most delightful and charming. There never was a kinder or more indulgent father, and I never saw a more devoted couple than General and Mrs. Grant." The trouble was, Grant was too indulgent to his children, or, more precisely, too unobservant of what was going on, just as he was with the rascals who swarmed about him as President. The Grants' son Jesse learned as a six-year old to exploit the lengthy receptions and by roaming from one room to another in the White House managed to cram in the equivalent of five or six meals a day. And when Grant allowed his son Ulysses Jr to run his business interests he ended up utterly ruined.

Even by the relaxed standards of the 19th century it was unusually easy to get to meet Grant both as a general and as President. During the Civil War non-combatant sightseers came to gape at him on the battle field, shake his hand and chat. In the White House anyone could gain access to him. He strolled or rode round Washington alone and quite unattended. Julia's family were frequent visitors, her two sisters, Mrs Sharpe and Mrs Casey, as well as her father and brother, becoming Washington residents. Grant's mother never visited Washington, even for her son's Inauguration, but his father Jesse frequently went there, staying in cheap hotels and only calling in at the White House.

Grant's son Fred, who despite rising to the rank of General was always known as 'Colonel', was a fellow New York Police Commissioner of Teddy Roosevelt's, but was duped into opposing the reformist Teddy with every obstructionist weapon in the old guard's armoury. Simplicity of outlook was evidently a Grant family characteristic.

BIOGRAPHICAL DETAILS AND DESCENDANTS

GRANT, (HIRAM) ULYSSES S(IMPSON), *b* Point Pleasant, Clermont Co, Ohio, 27 April 1822; *educ* Maysville Seminary, Ky., Presbyterian Acad, Ripley, Ohio, and West Point; farm worker 1829-39, Brevet 2nd Lt 4th Infy 1843, full 2nd Lt 1845, served Mexican War 1846-48, seeing action at Battles of Palo Alto, Resaca de la Palma and Monterey under Gen (later President) Taylor and at Vera Cruz, Cerro Gordo, Curubusco and Molino del Rey (for meritorious conduct during which he was promoted Brevet 1st Lt) and storming of Chapultepec (for meritorious conduct during which — as reported by Maj (as he then was) Robert E. Lee — Grant was promoted Brevet Capt) under Gen Winfield Scott, full 1st Lt Sept 1847, full Capt 1853, resigned commission 1854, farmer and realtor 1854-60, hardware and leather goods store assist 1860-61; 1861: rejoined US Army April, Col of 21st Illinois Regt June, Offr Cmmdg SE Dist Missouri July, Brig-Gen Aug (effective from previous May), Dist Cdr Cairo, Ill., Sept; 1862: Maj-Gen Volunteers Feb, won (with his kinsman by marriage Gen Buell) Battle of Shiloh April, 2nd-in-Cmmd to Gen Halleck, Union C-in-C, April, Offr Cmmdg Armies of Tennessee and Mississippi July, won Battles of Iuka, Miss., Sept and Corinth, Miss., Oct, Offr Cmmdg Dept of the Tennessee Oct, suffered reverses at Holly Springs, Miss., and Chickasaw Bayou, Miss., Dec; 1863: won Battles of Jackson, Miss., and Champion's Hill, May, received surrender of Vicksburg July, Maj-Gen Regulars July, C-in-C Western Theater Oct, won Battle of Chattanooga Nov; 1864: Offr Cmmdg entire Union land forces and Lt-Gen US Army March, drew (with Robert E. Lee) Battle of the Wilderness May, also unsuccessful candidate for (R) presidential nomination; 1865: received Lee's surrender Appomattox Court House, Va., April; 1866: Lt-Gen March, Gen (Four Star, first since Washington) of the Army July; US Sec of War ad interim 12 Aug 1867-13 Jan 1868, 18th President (R) of the USA 1869-77 (as well as being the R presidential candidate in 1872 President GRANT was the National Working Men's Convention's nominee), unsuccessful candidate for R presidential nomination 1880 (receiving over 300 votes in 36 consecutive ballots), fndr Grant & Ward, stockbrokers, 1881, Gen of the Army 1885, awarded Freedom of City of London (UK), author: *Personal Memoirs of U. S. Grant*, 2 vols (1885-86), *Battle and Leaders of the Civil War*, 4 vols (1887), *General Grant's Letters to a Friend 1861-1880*, ed James Grant Wilson (1897), *Letters of Ulysses S. Grant to his Father and his Youngest Sister, 1857-78*, ed Jesse Grant Cramer (1912) and *The Papers of Ulysses S. Grant, Volume I: 1837-1861*, ed John Y. Simon (1967); *m* St Louis, Mo., 22 Aug 1848 Julia Boggs (*b* White Haven, St Louis, 16 Feb 1826; author:*The Personal Memoirs of Julia Dent Grant*, ed John Y. Simon (1975); *d* Washington, DC, 14 Dec 1902, *bur* with her husband), est dau of Col Frederick Dent and his w Ellen Bray Wrenshall, and d Mount McGregor, New York, 23 July 1885 of throat cancer (bur Grant's Tomb, Riverside Park, New York), having had issue:

President Grant's son

I Frederick Dent GRANT, b St Louis 30 May 1850; educ West Point; ADC to Gen Philip Sheridan 1873-81, resigned commission after attaining rank of Lt-Col 1881, US Min to Austria-Hungary 1889-93, Police Commissioner New York City 1894-98, Brig-Gen Vols Spanish-American War 1898 then in Philippines, Brig-Gen Regular Army 1901, Maj-Gen 1906; m Chicago 20 Oct 1874 Ida Marie (b Louisville, Ky., 4 June 1854; d Washington, DC, 1930), dau of Henry Hamilton Honoré, of Chicago, and his w Elizabeth Carr, and d New York 11 April 1912, leaving issue:

Grandchildren

1 Julia GRANT, b the White House 7 June 1876; m Newport, Rhode Island, 25 Sept 1899 (divorce 1934) Maj-Gen Prince Michael Michaelovitch CANTACUZENE, 2nd Count SPERANSKY (b Odessa, Russia 29 April (Old Style) 1875; educ Cavalry Sch; succeeded father 25 March 1894, Col Horse Gds Regt, Ch of Staff to HIH Grand Duke Nicholas of Russia when latter C-in-C Russian Armies; d Sarasota, Fla., 25 March 1955), est s of Prince Michael Cantacuzene, 1st Count Speransky, allegedly descended from the Emperor JOHN VI of Constantinople (a descent which has been questioned in our own time but which was recognized as regards Sherban Cantacuzene, undoubted ancestor of Prince Michael mentioned above, by the Holy Roman Emperor LEOPOLD I shortly after the unsuccessful Turkish siege of Vienna in 1683), and his w Elisabeth Sicard, and d Washington, DC, 4 Oct 1975, having had issue:

Great-grandchildren

(1) Prince Michael CANTACUZENE, Count SPERANSKY, b St Petersburg, Russia, 21 July 1900; Chicago real estate executive; m 1st Nahant, Mass., 26 June 1921 (divorce 1935) Clarissa (b Boston 27 Nov 1899; d New York 30 Aug 1939), dau of Thomas Pelham Curtis and his w Frances Kellogg Small, and had issue:

Great-great-grandchildren

1a (Princess) Irina Cantacuzene (did not use the title), b Chicago 30 Dec 1925; m Wadsworth, Ill., 5 Oct 1945, as his 2nd w, Douglas ERICKSON (b Swampscott, Mass., 24 July 1915; m 1st Cohasset, Mass., 6 June 1942 Anne Whipple (divorce 1943); m 3rd 11 Nov 1990 Irene Harkins Hutchinson and d 18 Jan 1993), s of A. Wentworth Erickson and his w Cecile Macy, and d 12 Oct 1984, leaving issue:

Great-great-grandchildren's children

1b *Douglas Mihail ERICKSON [2 Elliot St, Thomaston, ME 04861, USA], b Santa Barbara, Calif., 29 June 1946; educ Miami-Dade Jr Coll and Hiram Scott Coll; real estate broker, manager and investor, fndr SoundVest Properties Inc (brokerage firm) 1992; m Montreal, Canada, 14 June 1969 *Pauline Janet (b Grandmere, Quebec, Canada, 17 Dec 1948), dau of James Stephen Oppé and his w Isabel Morgan, and has issue:

Great-great-grandchildren's grandchildren
1c *Irina ERICKSON, b Miami 17 Nov 1971
2c *Douglas Oppé ERICKSON, b Miami 14 March 1974; educ U of Southern Maine
3c *Ian Cantacuzene ERICKSON, b Miami 11 July 1976

Great-great-grandchildren's children

2b *Irina Erickson [Baroness Alexander von Korff, Schlipperhaus Weg 73, 4030 Ratingen 6, Germany], b Nassau, Bahamas, 30 Oct 1948; educ Everglades Sch and Western Coll; m Coconut Grove, Fla., 26 June 1971 *Baron Alexander von KORFF (b Madrid, Spain, 16 Nov 1946), s of Baron Arnt von Korff and his w Baroness Irina von Korff, and has issue:

Great-great-grandchildren's grandchildren
1c *Baron Alexei von KORFF, b Vienna, Austria, 25 Dec 1973
2c *Baron Sandro von KORFF, b Cologne, West Germany, 29 Oct 1975
3c *Baron Nicholas von KORFF, b Düsseldorf, West Germany, 2 Jan 1978

Great-great-grandchildren's children

3b *Michael Stråle ERICKSON [4 Rossi Ave, San Francisco, CA 94118-4218, USA], b Nassau 3 Feb 1952; educ Harvard (AB 1974) and Stanford Graduate Sch of Business (MBA 1977); entrepreneur and investor; m Miami 25 March 1984 *Wendy (b Boston 14 Oct 1959), dau of Stephen Sonnabend and his w Nancy Lelewer, and has issue:

Great-great-grandchildren's grandchildren
1c *Kelly Sonnabend ERICKSON, b San Francisco 14 Jan 1989
2c *Brett Lelewer ERICKSON, b San Francisco 22 April 1991

Great-great-grandchildren

2a *(Prince) Rodion CANTACUZENE (does not use title) [Capt Rodion Cantacuzene, USN (ret), 100 Timberlake Rd, Royal, AR 71968, USA], b Chicago 22 Oct 1928; educ US Naval Acad Annapolis; career offr US Navy, administrator Hillwood Museum, Washington, DC; m Ellicott City, Md., 24 Sept 1960 *Melissa (b New York 1 Feb 1939), dau of Merrill Macneille and his w Adelaide Close, and has issue:

Great-great-grandchildren's children

1b *Michael CANTACUZENE [Landfall Farm, Rte 1 Box 17, Aldie, VA 22001, USA], b Washington, DC, 12 July 1961; educ U of Virginia (AB 1981) and U of Southern California (MBA 1986); investor 1988-91, with Peace Corps

Botswana 1991-93

2b *Rodion CANTACUZENE [Suite 210, 203 W Wall St, Midland, TX 79701, USA], b Washington, DC, 7 Aug 1963; educ U of Texas at Lubbock (AB 1983, JD 1986); lawyer, co-fndr Cook & Cantacuzene, attys; m Midland, Tex., 25 May 1992 *Elizabeth Wolfe

3b *Clarissa Cantacuzene [Mrs Luis Echezarreta, Landfall Farm, Rte 1 Box 17, Aldie, VA 22001, USA], b Washington, DC, 6 Dec 1965; educ U of Virginia (AB 1985); professional polo-player and polo pony trainer; m Aldie, Va., 23 Nov 1991 *Luis ECHEZARRETA

Great-grandchildren

(1) Prince Michael Cantacuzene m 2nd Libertyville, Ill., 18 Oct 1941 Florence Bushnell Carr (b 12 Oct 189; d 5 July 1961); m 3rd Chicago 1971 Florence Clarke Hale (b 1899; d 1985) and d Lake Forest, Ill., 25 Dec 1972

(2) *Princess Barbara (Bertha) Cantacuzene [Mrs W D Siebern, 2707 Riedling Drive, Apt 2, Louisville, KY 40206, USA; 521 Zorn Ave., Louisville, KY 40206, USA], b St Petersburg, Russia, 27 March 1904; m 1st Washington, DC, 10 Oct 1926 (divorce 1933) Bruce SMITH (b Louisville 3 March 1901; d there 4 Oct 1942) and has issue:

Great-great-grandchildren

1a *Bruce Michael SMITH [620 Lucas Lane, Louisville, KY 40213, USA; 403 Wendover Avenue, Louisville, KY 40207, USA], b Louisville 7 Feb 1932; educ Yale (BS 1953) and Harvard Business Sch; 1st Lt USAF 1954-56, Sales Manager Louisville Paper Co 1956-69 (Pres 1969-72 and Pres and Chief Exec Offr from 1972); m Rockford, Ill., 18 June 1953 Dorothy Diane (b Geneva, Ill., 22 Dec 1932), dau of Robert Decker Frick and his w Dorothy May McConnell, and has issue:

Great-great-grandchildren's children

1b *Julia Elise SMITH, b Dayton, Ohio, 11 May 1955

2b *Mary Bruce SMITH, b Louisville 25 May 1957

3b *Barbara Grant SMITH, b Louisville 7 Jan 1959

4b *Bruce Michael SMITH, b Louisville 26 Aug 1961

Great-grandchildren

(2) (cont.) Mrs Barbara Smith m 2nd New Albany, Ind., 11 Nov 1934 William Durrell SIEBERN (b Cincinnati, Ohio, 28 Nov 1894; d Louisville, Ky., 6 Jan 1973), s of John Siebern and his w Orietta Durrell

(3) Princess Zenaida Cantacuzene, b St Petersburg, Russia, 17 Nov 1908; m Washington, DC, 1 Nov 1928 Sir John Coldbrook HANBURY-WILLIAMS, CVO (b Henley-on-Thames, UK, 28 May 1892; Gentleman Usher to King GEORGE V of Great Britain and Ireland, Emperor of India etc 1931, EDWARD VIII 1936, GEORGE VI 1937-46 (Extra Gentleman Usher 1946-52) and Queen ELIZABETH II 1952-65, Dir Bank of England 1936-63, one of HM's Lts for London 1936-65, High Sheriff of the County of London 1943 and 1958, Chm Courtaulds 1946-62; d London 10 Aug 1965), yr s of late Maj-Gen Sir John Hanbury-Williams, GCVO, KCB, CMG, Marshal of the Diplomatic Corps, and his w Annie Reiss, and d 17 Sept 1980, leaving issue:

Great-great-grandchildren

1a *Barbara Hanbury-Williams [Mrs James Edwards, Long Sutton House, Long Sutton, Langport, Somerset TA10 9LZ, UK], b London 6 Dec 1929; m 1st London 26 Jan 1950 (divorce 1963) her 1st cousin once-removed Prince Michael CANTACUZENE, Count SPERANSKY (b Poltava, Russia, 12 Oct 1913), only s of Prince Serge Cantacuzene, Count Speransky (yst brother of Maj-Gen Prince Michael Cantacuzene, for whom see above) and his w Marie Okoliszanyi, and has issue:

Great-great-grandchildren's children

1b *Prince Serge Michel CANTACUZENE, Count SPERANSKY [Dorking Tye House, Dorking Tye, nr Bures, Suffolk CO5 5JY, UK], b Paris, France, 13 May 1952; educ Harrow and U of N Carolina; coffee and commodity broker; m Eynsham Park, Oxon, UK, 26 July 1975 *Mary Jacqueline (b there 9 Dec 1952), dau of Capt Michael Henry Mason, RN, and his w Dorothy Margaret Sturdee, and has issue:

Great-great-grandchildren's grandchildren

1c *Prince Rodion Michael CANTACUZENE-SPERANSKY, b Colchester, UK, 22 June 1979

2c *Prince Alexei Peter CANTACUZENE-SPERANSKY, b Colchester 25 Feb 1981

3c *Princess Elizabeth (Erzsi) Irina CANTACUZENE-SPERANSKY, b Colchester 5 Sept 1984

Great-great-grandchildren's children

2b *Princess Alexandra Elizabeth Cantacuzene-Speransky [The Hon Mrs George Plumptre, The White House, Woodchurch, Ashford, Kent, UK], b London, UK, 16 June 1956; m 1st Ascot, UK, 6 Sept 1977 Capt Larry H. ROBERTSON, Irish Guards, yst s of Capt Ian Greig Robertson, of Forneth, Blairgowrie, Perthshire, Scotland, and his w Elizabeth Marion Aitken; m 2nd 1984 *Hon (Wyndham) George PLUMPTRE (b 24 April 1956), 3rd s of 21st Baron Fitzwalter (see BURKE'S PEERAGE & BARONETAGE) and his w Margaret Deedes, and with him has issue:

Great-great-grandchildren's grandchildren

1c *Wyndham James Alexander PLUMPTRE, b UK 14 March 1986

2c *Piers Harry Constantine PLUMPTRE, b UK 7 Nov 1987

3c *Hermione Amy Kathrine PLUMPTRE, b UK 26 Nov 1991

Great-great-grandchildren

1a (cont.) Barbara Cantacuzene-Speransky, *née* Hanbury-Williams, *m* 2nd London 31 July 1965 *James Valentine EDWARDS, CVO (*b* Bryn Arthur, St Asaph, Wales 4 Feb 1925; preparatory sch headmaster), yst s of late Capt Alfred Harold Edwards, OBE, and his w Eleanor Hayes, and has further issue:

Great-great-grandchildren's children
3b *Caroline Antonia EDWARDS, *b* Ascot 1 June 1966
4b *Charlotte Eleanor Marina EDWARDS, *b* Windsor 12 Sept 1968

Great-great-grandchildren

2a *Elizabeth Frances Hanbury-Williams [5 Pleasant St, Nantucket, MA 02554, USA], *b* London 6 Dec 1929; *m* 1st St James's, Spanish Place, London 24 July 1951 (divorce 1968) Brian Patrick Morgan KEELING (*b* London 10 July 1927 22 April 1990), 3rd and yst s of Sir John Henry Keeling, of Hurst House, Sedlescombe, Sussex, UK, and his w Dorothy May Finucane, and has issue:

Great-great-grandchildren's children

1b *Sara Elizabeth Keeling [Broad Farm, Salhouse, Norwich, Norfolk NR13 6HE, UK], *b* London 6 July 1954; *educ* Woldingham; teacher; *m* London 6 Feb 1982 *Henry Greville CATOR (*b* 26 March 1956), yr s of John Cator (himself gs through his mother of Sir George Cayley, 9th Bart, *see* BURKE'S PEERAGE & BARONETAGE) and his 1st w Elizabeth Kerrison (who *m* 2nd, as his 3rd w, Col Sir Robert Adeane, OBE, JP, and *d* 16 Nov 1992), and has issue:

Great-great-grandchildren's grandchildren
1c *Henrietta Elizabeth Anne CATOR, *b* Norwich 10 Oct 1983
2c Charlotte Lucinda CATOR, *b* Norwich 18 Oct 1985; *d* 6 March 1986
3c *Sabrina Mary CATOR, *b* Norwich 16 Jan 1987
4c *Thomas James CATOR, *b* Norwich 14 Oct 1989

Great-great-grandchildren's children
2b *Patrick James KEELING [27 Pembridge Sq, London W2 4DJ, UK], *b* London 31 May 1956; *educ* Eton and Buckingham U; banker

Great-great-grandchildren

2a (cont.) Mrs Elizabeth Keeling *m* 2nd London 6 June 1972 *John Grinnell Wetmore HUSTED (*b* 22 June 1926), er s of John Grinell Wetmore Husted, of David's Brook, Bedford, New York, and his w Helen Armstrong

3a *John Michael Anthony HANBURY-WILLIAMS [Huxley Lane Farm, nr Chester, Cheshire, UK], *b* London 7 July 1933; *educ* Eton; late 2nd Lt Green Howards, T/Capt Oxfordshire & Buckinghamshire Light Infantry, with Allied Provincial Securities Ltd, Manchester; *m* London 4 April 1956 *Diane (*b* London 28 Aug 1936), dau of Lister Hartley and his w Lucila D'Alkaine, and has issue:

Great-great-grandchildren's children
1b *Nicholas John HANBURY-WILLIAMS [51 Grove Park Rd, London W4 3RU, UK], *b* London 1 Jan 1957; *educ* Eton; *m* and has issue
2b *Charles Lister HANBURY-WILLIAMS, *b* London 18 Nov 1958; *educ* Eton; *m* and has issue
3b *Michael Anthony HANBURY-WILLIAMS, *b* London 28 June 1961; *educ* Eton; *m* and has issue
4b *Victoria Mary HANBURY-WILLIAMS, *b* Tarporley, Cheshire, UK, 27 Oct 1967

Grandchildren

2 Ulysses S. GRANT III, of Clinton, New York, *b* nr Chicago 4 July 1881; *educ* Theresianum, Vienna, Cutler Sch, New York City, Columbia U and West Point; served with US Army from 1903 (Col 1917-20 and Corps of Engrs 1934, T/Major-Gen 1943), awarded DSM and US Legion of Merit, also decorations of six foreign countries; *m* Washington, DC, 27 Nov 1907 Edith (*b* New York 1 Dec 1878; *d* Clinton, New York, 23 May 1962), only dau of Hon Elihu Root, US Sec of State, and his w Clara Frances Wales, and *d* Clinton 29 Aug 1968, leaving issue:

Great-grandchildren

(1) *Edith Grant [Mrs David Griffiths, 3016 N Pollard Street, Arlington, VA 22207, USA], *b* Clinton 9 Sept 1908; *educ* Bryn Mawr (AB, MA); *m* Governors Island, New York, 21 Nov 1936, as his 2nd w, Col David Wood GRIFFITHS (*b* Austin, Ill., 5 Nov 1896; served US Army; *d* Arlington, Va., 14 Feb 1967) and has issue:

Great-great-grandchildren

1a *John Grant GRIFFITHS [3016 N Pollard Street, Arlington, VA 22207, USA], *b* Little Rock, Ark., 15 July 1938; *educ* U of Iowa; with US Dept of Agriculture
2a *Frances Elizabeth GRIFFITHS [220 East 87th Street, New York, NY 10028, USA], *b* Galveston, Tex., 29 April 1941; *educ* Smith Coll (AB)
3a *Nancy Root Griffiths [Mrs Brian Price, No 5, 3801 Milan Drive, Alexandria, VA 22305, USA], *b* Galveston 5 Dec 1946; *educ* Beloit Coll (AB); *m* Clinton 6 Sept 1969 *Brian H. PRICE (*b* 19 Feb 1947)

Great-grandchildren

(2) Clara Frances Grant, *b* Clinton 4 Sept 1912; *educ* Bryn Mawr (AB); *m* Belmore, New York, 18 May 1935 *Maj-Gen Paul Ernest RUESTOW, USAF (ret) (*b* Rockville Center, New York, 29 Dec 1908), s of Ernest W. Ruestow and his w Louella Kiermaier, and has issue:

Great-great-grandchildren
1a *George Frederick RUESTOW [313 Rigby Road, Fairborn, OH 45324, USA], b San Antonio, Tex., 14 Jan 1936; educ U of Dayton (AB) and Auburn U (MA); m Dayton, Ohio, 12 June 1965 *Juanita Marie (b Minster, Ohio, Oct 1943), dau of Norbert Meyer and his w Wilma, and has issue:

Great-great-grandchildren's children
1b *Tanya René RUESTOW, b Alexandria, Va., 25 April 1966
2b *Kristin Marie RUESTOW, b Dayton 9 Dec 1967
3b *Kendra Frances RUESTOW, b Dayton 23 June 1969

Great-great-grandchildren
2a *Edward Grant RUESTOW [320 S 40th Street, Boulder, CO 80303, USA], b Honolulu, Hawaii, 30 Sept 1937; educ Pennsylvania (AB, MA), George Washington (MA) and Indiana Us (PhD); Assist Prof History U of Colorado; m Boulder 25 June 1973 *Carmen Gutierrez (b Longmont, Colo.)
3a *Claire Ruestow [Mrs George Telecki, 377 N Broadway, Yonkers, NY 10701, USA], b Utica, New York, 19 April 1945; educ Vassar (AB); m Clinton 2 May 1970 *George J. TELECKI (b Yugoslavia 26 May 1933), s of Joseph Telecki and his w Meta von Riesenfelder, and has issue:

Great-great-grandchildren's children
1b *Nicole TELECKI, b New York 23 June 1971

Great-grandchildren
(3) *Julia Grant [Mrs John Dietz, 402 Sedgwick Drive, Syracuse, NY 13203, USA], b New York 20 Jan 1916; m Clinton, New York, 18 Aug 1945 *John Sanderson DIETZ (b Albuquerque, N. Mex., 6 Aug 1919), s of Robert E. Dietz and his w Barbara, and has had issue:

Great-great-grandchildren
1a *John Edwin DIETZ [509 N Columbia Street, Chapel Hill, NC 27516, USA], b Syracuse, New York, 4 Jan 1948; educ U of N Carolina (AB); m Chapel Hill 29 June 1974 *Julia McMillan
2a Edith Root DIETZ, b Syracuse 25 Dec 1951; educ Stanford U; d New York 20 Oct 1971
3a *Ulysses Grant DIETZ, b Syracuse 22 July 1955; educ Yale
4a Edward Johnson DIETZ, b Syracuse 7 Aug 1956; d 17 June 1969

President Grant's son
II Ulysses S. GRANT, Jr, of San Diego, Calif., b Bethel, Clermont Co, Ohio, 22 July 1852; educ Harvard (AB 1874) and Columbia U (LLB 1876); admitted to Bar 1876, candidate for US Senate 1899, Delegate-at-Large Republican Nat Conventions 1896 and 1900, Presidential Elector-at-Large 1904 and 1908; m 1st New York 1 Nov 1880 (Fannie) Josephine (b Adrian, Mich., 16 Jan 1857; d San Diego 10 Nov 1909), yr dau of Jerome Bunty Chaffee, US Senator from Colorado, and his w Miriam Barnard Comstock, and had issue:

Grandchildren
1 Miriam Grant, b New York 26 Sept 1881; m 1st there 17 Oct 1904 Adml Ulysses Samuel MACY, USN, and had issue:

Great-grandchildren
(1) *Fannie Chaffee Grant Macy, b Salem Center, New York, 18 Oct 1905; m 1st 12 Sept 1932 William Jennings WALLACE and has issue:

Great-great-grandchildren
1a *Susan Grant WALLACE, b 11 July 1933
2a *Miriam WALLACE, b 21 May 1937

Great-grandchildren
(1) (cont.) Mrs Fannie Macy Wallace m 2nd *Edward C. HASSET
(2) Grant MACY; d in infancy

Grandchildren
1 (cont.) Mrs Miriam Grant Macy m 2nd John RICE
2 Chaffee GRANT, b New York 28 Sept 1883; m 1st Washington, Pa., 5 June 1907 (divorce 19—), as her 1st husb, Helen Dent (Nellie) Wrenshall (m 2nd Isaac Hart Purdy, former husb of her sister-in-law Fannie Grant, for whom see below) and had issue:

Great-grandchildren
(1) *Jane Grant, b 22 March 1908; m 1st 1930 Martin SMITH and has issue:

Great-great-grandchildren
1a *Peter Martin SMITH

Great-grandchildren
(1) (cont.) Mrs Jane Grant Smith m 2nd 1943 *Cormac de McCARTY and has further issue:

Great-great-grandchildren
2a *Grant Cormac McCARTY
3a *Dent Laurent McCARTY

Great-grandchildren
(2) Jerome Chaffee GRANT, b Aug 1913; m 1943 *Elizabeth Wurster and d Salem Center, New York, 1949

Grandchildren
2 (cont.) Chaffee Grant m 2nd Mrs Marion Potter, née Farnsworth
3 Julia Dent Grant, b New York 15 April 1885; m 8 Oct 1910 Edmund Cathcart KING and had issue:

Great-grandchildren
(1) *Fannie Chaffee King, b 23 July 1912; m 1 Jan 1948 *Henry CASTLETON and has issue:

Great-great-grandchildren
1a *Julia Dent CASTLETON, b 27 Jan 1949

Great-grandchildren
(2) *Grant KING, b 15 Nov 1913; m 4 March 1950 *Mary Lee and has issue:

Great-great-grandchildren
1a *Edmund Lee KING, b 7 Jan 1951
2a *Jessica Mary KING, b 10 Oct 1952
3a *Julia Eunice KING, b 10 Oct 1952

Great-grandchildren
(3) *Julia Dent King, b 7 Oct 1917; m Aug 1945 *William J. WATSON and has issue:

Great-great-grandchildren
1a *Stephen Lockeridge WATSON, b 6 May 1946
2a *Kirk William WATSON, b 20 Oct 1949
3a *Fannie Grant WATSON, b 20 June 1951

Grandchildren
4 Fannie Grant, b Salem Center, New York, 11 Aug 1889; m 16 Oct 1911 (divorce 19—) Isaac Hart PURDY (b 1887; m 2nd Helen Dent Wrenshall, for whom see above; d Salem Center 13 May 1956) and d 1943, leaving issue:

Great-grandchildren
(1) *Isaac Grant PURDY, b 1914

Grandchildren
5 Ulysses S. GRANT IV, b Salem Center 23 May 1893; Prof Geology U of Los Angeles; m 1st Oct 1917 (divorce 19—) Matilda Bartikofsky; m 2nd Frances Dean

President Grant's children
II (cont.) Ulysses S. Grant, Jr, m 2nd 1913 Mrs America Will, née Workman (b Santa Barbara, Calif., 1881; d San Diego 29 Oct 1942), and d San Diego 26 Sept 1929
III Ellen (Nellie) Wrenshall Grant, b Wish-ton-wish 4 July 1855; m 1st the White House, Washington, DC, 21 May 1874 Algernon Charles Frederick SARTORIS, JP Carmarthenshire, of Warsash House, Titchfield, Hants, UK (b London 1 Aug 1851; d Capri, Italy, 3 Feb 1893), yr s of Edward John Sartoris, JP, of Warnford Park, Bishops Waltham, Hants, UK, and his w Adelaide Kemble, singer, authoress of *Week in a French Country House* (1867) and *Medusa and Other Tales* (1868) and member of the theatrical family of Kemble which in her own generation included her sister the actress Fanny Kemble and a generation earlier her aunt Sarah Siddons, and had issue:

Grandchildren
1 Grant Greville Edward SARTORIS, b Elberon, New Jersey, 11 July 1875; d Titchfield, Hants, UK, 21 May 1876
2 Algernon Edward Urban SARTORIS, b Washington, DC, 17 March 1877; Capt US Volunteers Spanish-American War 1898; m Paris, France, 1904 Cécile Noufflard and d 17 Jan 1928, leaving issue:

Great-grandchildren
(1) *Herbert Charles Urban Grant SARTORIS, b Paris 17 Aug 1906; m 6 April 1929 *Alix Jeuffrain (b 1906) and has had issue:

Great-great-grandchildren
1a *Oliver Algernon SARTORIS, b 24 March 1930
2a *François Charles Henry SARTORIS, b 19 Nov 1931
3a Guy SARTORIS, b 3 Dec 1932; d 3 April 1933
4a *Claude SARTORIS, b 7 Sept 1934
5a *Jean Philippe SARTORIS, b 3 Nov 1937
6a *Antoine Greville SARTORIS, b 13 July 1944
7a *Anne SARTORIS, b 21 Jan 1947

Grandchildren
3 Vivien May Sartoris, b London, UK, 7 April 1879; m 1903 Frederick Roosevelt SCOVEL, of New York (d 27 July 1930), and d Dec 1933
4 Rosemary Alice Sartoris, b London 30 Nov 1880; m 29 Oct 1906 George Henry WOOLSTON, of Florida (b 1869; d 27 Jan 1930), and d 28 Aug 1914, leaving issue:

Great-grandchildren
(1) *Rosemary WOOLSTON, b 17 Jan 1909

President Grant's children
III (cont.) Mrs Nellie Grant Sartoris m 2nd 4 July 1912 Frank Hatch JONES, of Chicago, Assist US Postmaster-Gen, and d Chicago 30 Aug 1922
IV Jesse Root GRANT, of Sausalito, Calif., b Hardscrabble 6 Feb 1858; educ Cornell and Columbia Law Sch; author: *In the Days of My Father General Grant* (1925); m 1st San Francisco 30 Sept 1880 (divorce 18— or 19—) Elizabeth (b Minneapolis, Minn., 10 Jan 1858; d San Diego 28 Feb 1945), dau of William Smith Chapman and his w Sarah Armstrong, and had issue:

Grandchildren
1 Nellie Grant, b Elberon, New Jersey, 5 Aug 1881; m 15 May 1913 Capt William Piggott CRONAN, USN (b 9 Feb 1879; d 18 March 1929), and d La Jolla, Calif., June 1872, leaving issue:

Great-grandchildren
(1) *Elizabeth Grant Cronan, b 8 May 1915; m 21 April 1943 (divorce 19—) Donald Halliday WALLER, Jr (b 1915), s of Donald Halliday Waller, and has issue:

Great-great-grandchildren
1a *Marie WALLER, b 6 June 1945
2a *Carolyn WALLER, b 15 Aug 1946

Great-grandchildren
(2) *Nellie Grant Cronan, b 24 Feb 1917; m 13 Dec 1941 *Col Franklin D. ROTHWELL, US Army (b 9 May 1910), and has issue:

Great-great-grandchildren
1a *Theresa Lauren ROTHWELL, b 15 Aug 1944

Grandchildren
2 Chapman GRANT, b Salem Center, New York, 22 March 1887; educ Williams Coll (AB 1910); Maj US Army; m 21 Nov 1917 Mabel Glenn Ward (b 11 Feb 1892) and d 19—, having had issue:

Great-grandchildren
(1) *Mabel Chapman Grant, b 24 Aug 1918; m *Bruce R. HAZARD (b 1 Nov 1917) and has issue:

Great-great-grandchildren
1a *Terry Grant HAZARD, b 11 Jan 1943
2a *Polly Boulton HAZARD, b 19 April 1945
3a *Thomas Bruce HAZARD, b 16 Dec 1947

Great-grandchildren
(2) *Ulysses S. GRANT V, b 21 Sept 1920; m 5 March 1944 *Dorothy Jean Nichols and has issue:

Great-great-grandchildren
1a *Chapman Foster GRANT, b 15 Feb 1945
2a *Millard Ward GRANT, b 7 July 1948
3a *Bonnie Jean GRANT, b 22 May 1951

President Grant's son
IV (cont.) Jesse R. Grant m 2nd 26 Aug 1918 Lillian (b nr Warwick, Md., 1864; d New York 1 July 1924), widow of John Anthony Wilkins and only dau of Capt Owen Burns, USN, of Burnsville, N Carolina, and his w Martha Ann Armstrong, and d Los Altos, Calif., 8 June 1934

MALE LINE ANCESTRY AND COLLATERAL DESCENDANTS

Matthew GRANT, b 27 Oct 1601; said in some accounts to have been of Scots ancestry, but emigrated to America from Plymouth, Devon, in southwest England, 20 March 1630, disembarking at Nantasket, on the southern shore of Massachusetts Bay, 30 May 1630, rather than Boston, where the Captain of the ship *Mary and John*, in which the emigrants were voyaging, had agreed to take his passengers; this provoked a suit against him on the part of the said passengers, allegedly organized by Matthew Grant, who settled first at Matapan (later Dorchester), Mass., where became a Freeman by 18 May 1631, then c 1635 the Connecticut Valley (site of the subsequent Windsor, Conn.), where served as Town Clerk 1652-77, also Surveyor and Recorder; m 1st in England 16 Nov 1625 Priscilla —— (b 27 1601; d Windsor, Conn., 27 April 1644) and had six children — five s and one dau — one of whom may have predeceased her; m 2nd 29 May 1645 Susanna (b 5 April 1602; d 14 Nov 1666), widow of William Rockwell, by whom she is said to have had eight children, and dau of Bernard Capen, and d Windsor 16 Dec 1681, leaving (with other issue by his 1st w):

I Samuel GRANT, for whom *see below*
II John GRANT, the yst s, in the midst of whose family Matthew Grant died

The er of these two s,

Samuel GRANT, b Dorchester, Mass., 12 Nov 1631; m 27 May 1656 Mary (b England c 1638), dau of John Porter (1594-1648), of Felsted, Essex, England, and his w Ann White (1600-48), of Messing, Essex, and sister (a) of Samuel Porter (d 1689), whose ggdau Susannah m Aaron Cleveland, ggf of President CLEVELAND, also sister (b) of Sarah Porter, ancestress of President FORD; Samuel Grant d Windsor, Conn., 10 Sept 1718, having had issue (with four yr s and three daus):

Samuel GRANT, Jr, b Windsor 20 April 1659; m 1st 6 Dec 1683 Anna Filley (1644-86) and with her had one dau; m 2nd Windsor 11 April 1688 Grace (b Stratford, Conn., 20 Sept 1670; d 16 April 1753), dau of Capt John Miner (1635-1719) and his w Elizabeth Booth, and d 8 May 1710, having with his 2nd w had issue (together with four other s and three other daus) a 2nd s:

Noah GRANT, b Windsor 11 Dec 1693; m Tolland, Conn., 20 June 1717 Martha (b Norwich, Conn., 6 Dec 1696; m 2nd 7 Jan 1728/9 Capt Peter Buell; d Tolland probably 26 Aug 1779), dau of John Huntington (whose uncle Simon Huntington was ancestor of President FRANKLIN D. ROOSEVELT) and John Huntington's w Abigail Lathrop (whose bro Samuel was ancestor of President FRANKLIN D. ROOSEVELT and whose uncle Thomas Lathrop was ancestor of President BUSH), and d Tolland 10 Oct 1727, leaving (with a yst s and one dau):

I Noah GRANT, for whom *see below*
II Solomon GRANT; officer with his bro in French and Indian War of 1755; k on active service at the same time as his bro 1756

The er (?) s,

Capt Noah GRANT, Jr, b Tolland 12 July 1719; settled at Grant's Hill, Conn., Lt Capt Rodger's Scouts, saw action at the Battle of Lake George, New York State, 8 Sept 1755, Capt 7th Co, 2nd Connecticut Regt, 1756; m Tolland 5 Nov 1746, as her 1st husb, Susanna (b there 23 June 1724; d Coventry, Conn., perhaps 16 Aug 1806), 5th and yst dau of Jonathan Delano, Jr (1680-1752), whose yr bro Thomas was gggf of Sara Delano, mother of President FRANKLIN D. ROOSEVELT, and Jonathan Delano's w Amy Hatch (1684-1762), and was k in the French and Indian War 20 Sept 1756, leaving (with a yr s):

Capt Noah GRANT III, b Tolland 20 June 1748; offr Continental Army Revy War, fought at Battles of Lexington (19 April 1775) and Bunker Hill (17 June 1775), settled in Westmoreland Co, Pa., 1790 and in Ohio c 1799; m 1st Anna (d c 1787, though she is also said to have d while her husb was still serving in the army during the Revy War), widow of —— Richardson and dau of —— Buell, and had two s; m 2nd Greensburg, Westmoreland Co, Pa., 4 March 1792, Rachel (d Deerfield, now Maysville, Ohio, 10 April 1805), widow of —— Kelley and dau of —— Miller, and d Maysville, Ky., 14 Feb 1819, having with her had issue (together with three er daus and two yr s):

I Jesse Root GRANT, for whom *see below*
II A son; m and had issue:

1 Lawson Grant, proved by his uncle Jesse to be the heir to an entailed estate in Windsor, Conn.

The eldest s,

Jesse Root GRANT, b Greensburg, Pa., 23 Jan 1794; tanner and farmer, of Georgetown, Brown Co, Ohio; m Point Pleasant, Ohio 24 June 1820 or 1821 Hannah (b Horsham, Pa., 23 Nov 1798; d Jersey City, New Jersey, 11 May 1883), dau of John Simpson (c 1767-1837) and his 1st w Rebecca Weir (b c 1801-02), and d Covington, Ky., 29 June 1873, having had issue:

I ULYSSES S. GRANT, 18th PRESIDENT of the UNITED STATES of AMERICA
II Samuel Simpson GRANT, of Galena, Ill., b Georgetown, Ohio, 23 Sept 1825; merchant; d St Paul, Minn., 13 Sept 1861
III Clara Rachel GRANT, b Georgetown 11 Dec 1828; d Covington, Ky., 6 March 1865
IV Virginia Paine Grant, b Georgetown 20 Feb 1832; m Covington 13 May 1869, as his 2nd w, Hon Abel Rathbone CORBIN, of New York (b Otsego, New York, 24 March 1808; d 1881), s of Eliakim Lyon Corbin and his w Lodama, and d 28 March 1881, having had a dau (d in infancy)
V Orvil Lynch GRANT, b Georgetown 15 May 1835; m Bethel, Ohio, April 1857 Mary (b 1835; d 10 April 1894), dau of Asher Medary and his w Elizabeth Thornton, and d Elizabeth, New Jersey, 4 or 5 Aug 1881, leaving three s and one dau
VI Mary Frances Grant, b Georgetown 28 July 1839; m Covington 27 Oct 1863 Revd Michael John Cramer, DD (b Schaffhausen, Switzerland, 6 Feb 1835; US Min to Denmark 1871-81, Resident US Min and Consul-Gen Berne, Switzerland, 1881-85; d Carlisle, Pa., 23 Jan 1898), s of John Jacob Cramer and his w Magdalene Bowman, and d 23 Jan 1898, having had a s and dau

Great-great-great-great grandparents on the father's side   *Great-great-great-great grandparents on the mother's side*

Samuel Grant[1]
1631-1718

Mary Porter[2]
b c 1638

Samuel Grant, Jr
1659-1710

John Miner
c 1635-1719

Grace Miner
1670-1753

Elizabeth Booth
1641-1732

Christopher Huntington
c 1626-91

Ruth Rockwell
b 1633

John Huntington
1666—1695-1703

Samuel Lathrop
c 1622-1700

Abigail Lathrop
b 1665

Elizabeth Scudder
d a 1690

Philip Delano/
de Lannoy
c 1603-c 1681

Hester/Esther
Dewsbury

Jonathan Delano
c 1648-1720

Mercy Warren
1658-p 1727

Nathaniel Warren
c 1624/5-67

Sarah Walker

Jonathan Hatch
c 1625-1710

Joseph Hatch
1654-1737/8

Sarah Rowley

Amy Allen
1663-?1710/1

James Allen
c 1637-1714

Elizabeth Partridge
d 1722

?John Simpson
b c 1660

— —

Thomas Simpson
c 1683-1761

— —

[1] Son of Matthew Grant
(1601-81) and his w Priscilla
[2] Dau of John Porter
(1594-1648) and his w Ann
White (1600-48)

ULYSSES S. GRANT
FAMILY TREE

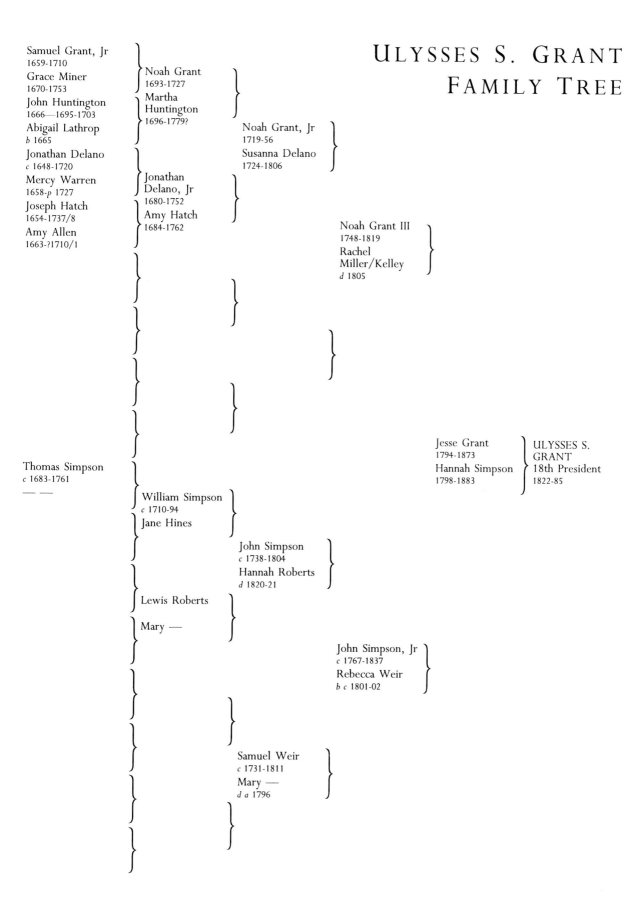

Samuel Grant, Jr
1659-1710

Grace Miner
1670-1753

John Huntington
1666—1695-1703

Abigail Lathrop
b 1665

Jonathan Delano
c 1648-1720

Mercy Warren
1658-p 1727

Joseph Hatch
1654-1737/8

Amy Allen
1663-?1710/1

Noah Grant
1693-1727

Martha
Huntington
1696-1779?

Jonathan
Delano, Jr
1680-1752

Amy Hatch
1684-1762

Noah Grant, Jr
1719-56

Susanna Delano
1724-1806

Noah Grant III
1748-1819

Rachel
Miller/Kelley
d 1805

Jesse Grant
1794-1873

Hannah Simpson
1798-1883

ULYSSES S.
GRANT
18th President
1822-85

Thomas Simpson
c 1683-1761
— —

William Simpson
c 1710-94

Jane Hines

John Simpson
c 1738-1804

Hannah Roberts
d 1820-21

Lewis Roberts

Mary —

John Simpson, Jr
c 1767-1837

Rebecca Weir
b c 1801-02

Samuel Weir
c 1731-1811

Mary —
d a 1796

Plate 59   Rutherford B. Hayes

RUTHERFORD B. HAYES

1822-93
19TH PRESIDENT OF THE UNITED STATES OF AMERICA
1877-81

The scandals of the Grant regime were such that everyone agreed the next President would have to be a new broom. Both the major parties nominated men of proved ability and honesty for the 1876 election: Samuel Tilden, a former associate of Martin Van Buren for the Democrats, Rutherford B. Hayes for the Republicans. Either man, it was reasonably believed, would make a good President of the type needed. Tilden had been one of the leaders in the battle against the corrupt machine of 'Boss' Tweed in New York; Hayes had been a brave and capable general in the Civil War and was serving his third creditable term as Governor of Ohio. Unfortunately the 1876 election proved to be the last and worst of the 'seventies' scandals.

On the surface it was a clear victory for the Democrats. Tilden won a comfortable majority of just under a quarter of a million in the popular vote and he had an equally comfortable majority in the electoral college. It was common knowledge that a large number of the Democratic votes had been obtained dishonestly by such tested methods as bribery and falsification, and the position in the South, where politics was radically distorted by the aftermath of the Civil War, made it impossible to believe in the reality of the elections in that region. So the Republicans, righteously overlooking their own dishonest practices, felt justified in resorting to any means available to claw back the presidency. The battle was bitter throughout the winter, but at the end of the day the Grand Old Party was victorious and Rutherford B. Hayes became President of the United States by a margin of one electoral vote.

Hayes appears to have convinced himself that he had become President honestly; it is doubtful if anyone else believed it. He was widely mocked as 'Rutherfraud' and 'His Fraudulency'. Doubters were not reassured by the scrupulous fashion in which he carried out one of the implied bargains which had given him the White House: he withdrew Federal troops from the South, which left the black population for two generations at the mercy of its white oppressors. But soon afterwards things changed. It was discovered that the President meant to be a reformer after all. He began to preach the virtues of a civil service that was not run entirely in the interests of the political parties and to practise what he preached. By so doing he not only struck at what was becoming an intolerable evil, one that milked the public purse for the private benefit of the politicians, he was beginning to emancipate the presidency itself from the control which Congress had exercised over it since the Johnson administration. No wonder the Congressional Republicans, bitterly divided though they were into factions — 'Stalwarts' and 'Half Breeds' — united against their nominal chief. The row was particularly violent when he dismissed Chester A. Arthur, Collector of the Port of New York, from his post on the grounds that Arthur, a notorious spoilsman, was running the New York Customs House for the benefit of the Republican party rather than the American public. Hayes, supported by the Democrats, was able to have his nominees to replace Arthur and his henchmen approved by the Senate. He was open to a charge of hypocrisy in that, if he challenged the Congressional leaders' exploitation of patronage, it was only in order to substitute his own. Hayes, who was so weak in Congress, would no doubt have retorted that reform could only come step by step and that, if anything was to be achieved, the presidency must be strengthened by whatever means. At least he could not be accused of low personal ambition. He had said that he would not be a candidate for a second term and he stuck to it. By the time of his retirement he was generally respected as an honest man and a worthy President.

He was helped by his wife. She was mocked as 'Lemonade Lucy' because, like Mrs Polk, she was a total abstainer. She was a much more genial character than Mrs Polk and initiated the practice of Easter egg rolling on the White House lawn, a happy tradition that has been kept up ever since.

Mention should also be made of the fact that Hayes had a town named after him. Nothing unusual about that for a US President, except that the town is in Paraguay. Hayes was called in as arbitrator to settle a frontier dispute which he did in favour of the Paraguayans. As a result he is much better known in that country than in his own.

RUTHERFORD B. HAYES' FAMILY

During Hayes's administration certain issues of the day, particularly as they affected the President's family, had a flavour that is recognizably modern. The Women's Movement, for instance, or Substance Abuse. Neither was called that of course. Feminism took the form of women's suffrage, a preoccupation with the 'New Woman' and how far the First Lady should promote her sex's cause with the President, substance abuse that of the Women's Christian Temperance Union. The forms these issues took were also modern. The WCTU, for instance, twisted language to disguise its illiberalism since it sought not temperance, *i.e.*, drinking in moderation, but total abstention. It was now that the term First Lady became current, supposedly coined by a female journalist (another sign of modern times), Mary Clemmer Ames. Mrs Ames likened Lucy's hair and eyes to those of a Madonna. Was she inspired to the phrase 'First Lady' by reference to 'Our Lady'? She wrote for a Protestant newspaper and was married to a Presbyterian clergyman, but the phrase is not exclusive to Catholics and Mrs Ames was not so dyed-in-the-wool Protestant as to be above poking mild fun at Methodism. She was not the only person to detect a virginal quality in Lucy. On the expiry of the Hayes presidency a Unitarian clergyman remarked that the White House was whiter and purer because Mrs Hayes had been its mistress.

The White House was certainly no midden in those years. Bible-readings, psalm-singing (the latter a favourite pastime of the Vice-President, William A. Wheeler, who was indulged in his personal whim as perhaps no other Vice-President has been), a catering policy that foreshadowed Prohibition — all flourished. But oddly enough it wasn't the Madonna of the White House who was behind it, for all that she got the credit. Or not principally. The President organized the psalm-sessions for Wheeler; the President was the one who thought up the ban on alcohol — he reckoned it would attract the 'temperance' vote. Less Lemonade Lucy than Root Beer Rutherford then.

Not that Lucy wasn't TT herself, but she was tolerant toward others. She did not object to fellow-passengers drinking claret cup when aboard a steamer, a lax attitude that caused the Lucy Hayes Temperance Society of Washington to expunge her name from its title. And her youthful feminism petered out as she got older, though two of her aunts remained staunch. It was the President, with as far as is known no prodding from her, who sent a women's delegation to the Paris Exposition and approved a bill letting women lawyers plead in the Supreme Court.

Lucy was actually one of the least interfering of First Ladies. Perhaps if she had stuck her oar in more, principle would not on one occasion have been sacrificed to expediency over the very item — drink — which the Hayeses so abhorred. Be that as it may, when the Russian Grand Dukes Alexis and

Plate 60   Lucy Webb Hayes

Constantine came to dinner in the White House wine appeared too. True, compared to the tergiversation of most administrations it was a small principle and a giant expediency. Luckily for non-Grand Ducal guests the food at the White House in Hayes's time was excellent; the President decreed that decorations and entertainment generally should be especially good to compensate for the lack of drink. He and Lucy evidently enjoyed offering hospitality. Friends and relatives, many of them young people, stayed at the White House for months on end, so that the Hayes's son Rud complained that on his own visits he never had a bedroom, even a bed, to himself. This reinforces one's impression that the Hayeses were not the type to force their teetotalism on others — not, anyway, outside the official residence of the chief executive. Indeed they were not puritans in the strict sense of the term at all. They spent so much of their own money on bonuses for the servants, upkeep of the stables and Lucy's particular passion, flowers (the hothouses swallowed a quarter of their entire housekeeping budget), that they left the White House with less than $1,000 in hand. Again, Lucy had a sweet singing voice; it is probable that she did not intone psalms out of a sense of duty so much as because she enjoyed making music. Her religion was sound as far as it went but she was a Methodist because her parents had been Methodists and they seem to have turned Methodist not because they were convinced of the sublime rightness of Wesley's teaching but because their Presbyterian minister in Chillicothe had supported slavery. (On that principle the WCTU should have become Muslims because Jesus Christ turned water into wine.) The wonder is that Lucy was so much the toast of the temperance movement.

Lucy was the first President's wife to have had a college education and perhaps because of this took a more intelligent interest in her husband's political career than many of her predecessors. She went to Washington to hear him speak in Congress, an unusual example of initiative for the time. When he was Governor of Ohio she helped raise funds for a veterans' orphans' home and a deaf mutes' school. Hayes was one of the more scholarly and cultivated Presidents. He had studied French and literature at Harvard as well as law. He built up an impressive collection of Americana and read for pleasure constantly. His other interests included genealogy (he held office in the New England Historic Genealogical Society) and he carried out research on his family during his trips round the country. He had a particular passion for visiting the Vermont of his mother's ancestors. He was able to indulge his interests since he inherited a legacy from his mother's brother, Sardis Birchard, a pioneer merchant and trader with the Indians at Lower Sandusky, Ohio, who took the place of Hayes's father after the latter's death (Hayes was born posthumously). Sardis also helped with the expenses of Hayes's education and early legal career. Lucy's father Dr James Webb died young too, while on a visit to Kentucky to free some slaves he had inherited, and her mother's brother Matthew Scott Cook helped with the expense of bringing up the young Webbs, one of whom, Joseph, was later surgeon in the Civil War to Hayes's regiment, the 23rd Ohio. Lucy had the sense to resist uncle Sardis's urging that she and Rutherford live with him in his house in Fremont, Ohio. When the Hayeses did eventually go there uncle Sardis was persuaded to go and live with a ward of his, Sarah Jane Grant.

Even if Hayes had not been an amateur genealogist he would surely have been aware of an odd strain in his family. His sister Fanny, who wrote him letters that read more like a lover's than a close relative's, seems to have suffered from periodic bouts of insanity, though as these occurred after giving birth they may not have amounted to much more than what we would now call postnatal depression. Nevertheless, Hayes sometimes feared he might go mad too (his paternal grandmother's grandfather married a cousin, and he may have worried about inbreeding.) There are curious parallels with Lucy's family. For a start, Lucy closely resembled Hayes's dead sister Fanny. Secondly, her mother and Hayes's died on the same day. Lastly, her brother died of what was called a 'mental malady'.

The Hayes's eldest son Birchard, like his father a bibliophile and a man with a taste for genealogy, was in general shyer and more introspective. He developed a gift for statistical analysis which led him to specialize in taxation law and real estate after qualifying as an attorney. The next eldest boy Webb Hayes seems to have been his father's favourite son. Less scholarly than Birchard, he acted not only as his father's secretary but as bodyguard after a person or persons unknown fired a shot into the family house at Columbus. As his father's secretary in the White House he regularly sat in on cabinet meetings. He also looked after the family property in Ohio while his father was tied down in Washington. More a man of action than a desk-bound type, he later served in the cavalry in Cuba, Puerto Rico, the Philippines, China, the Mexican border and on the Italian front in World War I, by which time he was over 60. With the third son Rud Hayes the bookish streak surfaced again. He helped organize the Ohio Library Association in 1895 and started up children's reading rooms and travelling libraries. Later he became a realtor. The daughter Fanny, one of whose best friends at school was President Garfield's daughter Mollie, became her father's chief prop after Lucy's death in 1889. The most bizarre fate was that of the youngest son to reach manhood, Scott Hayes, who never recovered from a breakdown in 1919 after an experience which sounds like something from a Werner Herzog film starring Klaus Kinski. Scott was shipwrecked off the Peruvian coast and, after floating around in one of two tankers into which the surviving passengers had been loaded, was picked up by another vessel, a Noah's Ark of a freighter carrying tigers, boa constrictors and other exotic beasts. These got loose in the stormy seas and spread terror among the recently rescued passengers. Scott died four years later. It was an odd coda to the history of one of the most respectable families to furnish the US with a President.

BIOGRAPHICAL DETAILS AND DESCENDANTS

HAYES, RUTHERFORD BIRCHARD, *b* Delaware, Ohio, 4 Oct 1822; *educ* Methodist Acad, Norwalk, Ohio, Isaac Webb's Sch, Middletown, Conn., Kenyon Coll, Gambier, Ohio (BA 1842, MA 1845), and Harvard Law Sch (LLB 1845); admitted to Ohio Bar 1845, Delegate to State Republican Convention 1855, Cincinnati City Slr 1857-59, served Civil War 23rd Regt Ohio Vol Infy (1861: Maj June, Judge Advocate Dept of Ohio Sept, Lt-Col Oct; 1862: wounded in the Battle for possession of the South Mountain, Md. (Union victory), 14 Sept, Actg Brig-Gen cmmdg Kanawha Div) and as commander Gen George

Crooke's 1st Infy Bde 1863-64 (Brevet Brig-Gen of Volunteers 1864, Brevet Maj-Gen of Volunteers 1865 for gallant and distinguished services at Union victories of Fisher's Hill, Va., and Cedar Creek, Va.), Memb US House of Reps from Ohio 1865-67, Govr Ohio 1868-72 and 1876-77, 19th President (R) of the USA 1877-81, Hon Memb New England Historic Genealogical Society 1877-93 (V-Pres 1879-89), Pres Nat Prison Assoc 1883-93 and John F. Slater Bd of Tstees (fund for promoting industrial education among Southern blacks), Memb Bd of Tstees Peabody Educn Fund (for promoting education in the South), author: *Diary and Letters*, 5 vols., ed Charles R. Williams (1922-26), *Diary of a President, 1875-1881*, ed Harry T. Williams (1964), and *Teach the Freeman: The Correspondence of Rutherford B. Hayes and the Fund for Negro Education, 1881-1887*, ed Louis D. Rubin (1959); *m* Cincinnati 30 Dec 1852 Lucy Ware (*b* Chillicothe, Ohio, 28 Aug 1831; *educ* Wesleyan Female Coll, Cincinnati, Ohio; Pres Woman's Home Missionary Soc of Methodist Episcopal Church; *d* Fremont 25 June 1889, *bur* initially Oakwood Cemetery, Fremont, remains subsequently reinterred with her husb's in Spiegel Grove State Park, Fremont), only dau of Dr James Webb (*d* 1833 of cholera) and his *w* Maria, dau of Judge Isaac Cook, of Ross Co, Ohio, and *d* Fremont 17 Jan 1893 after a heart attack, leaving issue:

President Hayes's children

I Sardis Birchard (later called Birchard Austin) HAYES, *b* Cincinnati 4 Nov 1853; *educ* Cornell U and Harvard Law Sch; practised law Toledo, Ohio; *m* Norwalk, Ohio, 30 Dec 1886 Mary Nancy (*b* Erie Co, Ohio, 15 May 1859; *d* Toledo 22 June 1924), dau of Nathan Gould Sherman and his *w* Elizabeth Otis, and *d* Toledo 24 Jan 1926, having had issue:

Grandchildren

1 Rutherford Birchard HAYES, *b* Toledo 2 Oct 1887; *d* there 27 Nov 1888

2 Sherman Otis HAYES, *b* Toledo 11 Oct 1888; Lt 14th US Infantry World War I; *m* 14 Feb 1912 Beatrice Henrietta (*d* 1939), dau of Royal F. Baker, of Corvallis, Oreg., and *d* Boston 27 Feb 1949, leaving issue:

Great-grandchildren

(1) Lucy Webb Hayes, *b* Portland, Oreg., 8 Jan 1915; *m* 17 April 1950 *Col Lloyd Webster HOUGH, US Army, and *d* Savannah, Ga., 30 July 1963, leaving issue:

Great-great-grandchildren

1a *Lucy Webb Hayes HOUGH, *b* Indiana 30 Sept 1952

2a *Lloyd Webster Hayes HOUGH, *b* 7 Feb 1954

Grandchildren

3 Webb Cook HAYES II, of Spiegel Grove, Fremont, *b* Toledo 25 Sept 1890; *educ* US Naval Acad (BS 1911); Ensign 1911, served World War I, transferred to USNR 1928, recalled to active duty 1941 (Dir Recruiting & Induction, Navy Dept, 1941-44, Commandant West Point 1944-45), Rear-Adml USN 1954 (BSM from President of the USA, Commendation with ribbon from Sec of Navy, Order of Avis (Portugal)), Pres Pemiscot Land & Cooperage Co 1930-57, Chm Baker Bros Machine Tool Co 1933-51, Tstee: Ohio Historical Soc, Memorial Hosp of Sandusky Co, Ohio, Birchard Library, Fremont, Pres Tstees Rutherford B. Hayes Fndn, Hon LLD Bowling Green State U; *m* 29 April 1919 *Martha Wilder (*b* Toledo 23 Dec 1896), dau of Arthur Ernest Baker, of Toledo, and *d* Fremont 10 July 1957, leaving issue:

Great-grandchildren

(1) *Webb Cook HAYES III [4401 Boxwood Road, Bethesda, MD 20816, USA; 8510 Longfellow Place, Chevy Chase, MD 20815, USA; c/o Baker & Hostetler, 1050 Connecticut Avenue, NW Ste 1300, Washington, DC 20036, USA], *b* Toledo 25 Sept 1920; *educ* Yale; lawyer; *m* 14 May 1945 *Betty (*b* 28 Aug 1923), dau of Norman B. Frost, of Chevy Chase, and has issue:

Great-great-grandchildren

1a *Webb Cook HAYES IV, *b* Washington, DC, 18 Aug 1946; *educ* Maryland U

2a *Norman Burke Frost HAYES, *b* Washington, DC, 2 Jan 1951

3a *Stephen Austin HAYES, *b* Washington, DC, 2 Jan 1953; *educ* Laurenceville

4a *Jeffrey Kent HAYES, *b* Washington, DC, 7 Dec 1955; *educ* Mercersburg Acad

Great-grandchildren

(2) *Arthur Baker HAYES, *b* Toledo 4 June 1924; *m* 20 Dec 1947 *June, dau of Charles A. Feltman, of Brooklyn, New York, and has issue:

Great-great-grandchildren

1a *Leslie June HAYES, *b* Cleveland, Ohio, 24 Dec 1950

2a *Arthur Baker HAYES, Jr [3214 Leyland Street, Chevy Chase, MD 20815, USA; 19310 Club House Road, Gaithersburg, MD 20879, USA], *b* Bay Village 29 March 1954

Great-grandchildren

(3) *Scott Birchard HAYES, *b* Washington, DC, 2 April 1926; *m* 27 Oct 1951 *Dorothy Deborah (*b* Worcester, Mass., 2 June 1931), dau of Harold John Walter, of Uxbridge, Mass., and has issue:

Great-great-grandchildren

1a *Scott Birchard HAYES, Jr, *b* Cleveland 19 Jan 1953

2a *James Walker HAYES, *b* Virginia, Minn., 11 Feb 1955

3a *Timothy Wheelock HAYES, *b* Royal Oak, Mich., 17 Jan 1958

4a *Michael Sherman HAYES, *b* Cleveland 10 Dec 1960

Grandchildren
4 *Walter Sherman HAYES, b Toledo 27 July 1893; Ensign USN, served World War I aboard USS *Utah*; m 19 Oct 1935 *Rachel (b Toledo 18 April 1908), dau of William Clifton Carr and his w Cora Elizabeth Crim, and has issue:

Great-grandchildren
(1) *Walter Sherman HAYES, Jr, b Toledo 26 Feb 1938; *educ* Wooster Coll; m 12 Sept 1964 *Jean (b 19 April 19—), dau of John Brand, of Wilmington, Del., and his w Dorothy, and has issue:

Great-great-grandchildren
1a *Elizabeth HAYES, b 21 April 1968

Great-grandchildren
(2) *Mary Elizabeth Hayes, b Toledo 30 March 1940; m 24 Aug 1963 *Gregg Wiley PARKS

Grandchildren
5 Scott Russell HAYES, b Toledo, 23 Sept 1895; 1st Lt Field Artillery in World War I; m 20 Oct 1934 Muriel (b Leonia, New Jersey, 2 Dec 1909), dau of William O. Gantz, and d Los Angeles 18 Nov 1968, leaving issue:

Great-grandchildren
(1) *Nancy Sherman Hayes, b Los Angeles 23 June 1938; m 18 June 1961 *Keith LEAVITT (b 4 Feb 1937), s of R. C. Leavitt, Jr, of Gorham, Maine, and has issue:

Great-great-grandchildren
1a *Scott Alan LEAVITT, b 29 June 1964

Great-grandchildren
(2) *Martha Jean Hayes, b Los Angeles 7 Dec 1940; m 18 June 1961 *Carl Edward LUSK (b 23 Sept 1937), s of Edward Lusk, of Los Angeles, and has issue:

Great-great-grandchildren
1a *Karen Marie LUSK, b 7 Dec 1963
2a *Robert Edward LUSK, b 8 April 1966

Great-grandchildren
(3) *Margaret Frances Hayes, b Los Angeles 19 Dec 1942; m 29 Dec 1964 *James CLARK (b 11 Nov 1942) and has issue:

Great-great-grandchildren
1a *Dorothy CLARK, b 21 Jan 1966

President Hayes's children
II James Webb (later called Webb Cook) HAYES, b Cincinnati, Ohio, 20 March 1856; *educ* Cornell U; confidential sec to his father when latter President, Lt-Col US Volunteers Spanish-American War 1898 (Congressional Medal of Honor), served Italy World War I with British and French brigades; m 30 Sept 1912 Mary Otis (b Fremont 11 April 1856; d Phoenix, Ariz., 3 March 1935), widow of —— Brinkerhoff and dau of Anson H. Miller and his w Nancy Otis, and d Marion, Ohio, 26 July 1935

III Rutherford (Rud) Platt HAYES, b Cincinnati 24 June 1858; *educ* Cornell U and Boston Polytechnic Inst; private sec to his father when latter President, banker, Tstee Birchard Library, Sec American Library Assoc; m 24 Oct 1894 Lucy Hayes (b Columbus, Ohio, 14 Sept 1868; d Clearwater, Fla., 4 Dec 1939), dau of William Augustus Platt, of Columbus and his w Sarah Follett, and d Tampa, Fla., 31 July 1927, having had issue:

Grandchildren
1 Rutherford Birchard HAYES, b Columbus Jan 1896; d Asheville, N Carolina, 2 Feb 1902
2 *William Platt HAYES, b Columbus 9 Dec 1897; served World War I; m 1st 28 June 1924 Sarah Taylor (b Waynesville, N Carolina, 23 Oct 1895; d Lansdowne, Pa., 17 Feb 1945), dau of Howard Taylor Rogers and his w Mary Ann Bavenson, and has issue:

Great-grandchildren
(1) *Lucy Roger Hayes, b Tampa 18 Oct 1926; m 25 Sept 1948 *Edward Scott LAWHORNE (b Philadelphia 10 Oct 1925), s of William B. Lawhorne and his w Emily, and has issue:

Great-great-grandchildren
1a *William Scott LAWHORNE, b 27 July 1949
2a *Sarah Hayes LAWHORNE, b 6 Aug 1951
3a *Katherine Rogers LAWHORNE, b 10 Sept 1954

Great-grandchildren
(2) *Rutherford Platt HAYES II, b Tampa 27 Dec 1928; m 24 June 1950 *Inge Christine (b Vienna, Austria, 12 Aug 1930), dau of Paul Peter Haas and his w Claire Marie Horry, and has issue:

Great-great-grandchildren
1a *Scott Taylor HAYES, b 19 Jan 1952
2a *Rutherford Platt HAYES III, b 29 Jan 1955

Great-grandchildren

(3) *William Taylor HAYES, *b* Philadelphia 15 Aug 1934; *m* 22 Dec 1956 *Sue (*b* Tulsa, Okla., 14 Oct 1933), dau of Paul Ward Cooper and his w Velna Iva Strout, and has three adopted children:

   a *Katherine Renee HAYES
   b *Kristin Ann HAYES
   c *William Dean HAYES

Grandchildren

2 (cont.) William P. Hayes *m* 2nd 9 Oct 1947 *Lillian (*b* Saginaw, Mich., 24 Feb 1899), widow of —— Kirk and dau of Augustus Burns Chalmers and his w Lillian Knight

3 Birchard Platt HAYES, *b* Asheville, N Carolina, 4 July 1902; *m* 24 June 1927 *Dorothy Ruth (*b* 24 Oct 1905), dau of Harry H. Toohey, of Milwaukee, Wis., and *d* nr Bamberg, S Carolina, 3 Jan 1958, leaving issue:

Great-grandchildren

(1) *Margaret Lucy Hayes, *b* Lakeland, Fla., 17 July 1928; *m* 18 Aug 1951 *Malcolm Alexander TAYLOR (*b* 23 Jan 1922), s of Alexander J. Taylor, of New Paltz, New York, and has issue:

Great-great-grandchildren

1a *Lucy Hayes TAYLOR, *b* Poughkeepsie, New York, 21 Sept 1953
2a Rutherford Van Wyck TAYLOR, *b* 25 Sept 1955; accidentally *k* New Paltz, New York, 29 June 1958
3a *Birchard Malcom TAYLOR, *b* Poughkeepsie 6 April 1957
4a *Scott Alexander TAYLOR, *b* Kingston, New York, 9 March 1960

Grandchildren

3 (cont.) Mr and Mrs Birchard P. Hayes also had five adopted children:

   a *Jonathan Bradbury HAYES
   b *Carolyn Bradbury HAYES
   c *Richard Platt HAYES
   d *Libby Lu HAYES
   e *James Birchard HAYES

President Hayes's children

IV Joseph Thompson HAYES, *b* Cincinnati 21 Dec 1861; *d* nr Charleston, W. Va., 24 June 1863
V George Crook HAYES, *b* Chillicothe, Ohio, 29 Sept 1864; *d* there 24 May 1866
VI Frances (Fanny) Hayes, *b* Cincinnati 2 Sept 1867; *educ* Miss Mittlebarger's Sch, Cleveland, and Miss Porter's Sch, Farmington, Conn.; *m* 1 Sept 1897 (divorce 18— or 19——) Capt Harry Eaton SMITH, USN (*b* Fremont, Ohio, 28 Dec 1869; *d* 1931), resumed her maiden name of Hayes and *d* Lewiston, Maine, 18 March 1950, having had issue:

Grandchildren

1 Dalton HAYES (born Dalton Hayes SMITH), *b* 22 June 1898; served with 165th Infantry (42nd Div) American Expeditionary Force World War I (wounded); *m* 17 April 1926 *Corinne (*b* Columbus 1 Jan 1906; *m* 2nd 1957 Charles William Schaub, of Fort Lauderdale, Fla.,), dau of Nicholas Daubeney Monsarratt and his w Jean Andrews, dau of Maj-Gen John Grant Mitchell, US Volunteers, and his w Laura, herself dau of William Augustus Platt and his w Fanny Arabella, sister of President HAYES; Dalton Hayes *d* Pompano Beach, Fla., 13 Jan 1950, leaving issue:

Great-grandchildren

(1) *Chloe Hayes, *b* Cape Town, S Africa, 24 Jan 1927; *m* 13 Dec 1952 *Harold Martin SCHROEDER and has issue:

Great-great-grandchildren
1a *Maude SCHROEDER, *b* Berkeley, Calif., 10 Dec 1953
2a *Jean SCHROEDER, *b* Highstown, New Jersey, 16 March 1955

Great-grandchildren

(2) *Jean Hayes [Mrs Edward Rogers II, 570 Park Avenue, New York, NY 10021, USA], *b* Cape Town, S Africa, 26 April 1928; *m* *Edward Sylvester ROGERS II (*b* 2 May 1923) and has issue:

Great-great-grandchildren
1a *Corinne ROGERS, *b* Albuquerque, N. Mex., 29 Dec 1954

President Hayes' children

VII Scott Russell HAYES, *b* Columbus 8 Feb 1871; *educ* Green Springs Acad and Cornell; railroad equipment mfr; *m* Sept 1912 Maude Anderson (*b* 7 July 1873; *d* San Francisco 19 Nov 1966) and *d* Croton-on-Hudson, New York, 6 May 1923
VIII Manning Force HAYES, *b* Fremont 1 Aug 1873; *d* there 28 Aug 1874

MALE LINE ANCESTRY AND COLLATERAL DESCENDANTS

George HAYES, *b* Scotland? (doubtful) *c* 1655; settled Windsor, Conn., 1680; *m* 1st 16— ——; *m* 2nd *c* 1685 Abigail (*b* Windsor 19 Jan 1666/7; *d* Simsbury (now Granby), Conn., after 1725), dau of Samuel Dibble, of Windsor, and his 1st w —— , dau of William Graves, of Newtown, Long Island, New York, and *d* Simsbury 2 Sept 1725, having with his 2nd w had (with other issue):

Daniel HAYES, *b* Windsor 26 April 1686; *m* Simsbury 4 May 1721 Sarah (*b* 24 April 1692; *d* Simsbury 13 July 1738), dau of John Lee, of Westfield, Mass., and his 2nd (?) w Elizabeth, dau of Dennis Crampton, of Guildford, Conn., and *d* Simsbury 23 Sept 1756, having with her had issue:

Captain Ezekiel HAYES, of Branford, Conn., and New Haven, Conn., *b* Simsbury 21 Oct or Nov 1724; blacksmith and innkeeper; *m* 1st Branford 26 Dec 1749 Rebecca (*b* New Haven, Conn., 6 Feb 1723; *d* there 27 May 1773), dau of Col-Judge John Russell, of Branford, and his w Sarah Trowbridge, and *d* New Haven 17 Oct 1817, leaving (with other issue):

Rutherford HAYES, of Brattleboro, Vt., *b* Branford 29 July 1756; *m* early in 1779 Chloe (*b* South Hadley, Mass., 10 Nov 1762; *d* Brattleboro 17 Feb 1847), dau of Col Israel Smith and his w Abigail Chandler, and *d* West Brattleboro 25 Sept 1836, leaving issue:

Rutherford HAYES, *b* Brattleboro 4 Jan 1787; farmer and storekeeper, moved from Dummerston, Vt., to central Ohio late 1817; *m* Wilmington, Vt., 13 Sept 1813 Sophia (*b* there 15 April 1792; *d* Columbus, Ohio, 30 Oct 1866), dau of Roger Cornwall alias Birchard, of Wilmington, and his w Drusilla Austin, and *d* Delaware, Ohio, 20 July 1822 of a fever, having had issue:

I A boy, *b* and *d* 14 Aug 1814
II Lorenzo HAYES, *b* 9 June 1815; *d* 20 Jan 1825
III Sarah Sophia HAYES, *b* 10 July 1817; *d* 9 Oct 1821
IV Fanny Arabella Hayes, *b* 20 Jan 1820; *m* 1839 William Augustus PLATT (*b* 1809; *d* 1882) and *d* 16 July 1856 in childbirth, having had two s and four daus (two of them newborn twins who *d* at the same time as her)
V RUTHERFORD BIRCHARD HAYES, 19th PRESIDENT of the UNITED STATES of AMERICA

George Hayes
c 1655-1725

Samuel Dibble
1643/4-1709/10
Abigail Dibble
1666/7-p 1725

— Graves
d a 1668

Walter Lee
d 1717/8
Mary —
d 1695/6
John Lee
1657-1711

Dennis Crampton
d 1689/90
Elizabeth Crampton
b 1662/7

Mary Parmelee
d 1667

Revd John Russell, Jr
c 1627-92
Rebecca Newberry
Revd Samuel Russell
1660-1731

Joseph Jacob
c 1673-1764

Revd John Whiting
c 1635-89
Abigail Whiting
c 1665-1733
John Lindsey
c 1640-c 1705
Sarah Lindsey
b 1674/5

Sybil Collins
c 1638-72
Mary Alley
1641/2-80/1

Thomas Trowbridge, Jr
c 1631-1702
Samuel Storrs
c 1640-66

Sarah Rutherford
1641-87
Thomas Trowbridge III
1663/4-1711
Mary Huckins
d 1683
Samuel Storrs
1677-1727

John Winston
c 1621-96/7
Mary Winston
1667-1742
John Burgess
fl c 1657
Martha Burgess
c 1671-1728

Elizabeth —
c 1617-80
Mary Worden

John Smith
c 1637-76 same as (a)
Richard Austin
c 1598-p c 1639

Mary Partridge
c 1638-83 same as (b)
John Smith, Jr
1665-1724
— —
Anthony Austin
1636-1708

John Root, Jr
c 1642-87
Mary Root
1667-1724
John Huggins
c 1609-70
Esther Huggins
1642/3-97/8

Mary Ashley
b 1644
Bridget —
c 1615-95

John Smith
(a)
Daniel Hovey
c 1618-92

Mary Partridge
(b)
Benjamin Smith
1673-1754/5
Abigail Andrews
d 1655
Thomas Hovey
c 1648-1739

Henry Buck
c 1625/6-1712
Ruth Buck
1681-a 1754
Aaron Cooke III
c 1640/1-1716
Sarah Cooke
1662-in/p 1739

Elizabeth Churchill
b 1642
Sarah Westwood
c 1644-1730

Thomas Chandler
c 1628-1702/3
Nathaniel Phelps
c 1627-1702

Hannah Brewer
1630-1717
Henry Chandler
1667-1737
Elizabeth Copley
d 1712
Nathaniel Phelps, Jr
1653-1719

George Abbott, Jr
c 1631-88/9
Lydia Abbott
1675-1748/9
William Martin
fl c 1645
Grace Martin
c 1656-1727

Sarah Farnum
b c 1638
Lydia Marsh
c 1624-p 1658

Thomas Hale, Jr
c 1650/1-1725
Thomas Merrick
c 1620-1704

Priscilla Markham
c 1654-82
John Hale
1680-1753
Elizabeth Tilley
d 1684
John Merrick
1658-1748

Isaac Gleason
c 1654-98
Abigail Gleason
1692-1721
Thomas Day
c 1638-1711
Mary Day
1666-1723

Hester Eggleston
b 1663
Sarah Cooper
c 1642-1726

RUTHERFORD HAYES
FAMILY TREE

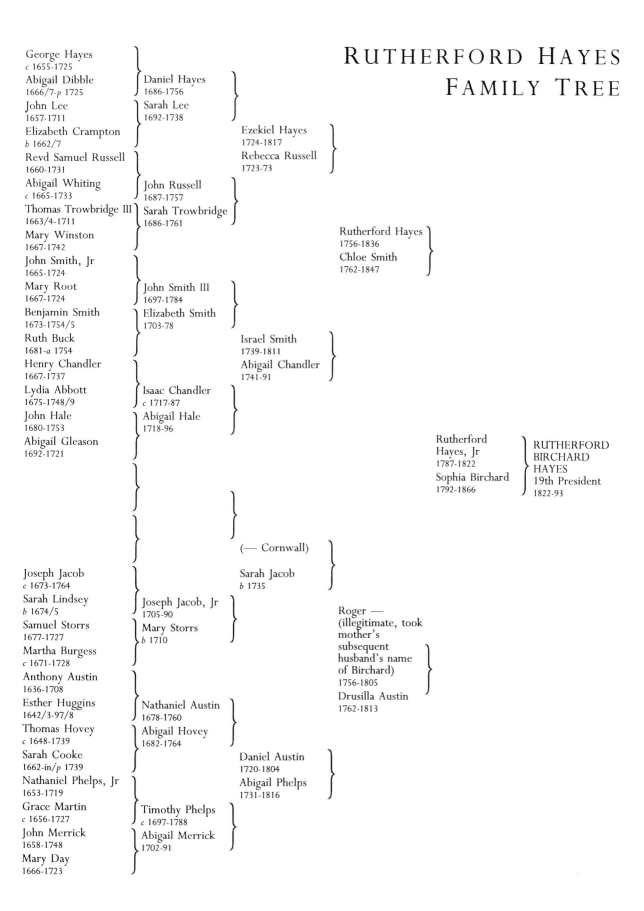

George Hayes
c 1655-1725

Abigail Dibble
1666/7-p 1725

John Lee
1657-1711

Elizabeth Crampton
b 1662/7

Revd Samuel Russell
1660-1731

Abigail Whiting
c 1665-1733

Thomas Trowbridge III
1663/4-1711

Mary Winston
1667-1742

John Smith, Jr
1665-1724

Mary Root
1667-1724

Benjamin Smith
1673-1754/5

Ruth Buck
1681-a 1754

Henry Chandler
1667-1737

Lydia Abbott
1675-1748/9

John Hale
1680-1753

Abigail Gleason
1692-1721

Daniel Hayes
1686-1756

Sarah Lee
1692-1738

John Russell
1687-1757

Sarah Trowbridge
1686-1761

John Smith III
1697-1784

Elizabeth Smith
1703-78

Isaac Chandler
c 1717-87

Abigail Hale
1718-96

Ezekiel Hayes
1724-1817

Rebecca Russell
1723-73

Israel Smith
1739-1811

Abigail Chandler
1741-91

Rutherford Hayes
1756-1836

Chloe Smith
1762-1847

Rutherford
Hayes, Jr
1787-1822

Sophia Birchard
1792-1866

RUTHERFORD
BIRCHARD
HAYES
19th President
1822-93

(— Cornwall)

Sarah Jacob
b 1735

Joseph Jacob
c 1673-1764

Sarah Lindsey
b 1674/5

Samuel Storrs
1677-1727

Martha Burgess
c 1671-1728

Anthony Austin
1636-1708

Esther Huggins
1642/3-97/8

Thomas Hovey
c 1648-1739

Sarah Cooke
1662-in/p 1739

Nathaniel Phelps, Jr
1653-1719

Grace Martin
c 1656-1727

John Merrick
1658-1748

Mary Day
1666-1723

Joseph Jacob, Jr
1705-90

Mary Storrs
b 1710

Nathaniel Austin
1678-1760

Abigail Hovey
1682-1764

Timothy Phelps
c 1697-1788

Abigail Merrick
1702-91

Roger —
(illegitimate, took
mother's
subsequent
husband's name
of Birchard)
1756-1805

Drusilla Austin
1762-1813

Daniel Austin
1720-1804

Abigail Phelps
1731-1816

Plate 61   James A. Garfield

JAMES A. GARFIELD

1831-81
20TH PRESIDENT OF THE UNITED STATES OF AMERICA
1881

Except that he had been a Republican leader in Congress and therefore could not have absolutely clean hands, James Garfield in 1880 was a man as like Hayes as the Republican leaders could well have found. He too had been born in Ohio, a crucial state; had been a lawyer before the Civil War; had attained military distinction during the war (he was made Major-General for his part in the Battle of Chickamauga) and had entered politics on the strength of his military reputation. He had some advantages over Hayes: he was much better looking and, as was dinned into the public ear during the presidential campaign, he had been born in a log cabin (perhaps the party made such a fuss about the fact because it guessed that Garfield would be the last President able to make the traditional boast). After his inauguration he proved that he too, like Hayes, knew that the times were changing; he fought a fierce battle over patronage against the great Republican boss of New York, Senator Roscoe Conkling, and won. Then, suddenly, he was murdered.

He died in two stages. First an obscure member of Conkling's 'Stalwart' faction, Charles J. Guiteau, who was mad, shot the President in the back. Secondly, the doctors probing the not particularly dangerous wound to extract the bullet, gave Garfield blood poisoning. He died of it after more than two months' agony. An old acquaintance of the Vice-President cried out in dismay and disbelief, "Chet Arthur President of the United States: Good God."

JAMES A. GARFIELD'S FAMILY

There was a Garfield family legend that they had a strong Saxon strain. Actually it would have been almost impossible to trace a single thread among the skein of genealogical ingredients constituting a 19th-century American, certainly not one so antique and ill-defined as 'Saxon'. But such romanticism was common then. It caused an early biographer of Garfield, Captain F. H. Mason (possibly a relative of Mrs Garfield through her mother Arabella Mason), to rhapsodize about the President's fair complexion and Germanic temperament. By this he meant an upright, dependable, strong character. Any consciousness among the Garfields of a Saxon/Germanic streak is only of practical consequence insofar as it encouraged James A. Garfield to learn German. (While in Congress he polished up his German and learned French also.) The language was highly useful when he campaigned among German-speaking settlers, on which occasions he was capable of saying things like "England is not the fatherland of the English-speaking people, but the ancient home; the real fatherland of our race is the ancient forests of Germany."

But Garfield was more than just a politician currying favour with ethnic groups. He was widely read, the more so because self-taught, carrying law books to study in the fields where he worked as an agricultural labourer. He taught Latin and Greek at the college of which he became President aged 26, and if the college in question was not quite up to Tübingen standards, it compensated by breadth of endeavour: he was also responsible for teaching higher mathematics, history, philosophy and rhetoric. The Disciples of Christ, the sub-Presbyterian sect which his parents had joined in 1833 and of which both he and his wife Lucretia were members (they first met at Disciples schools), was particularly active in education. Garfield preached the scriptures as a member of the Disciples, though he was never ordained. Later he became a distinguished orator in Congress. Clearly he could practise rhetoric as well as teach it.

What his party particularly liked about him when it came to campaigning was not just his log cabin birth but his early career as a canal bargee. This was the man-of-the-people stuff that won elections. Actually Garfield had wanted to run away to sea and become a salt water sailor, but he got no further than fresh water work for a cousin who owned a barge. Politically this was ideal because it combined the dignity of manual drudgery with local interest (the canal was a Midwest one) and even an element of family tradition. Garfield's father Abram had worked on the Ohio-Lake Erie Canal when he came west in 1826. Although Abram had saved money to begin with, inflation destroyed his savings and malaria added to the family's troubles: Abram contracted it, and the weakened state it put him in may have hastened his end when he caught a bad chill after fighting a forest fire that threatened his small-holding; Eliza his wife contracted it; Garfield himself contracted it, and had to return home from his life as a bargee in consequence; and as late as 1881 Lucretia Garfield was ill with it, for the disease lingers years in the system.

When Abram died aged only 34 Garfield's mother kept on his 30-acre small-holding (her elder son Thomas later abandoned it as too small to be profitable) and made clothes for her own and neighbouring children. The neighbours gave her shoes for her children in exchange. She was born Eliza Ballou, of a Huguenot family that had settled in New England a generation before the Revocation of the Edict of Nantes in 1685 (the cancelling by Louis XIV of an earlier toleration policy toward Protestants which sparked off the chief Huguenot emigration from France). She was not highly educated but she made up for it by her strong will, courage and piety. She was undoubtedly the formative influence on Garfield, intellectually as well as emotionally. After becoming a widow she first lived with her daughter then with Garfield. In 1871 Garfield took her and his Aunt Alpha, his mother's sister, to see their birthplace in Richmond, New Hampshire, combining with it a little research into the Ballou pedigree. Later she became the first mother of a President to live in the White House.

Lucretia Garfield, whom Garfield called Crete, was the daughter of yet another Disciple of Christ, Zeb Rudolph. Garfield had grave doubts about marrying her and there was a fairly sticky early period in their life together. He suffered acute depression; moreover at one time he seemed to have fallen for the charms of Kate Chase, the daughter of Lincoln's Secretary of the Treasury Salmon P. Chase. Later Garfield missed Lucretia so much when in Washington that he built a house there for them to live in. This was unusual at a time when legislators tended to stay in hotels, only seeing anything of their families back in their home state when Congress was not sitting. After she came to live with him in the capital Garfield curtailed his social life and stayed at home in the evenings to read and chat with his wife. Their favourite authors were Dickens and Scott and they probably took their pet name 'Trot' for their daughter Elizabeth from Betsy Trotwood in *David Copperfield*. Like Lucy Hayes, Lucretia Garfield had feminist sympathies, but unlike the Hayeses her husband did not share them at all. Judging from her photographs Lucretia was good-looking. Guiteau, Garfield's assassin, claimed to have put off an earlier attempt on the President's life on catching sight of her. After her husband's death she started a biography of him but soon abandoned it.

Sad to say, the fervour for educational self-improvement that had burned so brightly in Garfield failed to survive to the next generation. He complained that neither of his two eldest sons was interested in

Plate 62   Lucretia Rudolph Garfield

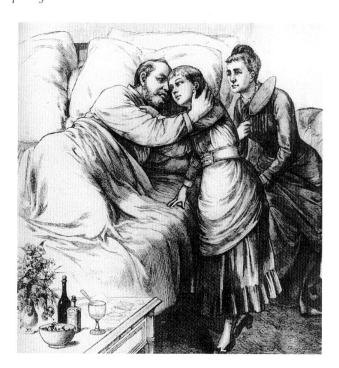

Plate 63   Mrs Garfield and Garfield's only surviving daughter Mollie
at the bedside of the mortally wounded President

his school books. Nevertheless Harry (a favourite name of Garfield's — he had given it to one of his horses) was an academic lawyer and political scientist for most of his life, first at Princeton then Williams College. In 1917 President Woodrow Wilson, a fellow academic, appointed him the USA's Fuel Administrator at a moment when the US was entering World War I. In this capacity he was responsible for introducing daylight saving and 'Fuelless Mondays' as well as closing non-essential factories to boost the nation's war effort. Garfield's second son, James Rudolph, was one of the leading progressive Republicans and as an Ohio state senator introduced legislation against corrupt campaign expenses there. His idealism caused the party machine to deny him its backing when he proposed running for Congress in 1900. Later Teddy Roosevelt made him Secretary of the Interior, where he was particularly involved in implementing his boss's conservation policies. He was also one of Roosevelt's 'lawn tennis' (or inner) cabinet. He was reckoned more popular among ordinary Ohio Republicans than the future President Warren Harding in the run-up to the party's 1910 gubernatorial nomination, but his lack of standing with the bosses led to Harding's selection. Lack of support by James Garfield and his progressives is the reason Harding lost.

President Garfield's daughter married his secretary Joseph Stanley Brown, who had worked for the President in that capacity while he was still a Congressman. Garfield was said to have particularly appreciated the man's skill in turning away importunate office-seekers, a field he was weak in himself. It is therefore ironic that Garfield's assassin Guiteau was, as well as mad, a disappointed office-seeker.

BIOGRAPHICAL DETAILS AND DESCENDANTS

GARFIELD, JAMES ABRAM, *b* Orange, Cuyahoga Co, Ohio, 19 Nov 1831; *educ* Geauga Seminary (subsequently Western Reserve Eclectic Institute and now Hiram Coll), Chester, Ohio, and Williams Coll, Williamstown, Mass. (BA 1856); carpenter and farmer, Prof Ancient Languages and Literature 1856-57 then Pres Western Reserve Eclectic Inst 1857-61, Memb Ohio State Senate from Portage and Summit Cos 1859, admitted to Ohio Bar 1860; 1861: Lt-Col 42nd Regt Ohio Volunteers Aug, Col Nov, commanded 18th Bde Army of Ohio at Big Sandy Valley Dec; 1862: saw action Battle of Middle Creek, Ky., and Paintville, Ky., and made Brig-Gen Jan, saw action Battle of Shiloh, Tenn., April; 1863: Chief of Staff to Gen William S. Rosecrans Feb, Maj-Gen Sept following gallantry at Battle of Chickamauga, resigned commission Dec; Memb from Ashtabula Dist of Ohio US House of Reps 1863-80 (Chm: Ctee on Military Affairs 1867, Ctee on Banking and Currency 1869, Ctee on Appropriations 1871, Speaker 1874, Memb Ways and Means Ctee 1875, Memb Electoral Commission investigating 1876 presidential election and unsuccessful Republican candidate for Speaker 1877), elected US Senator from Ohio Jan 1880 (never took seat for term due to commence March 1881 since elected President meanwhile), 20th President of the USA (R) 4 March-19 Sept 1881; author: *Great Speeches of James Abram Garfield* (1881), *Works*, ed Burke A. Hinsdale, 2 vols (1882-83), *Garfield-Hinsdale Letters*, ed Mary L. Hinsdale (1949), *The Wild Life of the Army: Civil War Letters of James A. Garfield*, ed Frederick D. Williams (1964), *Politics and Patronage in the Gilded Age: The Correspondence of James A. Garfield and Charles E. Henry*, ed James D. Norris and Arthur H. Shaffer (1970); *m* at her father's house in Hiram, Portage Co, Ohio, 11 Nov 1858 Lucretia (Crete) (*b* Hiram or Garrettsville, Portage Co, Ohio 19 April 1832; *educ* Geauga Seminary, Chester, Ohio, and Western Reserve Eclectic Inst, Hiram, Ohio; *d* South Pasadena, Calif., 13 March 1918 of pneumonia, *bur* the Garfield Memorial, Lake View Cemetery, Cleveland, Ohio), dau of Zebulon Rudolph, of Hiram, and his w Arabella Green Mason, and *d* Elberon, New Jersey, 19 Sept 1881 of wounds sustained when shot in the back at Baltimore and Potomac Railroad Station, Washington, DC, by Charles J. Guiteau 2 July 1881, having had issue:

President Garfield's children

I Eliza ('Trot') Arabella GARFIELD, *b* Hiram 3 July 1860; *d* there 1 Dec 1863

II Harry Augustus GARFIELD, of Washington, DC, and Williamstown, Mass., *b* Hiram 11 Oct 1863; *educ* St Paul's Sch, Concord, New Hampshire, Williams Coll (AB 1885, LLD 1934) and Columbia U Law Sch; admitted to the Bar 1888, Prof of Contracts Western Reserve U 1891-97, Prof of Politics Princeton 1903-08, Pres Williams Coll 1908-34, US Fuel Administrator 1917, Hon LLD Princeton and Dartmouth (1908), Amherst and Wesleyan (1909), William and Mary (1921), Harvard (1928) and Toronto (1933), LHD Whitman (1919); *m* Cleveland 14 June 1888 Belle Hartford (*b* there 7 July 1864; *d* 27 June 1944), dau of James Mason, of Cleveland, and *d* Williamstown 12 Dec 1942, leaving issue:

Grandchildren

1 James GARFIELD, *b* Cleveland 28 Oct 1889; *educ* Williams Coll (BA 1911); Capt Coastal Artillery World War I; *m* 20

Jan 1923 *Edith (*b* 17 Jan 1899), dau of Frederick De Peyster Townsend, of Mystic, Conn., and his w Katherine Jermain Savage, and had issue:

Great-grandchildren

(1) *John Robinson GARFIELD, *b* 11 May 1924; *m* 30 Dec 1944 *June Anne Merz (*b* 27 June 1925) and has issue:

Great-great-grandchildren
1a *Robin Burleigh GARFIELD, *b* 28 June 1953
2a *Johnathan Townsend GARFIELD, *b* 21 Oct 1956
3a *Alison Leigh GARFIELD, *b* 21 Aug 1963

Great-grandchildren

(2) *Elizabeth Ann Garfield, *b* 29 July 1926; *m* 27 Dec 1952 *Joseph Arthur GREENHOE (*b* 19 March 1924) and has issue:

Great-great-grandchildren
1a *Eliza GREENHOE, *b* 7 March 1954
2a *Samuel Chapman GREENHOE, *b* 15 Dec 1955
3a *Barbara Ann GREENHOE, *b* 9 Aug 1957

Great-grandchildren

(3) *Harry Augustus GARFIELD II [130 Mt Auburn St, Cambridge, MA 02138, USA], *b* 4 Aug 1932; *m* 1st 20 Aug 1955 Sara Ann Henry (*b* 28 Feb 1934) and has issue:

Great-great-grandchildren
1a *Harry Augustus GARFIELD III, *b* 23 Dec 1956
2a *James GARFIELD, *b* 2 July 1957
3a Ann Raleigh GARFIELD, *b* 8 Jan 1960; *d* 13 March 1987
4a *Amy Townsend GARFIELD, *b* 3 Nov 1961
5a *John Mason GARFIELD, *b* 20 July 1965

Great-grandchildren

(3) (cont.) Harry A. Garfield *m* 2nd 27 Oct 1979 *Janet L. Frothingham (*b* 15 Oct 1933)
(4) *Edith Townsend Garfield, *b* 3 Nov 1935; *m* 8 Sept 1956 *Donald Hartford CAMPBELL (*b* 12 Sept 1934) and has issue:

Great-great-grandchildren
1a *Deborah Leah CAMPBELL, *b* 19—
2a *Bonnie Ann CAMPBELL, *b* 19—
3a *Christine Townsend CAMPBELL, *b* 19—
4a *Jennifer Lynn CAMPBELL, *b* 19—

Grandchildren

2 Mason GARFIELD, *b* Cleveland 5 Oct 1892; *educ* Williams Coll (BA 1914) and Harvard (AM 1915); electronic engr and dairy farmer; *m* 1st 19 Feb 1916 (divorce 19—) Harriet Winchester (*b* Salem, Mass., 29 Oct 1894), dau of Gen William Alden Pew, of Salem, and his w Alice Huntington, and had issue:

Great-grandchildren

(1) *Alicia Rudolph Garfield, *b* 22 July 1917; *m* 1st 19— —— CABOT; *m* 2nd 21 Oct 1945 (divorce 1971) James Francis CONLAN (*b* 20 July 1916) and has issue:

Great-great-grandchildren
1a *Michael Rudolph CONLAN, *b* 28 Aug 1946; *m* June 1971 *——
2a *Peter Vosler CONLAN, *b* 26 July 1948; *m* 19— *——
3a *James Francis CONLAN, Jr, *b* 17 Dec 1952

Great-grandchildren

(2) *Louisa Huntington Garfield [Mrs Edward C Browne, PO Box 207, 906 Monument St, Concord, MA 01742, USA], *b* 16 Feb 1919; *m* 1946 *Edward Crowninshield BROWNE (*b* 5 Nov 1919) and has issue:

Great-great-grandchildren
1a *Charles Billings BROWNE, *b* 21 Jan 1949
2a *Edward Crowninshield BROWNE, Jr, *b* 25 Oct 1950
3a *Mason Garfield BROWNE, *b* 25 Oct 1950
4a *Louisa Huntington BROWNE, *b* 13 Aug 1953

Grandchildren

2 (cont.) Mason Garfield *m* 2nd *Mrs Alva Scott Mitchell and *d* Carlisle, Mass., 31 Aug 1945
3 Lucretia Garfield, *b* Cleveland 18 Jan 1894; *educ* Bryn Mawr; *m* 22 Dec 1925 John Preston COMER (*b* 6 Sept 1888; Prof of Govt Williams Coll; *d* 15 May 1976), s of Samuel Allen Comer, of Williamstown, and his w Amanda Bell Haskins, and *d* Charlottesville, Va., 23 Jan 1968, having had issue:

Great-grandchildren

(1) John Preston COMER, Jr, *b* Boston, Mass., 23 Oct 1926; *educ* MIT (MS) and Columbia (PhD); mathematical statistician; *m* New York 6 July 1963 *Lucette [Mrs John P Comer, 14947 SW 53rd Lane, Miami, FL 33185, USA] (*b* 1 Oct 1932), dau of Ray Landis Bowers and his w Ella Smith, and *d* Cincinnati, Ohio, 13 Oct 1969

(2) Mary Laura COMER, *b* Pittsfield, Mass., 17 July 1928; *d* Northern Italy 8 Jan 1931

Mr and Mrs John P. Comer also adopted a dau:

a Elizabeth Comer, *b* 3 Sept 1932; *m* Williamstown 19— *Neil Russell MARKS and *d* Charlottesville 26 Dec 1969, leaving issue:

  i *Russell Preston MARKS, *b* 19—

Grandchildren

4 Dr Stanton GARFIELD, *b* Willoughby, Ohio, 3 Aug 1895; *educ* Williams Coll; *m* 9 Sept 1922 Lucy Shaler (*b* 17 Feb 1900; *d* Washington, DC, 17 Nov 1987), dau of George Seymour Hodges, of Baltimore, Md., and his w Harriette Martha Goodwillie, and *d* Washington, DC, 5 March 1979, leaving issue:

Great-grandchildren

(1) Mary Barnett Garfield, *b* New Haven, Conn., 9 May 1924; *m* 16 Jan 1955 (divorce 21 Dec 1981) Hassler WHITNEY (*d* 10 May 1989) and *d* Washington, DC, 20 March 1988, leaving issue:

  Great-great-grandchildren

  1a *Sarah (Sally) Newcomb Whitney [Mrs George M Thurston, 22 Troy Rd, Belmont, MA 02178, USA], *b* Princeton, New Jersey, 28 April 1956; *educ* Oberlin Coll (AB 1978), Cornell (MS 1991) and Harvard; *m* 19 June 1988 *George Martin THURSTON (*b* 7 May 1956), s of Paul Ambrose Thurston and his w Helen Margaret Martt

  2a *Emily Baldwin WHITNEY [PO Box 474, Whitethorn, CA 95589, USA], *b* Princeton 10 May 1958 and has issue:

    Great-great-grandchildren's children
    1b *Amber Dawn POLLOCK, *b* 9 Oct 1980
    2b *Vincent Matthew POLLOCK, *b* 24 Aug 1989

Great-grandchildren

(2) *Stanton GARFIELD, Jr [9416 N Murray Rd, Newman Lake, WA 99025, USA], *b* New York 22 Oct 1925; teacher; *m* 1st 28 Dec 1956 (divorce 19—) Mary Matilda (*b* 4 June 1935), dau of James Weaver and his w Charlotte, and has issue:

  Great-great-grandchildren

  1a *Henry Addison GARFIELD [4967 Manfield, San Diego, CA 92116, USA], *b* Philadelphia, Pa., 4 Sept 1957; *m* 16 Nov 1984 *Brenda Stuart

  2a *Margaret Stanton Garfield [Mrs Michael T Overton, RR1 Box 244, Penobscot, ME 04476, USA], *b* Philadelphia 24 June 1959; *m* 11 Sept 1982 *Michael Terry OVERTON

  3a *Elizabeth Hodges Garfield [Mrs Larry Jordan, PO Box 812, Ellsworth, ME 04605, USA], *b* Philadelphia 29 Oct 1960; *m* 19— *Larry JORDAN

  4a *Martha Colburn Garfield [Mrs Thomas H Rochester, PO Box 146, Glen Cove, ME 04846, USA], *b* Philadelphia 6 May 1964; *m* 1989 *Thomas Haydon ROCHESTER

  5a *Katherine Weaver GARFIELD [3833 Grand Ave South #4, Minneapolis, MN 55409, USA], *b* Philadelphia 20 May 1965

Great-grandchildren

(2) (cont.) Stanton Garfield, Jr, *m* 2nd 29 Aug 1975, as her 2nd husb, *Norma, dau of Lawrence Alwin Servis and his w Mary McTaggart and formerly w of —— Pearson

(3) *George Hodges GARFIELD [3838 Piping Rock, Houston, TX 77027, USA], *b* Boston 17 March 1928; *m* 1st 13 Sept 1952 (divorce 18 April 1985) Barbara (*b* 29 Aug 1932), dau of Cloyd Young Kenworthy and his w Ethel Dorcas Kewley, and has issue:

  Great-great-grandchildren

  1a *George Hodges GARFIELD, Jr, *b* Stamford, Conn., 11 June 1957; *m* 8 Aug 1987 *Patricia Carol, dau of Richard Douglas Saunders

  2a *Susan Jennings Garfield [Mrs Edward Bowditch, 2076 Krameria St, Denver, CO 80207, USA] *b* Stamford 6 Oct 1959; *m* 1st 28 May 1988 Charles HIGGINSON, Jr (*d* Oct 1988); *m* 2nd 1992 *Edward BOWDITCH

  3a *Peter Stanton GARFIELD, *b* Stamford 18 July 1961

  4a *Sarah Kenworthy GARFIELD, *b* Stamford 23 Aug 1964

Great-grandchildren

(3) (cont.) George H. Garfield *m* 2nd 23 Dec 1987 *Nancy Elizabeth Wright

(4) *John Mason GARFIELD [14 Colonial Dve, North Haven, CT 06473-1238, USA], *b* Concord, Mass., 9 Aug 1934; *educ* Exeter, Williams Coll (AB 1956) and Wesleyan U; teacher and Dir Studies Hamden Hall Country Day Sch, Hamden, Conn., 1971-; *m* 15 July 1961 *Sylvia Marie (*b* 28 April 1938), dau of Thomas Carlyle Jones and his w Dorotha Anne Bratt, and has issue:

Great-great-grandchildren

1a *Andrew Mason GARFIELD, *b* Springfield, Mass., 31 Aug 1964

2a *James Robinson GARFIELD, *b* Springfield 7 Nov 1966

President Garfield's son

III James Rudolph GARFIELD, of Cleveland, Ohio, *b* Hiram 17 Oct 1865; *educ* St Paul's Sch, Concord, New Hampshire, Williams Coll (AB 1885) and Columbia Law Sch; admitted to the Bar 1888, Memb: Ohio State Senate 1896-1900 and US Civil Service Commission 1902-03, Commissioner of Corpn US Dept Commerce and Labor 1903-07, Sec of the Interior 1907-09, Hon LLD Howard U 1908 and Pittsburgh 1909; *m* 30 Dec 1890 Helen Newell (*b* Cleveland 12 Feb 1866; *d* 26 Aug 1930), dau of John Hills, of West Newbury, Mass., and his w Judith Poore, and *d* Cleveland 24 March 1950, having had issue:

Grandchildren

1 John Newell GARFIELD, *b* Chicago 3 Feb 1892; *educ* Williams Coll; Capt 34th Field Artillery US Army; *m* Cleveland 27 June 1916 Janet Sutherland (*b* Cleveland 6 Sept 1889; *d* Troy, New York, 6 March 1959), dau of Samuel D. Dodge and his w Jeannette M. Groff, and *d* Mentor, Ohio, 23 May 1931, leaving issue:

Great-grandchildren

(1) *Janet Dodge Garfield [Mrs Alexander Cushing Brown Jr, 16 Hamilton Gate Ct, Wickford, RI 02852, USA], *b* Cleveland 24 Sept 1917; *m* there 2 Jan 1939 *Alexander Cushing BROWN, Jr (*b* Cleveland 1 Dec 1913), s of Alexander Cushing Brown and his w Mary Bristol Dana, and has issue:

Great-great-grandchildren

1a *Alexander Cushing BROWN III [PO Box 511, Marlboro, CT 06447, USA], *b* Cleveland 8 Sept 1941; *educ* Union Coll; *m* Hartford, Conn., 27 June 1964 *Jean F., dau of Dr John G. Martin and his w Elizabeth Parsons, and has issue:

Great-great-grandchildren's children

1b *Elisabeth BROWN, *b* 24 Feb 1967

2b *Samantha Brown, *b* 15 Jan 1969; *m* 28 Dec 1991 *Theodore Godwin GOODRICH, s of Frederic P. Goodrich III and his w Shirley Godwin

Great-great-grandchildren

2a *Cornelia Brown, *b* Cleveland 10 Feb 1944; *m* Short Hills, New Jersey, 14 Dec 1968 *Robert Lawton ELMORE, Jr, s of Robert Lawton Elmore and his w Dorothy Woodbridge, and has issue:

Great-great-grandchildren's children

1b *Alexander Garfield ELMORE, *b* 6 Jan 1972

2b *Samuel Dodge ELMORE, *b* 2 Jan 1978

Great-grandchildren

(2) *James Rudolph GARFIELD II, *b* Cleveland 12 Jan 1920; *m* 1st 1941 (divorce 1950) Mary, dau of Alexander Cushing Brown and his w Mary Bristol Dana and sister of James Garfield II's brother-in-law (*see above*), and has issue:

Great-great-grandchildren

1a *James Rudolph GARFIELD III, *b* Dec 1942

2a *Edward Dana GARFIELD, *b* Oct 1946

3a *Dana Alexander GARFIELD, *b* June 1948

Great-grandchildren

(2) (cont.) James Rudolph Garfield II *m* 2nd 1950 *Esther MacGillicuddy and with her has issue:

Great-great-grandchildren

4a *Timothy Doane GARFIELD, *b* Feb 1952

5a *Sarah Elizabeth GARFIELD, *b* 11 June 1954

Great-grandchildren

(3) *Frances Sutherland Garfield [Mrs Charles Tillinghurst, 8754 Booth Road, Mentor, OH, USA], *b* Cleveland 19 Sept 1921; *m* 1942 Charles M. TILLINGHURST (*d* Oct 1981) and has issue:

Great-great-grandchildren

1a *Carolyn Dodge TILLINGHURST, *b* 28 Oct 1943

2a *Nancy Doan TILLINGHURST, *b* Jan 1947

Great-grandchildren

(4) *John Newell GARFIELD, Jr [19e Scott Street, Chicago, IL, USA], *b* Cleveland 5 Oct 1923; *educ* S Kent; real estate broker in Chicago; *m* 1st 9 March 1946 (divorce 1966) Christine (*b* 13 Sept 1927), dau of Horace Fuller Henriques and his w Christine Corlett, and has issue:

Great-great-grandchildren

1a *John Newell GARFIELD III, *b* Youngstown, Ohio, 11 April 1947

2a *Thames Corlett GARFIELD, *b* Youngstown 20 Oct 1948

3a *Christine Henriques Garfield, *b* Lake Forest, Ill., 9 Dec 1950; *m* 5 Aug 1972 (divorce 19—) David Wallace

YOUNG, s of George Webster Young
4a *Horace Fuller GARFIELD, b Sewickley, Pa., 3 July 1953

Great-grandchildren
(4) (cont.) John N. Garfield, Jr, m 2nd Lake Forest 1967 *Lynn (b Madison, Wisc., 1934), dau of Albert Hanson
(5) *Douglas Dodge GARFIELD, b 20 May 1927; m 1951 *Olivia Gardner Pattison and has issue:

Great-great-grandchildren
1a *Janet Dodge GARFIELD, b April 1952
2a *Douglas Dodge GARFIELD, Jr, b 1954
3a *Stephen Pattison GARFIELD
4a *Olivia GARFIELD
5a *Nina Royce GARFIELD

Grandchildren
2 James Abram GARFIELD II, b 18 April 1894; Maj 322nd Field Artillery US Army World War I; m 1st 31 Dec 1917 (divorce 1930) Edwina Forbes (b 24 July 1895), dau of Maj-Gen Edwin Forbes Glenn, of Chillicothe, Ohio, and had issue:

Great-grandchildren
(1) *Helen Louise GARFIELD [PO Box 945, West Palm Beach, FL 33402, USA], b Cleveland, Ohio, 23 Nov 1918
(2) *Elizabeth GARFIELD [PO Box 945, West Palm Beach, FL 33402, USA], b Cleveland 14 Feb 1921

Grandchildren
2 (cont.) James Abram Garfield II m 2nd *Marney Maxwell and d 2 July 1969
3 Newell GARFIELD, b Chicago 1 Aug 1895; Capt 322nd Field Artillery US Army World War I; m 7 Oct 1922 *Mary Louise Wyatt (b 10 May 1899) and d 19—, leaving issue:

Great-grandchildren
(1) *Newell GARFIELD, Jr [Hope Town, ABACO, Bahamas], b Rochester, New York, 8 July 1923; educ Yale; management consultant; m 1st 1946 (divorce 1960) Jane O. Day and has issue:

Great-great-grandchildren
1a *William Wyatt GARFIELD, b 12 July 1948; educ Vermont Acad, Tufts U and Dartmouth (MBA 1974); Lt USNR, corporate financial analyst; m Rollinsford, New Hampshire, 31 May 1975 (divorce 19—) Alexandra West, dau of Douglas Rollins, of Rollinsford
2a *Susan Garfield, b 8 July 1949; m 1st May 1971 (divorce 19—) John WILSON and has issue:

Great-great-grandchildren's children
1b *Cristian WILSON, b March 1972

Great-great-grandchildren
2a (cont.) Mrs Susan Wilson m 2nd 19— *Todd CHENY and has further issue:

Great-great-grandchildren's children
1b *Liza CHENY, b 19—

Great-great-grandchildren
3a *Newell GARFIELD III, b 19 April 1951; m 19— (divorce 19—) ——
4a *Stephen K. GARFIELD, b 25 Feb 1954

Great-grandchildren
(1) (cont.) Newell Garfield Jr m 2nd New York 16 Nov 1961 *(Mary) Jane Harrison (b New York 3 Nov 1929), only dau of James Blaine Walker, Jr, of New York, and his w Elizabeth, yst dau of President BENJAMIN HARRISON, and has further issue:

Great-great-grandchildren
5a *Eliza(beth) Newell GARFIELD, b New York 23 Nov 1962; descended from three US Presidents

Great-grandchildrn
(2) *Wyatt GARFIELD [Myrick Road, Princeton, MA 01541, USA], b 8 Oct 1924; m 1950 *Katherine D. Barney and has issue:

Great-great-grandchildren
1a *Sarah Brandegee GARFIELD, b 29 June 1951
2a *Louise Rich GARFIELD, b 19 Sept 1952
3a *Wyatt GARFIELD, Jr, b 11 July 1955
4a *Seth GARFIELD [1076 Horseneck Rd, Westport, MA 12790, USA], b 4 April 1957
5a *Angus L. GARFIELD, b 24 Nov 1959
6a *Benjamin GARFIELD, b 13 Dec 1962

Great-grandchildren
(3) *Sarah Winslow Garfield [Mrs Peter H Smith, University Lane, Manchester, MA 01744, USA], b Hartford 19 April 1929; m Concord 14 Dec 1957 *Peter Huntington SMITH (b St Louis, Mo., 30 Nov 1913), s of Huntington Smith and his w Caroline Lackland, and has issue:

Great-great-grandchildren

1a *Sarah Wyatt SMITH, b Guatemala City 9 May 1959

2a *Elise Griswold SMITH, b New Bedford, Mass., 20 Aug 1960

3a *Peter Huntington SMITH, Jr, b Boston, Mass., 29 July 1963

Grandchildren

4 Rudolph Hills GARFIELD, b Mentor, Ohio 13 Sept 1899; served USN World War I; m 26 Oct 1925 *Eleanor Borton [Mrs Rudolph Garfield, Mentor, Ohio 44060, USA] (b 20 March 1899) and d 1946, having had issue:

Great-grandchildren

(1) Molly Ann GARFIELD, b 20 Sept, d 23 Sept 1926

(2) *Rudolph Hills GARFIELD, Jr, b 16 July 1928; m 16 Oct 1954 *Jennifer Packard Barnes

(3) *Borton GARFIELD, b 5 April 1931

President Garfield's daughter

IV Mary ('Molly' or 'Mollie') Garfield, b Washington, DC, 16 Jan 1867; m Mentor 14 June 1888 Joseph Stanley BROWN (b Washington, DC, 19 Aug 1858; priv sec to his father-in-law President GARFIELD 1880-81; d Pasadena, Calif., 2 Nov 1941), s of Joseph Leopold Brown and his w Elizabeth Frances Marr, and d Pasadena 30 Dec 1947, having had issue:

Grandchildren

1 Rudolph STANLEY-BROWN, b Mentor 9 April 1889; educ Sheffield Scientific Sch, Columbia Sch of Architecture and Beaux Arts, Paris; served US Army World War I; m East Orange, New Jersey, 6 June 1922 Katharine Schermerhorn (b Philadelphia 30 April 1892; d Boston 15 April 1972), dau of Charles A. Oliver, of East Orange, and his w Mary Schermerhorn Henry, and d Augusta, Ga., 8 Feb 1944, leaving issue:

Great-grandchildren

(1) *Dr Edward Garfield STANLEY-BROWN [860 Roslyn Road, Ridgewood, NJ 07450, USA], b Cleveland 11 Nov 1923; educ S Kent Sch, Conn., U of Virginia and U of Pennsylvania Medical Sch; paediatric surg, Assoc Dir Surgery St Luke's Hosp New York City 1955-86; m Ridgewood 1 Nov 1952 *Jeanne Claire (b Ridgewood 12 July 1927), dau of Walter Rudolph Olson and his w Claire Drake, and has issue:

Great-great-grandchildren

1a *Jeanne Drake Stanley-Brown [Mrs Paul R Driscoll, 50 Oak Rd, Norwood, MA 02062-2035, USA], b New York 5 Sept 1954; educ Manhattanville Coll and U of Pennsylvania Sch of Nursing; Registered Nurse 1979-, currently with Children's Hosp, Boston; m Nantucket, Mass., 20 June 1987 *Paul Robert DRISCOLL, Jr, s of Paul Robert Driscoll and his w Genevieve Hatchfield, and has issue:

Great-great-grandchildren's children

1b *Sarah Hatchfield DRISCOLL, b Boston 19 May 1988

2b *Emily Garfield DRISCOLL, b Boston 25 July 1989

3b *Christopher Whitfield DRISCOLL, b Boston 25 May 1991

4b *David Reyer DRISCOLL, b Boston 16 Jan 1993

Great-great-grandchildren

2a *David Garfield STANLEY-BROWN [752 W Saddle River Rd, Ho-Ho-Kus, NJ 07423, USA], b New York 12 April 1956; educ Choate and Washington and Jefferson Colls; Dir of Sales VMX Inc 1987-; m Nantucket, Mass., 9 Sept 1989 *Kathleen Ann, dau of Edward John Martin and his w Marjorie Helen, and has issue:

Great-great-grandchildren's children

1b *Chelsea Alexandra STANLEY-BROWN, b Ridgewood, New Jersey 25 Dec 1991

Great-great-grandchildren

3a *Elizabeth Powell STANLEY-BROWN [214 West Avenue, Darien, CT 06820, USA], b New York 21 April 1958; educ Wheaton Coll, Norton, Mass. (BA 1980); V-Pres of Design Support Ralph Lauren Corp; m Nantucket Island, Mass., 6 Sept 1986 *Peter Garret HORAN, s of Edward Leo Horan and his w Mary Elizabeth, but uses maiden name, and with him has issue:

Great-great-grandchildren's children

1b *Mackenzie Elizabeth HORAN, b New York 9 Aug 1989

2b *Reilly Alexandra HORAN, b New York 2 Oct 1991

Great-grandchildren

(2) *Katharine Oliver Stanley-Brown [3 Tuck's Point Rd, Manchester, MA, 01944, USA], b Cleveland 2 March 1928; educ Vassar; m Boston 27 May 1955 *Gordon ABBOTT, Jr (b Boston 2 May 1927), s of Gordon Abbott and his w Esther Lowell Cunningham, and has issue:

Great-great-grandchildren

1a *Christopher Cunningham ABBOTT [1 Proctor St, Manchester, MA 01944, USA], b Boston 22 Oct 1956; educ St Lawrence U; with Merrill Lynch & Co 1980-90, now Sr V-Pres Putnam Investments; m Nantucket 24 June 1989 *Lexanne (b Philadelphia 4 June 1957), dau of Revd Stanley E. Johnson and his w Sally Hawes, and has issue:

Great-great-grandchildren's children:
1b *Lowell Cunningham ABBOTT, b Boston 11 March 1992

Great-great-grandchildren
2a *Katrina Schermerhorn ABBOTT, b Boston 29 April 1958
3a *Victoria McLane Abbott, b Boston 31 Jan 1961; m Manchester, Mass., 17 Aug 1991 *John Nicholas RICCARDI (b New York 7 July 1991), s of John Dominic Riccardi and his w Josephine Villamena
4a *Alexandra Garfield ABBOTT, b Boston 4 May 1967

Grandchildren
2 *Ruth Stanley-Brown [1161 Willa Vista Trail, Maitland, FL 32751, USA], b Mentor 3 Aug 1892; educ Vassar; m Mentor 25 March 1922 Dr (Albert) Herbert FEIS (b New York City 1893; Prof of Economics Kansas State U; d 2 March 1972), s of Louis J. Freis and his w Louise, and has an adopted dau:

a *(Mary) Felicia FEIS, b 1935

Grandchildren
3 Margaret Stanley-Brown, b Washington, DC, 2 Oct 1895; educ Vassar and Coll of Physicians and Surgs, New York (MD 1923); m 5 May 1950 Max K. SELLERS and d New Milford, Conn., 12 June 1958

President Garfield's son
V Irvin McDowell GARFIELD, of Boston, b Hiram 3 Aug 1870; educ Williams Coll and Harvard Law Sch; lawyer; m Boston 16 Oct 1906 Susan (b Boston 9 March 1878), dau of Nathaniel Henry Emmons, of Boston, and his w Eleanor Gassett Bacon, and d Boston 18 or 19 July 1951, leaving issue:

Grandchildren
1 *Eleanor GARFIELD, b 27 June 1908
2 *Jane Garfield [Mrs Charles E Cheever, 9 Lookout, Farm Rd, Natick, MA, USA], b 10 May 1910; m 1942 *Charles Ezekiel CHEEVER, and has issue:

Great-grandchildren
(1) *Charles Ezekiel CHEEVER, Jr, b 1943
(2) *Jane Wells CHEEVER, b 1945
(3) *Susan Emmons CHEEVER, b 1947

Grandchildren
3 *Irvin McDowell (Mike) GARFIELD, Jr [84 Main Street, Southboro, MA, USA], b 19 Jan 1913; m 19— *Elinor Fay and has issue:

Great-grandchildren
(1) *Michael Rudolph GARFIELD, b 1941
(2) *Richard GARFIELD, b 1942
(3) *Hester GARFIELD, b 1944
(4) *Irvin McDowell GARFIELD III, b 1945
(5) *James Abram GARFIELD III, b 1952
(6) *Anne GARFIELD, b 26 May 1955
(7) *Elizabeth GARFIELD, b 26 May 1955

President Garfield's son
VI Abram GARFIELD, of Cleveland, b Washington, DC 21 Nov 1872; educ Williams Coll (AB 1893) and MIT (BS 1896); architect; m 1st Cleveland 14 Oct 1897 Sarah Granger (b Cleveland 10 Jan 1873; d there 3 Feb 1945), dau of Edward Porter Williams, of Cleveland, and his w Mary Louise Mason, and had issue:

Grandchildren
1 Edward Williams GARFIELD, b Cleveland 17 May 1899; educ Williams Coll; m Milburn, New Jersey, 10 April 1928 Hope (b Summit, New Jersey, 20 June 1905; d 5 April 1977), dau of Frank D. Dillingham and his w Louise Bulkley, and d 25 Dec 1979, leaving issue:

Great-grandchildren
(1) *Louise Dillingham Garfield [Mrs Louise Muranko, 501 Lake Shore Drive Apt #103, Lake Park, FL, USA], b Cleveland 17 Jan 1929; m 1st 4 Sept 1948 (divorce 1961) Dr Paul Frederick GILLAN and has issue:

Great-great-grandchildren
1a *Bruce Paul GILLAN [501 Lake Shore Drive Apt #103, Lake Park, FL, USA], b Cleveland 12 Oct 1954; m 1st 4 April 1981 (divorce 1988) Lisa Ann Spangler; m 2nd 18 Nov 1990 (divorce 1991) Nina Russell
2a *Mary Louise Gillan [Mrs Richard Schmid, 1555 Holmden Ave, South Euclid, OH, USA], b Cleveland 9 Nov 1955; m 14 July 1984 *Richard William SCHMID (b Cleveland 25 Nov 1953) and has issue:

Great-great-grandchildren's children
1b *Danielle Anne SCHMID, b Cleveland 5 Nov 1985
2b *Ashley Rochelle SCHMID, b Cleveland 19 Nov 1987
3b *Eric William SCHMID, b Cleveland 21 July 1991

Great-grandchildren
(1) (cont.) Mrs Louise Gillan *m* 2nd 26 July 1963 (divorce 1986) Daniel Henry MURANKO (*b* Cleveland 19 April 1930)
(2) *Edward Williams GARFIELD, Jr [3579 Gottschee Court, Brunswick, OH 44212, USA], *b* Cleveland 23 Oct 1930; *m* 1st June 1956 (divorce 19—) June Cain and has issue:

Great-great-grandchildren
1a *Edward Williams GARFIELD III, *b* Cleveland 27 July 1957
2a *Marjory Ann GARFIELD, *b* Cleveland 2 Feb 1960
3a *Elizabeth Linda GARFIELD, *b* Cleveland, Ohio 19 April 1961

Great-grandchildren
(2) (cont.) Edward Williams Garfield, Jr, *m* 2nd 21 Oct 1967 *Dorothy Jane Andler (*b* Cleveland 27 Nov 1933) and with her has issue:

Great-great-grandchildren
4a *Susan Marie GARFIELD, *b* Cleveland 29 May 1969

Great-grandchildren
(3) *Dorothy Hope GARFIELD [Mrs Edward Stivers, 179 Almendral Av., Atherton, CA, USA], *b* Cleveland 17 May 1932; *m* Nov 1960 Edward Collier STIVERS (*b* Decatur, Ill., 30 Aug 1927; *d* London, UK, 18 June 1972) and has issue:

Great-great-grandchildren
1a *Katherine Ann STIVERS, *b* Boston 4 July 1961
2a *Sarah Marie STIVERS, *b* Atherton, Calif., 16 May 1963
3a *Christopher Collier STIVERS, *b* Atherton 1 June 1965
4a *Hope Marjorie STIVERS, *b* Atherton 1 Oct 1967

Grandchildren
2 *Marie Louise Garfield [Mrs Willian R Hallaran, 12564 Cedar Road, Cleveland, OH, USA], *b* Cleveland 5 July 1903; *m* there 7 Oct 1931 *Dr William Richard HALLARAN (*b* Ferszepore, India, 27 Dec 1904), s of William Hallaran, RAMC, and his *w* Mary Newton, and has issue:

Great-grandchildren
(1) *Sarah Newton Hallaran, *b* Cleveland 1 Oct 1934; *m* there 14 June 1957 *James William GRAMENTINE (*b* Akron 28 Sept 1927), s of James Gramentine and his *w* Helen Meier, and has issue:

Great-great-grandchildren
1a *James Garfield GRAMENTINE, *b* Cleveland 16 Aug 1960
2a *Helen Elizabeth GRAMENTINE, *b* Cleveland 12 Sept 1963

Great-grandchildren
(2) *Dr William Garfield HALLARAN, *b* Cleveland 2 Jan 1938; *m* there 30 March 1963 *Elizabeth Josephine (*b* Cleveland 22 March 1941), dau of Stanley Salter and his *w* Katherine Ottesen, and has issue:

Great-great-grandchildren
1a *William Patrick HALLARAN, *b* Cleveland 16 Dec 1965
2a *Timothy Richard HALLARAN, *b* Cleveland 2 Sept 1967

Great-grandchildren
(3) *Michael Terence HALLARAN, *b* Cleveland 25 April 1947; *m* N Granby, Conn., 21 June 1970 *Alice Warner (*b* N Granby 30 Jan 1947), dau of Willard Kellogg and his *w* Grace Hamilton

President Garfield's children
VI (cont.) Abram Garfield *m* 2nd Shaker Heights, Ohio, 12 April 1947 *Helen Grannis Matthews (*b* 1902) and *d* Cleveland 16 Oct 1958
VII Edward GARFIELD, *b* Hiram 25 Dec 1874; *d* Washington, DC, 25 Oct 1876

MALE LINE ANCESTRY AND COLLATERAL DESCENDANTS

Edward GARFIELD, GAFFIELD, GEARFFILD or GEARFIELD, *b* England? (there was a tradition in the Garfield family that they came from Wales or Chester, near the English-Welsh border in England, but there is no independent proof of that) *c* 1575?; emigrated to New England *c* 1630, was made a freeman by the Massachusetts Gen Court 6 May 1635 and was granted land as one of earliest proprietors of Watertown, Mass., 1636 (30 ac) and 1637 (12 ac), acquiring further plots in succeeding years so that by 1662 he had 100 ac in all; Selectman (memb of a board looking after local affairs) 1638, 1655 and 1662, Constable (tax-collector) 1661; *m* probably a 1st *w*, name unknown, and had issue:

I Samuel GARFIELD, *b* England in or before 1625; landowner by 1644, received 40 ac and £10 in his f's will of 1688; *m* 1st Susan —— (*d* on or before 10 May 1652) and had issue:

  1 Samuel GARFIELD, *b* Watertown by 1646; apprenticed 1 Nov 1653 to one John Flemming and lived 20 years in Salem and Cambridge, Mass., returning to Watertown *c* 1691
  2 John GARFIELD, *b* 8 Feb 1645/6; *bur* 15 Jan 1649/50
  3 Ephraim GARFIELD, *b* 20 Nov 1649; *d* Sudbury, Mass., 7 March 1722/3

I (cont.) Samuel Garfield *m* 2nd 28 Sept 1652 Mary Benfield (*d* Lancaster (now Harvard), Mass., 1709) and *d* Watertown 20 Nov 1684, having had further issue:

  4 Mary GARFIELD, *b* 30 June 1653; *d* young 5 Sarah Garfield, *b* 17 Jan 1654/5; *m* —— GUILE
  6 Rachel Garfield, *b* 23 Nov 1656; *m* John PRIEST, of Woburn and Lancaster, Mass., and *d* Harvard 17 May 1737, having had issue
  7 Elizabeth GARFIELD, *b* 8 Dec 1659; *d* young 8 Deborah Garfield, *b c* 1662; *m* —— BROOKS
  9 John GARFIELD, *b* 7 July 1664 10 Ruth GARFIELD, *b* 25 April 1666
  11 Lydia Garfield, *b* 31 Aug 1668; *m* 2 Jan 1693/4 Caleb BURBANK, of Rowley, Mass., and *d* 3 March 1697/8, having had issue at least one child, Hannah
  12 Daniel GARFIELD, *b* 5 Nov 1670; *d* 13 Feb 1683/4 13 Mary GARFIELD, *b* 4 June 1673
  14 Elizabeth GARFIELD, *b* 26 Sept 1676
  15 Ann, Anna or Hannah Garfield, *b* 16—; *m* Rowley, Mass., 6 Dec 1681 Jonathan JACKSON and had issue (all *b* between 1682 and 1705)
  16 Mercy Garfield; *m* —— BERREY

Edward Garfield *m* 2nd(?) Rebecca —— (*b c* 1606; *d* Watertown 16 April 1661) and had further issue:

II Joseph GARFIELD, *b* Watertown 11 Sept 1637; served King Philip's War 1675-76, in which a powerful Indian confederacy briefly threatened the very existence of the New England colony before most of the Indians concerned were exterminated; *m* 3 April 1663 Sarah Gale and *d* 14 Aug 1691, having had issue (all *b* between 1664 and 1688)
III Rebecca Garfield, *b* Watertown 10 March 1640/1; *m* 10 Jan 1660/1 Isaac MIXER or MIXTER and *d* 16 March 1682/3, having had issue (all *b* between 1662 and 1680, one of them being the ancestor of the Mormon pioneer Brigham Young)
IV Benjamin GARFIELD, for whom *see below*
V Abigail Garfield, *b* 29 June 1646; *m* John PARKHURST and *d* 18 Oct 1726, having had issue (all *b* between 1672 and 1690, one child being called Sara)

Edward Garfield *m* 3rd(?) 1 Sept 1661 Johannah, widow of Thomas Buckmaster or Buckminster, of Brookline, Mass., and *d* Watertown 14 June 1672

His yst s (and yr s by his 2nd marriage),
  Benjamin GARFIELD, of Watertown, *b c* 1643; Capt of Militia, admitted Freeman 18 April 1690, nine times Rep to Gen Court, Selectman for 20 years and Town Clerk of Watertown; *m* 1st 1673 Mehitabel Hawkins (*d* 9 Dec 1675) and had two s; *m* 2nd 17 Jan 1677/8 Elizabeth (*b* Cambridge, Mass., 17 Aug 1659; *m* 2nd 25 Oct 1720 Daniel Harrington), yst dau of Matthew Bridge, of Lexington, Mass., and his w Anne, dau of Nicholas Danforth, and *d* 28 Nov 1717, having with her had (with one other s and five daus) a 3rd s:

Thomas GARFIELD, of Lincoln, Mass., *b* 12 Dec 1680; Lt Lincoln Militia; *m* 2 Jan 1706/7 Mercy (*b* 1686; *d* 28 Feb 1744/5), dau of Joshua Bigelow and his w Elizabeth Flagg or Flegg and yr sister of Lt John Bigelow (gggf of Hon John Bigelow, US Min to France 1864-67 and literary executor of Samuel J. Tilden, the Democratic presidential contender against President GARFIELD's immediate predecessor President HAYES), and *d* Weston, Mass., 4 Feb 1752, leaving (with five other s and six daus) an est s:

Thomas GARFIELD, of Lincoln, *b* 28 Feb 1713; Lt Lincoln Militia; *m* 21 Oct 1742 Rebecca (*b* 2 Nov 1719; *d* 3 Feb 1763), dau of Deacon Samuel Johnson, of Lunenburg, Mass., and his w Rebecca, and *d* Lincoln 3 Jan 1774, leaving (with a yr s and three daus) a s:

Solomon GARFIELD, of Westminster, Mass., and of Cherry Valley, Otsego Co, New York, *b* Lincoln, Mass., 18 July 1743; served in the Revolutionary War with Noah Miles's Co and Whitcomb's Regt, fought at Concord 19 April 1775; *m* 22 Aug 1769 Sarah, widow of James Stimpson, of Sudbury, Mass., and probably dau of Abraham Bryant, of Sudbury and his w Sarah Frinks, and *d* Worcester, Otsego Co, New York, 1807 following a fall, having had (with a yr s and three daus) a s:

Thomas GARFIELD, of Worcester, New York, *b* Westminster 19 March 1773; *m c* 1794, as her 1st husb, Asenath Hill, of Schoharie Co, New York, (*b c* 1778; *m* 2nd Amos Boynton; *d* Newberg, Cuyahoga Co, Ohio, 5 Feb 1851), probably sister of Josiah Hill (*c* 1776-*c* 1864), and *d* Worcester 1801, leaving (with a yr s and two daus) a s:

Abraham (called Abram) GARFIELD, *b* Worcester 28 Dec 1799; farmer and canal construction supervisor 1826-28, moved to Western Reserve, Ohio, settling initially at Independence (now on the outskirts of Cleveland), later at Orange; *m* 3 Feb 1820 Eliza (*b* Richmond, New Hampshire, 21 Sept 1801; *d* Mentor 21 Jan 1888), dau of James Ballou, of Richmond, New Hampshire, farmer, and his w Mehitable, dau of Henry Ingalls, and *d* Otsego Co, New York, 3 May 1833 of pneumonia, having had issue:

  I Mehitable Garfield, *b* Ohio 28 Jan 1821; *m* 1837 Stephen D. TROWBRIDGE, of Solon, Ohio, and had three daus
  II Thomas GARFIELD, of Jamestown, Mich., *b* Ohio 16 Oct 1822; farmer, later moved to Michigan; *m* Jane Harper, and

had one s and one dau

III Mary Garfield, *b* Ohio 19 Oct 1824; *m* Marenus G. LARABEE, of Solon, and *d* 4 Nov 1884, leaving one s and three daus

IV James Ballou GARFIELD, *b* Ohio 31 Oct 1826; *d* 28 Jan 1929

V JAMES ABRAM GARFIELD, 20th PRESIDENT of the UNITED STATES of AMERICA

Benjamin Garfield[1]
c 1643-1717

Elizabeth Bridge[2]
b 1659

Joshua Bigelow
1655-1745

Elizabeth Flagg
1656-1729

Thomas Garfield
1680-1752

Mercy Bigelow
c 1686-1744/5

Samuel Johnson

Rebecca —
d 1731

Maturin Ballou
d 1661-73

Hannah Pike
d 1718/9

Valentine Whitman
d 1701

Mary —
d 1718

James Ballou
c 1652-*p* 1744

Susanna Whitman
1658-*c* 1725

Walter Cooke
d 1695/6

Catharine —
d 1695/6

John Rockwood
1641-1724

Joanna Ford

Nicholas Cook
1659/60-1730

Joanna Rockwood
1669-*c* 1710

John Ingalls
c 1626-1721

Elizabeth Barrett
d a 1718

Benjamin Ludden
c 1650-90/1

Eunice Holbrook
b 1658

James Wheeler
1667—1740-53

Grizell Squire
1668-*a* 1738

John West

Mehitable —
d p 1694

Benjamin Carpenter
1658-1727

Renew Weeks
1660-1703

John Martin
c 1652/3-1720

Mercy Billington
1651/2-1718

George Thompson
c 1638-74

Sarah —
d p 1674

Edmund Ingalls
fl c 1705

Eunice Ludden
b p 1726

James Wheeler, Jr
1697—1740-53

Elizabeth West
b 1694

Jotham Carpenter
1682-*c* 1760

Desire Martin
1684/5-1727

John Thompson
b 1660/1

Elizabeth —

[1 & 2] For generations further back *see* Male Line Ancestry section

JAMES A. GARFIELD
FAMILY TREE

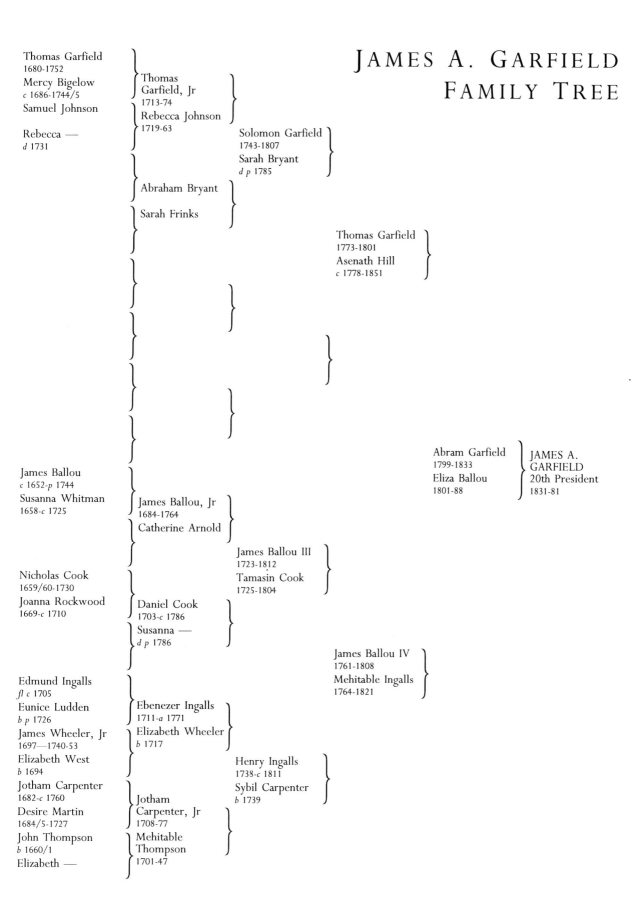

Thomas Garfield
1680-1752
Mercy Bigelow
c 1686-1744/5
Samuel Johnson

Rebecca —
d 1731

Thomas
Garfield, Jr
1713-74
Rebecca Johnson
1719-63

Solomon Garfield
1743-1807
Sarah Bryant
d p 1785

Abraham Bryant

Sarah Frinks

Thomas Garfield
1773-1801
Asenath Hill
c 1778-1851

Abram Garfield
1799-1833
Eliza Ballou
1801-88

JAMES A.
GARFIELD
20th President
1831-81

James Ballou
c 1652-p 1744
Susanna Whitman
1658-c 1725

James Ballou, Jr
1684-1764
Catherine Arnold

James Ballou III
1723-1812
Tamasin Cook
1725-1804

Nicholas Cook
1659/60-1730
Joanna Rockwood
1669-c 1710

Daniel Cook
1703-c 1786
Susanna —
d p 1786

James Ballou IV
1761-1808
Mehitable Ingalls
1764-1821

Edmund Ingalls
fl c 1705
Eunice Ludden
b p 1726
James Wheeler, Jr
1697—1740-53
Elizabeth West
b 1694
Jotham Carpenter
1682-c 1760
Desire Martin
1684/5-1727
John Thompson
b 1660/1
Elizabeth —

Ebenezer Ingalls
1711-a 1771
Elizabeth Wheeler
b 1717

Henry Ingalls
1738-c 1811
Sybil Carpenter
b 1739

Jotham
Carpenter, Jr
1708-77
Mehitable
Thompson
1701-47

Plate 64   Chester A. Arthur

CHESTER A. ARTHUR

1829-86
21ST PRESIDENT OF THE UNITED STATES OF AMERICA
1881-85

With Arthur's arrival in the White House there was reason for alarm. Arthur was well-known as a leading member of the faction led by New York's corrupt boss Senator Roscoe Conkling. He had been given the vice-presidential nomination in order to appease Conkling and his followers, known as the Stalwarts; reformers had consoled themselves with the fond thought that it was inconceivable that Garfield would die in office. To cap it all, Garfield's assassin had shouted out "I am a Stalwart and now Arthur is President!" It seemed likely that under Arthur the corruption of the Grant era would be revived.

It is immensely to Arthur's credit that it was not. On the contrary, he accepted the need for further reform and helped to pass the Pendleton Act of 1883, which laid the foundations for a non-partisan civil service. It did not stop the spoils system but it did stimulate the growth of a better way of administering the government and Arthur deserved the praise he got for it. He even paid the price of virtue: his party refused to nominate him for a second term in 1884: instead it turned to James G. Blaine, one of the most thorough spoilsmen of the age.

Undoubtedly Arthur tried to live up to the presidency. He tolerated no liberties from former cronies; he redecorated the White House; he renounced Conkling, though he continued to lean to the Stalwarts and was perhaps less austere in patronage matters than either his predecessor or his successor. For example, he did all he could to help the Stalwarts keep control of New York politics. When they picked a sufficiently pliant candidate for the Governorship of New York in 1883, Arthur appointed him Secretary of the Treasury to give him some prestige and visibility with the voters. (It may be said at once that this manoeuvre backfired badly; Grover Cleveland, the Democratic candidate, won the election handily.) But in essentials there was no backsliding from the modest gains of the Hayes years.

The reason for this pleasing disappointment was simple enough. Arthur was a loyal party man but he was not personally dishonest. He genuinely accepted the need for the spoils system, for it seemed to be the only way of keeping a party organization together and without the Republican party where would the Republic be? Such were his views until, perhaps, his dismissal from the Collectorship of New York by Hayes showed him that a new idea was awake. He was intensely gratified by the vice-presidential nomination, which Conkling wanted him to refuse, and when he got the presidency itself it was natural for this patriotic and cultivated lawyer to do the very best that he could. Perhaps in his own eyes he always had. The suggestion implied a degree of innocence hard to believe in a man who had lived at close quarters with the professional politicians of New York for so long, but perhaps innocence, in such cases, is just another word for muddle. If Arthur was too muddled to see that his notions of party loyalty and public spirit were inconsistent with each other, he was neither the first nor the last clever man of whom the same might be said.

CHESTER A. ARTHUR'S FAMILY

Compared with most of his immediate predecessors as President, who had had undistinguished fathers even if their mothers had sometimes been formative influences, Chester Arthur was unusual. His father, the Revd William Arthur, seems to have been a formidable personality. He was physically noticeable, with his dark hair and pronounced limp. In character he was blunt and opinionated to the point of being tactless. He was a late convert from Episcopalianism to the Baptist creed, with strong anti-slavery views and a broad Scots-Irish accent to deliver them in, to say nothing of his pungent addresses from the pulpit on less temporal matters.

Malvina Stone, the Revd William's wife, was the granddaughter of Major Uriah Stone, a veteran of the French and Indian Wars of the mid-18th century. Uriah had moved to Haverhill, New Hampshire, in 1763 and from there to Piermont, in the same state, where he farmed, operated a ferry on the Connecticut River and fathered 10 children. Five of them, Malvina's father George included, settled in the Vermont town of Berkshire. One of George's brothers, John, was a noted Baptist preacher too, being known as Elder Stone.

Given this Baptist background on both sides of the family, it seems strange that Chester Arthur tamely relapsed into Episcopalianism. But then he was of a sceptical turn of mind, and Episcopalianism, with its accommodation of both the fervent and the tepid, was perhaps on this account more congenial. He attended a black church twice after becoming President, but then settled down to regular divine service at St John's, Lafayette Square, where his dead wife Ellen had sung in the choir. (She also sang occasionally in concerts mounted by the Mendelssohn Glee Club, whose members felt sufficient tenderness toward her to flout their customary ban on such activities and sing at her funeral in New York.) Arthur presented St John's with a stained glass window in Ellen's memory, stipulating that it should be erected on the south side of the building so he could see it from the White House.

Since Arthur was single again by the time he entered the White House, it is not surprising that the place took on the air of a rather self-indulgent bachelor establishment, with servants who catered to his fads replacing blood relatives in importance. It is true that his sister Mary acted as his hostess, but she seems not to have cut much ice there otherwise, despite her taking on the responsibility of bringing up Arthur's daughter Nell. Meanwhile Arthur brought down a French chef from New York who had been used to tending the palates of that city's gourmets, also his old family cook Bridget Smith, perhaps to vary the *haute cuisine* with traditional fare. Actually he ate sparingly at breakfast and lunch, presumably holding back his appetite for an assault on dinner and the midnight supper which he liked to have on hand five hours later. Certainly he put on weight as President. Like his contemporary the Prince of Wales across the Atlantic, however, he was moderate in his consumption of alcohol, though his red face gave rise to rumours that he drank too much.

He liked other comforts besides food. His carriage, for instance, was a landau of dark green picked out in red, with morocco leather trimmings and cushions and doors embellished with heavy lace, the harness copiously adorned with silver. The coachman's lap robe was of green English box cloth, while the occupant's was otter fur from Labrador lined in dark green with the Arthur cipher worked in silk. Designed to Arthur's personal requirements, this equipage was said to be the finest ever seen in Washington. Arthur also took on a steward who had been in the New York political boss Roscoe Conkling's employ for 12 years (which argued considerable gifts as a confidential servant, given Conkling's energy and self-regard) and a black valet, Alec Powell, lent him by his New York Customs House crony Stephen B. French. Powell seems to have been a cross between Jeeves and Benson, the black majordomo in the 1970s television show *Soap*. When the President took Powell to Newport in the summer of 1884

Plate 65   Ellen Herndon Arthur

Plate 66   Mary Arthur McElroy, Arthur's sister
and hostess in the White House

the New York *Sun* rashly referred to him as "the servant", which provoked a stiff letter from Powell insisting that his status was that of messenger and concluding with the hope that the *Sun* would get his title right in future.

Once again the White House was in sore need of refurbishment — in Garfield's last months it had doubled as an infirmary. Soon the decor began to reflect the new Arthurian tone — Cosmos Club rather than Camelot — of quiet but considerable comfort. It must have been quite a contrast to the homeliness of the past few presidential families. This was the Gilded Age, however. What was a little odd, even given a widower President, was that Arthur oversaw the refurbishment himself: a Tiffany glass screen separating the entrance hall, which was very much a public thoroughfare, from the long corridor joining the East Room to the dining rooms and conservatory, where those living in the White House felt they were entitled to some privacy; an elevator (the first ever in the White House); new furniture; brass fire irons and fenders. It is somehow rather shocking that he could spare the time. In fact he was a conscientious President, perhaps not a frenetic worker on the lines of Polk or his immediate successor Cleveland, but a steady, if slow, despatcher of business.

While the White House was being done up Arthur lived on Capitol Hill and dined out often, breaching the taboo on Presidents being received at other people's houses. A member of the former Secretary of State James G. Blaine's family noted that when the President was a guest it could be a problem trying to wind up a dinner party before midnight (Washington was less dissipated than New York in the hours it kept), since protocol dictated that nobody must leave before him. Under Arthur, Washington was said to have experienced its only 'society' administration between the age of Buchanan and that of Teddy Roosevelt.

Nevertheless Arthur had been happily married and in all sorts of ways showed it. It is true that strain had developed between him and his wife Ellen during the Civil War, but this was common in North-South marriages (he came from New York-New England stock, she from Virginia). Ellen Herndon, as she had been before her marriage, had many Herndon and other relatives in the Confederate forces. Arthur was one of the men keeping the Union Army supplied. But he twice arranged the release of her cousin Dabney Herndon, who was captured by the Unionists three times. Dabney was an old room-mate of Arthur's from the New York days when he had started out to make a career as a lawyer; indeed it was through him that Arthur met Ellen in the first place. Arthur's name was mud in the South generally, however, since he had won his professional reputation by securing two landmark decisions, to the effect, first, that slaves in transit from one slave state to another via the free state of New York were ipso facto free, second, that blacks could use New York street cars on the same terms as whites.

Arthur kept a photograph of Ellen in a room at the White House and every day placed a fresh offering of flowers in front of it. News of his little ritual, but not of his idol's identity, leaked out. Washington gossip assumed the photograph represented a current flame and speculated on who the President might be intending to make the second Mrs Arthur. Victoria Sackville-West, the illegitimate daughter of the British Minister to Washington by his Spanish mistress, the dancer Pepita, claimed that President Arthur proposed marriage to her late at night after a White House banquet. Her grandson Nigel Nicolson in *Portrait of a Marriage* suggests the claim was true enough to have provoked the President's brother, William, to issue an official denial. Certainly a denial was issued, but it was expressed in terms which did not quite deny an offer had been made, merely that the President was not engaged to "Miss West". Something of the sort was probably necessary since Victoria was the British Minister's official hostess as well as love child. (Queen Victoria was allegedly amused by Lionel Sackville-West's request to instal his bastard daughter at the Legation in such a role.) Whether an official *démenti* increases the plausibility of Victoria's claim is a question best left to diplomats or linguistic philosophers. She was capable of making preposterous claims about other aspects of her family history. We will almost certainly never know Arthur's side of the story because he destroyed all his private papers shortly before his death. In any case he disliked others prying into his personal affairs. Hayes had wooed the 'temperance' vote; when a deputation lobbied Arthur to keep the White House dry he retorted that he might be the President of the United States but his private life was nobody's damn business.

He was the subject of preposterous claims himself. Over the period 1880 to 1881, during which time he was elected and inaugurated Vice-President, a certain Mr Hinman claimed that he had been born in Canada, which would have made him ineligible for the presidency. According to Hinman, Arthur had misappropriated a dead younger brother's birth certificate, which recorded a Vermont birthplace, and passed himself off as American-born. It is therefore untrue to say his eligibility for the presidency was never called in question. However, no modern authority pays Hinman's claim serious attention. It should be seen in the context of a whole series of absurd claims and irresponsible rumour-mongering about presidential contenders in an age when there was a mass of voters, some of them with very little education or sophistication, scattered across a huge country and with scant direct knowledge of national politicians.

Chester Crocker, the Assistant Secretary of State under President Reagan who was instrumental in negotiating the independence of Namibia and withdrawal of Cuban forces from Angola, is a distant relative of President Arthur's.

BIOGRAPHICAL DETAILS AND DESCENDANTS

ARTHUR, CHESTER ALAN, *b* Fairfield, Vt., 5 Oct 1829; *educ* Union Coll, Schenectady, New York (BA 1848, MA 1851); teacher 1848-53, Principal N Pownal Acad 1851-53, admitted New York Bar 1854, Judge Advocate 2nd Bde New York State Militia 1857, Engr-in-Ch on staff of Govr Edwin D. Morgan of New York with rank of Brig-Gen and Actg QMG New York State Militia 1860, QMG with rank of Brig-Gen July-Dec 1862, Sec Conference Govrs Loyal States 1862, Memb Republican City Exec Ctee 1867 (Chm 1868), Counsel to New York City Tax Cmmn 1869-70, Collector Port of New York 1871-78, Chm Republican New York State Convention 1876, Delegate-at-Large from New York to Republican Convention 1880, V-Pres USA 4 March-19 Sept 1881, 21st President (R) of USA 1881-85, unsuccessful candidate for Republican presidential nomination 1884, Pres New York Arcade Rlwy Co 1885-86; *m* Calvary Church, New York, 25 Oct 1859 Ellen Lewis (*b* Culpeper, Va., 30 Aug 1837; *d* New York 12 Jan 1880 of pneumonia, *bur* Rural Cemetery, Albany, New York), only child of Cdre William Lewis Herndon and his *w* Frances Elizabeth, dau of Col Joseph Hansbrough, of Culpeper, and *d* New York 18 Nov 1886 of cerebral haemorrhage and Bright's disease (*bur* with his *w*), having had issue:

President Arthur's sons
I William Lewis Herndon ARTHUR, *b* New York 10 Dec 1860; *d* Englewood, New Jersey, 7 July 1863
II Chester Alan ARTHUR, Jr, of Hobgoblin Hall, Colorado Springs, Colo., *b* New York 25 July 1864; *educ* Princeton (AB 1885); *m* 1st 8 May 1900 (divorce 1929) Myra Townsend (*b* New York 1 Jan 1870; *d* 11 Sept 1935), widow of —— Andrews and dau of Joel Adams Fithian, of Bridgeton, New Jersey, and his *w* Fannie Barrett Connolly, and had issue:

Grandchildren
1 Chester Alan ARTHUR III, of Moy Mell, Oceano, Calif., and 346 E 51st St, New York; *b* Colorado Springs 21 March 1901; *m* 1st London, UK, 29 June 1922 (divorce 19—) Charlotte (*b* 16 Aug 1897), dau of Charles S. Wilson, of Los Angeles; *m* 2nd 20 April 1935 (divorce 1961) Esther Knesborough (*d* Paris, France, Jan 1963), formerly *w* of (Evelyn) John St Loe Strachey, UK Sec of State for War 1950-51 (*see* BURKE'S PEERAGE & BARONETAGE, Strachie), and only dau of Patrick Francis Murphy, of New York; *m* 3rd 1965 *Ellen —— and *d* San Francisco 28 April 1972
2 Ellen Lewis Herndon ARTHUR; *d* young

President Arthur's children
II (cont.) Chester Alan Arthur, Jr, *m* 2nd 3 Nov 1934 Rowena (*b* 8 Nov 1894), widow of —— Graves and dau of Richard Edward Dashwood, of Colorado Springs, and *d* Colorado Springs 17 or 18 July 1937
III Ellen (Nell) Herndon Arthur, *b* New York 21 Nov 1871; *m* 1907, as his 1st *w*, Charles Pinkerton, of Mount Kisco, New York (*b* West Chester, Pa., 2 July 1871; *m* 2nd 1917 his 2nd cousin Sarah Harrison, a relation of the Harrison Presidents, and with her had two *s*, Charles Pinkerton, Jr, and Peyton R. H. Pinkerton; *d* Mount Kisco 31 Jan 1974, *bur* Rock Spring Cemetery, Rock Spring, Md.); she *d* Mount Kisco 6 Sept 1915

MALE LINE ANCESTRY AND
COLLATERAL DESCENDANTS

Gavin ARTHUR, of The Draen ('The Place of Blackthorns'), nr Ballymena, Co Antrim, Ireland, *b c* 1735; *m* Jane Campbell and had issue:

Alan ARTHUR, of The Draen, *b* 1766; *m* Eliza McHarg and had issue:

Revd William ARTHUR, MA, DD, *b* The Draen 5 Dec 1796; antiquary, author of *The Antiquarian* and *The Derivation of Family Names*, emigrated to Canada 1815, settling at Stanstead, Quebec, as a teacher, then to a school in Dunham, Quebec, and finally to Burlington, Vt., USA, *c* 1824, where he also taught and read law, brought up as Episcopalian but became a Baptist and ordained as Baptist minister 1827, becoming pastor of the North Fairfield Baptist congregation; *m* Dunham, Quebec, Canada, 12 April 1821 Malvina (*b* Berkshire, Franklin Co, Vt., 24 April 1802; *d* Newtonville, New York, 16 Jan 1869), dau of Revd George Washington Stone (1777-1854) and his w Judith Stevens (1771-1855), and *d* Newtonville 27 Oct 1875, leaving issue:

I Regina Malvina ARTHUR, *b* 8 March 1822; *d* 15 Nov 1910
II Jane ARTHUR, *b* 14 March 1824; *d* 15 April 1842
III Almeda ARTHUR, *b* 22 Jan 1826; *d* 26 March 1899
IV Ann Eliza ARTHUR, *b* 1 Jan 1828; *d* 10 April 1915
V CHESTER ALAN ARTHUR, 21st PRESIDENT of the UNITED STATES of AMERICA
VI Malvina Arthur, *b* 1832; *m* before 2 Aug 1864 Henry J. HAYNSWORTH, Confederate Govt official at Petersburg, Va., during Civil War and *d* 16 Jan 1920
VII William ARTHUR, *b* Hinesburg, Vt., 28 May 1834; *educ* Albany Medical Coll, New York; Maj and Paymr US Army (ret 1898), wounded in Confederate victory of Reams's Station, Va., (during Civil War temporarily commanded 4th New York Artillery 25 Aug 1864), later Commissioner Freedmen's Bureau, Florida; *m* Boston 6 June 1867 Alice Bridge (*b* Boston 25 Feb 1835; *d* Cohasset, Mass., 13 Feb 1916), est dau of Dr Charles Thomas Jackson, of Boston, pioneer of the use of ether in anaesthesia, and his w Susan Chapin and niece of Ralph Waldo Emerson, and *d* Cohasset 27 Feb 1915, having had issue:

President Arthur's nephews and nieces
1 William Campbell ARTHUR, *b* Fort Adams, Newport, Rhode Island, 1 July 1868; *d* Fort Pulaski, Ga., 9 May 1869
2 Alice Bridge ARTHUR, *b* Boston 29 Nov 1869; *d c* 1924
3 Susan Elizabeth ARTHUR, *b* Fort Riley, Kans., 13 Feb 1871; *d c* 1924
4 Robert Campbell ARTHUR, *b* and *d* Fort Hamilton, New York, 3 Feb 1875

VIII George ARTHUR, *b* 24 May 1836; *d* 8 March 1838
IX Mary Arthur, *b* 5 June 1841; acted as her brother's hostess at the White House; *m* 18— or 19— John Edward McELROY, of Albany, New York (*d* 1915), and *d* 8 Jan 1917, having had issue:

President Arthur's niece
1 May McElroy, *b* 18—; *m* 18— Charles H. JACKSON and had issue:

Great-nephew
(1) *Charles H. JACKSON, Jr [Rancho San Carlos, 2500 East Valley Road, Montecito, Santa Barbara, CA 93150, USA]; *m* *Ann Gavit and has issue:

Great-nephew's children
1a *Flora B. Jackson [Mrs Douglas Ramsey, 50 Moncada Way, San Rafael, CA 94901, USA], *b* 19—; *m* 1st 19— (divorce 19—) David BASHAM and has six children; *m* 2nd *Dr Douglas Elliott RAMSEY
2a *Palmer Gavit JACKSON, *b* 19—; *m* 19— *Joan ———— and has issue:

Great-nephew's grandchildren
1b *Palmer Charles JACKSON, *b* 19—

Great-nephew's children
3a *Peter JACKSON, *b* 19—; *m* 19— and has issue

Great-niece
(2) Jessie Jackson, *b* 18—; *m* 19— Hiland Garfield BATCHELLER (*d* 19 May 1961) and *d* 11 Dec 1966, leaving issue:

Great-niece's children
1a *Mary-Arthur Batcheller [Mrs John Doolittle, Menands Road, Menands, NY 12204 or 12211, USA], *b* Albany, New York, 7 Feb 1916; *m* there 20 June 1936 *John Quincy Adams DOOLITTLE, a descendant of President John ADAMS
2a *Elizabeth Batcheller [Mrs Woods McCahill, Menands Road, Menands, NY 12204 or 12211, USA], *b* 11 July 1918; *m* 21 June 1941 *Woods McCAHILL
3a Hiland Garfield BATCHELLER, Jr, *b* 7 April 1922; *ka* 16 April 1945
4a *Jessie Jackson Batcheller [Mrs Arnold Cogswell, 95 Old Niskayuna Road, Loudonville, NY 12211, USA], *b* Albany,

New York, 20 March 1928; *educ* Westover Sch and Vassar; *m* 11 July 1953 *Arnold COGSWELL, s of Ledyard Cogswell, Jr, and his w Dorothy Treat Arnold, and has issue:

> Great-niece's grandchildren
> 1b *Arnold COGSWELL, Jr [99 Redmond Rd, Portsmouth, RI 02871, USA], *b* Albany 24 Aug 1955; *educ* Williams Coll; museum administrator; *m* Columbia, S Carolina, 27 Sept 1986 *Cheryl Diana, dau of Richard Alexander Hinds and his w Lois Watts, and has issue:
>
> > Great-niece's great-grandchildren
> > 1c *Nathan Arnold COGSWELL, *b* Rhode Island 12 Jan 1992
>
> Great-niece's grandchildren
> 2b *Jessie Cogswell [Mrs Richard Tichko, 281 Southwest Rd, Canterbury, NH 03224, USA], *b* Albany 10 July 1957; *m* there 23 July 1983 *Richard TICHKO and has issue:
>
> > Great-niece's great-grandchildren
> > 1c *Parker Richard TICHKO, *b* 29 Jan 1988
> > 2c *Brant Cogswell TICHKO, *b* 12 Feb 1992
>
> Great-niece's grandchildren
> 3b *Elizabeth Ledyard Cogswell [Mrs James B Stone, Rolling Stone Ranch, Box 148, Ovando, MT 59854, USA], *b* Albany 9 March 1962; *educ* U of Montana; animal care technician 1986-93, basket weaver 1990-93; *m* Missoula, Mont., 28 Feb 1987 *James Bidwell STONE, s of John Stone and his w Jane Bidwell

President Arthur's nephews and niece
2 William McELROY, *b* 18— ; *d* 1892
3 Jessie McELROY, *b* 18—
4 Charles Edward McELROY *b* 1873; *m* Harriet Langdon, dau of Amasa J. Parker and his w Cornelia Kane Strong, and had issue:

Great-nephew and -niece
(1) Charles Edward McELROY, Jr, *b* 1904; *d* 1915
(2) Cornelia Kane McElroy, *b* 4 Sept 1905; *m* 22 Jan 1926, as his 1st w, Schuyler MERRITT II (*b* 9 April 1899; *d* 3 Sept 1983), s of Henry C. Merritt and his w Camilla von Bach, and *d* 10 Aug 1971, leaving issue:

> Great-niece's children
> 1a *Cornelia Kane Merritt [Mrs Norcross Tilney, 245 Pendleton Ave, Palm Beach, FL 33480, USA], *b* 29 Dec 1927; *m* 20 Oct 1951 Norcross Sheldon TILNEY (*b* 29 Dec 1913; *d* June 1987), s of I. Sheldon Tilney and his w Augusta Munn, and has issue:
>
> > Great-niece's grandchildren
> > 1b *Victoria Merritt Tilney, *b* New York 6 Oct 1953; *m* 1st 1978 (divorce 1985) Chips C. PAGE and with him has issue:
> >
> > > Great-niece's great-grandchildren
> > > 1c *William PAGE, *b* 1980
> >
> > Great-niece's grandchildren
> > 1b (cont.) Mrs Victoria Page *m* 2nd 1985 *David BEVAN and with him has issue:
> >
> > > Great-niece's great-grandchildren
> > > 2c *Christopher Tilney BEVAN, *b* 1988
> >
> > Great-niece's grandchildren
> > 2b *Schuyler Merritt TILNEY, *b* New York 27 Sept 1955; *m* 1981 *Elizabeth Arendall and with her has issue:
> >
> > > Great-niece's great-grandchildren
> > > 1c *Cornelia Lawrence TILNEY, *b* 1989
> > > 2c *Schuyler Bater TILNEY, *b* 1992
> >
> > Great-niece's grandchildren
> > 3b *Cornelia Kane TILNEY, *b* New York 10 Feb 1959
> > 4b *Augusta Munn TILNEY, *b* New York 6 Dec 1962
>
> Great-niece's children
> 2a *Harriet Parker Merritt [Mrs John F Garde, 139 Skunk's Misery Rd, Locust Valley, NY 11560, USA], *b* 3 Nov 1929; *m* 1st 19 May 1951 Lawrence Howland DIXON (*b* 3 Dec 1923; *d* Aug 1975), s of Courtlandt Palmer Dixon and his w Hortense H. Howland, and has issue:
>
> > Great-niece's grandchildren
> > 1b *Wendy Merritt DIXON, *b* Lawrence, New York, 7 May 1953
> > 2b *Meredith Howland DIXON, *b* Lawrence 17 Aug 1955
>
> Great-niece's children
> 2a (cont.) Mrs Lawrence Dixon *m* 2nd Dec 1981 *John F. GARDE

3a *Camilla Merritt [Mrs Robert McLane, 4 Cherrywood Rd, Locust Valley, NY 11560, USA], b Albany, New York, 5 July 1934; *educ* Miss Porter's Sch and Vassar; *m* 21 May 1955 *Robert Milligan McLANE (*b* Feb 1929), s of Allan McLane and his w Edith Pratt Maxwell, and has issue:

Great-niece's grandchildren

1b *Cornelia Gibb McLane [Mrs William W Burchfield, 1230 Vancouver Ave, Burlingame, CA 94010, USA], b Locust Valley 19 Jan 1957; *m* there 2 June 1984 *William Wulfhorst BURCHFIELD (*b* Feb 1956) and has issue:

Great-niece's great-grandchildren

1c *William McLane BURCHFIELD, *b* 16 Aug 1988

2c *Camilla James BURCHFIELD, *b* 27 Feb 1990

3c *Jennifer Gibb BURCHFIELD, *b* 22 Aug 1992

Great-niece's grandchildren

2b *Robert Milligan McLANE, Jr [33 Elm St, Hamilton, MA 01982, USA], b Locust Valley 9 Jan 1959; *m* Greenwich, Conn., 20 Oct 1990 *Gratia Lee (*b* Sept 1961), dau of Alexander J. Robertson and his w Mary Lee

Great-nephew

(3) *John Ewart McELROY [457 Devil's Lane, Naples, FL 33940, USA], b 25 Jan 1909; *educ* Taft Sch and Yale; *m* 1936 *Cornelia Sutherland, dau of Charles S. Ransom and his w Jessie Hamilton, and has issue:

Great-nephew's children

1a *Cornelia Sutherland McElroy [Mrs Richard M Leach, Box 1888 Maple Lane, New London, NH 03257, USA], b Albany, New York, 10 May 1939; *educ* Mt Vernon Jr Coll; florist; *m* 1st 1961 Morgan Dix WHEELOCK and with him has issue:

Great-nephew's grandchildren

1b *Timothy Dix WHEELOCK, *b* 28 Feb 1963

2b *Cornelia Sutherland Wheelock, *b* 26 Feb 1966; *m* 24 April 1993 *John Devin BERMINGHAM

3b *Morgan Dix WHEELOCK III, *b* 31 Jan 1969

Great-nephew's children

1a (cont.) Cornelia McElroy Wheelock *m* 2nd 8 July 1978 *Richard Malcolm LEACH, s of Walter Barton Leach and his w Florence Tower Sturgis

2a *Louise Parker McElroy [Mrs H Todd Spofford, Box 255 Dow St, Cobleskill, NY 12043, USA], b Cedar City, Utah, 28 March 1944; *educ* Westover Sch; *m* 19 Aug 1967 *H. Todd SPOFFORD, s of Homer Spofford and his w Rosamond, and has issue:

Great-nephew's grandchildren

1b *Christopher Todd SPOFFORD, *b* Boston 11 Feb 1970

2b *Bradley Parker SPOFFORD, *b* Cobleskill, New York, 10 Dec 1972

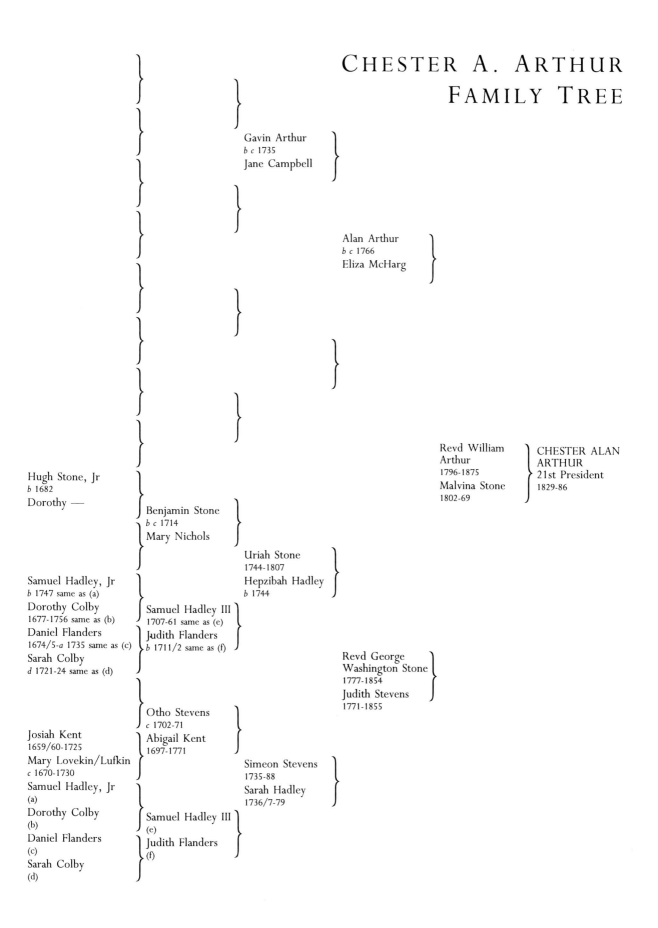

CHESTER A. ARTHUR
FAMILY TREE

Gavin Arthur
b c 1735
Jane Campbell

Alan Arthur
b c 1766
Eliza McHarg

Revd William
Arthur
1796-1875
Malvina Stone
1802-69

CHESTER ALAN
ARTHUR
21st President
1829-86

Hugh Stone, Jr
b 1682
Dorothy —

Benjamin Stone
b c 1714
Mary Nichols

Uriah Stone
1744-1807
Hepzibah Hadley
b 1744

Samuel Hadley, Jr
b 1747 same as (a)
Dorothy Colby
1677-1756 same as (b)
Daniel Flanders
1674/5-*a* 1735 same as (c)
Sarah Colby
d 1721-24 same as (d)

Samuel Hadley III
1707-61 same as (e)
Judith Flanders
b 1711/2 same as (f)

Revd George
Washington Stone
1777-1854
Judith Stevens
1771-1855

Otho Stevens
c 1702-71
Abigail Kent
1697-1771

Josiah Kent
1659/60-1725
Mary Lovekin/Lufkin
c 1670-1730

Simeon Stevens
1735-88
Sarah Hadley
1736/7-79

Samuel Hadley, Jr
(a)
Dorothy Colby
(b)
Daniel Flanders
(c)
Sarah Colby
(d)

Samuel Hadley III
(e)
Judith Flanders
(f)

Plate 67   Grover Cleveland during his 1st term of office

Plate 68   Grover Cleveland during his 2nd term of office

GROVER CLEVELAND

1837-1908
22ND AND 24TH PRESIDENT
OF THE UNITED STATES OF AMERICA
1885-89 AND 1893-97

The early 1880s were the years of the Mugwumps. This Indian word was applied in derision to those Republicans who could no longer tolerate their party's corruption. Like many such nicknames it became a term of honour. The Mugwumps might be accused of being impractical, disloyal and snobbish. Never mind, there were enough of them to win several decisive elections, including those which carried Grover Cleveland from comfortable obscurity in his law office at Buffalo, New York, to the presidency of the United States.

The Mugwumps were the leaders in the movement against political corruption that was still gathering strength. James G. Blaine, the Republican nominee in 1884, was the very embodiment of the system which they opposed. He had been Speaker of the House in the Grant years and leader of the Senate under Hayes; he was widely believed to have been corruptly involved with the great railroads. His denials were scoffed at in the chant "Blaine! Blaine! James G. Blaine! The continental liar from the state of Maine!". He was the Plumed Knight to his many devoted followers, but when the Republican convention gave in to sentiment and nominated him it became highly likely that the Mugwumps would bolt. When the Democrats nominated Cleveland, who had been a reform Mayor of Buffalo and a reform Governor of New York, the only question was, would enough Mugwumps change sides to swing the election?

Cleveland was anything but a glamorous candidate. He was a man strikingly of his generation which straddled the Civil War. Brought up on the old rural, patriotic, Protestant verities (his father was a minister) like Blaine himself, like J.P. Morgan, like John D. Rockefeller, he found it impossible to adapt sufficiently to the rapidly changing times. His rigid personal honesty, his zeal to do right, his devotion to hard work and a certain bull-like solidity of character (a solidity well symbolised by his corpulence — at one time he weighed 300 pounds) gave him great advantages over more flexible men. Cleveland was hard to move and impossible to shake. His economic and social views seem narrow, ungenerous, unimaginative to a later generation, but in his day he was a reassuring pillar of rectitude, just what the Mugwumps wanted.

Their faith in him was a little shaken during the campaign when it came out that some years previously he had fathered an illegitimate son on a merry widow. Cleveland's supporters were alarmed, but he sent them a message: "Above all tell the truth." The truth was that he had done the best he could for the boy, who was now a happily adopted member of a respectable family. The public, impressed by Cleveland's candour, accepted his explanation. The Mugwumps breathed again and when a Protestant minister injudiciously denounced the Democrats as the party of "rum, Romanism and rebellion" in Blaine's presence — in the heart of New York — and was not instantly repudiated, Cleveland's victory was assured. The Irish flocked to the polls to avenge the insult; the Democrats carried the state and the election.

It was a famous victory and in office Cleveland did not entirely disappoint his followers. He was more or less miserable as President. In June 1886 he improved his state by marrying, at the White House (he is the only President to have married there), Frances Folsom, the daughter of his former law partner. It was a happy union, but the White House remained intolerable as a home. Congress did not give the President enough money for the upkeep, by tradition it was open to all comers and as Washington grew larger there were too many of them. So the Clevelands bought a house of their own and the President used the great mansion only as an office. It was not even a very well run office. On occasion, since there was no one else to answer the door bell, the President did it himself. He had so little assistance that he had to write all his state papers in longhand himself. He never complained, but if the presidency was to carry out its functions effectively in the modern world, it would soon have to be radically reorganized.

Meantime there was the problem of corruption. No more than Hayes or Arthur could Cleveland abolish the spoils system in its entirety, but he could insist on honesty and efficiency in the government department. He appointed a good and diligent cabinet and worked like a dog himself to control Congressional extravagance — for example, the practice of granting pensions to all who could make a case, however bogus, that they had earned them by their services in the Civil War. Apart from that the President found himself rather short of ideas.

The fact was that Mugwumpery was already obsolete. "Public office is a public trust" had been Cleveland's slogan. It was a comment on the times that such a banality sounded like a challenge; much else was necessary that Cleveland simply did not understand. Industrialization and urbanization were galloping ahead; real power in society was falling more and more completely into the hands of monopolists and oligarchs — an unholy alliance between Wall Street and the US Senate, soon to be known as 'the millionaires' club'; the wild fluctuations of the business cycle, unemployment, low wages, long hours, a perennial crisis on the farms; these were the sort of things that needed tackling and Cleveland, from first to last, was incapable of doing so.

He tried. Slowly he overcame his old-fashioned belief that the President's only duty was to execute the laws that Congress passed. He began to take the lead in policymaking. Out of the dusty armoury of traditional policies he made two his own: a low tariff and a sound currency. The one was to wreck his first administration, the other his second.

The tariff was one of those questions which all parties and generations find baffling. The Democrats were supposed to be the low tariff party, the Republicans the protectionists, but whenever the subject came up for debate in Congress all party consistency was thrown to the winds in the scramble for special treatment. Every state, and therefore every congressional delegation, was split between protectionists and free traders; individual Senators and Congressmen voted as they thought would best please their constituents. No rational tariff was possible in the circumstances and, as Cleveland saw, the result was oppressive to consumers and helpful only to monopolists. When he came out in open opposition to the excessively high tariff he only injured himself. All the special interests turned against him. The election of 1888 was another close one: Cleveland actually increased his popular vote from 4,879,507 to 5,537,857 and had a larger majority, but he had only a minority in the electoral college. So Benjamin Harrison became President.

Cleveland's stand on the tariff seemed to be vindicated when the Republicans pushed through the notorious McKinley Tariff of 1890 which blatantly favoured the special interests; indignation about this was no doubt one of the reasons why Cleveland was reelected in 1892. The day after he took office there was a panic on Wall Street and the four years of his second term turned out to coincide exactly with those of the worst depression of the 19th century. Bank failures, farm mortgage foreclosures, soup kitchens and bread lines, bitter battles between capital and labour, all the symptoms of economic disaster plagued America. None of the nostrums advanced at the time would have done much good, but popular opinion fastened on the question of the currency. The West and South favoured cheap money in the form of a bimetallic currency of silver and gold. The East increasingly favoured gold alone and Cleveland became a passionately obstinate 'goldbug'. All his energy and courage were thrown into the battle to keep America on the gold standard. He succeeded but was nearly destroyed. Just when the crisis was at its worst and the government's credit tottering, he was found to have cancer of the jaw. A successful operation was carried out in the utmost secrecy (lest the stock market panic) on a yacht in New York harbour. Cleveland was never again as vigorous as he had been. The Democrats committed themselves, with passion equal to his own, to bimetallism. Cleveland was rejected and reviled by his own party and left office with a feeling of deep failure that he never quite threw off, though he lived for 11 years more. "I have tried so hard to do right" he said on his death bed. His tragedy was that though righteousness was necessary yet more was required of him.

GROVER CLEVELAND'S FAMILY

The first Cleveland to settle in America, the 22nd and 24th President's five-times great-grandfather Moses, was an artisan. By the time two generations had elapsed the Clevelands must have acquired some capital given that Aaron, Moses's grandson, was able to speculate in real estate in his native Massachusetts and operate as a contractor. Aaron was also able to educate his son, another Aaron, at Harvard, where the latter was a distinguished swimmer, wrestler and boxer. Aaron Junior later took Holy Orders but this muscular Christian was a touch flighty according to the Puritan tenets of New England. He converted from Presbyterianism to Episcopalianism in 1754, which necessitated his going to England to be ordained by the Bishop of London as there was no bishop available in America. Moreover he was a friend of Benjamin Franklin, a notorious freethinker, and died in Franklin's house. His son, yet another Aaron, introduced the first bill to abolish slavery in Connecticut history when a member of that state's legislature during the American Revolution, of which he was a supporter. He too was in holy orders, becoming a Congregationalist minister at the age of 53. His grandson Richard, Grover Cleveland's father, was also a Congregationalist minister, but far less distinguished. Unlike his grandfather Aaron, Richard published nothing, and although Congregationalism stressed the autonomy of each local church, so that no minister could climb an elaborate hierarchy to glory as dean, archdeacon or bishop in the way an Episcopalian might, there were nevertheless ways in which a gifted minister could attract attention outside his local congregation. The Revd Aaron had done this; the Revd Richard did not. Yet he was a good shepherd to his flock at parochial level.

Muscular Christianity, which as we have seen had long been present in the Cleveland family, reached its fullest flowering in the 19th century. But President Grover Cleveland was more muscular than Christian, perhaps because, like his immediate predecessor Chester Arthur, he was a son of the manse and had had his fill of religious observance in childhood. The Cleveland family in young Grover's day kept the Sabbath strictly from late on Saturday to sunset on Sunday and everybody had to be word perfect in the Westminster Catechism. As an adult Grover Cleveland was lax in attending divine service and refused to be married in church. It is true that late in life he became more punctilious, but this may in part have arisen from his cancer, which, necessitating as it did the fitting of a vulcanized rubber jaw to the lower half of his face, would have been enough to instil a sense of the hereafter in Robert Ingersoll (also the son of a Congregationalist minister as it happens).

Grover Cleveland's mother Anne Neal was the daughter of a Protestant of mixed Irish and English descent who had emigrated from Ireland for political reasons, possibly involvement in the abortive 1798 uprising against the British, and married a Quaker of German ancestry before dying in Baltimore. When Anne married Richard Cleveland she came north from Maryland, bringing a black maid and a gaudy collection of clothes, both of which possessions shocked the people of Windham, Connecticut. After Richard's death the local church people presumably either forgot this piece of profanity or overlooked it, for they offered to raise money to educate her younger children. Anne refused any money help, although she was happy to stay on in the minister's house rent-free. Some years afterward Lewis, Grover Cleveland's youngest brother, bought it for her.

Grover Cleveland's two Christian names were chosen by his parents to commemorate a predecessor of his father's as Congregationalist minister at Caldwell, Cleveland's birthplace, who was greatly admired both by them and the community generally. Among the most useful biographical sources on Grover Cleveland are his many letters to his sister Mary, to whom he was particularly close, although she married when he was only 16. Mary regularly acted as hostess for her brother while he was governor of New York and occasionally at the White House during his first two years as President, though in the latter case it was mostly the youngest Cleveland sister Libbie who did the honours. The Cleveland brothers were close too. In the Civil War Grover Cleveland hired a substitute rather than enlist — a legitimate action, if unheroic. It was just that he felt his obligation to support his widowed mother and sisters took priority. It did him no real harm in the presidential election of 1884 since for once the Republican candidate, in this case James G. Blaine, hadn't fought either. Cleveland's brother Lewis at first offered to be the substitute but Cleveland refused and hired a 32-year old Pole called George Brinske or Bennisky. Cleveland's political opponents later tried to claim Brinske/Bennisky had suffered frightful wounds, not to say general hardship, during his service as a mercenary, but it turned out he had injured his back after a relatively brief time with the 67th New York Regiment and had been assigned orderly duties in hospitals.

Unlike Grover, Lewis Cleveland and Richard, another brother, did enlist. Both were involved in fierce fighting, Richard serving under Grant himself. Lewis later entered the hotel business, acquiring the Royal Victoria Hotel in Nassau, in the Bahamas, a huge and luxurious establishment which had belonged to the British colonial government. He was lost at sea travelling out there when only 31, along with Richard, his assistant. Grover Cleveland managed the sizeable estate left by Lewis, keeping on the Nassau hotel although most of Lewis's wealth was inherited by their sister Margaret, who looked after their mother.

Of his other siblings there was William, the oldest boy, who secured a job right after his father's death teaching at the New York Institution for the Blind and procured Grover a teaching job there too. The oldest girl, Anna, also taught but then married a missionary; Margaret became for a while a governess on Long Island before marrying, in true Victorian novel tradition, above her station, her husband being Norval Bacon, descended from a great-uncle of the early 17th-century English philosopher, Lord Chancellor Francis Bacon. Grover Cleveland's next-to-youngest sister Susan was put through college at her President brother's expense.

Libbie Cleveland was one of the more intellectual First Ladies (if a mere sister of a President can be counted a First Lady), and what with her brains and her decisiveness, masculine manner and generous size rather overwhelmed visitors. She was said to prefer educated people to mere politicians — a sad comment on the Washington of the day — and to compensate for the tedium of shaking hands with visitor after visitor for an hour or more by mentally conjugating Greek verbs. She publicly expressed her admiration for the 'dry' regime instituted by the Hayeses, which irritated her brother the President since he was fond of washing down large helpings of German food with wine and beer and had been a lawyer for the Brewers' Association as well as shareholder in a brewery. Perhaps in consequence she never managed to eliminate wine from the White House. She was staunchly anti-Catholic and used to urge her brother not to appoint too many papists to public office. Her book *George Eliot's Poetry and*

Plate 69   Frances Folsom Cleveland

Plate 70   Rose Elizabeth Cleveland, Grover Cleveland's
sister and hostess in the White House

Other Studies appeared in June 1885, a few months after she had come to live in the White House, and went through 12 editions in a year, allegedly netting her over $25,000.

In his time as a bachelor President, Cleveland employed few servants. (The White House had recently been refurbished by President Arthur, so was in less need of attention than usual.) But it was by no means empty apart from the chief executive and officials. Cleveland enjoyed company. His house guests included his future wife, suitably chaperoned by her mother, and a Miss Van Vechten who had been engaged to the celebrated Civil War soldier General Sheridan and was now reckoned by contemporary gossip to be setting her cap at the President.

Cleveland was always very much a man's man, however, fit and beefy in youth, flabby when older, fond of blood sports, including fishing (when he was known to wear top hat and black coat), and ill at ease in drawing rooms. It was something of a marvel when he married. The White House wedding was very much a third choice as to venue since Cleveland's bride Frances had just lost her grandfather, in whose house the wedding had originally been planned, and Cleveland set his face against the alternatives of a church or a hotel. The ceremony was blessed by his brother William, by now in holy orders. Cleveland had known 'Frank', as he called his bride, from babyhood. Her father, who had died intestate in a carriage accident, had left Cleveland to administer his affairs. Frances was caustically described at the time as a girl less than half her husband's age and a third his weight but she was no china doll. Her engaging manner encouraged social activity and since Washington seemed to many onlookers to be getting socially smarter she got much of the credit.

The most interesting thing about Cleveland is how his political success was achieved despite a notorious sexual entanglement and how this runs completely counter, not only to the supposed prudery of the Victorian age but to the scandal-mongering of our own supposedly more liberal one. In 1874 Maria

Halpin, a pretty 36-yr old Buffalo widow, charged Cleveland with the paternity of her son, whom she christened Oscar Folsom Cleveland. (Cleveland's law partner and future father-in-law was called Oscar Folsom; quite why Maria called her son after him is not clear.) Cleveland couldn't be sure the baby was his (Maria was what was called 'fast' in those days, or, more crudely, promiscuous) but he took full responsibility, pointing out that he was the only bachelor involved. Nevertheless he refused to marry her. Maria took to drink, was put in an asylum and had to be relieved of Oscar, who was brought up by foster parents at Cleveland's expense. The episode gave rise to the famous doggerel in the 1884 election "Ma, Ma, where's my pa? Gone to the White House. Ha! Ha! Ha!" A respected Buffalo cleric investigated the affair the same year and declared that, apart from the initial sexual offence, Cleveland had been "singularly honourable".

Of his legitimate children, Esther, the second daughter, married William Bosanquet, member of a Huguenot family which had settled in England after the Revocation of the Edict of Nantes in 1685 and a second cousin once-removed of the British television news reader Reginald Bosanquet. Her mother-in-law was Philippa Bence-Jones, of the celebrated Anglo-Irish family which has produced the writer Mark Bence-Jones. In American terms the interest of the Bence-Joneses lies in their Winthrop connection, though it dates from way back in the 17th century. President Cleveland's son-in-law was descended from a first cousin of the half blood of John Winthrop, the 'Father of New England', Governor of Massachusetts and ancestor through his fourth wife of President John and John Quincy Adams. Esther's younger daughter is the distinguished philosopher Philippa Foot.

BIOGRAPHICAL DETAILS AND DESCENDANTS

CLEVELAND, (STEPHEN) GROVER, b Caldwell, Essex Co, New Jersey, 18 March 1837; clerk in store at Clinton, New York, assist teacher New York Institute for the Blind 1853-54, began studying law with Rogers, Bowen & Rogers, Buffalo, New York, 1855, admitted to New York Bar 1859, managing clerk Rogers, Bowen & Rogers 1859, Ward Supervisor Buffalo 1862, Assist Dist Atty Erie Co, New York, 1863-65 (unsuccessful candidate for Dist Atty 1865), formed law firm with Isaac K. Vanderpoel 1865, Sheriff Erie Co, New York, 1870-74, Mayor Buffalo 1882-83, Govr New York 1883-85, 22nd President (D) of the USA 1885-89, unsuccessful presidential candidate 1888, practised law New York 1889-93, 24th President of the USA 1893-97, apptd Henry Stafford Little Lectr in Public Affairs at Princeton 1899, Tstee Princeton 1901, Memb Tstee Ctee looking after majority of stock of Equitable Life Assur Co 1905, Rebate Referee Equitable Life and Mutual and New York Life Insur Cos, Pres Assoc of Presidents of Life Insur Cos 1907; author: *Principles and Purposes of Our Form of Government* (1892), *Writings and Speeches of Grover Cleveland* (1892), *Self-Made Man in American Life* (1897), *Independence of the Executive* (1900), *Presidential Problems* (1904), *Fishing and Shooting Sketches* (1906), *Good Citizenship* (1908), *Addresses-State Papers* (1909), *Venezuelan Boundary Controversy* (1913) and *Letters of Grover Cleveland* (1933); Grover Cleveland acknowledged as his (and paid for the upbringing of) a child born to Maria Halpin (b 1838; m 1st 18— ——, who d before 1871; m 2nd after 1874 ——; d in or after 1895), of Pennsylvania, shop assistant:

    I Oscar Folsom CLEVELAND, b Buffalo, New York, 14 Sept 1874; educ Protestant Orphan Asylum, Buffalo; adopted by a New York family

President Cleveland m the White House, Washington, DC, 2 June 1886, as her 1st husb, Frances (b Buffalo, New York, 21 July 1864; educ Central High Sch, Buffalo, and Wells Coll; m 2nd 10 Feb 1913 Thomas Jex Preston, Jr, Prof of Archaeology, Princeton; d Baltimore 29 Oct 1947, bur Princeton), dau of Oscar Folsom, attorney, and his w Emma Cornelia, dau of Elisha Harmon (himself ggs of Anan Harmon, whose w Elizabeth Bridgeman was gdau of John Bridgeman and his w Mary Sheldon, whose sister Ruth Sheldon was an ancestress of Nancy Davis, w of President REAGAN); President Cleveland d Princeton, New Jersey, 24 June 1908 of a heart attack, having had issue:

President Cleveland's daughters
    II Ruth CLEVELAND, b New York 3 Oct 1891; d Princeton 7 Jan 1904 of diphtheria
    III Esther Cleveland, b the White House, Washington, DC, 9 Sept 1893; m Westminster Abbey, London, UK, 14 March 1918 Capt William Sidney Bence BOSANQUET, DSO, Coldstream Guards (b 1893; d Redcar, Yorks, UK, 5 March 1966), yst s of Sir Frederick Albert Bosanquet, KC, of 12 Grenville Place, London SW, and Cobbe Place, Lewes, Sussex, UK, Common Serjeant of City of London, and his 2nd w Philippa Frances, yst dau of William Bence-Jones, JP, barrister and

author, of Lisselane, Clonakilty, Co Cork, Ireland, and 34 Elvaston Place, London SW, and *d* New Hampshire 25 June 1980, leaving issue:

Grandchildren

1 *Marion Frances Bosanquet [Mrs Peter Daniel, 5 Seaforth Place, Buckingham Gate, London SW1E 6AB, UK], *b* Lincs, UK, 28 Aug 1919; *educ* U Coll, London (BA 1950); *m* Westminster Register Office, London, 13 Dec 1973 *Prof Peter Maxwell DANIEL, MA, MB, BCh, DM, DSc, FRCP, FRCS, FCPath, FInstBiol, Prof of Neuropathology London U (*b* 1a Wimpole Street, London W1, 14 Nov 1910), s of Peter Daniel, FRCS, surg to Charing Cross Hosp, London, and his w Beatrice Laetitia Herskind

2 *Philippa Ruth Bosanquet [Professor Philippa Foot, 15 Walton St, Oxford, UK], *b* Owston Ferry, Lincs, UK, 3 Oct 1920; *educ* St George's Sch, Ascot, and Somerville Coll, Oxford (BA 1942, MA 1948, Hon Fellow 1989); Lectr in Philosophy Somerville Coll 1947-49, Fell and Tutor in Philosophy and U Lectr 1950-69, V-Pncpl Somerville 1967-69, Sr Research Fell 1970-88, sometime Visiting Prof: Cornell, MIT, U of California at Berkeley, Princeton, City U of New York and Fellow Center for Advanced Studies in Behavioral Sciences Stanford U 1981-82, Pres Pacific Div American Philosophical Assoc 1982-83, Griffin Prof UCLA 1988-91 (Prof of Philosophy from 1974), Griffin Prof Emeritus 1991-, FBA 1976, FAAAS 1983, author: *Virtues and Vices* (1978), ed. *Theories of Ethics* (1967); *m* London 21 June 1945 (divorce 1960) M(ichael) R(ichard) D(aniell) FOOT (*b* London 14 Dec 1919; historian specialising in Gladstone, British foreign policy and irregular warfare), s of Brig Richard Cunningham Foot, OBE, MC, TD, and his w Nina Raymond

President Cleveland's daughter

IV *Marion Cleveland [Mrs John Amen, 404 East 66th Street, New York, NY 10021, USA], *b* Buzzards Bay, Mass., 7 July 1895; *m* 1st Princeton, New Jersey, 28 Nov 1917 (divorce 192-) William Stanley DELL (*b* 1894) and has issue:

Grandchildren

1 *Frances Folsom Dell [Mrs David Payne, Christopher Road, Bedford, NY 10506, USA], *b* 1920; *m* 1st 1942 (divorce 194-) Rayford Wardlaw ALLEY, Jr, s of Rayford Wardlaw Alley, of Nassau County, New York, and his w Emily Dietrich, and has issue:

Great-grandchildren

(1) *Marion Alley, *b* 1944; took stepf's name of Payne; *m* 25 June 1966 *Alvin CARR and has issue:

Great-great-grandchildren
1a *Alvin CARR, Jr, *b* 1967
2a *Mathew CARR, *b* 1969
3a *William CARR, *b* 1971

Grandchildren

1 (cont.) Mrs Frances Alley *m* 2nd 1945 *David MacGregor PAYNE and has further issue:

Great-grandchildren

(2) *Margaret Appleton Payne, *b* 1947; *m* 21 June 1969 *Richard Stuart LANNAMANN, s of Frank Ellery Lannamann, of Cincinnati, Ohio, and his w, *née* Tomlinson

President Cleveland's daughter

IV (cont.) Mrs Marion Dell *m* 2nd Tamworth, New Hampshire, 25 July 1926 John Harlan AMEN (*b* Exeter, New Hampshire, 15 Sept 1898; US Attorney; *d* New York 10 March 1960), s of Harlan Page Amen and his w Mary Rawson, and has further issue:

Grandchildren

2 *Grover Cleveland AMEN, *b* June 1932; *m* Babette Sassoon (*d* 1971) and has issue:

Great-grandchildren
(1) *John Charles AMEN, *b* 1966

President Cleveland's son

V Richard Folsom CLEVELAND, of Baltimore, *b* Princeton, New Jersey, 28 Oct 1897; *educ* Princeton and Harvard Law Sch; attorney, with US Marine Corps World War I; *m* 1st Memphis, Tenn., 20 June 1923 (divorce 1940) Ellen Douglas (*b* 1897; *d* 17 Feb 1954), dau of Bishop Gailor, of Memphis, and had issue:

Grandchildren

1 *Ann Mary Cleveland [Mrs Bolling Robertson III, 4410 Atwick Road, Baltimore, MD 21210, USA], *b* Baltimore 15 Nov 1925; *m* there 30 April 1949 *(Thomas) Bolling ROBERTSON III (*b* Va. 26 June 1925), s of Rolfe Robertson, and has issue:

Great-grandchildren
(1) *Thomas Bolling ROBERTSON IV, *b* 13 Sept 1950
(2) *Elizabeth Averett Robertson, *b* 25 Sept 1952; *m* Baltimore 14 Sept 1974 *Laurence Ray ARNOLD, s of Clifford Emil Arnold, of St Albans, W. Va.
(3) *Ruth C. ROBERTSON, *b* 1 Sept 1955

Grandchildren

2 *Thomas Grover CLEVELAND [94 Center Street, Milton, MA 02186, USA; 2 Brook Road, Milton, MA 02186, USA],

b Baltimore 18 Oct 1927; *educ* Princeton and Virginia Theological Seminary; *m* Groton, Mass., 17 June 1950 *Charlotte B. (*b* 1927), dau of John Crocker and his w Mary Hallowell, and has issue:

> Great-grandchildren
> (1) *Thomas Grover CLEVELAND, Jr, *b* 1 April 1952
> (2) *John C. CLEVELAND, *b* 14 May 1953
> (3) *Sarah G. CLEVELAND, *b* 25 Oct 1955
> (4) *Ellen D. CLEVELAND, *b* 27 March 1957

Grandchildren

3 *Charlotte Gailor [Mrs David Look, Far Hills, NJ 07931, USA], *b* Baltimore 21 Jan 1930; *m* there 3 May 1958 *David T. LOOK (*b* New Jersey 1929), s of Edward Look and his w Carol, and has issue:

> Great-grandchildren
> (1) *Ellen D. LOOK, *b* 20 March 1959
> (2) *Carol T. LOOK, *b* 7 May 1961
> (3) *Charlotte C. LOOK, *b* 19 Oct 1963

President Cleveland's son

V (cont.) Richard F. Cleveland *m* 2nd 12 June 1943 *Jessie Maxwell [Mrs Richard Cleveland, 121 Woodlawn Road, Baltimore, MD 21210, USA] (*b* Baltimore 1 March 1919), dau of George C. Black and his w Jessie Maxwell, and *d* Baltimore 10 Jan 1974, having with her had issue:

Grandchildren

4 *Frances Black Cleveland [Mrs Frederick Corcoran, Rowley, MA 01969, USA; 17 Magnolia Avenue, Manchester, MA 01944, USA], *b* Baltimore 26 Jan 1946; *m* Tamworth, New Hampshire, 3 May 1969 *Frederick James CORCORAN (*b* 7 July 1944) and has issue:

> Great-grandchildren
> (1) *Richard Cleveland CORCORAN, *b* Wellesley, Mass., 24 June 1971
> (2) *Marion Maxwell CORCORAN, *b* Wellesley, Mass., 3 June 1972

Grandchildren

5 *George Maxwell CLEVELAND, *b* Baltimore 15 June 1952; *educ* Lenox Sch, Mass.
6 *Margaret Folsom CLEVELAND, *b* Baltimore 10 March 1956; *educ* Skidmore Coll

President Cleveland's son

VI *Francis Grover CLEVELAND, *b* Buzzard Bay, Mass., 18 July 1903; *m* 20 June 1925 *Alice (*b* 24 March 1904), dau of Revd Charles Erdman, of Princeton, New Jersey, and has issue:

Grandchildren

1 *Marion Cleveland, *b* 25 March 1926; *m* 10 March 1968 *Alfred COHEN

MALE LINE ANCESTRY AND COLLATERAL DESCENDANTS

E. J. and H. G. Cleveland, in *The Genealogy of the Cleveland and Cleaveland Families* (3 vols, 1899), claim for the family an origin in northeast England, where the North Yorkshire Moors contain a range called the Cleveland Hills and an ancient track called the Cleveland Way. The first known American member of the family was:

Moses CLEVELAND, *b* probably Ipswich, Suffolk, England, *c* 1624; emigrated (with his bro Aaron) as an apprentice indentured to a joiner from Ipswich to Plymouth, Mass., 1635, one of first settlers of Woburn, Mass., which was first established *c* 1638-40 and incorporated as a township 1642; *m* 26 Sept 1648 Ann, dau of Edward Winn, of Woburn, Mass., and his w Joanna, and *d* 9 Jan 1701/2, leaving (with other issue):

Aaron CLEVELAND, *b* Woburn, Mass., 10 Jan 1654/5; *m* there 26 Sept 1675 Dorcas (*b* 29 Jan 1657; *d* Cambridge, Mass., 29 Nov 1714), dau of John Wilson (*c* 1611-87) and his w Hannah James, and *d* Woburn 14 Sept 1716, leaving issue:

Aaron CLEVELAND, Jr, *b* Woburn 9 July 1680; tavern-keeper, building contractor and speculator in real estate; *m* Woburn 1 Jan 1701/2 Abigail (*b* there 29 Nov 1683; *d* probably Norwich, Conn., 6 Jan 1761), dau of Samuel Waters (1651/2-1729) and his w Mary Hudson (1653-1721), and *d* in that part of Cambridge which subsequently became separated from the larger parent town and incorporated with Medford *c* 1 Dec 1755, having had issue:

Revd Aaron CLEVELAND III, *b* probably Cambridge 29 Oct 1715; *educ* Harvard (graduate 1735); Presbyterian and later Episcopalian Minister, missionary with Society for the Propagation of the Gospel; *m* Medford 4 Aug 1739 Susanna (*b* there 26 April 1716; *d* Salem, Mass., 1 March 1788), dau of Revd Aaron Porter (1689-1721/2, *see* Grant, Male Line Ancestry and Collateral Descendants; the Revd A. Porter's aunt Sarah Cooke was an ancestress of President HAYES) and his w Susanna

Sewall (1691-1747), whose aunt *m* William Longfellow and with him was ancestor of both President FORD and the poet Henry Wadsworth Longfellow, author of *Hiawatha* etc; the Revd Aaron Cleveland *d* Philadelphia 11 Aug 1757, leaving issue:

Revd Aaron CLEVELAND IV, *b* East Haddam, Conn., 2 Feb 1744; hatter, with own manufacturing establishment (which he founded) at Norwich, Conn., single-term Memb Connecticut Legislature 1779, miscellaneous writer and versifier (works include the poem 'The Philosopher and Boy'), ordained Congregationalist minister 1797; *m* Norwich, Conn., 12 April 1768 Abiah (*b* there 27 Dec 1749; *d* there 23 Aug 1788), dau of Capt James Hyde (1707-93), whose gf Samuel Hyde was an ancestor of President FORD, and his w and 2nd cousin Sarah Marshall (1720-73), whose great-aunt Mary Post was an ancestress of President FILLMORE, and *d* New Haven, Conn., 21 Sept 1815, leaving issue (not necessarily in the order given):

I Charles CLEVELAND, Episcopalian missionary in London, UK

II William CLEVELAND, *b* Norwich 20 Dec 1770; *m* Westfield, Mass., 19 Dec 1793 Margaret (*b* there 25 Nov 1766; *d* Black Rock, New York, 10 Aug 1850), dau of Richard Falley, Jr (1740-1808), and his w Margaret Hitchcock (1741-1820), and *d* Black Rock 18 Aug 1837, leaving issue:

Revd Richard Falley CLEVELAND, *b* Norwich 19 June 1804; *educ* Yale (graduated 1824); Congregationalist minister at Windham, Conn.; *m* Baltimore 10 Sept 1829 Anne (*b* there 4 Feb 1806; *d* Holland Patent, New York, 19 July 1882), dau of Abner Neal (*b* Ireland; *d* Baltimore *c* 1826) and his w Barbara Reel (*d c* 1832), and *d* Holland Patent 1 Oct 1853 of peritonitis consequent upon a gastric ulcer, leaving issue:

I Anna Neal Cleveland, *b* 9 July 1830; *educ* Hamilton Coll; missionary and schoolteacher; *m* 9 March 1853 Revd Eurotas Parmalee HASTINGS, DD (*b* 1821; Pres Jaffna Coll, Manepay, Ceylon; *d* 1890), and *d* 1909, having had three s and four daus

II Revd William Neal CLEVELAND, *b* 7 April 1832; *educ* Hamilton Coll (graduated 1851); pncpl teacher Literature Dept New York Inst for the Blind from 1853; *m* 1860 Mrs Anita Marie Scholl, *née* Thomas (*b* 1835; *d* 1898) and *d* 15 Jan 1906, having had two s and one dau

III Mary Allen Cleveland, *b* 16 Nov 1833; *m* 1853 William Edward HOYT (*b* 1829; *d* 1901) and *d* 28 July 1914, having had two s and one dau

IV Richard Cecil CLEVELAND, *b* 31 July 1835; 2nd Lt 24th Indiana Regt Civil War; lost off the Bahamas 22 Oct 1872 in the burning of the steamer *Missouri*, outward bound from New York to Havana, Cuba

V (STEPHEN) GROVER CLEVELAND, 22nd and 24th PRESIDENT of the UNITED STATES of AMERICA

VI Margaret Louise Falley Cleveland, *b* 28 Oct 1838; governess; *m* 1873 Norval Baldwin BACON, of East Hamilton, New York (*b* 1837; architect; *d* 1913), s of Norval Comins Bacon and his w Janette Terry, and *d* 5 March 1932, leaving issue (with a dau):

1 Cleveland Frederick BACON, *b* 22 July 1874; *educ* Williams Coll (BA) and New York U Law Sch (LLB); lawyer, Memb: New York City Bar Assoc, New York County Lawyers Assoc, New York State Bar Assoc, American Bar Assoc, Soc of Colonial Wars; *m* 30 Nov 1914 Ethel Grace, dau of Wesley S. Thurston, and *d* 19—, having had issue:

(1) *Grover Cleveland BACON, *b* 8 April 1921

VII Lewis Frederick CLEVELAND, *b* 2 May 1841; served Army of the Potomac (32nd New York Vols) Civil War (1st Lt 1862), hotelier; lost 22 Oct 1872 with his brother Richard

VIII Susan Sophia Cleveland, *b* 2 Sept 1843; *m* 1867 Lucien Theron YEOMANS (*b* 1840; Memb New York State legislature; *d* 1906) and *d* 4 Nov 1938, having had two s and three daus

IX (Rose) Elizabeth (Libbie) CLEVELAND, *b* 13 June 1846; *educ* Haughton Seminary; teacher at Hamilton Coll and a collegiate inst at Lafayette, Ind., hostess for her brother at the White House, authoress: *George Eliot's Poetry and Other Essays* (1885); *d* 26 Nov 1918

Aaron Cleveland[1]
1654/5-1716

Dorcas Wilson[2]
1657-1714

　　　　　　　Aaron Cleveland, Jr
　　　　　　　1680-1755

Samuel Waters
1651/2-1729

Mary Hudson
1653-1721

　　　　　　　Abigail Waters
　　　　　　　1683-1761

Samuel Porter, Jr
1660-1722

Joanna Cooke
1665-1713

　　　　　　　Revd Aaron Porter
　　　　　　　1689-1721/2

Stephen Sewall
1657-1725

Margaret Mitchell
c 1664-1735/6

　　　　　　　Susanna Sewall
　　　　　　　1691-1747

Samuel Hyde
c 1637-67

Jane Lee
b c 1640

　　　　　　　John Hyde
　　　　　　　1667-1727

Caleb Abell
c 1646-1731

Margaret Post
1653-1700

　　　　　　　Experience Abell
　　　　　　　1674-1763

　　　　　　　Abiel Marshall
　　　　　　　d 1758

John Hough
1655-1715

Sarah Post
b 1659

　　　　　　　Abiah Hough
　　　　　　　1690-p 1720

　　　　　　　Richard Lamb
　　　　　　　d 1736-37
　　　　　　　— —

John Hitchcock
1642-1711/2

Hannah Chapin
1644-1719

　　　　　　　John Hitchcock, Jr
　　　　　　　1670-1751

Samuel Ball
1647/8-89

Mary Graves
c 1654-1727

　　　　　　　Mary Ball
　　　　　　　1673-1760

Edward Stebbins
1656-1712

Sarah Graves
c 1659-1700

　　　　　　　Thomas Stebbins
　　　　　　　1686/7-1758

Joseph Ely
1663-1755

Mary Riley
1665-1736

　　　　　　　Mary Ely
　　　　　　　1689-1770

[1] & [2] For generations
further back *see* Male
Line Ancestry section

GROVER CLEVELAND
FAMILY TREE

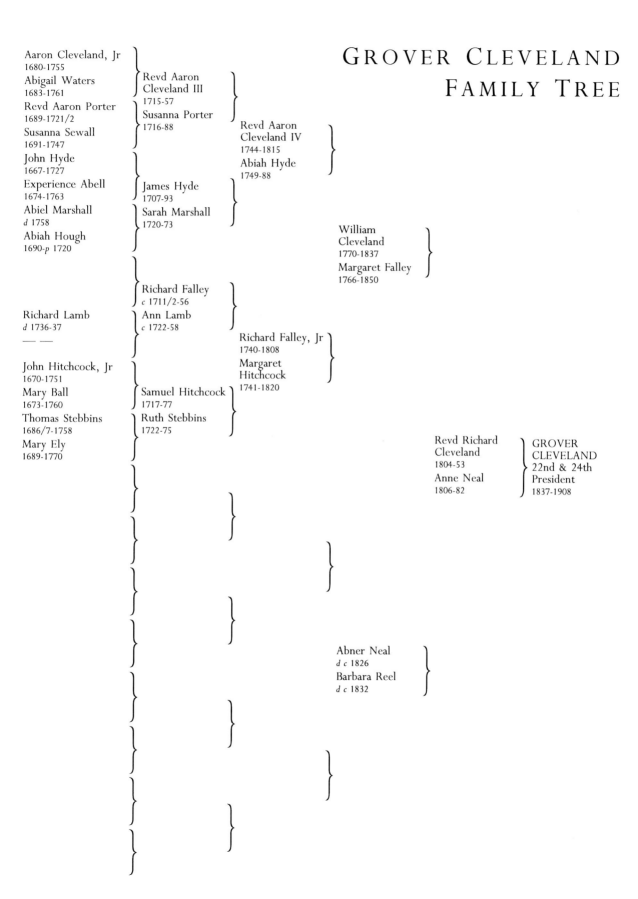

Aaron Cleveland, Jr
1680-1755
Abigail Waters
1683-1761
Revd Aaron Porter
1689-1721/2
Susanna Sewall
1691-1747
John Hyde
1667-1727
Experience Abell
1674-1763
Abiel Marshall
d 1758
Abiah Hough
1690-p 1720

Richard Lamb
d 1736-37
— —
John Hitchcock, Jr
1670-1751
Mary Ball
1673-1760
Thomas Stebbins
1686/7-1758
Mary Ely
1689-1770

Revd Aaron
Cleveland III
1715-57
Susanna Porter
1716-88

James Hyde
1707-93
Sarah Marshall
1720-73

Richard Falley
c 1711/2-56
Ann Lamb
c 1722-58

Samuel Hitchcock
1717-77
Ruth Stebbins
1722-75

Revd Aaron
Cleveland IV
1744-1815
Abiah Hyde
1749-88

Richard Falley, Jr
1740-1808
Margaret
Hitchcock
1741-1820

William
Cleveland
1770-1837
Margaret Falley
1766-1850

Abner Neal
d c 1826
Barbara Reel
d c 1832

Revd Richard
Cleveland
1804-53
Anne Neal
1806-82

GROVER
CLEVELAND
22nd & 24th
President
1837-1908

Plate 71   Benjamin Harrison, portrait by Eastman Johnson (1824-1906)

BENJAMIN HARRISON

1833-1901
23RD PRESIDENT OF THE UNITED STATES OF AMERICA
1889-93

The Republicans planned the election of 1888 very skilfully. Indiana had gone for the Democrats in 1884 because their vice-presidential candidate came from that state. So four years later the Republican nomination went to Indiana in the person of General Benjamin Harrison, grandson of William Henry Harrison. New York had also been counted for Cleveland, its Governor, but only by a few hundred votes. So the Republicans gave Harrison a New Yorker for running mate. Cleveland was on bad terms with the great Democratic machine at Tammany Hall and matters might have been left to take their course but a prudent manager contrived that a letter was written to the British minister, Lionel Sackville-West, as from an earnest and friendly citizen, asking if Cleveland was anti-British. The minister, not seeing the trap, wrote back saying that it would be quite all right from a British point of view to vote for Cleveland. This letter was released a few days before the election. Cleveland instantly asked for the minister's recall, but the damage was done. The President had been labelled a British puppet. The Irish vote went to his opponent, so did New York State, Indiana and the presidency.

The beneficiary of all this activity was a stout little man with a military beard and a straight back who had distinguished himself as a soldier, lawyer and Senator. He was a charming companion in private and an excellent public speaker. On paper he should have been a better President than any other Republican between Lincoln and Theodore Roosevelt. There was no taint on his election as there had been with Hayes. He was abler than Grant, Garfield or McKinley, and unlike Arthur had no spoilsman's record to live down. Although he can scarcely be blamed for accepting his party's nomination he was unsuited to the presidency. As a Civil War veteran he could not resist the demands of the veterans and the flood of unjustifiable pensions was renewed. He was a failure in other ways. He was cold and suspicious in his dealings with other politicians and, if he had not appointed the ever-popular Blaine to be his Secretary of State, might have had even more difficulty with Congress than he experienced. As it was he had no influence there. The only law of any importance passed in his administration was the McKinley Tariff, which was as unstatesmanlike as all the other tariffs passed between 1865 and 1912. His limitations of vision were as sharp as Cleveland's, but even if he had known what to do he would not have been able to do it, such was the hostility of Congress. 'Czar' Reed, the Speaker of the House of Representatives, said that having converse with President Harrison was like being in a dripping cave.

Meanwhile a spirit of revolt was beginning to sweep the West, where appalling climatic conditions were ruining the farmers. Harrison had nothing to offer them. In 1892 there was a brutal confrontation between the steelworkers and their employers at the Carnegie plant in Pittsburgh. Harrison, whose party was closely allied with the steel barons, suffered from the association. The country was in a mood for change and the President was palpably a stick-in-the-mud. It is no wonder he lost his bid for reelection. He did not mind very much.

While President he used to refer to the White House as his jail and his wife had died there after a long illness. In 1893 he went happily back to the law and later appeared very successfully for Venezuela when, under American pressure, the British finally agreed to arbitration of a boundary dispute between Venezuela and British Guiana. He married again and became a father once more, though he was already a grandfather, and wrote some amusing accounts of the Presidential life, not concealing what he took to be its horrors.

BENJAMIN HARRISON'S FAMILY

The coldness contemporary public figures noted in Benjamin Harrison — though he was warm enough in a small circle of friends and relatives — was very different from his grandfather William H. Harrison's geniality in the same circumstances. Perhaps this inability to handle official personages entered the family through William's wife Anna, who had always disliked the prospect of Washington life and wished her husband could have stayed on his farm. William and Anna's son Scott, who was also of course Benjamin's father, preferred seclusion from the great world too. Doubtless Scott's early experience of managing his father's farm while the latter was in Colombia as US Minister gave him a taste for rural life, particularly as his father subsequently made over to him 800 acres out of the 2,000-acre holding. But low prices for agricultural produce and the frequency of flooding (his farm was at the junction of the Ohio and Big Miami Rivers) brought money difficulties. And after his wife's death in 1850, a melancholy event in itself, finances grew even worse, what with his sons' schooling to pay for, and he borrowed money from his sister's husband, John Cleves Short. Eventually foreclosure on the family farm was only avoided by recourse to his son Benjamin, who as a successful lawyer was by then prosperous.

Scott was persuaded to run for Congress and even got elected, despite his lack of ambition. Not that he disliked public speaking, for he was in demand as a lecturer to local groups right up to his death. But he can have had few illusions as to the motives of his backers for political office. When in 1854 a group of Whigs suggested he make himself available for the presidential election in two years' time, he remarked that they had "calculated too largely on the potency of a name." His old-fashioned Whiggery — he backed Fillmore, to his son Benjamin's embarrassment, and helped scupper John C. Frémont's bid for the presidency by collecting evidence that he was a Catholic — conflicted with his son Benjamin's Republican sympathies from the early 1850s on. When Benjamin was asked to run for Republican City Attorney of Indianapolis in 1857 his father refused to visit him at his house and by the end of the decade Scott Harrison looked on Republicans as near-revolutionaries.

If Scott Harrison resembled his son in dealing with public figures, the circumstances surrounding his death resembled those of his father the 9th President in their touch of the ludicrous. His corpse was stolen by 'resurrectionists', as bodysnatchers supplying medical schools with material for dissection were called then. Benjamin urged the police forces of cities across the entire Midwest to search for it and even enlisted Pinkerton's Detective Agency. His son Russell talked to the press, public excitement became intense and a court case followed. (The dispute, a civil one between the Harrisons and the presumed culprits, seems to have been settled out of court.) It is curious to reflect that if medical students in that era had been given a better grounding in the vagaries of the human body (which need not necessarily have come about through the purloining of fresh corpses) Benjamin Harrison's first wife's tuberculosis might have been diagnosed sooner and not put down to the fatuously vague 'nervous prostration'.

Benjamin had always been the brightest of Scott Harrison's children. At school he was ahead of his elder brother Irwin and his mother had him held back. Irwin later offered to settle some money in his

Plate 72   Caroline Scott Harrison,
Benjamin Harrison's 1st wife

Plate 73   Mary Harrison McKee, Benjamin Harrison's
daughter by his 1st wife and his hostess in the White House

Plate 74   Mary Scott Lord Dimmick,
Benjamin Harrison's 2nd wife and his 1st wife's niece

will on Benjamin's second child if he, Irwin, remained single, but nothing came of it since he eventually married. He was Benjamin's favourite brother, although he had no monopoly of Benjamin's fraternal loyalty: Benjamin gave financial assistance to his youngest brother John Jr, who he said "couldn't make a dime".

Benjamin Harrison's first wife, Caroline or Carrie, spent much of her time in the White House doing needlework, cultivating orchids and painting. She was also a competent musician and had a passion for decorating chinaware, usually with four-leaf clovers. She collected any piece of china she could that had belonged to a former President. Although it is known that her last disease was tuberculosis leading to pleurisy, she was often ill with mysterious maladies when younger. It has been suggested that she was never the same after a nasty fall on ice in 1881; certainly she underwent an operation two years later. After the Harrisons had moved into the White House Carrie's father, the 90-year old Dr John Scott, and her elder sister Lizzie came to live there too. Lizzie's function was to help her sister but she died six months after Harrison's Inauguration and was replaced by her own daughter, Mary Dimmick (later Harrison's second wife). The plethora of Marys in the Harrison family was such that Mary Dimmick was called Mame. There was also Russell Harrison's wife Mary (the President's daughter-in-law), who was known as May. Yet another Mary was the President's daughter Mrs McKee, who with her two small children also came to live at the White House and was known as Mamie. Benjamin Harrison's grandchild Benjamin ('Baby') McKee became a national figure, providing journalists with heaven-sent human interest copy. He was said to have more influence than the entire Cabinet, toys were sent to the White House for him from all over the country, his grandfather allowed him the run of the house to such an extent that he was often to be found crawling around the legs of important public figures closeted with the President, and so on.

Despite Caroline's poor health, which culminated in her death a week before the 1892 presidential election and which in its last months is said to have cast such gloom over her husband that his whole campaign was affected, she seems to have possessed a good deal of energy. Appalled, like so many First Ladies, by the disrepair of the White House (there were only five useable bedrooms when the Harrisons moved in) she employed an architect to draw up three sets of plans, each more elaborate than the last. She ordered a thorough spring cleaning only weeks after her husband's Inauguration. It was long overdue, for green mould covered the walls due to bad plumbing, a cloacal miasma hung about the place on humid days due to the escape of gas from the sewers, and the fabric was often unsafe, with rotten floorboards, sometimes five layers deep in places, acting as the only protection between the unwary footfalls of a visitor and a crash through to the floor below. Electric light was introduced and splendid new bathrooms of white tile, porcelain and marble installed. Nor does she seem to have possessed the peevishness so often to be found in the terminally ill: she took no offence when Frances Cleveland, the former President's wife, boycotted the Inauguration, the traditional lunch at the White House which followed it and every Inaugural ball. The Inauguration period was particularly trying as the Harrisons had rashly extended a general invitation to visit them in the White House to all their Ohio acquaintance. A horde of Midwesterners, and no doubt other Americans, duly descended; Harrison reckoned he had shaken hands with 8,000 people between dawn and mid-afternoon on the day after the Inauguration. His tactic was to turn them over immediately afterward to his son-in-law Bob McKee, who took them for a tour of the White House.

It is pleasant to record that under Benjamin Harrison dancing was reintroduced to the White House on formal occasions — for the first time since Mrs Polk's ban, instituted almost half a century earlier. The wishes of the numerous young people living there were evidently too much for 50 years of a not particularly enticing tradition. It is less pleasant to record that Benjamin Harrison's second marriage, to his first wife's niece Mary (Mame), aroused hostility on the part of his son Russell and daughter Mary (Mamie). Harrison wrote Russell a rather plaintive letter pointing out how lonely he would have been had he remained a widower and adding that neither Russell nor Mary (Mame) was living under his roof and he hoped they would not want him to go on living alone. His social life became quite active after his second marriage, so loneliness was presumably kept at bay.

BIOGRAPHICAL DETAILS AND DESCENDANTS

HARRISON, BENJAMIN, b North Bend, Ohio, 20 Aug 1833; educ Farmer's Coll, nr Cincinnati, Ohio, and Miami U, Oxford, Ohio (BA 1852, AM 1855); admitted to Cincinnati Bar 1854, City Attorney Indianapolis 1857-60, Presbyterian Deacon 1857 and Elder of Session 1861-1901, Reporter Indiana Supreme Court 1860-62 and 1864-68, with 70th Indiana Infy (2nd Lt 1862, Capt 1862, Col 1862, Brig-Gen 1865) Civil War, unsuccessful gubernatorial candidate Indiana 1876, Memb Mississippi River Commission 1879, Chm Indiana Delegn to Republican Nat Conventn 1880, US Senator from Indiana 1881-87, 23rd President (R) of the USA 1889-93, Republican presidential candidate 1892, Ch Counsel Internat Tribunal of Arbitration at Paris representing Venezuela in boundary dispute with Great Britain 1898, Pres Ecumenical Conference of Foreign Missions in New York 1900, Memb Permanent Court of Arbitration 1900, author: *This Country of Ours* (1897), *Views of an Ex-President* (1901), *Public Papers and Addresses of Benjamin Harrison* (1893); m 1st Oxford, Ohio, 20 Oct 1853 Caroline (Carrie) Lavinia (b Oxford 1 Oct 1832; 1st Pres-Gen Nat Soc of Daughters of the American Revolution; d the White House 25 Oct 1892 of tuberculosis; bur Crown Hill Cemetery, Indianapolis, Ind.), 3rd dau of Revd Dr John Witherspoon Scott, Presbyterian Min and Prof of Mathematics and Natural Sciences, Miami U, and his w Mary Potts, dau of John Neal, and had issue:

President Benjamin Harrison's son
I Russell Benjamin HARRISON, b Oxford, Ohio, 12 Aug 1854; educ Lafayette Coll, Easton, Pa., and Pennsylvania Mil Acad; Lt-Col US Vols, served Spanish-American War of 1898, Memb (R) Indiana House of Reps 1921-23 and Indiana Senate 1925-29; m Omaha, Nebr., 9 Jan 1884 Mary (May) Angeline (b 16 Nov 1861; d Washington, DC, 28 Nov 1944), dau of Senator Alvin Saunders, Govr Nebraska Territory 1861-68, and d Indianapolis 13 Dec 1936, leaving issue:

Grandchildren
1 Marthena Harrison, b 18 Jan 1888; m 12 Feb 1912 (divorce 1927) Harry A. WILLIAMS, Jr, of Norfolk, Va. (b 12 Oct 1890; d 12 March 1958), s of Harry A. Williams, and d 22 Feb 1973, having had issue:

Great-grandchildren
(1) Surviller (Sally) Ann Williams, b 23 Oct 1913; m April 1937 William M. CONNORS, of Troy, New York (b 12 Sept 1911), and d in childbirth 13 Nov 1939
(2) *Mary Virginia Williams [Mrs Mary Devine, 1200 Corbin Court, McLean, VA 22101, USA], b 6 July 1916; m 21 April 1938 (divorce 1966) Dr John Leo DEVINE, Jr (b Sept 1911; d 1969), s of John Leo Devine, and has three adopted children:

   a *Richard Allen DEVINE
   b *John Michael DEVINE
   c *Mary Catherine DEVINE

Great-grandchildren
(3) *Marthena Harrison Williams [Mrs Gil Ellisor, 926 N Street, Washington, DC 20001 or 20002 or 20024, USA], b 10 Aug 1917; m 1st 18 April 1940 Paul Franklin TRAYNHAM (b 21 Oct 1917; d 17 March 1948) and has issue:

   Great-great-grandchildren
   1a *Mary Marthena Traynham, b 23 July 1942; adopted by stepfather (for whom see below) and assumed surname Ellisor; m 27 Sept 1969 *John Alfred EMMERLING (b 4 Nov 1939), s of Alfred C. Emmerling, of Franklin, Mich.
   2a *Paul Franklin Traynham, Jr, b 30 June 1947; adopted by stepfather and assumed surname ELLISOR

Great-grandchildren
(3) (cont.) Marthena Harrison Williams Traynham m 2nd 1 Feb 1957 *Julian Gillis (Gil) ELLISOR (b 14 Nov 1919) and has adopted his children by a previous marriage:

   a *Stephen ELLISOR
   b *Nancy ELLISOR

Grandchildren
2 William Henry HARRISON, b Terre Haute, Ind., 10 Aug 1896; educ Friends' Sch, Washington, DC, and Nebraska U (LLD Vincennes U); admitted to Indiana Bar 1925 and Wyoming Bar 1937, Memb Indiana House of Reps 1927 and Wyoming House of Reps 1945, 1947 and 1949, Memb US House of Reps from Wyoming 82nd-83rd, 87th-88th and 90th Congresses, Memb Renegotiations Bd 1968, Co-Chm Wyoming Republican Ctee 1948-50, State Committeeman 1946-48; m 19 Oct 1920 Mary Elizabeth Newton (b 2 April 1900; d 21 Jan 1978) and d 8 Oct 1990, leaving issue:

Great-grandchildren

(1) *Mary Elizabeth (Maribeth) Harrison [Mrs Forrest Rose, Box 503, Scottsbluff, NE 69361, USA], b Omaha, Nebr., 10 Sept 1921; *educ* Indiana U and Montana State U; teacher, writer of botanical articles, painter of botanical subjects; m 1st 1942 (divorce 19—) Gordon WILLIAMS and has had issue:

Great-great-grandchildren

1a Benjamin Harrison WILLIAMS, b 6 Oct 1943; d after an accident 12 April 1963
2a *Lynda Wrae Williams [11166 Front St, Logan, nr Manhattan, MT 59741, USA], b 1945; m 19— (divorce 1969) James BUCHHOLZ and has had issue:

Great-great-grandchildren's children

1b *James BUCHHOLZ [Box 6722, Bozeman, MT 59715, USA], b 16 Feb 1967
2b *Dawn Buchholz [Mrs Jerry Harper, Garton's Mobile Home Park #28, Knob Noster, MO 65336, USA], b 13 April 1968; m 19— *Jerry HARPER and has issue:

Great-great-grandchildren's grandchildren
1c *Steven James HARPER, b 1 Dec 1989

Great-great-grandchildren's children
3b Angela BUCHHOLZ, b March 1969; d April 1969
4b *Robert BUCHHOLZ, b 1974

Great-great-grandchildren

3a *Thomas William BREWER [Box 282, Broadus, MT 59317, USA] (b Williams but took stepf's name), b Sheridan, Wyo., 9 May 1947; *educ* Montana State U; range telephone centl office repair 1973-; m 1st 19— (divorce 1976), as her 2nd husb, Linda Adkinson; m 2nd 25 Nov 1978 *Verna Jo, dau of Albert M. Pikkula and his w Helen Irion, and has issue:

Great-great-grandchildren's children

1b *Lucas Harrison BREWER, b Sheridan 14 June 1980
2b *Ben(jamin) Albert BREWER, b Sheridan 9 July 1982
3b *Ty Edward BREWER, b Sheridan 9 June 1984
Mr and Mrs Thomas W. Brewer also have an adopted dau:
a *Jenny Mae Soong BREWER, b Seoul, S Korea, 21 Feb 1986

Great-grandchildren

(1) (cont.) Mrs Maribeth Harrison Williams m 2nd 1948 Walter BREWER and has further issue:

Great-great-grandchildren

4a *Margaret May Brewer, b 4 Dec 1949; m 1967 *Michael R. ANNALORA and has issue:

Great-great-grandchildren's children
1b *Matthew Anthony ANNALORA, b 23 Jan 1968

Great-great-grandchildren

5a *Miriam Elizabeth BREWER, b 7 July 1951
6a *Walter Thomas BREWER, b 20 Sept 1953
7a *Harrison Lee BREWER, b 28 Oct 1954

Great-grandchildren

(1) (cont.) Maribeth Harrison Williams Brewer m 3rd 12 April 1971 Robert PATRICK (d 11 Aug 1975); m 4th 30 Dec 1985 *Forrest ROSE, s of James Rose and his w Ida Mae Northern
(2) *William Henry HARRISON, Jr [4651 Massachusetts Avenue, Washington, DC 20016, USA], b 16 June 1923; m 10 Dec 1941 *Betty Alley (b 4 Jan 1924) and has issue:

Great-great-grandchildren

1a Ann ('Nancy') HARRISON, b 3 Dec 1942; d after an accident 30 Jan 1953
2a *William Henry HARRISON III, b 26 Jan 1945; m 20 Aug 1966 *Betty Anne Marosek and has issue:

Great-great-grandchildren's children

1b *John Benjamin HARRISON, b 14 Jan 1968
2b *Thomas Tyler HARRISON, b 21 Jan 1971

Great-great-grandchildren

3a *Barbara Jean Harrison, b 24 June 1949; m 26 April 1970 *John Alan SUNDAHL
4a *John Scott HARRISON, b 26 June 1957

President Benjamin Harrison's daughter

II Mary ('Marnie') Scott Harrison, b Indianapolis 3 April 1858; m there 5 Nov 1884 (James) Robert (Bob) McKEE (b Madison, Ind., 9 Dec 1857; d Greenwich, Conn., 21 Oct 1942), s of Robert S. McKee and his w Celine E. ———, and d Greenwich 28 Oct 1930, leaving issue:

Grandchildren

1 Benjamin Harrison McKEE, *b* Indianapolis 15 March 1887; *m* 1st Wimbledon, Surrey, UK, 5 April 1917 Constance Elizabeth Magnett (*d* Palm Beach, Fla., 23 Jan 1954) and had issue:

Great-grandchildren

(1) Patricia McKee, *b* Paris, France, 30 March 1921; *m* 1st 1944 (divorce 19—) Gerald ROHMER (*b* New York 27 March 1918), s of Gerald Rohmer and his *w* Beebe Bentley, and had issue:

Great-great-grandchildren

1a *Carole Laurie Rohmer, *b* Greenwich 5 Dec 1944; *m* Milwaukee, Wis., 19 Dec 1964 *Harold HOLBROOK, Jr (*b* Statesville, N Carolina, 1944), s of Harold Holbrook and his *w* Jane Brooks, and has issue:

Great-great-grandchildren's children

1b *Gerald McKee HOLBROOK, *b* Milwaukee, Wis., 13 Feb 1967

Great-grandchildren

(1) (cont.) Mrs Patricia Rohmer *m* 2nd Milwaukee 14 Nov 1953 *Richard E. MONAHAN [Mequon, WI 53092, USA] (*b* Monticello, Iowa, 13 June 1915), s of Michael Monahan and his *w* Eleanor Peil, and *d* Milwaukee 17 July 1956, leaving further issue:

Great-great-grandchildren

2a *Michael McKee MONAHAN, *b* Milwaukee 30 July 1955

Grandchildren

1 (cont.) Benjamin Harrison McKee *m* 2nd Nice, France, 24 Sept 1954 Marcelle Claudon (*b* 1903; *d* 1973) and *d* Nice 1 April 1958

2 Mary Lodge McKee, *b* Indianapolis 11 July 1888; *m* New York 15 Nov 1913 (divorce 1922) Curt Hugo REISINGER (*b* New York 27 Oct 1881; *d* there 17 Dec 1964), s of Hugo Reisinger and his *w* Edmée Busch, and *d* New York 2 March 1967, leaving issue:

Great-grandchildren

(1) Edmée Roberta Reisinger, *b* New York 18 June 1915; *m* Greenwich, Conn., 16 Feb 1937 Joseph Jenry MORSMAN, Jr (*b* Chicago 1 July 1912; *b* Stamford, Conn., 10 Jan 1982), s of Joseph Jenry Morsman and his *w* Helen Elizabeth Kimball, and *d* Darien, Conn., leaving issue:

Great-great-grandchildren

1a *Joseph Jenry MORSMAN III, *b* New York 11 Oct 1937; *educ* Yale and Mass U (MA); *m* Kenilworth, Ill., 26 Aug 1967 *Laura Cornell [Mrs Joseph J Morsman III, Box 81, Deerfield, MA 01342, USA] (*b* Chicago 26 Aug 1947), dau of Herbert Cornell De Young and his *w* Virginia Winston, and has issue:

Great-great-grandchildren's children

1b *Laura Winston MORSMAN, *b* Greenfield, Mass., 18 Feb 1969
2b *Joseph Jenry MORSMAN IV, *b* Greenfield 5 July 1970
3b *Virginia Harrison MORSMAN, *b* Greenfield 2 March 1972

Great-great-grandchildren

2a *Edmée Roberta Morsman, *b* New York 21 March 1943; *m* Darien, Conn., 9 June 1962 *David Robertson GEIS (*b* New York 30 March 1939), s of Philip Geis and his *w* Edythe Robertson, and has issue:

Great-great-grandchildren's children

1b *Edmée Elizabeth GEIS, *b* Stamford, Conn., 8 March 1964
2b *David Robertson GEIS, Jr, *b* Stamford 10 Feb 1970
3b *Alexandra Lynne GEIS, *b* Concord, Mass., 13 Aug 1971

Great-great-grandchildren

3a *Kimball Harrison MORSMAN, *b* New York 14 Dec 1946; *educ* Yale and Harvard (MBA); *m* Darien, Conn., 28 Dec 1968 *Ingrid Anne (*b* Cambridge, Mass., 15 Nov 1947), dau of Thomas Selmer Thompson and his *w* Nathalie Brown, and has issue:

Great-great-grandchildren's children

1b *Kristin Kjaer MORSMAN, *b* Landstuhl, West Germany, 9 April 1971
2b *Whitney Harrison MORSMAN, *b* Wellesley, Mass., 27 March 1974

Great-grandchildren

(2) *Mary Harrison Reisinger, *b* New York 3 Dec 1919; *m* 1st New York 7 March 1942 (divorce 194-) Albert OELSCHLAGER, s of Albert E. Oelschlager; *m* 2nd New York 31 May 1945 (divorce 19—) Bradford Lorin TOBEY (*b* Evanston, Ill., 9 May 1913), s of William Hayward Tobey and his *w* Myra E. Bates, and has issue:

Great-great-grandchildren

1a *Curt Reisinger TOBEY [50 Commonwealth Avenue, Apt 201, Boston, MA 02116, USA], *b* Evanston, Ill., 10 June 1946; *educ* Choate, Vermont U and Northwestern U Graduate Sch of Business Admin; financial analyst with New England Merchants Nat Bank, Boston; *m* Winnetka, Ill., 14 June 1969 *Barbara Warner (*b* Lake Forest, Ill.), dau of Morris R. Eddy and his *w* Barbara McNair

2a *Mary Harrison Tobey, b Evanston 25 Dec 1948; m Winnetka 31 Jan 1970 *Lt Rodney Wendell COOK (b Springfield, Va., 26 Nov 1946), s of Wendell Winfield Cook, of Burlington, Vt., and his w Lillian Casey, and has issue:

Great-great-grandchildren's children
1b *Kelly Harrison COOK, b Greensboro, N Carolina, 20 Dec 1973

Great-grandchildren
(2) (cont.) Mrs Mary Oelschlager Tobey m 3rd New York 6 Jan 1962 *Charles Joseph STEVENS (b Erie, Pa., 6 Oct 1906), s of George W. Stevens and his w Gertrude Zinck

President Benjamin Harrison's daughter
III A girl, d at birth 13 June 1861

BENJAMIN HARRISON m 2nd St Thomas's Protestant Episcopal Church, New York, 6 April 1896, as her 2nd husb, Mary (Mamie) Scott (b Honesdale, Pa., 30 April 1858; m 1st 22 Oct 1881 Walter Erskine Dimmick (d 14 or 16 Jan 1882); d New York 5 Jan 1948, bur Crown Hill Cemetery, Indianapolis), dau of Russell Farnham Lord, Ch Engr and Gen Manager Delaware & Hudson Canal Co, and his w Elizabeth Mayhew Scott (sister of the first Mrs Benjamin Harrison), and d Indianapolis 13 March 1901 of pneumonia, having had further issue:

President Benjamin Harrison's daughter
IV Elizabeth Harrison, b Indianapolis 21 Feb 1897; educ Westover Sch and New York U (LLB 1919, BS 1920); admitted to Indiana and New York Bars, Sec Ctee for Econ Devpt; m New York 6 April 1921 James Blaine WALKER, Jr, (b Helena, Mont., 20 Jan 1889; investment banker; d New York 15 Jan 1978), s of James Blaine Walker and his w Mary Gertrude Scannell, and d New York 25 Dec 1955, leaving issue:

Grandchildren
1 *Benjamin Harrison WALKER [108 East 82nd Street, New York, NY 10028, USA], b New York 27 Dec 1921; educ St Mark's Sch, Princeton (AB 1943) and Harvard Law Sch (LLB 1949); served reserve US Army and USAF 1942-57 (active service 1943-46 and 1951-52), Memb New York Bar, former Assist Gen Counsel Equitable Life Assur Soc of US; m New York 14 Jan 1956 *Elizabeth (b Rumson, New Jersey, 31 Aug 1916), dau of Henry Sillcocks and his w Ada Jackson, and has issue:

Great-grandchildren
(1) *James Harrison WALKER [91 Bonniefield Drive, Tiverton, RI 02878, USA], b New York 24 Feb 1957; educ Tabor Acad, Marion, Mass., and State U of New York (Maritime Coll) (BS 1979); Master Mariner Merchant Marine; m Newport, Rhode Island, 25 Aug 1984 *Elizabeth Maxfield (b there 26 April 1954), dau of Edward A. Sherman and his w Kirtley Maxfield, and has issue:

Great-great-grandchildren
1a *James Harrison WALKER, Jr, b Providence, Rhode Island, 5 Dec 1990
2a *William Henry Harrison WALKER, b Providence 27 May 1992

Great-grandchildren
(2) *Maj Benjamin Harrison WALKER, Jr, USAF [1707 Tipton Drive, Crofton, MD 21114, USA], b New York 8 Aug 1958; educ St Mark's Sch, Southborough, Mass., Bowdoin Coll (AB 1981) and Coll of Physicians and Surgeons of Columbia U (MD 1985); with Medical Corps USAF 1987- (attending physician in emergency medicine, Malcolm Grove Hosp, Andrews Air Force Base, Washington, DC)

Grandchildren
2 *Jane (formerly Mary Jane) Harrison Walker [Mrs Newell Garfield Jr, Box 669 Parker Point Rd, Blue Hill, ME 04614, USA], b New York 3 Nov 1929; educ Chapin, Westover, Bryn Mawr Coll (AB 1951) and Cornell Medical Sch (MD 1955); chest specialist, Assoc Prof Clinical Medicine New York U (ret); m New York 16 Nov 1961, as his 2nd w, *Newell GARFIELD, Jr (b Rochester, New York, 8 July 1923), s of Newell Garfield, of Concord, Mass., and his w Mary Louise Wyatt, and ggs of President GARFIELD, and has issue:

Great-grandchildren
(3) *Elizabeth Newell GARFIELD, b New York 23 Nov 1962; educ Chapin Sch, New York, Bowdoin Coll (AB 1985) and Harvard Sch of Educn (MA 1992); is descended from three US Presidents

MALE LINE ANCESTRY AND COLLATERAL DESCENDANTS

See Ancestry of President WILLIAM H. HARRISON

Great-great-great-great grandparents on the father's side		*Great-great-great-great grandparents on the mother's side*	
William Symmes 1626/7-91 Mary Chickering 1648-1720/1	Timothy Symmes *c* 1683-*c* 1765		?George Ramsey
Anthony Collamore *d* 1693 Sarah Chittenden 1646/7-1703	Elizabeth Collamore 1679-1758		?Isabel Littlejohn
John Cleves? *d* 1707 ?Eliza — *c* 1665-1740	John Cleves (Jr?) *c* 1686-1750		
	Mary —? *c* 1697-1784		
Henry Tuthill 1665-1750 Bethia Horton *c* 1674-1744	Henry Tuthill, Jr *c* 1690-1775		
	Hannah (Crouch?) *c* 1693-1715		
Barnabas Horton 1666-96 Sarah Wines *c* 1668-70—1733	Caleb Horton 1687-1772		
Nathaniel Terry *b* 1656 Mary Horton	Phebe Terry *c* 1698-1776		

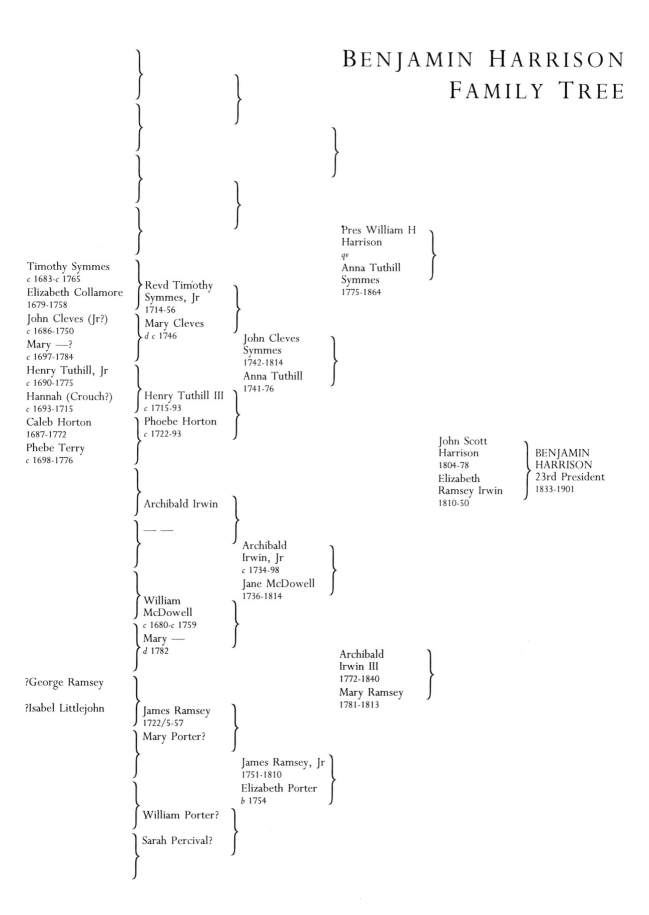

BENJAMIN HARRISON
FAMILY TREE

Pres William H
Harrison
qv
Anna Tuthill
Symmes
1775-1864

Timothy Symmes
c 1683-c 1765
Elizabeth Collamore
1679-1758
John Cleves (Jr?)
c 1686-1750
Mary —?
c 1697-1784
Henry Tuthill, Jr
c 1690-1775
Hannah (Crouch?)
c 1693-1715
Caleb Horton
1687-1772
Phebe Terry
c 1698-1776

Revd Timothy
Symmes, Jr
1714-56
Mary Cleves
d c 1746

Henry Tuthill III
c 1715-93
Phoebe Horton
c 1722-93

John Cleves
Symmes
1742-1814
Anna Tuthill
1741-76

John Scott
Harrison
1804-78
Elizabeth
Ramsey Irwin
1810-50

BENJAMIN
HARRISON
23rd President
1833-1901

Archibald Irwin

— —

Archibald
Irwin, Jr
c 1734-98
Jane McDowell
1736-1814

William
McDowell
c 1680-c 1759
Mary —
d 1782

Archibald
Irwin III
1772-1840
Mary Ramsey
1781-1813

?George Ramsey

?Isabel Littlejohn

James Ramsey
1722/5-57
Mary Porter?

James Ramsey, Jr
1751-1810
Elizabeth Porter
b 1754

William Porter?

Sarah Percival?

Plate 75   William McKinley

WILLIAM MCKINLEY

1843-1901
25TH PRESIDENT OF THE UNITED STATES OF AMERICA
1897-1901

McKinley was the last of the 19th-century Presidents and the first of the 20th century. The story of his administration points both forward and back but the same can be said of all administrations; it can hardly be that which makes his personality so elusive. Besides, he himself was in most ways a creature of the past: the last Civil War veteran to become President; another dependable lawyer-politician from Ohio with experience both in Congress and the governorship of his state; another Republican committed to a high tariff and the gold standard.

McKinley was the first President to make such extensive use of the telephone that he wrote very few letters and he seems to have made a point of destroying most of his papers. Yet these traits are not in themselves enough to make a man a mystery. If McKinley remains "the man without an angle or a tangle", as the poet Vachel Lindsay called him, the explanation must be sought in himself.

Some things are known. His marriage was even more poignantly disastrous then Lincoln's. Ida McKinley had been a young woman of exceptional beauty and considerable spirit. Then something went wrong during the birth of her second daughter. Doctors spoke of phlebitis; at all events she emerged a cripple and an epileptic, subject to frequent small fits and occasionally to major ones. To crown her desperate unhappiness her children died: first the new baby, then her elder daughter, aged four, of typhoid. McKinley paid for a few years of private happiness by devoting the rest of his life to what his biographer Margaret Leech has called "his secondary career of psychiatric nurse". His essential strength and goodness are demonstrated by the fact that he performed the role perfectly, carrying off the embarrassments of epilepsy with an amazing tact that spared the feelings of his wife and their friends as much as possible. When, at dinner for instance, Ida's hissing breath showed that she was about to have an attack, McKinley would insouciantly throw his napkin over her face until she recovered, and managed to do so with such a casual, everyday air that onlookers were almost convinced that nothing much had happened and were quite convinced that they should behave as if nothing had. Thanks to such loving stratagems Mrs McKinley was even able to play a small part in her husband's public life and she repaid him, not only with the sort of jealous, possessive clinging love that may be expected and forgiven in an invalid, but by broadening his horizons and diversifying his social round, which would otherwise have been passed exclusively in smoke-filled offices with other politicians. Nobody, probably, could have made McKinley cultured or have filled the gaps left by his scanty education, but Ida did at least stop him from getting coarse.

McKinley was not only an heroically loving husband, he was universally kind. Everyone noticed it and it seems to have been the secret of his charm. For charm he had, although it is hard to believe, looking at the photographs of a portly gentleman with a glassy expression, too pop-eyed it seems to be intelligent. In person he made a different impression. Everyone was captivated by him, from Mark Hanna, the Ohio industrialist who became his campaign manager, to small children visiting the White

House. It was a saying in Washington that when President Harrison gave a man a job he made him his enemy; when McKinley refused a job he made a friend. The biggest proof, perhaps, of McKinley's magnetism was the campaign of 1896. This is usually remembered for the saga of the losing candidate, William Jennings Bryan of Nebraska, who led an eloquent crusade for free silver and generated huge enthusiasm; still, he lost. One of the reasons for his defeat, usually overlooked, is that McKinley too was a great crowd pleaser. His obvious goodwill, his mellifluous voice and his blameless sentiments captivated the audience which flocked to hear him address them from the front porch of his home. This was no mean testimony to his power in an age which relished oratory and was a good judge of it. One of the reasons for Cleveland's defeat in 1888 was that he was such a tedious speaker.

McKinley was honest and McKinley was a thoroughly professional party politician, but he was not a particularly impressive President. His test came early when war fever mounted. The cause was Cuba, that island about which Americans have so seldom been rational. A rebellion against the colonial power, Spain, had been dragging on for years with ample assistance from private American citizens. Cleveland had done his utmost to keep the peace, but between an intransigent Spanish government and a bellicose, sentimental American public opinion he had had a hard struggle, and warned McKinley that time was against him. The new President scarcely needed the warning. He hated war worse than did Cleveland, probably because he had experienced it at first hand. He thought that firm diplomacy might induce Spain to concede independence to Cuba and that party discipline would keep Congress in hand. Both calculations were falsified by events. Spain's concessions always came too late and when an American warship, the *Maine*, blew up on a goodwill visit to Havana (the victim, possibly, of a mine planted by no one knows whom, but certainly not by the Spanish government), Congress too exploded. Public opinion, fanned by an irresponsible press, was clamouring for revenge; Congressional statesmen of both parties urged on the cause. McKinley's policy was brushed aside and there was a real possibility that Congress would declare war on Spain of its own accord. There was nothing the President could do but sail with the tide. He wept, he could not sleep, he struggled to avert a dishonourable war, or at least to give it a respectable appearance (his war message stressed the wrongs of Cuba, not the destruction of the *Maine*) but in the end he had to surrender. He had completely lost control of national policy because his amiable little arts of man-management were not enough. One must feel sorry for him but it is impossible to imagine certain other Presidents — Washington, say, or Lincoln, Jefferson or Jackson, even Madison or Cleveland — being forced into a policy of which they so deeply disapproved.

The war with Spain was short and successful. Cuba was given her independence; Puerto Rico, Guam and the Philippines became US colonies; the US Navy won a thumping victory over a Spanish fleet (three ships of which were made of wood) in Manila Bay and another at Santiago Bay in Cuba. McKinley was an adequate war President, even though he was ill-prepared for the task shortly before the outbreak of hostilities; he had confessed to the Secretary of the Navy that he did not know within 2,000 miles where the Philippines were. He soon learned.

What is difficult to decide is what else he learned. He worked extremely hard; he showed himself honest and patriotic on all occasions; but there is small trace of any large vision of America's future.

The war did not interfere with the rapid return of American prosperity and McKinley would clearly be a strong candidate for re-election in 1900, but his first running-mate had just died. So McKinley was joined on the ticket by one of the most notorious young jingoes in the country, Governor Theodore Roosevelt of New York. Bryan was again the Democratic candidate; again the Republicans won decisively; McKinley entered on his second term with every good prospect. Even the revolt of the Filipinos against their new masters was guttering out.

Then, in September 1901, he visited the Pan-American Exposition at Buffalo. There he was shot by a young man called Leon Czolgosz, a paranoid whose fantasies had been excited by revolutionist propaganda and the recent assassination of the King of Italy. Once more a wound that today would not have been lethal proved too much for the skill of the doctors, but McKinley's ordeal was shorter than Garfield's. He died eight days after the shooting.

Perhaps the truth about his character emerges most strongly from three of his last remarks. As he collapsed after being wounded he saw men beginning to beat up his assassin. "Don't let them hurt him," he said. Then as he realised how badly he was injured he murmured to his secretary, "My wife — be careful, Cortelyou, how you tell her — oh, be careful". A few days later he was the first to recognise that he was past saving. "It is useless, gentlemen," he told the doctors. "I think we ought to have a prayer."

WILLIAM MCKINLEY'S FAMILY

William McKinley's paternal ancestors were Scots-Irish and when we first hear of them were living at Dervock, some six or seven miles inland and to the south of the celebrated Giant's Causeway rock formation on the coast of Co Antrim, in Northern Ireland. Shortly after emigrating to America the 25th President's three times-great-grandfather swiftly contracted sufficient American patriotism to fight in the Revolutionary War. A generation later McKinley's paternal grandfather James moved west to Ohio to manage a charcoal furnace. His son William Sr was in the same line of business, though concentrating more on iron-production. William Sr, who was the future President's father, bought or rented two or three small furnaces in the Mahoning Valley, in northeastern Ohio, and kept up the family connection with Pennsylvania by going into partnership to produce iron with his younger brother Benjamin, who had stayed there. William Sr and his wife moved several times over the years but finally settled in Canton, Ohio, a little to the west of Mahoning County. Their eldest daughter Anna was already a teacher there (she became principal of the grammar school eventually) and did up a house for her parents to move into. Anna was also responsible for her brother William the future President, 13 years her junior, starting his law practice in Canton after his admission to the Ohio bar. He was already on a visit to her there and like her had taken up teaching, but only as a temporary way out of money difficulties when William Sr's business got into trouble.

The future President was a delicate youth, not very interested in sport. It is said to have been his Civil War service that toughened him up. Perhaps memories of his own delicate condition when young gave him the immense patience and tenderness he is so much remembered for in his dealings with his epileptic wife Ida. Her civilizing influence on him is acknowledged, though here too McKinley may have been induced not so much to change as to return to the more ethereal person he had been in his childhood, before enlisting as a soldier. His military service was moderately distinguished, however; he served on the staff of the future President General Rutherford B. Hayes, who commended his soldierly qualities warmly. And he had been an enthusiastic volunteer, thrilling to the seductive message of the recruiting meeting along with his cousin William McKinley Osborne. The cousins' gusto was no flash in the pan either: they had originally signed up for a three-month tour of duty, but when the time came for straightening out the paper work it appeared the three-month quota was full, so they signed on for three years or the duration. Osborne was later discharged sick but McKinley served throughout the war.

McKinley's attitude to drink was very different from that of his commanding general in the Union army, that other President-to-be Ulysses S. Grant. McKinley became a strong (if that does not sound paradoxical) 'temperance' agitator and was celebrated throughout Stark County, Ohio (where Canton was situated), for his speeches demanding total abstinence. As Stark County's Prosecuting Attorney he cracked down on the illicit sale of alcohol. Again it was Ida who toned down his hardline approach and once married to her he began to allow alcohol to be served at his table. He even, on special occasions, raised the odd glass to his own lips.

Plate 76   Ida Saxton McKinley

Of the four McKinley girls who survived to adulthood only two married. The two others became schoolmistresses, though Helen, the younger, sacrificed even that small degree of independence to act as a companion to her widowed mother Nancy. When McKinley's elder brother James died aged 56 he made his children James and Grace wards of McKinley, but they went to live with their grandmother old Mrs McKinley. Just after the Spanish-American War erupted, toward the end of McKinley's first term as President, James asked his uncle to pull strings so he could join the Canton Company of the Eighth Ohio Volunteers. McKinley's brother Abner was one of those perennial nuisances, the would-be 'fixer-cum-insider' exploiting his near kinship with the President to boast to outsiders of under-the-counter deals he could bring off. He cadged numerous favours from the White House staff, but McKinley kept him at arm's length. Abner was at least better behaved in his private life than most of the breed.

It is with Ida McKinley that for once a presidential family displays a truly macabre element. True, her epilepsy was not of her choosing, nor the early death of her children. But in her early twenties she had shown herself inconsiderate and unmanageable on a European tour with her sister Pina and a Canton schoolmistress, Jeanette Alexander. She had apparently resented from the start the proposed inclusion of Jeanette's brother as the girls' financial manager — because he was not among her admirers, Jeanette thought. From the early days of her marriage she was an absurdly bad loser. And not at croquet or tennis or poker or bridge, which pardonably arouse strong passions, but at that dreariest of parlour games cribbage, which the McKinleys used to play in the evenings. In short she was self-centred and probably trivial to boot (she had an obsession with clothes). Her headaches, which in charity one must assume were genuine, often obliged McKinley to spend an entire evening in darkness, for he felt he could not leave her in solitude. She had her good points. She was fond of children — extravagantly so — and had the knack of friendship. Among her intimates was Lucy Hayes's niece Emily Platt. But outbursts could be triggered at any moment, as when McKinley mentioned that he had seen a good-looking woman at a public gathering (President Garfield's funeral in this case) and Ida had hysterics, followed by one of her epileptic fits. McKinley is said to have used his wife's ill-health as an excuse not to campaign actively in 1896, and since he couldn't go to the crowds they had to come to him, with railroads running excursion specials to Canton, where McKinley presided benignly from his front porch over what were remarkably large gatherings for an obscure Midwest town. If he did at that moment exploit his wife's ill-health, it was the exception. So adroit was his general management of her that her own niece Kate Barber never discovered her aunt had been epileptic till told about it quite late in life, when she was at first affronted, thinking it Democratic Party propaganda.

It is odd that the McKinleys were so sociable a couple given the purely practical difficulties McKinley had in looking after her. To these was added, once he became President, the protocol awkwardness entailed by her having to be seated on his right at dinners so he could throw a napkin or handkerchief over her face when she had a fit. Handkerchiefs played an important role in their lives. When McKinley was Governor of Ohio he used to drop whatever he was doing at three o'clock sharp every afternoon and wave a handkerchief at his wife's hotel room from the state capitol. Given his death at the hand of an anarchist, to say nothing of Ida's brother George Saxton being shot by a jealous mistress (to both of which catastrophic occurrences Ida reacted with rather sinister self-control), the McKinley family circle was distinctly Dostoevskian.

Glamour and fuel for press gossip during the McKinley administration was supplied chiefly by McKinley's nieces. Pina's unmarried eldest daughter, Mary Barber, was a student at Smith and female higher education was still such a novelty that this added to her newsworthiness. Ida McKinley rather liked her but she did not return her aunt's affection, only staying at the White House to relieve her mother Pina of trouble. McKinley's next eldest sister Sarah (Mrs Andrew J. Duncan) had a younger daughter, also Sarah, who was training as a kindergarten teacher in Chicago. Grace McKinley, the niece who had been made McKinley's ward, was tall and blonde and thought to possess a commanding mien. Abner McKinley's daughter Mabel was a cripple, but with her fine mezzo-soprano voice overcame this handicap and eventually made a name for herself on the vaudeville circuit with hits like 'Nona from Arizona', 'Yankee Rose' and 'Honey, You Stay in Your Own Backyard' — the last title rather apposite given her uncle's presidential campaigning technique.

BIOGRAPHICAL DETAILS AND DESCENDANTS

McKINLEY, WILLIAM, b Niles, Trumbull Co, Ohio, 29 Jan 1843; educ Union Seminary, Poland, Ohio, Allegheny Coll, Meadville, Pa., and Albany Law Sch, Albany, New York; schoolmaster 1859, post office clerk 1861, Pte 23rd Ohio Vol Infy 1861, Commissary Sgt April 1862, 2nd Lt Sept 1862, 1st Lt Feb 1863, Capt July 1864, Brevet-Maj March 1865, honourable discharged with rank of Capt July 1865, admitted Ohio Bar 1867, Prosecuting Atty Stark Co, Ohio, 1869-71, Memb US House of Reps from Ohio 1877-84 and 1885-91 (Memb Ways and Means Ctee 1880, replacing James A. GARFIELD, who had just been elected President, and Chm 1889, also Republican Leader 1889, unsuccessful candidate for Speaker of House of Reps 1889), Chm Republican State Convention Ohio 1880 and 1884, Chm Ctee on Resolutions Nat Republican Convention 1888, unsuccessful candidate for re-election Congress 1890, unsuccessful candidate for Republican presidential nomination then Chm Republican Nat Convention 1892, Govr Ohio 1892-96, 25th President (R) of the USA 1897-1901, author: *Life and Speeches of William McKinley* (1896) and *The Tariff* (1904); m First Presbyterian Church, Canton, Ohio, 25 Jan 1871 Ida (b Canton 8 June 1847; d there 26 May 1907, bur next to Westlawn Cemetery there with her husband), er dau of James Asbury Saxton, banker, of Canton, and his w Catherine (Kate), dau of George Dewalt, proprietor of the Eagle Hotel, Canton, and d Buffalo, New York, 14 Sept 1901 of gunshot wounds sustained in an assassin's attack at Pan-American Exposition, Buffalo, 6 Sept 1901, having had issue:

President McKinley's children
I Katherine (Katie) McKINLEY, b Canton 25 Dec 1871; d there 25 June 1876 of typhoid fever
II Ida McKINLEY, b Canton 1 April, d there 22 Aug 1873

MALE LINE ANCESTRY AND
COLLATERAL DESCENDANTS

David McKINLEY or McKINLAY, *b* Ireland *c* 1705; weaver, emigrated 1743 to York Co, Pa.; *m* before 1728 Esther ———— and *d* Chanceford, York Co, *c* 1760/1, leaving (with two other s and one dau) an eldest s:

John McKINLEY or McKINLAY, *b* Ireland *c* 1728; weaver, blacksmith and distiller; *m* 17—, as her 1st husb, Margaret ———— (*b* 17—; *m* 2nd Thomas McColtagh; *d* before 1782) and *d* Chanceford 18 Feb 1779, having had issue (with four daus and three other children who *d* young):

David McKINLEY, *b* Chanceford 16 May 1755; fought as private in Revolutionary War; *m* 1st Westmoreland Co, Pa., 19 Dec 1780 Sarah (*b* 10 May 1760; *d* 6 Oct 1814), of Lancaster Co, Pa., dau of John Gray and his w Hannah Stevenson or Stephenson, and had five s and five daus; *m* 2nd 4 Sept 1815 Ellener McClean (*d* 16 Oct 1835); *m* 3rd Hannah C. Rose (*b* 1757; *d* 1840) and *d* Chatfield Township, Crawford Co, Ohio, 8 Aug 1840, leaving (with other issue) a 2nd s:

James Stevenson McKINLEY, *b* Wolf Creek, Pa., 19 Sept 1783; *m* Mercer Co, Pa., *c* 1805 Mary (*b* probably Hunterdon Co, New Jersey, or Bucks Co, Pa., 10/15 Nov 1788; *d* South Bend, Ind., 20 Aug 1847), dau of Andrew Rose and his w Hannah Chapman, and *d* South Bend 20 Aug 1847 also, leaving (with five other s and eight daus):

I William McKINLEY, Sr, for whom *see below*
II Benjamin McKINLEY, resided in Pennsylvania, ptnr with his er bro William in iron production

The est s,

William McKINLEY, Sr, *b* Wolf Creek 15 Nov 1807; moved to small town of Poland, nr Youngstown, Ohio, 1852, and to Canton 1869; *m* New Lisbon (now Lisbon), Columbiana Co, Ohio, 6 Jan 1829 Nancy Campbell (*b* nr New Lisbon 22 April 1809; *d* Canton, Ohio, 12 Dec 1897), dau of Abner Allison and his w Ann Campbell, and *d* Canton 24 Nov 1892, having had issue:

I David Allison McKINLEY, *b* Fairfield, Columbiana Co, 23 Nov 1829; sometime US Consul Honolulu and Hawaiian Consul-Gen San Francisco; *m* 1850 Nancy Minerva Scott and *d* 18 Sept 1892, leaving issue:

President McKinley's nephew and niece
1 William Perry Francis McKINLEY, *b* Niles, Ohio, 10 Sept 1852   2 Ida Helen McKinley *b* 18—; *m* David MORSE

II Anna McKINLEY, *b* Niles, Ohio, 24 Sept 1831 or 1832; schoolmistress, grammar sch pncpl in Canton, Ohioh; *d* Canton 29 July 1889/90
III James Rose McKINLEY, *b* Fairfield 27 Sept 1833; *m* San Francisco 4 May 1870 Eliza Howe Fuller and *d* 11 Oct 1889, leaving issue:

President McKinley's nephew and nieces
1 Hope McKINLEY, *b* 18—   2 James Fuller McKINLEY, *b* 18—   3 Grace McKINLEY, *b* 18—

IV Mary McKinley, *b* Fairfield 22 Sept 1835; *m* 18— David MAY and *d* 20 June 1868
V Helen Minerva McKINLEY, *b* Niles 8 March 1839; schoolmistress; *d* Cleveland, Ohio, 1924
VI Sarah Elizabeth McKinley, *b* Niles 1 Oct 1840; *m* 26 Feb 1867 Andrew Jackson DUNCAN (*b* 26 June 1836; *d* 30 May 1912) and *d* Cleveland 22 Nov 1931, leaving issue:

President McKinley's niece and nephew
1 Mary Duncan, *b* Pittsburgh, Pa., 20 Dec 1867; *m* ———— BOWMAN
2 William McKinley DUNCAN, *b* Pittsburgh 19 May 1873; lawyer; *m* Youngstown 19 Oct 1899 Anna Viola (*b* Sharpsburg, Pa., 23 March 1876: *d* 19—), dau of Dr John Deetrick, of Valencia, Pa., and his w Elizabeth Parks, and *d* 19—, having had issue:

Great-nephews
(1) *William McKinley DUNCAN, Jr, *b* Cleveland 16 Jan 1902
(2) *John Allison DUNCAN, *b* Cleveland 20 Dec 1903
(3) *Andrew Jackson DUNCAN III, *b* Cleveland 24 July 1908

President McKinley's niece and nephew
3 Sarah Duncan, *b* Pittsburgh 10 Feb 1875; *m* 18— or 19— ———— WONLOW
4 Andrew Jackson DUNCAN, *b* Pittsburgh 20 Oct 1877; electrical engineer; *d* 19—

VII WILLIAM McKINLEY, 25th PRESIDENT of the UNITED STATES of AMERICA
VIII Abbie Celia McKINLEY, *b* Niles 1 June 1845; *d* there 26 Jan 1846
IX Abner Osborn McKINLEY, *b* Niles 27 Nov 1847; lawyer; *m* 1876 Anna E. Endsley, of Johnstown, Pa., and *d* 1904, leaving issue:

President McKinley's niece
1 Mable McKinley, *b c* 1879; *m* the White House 1900 Dr Hermanus BAER, of Reading, Pa., and *d* 7 June 1937, leaving issue:

Great-nephew
(1) *Hermanus BAER, *b* 5 April 19—

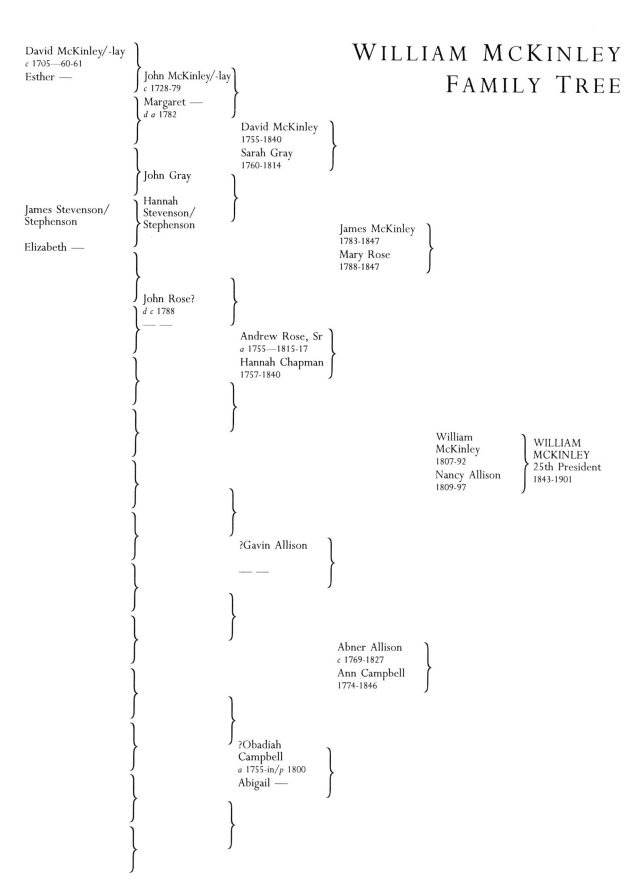

WILLIAM McKINLEY
FAMILY TREE

David McKinley/-lay
c 1705—60-61
Esther —

John McKinley/-lay
c 1728-79
Margaret —
d a 1782

David McKinley
1755-1840
Sarah Gray
1760-1814

John Gray

Hannah
Stevenson/
Stephenson

James McKinley
1783-1847
Mary Rose
1788-1847

James Stevenson/
Stephenson

Elizabeth —

John Rose?
d c 1788
— —

Andrew Rose, Sr
a 1755—1815-17
Hannah Chapman
1757-1840

William
McKinley
1807-92
Nancy Allison
1809-97

WILLIAM
MCKINLEY
25th President
1843-1901

?Gavin Allison

— —

Abner Allison
c 1769-1827
Ann Campbell
1774-1846

?Obadiah
Campbell
a 1755-in/*p* 1800
Abigail —

Plate 77   Teddy Roosevelt

THEODORE ROOSEVELT

1858-1919
26TH PRESIDENT OF THE UNITED STATES OF AMERICA
1901-09

Theodore Roosevelt is one of the legendary Presidents. Given his temperament, in which great abilities were forever boiling over into extravagant action, this is not very surprising. His legend is perhaps the most important thing about him. It makes the task of assessing his presidency extremely difficult. The folk hero obscures the statesman.

In one way he was admirably adapted to the office. He gave spontaneous expression to a side of the American character which steadier men such as Cleveland or McKinley could never do. The trouble is that, seen from this point of view, he appears too much the noisy, pigheaded, attitudinizing bully. He did all he could as Assistant Secretary of the Navy to thrust the United States into the ridiculous and unnecessary war with Spain; rushed off to raise a volunteer force — the 'Rough Riders' — when war broke out; and at the inconclusive battle of San Juan Hill in Cuba distinguished himself by hysterically cheering on his men to shoot down Spaniards as if they were rabbits. He displayed great personal courage, convinced his countrymen that San Juan Hill was a splendid victory, and was known as 'The Colonel' ever after. His fellow-citizens thought he was wonderful and promptly elected him to the governorship of New York. They went on thinking him wonderful to his dying day. The fact that they did so showed that they were still far from mature in their attitude to foreign countries. As for Teddy Roosevelt himself, he remained in many respects a rather nasty small boy all his life.

If that had been all he would scarcely be remembered today except as an embarrassment. Psycho-historians might argue uselessly over the question of whether his excesses were caused by some glandular malfunction or by a deep psychological wound. However, his career has a much larger significance, though it is to be noted that the demagoguery which his eccentricity made possible was a source of enormous political strength to him and showed the way to all subsequent Presidents. Ever since his time Presidents have dreamed of solving their problems by stirring up great waves of popular support. Few have been nearly so adept at it as Theodore Roosevelt.

Behind the brag, the horsemanship, the big-game shooting, the glorification of war, the fondness for wrestling, tennis and polo, lurked a very different personality. Roosevelt was an intellectual merely posing as a cowboy. He was a better historian than Woodrow Wilson, as good a writer as Thomas Jefferson and a better scholar than either.

He first attained prominence as a liberal Republican, all but a Mugwump. The evolution of his ideas over the next 30 years is a fascinating study. By 1912 his change was complete and he was sponsoring some of the most radical and valuable criticisms of American society then current. The ideas which he summed up as 'the new Nationalism' did not come to fruition until the administration of his nephew-by-marriage, Franklin Roosevelt, but the debt owed by the New Deal to Uncle Theodore's precept and example was enormous.

Even the intellectual in him was not his dominant trait. He was also a superb professional politician. From the very beginning he saw that to achieve anything it was necessary to attain power and, having attained it, to know how to wield it. With the energetic, single-handed application by which, as a boy, he had turned himself from a weakling into a thug, he studied the political art of which he eventually became a master. He saw, for example, that political power in America and especially in New York, his native state, could only be won through the party machines. The professional and business gentry of whom he was one despised the politicians as vulgarians, which they undoubtedly were; but to a man like Roosevelt, interested in power, this disdain seemed merely frivolous. He went among the politicians and learned from them the first lesson, party regularity at all costs. So he stuck to Blaine, whom he despised, in 1884, an action long remembered in his favour by the Republicans, which helps to explain his rapid rise to the top.

Roosevelt was far too self-assertive to become the bosses' tool; he was also too patriotic. He knew at first hand that the alliance between moneyed class and the political machines explained not only the perversion of American democratic politics, but such evils as the enormous slums of New York city.

He was not one of nature's democrats but he believed passionately in the greatness of his country and its institutions. He was also, in his curious way, a religious man. The rampant evils of American capitalist society revolted him on both counts and when he had power — when, for example, he became Governor of New York — he set about correcting them as much as he could. Naturally this enraged the bosses and it was they who arranged to get him out of the way by thrusting him into the vice-presidency. Then Czolgosz's bullet wrecked their calculations.

Three things stand out about Roosevelt's presidency. The first has already been touched on: his gift for exciting, amusing and interesting the country. His flair for the dramatic touch was well shown, for example, toward the end of his second term when, on a cruise down the Mississippi, he suddenly announced that he was inviting the governors of all the states to Washington for a conference on conservation. Since the presidential voyage was already attracting a great deal of attention, the Colonel had hit on an excellent means of publicizing a new policy; at the same time it showed he was a working President, not just a junketing one. Another episode demonstrates the Roosevelt touch even better. The Navy was one of his most frantic obsessions and he managed to double its size, making the United States a formidable naval power. Congress was always laggard in voting appropriations and foreign nations did not yet respect it as it deserved. So the President announced that the fleet would sail round the world, advertising American greatness to all nations, especially Japan, which was emerging as America's chief rival in the Pacific. The idea pleased the public, engendered pride in the new ships and increased public willingness to pay for them. Senators from eastern seaboard states were afraid that in the absence of the fleet Britain or Germany would instantly attack and one of them talked of cutting off appropriations for the voyage. Roosevelt announced that he had the money to send the fleet as far as the Pacific and go it would. Congress could leave it there if it liked. The Senate gave in and the Colonel had once more demonstrated his ascendancy.

A lesser incident worth mentioning was the occasion when Roosevelt went out hunting bears and failed to bag a single one. The cartoonists had a wonderful time and so the idea of the teddy bear was born. It will probably outlast all Roosevelt's other achievements but at the time he was not pleased. He made it a rule that in future when he accepted an invitation to hunt, game must be guaranteed and the first victim must fall to his rifle.

The second great feature of Roosevelt's presidency was the range of his interests and activities. He solved an old problem by inducing Congress to pay for new offices at the White House (he had good taste and architecture was going through one of its better phases, so the resulting extension was pleasing as well as convenient). He accomplished the dream of half a century by building the Panama Canal, though the achievement was sullied by the squalid political intrigue that made it possible. He intervened as arbitrator to make peace between Russia and Japan in 1905 and the next year was awarded the Nobel Peace Prize. He made himself the sponsor of every piece of reform legislation that went through Congress. He started to give some meaning to the Sherman anti-monopoly law by initiating prosecutions for its violation and successfully warned off the great banker J. P. Morgan from one of his biggest mergers in the Northern Securities case. In 1902 he intervened to settle a coal strike in favour of the miners — the first time that Federal power had ever been used in that way. In short, he instructed the American people very thoroughly in the notion that their President should be an activist.

Yet the third notable thing about his presidency was its pragmatism. Roosevelt, it has been observed, asserted his conservatism when he was doing something radical, his radicalism when he was doing something conservative. Either way he almost always succeeded. In his youth he laid down the maxim, "political expediency draws the line", and throughout his presidency he acted upon it. His study of the political art had not been in vain. His sense of political realities was unsurpassed among American Presidents; perhaps only Lincoln had it to the same degree. He knew the limits within which success was possible; better yet, he accepted them. For all his autocratic ravings he recognized the profound wisdom of the American constitutional system, which lays such emphasis on checks and balances. Power, he thought, was good and he greatly enjoyed using it, but power had to be restrained. Accordingly, though he loved being President, he made the most selfless decision of his career by refusing to run for a third term in 1908. The two-term tradition he thought was too valuable to be sacrificed even for him. He was to change his mind later when he found the inaction of retirement even less endurable than he had supposed. But in 1909 he gracefully left office and could congratulate himself on having left behind an excellent example, for all his successors, of how best to be a modern President.

THEODORE ROOSEVELT'S FAMILY

Teddy Roosevelt's Dutch ancestry has been discussed exhaustively (and is set down in the section on his lineage). That of his mother is just as interesting, arguably more so. Martha Bulloch had Southern ancestry, chiefly in Georgia, and beyond that forbears, the Baillies, who from at least the 15th century were lairds of Dunain, in the Scottish Highlands. Through the Baillies Teddy Roosevelt was a cousin, albeit very distantly, of several notables in British history generally and Scottish history specifically. There was Cuthbert Baillie, Lord High Treasurer of Scotland 1512-14; Robert Baillie, a late 17th-century radical and something of a republican to boot; a late 16th-century William Baillie who was a judge in the Scottish Court of Session (the highest judicial tier there); another William Baillie who was a Scottish general in the mid-17th century; the British Lords Burton, a leading brewing family ennobled in 1886; and the Baillies of Dochfour, who contributed several Members of Parliament to British public life, including a Privy Counsellor and Under-Secretary for India in mid-Victorian times. Most of these distant cousins' careers in fighting, the law or imperialist politics were paralleled, though in another time or place, by Teddy Roosevelt or his descendants.

Martha Bulloch's mother and sister were strongly pro-Confederate during the Civil War. Teddy Roosevelt's uncles James and Irvine Bulloch were excluded from the post-Civil War general amnesty for having financed, built and operated the Confederate warship *Alabama*. (After the Confederate defeat they went to England, remaining there even when their exclusion from the amnesty was reversed.) Uncle Irvine helped his nephew with technical information when the latter was writing his celebrated history on the naval war of 1812. He was not the only relative who improved Teddy Roosevelt's stock of knowledge. The future president's impoverished aunt Annie Bulloch lodged with her sister's family and paid for her keep by giving lessons to the Roosevelt children. And although Teddy Roosevelt never qualified as a lawyer, he studied the subject in his uncle Robert B. Roosevelt's office.

A family connection with the Confederacy was bound to embarrass people living in New York. During the Civil War, when Teddy Roosevelt was a child, his parents were wholly divided in their sympathies. But Theodore Sr, Teddy's father, was philanthropical rather than partisan and pressed Washington for a law to help soldiers in the field. He drafted a bill for appointing Allotment Commissioners who would visit military camps and persuade the troops to save part of their pay for family support. The law passed and Lincoln appointed Theodore Sr one of the three New York State commissioners.

Theodore Sr was also a US commissioner to the Vienna Exposition of 1873 and a founder of the Metropolitan and Natural History Museums. Civic-mindedness was acceptable, but by and large members of old families in New York did not get involved in politics. When President Rutherford B. Hayes nominated Theodore Sr Collector of the Port of New York in 1877 in his campaign for civil service reform it was partly a hit at Senator Roscoe Conkling, New York state's corrupt Republican machine boss, and was recognised as such, for the Senate rejected the nominee. Nevertheless Theodore Sr felt tainted by having to associate with men like Conkling at all and as late as 1896 one of Teddy Roosevelt's uncles refused on similar grounds to sit down to lunch with Mark Hanna, the McKinley era kingmaker.

To the urban patricians of the old East Coast cities in Teddy Roosevelt's early manhood this non-involvement reflected a feeling that politics had become a vulgar, corrupt business. Their fastidiousness was fairly new, however. Up to the Civil War the 'Knickerbocker' families of Dutch descent living in New York, of which the Roosevelts were a leading example, had been reasonably active in public affairs. Teddy Roosevelt's great-uncle James J. Roosevelt campaigned for Andrew Jackson and got elected to the New York state legislature and the US House of Representatives with Tammany Hall help. His family was scandalized, but apparently by the association with Tammany rather than political activity as such. When Teddy got involved in politics his family were horrified. "You will find at the meetings nobody but grooms, liquor dealers and low politicians" he was told. He answered "Well, if that is so, they belong to the governing class, and you do not. I mean if I can to be one of the governing class." Other Roosevelts had already taken part in post-Civil War public affairs, however, and not just in Theodore Sr's restricted fashion. The latter's brother Robert B. Roosevelt struck one of the first blows at corruption in New York by rousing citizens against the crooked ascendancy of 'Boss' Tweed. He did this through a series of editorials when co-editor of the *New York Citizen*, the official organ of the Citizens' Association, of which he was also secretary. Robert also at one time had ambitions to become mayor of New York. He was a Democrat, and though he and his nephew Teddy shared a love of hunting and the outdoor life the uncle disapproved of his nephew's Republican allegiance, even after the latter had become President.

This sort of family background helped launch Teddy's career. The political boss Joe Murray suggested he stand as a New York Assemblyman for the 21st District because of his father's local fame. This implies Teddy did not make the first move, but it has also been said he entered politics to avenge his father's death, supposedly brought on by Roscoe Conkling's hostility. With his cult of vigour, outdoors as well as in, Teddy Roosevelt appeared ludicrously extrovert, but his private life shows him to have been sensitive. After his first wife Alice's death he never mentioned her name either to his daughter or in his autobiography, though he did circulate among members of the family a memorial essay he had written on her when out West not long after her death. Like other fathers whose wives have died in childbirth, he seems to have developed almost a sense of horror toward his child by that wife. His sister Bamie brought up 'Baby Lee', as the child Alice was then known. Alice later became famous for outspokenness, an outspokenness that shaded into what one can only call impudence. Once when riding in her father's presidential carriage she thumbed her nose at passers-by. She was no respecter of other Presidents, calling Harding "just a slob" and saying of Coolidge that he looked as if he had been weaned on a pickle. Even in old age she remained acerb, remarking when President Lyndon Johnson lifted up

Plate 78   Teddy Roosevelt and his younger brother
Elliott on the North Dakota ranch about 1882

Plate 79   Alice Lee Roosevelt,
Teddy Roosevelt's 1st wife

Plate 80   Edith Carow Roosevelt,
Teddy Roosevelt's 2nd wife

his shirt to show the scars of his recent operation to anybody who cared to look (and doubtless many who did not), how lucky it was the President had not had piles.

To Teddy Roosevelt his daughter was not a figure who brought to mind flippancy, since her mother left this world two days after bringing her into it. The death of both his first wife and his mother (on the same day, 14 February 1884, something of a domestic St. Valentine's massacre) is said to have caused a certain disenchantment with East coast life. The trophies his brother Elliott brought back from India acted more positively and enticed him into hunting buffalo out West. His Hemingwayesque pursuit of big game, then and throughout the rest of his life, would in our present state of jaded sophistication be as likely to raise doubts about his masculinity as dispel them. But the suggestion that he never entirely grew up overlooks his gradually seeing the need for nature conservation. He developed in other ways: his dislike of being called 'Teddy' dated from his first wife's death.

In going out West he may also have wished to get away from his brother Elliott's dipsomania (supposedly induced by alcohol being prescribed for semi-epilepsy in Elliott's youth). Teddy was obliged to cope with major crises brought on by his brother's condition, however, notably negotiating with Elliott's mistress Katy Mann when she demanded $10,000 to hush up the existence of Elliott's illegitimate child by her. In contrast to his brother, Teddy Roosevelt hardly drank at all and Elliott's daughter Eleanor was famous for her horror of drink.

Teddy's second wife, Edith Kermit Carow, had been a childhood sweetheart. However, in his shattered state immediately after Alice's death he tended to avoid her. This was the more difficult because they were both members of the same small New York upper-crust society and she was a close friend of his two sisters Corinne and Anna. It was in Anna's house that he met her for the first time in many years in the autumn of 1885. They became engaged almost immediately, but by the time they got married she was living abroad, her father's business ventures having gone awry. Edith Carow Roosevelt was later called the White House's most brilliant entertainer since Dolley Madison and was rumoured to wield great power over her husband, especially in appointments. She acted as a part-time secretary to her husband, attending to state documents, incoming mail and the daily newspapers in case any item in them might be of interest to him. She later moved firmly to the right in politics and after her husband was dead came to detest Franklin Roosevelt's policies, but like many people in the 1920s and early '30s who otherwise upheld the rule of law she served alcohol at home throughout Prohibition.

Teddy's sister Anna made what from her brother's point of view was a particularly useful marriage to William Cowles, of the US Navy. He eventually attained Rear-Admiral's rank but when still a Lieutenant-Commander briefed his brother-in-law, by then Assistant Secretary of the Navy, on naval matters when Teddy was building up the US fleet prior to the Spanish-American War of 1898. After McKinley's assassination Mrs Cowles lent her brother her Washington house, 1733 North Street. Out of consideration for McKinley's epileptic widow, Teddy delayed moving into the White House proper and number 1733 became known as the 'Little White House'. Before marriage Anna had kept house in London for her distant cousin James Roosevelt, the future president Franklin's half-brother, when James was First Secretary at the US Legation there.

Teddy Roosevelt's eldest son, Theodore Roosevelt III, followed his father into New York state politics, being a member of the New York state assembly at the time his father died. He further emulated his father by going on to serve as Assistant Secretary of the Navy, being appointed less than a year after his distant cousin Franklin Roosevelt had left the same post. He was the Republican candidate for governor of New York state in 1924, being defeated by Al Smith, but of course New York was to have a Roosevelt as governor anyway only four years later — Franklin. Theodore III crowned his career by becoming Governor-General of the Philippines, a suitably proconsular post for the son of an expansionist President. He had another moment of glory when his distant cousin FDR in 1940 recalled him to

Plate 81   Teddy Roosevelt with family: l-r Quentin, the President, Theodore Jr, Archibald, Alice Roosevelt (subsequently Alice Roosevelt Longworth — his only child by his 1st wife), Kermit, his 2nd wife Edith Carow Roosevelt and Ethel (subsequently Ethel Roosevelt Derby), 1903

Plate 82   Teddy Roosevelt's eldest son Col Theodore Roosevelt Jr and the latter's youngest son Lt Quentin Roosevelt II during World War II

command his old World War I regiment. FDR hoped this would unite Republicans behind him at a time when he was trying to prepare Americans for war despite isolationist opposition.

Theodore III's wife, another Eleanor Roosevelt, was on at least one occasion confused with her namesake and cousin-in-law, FDR's wife, when she made a campaign contribution to the young Richard Nixon's 1950 senate bid. Nixon was debating against his Democratic opponent Helen Gahagan Douglas and read out a letter of support signed Eleanor Roosevelt which, given the famous Eleanor's equally famous progressive views, made the audience gasp. Nixon then revealed that it was the Eleanor Roosevelt from Oyster Bay, *i.e.*, Theodore III's wife. (Her conservative sister-in-law Alice Roosevelt Longworth always called her 'Eleanor the Good' whereas for everyone else 'Eleanor the Good' meant FDR's wife.) Nixon claims the ensuing hilarity in the audience helped swing support his way.

Subsequently this branch of the Roosevelts became somewhat enervated. They still had public service careers but in the lower reaches of the State Department or the Foreign Service, or again in state rather than national politics. Even their outlook on international affairs seemed to become narrower. Theodore III's youngest son, Quentin, was at college in the 1930s with Joe Jennedy Jr and joined with him in founding the Harvard Committee Against Military Intervention, an isolationist body. Quentin's brother Cornelius had a superficially adventurous job: he spent most of his career with the CIA. But he ended as chief of the Technical Services Division and whereas in its most melodramatic phase this body had devised contaminated suitings for Fidel Castro, under Roosevelt it was chiefly occupied with countering Soviet electronic surveillance.

Teddy Roosevelt's youngest son Quentin, a combat pilot, was shot down on the Western Front in the last months of World War I. It has been suggested that his boy's death killed in Teddy Roosevelt any lingering desire for the presidency, which could otherwise have been his for the asking in 1920. Teddy's words on the subject support this theory: "I am indifferent to the subject. I would not lift a finger to get the nomination. Since Quentin's death the world seems to have shut down on me." His grandson Kermit Jr also worked for the CIA, being the instigator of the 1953 coup against Iran's anti-Western leader Mossadegh. At any rate that is one side of the story. The British SIS (Secret Intelligence Service) version of events had it that Kermit Roosevelt did little more than turn up in Iran with CIA funds for agents the British had previously recruited and organized. Whoever is right, Kermit Jr wrote about the Middle East in two books, *Arabs, Oil and History* (1949) and *Countercoup: The Struggle for the Control of Iran* (1979).

Yet another member of the family served in the CIA: Archibald, Teddy Roosevelt's grandson by his third son Archibald Roosevelt Sr. As if to make matters more confusing, Archibald also operated in the Middle East, and at the same time as his cousin. He even organized a coup of his own, that against King Farouk of Egypt in the early 1950s. Perhaps a more spectacular feat still was his helping Alexander Barmein, the Soviet chargé in Athens, to defect. Barmein later married Archie's sister, Edith, but in intelligence terms was valuable for being the CIA's first major informant on Soviet covert operations abroad.

There have been artistically inclined Roosevelts too: Willard Roosevelt, Kermit Jr's composer younger brother; Archibald Jr's novelist sister, Theodora; Teddy Roosevelt's poetess younger sister, Corinne (who married a great-great-nephew of President Monroe). Corinne's grandsons, Joe and Stewart Alsop, were celebrated journalists, with Joe among the first people to inform American readers of Ambassador Joseph Kennedy's intimacy over in England both with the Prime Minister, Neville Chamberlain, and Lady Astor's insufficiently anti-Fascist 'Cliveden Set'. By 1940 Alsop was forecasting that Ambassador Kennedy would promote appeasement all over the US. Mrs Joseph Alsop, otherwise Susan Mary Jay, then Susan Mary Patten when married to her first husband (*see* the essay on John Quincy Adams), served on Jacqueline Kennedy's Special Committee for White House Paintings when the First Lady was working to render the White House a genuinely historic building, inside as well as out, in the early 1960s.

It has been said that Theodore Roosevelt was the first US President regarded as an equal by the crowned heads of Europe. He certainly mediated in disputes between foreign powers, negotiating both with the Prime Ministers who even then tended to make the really important decisions and the heads of state themselves. Indeed he was the choice as mediator both of Germany and Japan. As if to underline his quasi-monarchical position his only child by his first wife was known as 'Princess Alice'.

BIOGRAPHICAL DETAILS AND DESCENDANTS

ROOSEVELT, THEODORE, *b* New York 27 Oct 1858; *educ* Harvard (AB 1880) and Columbia Law Sch; Memb New York State Assembly 1882-85 (unsuccessful candidate for Speaker 1883, Republican Minority Leader 1883), Memb New York Delegn Republican Convention 1884, Dep Sheriff Billings Co, Dakota Territory, 1885, unsuccessful mayoral candidate New York City 1886, Pres and Fndr Boone and Crockett Club (body dedicated to exploration of American wilderness and nature conservation) and Chm Stockmen's Assoc, Little Missouri River, 1888, US Civil Service Commissioner 1889-94, Pres New York City Police Bd 1895, Assist Sec US Navy 1897-98, Lt-Col Roosevelt's Rough Riders (cavalry regt) Spanish-American War 1898, Govr New York 1899-1900, V-Pres USA March-Sept 1901, 26th President (R) of the USA Sept 1901-09, contributing ed *Outlook* magazine from 1909, US Representative at funeral of King EDWARD VII of Great Britain & Ireland 1910, Progressive wing of Republican Party nominee for presidency then unsuccessful Progressive Party presidential candidate 1912, Hon LLD: Columbia U 1899, Hope Coll and Yale 1901, Hon Degrees from Cairo U, Egypt, Christiania U, Norway, Berlin U, Germany, and Cambridge and Oxford Us, UK, Nobel Peace Prize 1906 (first American recipient ever), author: *The Naval Operations of the War between Great Britain and the United States — 1812-1815* (1882), *Personal Experiences of Life on a Cattle Ranch* (1885), *Hunting Trips of a Ranchman* (1886), *Thomas Hart Benton* (1887), *Gouverneur Morris* (1888), *Ranch Life and Hunting Trail* (1888), *Winning of the West*, 4 vols (1889-1896), *New York City* (1891), *The Wilderness Hunter* (1893), *Hero Tales, from American History*, with Henry Cabot Lodge (1895), *American Ideals and Other Essays*, 2 vols (1897), contributor to vol 6 of W. L. Clowes's *History of the Royal Navy of England* (1898), *The Rough Riders* (1899), *The Strenuous Life* (1900), *Oliver Cromwell* (1901), *The Deer Family*, with other authors (1902), *State Papers and Addresses* (1905), *Outdoor Pastimes of an American Hunter* (1905), *African Game Trails* (1910), *The New Nationalism* (1910) *African and European Addresses* (1910), *History as Literature, and Other Essays* (1913), *Theodore Roosevelt, an Autobiography* (1913), *Through the Brazilian Wilderness* (1914), *Life Histories of African Game Animals* (1914), *America and the World War* (1915), *Fear God and Take Your Own Part* (1916), *The Great Adventure* (1918), *The Foes of Our Own Household* (1917), *National Strength and International Duty* (1917) and *The Letters of Theodore Roosevelt*, ed Elting E. Morison & John M. Blum, 8 vols (1951-1954); *m* 1st the First Parish Church (Unitarian), Brookline, Mass., 27 Oct 1880 Alice Hathaway (*b* Chestnut Hill, Boston, 29 July 1861; *d* New York 14 Feb 1884 of Bright's Disease, *bur* Greenwood Cemetery, Brookline), 2nd dau of George Cabot Lee, banker, of Boston, and his w Caroline Watts Haskell, and had issue:

President Theodore Roosevelt's daughter
I Alice Lee Roosevelt, *b* New York 12 Feb 1884; author: *Crowded Hours* (1933); *m* the White House, Washington, DC, 17 Feb 1906 Nicholas LONGWORTH (*b* Cincinnati, Ohio, 5 Nov 1869; *educ* Harvard, Harvard Law Sch and Cincinnati Law Sch; Memb: Ohio House of Reps 1899-1901, Ohio Senate 1901-03, US Congress 1903-09, Speaker US House of Reps 1925-31; *d* Aiken, S Carolina, 9 April 1931), er s of Nicholas Longworth, Justice Ohio Supreme Court, and his w Susan, dau of Judge Timothy Walker, and *d* Washington, DC, 20 Feb 1980, having had issue:

Grandchildren
1 Paulina Longworth, *b* Chicago 14 Feb 1925; *m* 26 Aug 1944 Alexander McCormick STURM (*b* 1923; *d* Norwalk, Conn., 13 Nov 1951); er s of Justin Sturm, author, sculptor and playwright, of Westport, Conn., and his w Katherine McCormick, and was accidentally *k* Washington, DC, 27 Jan 1957, leaving issue:

Great-grandchildren
(1) *Joanna STURM [2009 Massachusetts Avenue, Washington, DC 20008, USA; 1618 29th St NW, Washington, DC 20007, USA], *b* 1946

THEODORE ROOSEVELT *m* 2nd St George's, Hanover Square, London, UK, 2 Dec 1886 Edith Kermit (*b* Norwich, Conn., 6 Aug 1861; *d* Oyster Bay, Long Island, New York, 30 Sept 1948), dau of Charles Carow and his w Gertrude Elizabeth, dau of Daniel Tyler, and *d* in his sleep at home, Sagamore Hill, Oyster Bay, Long Island, New York, 6 Jan 1919 (*bur* Young's Memorial Cemetery, Oyster Bay) of a coronary embolism, having with her had issue:

President Theodore Roosevelt's son
II Theodore ROOSEVELT, Jr, *b* Oyster Bay, Long Island, New York, 13 Sept 1887; *educ* Groton and Harvard (BA 1908, Hon MA 1919); business: banker 1912-17, Chm Bd American Express Co 1934 and 1935, V-Pres Doubleday, Doran & Co (publishers) 1935-44; politics: Memb New York State Assembly 1919-20, Assist Navy Sec 1921-25, Chm Internat Ctee Naval Experts Armaments Limitation Conference 1921-22, Republican candidate for Governor New York State 1924, Govr

Puerto Rico 1929-32, Govr-Gen Philippines 1932-33, Pres Nat Republican Club 1934-36; military: served 26th Infantry, 1st Div, AEF, World Wars I (wounded twice; Maj 1917, Lt-Col 1918-19) and II (Col cmmdg 26th Infantry, 1st Div, April 1941, Brig-Gen Dec 1941, 2nd-in-cmmd 1st Div, served Africa 1942-43, Sicily 1943, Ch Laison Offr between American 5th Army and French Expedy Corps, Italy, to March 1944, attached 4th US Infantry Div Normandy June 1944), awarded: Distinguished Service Medal, Distinguished Service Cross, Congressional Medal of Honour (posthumously), Purple Heart, Silver Star with Oak Leaf Cluster, Legion of Honour and Croix de Guerre with three palms (France), Grand Cross of Order of the Crown and Croix de Guerre with palms (Belgium), War Cross, Order of Knights of Danilo (Montenegro) and Order of Brilliant Jade (China); public service: organiser American Legion 1919, V-Pres Boy Scouts of America, Pres Nat Health Cncl 1934-36, Nat Chm Utd Cncl Civilian Relief China, Tstee Field Museum Nat History Chicago (jt head scientific expeditions Centl Asia 1925-26, China and Indo-China 1928-29), FRGS, Memb American Geographic Soc; author: *Average Americans* (1919), (with his bro Kermit Roosevelt) *East of the Sun and West of the Moon* (1926), *Rank and File* (1927), *All in the Family* (1928), (with Kermit Roosevelt) *Trailing the Giant Panda* (1929), (with Grantland Rice) *Taps* (war verse anthology) (1932), (with Harold J. Coolidge, Jr) *The Three Kingdoms of Indo-China* (1933), *Colonial Policies of the US* (1937), *The Desk Drawer Anthology* (1937), *Reader's Digest Reader* (1940); m New York 20 June 1910 Eleanor Butler (b New York 1889; d Oyster Bay 29 May 1960), dau of Henry Addison Alexander and his w Grace Green, and d on active service France 12 July 1944 of a heart attack induced by extreme exhaustion (bur American Military Cemetery, St Laurent, France), leaving issue:

Grandchildren

1 *Grace Green Roosevelt [Mrs William McMillan, Box 483B, Lutherville, MD 21071, USA; Glyndon, Baltimore, MD 21071, USA], b 1911; m 3 March 1934 *William McMILLAN (b Detroit 15 March 1905), s of Hugh McMillan and his w Josephine Warfield, and has issue:

Great-grandchildren

(1) *William McMILLAN, Jr [Glyndon, Baltimore, MD 21071, USA], b 29 Jan 1935; educ Princeton; m 24 March 1962 *(Martha) Elizabeth, dau of John Walden Myer, of Oyster Bay, Long Island, and his w Martha R. Humphrey, and has issue:

Great-great-grandchildren

1a *Martha Grace McMILLAN, b 8 Nov 1963
2a *Virginia Humphrey McMILLAN, b 11 Oct 1965
3a *Eleanor Warfield McMILLAN, b 16 March 1970

Great-grandchildren

(2) *Eleanor McMILLAN, b 11 Dec 1937

Grandchildren

2 *Theodore ROOSEVELT III [Silver Spring Farm, Paoli, PA 19301, USA], b New York 14 June 1914; educ Groton and Harvard (AB 1936); Lt-Cdr US Navy World War II (Air Medal for participation in US Navy air raids on Wake Island 27 June 1944), investment executive, Sec of Commerce of Pennyslvania 1949-51; m 1940 *Anne Mason Babcock and has issue:

Great-grandchildren

(1) *Theodore ROOSEVELT IV [1 Pierrepont St, Brooklyn, NY 11201, USA; Shearson Lehman, Hutton Inc., American Express Tower, World Financial Center, New York, NY 10285-1000, USA], b Jacksonville, Fla., 27 Nov 1942; educ Groton, Harvard (AB 1965) and Harvard Business Sch (MBA 1972); Lt-Cdr US Naval Reserve (served Vietnam 1965-67, Navy Commendation Medal), joined State Dept Aug 1967 (economic and commercial offr Ouagadougou 1968, detailed to Dept of Commerce 1970), managing director Shearson Lehman, Hutton 1985-; m Woods Hole, Mass., 7 Aug 1970 *Constance Lane (b New York 5 July 1944), dau of Charles E. Rogers and his w Doris Draper, and has issue:

Great-great-grandchildren

1a Theodore ROOSEVELT V, b 19—

Grandchildren

3 Cornelius Van Schaack ROOSEVELT, b New York 23 Oct 1915; educ Groton, Deutsch Segelflugschule, Harvard and MIT (BS 1938); mining engr 1938-41, herpetologist and archaeologist, served US Navy World War II (Special Devices Division of Bureau of Aeronautics), Pres and Dir: William Hunt & Co Fed Inc (Hongkong and Taiwan) 1949-50 and Internat Industries Inc 1949-50, V-Pres Far East Security Banknote Co Inc, Philadelphia, 1949-55, with CIA 1952-73 (ending as Ch Technical Services Division), Pres and Dir Linderman Engrg Co Inc (Washington, DC) 1954-68, Offr and Dir Columbia Research Co Inc (Washington, DC) from 1968; d before 16 Aug 1991

4 Quentin ROOSEVELT II, b 4 Nov 1919; served USAF World War, V-Pres China Nat Aviation Corpn; m 1944 *Frances B. Webb and was k in a flying accident nr Hong Kong 21 Dec 1948, leaving issue:

Great-grandchildren

(1) *Alexandra ROOSEVELT, b 15 Jan 1945
(2) *Anna Curtenius ROOSEVELT, b 1947
(3) *Susan Roosevelt, b 11 April 1948; educ Concord Acad, Mass., Radcliffe (BA 1970) and Harvard Law Sch; m Oyster Bay, Long Island, 7 June 1975 *William Floyd WELD, s of David Weld, of St James, Long Island (descendant of William Floyd, a 'Signer' of the Declaration of Independence)

President Theodore Roosevelt's son

III Kermit ROOSEVELT, *b* Oyster Bay 10 Oct 1889; *educ* Groton and Harvard; engr Brazil 1910-13, banker Argentina and Chile 1913-15, served World War I British Army (Capt Motor Machine Guns Mesopotamia 1915-17, awarded MC, War Cross, Order of Danilo (Montenegro)) and American Army (offr commanding battery of 75s, 1st Division, Western Front 1917-19), also World War II British Army (Maj Sept 1939 to March 1940 and June 1940 to May 1941, offr apptd to command British contingent Internat Vol Forces Finland 1940) and US Army (1942-43), explorer, Pres Roosevelt Steamship Co, V-Pres US Lines and Internat Mercantile Marine Co, author: *War in the Garden of Eden*, *The Happy Hunting Grounds*, *Quentin Roosevelt: a sketch, with letters,* (with his brother Theodore Jr, for whom *see above*) *East of the Sun and West of the Moon* (1926), *Cleared for Strange Ports*, *American Backlogs*, (with his brother Theodore Jr) *Trailing the Giant Panda* (1929); *m* Madrid, Spain, 10 or 11 June 1914 Belle Wyatt (*b* Baltimore, Md., 1 July 1892; *d* New York 30 March 1968), dau of Joseph Edward Willard, of Fairfax, Va., US Ambassador to Spain, and his *w* Belle Layton Wyatt, and *d* on active service Alaska 4 June 1943, leaving issue:

Grandchildren

1 *Kermit (Kim) ROOSEVELT, Jr [5062 Macomb St NW, Washington, DC 20016, USA; 1455 Pennsylvania Avenue, Washington, DC 20335, USA], *b* Buenos Aires, Argentina, 13 Feb 1916; *educ* Harvard (AB 1938); history teacher Harvard 1937-39 and California Inst Technology 1939-41, with OSS 1941-46, Consultant Middle Eastern and Communist Affairs to Sec of State 1947-57, Dir Govtal relations with Gulf Oil Corp 1958-60, V-Pres Kermit Roosevelt & Assocs Inc 1960-64 (Pres 1964), Sr V-Pres Downs & Roosevelt Inc, Dir Near East Foundation and American Friends of Middle East, Chm African Wild Life Leadership Fund, Cnclman Harvard Foundation, author: *Arabs, Oil and History* (1949), *A Sentimental Safari* (1963) and *Counter-Coup: The Struggle fo the Control of Iran* (1979); *m* Farmington, Conn., 28 June 1937 *Mary (Polly) Lowe (*b* 29 March 1917), dau of Houston Gaddis and his *w* Mary Avery, and has issue:

Great-grandchildren

(1) *Kermit ROOSEVELT III [5501 Hawthorne Place NW, Washington, DC 20016, USA], *b* Cambridge, Mass., 7 April 1938; *educ* Harvard (AB 1960) and Columbia Law Sch; *m* 1st 4 Feb 1961 (divorce 196-) Linda Ballantine, dau of John Cross, of Cambridge, Mass., and his *w* ——, *née* Ballantine; *m* 2nd New Haven, Conn., 7 May 1967 *Priscilla (*b* Baltimore, Md., 28 Jan 1942), dau of Prof Lloyd Reynolds, of Yale, and his *w* Mary Tracket, and with her has issue:

Great-great-grandchildren

1a *Corinne Avery ROOSEVELT, *b* New York 23 April 1969

2a *Kermit ROOSEVELT IV [4000 Cathedral Avenue NW, Washington, DC 20016, USA], *b* Washington, DC, 14 July 1971

Great-grandchildren

(2) *Jonathan ROOSEVELT [14 Gerry St, Cambridge, MA 02138, USA], *b* Pasadena, Calif., 30 Jan 1940; *educ* Groton, Harvard (AB 1962) and Harvard Law Sch (JD 1966); secondary sch techer Moshi, Tanganyika, 1962-63, served State Dept 1966-73 (political offr Kinshasa, Zaire, 1969-71 and Accra, Ghana, 1971-73), V-Pres Kermit Roosevelt & Assocs Inc 1973-86, realtor with LANDVEST, Boston, 1986-89, V-Pres and Manager Boston office of The Investigative Gp Inc 1989-; *m* Washington, DC, 14 June 1961 *Jae McKown (*b* 5 May 1941), dau of Joel Barlow, of Washington, and his *w* Eleanor Livingston Poe, and has issue:

Great-great-grandchildren

1a *Ashley Barlow Roosevelt, *b* Washington, DC, 2 Nov 1966; *m* May 1992 *John Jay ALTHOFF, s of Bernard Althoff and his *w* Peggy Lou Pease, of Rye, New York

2a *Jonathan ROOSEVELT, Jr, *b* Washington, DC, 31 Aug 1968

3a *Katherine ROOSEVELT, *b* Washington, DC, 31 Aug 1968

Great-grandchildren

(3) *Anne Cooper ROOSEVELT, *b* 24 Sept 1952

(4) *Mark ROOSEVELT, *b* 10 Dec 1955; *educ* Harvard

Grandchildren

2 *(Joseph) Willard ROOSEVELT [740 Poquatuck Lane, Orient, NY 11957, USA], *b* Madrid, Spain, 16 Jan 1918; *educ* Harvard and Hart Sch of Music; Lt-Cdr USNR World War II, composer (C=composed, R=revised, FP=first performed): *Scherzo for piano* (C, FP 1946), *Sonatina for piano* (C 1947, FP 1949), *Adagio for chamber orchestra* (C, FP 1948), *Concerto for piano and orchestra* (C 1948, R 1983, arrangement for two pianos FP 1988), *First suite for piano* (C, FP 1949), *Sonata #1 for piano* (C 1950, FP 1958, R 1977), *Dance suite for piano* (original title *Five studies*, C 1952, FP 1955, R 1982), *Sonata for violin and piano* (C, FP 1952, R 1973), *Sonata for 'cello and piano* (C 1953, R 1963, FP 1965), *'Serenade' for oboe, viola and 'cello* (C 1954, FP 1958), *Sonata #2 for piano* (C 1956, R 1977), *'The Leaden Echo and the Golden Echo'* (Hopkins) (C, FP 1957), *Suite for oboe, bassoon and strings* (C 1959, R 1979), *'May Song it Flourish'* (Joyce) for three voices and small orchestra (C 1960, FP 1961), *Concerto for 'cello and full orchestra* (C, FP 1963), *'Lament for Willie Thomas Jones' for four 'cellos* (from piano suite (C 1964), arranged 1977), *Songs with piano* (cummings, Frankenberg, E. McCarthy, Hopkins, L. Mitchell, D. Egan, C. Roosevelt) (C 1965 on, FP 1966 on), *'Amistad — Homenaje al gran Morel-Campos' for full orchestra* (C 1965, FP 1966), *'Song and dance suite' for two violas* (C 1970, arranged for oboe, clarinet and viola 1975 and FP in arrangement form 1989), *String Quartet* (C, FP 1974, R 1977), *'Judgement of Paris' and 'Paul Revere's Ride' for solo flute and optional mime* (C, FP 1975), *Songs with viola* (C, FP 1975 on, same songs also arranged for clarinet), *'And the Walls Came Tumbling Down'* (Loften Mitchell), opera in four scenes, one act; for five singers and chamber orchestra, also arranged for piano accompaniment (C 1974, FP 1976), *'Flute and*

Fiddle' duos for five flutes and violin/viola (C, FP 1975), and 'Our Dead Brothers Bid Us Think of Life' (Stephen Crane, O. W. Holmes, Jr) for soprano, narrator, dancer and small orchestra (C 1976, FP 1976; arrangement for soprano, narrator, oboe, piano and string quartet, entitled 'War is Kind' FP 1993), 'An American Sampler' four songs with french horn and piano (C, FP 1976), Three Songs for Poe with clarinet and piano (C 1977, FP 1988), Waltz for flute and piano (C, FP 1978, also for clarinet and piano), Suite for solo viola (C 1978, FP 1989), 'The Twinkle in His Eye' two pieces for band (C 1979) and Short suite for oboe, clarinet and bassoon (C 1982, FP 1991); m 1st Dec 1943 (divorce 1954), as her 1st husb, Nancy, dau of e. e. cummings, of New York, and has had issue:

Great-grandchildren
(1) Simon Willard ROOSEVELT, b 4 Sept 1945; m 2 Jan 1964 *Anne Whitney Alexander and was k in a car accident 1 May 1965, leaving issue:

   Great-great-grandchildren
   1a *Simon Cummings ROOSEVELT [138 W 13th, New York, NY 10011, USA], b 1 July 1964

Great-grandchildren
(2) *Elizabeth Françoise Roosevelt [Ms Elizabeth Aldred, PO Box 931, Brewster, MA 02631, USA], b New York 30 Aug 1947; journalist 1983-; m 8 Jan 1965 (divorce 1981) Derek C. ALDRED and has issue:

   Great-great-grandchildren
   1a *Charles W. ALDRED [1515 Alice St Apt 21, Oakland, CA 94612, USA], b London, UK, 17 May 1966
   2a *Axel C. ALDRED [PO Box 931 Brewster, MA 02631, USA], b Pittsfield, Mass., 30 April 1969

Grandchildren
2 (cont.) Willard Roosevelt m 2nd 29 May 1955 *Carol Adele Russell, of Cuttingsville, Vt., and with her has issue:

   Great-grandchildren
   (3) *Dirck ROOSEVELT, b 14 Dec 1955
   (4) Caleb Willard ROOSEVELT, b 15 March 1963; k July 1982 in a car accident
   (5) David Russell ROOSEVELT, b 18 Jan 1965; k June 1986 in a car accident

Grandchildren
3 *Belle Wyatt Roosevelt, b New York 8 Nov 1919; m 26 Dec 1942 *John Gorham PALFREY (b Boston 12 March 1919), s of John Gorham Palfrey and his w Methye Oakes, and has issue:

   Great-grandchildren
   (1) *John ('Sean') Gorham PALFREY [3 Cordaville Rd, Southborough, MA 01772, USA], b 19—; educ Harvard; m 19— *Judith S. Sullivan and has issue:

      Great-great-grandchildren
      1a *—— PALFREY, b Sept 1972

   Great-grandchildren
   (2) *Antonia Ford PALFREY [25 Nash Rd, Cummington, MA 01026, USA], b 5 April 1954

Grandchildren
4 Dirck ROOSEVELT, b New York 11 Jan 1925; d there 6 Jan 1953

President Theodore Roosevelt's daughter
IV Ethel Carow Roosevelt, b Oyster Bay 13 Aug 1891; sometime Pres Nassau Co (New York) Red Cross; m Oyster Bay 4 April 1913 Dr Richard DERBY (b New York 7 April 1881; d Brattleboro, Vt., 21 July 1963), est s of Dr Richard Henry Derby and his w Sarah Coleman Alden, and d Oyster Bay 3 Dec 1977, having had issue:

Grandchildren
1 Richard DERBY, Jr, b New York 7 March 1914; d there 2 Oct 1922
2 *Edith Roosevelt Derby [Mrs Andrew Williams, Mileta Farm, Burton, WA 98013, USA], b New York 17 June 1917; m 19— Andrew Murray WILLIAMS, Jr, s of Andrew Murray Williams, and has issue:

   Great-grandchildren
   (1) *Sarah Gilmore Williams, b 19—; m 1976 *Bruce Kerry CHAPMAN and has issue:

      Great-great-grandchildren
      1a *Adam Winthrop CHAPMAN, b 13 Feb 1978

   Great-grandchildren
   (2) *Andrew Murray WILLIAMS III [901 30th Avenue W, Anchorage, AK 99503, USA], b 19—; m 1977 *Joyce Hughes Entwistle
   (3) *Richard Derby WILLIAMS, b 23 Dec 1944; educ Harvard; m 21 June 1969 *Jeanne Adele, dau of George Gordon Strong, of Canton, Ohio, and has issue:

      Great-great-grandchildren
      1a *Helen Ogden WILLIAMS, b 9 April 1979

Grandchildren

3 *Sarah Alden Derby [Mrs Robert Gannett, RFD 2 Box 165, W Brattleboro, VT 05301, USA], b New York 11 Dec 1920; m 1941 *Robert T. GANNETT, attorney, and has issue:

Great-grandchildren

(1) *Sarah Alden Gannett, b 5 Sept 1947; m Middlebury, Conn., 1969 *Gustavus F. TAYLOR and has issue:

Great-great-grandchildren
1a *Ian TAYLOR, b 2 Feb 1978
2a *Graham G. TAYLOR, b 1980
3a *James D. Taylor, b 1983
4a *Camilla A. TAYLOR, b 1990

Great-grandchildren

(2) *Robert T. GANNETT, Jr, b 17 May 1950; educ Harvard; m 1982 *Joanne Ruvolo and has issue:

Great-great-grandchildren
1a *Jason E. GANNETT, b 1985
2a *Katherine R. GANNETT, b 1987
3a *Elizabeth D. GANNETT, b 1990

Great-grandchildren

(3) *William B. GANNETT, b 26 Sept 1952; educ Groton, Yale, Harvard Law Sch and Cornell (PhD 1984); m 1991 *Anna Carlson and has issue:

Great-great-grandchildren
1a *Theodore R. GANNETT, b 1992

Grandchildren

4 Judith Quentin Derby, b 1923; m 19— *Dr Adelbert AMES III [51 Nashoba Road, Concord, MA 01742, USA], s of Prof Adelbert Ames, Jr, and his w Fanny Vose Hazen, and d Concord 26 Sept 1973, leaving issue:

Great-grandchildren
(1) *Mark Adelbert AMES, b 16 Nov 1949
(2) *Judith Quentin AMES, b 27 Dec 1951
(3) *David H. AMES, b 31 March 1955

President Theodore Roosevelt's son

V Archibald Bulloch ROOSEVELT, b Washington, DC, 9 April 1894; educ Harvard (AB 1917); financier, Capt AEF (wounded) World War I and Lt-Col (wounded) World War II; m Boston 14 April 1917 Grace Stackpole (d Cold Spring Harbor, New York, June 1971), only dau of Thomas St John Lockwood, of Boston, and his w Emmeline Dabney Stackpole, and d Palm Springs, Fla., Oct 1979, leaving issue:

Grandchildren

1 Archibald Bulloch ROOSEVELT, Jr, b Boston 18 Feb 1918; educ Groton, Arizona Desert Sch, Tucson, and Harvard (AB 1939); jnlst 1939-42, Capt US Army Intelligence World War II, with Strategic Services Unit then CIA 1947-50 and 1951-74 (served as head of station Beirut, Istanbul, Madrid and London) also briefly with State Dept and VOA, V-Pres Chase Manhattan Bank, author: For Lust of Knowing — Memoirs of an Intelligence Officer (1988); m 1st New York 18 May 1940 (divorce 1950) Katherine Winthrop (b New York 16 Jan 1920), 2nd dau of Harrison Tweed, lawyer, of New York, and his w Eleanor (who m 2nd, as his 5th w, Count Paoli Pálffy, of Bratislava, Czechoslovakia), dau of William Roekler, of Greene Farm, East Greenwich, Rhode Island, and had issue:

Great-grandchildren

(1) *Tweed ROOSEVELT, b Berkeley, Calif., 28 Feb 1942; educ Millbrook Sch and Harvard; with Human Resources Admin and VISTA (Volunteers in Service to America)

Grandchildren

1 (cont.) Archibald Bulloch Roosevelt, Jr, m 2nd New York 1 Sept 1950 *Selwa ('Lucky') [Mrs Archibald B Roosevelt Jr, 3400 R Street NW, Washington, DC 20007, USA] (b Kingsport, Tenn., 13 Jan 1929; educ Vassar; Ch of Protocol State Dept during President REAGAN's administration, author: Keeper of the Gate: Behind the Scenes in the Reagan White House (1992)), dau of Salim Showker and his w Najla Choucaire, and d 31 May 1990

2 *Theodora Roosevelt [c/o A A Rauschfuss, PO Box 25, Patterson, NC 28661, USA], b New York 30 June 1919; novelist; m 1st 8 June 1945 (divorce 19—) Thomas KEOGH; m 2nd *Thomas O'TOOLE

3 *Nancy Dabney Roosevelt [Mrs William Jackson, 530 E 87th Street, New York, NY 10128, USA], b New York 26 July 1923; m 24 Sept 1944 *William Eldred JACKSON [1 Chase Manhattan Plaza, New York, NY 10005, USA], lawyer, s of Associate Justice Robert Houghwont Jackson and his w Irene Gerhardt, and has issue:

Great-grandchildren
(1) *Miranda D. Jackson, b 2 May 1948; m 19—
(2) *Melissa C. Jackson, b 25 March 1952; m 19—
(3) *Melanie E. Jackson, b 7 Dec 1954; m 19—

(4) *Melinda R. Jackson, b 31 Oct 1955; m 19—
(5) *Marina Quentin JACKSON, b 9 June 1959

Grandchildren
4 *Edith ROOSEVELT (has resumed maiden name), b New York 19 Dec 1926; educ Barnard Coll; m New York 1949 (divorce 1952) Alexander Gregory Barmine (b Russia 16 Aug 1899) and has issue:

Great-grandchildren
(1) *Margot Roosevelt Barmine (has assumed surname ROOSEVELT), b 13 Aug 1950; m 20 Dec 1969 *Ralph Hornblower III, s of Ralph Hornblower, Jr, and his w Phoebe M. Blumer

President Theodore Roosevelt's son
VI Quentin ROOSEVELT, b Washington, DC, 19 Nov 1897; educ Harvard; Offr Aviation Corps World War I; ka Cambrai, France, 14 July 1918

Male Line Ancestry and Collateral Descendants

Note: Surnames in the early generations of Roosevelts vary. This sometimes necessitates omission of surnames for members of the family whose line is not taken further.

Klaes or Claes Martenszen VAN ROSENVELT; emigrated from Europe to New Amsterdam (the Dutch settlement on the southern tip of what is now Manhattan) 1649, bought a farm in the middle of Manhattan Island by 1655; m 6 Aug 1655 Jannetje (d 1660), dau of Samuel Tomas or Tomas Samuels (the rarity of whose name being found in reversible forms in records has led to suggestions that he was English), and d probably after 2 Oct 1658 and certainly by 10 Dec 1660, having had issue:

I Christiaen, bapt New York Dutch Church 23 Oct 1650; d in infancy
II Elsje, bapt New York Dutch Church 11 Feb 1652; m c 1671 Hendrick GILLIS/JILLIS MEYER (b on or before 6 March 1650), s of Gillis Pieterszen and Elsje (Hendricks) Meyer and d after 24 Oct 1703, having had issue:

1 Elsje 2 Jannetje; m Abraham PROVOOST 3 Elsje; m Bernardus SMITH
4 Marritie; m 1st Hendrick van der HEUL; m 2nd Johannes D'HONEUR 5 Rachel 6 Catharina; m Harmanus RUTGERS
7 Hendrick 8 Johannes 9 Pieter

III Anna Margaret, bapt New York Dutch Church 29 Aug 1654; m Heyman ALDERTSE ROOSA, of Esopus, Ulster Co, New York, s of Aldert Heymansen Roosa and his w Wyntie Ariens de Jongh, and d before 23 Aug 1708, leaving issue:

1 Aldert 2 Jannetje; m Philip HOUGHTELING 3 Wyntie; m Willem CROM 4 Claes 5 Gysbert 6 Neeltje
7 Rachel; m Johannes Ten BROECK 8 Lea; m Anthony CRISPELL

IV Christina, bapt New York Dutch Church 30 July 1656; m 1st Nicasius de la MONTAGNE (b on or before 9 April 1659; d July 1702), s of Jan de la Montagne and Petronella Pikes, and with him had issue:

1 Johannes de la MONTAGNE 2 Samuel de la MONTAGNE 3 Jese/Josiah de la MONTAGNE

IV (cont.) Christina Van Rosenvelt de la Montagne m 2nd New York Dutch Church 24 Feb 1703 John HAMILL
V Nicholas ROOSEVELT

The yr s,
Nicholas ROOSEVELT, bapt New York Dutch Church 2 Oct 1658; settled Esopus between 1676 and 1680, returned to New York City c 1690, miller, New York Alderman of the Leislerian Party (named after a politician of Dutch background who agitated on behalf of the poorer classes against the propertied classes) 1698-1701 and Treasurer of New York City 1701, Elder of New York Dutch Church and slaveowner; m New York Dutch Church 26 Dec 1682 Heyltje Jans (b Albany, New York, 16—; d in or after 1730/1), dau of Jan Barentsen Kunst (d in or after 1670) and his w Jannetje Adriaens (d before 1663), and d New York 30 July 1742, having had issue:

I Jannetje Roosevelt, bapt Dutch Church, Kingston, New York, 11 Nov 1683; m New York Dutch Church 11 Nov 1699, as his 1st w, Johannes van der HEUL (b on or before 24 Dec 1673; m 2nd New York Dutch Church 3 Jan 1730 Sara Kip), s of Abraham and Tryntje Janszen and bro of Hendrick van der Heul (see above), and d 8 Oct 1728, leaving issue:

1 Abraham van der HEUL 2 Abraham van der HEUL 3 Catharina van der HEUL 4 Nicholas van der HEUL
5 Johannes van der HEUL 6 Helena van der HEUL

II Margarietje ROOSEVELT, bapt Kingston Dutch Church 11 Oct 1685
III Nicholas ROOSEVELT, bapt Kingston Dutch Church 28 Aug 1687; m New York Dutch Church 5 Feb 1710, as her 1st husb, Sarah (m 2nd 28 Feb 1718 Philip Schuyler and d 6 June 1730), dau of Barent Folleman and his w Catharina, of Flatbush, New York, and d before 3 Jan 1717/8, having had issue:

1 Catharina Roosevelt, *bapt* New York Dutch Church 7 Jan 1711; *m* there 9 May 1731, as his 1st w, Steenwyck de RIEMER (*b* on or before 23 April 1710; *m* 2nd 16 Jan 1742 Angel/Engeltje Anthony; *d* 1 Sept 1742) and *d* before 16 Jan 1742, having had issue:

(1) Isaac de RIEMER   (2) Sarah de RIEMER   (3) Nicholas de RIEMER   (4) Petrus de RIEMER
(5) Steenwyck de RIEMER

2 Hilletje ROOSEVELT, *bapt* New York Dutch Church 29 March 1713
3 Nicholas ROOSEVELT, *bapt* New York Dutch Church 6 Feb 1715; gold- and silversmith in New York City, Assist Alderman 1748-63 and Alderman 1763-68; *m* 1st New York Dutch Church 5 June 1737 Catherine (*b* on or before 18 Aug 1717), dau of Gerardus Comfort and his w Catharina Hennejon, and had issue:

(1) Catherine Roosevelt, *bapt* New York Dutch Church 22 March 1738; *m* c 6 Feb 1760 William KIRBY and *d* perhaps New York City Nov-Dec 1795
(2) Sarah ROOSEVELT, *bapt* New York Dutch Church 18 July 1740; *d* Chester, Orange Co, New York, 11 April 1794
(3) Gerardus Comfort ROOSEVELT, *bapt* New York Dutch Church 8 Sept 1742

3 (cont.) Nicholas Roosevelt *m* 2nd New York Dutch Church 24 Nov 1754 Elizabeth (*b* on or before 9 May 1725), dau of John Thurman and his w Elizabeth Wessels, and *d* before 1 May 1769, having had further issue:

(4) Elizabeth ROOSEVELT, *bapt* New York Dutch Church 26 Jan 1757; *d* young
(5) Nicholas ROOSEVELT, *bapt* New York Dutch Church 11 Oct 1758; *m* Lake George, New York, Margaret (*b* Staatsburg, New York, 10 March 1769; *d* Waterford, New York, 27 March 1832), dau of John Cramer and his w Catherine Ham, and *d* Johnsburgh, New York, 4 June 1838, leaving issue:

1a Nicholas ROOSEVELT   2a Robert G. ROOSEVELT   3a Catherine Roosevelt; *m* John D. DUNN

IV Johannes ROOSEVELT, for whom *see below*
V Elsie ROOSEVELT, *bapt* New York Dutch Church 1 Jan 1691
VI Jacobus ROOSEVELT, *b* 28 Feb 1692; merchant in New York City, real estate investor in New York City, New York State and New Jersey, invested in shipping with his bro Johannes, Ward-Assessor New York City, Elder New York Dutch Church; *m* New York 31 Jan 1713 Catharina (*b* 20 Feb 1694; *d* after 1739), est dau of Johannes Hardenbroeck (*bapt* Amsterdam, The Netherlands, 25 Sept 1665; *d* probably New York 1710-14) and his w Sara Van Laer (*d* probably New York on or before 17 Nov 1743), and *d* New York 4/5 May 1776, having had issue:

1 Johannes ROOSEVELT, *b* 23 Aug, *d* 27 Sept 1714
2 Johannes/John ROOSEVELT, *b* 14 Aug 1715; *m* Flatbush 8 Nov 1746 Ariantje, dau of Abraham Lequier and his w Antoinette Duryea, and *d* either before his father or 1806, leaving issue:

(1) Catherine Roosevelt; *m* c 26 Sept 1766, as his 1st w, Abraham VAN RANST (*b* c 18 July 1744; *m* 2nd 16 Feb 1797 Rebecca (Carhart) Ortenberger or Outenbogert; *d* Sept 1802-June 1803), s of Cornelius Van Ranst and his w Catherine Canon, and *d* on or before 11 Dec 1794, having had issue

3 Nicholas ROOSEVELT, *b* 9 Oct 1717; *m* Curaçao, Dutch West Indies, 23 March 1738 Wilhelmina Maria (*d* before 26 Jan 1739), dau of Cornelis Anderman van der Burgh; *m* 2nd New York 24 May 1740 Annetje (*b* c 9 Oct 1717), dau of Andries Brestede and his w Deborah Wessels, and *d* at sea 15 Aug 1740, leaving issue:

(1) Nicholas ROOSEVELT, *bapt* New York Dutch Church 1 Oct 1740; merchant in New York and Richfield, Conn., probably 1st Lt New York City Militia 1776; *m* New York 15 Dec 1761 Sarah (*b* c 6 Nov 1745), dau of Cornelius Van Ranst and his w Catherine Canon and sis of his future bro-in-law Abraham (*see above*), and *d* 10 Nov 1783, leaving at least one child:

1a James ROOSEVELT, aged under 21 at time of his f's death

4 Helena Roosevelt, *b* 8 Oct 1719; *m* 22 June 1737 Andrew BARCLAY, of New York and Curaçao (*b* Oct 1719; *d* 19 June 1775), s of Revd Thomas Barclay, chaplain to the garrison of Fort Orange, Albany, New York, 1708, and his w Anna Dorothea Drauyer and great-uncle of Susan De Lancey, whose 2nd husb was Gen Sir Hudson Lowe, GCMG, KCB, Governor of St Helena during NAPOLEON's exile there; Helena Roosevelt Barclay *d* 25 May 1772, leaving issue:

(1) Thomas BARCLAY   (2) Catherine BARCLAY   (3) Ann Dorothy Barclay; *m* Theophylact BACHE
(4) Catherine Barclay; *m* Augustus VAN CORTLANDT   (5) Sarah Barclay; *m* Anthony LISPENARD
(6) Ann Margaret Barclay; *m* 17 Nov 1773, as his 1st w, Frederick JAY (*b* 19 April 1747; *d* 14 Dec 1799), 7th s of Peter Jay, New York Alderman, and his w Mary Van Cortlandt, and bro of John Jay, Pres Congress 1778, Min to Spain 1779-82, a negotiator of peace with Britain 1783, Sec For Affairs 1784-89, 1st Ch Justice US Supreme Court 1789-95, Min Plenipotentiary to Britain 1794-95 and Govr New York 1795-1801
(7) James BARCLAY; *m* Maria van Beverhout and had issue:

1a Catherine Eliza van Beverhout, *b* New York 2 April 1784; *m* 7 Sept 1812, as his 2nd w, her cousin James Roosevelt (*see below*) and had issue

(8) Andrew BARCLAY   (9) Helena Barclay; *m* Thomas MONCREIFFE
(10) Henry BARCLAY   (11) John BARCLAY
(12) Charlotte Amelia Barclay; *m*, as his 2nd w, Dr Richard BAYLEY (*d* 1801), first Prof of Anatomy at Columbia Coll and health offr Port of New York (f by his 1st w Catherine Charlton of St Elizabeth Ann Seton (1774-1821), who founded

559

in 1809 and was the first Superior of the Order of Sisters of Charity in the USA and was canonized 1975), and had issue (with several other children):

1a Guy Carleton BAYLEY; *m* his cousin Grace Roosevelt (*see below*) and had issue:

1b James Roosevelt BAYLEY, *b* Rye, New York, 23 Aug 1814; *educ* Amherst Coll and Trin Coll, Hartford, Conn.; Episcopalian Rector St Peter's, Harlem, New York, 1835-41, converted to Catholicism 1842, ordained priest 1844, Prof and V-Pres Fordham Seminary (Actg Pres 1846), 1st Bp of Newark, New Jersey, 1853-72 and 8th Archbishop of Baltimore 1872-77, author: *A Brief Sketch of the Early History of the Catholic Church on the Island of New York* (1853) and *Memoirs of Simon Gabriel Bruté, First Bishop of Vincennes* (1855); *d* Oct 1877

5 Jacobus ROOSEVELT, *b* 14 Sept 1721; *d* 7 Aug 1771 6 Christopher ROOSEVELT, *b* 5 Feb 1724; *d* at sea Nov 1737 7 Isaac ROOSEVELT, *b* New York 8 Dec 1726; sugar refiner, Memb New York Provincial Congress 1775-76 and New York Provisional Convention 1776-77, New York State Senator 1777-86 and 1789-92, Delegate to New York Constitutional Convention 1788, a Fndr New York Hospital, Pres Bank of New York 1786-91; *m* Dutchess Co, New York, 22 Sept 1752 Cornelia (*b* Kingston, New York, 13 Aug 1734; *d* New York 13 Nov 1789), dau of Martin Hoffman (*b* Kingston 6 Feb 1706/7; *d* New York 29 Aug 1772) and his *w* Tryntje Benson (*b* Kingston 30 May 1712; *d* probably Dutchess Co 31 March 1765), and *d* New York 13 Oct 1794, having had issue:

(1) Abraham ROOSEVELT, *b* 13 Aug, *d* 2 Oct 1753 (2) Martinus ROOSEVELT, *b* 27 Oct 1754; *d* 20 Sept 1755 (3) Catherine ROOSEVELT, *b* 28 July 1756; *d* 19 May 1807 (4) Sarah ROOSEVELT, *b* 18 Nov 1758; *d* Red Hook, Dutchess Co, New York, 18 Dec 1777
(5) James ROOSEVELT, *b* 10 Jan 1760; *educ* Princeton; sugar refiner and gentleman farmer, Alderman New York 1809; *m* 1st New York 15 Nov 1786 Mary Eliza (*b* New York 15 March 1769; *d* there 22 March 1810), dau of Abraham Walton (*b* New York *c* 1739; *d* there 21 Dec 1796) and his *w* Grace Williams (*b c* 1745), and had issue ten children in all; two of their children (1a and 2a) were:

1a Grace Roosevelt; *m* Guy Carleton BAYLEY and had issue:

1b James Roosevelt BAYLEY; ArchBp of Baltimore (*see above*), was intended by his maternal gf James Roosevelt to inherit a large sum of money but on his converting to Catholicism was disinherited, it is said because his gf mistakenly believed a priest could possess no property
2b Richard BAYLEY 3b Carl(e)ton BAYLEY 4b William BAYLEY 5b Maria E. BAYLEY

2a Isaac ROOSEVELT, *b* New York 21 April 1790; *educ* Princeton and Columbia U (MD); *m* 26 April 1827 Mary Rebecca (*b* New York 20 Dec 1809; *d* there 24 Feb 1886), dau of John Aspinwall, Jr (*b* New York 10 Feb 1774; *d* there 6 Oct 1847), and his *w* Susan Howland (*b* Norwich, Conn., 20 May 1779; *d* New York 12 or 23 Dec 1852), and *d* Hyde Park, New York, 23 Oct 1863, leaving (with other issue):

1b James ROOSEVELT, *b* Mount Hope, New York, 16 July 1828; *educ* Dr Hyde's Acad, Lee, Mass., New York U, Union Coll, Schenectady (AB 1847), and Harvard; V-Pres Delaware & Hudson Railroad, lawyer and financier; *m* 1st 1853 his 2nd cousin Rebecca Brien (*b* 15 Jan 1831; *d* 21 Aug 1876), dau of Gardiner Greene Howland, and had issue:

1c James (Rosy) ROOSEVELT, *b* 27 March 1854; sometime 1st Sec US Legation London; *m* 1st 1878 Helen Schermerhorn (*d* 1893), 2nd dau of William Astor and his *w* Caroline Webster Schermerhorn, and had issue:

1d James Roosevelt ROOSEVELT, Jr (the repetition of the family name Roosevelt being a New York Dutch form of 'Jr'), *b* 1879; *educ* Groton and Harvard
2d Helen Rebecca Roosevelt, *b* 1881; *m* 1904 her 6th cousin Theodore Douglas ROBINSON (*b* 28 April 1883; Memb New York Assembly and New York Senate, Assist Sec Navy; *d* April 1934), est s of Douglas Robinson and his *w* Corinne Roosevelt (sister of President THEODORE ROOSEVELT), and *d* 19—, leaving issue:

1e *Helen Douglas Robinson, *b* 19—; *m* 19— *John Arthur HINCKLEY and has issue:

1f *John Arthur HINCKLEY, Jr, *b* 19—

2e Elizabeth Mary Douglas Robinson, *b* 19—; *m* 19—, as his 1st *w*, *Jacques Blaise DE SIBOUR [200 Ocean Lane Drive, Key Biscayne, FL 33149, USA] and had issue:

1f *Betsy Mary DE SIBOUR
2f *Jacques Blaise DE SIBOUR [3050 South Buchanan Street, Arlington, VA 22206, USA], *b* 19—; *educ* Princetown (BA 1954); *m* 19— *Diane L. Tate and has issue:

1g *Stephanie D. DE SIBOUR, *b* 19—

3e *Douglas ROBINSON, *b* 19—; *m* 1933 *Louise Miller
4e *Alida Douglas Robinson, *b* 19—; *m* 1933 *Kenneth Stewart WALKER

1c (cont.) James Roosevelt Roosevelt *m* 2nd 1915 Elizabeth R. Riley and *d* 7 May 1927

1b (cont.) James Roosevelt *m* 2nd Algonac, nr Newburgh, New York, 7 Oct 1880 Sara (*b* there 21 Sept 1854; *d* Springwood, Hyde Park, 7 Sept 1941), 5th and yst dau of Warren Delano, Jr (*b* Fairhaven, Mass., 13 July 1809; *d* Algonac 17 Jan 1898), and his *w* Catherine Robbins Lyman (*b* Northampton, Mass., 12 Jan 1825; *d* Algonac 10 Feb 1896), and *d* Hyde Park 8 Dec 1900, having with her had further issue:

2c FRANKLIN DELANO ROOSEVELT, 32nd PRESIDENT of the UNITED STATES of AMERICA

(5) (cont.) James Roosevelt *m* 2nd 7 Sept 1812 his cousin Catherine Eliza Barclay (*b* New York 22 April 1784; *d* there 15 Feb 1816), dau of James Barclay and his *w* Maria van Beverhout and gdau of Andrew Barclay and his *w* Helena Roosevelt, and with her had issue (with another child, possibly one of those mentioned below against 3a to 4a):

2a James Barclay ROOSEVELT

(5) cont.) James Roosevelt *m* 3rd New York 29 Jan 1821 Harriet (*b* 14 Sept 1784; *d* 18 April 1856), dau of Joseph Howland, of Boston (*b* 30 Sept 1749; *d* New York 11 March 1836), and his *w* Lydia Bill (*b* Norwich, Conn., 7 July 1753; *d* New York 1 May 1838) and sister of Susan Howland, Isaac Roosevelt's mother-in-law (*see above*), and *d* New York 6 Feb 1847; of his 10 children a further two (not necessarily in the order given) are known by name:

3a Susan ROOSEVELT   4a Richard V. ROOSEVELT; *m* Anna Maria —— and predeceased her

(6) Cornelia ROOSEVELT, *b* 29 April, *d* 1 June 1761

(7) Maria Roosevelt, *b* 5 Aug 1763; *m* New York 8 May 1786 Richard VARICK (*b* 25 March 1753; Mayor New York 1789-1801; *d* Jersey City 30 July 1831), s of John Varick and his *w* Jane Deyand *d* 19 July 1841

(8) Martin ROOSEVELT, *b* 22 May 1765; *educ* Princeton and *d* there 19 Sept 1781

(9) Cornelia Roosevelt, *b* 27 April 1767; *m* New York 16 Jan 1786 Dr Benjamin KISSAM (*b c* 1759; *educ* U of Edinburgh (MD 1783); Prof and Tstee Columbia Coll; *d* 14 July 1803), s of Benjamin Kissam and his *w* Catherine Rutgers, and *d* Rhinebeck, New York, 1 July 1818, leaving issue:

1a Cornelia Catherine Kissam; *m* Dr Caspar Wistar EDDY   2a Maria Ann KISSAM   3a Helena KISSAM
4a Amelia Charlotte KISSAM   5a Catherine Roosevelt KISSAM   6a Benjamin Roosevelt KISSAM
7a Richard Varick KISSAM

(10) Helena ROOSEVELT, 30 Aug 1768; *d* 7 Sept 1798

8 Abraham ROOSEVELT, *b* 25 Dec 1728; *d* 1 Feb 1747

9 Sarah Roosevelt, *b* 19 Dec 1730; *m* New York Dutch Church 29 Sept 1750, apparently as his 2nd w, Charles CROMMELIN (*b c* 29 Aug 1722), widower of Maria Brockholst, and with him had issue:

(1) Charles CROMMELIN   (2) James CROMMELIN

10 Peter ROOSEVELT, *b* 7 Oct 1732; *m* 1st New York Dutch Church 15 Nov 1753 Elizabeth (*b c* 7 Nov 1731; *d* 22 Oct 1757), dau of Joris Brinkerhoff and his 1st *w* Elizabeth Byvanck, and with her had issue:

(1) Elizabeth Roosevelt, *bapt* New York Dutch Church 30 Oct 1754

10 (cont.) Peter Roosevelt *m* 2nd Albany Dutch Church 3 June 1762, as her 2nd husb, Elizabeth (*b c* 3 Nov 1736; *m* 1st Revd Theodorus Frelinghuysen; *m* 3rd *c* 18 Oct 1770 William Lupton, with whom she had further issue; *d* Dec 1801), dau of Lancaster Symes and his *w* Margaretta Johanna Lydius, and *d* before 26 Nov 1762, leaving further issue:

(2) Peter ROOSEVELT, *b* 2 Aug(?) 1763; *m* Grace Church, Jamaica, Long Island, 17 Nov 1791 Judith Hallett (*b* 10 May 1769; *d* New York 20 July 1832), widow of Samuel Goodwin

11 Adolphus ROOSEVELT, *b* 18 May, *d* 9 July 1734

12 Adolphus ROOSEVELT, *b* 16 Oct 1735; settled at St Eustatius, Dutch West Indies; *m* there 31 Dec 1759 Elizabeth (*b c* 1740; *d* St Eustatius 3 Sept 1811), dau of Lucas Doeke Groebe and his *w* Anna Maria Heyliger, and *d* before 2 Feb 1799, having had issue:

(1) Anna Catherine Roosevelt, *b* St Eustatius *c* 1760; *m* either New York City Lutheran Church 16 Jan 1775 or St Eustatius Dutch Church after 3 Aug 1778, as his 1st *w*, William AMORY (*b c* 1755; *m* 2nd Hester Kortright; *d* before 21 July 1791) and had issue

(2) ?James ROOSEVELT; *d* young 1766

(3) Sarah Roosevelt, *bapt* St Eustatius Dutch Church 8 Nov 1771; *m* Dutch Church, St Croix, Danish West Indies, 8 July 1790 Jan de WINDT (*b c* 5 Oct 1765; *d* on or before 15 March 1803), s of Jan Jacob de Windt and his *w* Elizabeth Heyliger, and *d* Paris, France, 13 July 1850, having had issue:

1a Peter Herny Adolphus de WINDT   2a Elizabeth de WINDT

(4) Isaac Groebe ROOSEVELT, *bapt* Dutch Church, St Eustatius, 27 Feb 1776; *d* by 1799
(5) Maria Wilhelmina ROOSEVELT, *bapt* Dutch Church, St Eustatius, 7 Feb 1777; *d* by 1799

13 Christopher ROOSEVELT, *b* 24 Jan 1739; *m* New York Dutch Church 4 Oct 1769, as her 1st husb, Mary (*b c* 26 June 1751; *m* 2nd New York Dutch Church 5 Nov 1780 Thomas Stagg and *d* ?7 Sept 1784?), dau of Jacob Duryea and his *w* Sarah Van Nostrand and niece of Abraham Duryea (*see above*), and *d* 15 Jan 1772, leaving issue:

(1) James Christopher ROOSEVELT, *bapt* New York Dutch Church 18 Nov 1770; *educ* Princeton (AB 1791); *m* New York Dutch Church 5 Nov 1792 Catherine (*b c* 19 Sept 1773; *d* 18 Feb 1854), dau of Evert Byvanck and his *w* Mary Van Ranst and niece of Abraham Van Ranst (*see above*), and *d* 12 June 1840, leaving issue:

1a James H. ROOSEVELT
2a A dau; *m* —— BROWN and had issue:

1b James C. Roosevelt BROWN

VII Rachel ROOSEVELT, *bapt* New York Dutch Church 21 March 1694; *d* young

VIII Isaac ROOSEVELT, *bapt* New York Dutch Church 30 June 1697; *d* young

IX Rachel Roosevelt, *bapt* New York Dutch Church 23 April 1699; *m* there 9 Aug 1721 Peter LOW (*b c* 17 Oct 1697; *d* before 17 Oct 1750), s of Cornelius Low and his w Margrietje Van Borsum, and *d* on or before 21 Aug 1769, having had issue:

> 1 Helena Low; *m* Henry KIP   2 Margaret Low; *m* Cornelius LOW   3 Peter LOW
>
> 4 Jannetje Low; *m* probably John DURYEA, s of Jacob Duryea and his w Catharina Polhemus   5 John LOW
>
> 6 Rachel Low; *m* Cornelius CLOPPER
>
> 7 Elizabeth Low; *m* 3 Nov 1763, as his 2nd w, Abraham DURYEA (*b c* 16 Feb 1724; *m* 1st Elizabeth Low's 1st cousin Maria Roosevelt (*see below*) and *d* 7 April 1797), bro of John Duryea (*see above*)   8 Sara LOW

X Isaac ROOSEVELT, *bapt* New York Dutch Church 28 Feb 1701

Nicholas Roosevelt's 2nd s,

Johannes ROOSEVELT, *bapt* Dutch Church, Kingston, New York, 3 March 1689; merchant in New York, being granted a monopoly with Johannes van der Heul to produce linseed oil, investor in real estate, on occasion with his bro Jacobus (*see above*), Assist Alderman New York 1717-30, Alderman 1730-34 (memb various municipal ctees 1717-34); *m* New York Dutch Church 25 Sept 1708 Heyltje (*b c* 2 Sept 1688; was living 11 July 1751), dau of Olfert Sioerts and his w Margaret Clopper, and *d* 4 April 1750, having had issue:

I Margaret Roosevelt, *bapt* New York Dutch Church 8 May 1709; *m* there 5 May 1730 Willian DE PEYSTER (*b c* 8 May 1709; silversmith; *d* between 3 Nov 1780 and 19 Feb 1784), s of Johannes De Peyster, Mayor of New York, and his w Anna Bancker, and *d* ?16 Nov 1773, leaving issue:

> 1 Johannes DE PEYSTER   2 Heyltje De Peyster; *m* Dr Beekman VAN BEUREN   3 William DE PEYSTER
>
> 4 Gerardus DE PEYSTER   5 Nicholas DE PEYSTER   6 Abraham DE PEYSTER   7 Jacobus/James DE PEYSTER
>
> 8 Anna DE PEYSTER   9 Margaret DE PEYSTER   10 Margaret De Peyster; *m* James BLANCHARD

II Nicholas ROOSEVELT, *bapt* New York Dutch Church 8 Oct 1710; *m* there 7 Oct 1730 Maria, dau of Jeurian Bosch and his w Geesje Anna Bruyn, and *d* 22 Aug 1735

III Johannes ROOSEVELT, *bapt* New York Dutch Church 27 Aug 1712; *d* 22 Aug 1743

IV Heyltje ROOSEVELT, *bapt* New York Dutch Church 23 May 1714; *d* 25 Aug 1745

V Olfert/Oliver ROOSEVELT, *b* 7 Feb 1716; craftsman, chocolate-maker; *m* Elizabeth (*b* 15 April 1715/16; *d* 12 July 1796), dau of John Lounsberry, of Rye, New York, or Richard Lounsberry, of New York City, and *d* 17 Sept 1785, having had issue:

> 1 Heyla/Heyltje ROOSEVELT, *b* 25 April 1738   2 John ROOSEVELT, *b* 16 March 1740/41; *d* young
>
> 3 Altje ROOSEVELT, *b* 28 Feb 1743; *d* young   4 Maria ROOSEVELT, *b* 27 Sept 1744; *d* young   5 John ROOSEVELT, *b* 22 Jan 1746/47; *d* young   6 Cornelius ROOSEVELT, *b* 16 March 1748/49; *m*?; *d* ?18 June 1799
>
> 7 Margaret Roosevelt, *b* 13 Sept 1751; *m* New York Dutch Church 16 July 1774 John COZINE (*b* May 1749; New York Supreme Court Judge; *d* Flatbush 14 Sept 1798), s of John Cozine, and *d* after 10 Sept 1798, leaving issue:
>
> > (1) John Roosevelt COZINE   (2) Oliver Lettany COZINE   (3) Augustus Bayard COZINE   (4) Amelia COZINE
> > (5) Eliza COZINE
>
> 8 Oliver ROOSEVELT, *b* Jan 1754; *d* 19 June 1757
>
> 9 Elizabeth Roosevelt, *bapt* New York Dutch Church 6 Oct 1756; *m* 26 July 1783 Casimir Theodor GOERCK/GOERKE (*d* before 3 Dec 1798), Arty Lt and surveyor in New York City, and *d* after 20 Dec 1799
>
> 10 Oliver ROOSEVELT, *b* 31 July 1759; painter and glazier; *m* 1st on or after 6 May 1780 Rebecca Taylor (*b* 24 or 29 Sept 1759; *d* 15/16 July 1795); *m* 2nd New York 20 May 1804 Mary Knapp (*d* 16 March 1816 aged 45) and *d* 17 Oct 1815, having had issue

VI Jacobus ROOSEVELT, *bapt* New York Dutch Church 23 April 1718; *d* young

VII Maria Roosevelt, *bapt* New York Dutch Church 15 June 1720; *m* there 1 March 1744, as his 1st w, Abraham DURYEA (*see above*) and *d* 8 Aug 1755

VIII Jannetje ROOSEVELT, *bapt* New York Dutch Church 24 April 1723; *d* 11 Sept 1724

IX Jacobus ROOSEVELT, for whom *see below*

X Aeltje ROOSEVELT, *bapt* New York Dutch Church 26 Aug 1726; *d* 23 Sept 1727

XI A child; *d* 7 May 1728

XII Cornelius ROOSEVELT, *bapt* New York Dutch Church 11 July 1731; chocolate-maker, Assist Alderman New York 1759-63, Alderman 1763-67; *m* New York Dutch Church 10 Dec 1751 Margaret (*b c* 8 July 1733; *d* 6 Feb 1821), dau of Elbert Haring and his w Elizabeth Bogert, and *d* 13 March 1772, having had issue:

> 1 John ROOSEVELT, *bapt* New York Dutch Church 22 Aug 1753; *m* New York 28 June 1774 Ann (*b* 18 Feb 1756; *d* 15 Feb 1834), dau of Nathan Beardsley and his w Mary Beach, and *d* 11 Nov 1810, having had issue:
>
> > (1) Cornelius ROOSEVELT; *m* Ann Lockwood   (2) John ROOSEVELT; *m* Mary Wells
> > (3) Maria Roosevelt; *m* Dr Robert G. MERRITT   (4) Margaret Roosevelt; *m* Stephen HUNT
> > (5) Anna Louisa Roosevelt; *m* William Whitney BOGARDUS   (6) Betsy Roosevelt; *m* Jesse BROOKS

2 Cornelius C. ROOSEVELT, *bapt* New York Dutch Church 29 Oct 1755; Ensign American Revolutionary War; *m* 1st on or after 17 Oct 1781 Alida, dau of Winter Fargie and his w Eva Holland; *m* 2nd Fishkill, New York, 15 April 1789 Catherine (*b c* 18 Feb 1750; *d* 5 Dec 1807), dau of Matthew Van Alstyne and his w Sarah Lynch, and *d* New York 5 Feb 1814, leaving issue (by his 1st or 2nd w or both, and not necessarily in the order given):

(1) Ann Nicoll ROOSEVELT (2) Sarah ROOSEVELT (3) Eliza Roosevelt; *m* Walter VERSON, who predeceased her (4) Cornelius ROOSEVELT (5) William ROOSEVELT

3 Elizabeth ROOSEVELT, *bapt* New York Dutch Church 8 April 1757; *d* young
4 Maria ROOSEVELT, *bapt* New York Dutch Church 18 Feb 1759; *d* young
5 Maria, *bapt* New York Dutch Church 2 July 1760; *m* John DUFFIE (*b* New York 14 Dec 1763; *d* there 8 July 1808), s of Duncan Duffie and his w Mary Thompson, and *d* 17 May 1821, leaving issue (not necessarily in the order given):

(1) Cornelius Roosevelt DUFFIE (2) Margaret DUFFIE (3) Eliza Matilda DUFFIE (4) Cornelia Ann DUFFIE (5) Jane Antoinette DUFFIE (6) Maria Caroline Duffie; *m* William H. TODD

6 Cornelia ROOSEVELT (twin with Maria Roosevelt Duffie), *bapt* New York Dutch Church 2 July 1760
7 Margaret ROOSEVELT, *bapt* New York Dutch Church 7 March 1762
8 Peter ROOSEVELT, *bapt* New York Dutch Church 12 Feb 1764
9 Elizabeth ROOSEVELT, *bapt* New York Dutch Church 16 Oct 1765; *d* 21 April 1850

Johannes and Heyltje Sioerts Roosevelt's 9th child and 5th s,

Jacobus ROOSEVELT, *bapt* New York 9 Aug 1724; hardware merchant New York, admitted freeman of city 22 Feb 1748, is said by one source to have served as Private with New York Colonial Troops; *m* 1st New York 4 Dec 1746 Annetje (*bapt* New York 18 Aug 1728; *d* there 9 July 1773), dau of Jan Bogert and his w Annetje Peeck, and *d* 12 March 1777, having had issue (being also gggf through either his est s John or his yst Nicholas of Philip James ROOSEVELT; *b* 19—; *m* Tollington Park Baptist Church, Islington, London, UK, 24 Oct 1969 Philippa Buss, of Egerton Crescent, Chelsea, London, sister of Revd Michael Buss, the celebrant at the wedding and incumbent of Tollington Park):

I Anna/Hannah Roosevelt, *bapt* New York Dutch Church 18 July 1748; ?m New York 22 July 1771 Andries HEERMANCE and *d* before 12 Sept 1796
II John ROOSEVELT, *bapt* New York Dutch Church 16 Jan 1751; merchant in New York, Capt New York City Militia 1776; *m* Acquackanonk Dutch Church, Passaic, New Jersey, 23 Jan 1781 Mary (*b c* 1762), dau of John Schuyler, of Second River, Essex Co, New Jersey, and New Barbadoes, Bergen Co, New Jersey, and his w Ann Van Rensselaer, and *d* Troy, New York, 18 Aug 1820, having had issue
III Heyltje ROOSEVELT, *bapt* New York Dutch Church 22 Nov 1752
IV Margaret Roosevelt, *bapt* New York Dutch Church 12 March 1755; *m* there 3 Dec 1772, as his 1st w, Isaac VAN VLECK (*b* New York 22 Nov 1748; *m* 2nd Ann Green ; *m* 3rd ——; *d* New York 25 May 1804) and *d* Philadelphia 3 Feb 1783, having had issue
V Maria ROOSEVELT, *bapt* New York Dutch Church 12 Jan 1757; *d* young
VI Thomas ROOSEVELT, *bapt* New York Dutch Church 19 July 1758
VII James J. (Jacobus) ROOSEVELT, for whom *see below*
VIII Helena Roosevelt, *bapt* New York Dutch Church 19 Aug 1761; *m* 1st New York 24 Dec 1786 John RAY (*b* 10 Jan 1748; *educ* King's Coll (now Columbia U); Master in Chancery for New York State; *d* New York 28 Jan 1796), s of ?John Ray and his w Sarah Keeler, of Philadelphia and New York, with whom she had issue:

1 John RAY 2 James RAY 3 Elsey RAY 4 Helena RAY

VIII (cont.) Helena Roosevelt Ray *m* 2nd Kingston, New York, 22 Oct 1803 Henry MAURUS/MOWRIS/MOURITZ, widower, and *d* New York 18 Oct 1843
IX Maria Roosevelt, *bapt* New York Dutch Church 10 June 1763; *m* on or before 30 June 1782 her cousin James Alexander PROVOOST, s of John Provoost and Eva Rutgers and gs of Harmanus Rutgers and his w Catharina Meyer Rutgers, and *d* a widow 4 Aug 1798, having had issue
X Nicholas ROOSEVELT, *bapt* New York Dutch Church 27 Dec 1767; Dir New Jersey Copper Mine Assoc 1793, inventor and engr, constructed the *New Orleans* steamboat, which in 1811 made the first journey from Pittsburgh to New Orleans along the Ohio and Mississippi Rivers, taking only 14 days, granted a patent for vertical paddle wheels 1 Dec 1814, bought land and settled *c* 1825 Oswego Co, New York, moved to Skaneateles *c* 1840; *m* Washington, DC, 15 Nov 1808 Lydia (*b* London, Britain, 23 March 1791; *d* Skaneateles 29 June 1871), dau of Benjamin Henry Latrobe (1764-1820), the architect who completed Thomas Jefferson's designs for the Virginia state capitol (and helped him in designing pavilions for the U of Virginia), Surveyor of Public Buildings 1803, in which capacity he completed construction of the Capitol, Washington, DC, (and after the War of 1812 designed the rebuilding of the entire interior), a contributor to the designs of Baltimore Cathedral (over which his relative by marriage Archbishop Bayley later presided) and a highly capable engineer whose plans for supplying Philadelphia with running water were facilitated by his son-in-law Nicholas Roosevelt's steam engines (on the outbreak of the War of 1812 Latrobe also went into partnership with Roosevelt to build a steamboat which could negotiate the upper reaches of the Ohio River), and Latrobe's 1st w Lydia Sellon, and *d* Skaneateles, New York, 30 July 1854, having had issue (together with two other daus and four s who *d* young), not necessarily in the order given:

1 A dau; *m* —— FITCH and had issue:

(1) Laura FITCH

2 H. L. ROOSEVELT   3 Samuel ROOSEVELT; *m* and had issue

Jacobus Roosevelt *m* 2nd New York 15 July 1774 Helena/Eleanor Thomson, widow of —— Gibson, and *d* Red Hook, New York, 12 March 1777, having had further issue:

XI Ann ROOSEVELT, *bapt* New York Dutch Church 30 Jan 1775; *d* before 12 Sept 1796

Jacobus Roosevelt's 7th child and 3rd s,

James J. ROOSEVELT, was *bapt* as Jacobus Roosevelt at the New York Dutch Church 25 Oct 1759; Commissary New York Troops Revolutionary War; *m* Kinderhook, New York, 8 March 1793 Maria (*bapt* Kinderhook 8 Dec 1773; *d* New York 3 Feb 1845), dau of Cornelius Van Schaack, Jr, and his w Angeltje/Angelica Yates, and *d* New York 12/13 Aug 1840, leaving issue (not necessarily in the order given and including the father of a gs of James J. Roosevelt's called West Roosevelt):

I Cornelius Van Schaack ROOSEVELT, for whom *see below*
II James J. ROOSEVELT
III Catherine Roosevelt; *m?* —— BURKE and had issue:

1 Mary Roosevelt BURKE

IV William Henry ROOSEVELT; settled in Illinois; *m* and had issue:

1 James ROOSEVELT   2 Mary ROOSEVELT

James J. Roosevelt's est s,

Cornelius Van Schaack ROOSEVELT, *b* New York 30 Jan 1794; said to have been worth $500,000, Fndr Chemical National Bank of New York; *m c* 1822 Margaret (*b* 13 Dec 1799; *d* 23 Jan 1861), dau of Robert Barnhill and his w Elizabeth, dau of Thomas Potts, Memb New Jersey Provincial Congress, and *d* Oyster Bay, Long Island, New York, 17 July 1871, leaving (with other issue, which included two other er s):

I Silas Weir ROOSEVELT; *m* Mary West and had issue:

1 Hilborne Lewis ROOSEVELT, *b* 21 Dec 1849; organ-builder, pioneer in application of electricity to powering of organs, took out first patent for electrical action in operating an organ April 1869, invented various devices for Bell Telephone, principally an automatic switch hook; *m* 1 Feb 1883 Kate, dau of William Watson Shippen, of Hoboken, New Jersey, and *d* 30 Dec 1886
2 Frank H. ROOSEVELT; continued his bro's organ business till 1893

II Robert Barnwell (christened Barnhill but later took Barnwell as his 2nd name) ROOSEVELT, *b* New York 7 Aug 1829; lawyer, pro-Union Democrat in Civil War (Fndr Loyal Nat League and Union League Club), Sec Citizens' Assoc 1864, New York State Fish Commissioner 1866-68, Memb Ctee of 70 which exposed Tammany Hall corruption in New York, Memb (D) US House of Reps 1871-73, Commissioner Brooklyn Bridge 1879-81, Memb Bd New York Aldermen 1882, US Minister to the Netherlands 1888, Chm Relief Ctee during Spanish-American War of 1898, naturalist, author: *Game Fish of the Northern States of America, and British Provinces* (1862), *Superior Fishing* (1865), *The Game Birds of the Coasts and Lakes of the Northern States of America* (1866), *Five Acres Too Much* (1869), *Progressive Petticoats* (1874) (both satires), *Love and Luck* (novel) (1886), with Seth Green *Fish Hatching, Fish Catching* (1879) and *Florida and the Game Water-Birds of the Atlantic Coast and the Lakes of the United States* (1884); *m* 1st 1850 Elizabeth Ellis (*d* 1887), of New York, and with her had two s and two daus; *m* 2nd 18 Aug 1888 Mrs Marion T. Fortescue, *née* O'Shea, and *d* Sayville, Long Island, New York, 14 June 1906
II A son; *m* and had issue:

1 Emlen ROOSEVELT

III Theodore ROOSEVELT, for whom *see below*

Cornelius Roosevelt's yst s,

Theodore ROOSEVELT, *b* New York 22 Sept 1831; glass importer, Fndr Orthopaedic Hospital New York, nominated Collector Port of New York but nomination rejected by US Senate; *m* Roswell, Cobb Co, Ga., 22 Dec 1853 Martha (*b* Hartford, Conn., 8 July 1834; *d* New York 14 Feb 1884 of typhoid fever), dau of Maj James Stephens Bulloch and his 2nd w Martha, dau of Gen Daniel Stewart, and *d* New York 9 Feb 1878, leaving issue:

I THEODORE ROOSEVELT, 26th PRESIDENT of the UNITED STATES of AMERICA
II Anna ('Auntie Bye') Roosevelt, *b* New York 7 or 18 Jan 1855; *m* London, UK, 25 Nov 1895 Rear-Adml William Sheffield COWLES, US Navy (*b* Farmington, Conn., 1 Aug 1846; *d* 1 May 1923), s of Thomas Cowles and his w Elizabeth Sheffield, and *d* 25 Aug 1931, leaving issue:

President Theodore Roosevelt's nephew
1 William Sheffield COWLES, *b* 1898; *educ* Yale (BA 1921); *m* 1921 Margaret A. Krech (*d* 1984) and *d* 1986, leaving issue:

Great-nephew
(1) *William Sheffield COWLES III [Los Trigos Ranch, Rowe, NM 87562, USA], *b* Hartford, Conn., 18 March 1923; *educ* Yale (BA 1945) and MIT (BArch 1947); architect; *m* 27 May 1944 *Virginia F., dau of Wilton Lloyd-Smith and his w Marjorie Fleming, and has issue:

Great-nephew's children
1a *Cedar Cowles [Mrs Dan Backus, Box 84, Westfield, VT 05784, USA], *b* 19—; *educ* Marlboro Coll, Vt.; *m* 19—

*Dan BACKUS

2a *Thomas S. COWLES [Box 487, Putney, VT 05346, USA], b 19—; educ Lake Forest Coll, Ill., Sch for Internat Living, Brattleboro, Vt. (MA), and Boston U (MA); m 19— *Waew Kasatravatin

3a *Robert COWLES [The Pillars, Shelburne, VT 05482, USA], b 19—; educ Marlboro Coll

4a *Victoria L. S. Cowles [Mrs Nicholas Maravell, 8565 Horseshoe Lane, Potomac, MD 20854, USA], b 19—; educ Bennington; m 19— *Nicholas MARAVELL

5a *Nicholas Z. COWLES [Shelburne Orchards, Shelburne, VT 05482, USA], b 19—; educ Franconia Coll, New Hampshire, and Stowe; m 19— *Cindy Gokey

6a *Evan Roosevelt COWLES [148 Main St, Farmington, CT 06032-2241, USA], b Burlington, Vt., 9 March 1952; educ Groton, Hampshire and Columbia; coach leatherware merchant 1977-81, with Morgan Bank 1982-86, real estate investor 1986-; m 30 June 1979 *Brie Phoebe, dau of Ripley Quinby and his w Beverly, and has issue:

> Great-nephew's grandchildren
> 1b *Charlotte Clara COWLES, b New York 1 Dec 1984
> 2b *William Sheffield COWLES, b Hartford, Conn., 18 Sept 1986

III Elliott ROOSEVELT, b 28 Feb 1860; m 1883 Anna Rebecca (b 1863; d 7 Dec 1892 of diphtheria), dau of Valentine Hall and his w née Ludlow, and d 14 Aug 1894, having had issue:

President Theodore Roosevelt's niece and nephews

1 (Anna) Eleanor Roosevelt, b New York 11 Oct 1884; educ Mlle Souvestre's Sch at Allenswood, Wimbledon, London, UK; Memb Women's Div Democratic Ctee New York State, assist pncpl Todhunter Sch, Assist Dir Office Civilian Defense 1941-42, Dir Roosevelt & Sargent 1941, hon pres ctees for Yugoslav and Greek relief, worked with NAACP, US Rep UN Genl Assembly 1945-52 (Chm UN Human Rights Commission from 1947), board memb: Citizens Ctee for Children, American Assoc for UN, Brandeis U (also visiting lecturer there), US Delegn to UN Special Assembly 1961, Advsy Cncl Peace Corps 1961, Chm President KENNEDY's Commission on Status of Women 1961, posthumous recipient of first UN Human Rights Prize, newspaper columnist, author: When You Grow Up to Vote (1932), It's Up to the Women (1933), A Trip to Washington with Bobby and Betty (1935), This Is My Story (1937), My Days (1938), This I Remember (1950), India and the Awakening East (1953), On My Own (1959), ed The Moral Basis of Democracy (1940); m New York 17 March 1905 her 5th cousin once-removed FRANKLIN D. ROOSEVELT (32nd President, qv) and d New York 7 Nov 1962, having had issue

2 Elliott ROOSEVELT, b 1889; d 1893 of scarlet fever

3 (Gracie) Hall ROOSEVELT, b Neuilly, France, 28 June 1891; educ Groton and Harvard (AB 1913, MEE 1914); electrical engr, 2nd Lt Aviation Section Signal Corps and 1st Lt ASORC World War I; m 17 June 1912 Margaret (b Boston 29 May 1892; d 19—), dau of Prof Maurice Howe Richardson, MD, and his w Margaret White Peirson, and d 25 Sept 1941, leaving issue:

> Great-nephews and -niece
> (1) *Henry Parish ROOSEVELT, b Dawson City, Yukon, Canada, 11 April 1915
> (2) *Daniel Stewart ROOSEVELT, b Warren Co, New York, 26 July 1917
> (3) *Eleanor ROOSEVELT, b Schenectady, New York, 14 Nov 1919

IV Corinne Roosevelt, b New York 27 Sept 1861; Memb: Advsy Ctee to Presidents COOLIDGE and HOOVER and Exec Cncl Republican Nat Cttee, founded first Red Cross War Chapter Oct 1914, author: The Call of Brotherhood and Other Poems (1912), One Woman to Another, and Other Poems (1914), Service and Sacrifice, poems (1919), My Brother, Theodore Roosevelt (1921), The Poems of Corinne Roosevelt Robinson (1921) and Out of Nymph — poems (1930); m 29 April 1882 Douglas ROBINSON, of New York (b 3 Jan 1855; educ St Paul's and Ch Ch Oxford; d 12 Sept 1918), only s of Douglas Robinson (gs of George Robinson of Gask, Aberdeenshire, and his w Elizabeth Innes, herself sis of Sir John Innes, 9th Bart, see BURKE'S PEERAGE & BARONETAGE, Innes of Balvenie) and his w Frances (herself est dau of Col James Monroe, nephew of President MONROE), and d 17 Feb 1933, having had issue:

President Theodore Roosevelt's nephew and niece

1 Theodore Douglas ROBINSON, b 28 April 1883; m 1904 Helen Rebecca Roosevelt (for whom see above) and d April 1934, leaving issue

2 Corinne Douglas Robinson, b Orange, New Jersey, 2 July 1886; Memb Connecticut legislature; m Orange 4 Nov 1909 Joseph Wright ALSOP, of Woodford Farm, Avon, Conn. (b Middletown, Conn., 2 April 1876; d Charleston, S Carolina, 17 March 1953), s of Joseph Wright Alsop and his w Elizabeth Winthrop Beach, and d Avon 23 June 1971, leaving issue:

> Great-nephew and -niece
> (1) Joseph (Joe) Wright ALSOP, b 11 Oct 1910; educ Groton and Harvard; newspaper columnist, author: (with Adam Platt) I've Seen the Best of It (1990); m 1961, as her 2nd husb, *Susan Mary (author: To Marietta from Paris, 1945-1960 (1976)), dau of Peter Augustus Jay (sometime Sec US Legation, Paris, and US Embassy, Constantinople, and gggs of John Jay, 1st Ch Justice U Supreme Court etc (see above)) and widow of William Samuel (Bill) Patten, sometime Attaché US Embassies London and Paris, and d 28 Aug 1989
> (2) *Corinne Roosevelt Alsop [Mrs Percy Chubb II, Pottersville Rd, Chester, NJ 07930, USA], b 14 March 1912; m 28 May 1932 Percy CHUBB II (d 8 Oct 1982) and has issue:
>
> > Great-niece's children
> > 1a *Dr Hendon CHUBB [65 Johnson Rd, West Cornwall, CT 06796, USA], b New York 1 March 1933; educ St Paul's,

Yale and Adelphi U; served US Army 1954-56, exec Chubb & Son Inc and Chubb Corp 1957-74, psychologist Kings County Hosp, Brooklyn, New York, 1978-80 and in California 1980-87, Dir Brief Therapy Inst 1986- and psychologist in private practice 1988-; *m* 1st 1958 (divorce 1980) Nita Colgate and has issue:

Great-niece's grandchildren
1b *A. C. ('Amber') CHUBB, *b* 12 Dec 1960
2b *Oliver CHUBB, *b* 22 Sept 1965

Great-niece's children
1a (cont.) Dr Chubb *m* 2nd 12 June 1982 *Phyllis Lancaster, dau of William Boone Nauts and his w Helen Coley
2a *Percy CHUBB III [Carriage House, 431 Claremont Road, Bernardsville, NJ 07924, USA], *b* 1934; *m* 1956 *Sally G. Gilady and has issue:

Great-niece's grandchildren
1b *Percy L. CHUBB, *b* 1958
2b *Sarah C. CHUBB, *b* 1960
3b *Lucy Alsop CHUBB, *b* 1964

Great-niece's children
3a *Corinne Roosevelt Robinson Chubb [Mrs Warren Zimmerman, 96 Interpromontory Rd, Great Falls, VA 22066, USA], *b* New York 19 April 1937; *educ* Foxcroft Sch, Smith and Barnard Coll; artist; *m* 18 April 1959 *Warren ZIMMERMAN (*b* Philadelphia 16 Nov 1934; *educ* Yale (BA 1956) and Cambridge, UK (MA 1958); journalist, joined State Dept 1961, US Consul and political offr Caracas, Venezuela, 1962-64, political offr Belgrade 1968-70, Special Assist to US Sec of State 1973, Dep Counsellor Public Affrs US Embassy Moscow 1975-77, Counsellor Political Affrs US Embassy Paris 1980-81, Dep Ch Mission US Embassy Moscow 1984-85, Dep to Head US Delegn Nuclear and Space Arms Negotiations with personal rank of Ambassador Geneva, Switzerland, 1986-88, US Ambassador to Yugoslavia 1990-), s of Albert Walter Zimmerman and his w Barbara Shoemaker, and has issue:

Great-niece's grandchildren
1b *Corinne Alsop ZIMMERMAN, *b* Washington, DC, 18 May 1960
2b *Warren ZIMMERMAN, Jr, *b* Washington 26 Dec 1961
3b *Elizabeth Beach Zimmerman, *b* 13 April 1963; *m* London, UK, Sept 1989 *Charles METCALFE
4a *Joseph A. CHUBB [110 Riverside Drive, New York, NY 10023, USA], *b* 1940
5a *James P. CHUBB [PO Box 2312, Haley, ID 83333, USA], *b* 1946; *m* 19— *———— ———— and has two children
6a *Caldecot CHUBB [1542 North Courtney Dve, Los Angeles, CA 90046, USA], *b* 1951; *m* 19— *———— ———— and has two children

Great-nephew
(3) Stew(art) Johonnot Oliver ALSOP, *b* 17 May 1914; *educ* Groton and Harvard; political columnist, author: *The Centre and Stay of Exection* (1973), Lt KRRC (British Army) World War II; *m* 20 June 1944 *Patricia (Tish) Barnard (*b* 17 March 1926) [Mrs Stewart Alsop, 3520 Springland Lane NW, Washington 8 DC 20008, USA], only dau of Arthur Barnard Hankey (maternally gs of Revd Sir Edward Graham Moon, 2nd Bart, *see* BURKE'S PEERAGE & BARONETAGE) and his w Cecilia Mosley, and *d* Washington, DC, 26 May 1974, having had issue (with five other children):

Great-niece
1a *Elizabeth Alsop, *b* 19—; author; *m* 19— *Peter MAHONY, architect

Great-nephew
(4) *John de Koven ALSOP [95 Woodland Street, Hartford, CT 06101, USA], *b* Avon, Conn., 4 Aug 1915; *educ* Groton and Yale; Pres Covenant Gp, Republican Nat Commiteeman, Capt with OSS in occupied France and occupied China World War II; *m* Hartford 19 June 1947 *Augusta (Gussie) (*b* Hartford 24 Dec 1924), dau of Lucius Robinson, of Hartford, and his w Augusta McLane, and has issue:

Great-nephew's children
1a *Mary Oliver ALSOP, *b* Hartford 2 April 1948
2a *Augusta McLane ALSOP [18 Lancaster Street, Cambridge, MA 02140, USA], *b* Hartford 22 Aug 1950
3a *John de Koven ALSOP, Jr [c/o Postmaster, Palermo, ME, USA], *b* Hartford 20 Nov 1951

President Theodore Roosevelt's nephew
3 Monroe Douglas ROBINSON, *b* 19 Dec 1887; Capt US Army World War I; *m* 1915 (divorce 19—) Dorothy Jordan, of Boston, and *d* 7 Dec 1947, leaving issue:

Great-niece
1a *Dorothy ROBINSON, *b* 19—

President Theodore Roosevelt's nephew
4 Stewart Douglas ROBINSON, *b* 19 March 1889; *educ* Harvard; *d* there 22 Feb 1909

Father's side

Nicholas Roosevelt[1]
c 1658-1742

Heyltje Jans Kunst[2]
d in/*p* 1730/1

    { Johannes Roosevelt
    c 1689-1750

Olfert Sioerts
c 1661-*c* 1710

Margaret Clopper
c 1660-in/*a* 1703

    { Heyltje Sioerts
    c 1688—1751-52

Claes Bogart
c 1668-1727

Belitje Van Schaick
c 1672-1707

    { Jan Bogert
    1697-1775

Johannes Peeck
b c 1653

Elizabeth Van Imbroch
b c 1659

    { Annetje Peeck
    1696-1769

Emanuel Van Schaack
c 1680-1706

Maria Wyngaart
b c 1685

    { Cornelius Van Schaack
    1705-76

Hendrick Van Dyck
c 1665-1707

Maria Schuyler
1666-1742

    { Lydia Van Dyck
    1704-85

Christopher Yates
1684-1754

Catherine Winne
b c 1691

    { Johannes (John) Yates
    1716—75-76

Pieter Waldron
c 1675-1725

Tryntje Cornelis Van
Den Bergh
c 1684-1753

    { Rebecca Waldron
    b c 1719

    { Robert Barnhill

    { Sarah —

    { Daniel Craig
    fl c 1776

    { Margaret —
    d p 1776

David Potts
c 1670-1730

Alice Croasdale
1673-in/*a* 1730

    { John Potts
    1696-*p* 1766

Edmond McVeagh
d c 1739

Alice Dickinson
d in/*p* 1727

    { Elizabeth McVeagh
    c 1699-1791

Johann Lucken
c 1655—1741-44

Merken Gastes

    { William Lukens
    1688/9-1739/40

Rynear/Reiner
Tyson/Theissen
c 1659-1745

Margaret (?Streypers)
d in/*a* 1745

    { Elizabeth Tyson
    1690-*c* 1765

Mother's side

William/James Balloch
fl c 1687-90

Jean Reid/?Margaret
Leckie

    { James Bulloch
    c 1701-80

Revd Archibald Stobo
d in/*p* 1736/7

Elizabeth Park
d in/*p* 1747

    { Jean Stobo
    b c 1710

Andre De Veaux
d in/*p* 1754

— —

    { James De Veaux
    c 1710-85

Richard Fairchild
d 1721

Ann Bellinger
d in/*p* 1721/2

    { Anne Fairchild
    d 1765

Robert Irvine of Cults
c 1639-*c* 1728

Margaret Coutts
c 1665-*c* 1710

    { Charles Irvine
    c 1696-1779

John Douglas

Agnes Horn

    { Euphemia Douglas
    c 1711-66

John Baillie of Balrobert
d c 1747

Jean Baillie

    { Kenneth Baillie
    d 1766

    { Elizabeth Mackay

    { John Stewart

    { Hannah —
    d c 1780

[1] & [2] For generations
further back *see* Male
Line Ancestry section

THEODORE ROOSEVELT FAMILY TREE

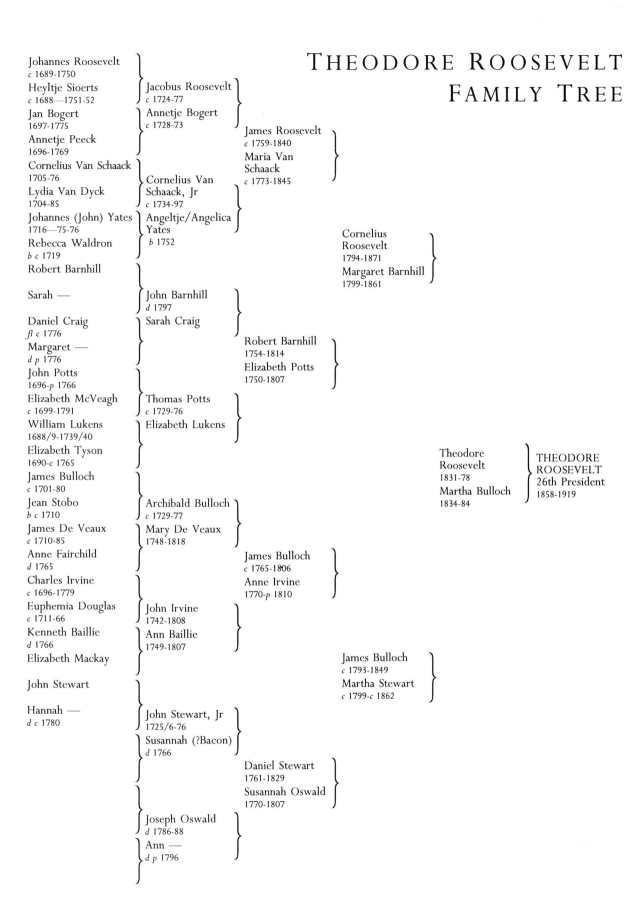

Johannes Roosevelt
c 1689-1750

Heyltje Sioerts
c 1688—1751-52

Jan Bogert
1697-1775

Annetje Peeck
1696-1769

Cornelius Van Schaack
1705-76

Lydia Van Dyck
1704-85

Johannes (John) Yates
1716—75-76

Rebecca Waldron
b c 1719

Robert Barnhill

Sarah —

Daniel Craig
fl c 1776

Margaret —
d p 1776

John Potts
1696-*p* 1766

Elizabeth McVeagh
c 1699-1791

William Lukens
1688/9-1739/40

Elizabeth Tyson
1690-*c* 1765

James Bulloch
c 1701-80

Jean Stobo
b c 1710

James De Veaux
c 1710-85

Anne Fairchild
d 1765

Charles Irvine
c 1696-1779

Euphemia Douglas
c 1711-66

Kenneth Baillie
d 1766

Elizabeth Mackay

John Stewart

Hannah —
d c 1780

Jacobus Roosevelt
c 1724-77

Annetje Bogert
c 1728-73

Cornelius Van Schaack, Jr
c 1734-97

Angeltje/Angelica Yates
b 1752

John Barnhill
d 1797

Sarah Craig

Thomas Potts
c 1729-76

Elizabeth Lukens

Archibald Bulloch
c 1729-77

Mary De Veaux
1748-1818

John Irvine
1742-1808

Ann Baillie
1749-1807

John Stewart, Jr
1725/6-76

Susannah (?Bacon)
d 1766

Joseph Oswald
d 1786-88

Ann —
d p 1796

James Roosevelt
c 1759-1840

Maria Van Schaack
c 1773-1845

Robert Barnhill
1754-1814

Elizabeth Potts
1750-1807

James Bulloch
c 1765-1806

Anne Irvine
1770-*p* 1810

Daniel Stewart
1761-1829

Susannah Oswald
1770-1807

Cornelius Roosevelt
1794-1871

Margaret Barnhill
1799-1861

James Bulloch
c 1793-1849

Martha Stewart
c 1799-*c* 1862

Theodore Roosevelt
1831-78

Martha Bulloch
1834-84

THEODORE ROOSEVELT
26th President
1858-1919

Plate 83   William H. Taft

WILLIAM H. TAFT

1857-1930
27TH PRESIDENT OF THE UNITED STATES OF AMERICA
1909-13

Not since Andrew Jackson put Van Buren in the White House had an American President been able to name his successor as Roosevelt named Taft. In neither case was the experiment successful. But whereas Van Buren was the victim of an economic crisis which was entirely outside his control, Taft was the victim of nothing so much as his own temperament. Left to himself he would never have tried for the presidency; what he wanted was a place on the Supreme Court. Beset by an ambitious wife and an exuberant Roosevelt, what could a fat, lazy, amiable man do? He succumbed to their importunity and was miserable for years as a result.

Not many men come to such high office in such circumstances. Taft owed his predicament to the fact that he was an ideal second-in-command. He was one of a generation which rose with extraordinary rapidity (other members were Roosevelt, Bryan and Woodrow Wilson, all born within a year or two of each other). In Taft's case it was his outstanding legal talent which made him Solicitor-General of the United States at the age of 33, a Federal judge at 35 and Governor of the Philippines at 43. In the latter post he came to Theodore Roosevelt's attention. Before very long he was installed at Washington, officially as Secretary of War (in which post he could continue to look after the Filipinos, for whom he had developed a great affection), but really as Roosevelt's indispensable assistant in everything. The two men became close friends and probably the deepest sorrow that his presidency brought Taft was his breach with his former chief.

At first he could not quite believe in his elevation. "When I am addressed as Mr President," he wrote in a letter to Roosevelt, "I turn to see whether you are not at my elbow." When the truth came home to him it did so dismally. The Republican party was in process of splitting between a conservative and a progressive wing; even the Colonel might have been unable to ride the storm; it was certainly beyond Taft. He was neither a radical nor a reactionary. Perhaps he liked the easy life a little too much (his predecessor had preached 'the strenuous life' at every turn), but he lacked the art of weaving and conciliating, so essential to a man trying to manage politicians. He soon found that he had alienated almost everybody. Gloomily he accepted defeat and turned to golf and eating for comfort. He was even fatter than Grover Cleveland; his belly was large enough to be made a national monument; when he was unhappy it became even more swollen. He put on a lot of weight in the White House.

Taft liked the tidy administrative structure of the law; he liked legal problems through which a trained and logical mind could thread its way to an intellectually satisfying solution that was at the same time socially valuable. He was quite ready to govern the United States on such terms and did in fact initiate many useful new laws and a fair number of anti-monopoly prosecutions (more than Roosevelt had done in fact). But his way was not what the country wanted. "It is a very humdrum, uninteresting administration," he wrote, "and it does not attract the attention or enthusiasm of anybody." He was resigned to being a single-term President and looked forward to laying down his burden.

He was destroyed by the man who had made him. Roosevelt convinced himself that Taft had become a spineless reactionary who ought to be driven from office. He tried to take the Republican nomination away from him in 1912 and, when that failed, launched an independent candidacy as the nominee of the new Progressive Party. Taft, who thought that the Colonel was now no better than a dangerous demagogue, stuck grimly to the battle, and although he had the mortification of coming third in the race (which Woodrow Wilson won for the Democrats) at least he had spoiled Teddy's chances.

It is pleasant to add that they were reconciled, in show at least, some years later. It is even more pleasant to record that Taft eventually had his dearest wish and was appointed Chief Justice of the United States by President Harding. As such he was a huge success; he even showed a dextrous hand in managing Congress when he needed legislation. He revelled in his work and lost a lot of flesh. He outlived the exponent of the strenuous life and all his other great contemporaries, dying a happier man than any of them. He was buried in Arlington National Cemetery — the first President ever to be laid there, but not the last and not the first President to be buried in Washington. That was the lot of his successor.

WILLIAM H. TAFT'S FAMILY

Once while actually in office Taft underlined his position as a nominee-President (Teddy Roosevelt's nominee) by referring to his predecessor as 'the President'. His wife Nellie did her best to remind him that what he meant was 'the ex-President'. "I suppose I do, dear", was Taft's answer, "but he will always be President to me and I can never think of him as anything else." Taft might regard himself as a stopgap, but the office itself in his time remained prestigious enough to be awarded a raise in salary from $50,000 to $75,000.

Taft's longing for high judicial office was in the family tradition, for his grandfather Peter Rawson Taft was a county court judge in his native Vermont, while his father Alphonso became a judge in his adoptive city of Cincinnati. Alphonso had once said that the post of Chief Justice of the Supreme Court was greater than the presidency and no doubt the observation stuck in his son's mind. A still older Taft family tradition was serving in militias. Taft's great-grandfather Aaron Taft and his great-great-grandfather Peter Taft were both minute men who saw action at Bunker Hill, while Peter's father Joseph was a captain of militia before the Revolution. This seems to have been about the limit of the family's outdoor activities and among President Taft's own generation only his sister Fanny, a first-class shot, showed any aptitude such as Teddy Roosevelt would have admired.

President Taft's two sons formed the law firm of Taft & Taft and the younger one, Charles, followed his father in being elected as prosecuting attorney in Hamilton County, Ohio. In fact, of President Taft's two half-brothers and three full brothers who survived to adulthood, three were lawyers or trained as lawyers; of the next generation of Taft males the tally was three out of six; and of the generation after that four out of 10. It is a remarkable record, even granted that upper-class Americans tend to do a spell as lawyers or law students as readily as the English upper class used to serve briefly in a good regiment.

Despite family leanings toward the law and his own ultimate success in the profession, Taft twice refused an appointment as a justice of the Supreme Court during the winter of 1902-3. His wife Nellie's opposition was decisive, but his other relatives were against the move too, though it is unclear how much their opinions counted. Pressure to decline the offer also came from the more conservative among the Filipinos, who wanted Taft to stay on as their governor. (He had resolved the problem of the religious orders' estates in the Philippines, which had been threatened with confiscation, and his influence among conservatives there was great.) On this occasion the Taft family went so far as to hold a conclave over·what advice to give him. Those present included his mother Louisa (who accompanied him to the

Plate 84   Helen Herron Taft

Plate 85   Helen Taft Manning, Taft's daughter and
hostess in the White House

Vatican in 1902 when he negotiated the price for the religious orders' estates with the Pope and who foretold the torment the presidency would inflict on his placid temperament), his aunt Delia, his half-brother Charles Phelps Taft together with Charles's wife Anne, and his full brother Henry Waters Taft. The participants in this family council took themselves so seriously they concurred in Henry drafting a report.

Charles Phelps Taft owned the Cincinnati *Times* and gave his half-brother a start in life by commissioning him to write law reports for the paper when a recent graduate from law school. He also served in the House of Representatives and continued his earlier generosity toward his half-brother by offering to subsidize his government salary by $6,000 a year when William became Secretary for War in 1904. By 1906 this had risen to $8,000 and was to go even higher. Charles also promised to raise $50,000 for William's 1912 re-election campaign and in the event provided at least half that sum. He even dropped all other commitments for a year to get his half-brother elected President in the first place. In the year that was accomplished, 1908, he also entertained hopes of becoming Senator from Ohio himself.

The family does not seem to have bulked quite so large in Taft's life after he became President, though he wrote regularly to Charles and Aunt Delia. The latter showed great enthusiasm for her nephew's bill to regulate child labour and may just conceivably have influenced him in appointing a woman head of the Children's Bureau — the first female bureau chief in US history. In general, however, Taft was one of many Presidents who have stressed the loneliness of the office. Whether out of a sense of isolation or overeating or plain lethargy (though he took exercise regularly) he had a tendency to fall asleep in working hours (as Ronald Reagan did also, for instance when he met the Pope). Nellie called her husband 'the Sleeping Beauty' but often covered up for presidential narcolepsy. She was a cultivated as well as an active woman, particularly in music, and is chiefly responsible for planting the mass of cherry trees whose blossom makes Washington so attractive in spring.

She was ambitious for her husband, not always in purely career terms either: on taking over the White House she replaced the frock-coated white ushers with azure-liveried black attendants and flouted precedent by riding back to the White House with her husband after his Inauguration. The Tafts' accord was seldom ruffled, exceptions being a difference over Prohibition (she was against it, Taft in favour) and female suffrage (she was against this also, Taft in favour). She kept a cow on the White House lawn, as had President Andrew Johnson's daughter Martha Patterson. (Under Woodrow Wilson sheep grazed there, but that was during World War I, when boosting production of food or clothing material, by whatever means, was patriotic.)

Like several other First Ladies she could be ruthless in settling old social scores. She got the US minister to France sacked in 1909 because he had once failed to invite her and her husband to a function attended by royalty and she refused to have President Benjamin Harrison's daughter Mrs McKee to the White House because of a past snub. Alice Roosevelt Longworth took umbrage at having to get a pass to enter the White House for the Inaugural luncheon on her father's leaving office and took it out on Mrs Taft, ridiculing her and mimicking her. In revenge Nellie Taft scotched any chance of Nicholas Longworth's becoming US Minister to China. Nellie's memory was capable of recollecting more than just insults, whether intentional or inadvertent. She could recall the White House in President Hayes's time, for as the daughter of his old friend and sometime law partner Judge John W. Herron she had first entered it at the age of 17. Unlike Hayes's wife Lucy she was partial to the odd glass of beer; she also smoked, a habit thought rather daring in women before World War I. With her liveliness and intellectual tastes, it must have seemed to her that a glorious prospect beckoned when her husband became President, but two months after his Inauguration she was felled by a stroke (only for about a year, fortunately, though the recovery was never quite complete). Meanwhile the Tafts' daughter Helen temporarily took over as hostess.

Plate 86   Senator Robert Taft, President Taft's eldest son, with family: l-r (with relationship to Senator) top row: John (grandson), the Senator, Martha Bowers Taft (wife), middle row: Blanca Noel Taft (daughter-in-law), Horace Taft (son), Barbara Bradfield Taft (daughter-in-law), Lloyd Taft (son), Virginia Stone Taft (daughter-in-law) holding her daughter Virginia, William H. Taft II (son, later William Taft III), bottom row: Martha Taft (granddaughter), William H. Taft IV (grandson), Deborah Taft (granddaughter), Robert Taft III (grandson), Maria Taft (granddaughter), Sarah Taft (granddaughter) and Louise Taft (granddaughter), early 1950s

Taft's elder son Robert was the Republican Party's favourite contender for the presidential nomination in 1952, being known as 'Mr Republican'. On the very eve of the GOP convention that year it was calculated he had over 100 more delegates than Eisenhower. He was actually less right-wing than his rival where domestic policies were concerned, but his dour, charmless manner obscured this. Nevertheless Margaret Truman, Harry Truman's daughter, reckoned him one of the shrewdest manoeuverers in the Senate; certainly he had great influence there, masterminding the cancellation of Lend-Lease immediately after World War II and getting the anti-labour Taft-Hartley Act passed over Truman's initial veto. Robert Taft's strength in the Republican party came from control of the party machine rather than widespread popular support. Like his father in 1912 he relied on having sewn up 'rotten borough' Republican clubs in areas such as the Deep South, where the party's strength amounted to little more than a handful of persons isolated from the population at large and where convention delegates were selected by party bosses. It was this sort of thing that led pro-Eisenhower Republicans in 1952 to wave banners saying "Graft with Taft" or "Rob with Bob".

It was Robert Taft who coined the celebrated description of Richard Nixon as "a little man in a big hurry". He wasn't the last man to write off Nixon prematurely. And it was Nixon who in the next decade transformed Republicanism in such places as the Deep South into something more genuinely representative. Arguably Robert Taft did his party his greatest service by showing once and for all how important it was to gauge a candidate's appeal through primaries. Robert Taft acted as a mediator between President Eisenhower and Congress over the Chip Bohlen affair, when Congressional hostility to Bohlen's appointment as Ambassador to Moscow had to be defused. His opposition to Eisenhower's first budget, when the deficit was slashed to $2.5bn, consisted of pounding the table, but this precursor of Khrushchev's outburst at the UN — boorish behaviour less forgiveable in a Taft than a Ukrainian peasant — achieved nothing.

Robert Taft's brother Charles, who was on the progressive wing of the Republican party, was the author of *You and I — and Roosevelt* (1936), a book which so impressed Alf Landon, the Republican candidate in the 1936 presidential campaign, that he appointed Charles one of his leading advisers. But Charles's progressive views made him acceptable also to FDR, who in 1941 appointed him to the President's Committee on War Relief Agencies. He also served as assistant director of the health and welfare section of the Federal Security Agency, a body whose responsibilities included curbing venereal disease among the troops, as a special adviser to the State Department and as adviser to the US delegation to the San Francisco conference which set up the United Nations. He supported Truman's tariff policy in 1945 whereas his brother was against it. Charles's education was at the Taft School in Watertown, Mass., which his uncle Horace had founded. In *This Side of Paradise* F. Scott Fitzgerald remarked of the Taft School that, along with Hotchkiss, it "prepared the wealth of the Middle West for social success at Yale".

BIOGRAPHICAL DETAILS AND DESCENDANTS

TAFT, WILLIAM HOWARD, *b* Cincinnati, Ohio, 15 Sept 1857; *educ* Woodward High Sch, Cincinnati, Yale (BA 1878) and Cincinnati Coll Law Sch (LLB 1880); admitted to Ohio Bar 1880, Assist Prosecutor Hamilton Co, Ohio, 1881, Collector Internal Revenue for 1st Dist of Ohio 1882-83, Assist County Slr Hamilton Co 1885, Judge Ohio Superior Court 1887-90, US Solicitor-Gen 1890 (helped draft Sherman Anti-Trust Act), US Fedl Circuit Court Judge 1892-1900, Dean Cincinnati Law Sch and Professor Law and Real Property 1896-1900, Chm then Pres Philippines Commn 1900-01, Govr-Gen Philippines 1901, US Sec of War 1904-08, Provisional Govr Cuba 1907, 27th President (R) of the USA 1909-13, Kent Prof of Law, Yale, 1913-21, Pres ABA 1913, Ch Justice US Supreme Court 1921-30; author: *Four Aspects of Civic Duty* (1906), *Present Day Problems, Addresses* (1908), *Political Issues and Outlooks* (1909) *Popular Government: Its Essence, its Permanence and its Perils* (1913), *Anti-Trust Act and the Supreme Court* (1914), *Ethics in Service* (1915), *Our Chief Magistrate and His Powers* (1915) and *Liberty Under Law* (1922); *m* Cincinnati 19 June 1886 Helen (Nellie) (*b* Cincinnati 2 June 1861; *educ* Miss Nourse's Sch Cincinnati and Miami U; author: *Recollections of Full Years* (1914); *d* Washington, DC, 22 May 1943, *bur* Arlington National Cemetery beside her husband), 3rd dau of Judge John Williamson Herron, of Cincinnati, and his w Harriet Anne Collins, and *d* Washington, DC, 8 March 1930, leaving issue:

President Taft's son

I Robert Alphonso TAFT, *b* Cincinnati 8 Sept 1889; *educ* Cincinnati and Manila (Philippines) public schs, Taft Sch, Watertown, Conn., Yale (BA 1910, MA 1936), and Harvard Law Sch (LLB 1913); lawyer with Maxwell & Ramsey, attys, Cincinnati 1913-17, Assist Counsel Food Admin World War I 1917-18, Counsel American Relief Admin Europe 1918-19, Memb Ohio House of Reps 1921-26 (Republican Floor Leader and Speaker), with law firm of Taft, Stettinius & Hollister 1920-38, Memb Ohio Senate 1931-33, US Senator from Ohio 1939-53 (Republican Floor Leader 1953), contender for Republican presidential nomination 1952, author: *A Foreign Policy for Americans* (1951); *m* Washington, DC, 17 Oct 1914 Martha Wheaton (*b* Winona, Minn., 17 Dec 1889; *d* Cincinnati 2 Oct 1958), dau of Lloyd Wheaton Bowers, US Slr-Gen, and his w Louise Bennett Wilson, and *d* New York 31 July 1953, leaving issue:

Grandchildren

1 William Howard TAFT III, *b* Bar Harbor, Maine, 7 Aug 1915; *educ* The Taft Sch, Yale (AB 1937) and Princeton (PhD 1942); instructor in English U of Maryland 1940-41, Haverford Coll 1941-42 and Yale 1945-48, civilian memb special branch US Army Intell 1942-45, Special Assist to Ch of Mission, Economics Cooperation Assoc in Ireland 1948-51, worked with CIA 1952-53, US Amb to Ireland 1953-57, Memb Dept of Policy Planning Staff 1957-60, Consul-Gen Lourenço Marques, Mozambique, 1960-62, apptd to Dept of State 1962, Office of Internat Scientific Affairs 1963, Pres Cleveland Park Citizens Assoc and Friends of Cleveland Park Library, Tstee Washington Internat Sch, Hon LLD Dublin (1959); *m* Grand Rapids, Mich., 27 June 1942 *Barbara Holt, PhD, MA [3101 35th Street NW, Washington, DC 20016, USA] (*b*

Grand Rapids 1917), dau of Thomas Bradfield and his w Irene Holt, and d Washington, DC, 23 Feb 1991 of prostate cancer, leaving issue:

Great-grandchildren

(1) *Maria Herron Taft [Mrs John Clemow, Eudarbieu, Touget, 32430 Cologue, France], b Washington, DC, 1943; m Paris, France, 1 Dec 1971 *John CLEMOW (b London, UK, 17 March 1921), s of Albert Clemow and his w Helen Edwards, and has issue:

Great-great-grandchildren
1a *Kieran TAFT, b 19—

Great-grandchildren

(2) *William Howard TAFT IV [3245 Cleveland Avenue NW, Washington, DC 20008, USA], b Washington, DC, 13 Sept 1945; educ St Paul's, Yale (BA 1966) and Harvard (JD 1969); admitted to DC Bar 1969, assoc Winthrop, Stimson, Putnam & Roberts, New York City, 1969-70, atty-adviser to Chm Fedl Trade Cmmn 1970, Pncpl Assist to Dep Dir Office of Management & Budget, Washington, DC, 1970-72 (Exec Assist to Dir 1972-73), Exec Assist to Sec Health, Education & Welfare, Washington, DC, 1973-76 (Gen Counsel 1976-77, Distinguished Service Award 1977), ptnr Leva, Hawes, Symington, Martin & Oppenheimer, attys, 1977-81, Gen Counsel Pentagon 1981-84, US Dep-Sec of Defense 1984-89, US Amb to NATO to 1992; m Washington, DC, 4 May 1974 *Julia (b New York 1942), dau of Antony Vadala and his w Shirley, and has issue:

Great-great-grandchildren
1a *Maria Consetta TAFT, b 19—
2a *William Howard TAFT V, b 19—
3a *Julia Harris TAFT, b 19—

Great-grandchildren

(3) *Martha Bowers Taft [Mrs Michael Golden, Rowly Barn, Rowly Drive, Cranleigh, Surrey GU6 8PL, UK], b New Haven, Conn., 25 Dec 1946; educ Bryn Mawr (BA 1969) and St Andrews U, Scotland, UK (MSc 1972); petroleum geologist with Pan Ocean Oil 1975-79, lecturer U of Calabar, Nigeria, 1975-79, tutor Open U, UK, 1980-; m St Andrews, Scotland, 21 Sept 1971 *Michael GOLDEN (b Greenock, Scotland, 1946), s of Michael Golden and his w Margaret Stephenson, and has four adopted sons:

a *Ian Taft GOLDEN, b Kingston-upon-Thames, UK, 5 March 1979
b *Scott Taft GOLDEN, b Kingston-upon-Thames 13 Feb 1980
c *Lawrence Taft GOLDEN, b London 12 Aug 1982
d *Gareth Taft GOLDEN, b London 3 Dec 1984

Great-grandchildren

(4) *John Thomas TAFT [1526 34th St NW, Washington, DC 20007, USA], b Dublin, Ireland, 7 July 1950; educ St Paul's, Yale (AB 1972) and Univ Coll, Oxford (BA 1974, MA 1979); stringer/writer for New Republic, Washington ed Harper's magazine, Pres Taft Assocs TV Production, of Washington, DC, Memb Editorial Bd Journal of Popular Film & Television, author: Mayday at Yale: A Case Study in Student Radicalism (1976) and American Power: The Rise and Decline of U.S. Globalism (1989); m Washington, DC, 26 June 1990 *Christine, dau of Edmond Loftin Rinehart and his w Barbara Young Lutz, and has issue:

Great-great-grandchildren
1a *Stephen Alexander Rinehart TAFT, b Washington, DC, 11 Dec 1990

Grandchildren

2 *Robert TAFT, Jr [4300 Drake Road, Cincinnati, OH 45243, USA; 2541 Waterside Drive NW, Washington, DC, USA], b Cincinnati 26 Feb 1917; US Naval Reserve 1942-46, Memb Ohio Bar, ptnr Taft, Stettinius & Hollister, attys, Cincinnati 1946-67, Memb Ohio House of Reps 1955-62 (Majority Floor Leader 1961-62), Memb 88th Congress at-large from Ohio, Memb 90th and 91st Congresses from 1st Dist of Ohio, US Senator from Ohio from 1971; m 1st 27 June 1939 Blanca Duncan (d Cincinnati 28 June 1968), dau of Louis W. Noel, of New York, and has issue:

Great-grandchildren

(1) *Robert Alphonso TAFT II [4373 Shire Creek Court, Hilliard, OH 43026, USA], b 1942; educ Yale; served with Peace Corps in Africa, Memb Ohio Bar and Ohio House of Reps 1976-80, Hamilton County Commissioner 1981-90, Sec of State of Ohio 1991-; m 17 June 1967 *Janet Hope, dau of Matthew H. Rothert, of Camden, Ark., and has one child

(2) *Sarah Butler Taft [Mrs Winfield Jones II, 1 East End Avenue, New York, NY, USA], b 1943; educ Radcliffe; m 1963 *Winfield Payne JONES II and has issue:

Great-great-grandchildren
1a *Eloise Dickey JONES, b 29 March 1967
2a *Natalie Duncan JONES, b 22 April 1969

Great-grandchildren

(3) *Deborah Taft, b 1946; m 19— *—— BOUTELIS, of France, and has issue
(4) *Jonathan Duncan TAFT, b 1954; m 19— *——

Grandchildren
2 (cont.) Senator Robert Taft *m* 2nd Indian Hill, Ohio, July 1969 *Katherine (*b* 1921), widow of John H. Perry and dau of —— Whitaker; *m* 3rd 1978 Joan M. Warner
3 Lloyd Bowers TAFT, *b* Cincinnati 1 Jan 1923; *educ* Yale (BA 1944); investment banker; *m* 28 June 1947 Virginia Ann Stone (*b* 1925; *d* 6 April 1982) and *d* 25 Oct 1985, leaving issue:

Great-grandchildren
(1) *(Ann) Louise Taft [Mrs Carleton P Cooke, 6797 Knollwood Rd, Fayetteville, NY 13066, USA], *b* 1949; *educ* Mount Holyoke; *m* 19 Dec 1970 *Carleton Perry COOKE III, s of Carleton Perry Cooke, Jr, of Buffalo
(2) *Virginia Stone Taft [Mrs Keith Carabine, 8 Ethelbert Rd, Canterbury, Kent CT1 3NE, UK], *b* 1950; *educ* Concord Acad, Radcliffe Coll, and U of Kent, Canterbury, UK (MA 1973); *m* 14 Sept 1974 *Keith CARABINE, s of George J. Carabine, of Manchester, UK, and has issue:

Great-great-grandchildren
1a *Edward S. CARABINE, *b* 28 Sept 1978
2a *Anna J. CARABINE, *b* 20 Nov 1980

Great-grandchildren
(3) *Lloyd Bowers TAFT, Jr [36 White, New York, NY, USA], *b* Cincinnati 29 Dec 1954; *educ* The Taft Sch, Hampshire Coll and Yale Sch of Architecture (March 1982); *m* 9 Dec 1978 *Mimi, dau of Paul Shanley and his w Isobel, and has issue:

Great-great-grandchildren
1a *Daniel Culley TAFT, *b* New York 30 Aug 1984
2a *Virginia Isobel TAFT, *b* New York 7 May 1986
3a *Bennet Stone TAFT, *b* New York 1988

Great-grandchildren
(4) *Julia Wilson Taft [Mrs Jeffrey R Jonathan, North Country School, Lake Placid, NY 12946, USA], *b* Cincinnati 13 May 1958; *educ* Taft Sch and Yale; teacher 1980-; *m* 1st 28 June 1980 John Alexander MACMULLEN; *m* 2nd 31 Oct 1985 *Jeffrey Robert JONATHAN, s of William R. Jonathan and his w Nancy Reppert, and has issue:

Great-great-grandchildren
1a *Elizabeth Taft JONATHAN, *b* 1 Aug 1991

Grandchildren
4 Horace Dwight TAFT, *b* Cincinnati 2 April 1925; *educ* Yale (BA 1950) and U of Chicago (MS 1953, PhD 1955); with US Army 1943-46, Prof Physics Yale from 1964, Master Davenport Coll 1966-71 (Dean from 1971), Tstee Taft Sch from 1966; *m* 9 Sept 1952 *Mary Jane, dau of Sherwin C. Badger and his w Mary Bancroft, and *d* 19——, leaving issue:

Great-grandchildren
(1) *John Godfrey TAFT [58½ Atwater, New Haven, CT 06511, USA], *b* 1954
(2) *Hugh Bancroft TAFT [7415 Birch Ave, Takoma Park, MD 20912, USA], *b* 1957
(3) *Horace Dutton TAFT, *b* 1962

President Taft's daughter
II Helen Herron Taft, *b* Cincinnati 1 Aug 1891; *educ* Bryn Mawr (BA 1915) and Yale (MA 1917, PhD 1924); Dean Bryn Mawr 1917-19 and 1925-41 and Actg Pres 1919-20; *m* Murray Bay, Canada, 15 July 1920 Frederick Johnson MANNING (*b* East Braintree, Mass., 1894; Prof History Swarthmore; *d* island of Nevis, West Indies, 7 Dec 1968) and *d* 21 Feb 1987, leaving issue:

Grandchildren
1 *Helen Taft Manning [Mrs Holland Hunter, 611 Spruce Lane, Villanova, PA 19085-1807, USA], *b* New Haven, Conn., 5 Oct 1921; *educ* Smith (AB 1943) and Harvard (PhD 1952); taught Bryn Mawr, Prof Emeritus, ret 1990; *m* 31 Jan 1946 *Holland HUNTER (*b* Evanston, Ill., 6 July 1921; PhD, Prof Economics Haverford Coll), s of Harry Holland Hunter and his w Hester Walrath, and has issue:

Great-grandchildren
(1) *Ann Herron HUNTER, *b* Cambridge, Mass., 16 Dec 1947
(2) *Barbara Walrath Hunter, *b* Bryn Mawr, Pa., 1 Aug 1949; *educ* Swarthmore; MD; *m* 14 July 1970 *John William CHAFFEE
(3) *Christine Manning Hunter, *b* 12 Aug 1952; *m* March 1974 *Louis VENECH
(4) *Timothy White HUNTER, *b* 14 Sept 1955; *m* July 1986 *Annie Schuster

Grandchildren
2 *Caroline Manning, *b* 1925; *m* 1947 *Frederic CUNNINGHAM, Jr (*b* Cooperstown, New York, 6 Sept 1921; PhD, Prof Mathematics Bryn Mawr), s of Frederic Cunningham and his w Mary Wardwell, and has issue:

Great-grandchildren
(1) *Sarah Evelyn CUNNINGHAM, *b* 1951
(2) *Mary Blair CUNNINGHAM, *b* 1954
(3) *Constance Lucy CUNNINGHAM, *b* 1960

President Taft's son

III Charles Phelps TAFT II, *b* Cincinnati 20 Sept 1897; *educ* The Taft Sch, Yale (BA 1918, LLB 1921) and Toledo U (LLD 1934); served 12th Field Arty 2nd Div American Expedy Force World War I (1st Lt 1919), Prosecuting Atty Hamilton Co, Ohio, 1927-28, ptnr: Taft, Stettinius & Hollister 1924-37, Headley, Sibbald & Taft 1946-59, Taft & Lavercombe 1959-66, Taft & Luken 1967, Chm Fedl Steel Mediation Bd 1937, Cincinnati City Cnclman (Majority Leader) 1938-42, 1948-51 and 1955-57, Dir: Community War Servs Fedl Security Agy 1941-43, State Dept Wartime Ec Affrs 1944 and State Dept Transport & Communications Policy 1945, Memb President's War Relief Control Bd 1941-46, Mayor Cincinnati 1955-57, Tstee: Twentieth Century Fund, Carnegie Inst of Washington, Ctee for Ec Devpt, Chm Info Dept WCC, Pres Fedl Cncl of Churches of Christ in America 1947-48, Medal for Merit 1946, Hon LLD: Rochester U, New York, Miami U, Ohio, Wesleyan U and Yale (1952), DCL Union Coll and DHL Hebrew Union Coll, author: *City Management: The Cincinnati Experience* (1933), *You and I — and Roosevelt* (1936), *Why I Am for the Church* (1947) and *Democracy in Politics and Economics* (1950); *m* Waterbury, Conn., 6 Oct 1917 Eleanor Kellogg (*b* Waterbury 9 Oct 1891; *d* Cincinnati 28 Aug 1961), 2nd dau of Irving Hall Chase, of Rose Hill, and his w Elizabeth Hosmer, dau of Gen Stephen Wright Kellogg, and *d* 24 June 1983, having had issue:

Grandchildren

1 *Eleanor Kellogg Taft [Mrs Donald Hall, 3655 Hunts Point Road, Bellevue, Seattle, WA 98004, USA], *b* Waterbury 16 Sept 1918; *m* Cincinnati 1941 *Dr Donald Thornton HALL (*b* 1910), s of Dr David C. Hall and his w Katherine, and has issue:

Great-grandchildren

(1) *Rosalyn Taft Hall [Mrs Ronald Barbieri, 177 Bolivar Lane, Portola Valley, CA 94025, USA], *b* 1943; *m* 1969 *Ronald BARBIERI

(2) *David C. HALL III [1111 E Columbia, Seattle, WA 98122, USA], *b* 1946; *m* 1970 *Anne Strathin and has one child

(3) *Katharine M. Hall [Mrs Mann, Pepper Pike, OH, USA], *b* 1948; *m* *Dr Leon MANN and has two children

(4) *Deborah HALL [3655 Hunts Point Road, Bellevue, Seattle, WA 98004, USA], *b* 1951

Grandchildren

2 *Sylvia Howard Taft [Mrs William Lotspeich, 514 Wellesly Road, Philadelphia, PA 19119, USA], *b* Narragansett Pier, Rhode Island, New York, 7 Aug 1920; *m* Cincinnati 13 June 1942 Dr William Douglas LOTSPEICH (*b* Cincinnati 30 May 1920; *d* 1968), s of Claude Lotspeich and his w Helen, and has issue:

Great-grandchildren

(1) *Sylvia F. LOTSPEICH [3311 Baring Street, Philadelphia, PA 19104, USA], *b* 1943

(2) *Charles Taft LOTSPEICH [Holyoke, MA, USA], *b* 1947; *m* 1st 1965 (divorce 19—) Laurie McDonald and has issue:

Great-great-grandchildren

1a *Christopher LOTSPEICH, *b* 19—

2a *Matthew LOTSPEICH, *b* 19—

Great-grandchildren

(2) (cont.) Charles T. Lotspeich *m* 2nd 19— *Phyllis Woolf

(3) *Steven LOTSPEICH, *b* 1952; *m* 19—

Grandchildren

3 *Seth Chase TAFT [6 Pepper Ridge Road, Cleveland, OH 44124, USA], *b* Cincinnati 31 Dec 1922; *educ* The Taft Sch, Yale (AB 1943) and Yale Law Sch (LLB 1948); Jr Lt US Navy, ptnr business law firm of Jones, Day, Reavis & Pogue, Cleveland, 1959-88, Commr Cuyahoga Co, Ohio, 1971-78, Republican gubernatorial candidate Ohio 1982; *m* New Haven, Conn., 19 June 1943 *Frances Bradley (*b* New Haven, Conn., 12 Dec 1921), dau of William E. Prindle, of New Haven, and has issue:

Great-grandchildren

(1) *Frederick Irving TAFT [2989 Washington Boulevard, Cleveland, OH 44118, USA], *b* New Haven 26 June 1945; *educ* Yale; *m* Cleveland 28 July 1973 *Susan Scott (*b* Cleveland 3 April 1945), dau of Kenneth Hoefflinger and his w June Reynolds and has two children

(2) *Thomas Prindle TAFT [1211 Meeting House Rd, Ambler, PA 19002, USA], *b* Cleveland 19 July 1948; *m* 19— *——— and has four children

(3) *Cynthia Bradley Taft [15a Traymore St, Cambridge, MA 02148, USA], *b* Cleveland 24 May 1950; *m* 19— *——— and has two children

(4) *(Seth) Tucker TAFT [14 Moon Hill Rd, Lexington, MA 02173, USA], *b* Cleveland 4 March 1953; *educ* Harvard; Ch Computer Scientist Intermetrics Inc 1980-; *m* 27 June 1982 *Phyllis Robin, dau of William Yale and his w Elaine, and has issue:

Great-great-grandchildren

1a *Rebecca Yale TAFT, *b* Boston 10 Oct 1986

2a *Maia Yale TAFT, *b* Newton, Mass., 15 June 1990

Grandchildren

4 Lucia Chase Taft, *b* Waterbury 9 June 1924; *educ* Vassar; *d* Cincinnati 29 Oct 1955

5 *Cynthia Herron Taft [Northampton, MA, USA], *b* Cincinnati 28 April 1928; *educ* Yale (PhD 1959); professor at Smith;

m Cincinnati 18 Sept 1955 (divorce 19—) Dr Donald Richard MORRIS (*b* Schenectady, New York, 26 April 1930), s of Ernest A. Morris, of Schenectady, and has issue:

Great-grandchildren
(1) *David Taft MORRIS, *b* Beirut, Lebanon, 14 March 1961
Dr and Mrs Donald Morris also adopted a child:
a *Michele MORRIS, *b* Nov 1967

Grandchildren
6 Rosalyn Rawson TAFT, *b* Cincinnati 6 June 1930; *d* Narragansett Sept 1941 of poliomyelitis
7 *Peter Rawson TAFT [17058 Avenida De Santa Ynez, Pacific Palisades, CA 90272, USA], *b* Cincinnati 3 March 1936; *educ* The Taft Sch and Yale (AB 1958, LLB 1961); law clerk for US Ch Justice Earl Warren 1962-63, with Munger Tolles Hills & Rickershauser, attys

MALE LINE ANCESTRY AND COLLATERAL DESCENDANTS

Robert TAFT, Sr (sometimes referred to as TAFFE), *b c* 1640; left England *c* 1678 and settled Braintree, Mass., was later one of the original settlers of Mendon when it was partitioned from Braintree, Memb First Bd of Selectmen 1680; *m c* 1670? Sarah ——— (*b c* 1640; *d* Nov 1725) and *d* Mendon 8 Feb 1725, having had issue:

I Robert TAFT, Jr, *b c* 1674; *m c* 1694/5 Elizabeth Woodward and *d* Uxbridge, Mass., 1748, leaving issue:

1 Israel TAFT, *b* Mendon, Mass., 26 April 1698/9; *m* there 19 Dec 1717 Mercy (*b* there 21 June 1700), dau of Jacob Aldrich (*b* 1677) and his *w* Margery Hayward, and *d c* 1753, having had issue:

(1) Huldah Taft, *b* Mendon 28 June 1718; *m* Upton, Mass., 25 Jan 1737/8 David DANIEL (*b* Mendon 4 or 5 1710; *d* there 21 May 1776), s of Eleazer Daniel and his *w* Mary Holbrook (whose mother Mary, *née* Pierce, had a brother Ephraim Pierce who was an ancestor of President BUSH) and had issue:

1a Chloe Daniel, *b* Mendon 13 Sept 1745; *m* there 20 Nov 1764 Seth DAVENPORT (*b* Milton, Mass., 2 Nov 1739; *d* there 28 March 1813), s of Samuel Davenport, of Dorchester, Mass., and his *w* Rebecca Holbrook, and *d* Mendon 19 May 1823, having had issue:

1b Anna Davenport, *b* Mendon 8 Sept 1765; *m* 1st Mendon 20 July 1788 William TORREY (*b* there 23 Nov 1754; *d* there 16 Sept 1817), s of Joseph Torrey, also of Mendon, and his *w* Deborah Holbrook; *m* 2nd Peter HOLBROOK and *d* Mendon 1 Aug 1842, having with her 1st husb had issue:

1c Samuel Davenport TORREY, *b* Mendon 14 April 1789; *m* Millbury, Mass., 27 Jan 1824 Susan Holman (*b* April 1803; *d* Millbury 3 Feb 1866), dau of Asa Waters, of Sutton, Mass., and his *w* Susan Trask Holman, and *d* Millbury 23 Dec 1877, having with her had issue:

1d Louisa Maria Torrey, *b* Boston 11 Sept 1827; *m* 1853 Alphonso TAFT (for whom *see below*)

II Joseph TAFT
Robert Taft, Sr's yr s,
Joseph TAFT, *b c* 1680; Capt of Militia Uxbridge, Mass.; *m c* 1708 Elizabeth (*b* Ipswich, Mass., 6 March 1686/7; *d* Uxbridge 10 March 1760), dau of James Emerson (whose uncle Nathaniel Emerson was an ancestor of President FILLMORE) and his *w* Sarah, and *d* Uxbridge 18 July 1747, leaving issue:

Peter TAFT, *b c* 1715; minute man at Bunker Hill; *m* Medfield, Mass., 20 April 1736 Elizabeth (*b* Medfield 21 Sept 1707; *d* Uxbridge 21 Sept 1783), dau of Josiah Cheney and his *w* Hannah, and *d* Uxbridge 12 Dec 1783, having had issue:

Aaron TAFT, *b* Uxbridge 28 May 1743; also a minute man at Bunker Hill; *m* Uxbridge 1 June 1769 Rhoda (*b* Uxbridge 4 Oct 1749; *d* Townshend, Vt., 9 June 1827), dau of Abner Rawson (a descendant of Edward Rawson, who left England *c* 1632 and was Sec of Colony of Massachusetts Bay 1650-81) and his *w* Mary Allen, and *d* Townshend 26 March 1808, leaving issue:

Peter Rawsom TAFT, of Windham Co, Vt., *b* Uxbridge 14 Apr 1785; settled Cincinnati, Ohio, 1841, Judge Superior Court; *m* 5 Dec 1810 Sylvia (*b* Townshend 17 Feb 1792; *d* 1866), dau of Levi Howard and his *w* Bethiah Chapin, and *d* Cincinnati 1 Jan 1867, leaving issue:

Alphonso TAFT, of Cincinnati, *b* nr Townshend 5 Nov 1810; *educ* Yale (AB 1833); Judge Cincinnati Superior Court 1865-72, Republican gubernatorial candidate Ohio 1875 and 1879, US Sec of War March-May 1876, US Atty-Gen 1876-77, US Min to Austria-Hungary 1882-84 and to Russia 1884-85; *m* 1st 29 Aug 1841 Fanny (*b* Townshend 28 March 1823; *educ* Misses Edwards Sch, New Haven, Conn.; *d* Cincinnati 2 June 1852 of tuberculosis), dau of Judge Charles Phelps, of Vermont, and had issue:

I Charles Phelps TAFT, *b* Cincinnati 21 Dec 1843; *educ* Yale (BA 1864, MA 1867) and Heidelberg U (JUD 1868); Hon LLD Cincinnati U and Lincoln Memorial U (1922), ed and publisher *Cincinnati Times-Star* from 1879, Memb US House of Reps 1895-97, Pres Bd Sinking Fund Tstees; *m* 4 Dec 1873 Anne, only dau of David Stinton, iron manufacturer, of Cincinnati, and *d* 31 Dec 1929, having had issue:

President Taft's half-niece

1 Jane Ellison Taft, *b* 1874; *m* 1895 Albert Stimson INGALLS (*b* 1874; *d* 1943) and had issue:

Half-great-nephew

(1) David Stinton INGALLS, *b* Cleveland, Ohio, 28 Jan 1899; *educ* Yale (BA 1920) and Harvard (LLB 1923); served USN World War I and Capt USNR 1942, Cdre 1945 (DSM, Légion d'Honneur (France), DFC (UK)), admitted to Ohio Bar 1923, Assoc Squire, Sanders & Dempsey, Cleveland, 1923-29, Memb Ohio House of Reps 1927-29, Assist-Sec US Navy for Aeronautics 1929-32, Dir Public Health and Welfare, Cleveland, 1933-35, V-Pres and Gen Manager Pan-Am Air Ferries Inc 1941-42 (Memb Bd 1949), with Pan-Am World Airways System, New York City, 1945-49; *m* 1st 27 June 1922 Louise (*b* 1898; *d* May 1978), dau of —— Harkness, of New York, and had issue:

Half-great-nephew's children

1a *Edith Ingalls [Mrs Paul Vignos, Appletree Farm, River Road, Chagrin Falls, OH, USA], *b* 1923; *m* 1946 *Paul J. VIGNOS (*b* 1919) and has issue:

Half-great-nephew's grandchildren

1b *Caren VIGNOS, *b* 1947

2b *Kathleen VIGNOS, *b* 1949

3b *Paul VIGNOS [Box 303, Molina, GA 30258, USA], *b* 1951; *m* 19— *Avril —— and has (with other issue):

Half-great-nephew's great-grandchildren:

1c *Stinton VIGNOS, *b* 19—

2c *Livingston VIGNOS, *b* 19—

Half-great-nephew's children

2a *Jane Ingalls, *b* 1926; *m* 1948 *Endicott P. DAVISON and has issue:

Half-great-nephew's grandchildren

1b Frederick Trubie DAVISON, *b* 1950; *d* 1953

2b *Endicott P. DAVISON, Jr, *b* 1951

3b *Jane DAVISON, *b* 1954

4b *David I. DAVISON, *b* 1955

5b *Malcolm Peabody DAVISON, *b* 1957

Half-great-nephew's children

3a *Louise H. Ingalls [Mrs Willard Brown, Fairmount Road, Chagrin Falls, OH, USA; 9111 Baldwin Road, Mentor, OH, USA], *b* 1928; *m* 1948 *Willard W. BROWN (*b* 1915) and has issue:

Half-great-nephew's grandchildren

1b *Willard H. BROWN, Jr, *b* 1948

2b *David I. BROWN [43 Ledyard Rd, West Hartford, CT 06117, USA], *b* 1951

3b *Alice BROWN, *b* 1952

4b *Barbara BROWN [65 Waterside Lane, Clinton, CT 06413, USA], *b* 1954

Half-great-nephew's children

4a *Anne Ingalls [Mrs John Lawrence, 8100 Buckingham Rd, Cincinnati, OH 45243, USA], *b* 1931; *m* 19— *John T. LAWRENCE, Jr (*b* 1928), and has issue:

Half-great-nephew's grandchildren

1b *John T. LAWRENCE III, *b* 1951

2b *Robert T. LAWRENCE, *b* 1952

3b *James P. LAWRENCE, *b* 1954

4b Louise H. LAWRENCE, *b* 1956; *d* 197-

5b *Anne I. Lawrence [Mrs Peter Mackenzie, 203 Skunk Lane, Wilton, CT 06897, USA], *b* 1960; *m* 19— *Peter MACKENZIE

Half-great-nephew's children

5a David Stinton INGALLS, Jr [Oak Hill Farm, Chagrin Falls, OH, USA; 20600 Chagrin Blvd, Cleveland, OH], *b* 1934; *m* 1st 19— Cynthia Robinson (*b* 1935) and had (with other issue):

Half-great-nephew's grandchildren

1b *Rebekah W. INGALLS [61 West Cedar St, Boston, MA 02114, USA], *b* 1961

2b *Louise H. INGALLS, *b* 1962

Half-great-nephew's children

5a (cont.) David S. Ingalls, Jr, *m* 2nd 19— *—— and *d* April 1993

Half-great-nephews
(1) (cont.) David S. Ingalls *m* 2nd 16 Feb 1979 *Frances W. Wrace and *d* 26 April 1985
(2) *Albert Stimson INGALLS, Jr, *b* 1900; *m* 1928 *Eileen Brodie (*b* 1903) and *d* 1955, leaving issue:

Half-great-nephew's children
1a *Albert Stimson INGALLS III, *b* 1930
2a *Eve Taft Ingalls, *b* 1936; *m* 19— *Heinrich von STADEN
3a *John Taft INGALLS

Half-great-niece
(3) Anne Taft Ingalls, *b* 1908; *m* 1929 Lt-Col Rupert E. L. WARBURTON, MC (*b* 1899; *educ* Cheltenham; *d* 18 March 1982), and *d* 24 March 1976, leaving issue:

Half-great-niece's children
1a *Wanda Annette Warburton [Mrs Denys Rowan-Hamilton, Killyleagh Castle, Co Down, Northern Ireland, UK], *b* 1930; *m* 1st 1950 Maj Ronald St George MAXWELL (*b.* 1919; *educ* Winchester, Magdalene Coll, Cambridge, and RMC Sandhurst; Maj 1st Bn The Black Watch; *d* 1960) and has issue:

Half-great-niece's grandchildren
1b *David Lindsay MAXWELL, *b* 8 April 1951; *educ* Eton, Jesus Coll, Cambridge, and Westminster Hosp (MD, MRCP); doctor, silver medal rowing (eights): World Championship ˙1974 and Olympic Games Montreal 1976; has issue:

Half-great-niece's great-grandchildren:
1c *Imogen Anne MAXWELL, *b* 17 Oct 1989
2c *Iona Jane MAXWELL, *b* 31 March 1991

Half-great-niece's grandchildren
2b Charles Rupert H. MAXWELL, *b* 22 July 1952; *educ* Eton, Trinity Coll, Cambridge, and Institut Européen d'Administration des Affaires; Capt The Black Watch, banker, barrister; *m* 1989 *Alexandra Della Casa [Mrs Charles Maxwell, 25 Favart Rd, London SW6, UK] and was *k* in Iraq 30 March 1991 while on location there with the BBC, leaving issue:

Half-great-niece's great-grandchildren
1c *Emerald Anne MAXWELL, *b* 30 April 1990
2c *Charlotte Wanda MAXWELL, *b* 13 Nov 1991

Half-great-niece's grandchildren
3b *Linda Margot Anne Maxwell [Mrs Linda Kulow, The Croft, Tullykin Rd, Killyleagh, Co Down, Northern Ireland, UK], *b* 22 July 1952; *educ* Wycombe Abbey; *m* 1972 (divorce 1985) Volkmar KULOW and has issue:

Half-great-niece's great-grandchildren
1c *Maximilian Robert KULOW, *b* 1973; *educ* Loretto
2c *Nikolai Alexander KULOW, *b* 1974; *educ* Loretto

Half-great-niece's grandchildren
4b *Ronald Taft Barry MAXWELL [5 Rothesay Mews, Edinburgh EH3 7SG, UK], *b* 25 March 1958; *educ* Eton and RMA Sandhurst; served 1st Bn The Black Watch; *m* 1993 *Miranda MacSwiney (*b* 1958)

Half-great-niece's children
1a (cont.) Mrs Ronald Maxwell *m* 2nd 16 Nov 1961 *Lt-Col Denys Archibald ROWAN-HAMILTON, MVO (1947), JP (1985), DL (Co Down, 1975) (*b* 26 April 1921; *educ* Wellington and RMC Sandhurst; commanded 4/5th Black Watch 1960-63, Defence Attaché British Embassy Damascus and Beirut 1964-67, High Sheriff of Co Down 1975), 2nd s of Brig Guy Rowan Hamilton, DSO, MC, DL (seventh in descent from Gawen Hamilton, yr bro of Sir James Hamilton, who was *cr* Viscount Claneboye in the peerage of Ireland 1622 and whose s James was promoted to be Earl of Clanbrassill 1647), and his w Phyllis Frances (dau of late Lord Blackburn, a Scottish Lord of Session, and his w Lady Constance Bowes-Lyon, est dau of 13th Earl of Strathmore (*see* BURKE'S PEERAGE & BARONETAGE) and great-aunt of HM Queen ELIZABETH II), and has further issue:

Half-great-niece's grandchildren
5b *Constance Orfla Rowan-Hamilton [Mrs Michael Criswell, 22 Rozel Rd, London SW4, UK], *b* 14 Oct 1962; *educ* Wycombe Abbey and St Catharine's Coll, Cambridge; *m* 1991 *Dr Michael CRISWELL
6b *Louisa Anne Rowan-Hamilton [Mrs Miles Nelson, 2/6 Gardner's Crescent, Edinburgh 3, UK], *b* 20 Nov 1963; *educ* Wycombe Abbey and St Andrew's U; *m* 1992 *Miles NELSON
7b *Gawn William ROWAN-HAMILTON [47 Crescent Lane, London SW4, UK], *b* 17 Oct 1968; *educ* Eton and Pembroke Coll, Cambridge

Half-great-niece's children
2a *Jane Warburton [Mrs John Haines, Longwood House, Churt, Farnham, Surrey, UK], *b* 1931; *m* 19— *John HAINES (*b* 1922) and has issue:

Half-great-niece's grandchildren
1b John HAINES, *b* 1951; *d c* 1990
2b *Timothy HAINES [18 Alexandra Ave, London SW11, UK], *b* 1953; *m* 19— *Caroline Lumley and has issue:

  Half-great-niece's great-grandchildren
  1c *Rosa HAINES, *b* 19—
  2c *A child, *b* 19—

Half-great-niece's grandchildren
3b *Kate Elizabeth Haines [Mrs James Hamilton, Brook House Farm, Avonbury, Bromyard, Hereford and Worcester HR7 4LB, UK], *b* Hobart, Tasmania, 24 Dec 1954; *m* 21 June 1975 *(Anthony) James HAMILTON, s of Anthony Norris Hamilton and his w Jean Philippa, and has issue:

  Half-great-niece's great-grandchildren
  1c *Ben(jamin) David HAMILTON, *b* Sherborne, Dorset, UK, 31 May 1976
  2c *Jessica Kate HAMILTON, *b* Dorchester, Dorset, UK, 31 May 1977
  3c *Edward James HAMILTON, *b* Plymouth, Devon, UK, 12 June 1980

Half-great-niece's grandchildren
4b *Anne Haines [Mrs Klaus Wegner, Königin-Sophie-Strasse 19, W-5340 Bad Honnet, Germany], *b* 1956; *m* 19— *Klaus WEGNER and has four children
5b *Richard HAINES [17 West End Grove, Farnham, Surrey GU9 7EG, UK], *b* 1956; *m* 19— *Mary —— and has issue:

  Half-great-niece's great-grandchildren
  1c *Holly HAINES, *b* 19—
  2c *George HAINES, *b* 19—

Half-great-niece's grandchildren
6b *Sally Haines, *b* 1959; *m* 19— *—— and has three children

Half-great-niece's children
3a *Evelyn Anne Warburton [Mrs Simon Kirby, 86 Westfield Rd, Edgbaston, West Midlands B15 3JG, UK], *b* Farnborough, Hants, UK, 6 June 1953; *educ* U of Pennsylvania (BA 1974) and Homerton Coll, Cambridge, UK (CertEd 1977); *m* 20 July 1974 *Simon Nicholas KIRBY, s of James and Margaret Kirby, and has issue:

  Half-great-niece's grandchildren
  1b *Thomas Edward KIRBY, *b* Birmingham, UK, 8 Feb 1980
  2b *William George KIRBY, *b* Birmingham 8 Sept 1981
  3b *Peter James KIRBY, *b* Birmingham 25 May 1983
  4b *John Rupert KIRBY, *b* Birmingham 19 Aug 1987
  5b *Charles Taft KIRBY, *b* Birmingham 16 April 1989

President Taft's half-nephew and -niece
2 David Stinton TAFT, *b* 1876; *d* 1891
3 Anna Louise Taft, *b* 1880: *m* 1917 Walter T. SEMPLE and *d* 1961, leaving issue:

  Half-great-nephew
  (1) Charles Taft SEMPLE, *b* 1919; *d* 1928

President Taft's half-nephew
4 Charles Howard TAFT, *b* 1882; *d* 1931

II Peter Rawson TAFT, *b* 12 May 1846; *m* 1876 Annie Matilda Hulbert (*b* 1858; *d* 1923) and *d* 4 June 1889, leaving issue:

President Taft's half-nephew
1 Hulbert TAFT, *b* 1877; *m* 1904 Nellie Leaman (*b* 1881; *d* 1927) and *d* 1959, leaving issue:

Half-great-nephew
(1) *Hulbert TAFT, Jr [8420 Shawnee Run Road, Cincinnati, OH, USA], *b* 1907; *m* 1933 Elizabeth Sutphin (*b* 1905) and has issue:

  Half-great-nephew's children
  1a *Mary Perin Taft, *b* 1935; *m* 1960 *Kenneth MAHLER
  2a *Nellie L. TAFT, *b* 1937
  3a *Dudley S. TAFT, *b* 1940

Half-great-niece
(2) *Katharine P. Taft [Mrs James Benedict, 439 Lafayette Avenue, Cincinnati, OH, USA], *b* 1909; *m* 1929 *James B. BENEDICT (*b* 1900) and has issue:

  Half-great-niece's children
  1a *James B. BENEDICT, Jr, *b* 1938; *m* 1959 *Diane Goude (*b* 1937) and has issue:

Half-great-niece's grandchildren
1b *William Logan BENEDICT, *b* 1960
2b *Robert James BENEDICT, *b* 1964

Half-great-niece
(3) *Margot Taft [Mrs John Tytus III, 8605 Indian Hill Road, Cincinnati, OH, USA; 753 Delta Ave, Mt Lkt, Cincinnati, OH, USA], *b* 1913; *m* 1937 *John B. TYTUS III, *s* of John Tytus, Jr, and has issue:

Half-great-niece's children
1a *Francis TYTUS, *b* 1938; *m* 1963 *Patricia Shinkle (*b* 1942)
2a *Denny T. TYTUS, *b* 1940; *m* 1960 *Lee Ault Carter (*b* 1938) and has issue:

Half-great-niece's grandchildren
1b *Margot L. TYTUS, *b* 1961
2b *Elizabeth Hill TYTUS, *b* 1963

Half-great-niece's children
3a *Hulbert T. TYTUS, *b* 1944

Half-great-nephew
(4) David Gibson TAFT, *b* 1915; *m* 1st 1946 Katharine Whittaker (*b* 1921) and had issue:

Half-great-nephew's children
1a *Dorothy W. TAFT, *b* 1946
2a *Katharine TAFT, *b* 1948
3a *Margot TAFT, *b* 1950
4a *David TAFT, Jr, *b* 1953
5a *Mary A. TAFT, *b* 1955
6a *James Whittaker TAFT, *b* 1957

Half-great-nephew
(4) (cont.) David G. Taft *m* 2nd 19— Virginia Kittredge (*b* 1928); *m* 3rd 19— *Eleanor Gholson (*b* 1946) and *d* 1962
III Mary TAFT, *b* and *d* 1848
IV Alphonso TAFT, *b* 1850; *d* 2 June 1851
V Alphonso TAFT, *b* 1851; *d* 1852

Alphonso Taft (cont.) *m* 2nd Millbury, Mass., 26 Dec 1853 his 4th cousin once-removed Louisa Maria Torrey (*b* Boston 11 Sept 1827; *d* Milbury, Mass., 7 Dec 1907), for whom *see above*, and *d* San Diego, Calif., 21 May 1891, having with her had issue:

VI Samuel Davenport TAFT, *b* Feb 1855; *d* 8 April 1856
VII WILLIAM HOWARD TAFT, 27th PRESIDENT of the UNITED STATES of AMERICA
VIII Henry Waters TAFT, of New York, *b* Cincinnati 27 May 1859; *educ* Yale (BA 1880, Hon MA 1905); Ptnr Cadwalader Wickersham & Taft, attys; *m* 28 March 1883 Julia Walbridge (*b* 1858; *d* 1942), dau of —— Smith, of Troy, New York, and *d* 11 Aug 1945, leaving issue:

President Taft's nephew
1 Walbridge Smith TAFT, of New York, *b* 1884; Ptnr Cadwalader, Wickersham & Taft; *m* 1st *c* 1909 (divorce 1918) ——; *m* 2nd 1923 *Elizabeth (*b* 1897), dau of —— Clark, of Detroit, Mich., and *d* 1951, leaving issue:

Great-niece
(1) *Lucie Clark TAFT, *b* 1924; *m* 1950 *S. Willetts MEYER (*b* 1921) and has issue:

Great-niece's children
1a *S. Willetts MEYER, Jr, *b* 1953
2a *Elizabeth Taft MEYER, *b* 1956
3a *Lucie Wing MEYER, *b* 1961

Great-nephew
(2) *Henry Waters TAFT, *b* 1926; *m* 1st 1949 (divorce 1958) Sylvia Babcock and has issue:

Great-nephew's children
1a *Charlotte Walbridge TAFT, *b* 1950
2a *Henry Waters TAFT, *b* 1952
3a *Laurie TAFT, *b* 1954

Great-nephew and -niece
(2) (cont.) Henry W. Taft *m* 2nd 1961, *June Clark Parks
(3) *Elizabeth Wing TAFT, *b* 1933; *m* 1st 1955 (divorce 19—) Leon LOURIÉ and has issue:

Great-niece's children
1a *Elizabeth S. LOURIÉ, *b* 1956

Great-niece
(3) (cont.) Mrs Elizabeth Lourié *m* 2nd 1960 (divorce 1962) Edward CHAPLIN

President Taft's nephew and niece
2 William Howard TAFT II, of New York, *b* 1887; *m* 19— Marguerite T. (*d* 1958), dau of —— O'Neill, of Pittsburgh, Pa., and *d* 1952
3 Louise Walbridge Taft, *b* 1888; *m* 19— George H. SNOWDON (*b* 1883; *d* 1931) and *d* 1926, leaving issue:

Great-nephew
(1) *Charles Taft SNOWDON, *b* 1911; *m* 1st 1947 Edith Thorn and has issue:

Great-nephew's children
1a *Taft SNOWDON, *b* 1950
2a *Mar-Lou SNOWDON, *b* 1952
3a *George SNOWDON, *b* 1954

Great-nephews
(1) (cont.) Charles T Snowdon *m* 2nd 1961 *Esther ——
(2) *Henry Taft SNOWDON, *b* 1912; *m* 1941 *Nancy Buckingham (*b* 1916) and has issue:

Great-nephew's children
1a *Nancy Louise SNOWDON, *b* 1944
2a *Henry Taft SNOWDON, Jr, *b* 1947

Great-niece
(3) Marion Louise Snowdon, *b* 1916; *m* 1940 James REED (*b* 1914; *d* 1962) and *d* 1961, leaving issue:

Great-niece's children
1a *Carolyn S. Reed, *b* 1940; *m* 19— *—— ORR
2a *Anica B. REED, *b* 1944
3a *James H. REED IV, *b* 1947

IX Horace Dutton TAFT, *b* Cincinnati 28 Dec 1861; *educ* Yale (BA 1883, MA 1893); admitted to Bar 1885, Fndr The Taft Sch 1890; *m* 29 June 1892 Winifred S. (*d* Dec 1909), dau of —— Thompson, of Niagara Falls, New York, and *d* 28 Jan 1943
X Frances (Fanny) Louise Taft, *b* Cincinnati 18 July 1865; *m* Dr William A. EDWARDS (her father's physician; *d* 1933) and *d* 5 Jan 1950

Father's side

Robert Taft
c 1640-1725 gf also of (a)
Sarah —
c 1640-1725
James Emerson
d 1756
Sarah —
c 1663-1732
→ Joseph Taft c 1680-1747 / Elizabeth Emerson 1686/7-1760

Joseph Cheney
1647-1704
Hannah Thurston
1650-90
→ Josiah Cheney 1685-1754 / Hannah — d 1717

Revd Grindall Rawson
1659-1714/5
Susanna Wilson
1664-1748
John Hayward
d 1710
Sarah Mitchell
1641-p 1731
→ Edmund Rawson 1689-1765 / Elizabeth Hayward 1683-1759

Nathaniel Allen
1648-1718
Mary Frizzell
1656-1745/6
Samuel Hill
c 1656-1723
Hannah Twitchell
c 1661-90
→ Ebenezer Allen 1694-?1778 / Mary Hill 1696-?1785

Samuel Hayward
d 1713
Mehitable Thompson
d a 1711
→ Benjamin Hayward b 1689 / Hannah —

Benjamin Wheaton
1661/2-?1726
Margaret —
Joseph Rockwood
1671-?1713
Mary Hayward
b c 1672?
→ Samuel Wheaton b 1693 / Mary Rockwood b 1690

Seth Chapin
1668-1746
Bethiah Thurston
b 1672
→ John Chapin 1695-1770 / Dorcas — 1694-1767

Benjamin Albee
fl c 1694
Abial —
→ Obadiah Albee b 1705 / Jean/Jane —

Mother's side

Angel Torrey
1657-1724/5
Hannah —
→ William Torrey 1700-79

Joseph Giddings, Jr
b 1672
Grace Wardwell
→ Susanna Giddings 1704-94

Peter Holbrook
1655/6-1712
Alice Godfrey
d 1705
Samuel Read, Jr
1669-1724/5
Deborah Chapin
b 1675/6
→ William Holbrook 1693/4-?1776 / Hopestill Read 1698-1762

John Davenport
1664-1725
Naomi —
→ Samuel Davenport 1697-1773

Daniel Holbrook
b 1676
Abigail Crafts
1673-1702
→ Rebecca Holbrook 1699-1777

Eleazer Daniel
1681-1772
Mary Holbrook
1686-1759
→ David Daniel 1710-76

Israel Taft[1]
1698/9-c 1753? (a)
Mercy Aldrich[2]
b 1700
→ Huldah Taft b 1718

Nathaniel Waters
1671/2-?1718
Elizabeth King
b 1671/2?
John Giles
1681-p 1738
Ann Andrews
→ Jonathan Waters 1715-86 / Mehitable Giles ?1716-99

Samuel Goodale
b 1669
Mary Buxton
b 1669
John Holbrook, Jr
1694-1756
Ruth Hill
d 1747
→ Samuel Goodale, Jr 1708-69 / Silence Holbrook b 1723/4

Solomon Holman
d 1753
Mary Barton
c 1673-1736
Richard Waters
1669-1725/6
Martha Reed
→ Solomon Holman, Jr 1697-1785 / Mercy Waters c 1697-p 1785

John Trask
b c 1678
Hannah Osborn
b 1679
Josiah Bond
1695/6-1781
Elizabeth Fuller
1701-86
→ Samuel Trask 1721-90 / Anna Bond 1732-c 1784

WILLIAM H. TAFT
FAMILY TREE

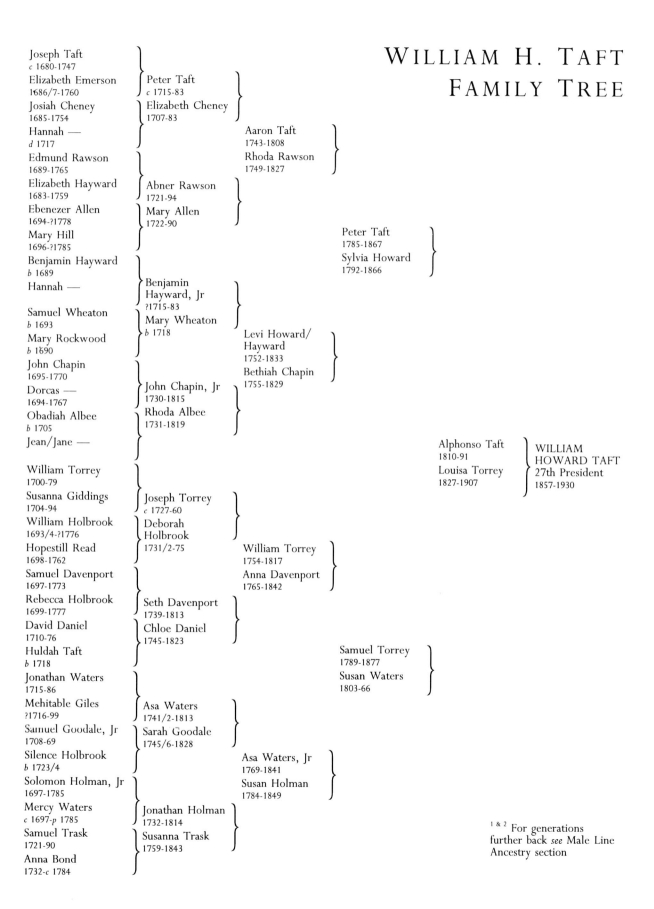

Joseph Taft
c 1680-1747

Elizabeth Emerson
1686/7-1760

Josiah Cheney
1685-1754

Hannah —
d 1717

Edmund Rawson
1689-1765

Elizabeth Hayward
1683-1759

Ebenezer Allen
1694-?1778

Mary Hill
1696-?1785

Benjamin Hayward
b 1689

Hannah —

Samuel Wheaton
b 1693

Mary Rockwood
b 1690

John Chapin
1695-1770

Dorcas —
1694-1767

Obadiah Albee
b 1705

Jean/Jane —

William Torrey
1700-79

Susanna Giddings
1704-94

William Holbrook
1693/4-?1776

Hopestill Read
1698-1762

Samuel Davenport
1697-1773

Rebecca Holbrook
1699-1777

David Daniel
1710-76

Huldah Taft
b 1718

Jonathan Waters
1715-86

Mehitable Giles
?1716-99

Samuel Goodale, Jr
1708-69

Silence Holbrook
b 1723/4

Solomon Holman, Jr
1697-1785

Mercy Waters
c 1697-*p* 1785

Samuel Trask
1721-90

Anna Bond
1732-*c* 1784

Peter Taft
c 1715-83

Elizabeth Cheney
1707-83

Abner Rawson
1721-94

Mary Allen
1722-90

Benjamin
Hayward, Jr
?1715-83

Mary Wheaton
b 1718

John Chapin, Jr
1730-1815

Rhoda Albee
1731-1819

Joseph Torrey
c 1727-60

Deborah
Holbrook
1731/2-75

Seth Davenport
1739-1813

Chloe Daniel
1745-1823

Asa Waters
1741/2-1813

Sarah Goodale
1745/6-1828

Jonathan Holman
1732-1814

Susanna Trask
1759-1843

Aaron Taft
1743-1808

Rhoda Rawson
1749-1827

Levi Howard/
Hayward
1752-1833

Bethiah Chapin
1755-1829

William Torrey
1754-1817

Anna Davenport
1765-1842

Asa Waters, Jr
1769-1841

Susan Holman
1784-1849

Peter Taft
1785-1867

Sylvia Howard
1792-1866

Samuel Torrey
1789-1877

Susan Waters
1803-66

Alphonso Taft
1810-91

Louisa Torrey
1827-1907

WILLIAM
HOWARD TAFT
27th President
1857-1930

[1 & 2] For generations
further back *see* Male Line
Ancestry section

Plate 87   Woodrow Wilson with his 2nd wife, Edith Bolling Galt, January 1916

WOODROW WILSON

1856-1924
28TH PRESIDENT OF THE UNITED STATES OF AMERICA
1913-21

Theodore Roosevelt called the presidency "a bully pulpit", but it was Woodrow Wilson who best used it as such. He once said of himself that he had, unmistakably, the orator's temperament. But his father was a Presbyterian minister and at the last it is the preacher's voice that is heard in his speeches, indeed a prophet's, sounding in the presidency for the first time since Lincoln's death. Wilson was not so generous in his sympathies as Lincoln; he once said that "it is not men that interest or disturb me primarily, it is ideas. Ideas live, men die." One cannot imagine Lincoln making such a shallow remark. In due course Wilson's presidency and his life reached their crisis and he was forced to face the pain and tragedy of history. Then it was that he began to speak as a prophet and nobody listened or, if they did, they soon forgot him.

It is Wilson's failure which first, in a chronological survey, lays bare the tragic dimension of the modern presidency. He aspired so high, he did so much, he fell so low. Nor was he the last. Most of his successors in fact have suffered similarly. It is as if the presidency had become too demanding, the instrument of a cannibal god, the Dagon of democracy who inexorably demands human sacrifice. Sometimes it is the President who pays, sometimes his family, usually both. Inevitably the question arises of whether any achievement is worth the price.

Wilson entered the world of politics much later than Bryan and Roosevelt, or even Taft. They were all a little younger than he but in 1902, the year that he became President of Princeton University, Roosevelt was already President of the United States; Bryan had twice been the presidential nominee of the Democratic party and Taft was Governor of the Philippines. However, to be President of Princeton was a great thing in itself, as Wilson lost no time in demonstrating. He was himself the product of a new professionalism in university education and scholarship and he knew that it was high time that Princeton was reformed. Other scholars fanning out across America from Johns Hopkins, the fount of the new learning, were also zealous to transform their colleges and universities, but none could equal the powers of leadership and inspiration that Wilson displayed. The word soon got around that he was an altogether exceptional man; a few even began to think of him as a future President of the United States.

It was perhaps as well for his chances that his new admirers did not have a very close knowledge of what happened next at Princeton. Wilson's zeal for reform and his distinctly high-handed way of pressing it began to make fewer friends than enemies (among them the elderly Grover Cleveland, a trustee of the university). He had a dangerous streak of stubbornness and a knack of seeing all criticism as a personal affront. But in 1910 these things mattered less than his prestige as President of Princeton. The bosses of New Jersey could not quite understand why such a man should want to leave the academic cloister for the low world of politics, but Wilson snatched at their invitation to run for Governor of New Jersey. He had always hankered for a political career like that of his great hero, the English statesman Gladstone (his mother was English-born). He fought a brilliant campaign and proved to be a great Governor. The gifts of leadership that he had displayed at Princeton once more had full scope. It is really no wonder that a little band of devoted admirers settled that he should be the next Democratic President and in due course brought it about.

He was swept into office in a year of hope. The forces which had split the Republican party had revivified the Democrats, not least because they knew that if they held together they could win the presidency for the first time in 16 years. There was an old guard among the Democrats as well as in the Grand Old Party but it was not allowed to stand in the way of victory. Bryan gave his blessing to Wilson's candidacy and the people gave their votes (Wilson led Theodore Roosevelt by more than two million). Buoyed up by this the new President felt authorized to push through a large and various legislative programme; first what in his campaign he had called 'the New Freedom' — lowering the tariff, a new Federally-supervised national banking system, new anti-monopoly legislation, a Federal Trade Commission — and then, as the 1916 election drew near, measures taken from Roosevelt's 'New Nationalism': a farm loan act, a child labour act, an eight-hour act. It was a remarkable record, solidly entitling Wilson to reelection, and in principle there seemed to be no reason why in his second term he should not be able to add to it, provided that America stayed at peace.

But that essential condition was unrealizable. Wilson actually won re-election on the slogan, launched almost accidentally by one of his supporters, 'He Kept Us Out Of The War'; to continue the feat was beyond him. Historians still argue about the nature and causes of World War I and about whether in 1917 Wilson had a choice. He himself thought that events had been too much for him and that by April 1917 there was nothing to be done but to ask Congress for a declaration of war on Germany, since Germany had resorted to unrestricted submarine warfare and was sinking American ships. One of his first innovations as President had been to review George Washington's practice of presenting his messages to Congress in person; now, on 2 April, he reviewed events before a joint session of both houses with the Supreme Court in attendance and the galleries crowded with the diplomatic corps. His speech was wonderfully eloquent but it consisted essentially of only two points: that imperial Germany was already making war on the United States and could only be checked by full-scale retaliation, and that the United States would fight, not just for the rights of neutrals, but "to make the world safe for democracy". Submarines and universal liberalism were America's reasons for going to war. This was a gross over-simplification and Wilson, had he not been so caught up in his prophesying, would have known it. But simplification is the prophet's weapon. It made great trouble for him and the world later on.

However, for the next two years he swept all before him. The Wilson administration organized the war effort superbly. The US Navy in partnership with the Royal Navy cleared the seas of U-boats. The US Army arrived in France in time to turn the tide against the Germans and deliver a good many of the smashing blows which induced Germany to ask for an armistice. American capital was lent lavishly to support the Allied economies. Woodrow Wilson sent forth from the White House a series of pronouncements telling the world how it ought to be reorganized after the war. Finally, his brisk diplomacy brought about an end to the hostilities in November 1918.

It was a record of which any man or nation might well be proud, but Wilson knew that it was necessary to crown it, if possible, with a lasting peace. Rightly deeming that this task of peacemaking was not one he could prudently delegate, he sailed for Europe in December 1918.

This is not the place to discuss the merits of the Treaty of Versailles, but it is important to understand Wilson's motives. At heart he was a deeply pacific man (Roosevelt had sneered at him because none of his family had fought on either side in the Civil War), and his central object throughout the negotiations was to try and create an international settlement which would make another world war impossible. He hoped that a League of Nations, into which all countries would eventually be gathered, would provide the mechanism for settling disputes. But underlying this proposal was his unswerving certainty that unless the United States committed itself irretrievably to the work of maintaining peace, another war would come. He understood the reality of power and the vision of peace very well, none better; unfortunately most of those who also understood power cared nothing for the vision, while those who shared the vision were utterly naive about the realities of power — nowhere more so than in the United States. Wilson and his work were to be destroyed between these crossfires and World War II came.

First he struggled. Nothing he saw in Europe weakened his detestation of war; indeed a pleading note now entered his oratory as he evoked the soldiers who had died. Unfortunately he was no longer the irresistible advocate that he had been. His health began to collapse during the peace conference. In the autumn of 1919, as he made a desperate cross-country speaking tour back in the US begging his countrymen to ensure the ratification by the Senate of his treaty, he had a complete breakdown and then, a few days later back in Washington, a stroke.

There ensued one of the most curious episodes in presidential history. Wilson was too proud, too convinced of his indispensability, to admit his incapacity, and neither the Constitution nor the law provided for such a contingency. It was not even clear that he could legally resign. So he lay incommunicado in his sickroom and Mrs Wilson became his sole link with the world of government and politics. She was his second wife, his first, the adored Ellen, having died in 1914. Edith Bolling, whom he married two years later, was an elegant, handsome widow of Virginian family, proud and devoted. She bore the burden, and people began to murmur that she was America's first woman President.

Gradually Woodrow Wilson regained strength, though he was never wholly to recover. He was able, however, to supervise the last battle in the Senate. Modifications were proposed in the Treaty. The Allies would have accepted them; had they been included they might have got the instrument through. Wilson rejected them and compelled his followers to do the same. The obstinacy and indignation of his Princeton battles was on him again, exacerbated no doubt by the nature of his illness. So in the end it was he himself who was largely responsible for killing the Treaty of Versailles and thereby committing America to that dreary path of isolationism which was to end in such ruin. The last months of his administration showed in other ways that he had lost command. Members of his Cabinet went their own way (the Attorney-General passed his time by launching a Red scare); the country suffered from a post-war depression. The Republicans won the presidential election of 1920.

Wilson did not leave Washington after the Inauguration of President Harding. He stayed there, a semi-invalid (though he was to outlive Harding) until his death in 1924. He is buried in the great Gothic cathedral whose tower forms one of Washington's more agreeable landmarks. The tomb, in a side chapel, looks somewhat like a mediaeval chantry, where masses for the dead should be recited daily; a curious end for a Presbyterian but, given the nature of Wilson's visions and foreboding and the guilt he felt for those he sent to their end in France, not inappropriate.

WOODROW WILSON'S FAMILY

The priest-king is not usually a subject for study by genealogists or historians of the USA, but with Woodrow Wilson something like a priest-king came to preside over the United States. He was not the first President to come from a long line of clerics — Cleveland had beaten him to it. Nor was he the only President with a love of moralizing, witness Jimmy Carter in our own time. But Wilson is the only President who could have stepped out of that classic of armchair anthropologizing *The Golden Bough*. It is hardly exaggerating to say that he had about him the aura of a member of a hereditary priesthood, with a minister for a father and a couple more on his mother's side of the family, the Woodrows. In Ellen Axson he married a minister's daughter and his father-in-law-to-be, together with his grandfather-in-law-to-be, both of them ministers too, officiated at the wedding. The Calvinism purveyed by these family connections ate deep into his personality and may have accounted for his refusal to compromise. In addition Wilson worshipped his father, consulting him on every matter of importance until well into middle age. The worship was returned, his father's letters to him being written in what was virtually liturgical language ("My precious Son, You deserve the place which you occupy within the house of my soul . . . you are yourself a sort of *magna pars* [great part] where there is so much that is great").

Onlookers were struck by Wilson's clerical manner at the time. One senator called him "a Presbyterian priest". As for the king side of it, when Wilson appeared before Congress — the first President to do so since John Adams — the gesture smacked to some of a speech from the throne, along the lines of English royalty. As his life swelled to a climax, so did the religious overtones. He was struck down at the zenith of his career as he repeatedly preached a nationwide sermon on his ideals, adherence to which he thought would prevent further wars. He was then kept veiled from public sightings like a sacred being within the holy of holies while a Logos in the shape of his second wife mediated between him and his subjects. When in addition one considers the Faustian parallels in his life — a scholar lured from his study by the prospect of temporal power and a weakness for pretty women (Wilson caught his first sight of Ellen in church, as Mephistopheles did Marguerite), while Dr Faustus's claim "The Emp'ror shall not live but by my leave, nor any potentate of Germany" perfectly describes Wilson's ascendancy in the winter of 1918-19 — it adds up to a combination both mythic and grandiose.

Wilson himself would have been slow to see things this way, for according to Charles Seymour, the Yale history professor who was a technical delegate at the Paris Peace Conference and wrote on Wilson's handling of the War, he was neither very learned, creative nor original. Moreover art and literature were closed books to him before Ellen opened them up, introducing him to Browning, Wordsworth and, rather surprisingly, Sterne. Instead he described himself as "a democrat, like Jackson, with aristocratic tastes". He was like Jackson in other ways. His paternal line can only be traced back to the grandfather, as with Jackson, and the grandfather in question came from Northern Ireland (Co Down in Wilson's case, Co Antrim in Jackson's). The aristocratic tastes could have been more accurately described as refined ones, but his mother's family the Woodrows certainly had aristocratic pretensions, for they looked back to Robert the Bruce as an ancestor. This was no very exclusive claim, however, since the Bruce had 13 children and lived 600 years ago, so that millions of Scots today (and every ancestor on Wilson's mother's side appears to be Scottish) descend from him.

Wilson's refinement probably arose from his relationship with his mother, which was every bit as close as that with his father. He self-deprecatingly described himself as a "laughed-at mamma's boy", and it was his mother's terror of the sea, as with George Washington and his mother, that kept Wilson from becoming a sailor — apparently a very real possibility at one point. Mrs Wilson had cause enough for her phobia: she was a first-generation American and had come out from Europe with her parents and seven brothers and sisters on an appalling voyage that found them within actual sight of Newfoundland before they were blown by storms all the way back across the Atlantic to Ireland.

Being "a laughed-at mamma's boy" did not make a cissy of Wilson, although his health was bad long before his gruelling experience while President, and he had to cut his studies short at more than one of his places of education. For instance, he was student director of athletic sport at Princeton (as his college was later renamed) and was both attractive to and attracted by women. He seems to have been capable of genuine friendship with women as well as more ardent feelings. His relationship from 1907 on with Mary Peck, a woman who was living apart from her husband, grew quite passionate, but as far as one can see only in epistolary form. He was an obsessive correspondent. (As President elect he is said to have answered personally the 15,000 letters he got from the public between election day and his Inauguration.) The Peck imbroglio may never have become physical but it caused Ellen disquiet all the same, despite Wilson's taking care to cultivate friendly relations between her and Mrs Peck. More

Plate 88   Ellen Axson, Woodrow Wilson's first wife

Plate 89   Margaret, Woodrow Wilson's eldest daughter and hostess in the White House

importantly, it was brought up by political opponents in the 1912 presidential election (and again, relatively discreetly this time, in 1916 by Wilson's aides, who exploited his anxiety on the subject to urge postponement of his second marriage on the grounds that it was too soon after Ellen's death).

Wilson owed his first wife more than just gratitude for her self-restraint over Mary Peck. Her frugal housekeeping in the early years of their marriage allowed him to live in modest comfort despite having virtually nothing but his university lecturer's salary to live on, and despite the help he gave his even more impoverished relatives. She looked over the proofs of his books and essays, helped compose his speeches, assisted him in learning German, and in particular was instrumental in securing William Jennings Bryan's goodwill just before the 1912 Democratic convention. She was the first presidential candidate's wife to campaign on what we would recognise as something approaching a modern scale. The women's suffrage movement was nearing complete victory, so this showed good timing. During her husband's presidency (though she only lived through the first year-and-a-half of it) she did social work, particularly in the Washington slums Goat Alley and Snow's Court, and put money into the Sanitary Housing Co and the Colored Social Settlement, two philanthropic ventures.

In the months after Ellen Wilson's death their eldest daughter Margaret acted as hostess at the White House, helped by her cousin Helen Woodrow Bones, through whom Wilson met his second wife Edith. After America entered World War I Margaret toured army camps giving singing recitals. Wilson's son-in-law, his daughter Jessie's husband Francis B. Sayre, was a YMCA worker with the troops overseas. Another son-in-law, William G. McAdoo, had been the Democratic convention acting chairman in 1912 and strongly pro-Wilson. He got his reward in 1913 when he was made Secretary of the Treasury (and a further reward, though presumably fortuitous rather than directly bestowed by Wilson, when he married the boss's daughter the following year). He took a leading part in erecting the new Federal Reserve Banks system and after America had entered the war he raised over $16 billion by means of Liberty Loans. He was momentarily the leading contender for the Democratic presidential nomination in 1924, with 431½ votes out of a necessary 731 on the first convention balllot, but his connection with past oil-leasing scandals and the opposition of both Al Smith and the Ku Klux Klan element scotched his chances. He swung crucial delegates to FDR in the 1932 Democratic convention and as a reward his acolyte Dan Roper was made Secretary of Commerce in 1933.

Daily records of White House entertaining under Wilson usually list just family guests, with reading aloud (Wilson enjoyed entertaining both his wives in this way) and non-political discussions after dinner. There was not even an inaugural ball when Wilson assumed the presidency. Walter Page, the US Ambassador to Britain, felt this restricted society was very bad for the President, who was reserved enough toward politicians as it was. But a somewhat conservative, family-dominated life suited the Wilsons — Wilson himself and both his wives were from the South after all. As Wilson put it, "The only place in the country, the only place in the world where nothing has to be explained to me is the South." His early memories of the destruction widespread in Virginia for years after the Civil War are said to have made him especially sensitive to the implications of sending American boys to fight in World War I. His second wife Edith Bolling's family had been ruined in the Civil War. Her father had even been obliged to anticipate the Emancipation Proclamation and let his slaves go since they were starving. The courtship between Wilson and Edith Bolling was conducted largely by letter, the correspondence amounting to the American equivalent of that across the Atlantic between Venetia Montagu and the British Prime Minister Asquith, Wilson's opposite number. As with Asquith to Venetia, Wilson mixed affairs of state with professions of intense affection. Once they were married she acted as a cipher clerk, decoding and encoding messages between her husband and his representatives overseas.

For all her Southern conservativism — she was always opposed to women's suffrage for instance — Edith Wilson was sufficiently staunch a republican to refuse to curtsey to Queen Mary when they met in England just after the end of the War. In Paris her descent from the Indian (or native American as

Plate 90   Jessie Wilson Sayre,
Woodrow Wilson's second daughter

Plate 91   Eleanor Wilson McAdoo,
Woodrow Wilson's youngest daughter, 1918

it is more fashionable to say nowadays) princess Pocahontas procured her the honour of an introduction to one of the more class-conscious duchesses of the Faubourg St Germain, a woman who otherwise looked down on Americans for having no aristocracy. Proust would have enjoyed that, particularly since on a visit Edith Wilson made to the duchess she and her hostess, as personages with royal blood, were the only ones allowed to have tea seated. Edith Wilson drew on her Pocahontas ancestry when asked during the war to rename captured German warships and the shoals of new ships being turned out of American yards (by energetic managers like Joseph Kennedy). Finding that so many American place names or physical features had already been used, she chose Indian (native American) ones.

James W. Gerard, the US Ambassador to Germany until war was declared, recalled Mrs. Wilson being present and asking "pertinent questions" one evening in late 1916 when he was making his report to the President. During the Paris Peace Conference Wilson's daily meetings with advisers to keep abreast of the Council of Four's latest developments were always held in Edith Wilson's room and she would contribute to the discussion. But she failed to persuade her husband to compromise with Congress over modifications to the Versailles Treaty. And she failed to stop him trying to get a Democratic Congress elected in 1918. This was fatal to acceptance of the Versailles Treaty because Wilson's renewed partisanship alienated independent Republicans who might otherwise have supported his programme. On the other hand she did dissuade him from demanding that the anti-Treaty senators should resign and seek re-election on a specific anti-League of Nations plank. She helped prevent Senator Albert Fall (later jailed for his part in the Teapot Dome scandal in Harding's administration) from misrepresenting the President's state of health after his stroke. In all she seems to have been truthful when she claimed in her *Memoirs* that she "never made a single decision regarding . . . public affairs." She added "The only decision that was mine was what was important and what was not, and the *very* important decision of when to present matters to my husband", which places her roughly in the position of the modern White House Chief of Staff. In other words one of enormous power.

Wilson's mother's Lake District childhood inevitably made him Anglophile, though this might not necessarily have ensured America entered the War on the Allied side if the Germans had not committed various provocations. But in Wilson's case Anglophilia extended to political science. He was fired by the style of debate of the British House of Commons. His anglophilia also survived trips to Britain, which is not always the case. He loved the Lake District landscape and made life-long friendships there. He felt a better American for having been to England in the sense that he thought all the good elements in American life were of English origin, a view not shared by many of the newer arrivals in America.

BIOGRAPHICAL DETAILS AND DESCENDANTS

WILSON, (THOMAS) WOODROW, b Staunton, Va., 28 Dec 1856; *educ* Davidson Coll, Davidson, N Carolina, Coll of New Jersey (now Princeton, BA 1879), U of Virginia Law Sch, Johns Hopkins U (PhD political science 1886); admitted to Georgia Bar 1882, Assoc Prof History Bryn Mawr 1885, Prof History Wesleyan U, Middletown, Conn., 1888-90, Prof Jurisprudence and Political Economy Coll of New Jersey 1890-92, Pres Princeton 1902-10, Govr New Jersey 1911-13, 28th President (D) of the USA 1913-1921, Nobel Peace Prize 1920, Polish Order of the White Eagle 1922, admitted to Bar Washington, DC, and New York City 1921; author: *Congressional Government in the United States, a Study in American Politics* (doctoral thesis) (1885), *The State: Elements of Historical and Practical Politics* (1889), *State and Federal Governments of the United States* (1889) *Division and Reunion 1829-1889* (1893), *An Old Master, and Other Political Essays* (1893), *Mere Literature, and Other Essays* (1896), *George Washington* (1896), *When a Man Comes to Himself* (1901), *A History of the American People*, 5 vols (1902), *Constitutional Government in the United States* (1908), *New Freedom* (1913), *On Being Human* (1916), *International Ideals* (1919), *President Wilson's Case for the League of Nations* (1923), *Robert E. Lee, an Interpretation* (1924), *Leaders of Men*, ed T.H.V. Motter (1952), *The Priceless Gift: The Love Letters of Woodrow Wilson and Ellen Axson*, ed Eleanor Wilson McAdoo (1962), *Papers*, ed Arthur S. Link (1966); *m* 1st Savannah, Ga., 24 June 1885 Ellen Louise (b there 15 May 1860; d the White House, Washington, DC, 6 Aug 1914, *bur* Myrtle Hill Cemetery, Rome, Ga.), est dau of Revd Samuel Edward Axson, Presbyterian Minister, and his w Margaret Jane, dau of Revd Nathan Hoyt, of Athens, Ga., and had issue:

President Wilson's daughters

I Margaret Woodrow WILSON, *b* Gainesville, Ga., 16 or 30 April 1886; *d* Pondicherry, India, 12 Feb 1944

II Jessie Woodrow Wilson, *b* Gainesville 28 Aug 1887; *educ* Goucher Coll; *m* the White House, Washington, DC, 25 Nov 1913 Francis Bowes SAYRE (*b* South Bethlehem, Pa., 30 April 1885; Prof Law Harvard Law Sch, Assist Sec of State and High Cmmr to the Philippines; *d* Washington, DC, 29 March 1972), 2nd s of Robert Heysham Sayre, Gen Manager Bethlehem Steel Works, and his w Martha Finley Nevin, and *d* Cambridge, Mass., 15 Jan 1933, leaving issue:

Grandchildren

1 *The Very Revd Francis Bowes SAYRE [3002 Glenview Road, Wilmette, IL 60091, USA], *b* the White House 17 Jan 1915; *educ* Williams Coll (AB 1937, Hon DD 1963) and Episcopal Theological Sch, Cambridge, Mass. (MDiv 1940); Hon LHD Wooster Coll (1956), Hon DD Virginia Theological Coll (1957), Wesleyan U, Conn. (1958), and Hobart Coll (1966), Hon STD Queens's U Belfast (1966), Hon LittD Lehigh U and Ursinus Coll (1973), ordained as Episcopalian clergyman 1940, Assist Min Ch Ch Cambridge 1940-42, Chaplain USNR 1942-46, Industl Chaplain Cleveland (Diocese of Ohio) 1946-51 and Rector St Paul's E Cleveland, Ohio, 1947-51, Dean of Washington 1951-78, Chm: Detroit Industl Mission 1956-68, US Commission for Refugees 1958-61 and Woodrow Wilson Memorial Commn 1962-68, Memb President's Commission on Equal Employment & Opportunity 1961-65, Memb Advsy Commission Bp of Armed Forces 1972-78, Memb Bd: Govrs Nat Space Inst and Dirs Presbyterian Ministers' Fund, Assoc Dir Woodrow Wilson Internat Center for Scholars, Washington, DC, 1978-79, Pres Martha's Vineyard Hosp 1981-83, Clergyman of the Year Award Religious Heritage of America 1976, Distinguished Public Serv Medal NASA; *m* 8 June 1946 *Harriet Taft Hart and has issue:

Great-grandchildren

(1) *Jessie Wilson SAYRE, *b* 1949

(2) *Thomas Hart SAYRE, *b* 1950

(3) *Harriet Brownson SAYRE *b* 19—

(4) *Francis Nevin SAYRE *b* 19—

Grandchildren

2 *Eleanor Axson SAYRE [23 Sibley Court, Cambridge, MA 02138, USA], *b* Philadelphia 26 March 1916

3 *Woodrow Wilson SAYRE [17 Loring Road, Springfield, MA 01105, USA], *b* Philadelphia 22 Feb 1919; *educ* Williams Coll (BA 1940) and Harvard (MA 1942, PhD 1957); Capt USAAF 1943-46, leader first US expedition north face Mt Everest 1962, Prof Philosophy Tufts U 1957-64 and Springfield Coll, Mass., 1965-; *m* 16 May 1942 *Edith Warren Chase [Edith Sayre, 71 Craig Drive West, Springfield, MA 01108, USA] and has two adopted daus:

Adoptive great-grandchildren

a *Jennifer Pomeroy SAYRE

b *Martha Nevin SAYRE

President Wilson's daughter

III Eleanor Randolph Wilson, *b* Middletown, Conn., 5 or 16 Oct 1889; *m* the White House, Washington, DC, 7 May 1914 (divorce 1935), as his 2nd w, Senator William Gibbs McADOO (*b* nr Marietta, Ga., 31 Oct 1863; *educ* U of Tennessee (AM); admitted to Bar 1885, Pres and Dir Hudson and Manhattan Railroad Co 1902-13, Delegate Dem Nat Conventn 1912, Sec of the Treasury 1913-18, Dir-Gen Railrds 1917-18, Chm Calif. Delegn to Dem Nat Conventn 1932, US Senator from Calif. 1933-39, Chm American President Lines, Pres Nat Aeronautics Assoc 1934-35, LLD, author: *The Challenge: Liquor and Lawlessness v. Constitutional Government* (1928) and *Crowded Years*, autobiography (1931); *m* 1st 1885 Sarah Houstoun Fleming, of Chattanooga, Tenn., (*d* 1912); *d* 1 Feb 1941), s of Judge William Gibb McAdoo and his w Mary Faith Floyd, and *d* Montecito, Calif., 5 April 1967, leaving issue:

Grandchildren

1 *Ellen Wilson McAdoo, *b* Washington, DC, 21 May 1915; *m* 1st 1934 (divorce 1937) Rafael LOPEZ DE ONATE (*b* Manila, Philippines, 13 April 1902; actor) and has issue:

Great-grandchildren

(1) *Richard Floyd McADOO [PO Box 39483, Los Angeles, CA 90039, USA], *b* Richard Floyd LOPEZ in Vienna, Austria, 27 July 1935; adopted by his gf Senator McAdoo; *m* 1st 30 June 1958 (divorce 1966) Johanna Hirth (*b* 21 Feb 1937) and has issue:

Great-great-grandchildren

1a *Lianne Margret McADOO, *b* 15 Oct 1964

Great-grandchildren

(1) (cont.) Richard Floyd McADOO *m* 2nd 8 Dec 1966 *Betsy Jane Shackleford (*b* 15 Oct 1937) and with her has issue:

Great-great-grandchildren

2a *Scott Gibbs McADOO, *b* 23 Oct 1969

Grandchildren

1 (cont.) Ellen Wilson McAdoo López de Oñate *m* 2nd 13 Sept 1938 (divorce 1943) William Alfred HINSHAW and has further issue:

Great-grandchildren
(2) *William Alfred HINSHAW, Jr, b 30 April 1941; m 10 June 1966 *Eileen Claire Johnson (b Westchester Co, New York, 14 Jan 1945) and has issue:

Great-great-grandchildren
1a *Shelby Lynn HINSHAW, b Van Nuys, Calif., 23 March 1967
2a *William Alfred HINSHAW III, b Encino, Calif., 7 July 1970

Grandchildren
2 *Mary Faith McAdoo, b New York 6 April 1920; m 1st 1946 Donald William THACKWELL (b 1912); m 2nd Nicholas HADDAD; m 3rd 13 Feb 1970 *Russell V. BUSH

President WOODROW WILSON m 2nd Washington, DC, 18 Dec 1915, as her 2nd husb, Edith (b Wytheville, Va., 15 Oct 1872; Hon V-Pres Girl Scouts of America; m 1st 30 April 1896 Norman Galt (d 28 Jan 1908); d Washington, DC, 28 Dec 1961, bur Washington, DC), only dau of Judge William Holcombe Bolling (himself ggs of John Bolling III, who m President JEFFERSON's sister Mary and was ggggs of the native American princess Pocahontas), of Wytheville, and his w Sallie or Sally White, and d Washington, DC, 3 Feb 1924 of a stroke (bur National Cathedral, Washington, DC)

MALE LINE ANCESTRY AND COLLATERAL DESCENDANTS

James WILSON, b Strabane, Co Down, Ireland, 20 Feb 1787; emigrated to America 1807; m Philadelphia 1 Nov 1808 Mary Anne Adams (b Co Down or Co Antrim c 1791) and d Steubenville, Ohio, 17 Oct 1850, having had (with six other s):

Revd Joseph Ruggles WILSON DD, b Steubenville 28 Feb 1822; educ Jefferson Coll, Pa. (AB 1844), and Coll of New Jersey (subsequently Princeton) (BD 1846); Theology Prof, Moderator Presbyterian Gen Assembly 1879; m Chillicothe, Ohio, 7 June 1849 Janet ('Jessie') (b Carlisle, Cumberland, UK, 20 Dec 1826; d Clarksville, Tenn., 15 April 1888), dau of Revd Thomas Woodrow (b Paisley, Scotland, 15 March 1793; Presbyterian Minister who emigrated to N America 1836 and was a missionary in Canada and in Ohio; d Columbus, Ohio, 25 April 1877) and his w Marion Williamson (1791-1836), and d Princeton, New Jersey, 21 Jan 1903, leaving issue:

I Marion Williamson WILSON, b 20 Oct 1850 or 18511; d 18— or 19—
II Annie Josephson Wilson, b 8 Sept 1853 or 1854; m 1874 Dr George HOWE (b 1848; d 1895) and d 15 Sept 1916, having had issue:

President Wilson's nephews and nieces
1 Joseph Wilson HOWE, b 1874; m 18— or 19— Virginia Peyton Knight
2 George HOWE, b 1876; m 1903 Margaret Smyth Flinn (b 1878) and d after 6 July 1912
3 Jessie Woodrow HOWE, b 1878; d 1884
4 Annie Josephson Howe, b 1891; m 19— Frank E. COMPTON

III (THOMAS) WOODROW WILSON, 28th PRESIDENT of the UNITED STATES of AMERICA
IV Joseph Ruggles WILSON, b Augusta, Ga., 20 July 1866 or 1867; d 18— or 19—

WOODROW WILSON
FAMILY TREE

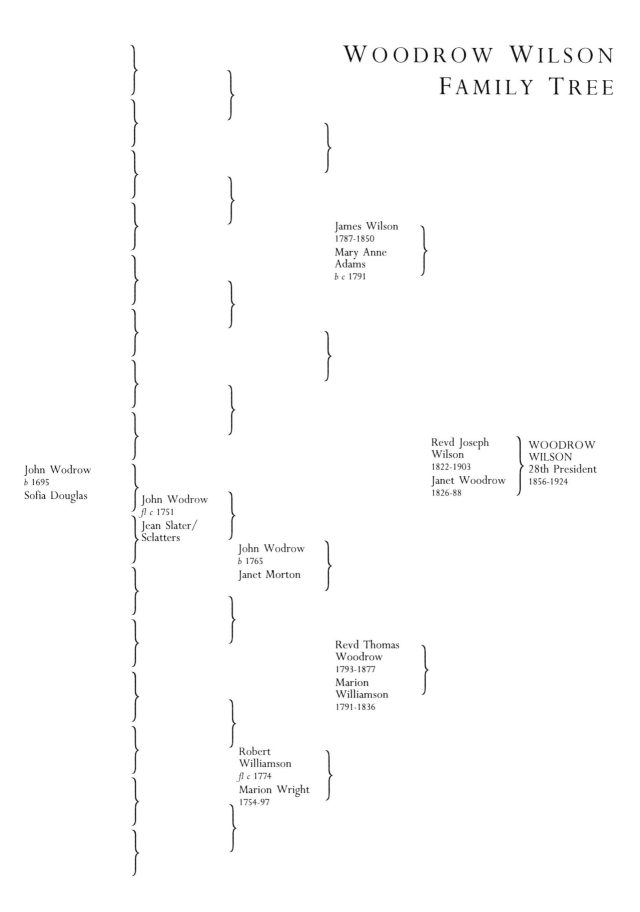

James Wilson
1787-1850
Mary Anne
Adams
b c 1791

Revd Joseph
Wilson
1822-1903
Janet Woodrow
1826-88

WOODROW
WILSON
28th President
1856-1924

John Wodrow
b 1695
Sofia Douglas

John Wodrow
fl c 1751
Jean Slater/
Sclatters

John Wodrow
b 1765
Janet Morton

Revd Thomas
Woodrow
1793-1877
Marion
Williamson
1791-1836

Robert
Williamson
fl c 1774
Marion Wright
1754-97

Plate 92   Warren G. Harding and his wife Florence Kling De Wolfe at the White House

WARREN G. HARDING

1865-1923
29TH PRESIDENT OF THE UNITED STATES OF AMERICA
1921-23

By 1920 the Americans were sick of Wilson and his preaching. More profoundly, they were sick of progressivism, of that positive attitude to reform which had characterized their leadership since the death of McKinley. In fact, they were sick of the modern world (though not of course, that side of it symbolized by Hollywood, the Model T Ford and radio). To make their feelings plain they voted in overwhelming numbers for the Republican candidate in the presidential elections. Senator Harding was a poor man's McKinley, if such a thing can be imagined. He too came from a small town in Ohio, was good at shaking hands, had a mellifluous voice and conducted a front-porch campaign. He exuded a comforting air of handsome Midwestern respectability (his warmer admirers said he looked like George Washington). He had a genius for confused language and popularized the awful word 'normalcy': "We must strive for normalcy to reach stability." It won instant public recognition. Normalcy — yes, that was exactly what the people wanted — synthetic normality. The word has not died yet.

Like so much respectability, Harding's was somewhat hollow. Before he took up politics he had been the editor of his town's newspaper and his favourite way of passing an evening was round the poker table with the boys, the air heavy with cigar smoke and a bottle of decent whisky close at hand. He had a passionate affair with a married woman and at the time of his election was deeply involved with a girl who had recently borne him an illegitimate daughter. But Harding was usually kept in order by his wife Florence Kling, 'the Duchess', who was six years older than he, richer and much tougher. Nobody ever liked the Duchess (she had only got Harding to the altar by bullying him), but she occasionally approached geniality by pouring out the drinks at the poker sessions. The Duchess's trouble was that she was no lady. When, after the election she went to inspect the White House, she and Edith Wilson (who was every inch a lady) loathed each other on sight. The Duchess went all over the mansion, from basement to attic. Mrs Wilson left her to it and went out; she was surprised when she came back some hours later to hear Mrs Harding's sharp voice coming up from the kitchen where she was cross-examining the cook.

Harding looked presidential and the country was in a mood for mediocrity. That is part of the explanation for his rise to fame. The rest was done by the Republican party managers. They were determined not to risk another progressive-conservative split, which meant that each faction could blackball the other's candidates. Harding was acceptable to both sides. The masters of the party knew that he would give them no trouble. They allowed themselves to be satisfied, rather too easily, with his less than frank assurance that there was nothing in his private life which might prove embarrassing and, in short, in a smoke-filled room, which gave a new phrase to presidential politics, they agreed to the nomination just as Harding's manager, Harry Daugherty, had predicted.

In all essentials poor Harding was the worst-prepared President since Grant, but he was superior to Grant in several respects. He did not, for one thing, regard the presidency as an opportunity to relax.

He was earnestly determined to do what he could to be worthy of the office. This entailed some comedy. For instance, the Prohibition amendment to the Constitution had come into force. It did not outlaw owning or drinking alcohol, but it was clearly unseemly for the President of the United States to do either, since he would thereby legitimize a habit which most people could only satisfy by dealing with a bootlegger or speakeasy. The point was put forcibly to Harding by the Anti-Saloon League. So first he had to give up drinking in public, then he had to drink only in his bedroom, and finally he was brought to the point, however reluctantly, of undertaking to give up booze entirely.

He showed himself a magnanimous man. Eugene Debs, the great socialist leader, had been imprisoned for making anti-war speeches and Wilson had refused to let him out. Harding not only pardoned him but insisted on receiving him at the White House, a healing gesture which did the President honour. He had also taken some pain with his appointments. It was he who made Taft Chief Justice, and his appointment of Andrew Mellon to the Treasury, Charles Hughes to the State Department and Herbert Hoover to the Department of Commerce won universal approval. He was not even wholly illiberal in foreign policy. Resisting the tide of isolationism, he began to recommend that the United States join the World Court at the Hague.

But the clouds were darkening. Harding's health was deteriorating and it was not improved by the discovery that members of his administration had been guilty of gross corruption. On one occasion a visitor to the White House opened a door to find the President shaking the Chief of the Veterans Bureau by the throat and shouting "You yellow rat! You double-crossing bastard!" The man soon resigned, but that was only the beginning of Harding's troubles.

He decided to go on a 'Voyage of Understanding'. He would cross the continent, making speeches on the World Court as he went, and then take a vacation in Alaska, which no President had yet visited. To begin with all went fairly well, but Harding's plea for the World Court had little more success than Wilson's for the League of Nations. In another way the trip began to resemble Wilson's last journey. The President's health was visibly poor and he was over-driving himself. The sea voyage to Alaska was ghastly. Harding insisted on endless bridge and Herbert Hoover, who was in the party, could never afterward bear the game. The Alaskan holiday exhausted the already weary President. He had a bad heart attack (not immediately recognized as such) in Seattle on the way home and a fatal one in San Francisco.

The return journey, which carried Harding's body back to Washington and then to burial in Ohio, was the occasion of demonstration of grief on a scale that had not been seen since Lincoln died. Three hundred thousand turned out to see the funeral car in Chicago. Americans had loved Harding ever since they had elected him. Yet very soon all the scandals of his administration, and his own weaknesses, were to be laid bare and he passed into myth, rather unjustly, as the worst of the Presidents. He was lucky in the moment of his death.

WARREN G. HARDING'S FAMILY

If there has been a dominant motive activating the Harding family in the last few generations it is anxiety to maintain the family's good name. This anxiety did not fade away with the death of President Harding in 1923, or even as the dust settled on the scandals that came to light in the years immediately following. In the 1960s President Harding's nephew George T. Harding prevented public access, even by historians of impeccable standing, to love letters between the President and one of his mistresses, Carrie Phillips. It was at a time when a new biography of Harding was being prepared. (And certainly one was needed.) The sad thing about the episode is not so much a relative's distaste for family dirty linen being washed in public. That is understandable. What was so shabby was the way the documents

*Plate 93   Nan Britton, Harding's last mistress
and mother of his child*

*Plate 94   President and Mrs Harding with General Pershing receiving Secretary of State
Hughes, Hughes's daughter Catherine and his wife at a White House reception for
disabled World War I veterans, 8 June 1922*

came to be sequestered. The process did not primarily involve George T. Harding, but rather an Ohio oligarchy putting petty considerations of local prestige above scholarship, and connivance at the suppression of documents of possibly national significance by persons who with their scholarly pretensions should have known better.

As it happens, the Harding-Phillips letters turned out to shed no light on purely political history. But no President is a purely political being, and they say much about the aridity of Harding's marriage. They also strengthen indirectly the allegations of another of Harding's probable mistresses, Nan Britton. The suppression of the letters showed how little had changed since the excessive concern of parochial Ohioans for surface respectability that had made Harding's home town of Marion such a whited sepulchre in his day.

Now no family need bother about its good name unless that good name is under attack. In the case of the Hardings there have been two kinds of attack, one unmerited, the other the fault of President Harding and to a lesser extent his close relatives in his own time. First the unmerited. A rumour had been circulating since the 1820s, when the Hardings first settled in Ohio, that they were descended from what the language of the age called negroes. The assault was most vehemently maintained during President Harding's lifetime by a demented academic from a dim Ohio college about 60 miles northeast of Harding's home town of Marion, reaching a climax at the time of Harding's presidential candidature. But it had been swirling around for years in less precise terms, like a swampy exhalation, and probably caused most misery to members of the Harding family in childhood, a time when taunts by others are most freely launched and most cruelly phrased. At one point President Harding's great-great-grandfather Amos Harding was said to have been the source of what would now be called the 'African-American' infusion. Actually he was said to have been a West Indies black, which shows how unsatisfactory the term 'African-American' can be. At other times it was supposedly the first wife of George T. Harding, the President's great-grandfather. This need have caused George's descendants little anguish as his children were all by his second wife, Elizabeth. Yet a third version had it that Elizabeth was a mulatto. The very imprecision of the rumour made it, as with most rumours, difficult to lay to rest.

Amos rather unconvincingly explained the story away as a malicious lie put about by a neighbour he had known as a bad hat back in Pennsylvania and who he had also caught stealing his corn in Blooming Grove, Ohio. Yet the Hardings were indisputably dark complexioned. On the other hand President Harding himself was so pre-eminently Caucasian in feature that he was compared with a classical Roman, and women found him classically handsome. Judging by photographs and paintings he certainly looks the most senatorially patrician of the Presidents.

To dwell on this aspect of family history may seem prurient. But it is of historical as well as genealogical interest because it must have helped turn Harding into the small-town rotarian good-fellow he always remained, conformist, platitudinous, intellectually lazy. Certainly it was not his fault he was from a narrow little backwater and inadequately prepared in the way of formal education. But so was Lincoln. When the Hardings replaced the Wilsons at the White House contemporaries spoke of Main Street having come to Washington. (Sinclair Lewis's novel of that title, his first big success, had just been published.) If it comes to that, so had Babbitt. Senator Boies Penrose of Pennsylvania, a powerful Republican Party boss, summed up his fellow senator Harding's limitations at the time of the 1920 primaries when he said "Harding isn't as big a man as I thought he was. He should have talked more about the tariff and not so much about playing cymbals in the Marion brass band."

Arguably the family legend about mixed race origins made Harding crave acceptance so avidly that it dulled his critical faculties toward the scoundrels surrounding him as President until it was too late. The legend was also a phenomenon with a national dimension electorally. In the 1920 presidential contest Harding genealogies of varying accuracy flew to and fro, the hostile ones rich in black antecedents, the friendly ones blanched to the point of anaemia in stressing Harding's Anglo-Saxon, Pennsylvania

Dutch and other Caucasian origins. To some extent the very nastiness of the charge, or more accurately the emotions it appealed to, worked in Harding's favour. Woodrow Wilson did not want the Democrats to make capital out of it, saying "We cannot go into a man's genealogy; we must base our campaigns on principles." Penrose reacted more cynically. When an eve-of-poll mention in the widely read *New York Herald* of the "conspiracy . . . to steal the election [by asserting] . . . that . . . Harding . . . is of Negro ancestry" was brought to his attention, he told the Republican National Committee chairman Will Hays to do nothing, adding that he gathered the Republicans had been having a lot of trouble holding the black vote recently. But it is doubtful if many blacks heard of the story. Even in white supremacist circles in the North the allegations were given relatively little publicity, hence did Harding little harm. (And most whites in the North were supremacist, differing only from their Southern fellow-whites in being less obsessed with the subject.)

How today would such a story, just as exploitative of visceral prejudice but harder to discuss honestly, affect the chances of a politician already selected by his party as its presidential candidate — roughly Harding's position as regards the wider public outside Marion, Ohio, in 1920? Realistically speaking, it is most likely that the allegation, even if furnished with the most copper-bottomed evidence, would be ignored by the media on grounds of sensitivity to race relations. The difference between now and 1920 is that according to orthodox modern opinion racial descent ought not to matter one way or the other, even though it almost certainly would. It is a depressing comment on modern America. People were less inhibited in 1920, on that score at least.

Second, the other attacks, those that were the fault of Harding and his close relatives. Because he came from a family that nursed, if not exactly a guilty secret, at any rate a sense that there was something to be covered up, Harding must have found it natural to conduct his life in separate, and hidden, compartments. Because he was uncertain of his social and ethnic position he was the readier to marry in Florence Kling, 'the Duchess', a wife of superior social and economic status, even though she was distinctly plain and a shrew. Moreover he married her — or perhaps it would be truer to say she married him — in the teeth of opposition by her plutocratic father, Amos. Amos Kling took years to become reconciled. Meanwhile he connived at a political rival's buying up Harding's debts and presenting him with a demand to repay $20,000 at a moment's notice. In 1897 he launched a rival newspaper to Harding's Marion *Star*, doubtless in part to drive Harding out of business. He secretly organised opposition to a local street-paving contractor. This had as a consequence one of his cat's-paws trying to do Harding physical violence (only the intervention of Harding's pugnacious father Tryon prevented utter mayhem). And as late as the 1899 campaign for Ohio state senator, which Harding eventually won, Kling was instrumental in persuading a rival to stand against him in the Marion caucus. The wonder is that Harding, who so liked to be liked (and who was a genuinely kindly man), should have entered the newspaper business with its incessant feuds at all. However, his Pollyana-ish code of reporting principles, which he issued to subordinates and which included such bromides as "Boost, don't knock" and "There's good in everybody", might have been designed to discourage investigative journalism of the Watergate kind. It certainly must have benefitted Harding, a persistent adulterer.

His adulteries were bound to be clandestine, but in his case the situation was made worse because he had an unusually watchful and suspicious wife in 'the Duchess'. As well as being suspicious of her husband she was pushy on his behalf. Her pushiness had its advantages. She was an admirable circulation manager of the *Star*. And although she initially opposed any bid by Harding for the presidency, preferring him to seek re-election as senator, a less hazardous undertaking, it was she who persuaded her husband to go for the bigger prize when he was within an ace of quitting during the early stages of the 1920 Republican national convention. During the campaign proper it was she who saw to it that he did not smoke or play cards in public view. Rather surprisingly, she proved a campaign asset, particularly among newly enfranchised women voters. Her abrasiveness in small gatherings evaporated before crowds and she played the perfect hostess to voters flocking to Marion (this was still the era of the front porch campaign), ignoring the way they trampled her garden to mud. Once in the White House her shrewishness reasserted itself. She bullied the housekeeper and Secret Service agents, using one of them to keep a record of who visited her husband in his office. Anybody who thinks Nancy Reagan's enslavement by astrology is unique in presidential history knows little of the Harding administration, for the same Secret Service man used to conduct Madame Marcia, a well-known Washington sybil of the day, to consultations with the Duchess. The truth is that the Duchess had ensnared Harding because for all his good looks he was passive, perhaps again because of insecurity about his position. It also looks as if Nan Britton, his young mistress while in the White House, ensnared him too.

The way his parents had developed into such tawdry figures did nothing for the name of Harding either. His obstetrician-cum-paediatrician mother's medical qualifications were largely bogus and his doctor father's, though in the undemanding Ohio of the day they had validity on paper, were ludicrously meagre. Tryon Harding kept a seedy consulting room in his son's newspaper office building and acted as a kind of unofficial janitor to the newspaper. It was fairly typical of the level of worldly achievements of the other members of the family. Even the limited progress they did make owed less to their own merits than to log-rolling by the one successful Harding, the man who became first a US senator then President. Heber Votaw, the husband of Harding's sister Carolyn, became his brother-in-law's senatorial assistant then Superintendent of Federal Prisons, in which post he swept evidence of narcotics abuse under the carpet. Carolyn was eased into a number of office jobs in Washington and hobnobbed with Charlie Forbes, one of the biggest crooks in Harding's administration. Even Harding's near-blind sister Mary owed her pathetically obscure position in life to fraternal pull. As Harding grew prosperous he was generous to his parents and brothers and sisters with money as well as patronage. (He was never massively rich, however, and at one point his presidential campaign might have ground to a halt had not his brother 'Deac' tided matters over with $500.) In general, whatever might be said about Harding's qualifications for the presidency, he was not a bad head of the family.

BIOGRAPHICAL DETAILS AND DESCENDANTS

HARDING, WARREN GAMALIEL (named after his mother's sister's husb, Warren Gamaliel Bancroft), *b* Corsica (otherwise known as Blooming Grove), Ohio, 2 Nov 1865; *educ* Ohio Central College, Iberia, Ohio (BSc 1882); teacher White Schoolhouse, nr Marion, Ohio 1882-83, employed by Marion *Mirror* 1883, bought Marion *Star* 1884, Memb: Republican Co Ctee 1886 and Marion Bd of Trade 1890, County Auditor Marion 1895, Ohio State Senator 1901-04 (Memb: Finance, Ditches and Drains, Medical Colls and Universities, Privilege and Elections Ctees and Chm Public Printings Ctee, Republican Floor Leader 1902), Lt-Govr Ohio 1904-06, Pres Tri-Metallic Mining, Refining and Smelting Co Jan-May 1905, Dir: Marion Lumber Co, Marion County Telephone Co and Home Bldg Savings & Loan Co, Pres Harding Publishing Co 1909, unsuccessful gubernatorial candidate Ohio 1910, US Senator from Ohio 1915-21, 29th President (R) of USA 1921-23, Hon LLD: Ohio Northen U 1910 and U of Alabama 1921, Hon Degree Princeton 1922, author: *Rededicating America* (1920) and *Our Common Country* (1921); *m* at his and his bride's house in Mount Vernon Avenue, Marion, 8 July 1891, as her 2nd husb, Florence Mabel (*b* Marion 15 Aug 1860; *educ* Cincinnati Conservatory of Music; sometime piano teacher; *m* 1st March 1880 Henry (Pete) De Wolfe (legal separation Sept 1884, divorce May 1886; he *d* 1894), by whom she had one s; *d* Marion 21 Nov 1924, *bur* Marion Cemetery with her 2nd husband, both bodies reinterred Harding Mausoleum, Marion, 1927), only dau of Amos H. Kling, of Marion, banker and merchant, and his 1st w Louisa M., dau of Harvey Bouton; President HARDING *d* Palace Hotel, San Francisco, 2 Aug 1923 of heart failure, leaving no legitimate issue

It has been claimed that Harding had a child (to whose support he certainly contributed) by Susan Pearle, dau of David McWilliams, of 322 East Center St, Marion, retired dry goods store proprietor, and estranged w of Thomas Harry Hodder:

   I Marion Louise Hodder, *b* Grand Island, Nebr., *c* 1895; *m* Arthur R. FLING and *d* New York 18 April 1917 of tuberculosis

President HARDING's mistress (Elizabeth) Nan Britton alias Christian, *b* Claridon, Ohio, 9 Nov 1896, yr dau of Dr Samuel Britton and his w Mary Williams; clerical worker, ptnr in Davis Personnel Service, versifier under the name Ninon Britton, author: *The President's Daughter* (1926) and *Honesty or Politics* (1932); *m* 5 Jan 1924 (annulment 1926) Magnus Cricken, sea captain, and previously had born a dau who she claimed was Harding's (and who Harding ackowledged as his in a Jan 1921 conversation with Nan's sister Elizabeth Willits):

II *Elizabeth Ann Christian, otherwise known as Elizabeth Ann Harding, but recorded as Emma Eloise Britton on her birth certificate, *b* Asbury Park, New Jersey, 22 Oct 1919; adopted by her mother's sister Elizabeth and mother's brother-in-law Scott A. Willits 15 March 1921 after a promise by Harding to pay them $500 a month for the child's upkeep; *educ* Sullivan High Sch, Evanston, Ill.; *m* 18 Sept 1938 *Henry El BLAESING, office-building manager, of Glendale, Calif., and has issue:

  1 *Warren BLAESING, *b c* 1940
  2 *James BLAESING, *b* 19—
  3 *Thomas BLAESING, *b* 19—

MALE LINE ANCESTRY AND COLLATERAL DESCENDANTS

Richard HARDING; Puritan, mariner and fisherman, emigrated from England to Braintree, Mass., 1623; *m* and had issue:

Stephen HARDING, *b* 1623; became a Baptist; worked as blacksmith, admitted Freeman of Providence, Rhode Island, 1669; *m* Bridget Estance and *d* 1698, having had issue:

Abraham HARDING, *b* 1656; *m* Deborah —— and *d* 1694, leaving (with other issue, including a s, Israel, who accompanied his bro Stephen to the Connecticut farm (*see below*)):

Stephen HARDING, *b c* 1677 (according to some sources the s of Stephen Harding, not of Abraham); originally a tanner and currier in Providence, by *c* 1707 a successful ship-builder and sea captain, settled *c* 1714 on a 400-acre farm in New London Co, Conn.; *m c* 1700 Jemima —— (*d* after 1734) and *d* after 1734/5, leaving issue:

I Stephen HARDING; Capt, commanded Fort Jenkins, Pa., in 1778, when his nephew Abraham, Jr, and family sought safety there from Indians and raiders loyal to the British crown; *m* and had issue:

  1 Benjamin HARDING; *k* by Indians 30 June 1778 ⎱ either of these may have been father of David HARDING,
  2 Stukely HARDING; *k* by Indians 30 June 1778 ⎰ who survived the 30 June massacre
  3 Stephen HARDING

II Abraham HARDING, *b* Providence *c* 1714; moved to Orange Co, New York, 1761, where he became a prosperous farmer, also elected highway master and fence viewer (officer charged with erecting and maintaining highway and boundary fences), 2nd Lt Continental Army Revolutionary War, 2nd Maj State Militia after Revolution; *m* 1st *c* 1741 Mercy (*b* New London 9 Jan 1715; *d* in or after 1755 but before 1779), dau of John Vibber (1689-*c* 1754) and his w Joanna Williams (*c* 1684-1754) and had six s (one of whom was called Lemuel and accompanied his bro Abraham to the Wyoming Valley, Pa. (*see below*)); *m* 2nd before 1779 Anna, dau of Isaac Dolson, but had no issue with her and *d* 1806 Susquehanna Co, Pa., leaving an eldest s by his 1st w:

  1 Abraham HARDING, Jr, *b* probably New London, Conn., 14 April 1744; farmed in Wyoming Valley, Pa., 1772-78, also serving as fence viewer and on a ctee to review land titles; *m* Conn. 9 July 1762 Huldah Tryon (*b c* 1743; *d* 1812) and *d* after 1778, having had issue at least three s:

    (1) Amos HARDING, for whom *see below* (2) John HARDING; *d c* 1776 (3) Joseph HARDING; *d* aged 11 *c* 1779

The est s,

  Amos HARDING, *b* Orange Co, New York, 19 March 1764; given half family farm by his father 1784, moved to Luzerne Co, Pa., 1800, where was co-fndr with Adam Miller of village of Clifford, moved to Blooming Grove, Richland Co (now Morrow Co), Ohio, 1821; *m* 1784 Phoebe, dau of William Tripp and his w Sarah Slocum, and *d* Blooming Grove 10 July 1839, having had (with five other children, one of whom was a s, William):

I George Tryon HARDING, for whom *see below*
II Salmon or Solomon HARDING, of legal age in 1817; built first church in Blooming Grove; *m*
III Mordecai HARDING, *b c* 1795; moved to Blooming Grove, Richland Co, Ohio, 1818, where officiated as deacon, later minister and fndr Bethel Baptist Church in Mount Gilead, Richland Co, Ohio; *m* twice, both wives predeceasing him
IV Ebenezer HARDING, Baptist preacher V Benjamin Franklin HARDING, pastor VI Abigail Harding; *m* —— STEARNES
VII Welthy Harding; *m* —— BAKER VIIII Huldah HARDING, drowned aged four IX Hilah HARDING, *b c* 1804
X John HARDING, *b c* 1807; wagon-maker in Laporte Co, Ind. XI Chauncey HARDING, *b c* 1808; *m*
XII Mahala HARDING, *b c* 1813

The est s,

  George Tryon HARDING, *b* Pittston, Pa., 15 June 1790; *m* 1st Anna Roberts; *m* 2nd 1816 Elizabeth (*b* 26 July 1800; *d* 6

Feb 1866), said to have been dau of William Madison and his w Mary Hooper, and d Blooming Grove 9 Jan 1860, having with her had issue:

I Huldah HARDING
II Phoebe Ann HARDING } one of these m —— MEREDITH and had issue at least one child, Helen Harding MEREDITH
III Mary Miranda HARDING
IV Jerusha Harding; m before 1849 David BUTLER, of Galion, Ohio, blacksmith
V William Oliver Perry HARDING
VI Charles Alexander HARDING

The yr s,

Charles Alexander HARDING, b Clifford, Pa., 8 April 1820; m 28 May 1840 Mary Ann (b probably Washington Co, Pa., 26 Aug 1823; d Blooming Grove 11 March 1895), dau of Joshua Crawford and his w Sophia Stevens, and d Blooming Grove 3 April 1878, having had issue (with three daus and another s, all of whom d in infancy, together with five daus — Phoebe, Sophia, Lydia, Margaret and Sarah — who survived into the 20th century) a 3rd child:

(George) Tryon HARDING, b Blooming Grove 12 June 1844; educ Iberia Coll, Iberia, Ohio (BA 1860), Ontario Acad and Western Coll of Homeopathy, Cleveland, Ohio (MD 1873); fifer 96th Ohio Volunteer Infy (invalided out with pleurisy after a few weeks) and drummer boy Co D 136th Regt Ohio Nat Gd during Civil War (honourable discharge due to typhoid), schoolmaster, physician, newspaper-owner; m 1st Galion, Ohio, 7 May 1864 Phoebe/Phebe Elizabeth (b nr Blooming Grove 21 Dec 1843; d Marion, Ohio, 20 May 1910), dau of Isaac Haines Dickerson, farmer, of Blooming Grove, and his w Charity Malvina, dau of William Van Kirk; m 2nd Anderson, Ind., 23 Nov 1911 (divorce 1916) Mrs Eudora Adella Kelley Luvisi, widow (b nr Bartonia, Ind., 25 Sept 1868; d Union City, Ind., 24 July 1955); m 3rd Monroe, Mich., 12 Aug 1921 (Mary) Alice Severns (b Marion 13 Nov 1869; d there 27 Nov 1864) and d Santa Ana, Calif., 19 Nov 1928, having had issue by his 1st w:

I WARREN GAMALIEL HARDING, 29th PRESIDENT of the UNITED STATES of AMERICA
II Charity (Chat) Malvina Harding, b Blooming Grove 1 March 1867; m 23 June 1886 Elton Elsworth REMSBERG, athletic club manager Santa Ana, Calif., and d 2 Nov 1951, having had issue:

President Harding's nephews and nieces
1 Nelle Marie REMSBERG, b c 1890
2 Edgar Harding REMSBERG
3 Helen Lucile REMSBERG
4 Katherine Elizabeth REMSBERG

III Mary Clarissa HARDING, b Blooming Grove 26 April 1868; kindergarten teacher Ohio Inst for the Educn of the Blind, Columbus, Ohio, from 1896; d 28 or 29 Oct 1913
IV Eleanor Persilla HARDING, b Blooming Grove 11 Nov 1872; d Caledonia, Ohio, 9 Nov 1878
V Charles Alexander HARDING, b Caledonia 8 April 1874; d there 9 Nov 1878
VI Abigail Victoria (Daisy) Harding, b Caledonia 31 May 1876; educ Marion High Sch and Vassar; elementary sch teacher, Marion (one of her pupils being Nan Britton, for whom see above under Harding Biographical Details), later at Harding High Sch, Marion; m 1924, as his 1st w, Ralph Tobias LEWIS (who m 2nd 1938 Mrs Hazel Kling Longshore, a niece of Mrs Warren G. Harding; d Fla. 27 March 1967) and d 21 March 1935
VII George Tryon ('Deac') HARDING, Jr, of Worthington, Ohio, b Caledonia 11 March 1878; educ Battle Creek Coll, Mich., and U of Michigan (MD 1900); superintendent Washington Branch Sanitarium, Washington, DC, 1906, proprietor Hartman Farm Home 1918; m 21 or 23 July 1903 Elsie (b 23 June 1881), dau of Jacob Charles Weaver, and d 13 or 18 Jan 1934, leaving issue:

President Harding's nephew
1 *George Tryon HARDING III [430 East Granville Road, Worthing, OH 43085, USA], b Columbus, Ohio, 27 May 1904; educ Columbia Union Coll (AB 1923) and Loma Linda U, Calif., (MD 1928); psychiatrist; m 2 June 1927 *Mary Virginia Woolley and has issue:

Great-nephews
(1) *Dr George Tryon HARDING IV [650 Andover Street, Worthington, OH 43085, USA; 445 E Dublin, Granville Road, Worthington, OH 43085, USA], b 19——
(2) *Dr Herndon Price HARDING [6580 Plesenton Dve, Worthington, OH 43085, USA], b 19——; m 19—— *Leola Janzen (b 14 Feb 1933) and has issue:

Great-nephew's son
1a *Herndon Price HARDING, Jr [332 Las Casas Ave, Pacific Palisades, CA 90272, USA], b Loma Linda, Calif., 11 Feb 1955; educ Loma Linda Medical Sch; Resident Harvard Medical Sch 1981-84, Medical Dir Dept Mental Health Ohio; m 21 Sept 1991 *Kellie Lee, dau of Fred Main and his w Sharon

Great-niece and -nephew
(3) *Ann Elizabeth Harding [Mrs Russell E Hoxte, 1107 Furman Place, Glendale, CA 91206, USA], b 19——; m 19—— *Russell Evan HOXTE
(4) *Dr Warren Gamaliel HARDING III [8430 Shawnee Run Rd, Cincinnati, OH 45243, USA], b Columbus, Ohio, 21 April 1941; educ Loma Linda U (BA 1963, MD 1967) and UCLA; orthopedic surg, Fellow American Coll of Surgeons

and American Acad of Orthopaedic Surgeons, Lt-Cdr Medical Corps USNR; *m* 6 Oct 1974 *Barbara Gibson, dau of Charles Shafor Crawford and his w Marian Dorsey, and has issue:

Great-nephew's children

1a *Warren Gamaliel HARDING IV, *b* San Diego, Calif., 20 June 1975

2a *James Shafor HARDING, *b* Cincinnati 31 Oct 1977

3a *Andrew Crawford HARDING, *b* Cincinnati 13 Sept 1980

Great-nephew

(5) *Richard Kent HARDING [220 Holliday Rd, Columbia, SC 29223, USA], *b* 19—

President Harding's nephews and nieces

2 *Dr Warren Gamaliel HARDING II, *b* Columbus, Ohio, 2 Nov 1905

3 *Ruth Virgina HARDING, *b* Columbus 5 April 1910

4 *Charles Weaver HARDING [970 High Street, Worthington, OH 43085, USA], *b* Columbus 22 Nov 1915

5 *Mary Elizabeth HARDING, *b* Columbus 17 May 1919

VIII Phoebe Caroline (Carolyn) Harding, *b* 21 Oct 1879; elementary sch teacher, Marion, Police Offr 2nd Class Women's Bureau Washington Dist Police Dept, welfare dir Dist of Columbia Police Dept, personnel dir Veterans' Bureau; *m* 4 July or 14 Aug 1903 Heber Herbert VOTAW, of Toledo, Ohio, travelling salesman, Seventh Day Adventist missionary Kemmendine, Rangoon, Burma, senatorial assist to his brother-in-law Warren G. Harding, Supt Fedl Prisons, and sec Seventh Day Adventist Religious Liberty Assoc, and *d* Washington, DC, 21 Oct 1951

Abraham Harding[1]
c 1714-1806
Mercy Vibber[2]
1715—55-79

Abraham Harding, Jr
1744-*p* 1778
Huldah Tryon
c 1743-1812

?Thomas Dickerson
1686-98—1725
?Abigail Reeve
a 1686-*p* 1737
?John Dickerson
c 1686-*c* 1758
?Abigail Reeve
p 1686-*p* 1758

?Joshua Dickerson
1718-25—70-77
?Mehitable Dickerson

Isaac Tripp
c 1704-78
Susannah Spencer
d in/*p* 1775
Joseph Slocum
1706-*p* 1768
Patience Carr
c 1705-*c* 1742/3

William Tripp
b c 1738
Sarah Slocum
1738-1808

Joseph Madison, Jr
1701-73
Eliza Stone

Revd John Madison
1729-1813
Jane Giddings

John Breese?
c 1713-1803
Dorothy Riggs?
c 1713-1803

John Van Kirk, Jr
c 1664-*c* 1724
Alsey —
b c 1675

Henry Van Kirk
c 1700-*c* 1776
Dorothy Morgan
c 1703-*c* 1745

[1] & [2] For generations
further back *see* Male
Line Ancestry section

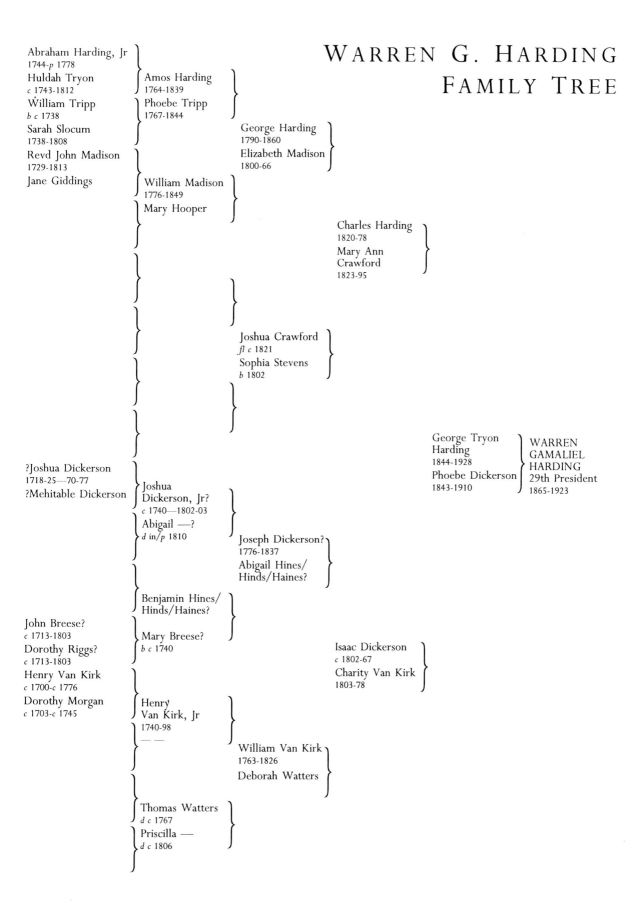

WARREN G. HARDING
FAMILY TREE

Abraham Harding, Jr
1744-p 1778

Huldah Tryon
c 1743-1812

William Tripp
b c 1738

Sarah Slocum
1738-1808

Revd John Madison
1729-1813

Jane Giddings

Amos Harding
1764-1839

Phoebe Tripp
1767-1844

William Madison
1776-1849

Mary Hooper

George Harding
1790-1860

Elizabeth Madison
1800-66

Charles Harding
1820-78

Mary Ann
Crawford
1823-95

Joshua Crawford
fl c 1821

Sophia Stevens
b 1802

George Tryon
Harding
1844-1928

Phoebe Dickerson
1843-1910

WARREN
GAMALIEL
HARDING
29th President
1865-1923

?Joshua Dickerson
1718-25—70-77

?Mehitable Dickerson

Joshua
Dickerson, Jr?
c 1740—1802-03

Abigail —?
d in/*p* 1810

Joseph Dickerson?
1776-1837

Abigail Hines/
Hinds/Haines?

Benjamin Hines/
Hinds/Haines?

John Breese?
c 1713-1803

Dorothy Riggs?
c 1713-1803

Henry Van Kirk
c 1700-c 1776

Dorothy Morgan
c 1703-c 1745

Mary Breese?
b c 1740

Isaac Dickerson
c 1802-67

Charity Van Kirk
1803-78

Henry
Van Kirk, Jr
1740-98
— —

William Van Kirk
1763-1826

Deborah Watters

Thomas Watters
d c 1767

Priscilla —
d c 1806

Plate 95   Calvin Coolidge with his wife Grace Goodhue

CALVIN COOLIDGE

1872-1933
30TH PRESIDENT OF THE UNITED STATES OF AMERICA
1923-29

If Harding had been a throwback to McKinley, his Vice-President was a throwback to the 18th century. He was born on the Fourth of July but there never was anyone less revolutionary, or more out of date. It was all symbolized in the manner in which he took the presidential oath of office. When Harding died it was early evening in San Francisco but in Plymouth, Vermont, one of the quietest corners of the United States, it was half past ten and the Coolidge family had just gone to bed. Not until midnight could the news be got through that the son of the house had inherited the presidency. Then there was some bustle, and at a quarter to three in the morning old Mr Coolidge, a notary public, administered the oath by the light of two oil lamps in his little country parlour. It was the sort of scene that Currier and Ives had delighted to illustrate in their prints: a scene of republican simplicity and virtue to go with little George Washington owning up about the cherry tree or Abe Lincoln splitting rails.

The scene was all the better for being perfectly genuine, but it was not uncalculated. Calvin Coolidge was too canny ever to act without deliberation. It suited him to make this picturesque debut. When he arrived in the White House he brought out his old rocking chair in the evening and sat on the front porch of the mansion as if he were still in the country. This little ploy rather backfired. It became one of the sights of Washington and after a few days the President, tired of being stared at, retreated indoors.

There was always something a little tricky about Coolidge. In his way he was as rocky as the Adams Presidents, but he also had more than a touch of the country boy's slyness when dealing with city slickers, whereas the Adamses, in spite of their love of Quincy, were essentially urban types. Compared to Coolidge they were flamboyantly outgoing. Not that 'Silent Cal' was at all taciturn in private, but he had a notion that a man was never hurt by what he hadn't said, and in public he was the great master of holding his tongue. Consequently, when he did speak, the effect was magnificent. He was Governor of Massachusetts when in 1919 the police in Boston went on strike. He did very little about it until the strike was nearly over; then he said "there is no right to strike against the public safety by anybody, anywhere, any time". It was enough; he was re-elected immediately by a huge majority and instantly became vice-presidential timber (some said presidential). Harding's death did the rest.

Masterly inactivity having got him so far, he figured that more of the same might be what was required now that he had arrived. He liked 12 hours' sleep at night and a long nap in the afternoon — so he literally spent more than half his presidency asleep. To clean up the Harding scandals he got him a new Attorney-General, since Harding's man, Daugherty, would be lucky to escape a jail sentence. He watched his reputation balloon, as the Americans grew fascinated by the anachronism at the head of their affairs. He was easily elected to a full term in his own right in 1924, and for the next four years did and said as little in public as possible. He enjoyed being President until his younger son, Calvin Jr, died of blood poisoning just before the election in 1924 and, according to his father, took the power and the glory of the presidency with him. In November Mrs Coolidge began to crochet a bedspread, eight squares long by six squares wide, one square for every month more they would have to spend in the White House. Each month she crocheted another square and they were that much nearer home.

Mrs Coolidge was a measureless asset to Calvin. Her beauty, her gaiety of heart, her kindness, her outgoing courage — she had all the things he had not. Of course she made a wonderful First Lady, making up for her husband's shyness and bad temper; she made an even better wife. The President was absolutely devoted to her. She was his prop and stay, though he refused ever to discuss politics with her. He did not even tell her that he was going to deliver one of his most famous oracular utterances — "I do not choose to run for President in 1928" — with which he startled the world in the summer of 1927.

Coolidge was a great character, but masterly inactivity was not at all what America and the world needed in the 1920s. Only the prosperity of the United States, 'Coolidge prosperity' as it was called, stood between humanity and fearful disaster, and that prosperity was much more fragile than the President realized. "I believe I can swing it," he told himself when he heard the news that he was President, but in truth the job was too big for him. There were plenty of people to inform him that the American economy was vulnerable and that something ought to be done. He preferred to listen to those who said that the regulation of the New York Stock Exchange was a state affair, not one for the federal government, and that all he need do was announce from time to time that prosperity was here to stay and that the price of stocks and shares was quite reasonable. In private he admitted that to his Vermonter mind the scramble for instant wealth on Wall Street was lunacy, but he felt that as head of the government he ought to say what his experts told him. If anything went wrong, his Secretary of the Treasury, Andrew Mellon, would fix it. So events took their course, while the President snooped about the kitchens and larders of the White House trying to figure out what happened to the ham after he and Mrs Coolidge had each had a slice at dinner and the butler had taken the rest away.

In spite of his renunciation he rather hoped that the Republicans would draft him for another term, and when they nominated Herbert Hoover instead he was distinctly sour ("That man has offered me unsolicited advice for six years, all of it bad"), but by March 1929 he had got most of his temper back. He left for his old home in Northampton, Massachusetts, and for the next four years watched in horror from the sidelines as his world crashed into an abyss whose existence he had never suspected. Then he died, like Harding, of sorrow and heart disease, and at much the same age.

CALVIN COOLIDGE'S FAMILY

During Coolidge's time in the White House it was not so much a question of whether the First Lady was encroaching on her husband's territory as whether he was encroaching on hers. Quite apart from his monitoring of the rate at which food disappeared, he vetted the guest lists and discussed the menus for forthcoming meals with the housekeeper, Mrs Jaffray, who had to get from the President script approval, as it were, before putting them into practice. He disliked the custard pies they made; Mrs Christy, wife of the man who painted his portrait, made good apple pies (implicitly better than the White House ones); and so on. Mrs Jaffrey had had much to put up with in the White House's previous chatelaine, 'the Duchess', who as it happened had taken a dislike to the Coolidges. Presumably the non-stop presidential probing, a sort of culinary precursor of McCarthy House Un-American Activities Committee investigations 25 years later, now proved the last straw, for Mrs Jaffray eventually resigned, even though she liked Grace Coolidge. (But then everyone, even Alice Roosevelt Longworth, liked Grace Coolidge — bar 'the Duchess' that is.)

The element of self-parody in Coolidge is stressed by many writers, but the touch of finicky old maid about him was genuine. There was his cheese-paring. For example, when he married Grace they

Plate 96   The Coolidge family: l-r Calvin Coolidge Jr, John Coolidge (the President's father),
John Coolidge Jr, and Grace Coolidge (Coolidge in foreground)

had planned a fortnight's honeymoon in Montreal; after a week he reckoned they had seen everything in Montreal worth seeing, so they went home and saved a further week's expenditure. There was his feminine interest in helping Grace shop for clothes (though he drew the line at helping her select her hats). There was his eccentricity. He used to walk round the White House with his pet kitten Tige or raccoon Rebecca curled round his neck. And there was the sheer number of his pet animals (dogs and birds as well as Tige and Rebecca). As with the archetypal spinster it seemed to some observers that he was more attentive to his pets than to human beings. A member of the public made him a present of a bear, which he turned over to the zoo out on Rock Creek and which he used to visit regularly to see how it was being looked after. With his love of sleep, tendency to growl and preoccupation with food he was himself a bit like a bear — one on the point of hibernating. As the humorous writer H. L. Mencken put it, Coolidge's "ideal day is one on which nothing whatever happens".

Though shy too, he was less shy than a bear. He rather took to being photographed. He was well aware of the political value of good pictures, for all his old-fashioned approach otherwise. He even allowed himself to be filmed by the new moving picture cameras. However, when the capricious Queen Marie of Roumania paid a state visit and used photographers at a reception she gave in the President's honour, breaching an express prohibition on them by the Coolidges, he said it made a confirmed republican of him. (A sly remark; what else could he have been as leader of the Republican Party and President of a Republic specifically set up in defiance of a European monarch?) But in general he so relished the cameras that one biographer suggests he was enjoying a belated boyhood. If so, it was well smothered in a performance that almost made a ritual of his position as head of the Coolidge household. While President he chose the guests to be invited aboard the presidential yacht the *Mayflower* and put his servants to unnecessary inconvenience to emphasise his position as their master. Perhaps it was a kind of childishness after all: he sometimes pressed all the bells on his desk simultaneously for the fun of hearing bells ring all over the White House. Never mind that it was an infernal nuisance for the staff.

His real boyhood had been overshadowed by the death when he was 12 of his mother after an illness that had lasted seven years. When it came to Coolidge's turn to die he was found to have carried her picture for years inside his old-fashioned waistcoat-pocket-watch-and-chain timepiece, which he carried next to his heart. Before his mother's death he had spent much of his time with his grandfather, a horsebreaker who taught him to ride and was famous locally for his practical jokes (source of the impishness which made Calvin Coolidge press all the buttons on his desk simultaneously?). Coolidge still went riding when President, though it is possible he overestimated his skill, since it was with difficulty that Grace and his Secret Service bodyguard Colonel Starling prevented him from trying out a wild horse. He did not like the idea of Grace riding, and said so. She dutifully obeyed, despite already having assembled the correct costume and started lessons. He also forbade her to dance in public, perhaps out of some dimly remembered obedience to his grandmother Sarah, who had bribed him with a dollar a time as a young man to shun dances.

He had great reverence for his father the Colonel, and despite his reputation for reserve in other relationships used to salute him with a kiss until well into his (Coolidge's) fifties. The Colonel refused to come and live at the White House, so that when he came down with his final illness Coolidge reached Vermont too late to see him alive. "It costs a great deal to be President", Coolidge said. It has been suggested that after his mother's death the boy Coolidge lavished the affection for women that would normally have gone to her on his sister Abigail. Unfortunately she too died after another five years. It is easy to assume that in earlier generations, when life was relatively uncertain and people often died so much younger, the surviving members of a family grieved less than we do today. With Coolidge that was certainly not the case. When his younger son Calvin Jr died after having played tennis in shoes but no socks, consequently developing a blister which led to blood poisoning, Coolidge mollycoddled the surviving son and was so shattered in his professional life he lost all appetite for the presidency and allowed future campaign plans to be neglected. Although his announcement that he would not seek re-election was issued to the public in 1927, he had already told his father a few weeks after Calvin Jr's death in the summer of 1924 that he would never again be a candidate for public office. (Given Calvin Jr's fate one begins to wonder if Jimmy Carter's determination 50 years later to control access to the White House tennis court was so very nit-picking after all.)

Coolidge was of good family. His Goddard ancestors stemmed from a younger son of the Goddards of Swindon in the English county of Wiltshire, who furnished over a period of 170 years no fewer than five Members of Parliament (the last of whom was sitting for Cricklade, virtually a family constituency, at the time Coolidge was born). The Goddards, like their famous cousin, seem to have pursued a political strategy of masterly inactivity. Though of honourable lineage the Coolidges were not rich, so that when the conservative Republican Henry Cabot Lodge was asked to nominate Calvin as Republican presidential candidate in 1920 he retorted "Nominate a man who lives in a two-family house! Never! Massachusetts is not for him!" Nevertheless in the Vermont of the 1870s both the Coolidges and the Moors, Coolidge's mother's family, were considered 'aristocratic'. Coolidge described Vermonters as people who belonged to themselves and lived within their income. Clearly he lived up to Vermont traditions. Yet it has been suggested his mother had Indian blood, an allegation Coolidge himself gave currency to. Recent genealogical research makes no mention of this, but it would have been appropriate if so, for it was during Coolidge's administration that native Americans (Indians in old-fashioned parlance) were first granted citizenship, provided they were born on US soil. And of course the photograph of Coolidge in Indian headdress is celebrated.

It was to be expected that Coolidge would be embarrassed by the headdress. But on other occasions he was not above mild dressing-up in the interests of getting elected. In the 1920 campaign he had his photograph taken pushing a plough and dressed in his grandfather's smock. The three elements involved — his quiet liking for publicity, his farm boy persona put in inverted commas and his implicit veneration for his grandfather — just about sum up Coolidge.

BIOGRAPHICAL DETAILS AND DESCENDANTS

COOLIDGE, (JOHN) CALVIN, *b* Plymouth, Vt., 4 July 1872; *educ* Black River Acad, Ludlow, Vt., St Johnsbury Acad, Vt., and Amherst Coll, Mass. (BA 1895); admitted Massachusetts Bar 1897, Memb Common Cncl Northampton, Mass., and V-Pres Nonatuck Savings Bank 1898, City Slr Northampton 1899-1902, Clerk of Courts for Hampshire Co, Mass., 1903-04, Chm Hampshire Co, Mass., Republican Ctee 1904, unsuccessful candidate Northampton Bd of Educn 1905, Memb Massachusetts House of Reps 1907-08, Mayor Northampton 1910-11, Massachusetts State Senator 1912-15 (Pres Massachusetts Senate 1914-15), Lt-Govr Massachusetts 1916-18, Govr Massachusetts 1919-21, Hon LLD Amherst, Tufts and Williams Coll 1919, V-Pres USA 1921-2 Aug 1923, 30th President (R) of the USA 2 Aug 1923-29, Pres American Antiquarian Soc 1930-32, author: *Have Faith in Massachusetts!* (1919), *The Price of Freedom* (1924), *America's Need for Education* (1925), *Foundations of the Republic* (1926) and *The Autobiography of Calvin Coolidge* (1929); *m* Burlington, Vt., 4 Oct 1905, Grace Anna (*b* there 3 Jan 1879; sometime Hon Pres Girl Scouts of America; *d* Northampton 8 July 1957, *bur* Plymouth, Vt.), dau of Andrew Issachar Goodhue, steamboat inspector, and his *w* Lemira Barrett, and *d* Northampton 5 Jan 1933 of coronary thrombosis (*bur* Notch Cemetery, Plymouth Notch, Plymouth, Vt.), having had issue:

President Coolidge's son
I *John COOLIDGE [48 Garden Street, Farmington, CT 06032, USA], *b* Northampton, Mass., 7 Sept 1906; *educ* Amherst Coll (BA), retired corp exec; *m* Plainville, Conn., 23 Sept 1929 *Florence (*b* Plainville 30 Nov 1904), dau of John H. Trumbull, Govr of Connecticut, of Plainville, Conn., and his *w* Maude Usher, and has issue:

Grandchildren
1 *Cynthia Coolidge [Mrs S Edward Jeter, 221 Deer Cliff Road, Avon, CT 06001, USA], *b* New Haven, Conn., 28 Oct 1933; *m* Farmington, Conn., 26 Sept 1964 *S. Edward JETER (*b* Hartford, Conn., 1 Sept 1937), s of Sherwood F. Jeter, Jr, and his *w* Edwina Pabst, and has issue:

Great-grandchildren
(1) *Christopher Coolidge JETER, *b* Hartford 3 Jan 1967

Grandchildren
2 *Lydia Coolidge [Mrs Jeremy Sayles, 1830 Walnut Avenue, Milledgeville, GA 31061, USA], *b* New Haven, Conn., 14 Aug 1939; *m* Farmington, Conn., 17 Sept 1966 *Jeremy Whitman SAYLES (*b* Schenectady, New York, 9 June 1937), s of Phil Whitman Sayles, of Scarsdale, New York, and his *w* Mildred Jones, and has issue:

Great-grandchildren
(1) *Jennifer Coolidge SAYLES, *b* Boston 27 July 1970
(2) *John Whitman SAYLES, *b* Fitchburg, Mass., 9 July 1974

President Coolidge's son
II Calvin COOLIDGE, *b* Northampton, Mass., 13 April 1908; *d* Washington, DC, 7 July 1924 of septicaemia

MALE LINE ANCESTRY AND COLLATERAL DESCENDANTS

Simon COOLIDGE, of Cottenham, Cambridgeshire, England; *m* Agnes Kingston and *d* in or after 1591, leaving (with other issue):

William COOLIDGE, of Cottenham; Churchwarden 1612; *m* Margaret —— (*d* in or before 1620) and *d* in or after 1618, leaving (with other issue):

John COOLIDGE, *bapt* Cottenham 16 Sept 1604; emigrated to Watertown, Mass., *c* 1630, Freeman 25 May 1636, Selectman many times between 1639 and 1677, Deputy to the General Court 1658; *m* ?1st Mary (1602-91), dau of Revd Richard Ravens (1562-1626) and sister of Grace Ravens (who with her 2nd husb Thomas Rogers was an ancestor of President BUSH) and had issue:

I Simon COOLIDGE, for whom *see* below

II John COOLIDGE, Jr, *b* 16—; *m* Hannah Livermore and had issue:

  1 Grace Coolidge; *m* Jonas BOND and with him was ancestor of President TAFT

John Coolidge the emigrant (or conceivably someone else of the same name) seems to have *m* ?2nd Mary Maddock, *née* Wellington, and(?)/or (a 3rd w?) Mary Maddock, and *d* Watertown 22 Aug 1691, leaving issue:

  III Jonathan COOLIDGE, Jr, *b* 1647; *m* Martha Rice and *d* 1724, leaving issue:

    1 John COOLIDGE, *b* 1690; citizen of Boston; *m* Hannah Ingram and *d* 17—, leaving issue:

      (1) Joseph COOLIDGE, Sr, *b* 1719; *m* 17— Marguerite Olivier and *d* 1771, leaving issue:

        1a Joseph COOLIDGE, Jr, *b* 1747; *m* Elizabeth Boyer and *d* 1820, leaving issue:

          1b Joseph COOLIDGE III, *b* 1773; *m* Elizabeth Bulfinch and *d* 1840, leaving issue:

            1c Joseph COOLIDGE IV, *b* Boston Oct 1798; *m* Monticello 27 May 1825 Ellen Wayles (*b* there 13 Oct 1796; *d* Boston 21 April 1876), dau of Thomas Mann Randolph, Jr, and his w Patsy Jefferson, herself dau of President JEFFERSON, and *d* 1879, leaving issue (*see* pp 142-160)

John Coolidge the emigrant's est s,
  Simon Coolidge, *b c* 1632; *m* 1st 15 Nov 1658 Hannah Barron (*b c* 1635; *d* Watertown 14 July 1680) and had issue; *m* 2nd 19 Jan 1681/2 Priscilla (*d* 1694), dau of John Rogers and his w Priscilla, and *d* 27 Dec 1693, leaving by his 1st w:

Obadiah COOLIDGE, *b* 20 July 1663; *m* 28 Feb 1686/7, as her 1st husb, Elizabeth Rose, Roose or Rouse, of Hartford, Conn., (*b* probably 1665; *m* 2nd 16 Feb 1714 John Cunningham and *d* before 6 Nov 1732) and *d* 1707, leaving (with other issue):

Obadiah COOLIDGE, Jr, *b* Watertown 27 Aug 1695; moved to Marlboro, Mass., cordwainer; *m* Watertown 24 July 1717 Rachel, dau of Josiah Goddard (gggs of Thomas Goddard and his w Anne Gifford, Anne in turn being gdau of Sir William Gifford and Eleanor Paulet, sister of 1st Marquess of Winchester, *see* BURKE'S PEERAGE & BARONETAGE), of Watertown, and his w Rachel Davis, and *d* after 1737, leaving (with other issue):

Josiah COOLIDGE, *b* 17 July 1718; *m* Brookline, Mass., 26 April 1742 Mary Jones and *d* Lancaster, Mass., 25 Dec 1780, leaving issue:

John COOLIDGE, *b* Bolton, Mass., *c* 1756; *m* Lancaster 8 Sept 1779 Hannah, dau of James Priest and his w Hannah Lawrence (ggdau of Nathaniel Lawrence and Sarah Morse; Sarah's aunt Mary Morse was an ancestor of President BUSH and another aunt, Elizabeth Morse, was an ancestor of President TAFT, while her ggf Thomas Morse's bro Richard Morse was an ancestor of President NIXON), and *d* Plymouth, Vt., 23 March 1822, leaving issue:

Calvin COOLIDGE, *b* Plymouth, Vt., 27 March 1780; *m* there 9 Dec 1814 Sarah (*b* Chester, Vt., 3 April 1789; *d* Plymouth 19 Nov 1856), dau of William Thompson and his w Dorcas Eaton, and *d* Plymouth 30 April 1853, leaving issue:

Calvin Galusha COOLIDGE, *b* Plymouth 22 Sept 1815; horsebreaker, left his gs Calvin Coolidge 40 ac, a colt and a heifer calf, further entailing the 40 ac to his gs's lineal descendants; *m* Plymouth 3 March 1844 Sarah Almeda (*b* Ludlow, Vt., 17 Dec 1823; *m* 2nd 15 April 1893 George W. Putnam; *d* Plymouth 2 Jan 1906), dau of Israel Brewer and his w Sarah or Sally Brown (ggggdau of Nathaniel Brown and Judith Perkins, whose bro Jabez Perkins was an ancestor of President FRANKLIN ROOSEVELT; Sally Brown was also gda of Adam Brown, Jr, and Priscilla Putnam, whose gggf Nathaniel Putnam had a bro Thomas Putnam, an ancestor of President HOOVER), and *d* Plymouth 15 Dec 1878, leaving issue:

Col John Calvin COOLIDGE, *b* Plymouth, 31 March 1845; notary public, politician, farmer and storekeeper, apptd aide to Govr Stickney 1900 with hon rank of Col; *m* 1st Plymouth 6 May 1868 Victoria Josephine (*b* there 14 March 1846; *d* there 14 March 1885), dau of Hiram Dunlop Moor and his w Abigail Franklin (ggggdau of James Franklin, Jr, and Martha Ormsby, herself dau of John Ormsby and Grace Martin, whose bro John was an ancestor of President GARFIELD), and had issue:

  I (JOHN) CALVIN COOLIDGE, 30th PRESIDENT of the UNITED STATES of AMERICA

  II Abigail Gratia Coolidge, *b* 15 April 1875; *educ* Black River Acad, Ludlow, Vt.; schoolteacher; *d* 6 March 1890 of appendicitis

Col John Calvin Coolidge *m* 2nd 9 Sept 1891 Caroline Athelia Brown (*b* probably Plymouth 22 Jan 1857; *d* there 18 or 19 May 1920) and *d* Plymouth 18 March 1926

Obadiah Coolidge, Jr[1]
1695-p 1737
Rachel Goddard[2]
b 1699

Josiah Coolidge
1718-80
Mary Jones

Joseph Priest, Jr
1678/9-1756
Margaret Childs
b c 1680
Jonathan Lawrence
1696-1773
Joanna Phillips
b 1697

James Priest
c 1720-50
Hannah Lawrence
b 1721/2

James Thompson, Jr
1680-1763
Abigail Hamlet
1689-1759
Ebenezer Jones
1699-1758
Elizabeth Dale
1693—1737-46

William Thompson
1723-1808
Abigail Jones
1729-57

Daniel Davis
1673-1740/1
Mary Hubbard
b 1682
John Lane, Jr
1691-1763
Katherine Whiting
c 1691-1731

Nathaniel Davis
1715-1802
Susanna Lane
b 1720

John Eaton
1696/7-1758/9
Abigail Roberts
c 1701-p 1758
John Boutwell, Jr
1702-23
Elizabeth Parker
b 1705/6

Thomas Eaton
1724/5-74
Betsey Boutwell
b 1723/4

John Harwood
1703-in/p c 1729
Mary —

John Harwood, Jr
1736-1800

Jonathan Brewer
1689-c 1753
Arabella Goulding
c 1692/3-c 1774
John Bent III
1689-1759
Hannah Rice
b 1691/2

Samuel Brewer
1716-in/p 1740
Martha Bent
b 1719/20

David Pulsipher, Jr
1708-in/p 1740
Elizabeth Stowell
b 1719

Mary Pulsipher
1744-1827

Philip Franklin
1707-97
Rachel Horton
1706-91

Aaron Frankin
1729-in/p c 1755
Margaret —

Comfort Starr, Jr
1696-1775
Elizabeth Perley
1705-42
Timothy Cooper
1706-in/p c 1730
Sarah Guile
b 1694/5

Comfort Starr III
1731-1812
Judith Cooper
1736/7-1815

Adam Brown
c 1721-75
Esther Parkman
b 1724
Tarrant Putnam, Jr
1716-94
Priscilla Baker
1724-1812

Adam Brown, Jr
c 1748-a ?1837
Priscilla Putnam
1751-1837

Silas Briggs
1732-1813
Esther Soper
1738-1812
James Paul
c 1725-c 1814
Sarah White
1729-c 1789

Asa Briggs
1755-1834
Elizabeth Paul
b c 1754

Stephen Grover, Jr
c 1682-c 1730
Elizabeth Bateman
1688-p 1730

Eleazer Grover
1728-in/p c 1756
Elizabeth —

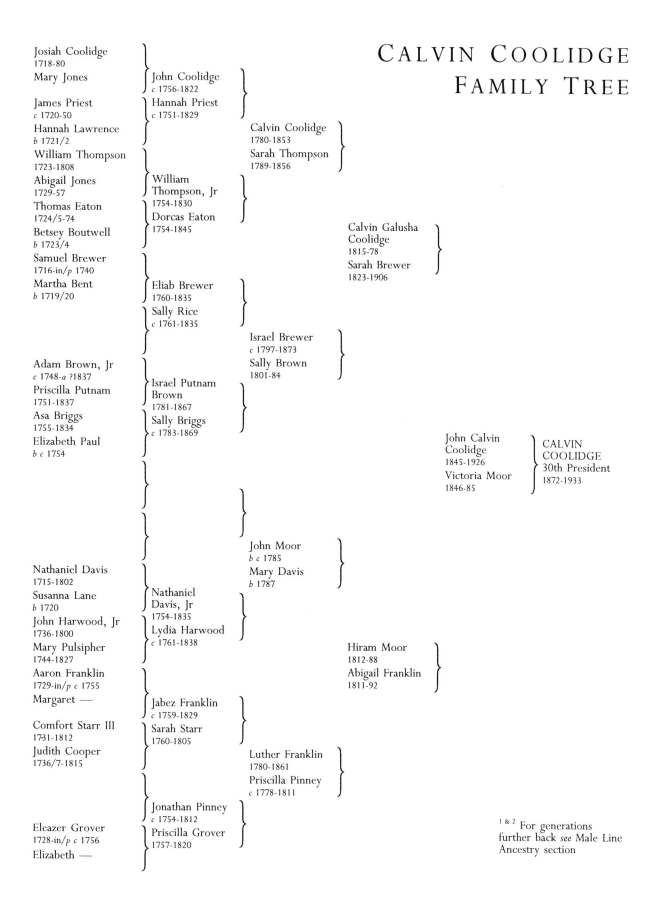

CALVIN COOLIDGE
FAMILY TREE

Josiah Coolidge
1718-80

Mary Jones

James Priest
c 1720-50

Hannah Lawrence
b 1721/2

William Thompson
1723-1808

Abigail Jones
1729-57

Thomas Eaton
1724/5-74

Betsey Boutwell
b 1723/4

Samuel Brewer
1716-in/p 1740

Martha Bent
b 1719/20

Adam Brown, Jr
c 1748-a ?1837

Priscilla Putnam
1751-1837

Asa Briggs
1755-1834

Elizabeth Paul
b c 1754

Nathaniel Davis
1715-1802

Susanna Lane
b 1720

John Harwood, Jr
1736-1800

Mary Pulsipher
1744-1827

Aaron Franklin
1729-in/p c 1755

Margaret —

Comfort Starr III
1731-1812

Judith Cooper
1736/7-1815

Eleazer Grover
1728-in/p c 1756

Elizabeth —

John Coolidge
c 1756-1822

Hannah Priest
c 1751-1829

William Thompson, Jr
1754-1830

Dorcas Eaton
1754-1845

Eliab Brewer
1760-1835

Sally Rice
c 1761-1835

Israel Putnam Brown
1781-1867

Sally Briggs
c 1783-1869

Nathaniel Davis, Jr
1754-1835

Lydia Harwood
c 1761-1838

Jabez Franklin
c 1759-1829

Sarah Starr
1760-1805

Jonathan Pinney
c 1754-1812

Priscilla Grover
1757-1820

Calvin Coolidge
1780-1853

Sarah Thompson
1789-1856

Israel Brewer
c 1797-1873

Sally Brown
1801-84

John Moor
b c 1785

Mary Davis
b 1787

Luther Franklin
1780-1861

Priscilla Pinney
c 1778-1811

Calvin Galusha Coolidge
1815-78

Sarah Brewer
1823-1906

Hiram Moor
1812-88

Abigail Franklin
1811-92

John Calvin Coolidge
1845-1926

Victoria Moor
1846-85

CALVIN COOLIDGE
30th President
1872-1933

[1] & [2] For generations further back see Male Line Ancestry section

Plate 97   Herbert Hoover

HERBERT HOOVER

1874-1964
31ST PRESIDENT OF THE UNITED STATES OF AMERICA
1929-33

Like Van Buren and Cleveland, Herbert Hoover was destroyed by an economic storm which he had not caused; he proved as impotent as they at ending it, but tried much harder. The storm itself was the most violent in American history and its sequel was the most deadly. Hoover was an early victim, but there were millions of others who suffered far worse. Yet it is impossible not to pity him.

The stock market crash of 1929 would in any circumstances have been a major disaster. It wiped out the savings of a generation, destroyed purchasing power, undermined the confidence of investors and managers. In such conditions capitalism cannot operate except at an invalid's pace and recovery takes years. Since the United States was the greatest capitalist nation and since the world money markets had been growing more and more closely intertwined for a century, the 1929 calamity was bound to have disastrous effects internationally. To make matters infinitely worse, by the autumn of 1929 the United States was the only major economy in the world which was not in the grip of deflation and under-production. Europe, Japan and the satellite economies of the British Empire had suffered grievously from World War I and attempts at recovery had repeatedly foundered (partly because Calvin Coolidge had refused to cancel the Allies' war debts: "They hired the money, didn't they? Let them pay it!"). The collapse of the United States removed the one element of hope and stability in the situation.

Under Harding and Coolidge the Americans had surrendered to the isolationist virus and abandoned all their international responsibilities, economic as well as political. Even before the crash there was hope that Hoover would do better. He was a self-made millionaire, a mining engineer whose business had taken him all over the world before 1914. During the war he had organized relief for Belgium and then for central and eastern Europe, with outstanding success. He had impressed all who met him at the Paris peace conference — especially J.M. Keynes, who described him as looking like a weary Titan. He had been an immensely successful Secretary of Commerce for eight years, in the course of which he had once again organized a successful relief programme when the Mississippi broke its banks in 1927. He had privately deplored the Wall Street boom and Coolidge's refusal to do anything about it, though when he became President he felt it was too late to do anything himself. No one could doubt Hoover's compassion or his sense of responsibility. If anyone could put things together again surely he could.

Desperately he tried to do so. During the four years of his presidency he sat labouring at his desk for endless hours until his broad shoulders were stooped, his face was grey and lined, his hands shook with palsy. He never lost faith in the country or in capitalism and said again and again "prosperity is just around the corner and the system is essentially sound." But he was defeated. In the autumn of 1932, when he stood for re-election, the economy was still prostrate. Production had not recovered and more than 12,000,000 were unemployed — 24 per cent of the work force.

Hoover is not to be blamed for failing where no one could have succeeded. It was not his fault, for example, that the French, by refusing to assist Britain and America in rescuing what was left of the

Austrian banking system, brought about a run on the pound that finally forced Britain off the gold standard. It was Congress which, obeying its traditional reflex for the last time, put up the US tariff to its highest ever level, thus dealing international trade, already reeling, another deadly blow. Hoover to be sure might have vetoed the tariff, but at least the mistake was not his alone and the battle with Congress, if he had used the veto, might have wasted energies badly needed elsewhere.

However, it can be said that Hoover did in other ways make things needlessly worse for himself. He was of Quaker stock and the pacific Woodrow Wilson was his hero; perhaps these traits explain why, when Japan invaded Manchuria, he was able to do nothing but bleat and wring his hands like Buchanan in 1861. He had written a book years before, called *American Individualism*, in which he identified the secret of his country's greatness as the opportunity it offered to every energetic young man to go out into the world and make something of himself, as young Herbert Hoover had done. This was a moral more than an economic doctrine, making it impossible for its author to agree relief payments to the unemployed. Such a dole would destroy their character. The fact that there was no work and no sign of any for even the most energetic young man in the Depression did not crack Hoover's dogmatism. Nothing is so immune to hard facts as ideology.

Above all Hoover failed as a political leader. He said he had faith in the American character, but he did nothing to elicit its resourcefulness, its courage, its capacity for hard work. Instead a heavy sad face, a weary voice spoke of hope and inevitable recovery. No recovery occurred; the administration seemed to be doing nothing and to have no ideas; inevitably the people turned away. The Democrats were clearly poised for victory in 1932 and some of them had dangerously radical ideas.

Hoover now emulated Woodrow Wilson in good earnest. He thought of himself as the last champion of American capitalism, of rugged individualism. The Democratic candidate had promised "a new deal for the American people". What horrors of socialistic innovation might not this imply? The President took his case to the voters and travelled up and down the country as devotedly and uselessly as Wilson and Harding before him. Election day came and he was overwhelmed. He had received 444 electoral votes in the landslide election of 1928; now Franklin Roosevelt received 472, Hoover 59. It was a conclusive rejection.

Gloomily he went back to Washington to finish his term. The banking system began to collapse, but there was nothing he felt able to do without the President-elect's assistance, and that assistance was not forthcoming. Still President, Hoover was little more than a ghost, impotently hoping against hope that his successor would see sense and adopt the Hoover policies.

HERBERT HOOVER'S FAMILY

Despite his German-Swiss ancestry in the male line, Hoover's kin include Presidents Pierce, Fillmore, Garfield, Cleveland, Taft, Coolidge, Nixon, Ford and Bush, all related through his mother, Hulda Minthorn. The relationship is reasonably close, that is to say a common ancestor occurs no longer ago than the 16th century and some common ancestors are found only a few generations back. Pierce and Hoover were fourth cousins, for instance.

Through Hulda, Hoover descended from Anne Bradstreet, *née* Dudley, who was America's first published poet and whom the great Congregationalist clergyman Cotton Mather called a "crown to her father". This father was Thomas Dudley, from whom of course Hoover also descended, and who was Governor of Massachusetts in 1634, 1640, 1645 and 1650, a co-founder of Cambridge, Mass., and an early promoter of the establishment of Harvard. Among Hoover's cousins through Anne were Oliver Wendell Holmes. The 19th-century American editor Rufus W. Griswold called Anne the "most celebrated poet of her time in America", which was a backhanded compliment as there were few rivals,

Plate 98   Lou Henry Hoover

and in any case Griswold's reputation as a critic is low nowadays. (However, his *Republican Court: or American Society in the Days of Washington* has some merit and is useful in reminding us of the extent to which the presidency under Washington established continuity with the ancien régime.)

Unlike Dudley, whose crown was poetic, Hoover and his wife Lou behaved in more substantially regal a fashion once he became President, much as Washington had done. Even when alone the two of them ate in the State Dining Room wearing formal evening dress. Old Guard Republicans privately referred to the President as 'Sir Herbert'. The Hoover family had lived for several years before World War I in England, his one-time residence in the London suburb of Walton-on-Thames being prophetically named the White House. He was therefore more or less bound to be suspected of being too pro-British, and with his personal admiration for Woodrow Wilson he was looked on as a crypto-Democrat as well. Yet his thoughts while in England often turned to America, and though he stayed on in London during the early war years it was in order to carry out sterling work in organising relief operations, not least for his fellow Americans. He never considered taking British citizenship, although Lord Kitchener, the British Secretary of State for War, asked him if he would, adding that the British government had it in mind that he could perform a great service for them. This probably meant making Hoover Minister of Munitions, perhaps with a seat in the Cabinet. Walter Page, the US Ambassador to London at the time, reckoned Hoover could have had a peerage as well if he had accepted the offer. Page was almost certainly right, since several other foreigners in those years acquired first British citizenship then a title, notably the Astors.

Despite having lived all over the world between graduating from Stanford and returning to head Wilson's Food Administration toward the end of the War, Hoover remained very American. In Australia he was known as '"Hail Columbia" Hoover' and in Britain as 'the star-spangled Hoover'. He recruited his mining engineers from America, including his brother Theodore; he kept up professional, family and college ties with his native country and often visited America for short periods. He could not have slipped so easily into high-level American politics if he had been a mere expatriate coming home after 15 years of no true contact with his native land. It was a great help to him in the 1928 presidential election against Al Smith, the city candidate, that he could refer to his family background in rural Iowa.

Even his Christian name was influenced by that background. His mother's sister Ann, recalling a book she had read in childhood about the Waldenses sect of early Protestants with a hero called Hubert, suggested he be called Herbert, which in her faulty memory she confused with Hubert. Other members of the family played crucial roles in his early life. His mother's brother had revived him when he was given up for dead after an attack of croup in early childhood. His aunt Laura had taught him all his early school subjects between the ages of 11 and 12. As Hoover became the most successful member of the family he tended to act on its members, rather than they on him. In China his wife Lou's sister lived with him and Lou. Hoover supported his elder brother Theodore while the latter was getting an education and Theodore followed him both into mining and mining finance. He even emulated his brother when it was a question of where to live, to the extent of settling for a while in London.

Lou Hoover was a geologist herself and was almost as much at home down a mine as her husband. In what was almost the burlesque of a Soviet socialist realist drama from the 1930s (boy meets girl meets tractor) the two were introduced by Hoover's teacher at Stanford, Professor Branner, over some chunks of rock in his laboratory. There was some question as to whether they were carboniferous or pre-carboniferous and Branner good-naturedly brought Hoover into the conversation as he explained their provenance to Lou. Lou's family had come out to California because her mother was thought to be tuberculous. They had done well there, so that when she first met Hoover he was the poor boy, she the relatively rich girl. That soon changed once they were married, with Hoover becoming very rich indeed. As a result the Hoovers were able to do a massive amount of entertaining long before they entered the White House, where Hoover continued to have breakfast, lunch and dinner guests almost every day, making up out of his own pocket the difference between the actual cost and his official entertainment allowance.

Lou had taste, and had started collecting porcelain when in China. She gathered all the empire furniture first purchased for the White House by Monroe in one place, the East Room, where it made a fine display. Her undoubted abilities as a hostess were much needed at times, for Hoover was little given to small talk. He could reel off an anecdote but not generate that sprightly give and take of conversation which arguably is the essence of civilised intercourse. Hoover's niece Hulda Hoover McLean reckoned the way both her father and her uncle were content to sit silently for long periods if they had nothing to say reflected their situation in childhood, when they were left early on without parents to teach them what the world calls good manners. It is also possible the Quaker tradition was at work, whereby one sits silent in assembly until moved by the spirit to speak. It is true that Hoover was not a strict Quaker in the way his parents's generation among the family had been. His mother, for instance, a well-educated woman for her day, spoke at numerous Quaker meetings beyond her home patch and was much in demand. She was also active in the anti-alcohol movement. Nevertheless it is interesting that what moved Hoover and his wife to unprecedentedly large-scale action was international relief, since it has become a peculiarly Quaker activity this century.

Lou Hoover was an able linguist. She learned far more Chinese than her husband did while they were stationed in Tientsin, although between them they had enough vocabulary to converse confidentially in later life when non-Chinese speakers were present. Her German, which Hoover was bad at, and Spanish came in useful on his other business trips abroad. But in the White House she communicated with the servants at big functions by hand signals disguised as natural gestures: if she patted her hair it meant dinner was to be announced, if she adjusted her spectacles the table was to be cleared and so on. The Hoovers were not particularly loved by their staff, though their generosity in material matters was acknowledged. When Lou Hoover came to show Eleanor Roosevelt round the White House she drew the line at entering the kitchen, saying she never went there and the housekeeper would have to conduct the new First Lady round it instead.

Lou Hoover supplemented her husband's career with contributions of her own in almost every field. In metallurgy she helped him with translating Agricola's work on medieval mining, a project she had first mooted anyway, and was a joint recipient with her husband of the Mining and Metallurgical Society of America's gold medal for the feat. When in Tientsin the foreigners were threatened by the Boxer Rising of 1900, Lou Hoover organised the women for defence just as her husband did the men. She also proved as able an organiser of relief work among women as he among men. She made speeches from the back of railroad cars during both his presidential campaigns. She went on a lecture tour to raise money for war relief and was as good at coaxing large sums of money from the rich for a charitable cause as her husband was at persuading hard-headed investors to sink large sums of money in purely self-interested ventures such as gold mines.

In a few matters she and her husband differed. She was a keen horsewoman; he had not ridden since his childhood, when his uncle's enthusiasm for carriage driving (along with much else in his uncle's character) had failed to rub off on him. She is the source for one particularly revealing glimpse into Hoover's own character: he could not stand bread queues. As early as 1914, during the Hoover-organised attempt to help Belgian war victims, she recorded how "My husband will not visit a bread-line unless literally compelled to, and . . . has his eyes near full of tears before he leaves." Even though Hoover's dislike of being confronted by the poor and homeless and hungry stemmed from too acute a sensibility rather than too blunt a one, it was just as fatal to a politician. One of his greatest failures as President stemmed from this. How interesting that we discover it first through his wife.

BIOGRAPHICAL DETAILS AND DESCENDANTS

HOOVER, HERBERT CLARK, *b* West Branch, Iowa, 10 Aug 1874; *educ* Friends Pacific Acad, Newberg, Oreg., Capital Business Coll, Salem, Oreg., and Stanford U, Calif. (AB 1895); miner Calif. 1895-96, mining engr in Australia, Canada, China, France, Germany, Hawaii, India, Malaya, New Zealand, Russia, UK and USA 1897-1914, Dir: Bewick, Moreing & Co 1903-08, Australian Exploration Co 1904-08, Chinese Engineering & Mining Co 1904, Zinc Corp 1905, Australian Smelting Corp 1905, Anglo-Continental Gold Syndicate 1908, Lake View Consols 1908, Oroya Leonesa 1910, Oroya Black Range, Maikop & Gen Petroleum Tst (also Fndr) 1910, Lake View & Star Ltd (also Fndr) 1910, Babilonia Gold Mines 1911, Granville Mining Co 1911 (also Fndr), General Petroleum Co 1912, Bishopsgate Syndicate, Burma Corp 1912 (Chm 1914), Fitzroy Mines 1912, Kyshtim Corp 1912, Maikop Apsheron Oil Co 1912, Mountain Queen, Inter-Argentine Syndicate 1912, Internat Mexican Syndicate 1913, Inter-Siberian Syndicate 1914, Irtysh Corp 1914, Camp Bird 1914, Inter-California Tst 1914, Inter Guaranty Syndicate 1914, Russo-Asiatic Corp 1914, Santa Gertrudis Co 1914, Yuanmi Gold Mines 1914, Natomas Land & Dredging Tst Co 1914-16 and Messina (Transvaal) 1914-16, Temp Chm Camp Birdmine, Colo., and Santa Gertrudis Mine, Mexico, 1914-16, Managing Dir and later Chm Oroya Exploration Co, Fndr Ctee of American Residents (aid for US citizens caught in Europe on outbreak of World War I) 1914-15, Fndr and Chm Commission for Relief in Belgium 1915-18, US Food Administrator 1917-19, Dir-Gen Relief and Reconstruction of Europe 1918, Chm Supreme Economic Cncl, Memb American Ctee Economic Advsrs Paris Peace Conf, Fndr Hoover Inst, Stanford U, 1919, US Secy of Commerce 1921-29, 31st President (R) of the USA 1929-33, Chm: US Grain Corp, US Sugar Equalisation Bd, Inter-Allied Food Cncl, Boys Club of America 1936, Polish Relief Commission and Finnish Relief Fund 1939, Ctee on Food for Small Democracies 1940, Belgian Relief Fund 1942, Co-ordinator Food Supply for World Famine 1946, Chm Commission on Govt Ops (2nd Hoover Commission) 1953-55, Memb Advsy BdWorld Bank Reconstruction and Devpt, held hon degrees from 85 universities round the world, 108 medals from organizations and socs worldwide and hon citizenship of over 12 cities worldwide, author: *Principles of Mining* (1909), translation (with Lou Hoover) of Georgius Agricola's *De Re Metallica* (1912), *American Individualism* (1922), *New Day* (1928), *Boyhood in Iowa* (1931), *Hoover After Dinner* (1933), *Challenge to Liberty* (1934), *The State Papers and Other Public Writings of Herbert Hoover*, ed William Star Myers, 2 vols (1934), *Addresses Upon the American Road*, 8 vols (1938-61), *America's Way*

Forward (1939), *Shall We Send Our Youth to War?* (1939), *Problems of Lasting Peace* (1942), *America's First Crusade* (1943), *Memoirs*: Vol I *Years of Adventure, 1874-1920* (1951); Vol II *The Cabinet and the Presidency, 1920-1933* (1952); Vol III *The Great Depression, 1929-1941* (1952), *The Ordeal of Woodrow Wilson* (1958), *An American Epic*, 3 vols (1959-61), *The Hoover-Wilson Wartime Correspondence, 1914-1918*, ed Francis W. O'Brien (1974); *m* Monterey, Calif., 10 Feb 1899 Lou (*b* Waterloo, Iowa, 29 March 1874; *educ* San Jose Normal Sch (now State U) and Stanford U; teacher, translator with her husb of *De Re Metallica*, Pres Soc of American Women in London 1914-15, Memb: Ctee of Mercy, Calif., 1915, Ctee American Women's War Relief Fund (and Sec-Treasurer American Women's War Relief Fund Economic Ctee 1915) and Citizens' Ctee, Chm Women's Division American Ctee, Chevalier Cross of Order of Leopold (Belgium); *d* New York 7 Jan 1944, *bur* Hoover Cemetery, West Branch), er dau of Charles Delano Henry, banker, and his w Florence Ida Weed, and *d* 20 Oct 1964 of an internal haemorrhage, leaving issue:

President Hoover's son
I Herbert Charles HOOVER, *b* London, UK, 4 Aug 1903; *educ* Stanford U (AB) and Harvard (MBA); mining engr 1925, researcher Harvard Buiness Sch 1928-29, communications engr Western Air Express 1929-31 and TWA 1931-34, teaching fellow California Inst Technology 1934-35, Pres: Utd Geophysical Co Inc 1935-52 (Chm 1952-54) and Consolidated Engrg Corp 1936-46, Special Adviser to US Sec of State 1953, US Under-Sec of State 1954-57; *m* Stanford 25 June 1925 Margaret Eva Watson (*b* San Francisco 28 March 1905; *d* 25 June 1982) and *d* Pasadena, Calif., 9 July 1969, leaving issue:

Grandchildren
1 *Margaret Ann Hoover [Mrs Richard Brigham, Wind O' Hill Farm, 1100 Meeting House Road, West Chester, PA 19382, USA], *b* Boston, Mass., 17 March 1926; *educ* Wellesley; *m* Pasadena 30 June 1949 *Richard Tatem BRIGHAM (*b* Boston 7 Nov 1925), s of Ferdinand Bennett Brigham and his w Mary Tatem, and has issue:

Great-grandchildren
(1) *Katharine Storrs BRIGHAM [331 West Miner St, West Chester, PA 19382, USA], *b* Boston 8 June 1950; *educ* Wellesley (BA 1972)
(2) *Ann Dyer Brigham [Mrs Glenn E Thomas, 2S 620 Eddie Rd, Glen Ellyn, IL 60137, USA], *b* Boston 13 Feb 1952; *educ* Mt Holyoke Coll (BA 1974) and U of S California Business Sch (MBA 1977); accountant 1977-78; *m* West Chester 15 June 1974 *Glenn E. THOMAS (*b* Chicago 26 Sept 1952), s of Lee Thomas and his w Dr Joan Thomas, and has issue:

Great-great-grandchildren
1a *Stephen Brigham THOMAS, *b* Wiesbaden, W Germany, 27 June 1980
2a *Nathan Hoover THOMAS, *b* Louisville, Ky., 9 July 1990

Great-grandchildren
(3) *Robert Hoover BRIGHAM [621 Madrone Av, Sunnyvale, CA 94086, USA], *b* Boston 2 July 1953; *educ* Amherst Coll (BA 1975) and Stanford U (PhD 1984); chemist; *m* Pittsburgh, Pa., 11 June 1977 Ellen (*b* 26 July 1953), dau of Albert McBride and his w Mary Ellen
(4) *Deborah Miles Brigham [Mrs Alan J Mesher, Box 6, Batesville, VA 22924, USA], *b* Wilmington, Del., 6 Feb 1959; *educ* Hollins Coll (BA 1981); trained horses and students 1981-87, massage therapist 1984-; *m* West Chester 20 Aug 1980 *Alan John MESHER (*b* 25 May 1948), s of Samuel Mesher and his w Frances, and has issue:

Great-great-grandchildren
1a *Matthew Emerson MESHER, *b* Austin, Tex., 7 Aug 1987

Great-grandchildren
(5) *Douglas Ward BRIGHAM [410 North Matlack St, West Chester, PA 19380, USA], *b* Wilmington, Del., 15 Feb 1960; *educ* Colorado State U (BA 1983); Pennsylvania State Police: Trooper April 1987, Patrolman Sept 1987-April 1990, with Narcotics Squad 1990-93, pilot 1993-; *m* 11 June 1984 (divorce July 1986) Kelleen Dee Selby

Grandchildren
2 *Herbert HOOVER [1520 Circle Drive, San Marino, CA 91108, USA], *b* Boston 5 Nov 1927; *educ* U of Arizona; *m* Virginia City, Nev., 8 Jan 1949 *Meredith McGilvray (*b* Palo Alto, Calif., 9 Dec 1927) and has issue:

Great-grandchildren
(1) *Stephen HOOVER, *b* Palo Alto 29 Aug 1949
(2) Michael HOOVER, *b* Tucson, Ariz., 13 March 1951; *d* 19—
(3) *Leslie HOOVER, *b* Palo Alto 17 Jan 1956

Grandchildren
3 *Joan Leslie Hoover [Mrs William Vowles, 28431 Southwest Mountain Rd, West Linn, OR 97086, USA], *b* Los Angeles 12 April 1930; *m* 29 June 1951 *William Leland VOWLES (*b* Oakland, Calif., 9 Feb 1926) and has issue:

Great-grandchildren
(1) *Mark Leland VOWLES, *b* San Jose, Calif., 21 Feb 1954
(2) *Aaron Clay VOWLES, *b* San Jose 2 Nov 1955
(3) *Brian Arthur VOWLES, *b* San Jose 24 Sept 1958

President Hoover's son
II *Allan Henry HOOVER [181 Clapboard Ridge Road, Greenwich, CT 06831, USA], *b* London, UK, 17 July 1907; *educ*

Stanford U (AB); sometime rancher in Calif.; *m* Los Angeles 17 March 1937 *Margaret (*b* Tucson 7 March 1911), dau of William Baylor Coberly and his w Winifred Wheeler, and has issue:

Grandchildren

1 *Allan Henry HOOVER, Jr [290 Via Lerida, Greenbrae, CA, USA], *b* Palo Alto 15 Nov 1938; *m* 21 Aug 1965 *Marion, dau of Dr C. H. Cutler, and has issue:

Great-grandchildren
(1) *Deborah H. HOOVER, *b* 1968
(2) *Allan Henry HOOVER III, *b* 4 Oct 1971

Grandchildren

2 *Andrew HOOVER, *b* Palo Alto 9 Nov 1940; *m* 28 Dec 1963 (divorce 1966) Victoria Louise Talman and has issue:

Great-grandchildren
(1) *Andrew HOOVER, Jr, *b* 20 July 1965

Grandchildren

3 *Lou Henry HOOVER, *b* Palo Alto 9 Jan 1943

MALE LINE ANCESTRY AND COLLATERAL DESCENDANTS

Georg HUBER, Untervogt (Deputy Sheriff) of Lenzburg, Canton of Aargau, Switzerland, and miller of Oberkulm, also in Switzerland; *m* and had issue:

Johann Heinrich HUBER, *b c* 1644; linen weaver of Oberkulm, moved because of religious persecution to Ellerstadt, near Dürkheim, Rhenish Palatinate (a few miles west of Mannheim in what is now southwest Germany); *m* Maria Margaretta Hoffman and *d* Oberkulm *c* 1706, leaving (with other issue):

Gregor Jonas HUBER, *b* Oberkulm, 6 July 1668; *m c* 1698 Anna Maria Kruetzer (*b c* 1675/6; *d* Ellerstadt 12 April 1756) and *d* Ellerstadt 23 April 1741, having had (with other issue, including two er s):

Andreas HUBER, *b* Ellerstadt 29 Jan 1723; emigrated to America 1738, joining his bros in Lancaster Co, Pa., then settled at Pipe Creek, Md., where he acquired 50 ac and worked as a miller and farmer, moved 1762 to Randolph Co, N Carolina, where he built a mill on the Uwharrie River, changed name to Andrew Hoover *c* 1763; *m* Pa. *c* 1745 Anna Margreta (Margaret) (*b* probably Zweibrücken, Rhenish Palatinate, *c* 1725; *d* N Carolina 1797), dau of Jacob Pfautz and his w Maria Elizabeth, and *d* Randolph Co, N Carolina, *c* 1783, leaving (with seven other s and five daus):

John HOOVER, *b* Uniontown, Md., *c* 1760; farmer and millwright, converted from Lutheranism to Quakerism and partly because of his Quaker opposition to slavery moved to West Milton, Miami Co, Ohio, 1802; *m* Randolph Co, N Carolina, *c* 1784 Sarah (*b* 20 Sept 1767; *d* Ohio 29 Dec 1843), dau of Christian Burkhard(t) and Anna Barbara Graeff, and *d* West Milton 18 Nov 1831, having had (with six other s and two daus) a 5th s:

Jesse HOOVER, *b* Uwharrie, N Carolina, 20 June 1799; settled Hubbard, Iowa, 1854; *m* West Milton, Ohio, 18 April 1819 Rebecca (*b* Ky. 3 Nov 1801; teacher; *d* West Branch, Iowa, 13 Aug 1895), dau of John Yount and his w Mary Lowe, and *d* West Branch 15 Dec 1856 after being injured in an accident, having had issue (with two other s and four daus):

I Eli HOOVER, for whom *see below* II John Y. HOOVER, Quaker evangelist III Benajah HOOVER, succeeded his nephew Jesse C. Hoover in the farm implements business

The est s,

Eli HOOVER, *b* West Milton 17 July 1820; *m* 1st Miami Co 20 Feb 1840 Mary (*b* 26 Oct 1820; farmer, carpenter and mason; *d* Miami Co 3 March 1853), dau of John Davis and his 1st w Lydia Coate, and had three s and two daus; *m* 2nd West Branch 17 Aug 1854 Hannah Leonard (*b* Ireland 14 Feb 1832) and *d* Hubbard, Iowa, 24 July 1892, having had with her two s and two daus; his sons by his 1st marriage:

I Davis HOOVER, took in his nephew Theodore (Tad) Hoover after his brother and sister-in-law's death
II Jesse Clark HOOVER, for whom *see below*
III Allen HOOVER, farmer, took in his nephew Herbert C. Hoover for a year and a half following the death of the latter's parents; *m* 18— Millie —— and had issue:

1 Walter HOOVER

The 2nd s,

Jesse Clark HOOVER, *b* Stillwater, Ohio, 2 Sept 1846; blacksmith and farm equipment merchant; *m* Iowa 12 March 1870 Hulda Randall (*b* Norwich, Ontario, Canada, 4 May 1848; *educ* U of Iowa; schoolteacher, West Branch sec Women's Christian Temperance Union, fndr Young People's Prayer Meeting of West Branch; *d* West Branch 22 Feb 1884 of typhoid and pneumonia), dau of Theodore Minthorn (ggs of William Minthorn, Jr, emigrant from England to New England, where he acquired a farm in Connecticut, and his w Mary Gilbert, herself gda of John Gilbert and Amy Lord, whose bro William Lord was an ancestor of President FORD) and his w Mary Wasley, and d West Branch 13 Dec 1880, leaving issue:

I Theodore (Tad) Jesse HOOVER, b West Branch 28 Jan 1871; educ Friends Pacific Acad, Newberg, Oreg., William Penn Coll, Iowa, and Stanford U (AB 1901); linotype operator for *Oakland Tribune*, mining engr then consulting engr, Dir: Minerals Separation to 1910, Mountain Queen Ltd (Australian mining company) 1910-11, Babilonia Gold Mines 1911 and Maikop Apsheron Oil Co, Oroya Links, Star Explorations, Trinidad-Cedros Oil, Zinc Corp and Lake View and Star Ltd 1912, Burma Corp 1914, Dean of Sch of Engrg Stanford U; m San Francisco 6 June 1899 Mildred Crew (b West Liberty, Iowa, 14 Feb 1872; d Palo Alto 3 Sept 1940), dau of Thomas Snowden Brooke, of Maryland, and his w Mildred Stanley; d Rancho del Oso, Santa Cruz, Calif., 5 Feb 1955, leaving issue:

President Hoover's niece
1 *Mildred Brooke Hoover [Mrs Cornelius Willis, 1 Carter Avenue, Sierra Madre, CA 91025, USA; Rancho Del Oso, Davenport, CA 95017, USA], b Palo Alto 13 May 1901; educ Stanford U; m Santa Cruz 27 Aug 1922 Cornelius Grinnell WILLIS (b Washington, DC, 26 Jan 1899; d Jan 1983), s of Dr Bailey Willis and his w Margaret Baker, and has issue:

Great-nephew
(1) *Theodore Hoover WILLIS [Rancho Del Oso, Davenport, CA 95017, USA], b Palo Alto 4 June 1925; educ Stanford U (BSEng 1948, MBA 1950); m 1st Stanford 30 Sept 1944 (divorce 1967) Jessie Beryl (b Grantsville, Utah, 7 Sept 1925), dau of Stanley William Rigsby and his w Jessie Tanner, and has issue:

Great-nephew's children
1a *Theodore Hoover WILLIS, Jr, b Stanford 13 Nov 1947; m Costa Mesa, Calif., 3 Dec 1973 *Ruth Ann Murray (b Inglewood, Calif., 9 July 1949) and has issue:

Great-nephew's grandchildren
1b *Trina Angela WILLIS, b Costa Mesa 16 May 1974
2b *Theodore Hoover WILLIS III, b Santa Cruz 4 Sept 1975
3b *Jonathon Cornelius WILLIS, b Twin Falls, Idaho, 27 May 1977
4b *Sarah Jane WILLIS, b Lakeview, Oreg., 13 Feb 1979
5b *Karen Ann WILLIS, b Lakeview 22 Oct 1980
6b *Diane Brooke WILLIS, b Butte, Mont., 8 May 1982
7b *Jacob Jesse Theodore WILLIS, b Butte 29 May 1989

Great-nephew's children
2a *Teryl Bailey Willis, b Stanford, Calif., 25 Sept 1949; educ Occidental Coll (BA 1973); m Tecate, Calif., 21 Oct 1973 (divorce 1978) Jeffrey KANNER
3a *Tracy Jane Willis, b Pasadena 29 Sept 1951; educ California State U; m Sierra Madre 22 March 1975 (divorce 1985) Nicolas LAREZ (b Santa Monica, Calif., 1 Feb 1949) and has issue:

Great-nephew's grandchildren
1b *Elisha Ann LAREZ, b Sierra Madre 29 Oct 1977
2b *Nicolas Jacob Theodore LAREZ, b Sierra Madre 29 July 1980

Great-nephews
(1) (cont.) Theodore Hoover Willis m 2nd Rancho del Oso 27 Dec 1975 *Agnes (b Los Angeles 6 March 1925), dau of Charles Oliver and his w Agnes McCormick and widow of Robert Victor Dobbs
(2) *David Grinnell WILLIS [98 Reservoir Road, Atherton, CA 94025, USA], b Palo Alto 7 Nov 1926; educ Stanford U (BSEng 1947, MS 1953, PhD 1954) and Harvard (MBA 1951); scientist; m Omaha, Nebr., 4 April 1953 *Jean Lee (b Omaha 8 April 1932), dau of James Allan and his w Gretchen Langdon, and has issue:

Great-nephew's children
1a *James Allan WILLIS, b Houston, Tex., 15 Oct 1956; educ Yale; m Dec 1989 *Astrid Lynne Johnson
2a *Cornelius Grinnell WILLIS, b Redwood City, Calif., 21 March 1961; m 27 Aug 1989 *Anne Louise Hartley
3a *Nathaniel Parker WILLIS, b Redwood City 9 May 1965; m 22 Aug 1992 *Anne Elizabeth Senti

Great-niece
(3) *Mildred Anne Willis [Mrs Robert Briggs, Rancho del Oso, Davenport, CA 95017, USA], b Los Angeles 9 Aug 1932; educ Stanford U; m 1st Sierra Madre 15 Nov 1952 (divorce 1969) John Richmond HUGENS (b Pasadena 29 Sept 1931), s of Earle Hugens (previously Huggins) and his w Mary Jacobs, and has issue:

Great-niece's children
1a *John Richmond HUGENS, Jr, b Pittsburgh, Pa., 22 Oct 1955; m Belmont, Calif., 19 Sept 1978 *Jennifer Sprinkle (b 28 Feb 1957)
2a *Daniel Willis HUGENS, b Pasadena 4 Sept 1957; m 18 June 1983 *Kathleen Joyce Hess
3a *Paul Brook HUGENS, b Pasadena 9 March 1961

Great-niece
(3) (cont.) Mrs Mildred Hugens m 2nd Rancho del Oso 27 June 1973 *Robert Owen BRIGGS (b Evansville, Ill., 7 Feb 1925), s of George Briggs and his w Evelyn Rist

President Hoover's niece

2 *Hulda Brooke Hoover [Mrs Charles McLean, 512 Walnut Avenue, Santa Cruz, CA 95060, USA], *b* Palo Alto 19 Aug 1906; *educ* Stanford U; artist and author; *m* Yuba City, Calif., 5 Dec 1925 Charles Alexander McLEAN, Jr (*b* Spokane, Wash., 13 April 1906; *d* 7 April 1981), s of Charles Alexander McLean and his *w* Lilian Robertson, and has issue:

Great-nephews

(1) *Charles Alexander McLEAN III [13805 Ginger Loop, Penn Valley, CA 95946, USA], *b* Palo Alto 19 Sept 1931; *educ* Stanford U (AB, MBA, MS); mining engr; *m* Kuala Lumpur, Malaya, 28 April 1962 *Mary Georgina (*b* Somerset, UK, 15 Nov 1939), yr dau of Rear-Adml George Arthur Thring, CB, DSO and bar, DL, of Alford House, Castle Cary, Somerset, and his *w* Betty Mary Blacker, JP

(2) *Allan Hoover McLEAN [512 Walnut Ave, Santa Cruz, CA 95060, USA], *b* Palo Alto 10 Oct 1935; *educ* U of Southern California (MS); Human Factors Engr; *m* Reno, Nev., 9 Oct 1954 (divorce 1973) Hazel Bassett and has issue:

Great-nephew's children

1a John David McLEAN, *b* Santa Cruz 4 Nov 1955; *d* there 4 June 1984

2a *Cheryln McLean, *b* Santa Cruz 20 Nov 1957; *m* 1st Rancho del Oso 1982 (divorce 1983) James HUGHES; *m* 2nd Carmel, Calif., 21 June 1986 *Tore FRANZEN and has issue:

Great-nephew's grandchildren

1b *Domenic Jason McLEAN, *b* 11 Oct 1972; *m* 1992 *Misti Cox and has issue:

Great-nephew's great-grandchildren

1c *Brooke McLEAN, *b* 19 Feb 1992

Great-nephew's grandchildren

2b *Lillian Brook Taylor McLEAN, *b* 10 Aug 1976

Great-nephew's children

3a *Skyelare Robertson McLEAN, *b* Santa Cruz 11 June 1959; *m* Rancho del Oso 11 Feb 1978 *Carol Knapton and has issue:

Great-nephew's grandchildren

1b *Felicia Lee McLEAN, *b* 13 July 1978

2b *Ambrin Brooke McLEAN, *b* 19 Oct 1983

3b *Jennifer Anne McLEAN, *b* 4 Oct 1989

Great-nephew's children

4a *Theodore Kirkland McLEAN [Teddo McLean, 11090 Redwood, Brookdale, Santa Cruz, CA 95007, USA], *b* Santa Cruz 27 March 1961; *m* Rancho del Oso 2 June 1990 *Kirsten Lynn and has issue:

Great-nephew's grandchildren

1b *Rose Marie McLEAN, *b* 20 Oct 1992

Great-nephew's children

5a *Allison Brooke McLEAN, *b* Santa Cruz 26 Sept 1963

6a *Rohanne Canna McLean, *b* Marietta, Ga., 22 March 1967; *m* Santa Cruz 1989 *Charles Randall JOHNSTON and has issue:

Great-nephew's grandchildren

1b *Hayley Jordan JOHNSTON, *b* 19 Nov 1992

Great-nephew

(3) *Robertson Brooke McLEAN [619 San Juan Avenue, Santa Cruz, CA 95060, USA], *b* Palo Alto 10 July 1939; *m* Santa Cruz 27 Feb 1960 *Rosanna Jean Branstetter and has issue:

Great-nephew's children

1a *William Stuart McLEAN, *b* Santa Cruz 16 Dec 1963; *m* 21 Aug 1987 *Judith Anne Moore

2a *Judith Ann McLEAN, *b* Santa Cruz 12 Nov 1965

President Hoover's niece

3 Louise Brooke Hoover, *b* London, UK, 29 March 1908; *m* 1st Stanford 21 June 1925 (divorce 1938) Ernest Albert DUNBAR (*d* 1969) and had issue:

Great-niece

(1) *Della Lou Dunbar [Mrs Wayne Swan, 240 Kellogg Ave, Palo Alto, CA 94301, USA], *b* Palo Alto 1 Aug 1926; *educ* San Jose State U and Colorado Coll; teacher; *m* 1 Jan 1950 *Wayne McIntyre SWAN, s of Thomas Edwards Swan and his *w* Ethel Means, and has issue:

Great-niece's children

1a *Jane Beatrice Swan, *b* Palo Alto 10 Dec 1953; *m* there 15 Aug 1992 *Arthur KECULAH

2a *Thomas Peter SWAN, *b* Shelbyville, Tenn., 7 June 1955

3a *Rachel Merelyn SWAN, *b* Vancouver, Canada, 6 Nov 1957

4a A dau; *d* in infancy March 1961

5a *Ernest William SWAN, *b* Palo Alto 6 March 1964

Great-niece

(2) *Judith Dawn Dunbar [Mrs Dan Wheeler, 483 Nicasio Way, Soquel, CA 95073, USA], b Palo Alto 27 May 1928; m 1st 1950 (divorce 19—) Louis CENTOFANTI; m 2nd 1992 *Dan WHEELER

President Hoover's niece

3 (cont.) Louise Brooke Hoover Dunbar m 2nd 1938 (divorce 19—) Harold FOUTS; m 3rd 1942 (divorce 19—) Kenneth STEVENSON; m 4th 1947 (divorce 19—) William HAUSELT and d 25 Feb 1985

II HERBERT CLARK HOOVER, 31st PRESIDENT of the UNITED STATES of AMERICA

III Mary (May) Hoover, b West Branch 1 Sept 1876; m Newburg, Oreg., 1899 Cornelius Van Ness LEAVITT (b 1 March 1874; d Santa Monica 7 April 1962) and d 7 June 1953, leaving issue:

President Hoover's nephew

1 *Van Ness Hoover LEAVITT [1617 Franklin Street, Santa Monica, CA 90404, USA], b San Francisco 1 July 1908; m 1st Santa Monica 30 Jan 1928 (divorce 19—) Dorothy Juanita Berry; m 2nd Santa Monica *Patricia Agnes Rheinschild (b 9 Nov 1914) and with her has issue:

Great-nephew

(1) *Michael Van Ness LEAVITT [2920 Kansas Avenue, Santa Monica, CA 90404, USA], b Santa Monica 13 March 1946; educ UCLA (BA); m 1970 *Joanne —— and has issue:

Great-nephew's children

1a *Thomas Van Ness LEAVITT, b Santa Monica 21 Jan 1972

2a *Gregory Charles LEAVITT, b Santa Monica 4 Feb 1974

Great-nephew

(2) *David LEAVITT, b Santa Monica 5 June 1951; m there 1973 *Bridget ——

Father's side		Mother's side	
Gregor Huber[1] 1668-1741		William Minthorn	
Anna Kruetzer c 1675/6-1756	Andrew Hoover 1723-c 1783	Mary —	William Minthorn, Jr c 1716-c 1805
Jacob Pfautz fl c 1727?	Anna Pfautz c 1725-97	Joseph Gilbert 1666-1751	Mary Gilbert b c 1712
Maria —		Elizabeth Smith 1672-1756	
Johannes Burkhart c 1710-c 1756			
— —	Christian Burkhardt fl c 1753		James Eldridge
	Anna Graeff		Elizabeth —
Andrew Yount b c 1717			
— —	George Yount c 1740-1810		
John Waywire c 1725-1801	Rosannah Waywire c 1751-1814		
— —			
		Jacob Winn, Jr	
		Sarah Buck b 1716	Jacob Winn III 1744-1809
		John Grout, Jr b 1731	Phoebe Grout 1751-1819
		Phoebe Spofford b 1733	
	Samuel Davis 1734-87		Francis Wasley fl c 1749
	Mary —	Samuel Bunting c 1692-c 1759	Phebe Bunting b c 1726
		Priscilla Burgess	
Moses Embree d 1748		John Scott, Jr b 1693	
Mary —	John Embree 1721-p 1768	Hannah Merrick b c 1707	Henry Scott b c 1739
	Mary —		Mary Dean c 1741-82
William Coate, Jr b c 1703		John Tool	
Rachel Budd b c 1705	Marmaduke Coate 1738-1822	Elizabeth Pugh	John Tool, Jr c 1756-91
Moses Coppock	Mary Coppock		Ruth Rankin
Martha Scarr			
William Hasket		George Haworth c 1681-1724	
Mary —	Isaac Hasket 1744-82	Sarah Scarborough 1694-1748	John Haworth c 1715-76
?Joseph Elliot d c 1788	Lydia Elliot	Hans Garner	Mary Garner
?Hannah Gordon		— —	

HERBERT HOOVER
FAMILY TREE

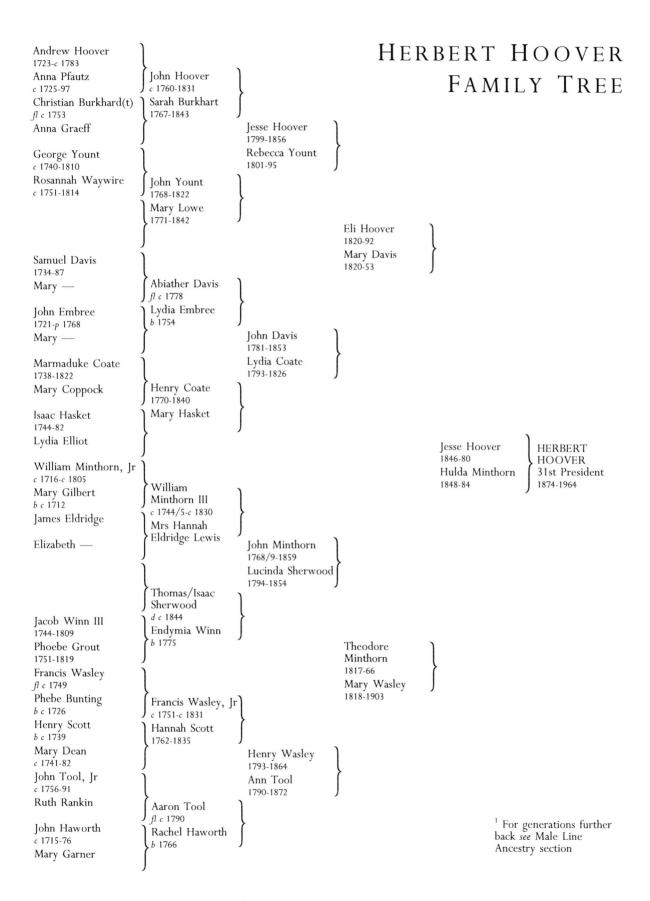

Andrew Hoover
1723-c 1783

Anna Pfautz
c 1725-97

Christian Burkhard(t)
fl c 1753

Anna Graeff

George Yount
c 1740-1810

Rosannah Waywire
c 1751-1814

Samuel Davis
1734-87

Mary —

John Embree
1721-p 1768

Mary —

Marmaduke Coate
1738-1822

Mary Coppock

Isaac Hasket
1744-82

Lydia Elliot

William Minthorn, Jr
c 1716-c 1805

Mary Gilbert
b c 1712

James Eldridge

Elizabeth —

Jacob Winn III
1744-1809

Phoebe Grout
1751-1819

Francis Wasley
fl c 1749

Phebe Bunting
b c 1726

Henry Scott
b c 1739

Mary Dean
c 1741-82

John Tool, Jr
c 1756-91

Ruth Rankin

John Haworth
c 1715-76

Mary Garner

John Hoover
c 1760-1831

Sarah Burkhart
1767-1843

John Yount
1768-1822

Mary Lowe
1771-1842

Abiather Davis
fl c 1778

Lydia Embree
b 1754

Henry Coate
1770-1840

Mary Hasket

William
Minthorn III
c 1744/5-c 1830

Mrs Hannah
Eldridge Lewis

Thomas/Isaac
Sherwood
d c 1844

Endymia Winn
b 1775

Francis Wasley, Jr
c 1751-c 1831

Hannah Scott
1762-1835

Aaron Tool
fl c 1790

Rachel Haworth
b 1766

Jesse Hoover
1799-1856

Rebecca Yount
1801-95

John Davis
1781-1853

Lydia Coate
1793-1826

John Minthorn
1768/9-1859

Lucinda Sherwood
1794-1854

Henry Wasley
1793-1864

Ann Tool
1790-1872

Eli Hoover
1820-92

Mary Davis
1820-53

Theodore
Minthorn
1817-66

Mary Wasley
1818-1903

Jesse Hoover
1846-80

Hulda Minthorn
1848-84

HERBERT
HOOVER
31st President
1874-1964

[1] For generations further
back see Male Line
Ancestry section

Plate 99   FDR with family: top row l-r Curtis Dall (son-in-law), James Roosevelt (son), middle row Elliott Roosevelt (son), Eleanor Roosevelt, Anna Roosevelt Dall (daughter), FDR, Sara Delano Roosevelt (mother), bottom row John Roosevelt (son) and Franklin Roosevelt Jr (son)

FRANKLIN D. ROOSEVELT

1882-1945
32ND PRESIDENT OF THE UNITED STATES OF AMERICA
1933-45

It would have seemed unlikely to the contemporaries of Theodore Roosevelt that there could ever be another President Roosevelt and quite inconceivable that the second would outdo the first in fame and in his impact, not just on the United States but on the history of the world. Yet so it was to be.

They were very distant cousins. Franklin's mother, Sara Delano, always insisted that her son took after her family entirely; certainly in youth Franklin looked very like her. Theodore Roosevelt, the Colonel, was such a commandingly interesting figure that an ambitious young man did not have to be related to him to think him a model worth emulating; indeed the middle-aged could learn from him too. It was Teddy Roosevelt's performance which showed Woodrow Wilson what a President might be. Franklin Roosevelt learned the lesson so well, emulated Theodore with such flair, that it is hard to resist the idea that like called to like, that there really was something apt in the Roosevelt blood.

Franklin got much closer to Theodore than mere cousinhood would have made possible by marrying the President's niece, Eleanor Roosevelt, a remarkable and attractive person in her own right. Later events make it likely that Franklin did not guess how strong-minded she was; she was shy and modest and his mother was strong-minded enough for two. He probably saw his early marriage as an opportunity for escape from the maternal thumb (mistakenly — Sara made the young couple live in a house next door to hers). He loved Eleanor spontaneously, for herself. But it cannot have diminished her appeal that by marrying her he would come into close contact with the most exciting politician America had produced for a generation.

The contact could occasionally be disconcerting. At the wedding reception in 1905 the guests all deserted the bride and groom so that they could go and listen to the President's killing jokes. Eleanor and Franklin were probably amused. Certainly Franklin was amused by a later incident, when during a visit to the White House he heard the Colonel roar out "Oh, if only I could only be President and Congress too for just 10 minutes!" In due course Franklin himself was to come very near to achieving that double state, and for rather longer than 10 minutes.

The influence of Teddy was so strong that the influence of Woodrow Wilson was at something of a discount. Yet Franklin was a Democrat and served Wilson for seven years as Assistant Secretary of the Navy, resigning only to run as the Democrats' Vice-Presidential candidate in 1920 (as which he was able, for the first time, to show how effective and charming he could be on the campaign trail). The strain of Wilsonian idealism was very powerful in him at that period, and though it was largely submerged during the 30s it rose to the surface again during World War II.

The Democratic defeat in 1920 was the first check that young Mr Roosevelt had met in his rapid rise to stardom. Perhaps it was time to take stock. A few years earlier he had fallen deeply in love with his wife's secretary, Lucy Mercer. He had contemplated leaving Eleanor but his mother had sworn to cut him off without a penny if he did, a divorce would have ended his political career, he thought a divorce would harm his children, and he still loved and respected his wife. So he renounced Lucy instead, but his marriage had been strained ever since.

At this point he contracted a bad case of polio. It took him out of public life for several years and left him with permanently disabled legs. In future this tall, handsome, self-confident man would only be able to stand for short periods, wearing leg-irons like a convict. His mother wanted him to give up politics, but Eleanor supported his determination not to be beaten. Underneath the easy charm he began to show, or to develop, qualities of will and endurance which no one had suspected before and which very few were to spot before he became President.

In 1928 his luck turned again. Governor Al Smith, the darling of New York, was the Democratic candidate for the presidency, so the state party needed a new candidate for the governorship. They turned to Roosevelt and in a Republican year, when Smith failed to carry his native state, Franklin Roosevelt won his election and entered on the final period of his apprenticeship.

He proved to be a good governor and won the presidential nomination in 1932 with rather less trouble than Wilson had experienced in 1912. He crushed Hoover in the election, but it is doubtful if any Americans knew what they were getting in exchange for that defeated figure. A change was necessary, they took what chance was offered them. As in 1860, it turned out that they had got themselves a hero.

Roosevelt's First Inaugural is legendary. The day before he delivered it the last banks in America had closed their doors; it seemed as if capitalist America might be done for. The President was stern; he knew that tens of millions of Americans were listening to him on the radio and his mission was to call up their strength, not to charm their feelings. His voice rang out: " . . . first of all let me assert my firm belief that the only thing we have to fear is fear itself — nameless, unreasoning, unjustified terror which paralyses needed efforts to convert retreat into advance. In every dark hour of our national life a leadership of frankness and vigour has met with that understanding and support of the people themselves which is essential to victory. I am convinced that you will again give that support to leadership in these critical days . . . For the trust reposed in me I will return the courage and devotion that befit the time. I can do no less . . .".

The reaction to that great voice was astonishing and well illustrates the relationship between Roosevelt and the American people which was to endure until his death. They felt summoned. They felt that here was a man actually concerned with them, actually speaking to them. He gave them back their belief in themselves and hope and courage for the future. Had he not himself overcome paralysis? A blizzard of letters reached the White House to assure the President that he had been heard — more letters than had ever been addressed to the President before. It was a renewed mandate making Roosevelt's point: "This nation asks for action and action now." He responded.

The New Deal of Franklin Roosevelt resolves into three strands. First there was rescue work: for example, the banking act which was hurried through Congress in eight hours flat, or the establishment of the Civilian Conservation Corps, which took unemployed young men out to work in the mountains and forests, or the Emergency Relief Act (12 May 1933) which pumped federal funds into the nearly bankrupt state unemployment relief agencies. This rescue work must be reckoned a success: the banks re-opened; the youth of America was redeemed, in thousands of cases, from the aimless drifting life of the tramp; help was continued to those who might otherwise have been without food, clothing or shelter.

But the New Deal also pledged recovery and reform. It achieved both these ends in some measure, but neither completely, because they conflicted. FDR had no intention of destroying the capitalist structure, if only because he had nothing to replace it with; but though the capitalists were willing, indeed eager, to get Federal help in reviving the economy, they did not in the least want to alter the ways which had laid it low in the first place. Consequently the politics of the first and second Roosevelt administrations became largely a running battle between conservatives and reformers in which, because neither side could be finally ignored, the outcome was invariably a compromise. Unemployment was reduced but not abolished; production increased but did not equal the 1929 level until 1937 or pass it until 1939, while the population had increased by seven per cent. A form of subsidy had been introduced which helped the large but not the small farmer; a social security system had been launched which omitted many categories of workers. Labour unions had been strengthened but would still have many bitter battles to fight.

However, the people never wavered in their affection for their President. They re-elected him by a record-breaking landslide in 1936. They forgave him his grosser blunders such as his losing battle with the Supreme Court in 1937. They trusted him. They also loved his wife. Eleanor was an immense help to her husband, one of his spare pairs of eyes, going everywhere, looking into everything, and always winning hearts and minds because of her palpable good will and good sense. She became a political force in her own right — the only President's wife to do so — and made sure that FDR did not lose touch with his more liberal and radical followers.

Beyond the domestic battles of the New Deal, however, loomed the new world crisis. By the late '30s it was plain that another great war was impending. The isolationists were still too strong to be fought openly, even if Roosevelt had been sure that they were wrong or had had an alternative policy to offer, but he began to move away from them. In 1939 the storm broke. It was this event which led the President to offer himself for a third term. He may also have been influenced by natural ambition and by the fact that, in his gigantic shade, no possible successor had grown up within the Democratic party. The key factor was undoubtedly his belief that in this new emergency America would need his strong leadership as much as ever. He shattered tradition by running and winning. In 1944 he was even elected to a fourth term, but after his death tradition was reasserted by the 22nd Amendment, which restricted future Presidents to two terms. The Amendment was planned by vengeful Republicans as a snub to FDR's memory, but it was nevertheless a good one. The presidency is too demanding an office for more than two terms to be prudent. America's chief executive ought always to be sound of health in mind and body; more than two terms would put both at risk. Roosevelt's third term destroyed his physical health so that he died suddenly in his fourth.

Before then he had conducted the United States safely through the greatest war in her history. There had been some fearful moments, above all the humiliating attack of the Japanese upon Pearl Harbor in 1941, but the jovial captain had weathered the storm. He left America at the top of her power, with her enemies about to collapse into total defeat. Well might his countrymen mourn him. But it is probable that it was the Roosevelt of the peace — 'Dr New Deal' as he once called himself — rather than 'Dr-Win-the-War' — they most regretted. It is doubtful if many Americans ever supposed for an instant that they would lose World War II, but many had feared they would lose the economic battle until FDR came along.

FRANKLIN D. ROOSEVELT'S FAMILY

The Roosevelts, though of Dutch origin, possessed a clannishness more usual among the Scots and FDR, who regarded himself as primarily Dutch, maintained an encyclopaedic knowledge of his genealogy. (His son Elliott records his conviction that the moment his father determined to seek a third term as President was when in May 1940 he received the news of Hitler's invasion of the Netherlands, which he took as an almost personal violation of ancestral territory.) Teddy Roosevelt, the 26th president, and FDR, the 32nd, were fifth cousins. Their most recent common ancestor had been born in the 17th century. Even in the much more static society of 19th-century England it is unlikely that such distant relatives would have ever met. Yet the many links between the two branches antedated Franklin's celebrated marriage to Eleanor, his fifth cousin once-removed and President Theodore's niece. To take just one example, Franklin's parents first met at the house of Theodore Roosevelt.

Moreover, other Roosevelts shared this Habsburg-like penchant for marrying among family connections. Franklin's grandfather Isaac Roosevelt married his own stepmother's niece. Franklin's father, James, married as his first wife his second cousin Rebecca Howland, and as his second wife another, remoter cousin, Sara Delano. James's son by Rebecca (in other words Franklin's half-brother) married a member of the Astor family whose aunt had married Sara Delano's uncle Franklin. It was this Delano great-uncle after whom FDR himself was named, for the great-uncle had no children and left some of the money he had acquired by marrying an Astor to his niece, Sara Delano. FDR's cousin-by-marriage Lord Astor, husband of the first woman MP in Britain, was a friend of Sara Delano's and Elliott Roosevelt claims he introduced FDR to the British economist Keynes's ideas about deficit financing.

Even Franklin's first political success, winning a New York state senate seat in 1910, derived from his family. This came about in at least two ways — three if one includes the conventional wisdom that Franklin wooed Eleanor in part because she was a highly dynamic president's niece. Franklin got his start in politics because New York State Democratic bosses were attracted to the idea of fielding a Roosevelt at a time when President Theodore had lent the name enormous lustre. The bosses also knew that Franklin's mother would pay his election expenses as well as contribute to party funds, an important consideration at the time. For instance, in 1880 a Democratic delegation had tried to persuade Franklin's father James to stand in Dutchess County, New York, because he could be relied on to meet his own expenses. Sara's expenditure on her son's election — $1,700, then a large sum — turned out to be five times that of any other candidate. She subsequently paid the rent on his house in Albany when he attended the state legislature. She even subsidized his stay in the White House, to the tune of $100,000 a year.

Sara Delano's sister's daughter Katharine took to politics too, serving as Republican Representative in Congress from New York from 1946 to 1964 and becoming the first woman to serve on the House Rules Committee. As a Republican she supported Dewey against her first cousin in 1944. A large family like the Roosevelts, with both anomalies and traditions, could throw up even odder results. A recent historical study suggests FDR's links with the China trade through his Delano ancestors led him to underrate Japanese military strength in 1941. He should have known better, perhaps did. The Roosevelts had their Japanese connections too, after all. His aunt Laura Delano had fallen in love as a girl with Saburu Kurusu, a member of a powerful family of Japanese industrialists and by chance one of the Japanese envoys in Washington in 1941. FDR tried to use this slender emotional link to prevent Japanese-American relations deteriorating even further as 1941 wore on to its devastating climax on 7 December.

Unlike Theodore, Franklin was of course no Republican. Yet Theodore with his radicalism resembled Franklin politically more than the difference in party labels suggests. In 1900, as a Harvard freshman, Franklin actually marched in support of the McKinley-Teddy Roosevelt ticket; in 1904 he cast his first and only Republican vote for his cousin. The two men even progressed to the White House via the same stepping stones — Assistant Secretaryship of the Navy and the Governorship of New York.

Perhaps Franklin's delight in reading to his family by the fireside inspired his famous 'fireside chats' to the American people during the Depression years. Certainly he made a prop of his family more literally than most politicians do. When he made his come-back at the Democratic national convention in 1924 after contracting polio three years earlier, it was his son James on whom he leaned as he awkwardly moved forward the few paces necessary to reach the microphones at Madison Square Garden. The 'Happy Warrior' speech he then made, nominating Al Smith as the Democrats' presidential candidate, was a great personal triumph. Would an entry in a wheel-chair have had the same initial effect? It is

Plate 100   Eleanor Roosevelt with grandchildren
on the occasion of General Eisenhower's placing a wreath
on FDR's grave, Hyde Park, New York, 1945:
l-r Chandler Roosevelt II, Bill Crawford (step-grandson
by Elliott Roosevelt's 3rd wife Faye Emerson),
David Roosevelt and Elliott Roosevelt, Jr,
holding Fala, FDR's scottie

Plate 101   Franklin Roosevelt, Jr, his 1st wife Ethel du
Pont and their elder son Franklin Roosevelt III at
commissioning of the aircraft carrier
USS Franklin D. Roosevelt

Plate 102   James Roosevelt, FDR's eldest son, addressing the 1948 Democratic
Convention, at which he was chairman of the Californian delegation

highly doubtful. Indeed it was never revealed to the American people just how badly crippled their 32nd President was.

Members of the Republican branch of the Roosevelts were just as prone to regard politics as a family business. When Franklin campaigned as the Democratic vice-presidential candidate in 1920, frequently being mistaken by rural voters for President Teddy Roosevelt's son, his distant cousin Theodore III, Teddy's actual son and a Republican member of the New York State Assembly, was stung into calling him a maverick, adding that he lacked the brand of the family. Four years later, when Theodore III was campaigning for the New York State governorship at a time when Franklin was supporting Al Smith for a third term, Congressman Nicholas Longworth, the husband of Alice Roosevelt Longworth, Theodore III's half-sister, called Franklin a "denatured Roosevelt". This was unjustifiable. The most politically prominent Roosevelt before Teddy Roosevelt embarked on his career had been a prominent Democrat. It was Teddy, if anyone, who was the maverick against a family adherence to the Democrats instituted a generation earlier, and in any case Teddy's son Kermit broke ranks and became a Democrat.

Of FDR's four sons who lived to become adults, three participated at one time or another in public life and even the one who didn't — the youngest, John — rates a mention in a book on presidential families because of his close friendship with Joseph Kennedy Jr while at Harvard. (He was also a secret Republican.) Sad to say, the activist sons quarrelled unbecomingly just after FDR's death as to who should have precedence in capitalizing on their father's name. James the eldest started early, managing his father's Massachusetts campaign headquarters in 1932 when aged only 25. Newspapers called him 'the Crown Prince' but his political career fizzled out, although he did become a six-term Congressman. But US representative to UNESCO under LBJ, his final post, was hardly the most glittering of prizes and his attempt to win the governorship of California in 1950 failed after a promising start with a win in the Democratic primary. His father took against him over his divorce of his first wife, vindictively arranging for one of the best New York lawyers to represent the aggrieved wife when it came to negotiating a settlement. James later alienated many members of his own party by joining the 'Democrats for Nixon' movement in 1972. Elliott Roosevelt, who like his brother John knew Joe Kennedy Jr, being a member of his air escort the day Joe's plane blew up in 1944, served as mayor of Miami Beach in the mid-1960s. Franklin Jr, or Frankie as he was known, was a three-term Congressman and served in the Kennedy and Johnson administrations. In the early 1950s he was a strong Averell Harriman supporter when the latter was trying for the Democratic presidential nomination, indeed was Harriman's floor manager at the 1952 convention. But Frankie was regarded as too openly ambitious and unreliable; despite his inheriting much of his father's charm, he made even more enemies.

Attempts by the children of a president to continue a family political tradition by electoral means were one thing. Much more of a throwback to the 19th century was the way James and Anna Roosevelt each acted as their father's secretary-cum-aide while he was in office. James took up his post in early 1937, though he had to leave it a year later after charges that he had taken unfair advantage of his position in business dealings. It has been said that when Joe Kennedy first sought the London embassy he approached James. (He also made approaches to Anna Roosevelt — amorous ones — chasing her in and out of gaps in the furniture in his hotel suite.) Kennedy had made a friend of James some years before and had already used him to importune the president for jobs, meanwhile keeping James sweet by putting business opportunities his way. In 1941 James, now back in favour, officially represented his father on a goodwill tour overseas. From December 1943 till the President's death Anna, who held no official position, nevertheless worked on everything from, as she put it, filling her father's cigarette case to planning the 1944 invasion of Normandy. She personally arranged for Vice-President Harry Truman to fly from Missouri and take part in the 1944 election victory parade.

Eleanor Roosevelt, however, was the supreme political dynast. It was her great achievement to demonstrate by her immense personal integrity that family need not be a blemish on politics. She was not actually a very good mother, but then she had never as a child experienced a stable family background; nor was she above personal vendettas, as Gore Vidal records in describing her triumph at having done down the New York City political boss Carmine De Sapio in revenge for the way he had destroyed Frankie's career. Her husband's tireless promoter and adviser, Louis Howe, got her into the women's division of the Democratic Committee of New York State so as to boost her husband's appeal among the newly enfranchised female voters and it has been said that she was chiefly responsible for persuading her husband to appoint as Secretary of Labor Frances Perkins, the first woman to reach the Cabinet. Once launched Eleanor quickly took on a political personality of her own, in 1928 convincing Governor Al Smith that the women Democrats of New York State should pick their own delegates to the Democratic Convention rather than acquiesce in male bosses making the selection. Even more important that year was her influence on her husband to run for the New York state governorship. He had been vacillating right up to the last minute. She also played a crucial role at the 1940 Democratic convention when FDR, operating by remote control from the White House, sought an unprecedented third term.

FDR even relied on relatives for non-sexual female companionship while his wife was away: his cousins Laura Delano and Daisy Suckley. Meanwhile Eleanor went on morale-boosting tours of US troops, even presenting decorations as if she were a queen consort. Her interest in politics — during the War she gave her own press conferences where she discussed public matters — made her at times something of a nuisance to the President, despite her being an asset overall, and when he went to Yalta he took Anna rather than his wife. Despite Eleanor's intense liberalism she could never shed an upper-class de haut en bas attitude to employees. In 1933 she even sacked six of the 32 White House staff shortly after moving in. It was excusable as an economy measure, but insensitive when unemployment was so high, particularly as she sometimes put her own protégés on the payroll.

After her husband's death Eleanor avoided relegation to the oubliette customary for former First Ladies. President Truman once said he really needed her involvement with his administration because of her influence with black voters. She served on the US delegation to the United Nations till Eisenhower's presidency but she was perhaps more important in domestic politics than as an international representative of her country. All the same, she was no figurehead at the UN: her chairmanship of the Human Rights Commission was firm, her management of Soviet delegates effective and her influence on the drafting of the Universal Declaration of Human Rights profound; even John Foster Dulles saluted her achievement. Despite her refusal to run for the Senate in 1946 — a proposal made by Democrats anxious to scotch a Dewey bid for the presidency as soon as possible — and again in 1948, as well as the failure of a group of delegates to the Democratic convention in 1952 to get her the Vice-Presidential nomination, she became a major moral force in the Democratic party. Her endorsement was sought by presidential contenders — including, famously, John F. Kennedy — because they knew the name Eleanor Roosevelt carried clout, not just because she transmitted FDR's approval from beyond the grave.

BIOGRAPHICAL DETAILS AND DESCENDANTS

FRANKLIN DELANO ROOSEVELT, *b* Hyde Park, New York, 30 Jan 1882; *educ* in Germany, Groton, Harvard (AB 1903) and Columbia Law Sch; admitted New York Bar 1907, Memb Hudson Fulton Celebration Commission 1909, New York State Senator 1911-13, Memb Plattsburg Centennial 1913, Assist-Sec Navy 1913-20, unsuccessful candidate Democratic senatorial primaries 1914, Overseer Harvard 1918-24, v-presdtl candidate 1920, ptnr Emmet, Marvin & Roosevelt, attys, 1920, V-Pres Fidelity and Deposit Co 1920-28, ptnr Roosevelt & O'Connor, attys, 1924-33, Chm Taconic State Park Commission 1925, Govr New York 1929-33, 32nd President (D) of the USA 1933-45, Pres American Nat Red Cross and Georgia Warm Spring Fndn, Congressional Medal of Honor awarded posthumously, Hon LLD: Yale 1934 and London (UK) 1943, Hon DCL Queen's U, Ontario, Canada, 1938, author: *Whither Bound?* (1926), *The Happy Warrior: Alfred E. Smith* (1928), *Government — Not Politics*

(1932), *Looking Forward* (1933), *On Our Way* (1934), *F.D.R., His Personal Letters, 1905-45*, ed Elliott Roosevelt, 3 vols (1948-50), *Public Papers and Addresses*, 13 vols (1938-50); *m* New York 17 March 1905 his 5th cousin once-removed (Anna) Eleanor (*see under* President THEODORE ROOSEVELT), only dau of Elliott Roosevelt and his w Anna Rebecca Hall, and *d* the Little White House, Warm Springs, Ga., 12 April 1945 of a cerebral haemorrhage (*bur* Hyde Park 15 April), leaving issue:

President Franklin Roosevelt's daughter

I Anna ('Sis') Eleanor Roosevelt, *b* New York 3 May 1906; *educ* Cornell; aide to her father Dec 1943-April 1945; *m* 1st Hyde Park, New York, 5 June 1926 (divorce 1934) Curtis Bean DALL, of New York, stockbroker, s of Charles Austin Dall, and had issue:

Grandchildren

1 *Anna ('Sistie' or 'Sisty') Eleanor Dall Boettiger [Mrs Van H Seagraves, 1813 Sheppard Street NW, Washington, DC 20011, USA], *b* 25 March 1927 (later adopted by her mother's 2nd husb, whose name she took); *m* Phoenix, Ariz., July 1948 *Van H. SEAGRAVES, sometime official with Mutual Security Admin, Paris, France, and has issue:

Great-grandchildren
(1) *Nicholas Delano SEAGRAVES [1813 Sheppard Street NW, Washington, DC 20011, USA], *b* Portland, Oreg., 7 Aug 1949
(2) *David Delano SEAGRAVES, *b* 195-
(3) *Anna Eleanor SEAGRAVES, *b* 16 Aug 1955

Grandchildren

2 *Curtis ('Buzz' or 'Buzzie') ROOSEVELT [41 Morton Street, New York, NY 10014, USA; Deia, Mallorca, Spain], *b* 19 April 1930 as Curtis Dall, later adopted by his mother's 2nd husb, whose name he added to Dall, later still took name Roosevelt in lieu of Dall Boettiger; *educ* Northwestern Mil & Naval Acad, Wis.; advertising exec and Ch of Non-Govtl Liaison Section, Public Info Dept, UNO; *m* 1st Santa Monica, Calif., 23 May 1950 (divorce 1954) Robin H., dau of James Burton Edwards, of Los Angeles, and has issue:

Great-grandchildren
(1) *Juliana ROOSEVELT, *b* 1952

Grandchildren

2 (cont.) Curtis Roosevelt *m* 2nd March 1955 (divorce 195- or 196-) Ruth W. Sublette; *m* 3rd 2 May 1961 *Jeanette Schlottman

President Franklin Roosevelt's daughter

I (cont.) Mrs Anna Dall *m* 2nd New York 18 Jan 1935 (divorce 1949) John BOETTIGER, Jr (*b* Chicago 25 March 1900; Washington correspondent of Chicago *Tribune*, exec assist Hays Office, newspaper publisher (with his w Anna), notably of the *Arizona Times*; committed suicide New York 31 Oct 1950), and had further issue:

Grandchildren

3 *John Roosevelt BOETTIGER [143 Woodbridge Street, South Hadley, MA 01075, USA], *b* Seattle 30 March 1939; Assoc Prof Human Devpt Hampshire Coll; *m* De Witt, New York, Aug 1960 *Deborah Ann Bentley (*b* 1938) and has issue:

Great-grandchildren
(1) *Adam BOETTIGER, *b* 19—
(2) *Sara Boettiger, *b c* 1968; *m c* Oct 1987 Duncan ('Champion Doug') VEITCH, Scots pop singer and record-producer, and has issue:

Great-great-grandchildren
1a Ernest VEITCH, aged five in Dec 1993

Great-grandchildren
(3) *Joshua BOETTIGER, *b* 19—

President Franklin Roosevelt's children

I (cont.) Mrs Anna Dall Boettiger *m* 3rd Malibu, Calif., 11 Nov 1952 *Dr James Addison HALSTED [RFD2, Hillsdale, NY 12529, USA], sometime Fulbright exchange scholar in Iran, and *d* 1 Dec 1975
II James ROOSEVELT, *b* New York 23 Dec 1907; *educ* Groton, Harvard and Boston U Law Sch; ptnr Roosevelt & Sargent, insur brokers, sec to his father 1937-38, intelligence offr 5th Div US Marine Corps ending as Col World War II, assist to Sam Goldwyn of MGM, unsuccessful candidate for Mayor of Los Angeles, Chm California Delegn 1948 Democratic Convention, Memb US House of Reps 84th-89th Congresses, US Rep to UN Economic and Social Council, Dir IOS, financial consultant, teacher U of California, author: *Affectionately FDR* and *My Parents: A Differing View* (1976); *m* 1st Brookline, Mass., 4 June 1930 (divorce 1940), as her 1st husb, Betsy (she *m* 2nd 1942 John (Jock) Whitney, US Amb to UK 1957-61), dau of Dr Harvey Cushing, of Boston, and had issue:

Grandchildren

1 *Sara Delano Roosevelt [Mrs Ronald A Wilford, 1120 5th Avenue, New York, NY 10028, USA], *b* Boston 13 March 1932; *m* 1st New York 12 June 1953 (divorce 1972) Anthony DI BONAVENTURA (*b* 1930), s of Fred di Bonaventura, and has issue:

Great-grandchildren
(1) *(Anthony Peter) Christopher DI BONAVENTURA [1120 5th Avenue, New York, NY 10028, USA], b Washington, DC, 10 June 1954
(2) *Andrea Isabelle DI BONAVENTURA [1120 5th Avenue, New York, NY 10028, USA], b 21 June 1956
(3) *Peter John DI BONAVENTURA, b 25 Nov 1957
(4) *Sarina Rosario DI BONAVENTURA, b 24 Aug 1959
(5) *Betsey Maria DI BONAVENTURA, b 22 May 1963

Grandchildren
1 (cont.) Mrs Sara di Bonaventura m 2nd 13 Jan 1973 *Ronald A. WILFORD
2 *Kate Roosevelt [Mrs William Haddad, 88 Central Park West, New York, NY, USA], b New York 16 Feb 1936; m there 17 Oct 1959 *William Frederick HADDAD (b Charlotte, N Carolina, 25 July 1928), s of Charles Frederick Haddad and his w Esther Nowack, and has issue:

Great-grandchildren
(1) *Andrea Whitney HADDAD, b 19—
(2) *Camilla Cushing HADDAD, b 19—
(3) *Laura Whitney HADDAD, b 19—

President Franklin Roosevelt's son
II (cont.) James Roosevelt m 2nd Beverly Hills, Calif., 14 April 1941 (divorce 1955) Romelle Theresa Schneider (b 1916), his former nurse, dau of Jerome M. Schneider, and with her had issue:

Grandchildren
3 *James ROOSEVELT, Jr [4120 Suitland Road 402, Suitland, MD 20034, USA], b Hollywood 9 Nov 1945; educ Harvard (AB 1968); m Cambridge, Mass., 15 June 1968 *Anna Martha, dau of Walter N. Conlon, of Cambridge
4 *Michael Anthony ROOSEVELT [1945 Broadway 401, San Fancisco, CA 94109, USA; c/o Heller, Ehrman, White & McAuliffe, 333 Bush Street, San Francisco, CA, USA], b Los Angeles 7 Dec 1946; educ Harvard and Columbia Law Sch; attorney with Heller, Ehrman, White & McAuliffe, of San Francisco; m Schenectady, New York, 21 Aug 1972 *Deborah Wilson, dau of F. Hubbard Horn, of Schenectady
5 *Anna Eleanor Roosevelt [Mrs Robert Johnston, Box 6068 College Station, Durham, NC 22708, USA], b Santa Monica, Calif., 10 Jan 1948; educ Stanford Univ; m 19— *Robert JOHNSTON

President Franklin Roosevelt's son
II (cont.) James Roosevelt m 3rd Los Angeles 2 July 1956 (divorce 1969) Mrs Gladys Irene Owens (b 1917); Mr and Mrs Roosevelt adopted a son:

a *Hall Delano ROOSEVELT, b June 1957

President Franklin Roosevelt's son
II (cont.) James Roosevelt m 4th Hyde Park, New York, 3 Oct 1969 *Mary Lena Winskill (b Birkenhead, Cheshire, UK, 5 June 1939) and d 31 Aug 1991, having with her had further issue:

Grandchildren
6 *Rebecca Mary ROOSEVELT, b 1971

President Franklin Roosevelt's sons
III Franklin Delano Roosevelt, Jr, b New York 18 March, d there 1 Nov 1909
IV Elliott ROOSEVELT, b New York City 23 Sept 1910; educ Groton; advertising exec with Kelly, Nason, Roosevelt of New York, aviation ed Los Angeles *Express*, radio commentator Mutual Broadcasting System network, rancher, Memb Texas Delegn Democratic Convention 1940, air intelligence offr 21st Reconnaissance Sqdn USAAF World War II (ended as Brig-Gen, DFC), Mayor Miami Beach 1965-67, Exec Dir Miami Beach Tourist Devpt Authority 1971, author: *As He Saw It* (1946), (with James Brough) *The Roosevelts of Hyde Park — an untold story* (1973) and several detective stories, notably *Murder and the First Lady* (1984), featuring his mother Eleanor Roosevelt as sleuth; m 1st Bryn Mawr, Pa., 16 Jan 1932 (divorce 1933) Elizabeth (Betty) Browning (b Pittsburgh 5 Dec 1911), dau of William Henry Donner, fndr Donner Steel Co of Pennsylvania, and had issue:

Grandchildren
1 *William Donner ROOSEVELT [Wilson Point, South Norwalk, CT 06854, USA], b New York 17 Nov 1932; educ Harvard; investment banker; m Denver Colo., 14 June 1957 *Karyl, dau of Thomas Kyle, of Denver, and has issue:

Great-grandchildren
(1) *Christopher Kyle ROOSEVELT, b Meeker, Colo., 2 Aug 1959; educ Malcolm Gordon Sch, Garrison, New York
(2) *Dana Donner ROOSEVELT, b 19—; educ St George's Sch, Newport, Rhode Island
(3) A son, b 19—

President Franklin Roosevelt's son
IV (cont.) Elliott Roosevelt m 2nd Burlington, Iowa, 22 July 1933 (divorce 1944) Ruth Josephine Googins (d 1974), of Forth Worth, Tex., and with her had issue:

Grandchildren

2 *Ruth Chandler Roosevelt [Mrs Henry D Lindsley III, 4604 Watauga, Dallas, TX 75209, USA; 4301 Westside Drive, Dallas, TX 75209, USA], b Forth Worth 9 May 1934; m there 21 April 1956 *Henry D. LINDSLEY III, s of Henry D. Lindsley, Jr, and has issue:

Great-grandchildren
(1) *Chandler LINDSLEY, b 19—
(2) *(Henry) Hays LINDSLEY [5525 Stonegate Rd, Dallas, TX 75209, USA], b Midland, Tex., 13 July 1958; educ Vanderbilt U (BS) and U of Texas (JD, MBA); m 19 March 1988 *Allyson, dau of Wade C. and Marilyn Smith, and has issue:

Great-great-grandchildren
1a *Hattie Smith LINDSLEY, b Dallas 27 Aug 1989
2a *Anne Marie LINDSLEY, b Dallas 17 March 1992

Great-grandchildren
(3) *Ruth Roosevelt LINDSLEY, b 19—

Grandchildren

3 *Elliott ROOSEVELT, Jr [9669 Jourdan Way, Dallas, TX 75230, USA], b Fort Worth 14 July 1936; educ Colorado State U (BS); served US Army 1959-60, with Ambassador Oil Corp 1960-65, owner General Petroleum and part-owner Texas Interstate Oil & Gas companies 1965-71, Exec V-Pres and Dir Shenandoah Oil Corp 1971-80, private oil and gas producer 1980-; m 24 Jan 1959 *Joanne, dau of John E. McFadden, of Evanston, Ill., and his w Josephine Hartman, and has issue:

Great-grandchildren
(1) *Laura Roosevelt, b Fort Worth 14 June 1960; m Dallas 25 Jan 1986 *Walid CHAMMAH
(2) *Elliott ROOSEVELT III, b Denver, Colo., 23 Feb 1963; m Texas 18 May 1990 *J. Elizabeth Coniglio
(3) *Elizabeth Roosevelt, b Denver 24 Aug 1965; m 31 Aug 1992 *Seth Thomas KELLY
(4) *David Anthony ROOSEVELT, b Denver 1 April 1970

Grandchildren

4 *David Boynton ROOSEVELT [Oyster Bay Road, Jericho, Long Island, NY 11753, USA], b Fort Worth 3 Jan 1942; educ Culver Mil Acad and Texas Christian U; stockbroker; m 1st (divorce) ——; m 2nd 28 April 1968 *Michele Josephine, dau of Alexander P. Chopen, of Greenvale, NY, and his w, née O'Connor, and with her has issue:

Great-grandchildren
(1) *Matthew Chopen ROOSEVELT, b Glen Cove, New York, 16 March 1972
(2) *Nicholas ROOSEVELT, b 19—

President Franklin Roosevelt's son

IV (cont.) Elliott Roosevelt m 3rd Grand Canyon, Colo., 3 Dec 1944 (divorce 1950) Faye Margaret Emerson (b Elizabeth, La., 8 July 1917; film actress); m 4th Miami Beach, Fla., 15 March 1951 (divorce 1960), as her 4th husb, Minnewa (b 1911), former w of Rex Ross and dau of Alonzo Bell; m 5th Qualicum, British Columbia, Canada, Nov 1960 *Patricia (Patty) Whitehead [Mrs Elliott Roosevelt, Quirita Dos Cedros, Pombois, Odivelas, Portugal] and d 27 Oct 1990, having with her had issue:

Grandchildren
5 Livingston Delano ROOSEVELT; d in infancy

President Franklin Roosevelt's son

V Franklin Delano ROOSEVELT, Jr [Clove Creek Farm, Poughquag, New York 12570, USA], b Campobello Island, New Brunswick, Canada, 17 Aug 1914; educ Groton, Harvard (AB 1937) and U of Virginia (LLB 1940); Cdr USNR (Silver Star), law clerk with Wright, Gordon, Zachry & Parlin, New York City, 1941, Nat V-Chm Americans for Democratic Action 1948, Memb US House of Reps 81st-83rd Congresses, Under-Sec Commerce 1962-65, Chm: Equal Employment Opportunity Commission 1965-66, Fiat-Roosevelt Motors, Mickleberry Corp; m 1st Wilmington, Del., 30 June 1937 (divorce 1949) Ethel (b Wilmington 1915; d Grosse Pointe, Mich., 24/25 May 1965), dau of Eugene Du Pont and his w Ethel, and had issue:

Grandchildren

1 *Franklin Delano ROOSEVELT III [404 Riverside Drive, New York, NY 10025, USA], b Wilmington 19 July 1939; educ St Mark's Sch, Yale (BA) and Columbia; economics teacher New Sch for Social Research; m 19— *Grace Ramsey (b Montclair, New Jersey, 1941), dau of Austin Goodyear, of New Canaan, Conn., and his w Louisa Robins, and has issue:

Great-grandchildren
(1) *Phoebe Louisa ROOSEVELT, b 19—
(2) *Nicholas Martin ROOSEVELT, b 19—
(3) *Amelia ROOSEVELT, b 19—

Grandchildren

2 *Christopher Du Pont ROOSEVELT [14 Middle Patent Road, Bedford, NY 10025, USA], b Philadelphia 21 Dec 1940;

educ St Paul's Sch; Assist US Attorney Southern Dist; *m* Concord, New Hampshire, 12 June 1965 *Rosalind, dau of Horace Havemeyer, Jr, and his w Rosalind Everdell, and has issue:

Great-grandchildren
(1) *Kate ROOSEVELT, *b* 27 Jan 1968
(2) *Emily ROOSEVELT, *b* 13 Aug 1969
(3) *Christopher Havemeyer ROOSEVELT, *b* 25 June 1972

President Franklin Roosevelt's son
V (cont.) Franklin Delano Roosevelt, Jr, *m* 2nd New York 31 Aug 1949 (divorce 1970) Suzanne, dau of Lee Perrin, of New York, lawyer, and with her had issue:

Grandchildren
3 *Nancy Suzanne ROOSEVELT [RDI, Box 212-A, Poughquag, NY 12570, USA], *b* New York 11 Jan 1952; *educ* Vassar (BA 1974)
4 *Laura D. ROOSEVELT [3065 University Terrace, Washington, DC 20016, USA], *b* Washington 26 Oct 1959

President Franklin Roosevelt's son
V (cont.) Franklin Delano Roosevelt, Jr, *m* 3rd New York 1 July 1970 (divorce 197-) Felicia Schiff, former w of Robert W. Sarnoff and dau of Paul Felix Warburg; *m* 4th Dutch County, New York, 6 May 1977 *Patricia Luisa Oakes [Mrs Franklin D Roosevelt Jr, 200 E 66th Street, New York, NY, USA; Clove Creek Farm, Poughquag, NY 12570, USA] and *d* 17 Aug 1978, having with her had issue:

Grandchildren
5 *A son, *b* New York Nov 1977

President Franklin Roosevelt's son
VI *John Aspinwall ROOSEVELT [333 East 57th Street, New York, NY 10022, USA], *b* Washington, DC, 13 March 1916; *educ* Groton and Harvard (AB 1938); stockbroker, Sr V-Pres and Dir Bache and Coluc, Lt-Cdr USN World War II (Bronze Star); *m* 1st Nahant, Mass., 18 June 1938 (divorce 1965) Anne Lindsay (*b* Concord, Mass., 13 July 1916; *d* New York 28 May 1973), dau of Franklin Haven Clark and his w Frances Sturgis, and has had issue:

Grandchildren
1 A son, *b* and *d* Boston 2 June 1939
2 *Haven Clark ROOSEVELT [305 Millwood Road, Chappaqua, NY 10514, USA], *b* Boston 5 June 1940; *educ* Millbrook Sch, Harvard (AB 1962) and Harvard Law Sch (LLD 1966); lawyer with Cadwalader, Wickersham & Taft; *m* Beverly Farm, Mass., 26 Nov 1966 *Hetty Archer (*b* April 1938), dau of John Elliott Knowlton, of South Dartmouth, Bermuda, and his w Hetty Archer, and has issue:

Great-grandchildren
(1) *Sara Delano ROOSEVELT, *b* 1968
(2) *Wendy Clark ROOSEVELT, *b* 1970

Grandchildren
3 *Anne Sturgis Roosevelt [Mrs Douglas S Luke Jr, Tower View, 3687 Kitzmiller Road, New Albany, OH 43054, USA], *b* San Diego, Calif., 15 Dec 1942; *educ* New Sch for Social Research; *m* Hyde Park, New York, 20 June 1964 *Douglas Sigler LUKE, Jr (*b* 1 Oct 1942), s of Douglas Sigler Luke, of Glen Falls, New York, and his w Joanne, and has issue:

Great-grandchildren
(1) *Haven Roosevelt LUKE, *b* 14 Jan 1967
(2) *David Russell LUKE, *b* 12 May 1969
(3) *Lindsay Anne LUKE, *b* 27 Dec 1973

Grandchildren
4 Sara (Sally) Delano ROOSEVELT, *b* Pasadena, Calif., 6 Dec 1946; *k* Old Forge, Utica, New York, 12 Aug 1960 in a riding accident
5 *Joan Lindsay ROOSEVELT, *b* Poughkeepsie, New York, 25 Aug 1952

President Franklin Roosevelt's son
VI (cont.) John Roosevelt *m* 2nd New York 28 Oct 1965 *Irene E. (*b* New York 8 March 1931), former w of Benjamin Brandreth McAlpin III and dau of James Hallam Boyd and his w Mary Elizabeth Watkins

MALE LINE ANCESTRY AND COLLATERAL DESCENDANTS

See Ancestry of President THEODORE ROOSEVELT

Great-great-great-great grandparents on the father's side | *Great-great-great-great grandparents on the mother's side*

Father's side

Nicholas Roosevelt
same as first two T
Roosevelt ancestors col. 1

Heyltje Jans Kunst

} Jacobus Roosevelt
1692-1776

Johannes Hardenbroeck
c 1665—1710-14

Sara Van Laer
d in/a 1743

} Catharina Hardenbroeck
1694-p 1739

Nicholas Hoffman
c 1680-1750

Jannetje Crispel
c 1686-1752

} Martin Hoffman
1706/7-72

Robert Benson
c 1686-c 1715

Cornelia Roos
c 1688-c 1760

} Tryntje Benson
1712-65

William Walton
c 1675-1747

Mary Santvoort
c 1678-1768

} Jacob Walton
1703-49

Gerardus Beekman
c 1653-1723

Magdalena Abeel
c 1657-1745

} Maria Beekman
1704-c 1794

} Charles Williams
c 1700-73

} Sarah —

Peter Aspinwall
c 1612-87

Remembrance Palfrey
c 1638-in/a 1701

} Joseph Aspinwall
1673-c 1743

Christopher Dean
d 1689

— —

} Hannah Dean

Henry Smith
1678/9-1766

Anna Shepard
1684/5-1735

} William Smith
1708-76

Henry Lloyd
1685-1763

Rebecca Nelson
1688-1728

} Margaret Lloyd
1713-56

Nathaniel Howland
c 1671-1746

Martha Cole
1669-1718

} Nathaniel Howland, Jr
b 1705

John Burt
b 1692

Abigail Cheever
b 1690

} Abigail Burt
1718-66

Samuel Bill, Jr
c 1690-in/a 1753

Hannah —
c 1692-1740

} Ephraim Bill
1719-1802

Joshua Huntington
1698-1745

Hannah Perkins
1701-45

} Lydia Huntington
1727-98

Mother's side

Jonathan Delano
c 1648-1720

Mercy Warren
1658-p 1727

} Thomas Delano
b 1704

Stephen Peckham
d 1724

Mary —

} Jean Peckham
b 1702/3

Eleazer Cushman
1656/7-p 1723

Elizabeth Coombs
1662-p 1723

} James Cushman
c 1695-1722

} Sarah Hatch

Nathaniel Church
1693-1717

Innocent Head

} Caleb Church
1728-c 1771

Lemuel Pope
1696-1771

Elizabeth Hunt
c 1697-1782

} Mercy Pope
1729/30-a 1780

Ebenezer Perry
1705/6-p 1775

Abigail Presbury
c 1703-49

} Samuel Perry
1731-1805

Jireh Swift, Jr
1709-82

Deborah Hathaway
1713-94

} Susannah Swift
c 1734-1806

Benjamin Lyman
1674-1723

Thankful Pomeroy
1679-1773

} Joseph Lyman
1699-1763

Nathaniel Lewis
1676-1752

Abigail Ashley
1681-1723

} Abigail Lewis
1701-c 1776

Thomas Sheldon
1661-1725

Mary Hinsdale
1665-1738

} Benjamin Sheldon
c 1697-1773

Ebenezer Strong, Jr
1671-1729

Mary Holton
1678-1705

} Mary Strong
1701-?76

Thomas Robbins
1703-91

Ruth Johnson
c 1703-37

} Revd Nathaniel Robbins
1726-95

Edward Hutchinson
1678-1752

Lydia Foster
b c 1687

} Elizabeth Hutchinson
1731-93

John Murray
1677-1728

Ann Bennet
1694-1737 (sis of)

} James Murray
1713-81

Andrew Bennet
c 1696-1745

Dorothy Collingwood
c 1695-1736

} Barbara Bennet
1724-58

FRANKLIN D. ROOSEVELT
FAMILY TREE

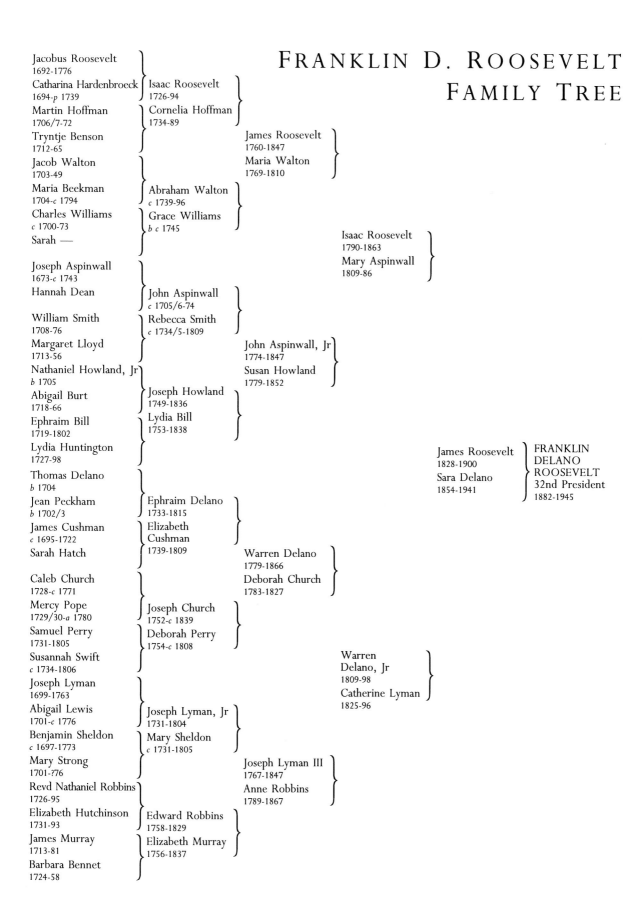

Jacobus Roosevelt
1692-1776

Catharina Hardenbroeck
1694-p 1739

Martin Hoffman
1706/7-72

Tryntje Benson
1712-65

Jacob Walton
1703-49

Maria Beekman
1704-c 1794

Charles Williams
c 1700-73

Sarah —

Joseph Aspinwall
1673-c 1743

Hannah Dean

William Smith
1708-76

Margaret Lloyd
1713-56

Nathaniel Howland, Jr
b 1705

Abigail Burt
1718-66

Ephraim Bill
1719-1802

Lydia Huntington
1727-98

Thomas Delano
b 1704

Jean Peckham
b 1702/3

James Cushman
c 1695-1722

Sarah Hatch

Caleb Church
1728-c 1771

Mercy Pope
1729/30-a 1780

Samuel Perry
1731-1805

Susannah Swift
c 1734-1806

Joseph Lyman
1699-1763

Abigail Lewis
1701-c 1776

Benjamin Sheldon
c 1697-1773

Mary Strong
1701-?76

Revd Nathaniel Robbins
1726-95

Elizabeth Hutchinson
1731-93

James Murray
1713-81

Barbara Bennet
1724-58

Isaac Roosevelt
1726-94

Cornelia Hoffman
1734-89

Abraham Walton
c 1739-96

Grace Williams
b c 1745

John Aspinwall
c 1705/6-74

Rebecca Smith
c 1734/5-1809

Joseph Howland
1749-1836

Lydia Bill
1753-1838

Ephraim Delano
1733-1815

Elizabeth
Cushman
1739-1809

Joseph Church
1752-c 1839

Deborah Perry
1754-c 1808

Joseph Lyman, Jr
1731-1804

Mary Sheldon
c 1731-1805

Edward Robbins
1758-1829

Elizabeth Murray
1756-1837

James Roosevelt
1760-1847

Maria Walton
1769-1810

John Aspinwall, Jr
1774-1847

Susan Howland
1779-1852

Warren Delano
1779-1866

Deborah Church
1783-1827

Joseph Lyman III
1767-1847

Anne Robbins
1789-1867

Isaac Roosevelt
1790-1863

Mary Aspinwall
1809-86

Warren
Delano, Jr
1809-98

Catherine Lyman
1825-96

James Roosevelt
1828-1900

Sara Delano
1854-1941

FRANKLIN
DELANO
ROOSEVELT
32nd President
1882-1945

Plate 103   Harry S. Truman

HARRY S. TRUMAN

1884-1972
33RD PRESIDENT OF THE UNITED STATES OF AMERICA
1945-53

At the best of times any man succeeding Franklin Roosevelt would have had a hard task, but circumstances made it peculiarly difficult for Harry Truman. He had been a valuable but not very conspicuous Senator until 1944, when he had reluctantly agreed to accept the Democratic vice-presidential nomination. He does not at that time appear to have guessed that FDR was unlikely to live out his fourth term, which in itself suggests how little he had seen of the President, for many people who met Roosevelt in the last year of his life were struck by his haggard and failing appearance. Nor does Roosevelt himself appear to have expected to die, certainly not as soon as he did. The result was that Truman was totally unprepared for his responsibilities.

However, as history has repeatedly demonstrated, it is character rather than preparation that makes a successful President and Truman's character was remarkable. He was an extraordinary mixture of modesty and assurance, of business-like attitudes and intellectual aspirations. He came of poor Missouri farming folk and had been unable to go either to college or to West Point as he would have liked. Yet as a boy he had aspired to be a concert pianist, and was deeply read in history. There were endless snobbish sneers at him as a 'little man' and 'failed haberdasher' from people who ought to have known better and were not evidently more intelligent than Truman. As a matter of fact, his experience had given him some excellent lessons. He had served as an officer in the artillery in France during World War I. He had put his savings into a haberdasher's business which had failed because of the postwar recession of the early 1920s. He had then served as a state judge, which had involved him in a substantial amount of administration (especially in road planning) as well as party politics and he had been a loyal New Deal Senator for 10 years. In sum, he had seen life and he had profound knowledge of American politics and government at both state and national level. If unprepared, he was by no means ill-equipped to be President and leader of the Democratic Party. It was his native qualities which served him best: his quick intelligence; his loyalty to his friends and colleagues; his courage; his unswerving devotion to his country; his sympathy with the ordinary man — with the farmer and the shopkeeper — that he had been himself. Dean Acheson, who served as his Secretary of State, rightly called him 'The Captain with the mighty heart', and as such he came to win a great deal of respect, both nationally and internationally.

His presidency was stormy. He had not been in office long when he had to decide whether to authorize the dropping of the atomic bomb on Japan. Truman, never one to shirk a decision (one of his faults in fact, was a tendency to over-value mere decisiveness) ordered the attack to go forward. He inherited deteriorating relations with the Soviet Union and by his somewhat unimaginative inflexibility may have helped to bring on a quarrel (but there would have been a break sooner or later, since Stalin was all too evidently bent on extending his tyranny over as much of Europe as possible). The first great stroke of his administration was the organization of Marshall Aid, which effectively rescued the shattered economies of western Europe. He resisted what he saw as Soviet expansion by sending American troops to the aid of South Korea in the face of communist invasion in 1950; he conspicuously reasserted civilian control over the military by dismissing General Douglas MacArthur from his command when that hero disregarded his commander-in-chief's orders once too often. The resultant row was appalling, but Truman never flinched.

The central event of his presidency, however, was undoubtedly the election campaign of 1948. This fixed the image of Harry Truman for ever. At the beginning of the year everyone was convinced that the Republicans were certain to win. Truman seemed unimpressive, the Republicans had captured Congress in 1946 for the first time since the Depression and the Democrats were badly split. Truman proved himself a bonny fighter, travelled up and down the country in his campaign train and made all the experts look foolish by soundly defeating the Republican candidate, Thomas E. Dewey of New York. Perhaps the best explanation of the upset was given by the newspaperman who noticed that in every crowd which gathered to hear the President there was a little man who looked just like him.

It was widely believed that Truman won because of his vigour in denouncing his enemies. "Give 'em hell, Harry!" was a slogan that still survives, as has Truman's caustic comment on the high-minded flinching of General Eisenhower from the rougher side of American politics: "If you can't stand the heat, get out of the kitchen." He also shocked the high-minded but delighted everyone else by his reaction to what he saw as a wanton attack on his daughter Margaret. She had inherited her father's musicality and wanted to be a singer. After one of her concerts a reviewer advised her, in unkind language, to forget it. The President sent the critic a letter threatening to punch his nose and black his eye at the first opportunity. This shocked the conventional almost as much as the garish ties he liked to wear, but it is doubtful if any President has ever done anything more endearing.

HARRY S. TRUMAN'S FAMILY

The first complete day for President and Mrs Truman and their daughter Margaret in the White House, 8 May 1945, was both his 61st birthday and VE Day. One stresses the first day for all three Trumans because, although the phrase 'First Family' only came to the fore in Kennedy's day, it would have been appropriate for these unusually close-knit Midwesterners. They were known by some White House domestic staff as 'The Three Musketeers'.

They were joined as long-term residents of the White House by Bess Truman's mother, Margaret Gates Wallace, whose formality was such that she was still calling her son-in-law "Mr Truman" after she had known him 26 years. Truman's own mother merely occupied the White House as a weekend guest, but her staunch Southern background allegedly made her refuse to occupy Lincoln's old bedroom. Considering she had been born in Jackson City, Mo., and was only 10 when the Civil War broke out this might seem pure affectation. But although Missouri itself had remained in the Union its Governor had been a secessionist and the secessionist rump had unilaterally set up a state capital-in-exile in Marshall, Tex. Civil War-vintage emotions therefore remained strong among Missourians.

Although Bess Truman was one of the most self-effacing of Presidents' wives (unlike Eleanor Roosevelt she never gave press conferences, much to the chagrin of the media), she worked alone with her husband for at least two hours practically every night, discussing his speeches or policies. One observer reckoned she had more say in political decisions than Eleanor Roosevelt on social questions. The fact that Truman himself called her "the Boss", though folksy, underlines this. Bess was socially the queen of Independence, Missouri, when she married Truman. Her childhood home, which continued as the Trumans' residence after her marriage, had been built by her great-grandfather before the Civil War. In Midwestern terms this amounted to venerable ancestral tradition. And Truman himself was not exactly from the wrong

Plate 104   Bess Truman

Plate 105   r-l Harry Truman, his daughter Margaret,
his 92-year-old mother, Martha Young Truman,
and his wife Bess, September 1945

Plate 106   Harry Truman, his daughter Margaret and wife Bess, April 1945

side of the tracks. His maternal grandfather had at one time had a farm of 2,000 acres. (This same grandfather, Solomon Young, was commemorated in Truman's middle name, the S standing for Solomon; Republicans spread rumours that Truman was Jewish during his 1940 senate election and in the 1944 presidential election.) Unfortunately Harry Truman's father speculated disastrously in grain in 1901 and in 1902 the family had to move from their relatively well-to-do neighbourhood in Independence to Kansas City nearby, a much less desirable address. Harry Truman had to give up his studies, especially the piano, and work in a bank, where one of his colleagues was Arthur Eisenhower, Ike's elder brother.

When Truman became president there was some rivalry, even a breaking of faith, by members of the ci-devant dynasty. James Roosevelt, FDR's eldest son, publicly called on Truman not to stand for election in 1948. As chairman of the Californian delegates to the Democratic convention that year, James also drew up with 18 other party bosses a round robin to the delegates generally urging them to caucus before the convention opened with a view to selecting the strongest and ablest man available — implicitly not Harry Truman. Truman was privately caustic about the whole Roosevelt clan, writing to his sister Mary that Teddy Roosevelt was happy to get Taft's support but then refused to reciprocate. Later in the 1948 campaign Eleanor Roosevelt became an enthusiastic Truman-supporter, but she was unable to persuade her three sons to follow her.

Truman was just as protective to his wife as to Margaret: on one occasion he wanted to have a foreign ambassador recalled from Washington because he thought the man had insulted Mrs Truman by peevishly cancelling an appearance at a diplomatic dinner. And the black Congressman Adam Clayton Powell was never invited to the White House in Truman's time because he had called Bess 'the Last Lady in the Land' following her attendance at a DAR function at a time when the DAR was taking a racist line.

Margaret Truman earned enough from her singing recitals, despite the hostile criticism at her debut, to finance a goodwill trip to Europe in 1951 on behalf of her father. Subsequently she published a number of thrillers set in Washington and, of more importance, a biography of her father, together with an edition of his letters and a biography of her mother. Her *White House Pets* was a coffee table book, while *Women of Courage*, which she wrote with Alice and Tom Fleming, was a collection of biographies of 12 American heroines inspired by President Kennedy's *Profiles in Courage*.

Truman made useful contributions to his party's pool of campaign tactics in both 1960 and 1964, pointing out for instance that many people outside America's big cities still didn't know where the local airport was, but everyone knew the railroad station, so let the presidential candidate make appearances at every railroad station across the nation. Johnson in particular profited by this. It must have been the last presidential election in which consumer lack of awareness about air travel was substantial. But then Truman and the family he came from represented an older America.

BIOGRAPHICAL DETAILS AND DESCENDANTS

TRUMAN, HARRY (named after his maternal unc Harrison Young) S., b Lamar, Barton Co, Mo., 8 May 1884; educ local schools in Independence, Mo., and Kansas City Sch of Law as adult; railroad construction timekeeper 1901-02, clerical work with Kansas City *Star* 1902, clerk and book-keeper 1903-04, enlisted Missouri Nat Gd 1905, farmer Grandview, Mo., 1906-17, Postmaster Grandview 1915, served with Batteries F (1st Lt 1917) and D (Capt 1918) 129th Field Artillery World War I (Maj 1919, Col USARC 1927), haberdasher Independence 1919, County Judge Eastern District, Jackson Co, Mo., 1922-24, Presiding Judge Jackson Co 1926-1934, US Senator 1935-45 (Memb: Appropriations, Enrolled Bills, Mily Affrs, Printing, Interstate Commerce and Public Bldgs & Gnds Ctees, V-Chm Senate Sub-Ctee investigating railroad financing 1937, Chm Ctee Investigating Defense Construction Program 1941), Vice-President of USA 20 Jan-12 April 1945, 33rd President (D) of the USA 12 April 1945-53, Hon Degree Kansas City U 1945, Hon LLD Fordham U and Washington College, Chestertown,

Md., 1946, had title 'Champion of Inter-American Solidarity' conferred on him by Pres Alemán of Mexico 1947, Woodrow Wilson Award 1951, Hon DCL Oxford (UK) 1956; author: *Addresses and Statements of H. S. Truman: a topical record from January 1935 to April 1945* (1945), *Memoirs: Year of Decisions, 1945* (1955), *Memoirs: Years of Trial and Hope, 1946-1953* (1956), *Mr Citizen* (1961), *Plain Speaking* (1974); m Independence 28 June 1919 Elizabeth (Bess) Virginia (b Independence 13 Feb 1885; d there 18 Oct 1982), dau of David Willock Wallace, farmer, of Independence, and his w Madge Gates (d 5 Dec 1952), and d Kansas City 26 Dec 1972 (bur Independence), leaving issue:

President Truman's daughter

I *(Mary) Margaret Truman [c/o Scott Meredith Literary Agency Inc, 845 3rd Avenue, New York, NY 10022, USA], b Independence 17 Feb 1924; educ Gunston Hall, Washington, DC, and George Washington U; singer, broadcaster (conducted own radio show *Authors in the News* 1950-57, co-hostess radio show *Weekday* 1955, (television) hostess *CBS International Hour* 1965), actress, author: *Souvenir — Margaret Truman's Own Story* (with Margaret Cousins) (1956), *White House Pets* (1968), *Harry S. Truman* (1972), *Women of Courage* (with Alice and Tom Fleming) (1976), *Murder in the White House* (1980), *Murder on Capitol Hill* (1981), *Murder in the Supreme Court* (1982), *Murder in the Smithsonian* (1983), *Murder on Embassy Row* (1984), *Murder at the FBI* (1985), *Murder in Georgetown* (1986), *Bess W. Truman* (1986), *Murder in the CIA* (1987), Tstee: Harry Truman Inst, George Washington U, Dir: Riggs Nat Bank, Seabury Press, Sec Harry S Truman Fndn, Hon Degrees: George Washington U, Wake Forest U and Rockhurst Coll; m Independence 21 April 1956 *E(lbert) Clifton DANIEL, Jr (b Zebulon, N Carolina, 19 Sept 1912, assoc ed *New York Times*), s of Elbert Clifton Daniel and his w Elvah Jones, and has issue:

President Truman's grandchildren
1 *Clifton (Kif) Truman DANIEL, b New York 5 June 1957
2 *William (Will) Wallace DANIEL, b New York 19 May 1959
3 *Harrison Gates DANIEL, b New York 3 March 1963
4 *Thomas DANIEL, b New York 28 May 1966

MALE LINE ANCESTRY AND COLLATERAL DESCENDANTS

William TRUMAN, of Bedford and Fanklin Counties, Va., m Nancy —— and had (with other issue):

William TRUMAN, b Va., 15 Jan 1783; m Woodford Co, Ky., 28 Aug 1807 Emma Grant (b St Mary's Parish, Caroline Co, Va., 29 Oct 1787; d Kentucky 21 June 1872), dau of Richard Shipp and his w Elizabeth Doniphan, of King George Co, Va., and d Shelby Co, Ky., 28 Nov 1863, having had issue (with 11 other children):

Anderson Shipp TRUMAN, b Shelby Co 27 Feb 1816; m there 13 Aug 1846 Mary Jane (b Kentucky 15 March 1821; d Missouri 5 Feb 1879), dau of Capt Jesse Holmes, of Shelby Co, and his w Ann Drusilla (Nancy) Tyler, and d Grandview, Mo., 3 July 1887, leaving issue (not necessarily in the order given and together with two other daus):

I A s, b 18——; m and had issue:

1 Ralph Emerson TRUMAN; Maj-Gen US National Guard; m and d Kansas City 1962, having had at least one child (together with at least one gs, Lawrence Truman, of Owensboro, Ky.), a s:

(1) Col Lou(is) TRUMAN; aide to commanding general at Pearl Harbor

II John Anderson TRUMAN

III Margaret Ellen Truman; m — NOLAND and had issue at least two children/grand-children, Ethel and Nellie

The yr (?) s,

John Anderson TRUMAN, b Jackson Co, Mo., 5 Dec 1851; farmer and livestock salesman; m Grandview, Mo., 28 Dec 1881 Martha Ellen (b Parish Farm, Jackson Co, Mo., 25 Nov 1852; d Grandview 26 July 1949), dau of Solomon Young and his w Harriet Louisa Gregg, and d Kansas City 3 Nov 1914, leaving issue:

I HARRY S. TRUMAN, 33rd PRESIDENT of the UNITED STATES of AMERICA

II (John) Vivian TRUMAN, b Harrisonville, Mo., 25 April 1886; Dir Federal Housing Authority; m Oct 1911 Louella Campbell and d Grandview July 1965, leaving four s (including Harry Arnold Truman, dairy farmer, and Gilbert Truman) and one dau

III Mary Jane TRUMAN, b Grandview 12 Aug 1889

Thomas Shipp
c 1707-52
Elizabeth —

Thomas Shipp, Jr
c 1727-77
Rachel —

Mott Doniphan
d c 1776
Rosanna Anderson
d a 1776
Thomas Monteith
c 1694-*c* 1747
Phillis Gallop

Anderson Doniphan
c 1718-20—60-61
Magdalin Monteith
d p 1792

John Holmes
d 1732-39
Mary —
d p 1739

James Holmes
d a 1782
Elizabeth —
d c 1803-05

James Lewis?

— —

Edward Tyler
1696-*c* 1726
Elizabeth Duvall
c 1696-*p* 1770

Edward Tyler, Jr
1719/20-1802
Ann Langley
c 1732-1820

HARRY S. TRUMAN
FAMILY TREE

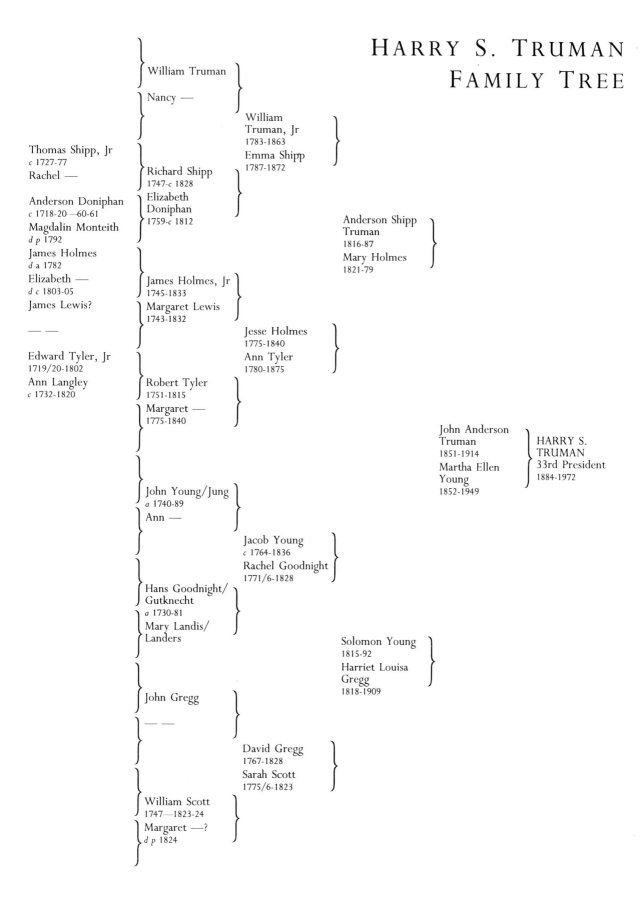

William Truman

Nancy —

William
Truman, Jr
1783-1863
Emma Shipp
1787-1872

Thomas Shipp, Jr
c 1727-77
Rachel —

Richard Shipp
1747-c 1828
Elizabeth
Doniphan
1759-c 1812

Anderson Doniphan
c 1718-20 —60-61
Magdalin Monteith
d p 1792

Anderson Shipp
Truman
1816-87
Mary Holmes
1821-79

James Holmes
d a 1782
Elizabeth —
d c 1803-05
James Lewis?

James Holmes, Jr
1745-1833
Margaret Lewis
1743-1832

— —

Jesse Holmes
1775-1840
Ann Tyler
1780-1875

Edward Tyler, Jr
1719/20-1802
Ann Langley
c 1732-1820

Robert Tyler
1751-1815
Margaret —
1775-1840

John Anderson
Truman
1851-1914
Martha Ellen
Young
1852-1949

HARRY S.
TRUMAN
33rd President
1884-1972

John Young/Jung
a 1740-89
Ann —

Jacob Young
c 1764-1836
Rachel Goodnight
1771/6-1828

Hans Goodnight/
Gutknecht
a 1730-81
Mary Landis/
Landers

Solomon Young
1815-92
Harriet Louisa
Gregg
1818-1909

John Gregg

— —

David Gregg
1767-1828
Sarah Scott
1775/6-1823

William Scott
1747—1823-24
Margaret —?
d p 1824

Plate 107   The Eisenhowers a few weeks before the 1952 presidential election: l-r Ike, his grandson David, his daughter-in-law Barbara Thompson Eisenhower holding her 8-month-old daughter Susan, his granddaughter Barbara and Mamie.

DWIGHT D. EISENHOWER

1890-1969
34TH PRESIDENT OF THE UNITED STATES OF AMERICA
1953-61

After Truman's victory in 1948 the Republicans grew desperate: they had not won a presidential election for 20 years. Some now turned to demagoguery, or sanctioned it, as Robert Taft, son of the 26th President, swallowing his conscience, sanctioned deplorable outbursts of the anti-communist rabble-rouser Senator Joe McCarthy. Perhaps a new Red Scare would drive out the Democrats. Others turned to an old remedy and resolved to nominate a military hero in 1952. MacArthur they felt was too eccentric, Marshall too closely involved with the Democrats, so they turned to General Eisenhower. He proved responsive, ran and was elected by a large majority. His backers had reason to be satisfied. Ike (as he was called) had even proved popular enough to bring in a slender majority of Republicans in both houses of Congress.

There is no great mystery about Ike's victory. He had been a highly competent Supreme Commander in Europe during World War II and his friendly personality had had the full benefit of wartime propaganda. He had become a familiar and reassuring figure to most Americans and his return to Europe as Supreme Commander for NATO in 1951 had given him the opportunity to display his military and diplomatic abilities afresh. The Democrats had involved the United States in the Korean War, which they seemed powerless to end. When, during the campaign, Ike promised to go to Korea if elected to study the problem at first hand, millions of voters took it as a guarantee that the problem would be solved, and so it proved. Ike indicated to the Chinese and North Koreans that if they wanted to avoid a renewed Western offensive, with the possible use of nuclear weapons, they had better come to a swift agreement; his prestige was such that they thought it as well to take the hint and an armistice was concluded in June.

In foreign affairs Ike acted with the same cool skill for the rest of his presidency. He had in John Foster Dulles a rash and reactionary Secretary of State for most of the time, but he never allowed Dulles to do any serious harm, though it may be argued that he let Dulles act as too much of a brake on his own impulse actively to seek a permanent peace with the Russians. For the rest, the dominant notes of foreign policy were prudence and goodwill. He was not a passive President. Anti-Americanism was a widespread emotion during the 1950s and Ike occasionally felt constrained to confront it directly, as when he engineered the overthrow of a hostile regime in Guatemala. He incurred intense hostility on the Right in Britain and France when in 1956 he put a stop to their invasion of Egypt. Then he himself sent an expeditionary force to the Middle East to support the government of Lebanon in 1958. But on the whole he was content to rely on the overwhelming strength of his country as a deterrent to aggressors and sought no adventures. His countrymen trusted his expertise and he was satisfied that the United States was under no serious military threat. Defence expenditures were high but he did his best to keep them from going higher and in the years immediately after the Korean War actually reduced them quite considerably.

In domestic affairs he was less successful. His long years on the government payroll had not weakened the conservative principles he had learned in his Kansas boyhood, perhaps because his army job saved him from the worst impact of the Depression. He believed in rugged individualism. He filled his cabinet with businessmen who would have found Herbert Hoover dangerously liberal, and although there was no serious attempt to dismantle the New Deal there was no attempt to build on it either. But America was in a conservative mood during the halcyon '50s, when all problems for the majority seemed to have resolved into ones of consumer choice — where to live? — what to buy? — so perhaps Ike's old-fashioned economic attitudes did not matter. His neglect of some other questions did. He regarded the rise of the civil rights movement with barely concealed distaste. Even his conservative Attorney-General, Herbert Brownell, was more enlightened than the President on this matter. Ike was far too slow to involve the Federal government in the attempt to equalize education for black and white in the South. The result was the crisis at Little Rock, Arkansas, in 1957, when troops had to be sent in to control a segregationist mob manipulated by the state's governor.

In the same year the Russians sent up Sputnik, the first man-made star. The little machine spun round the Earth, sending out its cheerful bleeps and Americans' complacency was shattered. They began to wonder if the Communists weren't catching up or overtaking, in science or weaponry or both, and they asked how such a state of affairs had come about. Perhaps his critics were right and their President did spend too much time playing golf.

Ike survived such episodes easily enough. More damaging was the failure of his foreign policy. After Dulles's death in 1959 he tried very hard, by a series of summit meetings, to reconcile America and Russia; at his invitation Nikita Khrushchev, the ruler of the Soviet Union, visited the United States and enabled millions to see that the master of the Kremlin did not actually have forked hoofs and a tail. But a bungled espionage mission by a U-2 plane, which the Russians shot down just before a full summit conference at Paris in 1960, hopelessly soured the atmosphere. Khrushchev denounced his recent host, cancelled his invitation to Moscow, and indicated that there would be no more serious diplomacy until Ike's successor was installed.

That would soon come about. Ike had been easily re-elected in 1956 and could certainly have won again in 1960 but he was debarred by the 22nd Amendment. In January 1961 he retired to his farm at Gettysburg, Pennsylvania, for a peaceful old age.

He had done well by his country; before long people would begin to miss the tranquillity of the Eisenhower years. Ultimately, however, his immense popularity depended less on his services than on his personality. Like that earlier statesman-soldier, Washington, he had a quick temper which he learned to control; apart from that, in his friendliness, his taste for western novels and golf, even in his hobby of painting badly in oils, he was thoroughly representative of a numerous class of Americans. It was this trait above all that made so many of them so ready to proclaim "I Like Ike". In some respects there was a strong likeness between Eisenhower and that other typical American, Harry Truman; perhaps that is why they took such a dislike to each other.

DWIGHT D. EISENHOWER'S FAMILY

The 34th President once told how, during World War II, Nazi propaganda had put it about that the Americans were so short of skilled military men they had had to appoint a Prussian — General Eisenhower.

Actually Eisenhower's male line ancestors were of Rhineland stock. The name had originally been spelled Eisenhauer, suggesting an ancestor who was a hewer of iron or blacksmith, and the family bearing it were devout Protestants who to avoid religious persecution moved first to Switzerland then to the

Plate 108   Eisenhower with Mamie in 1952,
the year he doffed uniform as General of the Army
and was elected Commander-in-Chief

Plate 109   Milton Eisenhower shortly before the 1964
Republican Convention

Plate 110   Mamie, Ike, David and Barbara on a tour of
Britain 1962; the railway carriage is the same one Ike
had used during World War II

Plate 111   John Eisenhower during the Senate Foreign
Relations Committee hearings over his appointment as
US Ambassador to Belgium in 1969

Netherlands and finally to America. In short the Eisenhowers were about as different from Prussians as a Texan is from a New England Yankee; moreover they had been in America since 1741. Nevertheless the German connection has led one of Eisenhower's more specious biographers to suggest it helped him realise how intransigent the enemy would be in fighting to the bitter end in World War II.

Protestant piety remained strong in the Eisenhowers well into the 19th century. Eisenhower's grandfather led a small Mennonite sect called the River Brethren, whose tenets included pacifism and avoidance of public office. His mother was publicizing her pacifist views as late as World War I, much to her family's embarrassment, particularly given their Germanic name, and the subject was raised again by the press in World War II. Few men, let alone Presidents, can so completely have run counter to ancestral tradition as Eisenhower.

In the late 1870s the Brethren's high moral attitude caused them to migrate west, for Pennsylvania, their original home, had become increasingly overrun by outsiders. Kansas, their destination, had cheap land and a seemingly beneficent climate. The first break with another family tradition, farming, now took place, but the culprit was Eisenhower's father David, who started a general store. It failed and he migrated south to Texas, where his third son, the future president, was born. Eisenhower always regarded himself as a native of Kansas rather than Texas, reasonably enough on the grounds that his father had returned north less than a year after his birth. On the other hand, he was perfectly capable of playing the Texas card if expedient. As President he used to cajole Sam Rayburn, the Democratic Speaker of the House, and Lyndon Johnson, then Senate Majority Leader, saying "us three Texans got to stand together". On a national scale there was little political mileage in being Texan, for until Johnson succeeded Kennedy it was assumed that nobody from that state could expect to become President.

As regards the sobriquet 'Ike', Eisenhower maintained in later life that it got bestowed on every boy in the Eisenhower family sooner or later. He added that he himself was called Ike at West Point when he had only been there a day, although he knew nobody at the academy beforehand. Other accounts have only two of the seven Eisenhower boys being called Ike, Edgar ('Big Ike') and the future President Dwight David ('Little Ike').

By the time of the North African landings late in 1942, the Nazis had changed their tune and began spreading word among the Arabs that 'the Jew Roosevelt' had dispatched 'the Jew Eisenhower' to place their fellow Jews in a position of power over the Arabs. Allied propagandists thereupon distributed photos of Eisenhower in profile, drawing attention to his little snub nose and adding a pedigree that demonstrated his 'Aryan' German origins. In this way genealogy, a subject of respect among the Arabs, played its own small part in both total war and high international politics.

Ten years later the nastier pro-Taft elements among Republicans in the US were not above spreading the charge that Eisenhower was Jewish in an attempt to sabotage his candidacy for the party's nomination. Not that Eisenhower was a convinced Republican any more than he was Jewish. He once told Elliott Roosevelt he thought it bad form for a soldier to vote at all, that a soldier should think only of his country, but that if he had voted he would have voted for FDR, a Democrat. Astrology as well as patriotism is said to have influenced Eisenhower. According to Alice Roosevelt Longworth, whose intelligence was not necessarily inaccurate for being so often lurid, he was quite keen on running for President in 1948 but his horoscope told him it would be a disaster and eventually he gave way, though reluctantly.

Sandwiched between presidents from the Roosevelt and Kennedy clans, where politics was a family business, Ike (as it will be more convenient to call him from now on so as to avoid confusion) nevertheless made his own small contribution to the dynastic presidency by relying heavily on his brother Milton. Milton Eisenhower is generally recognized as having been his brother's most trusted adviser, particularly on South America. (It was he who recommended Ezra Taft Benson as Secretary of Agriculture, Benson being cousin to Robert Taft, Ike's unsuccessful rival for the Republican presidential nomination in 1952.)

Milton's ascendancy is hardly surprising, for his ability as a government official acceptable to Republican and Democrat alike is shown by his winning the confidence even of the ultra-liberal Henry Wallace as well as being an adviser later on to Presidents Johnson and Nixon. Milton's true worth to his brother was his lack of an axe to grind.

Not that Milton's advice was always taken. To his credit, he wanted Ike to gun for Senator McCarthy openly rather than publicly holding aloof in the hope that McCarthy would overreach himself, though he later changed his mind and said Ike's was the correct strategy. He wanted his brother to drop extempore speech-making (he wrote some of Ike's 1952 campaign speeches), and given Ike's celebrated syntactical incoherence this might have seemed wise. But Ike's actual audiences thrilled to the tremendous warmth and sincerity of his ad-libbed addresses. Indeed it is hard to see how he could have been so successful both as a leader of men in the field and as presidential candidate had he been a lacklustre orator. The truth is that along with many other successful Presidents he possessed that special ability to make each individual in a crowd believe he or she was the focus of his attention. This is only a 'royal' gift in the sense that it is widespread in the British royal family, but royal or not it is a basic qualification for an elective President.

Milton's importance to Ike's career dated back way before the latter became President. When Ike was posted to Washington in 1927 as assistant to General Pershing on the Battle Monuments Commission, Milton, who had been a journalist at one time, helped him put together a guidebook to World War I battlefields in Europe. The success of the project boosted Ike's stock with Pershing. In addition, Milton's post in the Department of Agriculture brought him useful contacts and he was generous about letting Ike share in them. As late as the middle of 1942, when America had entered the War and Ike been given a major field command, he was still known in Washington as 'Milton's brother'. By the time of the Allied invasion of North Africa at the end of that year their positions were reversed. Yet even now Milton's support was crucial. Unlike Ike he was well known to FDR and he acted as a go-between in securing Administration approval of the pact Ike had made with the Vichy French commander Admiral Darlan over in Africa. Milton even flew there to propagandize on behalf of the pact. And in general he drew on his own long experience in public relations to help Ike captivate the press right from his first major appointment in mid-1942.

Milton Eisenhower is also a useful source for the history of his brother's presidency. In his book *The President Is Calling* (1974), for instance, he maintains that Ike was grooming Nixon for the presidency prior to 1956. Ike's general coolness toward his Vice-President notwithstanding, the assertion deserves to be noted. Presumably as a final return for all Milton had done, Ike recommended him as the Republican presidential nominee for 1964.

Mamie Eisenhower brought her husband a certain amount of money, which must have helped ease the discomfort of years in army married quarters. She was also an asset in political campaigning. But although she once attended a White House briefing on Ike's overthrow of President Arbenz of Guatemala, she does not rank among the 'political' First Ladies. Despite her naivety and emotional immaturity she was admired above all other women by Pat Nixon, who was in a good position to judge. As early as 1943 she was becoming famous in America because of her husband, who remarked on the way she was approaching royalty status. Once in the White House, however, her tendency to behave like the popular conception of a Southern belle (though she was not from the South), lying in bed for much of the morning and frittering away her time with cards, did nothing for her husband's reputation as a diligent chief executive. On the other hand she had had rheumatic fever as a child and ever afterward suffered from a slight heart murmur, so frequent rest was important. She is said by White House staff to have been an imperious mistress. She was undoubtedly a highly efficient hostess, meticulously superintending banquets and the like down to the tiniest details such as a place mat or place cards. Mamie's mother,

Mrs Doud, lived in the White House during the Eisenhowers' stay there and a sister, Frances, was one of Mamie's card-playing cronies.

The Eisenhowers were devastated by the death in childhood of their first-born son, Icky, and never really got over the tragedy. But their second son John had a distinguished career in his own right, first as a professional soldier then as Nixon's ambassador to Belgium. He also wrote books about his father. He served in Europe in World War II under General Omar Bradley, the latter of course one of Ike's subordinates. John Eisenhower could not undertake combat duties in case he was captured, though oddly enough he served in Korea when his father was about to become President, being called back to Washington for the 1953 Inauguration on Truman's initiative, a move which annoyed Ike. During his service years he was a comfort to his father even if a source of anxiety to Mamie. He accompanied his father on the latter's December 1959 goodwill tour of southern Europe and the Middle East.

Perhaps the most piquant aspect of Eisenhower family history is the way the descendants of two of what seemed then just about the most dissimilar Presidents joined in holy matrimony: David Eisenhower (Ike's grandson) and Julie Nixon, Richard Nixon's daughter. David Eisenhower's name was used by his grandfather in renaming the presidential retreat in the Catoctin Mountains of Maryland 'Camp David' instead of 'Shangri-La'.

BIOGRAPHICAL DETAILS AND DESCENDANTS

DWIGHT DAVID ('IKE') EISENHOWER, b Denison, Tex., 14 Oct 1890 as David Dwight Eisenhower; educ Abilene, Kans., High Sch, West Point (BSc 1933, degree conferred retroactively by Act of Congress); assigned to 19th Infy 1915, 1st Lt 1916, Capt 1917, trained troops in US for service in Europe in World War I 1917-18, organized and commanded Camp Colt for Tank Corps troops with rank Actg Lt-Col 1918 (Distinguished Service Medal 1918, later augmented by three oak leaf clusters), substantive Maj 1920, stationed Panama Canal Zone 1922-24 (DSM 1922), at Command & Gen Staff Sch Fort Leavenworth, Kans., 1925-26 (passed out 1st of class of 275), with Battle Monuments Commission Washington, DC, 1927, at Army War Coll, Washington, DC, 1928, on staff of Assist Sec of War 1929-32, on staff of Gen Douglas MacArthur, Army Ch of Staff, 1932-34 and in Philippines 1935-39 (Distinguished Service Star 1939), Full Lt-Col 1936, Regtl Exec Offr 15th Infy Regt, 3rd Infy Div, and Ch of Staff 3rd Infy Div 1940, Ch of Staff IX Army Corps with rank of Col then Ch of Staff III Army Corps with rank of Brig-Gen 1941; 1942: Assist Ch of Staff War Plans Div, War Dept, Feb, Actg Maj-Gen March, Commanding Offr European Theater of Ops (N Africa) June, Actg Lt-Gen July; 1943: Actg Gen Feb, Hon GCB (UK) June, Legion of Merit Nov, Supreme Cdr Allied Expedy Force Dec; 1944: nominated for promotion to newly created rank of General of the Army Dec (Congressional Act became law 1961), awarded Order of Suvorov (1st Class) by USSR; 1945: Freeman City of London and Hon OM (UK decoration in personal gift of sovereign — first American recipient ever) May, Govr US Mily Zone Germany July, Knight of Order of Elephant (Denmark) 1945, also Grand Cordon of Legion of Honour (France), Grand Cross of Order of Lion of the Netherlands, Order of White Lion of Czechoslovakia and Cross of Order of St Olav of Norway, DSM (Navy) 1947, Hon LLD Belfast (N Ireland), also Edinburgh (Scotland) and Cambridge (England) 1946, DCL Oxford (UK); US Army Ch of Staff 1945-48, DSM (US Navy) 1947, Pres and Tstee Columbia U 1948-53, Head Jt Chs of Staff and Pncpl Consultant to US Sec of Defense 1949, Supreme Cdr European Defence NATO 1951-52, 34th President (R) of the USA 1953-61, Pilgrims' Gold Medal 1963, author: Crusade in Europe (1948 — still selling well in 1980s, indeed said to have been second only to Spock in sales), Peace with Justice: selected addresses of Dwight D. Eisenhower (1961), The White House Years: Mandate for Change, 1953-1956 (1965), The White House Years: Waging Peace, 1956-1961 (1966), At Ease: Stories I Tell to Friends (1967), Dear General: Eisenhower's Wartime Letters to Marshall, ed James P. Hobbs (1971), Papers, ed Alfred D. Chandler (1970) and Letters to Mamie (1978); m Denver, Colo., 1 July 1916 Mary (Mamie) Geneva (b Boone, Iowa, 14 Nov 1896; educ Miss Walton's Sch, Denver; Co-Chm Republican Women for Nixon 1968; d Walter Reed Army Hosp, Washington, DC, 31 Oct 1979, bur with her husband Abilene, Kans.), est dau of John Sheldon Doud, of Denver, meat packer, and his w Elivera Mathilda Carlson, and d Walter Reed Army Medical Center, Washington, DC, 28 March 1969 (bur Abilene, Kans.) of heart failure, having had issue:

President Eisenhower's sons
I Doud Dwight ('Icky') EISENHOWER, b San Antonio, Tex., 24 Sept 1917; d Camp Meade, Md., 2 Jan 1921 of scarlet fever
II *John Sheldon Doud EISENHOWER [441 Timber Lane, Devon, PA 19333, USA], b Denver 3 Aug 1922; educ West Point (BS 1944 — graduated D-Day) and Columbia U (MA 1950); served: Gen Omar Bradley's staff World War II (2nd Lt 1944),

Army of Occupation Europe 1945, Korean War 1952-53 (Bronze Star 1953), Gen Staff 1957-58, on White House staff 1958-61 (Legion of Merit 1961), Lt-Col 1963, US Amb to Belgium 1969-71 (Order of the Crown of Belgium 1971), consultant to the President and Chm Interagency Classification Review Commission 1972-73, Brig-Gen US Army Reserve 1974, Chm President's Advsy Ctee on Refugees 1975, author: *The Bitter Woods* (1969), *Strictly Personal* (1974), *Allies* (1982) and *So Far From God* (1989), ed *Letters to Mamie* (1978); *m* 1st Fort Monroe, Va., 10 June 1947 (divorce 1986) Barbara Jean (*b* Fort Knox, Ky., 15 June 1926), dau of Col Percy W. Thompson, US Army, and his w Beatrice Birchfield, and has issue:

Grandchildren

1 *(Dwight) David EISENHOWER II, *b* West Point, New York, 31 March 1948; *educ* Phillips Exeter Academy and Amherst Coll; Head of Youth for Nixon 1968, joined US Naval Reserve 1970, sports writer with Philadelphia *Bulletin* 1973, author: *Eisenhower: At War 1943-1945* (1986); *m* Marble Collegiate Church, New York, 22 Dec 1968 *Julie (*b* Washington, DC, 5 July 1948), yr dau of President NIXON, and has issue:

Great-grandchildren
(1) *Jennie EISENHOWER, *b* San Clemente Gen Hosp, Calif., 15 Aug 1978
(2) *Alex Richards EISENHOWER, *b* 10 Oct 1980
(3) *Melanie Catherine EISENHOWER, *b* 18 June 1984

Grandchildren

2 *Barbara Anne Eisenhower [Mrs Wolfgang Flottl, 111 East 85th Street, New York, NY, USA], *b* West Point 30 May 1949; *m* 1st Valley Forge, Pa., 16 Nov 1968 (divorce) Fernando ECHAVARRIA URIBE, s of Hernan Echavarria, of Bogotá, Colombia, and his w, *née* Uribe, and has issue:

Great-grandchildren
(1) *Adriana ECHAVARRIA, *b* Bogotá 29 May 1969

Grandchildren

2 (cont.) Mrs Barbara Echevarria Uribe *m* 2nd 30 May 1992 *Wolfgang FLOTTL
3 *Susan Elaine Eisenhower, *b* Fort Knox, Ky., 31 Dec 1951; *m* 1st Gettysburg, Pa., 8 Jan 1971 (divorce 197-) Alexander Hugh BRADSHAW (*b* Cairo, Egypt, 18 March 1941; barrister), est s of Frederick John Bradshaw, Assist Sec-Gen Royal Commonwealth Soc, sometime British Consul Brussels, and his w Joan Pauline Beatrice Dagnall, and has issue:

Great-grandchildren
(1) *Caroline Louise BRADSHAW, *b* Middlesex Hospital, London, 29 March 1972
(2) *Laura Madeleine BRADSHAW, *b* London 29 Sept 1973

Grandchildren

3 (cont.) Susan Eisenhower Bradshaw *m* 2nd 9 June 1979 John Fraser MAHON (*b* 18 Aug 1931), s of John J. Mahon, of Syracuse, New York, and his w Amelia Fraser, and has further issue:

Great-grandchildren
(3) *Amelia Eisenhower MAHON, *b* 20 Aug 1981

Grandchildren

3 (cont.) Susan Eisenhower Bradshaw Mahon *m* 3rd 9 Feb 1990 *Roald SAGDEYEV, Soviet rocket scientist
4 *Mary Jean Eisenhower, *b* Washington, DC, 21 Dec 1955; *m* 1st 30 May 1976 (divorce) James Brewton MILLARD; *m* 2nd 1979 (divorce) Kenneth MOORE; *m* 3rd 19— (divorce) ———; *m* 4th 19— (divorce) Clifton WINDHAM; *m* 5th 19— *Ralph ATWATER, and has issue a child, *Merrill.

President Eisenhower's son
II (cont.) John S. Eisenhower *m* 2nd 9 April 1990 *Joanne Thompson

MALE LINE ANCESTRY AND COLLATERAL DESCENDANTS

Hans EISENHAUER; *b* c 1600; farmer in Heddesbach c 1646-48, later at Eiterbach, northwest of Heddesbach, 1659-71, in the Rhenish Palatinate (a virtually independent principality straddling the river Rhine about the middle of the westernmost part of Germany); *m* and had issue:

Johann Friedrich EISENHAUER, sometimes referred to as Hans Peter EISENHAUER, *b* between c 1650 and 1659; farm-hand employed by his 1st w's 1st husb to reclaim abandoned farm in forest near Eiterbach; *m* 1st 1672 Anne (*d* 1677), widow of Hans Brand and dau of —— Beckenbach, and had three s; *m* 2nd Anna Cat(h)arina Mildenberger and *d* Karlsbrunn, Saar (the region along the western side of which the modern French-German border runs), 28 Feb 1729, having with her had (together with six other children):

Johann Nicol EISENHAUER, sometimes referred to as Hans Nicol(aus) EISENHAUER, *b* Darmstadt, in the Palatinate, c 1695; lived for a while in the Odenwald, in Hessen, emigrated with his three s from Rotterdam on the ship *Europa* to Philadelphia, where he arrived 17 Nov 1741, then moved west to Bethel Township, Lancaster (from 1813 Lebanon) Co, Pa., and acquired a 168-acre farm in the area, building a house which was burnt by Indians Aug 1756; *m* 1st —— and had issue (with another child):

I John EISENHAUER, *b* 1713

Johann Nicol Eisenhauer *m* 2nd in or before 1721 Anna Margaretha Strubel, whose bro Friedrich had settled in Lancaster Co, Pa., 10 years before Johann Nicol/Hans Nicol(aus) Eisenhauer, and *d* after March 1760, having had with her further issue:

II (Johann) Peter EISENHAUER, for whom *see below*

III Johannes EISENHAUER, *b c* 1726; *m* 1st 7 Jan 1752 Veronica Meyer, of Bethel, and with her had issue:

1 Anna Margaretta Eisenhower, *b* 14 Feb 1753; m(?) 5 Jan 1772 Christian MEYER, of Bethel, and *d* probably by 8 Jan 1789, leaving three children

2 (George) Philip EISENHOWER, *b* 18 Dec 1754; Pte Capt Lewis Farmer's Co, Col Miles's Pennsylvania Rifle Regt Revolutionary War, seeing action at Battles of Long Island, White Plains, Trenton and Germantown and being discharged at Valley Forge 1 Jan 1778; *m* 1st Stouchsburg, Berks Co, Pa., Eva, dau of Albert Klinefelter, and had issue:

(1) Elizabeth EISENHOWER, *b* Fredericksburg 3 March 1781   (2) J. Philip EISENHOWER, *b* 2 Sept 1782
(3) Christina EISENHOWER, *b* 18 Feb 1784   (4) John EISENHOWER, *b* 26 March 1785
(5) Barbara EISENHOWER, *b* 15 July 1787   (6) Isaac EISENHOWER, *b* 25 Dec 1788
(7) Jacob EISENHOWER, *b* 5 Dec 1789

2 (cont.) Philip Eisenhower *m* 2nd before 6 April 1805 Elizabeth, dau of Peter Bixler, of Bethel, and *d* in or after 1819-20, having had further issue:

(8) Milly EISENHOWER, *b c* 1811   (9) Elizabeth EISENHOWER, *b c* 1813   (10) Joseph EISENHOWER, *b c* 1816
(11) Emely [*sic*] EISENHOWER, *b c* 1820

3 John EISENHOWER, *b c* 1755; served Revolutionary War; *m c* 1777 Barbara —— and *d* after 1810, having had issue:

(1) Adam EISENHOWER, *b* 4 Jan 1779   (2) Michael EISENHOWER, *bapt* Fredericksburg 27 March 1785; *d* young
(3) Michael EISENHOWER, *b* 23 March 1787

4 A child, *b c* 1756
5 Barbara Eisenhower, *b c* 1758; *m* 17— Balzer FETTEROLF and had issue:

(1) Elizabeth FETTEROLF, *b* 18 March 1781

6 Benjamin EISENHOWER, *b c* 1760; *m* Catherine Becker/Eisenbecker and *d c* 1823, having had issue:

(1) George EISENHOWER, *b c* 1790-91; *d* ?York Co, Pa., 12 April 1874?   (2) Mary Eisenhower; *m* John SCHULZ
(3) John EISENHOWER, *b c* 1795; *d* ?8 March 1861?   (4) Catherine Eisenhower, *b c* 1797; *m* John GLACE
(5) Henry EISENHOWER, *b* 27 April 1800; *d* 22 April 1849
(6) Esther Eisenhower, *b* 11 Nov 1802; *m* 18— John CHUBB (*b* 6 Oct 1793; *d* 17 March 1871) and *d* 30 Sept 1889
(7) Jacob EISENHOWER, *b c* 1804; *m* 18— Sarah —— and *d* before 1850
(8) Philip EISENHOWER, *b c* 1805-06; *m c* 1830 Elizabeth, probably dau of Elizabeth Martin, and *d* after 1850
(9) Benjamin EISENHOWER, *b* 25 July 1807; *d* 30 Oct 1875
(10) Peter EISENHOWER, *b c* 1812; *m* and moved to Missouri

7 Jacob EISENHOWER, *b c* 1762; signed Oath of Allegiance Berks Co, Pa., 18 July 1777; *m* Catherine —— and *d* 1851, having had issue:

(1) Henry EISENHOWER
(2) John EISENHOWER, *b* 10 Feb 1781; *m* 1st Elizabeth Bowman (*b* 11 Sept 1776) and had issue:

1a Susan EISENHOWER   2a Jacob EISENHOWER   3a John EISENHOWER

(2) (cont.) John Eisenhower *m* 2nd —— (*d* 29 Dec 1855) and *d* Ringtown, Pa., 16 Nov 1861, having had further issue:

4a Israel EISENHOWER   5a Abraham EISENHOWER   6a David EISENHOWER   7a Joseph EISENHOWER
8a Sarah EISENHOWER   9a Lucy EISENHOWER   10a Adam EISENHOWER   11a Betsey EISENHOWER

(3) Daniel EISENHOWER, *b* 21 Oct 1788; *m* Susanna —— (*b* 17 Aug 1802; *d* Middleburg, Pa., 25 July 1860) and *d* Middleburg 2 June 1874   (4) Jacob EISENHOWER   (5) David EISENHOWER

8 A child, *b c* 1764
9 Mary Eisenhower, *b c* 1766; m(?) Jackson, Lebanon Co, Pa., 21 Feb 1797 John Adam STUMP   10 A child, *b c* 1768
11 A child, *b c* 1770   12 Eva EISENHOWER, *b c* 1772   13 Catherine Eisenhower, *b c* 1774; *m* Henry EMERICH
14 Veronica Eisenhower, *b c* 1776; *m* Jackson 16 Sept 1797 Peter WENDEL

III Johannes Eisenhower *m* 2nd Stouchsburg, Pa., 15 March 1778 Barbara (*b* 2 April 1755; *d* in childbirth 5 Jan 1789), dau of Michael Strickback, and *d* of fever 23 Feb 1789, having had further issue:

15 Frencia EISENHOWER, *b c* 1779   16 Margaret EISENHOWER, *b c* 1780   17 A child, *b c* 1781
18 A child, *b c* 1782   19 Michael EISENHOWER, *b c* 1783-84; *m* by 1810 and probably had issue a s

IV Martin EISENHOWER, also known as IRONCUTTER, *b c* 1727; naturalized Philadelphia 11 April 1752; *m* Bethel 1 May 1748 Anna Margaret, dau of Hans Graff and sis of his bro Peter's w (*see below*), and *d* between 19 Dec 1759 and 24 March 1760, having had issue:

  1 Anna Maria Elizabeth IRONCUTTER, *b* 24 April 1750 2 John IRONCUTTER, *b* June 1752; living 1768
  3 George Martin IRONCUTTER, *b* March 1754 4 John Peter IRONCUTTER, *b* 17 March 1756; ?m and had issue?
  5 John Valentine IRONCUTTER, *b* 1759

  V Maria Magdalena Eisenhauer, *b c* 1730-35; *m* 17— Michael FISCHER

Johann Nicol Eisenhauer's 2nd s (but est by his 2nd marriage),
  (Johann) Peter EISENHAUER or EISENHOWER, *b* Forbach, Lorraine (5½ miles southwest of Saarbrücken in modern Germany), 1722; naturalized Philadelphia 11 April 1752, farmer Swatara Township, Lebanon Co, Pa., Constable at Bethel 1777; *m* 1st 1744 Elizabeth (*d c* 1764), dau of Hans Graff or Graef, and had issue:

  I Peter EISENHOWER, *b* 6 Sept 1745; *d* probably before 1790; *m* and had issue at least two children, including a s, Peter
  II Maria Barbara Eisenhower, *b* 22 Aug 1747; *m*? Christian MICHAEL
  III John Nicholas EISENHOWER, *b* 5 May 1749
  IV (George) Michael EISENHOWER, *b* 4 Aug 1751; *m* Catherine —— and had issue:

    1 J. Michael EISENHOWER, *b* 28 Aug 1774 2 Maria Elizabeth EISENHOWER, *b* 1 Sept 1776
    3 Jacob EISENHOWER, *b* 21 Sept 1778

  V (John) Frederick EISENHOWER, *b* 6 Oct 1753; enlisted spring 1777 as Cpl in Capt Benjamin Weisner's Co Northumberland Militia, saw action at Brandywine; *m* Sunbury, Northumberland Co, Pa., Nov 1775, as her 1st husb, Hannah or Anna Kleinan (*b c* 1755; *m* 2nd Gottlieb Roth) and *d* of gunshot wounds sustained while memb of a scouting party during Battle of Germantown 1777, leaving issue:

    1 John EISENHOWER, *b* Aug 1776; apprentice 1792; living 1830

  VI Maria Magdalena Eisenhower, *b* 7 March 1756; *m*? Christman COFFMAN
  VII Anna Maria Elizabeth EISENHOWER, *b* 25 April 1759; disinherited by her f
  VIII Samuel EISENHOWER, *b* 25 Nov 1763; living 1795

(Johann) Peter EISENHOWER *m* 2nd Bethel, Pa., 7 May 1765 Anna Maria Fischer (*d* probably before 29 Dec 1775) and had further issue:

IX John EISENHOWER, *b* 5 Feb 1774; served Pennsylvania Militia Revolutionary War and 5th Class Capt Henry Snevely's Co at the time of the Whiskey Rebellion 1794, bought his f's homestead of *c* 234 ac 2 Oct 1795 (where some of his descendants were still living in 1945); *m c* 1796 Catherine (*b* 25 Feb 1770; *d* 17 July 1845), dau of Jacob Plank, and *d* 21 June 1861, having had issue:

  1 Maria Elizabeth EISENHOWER, *b* 3 Nov 1797 2 David EISENHOWER, *b* 9 Sept 1799; *m*? Margaret, dau of Adam Koch, of Reading, Pa., soldier in Armand's Legion in Revolutionary War, and was *k* out riding, leaving a dau 3 Catherine Eisenhower, *b c* 1800; *m* 18— —— UNGER and *d* in or after 1850, having had issue at least one child, a s John 4 Mary Magdalena EISENHOWER, *b* 6 Nov 1802 5 Polly Eisenhower, *b* 16 Nov 1803; *m* 13 Dec 1820 Samuel SIEG and *d* 27 March 1838 6 Anna Margaret EISENHOWER, *b* 8 July 1804 7 John EISENHOWER

(Johann) Peter EISENHOWER *m* 3rd Stouchsburg 29 Jan 1777 Anna Margaret (*d* after Nov 1815), dau of Peter Dissinger (*fl c* 1776-81), of Stumpstown (now Fredericksburg), Pa., and *d* Lower Paxton Township, Dauphin Co, Pa., before 27 July 1802, having had further issue:

X John Jacob EISENHOWER, *b* 13 April 1777; shoemaker; *m* 13 June 1803 Anna/Nancy McDonald and *d* on or before 16 Feb 1813, having had issue:

  1 Betsey EISENHOWER, *b c* 1804 2 David EISENHOWER, *b* 24 May 1806; may have been the David Eisenhower who *m* Margaret Koch (*see above*) 3 Jacob EISENHOWER, *b* 10 March 1808 4 John EISENHOWER, *b* 25 Nov 1810; probably *d* young 5 Frederick EISENHOWER, *b* 24 May 1813

XI Catherine Eisenhower, *b c* 1779-80; *m* Philip BURRIS/BURROWS
XII Anna EISENHOWER, *b c* 1781-82; living 1795
XIII Christian EISENHOWER (dau), *b c* 1783; living 1795
XIV Barbara Eisenhower, *bapt* Shoop Church, nr Linglestown, Dauphin Co, Pa., 16 May 1784; *m* Zion Lutheran Church, Harrisburg, Pa., 4 Aug 1801 Conrad KNEPLEY
XV Margaret Eisenhower, *b c* 1787; *m* Salem Reformed Church, Harrisburg, 8 Oct 1808 George LININGER
XVI Peter EISENHOWER, *b* Shoop Church *c* 4 Jan 1790; *d* by 1826
XVII Frederick EISENHOWER, for whom *see below*
The yst child,
  Frederick EISENHOWER, *b* probably nr Linglestown, Dauphin Co, Pa., 15 July 1794; farmer in Lower Paxton Township, Pa.; *m c* 1816 Barbara (*b* 27 May 1789; *d* Elizabethville, Dauphin Co, Pa., 1 Jan 1862), dau of John Miller and his w Susanna Raysor, and *d* Abilene, Kans., 13 March 1884 (*bur* Belle Springs, nr Abilene), having had issue:

  I Polly Eisenhower, *b* 13 Aug 1817; *m* 18— Benjamin MILLER, of Elizabethville, and *d* 9 Dec 1863, having had issue:

1 John MILLER   2 Susan MILLER

II Anna Eisenhower, *b* 25 Aug 1819; *m* 18— Joseph NOVINGER and *d* 20 Dec 1846, leaving (with other issue):

1 Catherine NOVINGER, *b c* 1846

III John David EISENHOWER, *b* 6 Dec 1821; *d* unmarried Elizabethville 31 Dec 1840
IV Catherine Eisenhower, *b* Elizabethville 11 July 1824; *m* 9 April 18— Samuel PIKE and *d* 7 Nov 1907, leaving issue at least one child:

1 Anne Pike, *b* 22 May 18—; *m* 30 Dec 1863 Alfred FAIR and *d* 21 Sept 1929, having had issue:

(1) Alice FAIR   (2) Maud FAIR   (3) Mabel FAIR   (4) George FAIR

V Jacob Frederick EISENHOWER, for whom *see below*
VI Samuel Peter EISENHOWER, *b* 4 Feb 1831; *m* 18— Lydia Ornsdorf and *d* 30 June 1940, having had issue:

1 William Henry EISENHOWER, *b* Harrisburg 9 April 1858; moved to Kansas 1884 and settled near Abilene; *m* Millersburg, Pa., 16 June 1883 Amanda A. (*b* there 19 Oct 1864; *d* Navarre, Kans., 11 Nov 1940), dau of Jacob Hoover and his *w* Rebecca Kuppenhaver, and *d* Navarre 16 Jan 1926, having had 10 children
2 Leah Jane EISENHOWER, *b* 1864; *d* 1865
3 Elizabeth EISENHOWER, *b* 1868; *d* 1875

Frederick Eisenhower's 2nd s (but 5th child),
 Jacob Frederick EISENHOWER, *b* Elizabethville 19 Sept 1826; Minister Lykens Valley River Brethren, moved to Dickinson Co, Kansas, after Civil War and bought a farm two mi from Abilene, sold Pennsylvania farm for $8,500 1878; *m* Elizabethville 25 Feb 1847 Rebecca (*b* Pa. 18 March 1825; *d* Abilene 22 June 1890), 3rd dau of Henry Matter and his *w* Anna Mary, dau of Capt Jacob Dietrich (who served War of 1812), and *d* Abilene 20 May 1906, having had issue:

I John H. EISENHOWER, *b* 17 May 1848; *d* 4 April 1857
II Mary A. EISENHOWER, *b* 2 Sept 1849; *d* 27 April 1893
III Catherine A. EISENHOWER, *b* 25 Sept 1851; *d* 23 April 1924
IV Jacob F. EISENHOWER, *b* Sept, *d* Oct 1852
V Samuel F. EISENHOWER, *b* 30 Sept 1853; *d* 11 June 1854
VI Susan M. EISENHOWER, *b* 29 Oct 1854; *d* 1927
VII Peter A. EISENHOWER, *b* 27 Nov 1855; *d* 4 Aug 1856
VIII Lydia A. EISENHOWER, *b* 27 Aug 1857; *d* 15 Nov 1874
IX Emmy Jane EISENHOWER, *b* 3 Dec 1859; *d* 8 May 1860
X Hannah Amanda Eisenhower, *b* 11 Dec 1861; *m* 30 Nov 1884 C. O. MUSSER
XI David Jacob EISENHOWER, for whom *see below*
XII Abraham L. EISENHOWER, *b c* 1865; minister, ran an orphanage at Thomas, Kans., sold his er bro David Eisenhower, father of the future President, the second house in Abilene that David lived in; *d* Pasadena, Calif., 12 Dec 1944
XIII Ira EISENHOWER, *b* 30 July 1867; *d* Topeka, Kans., 2 April 1943
XIV Clinton EISENHOWER, *b* 30 July, *d* 10 Aug 1867

Jacob F. Eisenhower's 5th s and 11th child,
 David Jacob EISENHOWER, *b* Elizabethville 23 Sept 1863; *educ* Lane Coll, nr Lecompton, Kans.; general storekeeper, railroad employee, mechanic in creamery, gas company manager; *m* Hope, Dickinson Co, Kans., 23 Sept 1885 Ida Elizabeth (*b* Mount Sidney, Va., 1 May 1862; *educ* Lane Coll; *d* Abilene 11 Sept 1946), dau of Simon P. Stover and his *w* Elizabeth Ida, dau of William Link, and *d* Abilene 15 March 1942, having had issue:

I Arthur Bradford EISENHOWER, *b* Hope 11 Nov 1886; banker and sometime V-Pres Commerce Tst Co, Kansas City, Mo.; *m* 1st 1906 (divorce 1924) Alida B. ——; *m* 2nd 3 Sept 1926 *Louise Sandra, dau of Louis Grieb and his *w* Elise, and *d* Kansas City, Mo., 26 Jan 1958, having with her had issue:

President Eisenhower's niece
1 *Katherine Eisenhower, *b* 19—; *m* 19— *Berton RONECHE

II Edgar Newton EISENHOWER, *b* Denison, Tex., 19 Jan 1889; *educ* Michigan U; *m* 1st 19— Louise Alexander and had issue:

President Eisenhower's niece
1 *Janice EISENHOWER, *b* 19—

II (cont.) Edgar Eisenhower *m* 2nd 19— Bernice Thompson; *m* 3rd 19— (divorce 1967) Lucille —— (*b* 1920) and *d* 12 July 1971
III DWIGHT DAVID EISENHOWER, 34th PRESIDENT of the UNITED STATES of AMERICA
IV Roy Jacob EISENHOWER, *b* Abilene 9 Aug 1892; pharmacist Kansas City; *m* 18 Nov 1917 Edna Alice (*b* Ellis Co, Kans., 13 Sept 1891), dau of Alvin K. Shade and his *w* Laura Susan Straley, and *d* Junction City, Kans., 17 June 1942, having had issue:

President Eisenhower's nieces and nephews
1 *Patricia EISENHOWER, *b* Ellsworth, Kans., 17 July 1918
2 Roy Jock EISENHOWER, *b* Junction City 20 April, *d* 25 April 1921

3 *Peggy Jane EISENHOWER, *b* Junction City 12 April 1923
4 *Lloyd Edgar EISENHOWER, *b* Junction City 21 March 1925

V Paul Dawson A. EISENHOWER, *b* Abilene 12 May 1894; *d* there 16 March 1895 (*bur* Belle Springs)
VI Earl Dewey EISENHOWER, *b* Abilene 1 Feb 1898; electrical engr and sometime gen manager *Suburban Life*, a newspaper in La Grange, Ill.; *m* 19— Kathryn Snider and *d* Scottsdale, Ariz., 18 Dec 1968, leaving issue:

President Eisenhower's nephew
1 *Earl D. EISENHOWER, Jr, *b* 19—; *m* 19— and has issue:

  Great-nephew
  (1) *Earl D. EISENHOWER III

VI Milton Stover EISENHOWER, *b* Abilene 15 Sept 1899; *educ* Kansas State U (BS, ScD), and Edinburgh U; jr reporter 1917, ch reporter and managing ed 1919 and city ed 1920-21 *Abilene Daily Reflector*, Assist Prof Journalism Kansas State U 1924, US V-Consul Edinburgh (UK) 1924-26, assist to US Sec of Agric 1926-28, Dir Info Dept of Agric 1928-41, First Head of Office of Land Use and Planning 1937-42, Dir War Relocation Authority March-June 1942, Assoc Dir Office of War Info 1942-43, Memb: Famine Emergency Relief Ctee, UNESCO Exec Bd, President's Commission on Higher Educn 1946, Exec Ctee Assoc of Land-Grant Colleges and Universities 1944-47 and 1950-53 (Chm 1946-47 and 1952-53, Pres 1951-52), Presidential Advisory Ctee on Govt Organization 1953-60, Nat Advsy Ctee Inter-American Affrs 1960, Special Amb and US President's personal rep Latin American Affrs 1953 and 1957-60, Chm: Citizens Ctee's Critical Issues Cncl 1963 and President's Commission Causes and Prevention of Violence 1968, Pres: Kansas State U 1943-50, Pennsylvania State Coll (now U) 1950-56, Johns Hopkins U 1956-67 and 1971-72, Hon Alumnus Pennsylvania State U 1975 and Pres Emeritus 1976, sometime Dir or Tstee: Baltimore Museum of Art, Baltimore Medical Center, Johns Hopkins Hosp, American Acad Political Science, American Red Cross, Pan American Devpt Fndn, Nat Ctee Ec Devpt, Inst Internat Educn, Nat Commission Internat Devpt, Nat Cncl UN Assoc, Quaker Oats Co, New York Stock Exchange and Chicago Bd of Trade, Nat V-Pres: Nat Conference Christians and Jews, Soc for Advancement of Management, Fndr American Korean Fndn, co-author *The U.S. Department of Agriculture: Its Structure and Functions* (1930), author: *The Wine is Bitter* (1963); *m* Washington, DC, 12 Oct 1927 Helen Elsie (*b* New York 14 Aug 1904; *educ* George Washington U; *d* State Coll, Pa., 10 July 1954), dau of LeRoy Eakin and his w Mabel Gillespie, and *d* 2 May 1985, having had issue:

President Eisenhower's nephew
1 *Milton ('Buddy') Stover EISENHOWER, Jr [5 Roland Mews, Baltimore, MD 21210 USA; 4545 N Charles Street, Baltimore, MD 21210, USA; 191 Cheese Spring Road, Wilton, CT 06897, USA], *b* Washington, DC, 11 Dec 1930; *educ* Pennsylvania State U; IBM exec; *m* Florala, Ala., 17 Sept 1955 *Sally Ann (*b* there 9 Aug 1932), dau of Joseph I. Booth, Jr, and his w Aileen Casey, and has issue:

  Great-niece
  (1) *Jennifer EISENHOWER, *b* Glen Cove, New York, 9 Aug 1962

President Eisenhower's niece
2 *Ruth Eakin Eisenhower [Mrs Thomas W Snider, 1803 Indianhead Road, Ruxton, MD 21204, USA], *b* Washington, DC, 21 July 1938; *educ* Swarthmore Coll; *m* Baltimore, Md., Oct 1961 *Dr Thomas W. SNIDER (*b* Little Rock, Ark., 28 Dec 1933; Head Dept of Radiology Union Memorial Hosp, Md.), s of Harry C. Snider and his w Maureen Honan, and has issue:

  Great-nephews
  (1) *Thomas W. SNIDER, Jr, *b* Baltimore 29 July 1963
  (2) *Gordon Eisenhower SNIDER, *b* Baltimore 24 Sept 1964
  (3) *Michael LeRoy SNIDER, *b* Baltimore 19 April 1967

DWIGHT D. EISENHOWER
FAMILY TREE

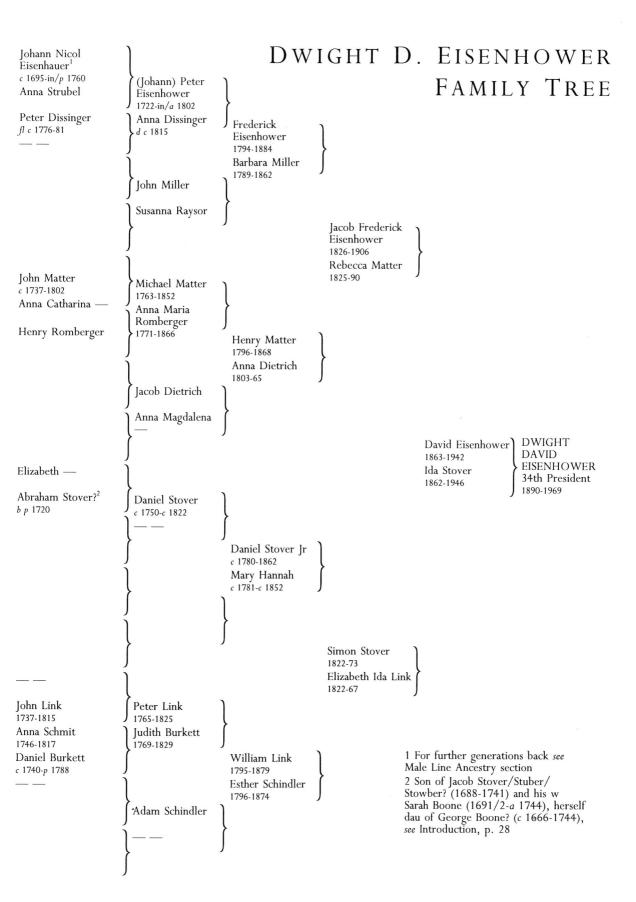

Johann Nicol
Eisenhauer[1]
c 1695-in/*p* 1760
Anna Strubel

Peter Dissinger
fl c 1776-81
— —

(Johann) Peter
Eisenhower
1722-in/*a* 1802
Anna Dissinger
d c 1815

Frederick
Eisenhower
1794-1884
Barbara Miller
1789-1862

John Miller

Susanna Raysor

Jacob Frederick
Eisenhower
1826-1906
Rebecca Matter
1825-90

John Matter
c 1737-1802
Anna Catharina —

Henry Romberger

Michael Matter
1763-1852
Anna Maria
Romberger
1771-1866

Henry Matter
1796-1868
Anna Dietrich
1803-65

Jacob Dietrich

Anna Magdalena
—

David Eisenhower
1863-1942
Ida Stover
1862-1946

DWIGHT
DAVID
EISENHOWER
34th President
1890-1969

Elizabeth —

Abraham Stover?[2]
b p 1720

Daniel Stover
c 1750-*c* 1822
— —

Daniel Stover Jr
c 1780-1862
Mary Hannah
c 1781-*c* 1852

Simon Stover
1822-73
Elizabeth Ida Link
1822-67

— —

John Link
1737-1815
Anna Schmit
1746-1817
Daniel Burkett
c 1740-*p* 1788
— —

Peter Link
1765-1825
Judith Burkett
1769-1829

William Link
1795-1879
Esther Schindler
1796-1874

Adam Schindler

— —

1 For further generations back *see*
Male Line Ancestry section
2 Son of Jacob Stover/Stuber/
Stowber? (1688-1741) and his w
Sarah Boone (1691/2-*a* 1744), herself
dau of George Boone? (*c* 1666-1744),
see Introduction, p. 28

Plate 112   John F. Kennedy

JOHN F. KENNEDY

1917-63
35TH PRESIDENT OF THE UNITED STATES OF AMERICA
1961-63

In 1961 the oldest President yet to have held office (but Ronald Reagan was to beat Ike's record) gave way to the youngest ever elected (Kennedy was 43, eight months older than Theodore Roosevelt had been when McKinley was shot). There was a mood of high expectation in the air, a mood dextrously encouraged by the new President in his Inaugural Address when he said, "Let the word go forth from this time and place, to friend and foe alike, that the torch has been passed to a new generation of Americans." The speaker also pledged his country to "pay any price, bear any burden, meet any hardship, support any friend, oppose any foe to assure the survival and success of liberty." The speech went down extremely well with everyone; in retrospect it seems to have been asking for trouble.

Kennedy was assassinated before any of his designs came to the test. The one conclusive moment of his administration was his showdown in 1962 with the Russians over the missile bases which they were secretly planting in Cuba. He forced the missile bases' dismantling, thereby inducing the Soviet Union to abandon the adventurism which had marked its diplomacy since 1958 and inducing in it a healthy respect for President Kennedy. The missile crisis also opened the way to the nuclear test-ban treaty of 1963, perhaps Kennedy's greatest achievement. But none of this was foreseen in 1961, when what lay behind Kennedy's ringing phrases was the mistaken belief that the Eisenhower administration had allowed America's defences to grow dangerously weak and had let the Soviet Union win too many diplomatic victories. The younger generation meant to put all that right, and promptly too.

What happened instead was that the new administration feebly allowed the CIA to go ahead with a hare-brained plan to send a force of Cuban émigrés to invade Cuba and overturn the revolutionary regime of Fidel Castro. This adventure ended in total fiasco in April 1961. It was followed in June by an unsuccessful meeting with Krushchev at which the Russian treated the American with something like contempt. It soon became clear that the so-called 'missile gap' against which the Democrats had thundered in the 1960 election campaign did not exist; in rocketry the United States was superior to the USSR.

These various embarrassments might have seriously injured the standing of other Presidents, but Kennedy survived them all unscathed. To his own wry amusement, his popularity was as unassailable as Eisenhower's. He seemed so young, so strong (his chronically bad back was a state secret), so handsome, so full of joie de vivre. His wife was so beautiful and chic. They made life in the White House elegant and amusing. They set the fashions and their glamour spilled over onto all their associates. Perhaps America felt it was time for a change from the unimaginative respectability of the Middle West. If so, the country got more than it bargained for. Kennedy was not quite all that he seemed. For one thing he was uncontrollably lecherous: he told the British Prime Minister that he got a headache unless he had sex every day and a compliant string of women was always at hand to oblige him. Worse, he had too many second-rate friends with links to Hollywood and Las Vegas and some of them even had links to organized crime. J. Edgar Hoover, the Director of the FBI, had to warn the President off when it turned out that he was sharing a mistress with a Mafia leader. It made matters no better when it turned out that this same gangster was being approached by the CIA to arrange the assassination of Fidel Castro, though in fairness to Kennedy it has never been proved that he knew of this particular project.

As he began to feel the true weight of his responsibilities, Kennedy apparently began to shake off his tawdry associates. But for the rest he had time only to start things. He launched a space programme to put an American on the moon by the end of the decade. He responded to the swelling progress of American blacks by sending a far-reaching civil rights bill to Congress, where it met heavy opposition. He substantially increased America's political and military commitment to the non-communist cause in South Vietnam, though he was able to disengage, more or less, from Laos.

Then he was shot. He was beginning his campaign for re-election by paying carefully managed visits to various parts of the country. He had been received ecstatically in the North-West, where he was greeted as a saviour because of the Test-Ban Treaty. In Florida, full of conservatives and disgruntled Cuban exiles, he had been warmly welcomed. They were cheering him in conservative Dallas too when the latest unstable successor to John Wilkes Booth put an end to all that grace and hopefulness.

JOHN F. KENNEDY'S FAMILY

The Kennedys were not the first family to try, as it seemed to impressionable onlookers, to make the presidency dynastic. The Roosevelts were every bit as prominent in national politics and possibly wielded more overall power in their heyday. Where the actual capture of the office is concerned nobody else has matched the achievement of the Adamses father and son, Harrisons grandfather and grandson or the Roosevelt cousins.

But the Kennedys had for a time in the 1960s a collective glamour, a 'charisma' as that era liked to call it, which no other modern American family has come within miles of. Moreover potential Kennedy Presidents were all of the same generation. In the early 1960s newspapers liked to speculate that the presidency might remain in the same family — first with JFK, then with Bobby, then with Teddy — till 1984, nearly a quarter of a century. The Kennedys' winning looks, marriage connections with the British aristocracy and Hollywood, the lurid ambition of Joe Kennedy and the tragic fates first of Joe Jr, 'Kick' and Rosemary, then of Jack and Bobby, made a heady cocktail. Though it became appallingly — and appallingly often — clear that the Kennedys were mortal, they had the consolation of seeming almost royal. Not only was Rose created a papal countess by Pius XII (himself the holder of an elective office which, like the American presidency, combines the headship of both state and government); even in little things there were royal parallels. There was the countess's insistence that no two Kennedy offspring should fly in the same aeroplane, so like the safety rules governing members of the British royal family. There was Jack Kennedy's habit of carrying no cash on his person, so like that of the Queen of England, for whom ladies-in-waiting make payments in shops. Even if actual royal rank eluded the Kennedys, they were undoubtedly noble. Rose's title of countess — the only rank of its kind created by Pius XII during his entire reign — was conferred on her for her life only. But when Joe Kennedy attended Pius XII's coronation in early 1939 he was created a Knight Grand Cross of the Order of Pius IX, which still conferred hereditary nobility by male primogeniture on its grantee and his successors (the articles of the order were reformed later that year). Hence although John F. Kennedy was not a nobleman when he was President, his son John inherited noble rank on the death of his grandfather in 1969.

Some historians have made too much of the Kennedys' Irishness. Loyalty and co-operation are just as natural, if less commented on, in any large, politically active family. Jack Kennedy's great-grandfather Patrick Kennedy was unlike the stereotyped Irish immigrant. He seems to have come to America not

Plate 113   *Jackie Kennedy Onassis*

Plate 114   *The Kennedys 1934: l-r Pat, Jack, Rose, Teddy (held by Joe, Sr),*
Jean, Joe, Bobby, Rosemary, Eunice, Kathleen

so much to escape the Irish Famine of the 1840s as to better himself economically. Some commentators have suggested that Patrick's son, P.J., was also an unusual Irishman in being a moderate drinker. And Joe Kennedy in his turn was unlike the Irish-American of popular lore. His pursuit of power lay along financial paths, whether in Wall Street or Hollywood (where however he claimed to use his wife and seven children as a first-hurdle review board to judge whether films he made would pass the Hays Office). His methods resembled those of buccaneer capitalists such as J. P. Morgan or Sam Goldwyn rather than the traditional political bosses of Irish extraction, of whom his father P. J. and father-in-law 'Honey Fitz' were epitomes. Finally, Jack's, Bobby's and Teddy's political careers were fuelled more by inherited wealth and a tradition of political service at national level than by Boston-Irish clannishness, even though Massachusetts was always important as their home patch. In this they resembled the Whig magnificos of 18th- and 19th-century England, from whom their sister Kick's husband the Marquess of Hartington was so notably descended, rather than the local personalities of New England two generations back, who could 'get the vote out' through exploiting a network of loyalties and obligations at ward and precinct level.

The English Whig resemblance could become almost ludicrously close. When Jack Kennedy became president in 1960, for instance, he vacated his senate seat. A *locum tenens* was installed to keep it warm until Teddy Kennedy was ready to take over, which he did two years later. This resembled nothing so much as the 18th-century practice in England where the patron of a generously-endowed church living would install some puppet as vicar until one of his younger sons came of age and stepped into the post. When Bobby Kennedy was elected in 1965 as Senator for New York he and Teddy became the first couple of brothers to serve simultaneously for a century. Brothers sitting simultaneously as legislators were quite common in 18th- and even 19th-century England. In the ruling families of 18th-century or Regency England boisterousness and an appetite for fleshly pleasures on the scale of the Kennedy men also were common.

It is because he so completely financed his sons' careers that Joe Kennedy may seem most important. But he is worth attention in his own right, for as a political influence he was an undoubted force during the New Deal era, even if his judgement was often flawed. He was an early supporter of Franklin Roosevelt, giving him $25,000 for his 1932 campaign and lending the Democratic National Committee $50,000. He was not only on the party's finance committee that year but an adviser to Roosevelt on more general matters. He was particularly useful in containing the awkward newspaper magnate Randolph Hearst, perhaps partly because of his own tendencies to isolationism. He claimed to have played a crucial role in persuading Hearst to pressure John Nance Garner into releasing his delegates to Roosevelt at the 1932 Democratic convention, although other forces were at work too. On the other hand not even Joe Kennedy could seduce the Irish of Boston away from Al Smith in the 1932 Massachusetts primary, although James Curley, Boston's mayor, was an exception. But in 1935 Joe Kennedy's Catholic background came in handy in minimizing attacks on Roosevelt by Father Charles Coughlin, the demagogic 'radio priest'. And in 1940, when FDR was running for an unprecedented third term, Joe Kennedy's endorsement helped win the Italian, German and Irish vote in New York. FDR's chief concern just then was to stop Joe Kennedy attacking him, however.

Once FDR was in office Joe restlessly sought a plum job, working through the president's son James as any good nepotist should. The pattern continued for years. He got FDR's son-in-law John Boettiger jobs in California and Seattle. As late as 1960 he roped in Franklin Roosevelt Jr to endorse Jack's primary campaign in West Virginia. To begin with, the only piece of presidential patronage to come Joe's way was the appointment of Rose Kennedy's uncle James Fitzgerald to a job in the Boston Federal alcohol tax office. Joe himself had to wait until Roosevelt's second term for his biggest reward, the London embassy. It is typical of the man that for all his pride in being Irish he turned down the ambassadorship

Plate 115   Mrs Kennedy, accompanied by members of the
family and President and Mrs Johnson, leaving the
Capitol after the funeral of her husband, November 1963

to Ireland itself, complaining that it lacked prestige. It is easy to sneer at this blend of inferiority complex and racial pride. All the same, it is very Irish.

So too was his sheer fecundity. The political utility of a large family in a sprawling country like the United States is considerable. In the crucial West Virginia Democratic primary of 1960 Hubert Humphrey, JFK's rival there, complained of feeling like a small shopkeeper fighting a chain store. He wasn't just referring to JFK's greater wealth; the sheer number of Kennedys overrunning the state swamped him. In early 1980, during the Teddy Kennedy campaign to win the Democratic presidential nomination, Teddy Jr at one point spoke successfully in place of his father, who was detained elsewhere. A family friend later wrote that this perfectly exemplified Kennedy campaigning — if one of them was not available another could take his place. Although Henry Ford (another Irish-American) started mass production of automobiles, the Kennedys introduced something like the standardized interchangeable component to that hitherto most human of activities, politics.

The ambivalent attitude to his ancestry which lay behind Joe Kennedy's refusing the Dublin embassy was underlined when he intrigued to secure the London one. (He subsequently appointed his two older sons, Joe Jr and Jack, as the ambassador's assistants, just as John Adams had done with his own son, John Quincy Adams, a century and a half earlier.) What was behind the President's offering the post, though? The orthodox explanation is, that FDR hoped Joe Kennedy would prove immune to the Anglophilia which had tainted other American ambassadors' judgement. (Compare Teddy Roosevelt's view of Robert Lincoln.) Unfortunately, Joe's tendency to harbour a passionate mixture of contempt and reverence for any closed society marred his judgement just as much, though in a different way. That the ambivalence existed cannot be doubted. It was something which had burnt within him as far back as Harvard, where his failure to win membership of clubs such as Porcellian shaped his life just as much as the extraordinary success of that other Irishman Cyril Connolly in making 'Pop' at Eton shaped his.

The tradition of old-fashioned political bossism on both sides of President Kennedy's ancestry was strong. His paternal grandfather P.J. served as a Massachusetts state senator in the late 1880s and early 1890s. He also seconded the re-nomination of President Grover Cleveland at the 1888 Democratic national convention. JFK's maternal grandfather, the famous 'Honey Fitz' (in whose honour the presidential yacht was rechristened after JFK took office), was also a Massachusetts state senator, though best known as a long-serving mayor of Boston. (His election to Congress was disallowed on grounds of electoral irregularity.) The moment Jack Kennedy took office members of the family circle were roped in to help shape the administration, just as they had been to win the election. The new President's brother-in-law, Sargent Shriver, was deputed to draw up lists of people to be considered for the chief appointments. His sister Jean Smith and her husband Stephen (who later ran for governor of New York) were included in a diplomatic mission to Saigon. Peter Lawford is said to have kept his brother-in-law well supplied with starlets. The term 'the First Family' came into vogue.

The women of the family played important political roles too. Rose, Joe's wife, had acted as hostess for her father the mayor from late girlhood and occasionally did so for her son when he was President and his wife absent. (Jacqueline Kennedy's mother also stood in for her daughter at a few functions.) Finally, a word must be said about the Kennedy male's notoriously predatory attitude to women, if only because by the time Teddy Kennedy campaigned for the Democratic presidential nomination in 1980 something of his father's and elder brother Jack's restless philandering, not to mention his own reputation, had been grasped by the public. His ex-alcoholic wife Joan's valiant and pathetic struggle to help her husband win votes thus had the effect of underlining the way Kennedys in the past had 'exploited' women. Now that women were politically assertive, such behaviour became a political liability.

The way Jacqueline Kennedy imprinted her personality on her husband's administration is all the more remarkable since his attitude to women might have seemed retrograde to an Ottoman sultan. She was the first First Lady — at any rate since Dolley Madison — to be truly chic, though one should add that not until the early 1960s were the American people ready for chic in the White House.

Much of this lingering mixture of awe and resentment toward chic arose from the American attitude to its country of origin, France. In Jacqueline Kennedy, née Bouvier, America now possessed its own little bit of France. Her triumph on the state visit to Paris in May 1961 was similar to that of Edward VII of England 57 years earlier. JFK said to the Paris Press Club on the last day of his visit "I am the man who accompanied Jacqueline Kennedy to Paris, and I have enjoyed it." (Nixon could be just as witty, once introducing himself as "General Eisenhower's grandson's father-in-law", but never got credit for it.) The public enjoyed Jackie too, though more vicariously. Her picture on a magazine cover, like the Princess of Wales 25 years later, sold thousands of extra copies.

She had a very French concept of the presidency, for as far back as Louis XIV the rulers of France have seen aesthetics as an instrument of government. She boosted the arts generally and the White House as social and cultural centre specifically. She set up a White House Fine Arts Committee and at her prompting a bill passed Congress making the White House a National Monument and creating the post of White House Curator. By autumn 1961 the physical embellishment of the White House was well under way. There was criticism of the cost, but that has cropped up every time a president's wife has redecorated, notably in the case of Mary Todd Lincoln. (Yet Lincoln's bedroom was the only major part of the building Jacqueline Kennedy left untouched.) She showed not just sophisticated taste but a sophisticated sense of public relations. She was instrumental in bringing out an official White House guidebook, setting up a non-profit organization, the White House Historical Association, to research and publish it. Her famous guided television tour of the building attracted an audience of 56,000,000, at that time a record, as well as raising over $2m toward the cost of refurbishment. She has been suggested as the person who first mentioned Camelot to Ted White after she had read *The Once and Future King* by T. H. White (no relation of Ted's). On the other hand he could have come up with the imagery himself, for the musical of the same name was first staged before Kennedy's Inauguration.

The visual arts were not the only ones cultivated. There were White House symphony concerts, Shakespeare readings, a Pablo Casals 'cello recital. Only somebody who refused to admit that state patronage of the arts has ever had any political effect, even though it has been practised with that very end in view by the ancient Roman Emperor Augustus, the Renaissance popes, Frederick the Great of Prussia, Napoleon and Presidents De Gaulle, Pompidou and Mitterrand of France, could maintain that all this made no contribution to the presidency's standing in America and America's standing in the world. Mrs Kennedy's own international standing certainly benefited. During her tour through Asia in 1962 she was treated like a queen, though she travelled in a private capacity and without her husband.

The immediate aftermath of her husband's assassination was perhaps her greatest moment, brutal though it sounds to say so. The dead President's funeral was arranged by her, and since there is no earl marshal in America with sole responsibility for state ceremonial she could select the very church it was held in, the music and bandsmen who piped him to his grave and the site of the burial ground itself (Arlington National Cemetery rather than the family plot in Brookline, Mass.). She once again showed her French sense of occasion by choosing an eternal flame to mark the grave. It is a matter of literary speculation as to whether her step-brother Gore Vidal was inspired by this when he wrote a novel about Artemisia, the 4th-century BC widow of Mausollus of Halicarnassus who by an artful display of mourning for her late husband, including the erection of the original mausoleum, managed to win the throne, rather as Catherine the Great was later to do in 18th-century Russia. Mid-20th-century America (outside Alabama) would not have been quite so manageable. On the other hand Mrs Kennedy was the first president's widow to be given protection by the Secret Service, also an office and secretarial help at the taxpayer's expense.

The subsequent history of the Kennedys, including Jacqueline, has been bathetic. Mrs Kennedy got caught up in café society, one brother was gunned down, the other pulled down by his own folly. Some of the younger generation succumbed to drugs and alcohol. When junior Kennedys campaigned politically the public failed to succumb wholeheartedly to the old magic. Joseph P. Kennedy II, Bobby's eldest son, has so far made the most impact in public life, securing the former House Speaker Thomas P. ('Tip') O'Neill's old Massachusetts seat in the House of Representatives against various opponents, including James Roosevelt Jr, the 32nd President's grandson. But at the same age (41) he is now (1993), his uncle Jack had been a Senator for six years and was within two years of making it to the White House, while his father Bobby had been US Attorney-General and was also a Senator. Joseph's sister Kathleen has considered running for Congress, but so far it has come to nothing. Their sister Kerry married the son and adviser of Governor Mario Cuomo of New York and their cousin-in-law, Arnold Schwarzenegger, the husband of Maria Shriver, campaigned so actively for George Bush in 1988 that he was made chairman of the President's Council on Physical Fitness and Sports in 1990. Edward Kennedy's youngest son Patrick became a member of the Rhode Island state legislature by the age of 23, which leaves him plenty of time to match his uncles' youthful feats. But all this, though cumulatively a sign of energy, is a pale reflection of the old Kennedy exploits.

BIOGRAPHICAL DETAILS AND DESCENDANTS

KENNEDY, JOHN FITZGERALD, *b* Brookline, Mass., 29 May 1917; *educ* Choate, LSE (UK), Princeton, Harvard (BS 1940) and Stanford U Grad Sch of Business Admin; aide to father when latter US Amb to UK 1939-40, Lt US Navy World War II (Purple Heart, Navy Medal and Marine Medal), journalist Internat News Serv 1945-46, Memb US House of Reps 1947-53, US Senator from Massachusetts 1953-60, candidate for nomination as Dem V-Pres candidate 1956, 35th President (D) of USA 1961-22 Nov 1963, awarded Presidential Medal of Freedom posthumously by President Lyndon B. JOHNSON, author: *Why England Slept* (1940), *As We Remember Joe* (1945), *Profiles in Courage* (1956, Pulitzer Prize 1957), *The Strategy of Peace* (1960) and *A Nation of Immigrants* (1986); *m* Newport, Rhode Island, 12 Sept 1953, as her 1st husb, *Jacqueline Lee [1041 Fifth Avenue, New York, NY 10028, USA; c/o Doubleday & Co Inc, 666 5th Ave, New York, NY 10103, USA] (*b* Southampton, Long Island, New York, 28 July 1929; *educ* Vassar, Smith, Sorbonne and George Washington U; journalist with Washington *Times-Herald*, Fndr JFK Memorial Library Harvard, consulting ed Viking Press 1975-77, with editorial staff Doubleday 1978-, Memb Alzheimer's Assoc Benefit Ctee; *m* 2nd island of Skorpios, Greece, 22 Oct 1968, as his 2nd w, Aristotle Socrates Onassis, shipowner (*b* Smyrna 15 June 1906; *d* the American Hosp, Paris, 15 March 1975)), er dau of John Vernou Bouvier III (*d* 1957), stockbroker, and his w Janet Lee, and was shot dead Dallas, Tex., 22 Nov 1963, having had issue:

President Kennedy's children
I A dau, stillborn 23 Aug 1956
II *Caroline Bouvier Kennedy, *b* New York 27 Nov 1957; *educ* Convent of Sacred Heart, 5th Avenue, New York City, Brearley Sch, New York City, Concord Acad, Mass., and Columbia U Sch of Law; Tstee John F. Kennedy Library, on staff of Metropolitan Museum of Art to 1985, author: *In Our Defense: The Bill of Rights in Action* (with Ellen Alderman, 1991); *m* Hyannis Port, Mass., 19 July 1986 *Ed(win) Arthur SCHLOSSBERG (*b c* 1945; *educ* Columbia U), designer and artist, s of Alfred Schlossberg, textile industrialist, and his w Mae, and has issue:

　Grandchildren
　1 *Rose SCHLOSSBERG, *b* 25 June 1988
　2 *Tatiana SCHLOSSBERG, *b* May 1990
　3 *John Bouvier Kennedy SCHLOSSBERG, *b* New York 19 Jan 1993

President Kennedy's sons
III *John (John-John) Fitzgerald KENNEDY, Jr, *b* Washington, DC, 25 Nov 1960; *educ* St David's, New York City, Collegiate Sch, New York City, Brown U and New York U Law Sch; Assist Dist Atty Manhattan 1989, admitted New York Bar 1990
IV Patrick Bouvier KENNEDY, *b* Otis Air Force Base, Mass., 7 Aug 1963; *d* there 9 Aug 1963 of respiratory distress syndrome

MALE LINE ANCESTRY AND COLLATERAL DESCENDANTS

Patrick KENNEDY, *b c* 1785; tenant farmer at Dunganstown, Co Wexford, Ireland; *m* Mary Johanna —— and allegedly had issue:

I John KENNEDY, *b c* 1809: *d* 1864　II James KENNEDY, *b c* 1815; *d* 1851
III Mary KENNEDY　IV Patrick KENNEDY

The yst s,
　Patrick KENNEDY, *b* Dunganstown *c* 1823; emigrated 1848 to Boston, where he worked as a cooper; *m* the Cathedral of the Holy Cross, Boston, 26 Sept 1849 Bridget (*b* Ireland *c* 1821; *d* Boston 20 Dec 1888), dau of Richard Murphy and his w Mary, and *d* Boston 22 Nov 1858 of tuberculosis (some sources say cholera), leaving issue:

I Mary Kennedy, *b* Boston 9 Aug 1851; dress-maker; *m* there 1 Jan 1883 Lawrence M. KANE (*b* Co Wexford, Ireland, 29 Nov 1858; teamster, labourer and pickle dealer; *d* East Boston 19 July 1905 of heat exhaustion and heart disease), s of Philip Kane and his w Margaret Murphy, and had issue:

　1 Joseph Lawrence KANE, *b* 29 Nov 1883; political activist alleged to have persuaded his cousin JFK to run for Congress; *d* Brookline, Mass., 19 March 1967
　2 A son, recorded (but almost certainly erroneously because identical with his er bro) as Joseph Lawrence KANE, *b* 29 Dec 1884
　3 Mary Margaret KANE, *b* 25 Aug 1885; *d* East Boston 14 Sept 1886 of entero-colitis
　4 George Philip KANE, *b* 8 Sept 1888; sign-painter; *d* Boston 6 July 1954

5 Gertrude Margaret Kane, *b* 26 May 1890; *m* Boston 29 Dec 1918 Charles Everett METCALF (*b* Chelsea, Mass., 1 Nov 1891; shipwright; *d* Boston 2 July 1955), s of William Metcalf and his w Rosa Jones, and *d* Boston 14 Jan 1969
6 Frederick KANE, *b* 1892; *d* Boston 15 Oct 1897 of diphtheria

II Jo(h)anna Kennedy, *b* Boston 27 Nov 1852; jute mill operative; *m* Boston 22 Sept 1872 Humphrey Charles MAHONEY (*b* Boston 12 Dec 1847; clerk, machinist, school caretaker; *d* Saratoga Springs, New York, 25 Aug 1928 after being hit by a car), s of Daniel Mahoney and his w Mary, and had issue:

1 Daniel MAHONEY, *b* East Boston 14 Oct 1873; *d* there 20 Nov 1875 of diphtheria
2 Mary E. MAHONEY, *b* East Boston 18 Oct 1875; *d* there 7 Dec 1875 of diphtheria
3 William Henry MAHONEY, *b* East Boston 17 May 1878; *d* there 10 May 1879 of tubercular meningitis
4 Frances Josephine Mahoney, *b* 2 March 1880; *m* Boston 20 June 1916 Louis Leo TWOMEY (*b* East Boston 12 Dec 1879; police patrolman and school caretaker; *d* Lynn, Mass., 14 Jan 1965) and *d* Lynn 13 April 1963, having had issue at least one child, a s:

(1) William TWOMEY; *d* Saratoga Springs 25 Aug 1928 in the same road accident as his gf

5 Annie MAHONEY, *b* East Boston 13 Feb 1883; *d* there 7 May 1889
6 Henry Joseph MAHONEY, *b* East Boston 15 Oct 1884; Boston City sch caretaker; *m* Chelsea, Mass., 30 June 1912 Mary Elizabeth (*b* McKeesport, Pa., 15 Oct 1884; *d* Boston 23 April 1949), dau of John A. Farley and his w Elizabeth Murphy
7 Gertrude MAHONEY, *b* East Boston 7 Oct 1886; *d* there 27 July 1887 of eclampsia
8 Frederick Louis MAHONEY, *b* East Boston 21 Aug 1890; *educ* Boston Coll; assist master Prince Sch, Boston; *d* Boston 26 Oct 1965

III John KENNEDY, *b* Boston 4 Jan 1854; *d* there 24 Sept 1855 of cholera infantum
IV Margaret Kennedy, *b* Boston July 1855; *m* there 21 Feb 1882 John Thomas CAULFIELD (*b* Weymouth, Mass., *c* Jan 1861; restaurateur, dry goods salesman and purchasing agent at Boston City Hall; *d* Lynn 12 July 1937), s of Patrick Caulfield and his w Mary McGovern, and *d* Revere, Mass., 2 April 1929, having had issue (with possibly another child, who presumably *d* young):

1 Mary Frances Caulfield, *b* East Boston 8 Feb 1884; *m* Boston 16 April 1906 Alexander G. CRAWFORD (*b* Liverpool, UK, *c* 1882; riveter and steamfitter) and *d* Revere 14 June 1938
2 Frederick CAULFIELD, *b* New York 20 June 1886; *d* young
3 Edith M. Caulfield, *b* New York 8 April 1888; *m* Boston 17 Feb 1920 Julius BAKER (*b* there Feb 1891; electrical supplier; *d* Boston 2 Dec 1928), s of Israel L. Baker and his w Annie Kohn, and *d* Boston 6 April 1943
4 Henry R. CAULFIELD, *b* New York May 1889; *d* Boston 27 April 1925
5 Florence J. CAULFIELD, *b* New York 19 Nov 1891; *d* East Boston 10 Aug 1892
6 Elsie G. CAULFIELD, *b* Bayonne, New Jersey, Oct 1894; *d* Revere, Mass., 8 Feb 1914 of diphtheria
7 Jeanette Dorothea Caulfield, *b* Bayonne Feb 1896; *m* Revere 4 Jan 1928 Frank William FLINKFELT (*b* Boston 16 Nov 1894; *d* Revere 3 Feb 1960), s of Frank C. Flinkfelt and his w Mary J. Starkey, and *d* Boston 1 June 1953
8 John Theodore CAULFIELD, *b* Winthrop, Mass., 3 June 1899; electrician; *m* Revere 29 Aug 1931 Hazel Elizabeth (*b* Lynn, Mass., 29 Nov 1902; *d* there 15 July 1968), dau of John D. Baker and his w Mary J. Metzger, and *d* Saugus, Mass., 18 Aug 1966

V Patrick Joseph KENNEDY

The yr s,

Patrick Joseph ('P. J.') KENNEDY, *b* East Boston 14 Jan 1858; brass finisher, saloon-keeper, hotelier and fndr P. J. Kennedy & Co, liquor importers, Memb Massachusetts House of Reps 1886-92 and Massachusetts Senate for two terms thereafter, seconded speech nominating Grover Cleveland presidential candidate at Democratic Convention 1888, sometime Boston Elections Commissioner, Boston Fire Commissioner and Actg Boston Fire Commissioner, an organizer of Columbia Tst Co 1895 and subsequently Memb Bd and Pres; *m* Boston 23 Nov 1887 Mary Augusta (*b* Boston 6 Dec 1857; *d* there 20 May 1923), dau of James Hickey, of Boston, and his w Margaret Martha Field, and *d* Boston 18 May 1929, having had issue:

I Joseph Patrick KENNEDY, for whom *see below*
II Francis Benedict KENNEDY, *b* Boston March 1891; *d* there 14 Jun 1892 of diphtheria
III Mary Loretta Kennedy, *b* Boston 6 Aug 1892; *educ* Boston Conservatory of Music, Radcliffe and Columbia U; teacher; *m* Winthrop, Mass., 12 Oct 1927 George William CONNELLY (*b* East Boston 10 June 1898; *educ* Harvard; ship broker, tanker-owner and dealer in oil in association with Beacon and Standard Oil Cos and realtor; *d* St Augustine, Fla., 29 Aug 1971), s of Michael John Connelly and his w Margaret Elizabeth Driscoll, and *d* Winfield, Ill., 18 Nov 1972, leaving issue:

1 *Mary Louise Connelly, *b* Winthrop, Mass., 21 Oct 1928; *m* St Augustine, Fla., 29 Dec 1951 *Matthew James McCARTHY (*b* Chicago 8 Feb 1926), s of Daniel Edward McCarthy and his w Helen Walsh

IV Margaret Louise Kennedy, *b* Boston 22 Oct 1898; *educ* Notre Dame Acad and Misses Guild and Evans Finishing Sch; Fndr with Rose Kennedy of Ace of Clubs (charity); *m* Winthrop, Mass., 14 June 1924 (divorce 19—) Charles Joseph BURKE (*b* Medford, Mass., 23 Aug 1899; served ambulance corps World War I also in World War II, salesman and tailor; *d* Boston 5 April 1967), s of Thomas Francis Burke and his w Alicia Augusta Mann, and *d* Brookline, Mass., 14 Nov 1974, leaving issue:

1 *Margaret Louise Burke, b Winthrop 2 April 1926; m *John Bernard DeVINE (b Ann Arbor, Mich., 5 Feb 1920), s of Frank Bernard DeVine and his w Elizabeth Doherty

2 *Charles Joseph BURKE, Jr, b Winthrop 5 May 1928; m Newton, Mass., 4 Feb 1976 *Claire (b Malden, Mass., 11 Nov 1935), dau of John Coliton and his w Edna Flynn

3 *Thomas Francis BURKE II, b Winthrop 25 May 1933; m Watertown, Mass., 18 June 1960 *Gertrude Ann (b Waltham, Mass., 10 Oct 1936), dau of George Miller and his w Mary Josephine Nelligan

The er s,

Joseph Patrick KENNEDY, b 151 Meridian Street, Boston, 6 Sept 1888; educ Boston Latin Sch and Harvard (AB 1912); Bank Examiner for Massachusetts 1912-14, Pres Columbia Tst Co, Boston, 1914-17, Assist Gen Manager Fore River Plant, Bethlehem Shipbldg Corp, 1917-19, Manager Boston branch Hayden-Stone (investment bankers) 1919-24, Pres and Chm Film Booking Offices of America 1926-29 and Pathé Exchanges Inc 1929-30, Chm: Bd of Dirs Keith Albee, Orpheum Theaters Corp and SEC 1934-35 and US Maritime Commission 1937, US Amb to UK 1937-41, Fndr Joseph P. Kennedy, Jr, Foundation 1945, Memb Commission on Organization Exec Branch Fedl Govt 1947, apptd by President EISENHOWER to Bd Consultants on Foreign Intelligence Activities 1956, Kt of Malta, Knight Grand Cross of Pius IX, Kt Equestrian Order of Holy Sepulchre 1946, Grand Cross Order of Leopold II (Belgium) 1959, Hon LLD Nat U of Ireland 1938 and Edinburgh, Manchester, Liverpool, Bristol and Cambridge (all UK) Us 1939, author: *The Story of the Films* (1927), *I'm for Roosevelt* (1936) and *The Surrender of King Leopold* (1959); m Boston 7 Oct 1914 *Rose Elizabeth (b North End, Boston, 21 July 1890; educ Dorchester High Sch, Manhattanville Coll of the Sacred Heart, New York, and Blumenthal Acad, Valls, Netherlands; cr Countess *ad personam* (i.e., not as a heritable title) by Pope PIUS XII 15 Oct 1951 in recognition of her charitable works, author: *Times to Remember* (1973)), est dau of John Francis ('Fitzie', later 'Honey Fitz') Fitzgerald, Mayor of Boston, Massachusetts State Senator and newspaper publisher, and his w and 2nd cousin Mary Josephine Hannon, and d Hyannisport, Mass., 18 Nov 1969, having had issue:

I Joseph Patrick KENNEDY, Jr, b Hull, Mass., 25 July 1915; educ Choate, LSE and Harvard (SB 1938); delegate Democratic Nat Convention 1940, Lt US Navy World War II (posthumous Navy Cross); missing (presumed dead) following explosion in air over Suffolk, UK, 12 Aug 1944

II JOHN FITZGERALD KENNEDY, 35th PRESIDENT of the UNITED STATES of AMERICA

III *Rosemary KENNEDY [St Coletta's School, Jefferson, WI, USA], b Brookline, Mass., 13 Sept 1918; educ Montessori Sch, Herts, UK

IV Kathleen ('Kick') Kennedy, b Brookline 20 Feb 1920; educ Sacred Heart Convent, Roehampton, UK; m Chelsea Register Office, London, UK, 6 May 1944 William John Robert Cavendish, Marquess of HARTINGTON (b 10 Dec 1917; ka Heppen, Belgium, 10 Sept 1944), er s of 10th Duke of Devonshire, KG, MBE, and his w Lady Mary Alice Gascoyne-Cecil (see BURKE'S PEERAGE & BARONETAGE, Devonshire), and was k in a flying accident Sainte-Bauzille, Ardèche, France, 13 May 1948

V *Eunice Mary Kennedy [Mrs Sargent Shriver, 1350 New York Avenue NW, Washington, DC 20005, USA], b Boston 10 July 1921; educ Sacred Heart Convent, Roehampton, Manhattanville Coll and Stanford U (BS 1943); Exec V-Pres Joseph P. Kennedy Jr Fndn and Fndr-Pres Special Olympics Inc 1968; m New York 23 May 1953 *(Robert) Sargent SHRIVER, Jr (b Westminster, Md., 9 Nov 1915; educ Yale; US Naval Reserve World War II, lawyer, Assist Gen Manager Merchandise Mart (Kennedy property) 1948-61, Dir Peace Corps 1961-66 and Office Econ Opportunity 1964-68 (also special assist to President JOHNSON), US Amb to France 1968-70, v-presdtl candidate 1972 and candidate for presdtl nomination Democratic Convention 1976, sr ptnr Fried, Frank, Harris, Shriver and Jacobson, Washington, DC), s of Robert Sargent Shriver and his w Hilda, and has issue:

President Kennedy's nephew and niece

1 *Robert (Bobby) Sargent SHRIVER III, b Chicago 28 July 1954; educ Yale and Yale Law Sch; former record-producer and journalist, financier

2 *Maria Owings Shriver [c/o NBC, 30 Rockefeller Plaza, New York, NY 10112, USA], b Chicago 6 Nov 1955; educ Sacred Heart Convent, Stamford, Conn., and Georgetown U (Memb Bd of Regents 1986-); television presenter (newswriter and producer KYW-TV Philadelphia 1977, WJ2-TV Baltimore 1978, *PM Magazine* 1981-83, CBS *Morning News* 1985-86, NBC's *Sunday Today* 1987, anchorwoman of prime time show *First Person with Maria Shriver*); m Cape Cod, Mass., 16 April 1986 *Arnold SCHWARZENEGGER [c/o Oak Productions, 321 Hampton Drive, Ste 203, Venice, CA 90291, USA; c/o Parker Public Relations, 11500 W Olympic Blvd, Ste 400, Los Angeles, CA 90064, USA] (b Austria or East Germany 30 July 1947; educ U of Wisconsin (degree in business and internat economics); winner Mr Europe title, Best-Built Man of Europe title and Internat Powerlifting Championship 1966, Mr Universe title 1967, 2nd in Mr Universe title 1968, Mr World, Mr Universe and Mr Olympia 1970, retd 1975, having won Mr Olympia title six times consecutively and Mr Universe title five times, emerged from retirement 1980 to win Mr Olympia title for unprecedented seventh time, winner biggest number of professional bodybuilding contests in world; film actor: (as Arnold Strong) *Hercules Goes to New York* (1970), *The Long Goodbye* (1973), *Stay Hungry* (1975; Golden Globe Award for Best New Actor), *Pumping Iron* (1977), *The Villain* (1977), *The Jayne Mansfield Story* (1980), *Conan the Barbarian* (1982), *Conan the Destroyer* (1983), *The Terminator* (1984), *Commando* (1985), *Raw Deal* (1986), *Predator* (1987), *The Running Man* (1987), *Red Heat* (1988), *Twins* (1988), *Total Recall* (1990), *Kindergarten Cop* (1990), *Terminator 2: Judgement Day* (1991) and *Last Action Hero* (1993), Chm President's Cncl on National Ftness and Sports 1990-, recipient Simon Wiesenthal Center's national Leadership Award 1991, author: *Arnold: The Education of a Body-Builder* (1977), *Arnold's Bodyshaping for Women* (1979), *Arnold's Bodyshaping for Men* (1981) and *Arnold's Encyclopaedia of Modern Bodybuilding* (1985)), yr s of Gustav Schwarzenegger (d 1972), police chief of Thal, Austria, and his w Aurelia Jedrny, and has issue:

Great-nieces
(1) *Katherine Eunice SCHWARZENEGGER, *b* 13 Dec 1989
(2) *Christina Aurelia SCHWARZENEGGER, *b* 23 July 1991

President Kennedy's nephews
3 *Timothy Perry SHRIVER, *b* Boston 29 Aug 1959; *educ* Yale
4 *Mark Kennedy SHRIVER, *b* Washington, DC, 17 Feb 1964; *educ* Holy Cross U
5 *Anthony Paul Kennedy SHRIVER, *b* Boston 20 July 1965; *educ* Georgetown U; Pres Best Buddies (charity for mentally ill)

VI *Patricia Kennedy, *b* Brookline, Mass., 6 May 1924; *educ* Sacred Heart Convent, Roehampton; sometime NBC employee and fndr with her husb of the Kenlaw Production Co (films and television); *m* New York 24 April 1954 (divorce 1966) Peter LAWFORD (*b* London 7 Sept 1923; actor; *d* Los Angeles 24 Dec 1984), s of Lt-Gen Sir Sydney Turing Barlow Lawford, KCB, Roy Fusiliers (*d* 15 Feb 1953), and his w Mary Somerville Bunny, and has issue:

President Kennedy's nephew
1 *Christopher Kennedy LAWFORD, *b* 29 March 1955; *educ* Tufts, George Washington U and Boston U Law Sch; actor (films include *The Doors* (1988), *Run* (1990) and *The Russia House* (1990)); *m* Bequia, West Indies, Dec 1984 *Jean (Jeannie) Edith (*b* Seoul, Republic of Korea, 24 Jan 1955), dau of Einar Valentine Olsson and his w Chae Ok Hee, and has issue:

Great-nephew and -niece
(1) *David LAWFORD, *b* 1988
(2) *Savannah LAWFORD, *b* 1990

President Kennedy's nieces
2 *Sydney Maleia Lawford, *b* 25 Aug 1956; *m* Barnstable, Mass., 17 Sept 1983 *James Peter McKELVY (*b* Pittsburgh 4 April 1955), s of William Sheldon McKelvy and his w Nancy Ryon
3 *Victoria Frances LAWFORD, *b* 4 Nov 1958; *educ* Mt Vernon Coll
4 *Robin Elizabeth LAWFORD, *b* 2 July 1961; *educ* Marymount Coll

VII Robert (Bobby) Francis KENNEDY, *b* Boston 20 Nov 1925; *educ* Milton Acad, Harvard (AB) and U of Virginia Law Sch (LLB); seaman 1944-46 USNR, reporter *Boston Post* 1948 (in Palestine), admitted Massachusetts Bar 1951, Atty Criminal Div, Dept Justice, 1951-52, Assist Counsel Senate Perm Sub-Ctee Investigations 1953, Assist Counsel Hoover Commission 1953-54, Ch Counsel Democratic Minority 1954, Ch Counsel and Staff Dir Democratic Minority 1955-59, Ch Counsel Senate Select Ctee Improper Activities Labor or Management Field 1957-59, US Atty-Gen 1961-64, US Senator (D) from New York 1965-68, author: *The Enemy Within* (1960), *Just Friends and Brave Enemies* (1962), *The Pursuit of Justice* (1964), *13 Days: The Cuban Missile Crisis, October 1962* (1969); *m* Greenwich, Conn., 16 June 1950 *Ethel (*b* 11 April 1928; *educ* Manhattanville Coll), dau of George Skakel, of Chicago, and his w Ann Brannack, and was shot dead Los Angeles 6 June 1968 (*bur* Arlington Nat Cemetery 8 June 1968), leaving issue:

President Kennedy's niece
1 *Kathleen Hartington Kennedy, *b* Greenwich, Conn., 4 July 1951; *educ* Radcliffe, Harvard and U of New Mexico Law Sch; ran Edward Kennedy's 1982 Senate re-election campaign; *m* Washington, DC, 17 Nov 1973 *David Lee TOWNSEND (*b* Baltimore 17 Nov 1947; *educ* Harvard), her tutor at Radcliffe and s of L. Raymond Townsend and his w Delores Fahey, and has issue:

Greate-nieces
(1) *Meaghan Anne Kennedy TOWNSEND, *b* Santa Fe, New Mexico, 7 Nov 1977
(2) *Maeve Fahey Kennedy TOWNSEND, *b* New Haven, Conn., 1 Nov 1979
(3) *Rose Katherine Kennedy TOWNSEND, *b* Weston, Mass., 17 Dec 1983

President Kennedy's nephew
2 *Joseph Patrick KENNEDY II [Office of House Members, House of Representatives, Washington, DC 20515, USA], *b* Boston 24 Sept 1952; *educ* U of Massachusetts, MIT and UCLA; worked for Robert F. Kennedy Memorial Fndn and San Francisco Public Health Dept, campaign manager Edward Kennedy's Senate re-election campaign 1976 and presidential nomination campaign 1980 in Iowa, with Community Servs Admin (Washington, DC), fndr Citizens Energy Corp, Memb (D) US House of Reps from 8th Massachusetts Dist 1986-; *m* Gladwyne, Pa., 3 Feb 1979 (divorce 1989) Sheila Brewster (*b* Brywn Mawr, Pa., 22 March 1949), dau of Rudolph Stewart Rauch, Jr, and his w Frances Stuart Brewster, and has issue:

Great-nephews
(1) *Joseph Patrick KENNEDY III, *b* Boston 4 Oct 1980
(2) *Matthew Rauch KENNEDY, *b* Boston 4 Oct 1980

President Kennedy's nephew
3 *Robert Francis KENNEDY, Jr, *b* Washington, DC, 17 Jan 1954; *educ* Harvard, LSE and U of Virginia Law Sch; Assist DA New York City, author: *Judge Frank M. Johnson, Jr: A Biography*; *m* Bloomington, Ind., 3 April 1982 Emily Ruth (*b* Bedford, Ind., 15 Oct 1957), dau of Thomas Allen Black and his w Elizabeth Armstrong, and has issue:

Great-nephew
(1) *Robert Francis KENNEDY III, *b* Mt Kisco, New York, 2 Sept 1984

President Kennedy's nephews and niece

4 David Anthony KENNEDY, *b* 5 Washington, DC, 15 June 1955; *educ* Harvard; *d* Palm Beach, Fla., 25 April 1984

5 *(Mary) Courtney Kennedy, *b* Boston 9 Sept 1956; *educ* Trin Coll, Dublin, Ireland; with AIDS Fndn for Immunology and Allergology; *m* 1st Washington, DC, 14 June 1980 Jeff(rey) Robert RUHE (*b* LaPorte, Ind., 21 Feb 1952; *educ* Stanford U; ABC-TV producer), s of Robert Werner Ruhe and his w Elva Jane Buckingham; *m* 2nd 26 June 1993 *Paul HILL (*b c* 1954; *m* 1st 1968 Marion Serravalli)

6 *Michael LeMoyne KENNEDY, *b* Washington, DC, 27 Feb 1958; *educ* Harvard and U of Virginia Law Sch; *m* New York 14 March 1981 *Victoria (Vicki) Denise (*b* Bakersfield, Calif., 20 Feb 1975; *educ* Boston Coll), dau of Frank Newton Gifford and his w Maxine Avis Ewart, and has issue:

Great-nephew and -niece
(1) *Michael LeMoyne KENNEDY, *b* Charlottesville, Va., 9 Jan 1983
(2) *Kyle Frances KENNEDY, *b* Washington, DC, 6 July 1984

President Kennedy's nieces and nephews

7 *(Mary) Kerry Kennedy, *b* Washington, DC, 8 Sept 1959; *educ* Brown U and Boston U Law Sch; lawyer, head of Robert F. Kennedy Memorial Center for Human Rights; *m* 9 June 1990 *Andrew CUOMO (*b c* 1958; lawyer and political advsr to his father), est s of Mario Cuomo, Govr New York 1983-, and his w Matilda Raffa

8 *Christopher George KENNEDY, *b* Boston 4 July 1963; *educ* Boston Coll

9 *(Matthew) Max(well) Taylor KENNEDY, *b* New York 9 Jan 1965; *educ* Georgetown U and U of Virginia Law Sch; *m* Aug 1991 *Vicki Strauss

10 *Douglas Harriman KENNEDY, *b* Washington, DC, 24 March 1967; journalist

11 *Rory Elizabeth Katherine KENNEDY, *b* (posthumously) Washington, DC, 12 Dec 1968

VIII *Jean Ann Kennedy, *b* Boston 20 Feb 1928; *educ* Sacred Heart Convent, Roehampton, and Manhattanville Coll; Fndr and Program Chairperson Very Special Arts (charity helping disabled express themselves creatively) 1974, recipient: Jefferson Award for Outstanding Public Service, Margaret Meade Humanitarian Award and Capital Children's Museum Humanitarian Award, US Amb to Ireland 1993-, author: (with George Plimpton) *Chronicles of Courage*; *m* New York 19 May 1956 Stephen Edward SMITH (*b* 24 Sept 1927; *educ* Georgetown U; with Devpt Loan Fund and State Dept 1961-62, with transport firm fnded by his maternal gf William Cleary; *d* Aug 1990), s of John J. Smith and his w Julia A. and gs of —— Smith, three-term New York Congressman, and has issue:

President Kennedy's nephews and adoptive nieces

1 *Stephen Edward SMITH, Jr, *b* 28 June 1957; *educ* Harvard and Columbia Law Sch
2 *William Kennedy SMITH, *b* Boston 4 Sept 1960; *educ* Duke U and Georgetown U
Mr and Mrs Smith also have two adopted daus:
a *Amanda Mary SMITH, *b* 30 April 1967
b *Kym Maria SMITH, *b* Vietnam 29 Nov 1972

IX *Edward (Teddy) Moore KENNEDY [3 Charles River Square, Boston, MA, USA; John F. Kennedy Federal Building, Boston, MA, USA], *b* Brookline 22 Feb 1932; *educ* Milton Acad, Harvard (AB 1956), Internat Law Inst, The Hague, and U of Virginia Law Sch (LLB 1959); admitted Massachusetts Bar 1959, Assist DA Suffolk Co, Mass., 1961-62, US Senator (D) from Mass. 1962- (Majority Whip 1969-71, Chm: Judiciary Ctee 1979-81 and Labor and Human Resources Ctee 1987-, Memb: Armed Forces Ctee and Jt Ec Ctee), on Bd Office of Technology Assessment, Pres Joseph P. Kennedy Jt Fndn 1961-, Tstee: John F. Kennedy Library, John F. Kennedy Center Performing Arts, Robert F. Kennedy Meml Fndn, author: *Decisions for a Decade* (1968), *In Critical Condition* (1972), *Our Day and Generation* (1979) and (with Senator Mark Hatfield) *Freeze: how you can help prevent nuclear war* (1982); *m* 1st 29 Nov 1958 (divorce 1983) (Virginia) Joan (*b* Riverdale, New York, 9 Sept 1936; *educ* Bronxville High Sch, Manhattanville Coll (Hon Doctorate Humane Letters) and Lesley Coll (MEd 1981); sometime Memb Bd Nat Symphony Orchestra), dau of Harry Wiggin Bennett, advertizing exec, and his 1st w Virginia Joan Stead, and has issue:

President Kennedy's niece and nephews

1 *Kara Anne KENNEDY, *b* Bronxville, New York, 27 Feb 1960; *educ* Tufts
2 *Edward (Teddy) Moore KENNEDY, Jr, *b* Boston 26 Sept 1961; *educ* Wesleyan U
3 *Patrick Joseph KENNEDY, *b* Boston 14 July 1967; Rhode Island state legislator

IX (cont.) Senator Edward Kennedy *m* 2nd 1992, as her 2nd husb, *Victoria (*b c* 1954; *m* 1st —— (divorce 1990) and has issue by her 1st husb a s, aged 10 in 1993, and a dau, aged seven in 1993), attorney specializing in banking law, of Washington, DC, dau of Judge Edmund Reggie, of Louisiana, and his w Doris

JOHN F. KENNEDY
FAMILY TREE

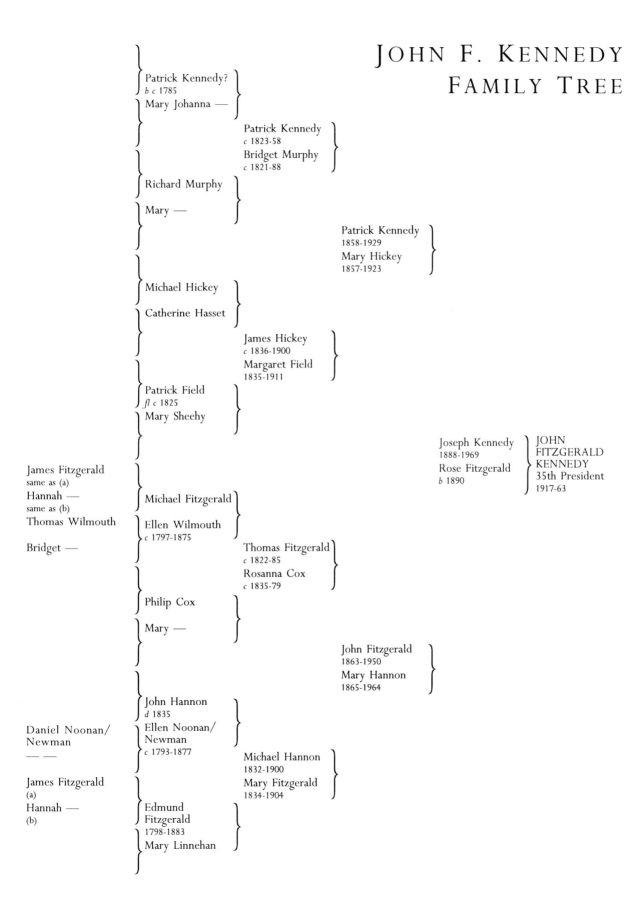

Patrick Kennedy?
b c 1785

Mary Johanna —

Patrick Kennedy
c 1823-58

Bridget Murphy
c 1821-88

Richard Murphy

Mary —

Patrick Kennedy
1858-1929

Mary Hickey
1857-1923

Michael Hickey

Catherine Hasset

James Hickey
c 1836-1900

Margaret Field
1835-1911

Patrick Field
fl c 1825

Mary Sheehy

Joseph Kennedy
1888-1969

Rose Fitzgerald
b 1890

JOHN
FITZGERALD
KENNEDY
35th President
1917-63

James Fitzgerald
same as (a)
Hannah —
same as (b)
Thomas Wilmouth

Bridget —

Michael Fitzgerald

Ellen Wilmouth
c 1797-1875

Thomas Fitzgerald
c 1822-85

Rosanna Cox
c 1835-79

Philip Cox

Mary —

John Fitzgerald
1863-1950

Mary Hannon
1865-1964

Daniel Noonan/
Newman

— —

James Fitzgerald
(a)

Hannah —
(b)

John Hannon
d 1835

Ellen Noonan/
Newman
c 1793-1877

Michael Hannon
1832-1900

Mary Fitzgerald
1834-1904

Edmund
Fitzgerald
1798-1883

Mary Linnehan

Plate 116   Lyndon B. Johnson

LYNDON B. JOHNSON

1908-73
36TH PRESIDENT OF THE UNITED STATES OF AMERICA
1963-69

Jack Kennedy had chosen his Vice-President for the usual reasons. He himself was a Catholic, so he needed a Protestant; from the North-East, so he needed a Southerner or Westerner; a newcomer whose success in winning the party nomination had upset the old hands, so he needed a veteran. All this added up to Lyndon Johnson of Texas, Senate Majority Leader, who had been runner-up for the presidential nomination. So the offer was made. Why Johnson accepted it is not so clear. One theory is that he knew that whoever won the election the post of Majority Leader would not again be what it had been under the easy-going Ike, when Johnson had been able to do pretty much what he liked and emerge as the biggest man in Congress. The new President, whether Democrat or Republican, would inevitably overshadow the Majority Leader. So LBJ (he was pathologically insistent on his initials and imposed them on his wife, his two daughters and his ranch) moved on to fresher pastures.

He hated the vice-presidency. Then Kennedy died. Being human LBJ could not suppress a thrill at the knowledge that his opportunity had come; being decent he hated himself for it. But he soon recovered and set to work.

What followed was the most impressive legislative performance since FDR's Hundred Days. Indeed Johnson, who had been a young New Deal congressman, took FDR for his model; the national grief and remorse over Kennedy's death gave him his opportunity. His own matchless congressional cunning did the rest. "Come, let us reason together" was the motto he found in the Bible, but as sheer relentless reasoning — some might call it nagging — did not work, Johnson was ready to exploit the political credit with individuals built up over a quarter of a century in Washington, or, if necessary, to use tougher forms of pressure. Perhaps his boundless energy and conviction were his greatest assets, though he paid for them in occasional bouts of melancholy and anxiety. However, by the opening of the 1964 election campaign (there had been no trouble about getting his party's nomination) the general outline of Johnson's 'Great Society' programme was clear. Many laws had either been passed or were about to be passed to realize it, of which the most important was the Civil Rights Act of 1964, which effectively outlawed racial discrimination. (It was supplemented in 1965 by an act to protect the right to vote of Southern blacks; as a result the balance of power in the South began to swing decisively in their favour.) Johnson's other laws showed that he was aware that the great American cities, labouring under a variety of painful burdens, now badly needed a reformer's attention, if only to make further progress in rescuing the Afro-Americans from degradation. The President was riding high and the folly of the Republicans in nominating Barry Goldwater, an amiable reactionary who was quite out of touch with the country's mood, completed the preparations for a triumph. Johnson won the election more sweepingly than any candidate since FDR in 1936.

Lyndon Johnson at his noontide was the most uninhibited occupant of the White House since Teddy Roosevelt, and the earthiest ever. He fascinated and appalled the press. There were stories of how the

President used to compel reporters to go swimming naked with him in the White House pool, or received them while sitting on the lavatory; there were stories (and photographs) of Johnson lifting his dogs by their ears to show them off, which outraged animal lovers; photographs of the presidential belly bared to display the scars of a recent operation. Salty wisecracks got into circulation, like his unkind observation about Gerald Ford, the leader of the Republicans in the House of Representatives. Johnson's vindictive streak occasionally showed, as when he kept Senator Hubert Humphrey dangling in humiliating anxiety for weeks before taking him on as his vice-presidential candidate in 1964. There seemed to be symptoms of something like persecution mania in his attitude to President Kennedy's brothers, Senator Robert of New York and Senator Edward of Massachussetts.

In short, there were weaknesses in Johnson's personality which prevented him from attaining the effortless ascendancy of the Roosevelts or of Jack Kennedy; they would not have destroyed him but for the fatal descent into the Vietnamese entanglement. A trap was waiting, into which he fell and from which he lacked the nous to extricate himself. His difficulty was rather like that of Herbert Hoover: his great gifts were useless in the particular difficulty in which he found himself.

Johnson's strong point was his understanding of the American domestic scene and what it required. As to foreign affairs, he saw things pretty much as they appeared in the days of Harry Truman, which was natural enough, for most of his advisers made the same mistake. Johnson did not see that the American armed forces had grown fat and incompetent since the end of the Korean War, or that the diplomatic establishment as presided over by the Secretary of State Dean Rusk was obsessed with the Russo-American competition to the exclusion of all other aspects of reality. Johnson knew quite well that war was usually unpopular nowadays and could wreck a President; after all, he had been elected with such a vast majority in large part because the voters saw him as the peace candidate. But the experts told him that the war in South Vietnam was just, which may possibly have been true, and in the interests of the United States, which was more than doubtful, and that America could win it easily and quickly, which was certainly false. When victory after all proved to be elusive, he was assured that to accept defeat and withdraw would undermine her allies' trust in America and their ability to withstand communist pressure; worse, that failure would disastrously diminish the nation's real strength. Believing what he was told, he pressed forward with the war, steadily increasing the commitment of US money, men and matériel; he felt he had no choice.

The rest was all downhill. American casualties grew until Vietnam ranked as the third most bloody war in national history. The war became enormously unpopular because young Americans, whose necks were on the line, believed as Washington did not that the game was not worth the candle and was therefore immoral. Only clear necessity could justify such a cruel policy, they believed. Such necessity was not clear to ever-growing numbers of Americans and had never been apparent to most of the rest of the world. Johnson's reputation collapsed in ruins. Eventually he accepted the criticism and acted in a way that shows his stature. In March 1968 he announced that he was suspending the bombing of North Vietnam; that he would not be a candidate for re-election; and that he was opening peace negotiations with the Vietnamese communists in Paris. Tragically this new departure led to nothing. The United States seemed to be tearing itself apart in a welter of riot and murder (both the great black leader, Martin Luther King, and Robert Kennedy were assassinated); the negotiations dragged on inconclusively; and the Republicans won the presidential election. Sad and tired, Lyndon Johnson turned over to Richard Nixon the problems that had defeated him and returned to Texas. There he abandoned the strict regime of the presidency, began to smoke again, to eat and drink unwisely; and there, as a result, he died only four years later.

Plate 117   LBJ flanked by his daughters Luci Baines
and Lynda Bird; Lady Bird far right

LYNDON B. JOHNSON'S FAMILY

There could hardly have been a greater personal contrast than between 'classy' Jack Kennedy and earthy Lyndon Johnson. But if length of time settled by male line ancestors in America goes for anything (and in Massachusetts it does, just as much as in Texas) Johnson was of better family. His forebear seven generations back, James Johnston, was living in Virginia in the 17th century. The Kennedys only came to America in the mid-19th century.

Johnsons also beat Kennedys by a generation where a tradition of public office was concerned. Jesse Johnson, the 36th president's great-grandfather, had been a sheriff, justice of the peace and minor judge in Georgia in the 1820s and 1830s. He died when his youngest son Samuel Ealy Johnson, LBJ's grandfather, was only 17 so that Samuel was too busy struggling to stay alive, whether as a Confederate soldier in the Civil War or trail-driver in Texas, to continue any family tradition as a public servant. But the underground stream surfaced again with LBJ's father Samuel Ealy Jr, who became a justice of the peace and served in the Texas House of Representatives from 1904 to 1909 and from 1917 to 1925. His re-election in 1906 went against local custom, for a kind of rotation operated and in the normal run of things his turn would have been over. His achievements included sponsoring the Alamo purchase bill (his portrait hangs inside that monument), a Confederate veterans' pension bill and a bill to provide homes for Confederate soldiers' widows. But his chief feat was to have set in train the defeat of the Ku Klux Klan in Texas.

Samuel Ealy's wife Rebekah Baines was daughter of the man he had succeeded in the Texas House of Representatives seat. In short, LBJ had legislators on both sides of the family. Rebekah's father also served as Secretary of State to the Governor of Texas. From Rebekah's grandfather George Washington Baines, president of Baylor College at the time of the Civil War, LBJ perhaps inherited the pedagogic streak that turned him briefly into a schoolteacher. Rebekah Johnson herself instilled the ambition that fuelled her son. She also taught him declamation so thoroughly that at college he won numerous debates and afterward was capable of teaching public speaking in a high school in Houston. More important in getting the young man a specific teaching job, however, was his uncle George Johnson, who taught history at the same school. As ingrained a lesson as any formal instruction that LBJ absorbed was the memory of his mother's swollen hands and problems in obtaining water, from which came his passion for rural electrification and water schemes.

Uncle George did more than get his nephew a job, though that was hard enough during the Depression. He acted as sounding board for the young man's ideas. He also helped him financially with a nest egg of $400-500 when LBJ ran for the House of Representatives in 1937. That sort of sum alone would not have gone far. Fortunately Lady Bird, LBJ's wife of only three years, got her father to advance her husband a loan of another $10,000 out of her inheritance from her mother (it was lucky for LBJ that he and his stepfather had hit it off from the moment they met). And so LBJ entered the House of Representatives.

Lady Bird Johnson was born Claudia Taylor. Her sobriquet appears to originate in her babyhood when a nurse said she was pretty as a ladybird. She was an only daughter and rather indulged by her widower father. Miraculously it did not make her spoiled. Rather the reverse: she used to polish LBJ's shoes, refill his fountain pen, serve him breakfast in bed and lay out his clothes for him to put on after his breakfast. If she had simply been a squaw with a deep pocket, however, her husband would not have got so far. What she did in 1942 was to mind his Congressional seat for him while he was away on US Navy business as a Lieutenant-Commander. Many other Congressmen's wives did the same, but observers reckon she put more into it than anyone else. Bobby Kennedy said she had carried Texas for the Democrats in 1960 (implicitly not LBJ, but then he disliked LBJ). Even allowing for Bobby Kennedy's malice it was a wholly plausible analysis. In 1964 she took the unusual step of making her own speeches at venues independent of the candidate himself. She concentrated on the South, and not just the big cities such as Atlanta and New Orleans, where the battle for civil rights was half-won already, but the small towns where it was an up-hill struggle. She played her Southern background and femininity for all they were worth. She was particularly effective at cajoling state governors.

She is thought to have been instrumental in building up the Johnson family's finances, particularly the broadcasting station in Austin. In recent years, however, the family's various business interests, which are gathered under the umbrella of a holding company, the LBJ Company, have lost awesome amounts of money. From the moment LBJ became Senate Majority Leader she developed from a shy, tongue-tied figure and by the time he was President she had become a formidable public speaker and fielder of questions at press conferences. The Johnsons had installed as a manager of their broadcasting station LBJ's brother-in-law Oscar Bobbitt. Connections on Lady Bird's side of the family had their uses too. During the 1960 presidential campaign she and her husband visited Alabama, where she had lived for a while as a child with her aunt Effie after her mother died. She made a speech in Montgomery which turned to triumph what had looked like being a very lacklustre occasion for the Kennedy-Johnson ticket, chiefly because of southern hostility to the civil rights plank in the Democratic platform. Simply by catching sight of several cousins in the audience and inviting them up onto the rostrum, she largely won the crowd over.

Once her husband became President Lady Bird started her beautification programme. So pervasive are today's 'green' concerns that it is easy to forget how radical this seemed at the time, especially since there were not only sneers but hostility from businesses that advertized widely by means of roadside hoardings. She continued the restoration of the White House started by her predecessor, Jackie Kennedy, and persuaded her husband to make the Curator of the White House an official post. The same executive order that did so also established a Committee for the Preservation of the White House. Lady Bird Johnson was honorary chairman of this committee, another of whose members was Jackie Kennedy, although she never attended any of its meetings.

Johnson's brother Sam Houston Johnson constituted another in the long line of family headaches born by Presidents down the decades. LBJ kept Sam Houston out of mischief as much as he could by installing him in the White House, where Secret Service agents could keep watch on him and where Sam cut out pieces from newspapers for use in a 1968 presidential re-election campaign which never materialized. The Johnsons' daughter Lynda Bird's wedding to Charles Spittal (Chuck) Robb was the first at the White House since 1914, when Eleanor, Woodrow Wilson's third daughter, had married Senator William McAdoo. Since then Robb has become Lieutenant-Governor of Virginia, with no little help from his mother-in-law, who came out of retirement to campaign once again, and then Governor. In 1988, the year he was mentioned as a possible Democratic Vice-Presidential candidate, he became the first Democratic senator from Virginia in 21 years, for Virginia is a conservative state and hostility to his father-in-law's Great Society had handicapped him when he first ran for state office. Robb's chief feat, it has been suggested, is to reunite Virginia's Democratic party. He met Lynda Bird when serving as a social aide at the White House, part of his duties as a Marine which included being stationed in Vietnam. His wife Lynda was appointed by President Carter to his Advisory Committee on Women. Robb's chances of securing the Democratic presidential nomination in 1992, at one time thought quite high, were destroyed after allegations in 1991 of adultery, drug-taking and wire-tapping.

BIOGRAPHICAL DETAILS AND DESCENDANTS

JOHNSON, LYNDON BAINES, b nr Stonewall, Tex., 27 Aug 1908; educ High Sch, Johnson City, Tex., Southwest Texas State Teachers' Coll (BSc 1930), Georgetown U Law Sch; rhetoric teacher Sam Houston High Sch, Houston, Tex., 1930-31, sec to Texas Memb US House of Reps Richard M. Kleberg 1931-35, Texas Dir Nat Youth Admin 1935-37, Memb US House of Reps from Texas 10th Congressional Dist 1937-48, Lt-Cdr US Navy World War II (Silver Star for gallantry in action 1942, remained Cdr US Naval Reserve to 1964), US Senator from Texas 1949-61 (Majority Whip 1951, Minority Leader 1953, Majority Leader 1955), V-Pres USA 1961-22 Nov 1963 (Chm: Presdtl Ctee on Equal Opportunity and Nat Aeronautics & Space Cncl 1961, also Peace Corps Advsy Cncl), 36th President of the USA (D) 22 Nov 1963-69, Hon LLD: Southwestern U 1943, Howard Payne U (Tex.) 1957, Brown U and Bethany Coll (W. Va.) 1959, Us of Hawaii and Philippines, also Gallaudet Coll (DC), E Kentucky Coll and Wm Jewell Coll (Mo.) 1961, Elon Coll (NC) and Southwest Texas State Teachers' Coll 1962, Wayne State U (Mich.), Jacksonville U (Fla.), McMurray Coll (Ill.), U of Maryland and Tufts 1963, Us of Texas and California, Syracuse and Georgetown Us and Swarthmore Coll 1964, U of Kentucky and Baylor (Tex.) and Howard (DC) Us, also Catholic U (DC) 1965, Princeton and U of Denver 1966, Texas Tech Coll 1967, Texas Christian U 1968, Hon DCL: Holy Cross Coll (Mass.) and U of Michigan 1964, U of Rhode Island 1966, Hon LLD Texas Christian U 1968, Hon DHL: Oklahoma City U 1960, Yeshiva U (New York) 1961, Hon Dr Letters: Glassboro State Coll (New Jersey) 1968, Hon DLit: St Mary's Coll (Calif.) 1962, Hon Dr Political Sci: Chulalongkorn U, Bangkok, 1966, author: My Hope for America (1964), A Time for Action (1964), This America (1966), The Choices We Face (1969), The Vantage Point: Perspectives of the Presidency, 1963-1969 (1971); m San Antonio, Tex., 17 Nov 1934 *Claudia Alta ('Lady Bird') [Mrs Lyndon B Johnson, LBJ Ranch, Stonewall, TX 78761, USA] (b Karnack, Tex., 22 Dec 1912; author: A White House Diary (1970)), dau of Thomas Jefferson Taylor and his w Minnie Pattillo, and d on way to San Antonio Hosp 22 Jan 1973 after a heart attack, leaving issue:

President Johnson's daughter

I *Lynda Bird Johnson, b 19 March 1944; educ U of Texas at Austin and George Washington U, Washington, DC; sometime memb staff McCall's magazine, contributing ed Ladies' Home Journal; m the White House 9 Dec 1967 *Maj Charles (Chuck) Spittall ROBB [The Honorable Charles S Robb, US Senator for Virginia, US Senate, 493 Russell, Senate Building, Washington, DC 20510-4602, USA; US Senate, 517 Hart, Senate Building, Washington, DC 20510-4602, USA] (b Phoenix, Ariz., 26 June 1939; educ Mount Vernon High Sch, Cornell, U of Wisconsin (BBA 1961) and U of Virginia (JD 1973); served Vietnam

US Marine Corps (Bronze Star, Vietnam Service Medal with Four Stars, Vietnam Cross of Gallantry with Silver Star), lawyer, Govr Virginia 1982-86 (Lt-Govr 1978-82), US Senator (D) from Virginia 1989- (Memb: For Rels, Budget and Commerce, Science & Transportn Ctees)), est child of James (Jim) Robb, of Milwaukee, Wis., and his w Frances Howard Woolley, and has issue:

Grandchildren
1 *Lucinda Desha ROBB, b Washington, DC, 25 Oct 1968
2 *Catherine Lewis ROBB, b Washington, DC, 5 June 1970
3 *Jennifer Wickliffe ROBB, b 20 June 1978

President Johnson's daughter
II *Luci (formerly Lucy) Baines Johnson [KLBJ Building, Suite 200 8309 North IH-35, Austin, TX 78753-5720, USA], b 2 July 1947; educ Georgetown U; sometime optometrist's assist; m 1st Shrine of the Immaculate Conception, Washington, DC, 6 Aug 1966 (divorce 1979) Patrick John NUGENT (b 8 July 1943), s of Gerard P. Nugent, of Waukegan, Ill., and his w —— Jocius, and has issue:

Grandchildren
1 *Patrick Lyndon NUGENT, b Austin 21 June 1967; m Sweden Feb 1992 *Nicole Tatum
2 *Nicole Marie Nugent, b Austin 11 Jan 1970; m there May 1992 *Brent COVERT
3 *Rebekah Johnson NUGENT, b Austin 10 July 1974
4 *Claudia Taylor NUGENT, b Austin 17 March 1976

President Johnson's daughter
II (cont.) Mrs Luci Johnson Nugent m 2nd Austin, Tex., 3 March 1984, as his 2nd w, *Ian Johnston TURPIN

MALE LINE ANCESTRY AND COLLATERAL DESCENDANTS

It has been suggested that the Johnsons ultimately descend from the Johnstons, of Annandale, Dumfriesshire, Scotland, the principal bearers of which family name are the Earls of Annandale and Hartfell. However, no records survive further back than:

James JOHNSTON, b c 1662; lived at Currowaugh, in Nansemond and Isle of Wight Cos, Va. (at the mouth of the James River); m c 1692 Mary (b Isle of Wight Co c 1674; d after 1747), dau of Robert Johnson (c 1643-1732/3), of the Lower Parish of Isle of Wight Co, planter, and his w Katherine Allen (c 1645-c 1693), and d Isle of Wight Co between 30 Jan 1745/6 and 11 June 1747, leaving (with five other s and five daus) a 2nd s:

John JOHNSTON, b Isle of Wight Co c 1696; m 1st —— and had issue; m 2nd Peninah —— (d 1799) and d Southampton Co (the southern part of Isle of Wight Co, formed into a separate county 1752) between 30 Jan and 8 May 1783, having had further issue with his 2nd w; his est s by his 1st w:

John JOHNSON, b Isle of Wight Co c 1724; hatter, moved to Franklin Co, N Carolina, c 1767; m 1st —— Holland, of Nansemond Co, and had two or three children; m 2nd before 19 June 1763 Elizabeth, dau of Robert Carr, of Nottoway Parish, Southampton Co, and his w Sarah, and with her had issue; m 3rd 28 Oct 1815 Martha (d 1816), widow of Elijah Denby, of Franklin Co, and dau of Patewells Milner and his w Jacobina, and d Franklin Co between 22 May and June 1829. His s by his 2nd w:

John JOHNSON, b Southampton Co 28 March 1764; settled in Oglethorpe Co, Ga.; m 1st c 1786 Ann (b Southampton Co 14 Sept 1763; d Oglethorpe Co 5 Jan 1815), dau of Samuel Eley or Ealy of Franklin Co, and his 1st w Mary Hillsman (d in or after 1784), and had five s and three daus; m 2nd Greene Co, Ga., 24 May 1823 Joicy, née Griffin, widow of William Fears, of Greene Co, and d Oglethorpe Co 14 Feb 1828. His 3rd s by his 1st marriage:

Jesse JOHNSON, b Oglethorpe Co 28 April 1795; lived Henry Co, Ga. (Sheriff 1822-31, Justice of the Peace and Judge of the Inferior Court there 1833-37), moved after 1837 to Randolph Co, Ala., and finally settled Caldwell Co, Tex.; m 14 Nov 1817 Lucy Webb (b probably Elbert Co, Ga., 14 Jan 1798; d Lockhart, Tex., 13 March 1857), dau of Leonard Barnett (c 1773-1828), of Ga., and his w Nancy Statham, and d Lockhart 15 May 1856, leaving (with one/two other s and five daus):

I (Jesse Thomas) Tom JOHNSON, b c 1838; cattle rancher in partnership with his yr bro Samuel E Johnson; drowned Brazos River 1877
II A son/sons, who was/were father(s) of:

1 Jesse JOHNSON   2 James JOHNSON   3 John JOHNSON

III Samuel Ealy JOHNSON, b Randolph Co, Ala., 12 Nov 1838; private Col DeBray's Regt, Confederate States Army, Battles of Galveston (Tex., 1863) and Pleasant Hill (La., 1864), in Civil War, started Johnson's Ranch on the Pedernales River, nr the present Johnson City (so named for the family), c 1888; m Lockhart 11 Dec 1867 Eliza Jane (b nr Russellville, Ky., 24 June 1849; d Stonewall, Tex., 31 Jan 1917), dau of Robert Holmes Bunton (1818-95) and his w Priscilla Jane

McIntosh (1821-1905), and *d* Stonewall 25 Feb 1915, leaving, with at least five other children, the following issue (not necessarily born in that order):

1 George JOHNSON   2 Tim JOHNSON   3 Samuel Ealy JOHNSON, Jr, for whom *see below*

4 A ninth child, Jessie Hermine JOHNSON; *d* 1973, having outlived her nephew, the 36th President, by a few weeks

The 3rd (?) child,

Samuel Ealy JOHNSON, Jr, *b* Buda, Hays Co, Tex., 11 Oct 1877; politician, teacher, farmer and real estate dealer, Justice of the Peace, Memb Texas House of Representatives 1904-09 and 1917-25; *m* Fredericksburg, Tex., 20 Aug 1907 Rebekah (*b* McKinney, Tex., 26 June 1881; wrote much of contents of her father's newspaper (*see below*), author: *A Family Album*, ed John S. Moursund, with an introduction by her s, the 36th President; *d* Austin, Tex., 12 Sept 1958), dau of Capt Joseph Wilson Baines (1846-1906), sometime lawyer and Texas Sec of State appointed by Govr John Ireland (in office 1883-87), also ed/publisher local newspaper, cattle rancher and Memb Texas State Legislature 1902(?)-04(?), of Blanco, Tex., and his w Ruth Ament Huffman (1854-1936), and *d* Austin 23 or 24 Oct 1937, leaving issue:

I LYNDON BAINES JOHNSON, 36th PRESIDENT of the UNITED STATES of AMERICA

II Rebekah (Becky) Luruth Johnson, *b* Stonewall 12 Sept 1910; *m* 10 May 1941 *Oscar Price BOBBITT [1505 Windsor Road, Austin, TX, USA] (manager Johnson-owned TV station KTBC), s of Oscar Price Bobbitt and his w Maude Wisner, and *d* 4 Feb 1978, leaving issue:

President Lyndon Johnson's nephew

1 *Philip Chase BOBBITT [1505 Windsor Road, Austin, TX, USA], *b* Temple, Tex., 22 July 1948; admitted Texas Bar 1977, Prof Law U of Texas at Austin 1979-, Assoc Counsel to the President, the White House, 1980-81, admitted to practice before the US Supreme Court 1989, Baker and Botts Law Prof 1989-, Counsellor to Legal Advsr State Dept Washington 1990-; *m* 19—— Selden Anne Wallace

III Josefa Hermine Johnson, *b* Stonewall 16 May 1912; *m* 1st Lake Charles, La., 16 May 1940 (divorce 1945) Lt-Col Willard WHITE; *m* 2nd Austin 23 April 1955 *Revd James B. MOSS, s of Mathew Moss and his w Alethea Whitacre, and *d* 1961, leaving an adopted s:

President Lyndon Johnson's adoptive nephew

a Rodney MOSS, *b* Biloxi, Miss., 14 April 1948; *d* 1989

IV *Sam Houston JOHNSON, *b* Johnson City 31 Jan 1914; *educ* Cumberland U (LLB 1934); *m* 1st Mattoon, Ill., 28 Dec 1940 (divorce 1944) Albertine SUMMERS and has issue:

President Lyndon Johnson's niece and nephew

1 *Josefa Roxanne JOHNSON, *b* Mattoon 28 Sept 1941

2 *Sam Summers JOHNSON, *b* Austin 5 Oct 1942

IV (cont.) Sam Houston JOHNSON *m* 2nd Vera Cruz, Mexico, 27 Jan 1955 *Mrs Mary Michelson Fish, dau of Michael A. Michelson and his w Jemmanetta MacFarlene

V *Lucia Huffman Johnson, *b* Johnson City 20 June 1916; *m* Lockhart 18 Sept 1933 *Birge Davis ALEXANDER, construction engr, of Johnson City, s of Kay Alexander and his w Helen Davis, and has issue:

President Johnson's niece

1 *Rebekah Sterling ALEXANDER, *b* Fort Worth, Tex., 13 Feb 1944

John Johnston[1]
c 1696-1783

— —

Robert Carr

Sarah —

Eli Eley
d a 1753
Ann —

Bennett Hillsman
d 1784-89

— —

Frank Barnett

Sukey Johnson

John Webb

Peggy —

John Bunton/Buntine
fl c 1762

— —

Robert Desha
b c 1715
Mary Everfieldt

Joseph Wheeler
c 1720-87
Maria Holmes

[1] For generations
further back *see*
Male Line Ancestry
section

John Johnson, Jr
c 1724-1829
Elizabeth Carr
d in/a 1815

Samuel Eley
c 1736-in/a 1771
Mary Hillsman
fl c 1784

Nathan Barnett
c 1729-*c* 1805
Lucy Webb
b c 1731

John Statham

— —

John Bunton, Jr
d in/p 1803
Mary McClure

Robert Desha, Jr
c 1738-1816
Elinor Wheeler
c 1740-*p* 1793

Levi Creecy

— —

James McCoy

— —

Louis Ogier
1726-80
Catherine Creuzé
1732-1808
Revd William/John
Martin
d in/a 1783
— —

John Huffman
c 1738-1802
Catherine —

Henry Lyter
c 1740-1807
Catharine Beaver
1743-1823

Thomas Jameson
1732-1830 same as (a)
Hannah Taggart
1740-1830 same as (b)

Thomas Jameson
(a)
Hannah Taggart
(b)

George Bains
1741-1802
Mary Creecy
1749-*p* 1802

William McCoy
d c 1795
Julia —
d p 1795

Louis Ogier, Jr
c 1753-1820
Susan(nah) Martin
c 1764-1827

John Huffman, Jr
c 1768-1826
Catharine Lyter
1771-1831

Philip Ament
c 1755-*c* 1836
Margaret —

Charles Perrin
d c 1850
Catherine Jameson
b 1773

George Kirby
fl c 1795
Helen/Eleanor Jameson
c 1775-*c* 1816

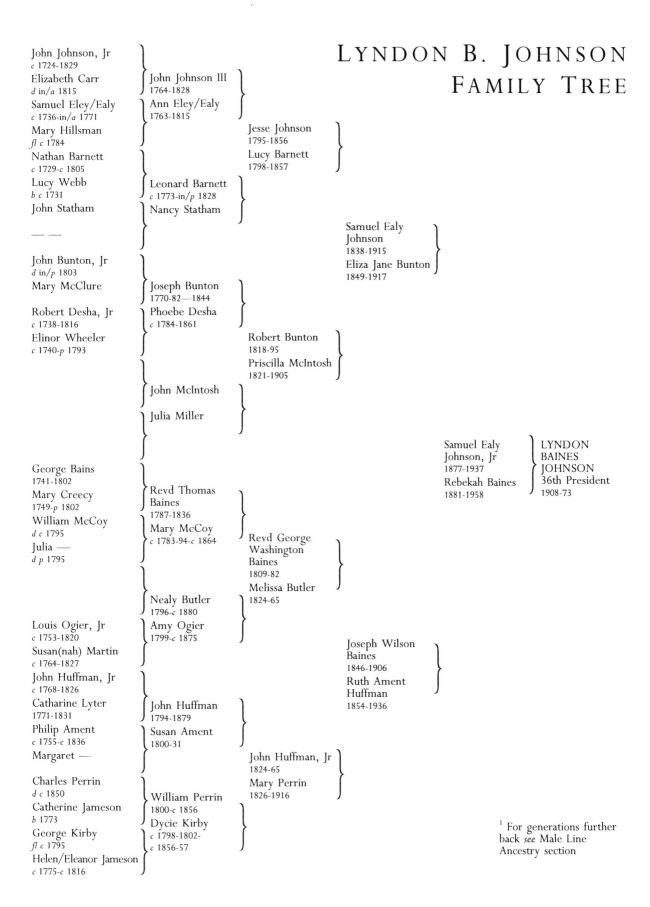

LYNDON B. JOHNSON
FAMILY TREE

John Johnson, Jr
c 1724-1829

Elizabeth Carr
d in/a 1815

Samuel Eley/Ealy
c 1736-*in/a* 1771

Mary Hillsman
fl c 1784

Nathan Barnett
c 1729-*c* 1805

Lucy Webb
b c 1731

John Statham

—— ——

John Bunton, Jr
d in/p 1803

Mary McClure

Robert Desha, Jr
c 1738-1816

Elinor Wheeler
c 1740-*p* 1793

George Bains
1741-1802

Mary Creecy
1749-*p* 1802

William McCoy
d c 1795

Julia ——
d p 1795

Louis Ogier, Jr
c 1753-1820

Susan(nah) Martin
c 1764-1827

John Huffman, Jr
c 1768-1826

Catharine Lyter
1771-1831

Philip Ament
c 1755-*c* 1836

Margaret ——

Charles Perrin
d c 1850

Catherine Jameson
b 1773

George Kirby
fl c 1795

Helen/Eleanor Jameson
c 1775-*c* 1816

John Johnson III
1764-1828

Ann Eley/Ealy
1763-1815

Leonard Barnett
c 1773-*in/p* 1828

Nancy Statham

Joseph Bunton
1770-82—1844

Phoebe Desha
c 1784-1861

John McIntosh

Julia Miller

Revd Thomas
Baines
1787-1836

Mary McCoy
c 1783-94-*c* 1864

Nealy Butler
1796-*c* 1880

Amy Ogier
1799-*c* 1875

John Huffman
1794-1879

Susan Ament
1800-31

William Perrin
1800-*c* 1856

Dycie Kirby
c 1798-1802-
c 1856-57

Jesse Johnson
1795-1856

Lucy Barnett
1798-1857

Robert Bunton
1818-95

Priscilla McIntosh
1821-1905

Revd George
Washington
Baines
1809-82

Melissa Butler
1824-65

John Huffman, Jr
1824-65

Mary Perrin
1826-1916

Samuel Ealy
Johnson
1838-1915

Eliza Jane Bunton
1849-1917

Joseph Wilson
Baines
1846-1906

Ruth Ament
Huffman
1854-1936

Samuel Ealy
Johnson, Jr
1877-1937

Rebekah Baines
1881-1958

LYNDON
BAINES
JOHNSON
36th President
1908-73

[1] For generations further
back *see* Male Line
Ancestry section

Plate 118   Nixon and family on his last full day in office, 8 Aug 1974:
l-r Edward Cox (son-in-law), Tricia Nixon Cox (daughter), the President, Pat Nixon,
Julie Nixon Eisenhower (daughter) and David Eisenhower (son-in-law)

RICHARD M. NIXON

1913-
37TH PRESIDENT OF THE UNITED STATES OF AMERICA
1969-74

The outstanding characteristic and fatal weakness of Richard Nixon was an almost inexhaustible capacity for self-deception. Absolute honesty with oneself is of course rare; absolute dishonesty is impossible outside prison or a mental hospital. But Nixon kept reality at bay for most of his career and it will take historians a long time to decide just how much harm he did as a result. It will not take them quite so long to decide if he did any good.

It was clear to friend and foe that the young Nixon owed his rise in politics to his success as a not-too-scrupulous Red-baiter and to some fortunate timing. He ran for the House of Representatives in 1946, a Republican year, insinuating that his opponent was a dangerous leftist. He won. A few years later he ran for the Senate, employed the same technique and won again. Between times he gained celebrity, if not fame, for helping to expose Alger Hiss, a former employee of the State Department, as a Russian agent. Doubts are entertained about Hiss's guilt to the present day, but the case against him is sufficiently strong to have convinced most people and it certainly convinced Nixon. Reality reinforced his fantasy. But he could not see that his other victories were less well earned. He had told extremely damaging lies about his opponents without realizing that they were lies — that is, deliberate, self-serving untruths. So he continued to see himself as an upright, serious, responsible public servant. This was to be the pattern to the end. Furthermore, credulous as he was about his own virtue, he was unable to believe in the virtue of others. He was always baffled by a stand genuinely taken on principle, for with him such a stand could only be the result of expediency. He believed in the honesty of those who agreed with him; the rest were simply men whose dishonesty had not yet been exposed. These were some of the delusions which would eventually destroy him.

In 1952 he was given the Republican vice-presidential nomination as a means of appeasing the right wing of the party, which had wanted Robert Taft for President. During the campaign it came out that some businessmen were supplementing Nixon's senatorial salary with a 'secret fund'. The Democrats cried bribery and corruption, so Nixon went on television to defend himself. He insisted that the fund was legitimate, being paid for political purposes only; but the essence of his defence, which swept the country, was his announcement that some admirer had given the Nixon family a dog, called Checkers, and even if it was wrong Checkers would not be given back because the Nixon children loved him so. The sentimentality of this pleased those who wanted to support Nixon and disgusted his opponents; in retrospect it is significant chiefly as showing how spontaneously he escaped from difficult questions into irrelevance. He believed that all problems could be solved by manipulating appearances — another fatal delusion.

He spent the Eisenhower years telling Republican audiences what they wanted to hear, and was rewarded in 1960 with the presidential nomination. But he underrated his opponent and in the election was narrowly defeated by John Kennedy. He ran for Governor of California in 1962 and lost again. In his bitterness he turned on the press: "You won't have Richard Nixon to kick around any more," and went to New York to make some money as a lawyer. But the attraction of politics was too great. He carefully cultivated the Republican party again and in 1968, a year of Democratic disarray, he again got his nomination. This time he was victorious.

During the campaign he had said that he had a secret plan for ending the war in Vietnam. This plan turned out to consist of withdrawing American troops while giving extensive military aid to the South Vietnamese. It was a scheme of extrication with honour and had the President pursued it singlemindedly might even have worked, for by 1973 the South Vietnamese were much better fitted to fight their war than formerly. But Nixon also wished to demonstrate his stature as a world statesman, which he had earned in his own eyes by becoming an expert in the Cold War fallacies that dominated official thinking in Washington. His Vietnamese policy, like Lyndon Johnson's, became hopelessly weakened and compromised by considerations of realpolitik and the balance of power; that was why he extended the war into Cambodia, possibly the most villainous single deed of any US President in history. In the end his devices were swept away by the Watergate Affair. The result of all this confusion was chaos and slaughter in Indo-China, persisting for years and years after the American withdrawal. Beside such an immense human disaster Nixon's petty diplomatic triumphs, such as his rapprochement with China, scarcely matter.

But his presidency was destroyed by its mistakes in domestic policy, not its war-making, though the two were closely intertwined. Nixon's attitude to the great office which he assumed was peculiar. In the first place he seems to have felt that he would not be a true President unless he indulged in conspicuous consumption. He bought himself sumptuous houses in Florida and California ('the White House West'); he cruised frequently in the presidential yacht; and he shuttled backward and forward between all these points, the true White House, and the official presidential retreat at Camp David in Maryland, riding the presidential plane, Air Force One. He ordered new uniforms for the White House police (the Watergate conspirator John Ehrlichman designed them), but they were laughed into oblivion for their banana republic effect. Nixon yearned for money. Like all too many other presidents since 1963 he was obsessed with the wealth and style of the Kennedys; he probably felt that the President ought to be a millionaire, like Lyndon Johnson. Above all, perhaps, he was trying to suppress a feeling of deep self-doubt, a dim recognition that he was ill-suited to the job. By slapping gilding on the externals of the presidency he could, he hoped, distract even his own attention from the internals.

Perhaps it was this lurking self-distrust that made him so obsessively secretive. He was appalled by the idea of government secrets being known, of government policies being revealed before their time. His attitude was not unjustified, but a healthy mind would have declined to brood on the matter, for Washington is the most indiscreet capital in the world and growing more so yearly. Nothing can be done about it, but Nixon doggedly pursued the talkers. He grew paranoid about them. He gave orders, or let it be understood, that they should be destroyed at all costs. This led directly to the setting up of the unit of 'plumbers' (to stop leaks), whose most famous exploit was to bug the headquarters of the Democratic party in the Watergate apartment complex in Washington and get caught doing so.

It is still not clear whether Nixon knew of the Watergate burglary in advance. What is clear is that once it had occurred he should have done all that he could to assist the investigation. Instead he thought that he could frustrate it, and hide not merely his own part in it, if any, but the involvement of far too many of his aides. Money would be no problem; there were lavish funds available from the 1972 presidential campaign (when he had won triumphant re-election).

This cover-up was the cause of Nixon's downfall. He never seems to have understood what he was doing. The President of the United States, who had taken a solemn oath faithfully to execute his office and to the best of his ability "to preserve, protect and defend the constitution of the United States", was now beginning to be looked upon as part of a conspiracy to pervert the course of justice. No wonder impeachment proceedings were started against him; no wonder he felt obliged, in the end, to resign. But it is doubtful even then that he saw himself as he was; even though the evidence was overwhelming; even though most of his chosen associates had to serve a spell in prison, or suffer other legal penalties. The utmost he ever confessed to was that he had mishandled the affair. When he appeared before the nation on television to announce his impending resignation, all he said was that he had lost his political support. The fact that he had dragged the presidency to the lowest point in its history, so that its utility as a policy making and executing institution would be seriously impaired for years, or that in some of his actions he had threatened the constitutional liberties and due processes of American republican government, were not acknowledged then or subsequently. Nixon clung instead to his image of himself as a good, religious man who loved his country. Perhaps he could not do otherwise and retain his sanity.

RICHARD M. NIXON'S FAMILY

Nixon's father Frank never completed his education, but had to leave school aged 11 after the sixth grade, his mother having died of tuberculosis when he was eight. The older he got the more tight-fisted, irascible and prone to hatred he became — character traits that later surfaced in his son. He could also be stubborn. He thought his son Harold had made some undesirable friends so packed him off to a spartan 'Bible' school in Massachusetts where cold showers at 5.30 in the morning were the norm. Some boys even arrived at breakfast with icicles in their hair. Harold already had a history of colds and bronchitis and when he returned home in early 1927 he had severe tuberculosis.

On the plus side, Frank was a good natural orator and according to Nixon's cousin Jessamyn West the best Sunday school teacher she ever had. (Nixon returned the compliment by saying that Jessamyn's father Eldo West was the best Sunday school teacher he ever had.) Frank Nixon pushed his son to excel as an orator and debater. Nixon himself has described how his uncle Philip Timberlake helped him win a high school debate by giving him facts to support his side of the argument. What Nixon says he chiefly learned from his father was the importance in debate of concentrating on a strong line of argument rather than dissipating one's cogency in several weaker ones.

Nixon's critics used to sneer at the contradiction between his Quaker ancestry and misdemeanours like the 1970 invasion of Cambodia, but similar jibes could have been launched at Eisenhower. A more fruitful approach would be to ask how much the Quaker tradition of impromptu speaking in religious assemblies shaped Nixon as an orator. Nixon's ability in that direction proved to be of some importance — no other President's career hinged so completely on a single speech in the way Nixon's did with the Checkers one. A television rerun of 'Checkers' would be deeply embarrassing now; it made even loyal Republicans squirm in the 1960s, not so many years after it was delivered. But most gems of oratory lack sparkle when studied away from the heat of the moment. Whether a speech palpably changed the course of history then and there is what matters. By that criterion 'Checkers' can match anything Demosthenes or Cicero threw off.

The episode is one of the best examples of exploitation of the family in the context of presidential politics. When in the election campaign of 1952 Nixon, then Ike's running mate, decided to riposte to accusations that he was enjoying the benefits of a secret fund, a Hollywood gossip columnist, Adela Rogers St. Johns, reminded him of Roosevelt's success with Fala only eight years earlier and suggested Nixon copy the Master. Nixon did so. In his television speech — broadcast live and without autocue, as was the practice in those days — Nixon told among other things how Checkers had been named by his daughters. He then introduced the topic of his wife, saying "I am not a quitter, and Pat's not a quitter. After all, her name was Patricia Ryan, and she was born on St Patrick's Day, and you know the Irish never quit." Some have thought it typical of Nixon that even now he told an untruth (Pat's birthday was 16 March, the day before St Patrick's).

He worked his wife into the speech in two other ways. It was known that the Democratic Vice-Presidential candidate John Sparkman employed his wife in his senate office at public expense. Nixon indirectly reminded the audience of this by saying that unlike some politicians he did not put his wife on the public payroll even though she worked in his office night and day. Another matter in the air at the time was the disclosure that there had been bribery of Democrats using fridges (in 1952 still rather a luxury) and mink coats. Nixon told his audience "Pat and I have the satisfaction that every dime we've got is honestly ours. I should say this, that Pat doesn't have a mink coat. But she does have a respectable Republican cloth coat, and I always tell her that she would look good in anything." One must of course remember that, quite apart from whatever gift of extempore speaking he got from his family background, Nixon was an able lawyer, one who would undoubtedly have made good in that profession had he not preferred politics. Here he gave a performance worthy of Clarence Darrow.

On Nixon's mother Hannah Milhous's side of the family as well as his father's there was a tradition of speech-making. Hannah's grandmother Elizabeth Milhous, née Griffith, used to travel to many Quaker meetings to speak. (She was the inspiration for Eliza Cope Birdwell in the novel *Friendly Persuasion* by Nixon's cousin Jessamyn West; it was filmed and became something of a Republican cult movie, for it was Mamie Eisenhower's favourite motion picture and was chosen by Nancy Reagan to show the Gorbachevs when they visited America in 1988.)

Hannah was called a saint by many people, not just her son Richard. One rather chilling view of her, however, suggests she was prone to fantasize about events and attribute them to the workings of Providence. Perhaps it was here Nixon got his distorted sense of reality. If indeed a saint, Hannah Nixon seems to have been less the contemplative than the practical sort, ministering to others. It is true that she retained a traditional Quaker element of apartness. Just as her mother Almira used the Quaker 'thee', 'thou' and 'thine' to her dying day, so she used 'thou' and 'thee' to her sisters (though not outside the family circle). But she was sufficiently of the world to teach her son Richard to read before he went to school and she instilled in him — what perhaps is the truly lasting lesson to posterity of Richard Nixon's career — the categorical imperative *never to quit*. It is of course easier not to quit if you have enormous inner strength. That she undoubtedly had. Nixon's father, who does not sound as if he was a particularly weak character, was a Methodist when he met the Quaker Hannah Milhous. They "compromised" (as their son sardonically put it) after their marriage and Frank Nixon became a Quaker too.

During Nixon's childhood his mother was away for three years in Arizona caring for her tuberculous son Harold until he died after a decade of treatment. A younger son, Arthur, died of tubercular meningitis aged seven. Nixon has claimed that it is as a direct result of such experiences that he has supported Federal help for grave illness. He has also claimed that when in 1971 he requested taxpayers' funding of $100 million for cancer research, it was because his wife Pat's mother had died of the disease when Pat was only 13.

Pat Nixon was frequently ignored by her husband in public. Back in 1946, during his bid for Congress, he walked through doors ahead of her; he never danced with her at Julie's wedding reception in 1968, though he did with Julie; and he never publicly kissed her at his Inauguration in 1969, though he was seen to kiss Mamie Eisenhower later in the proceedings. Nevertheless she submerged her life in her husband's to the point of pathos. She worked heroically during her husband's 1968 campaign to secure the Republican nomination, often at the dreariest tasks, such as churning out 50 handwritten letters a day. She is recorded as saying of her clothes, "I never buy anything because I like it. I think 'Will it pack?' 'Is it convenient?'" It was Hannah all over again and, again like Hannah, though she put others first she was by no means a doormat. She was something of a feminist in her way, for one thing. She

Plate 119   Richard Nixon when Vice-President with l-r Julie, Tricia and Pat, 1953

begged Nixon to nominate a woman to the Supreme Court as soon as he became President. (He came into office with two vacancies to fill there.) She even mentioned the matter to the press in an interview she granted off her own bat, adding that she was taking it up with her husband. Although one of the most discreet of First Ladies in voicing opinions on policy, she once said to the press that abortion ought to be a personal decision, whereas Nixon's position at the time was that abortion was an unacceptable way to control population increase. Pat Nixon always made a point of getting in touch with women's groups when travelling abroad with her husband, especially in countries where the inequalities between the sexes were most acute.

She is said to have been the most travelled First Lady in history. In 1970 she flew to Lima, Peru, where an earthquake had caused huge damage, arriving with the relief supplies and then touring the worst-hit spots with the President of Peru's wife Señora Velasco. American-Peruvian relations improved noticeably after that and she was publicly acclaimed as another and better Eleanor Roosevelt. In 1972 she became the first President's wife to represent the United States officially abroad when she attended the inauguration of the President of Liberia. Among her good works while First Lady was the 'Parks to the People' project, which aimed to provide open spaces for city dwellers. She was responsible for the White House being lit up at night and for adding some 500 antiques and other works of art to its public rooms. She also made more rooms open to the public than hitherto.

Don, Nixon's brother, was an embarrassment to him from the mid-1950s, when the (Howard) Hughes Tool Co made him a loan of $205,000 which was later dredged up during Nixon's California gubernatorial campaign in 1962. It was implied that the loan had involved a corrupt favour in return from Nixon, then the Vice-President. (Don Nixon went bankrupt, so the loan was of little ultimate use — to the Nixons at any rate; Howard Hughes got a tax-break worth millions, though a direct connection between the two events has never been established.) In early 1961 Bobby Kennedy as Attorney-General had the Justice Department investigate this episode; no hard incriminating evidence could be dug up.

In 1972 the Kennedy-instigated Justice Department probe was revealed by the *New York Times* and Nixon exploded in wrath against the dead former Attorney-General, claiming he had wanted to press charges against the Nixons' mother, Hannah, who had provided the security against the loan. Soon after Nixon became President, Don's loose mouth — not so much giving away White House secrets, for he had none to give, as boasting of the presidential favours he could get done — had caused Nixon to bug his telephone and have him spied on by Secret Service men. Donald's son, another Donald, was linked, like his father, with the notorious Robert Vesco, who left the US hurriedly for Costa Rica to avoid trial for fraud. Indeed Donald Jr slipped out of the country about the same time as Vesco, tirelessly proclaiming his admiration for the great financier.

When in late 1967 Julie Nixon got engaged to David Eisenhower, the former President's grandson, there was a faintly bitter taint for Nixon in that Ike declined to use the occasion to endorse his former 2nd-in-command for the Republican nomination, due next year. Ike was a pathological refuser of endorsements, but it seemed to the public that it was chiefly Nixon he did not wish to endorse, although back in 1960 he had campaigned readily enough on Nixon's behalf — so much so that Mamie Eisenhower rang Pat Nixon asking her to get Nixon to dissuade Ike from overexerting himself.

That Christmas in the winter of 1967-68 Nixon got momentarily so depressed he decided not to run for President, and David Eisenhower helped call him back to his usual keen ambition by reminding him of how even the Eisenhowers had had their heartaches in the rough and tumble of high politics. When Nixon was about to launch his campaign for the New Hampshire primary in early 1968 David turned up just before his initial press conference. Nixon was caught two ways, because he did not want to seem to be forcing Ike's hand in showing David to reporters, who would infer Ike's endorsement just from David's presence, yet feared to send him away since his arrival could not be kept secret and his subsequent absence might be taken as Ike's repudiation. Later David became a useful Nixon-Ike go-between, but although he himself wanted his grandfather to endorse Nixon before the 1968 Republican convention, he never succeeded in persuading him to. In the event Ike did endorse Nixon, and on the eve of the Republican convention what's more, but it was at the behest of Nixon himself and Admiral Lewis Strauss, an old friend and another Nixon-Ike go-between. Later, in the run-up to presidential election day itself, Ike wrote Nixon a warm letter regretting his absence from the fray due to ill-health but expressing pride that Mamie, their son John and grandson David were helping. It has rather unkindly been suggested that Ike was motivated at this point by desperation to see his grandson and Julie married before his own death. Nixon had David Eisenhower read the letter on television and in the closing moments of his telethon the night before the election had himself televised beside David to lend his inheritance of the Republican leadership a legitimist flavour.

Julie and Tricia, the Nixon daughters, attained twin status when their father renamed two presidential yachts *Patricia* and *Julie* three and a half weeks into his first administration, but in character were very different. Julie was more extrovert and partisan on her father's behalf, whereas Tricia particularly resented the lack of privacy in the White House. Both Julie and Tricia helped their father at times. For instance they handled incoming calls on the televised phone-ins that were part of Nixon's campaign during the crucial 1968 Oregon primary. But Julie was the better campaigner. She and David Eisenhower's visits to small towns throughout the spring of 1968 were especially useful in winning Nixon rank-and-file Republican support ahead of the convention. Nixon wanted them to wait till after the 1969 Inauguration to get married and have the ceremony in the White House, which would have suited his love of the trappings of greatness. Their insistence on a December date presumably reflected the natural impatience of all engaged couples mixed with concern lest Ike's death forestall them. Once her father was in office Julie used to show visitors round the White House. She and David represented Nixon at Expo '70 in Japan and Nixon wanted David to help him in his 1972 re-election campaign, ingeniously skirting the officers by suggesting he merely 'accompany' Julie when she made public appearances on her father's behalf.

Of all the Presidents Nixon must be by far the juiciest subject for a psycho-historian. There have been some fantastic attempts to account for his behaviour or personality by invoking the character of the dead brother Harold (fantastic, but even so more plausible than some of the stuff written about JFK and the dead war hero Joe Jr). There have been some reasonable theories too. Nixon's latest biographer suggests he deleted the expletives on the White House tapes to avoid shocking Hannah. Yet they were only profanities, not obscenities. Had he left them in he might have shocked the Bible Belt, it is argued, but not really the rest of America. As it was, the frequency of "expletive deleted" in the transcripts made Americans suspect their President was too foul-mouthed to live up to his high position and Nixon lost support rapidly. Certainly a close examination of the smoulderingly resentful Frank and the formidable Hannah goes far to explain this oddest of men.

BIOGRAPHICAL DETAILS AND DESCENDANTS

NIXON, RICHARD MILHOUS [577 Chestnut Ridge Road, Woodcliff Lake, NJ 07675, USA; c/o Simon & Schuster, Rockefeller Center, 1230 Avenue of the Americas, New York, NY 10020, USA; 26 Federal Plaza #1300, New York, NY 10001, USA; 142 E 65th Street, New York, NY 10021, USA], *b* Yorba Linda, Calif., 9 Jan 1913; *educ* Whittier Coll (AB 1934, Memb Bd Tstees 1939-68) and Duke U Law Sch (LLB 1937); admitted California Bar 1937 (resigned as practising lawyer 4 Oct 1974), Ptnr Bewley, Knoop & Nixon (attys) 1939 (joined firm when Wingert & Bewley 1937), Town Atty La Habra, Calif., 1939, with Office of Price Admin, Washington, DC, 1942, served USN World War II (Jr Lt 1942, Sr Lt 1943, Lt-Cdr 1945, Cdr USNR 1953) in Pacific and US; Memb US House of Reps 1947-51 (Memb Educn & Labor Ctee 1947, Chm Sub-Ctee House Ctee Un-American Activities 1948), US Senator 1951-53, V-Pres USA 1953-61, presidential candidate 1960, with Adams, Duque & Hazeltine, attys, Los Angeles, 1961-63, gubernatorial candidate California 1962, joined Mudge, Stern, Baldwin & Todd, attys, New York, 1963 (renamed Nixon, Mudge, Rose, Guthrie & Alexander with Nixon as ptnr Dec 1963), 37th President (R) of the USA 1969-1974 (resigned 9 Aug, granted full pardon by President Ford for any offences he might have committed against the US while in office 8 Sept), author: *Six Crises* (1962), *The Memoirs of Richard Nixon* (1978), *The Real War* (1980), *Leaders* (1982), *Real Peace: a strategy for the West* (1983), *No More Vietnams* (1986), *1999: Victory Without War* (1988), *In the Arena: A Memoir of Victory, Defeat and Renewal* (1990), *Seize the Moment: America's Challenge in a One Superpower World* (1992); *m* the Mission Inn, Riverside, Calif., 21 June 1940 Thelma Catherine ('Pat') (*b* Ely, Nev., 16 March 1912; *educ* Excelsior High, Artesia (now Cerritos), Calif., Fullerton Junior Coll and U of S California (degree in business studies 1937); sometime stenographer, x-ray technician, film extra, shop assistant, dental assistant and shorthand and typing teacher Whittier High Sch; *d* at home, Park Ridge, New Jersey, 22 June 1993 of lung cancer), only dau of William Ryan (*d* 1930 of silicosis) and his w Katharina (Kate) Halberstadt Bender (*d* 1925 of cancer), and has issue:

President Nixon's daughter

I *Patricia (Tricia) Nixon, *b* San Francisco 21 Feb 1946; *educ* Chapin Sch, New York City, and Finch Coll; *m* the White House, Washington, DC, 12 June 1971 *Edward Ridley Finch COX (*b* 2 Oct 1946; *educ* Princeton; sometime consumer researcher for Ralph Nader), s of Col Howard Elliott Cox and his w Anne C. D. Finch, and has issue:

Grandchildren
1 *Christopher COX, *b* New York 14 March 1980

President Nixon's daughter

II *Julie Nixon, *b* Washington, DC, 25 July 1948; *educ* Chapin Sch, New York City, and Smith; sometime ed with *Saturday Evening Post*, author: *Special People* (1977) and *Pat Nixon: The Untold Story* (1986); *m* Marble Collegiate Church, New York, 22 Dec 1968 *(Dwight) David EISENHOWER II (*b* West Point, New York, 31 March 1948), only s of Col John Sheldon Doud Eisenhower and his w Barbara Thompson and gs of President EISENHOWER, and has issue:

Grandchildren
1 *Jennie EISENHOWER, *b* San Clemente, Calif., 15 Aug 1978
2 *Alex Richards EISENHOWER, *b* 10 Oct 1980
3 *Melanie EISENHOWER, *b* 18 June 1984

MALE LINE ANCESTRY AND COLLATERAL DESCENDANTS

In the 17th century the 37th President's Nixon ancestors left Scotland and settled in Co Wexford, Ireland.

James NIXON, *b* Ireland *c* 1705; emigrated to America and is first heard of in Delaware 1731; *m* Mary —— (*d* after 1821) and *d* Brandywine Hundred, New Castle Co, Del., between 16 May 1773 (when his will, in which he left £60 to his w and £45 to his daus, was dated) and 26 June 1775 (when will probated), leaving (with two or more daus):

I George NIXON, for whom *see below*
II James NIXON, Jr, inherited two slaves under his f's will and fought in the Revolutionary War

The er (?) s,

George NIXON, *b* Brandywine *c* 1752; inherited a 100-acre farm from his f, fought in Revolutionary War (crossing the Delaware River with George Washington and seeing action at the Battle of Trenton (1776), Washington's first success against the British), settled first at Washington, Pa., 1803, then Clinton Co, Ohio, 1830, and finally Henry Co, Ill., 1842; *m* 1st Wilmington, Del., 17 Aug 1775 Sarah, dau of John Seeds, Jr (?) (1725-53) or Joseph Seeds (?) (1722-54), of Wilmington, and had issue; *m* 2nd Martha —— and *d* Colona Township, Henry Co, Ill., 5 Aug 1842, leaving a s by his 1st w:

George NIXON, Jr, *b* Brandywine *c* 1784; accompanied his father to Pennsylvania 1803, settled in Ohio 1844; *m* 1st Washington, Pa., *c* 1806 Hannah (*b* Delaware *c* 1790; *d* Washington, Pa., *c* 1827), dau of William Wilson (*c* 1764-1837) and his w Elenor Scothorn (*c* 1764-1819), and had issue; *m* 2nd Washington, Pa., 16 Nov 1830 Christine Pence and *d* Richland Township, Vinton Co, Ohio, after 1860, leaving a s by his 1st w:

George NIXON III, *b* Washington, Pa., *c* 1821; moved to Vinton Co 1853, joined Company B, 73rd Ohio Regt, in Civil War; *m* Washington Co, Pa., 10 Jan 1843 Margaret Ann (*b* Smith Township, Pa., *c* 1826; *d* Vinton Co 18 March 1865), dau of Anthony Trimmer (*c* 1781-1841) and his w Margaret Hunt (*b* Smith, Pa., *c* 1804; *m* 2nd Richard Howard; *d* Vinton Co 1876), and *d* Gettysburg, Pa., 14 July 1863 from wounds sustained at the battle there 1, 2 and 3 July 1863, leaving issue (with seven other children):

Samuel Brady NIXON, *b* Atlasburg, Pa., 9 Oct 1847; pottery factory operative, schoolteacher and mail deliveryman, bought a 40-acre farm; *m* 1st Hocking Co, Ohio, 10 April 1873 Sarah Ann (*b* there 15 Oct 1852; schoolmistress; *d* her father's house, Vinton Co, 18 Jan 1886 of tuberculosis), dau of Thomas Wiley Wadsworth (1826-79) and his w Mary Louise Moore (1832-1918), and had issue; *m* 2nd 1890, as her 1st husb, Lutheria Wyman (*b* 18 Oct 1863; *m* 2nd Dr W. V. Marshburn; *d* Calif. 1948) and *d* Vinton Co 28 April 1914, having with her had further issue; in all he had three s and two daus; his sons by his 1st w:

I Ernest NIXON, took a PhD and became a Professor at Penn State U
II Francis (Frank) Anthony NIXON, for whom *see below*

The yr s,

Frank NIXON, *b* Elk Township, Vinton Co, 3 Dec 1878; streetcar motorman for Columbus Railway & Light Co, farm hand, sheep-shearer, oil field handyman, carpenter (built family house at Yorba Linda, the future President NIXON's birthplace), grocer, moved to Calif. 1904, then back to Ohio and finally settled in Calif. 1907, where worked as motorman for Pacific Electric Railway Co; *m* Whittier 25 June 1908 Hannah (*b* nr Butlerville, Jennings Co, Ind., 7 March 1885; *educ* Whittier Acad and Whittier Coll; *d* Whittier 30 Sept 1967), dau of Franklin Milhous (1848-1919), nurseryman or truck garden proprietor, and his w Almira Park Burdg (1849-1943; her gggf Joseph Burdg's wife Sarah was sister of Job Morris, whose gdau Ann *m* Wiley Carter and was gggmother of President CARTER), and *d* La Habra, Calif., 4 Sept 1956, having had issue:

I Harold Samuel NIXON, *b* Yorba Linda, Calif., 1 June 1909; *d* Yorba Linda 7 March 1933 of tuberculosis
II RICHARD MILHOUS NIXON, 37th PRESIDENT of the UNITED STATES of AMERICA
III (Francis) Don(ald) NIXON, *b* Yorba Linda 23 Nov 1914; storekeeper and sometime restaurateur; *m* 9 Aug 1942 *Clara Jane Lemke [Mrs Donald Nixon, Whittier, CA, USA] and *d* before 1990, having had issue:

President Nixon's niece and nephews
1 *Lawrene Mae NIXON, *b* 18 July 1943
2 *Donald Anthony NIXON, Jr, *b* 12 Dec 1945; sometime aide to Robert Vesco
3 *Richard Calvert NIXON, *b* 28 Aug 1952

IV Arthur Burdg NIXON, *b* Yorba Linda 26 May 1918; *d* Whittier 10 Aug 1925 of tubercular encephalitis
V *Ed(ward)/Eddie Calvert NIXON, *b* Whittier 3 May 1930; telephone manager; *m* 1 June 1957 *Gay Lynne Woods and has issue:

President Nixon's nieces
1 *Amelia NIXON, *b* 4 June 1958
2 *Elizabeth NIXON, *b* 14 April 1960

Father's side

James Nixon
c 1705—1773-75
Mary —
d p 1821
} George Nixon *c* 1752-1842

?John/Joseph Seeds, Jr
1725-53/1722-54
—— ——
} Sarah Seeds

} William Wilson *c* 1764-1837

Nathan Scothorn, Jr
c 1730-*c* 1764
Hannah Twiggs
} Elenor Scothorn *c* 1764-1819

Anthony Trimmer
c 1724-54
Elizabeth ——
1723-81
} Paul Trimmer *c* 1750-1834

Moses McElwain
d 1760
Agnes Miller
d in/p 1762
} Jane McElwain

} William Hunt *fl* 1803-17

Christopher Andover
1755-1831
Margaret ——
} Margaret Andover

Thomas Wadsworth
fl c 1741
Rebecca Passmore
} Thomas Wadsworth, Jr 1747-*p* 1830

Matthew Wiley?
b 1730
—— ——
} Mary Wiley

Guy Lytle
d 1764
Elizabeth Webster
b 1723
} George Lytle *b c* 1759

Alexander McComas, Jr
fl c 1747
Deborah Hartley
} Elizabeth McComas

James Moore
d 1777
Elizabeth Dickinson
b 1739
} Joseph Moore 1759-1832

Thomas Clemson
c 1710-85
Elizabeth Strode
} Mary Clemson 1763-1817

Alexander Brown
a 1773-1816
Mary Bradford
} Isaac Brown 1771-1853

Thomas Clayton, Jr
c 1745-1813
Mary (?Walker)
} Mary Clayton 1777-1822

Mother's side

Thomas Milhous
1699-1770
Sarah Miller
1701-75
} William Milhous 1738-1826

Joshua Baldwin
1721/2-1800
Mercy Brown
1722-84
} Hannah Baldwin 1748-1825

Thomas Vickers
c 1720-93
Rebecca Dillon
} Thomas Vickers, Jr 1757-1829

Joshua Mendenhall
1727/8-1816
Lydia Mendenhall
} Jemima Mendenhall 1757-1851

William Griffith, Jr
1714-78
Esther Davis
c 1722-62
} Jacob Griffith 1757-1841

Recond Hussey
d 1784
Miriam Harry
d 1809
} Lydia Hussey 1757-1843

Samuel Price
1739-1825
Ann Moore
1744-84
} Daniel Price 1761-1846

John Hussey III
p 1713-70
Elizabeth ——
(2nd w)
} Elizabeth Hussey 1759-1847

Joseph Burdg
d in/p 1777
Sarah Morris
} Jacob Burdg 1743-*a* 1797

Anthony Smith
1723-1810
Lydia Willets
b 1726
} Judith Smith 1751-1836

Oliver Matthews
1721-1824
Hannah Johns
c 1728-91
} William Matthews 1755-1844

Isaac Griffith
b 1720/1
Ann Burson
b 1721
} Ann Griffith 1754-56—1792

Isaac Hemingway
1730-78
Elizabeth Haven
b 1736
} James Hemingway 1760-1822

Ephraim Armstrong
d 1788
Elizabeth McCulley
} Elizabeth Armstrong 1757-1837

John Malmsbury, Jr
1744-*p* 1797
Rebecca Doane
b 1754
} Benjamin Malmsbury 1779-1854

James Cattell, Jr
1743-1806
Hope Gaskill
b 1743
} Jane Cattell 1780-1853

RICHARD M. NIXON
FAMILY TREE

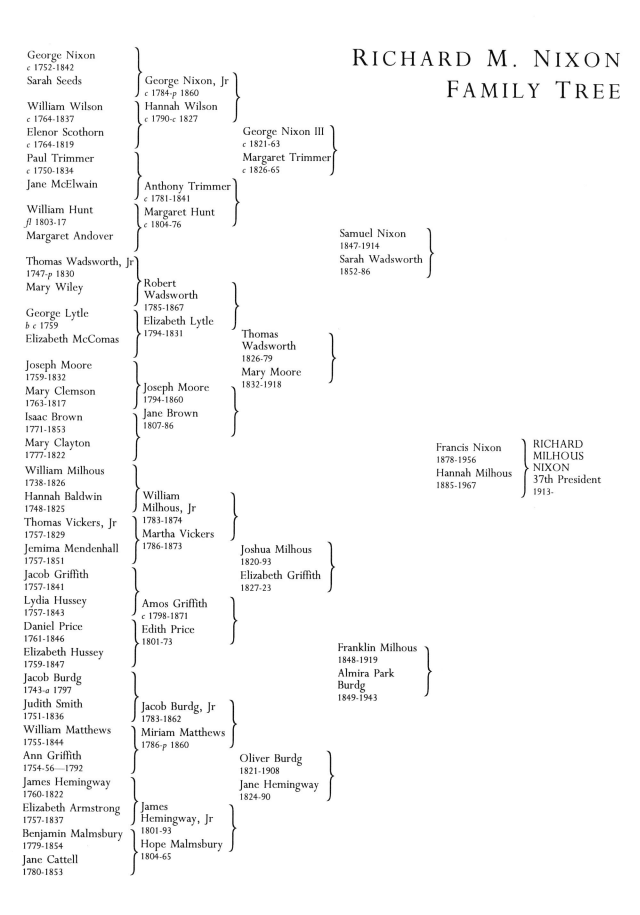

George Nixon
c 1752-1842
Sarah Seeds

George Nixon, Jr
c 1784-p 1860
Hannah Wilson
c 1790-c 1827

William Wilson
c 1764-1837
Elenor Scothorn
c 1764-1819

George Nixon III
c 1821-63
Margaret Trimmer
c 1826-65

Paul Trimmer
c 1750-1834
Jane McElwain

Anthony Trimmer
c 1781-1841
Margaret Hunt
c 1804-76

William Hunt
fl 1803-17
Margaret Andover

Samuel Nixon
1847-1914
Sarah Wadsworth
1852-86

Thomas Wadsworth, Jr
1747-p 1830
Mary Wiley

Robert Wadsworth
1785-1867
Elizabeth Lytle
1794-1831

George Lytle
b c 1759
Elizabeth McComas

Thomas Wadsworth
1826-79
Mary Moore
1832-1918

Joseph Moore
1759-1832
Mary Clemson
1763-1817

Joseph Moore
1794-1860
Jane Brown
1807-86

Isaac Brown
1771-1853
Mary Clayton
1777-1822

Francis Nixon
1878-1956
Hannah Milhous
1885-1967

RICHARD MILHOUS NIXON
37th President
1913-

William Milhous
1738-1826
Hannah Baldwin
1748-1825

William Milhous, Jr
1783-1874
Martha Vickers
1786-1873

Thomas Vickers, Jr
1757-1829
Jemima Mendenhall
1757-1851

Joshua Milhous
1820-93
Elizabeth Griffith
1827-23

Jacob Griffith
1757-1841
Lydia Hussey
1757-1843

Amos Griffith
c 1798-1871
Edith Price
1801-73

Daniel Price
1761-1846
Elizabeth Hussey
1759-1847

Franklin Milhous
1848-1919
Almira Park Burdg
1849-1943

Jacob Burdg
1743-a 1797
Judith Smith
1751-1836

Jacob Burdg, Jr
1783-1862
Miriam Matthews
1786-p 1860

William Matthews
1755-1844
Ann Griffith
1754-56—1792

Oliver Burdg
1821-1908
Jane Hemingway
1824-90

James Hemingway
1760-1822
Elizabeth Armstrong
1757-1837

James Hemingway, Jr
1801-93
Hope Malmsbury
1804-65

Benjamin Malmsbury
1779-1854
Jane Cattell
1780-1853

Plate 120   Gerald Ford

GERALD FORD

1913-
38TH PRESIDENT OF THE UNITED STATES OF AMERICA
1974-77

President Nixon's weakness for incompetent scoundrels landed him with a Vice-President who, at the height of the Watergate Affair, had to resign his office because he had been accepting bribes from a Baltimore businessman whom he had favoured in his days as Governor of Maryland. Spiro Agnew's disgrace and disappearance were however of some slight use to Nixon because he was able to replace him with a Vice-President of unquestioned honesty and general popularity. Gerald Ford was not widely known outside Republican circles and Congress, where he had led the party in the House of Representatives for nine years. But he had a knack for getting on with people, even political opponents, and there were absolutely no skeletons in his cupboard. The one slightly curious fact about him was that he was originally named Leslie Lynch King, but when his parents were divorced and his mother remarried he was adopted by his step-father, whose name he was given. He was only two when this happened.

His own family was a huge success. Mrs Ford especially became very popular with the American people, although the strain of the presidency and of her husband's campaign for election in his own right in 1976 severely strained her weak health. The Fords came as a breath of fresh air to the White House. But Washington is merciless. Lyndon Johnson's unkind jokes about Mr Ford were remembered and repeated; eager eyes looked for evidence that the new President was stupid or clumsy. In reality he was an accomplished athlete with excellent co-ordination but, like many athletes, he was accident-prone. Even former football players are fragile creatures compared with the ordinary unathletic slob, and every time President Ford stumbled, or hit his elbow, knowing voices cackled their superior pleasure.

None of this did him lasting harm. Much more serious was his decision to give Richard Nixon a free pardon only a month after the resignation. Ford defended his action on the ground that Nixon had suffered enough and was a spent force, and that the overriding public need was to think and talk about something other than Watergate. He was undoubtedly right; the spectacle of Nixon being dragged through the courts would have done nothing but harm. Unfortunately, the ex-President, not having been asked to give any undertakings before the pardon was issued, or, if asked, having refused, now showed what he was made of by trying, through legal processes, to get control of all the White House papers arising from his presidency. Other Presidents had usually taken their archives with them and all those since and including Harry Truman had been given handsome buildings in which to house them. But other Presidents were not suspected of wishing to tamper with the evidence. In the end it took an act of Congress to defeat Nixon's scheme. Worse still for Gerald Ford was the vindictiveness that many disillusioned Americans felt toward Nixon. They wanted his blood and they could not forgive Ford for frustrating them. It may have been their resentment which cost Ford the election of 1976.

He did not have much time to leave his mark on history. He presided with dignity over the celebrations marking America's bicentenary in 1976. He made a mess of the *Mayaguez* incident. This arose out of the fall of Cambodia to the Communists, which occurred in the spring of 1975. An American vessel, the *Mayaguez*, fell into the hands of the Communists. Ford threatened all sorts of frightfulness if the ship and her crew were not instantly restored to the United States and, without waiting to see how the ultimatum was received, launched a torrent of bombs on Cambodia. Only later was it learned that the men had been returned before the bombing started. It was the end. In 1976, for the first time for at least 11 years, America was a nation unequivocally at peace.

GERALD FORD'S FAMILY

Jerry Ford's strongest card was his air of sincerity. The American people were crying out for it. Lack of it in the previous President had caused his resignation. Yet although what Ford told was the truth he did not reveal the whole truth. All the years he was a Congressman, including his prominent ones as House Minority Leader, his biographical details never revealed either that his wife or his mother had had a previous husband before the one the world knew about. Only in the last year before he succeeded Nixon, when he became Vice-President, did these very mildly titillating details emerge. And in his memoirs Ford makes no mention of his wife's alcoholism. Fair enough, perhaps — it is an acutely distressing matter, after all — except that he does mention the drink problem of the wife of the then Senate Minority Leader, Howard Baker.

There may well have been good reason for this. Ford himself had once been a victim in childhood of a less than full disclosure of the truth. In adolescence it was revealed to him that he was not Gerald Ford Sr's real son but the product of an earlier marriage between his mother Dorothy and a man called Leslie Lynch King. There is some confusion as to his age at the time. Ford says his mother told him he was not Gerald Ford's son when he was 12, but adds that the matter was never really discussed, implying that no mention had been made of who precisely was his real father. He further says that he knew a Nebraska court had ordered his father to pay his mother $50-75 a month child support, but again makes no mention of the man's name or of his knowing the man's name. Ford's friend and White House Press Secretary Jerry terHorst states in his biography of him that the first Ford knew of his parentage was when Leslie King strolled unheralded into his life when he was 17. In either case the sudden appearance of a man calling himself his real father would have been a shock. But at least if he had been told something of his parentage five years earlier the shock would have been cushioned.

One can only conjecture what a youth after such a revelation would have thought of his mother and stepfather, a man who for at least his first twelve years he had assumed was his real father. In Ford's case they had dinned into him the injunction 'tell the truth' (one of a trinity of golden rules that included 'work hard' and ended in bathos with 'come to dinner on time'). Ford says his resentment was directed entirely toward King, however. At their brief meeting King gave his son $25 and said he had come east from Wyoming to collect a new Lincoln automobile. From this Ford inferred he was well-to-do. (He may have had this episode in mind when, on becoming President, he joked that he was a Ford not a Lincoln.) In contrast Gerald Ford Sr was doing badly in his paint business. Obviously the fact that Ford's stepfather had supported him all those years, treating him like a true son, would have predisposed Ford in his favour. In contrast King had shown no interest in him hitherto, not even paying the child support he owed (the shortfalls were made up by Ford's grandfather, Leslie King Sr, until he died). Moreover when Ford in his junior year at college was short of money and wrote to King asking for a loan, the latter made no reply. Nevertheless, the discovery that he was no blood relative of the man whose house he lived in and who paid for his upkeep must have been quite upsetting — all the more so, perhaps,

Plate 121   The Fords: l-r Susan Ford, Betty Bloomer Warren Ford,
Gerald Ford and the dog Liberty, October 1974

because it seems Jerry Ford felt toward Ford Sr exactly as a loving son would, talking over with him beforehand all his major steps in life. He even reckoned he looked like him (photographs bear this out). His step-father could scarcely have been more supportive in the chief move Ford did make in his career. He was not very active politically, although he became chairman of the Kent County Republicans. But he only did this to keep the position warm for his step-son, who was then away at the War. Ford Sr later resigned the chairmanship to campaign for his step-son's attempt at a Congressional seat. Ford's half-brother Tom acted as his campaign treasurer.

Even in youth there was more to Ford than his seemingly extrovert life as a public-spirited football-player and air of uncomplicated Middle-American normality. He was a bit of a loner. He was introspective. He had a stammer as a child (it cleared up when he was 10). He was also ambidextrous, left-handed when sitting down, right-handed when standing up. As was customary then, adults tried to force him to be right-handed. He got married at the advanced age of 34, long after his half-brothers had settled down. Indeed in his self-imposed role of ageing bachelor he seems to have caused his mother mild concern. Athletes are sensitive too, is the lesson Ford teaches us.

A few years after finding out about the great subterfuge that had been practised on him, Ford became a sports coach at Yale. His duties were to assist the coach of the football team and to coach in boxing on his own. He was proficient enough at football but originally knew nothing of boxing. So he had to practise a mild subterfuge himself to get the job, meanwhile acquiring what boxing skill he could from a former champion who lived locally before taking up his post. At Yale he wanted to study law as well as coach. The assessors thought he was incapable of combining the two activities. They underestimated him, as cerebral types so often do with athletes. It was a lesson in the value of not revealing too much about yourself if you want to avoid being pigeon-holed and get ahead in other ways. After the War Ford ran for Congress in a district heavily populated by members of the Dutch Reformed Church, one of the strictest of the Calvinist sects. He was intending to marry Betty Bloomer, who as a divorcee and dancer would not have gone down well with the Dutch Reformed, and in the early stages said nothing about his impending wedding. In this he showed he knew the value of selective reticence.

Ford could be revealing enough about others. He made comments of considerable interest, for instance, on Nixon's dislike of detail and Reagan's essential reserve (Ford said of him that he was one of the few politicians whose public speeches gave away more about him than his private conversations). His pithy summing up of Jimmy Carter is highly memorable ("His self-confidence, I thought, came very close to arogance."). And he had none of the false pride of American manhood about crying: he tells in his memoirs how he wept the night after Leslie King, his real father, had introduced himself in the diner where he was working and adds that in general "tears well up in my eyes very easily". In the mainstream America of Ford's generation — consider how crying on television destroyed Muskie in 1972 — perhaps only an ex-football star could make that statement publicly and get away with it.

Ford has been the readiest of the ex-Presidents to make very large sums of money from his position. By the early 1990s he was reckoned to be pulling in $3.2 million a year from directors' fees and his pension. Early in 1993 it was reported that he was charging $25,000 a time for the privilege of playing a round of golf with him. One wonders if he finds this sort of thing acceptable because he never got to be President by the usual channels, just as he became a Ford by unusual means too, a cuckoo in the nest twice over as it were. He is in fact the only President never to have been elected either as President or as Vice-President; indeed when he did put himself up for election he lost. Like Taft he had had quite another ambition orginally: Speaker of the House. Eventually, about the early 1970s, he realised he was never going to make it, whereupon he and Betty discussed their future plans. In 1973 they agreed he would run for Congress one more time then retire early in 1975. One reason for his decision to retire at 62 was Betty's poor health. A pinched nerve and arthritis had already put paid to her dancing, the activity she loved most.

While Ford was in the White House sincerity seemed a Ford family characteristic. The only obvious case of reticence seemed to be the staff, who to the Fords' surprise never responded to their 'good mornings' and 'thank yous' and so on. Eventually they discovered that Nixon had given orders that the staff were never to reply when the President or First Lady spoke to them. Things soon changed externally as well as internally. The frankness of Betty Ford's public utterances while in the White House became famous, and were probably an overall asset to her husband's administration, so that among the slogans in 1976 were "Elect Betty's Husband" and "Keep Betty in the White House". But Betty's frankness was a mite selective too. When a journalist asked her why she had not mentioned her first marriage she replied that she had never been asked. It was a disingenuous statement. As for her views, however frankly expressed, they do not seem particularly adventurous today. In the mid-1970s, however, they made her the target for anti-feminist agitation, a phenomenon which is scarcely conceivable now. She lobbied state legislatures across the nation on behalf of the Equal Rights Amendment. She pushed for more women in top jobs, conceivably tipping the scales over Carla Hills's appointment as Health, Education and Welfare Secretary and Anne Armstrong's as US Ambassador to Britain. She got her old dance teacher Martha Graham awarded a Presidential Medal of Freedom. Compared with a quasi-feminist like Pat Nixon she seemed almost revolutionary.

On the whole she enjoyed her stay in the White House, doubtless in part because for the first time in her married life she saw a reasonable amount of her husband. Marriage to a politician had never been easy: their honeymoon was interrupted by Jerry Ford attending a Dewey speech (this was during the 1948 election) and for years afterward she often only saw him on Sundays. She worked for him when he was in Congress, but in an unpaid position since the practice of employing relatives at public expense, while perfectly legal and indeed widespread, was judged imprudent. She was against her husband running for President in 1976, but it was only after the Fords left the White House that she subsided into alcoholism. Without getting caught up in arguments as to the pathology of alcoholism, one can at least observe that it seems to run in families. Betty Ford's father had been an alcoholic, a fact she only discovered much later.

All Ford's four children worked enthusiastically for him in the 1976 election, but especially Jack and Steve. Jack's first campaign speech on his father's behalf got a standing ovation and he organized his father's cheerleaders at the Republican convention. Steve represented his father at the convention while the President attended official engagements elsewhere. When Steve was charged with paternity of a child born to a Californian girl his father made a statement saying he accepted the child into the family. He could hardly have acted otherwise, but it was gracefully done. Indeed for all his tendency to stumble physically, Ford had the knack of seeming graceful in circumstances that would have embarrassed another man.

BIOGRAPHICAL DETAILS AND DESCENDANTS

FORD, GERALD (JERRY) RUDOLPH [PO Box 927, Rancho Mirage, CA 92270 USA], *b* Leslie Lynch King, Jr, Omaha, Nebr., 14 July 1913, adopted by stepfather and name changed to Gerald Rudolph Ford, Jr, 3 Dec 1935; *educ* South High Sch, Grand Rapids, Mich., Michigan U (football player Michigan U's national championship team 1932-33, AB 1935) and Yale Law Sch (LLB 1941); Assist Football Coach Yale Athletics Dept 1935-41, admitted to Michigan Bar 1941, ptnr Ford & Buchen, attys, 1941-42, Lt-Cdr USNR Pacific 1942-46, V-Pres Independent Veterans Assoc 1945-46, associate with law firm of Butterfield, Keeney & Amberg 1947-49 (subsequently with Amberg, Law & Buchen to 1953), Memb US House of Representatives from Michigan 5th Dist 1949-1973 (Memb: Public Works Ctee 1949-50 and Appropriations Ctee 1951-65, Defense Sub-Ctee, Minority Leader 1965-73), US-Canadian Interparly Gp, American Political Science Association's Distinguished Congressional Service Award 1961, Chm Republican Conference 1963, Memb Warren Commission investigating President KENNEDY's assassination 1963-64, Perm Chm Republican Nat Conventions 1968 and 1972, Dir: Bethlehem Rebar Industs Inc, Commercial Credit Co, IDS Mutual Funds Inc, Nova Pharmaceutical Corp, Pullman Co, Shearson Lehman Hutton Inc, Tesoro Petroleum Corp, Tiger Internat Corp, Pres Eisenhower Exchange Fellowship 1977-, Chm Acad of Educnl Devpt 1977-84, Fndr American Enterprise Inst World Forum 1982, Hon LLD: Michigan State U, Albion College, Mich., Aquinas College, Grand Rapids, and Spring Arbor Coll, Mich. (all 1965), V-Pres USA 6 Dec 1973-9 Aug 1974, 38th President (R) of the USA, 9 Aug 1974-77; author: (with John R. Stiles) *Portrait of an Assassin* (1965), *A Time to Heal* (1979), *Humor and the Presidency* (1987); *m* Grace Episcopal Church, Grand Rapids, 15 Oct 1948, as her 2nd husb, *Elizabeth (Betty) Ann (*b* Chicago 8 April 1918; *educ* Bennington and Bennington Sch of Dance; dancer Martha Graham Concert Gp, dance instructor, model and fashion co-ordinator, co-fndr Betty Ford Center for Drug and Alcohol Rehabilitation, Rancho Mirage, Calif., 1982, author: *The Times of My Life* (1978) and *Betty: A Glad Awakening* (1987); *m* 1st 1942 (divorce 1947) William G. Warren, insur salesman and furniture dealer, of Michigan), dau of William Stephenson Bloomer, rubber company representative, and his w Hortense Nehr, and has issue:

President Ford's son

1 *Michael Gerald FORD [Beverly, MA, USA], *b* Washington, DC, 14 March 1950; *educ* Wake Forest Coll and Gordon Conwell Theological Seminary, S Hamilton, Mass.; *m* Catonsville, Md., 5 July 1974 *Gayle Ann (*b* 1951; *educ* Wake Forest Coll), dau of Edward A. Brumbaugh, and has issue:

Grandchildren
1 *Sarah Joyce FORD, b Pittsburgh 22 April 1979
2 *Rebekah Elizabeth FORD, b Winston-Salem, N Carolina, 26 Feb 1982
3 *Hannah Gayle FORD, b Winston-Salem 17 Sept 1985

President Ford's sons
II *John (Jack) Gardner FORD, b Washington, DC, 16 March 1952; educ Utah State U; sometime forest ranger Yellowstone Park and television commentator; m La Jolla, Calif., 29 April 1989, *Juliann, dau of August Felando
III *Steven Meigs FORD, b 19 May 1956; educ T. C. Williams High Sch, Alexandria, Va., and Duke U; television actor; has issue by a California girl:

Grandson
1 A boy

President Ford's daughter
IV *Susan Elizabeth Ford, b Washington, DC, 6 July 1957; educ Holton Arms Acad, Bethesda, Md.; m 1st Palm Desert, Calif., 10 Feb 1979 (divorce 1988), as his 2nd w, Charles (Chuck) VANCE, sometime Secret Service agent protecting President and Mrs Ford, and with him has issue:

Grandchildren
1 *Tyne Mary VANCE, b Washington, DC, 15 Aug 1980
2 *Heather Elizabeth VANCE, b Washington, DC, 31 Jan 1983

President Ford's daughter
IV (cont.) Mrs Susan Vance m 2nd 25 July 1989 *Vaden BALES

MALE LINE ANCESTRY AND COLLATERAL DESCENDANTS

Lynch KING, of Pennsylvania, b 18—?; m Rebecca Shepherd, of Virginia or West Virginia, and had issue:

Charles Henry KING, b Pa. 12 March 1853; railroad pioneer Wyoming, settled in Los Angeles; m 18— Martha Alice Porter (b Ind. 17 Nov 1853; d Glendale, Calif., 14 July 1930) and d at his residence 1423 S Manhattan Boulevard, Los Angeles, 27 Feb 1930, leaving (with one other s and three daus) a s:

Leslie Lynch KING, b Chadron, Nebr., 25 July 1882; wool merchant in Omaha, Nebr., later dealt in lumber and real estate at Riverton, Wyo.; m 1st Harvard, Ill., 7 Sept 1912 (divorce 1915) Dorothy Ayer (b there 27 Feb 1892; educ Harvard, Ill., High Sch), dau of Levi Addison Gardner (1861-1916) and his w Adele Augusta Ayer (b 2 July 1867; ggdau of Samuel Ayer and his w Polly Chase, who was ggggdau of Aquila Chase and his w Ann Wheeler, one of whose bros, Henry Wheeler, was an ancestor of Presidents GARFIELD and BUSH, and another of whose bros, David Wheeler, was an ancestor of President HOOVER; d Los Angeles 10 Aug 1938), and had issue:

I LESLIE LYNCH KING, Jr, 38th PRESIDENT of the UNITED STATES of AMERICA as GERALD RUDOLPH FORD

Mrs Dorothy Gardner King m 2nd Grand Rapids, Mich., 1 Feb 1916 Gerald Rudolf FORD (b Grand Rapids 9 Dec 1890; railroad operative, salesman Grand Rapids Wood Finishing Co, Pres Ford Paint & Varnish Co, Head of Kent Co Civil Defense in World War II, Chm Kent Co Republican Ctee 1944-46; d 26 Jan 1962) and d there 17 Sept 1967, having had further issue:

II *Thomas Gardner FORD, b Grand Rapids 15 July 1918; educ U of Michigan (AB 1940); Lt-Cdr US Navy 1940-46, Representative (R) from Grand Rapids, Michigan Legislature, 1964-72, Senate Appropriations Ctee and House legislative audit co-ordinator, Michigan State Legislature; m 12 Sept 1942 *Janet Packer and has issue:

President Ford's half-nephew
1 *Thomas Gardner FORD, Jr, b 19—; educ Olivet Coll, Mich. (BS 1967), and U of Michigan Sch of Dentistry (DDS 1971); m 19— *—— and has issue:

Half-great-nephew
(1) *Cameron P. FORD, b 2 Oct 1973

President Ford's half-niece
2 *Julie G. Ford [Mrs Robert Foster, Berkley, MI 48072, USA; 547 Timberline Drive, Rochester, MI 48309, USA], b 10 March 1947; m 7 Aug 1971 *Robert Vern FOSTER

III *Richard Addison FORD [3440 Eagle Bluff NE, Grand Rapids, MI 49505, USA; RAF 7797 Esmeralda Way K-202, Naples, FL 33942, USA], b Grand Rapids 3 June 1924; educ U of Michigan (Bs, MS); Pres Ford Paint 1967-79; m 12 June 1947 *Ellen Priscilla, dau of Harrison William Platte and his w Helen Elizabeth Samuelson, and has issue:

President Ford's half-nieces and -nephew
1 *Linda Ford [Mrs Theodore Burba, 1955 Argentina Drive SE, East Grand Rapids, MI 49506, USA], b Grand Rapids 10

March 1948; *m* there 7 Aug 1971 *Theodore Vance BURBA
2 *Laurie Ann Ford [Mrs Richard W Jewell, 18404 Dorset, Southfield, MI, USA], *b* Grand Rapids 14 June 1953; *m* there 15 Jan 1987 *Richard William JEWELL
3 *Richard Platte FORD, *b* 6 April 1958; *educ* Grand Rapids High Sch, U of Michigan (BS 1977) and UCLA (MBA 1984); *m* Grand Rapids 30 Dec 1986 *Elizabeth Ann Baker

IV *James Francis FORD [2504 Ardmore Street SE, Grand Rapids, MI 49506, USA], *b* Grand Rapids 11 Aug 1927; *educ* Coll of Optometry, Chicago; optometrist; *m* 28 May 1949 *Barbara Brunner and has issue:

President Ford's half nieces and -nephews
1 *Martha Ford [Mrs Terry Hastings, Toledo, OH 43601, USA], *b* 9 March 1950; *m* 15 April 1972 *Terry HASTINGS
2 *Emily Clare Ford, *b* 13 Sept 1951; *m* 25 Aug 1979 *James TREMOULIS
3 *Robert J. FORD, *b* 19—; *educ* E Grand Rapids High Sch and Central Michigan U
4 *John Gregory FORD, *b* 19—; *educ* Woodcliff Sch, E Grand Rapids

Leslie Lynch King *m* 2nd Reno, Nev., 1919, as her 1st husb, Margaret Atwood of Los Angeles (*b* 1891; *m* 2nd 1949 Roy Mather (*d* 1954), copy editor on Los Angeles *Times*) and *d* Tucson, Ariz., 18 Feb 1941 (*bur* Forest Lawn Cemetery, Glendale, Calif.), having had further issue:

V *Marjorie B. King, *b* 1921; *m* 19— *Alton WERNER, of Cumberland, Md., Personnel Dir Kelly-Springfield Tyre Co, and has two children
VI Leslie ('Bud') Henry KING, *b* Glendale, Calif., 28 March 1923; manager Goodyear Rubber Center, Cookeville, Tenn.; *m* 14 Aug 1943 *Virginia Hodges and was *k* nr Lebanon, Tenn., 2 Dec 1976, having had issue:

1 *Leslie ('Buddy') Henry KING, Jr
2 *Craig Hodges KING
3 *Pam King; *m* *Hubie SMITH
4 *Kyra KING

VII *Patricia Jane KING [Balboa Island, CA 91380, USA], *b* 1925

John Gardner
fl c 1781

Alexander Hartridge   Janet Hartridge

Margaret Scott

William Brodie
fl c 1720
Janet Orr   Robert Brodie
                                       c 1735-1836

John Burns   Margaret Burns
                                       c 1744-*c* 1789

— —

Daniel Ayer
1743-1805
Sarah Adams   Samuel Ayer
b 1743   1777-1847
William Chase   Polly Chase
1756-1838   1784-1854
Abigail Gove
1761-1844

Wines Manney
1730-1811
Aeltje/Alida
Vanderburgh   John Manney
1741-1817   1763-1839
Hezekiah Collins, Jr   Elizabeth Collins
1739-*c* 1828   1774-1851
Rhoda Ricketson
1748-*c* 1828

                                       Daniel Butler

Anselm Comstock   Betsey Comstock
1762-1845   1795-1857
Elizabeth Jewett
1771-1860

Jonathan Gridley, Jr
b 1726
Martha Adams   Theodore Gridley
                                       c 1757-*c* 1826

Wells Ely   Amy Ely
c 1729-in/*a* 1804   *c* 1777-*c* 1876
Rebecca Selden
b c 1730-35

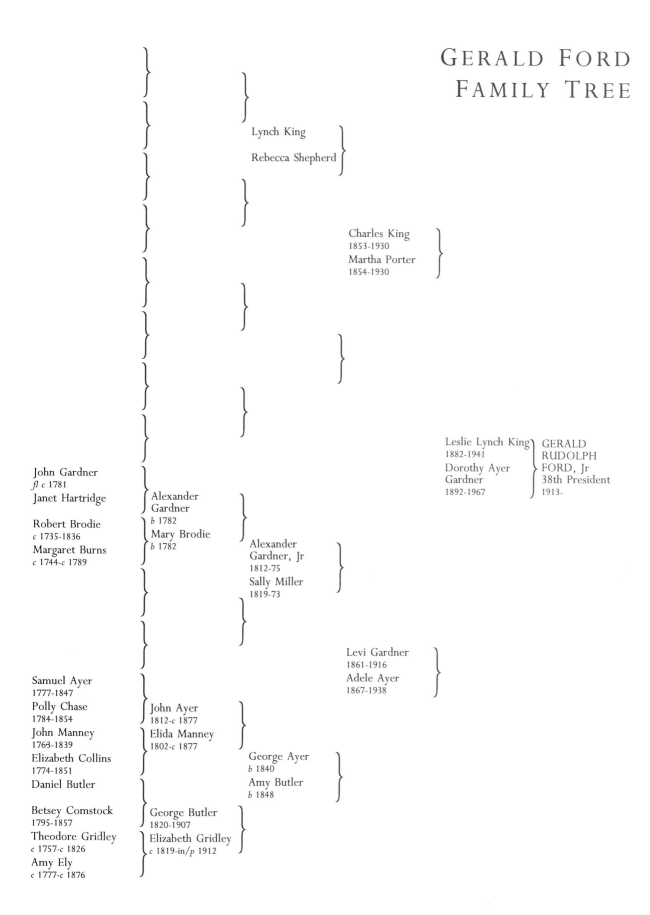

GERALD FORD
FAMILY TREE

Lynch King

Rebecca Shepherd

Charles King
1853-1930
Martha Porter
1854-1930

Leslie Lynch King
1882-1941
Dorothy Ayer
Gardner
1892-1967

GERALD
RUDOLPH
FORD, Jr
38th President
1913-

John Gardner
fl c 1781
Janet Hartridge

Robert Brodie
c 1735-1836
Margaret Burns
c 1744-*c* 1789

Alexander
Gardner
b 1782
Mary Brodie
b 1782

Alexander
Gardner, Jr
1812-75
Sally Miller
1819-73

Levi Gardner
1861-1916
Adele Ayer
1867-1938

Samuel Ayer
1777-1847
Polly Chase
1784-1854
John Manney
1763-1839
Elizabeth Collins
1774-1851

John Ayer
1812-*c* 1877
Elida Manney
1802-*c* 1877

George Ayer
b 1840
Amy Butler
b 1848

Daniel Butler

Betsey Comstock
1795-1857
Theodore Gridley
c 1757-*c* 1826
Amy Ely
c 1777-*c* 1876

George Butler
1820-1907
Elizabeth Gridley
c 1819-in/*p* 1912

Plate 122   Jimmy Carter

JIMMY CARTER

1924-
39TH PRESIDENT OF THE UNITED STATES OF AMERICA
1977-81

Nothing more surely marked the progress of America in certain respects than the election of Jimmy Carter to the presidency; nothing more surely showed what still needed to be done than his difficulties in that office.

In the first place, he could not have had the nomination without the new system for presidential primaries adopted by the Democratic Party. The most important new rule laid it down that convention delegates from each state must be apportioned according to the number of votes cast for each candidate; it was no longer to be a matter of winner take all. This meant that the candidate who had built up a nationwide organization patiently over the years and had somewhat pleased the voters could expect to bring a solid block of votes to the convention. In Jimmy Carter's case, because of the hopeless confusion and inefficiencies of his rivals, he was able to bring a majority.

Secondly, he would never have been elected but for the support of the blacks in the South. This was really remarkable, for Jimmy Carter was a Southern white. However, Lyndon Johnson's Voting Rights Act of 1965 had given the votes to the blacks and they had turned it into power. Even though Carter was a Georgian, the first candidate from the Deep South to have a chance of the presidency since Zachary Taylor, he was too palpably a liberal on the race issue for many Southern whites. But that was precisely his appeal to the Southern blacks. The number of whites who stayed with him was sufficient; he carried the South and with it the election.

Carter meant to be a new sort of President. He had earned his living for years as a peanut farmer, but his real identification was with the Navy. He had been through the Annapolis Naval Academy, he had been trained as a submarine officer and he had some knowledge of nuclear physics. He lived in a problem-solving world; his strong Baptist faith told him that goodness would carry him through. He had campaigned against Washington: against Watergate and all it stood for, against a remote Congress, a corrupt presidency and an unresponsive bureaucracy. He blew on his trumpets but when he got to Jericho after the election the walls were still standing.

He had not won by a very large majority and members of Congress, a good many of whom had been returned unopposed, could feel that they were as legitimate as he. They expected to be courted as in the past. For much of the time they were not; the President foolishly left them to the attentions of the ever more active lobbyists for special interests; when they were at last approached it was done without conviction. The sort of thing that the Washington press corps loves to gossip about — who is in, who is out of favour at the White House — did not matter very much. What did was that even when Carter was right and had a useful policy to propose he found it extremely difficult to get his way with Congress, though his own party was in a majority there. He did not understand its point of view and so was no good at getting it to share his. Meanwhile several nasty problems (economic ones especially) required concerted action and did not get it.

The impression that Carter was out of his depth spread from Washington to the whole country but since in spite of appearance he was a competent as well as a decent man, he might have bounced back, winning his countrymen's respect as Lincoln and Truman had done after equally uninspiring starts. He scored a great diplomatic triumph in 1978 when, after marathon negotiating sessions at Camp David, the president of Egypt and the Prime Minister of Israel signed agreements of peace and conciliation between their countries. But the following year, in the convulsions of the Iranian Revolution, a mob seized the US Embassy in Teheran and made hostages of the embassy staff. Neither negotiations nor force (a rescue expedition was botched) succeeded in rescuing the hostages and this event more than any other convinced the electorate that the country was not safe in Carter's hands. It was an impression reinforced when the President expressed surprise as well as outrage on hearing of the Soviet invasion of Afghanistan. For a while it seemed possible that his party would deny him renomination. He was spared that humiliation, but in the autumn of 1980 he was decisively rejected, and with what seemed like calculated cruelty the Iranians did not release the hostages, although negotiations continued uninterruptedly until the day after Carter's successor had taken the oath of office. Not since 1933 had a President gone so discredited into retirement.

JIMMY CARTER'S FAMILY

In his book *Why Not the Best?*, a mixture of autobiography and explanation of his political outlook, Jimmy Carter stressed the primitive conditions of farm life in his youth. Certainly there was no electricity until the late 1930s; that was true, however, for many country areas not only in the US but in Western Europe, not excluding the British Isles, where some areas were only electrified in the 1950s. Carter's mother Miss Lillian painted a more prosperous picture when she revealed that the family employed a cook and nanny, also that her husband had bought a 700-acre farm in 1927, when Jimmy was only three, and later added 3,300 acres to make up a holding of 4,000 acres. Though this might not be able to compete with the 825,000-acre King Ranch in Texas, it was substantial enough, particularly if the land was more fertile than in Texas. There was a history of land-ownership in the Carter family dating back to Kindred Carter, Jimmy's great-great-great-great-grandfather, who in the late 18th century owned a plantation of just over 300 acres in northeast Georgia, and descending through Kindred's eldest son James, who moved a little further southwest into Georgia and acquired a 500-acre plantation. This was slightly bigger than the average in that state at the time of his death just before the Civil War. Any family connection with Robert 'King' Carter, the 17th-century Virginia magnate, is probable rather than proven but if it is ever proven would add to the landowning tradition.

James's son Wiley was the first Carter to settle in Schley County, which lies some 20 miles north of Plains, and Jimmy Carter in his autobiographical writings mentions — with evident pride — that his children will eventually be the sixth generation to own the same land. A more distressing tradition was the Carter involvement in violence, though the involvement was often passive and the South is and always has been a violent place. Wiley Carter stood trial for murder, though he got off. His second son Littleberry Carter, Jimmy's great-grandfather, was killed in a brawl. Littleberry's son William Archibald Carter, Jimmy's grandfather, was shot fatally in the street by his former business partner Will Taliaferro. (Taliaferro had rented an office from William Carter but had then moved out, taking one of Carter's desks with him; the incident developed into a dispute and the dispute into a fight. Taliaferro stood trial for manslaughter three times but was never convicted.) Lastly, in our own time Jimmy's nephew William Tody Carter Spann was sentenced to 14 years in Soledad for armed robbery while intoxicated with drugs.

Plate 123 *The Carters shortly after Jimmy Carter's election as President:
l-r top: James Earl ('Chip') Carter III (son), Caron Griffith Carter (daughter-in-law),
John (Jack) Carter (son) holding Jason (grandson), Judy Langford Carter (daughter-in-law),
middle: Rosalynn Smith Carter, Jimmy Carter, Annette Jene Davis Carter (daughter-in-law),
Jeff Carter (son); seated at front Amy Carter (daughter)*

Plate 124 *President Carter concedes defeat in the 1980 election;
with him Rosalynn Smith Carter, Jason Carter (grandson) and Amy;
Jesse Jackson right background*

Jimmy Carter's family had some involvement in politics before his own spectacular one, though on a very minor scale. His father was an early director of the Rural Electrification Administration in their area, was on the county school board and served one year in the Georgia state legislature before dying young of cancer. After his premature death certain political bosses suggested to his widow that she serve out his term of office; 'Miss Lillian' refused. But then James Carter, Sr, had fairly conservative views, unlike his wife, who was to become the most celebrated woman liberal in a presidential family since Eleanor Roosevelt. Miss Lillian's father Jim Jack Gordy had political leanings and though he never ran for office he managed a successful bid for Congress by a fellow Georgian, Tom Watson; Watson later pushed through Congress Jim Jack's pet plan for free postal deliveries in rural areas. Miss Lillian attended the Democratic convention in 1964 and was co-chairman of the Sumter County campaign to elect LBJ. This needed courage in Georgia where LBJ, despite hailing from the South himself, was deeply unpopular with whites over his civil rights stance. During her son's presidential campaign she made over 600 speeches in support. Perhaps more importantly she advised him to moderate the rather sanctimonious tone of his own speeches. After Jimmy Carter became President she represented the US officially at the funerals of Presidents Fukhruddin Ali Ahmed of India and Tito of Yugoslavia. Among Jimmy Carter's generation his cousin Hugh Carter took over the Georgia state senate seat Jimmy vacated when he ran for governor. Jimmy's second son 'Chip' became a member of the Plains city council in the late 1970s. All three of Jimmy Carter's sons worked as unpaid assistants to their father when he was governor of Georgia.

Jimmy Carter reveals that one of the two chief reasons he joined the navy was his hero worship for his uncle Tom Gordy, naval lightweight boxing champion in the late 1930s. The other was the knowledge he would get a college education at Annapolis — the same motivation that operated with Eisenhower and Grant at West Point. He was a competent naval officer and the life of a navy wife appealed to Rosalynn. When Earl Carter died and she and Jimmy talked the future over, she was reluctant to head back to Plains and take over the family business. She was, Jimmy Carter claims, his first and only true love, indeed the girl next door inasmuch as she too had been brought up in Plains (she was a friend of his sister Ruth's). The statement is unexceptionable. But when he added later that he had committed adultery in his heart he became an object of ridicule.

Rosalynn's family had been settled in the Plains area since before the Civil War, the earliest ancestor to settle there being one Drury Murray, who was born in 1787. Her father had a very modest amount of public service experience as a Plains city councillor. Like her mother-in-law Miss Lillian among the Gordys Rosalynn seems to have been the first woman among the Smiths to go in for politics actively. She and her husband's political partnership has been described as without equal since that of the Franklin Roosevelts. Her staff as First Lady numbered 20, then an all-time high. When the Equal Rights Amendment came up for consideration across the various states Rosalynn wrote lobbying letters in support of it to state legislators. She sat in on Cabinet meetings during her husband's presidency and was in general considered one of his most influential advisers, persuading him, for instance, to appoint a 20-man Presidential Commission on Mental Health. (As the President's wife she couldn't be chairman so she was made honorary chairman instead.) She was also thought to have outshone her husband as a public speaker during the 1976 presidential campaign. In 1977 she toured various Caribbean and South American countries, with Washington stressing that her tour was much more than the usual goodwill trip by a First Lady — in fact a serious presidential initiative. She also represented the US at the inauguration of President Portillo of Mexico. At home she returned to the pre-Kennedy custom of serving only wine during White House functions. Under Carter there were more members of the President's family in residence at the White House than at any time since Franklin Roosevelt's day.

Billy Carter seems to have been the odd man out in the Carter family. He was the one who looked after the family business while the others worked to get Jimmy elected Governor of Georgia in 1966.

Desire to do business deals must have gone to his head, for in the middle of his brother's 1980 re-election campaign he accepted $220,000 from the Libyans to improve their country's image in America. It did nothing much for Libya's image and drove Billy's down to rock bottom. He spent the last two years of his life travelling round the country counselling people with fatal illnesses, though arguably it was his life story rather than any homilies he may have delivered that constituted the true lesson.

During his brother's presidency Billy stayed down in Georgia, so was less tractable than Sam Johnson, LBJ's errant brother. Amy, Jimmy and Rosalynn Carter's daughter, the youngest-born and it would seem their Benjamin, was a different matter. She was always being placed in some position or other by her parents. It would have been unfair to call it always a false position, but it must frequently have been a trying, even an uncomfortable one. When her father was Governor of Georgia she was put in the care of a parolee convicted of manslaughter. It showed her parents' faith in those who gave their pledge. The night her father won the Democratic presidential nomination she was woken up and shown to millions on television, yawning to the cameras in a way that was piteous to see. When her father became President she was sent to a tough inner-city school in Washington. It demonstrated her parents' freedom from prejudice. She showed her own freedom from hidebound attitudes by twice reading a book at table when a guest at official presidential dinners. In a televized debate a week before the 1980 presidential election her father quoted her opinion that nuclear weaponry and its control was the most important issue. His advisers had been against it but he thought it personalized things. Amy's opinion was a perfectly reasonable one, but the way her father brought it into public debate probably did him damage. It certainly made her seem precocious and priggish. She seemed more a symbol of her parents' devotion to ideals than their means of achieving limited but concrete improvement, even if only in one small corner of the world, and so appeared dehumanized. From having been the archetypal Awful Child she managed in her later career to acquire a reputation as the Awful Adolescent, getting herself arrested for taking part in demonstrations ("she was only arrested four times" her father said) and being asked to leave Brown University for hyper-activism (not to be confused with hyper-activity). The general feeling, unfortunately, was that the Carters had nobody to blame but themselves.

BIOGRAPHICAL DETAILS AND DESCENDANTS

CARTER, JAMES (JIMMY) EARL [The Carter Center, One Copenhill, Atlanta, GA 30307, USA], b Plains, Ga., 1 Oct 1924; educ Plains High Sch, Georgia Southwestern U and Georgia Inst of Technology, US Naval Acad Annapolis, Md. (BS 1947), and Union Coll, Schenectady, New York; served USN 1947-52 (Ensign 1947, Jr Lt 1950, Sr Lt 1952), peanut farmer and warehouseman 1953-77, Memb: Sumter Co Sch Bd 1955-62 (Chm 1960-62), Americus and Sumter Co Hosp Authority 1956-70, Sumter Co Library Bd 1961, Georgia State Senator 1963-67, Pres: Plains Devpt Corp and Sumter Co Devpt Corp 1963, Georgia Planning Assoc 1968, Chm West Centl Georgia Area Planning & Devpt Cmmn 1964, Dir Georgia Crop Improvement Assoc 1957-63 (Pres 1961), Govr Georgia 1971-75, Chm Congressional Campaign Ctee, Democratic Nat Ctee, 1974, 39th President (D) of the USA 1977-81, Fndr Carter Center, Emory U, Ga., 1982 (Chm Bd of Tstees, Carter Center Inc, 1986-), Distinguished Prof Emory U 1982-, Memb Bd Dirs Habitat for Humanity 1984-87, Chm: Carter-Menil Human Rights Fndn 1986-, Global 2000 Inc 1986-, official observer Nicaraguan Elections 1990, Hon LLD: Morehouse Coll 1972, Morris Brown Coll 1972, Notre Dame 1977, Emory U 1979, Kwansei Gakuim U, Japan, 1981, Georgia Southwestern U 1981, New York Law Sch 1985, Bates Coll 1985, Hon DE Georgia Inst of Technology 1979, Hon PhD: Weizmann Inst of Science 1980, Tel Aviv U 1983, Haifa U 1987, Hon DHL: Central U 1985, Connecticut State U 1985, awarded Internat Inst for Human Rights gold medal 1979, Harry S. Truman Public Service Award 1981, Wilderness Soc's Ansel Adams Conservation Award 1982, Southern Baptist Convention's Distinguished Service Award 1982, Internat League for Human Rights' Human Rights Award 1983, Albert Schweitzer Prize for Humanitarianism 1987, Philadelphia Liberty Medal 1990; author: *Why Not the Best?* (1975) (autobiography), *A Government as Good as its People* (1977), *Keeping Faith: memoirs of a President* (1982), *The Blood of Abraham* (1985), (with Rosalynn Carter) *Everything to Gain; making the most of the rest of your life* (1987), *An Outdoor Journal* (1988); m Plains 7 July 1946 *Rosalynn (b there 18 Aug 1927; educ Georgia Southwestern Coll; sometime memb Georgia Govr's Commission to Improve Service for the Mentally and Emotionally Handicapped, author: *First Lady from Plains* (1984)), dau of W(ilburn) Edgar Smith (*d* 22 Oct 1940, of leukaemia), of Plains, school bus driver, store assistant and mechanic, and his w Allathea ('Miss Allie') Murray, and has issue:

President Carter's son
I *John ('Jack') William CARTER, *b* Portsmouth, Va., July 1947; *educ* Georgia Inst of Technology and Georgia U Law Sch; served with US forces in Vietnam, attorney in Calhoun, Ga.; *m* 1st 1971 (divorce 19——) Judy Langford, of Calhoun, and has issue:

> Grandchildren
> 1 *Jason James CARTER, *b* 7 Aug 1975
> 2 *Sarah Rose Mary CARTER, *b* 19 Dec 1978

President Carter's sons
I (cont.) John W. Carter *m* 2nd *c* 1992, as her 2nd husb, *Elizabeth Brasfield (who *m* 1st —— Chuldenkl and with him has two children, John and Sarah), of Chagrin Falls, Ohio
II *James Earl ('Chip') CARTER III, *b* Honolulu, Hawaii, 12 April 1950; sometime Memb Plains City Cncl; *m* 1st 1973 (divorce 29 Feb 1980) Caron Griffin, of Hawkinsville, Ga., and has issue:

> Grandchildren
> 1 *James Earl CARTER IV, *b* Plains 25 Feb 1977

President Carter's son
II (cont.) James E Carter III *m* 2nd *c* 1982 *Ginger Hodges, of Americus, Ga., and has further issue:

> Grandchildren
> 2 *Margaret Alicia CARTER, *b* 23 Sept 1987

President Carter's son
III *(Donnel) Jeffrey (Jeff) CARTER, *b* New London, Conn., 18 Aug 1952; *educ* Georgia State U; *m* 1975 *Annette Jene Davis, of Arlington, Ga., and has issue:

> Grandchildren
> 1 *Joshua Jeffrey CARTER, *b* 8 May 1984
> 2 *Jeremy Davis CARTER, *b* 25 June 1987
> 3 *James Carlton CARTER, *b* 24 April 1991

President Carter's daughter
V *Amy Lynn CARTER, *b* Plains 19 Oct 1967; *educ* Brown U and art coll in Tennessee; sometime worker in bronze sculpture workshop

Male Line Ancestry and Collateral Descendants

Moore CARTER, *b* Isle of Wight Co, Va., *c* 1680; moved to Bertie Co, North Carolina, and *d* there *c* 1741. He has been described by the genealogist Gary Boyd Roberts as "probably" son of Thomas Carter, who *d* at some point after his will was completed in 1710, and Thomas's w Magdalene Moore. This Thomas Carter, the third of his name, was s of Thomas Carter, Jr, and a wife Eleanor, maiden name unknown. Thomas Carter, Jr, was in turn s of Thomas Carter, of Isle of Wight Co., Va., who *d* 1660. The genealogist Noel Currer-Briggs suggests there may be kinship between President Carter and Robert ('King') Carter, ancestor of the Harrison Presidents, through John Carter, brother of the first Thomas Carter and father of Robert. The brothers John and Thomas Carter may in their turn have been sons of John Carter, a wine-seller in Newgate Street, in the London parish of Christchurch, but this is not proven. The first Thomas Carter emigrated to Virginia in 1637, where he settled on the James River, Isle of Wight Co.

Moore CARTER *m* Jane —— and left issue:

Isaac CARTER, of Bertie County; *m c* 1742 Sarah Browne, widow of John Battle, also of Bertie Co, and dau of Samuel Browne (*d* Isle of Wight Co between 17 Oct 1739 and 23 June 1740), and *d* after 1790, leaving (with other issue):

Kindred CARTER, *b* probably in North Carolina *c* 1750; *m* —— and *d* Columbia Co (now McDuffie Co), Ga., *c* 1800, having had three s and one dau. The eldest s:

James CARTER, *b* North Carolina *c* 1773; *m* Columbia Co, Ga., 31 Jan 1798 Eleanor ('Nellie') (*b* probably Wilkes or Richmond Co, Ga., *c* 1780; *d* in or after 1820), dau of Jeremiah Duckworth, of Warren and Columbia Cos, Ga., and his w Christiana Ramsey, and *d* Schley Co, Ga., 19 July 1858, leaving (with four yr s and four daus):

Wiley CARTER, *b c* 1798; *m* 1st Warren County 18 Feb 1821 Ann (*b* Warren Co *c* 1801; *d* Warren Co *c* 1848), dau of Abel Ansley, of the Rock House, Warren Co, and his w Lydia, dau of Job Morris, and had four s and seven daus; *m* 2nd Warren

Co 1848 Mrs Sarah Wilson, widow, of Newton Co, Ga. (who *m* 3rd —— Ross and *d* 1870), and *d* Schley Co 4 March 1864, being the first Carter to be buried in the family plot. His 2nd s by his 1st w:

Littleberry Walker CARTER, *b* nr Plains *c* 1832; moved to Sumter Co, Ga., *c* 1860, enlisted Capt Cutts's Company, Sumter Flying Artillery, 1862 and served in Va. during Civil War; *m* Warren Co 5 Jan 1851 Mary Ann Diligent (*b c* 1838; *d* Sumter Co 27 or 28 Nov 1873 — the same night as her husb), dau of William Archibald Seals, of Warren Co, and his w Eliza Harris, and was *k* Warren Co 27 or 28 Nov 1873 in a brawl at a carnival, leaving (with an er s and two daus):

William Archibald CARTER, *b* 12 Nov 1858; *m* Abbeville Co, South Carolina, 8 Sept 1885 Nina (*b* Abbeville Co, 5 Dec 1863; *d* Plains 8 March 1939), dau of James Earl Pratt, of Abbeville Co, and his w Sophronia Cowan, and *d* Arlington, Ga., 4 Sept 1903 of gunshot wounds inflicted at Rowena, Ga. (five mi south of Arlington) following a dispute with his business partner, leaving (with three daus):

I Alton CARTER, *b c* 1888, antique dealer
II (James) Earl CARTER, for whom *see below*

The yr son,

(James) Earl CARTER, *b* Calhoun Co, Ga., 12 Sept 1894; *educ* Riverside Acad, Gainesville, Ga.; 1st Lt World War I, cowboy, farmer and peanut-broker; *m* Sumter Co 26 or 27 Sept 1923 (Bessie) Lillian (*b* Richland, Ga., 15 Aug 1898; fraternity house mother Auburn U, Ala., nurse, nursing home manager 1962-64, Peace Corps volunteer in India 1966-69; *d* Americus, Ga., 30 Oct 1983), 3rd dau of James Jackson (Jim Jack) Gordy, postmaster, and his w Mary Ida, dau of Nathaniel Nunn Nicholson, and *d* Plains 22 July 1953 of cancer, leaving issue:

I JAMES EARL CARTER, Jr, 39th PRESIDENT of the UNITED STATES of AMERICA
II Gloria Carter, *b* Plains 1926; art teacher; *m* 1st July 1945 (divorce 1949) 1st Lt William Everett HARDY (served USAF World War II, POW, awarded Presidential Citation, Air Medal, Purple Heart and four Bronze Stars) and had issue:

President Carter's nephew
1 *William Tody Carter SPANN, *b* 1947 as Hardy but later adopted by his stepf Walter Spann; was in the early 1980s serving 14 years in Soledad Prison, Calif., for armed robbery while under the influence of drugs

II (cont.) Gloria Carter Hardy *m* 2nd 1950 *Walter SPANN, of Plains, farmer, and *d* before 12 March 1990
III *Ruth Carter, *b* Plains 7 Aug 1929; evangelist; *m* 1948 *Robert (Bobby) STAPLETON, veterinarian, of Fayetteville, N Carolina, and has four children
IV William (Billy) Alton CARTER, *b* Plains 29 March 1937; *educ* Emory U; Private, Marine Corps, 1955-59; *m* 1955 *Sybil Spires (*b c* 1940; *educ* Plains High Sch) and *d* 25 Sept 1988, having had six children

Kindred Carter[1]
c 1750-*c* 1800

— —
   James Carter
   c 1773-1858

Jeremiah Duckworth
   Eleanor Duckworth
   c 1780-in/*p* 1820

Christiana Ramsey

Thomas Ansley
c 1737-1809

Rebecca Cox/Cocke
c 1733-1814
   Abel Ansley
   c 1761-62—1822

Job Morris
c 1740-86
   Lydia Morris
   c 1770-75—1838

Mary Ansley
c 1745-*c* 1815-17

William Seals
d c 1827

Judith (?Powell)
   Spencer Seals
   c 1780-*c* 1847

Henry Burnley
c 1756—1831-35
   Elizabeth Burnley
   c 1786-in/*a* 1831

Lucy Barksdale
c 1756-*c* 1803

   Nathan Harris
   d 1822

John Champion?
   Rhoda Champion
   d 1850

— —

William Pratt
c 1734-97

Mary Drennan?
d p 1797
   James Pratt
   1788-1828

Robert Lindsay
   Sara Lindsay
   1790-1840

— —

James Kay
c 1760-*p* 1820

Grace Elgin
c 1758-*p* 1820
   Revd James Kay
   1787-1857

Francis Clinkscales
c 1748-1837 same as (a)
   Elizabeth Clinkscales
   1788-1850

Mary Carpenter
d in/*a* 1831 same as (b)

Andrew Cowan
c 1742—86-89

Ann —
c 1745-*c* 1831
   Isaac Cowan
   c 1765-1831

James Seawright
c 1745—89-90
   Jane Seawright
   1771-1859

Elizabeth McCullough
d in/*a* 1789

Francis Clinkscales
(a)

Mary Carpenter
(b)
   Francis Clinkscales
   1786-1858

George Brownlee
c 1757-1836
   Eleanor Brownlee
   c 1791-1831

Sarah Caldwell
c 1758-1826

Peter Gordy, Jr
d a 1788

Ellinor —
d in/*a* 1797
   Peter Gordy III
   d c 1844

Samuel Wilson
d 1799-1803
   Ruth Wilson
   d p 1844

— —

Perry Scott
b 1755

Barbara —
   John R. Scott
   1776-1860

   Rebecca Radney
   1773-1851

George Helms
c 1720-25—48-49

Mary Falkenborough
b c 1735
   George Helms, Jr
   c 1758—1837-38

Thomas Pressley
d 1808
   Sarah Pressley
   d a 1837?

Sarah —

Charles Fisher
d in/*p* 1814

Barbara —
   William Fisher
   c 1760-1835

William Phillips
c 1730-in/*p* 1815
   Nancy Phillips
   d in/*a* 1849

Lussy —

William Nunn
c 1713-in/*p* 1787

Elizabeth Loftin
   John Nunn
   c 1745-46-*c* 1836

   Eliza Pratt

Jonathan Dawson
d c 1750

Frances Rouse
   Jonathan Dawson, Jr
   c 1750-in/*p* 1824

Wright Nicholson
c 1740-1807
   Repsy Nicholson

— —

John Brown
c 1760-*c* 1814

Mildred Gaines
b 1761
   Hollinger Brown
   1785-1859

Daniel Marcus
c 1763-*c* 1818
   Sarah Marcus
   1789-1851

Mary —
d in/*p* 1832

JIMMY CARTER FAMILY TREE

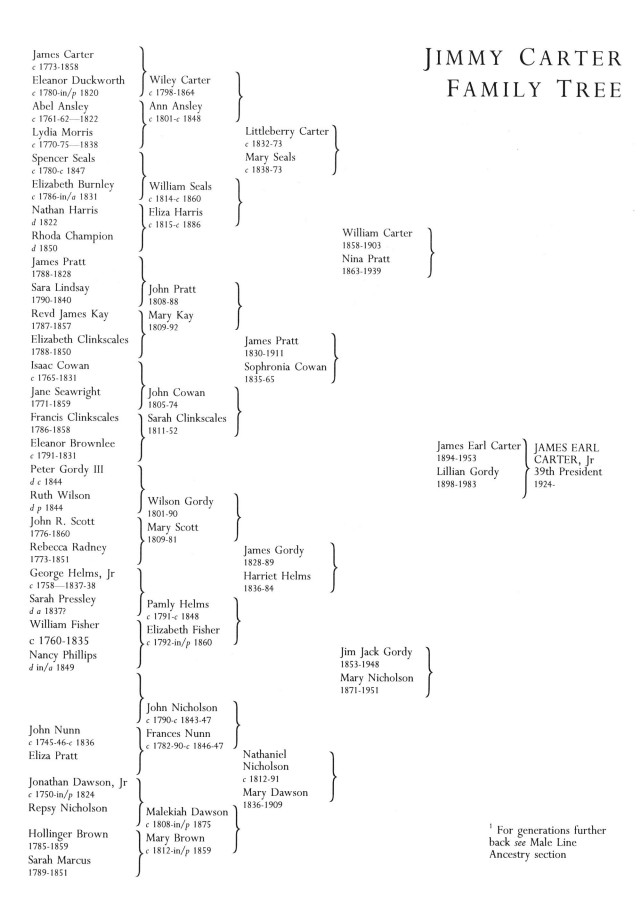

James Carter
c 1773-1858

Eleanor Duckworth
c 1780-in/*p* 1820

Wiley Carter
c 1798-1864

Abel Ansley
c 1761-62—1822

Ann Ansley
c 1801-*c* 1848

Lydia Morris
c 1770-75—1838

Littleberry Carter
c 1832-73

Spencer Seals
c 1780-*c* 1847

Mary Seals
c 1838-73

Elizabeth Burnley
c 1786-in/*a* 1831

William Seals
c 1814-*c* 1860

Nathan Harris
d 1822

Eliza Harris
c 1815-*c* 1886

William Carter
1858-1903

Rhoda Champion
d 1850

Nina Pratt
1863-1939

James Pratt
1788-1828

Sara Lindsay
1790-1840

John Pratt
1808-88

Revd James Kay
1787-1857

Mary Kay
1809-92

Elizabeth Clinkscales
1788-1850

James Pratt
1830-1911

Isaac Cowan
c 1765-1831

Sophronia Cowan
1835-65

Jane Seawright
1771-1859

John Cowan
1805-74

Francis Clinkscales
1786-1858

Sarah Clinkscales
1811-52

Eleanor Brownlee
c 1791-1831

James Earl Carter
1894-1953

JAMES EARL
CARTER, Jr
39th President
1924-

Peter Gordy III
d c 1844

Lillian Gordy
1898-1983

Ruth Wilson
d p 1844

Wilson Gordy
1801-90

John R. Scott
1776-1860

Mary Scott
1809-81

Rebecca Radney
1773-1851

James Gordy
1828-89

George Helms, Jr
c 1758—1837-38

Harriet Helms
1836-84

Sarah Pressley
d a 1837?

Pamly Helms
c 1791-*c* 1848

William Fisher
c 1760-1835

Elizabeth Fisher
c 1792-in/*p* 1860

Nancy Phillips
d in/*a* 1849

Jim Jack Gordy
1853-1948

Mary Nicholson
1871-1951

John Nicholson
c 1790-*c* 1843-47

John Nunn
c 1745-46-*c* 1836

Frances Nunn
c 1782-90-*c* 1846-47

Eliza Pratt

Nathaniel
Nicholson
c 1812-91

Jonathan Dawson, Jr
c 1750-in/*p* 1824

Mary Dawson
1836-1909

Repsy Nicholson

Malekiah Dawson
c 1808-in/*p* 1875

Hollinger Brown
1785-1859

Mary Brown
c 1812-in/*p* 1859

Sarah Marcus
1789-1851

[1] For generations further
back *see* Male Line
Ancestry section

Plate 125   Ronald Reagan and his 2nd wife Nancy Davis in the Blue Room of the White House

RONALD REAGAN

1911-
40TH PRESIDENT OF THE UNITED STATES OF AMERICA
1981-89

For 25 years or so Ronald Reagan was the loose cannon on the deck of American presidential politics. He emerged to a sudden national prominence with a highly effective speech supporting Barry Goldwater in the election of 1964. This convinced many rich Californian conservatives that they had found the man they needed to turn the tide of liberalism in the Golden State and, sure enough, he was elected and re-elected Governor in 1966 and 1970. He and his wife and his backers soon turned their thoughts to the White House. In 1980, at his third try, he won the Republican party's nomination and, thanks to President Carter's blunders and ill luck, the election. As President he became so popular that his re-election in 1984 was inevitable: he carried every state except Minnesota. In 1988 he was able to hand on the presidency to his chosen successor.

Reagan did not make this record of electoral success by playing conventional politics. He had been a fairly successful movie actor, though never a top-flight star, and while this profession had trained him in some invaluable skills (he was notably relaxed in front of the television cameras and knew how to exude warmth and sincerity), its chief benefit may have been in inducing his various opponents to underrate him. They seem to have found it impossible to take this ignorant, idle, naive and inexperienced man seriously and discovered their mistake much too late. Reagan only had a few political ideas but he stuck to them tenaciously and put them over convincingly. Like Jimmy Carter he was an anti-Washington candidate, only even more so. Government, he said, was not the solution, it was the problem. He hated Communism, despised liberalism and supposed that America's economic problems could be solved by cutting taxation heavily. These notions were widely shared, especially in the South-Western states; the tax-cutting programme, if enacted, would immediately benefit a great many families. Reagan thus always had a solid basis of political support; his inconspicuous mastery of the political arts of bargaining, intimidation and compromise (when necessary) did the rest. During his first term taxes fell, defence expenditure soared and so did the Federal budget deficit. Professional economists freely predicted that it would all end in tears, but most of the Reagan years were boom years and the voters felt correspondingly cheerful or, to use a key word of the period, comfortable.

He had his critics and they were not all liberal journalists and politicians. With the Reagans, Hollywood and the new rich of Southern California had captured Washington and they meant to enjoy their triumph. Life was one long party. Mrs Reagan was attacked for accepting gifts of expensive dresses from leading clothes designers (she said they were loans) and for spending $200,000 on a new dinner service for the White House (years later she explained she had no choice — the White House was steadily being stripped of china by guests helping themselves to souvenirs). More serious was the scale of corruption in the Reagan administration. It was worse than in the days of Harding and Grant. Reagan seemed blind and deaf to any suggestion that he was somehow to blame for all the sleaze, and the people, in their affection for him, let him get away with it. Early in his presidency he was gravely wounded by an assassin's gun. He behaved with conspicuous gallantry during the attack and the rush to hospital. Either he was very brave or he knew, as an old actor, how to appear very brave, and that was what the situation demanded. The incident should have convinced everyone that Reagan was no trifler when it mattered.

His second term was less trouble-free than his first. A White House plot was discovered which consisted of an attempt to redeem another band of American hostages from the Iranian revolution by agreeing to sell arms to the Iranians; the cash profits from the transaction were to be used to subsidize the 'Contra' rebels in Nicaragua, who were fighting to overthrow the Communist-dominated Sandinista government there. It was a murky affair and unsuccessful; the hostages were not redeemed and the Contras were not victorious. Worse, Reagan had repeatedly said that it was not US policy to barter for hostages; worse still, Congress had outlawed help for the Contras. Everyone's thoughts went back to Watergate; here was a fresh abuse of presidential power needing to be curbed.. But although the law suits resulting from the scandal dragged on for years afterward, no one could summon up the will or the energy to impeach President Reagan; he was a much less tempting target than President Nixon had been. However, he owed the rescue of his reputation to his own efforts and to Mikhail Gorbachev, the leader of the Soviet Union.

During his first term Reagan had famously denounced the USSR as an 'evil empire', and there had been enough ferocious Cold Warriors near him to plunge Soviet-American relations into alarming disarray. But then Gorbachev came to power and Reagan gradually formed the opinion that it was possible to make friends. The evident weakening of Soviet power and will convinced him that the Cold War was over and that America had won. Other forces were at work but it was undoubtedly Reagan who, by swallowing the words and attitudes of his entire public career, made the initial reversal of relations possible. He went to Moscow and the TV cameras showed him beaming amiably in Red Square. The administration launched the long, but ultimately successful, negotiations which began the disarmament of the superpowers and the liberation of Eastern Europe. Communism was now universally seen to be a bankrupt system, while the cult of western democracy seemed to be sweeping all before it. In retrospect it all looked inevitable, but it had taken political instinct of a high order to seize the opportunity when it offered, and it seems likely that in the end Reagan's many faults and weaknesses will not be thought to outweigh this single outstanding achievement.

RONALD REAGAN'S FAMILY

Ronald Reagan's father Jack was a second-generation Catholic Irish-American. He was also overfond of the bottle. Reagan's mother Nelle, a teetotaller of Scots-English ancestry, belonged to an obscure Protestant sect although she and Jack married in a Roman Catholic church. Their elder son Neil, known to the family as 'Moon' because he parted his hair in the middle like a comic-strip character called Moon Mullins, was baptized a Catholic but as Nelle's Protestant piety grew the younger boy Ronald was inducted into her church.

The Irish are popularly supposed to revel in story-telling and the 40th president loved anecdotes, often using one to break the ice when meeting a foreign head of state. He certainly relished his Irish background, frequently joking at Cabinet meetings with Don Regan, first his Treasury Secretary then his Chief of Staff, about their presumed common ancestor. Reagan's love of horses might be ascribed to his Irish ancestry too. While still a badly off young man he trained with the 14th Cavalry Regiment as a reserve officer, chiefly in order to get riding instruction cheaply.

But he was also very much his father's son in being a salesman, though notably successful where his father was not. (Perhaps Republicanism from the 1960s to the 1990s was inherently more marketable

Plate 126   Ronald Reagan and his 1st
wife, the actress Jane Wyman, with their
daughter Maureen, 1942

Plate 127   Reagan family Inaugural group portrait January 1981: l-r top: Nancy's nephew,
Dennis Revell (soon to be Maureen's husband), Michael Reagan holding his son Cameron,
the President, Neil Reagan (brother), Richard Davis (Nancy's brother), Ron Jr,
bottom: Nancy's niece, Maureen, Colleen (Michael's wife), Nancy, Bess Reagan
(Neil's wife), Mrs Richard Davis, Patti and Doria Reagan (Ron Jr's wife)

than shoes in the Depression.) It seems to have been his father who originated the sobriquet 'Dutch' in reference to Ronald's sturdy appearance as a baby, supposedly characteristic of a little Dutchman.

Nelle became more devout as she got older, but her brand of Protestantism tolerated the stage. She was active in a local amateur dramatic society and even persuaded her husband to join in. Ronald was therefore introduced to acting from an early age. By high school he easily surpassed his fellows as an actor. Equally valuable for Ronald's career were the good speaking voice and excellent memory for texts Nelle passed on to him. She used to travel the surrounding countryside giving public readings of poetry and plays. She also gave her younger son elocution lessons, which he built on when he studied rhetoric his first year at Eureka College. Although Ronald Reagan was a superb reader of prepared speeches, he was equally effective in ad-libbing. His experience as a radio sports commentator helped here, for not only are games among the least predictable of human activities but commentators in the 1930s were usually studio-based and had sometimes to make up what was going on when the wire service was out of action. Even to win the job in the first place he had had to create his own script as he went along.

Nancy Reagan has maintained her husband was on the verge of becoming a front-rank film star when the War interrupted his acting career. Less partisan accounts suggest he could never quite immerse himself in a role enough to become more than, as he himself engagingly put it, the "Erroll Flynn of the B movies". With one exception. He made four films as Brass Bancroft of the Secret Service and a decade later served in real life as an FBI informer. In a 1950s film he played an undercover army officer and in one of the General Electric Theater television shows he both compered and starred in he played an informer during the Irish Civil War of the 1920s. Few actors can so satisfyingly have merged reality and make-believe. There even seems to have been a family leaning toward undercover work. Ronald's brother 'Moon' prepared reports for the FBI in 1946, when there was allegedly Communist infiltration of the lobby group HICCASP (Hollywood Independent Citizens' Committee of Arts, Sciences & Professions). 'Moon' was one of the close family circle who urged Reagan to get into politics. He also helped prolong his brother's acting career at a time when it was in terminal decline.

By the time Ronald Reagan reached the White House he was also a highly experienced negotiator. Not only had this most conservative of Presidents been a trade union leader as President of the Screen Actors Guild (to which body he was introduced by his first wife Jane Wyman), he even led a successful six-month strike in 1959. And the man whose political career took off when the 'Silent Majority' became appalled by student unrest in the '60s had led a successful college revolt as a freshman in 1928. Margaret Truman remembers him as a rather left-wing Democrat at the time of her father's election campaign in 1948, and Maureen Reagan once reminded her father that she had been a Republican longer than he had. Once he got going, though, he quickly rose to the top of the Party. His adoptive son Michael records how his father's 1976 convention speech, which came after Ford's nomination, sparked an ovation and lingered in the minds of the faithful till 1980 (when the followers of Ford, following Reagan's nomination, are said by Michael Reagan to have tried to pressure Ronald Reagan into adopting Ford as a running mate, but with equal status, not as a junior partner).

Undoubtedly the most fascinating aspect of Ronald Reagan's presidency from the family point of view is his wife Nancy. Many are the accounts of her time as First Lady. Many are suspect. Don Regan, in contrast, comes across as authoritative. He claims Nancy intervened on such important matters as (1) a State of the Union speech, excising passages on Iran and abortion; (2) when to sack William Casey, head of the CIA, following his brain haemorrhage; (3) candidates for such senior White House staff positions as the Directorship of Communications; (4) the removal of the Secretary of Labor. He even says Nancy Reagan personally sacked a staff member on behalf of the President because the latter was too tender-hearted to do so himself. It now seems fairly clear she got Don Regan himself sacked. She was reported as having delayed her husband's endorsement of Bush in the spring of 1988 out of dislike and mistrust for Bush personally. At the time that looked like the typically feminine tendency to let personal feelings rule policy. Four years later her judgement of Bush's presidential qualifications looked reasonably sound. She certainly concerned herself over White House staff levels, wanting to keep attendants down to 18 instead of the much larger number usual in recent years.

Then there are the accounts of how she consulted astrologers and how presidential schedules had to be arranged to accommodate what star-gazers decreed as 'good' or 'bad' days for doing business. Florence Harding had dabbled in astrology during her husband's term of office but was not on the same plane of influence as Nancy, and Eisenhower is said by Alice Roosevelt Longworth to have consulted an astrologer before deciding whether to run for President in the first place. This was something else. Not since Rasputin guided the destinies of Tsar Nicholas II, his empire and his family, or possibly since table-turning at the court of Napoleon III, had the occult played such a part in governing a major power. Yet despite Nancy's absurdity, the deep mutual love of husband and wife undoubtedly kept Reagan relaxed. That this was important became obvious under Reagan's successor, George Bush, whose frenetic activity hampered his effectiveness. Michael Reagan reports that Nancy was always very intuitive, which makes one wonder why she needed an astrologer at all.

In purely family terms Nancy had a more extensive connection with acting than her husband: her mother was a professional stage actress and a great friend of the silent film star Alla Nazimova, who was Nancy's godmother. Other family friends included Walter Huston, the actor father of the film director John Huston, the character actress Zasu Pitts and Spencer Tracy. Zasu Pitts got Nancy her first break in showbusiness and indoctrinated her with anti-Communism. Her stepfather Loyal Davis's strong conservatism rubbed off on her too. Davis early on joined 'Moon' Reagan in suggesting his son-in-law enter politics, and was ready to raise $200,000 for a war chest. Nancy claims she met Ronald Reagan in 1949 at a time when strenuous efforts were being made to clear the film industry of supposedly Communist influence. The name Nancy Davis had apparently turned up in a list of Communist sympathizers. Nancy was anxious to establish that she knew nothing about politics and that this was just a namesake. To get acting union support she says she saw the then President of the Screen Actors Guild, the man who was to be her husband. Another source has their first meeting at a dinner party given by the MGM studio head Dore Schary.

For all the slightly shocking experience to old-fashioned Americans of having as president an ex-Hollywood film actor (and not even a major film actor), and for all the jokes made about him abroad, Ronald and Nancy Reagan's professional attention to smartness of turnout in public undoubtedly had its effect. On a state visit to Britain the President went riding with the Queen, a celebrated horsewoman, and turned in an impressive performance (he usually rode English-style anyway, wearing jodhpurs and boots). As far back as when he was Governor of California the Japanese, with what may have been typical canniness but could just as easily have been good luck, had recognized his potential and the Reagans became the first non-head-of-state guests to be received in audience by the Emperor.

There was distinct coolness toward Nancy on the part of the Reagan children, more so from her own flesh-and-blood than her stepchildren where politics was concerned. Patti, of whose relations even with her father a friend once said "They can hardly stand each other", was a political embarrassment with her membership of the anti-nuclear movement, although to be fair she cancelled an appearance at an anti-nuclear rally in 1979 so as not to harm her father's forthcoming bid for the Republican nomination. But after his election she was less restrained. In 1983 she even persuaded her father to give an audience at the White House to Dr. Helen Caldicott, the leader of the anti-nuclear organization Physicians for Social Responsibility. In a magazine article in late 1990 Patti claimed her father's budget cuts had increased homelessness. On another occasion she sold letters her father had written her as a means of raising cash. In contrast Mike and Maureen delivered speeches on behalf of their father from 1976 on. In the 1980 campaign Mike Reagan claims to have stumped 35 states; Ron Jr and Patti, he adds, didn't campaign at all. On the last night of the 1976 Republican national convention anti-Reagan elements took down pro-Reagan posters from the Reagan box, but Mike and Maureen went to the convention centre early next morning and pasted them up again. Maureen, who is the founder and chairman of the Republican Women's Political Action League, later represented her father's administration in an address to the UN explaining America's policy on women. In 1982 she entered the senatorial primary elections in California, and was still avid for a major position in national politics in 1992, when she announced she would seek the Republican nomination for a Congressional seat representing coastal Los Angeles County.

After Reagan's retirement, when reports of unsavoury activities during his administration began to lower his reputation, Nancy became involved too. The Inland Revenue investigated her tendency while First Lady to borrow expensive dresses and jewellery for functions, for in tax terms this amounted to interest-free loans. She had not reported the borrowings as required under the Ethics in Government Act and eventually was said to have had to pay several hundred thousand dollars in back taxes. On a more substantial level, critics of her memoirs noted how in attempting to defend her record she inadvertently showed her President-husband as even less in control than had been suspected at the time.

BIOGRAPHICAL DETAILS AND DESCENDANTS

REAGAN, RONALD WILSON [11000 Wilshire Blvd, Los Angeles, CA 90024, USA; 668 St Cloud Rd, Bel Air, Los Angeles, CA 90077, USA], *b* Tampico, Ill., 6 Feb 1911; *educ* Eureka Coll., Ill. (AB 1932); sports announcer radio station WHO, Des Moines, Iowa, 1932-37, film actor 1937-64: *Love Is On The Air* (1937), *Hollywood Hotel* (1938), *Swing Your Lady* (1938), *Sergeant Murphy* (1938), *Accidents Will Happen* (1938), *Cowboy From Brooklyn* (1938), *Boy Meets Girl* (1938), *Girls On Probation* (1938), *Brother Rat* (with Jane Wyman, for whom *see below*) (1938), *Going Places* (1939), *Secret Service of the Air* (1939), *Dark Victory* (1939), *Code of the Secret Service* (1939), *Naughty But Nice* (1939), *Hell's Kitchen* (1939), *Angels Wash Their Faces* (1939), *Smashing the Money Ring* (1939), *Brother Rat and a Baby* (with Jane Wyman) (1940), *An Angel From Texas* (with Jane Wyman) (1940), *Murder in the Air* (1940), *Knute Rockne — All American* (1940), *Tugboat Annie Sails Again* (with Jane Wyman and Neil Reagan, Ronald's brother) (1940), *Santa Fe Trail* (1940), *The Bad Man* (1941), *Million Dollar Baby* (1941), *Nine Lives Are Not Enough* (1941), *International Squadron* (1941), *Kings Row* (1942), *Juke Girl* (1942), *Desperate Journey* (1942), *This is the Army* (1943), *Stallion Road* (1947), *That Hagen Girl* (1947), *The Voice of the Turtle* (1947), *John Loves Mary* (1949), *Night Unto Night* (1949), *The Girl From Jones Beach* (1949), *It's a Great Feeling* (with Jane Wyman) (1949), *The Hasty Heart* (1950), *Louisa* (1950), *Storm Warning* (1951), *Bedtime for Bonzo* (1951), *The Last Outpost* (1951), *Hong Kong* (1952), *She's Working Her Way Through College* (1952), *The Winning Team* (1952), *Tropic Zone* (1953), *Law and Order* (1953), *Prisoner of War* (1954), *Cattle Queen of Montana* (1954), *Tennessee's Partner* (1955), *Hellcats of the Navy* (with Nancy Davis) (1957), *The Killers* (1964), television actor: G(eneral) E(lectric) Theater's "Long Way 'Round" (10 Oct 1954), "A Turkey for the President" (23 Nov 1958) and the episodes of "Money and the Minister" of 26 Nov 1961 and 7 Jan 1962, in all of which Nancy Davis also appeared, television producer: two episodes of G E Theater's "I Was a Spy" (18 & 25 March 1962) and two of the same sponsor's episodes "My Dark Days — Prelude" of 19 Aug 1962 and "My Dark Days — Aftermath" of 26 Aug 1962; 2nd Lt Cavalry Reserve US Army, subsequently Assist Army Air Force Public Relations World War II (1st Lt 1 Oct 1942, Capt USAAF 1945), Dir Hollywood Independent Citizens Ctee of Arts Sciences & Professions (HICCASP — a pro-FDR lobby group) 1946, six-term Pres Screen Actors Guild (SAG) 1947-52 & 1959-60 (board memb 1941-60, 3rd V-Pres 1946-47, subsequently life memb), two-term Pres Motion Picture Industry Cncl, sometime Hon Mayor Malibu Lake 1953, sometime Hon Mayor Thousand Oaks, mayoral candidate Hollywood; Democrat to 1962, Republican thereafter, sometime head re-election campaign LA mayor Fletcher Bowron, Govr California 1966-74, Chm State Govrs' Assoc 1969, 40th President of the USA 1981-89, Hon GCB (1989), Hon Doctorate George Washington U 1991, Hon Citizen Berlin, Germany, 1992, Hon Dr Mily Science Citadel Mily Coll, Charleston, S Carolina, 1993, author: *Where's The Rest of Me?* (with Richard G. Hubler) (1965) (published in UK as *My Early Life*, 1981), *Abortion and the Conscience of the Nation* (1984), *Speaking My Mind: selected speeches* (1989) and *An American Life* (1990); *m* 1st The Wee Kirk o' the Heather Church, Forest Lawn, Calif., 24/27 Jan 1940 (divorce 28 June 1948), as her 2nd husb, Jane Wyman (*b* St Joseph, Mo., as Sarah Jane Fulks 4 or 5 Jan 1914 or 28 Jan 1917; film actress, Oscar for best actress *Johnny Belinda* 1948, Oscar nominations: *The Yearling* 1947, *The Blue Veil* 1951, *Magnificent Obsession* 1954; *m* 1st New Orleans 29 June 1937 (divorce 10 Nov 1938) Myron Futterman; *m* 3rd 1952 (divorce 1954) and 4th 1961 (divorce 1965) the same man, Fred Karger, composer and musician), dau either of Richard D. Fulks (*d* 25 March 1928), sometime mayor of St Joseph, and his w Emma Reise or Reiss, or of Manning J. Mayfield (*b c* 1895; *d* 21 Jan 1922) and his wife Gladys Hope Christian, and has issue:

President Reagan's daughters

I *Maureen Elizabeth Reagan, *b* Los Angeles 4 Jan 1941; *educ* Marymount Coll, Va.; radio talk show hostess, Fndr and Chm Republican Women's Political Action League, Co-Chm Republican Nat Ctee, author: *First Father, First Daughter*; *m* 1st 1961 (divorce Montgomery, Ala., 1962) John FILIPPONE (*b* New York 1929, sometime memb Washington, DC, police); *m* 2nd Beverly Hills 8 Feb 1964 (divorce July 1968) Davis SILLS, atty and sometime Capt US Marine Corps; *m* 3rd April 1981 *Dennis REVELL

II Christina REAGAN, *b* prematurely 22 June, *d* 25 June 1947

Mr and the first Mrs Reagan also adopted 29 Nov 1945 a son:

a *Michael Edward REAGAN [Sherman Oaks, CA, USA], *b* as John L. Flaugher (s of Irene Flaugher, bit part actress under the name of Betty Arnold (*d* 26 Dec 1985), of Ky., by a USAAF Sergeant) 1942; *educ* San Fernando Valley State Coll, Arizona State U and U of S Calif.; outboard power boat racing world champion 1967, boat salesman, actor, radio reporter, fndr (with 2nd w) MCR International (firm raising funds for special events), author: *On the Outside Looking In* (1988), San Diego TV station chat show host in early 1990s; *m* 1st Hawaii 13 June 1971 (divorce 1973) Julie (*b c* 1953), of Atlanta, Ga., dentist, dau of former Los Angeles Rams football player Duane Putnam, and has issue

Adoptive grandson
i A boy, *b* Jan 1973

a (cont.) Michael E. Reagan *m* 2nd Anaheim, Calif., 7 Nov 1975 *Colleen Sterns and with her has issue:

Adoptive grandchildren
i *Cameron Michael REAGAN, *b* 30 May 1978
ii *Ashley Marie REAGAN, *b* 12 April 1983

RONALD REAGAN *m* 2nd North Hollywood 4 March 1952 (the actor William Holden being best man) Nancy Davis (*b* New York 6 July 1921 or 1923 as Anne Frances Robbins; *educ* Smith; film actress: *The Doctor and the Girl* (1949), *East Side, West Side* (1949), *Shadow on the Wall* (1950), *The Next Voice You Hear* (1950), *Night Into Morning* (1951), *Shadow in the Sky* (1951), *It's a Big Country* (1952), *Donovan's Brain* (1953), *Hellcats of the Navy* (see above), Bd Memb SAG 1951-50, Fndr Foster Grandparent Program (charity for the elderly) and Chairperson Child Help USA (charity for abused children), author: (with Bill Libby) *Nancy* (1980) and (with William Novak) *My Way* (1989)), dau of Kenneth Seymour Robbins, car salesman, and his 1st w Edith Luckett, stage actress (roles included Micah Dow and Lady Babbie in Sir James Barrie, Bart's *The Little Minister*, Ella Delchay in *Charley's Aunt*, Rory in a dramatization of Mark Twain's *Pudd'nhead Wilson*, Michaela in a dramatization of Prosper Mérimée's *Carmen*, Raina in Shaw's *Arms and the Man*, Lovey Mary in *Mrs Wiggs of the Cabbage Patch* and Dearest in a dramatization of Frances Hodgson Burnett's *Little Lord Fauntleroy*; Edith Luckett *m* 2nd 20 or 21 May 1929, as his 2nd w, Loyal Edward Davis, Hon FRCS London and Edinburgh, holder of US Legion of Merit medal, neurosurgeon, who adopted his stepdau Anne 1937; Edith Luckett *d* 1987); with his 2nd w Ronald Reagan has issue:

President Reagan's children

III *Patricia (Patti) Ann DAVIS [c/o Crown Publishers Inc, 225 Park Ave South, New York, NY 10003, USA], *b* 21/22 Oct 1952; *educ* Brentwood Town Sch, Los Angeles, Orme Sch, Ariz., Northwestern U and U of S California at Los Angeles; actress (appearances include roles in film *Curse of the Pink Panther* (1983) and on stage in a Birmingham, Ala., production of *The Pajama Game* (1984)), songwriter as Patti Davis, name she adopted 1974 (hits include "I Wish You Peace", co-written with Bernie Leadon, guitarist with The Eagles, which appeared on the platinum disc-winning Eagles album "One of These Nights" (1975)), author of autobiographical novels *Home Front* (with Maureen Strange Foster) (1984), *Deadfall* (1989) and *A House of Secrets* (1991), also of autobiography *The Way I See It* (1992, UK title: *Family Secrets*), television presenter for NBC's "The Midnight Special" 1981; *m* 14 Aug 1984 (divorce by Feb 1990) Paul Grilley, her yoga teacher

IV *Ron(ald) ('Skipper' or 'Skip') Prescott REAGAN, Jr, *b* 20 May 1958; *educ* Yale and Stanley Holden Dance Center, Los Angeles; dancer with Joffrey and Royal Ballets, sometime assoc ed *Playboy* magazine, reporter ABC TV's "Good Morning America" and presenter BBC TV's "Record Breakers" 1990 and MCA Fox TV's "The Ron Reagan Show" 1991, a topical chat show; *m* New York 24 Nov 1980 *Doria Palmieri (*b* 1951; literary researcher and dancer), dau of a Los Angeles set designer

MALE LINE ANCESTRY AND COLLATERAL DESCENDANTS

Thomas REAGAN, O'REGAN or RYAN, of Ballyporeen, Co Tipperary, Ireland; labourer; *m* Margaret Murphy and *d* before 31 Oct 1852. He may have been the identical Thomas Reagan who was father of:

Michael REAGAN, O'REGAN or RYAN, *bapt* Ballyporeen 3 Sept 1829; emigrated with his w to the USA via Canada, becoming a farmer in Fair Haven, Ill., with property worth $1,120 in 1860 and $3,000 by 1870; *m* St George's Cathedral, London borough of Southwark, 31 Oct 1852 Catherine (*b* Ireland Aug 1829; *d* after 1906?), dau of Patrick Mulcahey (*d* after 31 Oct

1852), also of Ireland, labourer, and *d* Fair Haven, Ill., 2 March 1884; he and his *w* may have been the same Mr and Mrs Michael Reagan who were parents of (along with two other children, who *d* in infancy):

I Thomas REAGAN, *b* Peckham, London, UK, 15 May 1852; *m* 18— Bridget ——— and was drowned (at a Fouth of July picnic?) Carroll Co, Ill., 4 July 1889

II John Michael REAGAN, for whom *see below*

III Margaret Reagan, *b* Peckham 1856; sold 13 Oct 1891 her nephew and ward William's land for $50; *m* 1894 Orson BALDWIN and settled in Buchanan, Iowa, by 1900

IV William REAGAN, *b* Fair Haven 23 Dec 1858; *d* Fulton, Ill., Oct 1883

V Mary Reagan, *b* March 1867; *m*? 18— Edward CHAPMAN (*d* by 1900), (?)s of Emerson Chapman, of Fulton, and his *w* Lorena, and *d* while her children were still young, leaving issue:

　1 William(?) CHAPMAN　2 Marguerite CHAPMAN

The 2nd s,

　John Michael REAGAN, *b* Peckham, London, UK, *c* 1854-55 (29 May 1854?); emigrated 1858 with his parents and became a farmer and worker on a grain elevator; *m* Fulton, Whiteside Co, Ill., 27/28 Feb 1878 Jennie or Jenny (*b* Dixon, Ill., *c* 1856-57; *d* Whiteside Co shortly after 19 Nov 1886 of tuberculosis), dau of Patrick Cusick (*b* Ireland *c* 1825-26; *d* shortly before 17 June 1891) and his *w* Sarah Higgins (*b* Ireland or New York *c* 1835; *d* before 1870), and *d* Fulton 10 Jan 1889 of tuberculosis, having had issue:

I Catherine REAGAN, *b* Fulton 14 July 1879

II William REAGAN, *b* Fulton 7/10 Jan 1881; committed to Watertown Hosp, Ill., 1919 suffering from paranoiac delusion arising from alcoholism, transferred to Dixon State Hosp 12 Aug 1921 and *d* there 19 Sept 1925

III John (Jack) Edward REAGAN, for whom *see below*

IV Anna REAGAN, *b* Fulton 14 May 1885

The yr s,

　John (Jack) Edward REAGAN, *b* Fulton 13 July 1883; shoe salesman; *m* St Emanuel's Catholic Church, Fulton, 8 Nov 1904 Nell(i)e Clyde (*b* Clyde Township/Fulton 24 July 1883; *d* Santa Monica, Calif., 24 or 25 July 1962), 7th and yst child of Thomas Wilson (*b* Clyde, Ill., 28 April 1844; prosperous farmer; *d* Whiteside Co(?) 12 Dec 1909) and his *w* Mary Ann Elsey (*b* Epsom, Surrey, UK, 28 Dec 1843; *d* Whiteside Co 6 Oct 1900), and *d* Hollywood, Calif., 18 May 1941, having with her had issue:

I *(John) Neil ('Moon') REAGAN [PO Box 413, Rancho Santa Fe, CA 92067, USA; 3941 Via Valle Verde, RSF CA, USA], *b* Tampico, Ill., 16 Sept 1908; *educ* Eureka Coll; employee State of Illinois, radio sports announcer, programme dir radio station WOC, Davenport, Iowa, bit parts in films (*see above* under list of President REAGAN's film appearances), delegate Nat Republican Convention 1976 and advertising exec with McCann, Erickson; *m* Adel, Iowa, 31 Aug 1935 *Ruth Elizabeth (Bess) (*b* Des Moines, Iowa 25 Dec 1908; *educ* Drake U), dau of Robert Hoffman and his *w* Fae Brown

II RONALD WILSON REAGAN, 40th PRESIDENT of the UNITED STATES of AMERICA

RONALD REAGAN
FAMILY TREE

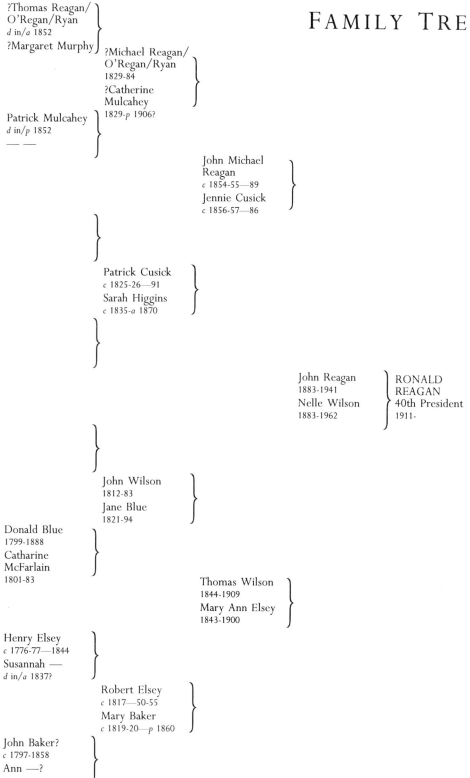

?Thomas Reagan/
O'Regan/Ryan
d in/a 1852

?Margaret Murphy

?Michael Reagan/
O'Regan/Ryan
1829-84

?Catherine
Mulcahey
1829-*p* 1906?

Patrick Mulcahey
d in/p 1852
— —

John Michael
Reagan
c 1854-55—89

Jennie Cusick
c 1856-57—86

Patrick Cusick
c 1825-26—91

Sarah Higgins
c 1835-*a* 1870

John Reagan
1883-1941

Nelle Wilson
1883-1962

RONALD
REAGAN
40th President
1911-

John Wilson
1812-83

Jane Blue
1821-94

Donald Blue
1799-1888

Catharine
McFarlain
1801-83

Thomas Wilson
1844-1909

Mary Ann Elsey
1843-1900

Henry Elsey
c 1776-77—1844

Susannah —
d in/a 1837?

Robert Elsey
c 1817—50-55

Mary Baker
c 1819-20—*p* 1860

John Baker?
c 1797-1858

Ann —?

Plate 128   George Bush

GEORGE BUSH

1924-
41ST PRESIDENT OF THE UNITED STATES OF AMERICA
1989-93

During his unsuccessful try for the Republican presidential nomination in 1980 George Bush advertised himself with the slogan, "A President we won't have to train." This was a sly dig at Jimmy Carter, who had taken so long to learn his way about Washington, and possibly a hint that if Ronald Reagan were nominated and elected he too might find himself at a loss. It was also an anything-but-sly assertion that Bush's rather limited experience in the Federal government (two terms in the House of Representatives, one year as head of the CIA and two diplomatic posts) qualified him for the top job of all. It was an insider's pitch, but 1980 was not an insider's year, and had Reagan not chosen Bush for his vice-presidential running-mate the world would probably have heard no more of him. But Bush served his President loyally, he assiduously courted the Republican right wing and in 1988 had his reward: with Reagan's blessing he received the presidential nomination. After an outstandingly nasty campaign, which did no credit to the candidate, he was convincingly elected President. At last he had his chance to show what his training had done for him.

Even before he took office it began to seem likely that Bush's central problem was not something that service in Washington could address. His knowledge of men and affairs needed to be directed by steady political conviction and what, in a characteristically lame phrase, he called 'the vision thing', and Bush had little of either. He was the authentic embodiment of old-style, high-and-dry New England Republicanism. His father had been an investment banker on Wall Street and a Senator from Connecticut; he himself was a graduate of Yale, married the daughter of another New York businessman and made his home, so far as he had one, at Kennebunkport in Maine, where he spent his summers. As a young man Bush made a half-hearted rebellion against this starchy background (perhaps his wartime service as an outstandingly brave fighter pilot opened doors in his imagination) and left New England to seek his fortune in the oil industry in Texas. He tried to take on the gaudy colouring of his new state but never did so convincingly, and even in Houston he got his start largely because of his family's wealth and connections. Nor did his political opinions ever advance beyond those which were (and are) the commonplaces of New England country clubs and cocktail parties. The New Right sensed the shallowness of his conversion to their views and accepted him only because they had no alternative; the voters at large made him President because he was the popular Reagan's chosen heir, the Democratic candidate was even less convincing, and the glow of the 'feel good' years was still in the sky. Bush, in short, had got to the top without believing in anything except the desirability of being President. It turned out to be a disastrous weakness.

He unguardedly admitted that he was bored by questions of domestic politics, so economic and social conditions were left to look after themselves, which they did not do with any marked success. The rich continued to get richer, the poor poorer, as under Ronald Reagan, and when a worldwide recession set in the middle class began to feel pinched. The vast Federal budget deficit inherited from Reagan was another problem, and Bush at length agreed to impose new taxes to mitigate its effect. Unfortunately for him his most famous campaign pledge had been that taxes would *not* be raised ("Read my lips") and he was not forgiven for this broken promise, not least because he never defended it candidly.

He did better over foreign policy. After some hesitation he continued the rapprochement with the Soviet Union. When in 1990 the dictator of Iraq, Saddam Hussein, invaded Kuwait, Bush successfully put together a military coalition under the auspices of the United Nations which turned him out again. This was a stunning victory, very popular in America, but it was not complete. Saddam continued in power in Baghdad, and having by his ambitions wrecked Kuwait, now wrecked his own country (already much damaged by UN bombing) by clinging to power. Since he was clearly still a danger to the peace the UN maintained its blockade and the Iraqi people had to endure disease and hunger while the American people wondered why Bush had not finished off Saddam when he had the chance. American journalists asked why the Reagan and Bush administrations had done so much to build up Saddam's military strength, even to the very eve of the Kuwait invasion. And the hope that the Gulf War victory and the end of Soviet-American rivalry would lead to a permanent peace in the Middle East seemed to have been another illusion: before long Israel and the Arab states were as unyielding to each other as ever.

If the successes of Bush's foreign policy were limited though real, the failures of his domestic policy, though limited, proved fatal. By 1992 the American people wanted a President who would effectively make economic recovery his first priority. Bush could not convince the voters that he was the man. They had come to know him too well. He made matters worse by bungling his re-election campaign from first to last: continuing his futile courtship of the reactionaries, he even allowed the Republican convention to be dominated by the fanatics of the religious Right, who alienated far more voters (women, environmentalists, homosexuals) than they could deliver. The maverick candidacy of the Texan billionaire Ross Perot split the Republican vote and exposed Bush to fire from two flanks. Bill Clinton, the Democratic candidate, won a comfortable majority in the electoral college, but his unimpressive share of the popular vote showed that the people were rejecting Bush rather than turning to anyone else. The President seemed totally discredited. But soon after the election the economy began perceptibly to recover, suggesting that, even in domestic matters, Bush had not been so incompetent a steward as his fellow-citizens had judged.

GEORGE BUSH'S FAMILY

George Bush as President seemed so anxious, so much of the time, to conceal what was thought of as his patrician background that it became something of a joke. Actually it was less his background, which as will be seen did not conform to the archetype of American privilege, than his mannerisms and habits, even physical appearance. Bush points out in his autobiography that much of the charge of 'preppiness' was insubstantial — he had not worn button-down Oxford cloth shirts for years, though he had an 'image problem' which said he did, while his other major marks of 'preppiness' seemed to amount to little more than tennis-playing and striped watch straps. All this, from having been mildly amusing, curdled however, for as his chances of retaining the presidency slipped ever further away throughout 1992 his attempts to play the man of the people took on an air of desperation, were even embarrassing. Since it is the Age of the Common Man, politics was always going to be behind Bush's passing himself off as something less than he was — all his swans geese as it were. But to many observers Bush seemed personally unhappy about his background. Unlike Franklin Roosevelt, say, he simply could not rise above it.

His family background was more interesting than the facile label 'patrician' suggests. Whereas the American people as a whole had tended to move west over the last few generations, notably the ancestors of Presidents such as Nixon, Eisenhower and Hoover, Bush's had come back to New England from the Mid-West and even as far away as the Pacific Coast. His father Prescott Bush had started out in Columbus, Ohio, his mother Dorothy in St Louis, Mo. Prescott Bush's great-grandfather had been one of the Forty-Niners who scrambled for sudden wealth in the Californian gold rush of the mid-19th century and according to his great-great-grandson had been intending to settle there with his family when he died at sea on his way east to fetch them.

Nor was Bush's background wholly WASP. His mother's father, George Herbert Walker, was born a Catholic and named after the 17th-century English devotional poet George Herbert. (Herbert, however, had been a Protestant, though not an extreme one.) In Herbert's poem 'The Church Militant' he refers to religion having emigrated from England to America, and it may have been this which inspired the Walkers to call their son after him. Bush was called after his grandfather, hence indirectly after the poet. Not even Bush's loyallest supporter can claim he has lived up to the name. True, the original George Herbert had early aspirations to political office and was briefly a Member of Parliament, but the contrast is painful between his prowess as Public Orator at the University of Cambridge and Bush's inarticulacy.

Bush's father Prescott could have entered the business run by his own father, Samuel Bush (a man active also in Ohio state politics, though as a Democrat), but was no more interested in doing so than George Bush was in the family profession of banking a generation later. According to George Bush, Prescott's initial involvement in Republican politics was confined to fund-raising and was an extension of his belief in good citizenship more than anything else. Later, when a Senator, he took an internationalist attitude, unlike the isolationist Republicans such as Robert Taft. His opposition to the gas deregulation bill during Eisenhower's presidency made the name of Bush mud down in Texas and George Bush was threatened with losing business opportunities if his father voted against it.

Prescott Bush had made his mark in business as an expert who could sort out a firm's financial problems. It was what George Bush was expected by the American people to do during his presidency. Unfortunately it always seemed as if he was keener on that other speciality of his father, foreign affairs. It was all the odder because he had studied economics at Yale and appreciated the importance of the average voter's paypacket when soliciting support: in his autobiography he tells how the Governor of Ohio gave him a lesson in the number one topic in politics by slamming down a wallet on the table between them and saying "That's what it's all about, George — *jobs, jobs, jobs.*"

For the major part of his career Prescott Bush was a banker. George Bush's maternal grandfather had been a banker too, so it could be said that banking was in the blood on both sides of the family. At any rate Bush was offered a job with his father's firm on leaving Yale. He turned it down, other jobs being easier to get in those days than during his presidency 40 years later. Instead he went to Texas, largely at the suggestion of an old family friend who offered him a job, and started in the oil business. When he set up his own company a few years later his uncle Herbert Walker, an investment banker, provided financial backing and financial expertise. One of Bush's biggest early investors was a man he had contacts with because he was a client of Prescott Bush's Wall Street bank. And when he was elected to Congress he was put on the Ways and Means Committee by its chairman Wilbur Mills, a Democrat, after Prescott Bush asked his old buddy Mills for help.

Another side to Bush's mother's family apart from banking was sport, which can be every bit as competitive as business. George H. Walker, the Catholic named after a 17th-century poet, was also an amateur boxing champion in his youth, later a six- or seven-handicap golfer and finally President of the US Golf Association. It was he who instituted the Walker Cup. In 1990, when President Bush was made an honorary member of the Royal & Ancient Golf Club, St Andrews, Scotland, his grandfather's services to the game were given fresh publicity. Bush himself did less well out of it because the Royal & Ancient had no women members and feminists back in the USA were affronted. Dorothy Bush was a very good golfer in her own right, as well as being expert at tennis, basketball and baseball. If Barbara Bush is to be believed, Dorothy had 10 times more influence on her son George than did his father. George Bush himself recalled his mother as being "a little like an Army drill-sergeant", and one of the most memorable sights during his presidency was his habit of pushing himself to the verge of extreme physical exhaustion as if he himself were the drill-sergeant of a platoon of undisciplined rookies.

Unfortunately Dorothy Bush also believed in sportsmanship — a fatal credo where politics is concerned — and although her son seems in many ways to have risen above this ancestral handicap, conducting his campaigns in 1988 and 1992 on a distinctly unpleasant personal level, there is evidence that he lacked the extra ounce of jugular-attacking aggression which, say, Nixon was never too squeamish to exert. For instance, in 1964 he passed up the chance of embarrassing his Democratic opponent Ralph Yarborough, who had accused the Republicans of not caring about the way nuclear weapons would cause leukaemia in babies. Bush of course had lost a child to leukaemia. Better still, he had launched a foundation for leaukaemia research. His campaign manager wanted him to deploy these facts and flatten Yarborough. Bush refused. Nixon at the same stage in his career would not have hesitated an instant.

George Bush shares with FDR the distinction of having the greatest number (15) of proveable kinships with other presidents. Among such kinships is Franklin Pierce, to whom his wife Barbara, née Pierce, is also related, being Pierce's fourth cousin four-times removed. During his early career she was not regarded as particularly active in politics, though in Texas she had written a monthly newspaper column on current events aimed at her husband's constituents. But by Bush's last year in office his wife's popularity ratings soared above his. Barbara Bush was more articulate than her husband, also more dignified. She had enjoyed a happy public reputation from the start, although as late as the 1988 campaign she was so little known to the public that a photographer yelled to "the woman in red" to get out of the picture so he could snap the presidential candidate entire. Her easy-going attitude to dress and deportment, whether truly upper-class, as was said, or no, was in sharp contrast to Nancy Reagan's anxiously parvenu one and there was by now a revulsion against the showiness of the Reagan era. As early as 1989, at the time of the American-Soviet summit in Malta, she presided cheerfully over a Kennedy Center ceremony honouring artistic achievement where Soviet military personnel performed alongside US sailors. Meanwhile her hapless husband was outmanoeuvered by Gorbachev and appeared almost ridiculous when he became the victim of stormy weather in the Mediterranean. When the Gulf War was starting she won new plaudits with her decision to defy terrorism, encourage domestic airline companies and set a good example by taking scheduled flights rather than continue using Air Force One.

Every First Lady these days has a pet charitable project. Barbara Bush's was literacy, a cause dear to her heart because her son Neil was dyslexic. She argued that her Barbara Bush Foundation for Family Literacy was right to emphasize the role of the family in overcoming illiteracy. Her other charity also had a family connection, a tragic one this time. After the Bushes' elder daughter Robin died of leukaemia aged three, Barbara worked on behalf of the Leukaemia Society of America. Her famous white hair turned that colour as a result of the shock of losing the child, although up till 1970 she dyed it brown, at the request of her mother-in-law. She denied having influence on her husband, but during the 1988 presidential election she is said to have advised him to soften his attacks on Dukakis. When Bush formed his administration he appointed three Barbara Bush favourites to top positions: Louis Sullivan as Health and Human Services Secretary, Jack Kemp as Housing Secretary and William Bennett as head of the anti-drug campaign. In 1989 she said publicly that semi-automatic rifles should be banned (she had once found her husband in her sights when shooting birds and had not handled a gun since); the President then approved an embargo on import of the weapons.

Bush continued the tradition of using close relatives to perform some ceremonial functions of the presidency, just as he had had the benefit of help from his children in his campaign for the Republican presidential nomination in 1980, with Neil Bush active in New Hampshire, Marvin Bush at the Iowa

Plate 129   Barbara Pierce Bush

*Plate 130   George Bush with his wife Barbara, children and grandchildren,
holding up his grandson George P. Bush's hand on his acceptance of the
Republican presidential nomination for the second time, August 1992*

caucus and Jeb Bush and his Mexican wife, both of whom spoke Spanish, among Hispanic voters in Florida, Texas and Puerto Rico. After Bush was elected, Jeb and his son George Prescott flew to Soviet Armenia as goodwill ambassadors. In 1988 a stockmarket panic was sparked by rumours that the *Washington Post* was about to publish allegations of marital infidelity by Bush. The Bush campaign manager Lee Atwater got his boss's eldest son George Jr to deny it and Wall Street regained its nerve. Bush sent his brother William ('Bucky') Bush to Malta in 1989 to represent the US at Malta's independence celebrations and to Britain in 1992 to attend a dinner celebrating the fortieth anniversary of the Queen's accession. It was because William Bush was such a success in Malta that his brother chose it as the venue for the summit with President Gorbachev later in 1989. When the Greek government celebrated 2,500 years of democracy in September 1991, the President sent his sister Nancy Ellis as America's representative.

A more distressing tradition was the embarrassing relative. Bush had more than his fair share of them. One was his son Neil, who was director of the Silverado Banking, Savings & Loan Association in Denver when it allegedly made loans to a business associate of his. The Silverado Association later collapsed. By August 1990, in the wake of the Iraqi invasion of Kuwait, the role had been taken over by George Jr, who while being televised at the first tee of a golf course complained in true Marie Antoinette style that reporters' questions about American hostages were affecting his backswing. By July 1991 unwelcome attention had shifted to the President's elder brother Prescott Bush, who was being investigated by the Securities & Exchange Commission over alleged business links with Japanese gangsters. Later the same month the family stockbroking firm of J. Bush & Co., which was owned by another brother, Jonathan Bush, was reported as having been fined $30,000 and banned from trading with the general public for a year for infringing regulations. By the spring of 1992 attention had swung back to George Jr, who was being accused by a news magazine of insider trading in relation to a Dallas oil company. George Jr's advice was still influential during the 1992 campaign, however. After the New Hampshire primary in February, the President asked his son for his views before recanting part of his 1990 budget policy. Another son, Jeb Bush, ran the Florida campaign on his father's behalf.

Privileged family background alone would have been no strong reason for Bush losing popularity as the 1992 election drew closer. The problem was economic. But it is easier for a man from a privileged background to project concern for ordinary Americans in such circumstances if he is a Democrat. At one point in his career Bush plaintively asked a media analyst why the two Roosevelts, the two Tafts and John F. Kennedy hadn't been called elitist when they had gone to Ivy League schools too. The media analyst said he had no idea but that it was a question of 'perceptions' of Bush. The real answer is surely that 'elitist' and 'elitism' didn't exist as undesirable qualities in earlier times, even though the term 'aristocrat' had been used as one of abuse from the early 19th century on. Bush, the supposed WASP, had entered presidential politics in an era of more jumbled-up culture than he was capable of handling. But in the same way that the economy began to show signs of reviving just as he stepped down, so there seemed to be renewed respect for WASPs.

BIOGRAPHICAL DETAILS AND DESCENDANTS

BUSH, George Herbert Walker, *b* Milton, Mass., 12 June 1924; *educ* Phillips Acad, Andover, Mass., and Yale (BA Econs 1948); Lt USNR World War II (DFC 1944, three Air Medals), equipment clerk then salesman Dresser Industs/Ideco 1948-51, Co-Fndr Bush-Overbey Devpt Corp (oil and gas) 1951-53, joined Hugh and William Liedtke to found Zapata Petroleum Corp (Dir 1953-59), which absorbed Bush-Overbey and devpd offshore drilling equipmnt, Co-Fndr & Pres Zapata Offshore Co, Houston, 1954 (Pres 1956-64, Chm 1964-66), Republican Pty Chm Harris Co, Tex., 1963-64, candidate for US Senate 1966 and 1970, Memb US House of Reps for Texas 7th Dist 1967-71 (Memb Ways and Means Ctee), Perm Rep to UN 1971-73, Chm Republican Nat Ctee 1973-74, Ch US Liaison Office Peking 1974-75, Dir CIA 1976-77, Chm Exec Ctee First Internat Bank of Houston 1977-78, Adjunct Prof Business Rice U 1977-78, V-Pres USA 1981-89, 41st President (R) of the USA 1989-93, Hon LLD: Beaver Coll and Adelphi U (1972), N Michigan U (1973), Franklin Pierce Coll, New Hampshire, and Allegheny Coll, Pa. (1976), U of New Haven, Conn. (1979), Tuskegee Inst, Ala., Dusquesne U, Pa., Howard U, DC, Sacred Heart U, Conn. (1981), Miami U, Ohio, Boston Coll, Mass., Bowdoin Coll, Maine (1982), Furman U, S Carolina, New England Sch of Law, Mass., Texas Christian U, U of Delaware, Rochester U, New York (1983), Wheaton Coll, Ill., Hampden-Sydney Coll, Va., Bar-Ilan U, Israel, Yeshiva U, New York City (1985), Westminster Coll, Mo. (1986), Albion Coll, Mich., U of New Hampshire, Northwestern Coll, Iowa (1987), Texas A & M, Boston U, Mass. (1989), U of S Carolina, U of Texas at Austin (1990), U of Michigan at Ann Arbor, Princeton, Hampton U, Va., Yale (1991), Notre Dame U (1992), Hon DHL: Texas Southern U (1981), Ohio State U, Medical U of S Carolina (1983), Milwaukee Sch of Engrg (1986), Centl State U, Ohio (1988), Johns Hopkins, Texas A & I (1990), SMU, Tex. (1992), Hon Dr Humanities: Austin Coll, Tex. (1973), Liberty U, Va. (1990), Hon Dr Business Admin Southern Baptist U, Mo. (1982), Hon DCL U of the South, Tenn. (1985), Hon Dr Legal Laws U of St Louis, Mo. (1987) Hon DEcon Oklahoma State U (1990), Hon Dr of Public Serv Florida Internat U, Miami (1992), Hon DPhil Kuwait U (1993), Hon Fellow U of Georgia (1984), Hon Distinguished Prof Political Economy U of Mississippi (1985), recipient (with Mrs Bush) of UN Albert Schweitzer Leadership Award, author: (with Victor Gold) *Looking Forward* (autobiography) (1988); m Rye, New York, 6 Jan 1945 *Barbara (b there 8 June 1925; educ Ashley Hall, Charleston, S Carolina, and Smith (Capt Freshman Soccer Team); Hon Pres Girl Scouts of America, Hon Chm: Advsy Bd Reading Is Fundamental (body promoting literacy among children), Nat Assoc Ptnrs in Educn, Washington Parent Gp Fund and Leukemia Soc, Hon Memb: Bd Dirs Business Cncl Effective Literacy, Bd Children's Oncology Servs of Washington, DC, Inc, Bd Memb Ronald McDonald House and Morehouse Sch of Medicine, established Barbara Bush Fndn for Family Literacy March 1989, Hon Degrees: Stritch Coll, Wis., and Mt Vernon Coll, Wash. (1981), Hood Coll, Md. (1983), Howard U, Wash. (1987), Jackson Coll, Ala. (1988), Hon DHL: Bennett Coll, NC, Smith and Morehouse Sch Medicine (1989) and St Louis U, Mo., 1990, Hon LLD U of Pennsylvania, author: *C. Fred's Story: A Dog's Life* (1984) and *Millie's Book* (1990)), yr dau and 3rd child of Marvin Pierce (b 1893; exec with McCall Corp (V-Pres 1926, Pres 1946); d 1969), of New York, and his 1st w Pauline Robinson (b 1896; d Oct 1949 in a car accident), and has issue:

President Bush's son
I *George Walker BUSH, Jr [c/o Texas Rangers, 1205 E Copeland Rd, Arlington, TX 760011-4949, USA], b 6 July 1946; *educ* Yale (BA History, 1968) and Harvard Business Sch (MBA 1975); jet pilot Texas Air Nat Gd, Dir and Consultant Harken Energy Corp (oil drilling company), which merged with Spectrum 7 Energy Corp (of which Fndr and Manager) 1986, managing part-owner Texas Rangers Baseball Club 1989-; m 19— *Laura Welch (b 4 Nov 1946) and has issue:

    Twin grandchildren
    1 *Jenna Welch BUSH, b 25 Nov 1981
    2 *Barbara Pierce BUSH, b 25 Nov 1981

President Bush's children
II (Pauline) Robin(son) BUSH, b Compton, Calif., 20 Dec 1949; d 11 Oct 1953 of leukaemia
III *John ('Jeb') Ellis BUSH, b 11 Feb 1953; *educ* U of Texas at Austin (BA Latin American Studies); sometime Sec of Commerce Florida, with Texas Commerce Bank, Chm/owner Bush-Klein Realty 1988-, Pres Codina-Bush Gp (real estate and investment banking), Florida campaign manager for his father's re-election bid 1992, Chm Florida Republican Pty; m 19— *Columba Garnica (b 17 Aug 1953), of Mexico, and has issue:

    Grandchildren
    1 *George Prescott BUSH, b 24 April 1976
    2 *Noelle Lucila BUSH, b 26 July 1977
    3 *John Ellis (Jebby) BUSH, Jr, b 13 Dec 1983

President Bush's son
IV *Neil Mallon BUSH, b 22 Jan 1955; *educ* Tulane U (MBA 1980); Non-Exec Dir Silverado Banking, Savings & Loan Assoc 1985-Aug 1988, owner of JNB Exploration (oil company); m 19— *Sharon Smith (b 19 May 1952) and has issue:

    Grandchildren
    1 *Lauren Pierce BUSH, b 25 July 1984
    2 *Pierce Mallon BUSH, b 15 March 1986
    3 *Ashley Walker BUSH, b 7 Feb 1989

President Bush's son
V *Marvin Pierce BUSH, b 22 Oct 1956; *educ* U of Virginia (BA English); accountant, spokesman Crohn's and Colitis Fndn of America; m 19— *Margaret Molster (b 2 March 1959); Mr and Mrs Marvin Bush have an adopted dau:

    a *Marshall Lloyd BUSH, b 14 May 1986

Mr and Mrs Marvin P. Bush also have issue:

    1 *Charles Walker BUSH, b 1989

President Bush's daughter
VI *Doro(thy) Walker Bush, b 18 Aug 1959; *educ* Boston Coll (BA Sociology); formerly with Maine Office of Tourism,

Communications and Devpt Office Nat Rehabilitation Hosp, Washington, DC; *m* 1st 19— (divorce before 27 June 1992) William Heekin LeBLOND (*b* 11 Jan 1957) and has issue:

Grandchildren
1 *Samuel Bush LeBLOND, *b* 26 Aug 1984
2 *Nancy Ellis (Ellie) LeBLOND, *b* 19 Nov 1986

President Bush's daughter
VI (cont.) Mrs Dorothy Bush LeBlond *m* 2nd Camp David, Md., 27 June 1992 *Robert (Bobby) P. KOCH, sometime aide to Dem House Majority Leader Richard Gephardt

MALE LINE ANCESTRY AND COLLATERAL DESCENDANTS

Richard BUSH, *b* 16— or 17—; probably *m* on or after 25 Jan 1726 Mary (*b* 22 Aug 1699; *d* Bristol, Rhode Island, 7 May 1743), dau of Jeremiah Fairbanks (1674-1735, whose uncle George Fairbanks was an ancestor of President TAFT), of Dedham, Mass., and Bristol, and his w Mary Penfield (*b* 1678), and *d* Bristol 27 Sept 1732; Richard and Mary Bush may have been parents of:

Timothy BUSH, *b* 17—; served French and Indian Wars 1755-57, settled after his first five children were born at Norwich, Vt., and served as a Capt Revolutionary War; *m* Hebron, Tolland Co, Conn., 12 April 1759 Deborah (*b* Lebanon, Conn., 6 April 1742; *d* Springport, New York, *c* 1819), dau of John House (1715-1805, whose mother's father Jonathan Davenport had a brother, John, who was ancestor of President TAFT), of Little Compton, Rhode Island, and his w Deborah Guile or Guild (1715-83), and *d* Springport *c* 1815, having had issue (with at least four other children):

Timothy BUSH, Jr, *b* probably Lebanon, Conn., 1 April 1766; blacksmith; *m* Penfield, Monroe Co, New York, 26 July 1791 Lydia (*b* 28 April 1763; *d* Penfield 14 Sept 1835), dau of Daniel Newcomb and his w Elizabeth May; (Elizabeth's ggf John May *m* Sarah Brewer, whose brother Daniel was ancestor of President PIERCE and whose probable sister was ancestor of President HAYES), and *d* Rochester, New York, 4 May 1850, having had issue:

Obadiah Newcomb BUSH, *b* 28 Jan 1797; merchant; *m* Rochester 8 Nov 1821 Harriet (*b* Cambridge, New York, 12 May 1800; *d* Cincinnati, Ohio, 21 June 1867), dau of Dr Sanford Smith and his w Priscilla Whippo or Whipple, and *d c* 1851 at sea en route from California to the East Coast of America, having had issue:

Revd James Smith BUSH, *b* Rochester 15 June 1825; *m* 1st 18— ———; *m* 2nd New York 24 Feb 1859 Harriet Eleanor (*b* Savannah, Ga., 29 Oct 1829; *d* Boston 27 Feb 1924), dau of Samuel Howard Fay and his w Susan Shellman, and *d* Ithaca, Tompkins Co, New York, 11 Nov 1889, having had issue:

Samuel Prescott BUSH, *b* Brick Church, New Jersey, 4 Oct 1863; Pres Buckeye Steel Casting, Columbus, Ohio; *m* Columbus 20 June 1894 Flora (*b* Franklin Co, Ohio, 17 March 1872; *d* Rhode Island 4 Sept 1920), dau of Robert Emmet Sheldon (1845-1917) and his w Mary Elizabeth Butler (1850-97), and *d* Columbus 8 Feb 1948, having had issue:

I Prescott (Pres) Sheldon BUSH, for whom *see below*
II Herbert BUSH, part-owner New York Mets Baseball Team

The er s,

Prescott Sheldon BUSH, *b* Columbus 15 May 1895; *educ* Yale (MA 1917); Capt Field Artillery American Expedy Force Western Front 1917-19, with Simmons Hardware Co, St Louis, Mo., then US Rubber Co, Managing Ptnr Brown Bros, Harriman & Co (Wall Street bankers) 1930-72, sometime Tstee Westminster Choir Coll and Dir CBS and Prudential Insur Co of America, Chm Nat War Fund Campaign 1943-44, Connecticut Republican Finance Ctee and Delegate-at-large Republican Nat Convention 1948, US Senator from Connecticut 1953-63; *m* Kennebunkport, Me., 6 Aug 1921 Dorothy (*b* nr Walker's Point, York Co, Me., 1 July 1901; *d* 19 Nov 1992), dau of George Herbert Walker (*b* St Louis, Mo., 11 June 1875; built the family house of Walker's Point at Kennebunkport; *d* New York 24 June 1953) and his w Lucretia ('Loulie') Wear (*b* St Louis 17 Sept 1874; *d* Biddeford, Me., 28 Aug 1961), and *d* New York 8 Oct 1972 of lung cancer, having had issue:

I *Prescott (Pres) Sheldon BUSH, Jr, *b* 10 Aug 1922; owner of Prescott Bush & Co (property company); *m* 19— *Elizabeth Louise Draper Kauffman and has issue:

President Bush's nephew and niece
1 *Prescott S. BUSH III, *b* 4 Nov 1945
2 *Kelsey Bush, *b* 4 June 1947; *m* 19— *Philip NADEAU and has issue:

Great-nieces and -nephews
(1) *Elizabeth NADEAU, *b* Nov 1978
(2) *Kate NADEAU, *b* Nov 1980
(3) *William NADEAU, *b* 27 July 1986
(4) *Prescott NADEAU, *b* 27 July 1986

President Bush's nephew

3 *James L. BUSH, *b* 23 July 1955; *m* 19— *Susan ―――― and has issue:

Great-niece and -nephew
(1) *Sarah BUSH, *b* 1983
(2) *Sam BUSH, *b* 15 Nov 1985

II GEORGE HERBERT WALKER BUSH, 41st PRESIDENT of the UNITED STATES of AMERICA
III *Nancy Bush, *b* 3 Feb 1926; *m* 19— Alexander (Sandy) ELLIS, Jr (*d* Dec 1989) and has issue:

President Bush's niece
1 *Nancy (Nandy) Walker Ellis, *b* 19—; *m* 19— *Tom BLACK and has issue:

Great-niece
(1) *Sophie Ellis BLACK, *b* 11 Jan 1986

President Bush's nephew
2 *Alexander ELLIS III, *b* 19—; *m* 19— *Robin Rand and has issue:

Great-nephews
(1) *Alexander ELLIS IV, *b* April 1979
(2) *Christopher ELLIS, *b* April 1982
(3) *Walker Bush ELLIS, *b* 1985

President Bush's nephews
3 *John P. ELLIS, *b* 19—; *m* 19— (divorce 19—) *Joan Kenyon
4 *Josiah Wear ELLIS, *b* 16 Nov 1957; *m* 19— *Ann Corning Woodworth (*b* 19 Jan 1960) and has issue:

Great-nephew
(1) *Josiah Wear ELLIS, Jr, *b* 19 June 1992

IV *Jonathan James BUSH, *b* 6 May 1931; owner J Bush & Co (stockbrokers); *m* 19— *Josephine (Jody) Bradley (*b* 21 Aug 1939) and has issue:

President Bush's nephews
1 *Jonathan James BUSH, Jr, *b* 10 March 1969
2 *William Hall (Billy) BUSH, 13 Oct 1971

V *William ('Buck' or 'Bucky') Henry Trotter BUSH, of St Louis, Kans., *b* 14 July 1938; banker; *m* 19— *Patricia (Patty) Lee Redfern (*b* 8 April 1938) and has issue:

President Bush's nephew and niece
1 *William Prescott (Scott) BUSH, *b* 5 Feb 1964; *m* 19— *Lindsay Whitaker
2 *Louisa BUSH, *b* 6 May 1970

Timothy Bush
d c 1815

Deborah House
1742-*c* 1819
}
Timothy Bush, Jr
1766-1850

Daniel Newcomb
1729-*a* 1789

Elizabeth May
1730-*p* 1789
}
Lydia Newcomb
1763-1835

Ephraim Smith
1704-74

Lucy Stevens
c 1717-1806
}
Sanford Smith
1760-1815

Priscilla Whippo
c 1763-1838

Jonathan Fay, Jr
1752-1811

Lucy Prescott
1757-92
}
Samuel Fay
1778-1856

Samuel Howard
c 1752-97

Anna Lillie
c 1760-1804
}
Harriet Howard
1782-1847

John Shellman/
Schellman
c 1723-1816

Maria Margareth Fout/
Fought/Fauth
1732-95
}
John Shellman, Jr
1756-1838

Robert Munford/
Montfort
d 1771-78

Anne Brodnax
d p 1780-82
}
Clarissa Montfort
d 1845

}
Michael Sheldon

}
Mary —

}
James Uncles
1794-1835

}
Elizabeth
Criswell/Kiswell

Revd Nathaniel Butler
1761-1829

Sarah Herrick
?1764-*c* 1823
}
Samuel Butler
1785-1851

Gilbert Livingston
1758-1833

Susannah Lewis
1761-1822
}
Judith Livingston
1785-1858

Isaac Pierce
1763-1849

Anna Fitch
1763-1809
}
Levi Pierce
1797-1838

Jarvis Wheeler
1774-1852

Sarah Horton
1777-1856
}
Betsey Wheeler
1800-81

}
Thomas Walker
d c 1798-1800

Catharine McLelland

Robert Mercer, Jr
b 1737

— —
}
John Mercer
fl c 1793

Richard Davis
b c 1745

— —
}
Rebecca Davis

Victor Emanuel Bechi

— —
}
Joseph Beaky

Catharine Shriner

Lemuel Bangs
1739-1824

Rebecca Keeler
1751-1812
}
Elijah Bangs
1780-1856

Amos Stackhouse
1757-1825

Mary Powell
1763-1841
}
Esther Stackhouse
1787-1819

Jonathan Weir
c 1750-60-*c* 1832

Mary —
c 1758-*c* 1848
}
James Weir
1789-1832

Jonathan Gault

— —
}
Elizabeth Gault

Jechonias Yancey
fl c 1793

Mildred Wood
}
David Yancey
fl c 1815

John Field
fl c 1795

Sally Wood
}
Mildred Field

William Holliday
c 1755—1811-12

Martha Patton?
}
Joseph Holliday
1789-1870

}
Nancy R. McCune
1799-1834

Samuel Dawson

— Montjoy/Mountjoy
}
Peter Foree
fl c 1816

Eliza Dawson

GEORGE BUSH FAMILY TREE

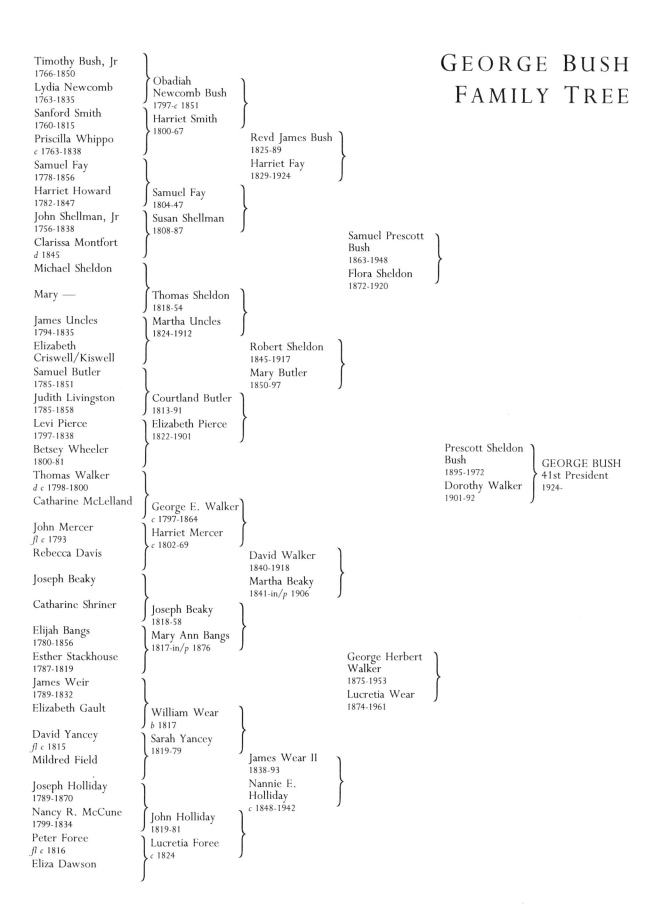

Timothy Bush, Jr
1766-1850

Lydia Newcomb
1763-1835

Obadiah
Newcomb Bush
1797-c 1851

Sanford Smith
1760-1815

Harriet Smith
1800-67

Priscilla Whippo
c 1763-1838

Revd James Bush
1825-89

Samuel Fay
1778-1856

Harriet Fay
1829-1924

Harriet Howard
1782-1847

Samuel Fay
1804-47

John Shellman, Jr
1756-1838

Susan Shellman
1808-87

Clarissa Montfort
d 1845

Samuel Prescott
Bush
1863-1948

Michael Sheldon

Flora Sheldon
1872-1920

Mary —

Thomas Sheldon
1818-54

James Uncles
1794-1835

Martha Uncles
1824-1912

Elizabeth
Criswell/Kiswell

Robert Sheldon
1845-1917

Samuel Butler
1785-1851

Mary Butler
1850-97

Judith Livingston
1785-1858

Courtland Butler
1813-91

Levi Pierce
1797-1838

Elizabeth Pierce
1822-1901

Betsey Wheeler
1800-81

Prescott Sheldon
Bush
1895-1972

Thomas Walker
d c 1798-1800

GEORGE BUSH
41st President
1924-

Catharine McLelland

George E. Walker
c 1797-1864

Dorothy Walker
1901-92

John Mercer
fl c 1793

Harriet Mercer
c 1802-69

Rebecca Davis

David Walker
1840-1918

Joseph Beaky

Martha Beaky
1841-in/p 1906

Catharine Shriner

Joseph Beaky
1818-58

Elijah Bangs
1780-1856

Mary Ann Bangs
1817-in/p 1876

Esther Stackhouse
1787-1819

James Weir
1789-1832

George Herbert
Walker
1875-1953

Elizabeth Gault

Lucretia Wear
1874-1961

William Wear
b 1817

David Yancey
fl c 1815

Sarah Yancey
1819-79

Mildred Field

James Wear II
1838-93

Joseph Holliday
1789-1870

Nannie E.
Holliday
c 1848-1942

Nancy R. McCune
1799-1834

John Holliday
1819-81

Peter Foree
fl c 1816

Lucretia Foree
c 1824

Eliza Dawson

Plate 131 Bill Clinton

BILL CLINTON

1946-
42ND PRESIDENT OF THE UNITED STATES OF AMERICA
1993-

BILL CLINTON'S FAMILY

An institution usually becomes a political debating topic only when it has been badly damaged or is in decline. The family is no exception. Once so much a keystone of society that it was never mentioned in presidential elections, it is now cracking up as divorce, absconding breadwinners, illegitimate births and investigations into cases of incest multiply. It was therefore not surprising when the struggle between Bill Clinton and George Bush in 1992 revolved around 'family values' to a greater extent than any other in American history. Bush was the conservative and belonged not only to a large family but an old one, so should have had the upper hand. Yet the questionable business dealings of some of his brothers and sons were a drawback. His wife on the other hand was an asset. Clinton had only one embarrassing blood relation, his ex-drug dealer half-brother Roger. But his wife, unlike Bush's, was his greatest liability — apart perhaps from himself. The personality of a candidate's wife had never mattered in the 19th century. If it had, Lincoln would not have become President. The obsession with Mrs Clinton was a sign of political naivety, because it assumed a President's wife would only be a major influence on him him if she had a career of her own. But if you don't want a President whose wife pushes him around you shouldn't vote for him at all. The wife's specific attitude to civics hardly matters. It is more important not to elect a weak chief executive, for if a President can be dominated by his wife he may be dominated by anybody.

Clinton was also handicapped by the feeling among many people that he was dishonest. Before his election this was chiefly because of his evasion of military service, in which it turned out a step-uncle with political pull, Raymond Clinton, had tried to help by getting a Naval Reserve post created for his step-nephew where none had existed before, thus buying time while the local draft board was pressured into letting Clinton go to Oxford. The draft-dodging charge became complicated by numerous minute details and never really stuck. What was shabby was the prevarication by Clinton over the specific allegation concerning his step-uncle: first he said in September 1992 that he'd never known about it, then two days later that he had known since March. After the election, and particularly as Inauguration loomed, his broken campaign pledges became the embarrassment: an economic programme that would start with tax cuts for the middle class, the deficit cut by half by 1997, the economic plan submitted to Congress the day after his Inauguration, his implied support for letting in Haitian refugees (the muddle regarding which one might call — in Bush-speak — Voodoo immigration policies), a White House staff cut of a quarter — all betrayed.

With Hillary it was the other way round. She had been unpopular because she was not dishonest enough. The frankness of the Clintons' sales pitch — that if you elected him you got her too — brought into the open what any student of the presidency has known all along, that a President's wife is in a uniquely strong position to influence her husband. Abigail Adams, Julia Grant and Edith Wilson showed that, let alone the cases of Eleanor Roosevelt and Rosalynn Carter, who were all most journalists writing about the Clintons seemed to have heard of. Since any President has his inner circle of influential advisers, many of them personal associates of long standing unknown to the public and without high official position, an avowedly influential wife, who had at least been shown to the people for their approval, was relatively a step forward.

For someone of Hillary Clinton's abilities and interests in such things as children's rights the choice was never between baking cookies at home and earning a large salary as a lawyer, but between campaigning openly as a co-candidate and manipulating her husband discreetly once he became President. To her credit she chose to advertise her power — pushing her husband into reorganizing his campaign team in June 1992, sitting in on transition meetings between election day and Inauguration — rather than practise traditional petticoat government, with all its furtiveness. Republicans exploited her interest in children's rights to suggest she was a threat to family cohesion, citing a paper she had written years before in which she argued children should be able to sue their parents. That looked a lot less revolutionary if one was in Bill Clinton's position. Here was a man who had grown up first with no father, then for five years with no mother while she left him with his grandparents to train as a nurse 350 miles away, and lastly with a drunken brute of a stepfather with whom his mother was so wrapped up that she remarried him a few months after divorcing him. Clinton himself referred to his dislike of conflict as being caused by growing up in a household the head of which was a violent alcoholic. And when it came to the way Hillary ran her own family the Republicans could uncover nothing damning. In some ways the Clintons were suffocatingly close-knit: Hugh and Dorothy Rodham, Hillary's parents, had accompanied their daughter and son-in-law on their honeymoon. They also left Chicago to go and live in Little Rock. The Clintons' refusal to make an electoral tool of their daughter in the way Jimmy Carter had with Amy Carter also spoke in their favour. By March 1993 the most popular girl's name in the English county of Essex (the heartland of Bubbadom in the British nation) was Chelsea, so the Clintons were evidently striking a chord there too.

Clinton, with his poorish white Southern background, was inevitably compared with Carter. But Clinton had nothing of Carter's religiosity. One of his baptismal names was Jefferson and it was by Jefferson's radicalism that he was clearly inspired, though he may not have been as sceptical toward religion as the great man himself. At any rate, Clinton chose to descend on Washington from Monticello at the time of his Inauguration. And it is of some interest that a branch of Jefferson's descendants, the Ruffin Marshalls, settled for a time in Hope, Ark., around the time of Clinton's birth there. In such a small place it is unlikely that knowledge of a neighbour's Jeffersonian antecedents would have stayed concealed for long. Was this a reason Clinton's parents christened him William Jefferson?

Clinton admitted that he and his wife discussed everything except her legal cases, which would have breached legal ethics about client confidentiality. And as President he would be handling numerous public issues, on which Hillary Clinton had as much right to comment as any citizen (though infinitely more opportunity). Yet in the most delicate matters he would be like a confidential man of business to 240 million clients — the American people — to say nothing of America's allies round the world, and to discuss matters of that sort with a third party, even if she was his wife, would breach the ethics of high statesmanship. Of course nobody expected a politician to keep things from his wife, even though a lawyer was expected to from her husband. Why was that? If Clinton, or any other politician, had asked himself the question, the perennial influence of the family on American Presidents might have been faced squarely and this book would not have had to be written. In the event the suggestion that there would be strong family influence on Clinton did him no real harm in the election, though he won a relatively small percentage of the total vote. But Clinton did overwhelmingly well among women and

Plate 132   Bill Clinton with his daughter Chelsea   *Plate 133   Hillary Rodham Clinton speaking to the*
media on health care reform; Senate Majority Leader
George Mitchell on left

Bush, who in opposing abortion might have cornered the foetus vote if there had been one, went down to defeat.

Hillary Clinton was obliged to dissemble somewhat as the campaign progressed. She was less of a Washington outsider than she seemed. She had even been a Republican in her youth. Through her work she had made numerous Washington acquaintances, starting in the early 1970s when she was taken on as a Congressional counsel to prepare possible impeachment proceedings against Nixon. Her take-it-or-leave-it attitude to questions about her influence was repeated when she and her husband were quizzed about his alleged affair with a personable chanteuse, Gennifer Flowers. Clinton denied Ms Flowers's specific charge that they had had an affair but hinted at something he called past "wrongdoing" in his marriage. Hillary Clinton in effect said that if she could let bygones be bygones the public ought to be able to. Amazingly, it worked. Perhaps Americans were bored with seeing politicians destroyed by sex. Perhaps an alleged affair that had lasted 12 years suggested a perverse kind of fidelity — after all many marriages were less durable.

After the Inauguration — at which Clinton had played his saxophone although his half-brother Roger the rock musician did not perform (whereas he had sung a solo at the Democratic Convention) — the Clintons showed signs of acquiring presidential dignity. A certain amount of name-changing took place, rather as happens with the British monarchy where the new sovereign adopts a reign name that may be different from his or her baptismal one. Bill Clinton, known in childhood as Billy Blythe, became William J. Clinton. Hillary briefly let it be known that she wished to be called the Presidential Partner, but soon it was back to First Lady. Her maiden name resurfaced, however, and she became Hillary Rodham Clinton. She banned smoking in the White House, a far cry from the situation under Grant and an ordinance that appeared to rule out a visit by the Chinese leader Deng Xiaoping. (A few months later her husband was photographed revolving a cigar in his mouth and though White House spokesmen claimed he was chewing on it rather than smoking it, a close examination of the presidential jaw as reproduced in the picture suggests he was actually sucking on it — preparatory to lighting up? It would be dangerous to speculate.)

Hillary was put in charge of a 'task force' — a favourite device of Clinton's and his hero JFK — to sort out the expensive chaos of the health system, with six Cabinet officers reporting to her, and to help her as First Lady had a staff five of which enjoyed presidential assistant rank. One had been the maximum for her predecessors. In the summer of 1993 her position was clarified by a US District of Columbia Court of Appeals ruling that her status was that of a Federal official.

Already commentators are speculating that Hillary Clinton may run for President in 1996 or 2000. It would be more than a replay on a national scale of the Alabama gubernatorial elections of 20 years ago, when Lurleen Wallace succeeded her husband George. Hillary Clinton is clearly no stalking horse for her husband. Yet inasmuch as the Clintons hail from the South, it would show that the South has come of age.

BIOGRAPHICAL DETAILS AND DESCENDANTS

CLINTON, WILLIAM JEFFERSON [President William Clinton, The White House, 1600 Pennsylvania Avenue NW, Washington, DC 20500, USA; 1800 Center St, Little Rock, AR 72206, USA], b William (Bill or Billy) Jefferson Blythe, Hope, Ark., 19 Aug 1946, legally adopted by stepf Roger Clinton 1950; educ Miss Mary's Kindergarten, Hope, Georgetown U, University Coll, Oxford, UK (Rhodes Scholar), and Yale (JD 1973); Staff Atty US House of Reps Judiciary Ctee 1972-73, Prof Law U of Arkansas Law Sch at Fayetteville, also practice as lawyer, 1973-76, candidate US House of Reps from 3rd Arkansas Dist 1974, Atty-Gen Arkansas 1977-79, Govr Arkansas 1979-81 and 1981-92, with law firm Wright, Lindsey & Jennings, Little Rock, 1981-82, Chm Southern Growth Policies Bd 1985-86, Chm and Memb Steering Ctee Educn Commission of the States 1986-87, Chm Dem Ldrship Cncl 1990-, Hon Fellow University Coll, Oxford, UK, 1992, 42nd President (D) of the USA 1993-, Hon Degree Northeastern U, Boston, 1993, Memb: Carnegie Fndn Task Force on Adolescent Educn, ABA, Arkansas Bar Assoc, Nat Govrs Assoc (V-Chm 1986, Chm 1986-87, Co-Chm Educn Task Force 1990-, Memb: Exec, Finance, Human Resources, Internat Trade & For Rels, Rural Devpt Ctees), author: *Putting People First*; m 1975 *Hillary (b between 24 and 31 Oct 1947; educ Wellesley and Yale Law Sch; ptnr Rose Law, attys, of Little Rock, Ark., Chm Children's Defense Fnd, Washington, DC, former head Arkansas Educn Standards Ctee, Chm Presidential Task Force on National Health Reform 1993-, recipient Lewis Hine Award for services to children, Hon Dr of Laws U of Michigan 1993), dau of Hugh Rodham, clothing store-proprietor, of Chicago, and his w Dorothy, and has issue:

President Clinton's daughter
I *Chelsea CLINTON, b 1980; educ Mann Magnet Sch, Little Rock, Ark., and Sidwell Friends Sch, Washington, DC

MALE LINE ANCESTRY AND COLLATERAL DESCENDANTS

Andrew J. BLYTHE, b S Carolina c 1801; was living Marshall Co, Miss., 1850; m 18— Jane —— (b Tennessee c 1808, living in Tippah Co, Miss., as late as 1870) and d in or before 1860, leaving issue:

Thomas Jefferson BLYTHE, b Alabama 1 Aug 1829; living in Marshall Co, Miss., by 1850 and Tippah Co, Miss., by 1860, Pte Mississippi Infy Confederate States Army Civil War; m 1st Marshall Co 1 Jan 1849 Esther Elvira (b probably Rutherford Co, Tenn., c 1825; d c 1865), dau of Moses Baum (b N Carolina 25 Feb 1804; d Marshall Co, Miss., 4 May 1853) and his w Mary —— (b Kentucky 3 July 1802; d Marshall Co, Miss., 24 Nov 1862); m 2nd Nov 1867, as her 2nd husb, Elizabeth Melvinia (1831-1906), dau of Elias Hines and his w Polly, of Tippah Co, and widow of Thomas Franklin Lockhart (k Battle of Atlanta 22 July 1864); Thomas J. Blythe d Tippah Co 6 Aug 1907, having with his 1st w had issue (with another s William Jefferson Farr BLYTHE, after whom the latter's nephew was named — see below):

Henry Patton Foote BLYTHE, b Tippah Co 18 Sept 1851; m Ripley, Miss., 29 Oct 1874 Frances Ellen (Fannie) (b Tippah Co 2 Dec 1857; d Grayson Co, Tex., 11 July 1936), dau of John F. Hines (b Tenn. c 1833, bro of Thomas J. Blythe's 2nd w

— *see above*; *d* Parker Co, Tex., 11 Nov 1902) and his w Eliza Emily Lockhart (*b* N Carolina 18 Oct 1832; *d* Tippah Co 27 Dec 1904), and *d* Tippah Co 3 July 1898, leaving issue:

William Jefferson BLYTHE II, *b* Tippah Co 21 Jan 1882 or 1884; *m* there 19 Aug 1906 Lou Birchie (*b* Tippah Co 9 Feb 1893; *d* Sherman, Grayson Co, Tex., 15 Feb 1946), dau of Simpson Green ('Dick') Ayers (*b* Georgia 27 Oct 1820; *d* Tippah Co 27 May 1897) and his w Hattie Hayes (*b* either Florida or at sea 1852 or 23 July 1858; *d* Kossuth, Alcom Co, Miss., 16 Aug 1935) and *d* Grayson Co 5 Feb 1935, leaving issue (with a dau, *Vera, aged 69 in June 1993; *m* 19— *— RAMEY):

William Jefferson BLYTHE III, *b* Sherman, Grayson Co, Tex., 27 Feb 1918; travelling salesman; *m* 1st Dec 1935 (divorce *c* 1937) Adele Gash Coffelt (*b* 21 June 1918; *m* 2nd California 19— Charles Ritzenthaler, police chief of Brawley, Calif.) and had issue:

I *Henry Leon RITZENTHALER, *b* Blythe 17 Jan 1938 but changed name aged *c* eight years old; former owner of caretaker business; *m* 19— *Judith ——

William J. Blythe III *m* 2nd 19— *Faye Coffelt, his 1st w's sister; *m* 3rd? 1941 (divorce 194-) *Wannetta — and with her had issue:

II *Sharron (later changed name to Sharon) Lee Blythe, *b* Kansas City 11 May 1941; *m* 19— *Bob PETTIJOHN

William J. Blythe III *m* 3rd/4th Texarkana, Ark., 3 Sept 1943, as her 1st husb, *Virginia Dell (*b* Bodcaw, Nevada Co, Ark., 6 June 1923; nurse and anaesthetist), dau of (James) Eldridge Cassidy (*b* Parker Township, Nevada Co, Ark., 19 Aug 1898; store-keeper and night watchman; *d* Hope, Hempstead Co, Ark., 11 March 1957) and his w Edith Vallie or Valeria Grisham (*b* Bodcaw, Ark., 2 Nov 1901; *d* Hope 17 Jan 1968), and *d* nr Sikeston, Scott Co, Mo., 17 May 1946 by drowning in a rain-filled ditch following a road accident, leaving issue:

III/I WILLIAM (BILL) JEFFERSON BLYTHE IV, took stepf's name of CLINTON 12 June 1962, 42nd PRESIDENT of the UNITED STATES of AMERICA

Virginia Cassidy Blythe *m* 2nd 1950 (divorce May 1962) Roger CLINTON, car salesman (*b* 25 July 1909; *d* Nov 1967 of cancer), who adopted his stepson, and with him had issue:

II *Roger CLINTON, Jr, *b c* 1957; sentenced 1984 to one year in prison for drug-dealing; television production assist

Mrs Virginia Cassidy Blythe Clinton *m* 3rd Aug 1962 (for the 2nd time) Roger CLINTON; *m* 4th 1968, as his 2nd w, Jeff DWIRE (hairdresser; *m* 1st 19— —— and had at least one child, a dau Dianne, *b c* 1947, who *m* before 1968 Buford Welch, oil company owner, and served six years imprisonment 1986-92 of a 45-year sentence for drug offences and armed robbery; Jeff Dwire *d* 1974 of diabetes); *m* 5th 1986 *Richard (Dick) KELLEY, sometime food wholesaler

BILL CLINTON FAMILY TREE

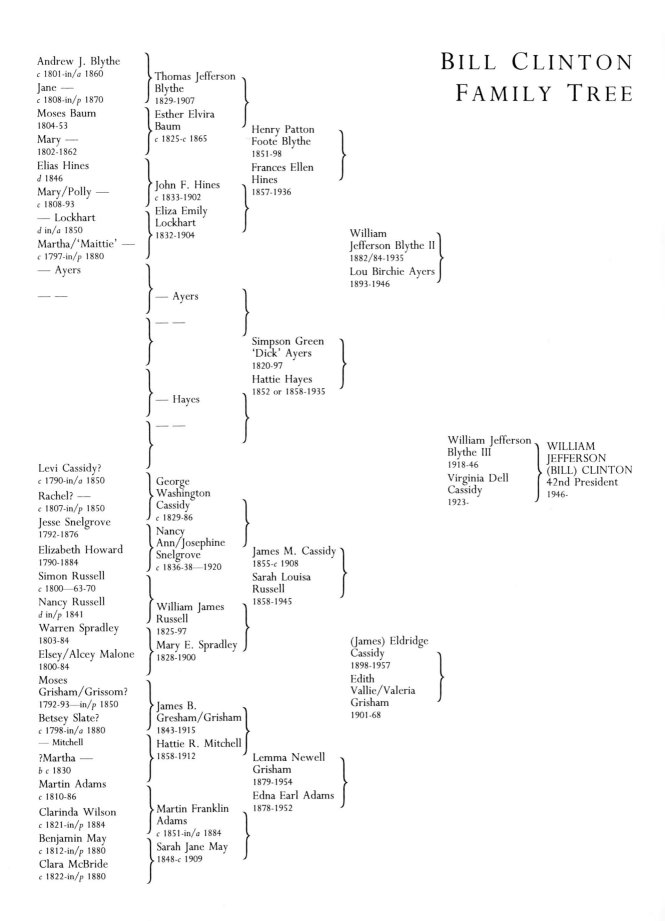

Andrew J. Blythe
c 1801-in/*a* 1860

Jane —
c 1808-in/*p* 1870

Moses Baum
1804-53

Mary —
1802-1862

Elias Hines
d 1846

Mary/Polly —
c 1808-93

— Lockhart
d in/*a* 1850

Martha/'Maittie' —
c 1797-in/*p* 1880

— Ayers

— —

Levi Cassidy?
c 1790-in/*a* 1850

Rachel? —
c 1807-in/*p* 1850

Jesse Snelgrove
1792-1876

Elizabeth Howard
1790-1884

Simon Russell
c 1800—63-70

Nancy Russell
d in/*p* 1841

Warren Spradley
1803-84

Elsey/Alcey Malone
1800-84

Moses Grisham/Grissom?
1792-93—in/*p* 1850

Betsey Slate?
c 1798-in/*a* 1880

— Mitchell

?Martha —
b c 1830

Martin Adams
c 1810-86

Clarinda Wilson
c 1821-in/*p* 1884

Benjamin May
c 1812-in/*p* 1880

Clara McBride
c 1822-in/*p* 1880

Thomas Jefferson Blythe
1829-1907

Esther Elvira Baum
c 1825-*c* 1865

John F. Hines
c 1833-1902

Eliza Emily Lockhart
1832-1904

— Ayers

— —

— Hayes

— —

George Washington Cassidy
c 1829-86

Nancy Ann/Josephine Snelgrove
c 1836-38—1920

William James Russell
1825-97

Mary E. Spradley
1828-1900

James B. Gresham/Grisham
1843-1915

Hattie R. Mitchell
1858-1912

Martin Franklin Adams
c 1851-in/*a* 1884

Sarah Jane May
1848-*c* 1909

Henry Patton Foote Blythe
1851-98

Frances Ellen Hines
1857-1936

Simpson Green 'Dick' Ayers
1820-97

Hattie Hayes
1852 or 1858-1935

James M. Cassidy
1855-*c* 1908

Sarah Louisa Russell
1858-1945

(James) Eldridge Cassidy
1898-1957

Edith Vallie/Valeria Grisham
1901-68

Lemma Newell Grisham
1879-1954

Edna Earl Adams
1878-1952

William Jefferson Blythe II
1882/84-1935

Lou Birchie Ayers
1893-1946

William Jefferson Blythe III
1918-46

Virginia Dell Cassidy
1923-

WILLIAM JEFFERSON (BILL) CLINTON
42nd President
1946-

AMERICAN ORDERS
OF CHIVALRY

BY DUANE L.C.M. GALLES

It is said that there are some 300,000 members of the French Legion of Honour, founded by Napoleon in 1802. Moreover, an estimated one Frenchman in six possesses the right to some order or decoration. Indeed, until quite recently a Frenchman was considered rather a failure in life if he had not been appointed to the Legion of Honour by the time he was forty years of age.[1]

Yet titles and decorations are things that few Americans have had to contend with, thanks to the Federal Constitution of 1787. The furore which followed the establishment of the Society of the Cincinnati in 1783 left an indelible mark on America. The opposition to that association of veteran officers of the Continental Army of the United States was so strong that to this day it remains enshrined in three clauses of the United States Constitution of 1787. One clause forbids the Federal Government to grant titles of nobility. Another clause lays the same prohibition on state governments. A third clause forbids Federal officials, without the consent of Congress, to accept titles or honours "from any king, prince or foreign state".[2]

The prohibitions were so rigidly adhered to that even medals for the reward of civil or military service were created by the United States with the greatest reluctance. It was only the great cataclysm of the Civil War that moved Congress to institute the Congressional Medal of Honor, America's counterpart to the Victoria Cross. And it was not until this century that the Legion of Merit, counterpart of the Order of the Bath, and the Presidential Medal of Freedom, counterpart of the Order of the British Empire, were created. The Legion of Merit dates only from 1942. The Medal of Freedom dates only from 1945 and, in its present form, from 1963. Even the Military Order of the Purple Heart, instituted in 1782 by General Washington, was permitted thereafter to fall into abeyance. It was only revived by Congress in 1932 during the celebration of the bicentenary of the birth of Washington. Today it is bestowed on members of the armed forces wounded in action or killed in battle.[3]

Nevertheless, America has not been without a number of Orders. Some of these antedate the 1787 constitutional provisions. Others were created by territories before their incorporation into the United States. The creation of these American orders tended to coincide with two modern bursts of activity in Europe along the honours front. The first wave began in 1687 with the creation of the Scots Order of the Thistle. The following year began a series of wars over the succession of the British and Spanish thrones, which ended only in 1715 with the Peace of Utrecht. During those two and a half decades of war European princes found it expedient to create eleven new orders. By contrast, the previous two centuries had witnessed the creation of very few new orders, and from Utrecht until the advent of the French Revolution relative quiet returned to the honours front.

The second burst of honours activity was set off by the creation in 1802 of the Legion of Honour. Child of the French Revolution, the new honour did not confer nobility on the recipient. Rather, it was an honour to recognize the personal merit of the recipient. This new type of honour often used a laurel wreath in place of a military trophy as a device to suspend its badge from the ribbon. It endeavoured to reform the honours system in accordance with the revolutionary concept of the career open to talent.[4]

I. THE NOBLE ORDER OF THE SUN (1705)

The Order of the Sun was created in 1705 by His Excellency the Palatine of Carolina and the other Lords Proprietors of that province. The act of creation formed part of the patent of office by which their lordships created Lawrence Cromp, already York Herald, "principal herald of the whole province of Carolina, by the name of Carolina Herald". In that same patent their lordships authorized Cromp to invest the Carolina provincial nobility, called landgraves and caciques, with a "purple ribbon or gold chain with the Sun in its Glory pendent at the same, with this Motto about the face of the said sun, *Videt quae Deus hanc lucem esse bonum* ("and God saw that this light was good"). The patent went on to confirm the landgraves and caciques of Carolina "and their Heirs for ever all the above-mentioned Honorable Distinctions of Nobility". Further, the Carolina nobility were enjoined and required always to appear wearing this distinction.

The Carolina provincial nobility thus formed a distinct and hereditary juridical order and from 1705 they possessed a special badge or emblem as well. Their badge is reminiscent of the badge of the Baronets of Nova Scotia, which was suspended from an orange tawny ribbon. In that both orders were hereditary, there is a further parallel. Finally, one might note that originally the Baronets of Nova Scotia were charged with settling or financing the settlement of the province of Nova Scotia. The nobility of the province of Carolina had a similar task.[5]

Since the Order was created as an hereditary order, it may still be in existence today. Several grants of the title of landgrave and cacique are known to have been made. It would only be necessary to review the terms of the grant and prove the appropriate descent through a line entitled to inherit under it in order to lay claim to the Order. The problem is that Carolina Herald does not exist today to pass on claims to these titles.[6] Thus there would not seem to be any forum in which a claimant could vindicate his claim. Nevertheless, the Order of the Sun remains of interest as the first American order.

II. THE ORDER OF THE GOLDEN HORSESHOE (1716)

The Order of the Golden Horseshoe was founded shortly after the Carolina order in neighbouring Virginia. It owes its founding to His Excellency Colonel Alexander Spotswood, Governor of the province. Colonel Spotswood was Quartermaster General of the British Army during the War of the Spanish Succession. Then in 1710 at the age of thirty-four he was appointed Deputy Governor of Virginia. Spotswood was a builder. He contributed generously to the rebuilding of Bruton parish church in the provincial capital of Williamsburg. Very conscious of his vice-regal dignity, Spotswood had constructed in the restored church a special gubernatorial pew, raised above the floor of the church on a platform and covered with a canopy. Around the interior in gilt letters he emblazoned his name.

Governor Spotswood also took direct charge of the construction of the Governor's Palace, as Government House in Virginia was called. "A magnificent structure", declared the Reverend Hugh Jones in 1724, "built at public Expense, furnished and beautified with Gates, fine gardens, Offices, Walks, a fine Canal, Orchards". At Government House we are assured royal birthdays and other occasions were celebrated as "splendid entertainments" during Spotswood's time.

But Spotswood was not only a builder. He had also the strategic vision of a general. Already in 1710 he was writing the Board of Trade in London, which had oversight of the British overseas empire, advising them not to permit the French settlements in Quebec and Louisiana to establish land communications between them. He proposed a "Tramontine Expedition" to explore the trans-Appalachian region. Six years later he returned to the idea and himself organized an expedition to cross the Appalachian Mountains. He hoped to find a route through the mountains to enable the British to colonize the trans-Appalachian region and thus steal a march on the French, who were fast approaching from both the north and the south. He set out with a small band of associates on 20 August 1716, on what proved to be a month-long expedition. On 5 September the expedition reached "the very top of the Appalachian Mountains" and there they drank "King George's health and all the Royal Family's". The next day they crossed the Shenandoah River and there Governor Spotswood buried a bottle in which he had enclosed a proclamation taking possession of the land in the name of George I. The site was near the present Elkton, Virginia.

To commemorate the event Governor Spotswood bestowed on each of the Gentlemen Adventurers who accompanied him a miniature golden horseshoe. On the obverse it was inscribed, *Sic juvat transcendere montes*. On the reverse was written "Tramontine Order". Those so decorated were called "Knights of the Golden Horseshoe". The motto referred to the large quantity of spare horseshoes carried by the expedition in order to negotiate the mountainous terrain. The Order was and remained commemorative in nature and there is no indication of any creations beyond the original ones.

Its name, however, recalled several predecessor orders. Shortly after his accession in 1603 King James I and VI of England and Scotland had instituted a British Order of Golden Knights. The Order had as its corporate purpose the finance of the search for precious metals in Britain. Two knights had actually been appointed before Secretary of State Robert Cecil was able to persuade the King to abandon the project.

Perhaps the most famous of the *equites aurati* or golden knights were those created by the popes. The name derived from the golden spurs which knights customarily received when made knights, and papal creations of golden knights date from the second half of the 14th century. From the 17th century papal Knights of the Golden Spur wore a Maltese cross of gold, enamelled white and suspended from a red neck ribbon.[7] It is of interest that the Virginia order preceded by a decade the creation of the British Order of the Bath.

III. THE SOCIETY OF THE CINCINNATI (1783)

The Society of the Cincinnati was instituted in 1783 as a society of officers of the Continental Army and their male descendants. Officers of the allied French expeditionary army were also included in membership. While its founding document, the "Institution", calls it merely "one Society of Friends" and states that its purpose was "to render permanent the cordial affection subsisting among the officers", the Society of the Cincinnati quickly became more than a mere club. Foreigners quickly came to view it as an official American order and, for Americans during its first century, it functioned as though it were one. Its enemies claimed it would transform itself into an American nobility and Thomas Jefferson called for its abolition. But King Louis XVI gave his approval to the order and undertook to serve as its patron. He authorized Frenchmen to wear its decoration and many, including the Marquis de Lafayette, enthusiastically did so. Czar Alexander I expressly requested Baron Gustavus de Rosenthal to wear the decoration. As "Major John Rose" the Baron had served in the Continental Army before returning to Russia at the close of the Revolutionary War. Today the Grand Chancellery of the Legion of Honour, while not recognizing it as an order, permits French citizens to wear its decoration on the right lapel.

The decoration consists of an eagle in gold charged with a medallion showing three senators presenting Cincinnatus with a sword and including the motto, *Omnia relinquit servare rem publicam,* "he left all to serve the commonwealth". The 'eagle', as the decoration is called, is suspended from a blue ribbon, edged white, symbolic of the Franco-American alliance during the Revolutionary War. Washington was its first head with the title of 'President General' and the French members presented him with an eagle set with diamonds. This diamond eagle was presented by his widow to his successor in office, Alexander Hamilton, and has since become an heirloom of office, passing in succession to each head of the organization. Today there are some 3,000 members.

While never actually an official American order, it quickly came to function as though it were. The leading officers of the War of 1812, for example, were elected to honorary membership, entitling them to wear the eagle. Commodore Oliver Hazard Perry and Thomas Macdonough not only wore the eagle as though it were a national decoration, they also had their portraits painted wearing it. After the Mexican War Commodore Matthew C. Perry and General Zachary Taylor in 1847 likewise were made honorary members. Until the advent of the Congressional Medal of Honour in the 1860s the Cincinnati eagle thus enjoyed the quasi-official status of an American order.[8]

IV. THE ORDER OF SAN JACINTO (1843)

In 1838 the Republic of Texas established its independence from Mexico as the number of its English-speaking residents expanded. The new republic quickly achieved recognition by the great powers and the exchange of diplomats followed. But as a sparsely settled country without capital or industry its financial resources were slender. Not able to reward its friends with cash, Texas adopted the time-honoured expedient of creating and dispensing honours. During the previous century Oliver Goldsmith had pointed out this useful aspect of honours. He maintained that "while a European king has a yard of blue or green ribbon left, he need be under no apprehension of wanting statesmen, generals, and soldiers". His contemporary, Horace Walpole, called the Most Honourable Order of the Bath, created in 1725, "an artful bank of thirty-six Ribbands to supply a fund of favours in lieu of places".[9]

And so in 1843 Sam Houston, as President of the Republic of Texas, created the Order of San Jacinto. He announced its creation in a letter to William Hendry Daingerfeld, Texas's chargé d'affaires to The Netherlands. The letter announced that Daingerfeld was created a Knight of San Jacinto, as was Colonel Ashbel Smith, Texas's envoy to Britain and France. The ensign of the Order consisted of a green ribbon worn in the buttonhole of the coat. It does not appear that the Order possessed any badge, and no other grade than that of knight was mentioned. Presumably, as President of the Republic and creator of the Order, Sam Houston was also a member and its grand master. Houston explained that the Order was created as "some reward for the worthy, as we have no cash, to encourage Gentlemen in preserving order".

Only two years later, in 1845, Texas was annexed to the United States. There is no indication if any further honours were bestowed after the initial creations. It would appear that after Texas became part of the United States the Order of San Jacinto fell into abeyance.[10]

V. THE ORDER OF KAMEHAMEHA (1865)

Early in the 19th century the Hawaiian kingdom came under British influence, as can be seen from the presence of the British Union Jack in Hawaii's flag. In 1862 Queen Victoria became the godmother to King Kamehameha's son and the British influence was soon apparent in the Hawaiian orders. The order of Kamehameha was created in 1865 by the great Hawaiian king Kamehameha V (1863-72). It commemorated the other great Hawaiian monarch of the same name who in 1810 had united the eight Hawaiian Islands under a single sovereign. The King of Hawaii was to be grand master of the new order. It consisted of three grades. There were to be twelve knights grand cross, thirty knight commanders and fifty knights. Foreign members did not count toward these limits. The order could be awarded for all types of meritorious service.

Its badge was a white enamelled Maltese cross in gold surmounted by a Hawaiian royal crown. In the centre was a medallion in blue enamel bearing the cipher 'K' and surrounded by a fillet inscribed "Kamehameha". Between the arms of the cross were a number of pencil rays in gold. The ribbon of the order was red edged white for knights grand cross. For knight commanders and knights it was of alternate red and white stripes. The star of the order for grand crosses was in the same design as the badge but without the crown. Queen Victoria and the Japanese Emperor Mutsuhito were grand crosses of the order.[11]

VI. THE ORDER OF KALAKAUA (1875)

A decade after the creation of the Order of Kamehameha, the Order of Kalakaua was established by the newly-elected King Kalakaua (1874-91). It marked the accession of a new dynasty. This order consisted of four grades: grand cross, grand officer, knight commander and knight companion.

The badge of the order was a blue enamel Maltese cross with a white enamel border surmounted by the Hawaiian royal crown. Between the arms of the cross were four golden club-sceptres and in the centre was a blue enamel medallion charged also with a club-sceptre within a white fillet inscribed "Kalakaua".

The ribbon consisted of four blue stripes alternated with four white ones. The star of the order for grand crosses was identical to the badge but was without the crown above the cross. The sugar magnate Claus Spreckels was a knight commander of the Order of Kalakaua.[12]

VII. THE ORDER OF KAPIOLANI THE GREAT (1881)

The Order of Kapiolani the Great was created in 1881, although its statutes, printed in 1883, bore the date 30 August 1880. It appears that the order became a public decoration during King Kalakaua's world tour in 1881, whereas previously it had been a personal, unofficial decoration. The King's consort,

Queen Kapiolani, was the granddaughter of Kaumualii, the last King of Kauai. The order was established to reward distinguished services to the crown, the state, or the people of Hawaii as well as to recognize distinguished achievements in the arts and sciences. The order was the first Hawaiian order to make provision for the admission of women. It was divided into seven grades. These were grand cross, high grand officer, grand officer, commander, officer, companion and lady companion. Foreigners were eligible for membership.

The badge of the order consisted of a Maltese cross, enamelled red and edged gold, and on a red centre medallion was the monogram 'K' within a white fillet inscribed "Kulia i Kanuo". On the upper arm of the cross was a golden medallion bearing a portrait of Queen Kapiolani and atop the arm rested a golden regal crown. Between the four arms of the cross were four golden regal crowns. The star for grand crosses was similar but lacked the crown atop the cross. The ribbon was yellow, edged white, red and blue. The authoress Lady Brassey (1839-87), who was also a Dame of the Venerable Order of Saint John of Jerusalem, was a lady companion of the order. Likewise Isabella Bird Bishop.[13]

VIII. THE ORDER OF THE CROWN OF HAWAII (1882)

The Order of the Crown of Hawaii was created on 12 September 12 1882. It was divided into five grades, namely, grand cross, grand officer, commander, officer and knight. Foreigners were eligible to receive it.

The badge of the order was a white enamelled cross surmounted by a golden regal crown with a central medallion also charged with a crown and surrounded by a circlet inscribed "Order Crown of Hawaii".[14]

IX. THE ORDER OF THE STAR OF OCEANIA (1886)

The Order of the Star of Oceania was created by King Kalakaua on 16 December 1886 and was intended to reward foreigners for services to the Hawaiian state. In fact, it formed part of the King's vision of a Polynesian federation to include Hawaii, Samoa and Tonga - the Pacific nations not yet claimed by European powers. A Samoan-Hawaiian treaty of political alliance and confederation was in fact signed and on 7 January 1887 the insignia of the grand cross of the Order of the Star of Oceania were presented by an Hawaiian emissary to King Malietoa of Samoa. But the king's project foundered when four German warships arrived in Samoa. King Malietoa was forced into exile and a German puppet ruler was installed in his stead.

The order was divided into five grades, namely, grand cross, grand officer, commander, officer and knight. The badge of the order was a green, white-edged and five-pointed star with gold balls at the points and gold rays between the arms. In the centre was a medallion enamelled white and bearing the Hawaiian banner and surrounded by the inscription, "Ka. Koku o Osiania", the star of oceania. The badge was summounted by a royal crown.

The ribbon of the order was green, edged white. It and the other Hawaiian orders apparently ceased to be conferred after the overthrow of the monarchy in 1893. In 1898 the Republic of Hawaii was annexed by the United States.

NOTES

1. Sir Ivan de la Bere, The Queen's Orders of Chivalry (London, 1964), p. 15.

2. U.S. Constitution, article I, sections 9, 10.

3. Robert Werlich, Orders and Decorations of All Nations (Washington, 1974), pp. 1-4, 9, 15-17.

4. D'Arcy Jonathan Dacre Boulton, *The Knights of the Crown: The Monarchical Orders of Knighthood in Later Mediaeval Europe, 1325-1520* (New York, 1987), pp. 499-500. This article deals only with orders, not with titles or decorations. For a taxonomy of orders, *see* Boulton, pp. xvii-xxi. He divides orders of knighthood into two broad categories, secular and religious orders. Secular orders he divides into 'True Orders' (those with a rule or statutes to govern daily life and corporate activities) and 'Pseudo Orders' (those with no rule or statutes). 'True Orders' are further divided into monarchical, confraternal, fraternal, or votive orders. 'Pseudo Orders' might be 'cliental' or 'honorific'; the former bound the members by an oath of clientship to a prince who bestowed the 'order' in the form of a badge; the latter bore no special obligations for their members and were the predecessors of the present orders of merit, like the Legion of Honour. This study includes only orders created by public authority and thus does not include any of the numerous private organizations which are merely non-profit corporations, organized under the general nonprofit corporation law of some jurisdiction employing the word 'Order' in their corporate style, unless there has been further recognition by a public authority, as in the case of the Society of the Cincinnati.

5. Joseph I. Waring, "The Carolina Herald", *South Carolina Historical Magazine,* 72 (July, 1971), 161; Francis W. Pixley, *A History of the Baronetage* (London, 1900), p. 200. It may be significant that the Joint Committee on Flag and Seal of the Senate and House of Representatives of the Confederate States of America on 19 April 1862 introduced into the Confederate Congress a joint resolution that the Confederate flag be "a red field charged with a white saltire, having in the center the device of a sun in its glory on an azure ground [shield], the rays of the sun corresponding with the number of the States composing the Confederacy". Devereaux D. Cannon, *The Flags of the Confederacy: An Illustrated History* (Memphis, 1988), p. 14. Had this joint resolution been adopted, the Order of the Sun might have been revived as a Confederate order of merit or decoration.

6. For a blueprint for the revival of the office of Carolina Herald, see D. Galles, "A Southern Call to Arms: An Armorial Compact", *William Mitchell Law Review,* 16 (1990), 1281-1291.

7. Armistead C. Gordon, "Governor Alexander Spotswood and the Knights of the Golden Horseshoe" in *Men and Events: Chapters of Virginia History* (Staunton, Va., 1923), pp. 122, 126-129, 135-136, 143, 148; H. C. de Zeininger, "L'Ordre de l'Eperon d'Or", *Archives Heraldique Suisses* 52 (1939), 91, 94; George Pratt Insh, *Scottish Colonial Schemes 1620-1686* (Glasgow, 1922), p. 62.

8. Minor Myers, Jr., *Liberty Without Anarchy: A History of the Society of the Cincinnati* (Charlottesville, Va., 1983), pp. 49, 56, 162, 200, 212, 238, 255, 256, 259, 262.

9. Oliver Goldsmith, *Happiness and Show,* quoted in Michael De-la-Noy, *The Honours System* (London, 1985), p. 5; James C. Risk, *The History of the Order of the Bath* (London. 1972), p. 1.

10. Amelia W. Williams and Eugene C. Barker (eds.), *The Writings of Sam Houston, 1813-1863* (Washington, 1940) III, p. 311.

11. J. H. Lawrence-Archer, *The Orders of Chivalry* (London, 1887), p. 317; H. Gourdon de Genouillac, *Nouveau Dictionnaire des Ordres de Chevalerie* (Paris, 1891), p. 150; Ralph S. Kuykendall, *The Hawaiian Kingdom: Volume III, 1874-1893; The Kalakaua Dynasty* (Honolulu, 1967), p. 229.

12. Lawrence-Archer, p. 318: Gourdon de Genouillac, p. 149; Kuykendall, p. 229, 298; Spreckels was also a grand officer in the Order of Kapiolani and in the Order of the Crown of Hawaii. *Ibid. p. 297.*

13. Lawrence-Archer, p. 319; Gourdon de Genouillac, p. 151; Kuykendall, p. 220. [Isabella Bird Bishop (1831-1904) was an explorer and author of *The Hawaiian Archipelago* (1875) — Ed]

14. Gourdon de Genouillac, p. 74

15. *Ibid.,* 123; Kuykendall, p. 327: Vaclav Mericka, *Orders and Decorations* (London, 1967), p. 101.

PRESIDENTIAL
COATS OF ARMS

(see endpapers)

Only two Presidents have been granted or officially assumed coats of arms: Eisenhower and Kennedy. Others may have been of armigerous families (Monroe or Buchanan, for instance) but they would have had to furnish better proof of their descent than currently exists before they could legitimately display the Monroe or Buchanan coat of arms. And even then, since they were from a junior branch (if any), the arms would have had to bear a mark of 'difference' to show this. That holds true even of Washington, whose ancestors were undoubtedly armigerous but who himself was of a junior line.

President Eisenhower was created a Knight of the Order of the Elephant by Christian X of Denmark in 1945. Normally no coat of arms is granted simultaneously (Denmark has no College of Arms, King of Arms or official rules regarding the use and display of arms). Instead, the new knight is asked to deliver an armorial device to be used on his stall plate in Frederiksborg Castle. This can be either an existing one or a new one. In Eisenhower's case we are informed by the Societas Heraldica Scandinavica that an old German coat of arms of the family was used. It seems, however, that the Eisenhower coat of arms was designed for the General (as he then still was) by Dom Wilfrid Bayne (1893-1974), of St Gregory's Abbey, Portsmouth, Rhode Island, a leading American heraldic designer and descendant of the Carters of Virginia (hence kin to the Harrison Presidents and also possibly to Jimmy Carter). Eisenhower then assumed them for the purpose of display in his stall at Frederiksborg. According to Danish convention the arms are heritable by both President Eisenhower's male and female descendants.

The arms — *Or, an anvil azure* — and crest — *An orle of five mullets argent* — refer to the Pennsylvania German word *eisenhauer*, meaning 'iron-beater' or 'iron-hewer', hence are what is called 'canting'. The tincture (colour) of the anvil recalls the 'dress blues' uniform of a US Army officer, the mullets on the crest the badge of a five-star general. The arms are shown inside the front cover of this book.

President Kennedy referred to heraldry in his first State of the Union message to Congress on 30 Jan 1961. He said "On the presidential Coat of Arms, the American eagle holds in his right talon the olive branch, while in his left is held a bundle of arrows. We intend to give equal attention to both."

The Chief Herald of Ireland designed a coat of arms for President Kennedy which incorporated the three helmets of the O'Kennedys of Ormonde. This motif is also canting, in that the Gaelic *Ó Cinnéide* means 'helmet-headed'. The border of red and ermine introduces elements traditionally associated with the Fitzgeralds of Desmond (President Kennedy's mother's family name being of course Fitzgerald).

The crest refers generally to the US eagle claws and their arrows and olive branch and specifically to the speech quoted above. The coat of arms with crest is shown inside the back cover of this book.

In heraldic language President Kennedy's arms are *Sable three helmets in profile or within a bordure per saltire gules and ermine* and the crest is *Between two olive branches a cubit sinister arm in armour erect, the hand holding a sheaf of four arrows, points upwards, all proper, mantled gules doubled argent.*

INDEX

Brown, Janet Dodge Garfield, 493
Brown, Jean F. Martin, 493
Brown, Kate Deming, 90
Brown, Louise H. Ingalls, 581
Brown, Mark Alan, 195
Brown, Mary Patricia Wiley, 66
Brown, Nancy Lee Fitzhugh, 335
Brown, Philip Henry, 121
Brown, Rodney, 185
Brown, Sarah Fuller, 90
Brown, Willard W., 581
Brown, Jr, Willard H., 581
Browne, Abigail Adams Mason, 282
Browne, Jr, Alfred L., 282
Browne III, Alfred L., 282
Browne, Charles Billings, 491
Browne, Edward Crowninshield, 491
Browne, Jr, Edward Crowninshield, 491
Browne, Frances Ann Kiehn, 106
Browne, Louisa Huntington, 491
Browne, Louisa Huntington Garfield, 491
Browne, Mary Langdon, 106
Browne, Mason Garfield, 491
Browne, Priscilla Crowninshield, 282
Browne, William Prichard, 106
Bruce, Graeme Grant, 164
Bruhn, Elizabeth McClaughry Henry, 430
Bryan, Catherine Augusta, 161
Bryan, Elizabeth Walker, 161
Bryan, John Edward, 161
Bryan, John Randolph, 161
Bryan III, Jonathan, 161
Bryan, Judy Lynn Blackwell, 161
Bryan, Robert Carter, 161
Bryan, Robert Coalter, 161
Bryan, Susan Carter Agnor, 161
Bryan, Will Hamilton, 161
Bryant, Clara Irene Harrison Tanner, 323
Bryant, William, 323
Buchholz, James, 530
Buchholz, Lynda Wrae Williams, 530
Buchholz, Robert, 530
Burba, Linda Ford, 714
Burba, Theodore Vance, 715
Burbank, Ellen Randolph Coolidge, 204
Burbank, Peter Jefferson, 204
Burbank, Stephen Bradner, 204
Burchfield, Camilla James, 510
Burchfield, Cornelia Gibb McLane, 510
Burchfield, Jennifer Gibb, 510
Burchfield, William McLane, 510
Burchfield, William Wulfhorst, 510
Burgess, Angel Marie, 181
Burgess, Christina Rachelle, 181
Burgess, Evelyn Joyce, 181
Burgess, Larisa Jane, 181
Burgess, Lisa Grace, 181
Burgess, Sharon Nicole, 181
Burgess, Susan Jane, 181
Burgess, Susan Jane Lancaster, 181
Burgess, Thomas, 181
Burgess, Jr, Thomas, 181
Burgess, Thomas Walter, 181
Burke, Agnes Hayes Honeycutt, 211

Burke, Chaffee Kem Shackelford, 187
Burke, Jr, Charles Joseph, 682
Burke, Claire Coliton, 682
Burke, Claire Juliette Geszty Gardiner, 211
Burke, Cornelia Lee Baum, 212
Burke, Daniel, 114
Burke, Gertrude Ann, 682
Burke, Harriet Holland Hackett, 212
Burke, James Stuart Chaffee, 187
Burke, Jane Randolph, 212
Burke, Joan Ruth Arnold, 212
Burke, Margot Stuart Shackelford, 187
Burke, Mary Gascoigne Lyne Shackelford, 187
Burke, Mary Weeden, 211
Burke, Nicholas Gordon Trist, 212
Burke, Nicholas Randolph, 211
Burke, Pamela DeWindt, 114
Burke II, Thomas Francis, 682
Burleigh, Christopher Medlicott, 363
Burleigh, John Medlicott, 363
Burleigh, Lane Shattuck, 363
Burleigh, Pamela Shattuck, 363
Burlinson, Alice Pell, 310
Burlinson, Ellen Van Buren Thomson, 310
Burlinson, Lucy Ellen, 310
Burlinson, Paul Scott, 310
Burnett, Celeste, 399
Burnett, Medora, 399
Burnett, Norma, 399
Burnett, Peter, 399
Burnette, Ann Randolph Bradley, 219
Burnette, R. Bradford, 219
Burns, Douglas Mackey, 151
Burns, Jeffrey Douglas, 151
Burns, Jessica Leigh, 151
Burns, Mary Leigh Bankhead, 151
Burton, Caroline, 106
Burton, John R., 106
Bush, Ashley Walker, 745
Bush, Barbara Pierce, 745
Bush, Charles Walker, 745
Bush, Columba Garnica, 745
Bush, Elizabeth Louise Draper Kauffman, 746
Bush, George Herbert Walker, 744
Bush, George Prescott, 745
Bush, Jr, George Walker, 745
Bush, James L., 747
Bush, Jenna Welch, 745
Bush, John ('Jeb') Ellis, 745
Bush, Jr, John Ellis, 745
Bush, Jonathan James, 747
Bush, Jr, Jonathan James, 747
Bush, Josephine Bradley, 747
Bush, Laura Welch, 745
Bush, Lauren Pierce, 745
Bush, Lindsay Whitaker, 747
Bush, Louisa, 747
Bush, Margaret Molster, 745
Bush, Marshall Lloyd, 745
Bush, Marvin Pierce, 745
Bush, Mary Faith McAdoo Thackwell Haddad, 598
Bush, Neil Mallon, 745
Bush, Noelle Lucila, 745

Bush, Patricia (Patty) Lee Redfern, 747
Bush, Pierce Mallon, 745
Bush, Jr, Prescott Sheldon, 746
Bush III, Prescott S., 746
Bush, Russell V., 598
Bush, Sam, 747
Bush, Sarah, 747
Bush, Sharon Smith, 745
Bush, Susan, 747
Bush, William ('Buck'/'Bucky') Henry Trotter, 747
Bush, William Hall, 747
Bush, William Prescott (Scott), 747
Butcher, Kevin Edward Roland, 164
Butcher, Nicholas Truscott, 164
Butcher, Thomas Randolph, 164
Butcher, Virginia Anne Truscott, 164
Butler, Boyd Evelyn Phillips, 182
Butler, Eddy Louise Hood, 181
Butler, Miriam Elizabeth, 180
Butler, Vance, 330

Caldwell, Cary Randolph, 144
Caldwell, Jr, David Pollard, 330
Caldwell, Elizabeth Maynard Henry Whalley, 429
Caldwell, Iris Jean Bankhead, 144
Caldwell, Katherine Louise Harrison, 330
Caldwell, Jr, Lafayette Hardwick, 430
Caldwell, Randolph Cameron, 144
Caldwell, Roxanne Kay Garlick, 144
Caldwell, Sue Etrick, 330
Caldwell, Terrill Cameron, 144
Camp, David Sumner, 410
Camp, Jr, Guy William Arthur, 410
Camp III, Guy William Arthur, 410
Camp, Helen Blakemore, 410
Camp, Helen Elizabeth, 410
Camp, Millard Fillmore, 410
Camp, Ruth Roth, 410
Campbell, Archibald Bruce Duchesnay, 396
Campbell, Betty Cantelli, 182
Campbell, Bonnie Ann, 491
Campbell, Bruce John Charles, 396
Campbell, Carol Ann Eleanor, 396
Campbell, Charles Carroll Wood, 396
Campbell, Charles Colin Robin, 396
Campbell, Christine Townsend, 491
Campbell, Deborah Leah, 491
Campbell, Donald Hartford, 491
Campbell, Duncan Archibald Edmund, 396
Campbell, Edith Townsend Garfield, 491
Campbell, Elizabeth Eva, 182
Campbell, Isabel Jean MacKay, 396
Campbell, Jacqueline Louise Ennette Katherina Burns, 396
Campbell, Jennifer Lynn, 491
Campbell, Karen Louise, 396
Campbell, Kristen Marie, 182
Campbell, Lola Henrietta, 396
Campbell, Martin Bradburn, 182
Campbell, Michael Raymond, 182
Campbell, Miriam Alberta Harrop, 396
Campbell, Nellie Kate Robbins, 396

Campbell, Jr, Raymond Henry, 182
Campolattaro, see Capomazza di Campolattaro, 398
Canavan, Carl Francis, 165
Canavan, Helen Augusta Randolph, 165
Candler, Jr, Charles Murphey, 299
Candler, Edith Eudora Lawrence, 299
Canfield, David E., 309
Canfield, Sarah Duer, 309
Cantacuzene, Count Speransky, Prince Serge Michel, 466
Cantacuzene, Countess Speransky (Mary Jacqueline), 466
Cantacuzene, Elizabeth Wolfe, 466
Cantacuzene, Melissa Macneille, 465
Cantacuzene, Michael, 465
Cantacuzene, Rodion, 465, 466
Cantacuzene-Speransky, Prince Alexei Peter, 466
Cantacuzene-Speransky, Prince Rodion Michael, 466
Cantacuzene-Speransky, Princess Elizabeth Irina, 466
Canton, Charles B., 264
Canton, Eleanor Agnes Richardson, 264
Canton, Geraldine, 264
Capomazza di Campolattaro, Carlo, 398
Capomazza di Campolattaro, Carlo-Emilio, 398
Capomazza di Campolattaro, Rosemonde Kuntz, 398
Capomazza di Campolattaro, Stefano, 398
Carabine, Anna J., 578
Carabine, Edward S., 578
Carabine, Keith, 578
Carabine, Virginia Stone Taft, 578
Carnes, Deborah Gail Hubard, 214
Carnes, Nicole Rochelle, 214
Carnes, Steve, 214
Carnesale, Carrie Lee, 171
Carnesale, John Lawrence, 171
Carnesale, Louis John, 171
Carnesale, Louis Vincent, 171
Carnesale, Lucie Bronaugh Taylor, 171
Carnesale, Virginia Powell, 171
Carpenter, Karen Louise Brown, 335
Carpenter, Kary Louise, 335
Carpenter, Kinsey Leas, 335
Carpenter, Jr, Kinsey L., 335
Carr, Alvin, 519
Carr, Jr, Alvin, 519
Carr, Marion Alley/Payne, 519
Carr, Mathew, 519
Carr, William, 519
Carroll, Alberta Lee Eppes, 223
Carroll, Allison LeAnne, 224
Carroll, Teresa Willa Hornsby, 224
Carroll, Jr, William Thomas, 224
Carroll III, William Thomas, 224
Cartee, Alicia Faye Woods, 230
Cartee, Christopher, 230
Cartee, David, 230
Carter, Amy Lynn, 724
Carter, Annette Jene Davis, 724

Gannett, Sarah Alden Derby, 557
Gannett, Theodore R., 557
Gannett, William B., 557
Garde, Harriet Parker Merritt Dixon, 509
Garde, John F., 509
Gardner, Caroline DeWindt, 115
Gardner, Deborah Ann, 115
Gardner, Joan Carolyn Arnold, 115
Gardner, William Alfred, 115
Gardner, Jr, William Alfred, 115
Garfield, Alison Leigh, 491
Garfield, Alva Scott Mitchell, 491
Garfield, Amy Townsend, 491
Garfield, Andrew Mason, 493
Garfield, Angus L., 494
Garfield, Ann Raleigh, 491
Garfield, Anne, 496
Garfield, Benjamin, 494
Garfield, Borton, 495
Garfield, Brenda Stuart, 492
Garfield, Dana Alexander, 493
Garfield, Dorothy Jane Andler, 497
Garfield, Douglas Dodge, 494
Garfield, Jr, Douglas Dodge, 494
Garfield, Edith Townsend, 491
Garfield, Edward Dana, 493
Garfield, Jr, Edward Williams, 497
Garfield III, Edward Williams, 497
Garfield, Eleanor, 496
Garfield, Eleanor Borton, 495
Garfield, Elinor Fay, 496
Garfield, Eliza Newell, 494
Garfield, Elizabeth, 494, 496
Garfield, Elizabeth Linda, 497
Garfield, Elizabeth Newell, 532
Garfield, Esther MacGillicuddy, 493
Garfield, George Hodges, 492
Garfield, Jr, George Hodges, 492
Garfield II, Harry Augustus, 491
Garfield III, Harry Augustus, 491
Garfield, Helen Louise, 494
Garfield, Henry Addison, 492
Garfield, Hester, 496
Garfield, Horace Fuller, 494
Garfield, Jr, Irvin McDowell, 496
Garfield III, Irvin McDowell, 496
Garfield, James, 491
Garfield III, James Abram, 496
Garfield, James Robinson, 493
Garfield II, James Rudolph, 493
Garfield III, James Rudolph, 493
Garfield, Jane Harrison Walker, 494, 532
Garfield, Janet Dodge, 494
Garfield, Janet L. Frothingham, 491
Garfield, Jennifer Packard Barnes, 495
Garfield, John Mason, 491, 492
Garfield, Jr, John Newell, 493
Garfield III, John Newell, 493
Garfield, John Robinson, 491
Garfield, Jonathan Townsend, 491
Garfield, June Anne Merz, 491
Garfield, Katherine D. Barney, 494
Garfield, Katherine Weaver, 492
Garfield, Louise Rich, 494
Garfield, Marjory Ann, 497
Garfield, Marney Maxwell, 494
Garfield, Michael Rudolph, 496
Garfield, Nancy Elizabeth Wright, 492

Garfield, Nancy Greenleaf, 109
Garfield, Jr, Newell, 494, 532
Garfield III, Newell, 494
Garfield, Nina Royce, 494
Garfield, Norma Servis Pearson, 492
Garfield, Olivia, 494
Garfield, Olivia Gardner Pattison, 494
Garfield, Patricia Carol Saunders, 492
Garfield, Peter Stanton, 492
Garfield, Richard, 496
Garfield, Robin Burleigh, 491
Garfield, Jr, Rudolph Hills, 495
Garfield, Sarah Brandegee, 494
Garfield, Sarah Elizabeth, 493
Garfield, Sarah Kenworthy, 492
Garfield, Seth, 494
Garfield, Jr, Stanton, 492
Garfield, Stephen K., 494
Garfield, Stephen Pattison, 494
Garfield, Susan Marie, 497
Garfield, Sylvia Marie Jones, 492
Garfield, Thames Corlett, 493
Garfield, Timothy Doane, 493
Garfield, William Ernest, 109
Garfield, William Wyatt, 494
Garfield, Wyatt, 494
Garrabrant, Laura Wayles, 221
Garrabrant, Patricia Hebb Kennedy, 221
Garrabrant, Peter Buckley, 221
Garrabrant, Robert Bayard, 221
Garrabrant, Samuel Robert, 221
Garrison, Jr, Norman Asa, 154
Garrison, Terry Jo Bankhead Mitchell, 154
Garvey, Deborah, 108
Garvey, Mary Jane Cajka, 108
Garvey, Richard Scott, 108
Garvey, Ruth Carlisle Scott, 108
Garza, Maria de Lourdes Arzac, 87
Garza, Rodolfo, 87
Garza Arzac, Alfredo, 87
Garza Arzac, Rodolfo, 87
Gatchell, Catharine Allen, 266
Gatchell, Elizabeth Emory, 266
Gatchell, Elizabeth Kortright Monroe Emory, 266
Gatchell, Esther Allen, 266
Gatchell, Jr, G. Gordon, 266
Gatchell, Margaret Parsons, 266
Gatchell, Monroe Tyler, 266
Gatchell, Richard Emory, 266
Gatchell, Jr, Richard Emory, 266
Gatchell, Susan Miller Rowe, 266
Gatchell, William Hugh, 266
Gates, Althea Ora, 111
Gates, Andrea Lins, 111
Gates, Jonathan Hubert, 111
Gates, Linda de Windt Dunkerton, 111
Gates, Quintin Garner, 111
Geannini, Curtis, 155
Geannini, David Curtis, 155
Geannini, Ellen Olivia Bailey, 155
Geannini, Giles Anderson, 155
Geannini, Stephen Philip, 155
Geis, Alexandra Lynne, 531
Geis, David Robertson, 531
Geis, Jr, David Robertson, 531
Geis, Edmée Elizabeth, 531

Geis, Edmée Roberta Morsman, 531
Gerard, Peter Charles Rupert, 161
Gerard, Sophie Christine May, 161
Gerfen, Anne Randolph Block, 189
Gerfen, Earl, 189
Gerfen, Grace Virginia, 189
Gerfen, Peter Morson, 189
Gibbs, Janet Sherwin, 309
Gibbs, Jr, Wolcott, 309
Gibson, Corwin Henry, 337
Gibson, Mary Virginia, 337
Gibson, Virginia Berkeley Badger, 337
Gielow, Diane Lewis Hammond, 179
Gielow, George Roger, 179
Gielow, James Randolph, 179
Gielow, Mary Elizabeth, 179
Gilbert, Carl Joyce, 283
Gilbert, Helen Amory Homans, 283
Gilbert, Margaret Helen Bay, 283
Gilbert, Thomas Tibbots, 283
Gile, Bradford Willis, 167
Gile, Jr, Bradford Willis, 167
Gile, Emily Hume, 167
Gile, Emily Hume Taylor, 167
Gillan, Bruce Paul, 496
Gillespie, Adam Stuart, 157
Gillespie, Anne Marie Varn, 157
Gillespie III, Campbell Houston, 157
Gillespie, Cary Ruffin, 157
Gillespie, Clark Patton, 157
Gillespie, Dorothy Hastings Wellman, 157
Gillespie, Elizabeth Lowell Barton, 204
Gillespie, Garrett Gregory, 204
Gillespie, Jr, Garrett Gregory, 205
Gillespie, James Campbell, 157
Gillespie, Kelly Elizabeth, 157
Gillespie, Layle Christine, 157
Gillespie, Layle Church, 157
Gillespie, Mary Bert Patillo, 157
Gillespie, Mary Ruffin, 157
Gillespie, Mary Ruffin McMurdo, 173
Gillespie, Maryanna Keeval, 157
Gillespie, Melanie L., 204
Gillespie, Patricia DeAnne, 157
Gillespie, Robert McMurdo, 157
Gillespie, Stuart Edgar, 157
Gillespie, Susan Estes Robinson, 157
Gillespie, Teresa Marie, 157
Gillespie, William Bennett, 157
Gillespie, William Stuart, 157
Glasgow, Jr, Arthur Charles, 236
Glasgow, Marguerite Eppes, 236
Glasgow, Virginia Anne, 236
Glenn, Janet Elizabeth Hutchison, 146
Glenn, Jr, Robert Carson, 146
Glenn, Robin Casey, 146
Glenn, Roger Christopher, 146
Glockner, David A., 166
Glockner, Margaret Elizabeth Randolph, 166
Goldberg, Raleigh Fox, 174
Goldberg, Samuel Allen, 174
Golden, Gareth Taft, 577
Golden, Ian Taft, 577
Golden, Lawrence Taft, 577
Golden, Martha Bowers Taft, 577
Golden, Michael, 577
Golden, Scott Taft, 577

Goodrich, Samantha Brown, 493
Goodrich, Theodore Godwin, 493
Goodwin, Bessie Van Lear Washington, 71
Goodwin, Carrie Lisa, 76
Goodwin, Constance Anne Meehan, 72
Goodwin, Harry Washington, 72
Goodwin, James Andrew, 72
Goodwin, Jennifer Anne, 72
Goodwin, Suzanne Scott, 76
Goodwyn III, Albert Taylor, 362
Goodwyn, Alice McGehee Thomas, 360
Goodwyn, Alison Coats, 361
Goodwyn, Elizabeth Hudson Hill, 361
Goodwyn, Elizabeth Lancaster, 362
Goodwyn, Elizabeth Lee Valentine, 254
Goodwyn, Foy Glen Gilmore, 361
Goodwyn, Jr, Gardner F., 363
Goodwyn III, Gardner F., 363
Goodwyn, George Thomas, 361
Goodwyn, Jr, George Thomas, 361
Goodwyn III, George Thomas, 361
Goodwyn, Jean Elizabeth Fleming, 361
Goodwyn, John Fleming, 361
Goodwyn, Judith Millar, 361
Goodwyn, Leslie Alison Coats, 361
Goodwyn, Margaret Myrtle Williams, 363
Goodwyn, Margaret Priscilla, 364
Goodwyn, Jr, Marvin William, 364
Goodwyn, Mary Jeanette Johnson, 361
Goodwyn, Mary Lindsey, 361
Goodwyn, Philip Lightfoot, 361
Goodwyn, Reid Millar, 361
Goodwyn III, Robert Tyler, 360
Goodwyn IV, Robert Tyler, 361
Goodwyn, Tyler W., 364
Goodwyn, Warren Hudson, 362
Goodwyn, Jr, Wilfred Lacy, 254
Goodwyn, Jr, William Bibb, 361
Goodwyn III, William Bibb, 361
Goodwyn IV, William Bibb, 361
Goodwyn, Winifred Hutchison Lightfoot, 361
Goodwyn, Winifred Lightfoot, 361
Gould, Isabel Cynthia, 65
Gould, Jr, Lyttleton Bowen Purnell, 65
Gould III, Lyttleton Bowen Purnell, 65
Gould, Mary Esther Krech, 64
Gouverneur, Abigail Josephine, 265
Gouverneur, Caroline Erickson Jeffress, 265
Gouverneur, Carolyn Marie Wortendyke, 265
Gouverneur, Jacob Reynier, 265
Gouverneur, Jeffress, 265
Gouverneur, Minor Fairfax Heiskell, 265
Gouverneur, Sallie Thornton, 265
Gower, April, 115
Gower, Bretton Lee, 115
Gower, Candice, 115
Gower, Carol Gardner, 115